Science Fiction, Fantasy and Horror Film Sequels, Series and Remakes

An Illustrated Filmography, with
Plot Synopses and Critical Commentary

by KIM R. HOLSTON *and*
TOM WINCHESTER

with a foreword by INGRID PITT

McFarland & Company, Inc., Publishers
Jefferson, North Carolina, and London

ALSO BY KIM R. HOLSTON

The Marching Band Handbook, 2d ed.
(McFarland, 1994)

*The English-Speaking Cinema:
An Illustrated History, 1927–1993*
(McFarland, 1993)

*Starlet: Biographies, Filmographies, TV Credits and
Photos of 54 Famous and Not So Famous Leading Ladies of the Sixties*
(McFarland, 1988)

WITH WARREN HOPE

*The Shakespeare Controversy: An Analysis of the Claimants
to Authorship, and Their Champions and Detractors*
(McFarland, 1992)

British Library Cataloguing-in-Publication data are available

Library of Congress Cataloguing-in-Publication Data

Holston, Kim R., 1948–
Science fiction, fantasy and horror film sequels, series and
remakes : an illustrated filmography, with plot synopses and
critical commentary / by Kim R. Holston and Tom Winchester ;
with a foreword by Ingrid Pitt.
p.   cm.
Includes bibliographical references and index.
ISBN 0-7864-0155-9 (library binding : 50# alkaline paper) ∞
1. Science fiction films — Catalogs.   2. Fantastic films — Catalogs.
3. Horror films — Catalogs.   4. Motion picture sequels.
5. Motion picture remakes.   I. Winchester, Tom.   II. Title.
PN1995.9.S26H59   1997
016.79143'615 — dc21   96-51433
                                                            CIP

Manufactured in the United States of America

*McFarland & Company, Inc., Publishers
Box 611, Jefferson, North Carolina 28640*

Contents

Acknowledgments
vi

Foreword by Ingrid Pitt
1

Preface
5

Introduction
11

The Films
15

Bibliography
529

Index
535

Acknowledgments

We wish to thank Hazel Court and Ingrid Pitt; Jim Murray of the Movie Poster Place; Kristine Krueger of the National Film Information Service; Gayla Rauh and Film Favorites; Cinema Collectors; the Spicciati family; Elena Watson; Jerry Ohlinger's Movie Material Store; Floyd "Chunk" Simmons; Michael Betz; Albert and Jean Holston.

Last but not least, we must thank Nancy Holston for her suggestions. And we can't resist relating an insightful moment from Michael Holston. When he was eight years old, his father, Kim, told him proudly, "Daddy knows more about monster movies than anyone you'll ever meet." Michael responded succinctly: "Why?" We also like to recall Courtney Holston's exasperated answer to her mother's question about Daddy's whereabouts: "He's watching *another* Dracula movie."

Foreword
by Ingrid Pitt

I've never been asked to write a Foreword before. I don't remember ever having read one either. So perhaps you will forgive me if this is a bit off the wall.

It's always difficult to find a niche in a medium as copiously covered as horror and science fiction, but in this offering Kim Holston and Tom Winchester have done just that.

I approached the material with a bit of a jaundiced eye. Who cares what makes a science fiction sequel or a horror series function? Then I thought, hang on — I do! Several things that have been very helpful to me over my career can be included in this bracket, although, sadly, not necessarily in this book. (*Vampire Lovers* is in, of course, but *Wild Geese 2* doesn't make it, although that was a bit of a horror after Richard Burton kicked the bucket the night before shooting started and a hastily revamped script was substituted.)

The format of *Science Fiction, Fantasy and Horror Film Sequels, Series and Remakes* has been well thought out. Not sure that I like the critics strutting their stuff so prominently, but as they have always been kind to me I guess I shouldn't envy them their moment in the spotlight.

What is particularly interesting is the "Analysis" section. This is succinct and shows exceptional insight. Insight not being my thing, I was grateful to the authors for explaining to me what *Vampire Lovers* was all about. Lesbianism, eh? Nobody told me! It's a pity they didn't analyze my two TV *Dr. Who* appearances — I'm still trying to figure out my motivation. It couldn't just be money — could it?

When a screenwriter comes up with a brilliant idea, he usually mulls it over for a year or two, rewrites it every time he gets a rejection or an unfavorable criticism, and finally comes up with a finely honed concept and, ideally, a perfect script. It then goes through the sausage machine of a production company, where the sacrilegious hands of other writers are laid on it. When it finally hits the screen it is (possibly) in its ultimate form. The box-office is a bit good and, hey presto, a sequel is cobbled together.

Very rarely does the follow-up match the inceptor. For one thing, the magic's gone, and for another it isn't easy to spring surprises that weren't foreshadowed in the original. Take *Jaws* as an example. Who didn't scream when the bloated head emerged from the bottom of the boat? Who (since then) hasn't

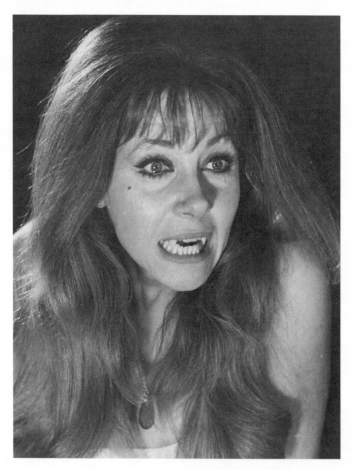

Ingrid Pitt, *The
Vampire Lovers*
(Hammer, 1970)

had a momentary thought, when swimming in the sea, that at any moment a
pain in the nether regions might be the prelude to being a shark's breakfast? Yet
the follow-ups to *Jaws* are very much like the contents of the sharks' stomach:
interesting in detail, but not something to linger over.

    Raiders of the Lost Ark was exciting and highly entertaining. *Temple of Doom*
re-dug the same cabbage patch. The third episode, *The Last Crusade*, lived up
to the first, but that success is mainly due to bringing in a top star, Sean Connery, and to Harrison Ford's intelligence in letting it work for him.

    Dracula goes on forever because he is simultaneously so repulsive and so
attractive that the fascination, like the monster, never dies. The warmed-over
Damien films, *Alien*, the *Back to the Future*, and *Robocop* definitely suffer from
too much money and not enough inspiration.

    The Karnstein Trilogy falters with a slightly different malady. *Vampire Lovers*
is well-scripted and innovative, the sequels and prequels thrash around
desperately looking up something to hang on to but are left floundering because
all the best material has been used up. Lucky me!

Series have a different problem. The mainstay of the continuous play is the characters created by the actors. They benefit from the fact that when a writer knows he is going into a series he doesn't leave hostages to fortune in the first script that can shoot him in the foot in a subsequent episode. How to keep the material fresh? For me all the *Star Treks* seem to be concerned with looking for Spock. The aging of the actors doesn't help focus the mind on higher things like "Live long and prosper" when the prospering can be seen in the solidly bulging waistlines and increasingly aggressive "syrups" (wigs) of the actors.

So why make sequels and series? Well, the attraction of series is easy to understand. Like the variation on a favorite musical theme you are familiar and comfortable with the basic premise. You nod benignly to well-known characters and overlook their faults (unless they are unfaithful to the original). As for sequels — who wants them? I guess somebody does, or money-conscious producers wouldn't stuff multi-million bucks into making them.

But why take my word for anything when you have everything laid out and analyzed for you in this magnificent edition of *Science Fiction, Fantasy and Horror Film Sequels, Series and Remakes*.

Enjoy!

Preface

This book catalogs and evaluates more than 400 science fiction, fantasy and *supernatural* horror films released from 1931 through 1995. Movies of *merely* mental aberration, e.g., *Psycho*, are not included. Nor are "thrillers." The monstrous great white shark of *Jaws* is not a supernatural creature. The James Bond series uses futuristic equipment, so some might argue those films deserve inclusion; yet we categorize 007 as "thriller/espionage/crime/adventure" (some say spoof). Besides, Bond receives plenty of literary coverage elsewhere.

It crossed our minds to omit *Friday the 13th*. Jason Voorhees, after all, is hardly preternatural in his first outing. There is little rationale supplied for his existence. Not even an implausible explanation is offered in the early films of the series. Later on, however, we see him resurrected via "Frankenstein" methods — lightning, for instance. Voilà, a science fiction explanation! Likewise, *Halloween*'s Michael Myers is hardly recognized as a supernatural entity in his first films. Only the doctor played by Donald Pleasence has an inkling of his nemesis's true identity and power, and we look upon this as a plot contrivance to impart some rationality. Eventually, though, Myers is termed evil incarnate.

At first glance, the Indiana Jones trilogy seems tied to the adventure genre. Yet a strong supernatural element infuses each film: the spirits of the Lost Ark, the Kali worshippers of the Temple of Doom, the Holy Grail of *Last Crusade*. We have, then, included these films.

Besides sequels, remakes, and true series, we include films in which the character that appeared in one film resurfaces in another, like Dracula and Frankenstein. We have also included some phony sequels. *The Curse, Curse II: The Bite*, and *Curse III: Blood Sacrifice* are related only by title, not characters or content. "Hidden" sequels are also attended to. For instance, *The Mind Benders* and *Altered States* are variations on the Jekyll-Hyde theme.

Our basic criteria: The progenitor movie must be a live-action, theatrical, English-language sound film. TV movies and TV movie sequels to theatrical films are not included. To us it is patently obvious that "movies" made for television are victims of censorship, tight budgets, fast shooting schedules, and second or no-rank stars. In short, we do not trust their production — or entertainment — values. Made for video? We don't trust their production values either, but at this stage in cinema history it is often difficult to determine if a production was made exclusively for video or cable television. Perhaps it was made for theaters but the producers or studio had second thoughts and sent it direct to video. We've thrown up our hands in video stores when discovering more and more sequels based on an original of which we've not heard. Purists at heart, we've nevertheless included a few video-only sequels, series, and remakes.

In those instances when we've been unable to examine a movie ourselves, we have relied on our memories and trusted sources to construct synopses and analyses. Some films, like Elizabeth Taylor's *The Blue Bird*, are not yet on video and have not appeared on broadcast or cable television — at least not in the three years during which we've worked on this book. When there is no rating or synopsis, it means we have no good sources to rely on and have not located the film.

If the reader wonders why some bad movies have a longer synopsis than good ones, it's because we've chosen to follow the perambulations of the plot. Some plots whisk the audience hither and yon and back again.

We believe no other book examines sequels, series, and remakes of the fantastic cinema in this depth. Nor does this book duplicate the Robert A. and Gwendolyn Wright Nowlan book *Cinema Sequels and Remakes, 1903–1987*, which purposely omits the "fantasy" cinema.

About Reviews

We have made every attempt to locate reviews contemporary with the release of the films, and we believe we've accomplished that for over 90 percent of the movies examined. The farther back one goes, the less likely one is to find a review. Often *The New York Times* comes to the rescue, but sometimes a film was not released in New York, or else it was reckoned insignificant and not reviewed. As fantasy films gained in popularity and proved to be more than a *divertissement*, more critics paid attention. Sometimes, however, the second and succeeding films in a series received more recognition than the original, which had been dismissed as a minor entry. It is frequently illuminating, even amazing, to read contemporary reviews. In 1939, *The Wizard of Oz* was hardly recognized as the classic it would become. It astounded us to find so many negative reviews of *Alien* when we recalled almost universal praise when it opened in 1979. Obviously some of the positive reviews were in periodicals and newspapers that are not standard in library collections. As well as time, one must consider the reviewing organ's slant and audience. *The New Yorker, Village Voice*— these are "highbrow" periodicals. *Christian Century* and *Commonweal* will bring a religious orientation to their reviews. Certain (most?) established critics have little truck with the fantastic cinema and are often unduly harsh on such films, while the genre periodicals like *Fangoria* and *Starlog*, just by publishing profusely illustrated articles on forthcoming films, will seem to extol them. *Variety* will consider a film from the perspective of expected box office receipts as well as from technical, script, and dramatic standpoints. A note: When we cite only

Variety (without name of reviewer or issue date), the review is from the edited compilation *Variety Movie Guide.*

Our own rating system is somewhat arbitrary. After all, is *½ really any better than *? The liberalism of one author has been somewhat tempered by the other's harder line. In any case, a film will score some points with us for not being boring. Our ratings are as follows:

*	= poor	***Bomb	= awful but highly entertaining
**	= fair	****	= excellent
***	= good	nv	= not available on video

About Home Video and Special Editions

Modern video technology has made it possible to view innumerable treasures (and more than a few "booby prizes") of the past that were once thought forever lost. It has also given motion picture directors the opportunity to offer the public their original thoughts, or their second thoughts, on some of their work. It's a well-known fact that considerably more film is shot for a feature than actually turns up on screen; "the cutting-room floor" is the repository of much footage that has actually been lensed, and, until relatively recently, that repository was the last stop for those minutes of film. In the 1970s, television showings of a number of features made the claim, "containing scenes never before shown," or words to that effect, implying that the film was somehow more complete. A typical case would be the early–'80s premier telecast of *Superman* which was touted to contain some fifteen minutes of footage not shown in the theatrical release. Since that time, it seems that almost every other "hit," when shown on TV, has been promoted as restoring similarly "lost" footage. Such promotions should be viewed with some skepticism, since in the great majority of cases the restored minutes of film simply pad the running time to fill a given slot and, consequently, sell more advertising. (Exceptions exist. When the Dino De Laurentiis/David Lynch version of Frank Herbert's mammoth *Dune* was televised, nearly an *hour* of deleted footage was restored to what had been a sometimes incoherent narrative. The resulting film was still not the masterpiece some cultists insisted it was, but it did emerge in somewhat better shape than the theatrical version.) Video releases of theatrical films fare somewhat differently. In the majority of cases, the video releases are identical to the theatrical original. In some instances, the soundtrack may be altered for reasons of music copyright, but that's usually all. (The videotape release of John Carpenter's remake of *The Thing* contains a small note reading, "Some Music Re-scored for Home Video." This, fortunately, does not refer to Ennio Morricone's superb score, but to some incidental rock music played in the film by one of the characters. Interestingly, the original rock music was restored in the laser disk version of the film.) In the last few years, with the increased awareness of the "pan and scan" limitations of the typical television screen, many video versions have been released in "letter-box" format, a technique that "crops" the top and bottom of the viewing area so that the proportions of the original screen showing are duplicated. Not infrequently, home video versions of genre hits are released with "enhanced" soundtracks (e.g., the video release of Lucasfilms' *Indiana Jones and the Last Crusade*). All in all, the video versions of most theatrical films remain true in spirit to the original, and frequently, as in the case of those that feature augmented sound, actually manage to enhance the experience.

In the early 1990s, director James Cameron produced a version of his hit sequel *Aliens* for laser disk, entitled *Aliens: Special Edition*. This deluxe letterboxed edition of the film restores nearly twenty minutes of footage that were deleted prior to the film's premiere in order to bring the film in at two hours and fifteen minutes. Far from being of ephemeral interest, the restored footage in *Special Edition* truly reinforces the already electrifying experience of the film. In addition to the reconstruction of the film, *Special Edition* provides much supplementary material: an interview with James Cameron, and behind-the-scenes material on the making of his film (which includes excerpts from the shooting script, design drawings, cast photos, and publicity stills), as well as insights about how the script progressed from the beginning. Similarly, after the initial home video release of his 1992 *Terminator 2: Judgment Day* came the special (laser) edition of that film. As with *Aliens: Special Edition*, the scenes new to this edition of *Terminator 2* primarily serve to amplify what we already know about the characters involved, rather than shedding any new light on the story itself. Cameron is one director who seems especially fond of utilizing the home video format to expand on his cinematic statements, as his last three films have seen considerable expansion when released on the laser format (the special edition of his undersea opus *The Abyss* contains some forty minutes of additional footage), but he is by no means the only one.

All of which leads us to ask: which version of a film should be considered definitive?

Well, each film needs to be judged separately, and on its own merits, to be sure. But generally, it is safe to consider the original theatrical release as definitive. There are certainly exceptions, but it's a good rule of thumb. However much restored footage adds to the effect of a film, seldom does restored footage do more than enhance the effect. Even the restored footage of so revered a classic as *Lawrence of Arabia* does not raise the David Lean film so far above the original version as to render it shoddy or inferior.

For this book, "special editions" (and their equivalent, the "director's cut") will be considered just that: special, quite separate from the original theatrical release.

About the Arrangement

This book is arranged as an alphabetical listing of original films — that is, each alphabetically listed entry is the first in a series, or the original work that spawned one or more remakes. Beneath the original film, its offspring are listed in chronological order.

Any sequel or remake whose title departs from that of the parent film has been cross-referenced to the original (e.g., "Freddy's Dead: The Final Nightmare *see under* Nightmare on Elm Street"). These cross-references should prove especially helpful in cases where a sequel or remake attained more recognition than the original. For example, many people are familiar with the 1953 movie *Donovan's Brain*, but few may be aware that the novel of the same name was first filmed in 1944 under the title *The Lady and the Monster*. For this reason, anyone searching our D section for *Donovan's Brain* will find a cross-reference to its precursor: "Donovan's Brain *see under* The Lady and the Monster."

Those who have trouble remembering exact titles but can recall a "hook" word or phrase — "What were all those films about that nasty kid named Damien?" — will find help in the book's index (where the entry "Damien" leads the searcher to *The Omen* and its sequels).

We hope you'll find the book easy to use and that you'll turn to it the way audiences and filmmakers turn to their favorite fantastic subjects: again and again!

Introduction

In 1931, four years after the advent of "talkies," four films of a "fantastic" nature were released that would initiate series, have sequels, or be remade many times in the ensuing decades: *Alice in Wonderland, A Connecticut Yankee, Dracula,* and *Frankenstein.* The success of *Frankenstein* and the sequels that followed in 1935 (*Bride of Frankenstein*) and 1939 (*Son of Frankenstein*) led to further, if lesser, outings for the monster through the 1940s; Dracula, too, enjoyed success in new forms (*Dracula's Daughter,* 1936, and the reappearance of Bela Lugosi's count in 1948). It has been suggested that audiences took to movie monsters because, especially in the Frankenstein monster's case, people living through the Great Depression could empathize with victims. Evidently the empathy value of a good victim has never declined, for the horror genre is still one of the most fertile fields for the growth of cinemas, sequels, and remakes. Audiences of the thirties and forties couldn't seem to get enough of Dracula; in the 1980s, quasi-supernatural villains like Jason Voorhees and Freddy Krueger inspired the same sort of addiction. Fantasy and science fiction likewise offered rich possibilities for remakes and sequels from the start of the sound era. All told, the 1930s saw the release of 25 films that were either progenitors, sequels, or remakes in the fantastic cinema realm.

Into the early 1940s Universal remained *the* studio for supernatural horror. Once they discovered a viable character, they made more films with it. (We're not sure how artistically viable *Captive Wild Woman* was, but back then grist was needed for the theatrical mill.) Werewolves and mummies populated the Universal lot throughout the decade, but in 1948 that studio's *Abbott and Costello Meet Frankenstein* put a temporary end to the horror cycle. Meanwhile, RKO threatened to overtake Universal, achieving renown with its subdued Val Lewton–produced horror films during World War II. *The Cat People* and *The Curse of the Cat People* are Lewton's films represented here.

Overall, the 1940s produced 31 supernatural series or sequel films, plus two remakes: the 1941 *Dr. Jekyll and Mr. Hyde* and the 1949 *A Connecticut Yankee in King Arthur's Court.*

Prompted by the A-bombs of 1945, postwar hydrogen bomb development and testing, subsequent fears of radioactive mutants (or "mu-tants" as they were often called in fifties science fiction movies) and reports of flying saucers, science fiction supplanted horror as viable fantastic film material at mid-century. Classics and near-classics like *The Thing from Another World, Invaders from Mars, Invasion of the Body Snatchers* and *The Blob* would be remade in the 1970s and 1980s. Universal managed to add another memorable monster to their canon when they introduced the prehistoric Devonian Age Gill Man in 1954's *Creature from the Black Lagoon.*

Just as science fiction films declined in quality in the late fifties, a successful revival of supernatural horror began in England. Hammer Studios took the Universal characters, but to avoid litigation for patent infringement, they employed new makeup and, to the consternation of some, filmed their exploits in color. *The Curse of Frankenstein* in 1957 was followed by the even more successful *Horror of Dracula* in 1958 and *The Mummy* in 1959. So successful were they that a plethora of sequels ensued, and Hammer became a studio to reckon with, adding to its canon all the way into the early 1970s. All this hammering led to even more sequels and series films in the 1950s than in previous decades; in all, 51 were released.

The 1960s saw 47 sequels, thanks to American International Pictures, where James Nicholson and Samuel Arkoff began producing low-budget, drive-in, teenage-oriented films, sometimes taking old familiar monsters. Unlike Hammer, AIP moved them out of Gothic and into modern settings. Early in the decade, AIP's prolific director Roger Corman and star Vincent Price strove for a note of elegance with their well-regarded series of films based on the works of Edgar Allen Poe. By the end of the decade, however, the pendulum (over the pit?) had swung in the opposite direction, thanks to George Romero and his champion 1968 gross-out, *Night of the Living Dead*. Condemned by mainstream critics, this cheaply made, black-and-white film became a drive-in and cult favorite eventually recognized as a seminal horror film. Strangely, its first sequel, *Dawn of the Dead*, did not appear till 1979.

In contrast with the shoestring-budgeted *Night of the Living Dead*, 1960s science fiction went big budget in a big way, giving rise to the megahits *Planet of the Apes* and *2001: A Space Odyssey. Planet of the Apes* spawned an immediate series, *2001* a sequel sixteen years later.

By the 1970s, the Baby Boomers had grown up into filmmakers like George Lucas and Steven Spielberg, and as a result, the science fiction and comic-book dreams of 1950s childhoods suddenly exploded onto movie screens. The unforeseen and phenomenal success of 1977's *Star Wars* finally gave science fiction credibility with studios and spawned a trilogy. Likewise, the first *Star Trek* movie (1979) gave birth to a long series. Special effects became state-of-the-art, and organizations like Industrial Light and Magic took center stage, basing outer space creations on the standard that had been set with 1968's *2001: A Space Odyssey*. Meanwhile, comic-book heroes such as Superman and Flash Gordon had their outings, and subsequent encores, on the screen; Batman would follow in the next decade. The 1970s' score for sequels and sequel-makers: 82.

Led on by the 1978 remake of 1956's *Invasion of the Body Snatchers*, fifties genre classics were often remade in the eighties, to generally ho-hum audience response. Films such as *Invaders from Mars*, *The Blob*, and *Not of This Earth* were hyped in magazines but frequently pulled within a week from the few area theaters in which they were playing. Their audiences awaited them on video and cable television. Meanwhile, new series proliferated, featuring both supernatural stories (*The Howling*) and slasher stories with phony supernatural elements as a rationale for the most unbelievable plotlines. With the burgeoning popularity of such series as *Friday the 13th* and *Nightmare on Elm Street*, the 1980s was nearly overwhelmed with sequels, remakes, and series films. An amazing 145 were released, 23 in 1988 alone.

By the 1990s, such series seemed to be sputtering to a halt, while others — *The Amityville Horror*, *Living Dead*, *Puppet Master*—seemed destined to continue successfully on video. Meanwhile, the supernatural films of the past were making a comeback, with Francis Ford Coppola remaking *Dracula* and a new *Frankenstein* from director-actor Kenneth Branagh. What goes around comes around — and (in the sequel and remake business) around, and around, and around again. But who's complaining? It's a very diverting ride.

The Films

Abbott and Costello Meet Dr. Jekyll and Mr. Hyde *see under* **Dr. Jekyll and Mr. Hyde**

Abbott and Costello Meet Frankenstein *see under* **Frankenstein**

Abbott and Costello Meet the Invisible Man *see under* **The Invisible Man**

Abbott and Costello Meet the Mummy *see under* **The Mummy**

The Abominable Dr. Phibes
(AIP, 1971; 94 min.) ***½

Produced by Louis M. Heyward, Ronald S. Dunas. Directed by Robert Fuest. Screenplay, James Whiton, William Goldstein. Edited by Tristam Cones. Director of Photography, Norman Warwick. Color, Movielab. Music, Basil Kirchen, Jack Nathan. Set Decoration, Brian Eatwell. Makeup, Trevor Crole-Rees. Special Effects, George Blackwell.

Cast: Dr. Anton Phibes (Vincent Price), Dr. Vesalius (Joseph Cotten), Vulnavia (Virginia North), Inspector Trout (Peter Jeffrey), Dr. Longstreet (Terry-Thomas), Rabbi (Hugh Griffith), Victoria Regina Phibes (Caroline Munro), Goldsmith (Audrey Woods), Nurse Allan (Susan Travers), Dr. Hargreaves (Alex Scott), Dr. Dunwoody (Edward Burnham), Dr. Kitaj (Peter Gilmore), Dr. Whitcombe (Maurice Kaufman), Schenley (Norman Jones), Waverley (John Cater), Crow (Derek Godfrey), Lem (Sean Bury), Ross (Walter Horsbrugh), Mrs. Frawley (Barbara Keogh), Police (Dallas Adams, Alan Zipson).

Synopsis: Inspector Trout and Scotland Yard are puzzled by the mysterious murders of several surgeons. One was killed by Malayan bats, another by a constricting frog mask at a ball, a third by having his blood siphoned off. Unknown to the authorities, Dr. Anton Phibes and his mute assistant, Vulnavia, are the perpetrators, venturing from his home, the repository of his unique lifesize clockwork automatons, to commit the heinous deeds. Trout queries Dr. Vesalius, who knew the late physicians, and a rabbi who theorizes that the murderer is basing his deeds on the ten "plagues of the Pharaohs." Dr. Vesalius discovers that the only time he supervised an operation in which the dead men participated was the case of Victoria Regina Phibes. That was 1921. She died, and her husband, the famous organist Anton Phibes, apparently was killed in a car crash returning from Switzerland. The police are powerless to stop the murder spree, which continues by such bizarre means as a catapult-thrown unicorn head and locusts which eat the flesh from the nurse. When only Vesalius is left, he and Inspector Trout realize that the madman will use the plague of the death of the first born — Vesalius's son. True, Vesalius's son has been kidnapped, and by Phibes, who is quite alive. In his home in Maldine Square, he gives Vesalius one chance to save his son. In six minutes he must operate to remove a key that Phibes inserted into the boy, unlock a chain and push the table from beneath the acid containers. Vesalius is successful, but Vulnavia accidentally suffers the acid "bath." Phibes has already disappeared, embalming himself for an eternal rest by the side of his beloved wife

15

in a hidden underground chamber that is sealed as the police and Vesalius enter the basement.

Reviews: "A pretty good, sometimes oddly amusing collage of straight horror, sudden farce, and high camp.... has a slushy, rather weak middle [but] the climactic scenes are marvelously handled...." (Dale Winogura, *Cinefantastique*, Fall 1971, p. 40) ¶"Anachronistic period horror musical camp fantasy.... Price's makeup ... is outstanding...." (Murf., *Variety*, May 26, 1971, p. 23)

Analysis: This was an unexpected pleasure whose "Love Means Never Having to Say You're Ugly" ad gave an indication of the black comedy to come by poking fun at the previous year's *Love Story* ("Love means never having to say you're sorry"). It's marvelously stylish and tailor-made for the theatrics of Price, whom *Cinefantastique* praised for his "grotesque charm." The *New York Times* (August 5, 1971, p. 25) complained that the campy tone had a "steamroller" effect on the fun, but in fact it's all played straight — the best way. Hugh Griffith will appear in the sequel as a different character.

Dr. Phibes Rises Again
(AIP, 1972; 88 min.) ***½

Produced by Louis M. Heyward. Directed by Robert Fuest. Screenplay, Robert Fuest and Robert Blees. Edited by Tristan Cones. Director of Photography, Alex Thomson. color. Music, John Gale. Art Direction, Brian Eatwell.

Cast: Dr. Anton Phibes (Vincent Price), Vulnavia (Valli Kemp), Biederbeck (Robert Quarry), Waverley (John Cater), Inspector Trout (Peter Jeffrey), Ambrose (Hugh Griffith), Diana (Fiona Lewis), Shavers (John Thaw), Stuart (Keith Buckley), Baker (Lewis Flander), Hackett (Gerald Sim), Manservant (Milton Reid), Captain (Peter Cushing), Miss Ambrose (Beryl Reid), Lombardo (Terry-Thomas), Victoria (Caroline Munro).

Synopsis: Three years have passed when Dr. Anton Phibes rises from his tomb, calls forth trusty servant Vulnavia, and seeks his safe with the papyrus map that will be instrumental in resurrecting his dead wife, Victoria. To his consternation, his home in Maldine Square has been razed and the safe is empty. Biederbeck has the map and also intends going to Egypt — to maintain his youth. The elixir he has been taking is almost gone. Phibes recovers the map by killing Biederbeck's manservant. Both Phibes and Biederbeck take ship together. During the journey Phibes tosses overboard Ambrose, an inquisitive associate of Biederbeck. The body washes ashore, and the Scotland Yard policemen who'd previously investigated Phibes now realize their nemesis lives. Phibes and Vulnavia enter the tomb the doctor knows will lead him to the river of life. There remain obstacles: Biederbeck's crew discover the sarcophagus in which Phibes placed Victoria, but Phibes disposes of them and kidnaps Biederbeck's fiancee, Diana. In exchange for the key to the river's gate, Phibes lets Biederbeck rescue Diana. Biederbeck rushes back too late to share in Phibes' victory — the water gate closes behind Phibes, who poles his boat and wife down the river of life. An aging Biederbeck hangs on the gate.

Reviews: "Displays a good deal of wit in its amused affection for awful movie styles of the 1930's." (Vincent Canby, *New York Times*, February 4, 1973, Section II, p. 1) ¶"Vincent Price ... delivers one of his priceless theatric performances, and Quarry is a properly ruthless rival who nearly matches Phibes in knowledge and cunning." (Whit., *Variety*, July 19, 1972, p. 14)

Analysis: This is better than its progenitor. The sandblasted victim, the Scottish fusiliers, Phibes hiding amongst the tomb skeletons, Vulnavia and the sousaphone... It's a great parody. We congratulate whoever realized that Peter Jeffrey and John Cater, who had a few scenes together in the first film, would make a great detective team. How many times must they have broken up while straightforwardly delivering those lines about such improbable incidents? It's too bad there wasn't another entry in this series — with the divine Ms. Kemp. There's no explanation for her return from the acid bath she took at the end of *The Abominable Dr. Phibes*. We assume Phibes found a substitute or that he restored her face. After all, he recreated his own. As Vincent Canby pointed out in the *New York Times* (January 11, 1973, p. 35),

Dr. Phibes (Vincent Price, right) with his trusty servant Vulnavia (Valli Kemp) in *Dr. Phibes Rises Again* (AIP, 1972).

the film's "respect for fantasy" prevented it from becoming too entangled in attempts to explain things.

The Absent Minded Professor

(Buena Vista, 1961; 97 min.) ***

Produced by Walt Disney. Associate Producer, Bill Walsh. Directed by Robert Stevenson. Assistant Director, Robert G. Shannon. Screenplay, Bill Walsh. Based on a story by Samuel W. Taylor. Edited by Cotton Warburton. Director of Photography, Edward Colman. Music, George Bruns. Sound, Dean Thomas. Art Direction, Carroll Clark. Special Effects, Peter Ellenshaw and Eustace Lycett.

Cast: Ned Brainard (Fred MacMurray), Betsy Carlisle (Nancy Olson), Biff Hawk (Tommy Kirk), Alonzo Hawk (Keenan Wynn), Shelby Ashton (Elliott Reid), Fire chief (Ed Wynn), President Rufus Daggett (Leon Ames), Coach Elkins (Wally Brown),

Professor Ned Brainard (Fred MacMurray) and his fiancee, Betsy (Nancy Olson), arrive in Washington, D.C., in a flubberized car in *The Absent Minded Professor* (Buena Vista, 1961).

Defense secretary (Edward Andrews), First referee (Alan Carney). With Ray Teal.

Synopsis: So impassioned about his work is Professor Ned Brainard of Medfield College of Technology that he's missed his wedding twice. Betsy gives him one more chance, but an explosion in his garage lab reveals a new energy inherent in what Brainard dubs "flubber"—flying rubber, which he learns to control through gamma ray bombardment. When Brainard tries to explain to Betsy why he once again missed the nuptials, he is interrupted by the arrival of Alonzo Hawk, owner of the Auld Lang Syne Finance Company. Hawk's loan to Medfield College is outstanding, and he longs to turn the campus into a housing development. He's also angry with Brainard because the professor flunked his son Biff, a star basketball player who now cannot play in the big game against rival Rutland. Brainard tells Betsy flubber can save the college. He installs flubber in his

Model T, but before he can demonstrate, Shelby Ashton of Rutland whisks Betsy off to the game. Brainard arrives at the gym and witnesses a solid thrashing of Medfield by Rutland. He sneaks into Medfield's locker room, removes the extra sneakers and in his lab irons on flubber. He returns, leaves the new sneakers, and gives the players a pep talk. Subsequently, they bound and leap over the opposing team and win the game by a point. Alonzo Hawk and son Biff spot Brainard's flying car in the moonlight, and the senior Hawk tries to make a deal. Instead, Brainard calls the federal government, finally getting through to the Defense Department. Representatives of the army, navy and air force come to Medfield to inspect the "anti-gravity" discovery. Meanwhile, Biff and his dad substitute an unflubberized Model T for Brainard's while the latter impresses Betsy at the dance—he's put flubber on his shoes. When the military arrives and

Brainard shows them his car, nothing happens and he's considered a nut. But Betsy begins to believe him. Brainard realizes Hawk switched cars and gives him flubberized shoes, ostensibly to prove how they can make a fortune selling such footwear. However, the real motive is to get Hawk jumping uncontrollably until he tells them the car's location. It's in his warehouse, guarded by two flunkies. Brainard retrieves it in his own flubberized shoes. Hawk is finally brought to ground, and with Biff and his henchmen, he chases Brainard and Betsy. They crash into a police car and are arrested. Brainard and Betsy head for Washington, D.C., and land at the White House. All units of the military will share in the discovery. Brainard and Betsy finally marry and take off for their honeymoon in his flying car.

Reviews: "Amiably wacky comedy.... MacMurray invests the hero with a combination of ingenuity, befuddlement and unshakable good will...." (Moira Walsh, *America*, April 1, 1961, pp. 25-26) ¶"Delightful, highly diverting fantasy-comedy, with satirical touches." (F. Maurice Speed, ed., *Film Review 1962-63*, p. 99)

Analysis: How cute it was! Who will forget the flying car, the basketball game, or the dance? That overshadowed the total ludicrousness of the film's contention that Medfield's basketball team would beat Rutland if Biff were allowed to play. All of the Rutland players are bruisers a foot taller than the Medfield team members. The fifth highest grossing film of the year, it received Academy Award nominations for black and white cinematography, black and white art direction-set decoration, and special effects. (Edith Oliver of *The New Yorker* [April 1, 1965, p. 215] said the trick-effect technicians were the "real stars.")

Son of Flubber

(Buena Vista, 1963; 100 min.) ***

Produced by Walt Disney. Co-Producer, Bill Walsh. Directed by Robert Stevenson. Screenplay, Bill Walsh and Don Da Gradi. Based on a story by Samuel W. Taylor and on books by Danny Dunn. Edited by Cotton Warburton. Director of Photography, Edward Colman. Music, George Bruns. Art Di-

rection, Carroll Clark, Bill Tuntke. Set Decoration, Emile Kuri, Hal Gausman.

Cast: Ned Brainard (Fred MacMurray), Elizabeth Brainard (Nancy Olson), Biff Hawk (Tommy Kirk), Alonzo Hawk (Keenan Wynn), A.J. Allen (Ed Wynn), President Rufus Daggett (Leon Ames), Shelby Ashton (Elliott Reid), Desiree/Mary Lee Spooner (Joanna Moore), Humphrey Hacker (Leon Tyler), Mr. Hurley (Ken Murray), Judge Murdock (Charlie Ruggles), Mr. Hummel (William Demarest), Radio announcer (Paul Lynde), Coach (Stuart Erwin), Harker (Bob Sweeney), Sign painter (J. Pat O'Malley), Rex Williams (Joe Flynn), Mrs. Daggett (Harriet MacGibbon), Pentagon official (Edward Andrews), Mr. Barley (Jack Albertson), Officer Kelly (Forrest Lewis), Officer Hanson (James Westerfield).

Synopsis: Government red tape and Pentagon stonewalling force Professor Ned Brainard to return home without funds to help Medfield College pay off its $350,000 loan to Alonzo Hawk — or to pay the Brainards' bills. Nevertheless, Brainard thinks the residue of flubber, "flubbergas," may yet make his fortune. He devises a weather gun and creates a kitchen cloudburst from teapot steam. The gun fails to work on a distant cloud, however, and the unexpected side effect is broken glass all over Medfield. Made jealous by the arrival of Ned's old flame, Mary Lee Spooner, and fed up with lack of money, Elizabeth leaves to think things out. Spurning Hawk's scheme to buy glass companies and then use his machine to break glass, Brainard consults with Biff and Humphrey about winning the upcoming football game. Humphrey dons a special flubbergas-filled suit and is kicked and thrown for touchdowns. But as time runs out, the game must be won with the ball and a field goal — a 96-yarder! The police arrest Brainard. A criminal damage suit comes to trial. Brainard acts in his own defense, claiming that everyone is selling fear. To gain time, Elizabeth testifies. When county agricultural agent A.J. Allen testifies that Brainard's rays ("dry rain") have produced giant produce — and he displays said fruit and vegetables — the judge dismisses the case. Betsy and Ned take an airborne ride in the car. Flying beyond them to join the satellites is the football that won the game.

Reviews: "Not entirely disastrous.... Some of the sight gags ... are fairly fresh and ingenious." (Moira Walsh, *America*, March 2, 1963, p. 316) ¶"The humor is still the old gasser about how stupid scientist types really are — but they should be tolerated in a democratic nation ... because scientists win ball games." (*Newsweek*, January 21, 1963, p. 91)

Analysis: It's about as good as the first. After we saw this in the theater back in '63, a heated lunchtime discussion took place comparing the football game here with the basketball game in *The Absent Minded Professor*. Don't look too close: there are incidents of cheating and experiments dangerous to bystanders. What was going on to inspire MacMurray's court testimony that everyone is selling fear? The Cuban missile crisis? The Disney people could have continued this series. (Maybe they did: see the *Honey, I Shrunk the Kids!* duo, with scientist Wayne Szalinski and his gizmo.) MacMurray and Demarest would shortly be a team on TV's *My Three Sons.*

The Addams Family
(Paramount 1991; 100 min.) **½

Produced by Scott Rudin. Directed by Barry Sonnenfeld. Screenplay by Caroline Thompson and Larry Wilson. Based on characters created by Charles Addams. Edited by Dede Allen and Jim Miller. Director of Photography, Owen Roizman. Music, Marc Shaiman. Dolby Stereo. Song "Mamushka" music, Marc Shaiman. Lyrics, Betty Comden and Adolph Green. Choreography, Peter Anastos. Makeup, Fern Buchner. Visual Effects Supervisor, Alan Munro. "Thing" Prosthetics and Puppets, David Miller Studio.

Cast: Gomez Addams (Raul Julia), Morticia Addams (Anjelica Huston), Uncle Fester (Christopher Lloyd), Tully Alford (Dan Hedaya), Abigail Craven (Elizabeth Wilson), Granny (Judith Malina), Lurch (Carel Struycken), Wednesday Addams (Christina Ricci), Pugsley Addams (Jimmy Workman), Margaret Alford (Dana Ivey), Judge Womack (Paul Benedict), Thing (Christopher Hart), Cousin It (John Franklin), Digit Addams (Tony Azito), Dexter Addams (Douglas Brian Martin), Donald Addams (Steven M. Martin), Flora Amor (Maureen Sue Levin), Fauna Amor (Darlene Levin), Swedish blonde (Victoria Hall), Sally Jesse Raphaël (Herself).

Synopsis: Uncle Fester Addams has disappeared. Abigail Craven convinces her son that he can pass for Fester and, after worming his way into the eccentric family's household, make off with the treasure horde in their basement. She convinces the Addams family solicitor, Tully, to help. Pretending to be a psychiatrist, she explains Fester's disappearance and reappearance. Gomez and Morticia give a grand ball to welcome Fester back. With "Fester" safely ensconced in the family's good graces, Abigail has him kick Gomez out of the house. Finally the real Fester realizes he has had amnesia and is in fact Gomez's brother. Abigail is propelled from the house to a grave and the family is reunited.

Reviews: "The plot is lame; the jokes are often broad.... the movie doesn't descend into camp." (Cathleen McGuigan, *Newsweek*, November 25, 1991, p. 56) ¶"Turns voodoo into visual wit." (Richard Corliss, *Time*, November 25, 1991, p. 96)

Analysis: We don't recall public clamor for this theatrical film based on the sixties TV series starring Carolyn Jones and John Astin. Nevertheless, it became a success. True, the casting is inspired, but the story stinks, getting off to an implausible start as the Addams family solicitor allows himself to betray his clients. Why? They pay him exceedingly well — gold doubloons! It's nonsense, just contrived, and taints the rest of the film. It would have been better to explore Addams family origins.

Addams Family Values
(1993; 100 min.) **½

Produced by Scott Rudin. Directed by Barry Sonnenfeld. Screenplay, Paul Rudnick. Based on characters created by Charles Addams. Edited by Jim Miller and Arthur Schmidt. Director of Photography, Donald Peterman. Color by DeLuxe. Music, Marc Shaiman. Addams Family Theme, Vic Mizzy. Dolby Stereo. Art Direction, William J. Durrell, Jr. Set Decoration, Marvin March. Opticals/Visual Effects, Peter Kuran.

Cast: Gomez Addams (Raul Julia), Morticia Addams (Anjelica Huston), Fester (Christopher Lloyd), Wednesday Addams (Christina Ricci), Granny (Carol Kane), Debbie Jellinsky (Joan Cusack), Lurch (Carel Struycken), Pugsley Addams (Jimmy Workman), Joel

Glicker (David Krumholtz), Gary Granger (Peter MacNichol), Becky Granger (Christine Baranski), Dementia (Carol Hankins), Young Debbie (Haley Peel).

Synopsis: Wednesday and Pugsley feel neglected after Morticia has a baby boy, Pubert. Attempts at infanticide are interrupted when Morticia and Gomez hire nanny Debbie Jellinsky. Little do they know that this perky blonde is a notorious "black widow" murderess now after Fester's hand — and money. In order to get the suspicious Wednesday out of her way, Debbie convinces Gomez and Morticia that their older children really want to go to summer camp. While they are being miserable at Camp Chippewa, Debbie obtains Fester's affection. They marry and honeymoon in Hawaii, where Debbie trades sexual favors for Fester's promise never to see his family again. Wednesday and Pugsley finally escape Camp Chippewa and reach home. Unsuccessful in blowing up Fester, Debbie follows him back to his family and, shotgun in hand, locks them up and prepares to electrocute them. Having momentarily forgotten Pubert, she finds him on the floor connecting the cables and it is she who is fried. The Addamses celebrate Pubert's first birthday. Amongst the guests is Joel, a nerdy boy befriended by Wednesday at camp.

Reviews: "This sequel is a wittier and more consistent black farce.... If there's a problem ... it's how to make an Addams Family movie something more than a rhythmless string of gags." (Owen Gleiberman, *Entertainment Weekly*, November 26, 1993, p. 45) ¶"An uproarious confection whose strengths overshadow its shortcomings.... great mindless fun." (Marshall Fine, *News Journal* [Wilmington, DE], November 19-21, 1993, p. 7)

Analysis: Again, the story is a clunker. Because it is fragmented into scenes at summer camp, Fester's honeymoon, and the Addams manse, we don't get enough of any character, especially Gomez and Morticia, upon whose broad shoulders the movie should rest. The story of Fester's courtship by mankiller Debbie differs little from the first film (in which Abigail Craven used Fester to get at Addams

Family money). Not that there aren't a lot of laughs. There are certainly plenty of in-jokes, including a prescient barb directed at Michael Jackson, who got into hot water after this film was released. Christina Ricci makes Wednesday a commanding character.

Alice in Wonderland
(Unique Foto Film, 1931) nv

Directed by Bud Pollard.

Cast: Alice (Ruth Gilbert), Mad Hatter (Leslie T. King), White Rabbit (Ralph Hertz), Queen of Hearts (Vie Quinn), King of Hearts (N. R. Cregan), Knave of Hearts (Pat Glasgow), Duchess (Mabel Wright), Cook (Lillian Ardell), Cheshire Cat (Tom Corliss), March Hare (Meyer Beresen), Dormouse (Raymond Schultz), Gryphon (Charles Silvern), Mock Turtle (Gus Alexander), Caterpillar (Jimmy Rosen).

Review: "[Despite] poor photography and ... vocal recording, ... [it] possesses something of the charm Lewis Carroll gave to his memorable work...." (Mordaunt Hall, *New York Times*, December 28, 1931, p. 22)

Analysis: This is so obscure most cinema histories do not even list it. In fact, the only reference we found was the *New York Times* review, which indicates it was filmed in an old studio in Fort Lee, New Jersey. Apparently an effort was made to recapture the original illustrations by Sir John Tenniel; the *New York Times* reviewer commented that at times those illustrations seemed to have "staggered to life" on the screen.

Alice in Wonderland
(Paramount, 1933; 75 min.) ***

Produced by Louis D. Lighton. Directed by Norman Z. McLeod. Screenplay, Joseph L. Mankiewicz and William Cameron Menzies. Based on the novel by Lewis Carroll. Directors of Photography, Henry Sharp, Bert Glennon. Music, Dimitri Tiomkin.

Cast: Alice (Charlotte Henry), Humpty Dumpty (W. C. Fields), Mock Turtle (Cary Grant), White Knight (Gary Cooper), Red Queen (Edna May Oliver), Queen of Hearts (May Robson), Mad Hatter (Edward Everett Horton), Tweedledum (Jack Oakie), Uncle (Leon Errol), March Hare (Charles Ruggles),

White Queen (Louise Fazenda), Caterpillar (Ned Sparks), Duchess (Alison Skipworth).

Synopsis: During an outing, Alice falls asleep and finds herself following a large white rabbit. Falling down a shaft, she finds a bottle with "Drink Me" on a note. Sipping it, she grows tiny. With an "Eat Me" cookie she becomes huge. Seeing the White Rabbit again, she follows and meets a mouse and other animals in the forest. At the house of the White Rabbit, she drinks and grows huge, then smaller. Back in the forest, she meets the Caterpillar, who tells her eating one side of the mushroom will increase, the other decrease her size. She takes pieces. After dancing about with Tweedledum and Tweedledee, she encounters the Duchess, who receives an invitation to the Queen of Hearts's croquet tournament. Before Alice can get there she meets the Mad Hatter, March Hare and Dormouse. Leaving that madcap party, she takes a yellow door in a tree and finds herself once again in the hall where the small door is located. She eats the mushroom to shrink and enters the Queen of Hearts's kingdom. The Queen constantly wants to chop off peoples' heads. After the croquet match, Alice is taken to the Mock Turtle where she and he and the Gryphon engage in the Lobster Quadrille. At a trial of the Knave of Hearts, Alice begins growing. Just as the Queen shouts "Off with her head!" Alice wakes and returns home.

Review: "A marvel of camera magic and staging.... William Cameron Menzies never disappoints one.... [This version is] very welcome." (Mordaunt Hall, *New York Times,* December 23, 1933, p. 19)

Analysis: It's an all-star cast production and in that respect can be compared to this film's credit with 1972's *Alice's Adventures in Wonderland.* Ida Lupino was supposed to have played Alice, and in retrospect that might have been wise. Charlotte Henry is generally reckoned bland; the *New York Times* reviewer called her "attractive" but "limited."

Alice in Wonderland

(Souvaine, 1951; 83 min.) nv

Produced by Lou Bunin. Directed by Dallas Bower. Screenplay, Henry Myers, Albert Lewin, Edward Eliscu. Based on the story by Lewis Carroll. Ansco-Color.

Cast: Lewis Carroll (Stephan Murray), Alice (Carol Marsh), Queen Victoria (Pamela Brown), Dr. Liddel (Felix Aylmer), Vice Chancellor (Ernest Milton), Prince Consort (David Read), Tailor (Raymond Bussieres), Lorena (Elizabeth Henson), Edith (Joan Dale). Lou Bunin Puppets.

Review: "Motley visualization.... almost Tolstoyian in mood.... The sets are uncomfortably tasteless...." (Bosley Crowther, *New York Times,* July 27, 1951, p. 15)

Analysis: This U.K.-U.S.-French co-production featured puppets that the *New York Times* review called "ugly and lifeless." It was released the same year as Disney's animated version and eclipsed by that. Carol Marsh will surface in *Horror of Dracula.*

Alice's Adventures in Wonderland

(American National/Gold Key Entertainment, 1972; 96 min.) **

Produced by Derek Horne. Executive Producer, Josef Shaftel. Directed by William Sterling. Assistant Director, Bert Batt. Screenplay, William Sterling. Based on the novel by Lewis Carroll. Edited by Peter Weatherley. Director of Photography, Geoffrey Unsworth. Eastmancolor. Todd-AO. Music, John Barry. Lyrics, Don Black. Art Direction, Norman Dorme. Makeup, Stuart Freeborn. Special Effects, Ted Samuels, Doug Ferris, Roy Whybrow.

Cast: Alice (Fiona Fullerton), White Rabbit (Michael Crawford), Caterpillar (Ralph Richardson), Queen of Hearts (Flora Robson), March Hare (Peter Sellers), Mad Hatter (Robert Helpmann), Dormouse (Dudley Moore), Mock Turtle (Michael Hordern), Dodgson (Michael Jayston), Duckworth, (Hywell Bennett), Duchess (Peter Bull), King of Hearts (Dennis Price), Tweedledum and Tweedledee (Frank and Freddie Cox), Gryphon (Spike Milligan).

Review: "Proves Americans don't have a monopoly on making bad children's musicals. Waste of a good cast." (Leonard Maltin, ed., *Movie and Video Guide 1993,* p. 19)

Analysis: With this cast and these credits, one expects more than a slightly boring musical. The adventure is entered into rather too quickly. Apparently, it was never theatrically released in the U.S. Fiona Fullerton is a good Alice. Most of the famous performers are unrecognizable in their costumes. The musical score is by prolific film score composer John Barry, famous for *Zulu, Born Free,* and the James Bond movies. He provides a nice lilting theme.

Notes of Interest: Lewis Carroll's *Alice's Adventures in Wonderland* and *Through the Looking Glass* were published in 1865 and 1872, respectively. There was a 1921 silent film version. The most famous cinematic version is Walt Disney's 1951 animated film, whose success obscured the live-action international co-production that year.

Alice's Adventures in Wonderland *see under* **Alice in Wonderland**

Alien

(20th Century–Fox, 1979; 125 min.)****

Produced by Gordon Carroll, David Giler, and Walter Hill. Executive Producer, Ronald Shusett. Directed by Ridley Scott. Assistant Director, Paul Ibbetson. Screenplay, Dan O'Bannon. Edited by Terry Rawlings. Director of Photography, Derek Vanlint. Panavision. Eastmancolor. Music, Jerry Goldsmith. Art Directors, Les Dilley, Roger Christian. Design, Michael Seymour. Special Effects, Brian Johnson, Nick Alider, Carlo Rambaldi. Costumes, John Mollo. Alien Design, H. R. Giger.

Cast: Ripley (Sigourney Weaver), Dallas (Tom Skerritt), Ash (Iam Holm), Kane (John Hurt), Brett (Harry Dean Stanton), Parker (Yaphet Kotto), Lambert (Veronica Cartwright).

Synopsis: The mining ship USS *Nostromo* is returning to earth from deep space. The hibernating crew is awakened prematurely to investigate signals from a nearby planet, where they discover the huge wreck of some extraterrestrial spacefaring civilization. Inside the craft Kane is attacked by a parasite which attaches itself to his face. The crew cannot dislodge it because its "blood" is so acidic it burns through the bulkheads. Later, for no apparent reason, the crablike creature removes itself and dies. Kane seems fully himself until dinner

when a hideous snake-like creature erupts from his body and darts away into the bowels of the *Nostromo.* All efforts to destroy the ever-growing monster fail, and one by one the crew members become victims. To make matters worse, Ash, who disobeyed orders when he allowed the infected Kane back on board, has his own agenda. He attempts to kill Ripley, but with Parker's help is subdued, at which time they learn that he's a robot. Eventually only Ripley remains. With Jones the cat she programs the mother ship to self-destruct and enters the escape craft. Rocketing away from the explosion that destroys the *Nostromo,* Ripley finds that the alien, now more than man size, has hidden behind the consoles. Gingerly donning her space suit and helmet, she attracts the creature, then opens the hatch but it latches onto the port sides before it can be sucked out. Ripley shoots it with a dart and it falls away to hang by its tail. Ripley blasts it with the engines. She steps into a hibernating chamber. Perhaps a rescue ship will pick her up.

Reviews: "An extremely small, rather decent movie set inside a large, extremely fancy physical production.... executed with a good deal of no-nonsense verve. (Vincent Canby, *New York Times*, May 25, 1979, p. C16) ¶"My health had far more to fear from boredom than from heart failure." (*New Yorker*, June 11, 1979, p. 154) ¶"Quite unintentionally one aspect of the film is as disturbing as the most chilling tale of terror. I refer not to the alien but to the picture's conception of the human species. The characters of *Alien* range all the way from the insipid to the banal." (Harry M. Geduld, *Humanist*, September/October, 1979, p. 63)

Analysis: Ridley Scott's remarkable film details how a lone, courageous soul takes on an almost literal fiend from hell, goes through her own hell in doing so, and emerges victorious in the end. Although the film's lineage can be traced to *The Thing* (1951) and *It, The Terror from Beyond Space* (1959) as well as the fiction of A. E. Van Vogt (*The Voyage of the Space Beagle,* for instance), *Alien* seemed like a bolt from the blue when it appeared in 1979. It attracted a non–science fiction audience as well as inveterate horror and s-f fans. Virtually unknown, Sigourney Weaver was, like Genevieve Bujold in the previous year's *Coma*, an intelligent, strong, resourceful female protagonist. The grotesque scenes were much commented upon. The ad worked: "In space no one can hear you scream." On TV and in an interview with Dan O'Bannon, it was revealed that the cast had little idea of what to expect in the famous scene in which the alien spawn erupts from John Hurt's abdomen. O'Bannon: "The amount of blood was just unparalleled. I saw Veronica Cartwright get drenched from head to toe in blood and scream her fool head off and fall backwards over a table and brain herself." (Sunden, Ed, II, interview, "Dan O'Bannon on Alien," *Fantastic Films*, September 1979, p. 29)

Variety (May 23, 1979) cracked that the script had "more loose ends than the Pittsburgh Steelers," though the critic felt that the relentless, rollercoaster pacing more than compensated. Nevertheless, it is true that the story raises questions. Our feeling is that the Company knew something was up on that alien planet (the one it eventually sought to terraform) even before the *Nostromo* left earth for its ostensible mining mission, the tip-off being the last-minute substitution of the android Ash for the ship's first science officer. It wouldn't seem likely that the Company could secret an android on every deep space tug, just on the most far-flung assumption that the ship would intercept some message that would lead to an alien. *How* the Company could have this information is something that's never made terribly clear, but it seems plain from all three movies (abundantly plain in *Alien 3*) that the Company is doing a lot of furtive behind-the-scenes manipulating here. Whether the conspiracy to transport these alien creatures back to earth (a recurrent theme in all three films) is some sort of policy or the work of clandestine elements within the Company is just speculation, but we think a re-viewing of *Alien* indicates that someone at the top knew of this alien life-form and the fact that it had military value. Academy Award for visual effects. Nomination for art direction-set decoration. *Alien: Special Widescreen Collector's Edition* consists of three laser disks from Fox Video. Footage eliminated from the original film is included as well as behind-the-scenes material.

Aliens
(1986; 137 min.) ****

Produced by Gale Anne Hurd. Directed by James Cameron. Screenplay, James Cameron. Story, James Cameron, David Giler, and Walter Hill. Based on characters created by Dan O'Bannon, Ronald Shusett. Edited by Ray Lovejoy. Director of Photography, Adrian Biddle. Color, Eastman Kodak. Print, De-Luxe. Music, James Horner. Sound, Roy Charman. Dolby Stereo. Alien Effects, Stan Winston. Visual Effects, Robert Skotak, Dennis Skotak, Brian Johnson. Alien Design, H.R. Giger. Special Effects, John Richardson. Art Direction, Terence Ackland-Snow, Bert Davey, Fred Hole, Michael Lamont, Ken Court. Set Decoration, Crispian Sallis. Costumes, Emma Porteous.

Cast: Ripley (Sigourney Weaver), Corporal Hicks (Michael Biehn), Bishop (Lance Hendriksen), Burke (Paul Reiser), Newt (Carrie Hehn), Private Vasquez (Jenette Goldstein), Private Hudson (Bill Paxton), Lieutenant Gorman (William Hope), Sergeant Apone (Al Matthews), Private Drake (Mark Rolston), Private Frost (Ricco Ross), Corporal Ferro (Colette Hiller), Private Spunkmeyer (Daniel Kash), Corporal Dietrich (Cynthia Scott), Private Wierzbowski (Trevor Steedman), Private Crowe (Tip Tipping), ECA Rep (Valerie Colgan), Van Leuwen (Paul Maxwell), Insurance man (Alan Polonsky), Doctor (Blain Fairman), Alien warrior (Carl Toop), Med tech (Alibe Parsons), Cocooned woman (Barbara Coles), Power loader operator (John Lees).

Synopsis: Picked up by an earth ship after hibernating in the *Nostromo's* escape craft for a half-century, Ripley can't seem to convince her company that she blew up the *Nostromo* because of a deadly alien. She is shocked to learn that colonists have been terraforming the planet where her crew found the alien. Communication has been lost, so the sympathetic Burke convinces Ripley to accompany himself and a Marine squad to investigate. Only a child, Newt, is found initially mute but obviously an expert at hiding from something. Monitoring

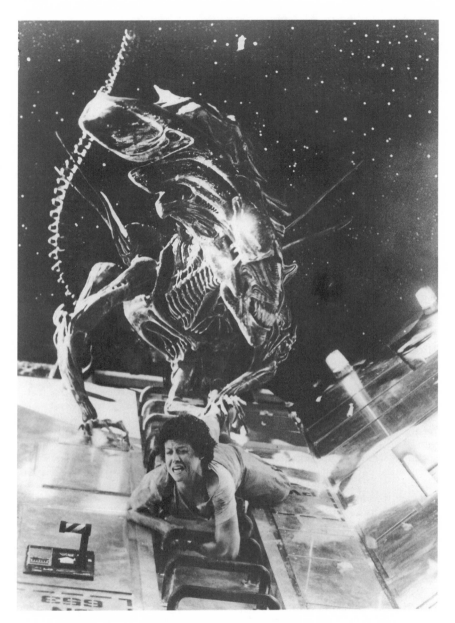

Ripley (Sigourney Weaver) battles the mother alien in *Aliens* (Twentieth Century–Fox, 1986).

devices indicate that there is life under the main building near the nuclear reactor. Descending level by level, the Marines find colonists encased in cocoons and impregnated with the second stage of the alien lifeform. Only Hicks, Vasquez, and Hudson make it back to the armored personnel carrier, of which Ripley has taken command. When the lieutenant is knocked unconscious, Corporal Hicks agrees with

Ripley that they should return to their main spacecraft and nuke the complex. Burke, concerned about dollars and the effect an alien could have on biowarfare, disagrees but is overridden. A landing craft is called to pick up Ripley and the others, but an alien enters and kills the crew, causing the craft to crash and explode. Without a means of leaving the planet, Ripley and the Marines retreat inside the colonists' buildings and decide how best to survive until relief arrives in approximately 17 days. But they won't have that long. As the android Bishop points out, the landing craft's explosion did severe damage to the nuclear plant. Venting indicates a general explosion will occur in four hours. Bishop volunteers to crawl through an air tunnel to a satellite dish he hopes to fix and bring down the second landing craft. While resting with Newt, Ripley awakes to find herself and the child locked in the lab, her weapon gone. The first stage of the alien is loose. Ripley sets off the fire alarm, and Hicks and Hudson arrive just in time. Burke is the responsible party; he planned to transport an alien back to earth through quarantine by having Ripley or Newt impregnated. Before Bishop can bring down the landing craft, the aliens attack, losing many to programmed corridor machine guns but entering the command center between the ceiling and upper floor. The humans make a fighting withdrawal into corridors familiar to Newt, but Hudson, Vasquez, the lieutenant and Burke are killed. Newt is captured by an alien. Ripley and Hicks rendezvous with Bishop. Ripley has the android guide the craft into the main complex. Via Newt's wristband monitor, Ripley tracks her into the depths of the building and frees her from a cocoon. There they encounter a queen alien laying eggs. Ripley torches the pods and flees, ignorant of the fact that the mother alien has broken free of its procreative sack. Only minutes are left until the entire complex will explode. The alien faces Ripley and Newt on the landing platform, but Bishop arrives to whisk them from the holocaust. On the main ship's deck, the trio note a drip mark beneath the landing craft. Bishop is impaled on the tail of the mother

alien, which had secreted itself under the craft. It rips him in two, Newt hides, and Ripley runs into a compartment, emerging armored in a forklift suit. She and the alien "bitch" fight to the death. The alien is sucked into space. Bishop's torso and head, still functioning, save Newt from a similar fate. Later, while putting the wounded Hicks and Bishop into hibernation, Ripley agrees that Newt can dream now.

Reviews: "Cameron restores conviction to a debased genre [action movie] ... by playing it straight." (David Ansen, *Newsweek*, July 21, 1986, p. 64) ¶"More mechanical than the first film — more addicted to 'advanced' weaponry and military hardware.... Weaver gives the movie a presence." (Pauline Kael, *The New Yorker*, August 11, 1986, p. 79)

Analysis: James Cameron pulled off an almost unthinkable feat with this film, fashioning a sequel superior to Ridley Scott's outstanding original. This is a great science fiction film full of compelling characters, impressive sets, great action, horrendous monsters. Some called *Alien* the fun house, *Aliens* the rollercoaster. In truth, the last half hour of this stands unequaled for edge-of-seat excitement. Great scene: the opening of Ripley's pod at the beginning. One can imagine the people who are about to enter wary of what they might find, and for all the audience knows those *entering* might not be human. Some impressive scenes are negated by typical TV presentation. Letterboxing would restore the majesty of Bishop's lone, vulnerable figure working outside on the satellite dish with the nuclear reactor venting in the background. There are a couple of negatives: the Marines seem too cocky, and a typical Hollywood ploy is introduced, to wit: the presence of a saboteur (Reiser). Why do we need this character in a film already incredibly exciting and tense? Reiser is the Donald Pleasence character of *Fantastic Voyage.*

Much blood was shed in these sagas, and numerous lives were lost. But withal, relationships emerge at the end of the second film that are remarkable, Ripley outmarining the marines and besting the demon-spawn in their labyrinth and the she-demon herself on the *Sulako*. In the process, we came to care about all those involved: Ripley, Newt, Hicks, Hudson, Vasquez, even the android Bishop, just as we cared about the ill-fated crew of the *Nostromo*. When Ripley, Newt and Hicks survived their ordeal, we cared, and it was special. Considering the nature of the relationship between Ripley and Newt, a relationship that's far more apparent in the "uncut" *Aliens*, to think that their coming together will last only briefly and end so tragically (and pointlessly) in *Alien 3* is a bitter pill.

As different as they are — just as different as the wildly divergent styles of Ridley Scott and James Cameron could make them — *Alien* and *Aliens* are both films whose superior qualities are evident throughout and from almost every angle. The ensemble acting in both is equally superior and memorable. Tom Skerritt's rather world-weary Captain Dallas, the laid-back banter of Parker and Brett (Yaphet Kotto and Harry Dean Stanton), the nervous wise-cracking of Lambert (Veronica Cartwright) — these were quite vivid characterizations in the Ridley Scott film (despite the fact that the dialogue generally didn't lend itself to vivid characterization). At least as much can be said for the character parts in *Aliens*: Bill Paxton is perfect for Hudson, the marine whose tendency to whine nicely offsets his wiseacre bravado. Likewise, Pvts. Vasquez and Drake come across as tough troops, she as macho as he, and each with a fancy for the other. Sgt. Apone is as tough a marine sergeant as any we can remember (in movies), and, of course, Cpl. Hicks is the logical choice for Ripley to identify with romantically. Winner of Academy Awards for Visual Effects and Sound Effects Editing.

While we feel many of the "expanded editions," "director's cuts," and other "special" versions of various films that have appeared in recent years to be of dubious value, the *Aliens* "special laser disk edition" that appeared in 1991 is a welcome addendum to an already fine film. Due to constraints imposed upon him by Twentieth Century–Fox to keep the film to as close to a two-hour running time as possible, director James Cameron ultimately delivered his theatrical cut at just over two-and-a-quarter hours, a time that satisfied the studio but left what the director felt to be much crucial material on the cutting-room floor. When the time came to put together a deluxe version of *Aliens* for laser disk, Cameron and producer Gale Anne Hurd were delighted to be able to restore the "lost" footage to its rightful place in the film.

The special edition laser disk runs about 17 minutes longer than the theatrical release of *Aliens*. Unlike the excised material that frequently makes its way back into a feature film when it is shown on television, the restored footage here actually accomplishes something: It fleshes out the character of Ripley and the family she lost during her 57-year hypersleep between *Alien* and *Aliens*. The discovery of the alien space craft by the colonists of LV246 is depicted, and we're introduced to Newt's doomed family. Most important, perhaps, is the depth that's added to the relationship between Ripley and Newt. This director's cut is truly a special edition in every sense of the term. Twentieth Century–Fox should make arrangements to distribute *this* version as widely as possible, namely on a tape format and without the deluxe packaging of the laser format.

Alien 3
(1992; 115 min.) **

Produced by Gordon Carroll, David Giler and Walter Hill. Co-producer, Sigourney Weaver. Directed by David Fincher. Screenplay, David Giler, Walter Hill and Larry Ferguson. Story, Vincent Ward. Based on characters created by Dan O'Bannon and Ronald Shusett. Edited by Terry Rawlings. Director of Photography, Alex Thomson. Panavision. Color, Rank Laboratories. Music, Elliot Goldenthal. Dolby Stereo. Art Direction, James Morahan. Set Decoration, Belinda Edwards. Visual Effects produced by Richard Edlund. Alien 3 Creature Design, H. R. Giger. Alien Effects designed and created by Alec Gillis and Tom Woodruff, Jr. Special Effects Supervision, George Gibbs.

Cast: Ripley (Sigourney Weaver), Dillon (Charles S. Dutton), Clemens (Charles Dance), Andrews (Brian Glover), Aaron (Ralph Brown), Bishop II (Lance Hendriksen), Golic

(Paul McGann), Morse (Danny Webb), Rains (Christopher John Fields), Junior (Holt McCallany), Murphy (Chris Fairbank), Frank (Carl Chase), Boggs (Leon Herbert), Corporal Hicks (Michael Biehn), Newt (Danielle Edmond).

Synopsis: Emergency monitors detect a life-threatening situation aboard the *Sulako*, the Space Marine vessel returning from LV426 with the survivors of the ill-fated expedition there. Ripley, Corporal Hicks and young Newt lie in suspended animation. Unknown to anyone, an alien "face-hugger" has managed to secrete itself aboard the *Sulako*. It causes an explosive malfunction that causes the hypersleep pod to be ejected. It crashes on Fiorina 161 "Fury"—a prison world that over time has become a toxic waste dump. Only two dozen inhabitants, convicts all, maintain the facility. The crashed pod is hauled out of the nearly frozen ocean. Both Hicks and Newt are dead. After recovering, Ripley strikes up a relationship with Dr. Clemens. She's bothered by the seemingly inexplicable malfunction aboard the *Sulako* and insists that autopsies be performed on the bodies of Hicks and Newt, afterward having their remains cremated. The face-hugger has meanwhile infected a dog, and a new alien creature bursts forth from the dog's chest cavity. The alien's first victim is a hapless inmate caught unawares as he scrubs down the interior of a ventilation tube. Ripley is not quite sure he was killed by fan blades, but her warnings meet with indifference and outright hostility from Golic, the establishment chief. Ripley, the only woman on the planet, is advised to remain quiet and out of sight until a rescue ship arrives. She nevertheless attempts to come to *some* kind of terms with Dillon, the chief inmate and the one to whom the others look for real leadership. Dillon will have nothing to do with her. Determined to resolve the mystery of the *Sulako*'s destruction, she looks through the compound's refuse for the remains of the discarded android Bishop. She is assaulted by one of the back-sliding "brothers," but rescued by Dillon. Locating the limbless torso of the android, Ripley jury-rigs its CPU and probes for answers. She learns of the alien that breached the hypersleep pods and

caused an electrical fire. Most appalling to Ripley is the discovery that the organism was of the queen alien, and that she herself might have been impregnated. More deaths occur, and the monster bursts in on Ripley and the doctor as they question an earlier near-victim. Clemens and the patient are dispatched, but Ripley is left unharmed, and the creature retreats into the ventilator. With no weapons, the inmates are panic-stricken. They cannot even track the alien. Ripley uses scanners in the escape pod and learns that she indeed is the host for an alien embryo. She seeks death at the talons of the adult, but it will not harm her. She makes a deal with Dillon: kill her in exchange for help killing the monster. They lure the creature into the huge lead-smelting kiln, but it springs from the lava-like mass. But Number 89, watching from a safe vantage point, throws a lever that triggers the fire-extinguishing system. When the frigid water hits the superheated alien, the beast explodes. The rescue ship arrives. Disembarking are two dozen or more armed men led by another, this one cloaked and apparently unarmed, his features obscured by a large visor. It's the human Bishop, there to procure the alien for the weapons-research division. Ripley slams a locked grate between herself and the newcomers. Although they want to remove the embryo and save her, she does not trust the Company, period. Backing up on the catwalk above the channel of molten ore, deaf to the desperate cries of Bishop, Ripley calmly steps backward into nothingness. Even as she falls toward immolation, the young alien bursts from her torso. Ripley clutches the writhing beast to her as both descend into the fire.

Reviews: "Maybe you've seen it before, but the scare potential is still there." (Jim Welsh, *Delaware Beachcomber*, July 3, 1992, p. 78) ¶"A dark, dank horror film that begs to be taken as a quasi-religious passion play.... doesn't know how to deliver the goods." (David Ansen, *Newsweek*, June 1, 1992, p. 73) ¶"Doesn't seem to have the skill to make even the simplest action sequences coherent, or the patience to give the audience the narrative information it needs." (Terrence Rafferty, *New Yorker*, June 1, 1992, p. 61)

Analysis: The overwhelming sense of gloom and defeat *Alien 3* generates is so pervasive that it threatens enjoyment of the first two films, and this is a wretched comment indeed. Perhaps the film's ambiance was affected by the atmosphere on the set, for *Alien 3* had a troubled production from the very beginning, as far back as its concept. It went through a number of writers and even more written versions before the final script was arrived at and shooting began. Renny Harlin (*Die Hard 2*) was among the directors considered for this third film in the *Alien* cycle, but ultimately it was the largely untried and unproven David Fincher who was luckless enough to be saddled with this project; prior to *Alien 3*, Fincher's major accomplishments had been in the field of music video (e.g. Madonna's "Vogue"). The result, according to Terrence Rafferty in the *New Yorker* (June 1, 1992, p. 61), was incoherent action sequences and an appalling lack of "narrative information." The decision to drop Ripley into an environment of criminals was made at the outset, according to the producers, who saw an opportunity here to exploit the same sort of thinking that had produced two previous hits. If "truck drivers in space" (*Alien*) had been a hit, and "soldiers in space" (*Aliens*) an even bigger one, then "convicts in space" would *have* to be a winner. It wasn't. *Alien 3*, despite two fabulously successful preceding films and a ready-made audience clamoring to see it, proved to be the biggest disappointment of the 1993 summer movie season. This vision of a hellishly derelict world is convincingly portrayed, the alien effects are about as well-done as ever, and the cast, heavily weighted in the British direction, is more than capable. For all his comparative youth and inexperience, David Fincher doesn't do a bad job of translating his troubled script to the screen, but his lack of seasoning does show in the film's final quarter, where there is much running about and much happening that is never really made clear. Ripley's death, an unhappy choice in any event, seems unnaturally rushed and abrupt. One source has it that the producers were not happy with the scene, but at that point

Sigourney Weaver had moved on to another project and refused to shave her head for any re-shoots. Reaction of both critics and the public was very nearly uniform: *Alien 3* was reckoned the best-made *bad* movie to come along in quite a while, outdoing even John Frankenheimer's 1982 flop, *Prophecy*. One could speculate endlessly as to just how *Alien 3* ever came to be made, as it's hardly conceivable that anyone involved in the project actually felt that it was going to be worthwhile. After all, film projects have been abandoned midway through before, and probably will again. With *Alien 3* it was probably a case of too much money being tied up in the project even before any film was exposed, which is the nature of movie-making these days.

For fans of the first two films, *Alien 3* is lost in the first few minutes with the deaths of Newt and Hicks. Presumably this was written into the script to give the film some heavy emotional impact early on. Instead, it is a major miscalculation that alienates (no pun intended) much of its audience from the beginning. The first two films are full of memorable, identifiable characters (despite claims to the contrary by some critics), and this is another area where *Alien 3* misses the boat; everybody here looks, acts and talks alike (even Ripley, after a bit). Despite the carnage in the Ridley Scott and James Cameron films, those works leave their viewers feeling exhilarated. *Alien 3* leaves one merely drained, disappointed and maybe as grimy as Ripley and her cohorts on Fury 161. It is, as the *Encyclopedia of Science Fiction* (John Clute and Peter Nicols, p. 19) puts it, "one of Hollywood's occasional, strange films so unmitigatedly uncommercial that it is impossible to work out why it was ever made."

Altered States *see under* **Dr. Jekyll and Mr. Hyde**

Always *see under* **A Guy Named Joe**

The Amazing Colossal Man
(AIP, 1957; 68 min.) **½

Produced and directed by Bert I. Gordon. Screenplay, Mark Hanna and Bert I. Gordon. Edited by Ronald Sinclair. Director of Photography, Joe Biroc. Music, Albert Glasser. Set Decoration, Glen Daniels. Sound, Chuck King. Special Effects, Bert I. Gordon. Special Props, Paul Blaisdell.

Cast: Colonel Glenn Manning (Glenn Langan), Carol Forrest (Cathy Downs), Dr. Paul Lindstrom (William Hudson), Colonel Hallock (James Seay), Dr. Eric Coulter (Larry Thor), Richard Klingman (Russ Bender), Typist (Diana Darrin), Sergeant Taylor (Lyn Osborn), Control officer (William Hughes), Briefing room lieutenant (Jack Kosslyn), Girl in bath (Jean Moorhead), Reception desk sergeant (Jimmy Cross), Henry (Hank Patterson), Delivery man (Frank Jenks), Army guard (Harry Raybould), Sergeant Lee Carter (Scott Peters), Captain Thomas (Myron Cook), Police Lieutenant Keller (Michael Harris), Lieutenant Peterson (Bill Cassady), Sergeant Hanson (Dick Nelson), Dr. McDermott (Edmund Cobb), Attendant (Paul Hahn), Robert Allen (Judd Holdren), Nurse (June Jocelyn), Lieutenant Kline (Stanley Lachman).

Synopsis: Near Desert Rock, Nevada, Colonel Glenn Manning is caught in a plutonium bomb explosion when he rushes out of his trench to rescue the pilot of a crashed civilian plane. He suffers third-degree burns over most of his body, and Dr. Paul Lindstrom gives him little hope for survival. But next day his skin has regenerated. Plutonium expert Klingman is quizzed. Manning's fiancee, Carol, tracks him to the U.S. Army Rehabilitation Research Center, where she finds he has become an eighteen-foot giant — and continues to grow! As he increases in size, a circus tent is brought in to house him. When he's shown the newspaper headline, "Man Lives Through Plutonium Blast," Manning responds, "That's a great joke, isn't it, Sergeant? They call this living." Dr. Lindstrom tells Carol that Manning's heart isn't increasing at the same rate as the rest of his body. Unless they find an antidote, "his mind will go first, and then his heart will literally explode." Manning runs away, and while the army searches for him, Dr. Coulter finds the secret of Manning's growth in the bone marrow. He proposes they inject him with sulpha-hydro compounds to stop the growth and stimulate the pituitary gland to reduce his size. It has worked with a camel and an elephant. Manning is spotted entering Las Vegas and cornered near Boulder Dam. Extracting the giant hypodermic needle Lindstrom and Coulter stab into his ankle, Manning impales Coulter and grabs Carol. After Manning is induced to put her down, troops open up with rifles and bazookas, and Manning falls into the roaring river.

Reviews: "The Army mows him down with bazookas. So, you see science couldn't do any more for the 'Amazing' man than it could for his 'Shrinking' predecessor." (Richard W. Nason, *New York Times*, October 26, 1957, p. 19) ¶"Imaginative story premise.... Glenn Langan delivers persuasively.... Technical departments are well handled." (Whit., *Variety*, September 4, 1957)

Analysis: Only two helicopters are used initially to search for the missing and top secret giant! Yeah, right. We guess it's no surprise that the science is generally faulty. Why would the giant's heart explode rather than merely fail? The fall from the dam is the least impressive special effect. For some reason, veteran Hollywood actor Glenn Langan is "Glen" in the credits.

War of the Colossal Beast
(AIP, 1958; 68 min.) **

Produced and directed by Bert I. Gordon. Screenplay, George Worthing Yates. Story, Bert I. Gordon. Edited by Ronald Sinclair. Director of Photography, Jack Marta. Music, Albert Glasser. Sound Effects Editor, Josef von Stroheim. Art Direction, Walter Keller. Set Decoration, Maury Hofman. Special Makeup, Jack H. Young. Special Effects, Bert I. Gordon. Assistant Technical Effects, Flora M. Gordon.

Cast: Joyce Manning (Sally Fraser), Colonel Glenn Manning (Dean Parkin), Major Baird (Roger Pace), Dr. Carmichael (Russ Bender), Captain Harris (Charles Stewart), John Swanson (George Becwar), Miguel (Robert Hernandez), Sergeant Luis Muillo (Rico Alaniz), Army officer (George Alexander), Mexican doctor (George Navarro), Neurologist (John McNamara), Pentagon correspondent

(Bob Garnet), Medical corps officer (Howard Wright), Mayor (Roy Gordon), Switchboard operator (Warren Frost), General Nelson (George Milan), Bus driver (Bill Giorgio), Joan (Loretta Nicholson), Mrs. Edwards (June Jocelyn), Newscaster (Jack Kosslyn), TV announcer (Stan Chambers).

Synopsis: When Colonel Glenn Manning's sister Joyce hears a news item about a missing truck in Mexico, she contacts the owner, Mr. Swanson, who's come north to collect insurance. She and Major Baird quiz him about any strange footprints in the area of the missing vehicle made by a man ten times his size! In Mexico, Joyce, Dr. Carmichael and Major Baird find a footprint. Perhaps the giant went into the mountains, says Sergeant Murillo. Joyce and the major find Manning, now scarred and missing an eye from his fall from Boulder Dam. He's been raiding trucks for food. They feed him drugged bread, and they fly the unconscious Manning to the States, but no government department wants responsibility for housing and feeding the giant. Nor does the public want him. Finally, the mayor of Los Angeles allows the plane to land. Manning is roped down in a airplane hangar but breaks free. Carmichael suggests anesthetic and when Manning is recaptured and chained, Carmichael tries to determine whether he has amnesia or brain tissue damage. "GIANT FAILS LAST CHANCE" reads a newspaper headline after the doctors fail to communicate with Manning. Before the army can isolate him on an uninhabited island, Manning breaks loose again with Carmichael killed during the escape. Manning is spotted in Griffith Park, where he raises a filled school bus above his head, until Joyce reasons with him. After putting the bus down, he calls her name, then electrocutes himself on high-tension lines.

Review: "Invention seems to have been exhausted." (Powe., *Variety*, August 20, 1958)

Analysis: This has several earmarks of below-average fifties science fiction. For one thing, people are not worried enough, and for another, the heroine wears a dress when trekking into the wilderness. The major carries neither canteen nor hardware. Everyone thinks they'll be back by nightfall in these films — and they're usually right. What also seems strange now is the military's difficulty getting permission to house the giant! Where are all the scientists who should be interested? This is a low budget ship with Bert Gordon at the helm, so the special effects are unsurprisingly average; one always knows the "giant" was filmed separately and mixed in with other shots. Paired with, somewhat appropriately, *Attack of the Puppet People.*

The Amityville Horror
(AIP, 1979; 126 min.) **½

Produced by Ronald Saland and Elliot Geisinger. Executive Producer, Samuel Z. Arkoff. Directed by Stuart Rosenberg. Screenplay, Sandor Stern. Based on the book by Jay Anson. Edited by Robert Brown. Director of Photography, Fred J. Koenekamp. Movielab Color. Music, Lalo Schifrin. Art Direction, Kim Swados.

Cast: George Lutz (James Brolin), Kathleen Lutz (Margot Kidder), Father Delaney (Rod Steiger), Father Bolen (Don Stroud), Father Ryan (Murray Hamilton), Father Nuncio (John Larch), Amy (Natasha Ryan), Greg (K. C. Martel), Matt (Meeno Peluce), Jeff (Michael Sacks), Carolyn (Helen Shaver), Jackie (Amy Wright), Sergeant Gionfriddo (Val Avery), Aunt Helena (Irene Dailey), Jimmy (Marc Vahanian), Mrs. Townsend (Elsa Raven), Bride (Ellen Saland), Agucci (Eddie Barth).

Synopsis: Without apparent motive, on November 13, 1974, in Amityville, Long Island, a son shoots to death his mother, father and four siblings. A year later George and Kathy Lutz move into the house with their children. "Houses don't have memories," George says when Kathy mentions the previous owners. A month later Father Delaney visits when the family is out. Inside, he senses a presence and a voice cries, "Get out!" He leaves; later, he phones the Lutz house and gets an electric shock. Kathy's Aunt Helena, a nun, has a similar experience. Strange things begin happening to the Lutz family. Kathy wakes screaming, her brother loses his money, there's black fluid in the toilet, the babysitter gets locked in the closet. Little Amy tells her mother that she has an invisible friend, Jody. Father Delaney, who with young priest Father

Bolen suffers a car wreck on the way to the Lutz house, fails to convince a panel that the Lutz family is in danger from satanic forces. On the Lutzes' eighth day in their new home, the front door breaks open. Police sergeant Gionfriddo, who investigated the killings at the house, is startled to find that George looks like someone in the deceased family. On the twelfth day Jeff's girlfriend, Carolyn, tells George about the house's history of devil worship. In the meantime, Kathy sees eyes looking in the window of Amy's room. Carolyn and Jeff accompany George home. In the basement, where the Lutz family dog, Harry, has been scratching, is the origin of the force, says Carolyn. Taking a pickax to the wall, George sees a visage that looks like him! Carolyn says the demons come and go through there and screams. Gionfriddo asks Father Bolen about Father Delaney, who's gone blind. Kathy checks microfilm of old newspapers and sees George's face. She races back to the house and sees George coming up from the boathouse. He sees a demonic face in the window. The house begins "bleeding," lightning strikes, the house shakes. When Kathy screams at the ax-wielding George, he recovers from his trance. The family piles into their van, but Harry has been left behind. When George returns, he falls through the basement stairs into a pit of black goo, but with Harry's help, he escapes. An end title tells us that the Lutzes move to another state, never returning to the house or reclaiming their belongings.

Reviews: "Inflates gullibility into horror with cheap tricks." (Veronica Geng, *New Yorker*, August 13, 1979, pp. 97–98) ¶ "The movie's creators should either have stuck to the facts, ma'am, or they should have invented something to scare the pants off us. As it is, they have managed merely to bore them off." (R. S., *Time*, September 17, 1979, p. 102)

Analysis: This is a strange hybrid, a mix of large and small scale. On the one hand it has major film composer Lalo Schifrin, on the other producer Samuel Z. Arkoff, more often associated with low-budget AIP. It's an *Exorcist* clone with Val Avery playing Lee J. Cobb, Rod Steiger as Max Von Sydow, and James Brolin/Don Stroud as Jason Miller. *Time* complained of Brolin's "eye-rolling" and called Rod Steiger's performance "overripe." The nun's vomiting scene is ludicrous. In *Danse Macabre*, Stephen King hits the nail on the head: *The Amityville Horror* is about the horror of impending financial ruination, caused in this case by a possessed dwelling.

Amityville II: The Possession
(Orion, 1982; 104 min.) ★★

Produced by Ira N. Smith and Stephen R. Greenwald. Directed by Damiano Damiani. Screenplay, Tommy Lee Wallace. Based on the book *Murder in Amityville* by Hans Holzer. Edited by Sam O'Steen. Director of Photography, Franco DiGiacomo. Technicolor. Music, Lalo Schifrin. Art Direction, Ray Recht. Set Decoration, George Detitta, Jr. Costumes, Bill Kellard. Special Makeup, John Caglione, Jr.

Cast: Father Frank Adamsky (James Olson), Anthony Montelli (Burt Young), Delores Montelli (Rutanya Alda), Sonny (Jack Magner), Patricia (Diane Franklin), Father Tom (Andrew Prine), Chancellor (Leonardo Cimino), Mark (Brent Katz), Jan (Erica Katz), Mrs. Greer (Petra Lea), Attorney (Ted Ross), Movers (Danny Aiello III, Gilbert Stafford), Police chief (John Ring), Cab driver (Peter Radon), Detective Turner (Moses Gunn), Demons' voices (Anita Keal, Sondra Lee, Alice Playten).

Synopsis: Anthony and Delores Montelli move into their new house with their teenage son and daughter, Sonny and Patricia, and their younger children, Mark and Jan. Investigating a hidden room off the basement, a moving man finds flies and gunk falling from the ceiling. Delores feels a presence. At dinner the large mirror falls over. That night there is a loud knocking at the door, but no one is there. Jan and Mark watch a brush paint a hideous figure on their wall. Anthony takes his belt to the children and slugs Delores. The fight stops when Sonny points a rifle at his father. Next day Delores asks Father Adamsky to bless their house, but when he arrives the kitchen cupboards disgorge their contents. Anthony thinks Jan did it and strikes her. Leaving, Adamsky finds a shredded Bible in his car. While Delores and Anthony go to apologize, Sonny stays behind, hears things and enters the basement room with a rifle. He thinks he sees an arm in the wall. Upstairs, he hears laughing, and the rifle is taken out of his hand. An unseen presence forces him into the bed. When the family returns, Sonny goes to Pat's room and seduces her. She makes a partial confession to Father Adamsky. He returns to the house to bless it, but in so doing his holy water turns to blood or does it? He consults with the monsignor about an exorcism. During his birthday party, Sonny hears a voice telling him to kill his pathetic family. That night Sonny shoots them all. Later, Sonny tells Adamsky he doesn't remember anything. "Who is inside you?" Adamsky asks. At the family funeral, Adamsky tells Father Tom he feels responsible for the murders. He is turned down by Detective Turner when he suggests he be allowed to take Sonny to church. Visiting the Montelli house, Adamsky sees Patricia in the doorway. A librarian shows him old records about a woman expelled from Salem for witchcraft and the desecration of an Indian burial ground where the Montelli house is located. Adamsky gets a phone call — from Patricia. At Sonny's trial the judge won't accept the defense plea of possession. After Adamsky and Turner see "SAVE ME" imprinted on Sonny's arm, Turner helps the priest take Sonny away. Sonny escapes from Adamsky and returns to his house. Adamsky follows and in the basement sees strange man-like creatures leaving the secret room. Taking the form of Patricia, Sonny accuses Adamsky of desiring her. Adamsky asks God to save the boy and let him be taken by the spirit. As is evidenced by his gnarled hand, the wish is granted.

Review: "Manages even to make sensation, blood, sex and suspense become a monotonous way of life." (Richard F. Shepard, *New York Times,* September 24, 1982, p. C20)

Analysis: If you fail to notice during the credits the title of the book upon which this is based, you nevertheless will recognize that this is a prequel one-half hour after it starts. It explains why the house was possessed when James Brolin and Margot Kidder moved in. The *New York* *Times* review called some of the acting "reasonably competent," but the characters are problematic. Burt Young builds on his role in *Rocky* (1976) to become an incredibly irritating character. Until the conclusion, James Olson's priest is rather stiff and unbelievable. He won't answer the phone because he's got to go on vacation with fellow clergyman Prine? Speaking of farfetched, would a detective tell a priest to knock him out with the butt of his pistol? Would a priest do it? Would a detective permit a clergyman to take a mass murderer from the jail? Some of the roaming around the house gets boring. There are obvious *Exorcist* parallels. Filmed in New Jersey and Mexico.

Amityville 3-D
(Orion, 1983; 105 min.) *½

Produced by Stephen F. Kesten. Directed by Richard Fleischer. Assistant Director, Joe Reidy. Screenplay, William Wales. Edited by Frank J. Urioste. Director of Photography, Fred Schuler. ArriVision 3-D. 3-D Coordinator, Tibor Sands. Color. Music, Howard Blake. Art Direction, Giorgio Postiglione. Set Decoration, Justin Scoppa. Makeup Illusions, John Caglione, Jr. Costumes, Clifford Capone.

Cast: John Baxter (Tony Roberts), Nancy Baxter (Tess Harper), Dr. Elliott West (Robert Joy), Melanie (Candy Clark), Susan (Lori Loughlin), Lisa (Meg Ryan), Harold Caswell (John Beal), Emma Caswell (Leora Dana), Clifford Sanders (John Harkins), Jeff (Neill Barry), Roger (Pete Kowanko), Elliot's Assistant (Rikke Borge), David (Carlos Romano), Dolores (Josephina Echanove), Van driver (Jorge Zepeda), Sensory woman (Raquel Pankowsky), Maintenance man (Paco Pharres).

Synopsis: After exposing shyster psychics in the "haunted" Amityville house, *Reveal* magazine writer John Baxter decides to buy the dwelling in order to have a quiet place to work. He's separating from his wife, Nancy. The realtor dies, apparently of a stroke, but he'd been attacked by a horde of flies in the attic before John found him. When Melanie, John's partner at *Reveal,* develops photos of the realtor, she finds his face distorted. Later, while waiting in the house for John, she becomes hysterical and next day tells John she'll never return. She never does after discovering a horrible little face on a photo, jumps in the car, loses control and crashes. Her briefcase catches on fire and so does she. Later, John's daughter Susan agrees to have a seance with friend Lisa and two boys. During the seance, Susan is told she's in danger. She drowns when the foursome take a boat out on the river. But her mother, Nancy, swears she saw Susan in the house and keeps vigil while Dr. West and his team set up their equipment to find if there really is a psychic presence. Susan's voice and an apparition guide Nancy to a basement well. Dr. West is pulled in by a monster. John and Nancy and the other investigators escape as the house self-destructs. Another being escaping is a flying "bug" whose face Melanie had seen in a photograph.

Review: "The cast is good, but the characters are idiots." (Janet Maslin, *New York Times*, November 20, 1983, p. 68)

Analysis: There's nothing new here, and there's no real underlying rationale for the goings-on. What's that darned flying bug, anyway? How come her father or friends didn't try any CPR on the drowned Susan while waiting for the paramedics? Compare the psychic investigations here with *Poltergeist*. Is this plot really suitable for 3-D? (The *New York Times*'s Maslin called 3-D "the stuff of which headaches are made.") Check out the secondary cast, which includes future leading lady Meg Ryan and TV sitcom star Lori Loughlin. John Beal was *The Vampire* in 1957. It's another odd film for veteran director Richard Fleischer, who'd helmed *The Narrow Margin*, *20,000 Leagues Under the Sea*, and *The Vikings*.

Amityville 92: It's About Time
(Republic, 1992; 95 min.) **

Produced by Christopher DeFaria. Directed by Tony Randel. Screenplay, Christopher DeFaria and Antonio Toro. Inspired by the book *Amityville: The Evil Escapes* by John G. Jones. Edited by Rick Finney. Director of Photography, Christopher Taylor. Color. Music, Daniel Licht. Set Decoration, Natalie Pope. Special Makeup Effects, Kurtzman, Nicotero, Berger EFX Group. Visual Effects, VCE, Inc./Peter Kuran.

Cast: Jacob (Stephen Macht), Andrea (Shawn Weatherly), Rusty (Damon Martin), Lisa (Megan Ward), Iris Wheeler (Nita Talbot), Leonard (Jonathan Penner), Mr. Anderson (Dick Miller).

Synopsis: Jacob returns to Burlwood Estates from a business trip with an antique clock from a development his company demolished. During the night the clock drills into the mantel. Teenage son Rusty flips a light switch in the hall outside the room and sees another room. He relates this to neighbor Iris Wheeler. Having passed the house the night before, she knows something's afoot and tells Rusty the house is trying to communicate with him. While jogging, Jacob is attacked by the German shepherd Peaches. Housesitter and sometime lover Andrea agrees to stay a few more days to change his bandages. She is surprised to find that Peaches, whom Jacob said he injured with a glass bottle, is not marked and her owner is ignorant of the attack. Thick black goo appears in Andrea's bed and filters into the bathtub where Andrea's teacher/psychiatrist Leonard is relaxing. In the kitchen, he is shocked when Jacob appears out of nowhere and threatens him with a gun for sleeping with Andrea. The normally demure Lisa becomes a tease and lures her boyfriend to the garage, where he is sucked into the goo. Rusty consults with Iris, and they find two books containing pictures of rooms with the clock that's now in Rusty's home. Rusty recalls that the clock came from Amityville on Long Island. Iris says the evil is trying to find a new home, but before she can do more she is impaled by the stork on a diaper delivery truck. Rusty eventually convinces Andrea that they must leave the house, but the possessed Jacob hangs Leonard and tries to kill Andrea. Andrea fights Jacob off, then faints; when she awakes, she relives Jacob's homecoming. She smashes the clock and leaves the stunned household.

Review: "Halfway decent horror film with high-grade special effects, and much, much better than previous Amityville sequels, which isn't saying much." (*Video Hound's Golden Movie Retriever 1994*, p. 102)

Analysis: This presumably made-for-video film is entirely watchable, and we

relish the skeptical psychiatrist's consternation when *he* is under the evil gun. Note
Dick Miller in a small role. Nita Talbot was
a familiar female sidekick in '60s comedies.
Shawn Weatherly was Miss Universe 1980.

Amityville: A New Generation
(Republic, 1993; 92 min.) *½

Produced by Christopher Defaria. Directed
by John Murlowski. Screenplay, Christopher
Defaria and Antonio Toro. Inspired by the
book *Amityville: the Evil Escapes* by John G.
Jones. Edited by Rick Finney. Director of
Photography, Wally Pfister. Color, CFI. Music,
Daniel Licht. Art Direction, Kurt Meisen-
bach. Set Decoration, Michael Stone. Special
Visual Effects, Cruse and Company.

Cast: Keyes Terry (Ross Partridge), Suki
(Julia Nickson-Soul), Dick Cutler (David
Naughton), Detective Clark (Terry O'Quinn),
Franklin Bronner (Jack R. Orend), Pauli
(Richard Roundtree), Jane (Barbara Howard).
With Lala Sloatman.

Synopsis: A derelict gives photographer
Keyes Terry a weirdly framed mirror, and
strange things start happening in the
building Terry shares with artist Suki and
landlord Dick Cutler. Suki's ex-boyfriend
sees the mirror and is killed after stumbling into a window. After painting demons and seeing a fleeting green apparition, Suki is found hanged. Keyes has bad
dreams and eventually learns that the now-
dead derelict was his father, Franklin Bronner. Worse, as detective and psychopa-
thology unit member Clark explains, years
before Bronner had killed his whole family in Amityville, New York. The night of
a house art show, Dick is killed by Suki's
spirit, but Keyes breaks the spell by blasting the mirror.

Review: "And the bad sequels just go on
and on and on." (*Video Hound's Golden
Movie Retriever 1994*, p. 146)

Analysis: It's confusing and boring. Lala
Sloatman should get second billing, but we
couldn't tell what her name was and the
credits were too small to read. Baldpated
here, Richard Roundtree could pass for
Lou Gossett.

Notes of Interest: The novel *The Amityville Horror* was a bestseller. *Amityville 4:
The Evil Escapes* was a 1989 TV movie starring Patty Duke. *The Amityville Curse*

(1990) was not theatrically released and is
hard to find on video. *Amityville: A New
Generation* was a video release scheduled
for 1994. Compare this series to the *Poltergeist* trilogy.

Angels in the Outfield
(MGM, 1951; 99 min.)***

Produced and directed by Clarence Brown.
Screenplay, Dorothy Kingsley and George
Wells. Based on a story by Richard Conlin.
Edited by Robert J. Kern. Director of Photo-
graphy, Paul C. Vogel. Music, Daniele Amfi-
theatrof.

Cast: Guffy McGovern (Paul Douglas),
Jennifer Paige (Janet Leigh), Fred Bayles
(Keenan Wynn), Bridget White (Donna Cor-
coran), Arnold P. Hapgood (Lewis Stone),
Saul Hellman (Bruce Bennett), Sister Ed-
witha (Spring Byington), Timothy Durney
(Marvin Kaplan), Sister Veronica (Ellen
Corby), Dave Rothberg (Jeff Richards), Mc-
Gee (King Donovan), Reynolds (John Gal-
laudet), Rube Ronson (Don Haggerty), Tony
Minelli (Paul Salata), "Chunk" (Fred Gra-
ham), Bill Baxter (John McKee), Patrick J.
Finley (Patrick J. Molyneaux). With Bing
Crosby, Joe DiMaggio, Ty Cobb, Harry Ruby.

Synopsis: While searching for a lost
lucky piece in the Forbes Field infield,
Pittsburgh Pirates coach Guffy McGovern
encounters an angel. A deal is made: in exchange for a cessation of blasphemy and
mean-spiritedness by Guffy, his baseball
team will start to win games. That would
be a novelty for the cellar-dwelling club.
When the team goes on a winning streak,
orphan Bridget White says she sees an
angel behind each player. Jennifer Paige,
the newspaper's household hints reporter,
hears of this, and before long it's a feature
story. However, the press and at least one
radio announcer think Guffy is crazy. Guffy
keeps up his side of the bargain nevthe-
less, and the team continues its winning
ways. Even the terminally ill pitcher Saul
Hellman summons up enough of his failing strength to save the season.

Review: "A heart-warming and edifying
amalgam which can pass the test of what is
traditionally termed entertainment." (A. H.
Weiler, *New York Times*, October 18, 1951,
p. 32)

Analysis: So infrequently televised, we

found hardly anyone knew the 1994 film was a remake. It's cute and offers Paul Douglas yet another role suited to his bluff, blustering and essentially kind-hearted persona.

Angels in the Outfield
(Walt Disney Pictures, 1994; 105 min.) **½

Produced by Irby Smith, Joe Roth, Roger Birnbaum. Directed by William Dear. Screenplay, Dorothy Kingsley, George Wells, Holly Goldberg Sloan. Based on the 1951 film of the same name. Edited by Bruce Green. Director of Photography, Matthew F. Leonetti. Technicolor. Music, Randy Edelman. Visual Effects Supervisor, Giedra Rackaukas.

Cast: George Knox (Danny Glover), Roger (Joseph Gordon-Levitt), Al the Angel (Christopher Lloyd), Mel Clark (Tony Danza), Maggie Nelson (Brenda Fricker), Hank Murphy (Ben Johnson), Ranch Wilder (Jay O. Sanders), J. P. (Milton Davis, Jr.), David Montagne (Taylor Negron), Triscuitt Messmer (Tony Longo), Kesey (Carney Lansford), Angels Player Mapel (O.B. Babbs), Angels Player Abascal (Mitchell Page), Angels Player Norton (Mark Cole).

Synopsis: Left in a foster home by his biker father, young Roger forms a friendship with another boy, J. P., and they attend California Angels baseball games. One day Roger encounters angels and tells the team's coach, George Knox. The angels are helping the last-place team win. Roger says that he will wave his arms to show when the angels are present. Knox begins to believe in the angels, but a press conference is called for him to put the story to rest. But his teams sticks up for him. The playoffs begin. The Angels' main pitcher, Mel Clark, is terminally ill, and an angel tells Roger. At the last game the angels are nowhere to be found, so George and Roger pretend they are, flapping their arms to get the crowd to do likewise and give Mel and the team confidence. Mel summons up all his strength and gumption and with his team's help, wins the game. Afterward, the boys' foster mother, Maggie, tells them Roger is to be adopted, which causes J. P. grief until he learns that both are being adopted by George. Al flies by the window.

Review: "An unaccountable remake of the less-than-classic 1951 film of the same title, faithful right down to its dreary pace and ham-handed style." (Ralph Novak, *People,* July 25, 1994, p. 18)

Analysis: Children like it, as do some adults. Others, like us, who've seen perhaps too many movies, find it derivative and slightly boring.

The Armageddon *see* **Warlock: The Armageddon** *under* **Warlock**

Army of Darkness *see under* **The Evil Dead**

Attack of the Killer Tomatoes
(N.A.I. Entertainment/Four Square, 1978; 87 min.) *½

Produced by Steve Peace and John De Bello. Directed by John De Bello. Screenplay, Costa Dillon, Steve Peace and John De Bello. Edited by John De Bello. Director of Photography, John K. Culley. Music, Gordon Goodwin and Paul Sundfor.

Cast: Mason Dixon (David Miller), Jim Richardson (George Wilson), Louise Fairchild (Sharon Taylor), Agriculture official (Jack Riley), Wilbur Finletter (Rock Peace), Senator Polk (Eric Christmas), Janitor (John De Bello), Housewife (Cindy Charles), President (Ernie Myers), Singing soldier (Tom Coleman).

Synopsis: When tomatoes leave their patches and gardens to kill humans, the president authorizes an investigation, which he hopes can be conducted without frightening the populace. Special investigator Mason Dixon is put in charge. Louise Fairchild tracks him, hoping to get a newspaper scoop. Some tomatoes grow very large. Several states, including Arkansas, are lost to the fruit before Dixon discovers that they can be stopped and shrunken by playing a Donny Osmond record. Saving Louise from a giant tomato wearing earmuffs by showing it the printed song lyrics, Mason and Louise realize they are meant for each other. At fadeout a carrot rises from the garden. A new invasion?

Review: "If this item can make it to the

screen, the exhibitors must be more desperate than anyone supposes." (*Variety*, January 31, 1979)

Analysis: While primitive, it is not entirely insufferable. Accidentally but fortuitously, the funny scenes are spaced well. Howls can be elicited by the meeting room that's so small the brass, scientists and investigators must crawl over the table to their folding chairs. The soldiers carry M1s, not M16s. Did the producers not have the cooperation of the modern military?

Return of the Killer Tomatoes
(Four Square Productions/ New World, 1988; 99 min.)*½

Produced by J. Stephen Peace. Directed by John De Bello. Screenplay, Constantine Dillon, J. Stephen Peace, John De Bello. Director of Photography, Stephen Kent Welch. Color, Foto-Kem. Edited by Stephen F. Andrich, John De Bello. Music, Rick Patterson, Neal Fox. Art Director, Roger Ambrose. Set Decorator, Melinda Ritz.

Cast: Chad Finletter (Anthony Starke), Tara (Karen Mistal), Matt (George Clooney), Professor Gangreen (John Astin), Igor (Steve Lundquist), Charlie Jones (Charlie Jones), Wilbur Finletter ("Rock" Peace), Sam Smith (Frank Davis) Greg (Ian Hutton), Girl in Matt's bed (Teri Weigel), Jim Richardson (Rick Rockwell).

Synopsis: After the great tomato war, Professor Gangreen turns tomatoes into Rambo-like men in his home lab with the assistance of his young lover and housekeeper, Tara. Wilbur Finletter recalls the conflict and how the song "Puberty Love" saved the day. Tara saves a mutant tomato she calls "FT" (fuzzy tomato). She approaches Chad and offers sex — or cleaning. She says she ran away and came to him because he was the only person she knows. First he stops at the prison to speak with Richardson. While shopping, Chad and Tara see a smuggler trying to sell the now illegal tomato to a store owner. While Chad is out of the dining room during dinner, a violinist plays, and Tara briefly turns into a tomato. Next day, FT falls out of the window and rolls down the street. People try to kill it, but Tara comes to the rescue. Chad realizes the garbage truck driven by Igor is tailing them and follows it to a hazardous

waste site; there Igor obtains a container of toxic liquid, which he takes to Professor Gangreen. Back at his apartment, Chad finds Tara eating plant food spikes. Running off, she is kidnapped by Igor. Finally Chad realizes he should return to Gangreen's. Matt accompanies him. Overcome by the professor and Igor, the two are locked in a room with Tara. Slipping FT a note, they inform Uncle Wilbur of their predicament. Gangreen, Igor and Tara head for the prison while Finletter and his men rescue Chad and Matt. At the prison, Gangreen gases Tara even as FT jumps on a grenade. But Tara survives because she's not human. Yet the gas has made her human. And FT has survived. At the heroes' welcome, FT replicas are sold to children. Chad and Tara drive off. Matt, meanwhile, has created his own beautiful blonde from a Gangreen tomato. Armed, man-size carrots appear.

Review: "An improvement, but still nothing much.... Too long, too silly, but has its moments." (Leonard Maltin, *Movie and Video Guide 1993*, p. 1025)

Analysis: It's more professional though more senseless than the first, with some "names," like John Astin. Starke would play the young priest in *Repossessed*. Cute Karen Mistal is a treat for the eyes. There are occasional, more or less irritating, digressions where we see and hear the film crew. Nevertheless, some yucks are provided by the "product placement" episodes, e.g., the Kellogg's Corn Flakes box a hand puts on the table between Starke and Clooney. George Clooney has good comic timing. The briefly seen Teri Weigel went on to become a porn star.

Killer Tomatoes Strike Back!
(Four Square/20th Century–Fox, 1990; 87 min.) **

Produced by J. Stephen Peace, John De Bello. Directed by John De Bello. Screenplay, Constantine Dillon, Rick Rockwell, John De Bello. Edited by Beth Accomando. Director of Photography, Stephen F. Andrich. Ultra-Vision. Color, Foto-Kem Laboratories. Music, Rick Patterson and Neal Fox. Art Direction, Jonathan A. Carlson. Killer Tomato Puppets designed and created by Andrew R. Jones.

Cast: Detective Lt. Lance Boyle (Rick Rockwell), Dr. Kennedy Johnson (Crystal Carson), Igor (Steve Lundquist), Evan Rood (John Witherspoon), Professor Gangreen (John Astin), Bank teller (Kevin West), Captain Wilbur Finletter (Rock Peace), Charlie Jones (Charlie Jones), Charles White (John De Bello).

Synopsis: A hockey-masked maniac chasing a woman is surprised by tomatoes wearing hockey masks. Detective Boyle investigates as does the pretty tomatologist Dr. Johnson. Her lab is attacked by tomatoes she wards off and freezes with a fire extinguisher. "Jeronahew," the latest "lord of tabloid television," is in fact Dr. Gangreen, who is concocting a grand scheme with the help of longtime assistant Igor. Detective Captain Finletter, Dr. Johnson and Fuzzy Tomato come on his show. Jeronahew claims there are no *killer* tomatoes while in secret using them to rob and terrorize. Dr. Johnson survives a shower attack. During Media Appreciation Day, members of the TV medium are kidnapped by Igor and tomatoes. After leaving Johnson's lab, Boyle is warned by tomatoes to stay away from Johnson's lab. He thinks Fuzzy Tomato is behind it and follows Johnson and FT to the San Diego Zoo, where the tomato performs at the outdoor marine exhibit. That night, Gangreen sends two tomatoes to kill Johnson, but Boyle hears her screams, breaks in, and beats them off her chest with a golf club. Gangreen kidnaps a bank teller and Rood, Boyle's buddy. Boyle and Johnson go to the Slip Inn, where Captain Finletter said Boyle might get some information on tomatoes. In fact, only rough-looking tomatoes frequent the joint. Learning that Finletter sent them, the bartender directs them to a booth where Johnson translates what the tomato is saying: "Follow the stars." Finally they see such a sign on a bus. They enroll in Camp Broadcasting School, where FT is already snooping around. They find Rood in the brainwashing room, but Boyle and Johnson are attacked and the latter dragged off. Jeronahew's next program is about hostages, and the bound and gagged Johnson is one of the guests. Boyle tracks her to Gangreen's lair, where she is placed on a giant sandwich for the killer

tomatoes' delectation. By keeping Gangreen talking about using TV to control the world, Johnson and Boyle enrage the tomatoes and manage an escape. They interrupt the Jeronahew show and warn the world. The jig being up, Gangreen admits his goals but falls on fertilizer, and the tomatoes inundate him.

Review: "Beyond corny, this reduces the original vicious tomato spoof to an all-time low." (Mick Martin and Marsha Porter, *Video Movie Guide 1994*, p. 301)

Analysis: Similar to a *Naked Gun* movie, it makes telling jabs at television (Astin: "The power of really bad television. It's universal.") and pays tribute to or parodies movies like *Psycho* and *Friday the 13th*. Perhaps the funniest scene is when Rockwell breaks open the ketchup case and the bottle won't disgorge its contents because it's the good brand. Aka *Attack of the Killer Tomatoes 3*. Coming: *Killer Tomatoes Eat France*.

Babes in Toyland
(MGM, 1934; 77 min.) ***

Produced by Hal Roach. Directed by Gus Meins and Charles Rogers. Screenplay, Nick Grinde and Frank Butler. Original book, Glen MacDonough. Director of Photography, Art Lloyd and Francis Corby. Music, Victor Herbert.

Cast: Oliver Dee (Oliver Hardy), Stanley Dum (Stan Laurel), Bo-Peep (Charlotte Henry), Silas Barnaby (Henry Kleinbach, later Brandon), Tom-Tom Piper (Felix Knight), Widow Peep (Florence Roberts), Toymaker (William Burress), Santa Claus (Ferdinand Munier). With Johnny Downs, Marie Wilson.

Synopsis: Silas Barnaby holds the mortgage to the Widow Peep's home in Toyland. He will release her from her financial obligation if her daughter Bo-Peep marries him. To save her mother from destitution, Bo-Peep agrees. However, on the wedding day the veiled bride turns out to be Stanley Dum, and Oliver Dee has torn up the mortgage. Barnaby vows revenge. He steals Little Elmer Pig and incriminates Bo-Peep's boyfriend, Tom-Tom Piper. Tom-Tom is relegated to Bogie Land, and Bo-Peep follows him there. Stanley and

Oliver find the missing Elmer Pig, and Barnaby flees. In Bogie Land he fights with Tom-Tom, then summons the half-man, half-animal bogies. They pursue Tom-Tom, Bo-Peep, Stanley and Oliver back to Toyland. Although they were poor toymakers, Stanley and Oliver prove their worth now by batting darts into the bogies' hides and releasing 100 six-foot-tall wooden soldiers. The bogies and Barnaby are routed.

Review: "An authentic children's entertainment and quite the merriest of its kind...." (Andre Sennwald, *New York Times*, December 13, 1934, p. 28)

Analysis: For the most part, Laurel and Hardy's feature-length sound films are reckoned inferior to their silents and shorts. This is an exception: a fast-moving, enjoyable fairy-tale fantasy. Warning: the hideous bogies may be too much for younger children. As impressive as Henry Kleinbach is as Barnaby, it would be years before the German-born actor impinged on audiences in like fashion. In the 1950s, now as Henry Brandon, he was a great portrayer of formidable American Indians, notably Chief Scar in John Ford's *The Searchers*. There is some animation. It's been colorized. Aka *March of the Wooden Soldiers*.

Babes in Toyland
(Buena Vista, 1961; 105 min.) **

Produced by Walt Disney. Directed by Jack Donohue. Screenplay, Joe Rinaldi, Ward Kimball, Lowell S. Hawley. Based on the operetta by Victor Herbert and Glen MacDonough. Original Score, Victor Herbert. Lyrics, Mel Leven. Music adapted by George Bruns. Choreography, Tom Mahoney. Director of Photography, Edward Colman. Technicolor. Art Direction, Carroll Clark, Marvin Aubrey Davis. Set Decoration, Emile Kuri, Hal Gausman. Costumes, Bill Thomas. Special Effects, Eustace Lycett, Robert A. Mattey, Bill Justice, Xavier Atencio, Yale Gracey.

Cast: Mary Contrary (Annette Funicello), Tom Piper (Tommy Sands), Barnaby (Ray Bolger), Toymaker (Ed Wynn), Gonzorgo (Henry Calvin), Roderigo (Gene Sheldon), Grumio (Tommy Kirk), Mother Goose (Mary McCarty), Boy Blue (Kevin Corcoran), Willie Winkee (Brian Corcoran), Bo Peep (Ann Jillian), Twins (Marilee and Melanie Arnold).

Synopsis: Sylvester J. Goose introduces Mother Goose, who invites the audience to Mother Goose village for the marriage of Tom and Mary. Villainous Barnaby schemes to do away with Tom so he may marry Mary and gain access to her inheritance. For cash, Gonzorgo and Roderigo will assist him. They bop Tom on the head and cart him away and tell Mary he was lost at sea. They recite from a letter telling her to forget him. At Barnaby's direction, they steal the sheep. Meanwhile, Barnaby tries to impress himself upon Mary but is rejected. Bo Peep is distraught to find that her sheep is in the Forest of No Return. To prevent further mischief, Mary agrees to marry Barnaby. But Tom appears in the midst of a visiting gypsy troupe! After finding a note that Bo Peep and the other children have entered the Forest of No Return to retrieve the sheep, Mary and Tom find them and settle down in the forest for the night. Barnaby and his minions spy on them, and in the morning the trees tell the interlopers that the Toymaker will decide what to do with them. In Toyland the Toymaker's assistant, Grumio, shows him how automation can eliminate the need for hand tools, but his machine is overloaded by the Toymaker and explodes. Tom offers his and the children's help in making toys for the Christmas deadline. Grumio develops a device that shrinks — or destroys — things. Barnaby gets hold of it and shrinks the Toymaker and Gonzorgo and Roderigo when they refuse to help him any longer. He produces a shrunken Tom for Mary, and to help Tom out of his predicament, she again agrees to marry Barnaby. While the Toymaker conducts the ceremony, Barnaby's erstwhile minions loosen Tom's bonds, and he summons toy soldiers with a bugle. Barnaby fends off the toy army for a while but succumbs when Mary shoots him with a toy cannon while he holds the shrinking weapon. He and Tom duel with swords. Tom drives him off a block into a box. Grumio restores the tiny people to their original size with a new device. Mary and Tom wed.

Review: "A garden of dreams to delight every child." (A. H. Weiler, *New York Times*, December 15, 1961, p. 49)

Analysis: With little menace and a surfeit of singing and dancing (it's an operetta, after all), many adults will find this hard to watch. The battle between the toy army and Barnaby is an exception. The *New York Times* review found Annette Funicello and Tommy Sands a disspirited twosome. Ms. Funicello, in the credits billed merely as "Annette," was maturing out of her *Mickey Mouse Club* TV days. She'd make more Disney films before starring in most of the AIP "beach" movies that began with *Beach Party* in 1964. Gene Sheldon and Henry Calvin are the Laurel and Hardy characters of the 1934 version. They were having success in Disney's TV series *Zorro.* As in that, Sheldon is mute. After playing Bo Peep, Ann Jillian would go on to some fame in movies on TV. Tommy Kirk's toymaking machine is controlled by an interesting "computer."

There is a 1986 TV movie version of this venerable Victor Herbert operetta directed by Clive Donner and starring Drew Barrymore. It's on video.

Back to the Future

(Universal 1985; 116 min.) ***½

Produced by Bob Gale and Neil Canton. Directed by Robert Zemeckis. Screenplay, Robert Zemeckis and Bob Gale. Edited by Arthur Schmidt and Harry Keramidas. Director of Photography, Dean Cundey. Panavision. Technicolor. Music, Alan Silvestri. Song "The Power of Love" performed by Huey Lewis and the News. Choreography, Brad Jefries. Dolby Stereo. Art Direction, Todd Hallowell. Set Decoration, Hal Gausman. Visual Effects, Industrial Light & Magic. Makeup, Ken Chase. Costumes, Deborah L. Scott. Special Effects, Kevin Pike.

Cast: Marty McFly (Michael J. Fox), Dr. Emmett Brown (Christopher Lloyd), Lorraine Baines (Lea Thompson), George McFly (Crispin Glover), Biff Tannen (Thomas F. Wilson), Jennifer Parker (Claudia Wells), Dave McFly (Marc McClure), Linda McFly (Wendie Jo Sperber), Sam Baines (George DiCenzo), Stella Baines (Frances Lee McCain), Mr. Strickland (James Tolkan), Skinhead (Jeffrey Jay Cohen), 3-D (Casey Siemaszko), Match (Billy Zane), Marvin Berry (Harry Waters Jr.), Goldie Wilson (Donald Fullilove), Babs (Lisa Freeman), Betty (Cristen Kaufman), Clocktower lady (Elsa Raven), Pa Peabody (Will Hare), Ma Peabody (Ivy Bethune), Sherman Peabody (Jason Marin), Peabody's daughter (Katherine Britton), Milton Baines (Jason Harvey), Sally Baines (Maia Brewton), Dixon (Courtney Gains). With Huey Lewis.

Synopsis: One day in 1985, teenage Marty McFly receives a call from Dr. Emmett Brown asking him to meet him at 1:15 next morning at Twin Pines Mall. In the parking lot Brown shows Marty the DeLorean car he's turned into a time machine via plutonium and his invention, the Flux Capacitor. He uses a remote to test it with his dog, Einstein, inside. When it reaches 88 mph the car disappears, then reappears a minute later according to the program. Doc got the plutonium from Libyans and they now discover him and shoot him. Marty dives into the car, accelerates to 88 mph and finds himself in November 5, 1955. The car is empty of plutonium, so Marty pushes the car behind a sign. In town he's amazed to see the movie *Cattle Queen of Montana* playing at the local theater, the songs "The Ballad of Davy Crockett" and "16 Tons" the current hits. In the soda fountain, Marty meets his own younger, nerdy father. Outside he is knocked unconscious by a car and taken in by the teenage Lorraine his future mother. Later he locates Doc Brown at 1640 Riverside and convinces him that he's come through time. They retrieve the DeLorean. Without plutonium, Doc figures they need 1.21 gigawatts to power the car, and that can only come from lightning. Marty has a flyer from the future that indicates the clock tower will be struck by lightning the coming Saturday night. It can't come too soon, because a snapshot shows Marty's brother disappearing. He must get George McFly to meet Lorraine, but she's more interested in Marty. Putting on his yellow radiation suit, Marty orders George to find Lorraine and take her to the Saturday night "Enchantment Under the Sea" dance. Marty plans for George to interrupt him making a play for Lorraine but when that moment comes, Lorraine is not averse to Marty. However, school bully Biff's chums spirit Marty away while Biff harasses Lorraine. George shows and flattens Biff. In the town square, Doc refuses to read the

Jennifer Parker (Claudia Wells) and Marty McFly (Michael J. Fox) contemplate their situation in *Back to the Future* (Universal, 1985).

note Marty wrote to warn him about the Libyans in 1985. The storm arrives, and after trials, Doc connects the cable to the town hall. Marty rides past, and the car returns to 1985. Although Marty programmed the car to arrive a few minutes early so he could warn Doc, the shooting occurs. But Doc is okay; he had pieced back the note in 1955 and is wearing a bulletproof vest. Doc says he's going to go thirty years into the future. At home, Marty discovers that his family has gotten cool. Doc shows up and says they need to do something about Marty's kids. He, Marty and Jennifer take off in the DeLorean. "To Be Continued."

Reviews: "Freewheeling blend of sitcom and science fiction.... Its personality is cheerfully split between H. G. Wells and *Revenge of the Nerds.*" (David Sterritt, *Christian Science Monitor*, July 3, 1985, p. 23) ¶"Even as you're saying to yourself, 'This is dumb,' you're also enjoying the movie." (David Denby, *New York*, July 15, 1985, p. 64)

Analysis: The "Flux Capacitor" is a sort of Macguffin as well as an implausible plausibility. They've done a good job of recreating a 1955 small town. A standout among many funny scenes is the hilarious one in which Fox pretends to be Darth Vader from the planet Vulcan and plays a Van Halen tape into Crispin Glover's startled ears. Christopher Lloyd is a very appropriate "mad" scientist. Why haven't we seen more of peachy Claudia Wells? *Back to the Future* was the highest grossing film of 1985. Academy Award for Sound Effects Editing. Nominations for Screenplay, Sound, Song ("Power of Love").

Back to the Future Part II
(1989; 107 min.) **½

Produced by Bob Gale and Neil Canton. Executive Producers, Steven Spielberg, Frank Marshall, Kathleen Kennedy. Directed by Robert Zemeckis. Screenplay, Bob Gale. Story, Robert Zemeckis and Bob Gale. Based on characters created by Robert Zemeckis and Bob Gale. Edited by Arthur Schmidt and Harry Keramidas. Director of Photography, Dean Cundey. Panavision. Deluxe Color.

Music, Alan Silvestri. Dolby Stereo. Art Direction, Margie Stone McShirley. Set Decoration, Linda DeScenna. Visual Effects Supervisor, Ken Ralston. Special Visual Effects, Industrial Light & Magic. Costumes, Joanna Johnston. Makeup, Ken Chase.

Cast: Marty McFly/Marty McFly Jr./Marlene McFly (Michael J. Fox), Dr. Emmett Brown (Christopher Lloyd), Lorraine (Lea Thompson), Biff Tannen/Griff (Thomas F. Wilson), Jennifer (Elizabeth Shue), Marvin Berry (Harry Waters, Jr.), Terry (Charles Fleischer), Western Union man (Joe Flaherty), Needles (Flea), Strickland (James Tolkan), George McFly (Jeffrey Weissman), 3-D (Casey Siemaszko), Match (Billy Zane), Skinhead (J.J. Cohen), Michael Jackson (E. Casanova Evans), Ronald Reagan (Jay Koch), Ayatollah Khomeini (Charles Gherardi), Data (Ricky Dean Logan), Spike (Darlene Vogel), Whitey (Jason Scott Lee), Video game boys (Elijah Wood, John Thornton), Hoverboard girls (Theo Schwartz, Lindsey Bary), Antique store saleswoman (Judy Ovitz), Officer Foley (Stephanie E. Williams), Babs (Lisa Freeman), Cab driver (Marty Levy), Fujitsu (James Ishida), Loretta (Nikki Birdsong), Dad (Al White), Mom (Junior Fann), Harold (Shaun Hunter), Bum (Buck Flower), Museum narrator (Neil Ross), Jacuzzi girls (Tamara Carrera, Tracy D'Aldia), Baseball kids (Jennifer Brown, Irina Cashen, Angela Greenblatt, Cameron Moore, Justin Mosley Spink), Radio sportscaster (John Erwin), Starlighters (David Harold Brown, Tommy Thomas, Lloyd L. Tolbert, Granville "Danny" Young), CPR kid (Wesley Mann), Einstein (Freddie).

Synopsis: Doc Brown reappears in his time-traveling DeLorean on Saturday, October 26, 1985. He tells Marty they must go into the future and visit Hill Valley on October 21, 2015. Doc renders Jennifer unconscious so he and Marty can thwart Griff Tannen's plot to have Marty's son help in a robbery. Jennifer wakes up too soon and sneaks around her future home till Doc finds her. Biff Tannen, meanwhile, steals Doc's car. He returns it and Doc, Marty and Jennifer go to what they think is 1985. But something's wrong: another family inhabits Marty's house, there's rampant crime in the streets, Biff owns a gambling palace—and is married to Marty's mom. Marty's father was killed. Doc finally realizes that Griff stole the car and took Marty's sports almanac back to Biff, who used its knowledge of future athletic contests to become a millionaire. In order to change this future, they must return to November 12, 1955, and get the almanac from Biff without letting Griff know. Marty finally obtains and burns the magazine. But Doc's car is struck by lightning and disappears. A man delivers a letter to Marty, telling him the message has been around for 70 years. In the letter Doc reveals that he's living in 1885. In town, Doc connects the wire that lightning strikes to power Marty and the DeLorean in 1985. The "new" Marty confronts Doc. "To Be Concluded."

Reviews: "Doesn't stay fresh and surprising all the way through." (David Sterritt, *Christian Science Monitor*, December 4, 1989, p. 10) ¶"Satirically acute, intricately structured and deftly paced, it is at heart stout, good and untainted by easy sentiment." (Richard Schickel, *Time*, December 4, 1989, p. 101) ¶"Allegorizes the story of American postwar rise and decline.... grandiose as well as pragmatic, at once jerry-built and overweening." (J. Hoberman, *Village Voice*, December 5, 1989, p. 117)

Analysis: It's fairly entertaining, but all the running around gets tiresome. (The *Christian Science Monitor* review complained that an excess of chase scenes was the filmmakers' attempt to compensate for a plot that "gets too tricky.") Perhaps the pace is to prevent the audience from examining the plausibility of Doc's schemes. It works. The real reason we can't give this an unqualified good rating is that while *Back to the Future* contained several scenes that made us laugh out loud, this has nary a one. It's basically a bridge to the third in the series.

Back to the Future Part III
(1990; 118 min.) ***

Produced by Bob Gale and Neil Canton. Executive Producers, Steven Spielberg, Frank Marshall, Kathleen Kennedy. Directed by Robert Zemeckis. Screenplay, Bob Gale. Story, Robert Zemeckis and Bob Gale. Based on characters created by Robert Zemeckis and Bob Gale. Edited by Arthur Schmidt and Harry Keramidas. Director of Photography,

Dean Cundey. Panavision. DeLuxe Color. Music, Alan Silvestri. Song: "Doubleback" written and performed by ZZ Top. Dolby Stereo. Art Direction, Marjorie Stone McShirley, Jim Teegarden. Set Decoration, Michael Taylor. Visual Effects Supervisors, Ken Ralston, Scott Farrar. Special Effects, Industrial Light & Magic. Stunts, Walter Scott. Costumes, Joanna Johnston.

Cast: Marty McFly/Seamus McFly (Michael J. Fox), Dr. Emmett Brown (Christopher Lloyd), Clara Clayton (Mary Steenburgen), Buford "Mad Dog" Tannen/Biff Tannen (Thomas F. Wilson), Maggie McFly/Lorraine McFly (Lea Thompson), Jennifer (Elizabeth Shue), Bartender (Matt Clark), Barbwire salesman (Richard Dysart), Saloon old timers (Pat Buttram, Harry Carey, Jr., Dub Taylor), Marshal Strickland (James Tolkan), Dave McFly (Marc McClure), Linda McFly (Wendie Jo Sperber), George McFly (Jeffrey Weissman), Buford Tannen's gang (Christopher Wynne, Sean Gregory Sullivan, Mike Watson), Mayor (Hugh Gillin), Colt gun salesman (Burton Gilliam), Engineer (Bill McKinney), Deputy (Donovan Scott), Needles (Flea), Needles' gang (J.J. Cohen, Ricky Dean Logan), Mortician (Marvin J. McIntyre), Strickland's son (Kaleb Henley), Jules (Todd Cameron Brown), Verne (Dannel Evans), Celebration man (Leslie A. Prickett), Photographer (Dean Cundey), Pie lady (Jo B. Cummings), Festival men (Steve McArthur, John Ickes), Festival dance caller (James A. Rammel), Eyepatch (Brad McPeters), Townsmen (Michael Klastorin, Michael John Mills, Kenny Myers), Toothless (Phinneas D.), Ticket agent (Rod Kuehne), Conductor (Leno Fletcher), Joey (Joey Newington), Train fireman (Larry Ingold), Barbwire salesman's companion (Tim Konrad), Boy with gun (Glenn Fox), Copernicus (Foster), Einstein (Freddie), Musicians (ZZ Top).

Synopsis: Marty McFly confronts Doc Brown on Saturday, November 12, 1955, at 10:03 p.m. — after the scientist thought all was well and Marty was sent back to 1985 in the DeLorean. On November 13, 1955, Marty shows Doc the 1885 letter he, Doc Brown, had sent him. It provides directions to the DeLorean to be found in 1955. It urges Marty not to come back to 1885 and to destroy the time machine. Marty and Doc dynamite a mineshaft and find the car. After discovering a photo showing a September 7, 1885, tombstone with Doc's name on it — he'd been shot by Buford

Tannen — Marty says he must go back to bring Doc home. When he arrives in the Old West, Marty finds himself in the midst of Indian warriors, then the pursuing cavalry. He hides the DeLorean in the cave. Chased by a bear, Marty falls and is knocked unconscious. When he comes to, he finds himself in the farmhouse of relatives: Seamus and Maggie McFly. Marty says his name is Clint Eastwood. In Hill Valley next day, Marty is found by Doc, but not until the uncouth "Mad Dog" Tannen almost lynches him. Doc is a blacksmith. Marty shows him the photo of the tombstone. They'll need gas to power the DeLorean to 88 mph, but there is none. They concoct a scheme whereby a locomotive will push the car to that speed. Flies in the ointment include the arrival of Clara Clayton, to whom Doc is immediately drawn, and Tannen's challenge to Marty. Doc says he's staying with Clara, but he changes his mind and tells Clara he must leave. In the saloon, Doc takes a swig of whiskey and falls unconscious. Bartender helps Marty revive him with "wake up juice," but it's too late to circumvent Tannen. The outlaw holds Doc hostage until Marty comes into the street. Marty refuses to draw and is gunned down. But he was wearing a stove door under his poncho! He gets up and beats Tannen to a pulp. The tombstone disappears from the photo. Meanwhile, Clara has boarded a train for San Francisco. When she overhears two men talking about the lovestruck blacksmith, she stops the train and returns to town. On horseback, she chases Marty and Doc, finally locating them aboard the engine they've commandeered to push the DeLorean toward Clayton Ravine. Doc must rescue Clara, and Marty must go back to the future by himself. He arrives in 1985 across what is now Eastwood Ravine and leaps out as a train bears down on and smashes the DeLorean. Marty finds Jennifer still asleep on her porch swing. He takes her to the DeLorean where, amazingly, Doc and Clara and their two children, Jules and Verne, appear in a steam-powered train engine time machine. Before leaving, Doc tells Marty and Jennifer they can make the future whatever they like.

Reviews: Sprightly and inoffensive.... satisfyingly ties up the various plot strands." (Peter Rainer, *Los Angeles Times Calendar*, May 25, 1990, p. 1) ¶"Some excellent special effects and much quick-witted dialogue." (Mark Kermode, *Monthly Film Bulletin*, July 1990, p. 192)

Analysis: Like the first but not the second film in the trilogy, this one elicits laughs and chuckles, notably in Fox's Clint Eastwood parody. There are excellent effects, not the least of which is the use of two Michael J. Fox's in one scene. We quibble with the final locomotive wreck. Was it really necessary to enhance the explosion "in the camera"?

Badge of Silence *see* **Maniac Cop 3 under Maniac Cop**

The Barbaric Beast of Boggy Creek, Part II *see* **Boggy Creek II under The Legend of Boggy Creek**

Basket Case
(Analysis, 1982; 90 min.) ***

Produced by Edgar Ievins. Executive Producers, Arnie Bruck, Tom Kaye. Directed by Frank Henenlotter. Screenplay, Frank Henenlotter. Edited by Frank Henenlotter. Director of Photography, Bruce Torbet. Color. Music, Gus Russo.

Cast: Duane Bradley (Kevin Van Hentenryck), Sharon (Terri Susan Smith), Dr. Kutter (Diana Browne), Casey (Beverly Bonner), Dr. Needleman (Lloyd Pace) Young Duane (Sean McCall), Doctor (Bill Freeman), Hotel manager (Robert Vogel), O'Donovan (Joe Clarke).

Synopsis: Duane Bradley arrives in New York with a pack and a large rectangular basket. He visits Dr. Needleman's office to get Dr. Kutter's address. When the receptionist is gone, Duane opens the basket and lets a strange misshapen creature kill the physician. The creature — a head and two arms, not much of a body, no legs — turns out to be Duane's brother, a "twin" separated from his side when he was twelve years old. The brother, Belial, communicates with Duane telepathically. He loves hamburgers and raw hotdogs. The doctors murdered are those that separated the two.

Distressed that Duane wants a private life and a girlfriend, Belial leaps upon him and in the fight both fall from the Hotel Broslin's window onto the neon sign before dropping to the street.

Reviews: "Scary, quirky, morbidly funny.... made with an obvious regard, one approaching reverence, even, for the genre." (Charles Balun, *The Connoisseur's Guide to the Contemporary Horror Film*, p. 13) ¶"Cheap, sick, and thoroughly entertaining oddity.... bolstered by several surprisingly strong performances,.... one of the most compelling blackly comic scare pics of recent vintage and an ideal late-night video treat." (Phantom of the Movies, *The Phantom's Ultimate Video Guide*, p. 125) ¶"Twisted gem.... With animated sequences, gore, humor, and lots of surprises for horror fans." (Michael Weldon, *The Psychotronic Encyclopedia of Film*, p. 36)

Analysis: This may be the strangest series in this book, and much of the populace will find it goofy, to say the least; more likely loathsome, incredible, weird. For a tolerant audience, it is fascinating. The first film is both amusing and frightening. But what is the green light in Belial's eyes late in the film? He's not a mere mortal?

Basket Case II
(Shapiro Glickenhaus Entertainment, 1990; 90 min.) ***

Produced by Edgar Ievins. Executive Producer, James Glickenhaus. Written and directed by Frank Henenlotter. Edited by Kevin Tent. Music, Joe Renzetti. Dolby Stereo. Director of Photography, Robert M. Baldwin. Color, TVC. Special Makeup Effects, Gabe Bartalos. Special Effects, Patrick Shearn, George Bernota, Gregory Ramoundos.

Cast: Duane Bradley (Kevin Van Hentenryck), Granny Ruth (Annie Ross), Susan (Heather Rattray), Marcie Elliott (Kathryn Meisle), Editor Lou (Jason Evers), Phil (Ted Sorel), Artie (Matt Mitler), Braniac (Jody Oliver), News Woman (Judy Grafe).

Synopsis: Both Duane Bradley and his separated "Siamese twin" Belial survive a fall from their New York hotel window and are taken to a hospital. Duane and Belial escape the hospital with the help of Granny Ruth and Susan, who'd seen the story on TV and realize they can provide a safe haven for the pair on their Staten Island estate. Granny Ruth has taken in many "freaks" from distraught parents or sideshows. She advises Belial that "ripping faces off people may not be in your best interest." Once he's recovered and knows that Belial is better, Duane states his intention to join the real world. However, a reporter, a photographer and a private detective get in the way. Duane helps Granny Ruth and her house guests kill the three interlopers. Duane wants to leave with Susan until Susan reveals that she's pregnant with a hideous serpent-like creature that erupts from her abdomen on occasion. Duane finds Belial, knocks him out with a baseball bat and sews him back to his side. They are together again.

Reviews: "Outrageous dark humor, bizarre horror, driving energy and genuine pathos. It also looks and sounds great thanks to cinematographer Robert M. Baldwin and composer Joe Renzetti." (Kevin Thomas, *Los Angeles Times Calendar*, April 13, 1990, p. 6) ¶"Mildly amusing if occasionally tedious affair, with ambitions far beyond its achievements." (Mark Kermode, *Monthly Film Bulletin*, September 1990, p. 253) ¶"Agreeable in spurts." (David Edelstein, *New York Post*, March 2, 1990, p. 23) ¶"Unexpectedly weird narrative twists lend the film a humanist morality almost in spite of its queasy castration-fear underpinning." (Richard Gehr, *Village Voice*, March 6, 1990, p. 69)

Analysis: More tongue-in-cheek (for instance, the handicapped license plate on Granny Ruth's van) than the first in the series, it's almost as good. The audience empathizes with Granny Ruth on one hand, but is concerned when she uses Belial to murder those who would disrupt their community. It's a problem without a good solution.

Basket Case 3: The Progeny
(Shapiro Glickenhaus Entertainment, 1992; 90 min.) ***

Produced by Edgar Ievins. Executive Producer James Glickenhaus. Directed by Frank Henenlotter. Screenplay, Frank Henenlotter and Robert Martin. Director of Photography, Bob Paone. TVC Color. Edited by Greg

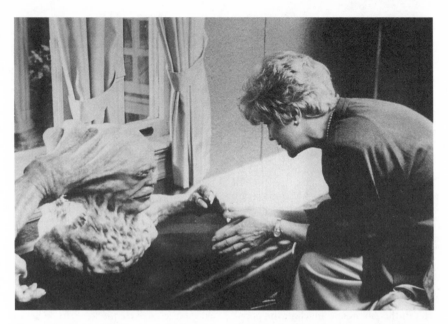

Granny Ruth (Annie Ross) counsels the monster twin Belial in *Basket Case II* (Shapiro Glickenhaus, 1990).

Sheldon. Music, Joe Renzetti. Production Design, William Barclay. Art Direction, Caty Maxey. Costumes, Carleen Rosado. Production Manager, Bob Baron. Creatures and Makeup Effects, Gabe Bartalos, David Kindlon. Sound, Palmer Norris.

Cast: Granny Ruth (Annie Ross), Duane (Kevin Van Hentenryck), Uncle Hal (Dan Biggers), Sheriff (Gil Roper), Opal (Tina Louise Hilbert), Little Hal (James O'Doherty). With Carla and Carmen Morrell.

Synopsis: Duane is straitjacketed and Belial once again removed from his side. While Duane tries to convince Granny Ruth he's okay and wants to speak to Belial, Belial is unwilling to converse or even see his brother. The similarly malformed female with whom Belial mated is pregnant, and Granny Ruth decides to take her to Uncle Hal, a doctor in Georgia. In a school bus they make their way south. Uncle Hal has raised Granny Ruth's son, Little Hal, now a "man" although he too is malformed from the chest down. Recalling the time when he was twelve and removed from Duane, Belial attacks Uncle Hal but is subdued by the others and locked in his basket while the delivery is

made by Granny Ruth. Twelve misshapen little Belials are produced. Meanwhile, Duane has contacted the sheriff's daughter, but is jailed by two policemen who learn that there is a million dollar reward for locating the Times Square mutant twins. They scout out Hal's house, observe the strange inhabitants celebrating the births, shoot Eve and kidnap the babies. Granny Ruth sends her family to retrieve the babies. Belial kills three policemen, and the sheriff's daughter is accidentally shot and killed. Duane escapes but can't get the babies. The sheriff returns, finds the carnage and makes a deal: He'll trade the babies for Belial. Meanwhile, Duane and Little Hal develop a machine to encase Belial and give him mobility. The sheriff arrives and does battle with Belial. Belial wins. Granny Ruth is convinced that her family must come out of the closet. They invade a TV talk show and announce this intention to the viewing audience. "Have a nice day."

Review: "Henenlotter's mix of wild overacting, cartoon color scheme and heavy-handed message regarding tolerance is tough to take for the uninitiated. Creature effects are quite inventive." (Lawrence Cohn, *Variety*, February 24, 1992, p. 249)

Analysis: They've gone for humor at the expense of a hard edge. Best touch: "No One You Know" sign on the bus. Some scenes go on too long. Nevertheless, it's mostly engrossing.

Batman
(20th Century–Fox, 1966; 105 min.)
**

Produced by William Dozier. Directed by Leslie H. Martinson. Screenplay, Lorenzo Semple, Jr. Based on characters appearing in comic strips by Bob Kane. Edited by Harry Gerstad. Director of Photography, Howard Schwartz. DeLuxe Color. Music, Nelson Riddle. Batman Theme, Neil Hefti. Set Decoration, Walter M. Scott, Chester L. Bayhi. Makeup, Ben Nye. Special Photographic Effects, L. B. Abbott.

Cast: Bruce Wayne/Batman (Adam West), Dick Grayson/Robin (Burt Ward), Catwoman (Lee Meriwether), Joker (Cesar Romero), Penguin (Burgess Meredith), Riddler (Frank Gorshin), Alfred (Alan Napier), Commissioner Gordon (Neil Hamilton), Chief O'Hara (Stafford Repp), Aunt Harriet Cooper (Madge Blake), Vice Admiral Fangschliester (Milton Frome), Commander Schmidlapp (Reginald Denny), Colonel Terry (Sterling Holloway), Bluebeard (Gil Perkins), Morgan (Dick Crockett), Quetch (George Sawaya).

Synopsis: Batman and Robin have difficulty making a rescue at sea when a yacht disappears. It was an illusion, a ruse allowing Catwoman, the Joker, the Penguin, and the Riddler to hijack a second yacht, belonging to an inventor of a dehydrator which turns humans into ashes that can be restored to human form with water. Batman and Robin have difficulty capturing the villains. The Penguin visits the United Nations Security Council and turns a number of diplomats into ash, which he stores in test tubes. Batman and Robin capture the heinous quartet. Because the inventor scatters the ashes with his sneeze, when they are reconstituted, each diplomat speaks a language previously unknown to him.

Review: "Excellent color.... pretty good

for half an hour." (H. T., *New York Times*, August 25, 1966, p. 42)

Analysis: Batman's first appearance on the big screen was actually in 1943, with the release of Columbia's serial, *Batman*, which starred Lewis Wilson as Batman and young Douglas Croft as Robin. A second Columbia serial, *Batman and Robin*, appeared in 1949, this time with Robert Lowery and Johnny Duncan as the Dynamic Duo. The pair was then absent from the screen until the "Batman" television show became the surprise hit of the 1966 season. This hastily made theatrical spin-off was released later that year, but by that time the batmania had peaked and interest had already dropped off.

It's hard to make the plot of this film sound sensible in writing. It's as silly as the television series that inspired it. At least they didn't string together TV episodes and call it a movie. Some viewers find the number of villains overbearing.

Batman
(Warner Bros., 1989; 126 min.) ***½

Produced by Jon Peters and Peter Guber. Directed by Tim Burton. Screenplay, Sam Hamm and Warren Skaaren. Based on characters created by Bob Kane in DC Comics. Edited by Ray Lovejoy. Director of Photography, Roger Pratt. Technicolor/Eastmancolor. Music, Danny Elfman. Songs, Prince. Dolby Stereo. Sound, Don Sharpe and Tony Dawe. Art Direction, Terry Ackland-Snow, Nigel Phelps. Set Decoration, Peter Young. Makeup, Paul Engelen. Joker Makeup Design, Nick Dudman. Costumes, Bob Ringwood, Linda Henrikson. Visual Effects, Meddings Magic Camera Company. Special Effects Supervisor, John Evans. Stunts, Eddie Stacy. Production Design, Anton Furst.

Cast: Bruce Wayne/Batman (Michael Keaton), Jack Napier/Joker (Jack Nicholson), Vicki Vale (Kim Basinger), Alexander Knox (Robert Wuhl), Commissioner Gordon (Pat Hingle), Harvey Dent (Billy Dee Williams), Alfred (Michael Gough), Carl Grissom (Jack Palance), Alicia (Jerry Hall), Bob the Goon (Tracey Walter), Mayor (Lee Wallace), Eckhardt (William Hootkins), Goons (Richard Strange, Carl Chase, Mac MacDonald, Terence Plummer, George Lane Cooper, Phil Tan), Accountant (John Sterland), Rotelli (Edwin Craig), Crimelords (Vincent Wong,

Joel Cutrara), Ricorso (John Dair), Nic (Christopher Fairbank), Eddie (George Roth), Young Bruce Wayne (Charles Roskilly), Young Jack Napier (Hugo E. Blick), Mom (Liza Ross), Dad (Garrick Hagon), Scientist (Michael Balfour), Cartoonist Bob (Denis Lill).

Synopsis: Gotham City is held under the thumb of crime boss Carl Grissom's gang, despite the posturing of city officials. Jack Napier, Grissom's chief lieutenant and enforcer, pledges to hand Grissom the lungs of anyone unwise enough to stand in their way, and that includes some character known as "the Bat" who's been putting the quietus on many small-time hoodlums. Napier has also been spending time with Grissom's mistress, Alicia, a fact that Grissom has become privy to. Reporter Alexander Knox and photo-journalist Vicki Vale throw in together on the mysterious crimefighter story. They attend a charity ball thrown by millionaire philanthropist Bruce Wayne, finding him as personable as he is enigmatic. Wayne overhears a message whispered to Police Commissioner Gordon that there has been a burglary at Axis Chemical Company. He makes a discreet exit. The break-in at Axis is a set-up engineered by Grissom to neatly eliminate Napier. The police arrive and a shootout ensues. Napier draws a bead on Commissioner Gordon, but a cowled, caped figure kicks the gun from his hand. "I'm Batman," says the newcomer. In the fracas that follows, Napier plummets into a vat of chemicals. Batman departs as mysteriously as he arrived. Vicki Vale accepts an invitation to dinner at the Wayne home the next evening. The two hit it off very well and have a stimulating chat with butler Alfred as well. Tipsily, Wayne and Vicki stagger off to the master bedroom. Not so cozy is the basement office of the back alley quack where Jack Napier is having bandages taken off his scarred, discolored face. Demanding a mirror, Napier cackles with crazy mirth at the face baring an undeniable resemblance to the joker card of the lucky deck he always carries. Napier repays his former boss's treachery by killing him and declares himself crime boss of Gotham City. He announces his presence as the Joker to Gotham at large the next day when

murdering a rival crime lord in front of City Hall. The occasion affords him his first look at both Bruce Wayne and Vicki Vale. The latter piques his interest. Access to Axis Chemicals provides the Joker with the wherewithal for his next big caper: contaminating cosmetics with "Smilex," a deadly concoction that throws its victims into laughing fits before killing them. Pandemonium reigns as the terrified Gothamites fear to take showers or brush their teeth. Vicki receives a mysterious invitation instructing her to meet "someone special" at a local museum. After she arrives, a deadly looking green gas begins to fill the chamber. Only the timely receipt of a protective mask prevents Vicki from succumbing. In walks the Joker, pitching some woo and inquiring about Batman. She tosses a pitcher of cold water in the harlequin's face. A crash from above announces the entrance of Batman, who snatches up the surprised photo-journalist and makes a hasty exit to the Batmobile. It's a nightmare pursuit through traffic bedlam. Trapped in an alley, Batman goes hand-to-hand with a half-dozen of Joker's henchmen, routing them in short order. Later he gives Vicki the solution to Joker's Smilex stratagem: He's only tampered with *certain* products, that, taken in combination with other products (hairspray *plus* toothpaste, or deodorant *plus* shaving cream, for instance), produce lethal results. With his plan to wreak havoc foiled, the Joker again appears on TV and challenges the "winged freak" to a one-on-one contest. To insure a huge turnout, the Joker promises to fling millions of dollars to the crowd. He doesn't mention that his huge clown balloons are equipped with Smilex gas. Bruce Wayne, of course, witnesses the Joker's tirade. He has also come to possess information revealing that it was, in fact, a young Jack Napier who murdered Bruce Wayne's parents many years earlier. Butler Alfred, ever concerned with his employer's well-being, reveals the secret of Bruce's other identity to Vicki. The Batmobile roars into Axis Chemicals and is immediately beset by a platoon of the Joker's lackeys. Their ordnance fails to dent its armor. The car responds by ejecting a

Michael Keaton is *Batman* (Warner Bros., 1989).

small sphere. The building is rocked by a series of explosions. The Batmobile returns to the remote-controlling Batman. But a mocking cry reveals that the Joker was not present when the building fell apart. At the Bicentennial parade, the Joker is as good as his word and throws fistfuls of greenbacks to the hysterical crowd. But reporter Knox foils the gas plan by yelling a warning. The mad jester is further outraged when the Batplane appears overhead, towing away his precious balloons. Returning, Batman destroys his enemy's deadly floats. He is thwarted, however, by the Joker's firing an armor-piercing round into the Batplane, causing it to skid to a flaming crash. The Joker drags Vicki into Gotham Cathedral while a stunned Batman follows. After beating off a trio of opponents, Batman turns upon the Joker, who turns the tables. Batman and Vicki find themselves hanging from the bell tower's crumbling parapet. The Joker is about to make his helicopter getaway when Batman hurls a Batarang that ensnares his foe's ankle with a carved gargoyle. The gargoyle is pulled

from its moorings on the cathedral roof. The weight is too much for the Joker to support; his fingers lose their grip on the rope ladder, and he falls to his death.

Reviews: "The story continues long after its ideas have started to sag.... haunting tone." (David Sterritt, *Christian Science Monitor*, June 29, 1989, p. 10) ¶"Disastrously low on the sort of wit that can make a gargantuan movie lovable." (Sheila Benson, *Los Angeles Times Calendar*, June 23, 1989, p. 1) ¶"One of the great strengths of the film is the utter conviction the actors bring to their roles." (Mike McGrady, *Newsday*, June 23, 1989, Part III, p. 3) ¶"Not about much of anything but its own ambitions." (David Denby, *New York*, July 17, 1989, p. 45) ¶"Doesn't have the courage of its own perversity." (J. Hoberman, *Village Voice*, July 4, 1989, p. 69)

Analysis: Batman was easily the biggest hit of 1989's summer season, though its director had only *Pee Wee's Big Adventure* and *Beetlejuice* to his credit, and Michael Keaton was nobody's idea of a superhero. The millions spent on promotion — months before the film premiered — were hardly wasted. *Batman* opened to record box-office, and positive word-of-mouth guaranteed that Warner's gamble on both Burton and Keaton had paid off. To the theatergoing public at large, the only Batman was the campy figure of sixties Bang! Whap! Zowie! fame. *That* Batman was the product of a decade and a half of kiddie-oriented sci-fi/fantasy fare. Considering director Tim Burton's predilection for subjects of a zany nature, theatergoers in 1989 were probably surprised *not* to get a Batman reminiscent of William Dozier's camp sixties rendering. Actually, however, Burton's Batman was a return to the original comic book rendering of "the Batman" as a dark avenging angel (see Notes of Interest). At any rate, audiences seemed to take to this masked loner and flocked to the theaters, lining up to see this exploit with the Joker time and again.

Michael Keaton seemed a peculiar choice for both the millionaire playboy and the costumed crimefighter in this megabucks extravaganza, but he and the director seem to have enjoyed a certain rapport occasioned by the filming of *Beetlejuice*. There can be no denying that, in this instance particularly, clothes *do* make the man, and after a bit Keaton does fill the bill of superhero. Unarguable, too, is the fact that this show is really Jack Nicholson's, whose Joker, while perhaps not supplanting Cesar Romero's memorable portrayal of the sixties, is unquestionably unique. While not entirely avoiding the camp mannerisms that would seem inherent in this comic book personality, Nicholson plays to the tenor of the film by emphasizing the character's *noir* qualities. In addition to the principals, veterans Michael Gough and Pat Hingle appear as Alfred the butler and Commissioner Gordon, respectively. Composer Danny Elfman, another Burton favorite, provides a rousing and atmospheric score.

What sets *Batman* apart from the superhero films that have preceded it, however, is the uniquely bizarre *noir* cityscape of Gotham City. Tim Burton's Gotham is the handiwork of production designer Anton Furst. This looming gothic metropolis, clustered with great brooding skyscrapers and mournful statuary, occupies a warp in time someplace between the 1920s and the 1980s, positioned somewhere on the map between Fritz Lang's *Metropolis* and Mervyn Peake's *Gormenghast*. The Gotham weather man probably never has to predict pleasant weather; the meteorological situation here makes London look like Tahiti. It's quite obvious that there was never a better home for the nocturnal crimefighter. Academy Award for Art Direction.

Batman Returns
(Warner Bros., 1992; 126 min.) ***½

Produced by Denise Di Nove and Tim Burton. Executive Producrs, Jon Peters, Peter Guber, Benjamin Melniker, Michael Uslan. Directed by Tim Burton. Screenplay, Daniel Waters. Story, Daniel Waters and Sam Hamm. Based on characters created by Bob Kane in DC Comics. Director of Photography, Stefan Capsky. Technicolor. Music, Danny Elfman. Penguin Effects, Stan Winston.

Cast: Bruce Wayne/Batman (Michael Keaton), Selena Chase/Catwoman (Michelle Pfeiffer), Penguin (Danny DeVito), Max Shreck (Christopher Walken), Alfred (Michael Gough), Mayor (Pat Hingle). Mayor (Michael Murphy).

Synopsis: Sometime in the past, shortly before Christmas in Gotham City, the wealthy Cobblepotts enjoy a not-so-blessed event and welcome a freakish scion into the world. Ugly and diminutive, with deformed, flipper-like hands, and showing a nasty disposition, this awful offspring is trundled to a park and pushed into a rivulet leading through a culvert into the underground. Years later, wealthy businessman Max Shreck is addressing a Yuletide crowd with the mayor when the festivities are interrupted by a bizarre assortment of criminal party-crashers. The Batman routs the scoundrels, including those who would mug Shreck's mousy personal secretary, Selena Chase. Shreck, meanwhile, has been kidnapped and ushered before a throne in Gotham's subterranean depths. There sits the Penguin, a mystery figure mentioned in rumor. "What you hide, I discover," prattles the criminal to the millionaire. "What you put in your toilet, I place on my mantle." Penguin has the goods on Shreck: his shady business deals, the toxic waste produced by his textile plant, his missing business partner. Penguin wants only to learn the truth of his origin and knows that Shreck can fund his search. Returning to his office, Shreck finds Selena going through private papers she came upon while fetching the Bruce Wayne files for an upcoming meeting. Shreck throws Selena through the window, but her fall is broken by awnings and she lands stunned on the snow-covered pavement. Licked back to consciousness by a multitude of stray alley cats, Selena stumbles to her apartment. She ultimately undergoes a bizarre transformation, trashing her flat in a frenzy and fashioning for herself a black leather outfit, skintight and glistening, equipped with razor-like talons. Next day the mayor is addressing a holiday crowd when his party is assaulted by a tumbling acrobat. The miscreant gymnast scoops up His Honor's young child and vanishes into a manhole. To the crowd's delight, the child reappears in the protecting arms of ... the Penguin, who is hailed as a hero and whose cause is championed by Max Shreck. The millionaire is having his own problems with the mayor, who (along with Bruce Wayne) blocks the building of a proposed Gotham Power Plant. Penguin learns that he is actually Oswald Cobblepott. Meanwhile, a leather-garbed female appears to beat up some muggers. Later she encounters Batman and ends up hurtling from a great height, to land, fortuitously, in a truckload of sand. While Batman and Catwoman seem natural enemies, the opposite can be said for Bruce Wayne and Selena Chase. They seem curiously attracted to one another. As they struggle with this attraction, the wily Shreck convinces Oswald that he would be an ideal mayoral candidate. Throwing in with Catwoman, they plan to neutralize Batman's effectiveness. Kidnapping Miss Gotham, the trio pin the deed on Batman. Further damage is done to the Caped Crusader's reputation when Miss Gotham is killed and his car comes under the remote control of Penguin and races recklessly about town. But when a crowd hears a tape of Penguin confessing his part in the shenanigans, they turn into an angry mob. Penguin is forced back to the sewers and launches a plot to destroy Gotham, first by kidnapping the children of Gotham society, then by attacking city center with his missile-armed penguins. Batman, however, scrambles the telemetry even as Penguin races up to intercept them. He and Batman come to blows in the park; the penguins loose their missiles, and the park erupts in a multitude of fiery blasts. Penguin falls through a fissure into his lair below. Batman follows and finds Shreck and Catwoman, now revealed as Selena. Selena stalks the magnate with her deadly whip, closing the distance between them even as he squeezes off rounds from his revolver. Finally, she takes him in an embrace, thrusting both into coils of live electrical conduit. Batman finds the charred remains of Max Shreck. Of the Catwoman, there is no sign.

Reviews: "Spellbinding.... As in Burton's distinctive *Edward Scissorhands*, the theme here is duality and psychological nonintegration.... Fantasy and realism swirl around each other in this classic tale whose depths Burton plumbs with his unique, subversive vision." (Anne Swigart, *Film Ex*, Summer 1992, p. 8) ¶"More fun than the first film.... Its strong points — the look, the music, the performances — are all immediate pleasures. But ... its virtues are increasingly overshadowed by its flaws — sloppy storytelling, limp structure, and the lack of any real focus." (Andy Klein, *We Mbl*, July 13-26, 1992, pp. 9, 12.)

Analysis: More than satisfactory, despite the absence of the first movie's designer, Anton Furst. One great appeal of the original film was its unique look — "urban Gothic" — and the Gothic look is amplified, if anything, in the sequel. There was also concern abut the perceived absence of the Kim Basinger character, Vicki Vale. Basinger may or may not be one of those manufactured starlets, but her role in *Batman* was on a par with others she's had, and she delivered the goods nicely. At the end of that film, Vale and Bruce Wayne seemed destined for something. We feared that Vicki Vale would simply be forgotten in the sequel, but such is not the case, and her absence is satisfactorily explained.

Batman Returns is a "busier" film than

the first, less monothematic, which, with its three villains, is hardly surprising. It's a visually bustling movie, also, with things happening all over the place. This is a blue-green film (more of the former than the latter), one in which the sun makes few appearances, and one that seems to spend much of its time either on the rooftops or down in the sewers of Gotham (which are even more picturesque than those of Paris). There's more action here than in the first film, which is welcome; the Batman is definitely a crime *fighter* here, and even though Michael Keaton is hardly anybody's idea of a superhero, the image of a larger-than-life character actually capable of this far-out daring-do is brought off with surprising acumen. Images are definitely important to this kind of cinema, and Burton has clear ideas about the kind of images he wants to film. Bat images, cat images, penguin images … all very phallic or Freudian or Jungian or something. All the principals do quite well. We initially wonder why they'd want to name a character after an obscure German actor of yesteryear, but then we realized Max Schreck did play the vampire Nosferatu, the screen's original "bat-man." Overall, *Batman Returns* is a worthy sequel, not better than the original maybe, but in the same league. The negative comments are understandable. Even though the great majority of action/adventure movie conventions are observed, Burton's vision is still a unique one and probably not for every taste.

Batman Forever
(Warner Bros., 1995; 121 min.) ***

Produced by Tim Burton and Peter Mac-Gregor-Scott. Directed by Joel Schumacher. Screenplay, Lee Batchler, Janet Scott Batchler and Akiva Goldsman. Story, Lee Batchler and Janet S. Batchler. Based on characters created by Bob Kane in DC Comics. Edited by Dennis Virkler. Director of Photography, Stephen Goldblatt. Panavision. Technicolor. Music, Elliot Goldenthal. Dolby sound. Art Direction, Chris Burian-Mohr, Joseph P. Lucky. Set Decoration, Elise "Cricket" Rowland. Project Consultant, Bob Kane. Special Makeup, Rick Baker. Visual Effects Supervisor, John Dykstra.

Cast: Bruce Wayne/Batman (Val Kilmer),

Dr. Chase Meridian (Nicole Kidman), Harvey Dent/Two-Face (Tommy Lee Jones), Edward Nygma/Riddler (Jim Carrey), Dick Grayson/Robin (Chris O'Donnell), Alfred (Michael Gough), Commissioner Gordon (Pat Hingle), Spice (Debi Mazar), Sugar (Drew Barrymore), Dr. Barton (Rene Auberjonois), Fred (Ed Begley, Jr.), Bank guard (Joe Grifasi), Newscaster (Philip Moon), Gang leader (Don "The Dragon" Wilson).

Synopsis: Called to Gotham to foil a crime, Batman meets psychiatrist Dr. Chase Meridian, who is lending her insight into the criminal mind at Commissioner Gordon's request. She and Batman feel a mutual attraction. Batman exits to do his duty: stop an apparent robbery by ex–D.A. Harvey Dent. Now known as Two-Face, he blames Batman for not preventing a mobster from scarring him with acid during a trial. He tricks Batman into a vault with the bound guard. Batman escapes and climbs into Dent's helicopter. Dent parachutes to safety as the chopper crashes into the Statue of Liberty. Batman survives his fall into the sea. Later, in his daytime guise as millionaire Bruce Wayne, Batman visits Wayne Enterprises and meets the eccentric Edward Nygma. Miffed by Bruce's negative response to his brainwave machine, Nygma plans revenge. Seeing the bat signal that night, Batman finds Chase using it merely to meet him again. Upon leaving, he eludes Two-Face and his henchmen. After receiving a bizarre note, Bruce seeks an explanation from Dr. Meridian. She offers the opinion that a wacko sent it. Although she intimates she is starting an affair with someone, she agrees to attend the circus with Bruce. To everyone's consternation, Two-Face appears as ringmaster and demands that Batman step forward or else he'll detonate dynamite. Bruce steps up to announce his true identity, but the crowd is so raucous no one notices. He manages to disable some of Two-Face's henchmen while the Graysons, highwire artists, attempt to defuse the bomb. Young Dick Grayson manages to roll the bomb off the roof into the river, but his family falls to their deaths inside. In the guise of the Riddler, Nygma approaches Two-Face with a plan to wreak havoc in Gotham and demonstrates his brainwave machine using

Two-Face's lovely mistresses, Sugar and Spice. Taken in by Bruce, Dick Grayson learns of his benefactor's true identity after falling into the Batcave. He wants to work with Bruce, specifically to kill Two-Face. With stolen monies, Nygma succeeds in manufacturing and marketing his device to the citizens of Gotham, who attach it to their televisions. His success rivals that of Wayne Enterprises, and at his party at the Ritz Gotham, he taunts Bruce. Thinking he's got the key and can prevent any mind-reading, Bruce enters Nygma's demonstration chamber. But Sugar has the real key, and Nygma and Two-Face do learn Bruce's secret. Before that, however, Two-Face, Spice and his gang take the partygoers hostage. Bruce escapes and changes into his Batman garb. Dick dons his highwire garb to help and rescues Batman from being buried alive in a subway collapse. Haunted by his own past, Bruce doesn't want Dick to help. Bruce consults with Chase and recalls the deaths of his parents, finally remembering how he'd found his father's journal, trudged through the rain and fallen into a pit. He saw a bat and decided to use its image to help others. Pretending to be Halloween trick-or-treaters, Riddler and Two-Face gain entrance to Wayne Manor, knock out Alfred the butler, and after wounding Bruce, kidnap Chase. Nygma blows up most of the Batcave, but the airplane and boat remain as well as Batman's prototype sonar-equipped suit. With Dick, now as Robin, Batman heads for Nygma's island. Nygma and Two-Face use depth charges and other weapons to delay them. On the island, inside a central cylinder, Batman seems destined to be crushed but he breaks a cable and emerges to find the Riddler waiting. Below, Robin had bested Two-Face in hand-to-hand combat but couldn't let him fall to his death. Two-Face pulled a gun, and now Robin and Chase are imprisoned in separate glass containers. After a tense parlay, Batman breaks Nygma's master brainwave machine, causing its inventor to rapidly lose his power. Batman dives into the pit after the falling Chase and Robin and with his hooks and ropes saves both. Two-Face gets the drop on the trio,

but when Batman reminds him of his penchant for tossing his coin before taking any major action, Two-Face flips it skyward. Batman throws up his own coins and while reaching out, Two-Face falls to his doom. A shell of his former self, Riddler is placed in the Arkham Asylum, where he comes to believe he is Batman.

Review: "A long way from the dark poetry of Tim Burton's 1989 original.... catches the campy innocence of the Batman TV series of the '60s.... For all the homogenizing, *Batman Forever* still gets in its licks. There's no fun machine this summer that packs more surprises.... Subversive humor keeps bubbling under the surface." (Peter Travers, Rolling Stone, July 13, 1995, pp. 114–115) ¶"The only thing Schumacher and his scrupulous craftsfolk forgot to give the movie was life — the energizing spirit of wit and passion that make scenes work and characters breathe." (Richard Corliss, *Time*, June 26, 1995, p. 79)

Analysis: We initially agreed with whoever said that *Batman Forever* was forgotten five minutes after leaving the theater, but the biggest grossing movie of 1995 seems better when viewed a second time on video. It touches all the right comic book superhero buttons and moves at a brisk pace. Kilmer makes a good Batman, O'Donnell a traditional Robin. What happened to Mazar and Barrymore during the collapse of Riddler's empire? Not to ask. They were just window dressing like Pat Hingle's Commissioner Gordon. Does anyone remember when instead of helping the good guys, Michael Gough was playing villains, notably in *Konga* and *Horrors of the Black Museum*? Nygma's brainwave device is no more than a Hitchcockian MacGuffin. How does it really work? What's it good for? Would people actually buy it?

Notes of Interest: The Batman (originally, the definite article was part of the name) was created by a fledgling cartoonist named Bob Kane. The Dark Knight, as the Batman was also known, originally appeared in the anthology *Detective Comics* (#27, May 1939) and had his own comic magazine in 1940. These early stories had a hard edge to them, with the Batman dealing out justice in as harsh a manner as he deemed necessary. To soften this edge a bit and make the character more human and approachable, he was given a youthful sidekick named Robin, and the two waged a kinder, gentler war on crime. Through the passing years, Batman and Robin have gone through numerous mutations, from the *noir* crimefighters of the forties, to the science fiction and fantasy–oriented duo they became in the fifties and early sixties, to the campy do-gooders they were in the middle to late sixties (as a result of the high camp "Batman" television show). In the 1970s, Batman returned to his loner roots, once more the Dark Knight fighting crime alone. Batman is one of the very few comic book heroes to have actually endured, without a break in publication, from the very beginning of what is generally called the golden age of comic book superheroes.

Batman Forever *see under* **Batman**

Batman Returns *see under* **Batman**

Battle for the Planet of the Apes *see under* **Planet of the Apes**

The Beastmaster
(MGM/United Artists/Leisure Investment Company, 1982; 120 min.) ***

Produced by Paul Pepperman and Sylvio Tabet. Directed by Don Coscarelli. Screenplay, Don Coscarelli and Paul Pepperman. Based on the novel by Andre Norton. Edited by Roy Watts. Director of Photography, John Alcott. Color. Music, Lee Holdridge. Dolby Stereo. Costumes, Betty Pecha Madden. Special Visual Effects Consultant, Michael Minor. Special Effects, Roger George, Frank DeMarco. Dar's Sword, Victor Anselmo.

Cast: Dar (Marc Singer), Kiri (Tanya Roberts), Maax (Rip Torn), Seth (John Amos), Tal (Josh Milrad), Zed (Rod Loomis), Young Dar's Father (Ben Hammer), Young Dar (Billy Jacoby), Witchwoman #1 (Janet De-May).

Synopsis: After King Zed banishes the bloodthirsty priest Maax, the king and his pregnant bride are placed under a witch's spell that transfers their unborn child to a cow's womb. The enchantress removes the

baby from the bovine, brands its hand with a symbol, and prepares to murder it. Providentially for the babe, a passing farmer kills the witch and saves the child. The child is named Dar and grows to manhood, during which time he finds that he has an uncommon affinity with animals. When the Juns attack Dar's village and massacre the inhabitants, Dar's dog pulls him to safety. Accompanied by an eagle, two ferrets and a great cat, Dar pursues the Juns. He meets Kiri, a slave girl of the temple, and follows her to the city, on the way encountering a strange bird-like people who allow him to go free when the eagle appears. Maax realizes a deadly enemy is at hand and sends out assassins. Dar meets Seth, once an intimate of King Zed, now guardian of Tal, Zed's young son. He also learns that Kiri is actually a princess and Tal's cousin. Entering the temple, Dar, Tal and Kiri find a blinded Zed. Maax's witch blinds Dar, but he kills her when his tiger's eyes substitute. Zed will not listen to reason and wait for Seth to gather a rebel army. He rejects Dar and is captured in the abortive attack. Dar returns, frees Kiri, Seth and Tal and fights his way to the top of the sacrificial pyramid, but he sees Maax kill Zed. Maax himself falls into the fiery pit along with one of Dar's ferrets, which sacrifices itself to save its human master. The people rise up, but the Juns arrive. Dar defeats the Jun leader, and the battle is won when the bird people swoop down and destroy those Juns that have survived the fiery moat. Dar leaves Tal to rule. Kiri follows him.

Reviews: "Much scope and unflagging vitality.... Singer is an appealing hero." (Kevin Thomas, *Los Angeles Times Calendar*, August 19, 1982, p. 4)¶"Rambles addlepatedly through a rehash of *Conan the Barbarian*. In its crude way, ... it is marginally livelier than the Milius film." (Tom Milne, *Monthly Film Bulletin*, April 1983, p. 93) ¶"Laughable, romantic, big on animals and terribly juvenile." (Archer Winsten, *New York Post*, August 20, 1982, p. 49)

Analysis: There is much to recommend: the scenery of desert, forest, and field. It was filmed in California's Simi Valley. Tanya Roberts' tasteful woodland bathing scene is excised from network television airings. The best line is Dar's "Which way did the Jun horde go?" The Juns are more like a Gary Larson Far Side hordette. The film is about 15 minutes too long.

Beastmaster 2: Through the Portal of Time

(New Line Cinema, 1991; 107 min.) **

Produced and directed by Sylvio Tabet. Screenplay, R.J. Robertson, Jim Wynorski, Sylvio Tabet, Ken Hauser, Doug Miles. Story, Jim Wynorski and R.J. Robertson. Adapted from characters created by Andre Norton. Edited by Adam Bernardi. Director of Photography, Ronn Schmidt. Color. Music, Robert Folk. Costumes, Betty Madden. Special Effects, Frank Isaacs and Mel. Stunts, Brian McMillan.

Cast: Dar (Marc Singer), Jackie Trent (Kari Wuhrer), Arklon (Wings Hauser), Lyranna the Witch (Sarah Douglas), Lead (Charles Young), Inquisitor (Charles Hyman), Creature (John Fifer), Exeter (Eric Waterhouse), Policemen (Dan Woren, Carl Ciarfalio), Zavik (Robert Z'Dar), Admiral Binns (Larry Dobkin), Herbert Trent (Mark Roberts).

Synopsis: Upon the death of Maax, Dar leads the rebels against Arklon. Captured, Dar escapes with the assistance of an eagle and tiger. Arklon's attention is diverted by the witch Lyranna, who shows him the portal to the future. In that future a young woman speeding away from police crashes into Arklon's world. Arklon finds cars fascinating and orders his men to pursue the fleeing woman, whose name is Jackie. Captured after she meets Dar, Jackie enters the portal into modern Los Angeles with Lyranna and Arklon. Dar follows with eagle, tiger and ferrets. Confronting each other in an alley, Arklon and Dar spy a symbol on each other's palms. They are brothers. Nevertheless, Arklon will have the neutron detonator and prevents Dar from following him. Dar is subdued by the police, his tiger taken to a zoo. He breaks free, however, and is picked up by Jackie, who escaped from Arklon in a department store and who takes Dar to the mansion of her father, a United States senator. Jackie shows Dar the sights of the twentieth century. Meanwhile, Lyranna falls in with Arklon, who masquerades as a military man and steals the neutron detonator from the local military base. Cast aside later, Lyranna joins Dar and Jackie. At the zoo Dar and Arklon battle. Arklon uses his "laser" beam to open the earth, but Dar pulls Arklon into the crevice. A general disarms the detonator with one second left. Dar and his animal pals reenter the portal to their parallel universe, where pilgrims begin worshipping Jackie's red sports car.

Review: "Gets off to a suitably campy start.... but quickly fades to a series of tired new-alien-in-town jokes.... Even fans of the genre are likely to be disappointed." (Randy Pitman, *Library Journal*, March 15, 1992, p. 141)

Analysis: It's mildly entertaining with a few good in-jokes, e.g., Sarah Douglas chiding Arklon for his weak power beam. Recall General Zod's flame balls in *Superman II* in which Douglas was Ursa, one of Zod's helpers. Nevertheless, the tongue-in-cheekness of this sequel is probably a mistake.

Ben *see under* **Willard**

Beneath the Planet of the Apes *see under* **Planet of the Apes**

Beware! The Blob *see under* **The Blob**

Beyond Thunderdome *see* **Mad Max: Beyond Thunderdome** *under* **Mad Max**

Bill and Ted's Excellent Adventure

(Orion, 1989; 90 min.) ***

Produced by Scott Kroopf, Michael S. Murphy, Joel Soisson. Directed by Stephen Herek. Screenplay, Chris Matheson and Ed Solomon. Edited by Larry Bock and Patrick Rand. Director of Photography, Timothy Suhrstedt. Panavision. Technicolor. Music, David Newman. Dolby Stereo. Art Direction, Gordon White. Set Decoration, Jennifer Williams. Neanderthal Makeup, Kevin Yagher. Visual Effects Supervisor, Barry Nolan. Costumes, Jill Ohanneson.

Cast: Ted "Theodore" Logan (Keanu Reeves), Bill S. Preston (Alex Winter), Rufus

(George Carlin), Napoleon (Terry Camilleri), Billy the Kid (Dan Shor), Socrates (Tony Steedman), Genghis Khan (Al Leong), Freud (Rod Loomis), Joan of Arc (Jane Wiedlin), Abraham Lincoln (Robert V. Barron), Beethoven (Clifford David), Mr. Ryan (Bernie Casey), Captain Logan (Hal Landon, Jr.), Missy/Mom (Amy Stock-Poynton), Princess Joanna (Diane Franklin), Princess Elizabeth (Kimberley LaBelle), Ox (Will Robbins), Randolf (Steve Shepherd), Deacon (Frazier Bain), Mr. Preston (J. Patrick McNamara), Buffy (Anne Machette), Jody (Traci Dawn Davis), Bartender (Duncan McLeod), Tattooed cowboy (John Clure), Bearded cowboy (Jim Cody Williams), Kerry (Heather Pittman), Daphne (Ruth Pittman), Old West ugly dude (Dusty O'Dee), Neanderthal #1 (Mark Ogden), Neanderthal #2 (Tom Dugan), Three most important people in the world (Martha David, Clarence Clemons, Fee Waybill).

Synopsis: Bill and Ted, well-meaning intellectual pygmies attending school in San Dimas, California, are visited by Rufus, a man from A.D. 2680. He has been sent to help them along in life so their contribution to the future preserves that future. It is endangered by the fact that they'll flunk school if they don't get an A+ on their oral history report. Ted's father is set to send him to military school in Alaska. With a special phone book and booth, Bill and Ted stop first in Austria in 1805 and pick up Napoleon. In New Mexico in 1879 they escape a shootout with Billy the Kid. In Athens, 410 B.C., they abduct Socrates. They arrive in England in the fifteenth century, are captured and about to be executed but are saved by Billy and Socrates. They mistakenly go to A.D. 2680 and meet Rufus's cohorts. "Be excellent to each other," says Bill. "Party on, dudes," says Ted. Meanwhile, in San Dimas, Napoleon is being attended to by siblings. Bill and Ted head for Vienna and pick up Sigmund "Frood" in 1901. Next it's Kassel, Germany, in 1810: Beethoven. In 1429 they grab Joan of Arc in Orleans, France. In Outer Mongolia, 1209, they find Genghis Khan. Abraham Lincoln is abducted from the White House in 1863. Because their antenna is broken, Bill and Ted find themselves in 1,000,000 B.C. until Bill patches it up. Back to San Dimas, they situate their charges in

the mall while they look for Napoleon. He's found at the Waterloo waterslide park. Meanwhile, the other historical personages have been arrested. Ted gets his father's keys and releases them. At school, Bill and Ted put on a demonstration that gets them the A+. Rufus brings them the princesses from England and says they will indeed form the band the Wyld Stallyns, which will provide the music of the future, stop war and align the planets. Rufus presents them with guitars and jams with them.

Reviews: "Incredibly, almost any line of dialogue could have been spoken by any one of the characters." (Randy Pitman, *Library Journal*, September 1, 1989, p. 229) ¶"Meant to be funny, but it only swells the sinus passages." (Vincent Canby, *New York Times*, February 17, 1989, p. C12)

Analysis: The *Library Journal* ranked the plot just above protozoan life-forms for intelligence, but hey, it's amusing enough for our passing grade. It engenders some yucks, e.g., when our hosts introduce their historical personages on their "1988 World Tour." The continuity person flubbed. Genghis Khan is originally located in 1209, but when the presentation is made at school, Bill says the Mongol leader came from 1269. The real Genghis died in 1227. Amazingly, Keanu Reeves survived this and miscasting in *Bram Stoker's Dracula* (1992) and *Much Ado About Nothing* (1993) before finding his milieu in a hit action film of modern mien, *Speed* (1994).

Bill and Ted's Bogus Journey
(Orion, 1991; 95 min.) ***

Produced by Scott Kroopf. Directed by Pete Hewitt. Screenplay, Chris Matheson and Ed Solomon. Edited by David Finfer. Director of Photography, Oliver Wood. Panavision. Deluxe color. Music, David Newman. Dolby Stereo. Art Direction, Greg Pickrell. Set Decoration, Robin Peyton. Costumes, Marie France. Costumes and Makeup Effects, Kevin Yagher. Visual Effects, Richard Yuricich, Gregory L. McMurry.

Cast: Ted Logan (Keanu Reeves), Bill Preston/Granny Preston (Alex Winter), Grim Reaper (William Sadler), De Nomolos (Joss Ackland), Ms. Wardroe (Pam Grier), Rufus (George Carlin), Sir James Martin (Jim Martin), Missy (Amy Stock-Poynton), Captain

Bill (Alex Winter, left) and Ted (Keanu Reaves, right) fail to impress the Grim Reaper (William Sadler) in *Bill and Ted's Bogus Journey* (Orion, 1991).

Logan/Thomas Edison (Hal Landon, Jr.), Joanna (Sarah Trigger), Elizabeth (Annette Azcuy), Colonel Oats (Chelcie Ross), Gatekeeper (Taj Mahal), Bach (Robert Noble), Young Ted (Brendan Ryan), Young Bill (William Thorne), Albert Einstein (John Ehrin), Benjamin Franklin (Don Forney), Good Robot Bill (Michael "Shrimp" Chambers), Good Robot Ted (Bruno "Taco" Falcon), George Washington Carver (Ed Cambridge), Confucius (Tad Horino), Captain James Tiberius Kirk (William Shatner), The Smoker (Max Magenta), Kate Axelrod (Tanya Newbould).

Synopsis: A half-millennium in the future, De Nomolos hatches a scheme to prevent the twentieth century's Bill and Ted from affecting his future with their music and lifestyle. He sends Bill and Ted automatons back in time to disrupt their models' lives. The real Bill and Ted are preparing Wyld Stallyns for the annual Battle of the Bands. Evil Bill and Evil Ted take their twins into the desert and push them from a cliff. Finding themselves dead, Bill and Ted foil the Grim Reaper and return to San Dimas. Learning that Missy, now Ted's stepmother, is conducting a seance, they intrude but are whisked into a black void where they encounter Beelzebub. Escaping, they find themselves once more in the presence of the Reaper. He says they'll play a game of their choosing. If they win, they go back to San Dimas. If he wins, they stay in Hell. They beat the Reaper at Battleship. "Two out of three," he says. They continue to defeat him, and after he loses at Twister, he agrees to take them to Heaven. God sends them to scientists, and they pick two Martians, who accompany them to Earth and build them Good Bill and Ted robots. On stage, the good automatons destroy the bad ones. De Nomolos appears, but he is vanquished, partially because Bill and Ted's agent, Ms. Wardroe, is none other than Rufus, their futuristic mentor. Reunited with their princess band members Joanna and Elizabeth, Bill and Ted take a 16-month course in guitar and return to rock the auditorium.

Reviews: "If there's one bright spot ... it's William Sadler, who has a field day playing 'Your Royal Deathness.'" (Audrey Farolino, *New York Post*, July 19, 1991, p. 29) ¶"Hugely enjoyable sequel." (Mark

Kermode, *Sight and Sound*, January 1992, p. 38)

Analysis: Bill Sadler's performance as the Grim Reaper puts this into the passable category. In fact, it's as good (or as bad, some would say) as the original. The ad read: "Once ... they made history. Now ... they are history."

Billy the Kid vs. Dracula *see under* **Dracula**

The Bite *see* Curse II *under* **The Curse**

Blackenstein: The Black Frankenstein *see under* **Frankenstein**

Blacula

(1972; 92 min.) *****

Produced by Joseph T. Naar. Executive Producer, Samuel Z. Arkoff. Directed by William Crain. Assistant Director, Phil Cook. Screenplay, Joan Torres and Raymond Koenig. Edited by Allan Jacobs. Director of Photography, John Stevens. Movielab Color. Music, Gene Page. Songs, Wally Holmes. Art Direction, Walter Herndon. Special Effects, Roger George.

Cast: Mamuwalde/Blacula (William Marshall), Dr. Gordon Thomas (Thalmus Rasulala), Luva/Tina (Vonetta McGee), Michelle (Denise Nicholas), Sam (Elisha Cook), Lt. Peters (Gordon Pinsett) Dracula (Charles Macaulay), Nancy (Emily Yancy), Swenson (Lance Taylor, Sr.), Bobby (Ted Harris), Billy (Rick Metzler), Skillet (Jitu Cumbuka), Barnes (Logan Field), Juanita Jones (Ketty Lester), Real estate agent (Eric Brotherson).

Synopsis: Transylvania, 1780: On their mission to convince European leaders to stop the slave trade, African prince Mamuwalde and his bride, Luva, are beset by Count Dracula, who walls up Luva with her vampirized husband after cursing him: "You shall pay, black prince. I shall place a curse of suffering on you that will doom you to a living hell, a hunger. A wild, gnawing, animal hunger will grow in you, a hunger for human blood. Here you will starve for an eternity, torn by an unquenchable lust. I curse you with my name. You shall be — Blacula!" Transylvania, present day: Bobby and Billy, gay American antique dealers, buy the contents of Castle Dracula and ship them to the Port of Los Angeles. In the Andrews Brothers Warehouse they are vampirized by Blacula. In Swenson's funeral parlor, where Bobby is laid out, Blacula sees Tina, a dead ringer for his long-dead bride. He accosts her on the street but she flees, dropping her purse. He loses her when a taxi knocks him down. He vampirizes the cabby, Juanita Jones. Examining her body, Dr. Gordon Thomas sees strange neck wounds but says to himself, "That's ridiculous." At a club where Thomas and Tina are celebrating Michelle's birthday, the strange black-caped man who'd frightened Tina introduces himself as Mamuwalde. Photographer Nancy takes pictures of the party, but when she develops them finds that Mamuwalde is missing. She can't warn anyone because Blacula makes her his next victim. Mamuwalde visits Tina and tries to explain that she is his reincarnated wife. Meanwhile, Thomas enlists Michelle's aid and digs up Billy's grave. Billy erupts from the coffin, but Thomas beats him back and impales him with a wooden stake. He realizes Juanita Jones may be a vampire and calls the morgue. Sam rolls the body out but fails to lock the door as directed and is attacked. Arriving later, Lt. Peters is convinced that vampires exist when Juanita is killed a second time — by sunlight. At the club, Thomas quizzes Mamuwalde on the black arts. Hearing that Nancy hasn't been seen, he goes to her place and in her darkroom finds negatives showing Tina — without Mamuwalde. Thomas, Peters and other policemen track Bobby to the Andrews Brothers Warehouse, but only Thomas and Peters escape from the host of vampires they manage to stake or set afire. Mamuwalde confronts them outside but changes to a bat and flies off. He calls Tina to his new abode at the chemical plant. When she's mortally wounded by a policeman, Mamuwalde vampirizes her to save her and goes on the rampage, killing many police. When his coffin is found containing Tina, Lt. Peters puts a stake into her heart. Blacula is bereft and ascends to the sun-scorched roof, where he decays.

Reviews: "Well developed and catches the spirit of past [vampire] renderings...."

Marshall portrays title role with a flourish." (Whit., *Variety*, August 2, 1972, p. 18)

Analysis: Only in America could a movie with this title and plot be devised. And it's a very good blaxploitation/horror film that in a retrospective would be well paired with *Shaft*. As the *New Yorker* pointed out in "On Old Broadway" (September 9, 1972, pp. 29–30), the film was unusual both for its "warm, human relationship" between vampire and non-vampire and for the previously unexplored idea of vampire suicide. Marshall, a Shakespearean actor memorable as a gladiator in 1954's *Demetrius and the Gladiators*, is big and imposing. Thalmus Rasulala is his formidable foil. He had another leading role in *Cool Breeze*, the blaxploitation version of *The Asphalt Jungle*. Sadly, Rasulala died at age 55 in 1991.

There are numerous funny scenes, e.g., the cabby confronting the vampire: "Imbecile? Who the hell you callin' an imbecile? You the nut that ran in front of my cab! You the only imbecile on this street — boy!" Skillet: "Say man, that is one strange dude." Mamuwalde: "Make it a Bloody Mary." There are horrific scenes, e.g., Rasulala battling a vampire in a grave and during the warehouse fracas diving onto one with a stake. These vampires are active and aggressive and must be dealt with promptly. The credits are among the best ever: against a black and white background, an animated bat pursues and feeds on a blood-red maiden.

Scream Blacula Scream
(AIP, 1973; 95 min.) ***

Produced by Joseph T. Naar. Directed by Bob Kelljan. Assistant Director, Reuben Watt. Screenplay, Joan Torres, Raymond Koenig and Maurice Jules. Story, Joan Torres and Raymond Koenig. Edited by Fabien Tordjmann. Director of Photography, Isidore Mankofsky. Movielab Color. Music, Bill Marx. Title Song: "Torment." Art Direction, Alfeo Bocchicchio. Set Decoration, Chuck Pierce. Special Effects, Jack De Bron, Jr.

Cast: Mamuwalde/Blacula (William Marshall), Justin Carter (Don Mitchell), Lisa Fortier (Pam Grier), Sheriff Harley Dunlop (Michael Conrad), Willis Daniels (Richard Lawson), Denny (Lynn Moody), Gloria (Jane Michelle), Elaine (Barbara Rhoades), Ragman (Bernie Hamilton), Louis (Arnold Williams), Professor Walston (Van Kirksey), Pimp #1 (Bob Minor), Pimp #2 (Al Jones), Milt (Eric Mason), Librarian (Sybil Scotford), Maggie (Beverly Gill), Doll man (Don Blackman), Prostitute (Judith Elliotte), Cop (Dan Roth), Dennis (Nicholas Worth), Joe (Kenneth O'Brien), Sarge (Craig Nelson), Attendant (James Payne), Cop #1 (Richard Washington), Cop #2 (Bob Hoy), Sergeant Williams (James Kingsley), Woman (Arnita Bell).

Synopsis: When he learns that he will not automatically succeed his deceased mother as head of a voodoo cult, Willis Daniels vows revenge on Lisa Fortier. A one-time voodoo priest gives Willis a bag of bones and directions for a ceremony that will release power beyond that of common man. Willis raises Mamuwalde, aka Blacula, from the dead and is turned to a vampire himself. Mamuwalde recalls the curse of vampirism placed on him by Count Dracula. He attends the party Willis was supposed to attend and shares his knowledge of the African artifacts on display. He knows they come from the Sabu River region of Africa. Learning that Lisa understands voodoo, he asks her if the inner being can be controlled and a man's destiny changed? He bids adieu when Lisa must attend to Gloria, who cut her hand. Reentering the house through the garage, he attacks Gloria. Then as a bat, he flies into town and vampirizes two pimps who threaten to take his "bread." Sheriff Harley Dunlop questions Lisa about Gloria's murder, thinking that maybe a snake was responsible. While Lisa watches over Gloria's coffin, the dead woman rises and calls Lisa to her. Blacula appears and saves Lisa from the undead. He tells her he is at the mercy of powers beyond his control and needs her help. At his residence, he warns his minions not to harm Lisa. Justin, Lisa's boyfriend and formerly a police detective, reads up on the occult and tries to convince Harley vampires may be responsible for the recent murders. Reluctantly, Harley and his men accompany Justin to Willis's house. Inside, Lisa uses a voodoo doll to help exorcise Blacula's demon. But just as success seems assured, Justin breaks in. Promising to begin the ceremony again, Lisa flees with Blacula. Mamuwalde is

William Marshall is Mamuwalde, also known as Blacula, in *Scream Blacula Scream* (AIP, 1973).

overcome by his demonic self, kills several policemen, and is about to do in Justin when Lisa plunges an arrow into the voodoo doll. Blacula writhes in agony and screams to the sky.

Review: "Marshall displays the same flourish.... frequent high suspense." (Whit., *Variety*, July 4, 1973, pp. 18, 30)

Analysis: As good as its predecessor, it has similar humorous asides and scary vampire attacks. The finale, when the police assault and are assaulted by Blacula's minions, is just great. The drums in the background contribute to the tension. Without being preachy, it also makes some points about slavery: Blacula is subject to a curse, as were his modern African-American kinsmen. He makes this clear when confronted by two pimps: He tells them that by subjugating women, they are merely aping their former masters. Richard Lawson has the best monologue. After becoming undead, he dresses to the nines in perhaps the worst jive suit ever. But he can't see how he looks in the mirror and

turns to Blacula: "Hey look man, I don't mind being a vampire and all that shit but, but this really ain't hip. I mean, a man has got to see his face! Shit!" With the *Count Yorga* director Kelljan, we have a man who knows how to deliver a quality action-exploitation film. See also his *Rape Squad* (aka *Act of Vengeance*). We'd like to think Blacula *was* exorcised. He was a noble villain. The June 27th *Variety* had a full-page ad on page 21: "The Black Prince of Shadows Stalks Earth Again!/William Marshall ... as Dracula's Blood brother, sets a death-trap for revenge!/ALL NEW!/Pam Grier ... that 'Coffy' spitfire is a Voodoo Priestess now!"

The Blob

(Paramount/Tonylyn Films, 1958; 85 min.) ***

Produced by Jack H. Harris. Directed by Irvin S. Yeaworth, Jr. Assistant Director, Bert Smith. Screenplay, Theodore Simonson and Kate Phillips. Edited by Alfred Hillmann.

Director of Photography, Thomas Spalding. Color, DeLuxe. Music, Ralph Carmichael, Burt Bacharach, Hal David. Sound, Godfrey Buss, Robert Clement. Art Direction, William Jersey, Karl Karlson. Special Effects Supervisor, Bart Sloane.

Cast: Steve Andrews (Steven McQueen), Jane Martin (Aneta Corseaut), Lt. Dave (Earl Rose), Dr. T. Hallen (Steven Chase), Sergeant Burt (John Benson), Old man (Olin Howlin), Diner owner (Vince Barbi), Mrs. Martin (Audrey Metcalf), Mrs. Porter (Elinor Hammer), Danny Martin (Keith Almoney), Sally (Julie Cousins), Tony Gressette (Robert Fields), Mooch Miller (James Bonnet), Al (Anthony Granke). With Jasper Deeter.

Synopsis: Outside Downingtown, an old man probes a small meteorite, which disgorges a painful goo onto his arm. Found by teenager Steve Andrews and Jane Martin, he is taken to Dr. Hallen. The doctor is mystified by the growth, and the man is engulfed — eaten — by the "blob." Dr. Hallen's nurse throws acid on it — to no effect — and is killed. Steve sees Hallen thrashing around through the window but can't convince the authorities, although policeman Dave is sympathetic. After being chased by the blob in Steve's father's market and hiding in the freezer, Steve and Jane gather their friends and rouse the town. The police arrive and find no monster, but a crowd rushes screaming down the street. The now gigantic blob has chased them from the movie theater. Steve and Jane hole up in the diner with Jane's young brother, the cook, and the waitress. The building is surrounded by the creature. When the police try to electrocute it, they start a fire instead. In the basement, Steve finds that a CO2 fire extinguisher deters the blob, which withdraws from the cold. Yelling upstairs to the still connected phone, Steve makes his discovery known. Teenagers and firemen gather up all the fire extinguishers they can and force the blob away from the diner. Steve and Jane are rescued, and the blob is airlifted to the arctic. "The End ?"

Reviews: "Talks itself to death.... Most of the trick effects ... look pretty phony." (Howard Thompson, *New York Times*, November 7, 1958, p. 23) ¶"Good prospects of turning a profit.... McQueen ... makes with the old college try." (Gilb., *Variety*, September 10, 1958)

Analysis: Filmed in southeastern Pennsylvania at Valley Forge Studios, this very famous piece of pop culture is a model of a decent movie on a small budget. Everything takes place at night. The Downingtown Diner was used for some shots and Phoenixville's Colonial Theatre (hanging on still in the 1990s) for others. Miniatures were also employed. Is it the original "feel good" film? Although some policemen and parents are harsh on the teens initially, they come around and even contribute. Note the principal who hesitates but decides it's okay to break the window of the school door so they can get the fire extinguishers. And the cop who's been a jerk gets to use his marksmanship to try electrocuting the blob. One can analyze this on a Cold War level as well. A humorous interlude involves an older man who rises at the sound of the horns and sirens, wondering if it's an air raid or a fire and which helmet he should wear. This was not Steve McQueen's first film, but it was his first leading role. His acting is as natural as can be. Working titles: *The Molten Meteor, The Glob*. Double-billed with *I Married a Monster from Outer Space*.

Beware! The Blob
(Jack H. Harris Enterprises, 1972; 88 min.) **½

Produced by Anthony Harris. Directed by Larry Hagman. Screenplay, Jack Woods and Anthony Harris. Story, Richard Clair and Anthony Harris. Edited by Tony De Zarraga. Director of Photography, Al Hamm. Color, DeLuxe. Music, Mort Garson. Animal Sequences, Dean Cundey. Special Effects, Tim Baar.

Cast: Bobby (Robert Walker), Lisa Clark (Gwynne Gilford), Chester (Godfrey Cambridge), Sheriff Jones (Richard Webb), Joe's girlfriend (Carol Lynley), Barber (Shelley Berman), Marion (Marlene Clark), Joe (Gerrit Graham), Lisa's friend (Cindy Williams), Scoutmaster (Dick Van Patten), Drunks in barn (Larry Hagman, Burgess Meredith). With Richard Stahl.

Synopsis: After laying pipeline in the permafrost, Chester returns with a canister turned up by a bulldozer. Taken from the freezer, its lid pops off and a red goo emerges — and devours a fly, a kitten,

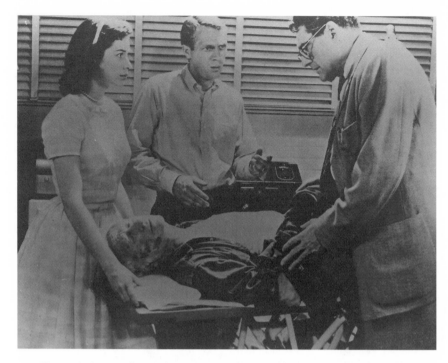

An old man (Olin Howlin, reclining) is much the worse for his encounter with a meteorite; teenagers Steve (Steve McQueen) and Jane (Aneta Corseaut) press Dr. Hallen (Steven Chase) for explanations in *The Blob* (Paramount/Tonylyn, 1958).

Chester's wife Marion, and Chester while he's watching *The Blob* on TV. Lisa Clark arrives in time to see Chester engulfed. She finds boyfriend Bobby. When they return there's no body, no blob. Sheriff Jones quizzes the duo. People begin disappearing around town, but Jones thinks they're at the bowling tournament. Trapped in their truck by the blob, Bobby and Lisa accidentally trip the air conditioner, and the blob draws back. They try to locate the sheriff at the bowling alley, but along with the owner they are trapped in the adjacent uncompleted ice rink by the now enormous blob. The blob oozes into the booth, but retreats when ice from a portable refrigerator spills onto it. Realizing the cold deters it, Bobby climbs a rope to the switch that will cause ice to form in the rink. He succeeds, the press arrives, and out on the frozen creature Sheriff Jones expounds on the danger mankind faced and defeated. A lamp thaws some ice, and a bit of the blob

flows down to the sheriff's boot. He looks down and exclaims, "What?"

Reviews: "Plenty of suspense.... Direction is sufficiently high-tempoed...." (Whit., *Variety*, June 7, 1972, p. 18.)

Analysis: Now viewed as a relic of mid to late hippiedom, this was first seen by your authors in the U.S. Army & Air Force Theater at Coleman Barracks in Sandhofen, West Germany, in 1972. Our opinions are colored by that unique experience. It seemed a riot. Check out the guy trying to keep the blob at bay with a crucifix! It's actually more primitive than the original, but it's a good bit of fun. It has the oddest cast: Carol Lynley, her heyday over; Godfrey Cambridge, who was making big films like *Cotton Comes to Harlem*; director Larry Hagman between hit TV series *I Dream of Jeannie* and *Dallas*; pre–*American Graffiti* Cindy Williams; Burgess Meredith slumming. Richard Webb, TV's Captain Video of the 1950s, steals the show, and his "What?" line is priceless. How are the effects? Not good, but not pitiful. There's some tension, and some nods to the predecessor. There *is* too much footage that's not germane, e.g., the barber shop, the sewer drain. Aka *Son of Blob.*

The Blob
(Tri-Star, 1988; 92 min.) ***

Produced by Jack H. Harris and Elliott Kastner. Directed by Chuck Russell. Screenplay, Chuck Russell and Frank Darabont. Edited by Terry Stokes and Tod Feuerman. Director of Photography, Mark Irwin. Color. Music, Michael Hoenig. Sound, Robert J. Anderson, Jr. Art Direction, Jeff Ginn. Set Decoration, Anne Ahrens. Makeup, Tony Gardner. Special Effects, Dream Quest Images. Visual Effects Supervisor, Hoyt Yeatman. Creature Effects Design, Lyle Conway. Additional Creature Effects Supervisor, Stuart Ziff.

Cast: Meg Penny (Shawnee Smith), Brian Flagg (Kevin Dillon), Paul Taylor (Donovan Leitch), Sheriff Briggs (Jeffrey DeMunn), Fran Hewitt (Candy Clark), Mr. Penny (Art La Fleur), Mrs. Penny (Sharon Spelman), Reverend Meeker (Del Close), Scott Jeskey (Ricky Paul Goldin), Deputy Briggs (Paul McCrane), Can man (Billy Beck), Dr. Meadows (Joe Seneca), Kevin Penny (Michael Kenworthy), Vicki (Erika Eleniak).

Synopsis: Outside Arborville in Fayette County, a hermit pokes the crater created by a meteor. A thick ooze speeds up the stick onto his arm. Town punk Brian, high school football jock Paul and cheerleader Meg take the man to the hospital, where the doctor finds the patient's lower extremities eaten away. The physician and Paul are engulfed by the horrible culprit. Meg escapes and tries to explain what she saw to Brian. Meanwhile, the blob consumes teenagers necking in a car on a lover's lane and sucks a cook into a sink. Again, Meg escapes, but Fran stops to make a phone call and is taken. Reverend Meeker picks up frozen pieces of the alien, pieces left when it withdrew from the freezer where Meg and Brian took refuge. Men attired in white anti-contamination suits arrive and inspect the crater. Suspecting they are hiding something, Brian refuses to go along with their suggestions and gets away. Meg goes to the movie theater to get her young brother Kevin. The now giant blob enters the projectionist's booth, then the auditorium. Meg and her brother flee into the sewer. Brian learns that the meteor was actually a satellite and that it returned to earth with an experimental virus that hunts prey and grows geometrically. Brian finds Meg after she helps Kevin escape, but Brian, a government man and Meg are closed in the sewer on purpose by Dr. Meadows. Using a LAW rocket, Brian breaks them out. Disrupting the three-way armed confrontation between Brian, Meadows and the town police, the blob drags Meadows down. "Let's frag that son-of-a-bitch!" concludes the colonel. But grenades merely goad it into the street. Meg uses a fire extinguisher to keep it at bay until Brian finds a snow-making truck. Meg blows it up and the "snow" covers the creature, which seems destined for an ice house. Outside town, Reverend Meeker tells listeners in a tent revival that the day of reckoning is near. He observes the small, living blob in his jar.

Review: "Blob effects ... are pretty neat.... Like all the best weirdies, *The Blob* '88 covers more than towns and teenagers: underneath the gooey glob is a political subsurface." (Thomas Doherty, *Cinefantastique*, January 1989, pp. 98-99)

Analysis: It's a true remake in the sense that many elements of the first — and second — movies are recapped. Are there no other interesting venues besides a diner, a movie theater, and a sewer? That carping aside, we do like "sewer/confined spaces" movies and wish this one had spent more time underground. This blob moves fast and provides some chilling and gruesome moments. The film itself has a brisk pace. Some of us object to the constant cinematic harping on a government conspiracy behind the apparent raison d'être. Maybe it was even there in the past (the old civil defense man in the original *Blob*), but it becomes irritating when the filmmakers use it like a sledgehammer. Note Erika Eleniak in the small part of a teenager smooching on lover's lane. She'd become a *Playboy* Playmate and co-star of bigger productions, like *Under Siege* (1992) and *The Beverly Hillbillies* (1993).

Blood from the Mummy's Tomb

(Hammer, 1971; 90 min.) ***

Produced by Howard Brandy. Directed by Seth Holt and Michael Carreras. Screenplay, Christopher Wicking. Based on Bram Stoker's novel *The Jewel of the Seven Stars*. Edited by Peter Weatherley. Director of Photography, Arthur Grant. Color. Music, Tristram Cary. Art Direction, Scott MacGregor. Special Effects, Michael Collins.

Cast: Margaret/Tera (Valerie Leon), Fuchs (Andrew Keir), Corbeck (James Villiers), Dandridge (Hugh Burden), Berigan (George Coulouris), Tod Browning (Mark Edwards), Helen Dickerson (Rosalie Crutchley), Dr. Putnam (Aubrey Morris), Doctor (David Markham), Mrs. Caproal (Joan Young), Male nurses (James Cossins, David Jackson), Saturnine young man (Jonathan Burn), Youth in museum (Graham James), Veronica (Tamara Ustinov).

Synopsis: Margaret Fuchs has nightmares of ancient Egypt and the burial of a beautiful woman. Her father, an archaeologist, gives Margaret a talisman: a large red ring with unusual elements. Margaret and her boyfriend Tod Browning soon learn that while part of an expedition, Professor Fuchs found the sarcophagus of one Tera, perceived by her contemporaries as an evil being. Her right hand had been severed to curtail her power, but that hand — and the red ring — were found near the remarkably well preserved body. As Fuchs was uncovering Tera, his wife died giving birth to Margaret in England. Corbeck, another member of the expedition, wants to resurrect Tera, whose astral spirit roams the universe. As seven stars come into alignment, that time is nigh. Other expedition members Dandridge, Berigan, and Dickerson die, and Tod is killed when his car crashes into a tree. While Corbeck reads the Scroll of Life over Tera and the severed hand becomes reconnected, Fuchs has second thoughts and tries to stop the ceremony. Although they manage to kill Corbeck, Fuchs and Margaret must grapple with a risen Tera. Margaret succeeds in driving a knife into the body. The building then crashes down. In the hospital, Margaret — or Tera — awakes — bandaged and unable to speak.

Reviews: "Fulsome melodrama.... chill effects that often approach the class of *The Beast with Five Fingers*.... Valerie Leon ... fills out her dual role as amply as could be wished." (Gordon Gow, *Films and Filming,* January 1972, p. 62) ¶ "Is for almost its entire length tremendous fun, skillful and wonderfully energetic.... [It shows] a fine respect for the horror heritage, a young hero named Tod Browning, and for a heroine a millennium's old free-floating astral spirit named Tera — who, as currently embodied in Miss Valerie Leon, is a 500 per cent knockout." (Roger Greenspun, *New York Times,* May 18, 1972, p. 55) ¶ "Polished and well-acted but rather tame...." ("Jock.," *Variety,* October 27, 1971, p. 18)

Analysis: There's no bandaged mummy monster and few obvious chills. Nevertheless, it is engrossing and consistently entertaining. The role was perfect for Valerie Leon, stunning in her nightdress. Why wasn't she in more horror films? Note the character name in-joke: the real Tod Browning directed *Dracula.*

The Awakening

(EMI/Orion/Warner Bros., 1980; 102 min.) ***

Produced by Robert Solo. Directed by Mike Newell. Screenplay, Allan Scott, Chris Bryant and Clive Exton. Based on Bram Stoker's novel *The Jewel of Seven Stars.* Edited by Terry Rawlings. Director of Photography, Jack Cardiff. Panavision. Color, Technicolor. Music, Claude Bolling. Dolby Stereo. Art Direction, Lionel Couch. Set Decoration, Tessa Davies. Makeup, George Frost. Main Title Graphics, Maurice Binder. Special Effects, John Stears.

Cast: Matthew Corbeck (Charlton Heston), Jane Turner (Susannah York), Anne Corbeck (Jill Townsend), Margaret Corbeck (Stephanie Zimbalist), Paul Whittier (Patrick Drury), Dr. Khalid (Bruce Myers), Dr. El Sadek (Nadim Sawalha), Dr. Richter (Ian McDiarmid), Yussef (Ahmed Osman), John Matthews (Leonard Maguire).

Synopsis: "Eighteen Years Ago": Archaeologist Matthew Corbeck and his assistant Jane search for the tomb of an Egyptian queen. Corbeck's pregnant wife feels abandoned back at the base. Away from the main dig, Corbeck and Jane discover the tomb they've sought. Jane finds hieroglyphs that repeatedly say, "Live again." The closer they get to the sarcophagus, the closer Corbeck's wife gets to bearing her child. She is in fact rushed to a hospital. The baby seems stillborn, but after the doctors give up, it evinces life. Corbeck has a problem with an Egyptian official who tries to stop the removal of the artifacts, but a snapped wire kills the official. Most artifacts are studied in a Cairo museum, but Corbeck is given a large ankh, which finds its way to his daughter. Time passes. Corbeck and Anne divorce. Living in New York, Margaret reaches the age of eighteen and feels the need to see her father in England. Meanwhile an eclipse has caused changes in the mummy in Cairo. The officials think perhaps bacteria has invaded the body and want to extract a portion of the flesh to examine. Corbeck objects and says he'll take it to England. The man standing in his way is killed by a truck. Margaret arrives, and her father takes her to Egypt, where they find the canopic jars containing the vital organs of the long-dead queen. Matthew secretes them in his luggage. At an English observatory he verifies that there have been 31 eclipses since the queen's entombment and that Ursa Major is aligned as it was then. He is fearful of what he might unleash and phones Jane to break the canopic jars. While attempting the deed, Jane falls from a window and is killed by a shard of glass. After Jane's funeral and after Margaret evinces strange behavior and illness, Matthew realizes he must try to resurrect the ancient queen if for no other reason than to save his daughter. He takes the canopic jars to the museum, where he invokes ancient Egyptian deities. Margaret urges him on. When he cuts open the mummy's bandages and touches the dried flesh while reciting incantations, nothing happens. He thinks he's failed until Margaret's personality changes. Realizing too late that the mummy's spirit has passed into his daughter, Matthew is crushed by a statue.

Review: "An eerie, sporadically frightening film.... stands a notch above the recent trend of low-budget scare pictures. Charlton Heston ... surmounts the twin obstacles of an offbeat role and occasionally silly dialogue simply by underplaying." (Raymond Pignone, *Cinemacabre* no. 4, pp. 37-39)

Analysis: Needless to say, with Jack Cardiff as the cinematographer, the Egyptian locales are well photographed. A solid double feature would include this and 1976's *The Omen.* The transformation (makeup, sneer, expression, laugh) of Stephanie Zimbalist into the resurrected Egyptian queen is very well done. Befitting occult films of this period, evil wins, but in this instance it is acceptable.

Blood of Dracula's Castle *see under* **Dracula**

Blood Sacrifice *see* Curse III *under* **The Curse**

The Blue Bird
(20th Century–Fox, 1940; 98 min.)
***

Produced by Gene Markey. Directed by Walter Lang. Screenplay, Ernest Pascal. Additional Dialogue, Walter Bullock. Based upon the play by Maurice Maeterlinck. Edited by Robert Bischoff. Directors of Photography, Arthur Miller, Ray Rennahan. Technicolor. Music, Alfred Newman. Art Direction, Richard Day, Wiard B. Ihnen. Set Decoration, Thomas Little. Costumes, Gwen Wakeling. Special Effects, Fred Sersen.

Cast: Mytyl (Shirley Temple), Tyltyl (Johnny Russell), Tylette the Cat (Gale Sondergaard), Tylo the Dog (Eddie Collins), Light (Helen Ericson), Mummy Tyl (Spring Byington), Angela Berlingot (Sybil Jason), Daddy Tyl (Russell Hicks), Mr. Luxury (Nigel Bruce), Mrs. Luxury (Laura Hope Crews), Wild Plum (Sterling Holloway), Fairy Berylune (Jessie Ralph), Oak (Edwin Maxwell), Footman (Brandon Hurst), Little sister (Ann Todd), Child (Scotty Beckett), Mrs. Berlingot (Leona Roberts), Father Time (Thurston Hall), Cypress (Dorothy Dearing), Studious boy (Gene Reynolds), Grandpa Tyl (Al Shean), Granny Tyl (Cecilia Loftus), Wilhelm (Stanley Andrews), Major Domo (Keith Hitchcock), Footman (Herbert Evans), Caller of Roll (Frank Dawson), Royal Forester (Dewey Robinson), Child (Payne Johnson), Boy inventor (Buster Phelps), Little girl (Diane Fisher), Lover (Dorothy Joyce).

Synopsis: Mytyl and her younger brother Tyltyl capture a bird in the forest and return late for dinner. Having passed a home in which children are enjoying a sumptuous Christmas party, Mytyl complains of being poor and sad. Her mother calls her an ungrateful child. During dinner a messenger arrives to tell Mytyl's father that the army must mobilize against Napoleon. Mytyl's mother is grief-stricken, fearing her husband will not return. During the night, Mytyl and Tyltyl hear a knock at the front door and find themselves greeting an old lady who claims to be Fairy Berylune. She uses her magic powers to dress them for a journey to find the bluebird and be happy. She changes their dog Tylo into a man and cat Tylette into a woman to accompany them and sends Light in the form of a beautiful woman to guide them. Light takes the foursome to a graveyard and tells them to enter, but they must return in an hour or they'll remain in the past. Mytyl and company find themselves in the presence of her grandparents, who awake whenever someone they've left behind thinks of them. Mytyl finds no bluebird in Granny's aviary, and although the devious Tylette turns back the clock hands, Mytyl leaves in time to find Light. Mytyl proceeds to the Land of Luxury, warned by Light not to spend too much time. Tylette enjoys this journey, but when Mytyl, with Tylo's help, gets ready to leave, Tylette informs the forest that they must stop her. The trees decide to destroy the children, going so far as to enlist the aid of their ancient enemies, wind and lightning. But Tylette is the victim of the fiery holocaust; Mytyl, Tyltyl and Tylo escape, and Light sends them to the Future. They see children waiting to be born, including their own sister. Light guides them home, and Mytyl and Tyltyl wake in their beds. The house seems light and airy, and their father doesn't have to go to war because of a truce and impending treaty. Even Tylette is still alive. And the bird Mytyl caught in the forest is now blue. She takes it to Angela, who almost miraculously recovers from her illness. But the bird flies free when Angela holds it. She's distraught, but Mytyl tells her they can find it again

because they know where it is. "Don't we?" she asks the audience.

Review: "Acceptable.... Edifying and moralistic and not too frightening...." (Frank S. Nugent, *New York Times*, January 20, 1940, p. 11)

Analysis: The film is good but was not a financial success, and some say it was a harbinger of doom for Temple, who nevertheless did have some nice teenage roles in the forties, e.g., *The Bachelor and the Bobby-Soxer, Fort Apache*. The switch from black and white to color occurs when Mytyl is awakened by the fairy. This was supposed to be Fox's answer to *The Wizard of Oz*, which before Judy Garland became Dorothy was to have starred Shirley Temple on loan from Fox. Academy Award nomination for Cinematography.

The Blue Bird
(20th Century–Fox, 1976; 100 min.) nv

Produced by Edward Lewis. Directed by George Cukor. Screenplay, Hugh Whitemore and Alfred Hayes. Based on the play *The Blue Bird* by Maurice Maeterlinck. Edited by Ernest Walter. Director of Photography, Freddie Young, Ionas Gritzus. Panavision. Deluxe Color. Music, Irwin Kostal. Songs and Ballet Numbers, Andrei Petrov. Lyrics, Tony Harrison.

Cast: Mother/Maternal Love/Light/Witch (Elizabeth Taylor), Luxury (Ava Gardner), Cat (Cicely Tyson), Night (Jane Fonda), Myltyl (Patsy Kensit), Tvityl (Todd Lookinland), Oak (Harry Andrews), Grandfather (Will Geer), Grandmother (Mona Washbourne), Dog (George Cole), Bread (Richard Pearson), Blue Bird (Nadia Pavlova), Sugar (George Vitzin), Milk (Margareta Terechova), Fat Laughter (Oleg Popov), Father (Leonid Nevedomsky), Water (Valentina Ganilai Ganibalova), Fire (Yevgeny Scherbakov). With Leningrad Kirov Ballet.

Reviews: "So bad you might suspect that the Chinese communists made it." (Vincent Canby, *New York Times*, January 2, 1977, Part II, p. 1)

Analysis: This was a miscalculated U.S./ U.K./U.S.S.R. co-production that nobody seems to have seen. The *New York Times* reckoned it a bore for all ages.

Body Snatchers *see under* **Invasion of the Body Snatchers**

The Boogey Man
(Interbest American Enterprises,
1980; 86 min.) ***

Produced and directed by Ulli Lommel.
Screenplay, Ulli Lommel, Suzanna Love, and
David Herschel. Edited by Terrell Tannen.
Directors of Photography, David Sperling,
Jochen Breitenstein. Color. Music, Tim Krog.
Art Direction, Robert Morgan. Set Decora-
tion, David Weiss. Special Effects, Craig Har-
ris.

Cast: Lacy (Suzanna Love), Jake (Ron
James), Willy (Nicholas Love), Dr. Warren
(John Carradine), Kevin (Raymond Boyden),
Uncle Ernest (Bill Rayburn), Helen (Felicite
Morgan), Father Reilly (Llewelyn Thomas),
Young Lacey (Natasha Schiano), Young Willy
(Jay Wright), Mother (Gillian Gordon),
Lover (Howard Grant), Jane (Jane Pratt),
Susan (Lucinda Ziesing), Timmy (David
Swim), Katy (Catherine Tambini), Teenagers
(Katie Casey, Ernest Meier, Stony Richards,
Claudia Porcelli).

Synopsis: Young Willy knifes his mother's abusive boyfriend while sister Lacey
watches. Twenty years later, Willy still
can't speak, and Lacey, though happily
married and the mother of Kevin, continues to have nightmares. Dr. Warren, a
therapist, advises Lacey's husband, Jake, to
take Lacey to the house she grew up in,
thus to exorcise the "ghosts." Meanwhile,
Willy paints all the mirrors in their farmhouse black. At her old house, in an old
mirror, Lacey sees an image of the man her
brother killed. She smashes it and Jake
picks up the pieces, taking them and the
frame home. He glues it together to prove
to Lacey that there's no one in it. That
night a piece of glass left behind on the
floor begins glowing. Timmy sees a shadow. His sister is possessed and stabs herself in the neck. Timmy is crushed by a
window frame, and his other sister is also
killed. Dr. Warren tells Lacey that destroying the mirror destroyed the ghost.
When Lacey finds Willy in the barn, she
sees a pitchfork almost impale him. When
Lacey takes Kevin to a pier to fish, neither
is cognizant that on the bottom of the boy's
shoe is a piece of the mirror. Its reflection
across the river causes the death of two
teenage picnickers. Back home, Lacey is attacked by an invisible presence, and Jake

cannot force a piece of the mirror back into
its place. He begins to believe the mirror
has an evil power and calls Father Reilly.
When the priest touches the mirror, it
glows. A scream is heard from the barn,
and when Lacey and Willy investigate, they
find the dead bodies of Uncle Ernest and
Aunt Helen. The former was impaled by a
pitchfork, the latter strangled by a hose.
Back at the house, Lacey becomes possessed by a piece of glass that attaches itself to her right eye and causes her to "levitate." Father Reilly dislodges it, and though
he is dying, he destroys it in sink water.
Jake and Willy toss the mirror in the well,
causing a jet of flame to shoot into the sky.
At the cemetery, unknown to all, the piece
of glass on Kevin's shoe falls off and begins
glowing.

Reviews: "Most movies of this ilk don't
name the unnameable horror lurking behind crime. *The Boogey Man* does: fear of
sex." (Carrie Rickey, *Village Voice,* December 17-23, 1980, p. 70) ¶"Unpretentious
and confidently told hokum." (Tim Pulleine, *Monthly Film Bulletin,* July 1981, p.
133)

Analysis: This is a somewhat primitive
(low-budget) film built around a very interesting concept. It took us a while to
figure out that water destroyed the mirror's power.

Boogeyman II
(New West Films, 1983; 79 min.) *

Produced by Bruce Starr and Ulli Lommel.
Directed by Bruce Starr. Screenplay, Ulli
Lommel and Suzanna Love. Edited by Terrell
Tannen. Directors of Photography, Philippe
Carr-Forster, David Sperling. Color, Pacific
Film Lab. Music, Tim Krog. Special Effects,
CMI Ltd., Craig Foster.

Cast: Lacey (Suzanna Love), Bonnie
(Shannah Hall), Mickey Lombard (Ulli Lom-
mel), Joseph (Shoto von Douglas), Bernie
(Bob Rosenfarb), Miss Arizona (Leslie
Smith), Kathy (Sarah Jean Watkins). With
Rock MacKenzie, Ashley Dubay, Rhonda
Aldrich.

Synopsis: Lacey visits childhood friend
Bonnie in the home of her Hollywood director husband Mickey Lombard. Lacey
tells her hosts about the "murderer" who
won't be caught and recaps the childhood

incident when her brother killed their mother's boyfriend. She tells of the psychiatrist and of the strange mirror. Bonnie thinks Lacey's story would make a great movie, but Mickey feels it would be exploiting her friend. Lacey shows them a small box that contains a St. Benedict medal, charms from the Chincoteague Indians back East, and a piece of the mirror. Only she is immune to it, she explains. Butler Joseph steals it. During a nighttime pool party to which promoters, actors and actresses are invited, the possessed Joseph helps cause their deaths. Finally Lacey realizes what is happening, and she and Bonnie drown Joseph in the pool. Lacey realizes the mirror was used against those who would exploit it. Lacey has Mickey drive her to Joseph's rude grave. His hand emerges, shines the mirror toward Bonnie's car, and it explodes. The hand withdraws into the earth.

Review: "Moronic slasher film.... almost laughable." (Leonard Maltin, *TV Movies and Video Guide 1989*, p. 115)

Analysis: It's shameful the way the filmmakers used so much footage from the original to pad this out. It's audience exploitation in the worst sense. Maybe it's really about Hollywood promoters, con men, and naive actresses. Maybe it's tongue-in-cheek. Take the murders: by corkscrew, barbecue rods, electric toothbrush, and, get this, shaving cream! If not a spoof, it's ludicrous. In any event, it's terrible. Aka *Revenge of the Boogeyman.*

The Brain *see under* **The Lady and the Monster**

Bram Stoker's Dracula *see under* **Dracula**

The Bride *see under* **Frankenstein**

Bride of Frankenstein *see under* **Frankenstein**

Bride of Re-Animator *see under* **Re-Animator**

Brides of Dracula *see under* **Dracula**

Bud the CHUD *see* C.H.U.D. II *under* **C.H.U.D.**

Captain Nemo and the Underwater City *see under* **20,000 Leagues Under the Sea**

Candyman
(TriStar, 1992; 101 min.) ***

Produced by Steve Golin, Sigurjon Sighvatsson, Alan Poul. Directed by Bernard Rose. Screenplay, Bernard Rose. Based on the short story "The Forbidden" by Clive Barker. Edited by Dan Rae. Director of Photography, Anthony B. Richmond. Panavision. Color, DeLuxe. Music, Philip Glass. Special Makeup Effects, Bob Keen.

Cast: Helen Lyle (Virginia Madsen), Candyman (Tony Todd), Trevor Lyle (Xander Berkeley), Bernadette Walsh (Kasi Lemmons), Anne-Marie McCoy (Vanessa Williams), Clara (Marianna Eliott), Jake (DeJuan Guy), Billy (Ted Raimi), Monica (Ria Pavia), Student (Mark Daniels), Diane (Lisa Ann Poggi), Danny (Adam Philipson), Harold (Eric Edwards), Stacey (Carolyn Lowery), Baby Anthony (Latesha and Lanesha Martin).

Synopsis: Graduate student Helen Lyle is researching a thesis on urban legends with friend Bernadette Walsh when their studies lead them to Chicago's crime-infested Cabrini-Green housing project. Interviews with the locals keep bringing the name "Candyman" to the surface. Allegedly a black slave who unwisely fell in love with a white woman, Candyman earned his name when a white mob sawed off his right hand, smeared him with honey and threw him into a beehive. Say his name five times before a mirror in a darkened room, the story goes, and he'll appear behind you. Not that you'd want him to, mind; a visit from the Candyman is the last one you'll ever receive. Reputedly armed with a vicious hook that takes the place of his missing right hand, Candyman's victims are invariably found dead, split from "groin to gullet." Investigating the Cabrini-Green tenements, the women come to know a young single mother, Anne-Marie McCoy, and her neighbor, 10-year-old Jake. The boy shows Helen what "sights" the neighborhood can boast, including the vacant lot which has a growing mound of refuse that will soon make up an annual bonfire celebrated in the Green. Accompanying the

boy through the slums, Helen is assaulted
by thugs whose leader mimics the *modus
operandi* of the legendary Candyman. Helen
survives the attack and attains some notoriety as her testimony leads to the arrest of
the perpetrator. Shortly thereafter, however, the woman is accosted by the *real*
Candyman, who sets in motion a series of
events which begins Helen's descent into
nightmare. When she is found, bloody and
disoriented, in Anne-Marie's apartment,
the woman's guardian Rottweiler beheaded
and McCoy screaming hysterically about
her infant son who is missing, Helen is suspected of being the kidnapper. Barely
home on bail, she is again visited by Candyman. Helen's and Bernadette's work, he
tells her, has put his very existence in
jeopardy. His people, the inhabitants of
Cabrini-Green and adjacent locales, are
ceasing to believe in him. He has taken
Anne-Marie's son and will kill the infant if
Helen doesn't agree to die in his place.
Helen is torn between the terrible prospect
of dying or seeing the child die when
Bernadette appears. Candy kills Bernadette, and the police, attracted by Helen's
screams, arrive to find her wielding a
bloody butcher knife. Institutionalized,
Helen is challenged by the hospital's chief
of psychiatry to produce Candyman.
When she does, the fiend kills the doctor.
Helen escapes and returns home only to
find that husband Trevor has taken a
teenage lover. Dispirited and broken,
Helen returns to Cabrini-Green determined at least to save Anne-Marie's baby.
She finds the infant secreted in the interior of the veritable mountain of debris.
At night, as the slum denizens set the
mound ablaze, not knowing of those in its
center, Helen drives a fiery brand into the
approaching Candyman. She snatches the
wailing infant and hurls him to safety in
the milling crowd. Burned beyond recognition, Helen stumbles from the flames
and collapses. Inside the conflagration, the
Candyman is consumed.

Review: "Virginia Madsen gives a gutsy
performance.... sacrifices cheesy special
effects in favor of interesting characterizations and bizarre set designs, making this
an enduring horror movie for the art-house

set." (Bleiler, David, ed., *TLA Film & Video
Guide 1996-1997*, p. 80)

Analysis: *Candyman* applies the usual
trappings of the genre to an urban ghetto
setting that hardly needs these accouter-
ments. Cabrini-Green has enough real-life
horrors to make a phantom like Candyman
seem lost in the crowd. The film makes this
premise work; *Candyman* is a genuinely
scary movie. The production is slick and
professional, the performances uniformly
excellent. One attractive element of *Candyman* is the hypnotic, evocative score by
noted minimalist composer Philip Glass.
The general logic of the film requires some
stretch on the audience's part, however. If
one *could* summon Candyman by saying his
name aloud five times in a darkened room
before a mirror, why in the world would
anyone want to? And the implied suggestion that the specter/killer sees Helen Lyle
as some sort of reincarnation of his lost love
seems specious, as the woman would seem
to have no discernible connection to the
Candyman's history. And, too, the film's
basic premise seems skewed: A death-dealing black boogeyman with a hook for a
hand is a frightening image, but his victims
and those others who fear him are as likely
as not to be poor, black, and ignorant—
hardly the type who should be targets of his
rage. Like Stephen King, Clive Barker is
something of a cottage industry among
horror writers. A best-selling author, his
Hellraiser became an instant genre favorite
and has spawned (to date) three sequels.
Barker's style is both literate and gruesome,
and his hallmark is an unusual seriousness
of purpose. Like King, Barker's efforts have
mined the more traditional horror digs.
Candyman aspires to a higher level than
many recent ventures in horror cinema,
most of which rely on a strong tongue-in-
cheek approach, even venturing into parody. *Candyman* is less derivative than most,
despite the slasher elements. In generating
the fright and suspense of Helen Lyle's terrifying plight, *Candyman* is a winner.

Candyman: Farewell to the Flesh
(Polygram Filmed Entertainment,
1995; 95 min.) ***

Produced by Sigurjon Sighvatsson and

Gregg Feinberg. Directed by Bill Condon. Screenplay, Rand Ravich and Mark Kruger. Story, Clive Barker. Edited by Virginia Katz. Director of Photography, Tobias A. Schliessler. Color. Music, Philip Glass.

Cast: Candyman/Daniel Robitaille (Tony Todd), Annie Tarrant (Kelly Rowan), Ethan Tarrant (William O'Leary), Reverend Ellis (Bill Nunn), Thibideaux (Matt Clark), Detective Ray Levesque (David Gianopoulos), Pam Carver (Fay Hauser), Matthew (Joshua Gibran Mayweather), Phillip Purcell (Michael Culkin), Paul McKeever (Timothy Carhart), Octavia (Veronica Cartwright).

Synopsis: Daniel Robitaille, the son of slaves and an artist by trade, was unfortunate enough to fall in love with and impregnate the daughter of a wealthy white landowner. The outraged father had Robitaille's right hand sawed off, his body smeared with honey for frenzied bees, and left for dead. Robitaille perished, but his specter — a one-handed apparition wielding a hook in place of his missing hand — appears "in the most desperate areas." Candyman, as the specter is called, is filled with sadness and hate, and murders in his name appear even in the Big Easy, a hundred years after his passing. The tale is told by Phillip Purcell, who is in New Orleans touting his book about this "urban legend." Among the attendees of the lecture is Ethan Tarrant, whose father's death the young Tarrant attributes to bad advice from Purcell. When the author is killed gruesomely in a filthy tavern restroom, there are no witnesses to see the tall black man with a hook for a hand. Tarrant is the immediate suspect and jailed. Ethan's sister Annie knows her brother is innocent, but the police are quite convinced they have Purcell's murderer as well as the culprit behind a number of earlier killings, possibly including Ethan and Annie's own father. Hoping to find some connection between this murder and her father's, Annie and husband Paul return to the Tarrant estates, a once stately colonial mansion, now the abode of derelicts and transients. Annie is shocked by the graffiti and violent street art that adorns the walls. A central theme is a tall, hook-brandishing black figure looming large amid scenes of panic and terror. Disturbingly similar scenes are sketched by Matthew, one of Annie's students. To prove that Candyman is merely a modern boogeyman, Annie unwisely utters his name four, then five, times. That evening Candyman appears and kills Paul and entreats Annie to join him, but she faints. Her story is met with skepticism by the police, who suspect that Paul's murderer is more likely a Mardi Gras celebrant than any supernatural visitor. Retreating to the home of her alcoholic mother, Octavia, Annie finds no answers to questions that plague her. When Matthew disappears, Annie seeks out his widowed father, Reverend Ellis. Matthew's sketchbooks contain further evidence that the Candyman has loomed large in the boy's imagination. Annie later visits the Cajun, Thibideaux, who reveals to her that her father knew that the Candyman's story began in New Orleans with his tryst with Caroline Sullivan, a white plantation-owner's daughter. Through Thibideaux, Annie learns that she is of Robitaille's blood. The issue of Robitaille's liaison with Caroline Sullivan was Isabel Sullivan, Annie's grandmother. Annie's parents knew this, and her father died trying to dispel Candyman's evil. Annie learns that the key to Candyman's apparent immortality is the hand mirror owned by Caroline Sullivan. Daniel Robitaille's spirit entered the glass at the moment of his death, and it was to be through this universal portal that his spirit could reenter the world of the living. In the ruined slave quarters, Annie eventually finds Matthew *and* the mirror of Caroline Sullivan. Together, the two of them smash the mirror and end (they hope) Candyman's terror.

Review: "Relies less on mysticism than on sheer blood and guts horror.... Philip Glass's mesmerizing and passionate score adds just the right note of poetic justice to this tragic tale." (Bleiler, David, ed., *TLA Film & Video Guide 1996-1997*, p. 80)

Analysis: Despite some reviews that hailed it as "scarier" than the original, *Candyman: Farewell to the Flesh* doesn't quite reach that pitch of intensity. Tony Todd recreates his role as the title character, and Helen Lyle is referred to in passing in the introduction by Michael Culkin. Otherwise, this film doesn't owe much to its predecessor. On the positive side, more of the Candyman's background is given this time around, filling in the blanks and tying him to a milieu that was mostly left vague. Also, Candyman's viciousness is more focused here than before, and a rationale for his rage is given. Good location photography and capable performances make this a better-than-average supernatural thriller.

Captive Wild Woman
(Universal 1943; 61 min.) **

Produced by Ben Pivar. Directed by Edward Dmytryk. Screenplay, Henry Sucher and Griffith Jay. Story, Ted Fithian, Neil P. Varnick, Maurice Pivar. Edited by Milton Carruth. Director of Photography, George Robinson. Art Direction, John B. Goodman, Ralph M. DeLacy. Set Decoration, Russell A. Gausman, Ira S. Webb. Makeup, Jack P. Pierce.

Cast: Beth Colman (Evelyn Ankers), Dr. Sigmund Walters (John Carradine), Paula Dupree (Burnu Acquanetta), Dorothy Colman (Martha [Vickers] MacVicar), Fred Mason (Milburn Stone), John Whipple (Lloyd Corrigan), Miss Strand (Fay Helm), Curley Barret (Vince Barnett), Gruen the feeder (Paul Fix), Cheela the ape (Ray "Crash" Corrigan), Narrator (Turhan Bey).

Synopsis: Dr. Sigmund Walters uses his Crestview Sanitarium laboratory to develop a superior race via the introduction of female sex hormones into the gorilla Cheela. Because his nurse, Miss Strand, objects, he kills her and places her brain into the ape. The new creature, seemingly an exotic but attractive woman, is dubbed Paula Dupree. Walters takes her to the circus, where she is attracted to the animal tamer and demonstrates great control over the animals. After saving Fred Mason's life, she's hired as an assistant. But Paula's animal instincts occasionally come to the fore. She becomes jealous of Beth Colman but only manages to kill a bystander. Beth begins to understand something of Paula's condition, but she can't convince Fred. Eventually Paula reverts to Cheela and Walters grabs Beth, intending to use her brain. But Beth releases Cheela from her cage. The ape kills Walters and, finding Fred attacked by his big cats, rescues him.

But a policeman thinks she's harming the man and shoots her.

Review: "Nothing to recommend.... decidedly bad taste." (Thomas M. Pryor, *New York Times*, June 7, 1943, p. 9)

Analysis: Anything is grist for the cinematic mill. Get a load of the director, a major filmmaker (*Crossfire*, 1947; *Warlock*, 1959) fulfilling his apprenticeship. Acquanetta was a guest at FANEX 6 (1992) in Baltimore.

Jungle Woman
(1944, 54 min.) *½

Produced by Will Cowan. Directed by Reginald LeBorg. Screenplay, Henry Sucher, Bernard Schubert and Edward Dein. Based on a story by Bernard Sucher. Edited by Ray Snyder. Director of Photography, Jack Mackenzie. Art Direction, John B. Goodman, Abraham Grossman. Set Decoration, Russell A. Gausman, Edward R. Robinson. Makeup, Jack P. Pierce. Special Effects, Red Guthrie.

Cast: Paula Dupree (Acquanetta), Dr. Carl Fletcher (J. Carrol Naish), Beth Colman (Evelyn Ankers), Fred Mason (Milburn Stone), Joan Fletcher (Lois Collier), Bob Whitney (Richard Davies), Willie (Eddie Hyams, Jr.), George (Christian Rub), District Attorney (Douglas Dumbrille), Dr. Meredith (Pierre Watkin), Nurse (Nana Bryant), Coroner (Samuel S. Hinds), Caretaker (Alec Craig), Fingerprint man (Richard Powers), Girl (Julie London).

Synopsis: Outside a sanitarium, Dr. Carl Fletcher is attacked by a strange humanoid form into which he jabs a hypodermic needle. The incident is not a secret, and newspapers pick up the story. The district attorney wants Fletcher prosecuted for murdering Paula Dupree. To the coroner, Fletcher reveals the facts, recalling the Whipple Circus, the mauling of Fred Mason, and the shooting of the ape Cheela by a cop. Fletcher obtained possession of the ape, found it was not dead, and doctored it back to health. In the old lab, Fletcher continued the late Dr. Walters' experiments. Cheela escaped. Right after that a strange woman was found on the grounds. She seemed to be in shock. Recovering, she said she was Paula Dupree. She found herself attracted to Bob Whitney, the fiancé of Joan Fletcher, the doctor's daughter, and tried to drown the woman but failed. Dr. Fletcher finally deduced that Paula and Cheela were one and the same. Tracking her down, he found her as the ape and used his hypodermic, so loaded with a drug it killed her. The district attorney can't believe this story when he hears it in court and calls for an autopsy. When the jurors find Paula's corpse to be half ape, Fletcher is exonerated.

Review: "Apparently Universal couldn't leave bad enough alone." (Bosley Crowther, *New York Times,* July 15, 1944, p. 19)

Analysis: If nothing else, it has a fine cast of contract players and character actors. As one can see from the plot synopsis, there's no jungle.

Jungle Captive
(1945, 64 min.) *½

Produced by Morgan B. Cox. Directed by Harold Young. Screenplay, M. Coates Webster and Dwight V. Babcock. Edited by Fred R. Feitshans, Jr. Director of Photography, Maury Gertsman. Musical Direction, Paul Sawtell. Art Direction, John B. Goodman, Robert Clatworthy. Set Decoration, Russell A. Gausman, Andrew J. Gilmore.

Cast: Paula Dupree (Vicky Lane), Dr. Stendahl (Otto Kruger), Ann Forrester (Amelita Ward), Don Young (Phil Brown), Moloch (Rondo Hatton), Jim (Ernie Adams), Inspector Harrigan (Jerome Cowan), Bill (Eddie Acuff), Fred (Charles Wagenheim), Detective (Jack Overman), Motor policeman (Eddy Chandler).

Synopsis: Dr. Stendahl, a biochemist, uses electricity and blood transfusions to successfully restore the heart of a dead rabbit. Meanwhile, in the morgue, the ugly Moloch hands in a note for the body of Paula the Ape Woman to be released to him. Although the attendant, Fred, is suspicious, he cannot prevent it because Moloch strangles him. Moloch takes the corpse to a house on Old Orchard Road, where Stendahl now takes assistant Ann. He intends to use Ann's blood to restore the ape woman's life. The transfusion does in fact revive the ape form. Stendahl must now change her into Paula Dupree, and he sends Moloch to steal the notes of the late Dr. Walters. Learning that he needs female hormones to do the deed, Stendahl procures

them from Ann, and Paula Dupree is "reborn." But her brain is not right; she still seems an animal. So Stendhal plans to put Ann's brain in Paula's cranium. Before that can occur, Paula leaves the house. Moloch tries to inform Stendhal. Assistant Don Young notices that Moloch is wearing a pin he gave to Ann and tracks the brute to the old house. Moloch captures him, however, and he has to watch preparations for the brain transplant. Only now finding out about the transplant, Moloch is maddened and must be shot by Stendhal. The ape woman kills Stendhal during the battle. The police arrive and plug her as she's about to kill Ann.

Review: "Vicky Lane plays the brainless woman with monosyllabic finesse." (J. Littauer, *New York Times,* July 7, 1945, p. 7)

Analysis: It's a bit better than the second but not as "good" as the first. A.k.a. *Wild Jungle Captive.*

Cat Girl *see under* **The Cat People**

The Cat People
(RKO, 1942; 73 min.) ***

Produced by Val Lewton. Directed by Jacques Tourneur. Screenplay, DeWitt Bodeen. Edited by Mark Robson. Director of Photography, Nicholas Musuraca. Music, Roy Webb. Art Direction, Albert D'Agostino, Walter E. Keller. Set Decoration, Darrell Silvera, Al Fields. Gowns, Renie.

Cast: Irena Dubrovna (Simone Simon), Oliver Reed (Kent Smith), Dr. Judd (Tom Conway), Alice Moore (Jane Randolph), Commodore (Jack Holt), Carver (Alan Napier), Barbara Farren (Elizabeth Russell), Zookeeper (Alec Craig), Mounted policeman (Bud Geary), Blondie (Mary Halsey), Miss Plunkett (Elizabeth Dunne), Caretaker (Murdock MacQuarrie), Minnie (Theresa Harris), Organ grinder (Steve Soldi), Taxi driver (Donald Kerr), Mrs. Hansen (Betty Roadman), Mrs. Agnew (Dot Farley), Woman (Henrietta Burnside), Bus driver (Charles Jordan), Policeman (Eddie Dew), Cafe proprietor (John Piffl), Patient (Leda Nicova).

Synopsis: Oliver Reed, a draftsman for the C. R. Cooper Ship and Barge Construction Company, meets Irena Dubrovna, a beautiful but odd young lady from Serbia.

Irena (Simone Simon, right) raises a toast with her husband, Oliver (Kent Smith, left), and Oliver's co-worker Alice (Jane Randolph) in *The Cat People* (RKO, 1941).

She provides him with the history of her land, which includes Satan worship. Oliver disdains these fairy tales of witches and cat people, even when in the Belgrade restaurant a strange woman calls Irena "sister." "Oh Irena, you crazy kid," says he. They marry but maintain separate bedrooms. Irena decides she needs professional help, and Oliver sends her to psychiatrist Dr. Judd. He thinks childhood tragedies are responsible. When Irena finds that Oliver told co-worker Alice about his problems, she follows Alice. Alice realizes someone is behind her as she walks through a tunnel. At the height of her terror a bus pulls up. Nearby a farmer finds some dead sheep. "Don't touch me," the exhausted Irena tells the concerned Oliver and weeps in the bathtub. Later she dreams of cats, Dr. Judd's pronouncements, and a key. Next day she removes the key from the panther's cage at the zoo. That evening Irena, Oliver and Alice tour a museum. Alice returns to her hotel for a late-night swim. Alice hears growling and dives into the pool, treading water while something prowls in the shadows. She screams, but when the light comes on she finds Irena, who inquires after Oliver's whereabouts. Afterward, the hotel attendant shows Alice her shredded bathrobe. Alice asks Dr. Judd about cat people and Irena's stories. Judd dismisses Alice's suspicions that she's being followed by the cat form of Irena, but Alice advises him to be careful. Judd warns Irena that her hallucinations border on insanity. Forget the legends, rid yourself of cat items, he says. Irena prepares a dinner for Oliver and says she's changed, but Oliver tells her it's too late; he loves Alice. Irena urges him to leave. Judd tells Oliver to either put Irena away *or* have the marriage annulled. Wanting to help Irena, Oliver agrees to commit her. Oliver and Alice return to their office while Judd surreptitiously leaves Oliver's door unlocked. At the office Oliver and Alice are stalked by a panther. "In the name of God, leave us in peace," says

Oliver while grasping a T-square in a crucifix-like position. The cat leaves. In the lobby they smell Irena's perfume. Irena returns home and finds Judd, who kisses her. She is transformed and kills him. Injured by the blade in Judd's walking stick, she heads for the zoo and opens the panther cage. The cat knocks her down when it leaps past. A police car runs over the cat. Alice and Oliver find Irena's body.

Reviews: "Labored and obvious attempt to induce shock." (Bosley Crowther, *New York Times*, December 7, 1942, p. 22) ¶ "Not quite so horrifying as its makers wanted it to be because Simone Simon does not give people real feline shudders." (*Time*, January 4, 1943, p. 86)

Analysis: This and its sequel are the epitome of the solid B movie: On a limited budget the filmmakers have concocted engrossing fare. Famous fright scene: Jane Randolph treading water in a darkened indoor pool as shadows and growls surround her. At least as unsettling is the scene in which Kent Smith approaches his office and hesitates at the revolving door which seems to move of itself. He looks down and sees the cleaning lady scrubbing the floor.

The Curse of the Cat People
(RKO, 1944; 70 min.) ***

Produced by Val Lewton. Directed by Robert Wise and Gunther V. Fritsch. Screenplay, DeWitt Bodeen. Edited by J. R. Whittredge. Director of Photography, Nicholas Musuraca. Music, Roy Webb. Art Direction, Albert D'Agostino and Walter E. Keller. Set Decoration, Darrell Silvera, William Stevens. Gowns, Edward Stevenson.

Cast: Irena Dubrovna (Simone Simon), Oliver Reed (Kent Smith), Alice Reed (Jane Randolph), Julia Ferren (Julie Dean), Amy Reed (Ann Carter), Barbara Ferren (Elizabeth Russell), Miss Callahan (Eve March), Edward (Sir Lancelot), Donald (Joel Davis), Lois (Juanita Alvarez).

Synopsis: In Tarrytown, New York, Amy Reed is a child who daydreams. Oliver Reed tells his wife, Alice, that Amy could almost be the child of his first wife, Irena. The day after a birthday party to which no children came because Amy put the invitations in the "magic mailbox"—a tree— Amy is called by a voice from an upstairs

window in the old Ferren house. A handkerchief with a ring is tossed out to her. A lady emerges and takes the hankie away. Oliver dismisses Amy's tale of the voice. Outside, Amy says, "I wish for a friend," and runs about as if with a playmate. Amy tells her mother about the Ferrens, and Alice says she must return the ring. Amy returns to the house and meets old Julia Ferren, an ex-actress, who refuses to take the ring back. Julia says the young woman in the house, Barbara, is not who she claims — her daughter. The Reeds' housekeeper arrives and takes Amy home. Amy has a nightmare, wakes, and wishes on her ring for a friend. The next day Amy finds a photo of Irena in a drawer. Later Irena appears to Amy in the garden. Both want a friend. Irena makes Amy promise not to tell anyone about her. Time passes. It's Christmas. Amy gives Irena a star pin and Julia Ferren a ring. Amy finds another photo of Irena, this one with Oliver. She admits that this is the friend she sees outside. Oliver punishes her for what he believes is pure intransigence. Amy's teacher discusses the unseen friends of children. Amy sneaks out of the house and enters the woods seeking Irena. The police are called in to search for her. Amy finds her way to the Ferrens' where Julia collapses on the steps. Barbara, who'd vowed to kill the child if she returned, is mollified when Amy hugs her. Amy had seen Irena there. Back home, Amy says she still sees Irena in the garden, and Oliver, though he does not look that way, says he does, too.

Reviews: "Masquerading as a routine case of Grade B horrors ... the picture is in fact a brave, sensitive, and admirable little psychological melodrama." (James Agee, *Nation*, April 1, 1944, pp. 401-2) ¶ "The box-office connection it makes to the earlier *Cat People* and its use of a conventional plot-enlivener about a haunted house are too melodramatic for the picture's needs, but even with these there has been a real effort to work them into the theme with convincing psychological presence and relationship." (Manny Farber, *New Republic*, March 20, 1944, pp. 380-81)

Analysis: There's more light to this than the original, and it is in fact a gentler film.

There are no cat people, even though four of the principals from the earlier film are on hand. The Irena music motif is good. Recommended.

Cat Girl
(Insignia, 1957; 75 min.) ***

Produced by Herbert Smith. Directed by Alfred Shaughnessy. Screenplay, Lou Rusoff. Story, Peter Hennessey. Edited by Jocelyn Jackson. Director of Photography, Peter Hennessey. Makeup, Philip Leakey.
Cast: Lenora (Barbara Shelley), Dr. Brian Marlowe (Robert Ayres), Dorothy Marlowe (Kay Callard), Cathy (Patricia Webster), Edmund (Ernest Milton), Anna (Lilly Kann), Allan (John Lee), Richard (Jack May), Roberts (John Watson), Cafferty (Martin Boddey). With Edward Harvey.
Synopsis: Lenora's Uncle Brant awaits the arrival of his niece at his rural manse. On her part, Lenora is filled with trepidation. Stopping off at a pub, she is recognized by Dr. Brian Marlowe, whom she knew when she was younger. While they talk, her husband, Richard, flirts with Cathy. Cathy's husband, Alan, is oblivious. Meanwhile, Lenora's uncle goes out into the woods with his leopard, which kills a rabbit the man then skins. When Lenora and her party arrive at her uncle's house, the housekeeper, Anna, says she was to have come alone. Exploring the outside environs, Richard and Cathy come across the returning uncle and leopard. The uncle confronts Lenora, who is told to sleep alone. Later that night, Anna wakes Lenora and takes her downstairs. Her uncle is reading from an old book about transferring the 700-year-old curse of the Brants. Lenora thinks he's mad. He warns her not to bear children; the line must cease. She runs into the woods. He lets the big cat out and tells it to kill her. When the leopard comes to Lenora, she takes pleasure touching the blood on it, then faints. The police institute a three-county search for the beast. Dr. Marlowe arrives, and Lenora informs him that the leopard is her other self. When Richard is killed, Lenora tries to convince the authorities that she's to blame. But Marlowe persuades her to go to a sanitarium. There she hears the leopard and at night transforms into a cat person.

The next night she tries to bring the leopard so Brian will believe her, but a guard's flashlight disrupts the process. Brian says she should move into a hotel for a few days and mingle with normal people. Brian's wife, Dorothy, entertains Lenora. Wishing Dorothy dead so that she can have Brian, Lenora gives Dorothy incorrect directions to the Riverview Grill in the East End, where Brian is waiting for them. She follows the leopard, which stalks Dorothy. The police are called by some passersby, and the leopard is killed by Brian's car when he learns where Dorothy really is. The police find the dead body of Lenora nearby.
Review: "British-made and cheap, but Shelley is a good actress, better than the material." (Steven H. Scheuer, *Movies on TV*, p. 61.)
Analysis: This solid, atmospheric little film owes something to *The Cat People*, but it's not a scene-for-scene remake, which is all the better. Barbara Shelley is terrific. When we see her in bed we find it startling that her shoulders are bare. She sleeps in the nude! This is proven when she sits up and we see a bare back. Of course it fits her character's feline nature, but it's still unusual for 1957, when most heroines from Mala Powers to Coleen Gray wore nightgowns. Shelley would gain a large following over the years. See *Dracula, Prince of Darkness, Quatermass III,* and *Village of the Damned.*

Cat People
(Universal/RKO, 1982; 118 min.)
**½

Produced by Charles Fries. Directed by Paul Schrader. Screenplay, Alan Ormsby. Based on a story by DeWitt Bodeen. Edited by Bud Smith and Jacqueline Cambas. Director of Photography, John Bailey. Panavision. Technicolor. Music, Giorgio Moroder. Theme Lyrics written and performed by David Bowie. Dolby Stereo. Art Direction, Edward Richardson. Set Decoration, Bruce Weintraub. Costumes, Daniel Paredes. Special Effects, Albert Whitlock and Tom Burman.
Cast: Paul Gallier (Malcolm McDowell), Irena Gallier (Nastassia Kinski), Oliver Yates (John Heard), Alice Perrin (Annette O'Toole),

Female (Ruby Dee), Joe (Ed Begley, Jr.), Billie (Tessa Richarde), Taxi driver (Patricia Perkins), Sandra (Berry Berenson), Bill (Scott Paulin), Detective Brandt (Frankie Faison), Detective Diamond (Ron Diamond), Ruthie (Lynn Lowry), Bronte (John Larroquette), Otis (Fausto Barajas), Massage parlor manager (John H. Fields), Yeatman (Emery Hollier), Moonie (Stephen Marshall), Ted (Robert Pavlovitch), Carol (Julie Denney), Indian village mother (Arione de Winter), Church woman (Francine Segal), Agent (Don Hood), Man in bar (David Showacre), Cat woman (Neva Gage), Indian girls (Marisa Folse, Danelle Hand), Police officer (John C. Isbell).

Synopsis: In a wild, orange-hued landscape, a young woman is tied to a tree. A black leopard appears. Next day the woman is brought into a cave with the leopard. Her face becomes that of Irena Gallier, who has arrived at the New Orleans airport to meet long-lost brother Paul. That evening Paul sits catlike on the sleeping Irena's bedstead. A prostitute is mauled by a black leopard. Oliver Yates, zoo curator, sedates the mysterious cat. Visiting the zoo, Irena is fascinated by the big cat and stays all day. Oliver discovers her after hours; the two have dinner. Zookeeper Joe dies from blood loss after the leopard tears off his arm, but before Oliver can shoot the beast it disappears, leaving behind a strange goo on the floor of the cage. Paul tells Irena he's been in prison, praying. He taunts her, saying only they can touch each other. She rushes outside. A police dog leads the cops to the basement of the Gallier home. Skeletons and a cage are found. Perhaps some horrendous ritual has been carried out. Oliver gives Irena a place to stay and drives her to a house he uses for fishing. Meanwhile, Paul picks up blonde and buxom Billie. When he wakes, the girl is a bloody pulp. He finds Irena and tells her the killing will stop only if they mate. He informs her that their parents were also brother and sister. "I'm not like you!" she protests, cutting him with a piece of glass and rushing from the room. He begins changing. A black leopard stalks Oliver, but Alice gets his shotgun. The cat leaps through the window and lands in the street, dead. Oliver's autopsy reveals a human arm within the

cat's cadaver! Female, Paul's housekeeper, tells Irena to live as Paul did and never love. Irena dreams of Paul and learns of their ancestors, how children were sacrificed to leopards and grew inside them till the leopards became human, or gods. At the health club Alice dives into the pool to escape what she believes is a leopard — but it's Irena. Later, Irena and Oliver make love. She turns into a cat but does not kill Oliver. The leopard is cornered on a bridge but leaps into the river. Oliver suspects its destination and drives to his summer cabin, where he finds Irena. She asks him to make love to her again. "I want to live with my own." He ties her up and accedes to her request. Later, at the zoo, Oliver hand feeds a black leopard.

Reviews: "Confusingly put together.... With the possible exception of McDowell's, the performances are of no interest." (Pauline Kael, *New Yorker*, May 3, 1982, pp. 130-31) ¶"Bodeen's little story has been crassly refashioned so as to produce juicy Freudian horrors.... but it's a rhythmless, inexpressive mess." (David Denby, *New York*, April 12, 1982, pp. 60-61)

Analysis: The first time we saw this we gave it a "good" rating, but a second viewing years later reveals a confusing story negating the film's undeniable style. Is McDowell really killed? Is it a dream when he reveals ancestry to Kinski? It takes much too long to wind up. It does pay homage to the original with the swimming pool scene (which is actually needless here) and the strange woman in the restaurant. David Denby of *New York* found Kinski "more feline than Simone Simon." There are two horrific scenes: the death of Ed Begley, Jr., and the autopsy. Sound (the snapping of the vertebrae) and visuals combine for a sickening, shocking revelation.

Cat-Women of the Moon
(Astor, 1953; 64 min.)***Bomb

Produced by Jack Rabin and Al Zimbalist. Directed by Arthur Hilton. Screenplay, Roy Hamilton. Story, Jack Rabin and Al Zimbalist. Edited by John Bushelman. Director of Photography, William Witley. 3-D. Music, Elmer Bernstein. Art Direction, William Glasgow. Set Decoration, Fay C. Babcock. Special

Effects, Jack Rubin and Al Zimbalist. Mechanical Effects, Willis R. Cook.

Cast: Lt. Kip Reisler (Victor Jory), Laird Grainger (Sonny Tufts), Helen Salinger (Marie Windsor), Douglas Smith (William Phipps), Walt Willis (Douglas Fowley), Alpha (Carol Brewster), Lambda (Susan Morrow), Zeta (Suzanne Alexander), Cat-women (Betty Allen, Judy Walsh, Ellye Marshall, Roxann Delman).

Synopsis: Moon Rocket 4 has a crew of five: four men and one woman. While radioing in to White Sands, Helen, the navigator, makes a strange reference to "Alpha." Recovering from his efforts to mitigate the effects of a meteor strike, Kip tells Helen, "You can't turn love on and off like a faucet. Believe me, baby, if I ever fell in love with you I'd chase you across the world, around the moon, and — all the way stations in between." Helen designates a landing spot on the dark side of the lunar surface and directs her companions to a cave in which they find oxygen — and giant spider-things Kip shoots with his pistol. Finding their space suits stolen, the humans proceed and discover a city inhabited by women, including Alpha, Beta and Lambda. The lunar ladies can project their thoughts; that's why Helen found them so easily. They tell her they desire to go to Earth. Their goal is conquest via their telepathic powers. Walt is killed in the caverns. Lambda, who has fallen in love with Doug, warns him, and Kip reveals to Laird that Helen has been under the cat-women's spell. Lambda procures space suits for Kip and Doug but is killed by her compatriots. Kip shoots the two cat-women making for the rocket with Helen. Kip, Laird, Helen and Doug head for home.

Review: "About earth explorers on the moon. There, says producer Al Zimbalist, they find 'ugly-looking things like giant spiders with four eyes, and they blow poisonous fumes.'" (*Time,* October 19, 1953, p. 112)

Analysis: The effects are primitive, the rocket interior so very unrealistic. There's no explanation why the rocket cabin's gravity is the same as earth's. This is the film in which three of the crew don't have oxygen tanks on their space suits when they leave the rocket! The strangest casting of all time

makes legendary screen villain Victor Jory a romantic lead. Future maestro of film music Elmer Bernstein served his apprenticeship with this and *Robot Monster.* A.k.a. *Rocket to the Moon.*

Missile to the Moon
(Astor, 1958; 78 min.)***Bomb

Produced by Marc Frederic. Directed by Richard Cunha. Screenplay, H. E. Barrie and Vincent Fotre. Edited by Everett Dodd. Director of Photography, Meredith Nicholson. Music, Nicholas Carras. Art Direction, Sham Unlimited. Set Decoration, Harry Reif. Special Effects, Ira Anderson. Visual Effects, Harold Banks.

Cast: Steve Dayton (Richard Travis), Gary (Tommy Cook), Lon (Gary Clarke), June Saxton (Cathy Downs), Dirk Green (Michael Whalen), The Lido (K. T. Stevens), Alpha (Nina Bara), Zeema (Marjorie Hellen), Lambda (Laurie Mitchell), Moon women (Marianne Gaba, Pat Mowry, Sandra Wirth, Lisa Simone, Mary Ford, Renata Hoy, Tania Velia, Sanita Pelkey).

Synopsis: About to have his homemade rocket impounded by the government, Dirk Green uses two young escaped convicts, Lon and Gary, to help him blast off for the moon. Climbing aboard at the last minute are Dirk's associate, Steve Dayton, and his fiancée, June Saxton. During a meteor shower — after a fight with Gary — Dirk is mortally injured. Steve lands the craft safely, and the four don oxygen suits to explore. Menacing rock creatures force the humans to take shelter in a cave, where they discover breatheable air and, farther on, a race of women ruled by the Lido. Because Steve has Dirk's amulet, the blind Lido believes him to be Dirk, who left the moon many years ago. She informs Steve that the moon's oxygen supply is almost gone, that they must use his rocket to find refuge on another planet. Initially failing to overcome the Lido in a test of wills, Alpha stabs the ruler and becomes the new Lido. She puts Steve into a trance and sends June into the tunnels to be exterminated by "the Dark Ones," giant spider-like monstrosities. June is saved through the efforts of Zeema, Lon and Gary. Zeema then challenges Alpha while Steve rejoins the others and makes his way outside. Although

Alpha tries to call him back with her tele-pathic powers, Zeema detonates a bomb which leads to the loss of all oxygen. Gary, weighted down with diamonds and back-ing away from the rock creatures, is blasted into a skeleton by the sun's rays. Steve, June and Lon make it to the rocket and lift off for Earth.

Review: "[A double bill with *Franken-stein's Daughter* is] 163 minutes of near agony." (Howard Thompson, *New York Times*, November 17, 1958, p. 37)

Analysis: It's a low-budget, scientifically inaccurate hoot, quite on a par with its 1953 inspiration; but while this cast is not a bunch of nobodies, it's not as "good" as that of *Cat-Women of the Moon*. Nor is the dialogue as priceless. But for the fact that the rock creatures are too slow to catch anyone, they aren't bad "effects." In fact, one of your authors recalls getting a slight chill from them upon viewing the film at the Congress Theater in Marcus Hook, Pa., when he was about 10 years old. The large spiders, on the other hand, are laughable puppets, probably the same ones used in *Cat-Women*. Moon woman Marianne Gaba became *Playboy's* Miss September, 1959.

Children of the Corn

(New World, 1984; 93 min.) **½

Produced by Donald P. Borchers and Ter-rence Kirby. Directed by Fritz Kiersch. Screenplay, George Goldsmith. Based on the short story by Stephen King. Edited by Harry Keramidas. Director of Photography, Raoul Lomas. Color, CFI. Music, Jonathan Elias. Art Direction, Craig Stearns. Set Decoration, Cricket Rowland. Special Visual Effects, Max W. Anderson.

Cast: Dr. Burt Stanton (Peter Horton), Vicky (Linda Hamilton), Diehl (R. G. Arm-strong), Isaac (John Franklin), Malachai (Courtney Gains), Sarah (Anne Marie Mc-Evoy), Job (Robby Kiger), Rachel (Julie Mad-dalena), Joseph (Jonas Marlowe), Amos (John Philbin), Boy (Dan Snook), Dad (David Cowan), Mom (Suzy Southam), Hansen (D. G. Johnson).

Synopsis: Years after adults are massa-cred in Gatlin, Nebraska, Dr. Burt Stan-ton and girlfriend Vicky are driving through Nebraska on their way to his new job. Suddenly a young boy appears in the highway, and they hit him. Burt follows a trail of blood into the corn and finds a suit-case. At a gas station, they are advised by the owner to go to Hemingford and bypass Gatlin, it's got nothin' but religious folk who don't cotton to outsiders. After they leave, the man is killed. In the corn, young Isaac gathers his youthful flock for the final test. Outlanders will soon arrive and will be sacrificed like the "blue man," a police-man's corpse on a homemade crucifix. They are observed by two younger chil-dren — Sarah and Job — who helped the boy, Joseph, who was hit by Stanton. Burt and Vicky find Gatlin desolate. Sarah tells them Isaac is their leader. Vicky is ab-ducted while Burt walks into town and finds a drawing of a dragon in a cornfield. Isaac tells the older and bigger Malachai to bring the woman's husband so they can be sacrificed that evening. In town, Burt in-terrupts a bizarre church service. All who become 19 are sacrificed. He is stabbed, es-capes and is helped by Job. In the corn, Malachai wrests control from Isaac, who replaces Vicky on the cross. Sarah and Job lead Burt to a hayloft from which he can see the sacrificial clearing. Burt rescues Vicky, fights off Malachai, and tries to rea-son with the children. An underground force that took the 19-year-old Amos courses into Isaac and blasts his cross into the air. He returns and strangles Malachai. Bert and Vicky fly to the barn and learn from Job that Malachai stopped Officer Hotchkiss's attempt to defeat the monster by fire. Burt pulls a gas line into the irri-gation system and fires the field. The de-mon seems to be destroyed. Burt knocks out the teenage girl who attempts to kill him. With Vicky, Job and Sarah, he sets out for Hemingford.

Reviews: "As gory as it is silly…. bloodbath of a film." (Kevin Thomas, *Los Angeles Times Calendar*, March 9, 1984, p. 13) ¶"Mean, angry stuff without a drop of poetry in it." (Leo Seligsohn, *Newsday*, March 16, 1984, Part II, p. 3) ¶"[had] tried for a more lyri-cal texture. Choppy and dawdling, and like most of King's work, it's not going any-where very interesting." (David Edelstein, *Village Voice*, March 27, 1984, p. 52)

Analysis: We expected a film in which no one survives, but we should have remembered that in his novels, if not his short stories, Stephen King often provides a finale in which the supreme evil is defeated, as it is here. We can imagine another story in which a child who witnesses slaughter returns as an adult to annihilate the culprits. Compare to *Necromancy.* Underground creatures are more fully explored in *Tremors.* Filmed in Iowa. Linda Hamilton had a bigger success the same year in *The Terminator.*

Children of the Corn II
(Paramount/Miramax, 1993; 93 min.) *½

Produced by Scott Stone, David Stanley, Bill Froelich. Directed by David Price. Screenplay, A. L. Katz and Gil Adler. Based on the short story "Children of the Corn" by Stephen King. Edited by Barry Zetlin. Director of Photography, Levie Isaacks. Color, Foto-Kem. Music, Daniel Licht. Set Decoration, Natalie Pope. Special Visual Effects, Calico, Ltd.

Cast: John Garrett (Terence Knox), Danny Garrett (Paul Scherrer), Angela (Rosalind Allen), Lacey (Christie Clark), Frank Red Bear (Ned Romero), Micah (Ryan Bollman), Mordechai (Ted Travelstead), Mrs. Burke (Marty Terry), Mrs. West (Marty Terry), Dr. Appleby (Ed Grady), Sheriff (Wallace Merck).

Synopsis: Hoping to get a scoop for the *World Inquirer,* John Garrett and his teenage son Danny arrive in the town of Hemingford, where the surviving children of fifty murdered Gatlin adults are staying in foster homes. Mordechai tells the other children they must wait for He Who Walks Behind the Rows. Micah, who has returned from the void where he was infested with a demonic force, urges them to rid the world of those who defile the corn. One of their first victims is Mrs. Burke, crushed beneath her house. Micah carves up a wooden doll and a man bleeds to death in church. At the Gatlin Elementary School, Garrett meets Frank Red Bear, a professor from a nearby college who believes life is out of balance. He shows Garrett a boulder covered with ancient drawings and relates the tale of a farm tribe whose parents became lazy and abused the land. Their

children rebelled. Back in Hemingford, Dr. Appleby is killed with hypodermics and a knife, and Danny is invited into the cult. He and Lacey, a "normal" teenager, discover more bodies. Red Bear and Garrett find corn with toxins on it. The sheriff confirms that it was to be sold anyway, ties the two up and sets a combine on them, but they roll free. A town meeting is surrounded, the house set afire. Angela and Christie are abducted for that night's sacrifice. A light approaches the clearing, but it's the combine driven by Red Bear. Although mortally wounded by an arrow, Red Bear grinds up Micah, whose demon spirit manages to escape the body. Something churns through the earth. Garrett and Danny rescue Angela and Christie and leave town next day. In the woods, Red Bear's spirit passes the carved rock.

Review: "So poorly conceived that its symbolism has no internal logic." (Stephen Holden, *New York Times,* January 30, 1993, Sec. I, p. 16)

Analysis: This is really a remake, witness the plot and its announced basis Stephen King's short story and the fact that He Who Walks Behind the Rows is still around. The children are not as frightening as those in the first film. It's yet another film whose TV ads suggested living flesh (the delicious Christie Clark) but whose R-rating is actually for severed appendages. There is one novel scene: the leader of the bad children infected by the demon — his molecular structure seemingly rearranged. Filmed in North Carolina.

Children of the Corn III: Urban Harvest
(Miramax, 1994; 91 min.) **

Produced by Gary Depew, Brad Southwick. Directed by James D. R. Hickox. Screenplay, Dode B. Levenson. Based on the short story "Children of the Corn" by Stephen King. Edited by Chris Peppe. Director of Photography, Gerry Lively. Color, Foto-Kem. Music, Daniel Licht. Set Decoration, Susanna Vertal. Creature Makeup Effects, Screaming Mad George.

Cast: Eli (David Cerny), Joshua (Ron Melendez), William Porter (Jim Metzler), Amanda (Nancy Lee Grahn), Maria (Mari

Morrow), Father Frank Nolan (Michael Ensign), Malcolm (Jon Clair), Arnold (Rif Hutton), Earl (Duke Stroud), Diane (Gina St. John), Employer (Rance Howard), Jake (Brian Peck), Derelict man (Johnny Legend), Samantha (Yvette Freeman).

Synopsis: In a Gatlin cornfield, young Eli uses his strange powers to destroy Joshua's drunken father. Joshua and Eli are then adopted by William and Amanda Porter of Chicago. Discovering an abandoned factory with plenty of yard space adjacent to his new home, Eli sprinkles kernels that sprout into a full-grown field in four weeks. Easily angered, Eli causes bad dreams for Amanda and his school principal, Father Nolan, who experienced a massacre of adults in Gatlin. Nor is Eli pleased when Joshua makes friends with Malcolm and his sister Maria. Amanda discovers his cornfield, as does a bum who is dragged underground by roots. Finding that the corn is sweet and impervious to pests, William dreams of making a fortune on the world market. Joshua finds Eli's drawing on which the Amanda character is X-ed out after she'd tried to cut the corn, was attacked, fell backward onto a pipe and died. Joshua and Malcolm see a picture in a 1964 Gatlin newspaper in which Eli seems to be the same age as he is now. Eli has Father Nolan killed, but before dying the priest reveals to Joshua and Malcolm that Eli's old Bible holds the key to his power. Joshua and Malcolm drive back to Gatlin and find the book where Eli had left it beneath a scarecrow. But a second scarecrow is the demonic form of Joshua's father, which Joshua dispatches with a scythe. The corn impales Malcolm, but Joshua escapes with the book. On the night of the harvest moon, Eli mesmerizes his classmates and kills William with a scythe. Joshua arrives and reveals that the book is Eli's other half. Destroying one will not destroy the other. Eli uses fire bolts against Joshua, who bounces them back off the book. Eli grabs Maria, but when Joshua tosses him the book, Maria knocks it down. Joshua puts a scythe through the book into Eli, who disappears. The crowd comes out of its trance, but a hideous, giant monster emerges from the furrows and begins killing the students. It swallows Maria, but Joshua cuts her out of its tail and severs its root. They watch the thing crumple to the ground. Later, in Hamburg, Germany, a crate of corn cobs is unloaded.

Review: "Contrived premise but lots of nifty special effects." (*Video Hound's Golden Movie Retriever 1997*, p. 150)

Analysis: Once again filmmakers make the fatal mistake of transferring a rural horror tale to an urban setting. At least Eli gets to plant a cornfield that for all intents and purposes puts the characters in that scarier environment. The parochial high school isn't realistic: There is no dress code. How did Eli and Joshua get themselves adopted by a Chicago couple? Why did Eli slip his adoptive mother some tongue when he preached purity? Perhaps this is explained when Eli comes out of the closet as a demonic-type being. The credits list the character Amanda as "Alice." The monster is a frightening creation, and the in-your-face camera work during the battle with it is gripping. The death of Malcolm, as the corn pulls his head and spinal cord out of his body, must rank with the most grotesque scenes in the annals of the cinema.

Children of the Damned *see under* **Village of the Damned**

Child's Play
(United Artists, 1988; 87 min.) ***

Produced by David Kirschner. Directed by Tom Holland. Story and screenplay, Don Mancini. Edited by Edward Warschilka and Roy E. Peterson. Director of Photography, Bill Butler. Technicolor. Music, Joe Renzetti. Dolby Stereo. Set Decoration, Cloudia. Special Effects, Richard O. Helmer and James D. Schwalm. Visual Effects, Apogee Inc. Chucky doll created by David Kirschner. Chucky doll designed by Kevin Yagher.

Cast: Karen Barclay (Catherine Hicks), Andy Barclay (Alex Vincent), Mike Norris (Chris Sarandon), Charles Lee Ray (Brad Dourif), Maggie Peterson (Dinah Manoff), Jack Santos (Tommy Swerdlow), Dr. Ardmore (Jack Colvin), Peddler (Juan Ramirez), Mr. Criswell (Alan Wilder), Dr. Death (Raymond Oliver), Mona (Tyler Hard), George (Ted Liss), Lucy (Roslyn Alexander).

Synopsis: Chicago policeman Mike Norris tracks and kills criminal Charles Lee Ray, who chants an incantation to Damballa before expiring. His soul enters the doll Chucky. Karen Barclay buys said doll for her small son Andy. Chucky communicates with Andy but no one else. He hits baby-sitter Maggie with a hammer, and she falls to her death from the window. He uses Andy to locate his ex-partners and exterminate them. Eventually Karen realizes that her son is telling the truth — Chucky is alive. After all, he's talking without batteries! Both Karen and Norris are attacked by the doll. Chucky learns that he is becoming more human each minute and can in fact be hurt by bullets unless he transports himself into the first person he met when he came to life in the doll. This means Andy, who's under observation in an institution. Andy flees back home, where a knock-down, drag-out battle is waged between himself, his mother, Norris and the crazed doll. "This is the end, friend," says Chucky. "Hi, I'm Chucky. Wanna play?" Incineration delays him for but a few moments, and only a bullet into the heart of his decapitated body seals his fate.

Reviews: "Moves with the speed of a bullet train and with style to burn." (Kevin Thomas, *Los Angeles Times Calendar*, November 9, 1988, p. 3) ¶"Is it scary? Golly, yes. You won't go to bed with those stuffed animals staring at you from the dresser anymore." (Jami Bernard, *New York Post*, November 9, 1988, p. 41) ¶"Predictable enough…. But the movie certainly managed to scare me shitless." (Renee Tajima, *Village Voice*, November 15, 1988, p. 70)

Analysis: This is a solid, not overlong thriller. Its most distressing point is the hammer in the face of Dinah Manoff, an actress who deserves better things.

Child's Play 2
(Universal, 1990; 84 min.) **½

Produced by David Kirschner. Directed by John Lafia. Screenplay, Don Mancini. Based on characters created by Don Mancini. Edited by Edward Warschilka. Director of Photography, Stefan Czapsky. Color, DeLuxe. Music, Graeme Revell. Dolby Stereo. Art Direction, Donald Maskovich. Set Decoration, Debra Combs. Chucky doll created by David Kirschner. Chucky doll designed by Kevin Yagher.

Cast: Andy Barclay (Alex Vincent), Joanne Simpson (Jenny Agutter), Phil Simpson (Gerrit Graham), Kyle (Christine Elise), Voice of Chucky (Brad Dourif), Grace Poole (Grace Zabriskie), Miss Kettlewell (Beth Grant), Sullivan (Peter Haskell), Social worker (Raymond Singer), Van driver (Charles C. Meshack), Homicide investigator (Stuart Mabray), Policeman (Matt Roe), Liquor store clerk (Herb Braha), Voice of Tommy doll (Edan Gross), Technicians (Don Pugsley, Ed Krieger, Vince Melocchi), Rick Spires (Adam Ryen), Sammy (Adam Wylie), Adam (Bill Stevenson).

Synopsis: While his mother undergoes psychiatric care, Andy Barclay is housed at a Chicago crisis center before taken in by foster parents Joanne and Phil Simpson. Meanwhile, at the Good Guys toy plant, Sullivan hopes to learn what went wrong with Andy's doll. A technician is electrocuted during the doll's refurbishing, and Sullivan wants the affair hushed up and asks his manager to dispose of the doll. But the doll Chucky uses the manager's car phone directory to locate Andy, smothers the manager, and locates the Simpson house, where he buries the Tommy doll and takes its place. That night Andy wakes up tied to his bed. Chucky begins reciting the incantation that will remove Charles Lee Ray's soul from the doll and place it in Andy's body. Interrupted by Kyle and Mr. Simpson, Chucky pretends to be inanimate, and Mr. Simpson tosses the doll down the cellar steps. After Chucky kills his teacher, Miss Kettlewell, Andy takes an electric carving knife into the basement. When Mr. Simpson investigates the commotion, Chucky trips him and he falls to his death. About to be returned to the crisis center, Andy warns Kyle. Kyle deposits the doll in the trash can but while swinging unearths the Tommy doll. She examines the trash, but the other doll has disappeared. Finding Joanne strangled upstairs, she is held at knife point by Chucky, who makes her drive to the crisis center. Nearing the building, Kyle jams on the brakes and Chucky goes through the windshield. But after trying to ram the doll, Kyle's car stalls, and she's recaptured. Chucky sets off the fire alarm to evacuate the center. Inside he kills Grace and escapes with Andy to the Good Guys factory. Kyle follows. Chucky starts his incantations, but he's too late; he's become "human." On the rampage, he chases Andy and Kyle. Rendered legless, Chucky continues his fight until Andy inundates him with a molten mixture. Still, he rises from the goo. Kyle stuffs a hose into his mouth and his head explodes.

Review: "Handsomely produced but morbid and not in the least amusing to watch." (Kevin Thomas, *Los Angeles Times Calendar*, November 9, 1990, p. 8) ¶"Instead of inner demons, the film-makers confront the miraculously well-adjusted Andy with a three-foot tall serial-killer, a pair of highly unintelligent guardians, and a string of ludicrous plot contrivances." (Farrah Anwar, *Monthly Film Bulletin*, January 1991, p. 13)

Analysis: Jenny Agutter (*The Railway Children, Walkabout, Equus, Logan's Run, An American Werewolf in London*) may want to omit this from her resume. But actors and actresses have to act. It's not all that bad, but the accomplished Agutter has little to do and suffers a standard fate. When all is said and done, it's the Alex Vincent/ Christine Elise/Chucky show. Straining credulity are the rapidity with which Chucky gets to Andy's foster home, the clouds that form over the toy factory when Chucky says the incantation (if Charles Lee Ray could do this, he would have been master of the universe instead of a small-time hood), Kyle's car starting when she returns to it. Some events are telegraphed: the Tommy doll's burial we knew would be short-lived. What was that hose or cord Kyle stuck in Chucky's mouth that made it explode? Gas? Electricity?

Child's Play 3
(Universal, 1991; 90 min.) **

Produced by Robert Latham Brown. Executive Producer, David Kirschner. Directed by Jack Bender. Screenplay, Don Mancini. Edited by Edward A. Warschilka, Jr., Scott Wallace. Director of Photography, John R. Leonetti. Color, Deluxe. Music, Cory Lerios, John D'Andrea. Dolby Stereo. Set Decoration, Ethel Robins Richards. Chucky doll created by David Kirschner. Chucky doll designed and engineered by Kevin Yagher.

Cast: Andy Barclay (Justin Whalin), Christine De Silva (Perrey Reeves), Tyler (Jeremy Sylvers), Cadet Lt. Colonel Shelton (Travis Fine), Harold Whitehurst (Dean Jacobson), Sullivan (Peter Haskell), Colonel Cochrane (Dakin Matthews), Sergeant Botnick (Andrew Robinson), Voice of Chucky (Brad Dourif), Ivers (Donna Eskra), Sergeant Clark (Burke Byrnes), Ellis (Matthew Walker), Voice of Good Guy doll (Edan Gross), Patterson (Richard Marion), Ghoul (David Elzey), Mother (Kim Stockdale).

Synopsis: During the cleanup of the abandoned Good Guys toy factory, a headless doll is transported across a vat of molten rubber into which its "blood" drips. At an executive meeting, Sullivan gives the go-ahead to make more Good Guy dolls. After all, it's a business and children are "consumer trainees." Sullivan receives the first new doll, which kills him that night. It's Chucky reborn! Chucky uses Sullivan's computer to locate Andy Barclay at the Kent Military School. His mother is still under special care. A package arrives at the school for Andy, but young Tyler absconds with it once he discovers its contents: a Good Guy doll. Chucky ingratiates himself with Tyler while Andy makes friends with De Silva and Whitehurst. Chucky decides to invade Tyler's body, but he is interrupted, and Colonel Cochrane tosses him in the trash. Climbing out of the garbage truck, Chucky crushes the driver inside. Chucky confronts Andy, but they are interrupted by Cadet Lt. Col. Shelton. After Chucky causes Col. Cochrane to die from a heart attack, Andy tries to convince Tyler that Chucky is a bad guy. Whitehurst sees Chucky slashing barber Botnick but won't talk about it to Andy. War games begin. Chucky substitutes real bullets in some of the rifles, and Shelton is one of the victims. Chucky finds Tyler, who finally realizes the doll is bad and stabs it with a penknife. Whitehurst sacrifices himself on a grenade tossed by Chucky. Chucky chases Tyler into a traveling carnival's "Devil's Lair" haunted house. With the security guard's extra gun, Chucky wounds De Silva, but as he recites his incantation over Tyler, he is shot twice by Andy, loses a hand and falls into a large fan.

Review: "From the start, this ... has been a mean-spirited and silly horror concept.... You'll find yourself expecting certain ultra-obvious clichés, and saying to yourselves, 'They wouldn't *dare*.' And, still, they do it." (Jack Garner *Wilmington* [DE] *News Journal*, Aug. 30-Sep. 1, 1991, p. 7)

Analysis: It doesn't make much sense for Chucky to seek out Andy again when he couldn't make the incantation work that last time out. But then, Chucky's got a new doll body. Perhaps his spell will work now? Also senseless is Chucky's decision to confront Andy when he'd already decided to transfer his soul to Tyler. Having Whitehurst dive on a grenade is implausible, and all the chasing around during the war games is unlikely. This military school is too strict. The student officers are too nasty and vulgar.

A Christmas Carol *see under* **Scrooge**

C.H.U.D.
(New World, 1984; 90 min.) ***

Produced by Andrew Bonime. Directed by Douglas Cheek. Assistant Directors, Lewis Gould, Stephen Wertimer. Screenplay, Parnell Hall. Story, Shepard Abbott. Edited by Claire Simpson. Director of Photography, Peter Stein. Panavision. Color, TVC Labs. Music, Cooper Hughes. Art Direction, Jorge Luis Toro. Special Makeup, John Caglione, Jr.

Cast: George Cooper (John Heard), "Reverend" A. J. Shepard (Daniel Stern), Lauren Daniels (Kim Greist), Francine (Brenda Currin), Justin (Justin Hall), Captain Bosch (Christopher Curry), Hays (Vic Polizos), Sanderson (Cordis Heard), Flora Bosch (Laure Mattos), Fuller (Michael O'Hare), Crespi (Sam McMurray), Cop (Frank Adu), Mrs. Monroe (Ruth Maleczech), Murphy (J. C. Quinn), Ad woman (Patricia Richardson), Ad man (Raymond Baker), Doris (Beverly Bentley), Val (Graham Beckel), Jackson (Gene O'Neill), Wilson (George Martin), Gramps (Peter Michael Goetz), Shadow (John Bedford-Lloyd), Commissioner (John Ramsey), Coroner (Henry Yuk), Cops in diner (John Goodman, Jay Thomas).

Synopsis: In the Lafayette Street area of New York City, derelicts and bag ladies especially those who live in the sewers and subways begin disappearing. "Reverend" Shepard, who runs a soup kitchen, is worried and talks to police captain Bosch. Bosch tells Shepard that his wife, Flora Bosch, is missing, too. Shepard thinks an EPA probe is ongoing and takes Bosch underground, where they find a Geiger counter. They hear a roar in the distance. Bosch meets with higher authorities, including nuclear regulatory authority commission representative Wilson. Murphy, a reporter, is snooping around and follows photographer George Cooper, who's taken pictures of the street people for an article. He convinces Cooper something important is afoot. Shepard and Bosch confront Wilson, who admits that a mutated CHUD, a "cannibalistic humanoid underground dweller," was killed by a gas leak. Police and Wilson's men enter the tunnels and are killed. There must be other CHUDs! Cooper and Murphy explore the tunnels, and Murphy is killed. Shepard discovers several CHUDs but escapes. Meanwhile, Cooper's girlfriend Lauren manages to decapitate a CHUD in her apartment building. Hoping to keep Shepard from going to the newspapers, Wilson makes sure Shepard is locked underground as the gas mains are prepared to discharge into the tunnels. Cooper and Shepard find toxic waste, Wilson's "poison dump." Stumbling on a video camera dropped by the dead police team, they communicate with Bosch, who realizes that CHUD really means "Contamination Hazard Urban Disposal." When Bosch attempts to rescue Shepard and Cooper, Wilson shoots him. Nevertheless, Shepard and Cooper get out of the sewer, and Shepard shoots Wilson in his truck, which explodes. The CHUD menace is not over, as two policemen and the customers of a diner discover to their horror.

Reviews: "The CHUDs are gruesome but in such a literal and transparently make-believe way that they're likely to frighten only small fry.... well photographed." (Kevin Thomas, *Los Angeles Times Calendar*, August 31, 1984, p. 6) ¶"The heroes are an interesting and varied bunch, allowing Heard, Stern and Christopher Curry a little more characterization than is usual in this sort of thing." (Kim Newman, *Monthly Film Bulletin*, February 1985, p. 45)

Analysis: There are tense spots, particularly when Stern stumbles on a nest of CHUDs. We wish there had been more underground action. As it is, about two-thirds of the film takes place above ground, one-third below. We'd reverse that to make it a true "confined spaces" movie. Pair it with *Wolfen.*

C.H.U.D. II: Bud the CHUD
(Vestron Video/Lightning Pictures, 1989; 84 min.) **

Produced by Jonathan D. Crane. Directed by David Irving. Screenplay, M. Kan Jeeves. Edited by Barbara Pokras. Director of Photography, Arnie Sirlin. Panavision. Color. Music, Nicholas Pike. Art Direction, Don Day. Set Decoration, Nancy Booth. Special Makeup Effects, Makeup & Effects Laboratories.

Cast: Steve (Brian Robbins), Kevin (Bill Calvert), Katie (Tricia Leigh Fisher), Bud (Gerrit Graham), Colonel Ted Masters (Robert Vaughn), Graves (Larry Cedar), Sam (Judd Omen), Doctor (Larry Linville), Tyler (Norman Fell), Gracie (June Lockhart), Velma (Bianca Jagger), Barbershop customer (Rich Hall), Dr. Kellaway (Clive Revill). With Jack Riley, Sandra Kerns.

Synopsis: CHUD research has been discontinued and the last mutant is to be terminated, but it escapes, to the great glee of Colonel Masters. He wants to use CHUDs as soldiers. He freezes "Bud" and transports him to the Winterhaven Disease Control Center. As scientists realize the "chudified" brain can be kicked into a second life, two high school students, Kevin and Steve, steal the body to replace a cadaver they accidentally lost. Bud comes alive when an electric cord falls into the bathtub with him. He escapes, and each time he bites a human or animal, the victim becomes a CHUD. The CHUDs gather and enter the auditorium, where a Halloween dance is underway. Steve, Kevin and Katie hatch a plan to destroy the CHUDs. In a sexy swimsuit, Katie lures Bud and the other monsters to the pool. After they fall in, the water is frozen and electrified, at which time the creatures explode because they are now a closed system. Having been bitten by a CHUD, Steve leaves town, hitching a ride with a woman. In the back of the pickup is the chudified Colonel Masters.

Review: "Graham excels as the kidnapped corpse, but this horror-comedy is consistently repellent." (*Video Hound's Golden Movie Retriever 1994*, p. 210)

Analysis: This crosses the boundary from merely tongue-in-cheek into outright comedy. True, some of it's amusing, and the filmmakers milk the situation as well as can be expected. However, we're not enamored of comedic sequels. What's Clive Revill doing in this? Such a small part, that is.

Cinderfella *see under* **The Glass Slipper**

Cocoon
(20th Century–Fox, 1985; 117 min.) ***

Produced by Richard D. Zanuck, David Brown, Lili Fini Zanuck. Directed by Ron Howard. Screenplay, Tom Benedek. Story, David Saperstein. Edited by Daniel Hanley and Michael J. Hill. Director of Photography, Don Peterman. Panavision. DeLuxe Color. Music, James Horner. Dolby Stereo. Special Music and Dance Coordination, Gwen Verdon. Set Decoration, Jim Duffy. Visual Effects, Industrial Light & Magic, Joseph Unsinn, Ken Ralston, Mitch Suskin. Cocoons-Dolphin Effects, Robert Short Productions, Inc. Alien Creatures Effects, Greg Cannom. Special Creature Consultant, Rick Baker. Special Music-Dance Coordinator, Gwen Verdon. Alien Choreography, Caprice Rothe.

Cast: Art Selwyn (Don Ameche), Ben Luckett (Wilford Brimley), Joe Finley (Hume Cronyn), Walter (Brian Dennehy), Bernie Lefkowitz (Jack Gilford), Jack Bonner (Steve Guttenberg), Mary Luckett (Maureen Stapleton), Alma Finley (Jessica Tandy), Bess McCarthy (Gwen Verdon), Rose Lefkowitz (Herta Ware), Kitty (Tahnee Welch), David (Barret Oliver), Susan (Linda Harrison), Pillsbury (Tyrone Power, Jr.), John Dexter (Clint Howard), Pops (Charles Lampkin), Doc (Mike Nomad), Lou Pine (Jorge Gil), DMV clerk (Jim Ritz), Smiley (Charles Rainsbury), Aliens (Wendy Cooke, Pamela Prescott, Dinah Sue Rowley, Gabriella Sinclair), Teller (Cyndi Vicino), Doctor (Russ Wheeler), Reverend (Harold Bergman), Salvatore (Mark Cheresnick), Dock master (Fred Broderson), Waitress (Ivy Thayer).

Synopsis: Art, Ben and Joe of the Sunny Shores, St. Petersburg, retirement community are put out when Walter, two other men and Kitty rent the empty estate with the indoor pool the three use each day. Nevertheless, they continue to frequent the pool when the newcomers take ship on Jack Bonner's boat. They have rented the *Manta III* for 27 days and dive for objects they cover before boarding. But one night Jack sees Kitty remove her human skin. Walter explains that he and the others are Antareans, who a hundred centuries before had an outpost on Earth. A seismic upheaval forced them to leave, but twenty volunteered to remain behind. This "ground crew" are in cocoons, which Walter and friends retrieve from the ocean floor and store in the pool. Unbeknownst to Walter, the life force permeating the pool has rejuvenated Art, Ben and Joe. Hiding in a dressing room when Walter returns unexpectedly, they observe and are observed by the aliens. Ben secures from Walter a promise that they can continue to use the pool if they do not disturb the cocoons. They introduce their wives to the pool, but when Bernie makes mention of the pool in the cafeteria, all the retirement community men and women rush over and dive in, using up the life force. Walter opens a cocoon and finds a dying Antarean. Ben offers to help replace the cocoons in the ocean until the aliens can return. Walter offers passage on his ship for the three couples and about thirty of their friends. They agree to go where they will be students *and* teachers and live "forever." Evading the authorities, the *Manta III* is pulled up into the immense alien craft.

Reviews: "An outgoing filmmaker with a good sense of comic timing, [Ron Howard] makes the most of both *Cocoon* story lines and integrates the large cast into a smooth ensemble." (David Sterritt, *Christian Science Monitor*, June 20, 1985, p. 25)¶ "Succeeds in being condescending to the elderly, creatures from outer space, dolphins and the audience." (Lenny Rubenstein, *Cineaste* Vol. XIV, No. 2 [1985], p. 60)

Analysis: Certainly many will find it simple-minded, but it's entertaining and given high-class treatment. Linda Harrison? Last we saw her she was killed in *Beneath the Planet of the Apes.* Academy

Awards for supporting actor (Don Ameche) and visual effects.

Cocoon: The Return
(20th Century–Fox, 1988; 116 min.)
*½

Produced by Richard D. Zanuck, David Brown, Lili Fini Zanuck. Directed by Daniel Petrie. Screenplay, Stephen McPherson. Story, Stephen McPherson and Elizabeth Bradley. Based on characters created by David Saperstein. Edited by Mark Roy Warner. Director of Photography, Tak Fujimoto. Panavision. Color, DeLuxe. Music, James Horner. Dolby Stereo. Set Decoration, Frederick C. Weiler, Jim Poynter. Cocoons, Robert Short. Special Effects, Richard Jones. Visual Effects, Industrial Light & Magic. Special Alien Creatures and Effects, Greg Cannom.

Cast: Art Selwyn (Don Ameche), Ben Luckett (Wilford Brimley), Joe Finley (Hume Cronyn), Bernie Lefkowitz (Jack Gilford), Jack Bonner (Steve Guttenberg), Kitty (Tahnee Welch), Sara (Courteney Cox), David (Barret Oliver), Mary Luckett (Maureen Stapleton), Ruby Feinberg (Elaine Stritch), Alma Finley (Jessica Tandy), Bess McCarthy (Gwen Verdon), Walter (Brian Dennehy), Susan (Linda Harrison), Pillsbury (Tyrone Power, Jr.), Doc (Mike Nomad).

Synopsis: Bernie Lefkowitz mourns his late wife, Rose. Jack Bonner conducts cheesy boat tours. David's TV keeps coming on, and his grandfather Ben appears, telling him he'll be visiting. Dolphins welcome the returning Antarean spacecraft. Believing they were lost at sea, David's mother faints when Ben and Mary ring the doorbell. Bernie is shocked to find Art, Joe, Alma and Bess at *his* door. Kitty tells Jack their sensor indicates the remaining cocoons are in danger. They have four days to accomplish their mission before another spaceship returns for them. While the aliens are diving, Jack observes the St. Petersburg Oceanographic Institute boat hauling up a cocoon. Jack and his visitors break into the Institute. While one of the aliens observes the tests on the cocoon, scientist Sara sees a life-form inside. Meanwhile, Art introduces Bernie to Ruby Feinberg. During a basketball game against some young dudes, Joe gets a pain in his side. Bess collapses while trying on dresses.

At the Institute the cocoon is opened, and Sara tells the alien not to be afraid. Jack is told the alien will be okay for a while but will need an infusion of life force. Art learns that Bess is pregnant and Joe that his leukemia has returned. Sara is worried when the military wants to transport the alien to a more secure facility. Alma is hit by a car and hospitalized. The doctor doesn't expect her to live. Joe uses his healing power to aid her, tells her to take that daycare job, and says his time has run out. Kitty, Art and Ben secrete themselves in a truck and gain access to the Institute, where Art dons a guard's uniform and the other two pretend to be doctors. Kitty takes on her alien form to distract the scientists as Ben rescues her companion. They motor out to the *Manta IV*, where Ben and Mary decide to remain on Earth with their grandson David. The spacecraft arrives and Walter appears on deck. The aliens, Art and Bess ascend into the spaceship. Bernie goes to Ruby's house. Jack meets Sara, who reminds him of a woman Kitty showed him in a vision.

Review: "The net effect is one of being on a cruise ship to hell." (Janet Maslin, *New York Times*, November 23, 1988, p. C15)

Analysis: There are two stories at work: the rescue of the cocoons and the adventures of the old folks at home. There are some pretty goofy tests given the obviously intelligent alien at the Institute. The other aliens and their human friends take their sweet old time thinking up a way to retrieve their friend. Kitty even has time for a dinner date with Jack! The Brian Dennehy character should have returned earlier to be a stabilizing influence. The lack of imagination that some of the codgers evince is galling to those of us interested in other worlds and space travel. The *New York Times* dismissed the whole thing as "tired."

Conan the Barbarian
(Universal, 1982; 129 min.)***

Produced by Buzz Feitshans and Raffaella DeLaurentiis. Directed by John Milius. Assistant Director, Pepe Lopez Rodero. Screenplay, John Milius and Oliver Stone. Based on the character created by Robert E. Howard. Edited by C. Timothy O'Meara. Director of Photography, Duke Callaghan. Todd-AO. Technicolor. Music, Basil Poledouris. Art Direction, Pierluigi Basile, Benjamin Fernandez. Costumes, John Bloomfield.

Cast: Conan (Arnold Schwarzenegger), Valeria (Sandahl Bergman), Thulsa Doom (James Earl Jones), King Osric (Max von Sydow), Conan's father (William Smith), Rexor (Ben Davidson), Witch (Cassandra Gavioila), Subotai (Gerry Lopez), Akjiro the Wizard (Mako), Princess (Valerie Quennessen), Red Hair (Luis Barboo), Pictish scout (Franco Columbo), Snake Girl (Leslie Foldvary), Guard (Gary Herman), Officer (Erick Holmey), General (Akio Mitamura), Conan's mother (Nadiuska), Young Conan (Jorge Sanz), Priest (Jack Taylor), Sword master (Kiyoshi Yamasaki), Thorgrim (Sven Ole Thorsen).

Synopsis: In a pagan age, young Conan is advised by his father to worship Cram, god of the Earth, and to learn the discipline of steel for it alone can be trusted. After witnessing the death of his father and the beheading of his mother during a raid by Thulsa Doom, Conan is enslaved. He grows to manhood pushing a huge mill wheel, knowing strength but little else. Taken away from the grindstone, he achieves renown in mini-gladiatorial games and acquires the rudiments of language and literature. One day his captor frees him. Fleeing pursuing dogs, he falls into a cave filled with ancient runes, statues and skeletons. He obtains a sword — by Cram! — and begins his quest to bring justice to Thulsa Doom. A witch woman foretells that he will be a conqueror. He meets Subotai, an archer, and they journey together. Valeria, a woman warrior, helps them steal priceless gems during a ceremony. Conan and Subotai dispatch the giant snake to which the virgin was to be sacrificed. Afterward, Conan and Valeria make love. King Osric the Usurper has the trio brought before him and salutes the barbarian for having the gall to rob Thulsa Doom. Osric asks Conan to retrieve his daughter from the snake cult. Although Valeria argues against it, she finds Conan gone next morning. Conan meets a wizard and with him leaves his horse and sword. Masquerading as a disciple of Doom, he observes a ceremony but is found out because of the amulet he carries. Tortured, Conan cries out that Thulsa Doom killed his parents. He is crucified on the Tree of Woe, but rescued by Subotai and Valeria. Unconscious and near death, he is taken to the wizard. He is anchored to stakes and his face painted with mystic runes to ward off the demons that surely will come for him. Valeria and Subotai weather the demonic forces, and Conan recovers. They ride to a gorge behind the mountains, enter a cave and observe an orgy and the eating of a broth of human flesh before Thulsa Doom. Doom becomes a snake himself and crawls off into a tunnel. Behind, Conan and company raise havoc and retrieve Osric's daughter. Outside, they mount up and ride, but Thulsa Doom looses a magic snake arrow and hits Valeria, who dies. Conan gives her a warrior's funeral on a burning pyre. Then he and Subotai prepare a defense. Thulsa Doom leads his minions against the barbarian, but only Thulsa Doom himself survives. Conan pursues him to his temple. Before the multitude of admirers, Thulsa Doom tells Conan that he, Doom, is the wellspring from which Conan flows. Nevertheless, Conan beheads him. The crowd disperses while Conan mulls over the end of his quest.

Reviews: "Restores violence to its former Hollywood appellation of action…. The casting of the title role must have discouraged film producers until the arrival of Arnold Schwarzenegger on the entertainment scene…. The physique is role-perfect." (Carlos Clarens, "Barbarians Now," *Film Comment*, May-June 1982, pp. 28) ¶"Casting couldn't have been more on the money…. could have been a movie with real substance, sort of a *Seventh Seal* with muscles and viscera." (Jeff Rovin, *The Laserdisc Film Guide, 1993-1994 Edition*, p. 55) ¶"Frequently incoherent, ineptly staged." (Vincent Canby, *New York Times*, May 15, 1982, p. 13)

Analysis: This film version is true to its pulp source. The excellent opening credits are enhanced by Basil Poledouris' music. It's nice to see William Smith, king of the bikers, in something completely different. There are moments that drag when we wish

for some sword-wielding. Then it comes in a slam-bang battle of three against, what, thirty-three? The carnage is great — with villains who deserve slaughter. Is it a fact that animals were treated badly in this film? The big snake is a prop. Arnold does seem to slug a camel. Horses do take bad falls.

Conan the Destroyer
(Universal, 1984; 103 min.) **½

Produced by Raffaella De Laurentiis. Directed by Richard Fleischer. Screenplay, Stanley Mann. Story, Roy Thomas and Gerry Conway. Based on the character created by Robert E. Howard. Edited by Frank J. Urioste. Director of Photography, Jack Cardiff. J-D-C Widescreen. Technicolor. Music, Basil Poledouris. Art Direction, Kevin Phipps, Jose Maria Alarcon. Visual Special Effects Coordinator, Charles Finance. Dagoth Created by Carlo Rambaldi. Stunt Coordinator, Vic Armstrong.

Cast: Conan (Arnold Schwarzenegger), Bombaata (Wilt Chamberlain), Princess Jehnna (Olivia D'Abo), Zula (Grace Jones), Akjiro "The Wizard" (Mako), Malak (Tracey Walter), Queen Taramis (Sarah Douglas), Man Ape/Thoth-Amon (Pat Roach), Grand Vizier (Jeff Corey), Togra (Sven Ole Thorsen), Village heckler (Bruce Fleischer), the Leader (Ferdinand Mayne).

Synopsis: Although on foot, Conan makes mincemeat of the horse soldiers sent against him by Queen Taramis of Shadazar. It's a test. Taramis promises to restore Valeria to life if Conan helps her. He is entrusted with Taramis's niece, Princess Jehnna, who must undertake a perilous journey. "What good is a sword against sorcery?" inquires Conan, who nevertheless undertakes the mission along with his friend Malak. Taramis sends Bombaata to guard Jehnna's virginity. He is also instructed to kill Conan once Jehnna possesses the magic horn of Dagoth. The quest begins. Conan's old friend, the wizard Akjiro, joins the company after being saved from cannibals and the tall black woman bandit Zula after demonstrating her skill with the staff. Arriving at a castle surrounded by a lake, Conan urges a rest. During the night, the castle's wizard turns into a great flying beast and abducts the princess. Conan and company row to the island and enter the castle proper via an underwater tunnel. Conan is separated from the others and must deal with a large man with the face of a black beast. The man-beast is defeated when Conan breaks the mirrors ringing the room. Conan sends his sword through one mirror, into the wizard. Jehnna awakes and takes the magic crystal. The castle crumbles as Conan rows his people to the mainland. The Taramis soldiers attack but fail to take Jehnna. Conan avoids the club of Bombaata, who claims he thought Conan was going to hurt the girl. That evening, Jehnna speaks with a drunken Conan about his desire: the warrior woman Valeria. Zula begins to instruct Jehnna in the use of the staff. Next day, each proceeds single file through a crevasse to a temple. Putting his shoulder to the door, Conan forces an entrance. In a brazier-lit room while Akjiro reads wall inscriptions, Jehnna places the crystal key on a pedestal. A statue's mouth opens and Jehnna walks into the flames, passing into another room where the magic horn is located. The keepers of the horn appear. Conan refuses to give up the girl, and they wage a running battle back to the crypt. Jehnna thinks she knows a way out. Conan observes Bombaata's true colors when the large man causes a cave-in. Bombaata and Jehnna exit the temple and find their horses. Conan realizes Taramis's perfidy but rides to stop the sacrifice of Jehnna. Malak takes Conan to a secret entrance to Shadazar behind a waterfall. Jehnna places the bejeweled horn upon the forehead of Dagoth's statue. As she is prepared for the sacrifice, Conan fights and kills Bombaata. Dagoth comes alive and impales Taramis. To defeat the god monster, Conan tears out the horn. The kingdom is inherited by Jehnna, who rewards her erstwhile quest companions. Zula becomes captain of the guard, Malak the court jester, Akjiro the wise consultant. As for Conan, he wants his own kingdom and queen. Jehnna kisses him goodbye.

Reviews: "Nothing is imaginative, or fun, or particularly smart; a lot of the picture is spent watching 3,000-pound doors open and close." (Sheila Benson, *Los Angeles Times*

Calendar, June 29, 1984, p. 1) ¶"Conan seems more at home in the cinema in his second installment.... It's somewhat disappointing ... [Fleisher] couldn't deliver a barbarian movie with more gristle." (Richard Combs, *Monthly Film Bulletin*, October 1984, p. 303)

Analysis: It's 26 minutes shorter than the first film but seems just as long. Not that it's boring. Questions do arise: After seeing how Conan routed a dozen of her elite, what made Taramis think four of her guards would be able to overcome him later? Have the residents of Hyperborea forgotten the use of the bow? What exactly is Schwarzenegger's attitude toward animals? Again, he bops a camel and slugs a horse. It is of course ironic now to see that basketball great Wilt Chamberlain protecting a young lady's virtue. A few years ago he'd claimed to have slept with thousands of women. Olivia D'Abo is very cute, Sarah Douglas sexy as usual. Filmed in Mexico. In *Red Sonja* (1984) Arnold Schwarzenegger was supposed to play Conan, but he and Sandahl Bergman played different characters.

Notes of Interest: Like those of his contemporary H. P. Lovecraft, Robert E. Howard's writings were not widely appreciated in his lifetime. Howard wrote one novel (*The Hour of the Dragon/Conan the Conqueror*)) plus novellas of this hero of the Hyperborian Age. His works were akin to those of Edgar Rice Burroughs. He committed suicide in 1936 at the age of 31. Conan has become his most famous creation although he wrote numerous adventures with other protagonists: Solomon Kane, King Kull, Bran MakMorn. Conan comes from Cimmeria, in Hyperborea, before the last ice age.

A Connecticut Yankee
(Fox, 1931; 96 min.)***

Directed by David Butler. Screenplay and Dialogue, William Conselman. Based on Mark Twain's novel *A Connecticut Yankee in King Arthur's Court*. Edited by Irene Morra. Director of Photography, Ernest Palmer. Sound, Joseph E. Aiken. Settings, William Darling. Costumes, Sophie Wachner. Special Effects, Fred Sersen, Ralph Hammeras.

Cast: Hank/Sir Boss (Will Rogers), Queen Morgan Le Fay (Myrna Loy), Alisande (Maureen O'Sullivan), Clarence (Frank Albertson), King Arthur (William Farnum), Merlin (Mitchell Harris), Sagramor (Brandon Hurst).

Synopsis: On a stormy night Hank Martin of Hank Martin Radio Supplies and the WRCO radio station runs a battery up to a mansion, where he encounters a variety of strange residents. He connects the battery to the master's console and is told that the machine will pick up sounds from past ages. He seems to hear the Arthurian era. A statue falls on Hank. When he awakes he asks of Sir Sagramor, "Where in the helleth am I?" It's Camelot, A.D. 528. Although he claims only to be a Democrat, Hank is imprisoned as a magician. Arthur is impressed but court sorcerer Merlin is not pleased when Hank demonstrates a lighter. Arthur consigns Hank to the pyre, but Hank notices in his notebook that an eclipse is imminent. He brings on this "Yankee Curse," and, cowed, Arthur knights Hank "Sir Boss" after he restores the sun. Hank proceeds to bring modern industry to Camelot, installing a phone system and an armor cleaning and maintenance shop. Merlin remains antagonistic, however, as does Sir Sagramor, who insults Hank. In a joust, Hank uses his wild west skills and a lariat to defeat his opponent. Then he and Arthur set out to rescue the king's daughter, Alisande, from the king's evil sister, Morgan Le Fay. Merlin and Sagramor conspire and waylay the duo. The king is shorn of his beard so that his sister won't recognize him. She consigns him to the dungeon and makes a pass at Sir Boss, whom she dresses in fine raiment. When he learns that she won't release the prisoners in the dungeon, he takes matters and a pistol into his own hands. Still, there are too many men at arms for him; he is captured and, along with Arthur and Alisande, scheduled for execution. However, a page named Clarence leads the Knights of the Round Table to the rescue. They invade in twentieth-century cars and an armored tank. Bombs are dropped on Morgan's castle and Sir Boss is knocked out. He comes to back in Connecticut, where he finds that he's been in the presence of a lunatic whose doctor looks like Merlin. He rushes out and finds "Clarence" and "Alisande" in the back of his truck. He helps them elope and walks toward home.

Review: "A thoroughly merry entertainment.... Mr. Rogers fits his role marvelously." (Mordaunt Hall, *New York Times*, April 13, 1931, p. 17)

Analysis: The sets and matte work are more impressive than those in the 1949 version. Rogers makes several funny references to the United States and the world of the 1930s, at one point saying he'd like to be the Boss, like Mussolini. Equally amusing is his initiation of the Industrial Revolution, and the rescue by modern means and tommy guns is a riot. In these days before she'd be Nora Charles to William Powell's Nick, Loy is overtly sexy and radiant. Another radiant lass, Maureen O'Sullivan, has too little to do. The next year she'd remedy that as Jane in *Tarzan the Ape Man*. Re-released in 1936.

A Connecticut Yankee in King Arthur's Court
(Paramount, 1949; 106 min.) ***

Produced by Robert Fellows. Directed by Tay Garnett. Screenplay, Edmund Beloin. Based on the novel by Mark Twain. Edited by Archie Marshek. Director of Photography, Ray Rennahan. Technicolor. Technicolor Direction, Natalie Kalmus. Music, Victor Young. Songs, Johnny Burke and Jimmy Van Heusen. Art Direction, Hans Dreier, Roland Anderson. Set Decoration, Sam Comer, Bertram Granger. Makeup, Wally Westmore. Costumes, Mary Kay Dodson. Special Photographic Effects, Gordon Jennings, Jan Domela, Irmin Roberts. Process Photography, Farciot Edouart.

Cast: Hank Martin (Bing Crosby), Alisande LaCarteloise (Rhonda Fleming), Sir Sagramore (William Bendix), Merlin (Murvyn Vye), King Arthur/Lord Pendragon (Cedric Hardwicke), Morgan LeFay (Virginia Field), Sir Lancelot (Henry Wilcoxon), Sir Logris (Joseph Vitale), Sir Galahad (Richard Webb), Lady Penelope (Julia Faye), High executioner (Alan Napier), Peasant girl (Ann Carter).

Synopsis: In 1912, Hank Martin visits Pendagon Castle in England and regales Lord Pendragon with a strange tale that began in Connecticut: While riding a horse in a rainstorm, Hank was knocked unconscious by a tree limb. He awoke as the prisoner of the knight Sir Sagramore in A.D. 528. Taken to Camelot, Hank was considered a monster and ordered burned at the stake. Using a glass watch face, he started two small blazes that secured his freedom. King Arthur granted him a blacksmith shop and Sir Sagramore as squire. Achieving rapport with the king's niece Alisande, Hank, by then known as Sir Boss, was perturbed to learn that she was engaged to Sir Lancelot. That knight challenged him to a joust, which Sir Boss won via pinto and lariat. Sir Boss told Arthur that he should visit his people, for they were sore in need. In disguise, Sir Boss, Arthur and Sagramore set out, but Merlin had them followed and captured. Imprisoned, Sir Boss used a magnet to retrieve the keys after Sagramore choked a guard unconscious. But only Sagramore escaped the castle. Alisande, who was also imprisoned, had a premonition and gave Sir Boss an amulet. Approaching the executioner's block, Sir Boss read in his almanac that an eclipse was imminent. He used this knowledge to cowl the multitude and secure his freedom. He rode to Merlin's castle and, with the pistol he'd made that Sir Sagramore had brought to him, shot the knight trying to kill him. Nevertheless, Sir Boss was knocked unconscious again. He woke in the present day. Lord Pendragon sends Hank to a parapet for a great view — and to meet his niece, a dead ringer for Alisande.

Review: "It is Bing in the role of the Yankee who gives this film its particular charm." (Bosley Crowther, *New York Times*, April 8, 1949, p. 31)

Analysis: There are enough songs to qualify it as a musical as well as a fantasy. The *New York Times* roundly praised the cast. Rhonda Fleming's introduction, where she lilts about the castle hall, is kind of goofy. The novel's Sagramore and Clarence are combined into one person here. Why is this Merlin not afraid of Sir Boss's powers after he'd seen them work? Hank doesn't get to use enough of his Yankee ingenuity.

Unidentified Flying Oddball

(Buena Vista, 1979; 93 min.) **½

Directed by Russ Mayberry. Screenplay, Don Tait. Edited by Peter Boita. Technicolor.

Music, Ron Goodwin. Art Direction, Albert Witherick. Special Photographic Effects, Cliff Culley.

Cast: Tom Trimble (Dennis Dugan), King Arthur (Kenneth More), Sir Mordred (Jim Dale), Alisande (Sheila White), Merlin (Ron Moody), Sir Gawain (John LeMesurier), Clarence (Rodney Bewes), Senator Milburn (Robert Beatty), Dr. Zimmerman (Cyril Shaps), Oaf (Pat Roach), Winston (Kevin Brennan), Prisoner (Reg Lye), Watkins (Ewen Solon).

Synopsis: When Senator Milburn objects to sending a human into deep space aboard NASA's *Stardust*, Dr. Zimmerman directs Tom Trimble to create a robot. However, when Trimble boards the craft to assure his duplicate, "Hermes," about the mission, lightning ignites the rockets. Trimble has to take control but finds himself landing in sixth century Britain, where he is captured by Sir Mordred and displayed before King Arthur. Arthur orders the "monster" burned, but the asbestos suit protects him. Still, Trimble is pursued at Arthur's behest. Magnetizing Mordred's sword, Trimble survives the duel but must engage in a joust with Mordred. Later, Trimble discovers documents that incriminate Mordred in a plot to overthrow Arthur, and Mordred flees. Trimble shows Arthur a laser gun, which Merlin steals. He also kidnaps Alisande. Trimble rescues Alisande and returns to the besieged castle via jet backpack. Hermes in the *Stardust* helps repel the attackers with rocket jets and magnetism. Mordred's forces are defeated, and "Sir Tom Trimble" is carved on the Round Table. Trimble hopes to return to twentieth-century earth. On the trip he finds Alisande's goose, which isn't aging. Realizing Alisande could come with him, he turns about.

Review: "Dale plays a villain, for once, as Mordred, while Moody Faginizes Merlin." (Steven H. Scheuer, ed., *Movies on TV: 1982-1983 Edition*, p. 702)

Analysis: Although it compresses characters and makes the protagonist an astronaut, it maintains the spirit of the Twain book. The funniest scenes and best reactions come from a deadpan John Le Mesurier. Ironically, Jim Dale is a villain, as he was in Disney's 1977 release *Pete's*

Alisande (Sheila White) presents Tom Trimble (Dennis Dugan) with a goose feather to wear as a talisman during a joust in *Unidentified Flying Oddball* (Buena Vista, 1979).

Dragon. On Broadway Dale is a Tony winner for the title role in 1980's *Barnum.* He was also the lead in *Me and My Girl* on the Great White Way. Sheila White played Messalina in the acclaimed public television production *I, Claudius.* Both she and Ron Moody had been in 1968's *Oliver!* Kenneth More had been a leading man of many British productions. Dennis Dugan has directorial credits, e.g., *Problem Child.* As you can see, the cast is above average, and in fact, the location shooting in England bespeaks a higher budget than many of the Disney films of this era. A.k.a. *The Spaceman and King Arthur/A Spaceman in King Arthur's Court.*

Notes of Interest: There was a 1920 silent version of the Mark Twain novel, which was published in 1889, a decade or so after Alexander Graham Bell patented the telephone.

A Kid in King Arthur's Court
(Walt Disney Pictures, 1995; 89 min.) **
Produced by Robert L. Levy, Peter Abrams,

J. P. Guerin. Directed by Michael Gottlieb. Screenplay, Michael Part and Robert L. Levy. Edited by Michael Ripps and Anita Brandt-Burgoyne. Director of Photography, Elemer Ragalyi. Technicolor. Music, J.A.C. Redford. Art Direction, Beata Vaurinecz.

Cast: Calvin Fuller (Thomas Ian Nicholas), King Arthur (Joss Ackland), Lord Belasco (Art Malik), Princess Katey (Paloma Baeza), Princess Sarah (Kate Winslet), Merlin (Ron Moody), Master Kane (Daniel Craig), Ratan (David Tysall), Blacksmith (Barry Stanton), Coach (Shane Rimmer).

Synopsis: After striking out for the Knights baseball team, Calvin Fuller finds himself in the dugout during an apparent earthquake. He falls into a fissure and emerges in the Middle Ages, toppling the Black Knight from a horse. The shocked knight flees the scene, and so does Calvin. In the nearby castle he is captured and brought before King Arthur. When challenged to combat by Arthur's adviser Lord Belasco, Calvin selects his CD player as a weapon. After a demonstration of its decibel power, Belasco leaves the hall. Princess Katey takes Calvin to the Well of Destiny, where the boy learns from the visage of the magician Merlin that he must prevent the collapse of Camelot. Merlin guarantees a trip home if Calvin can foil Belasco, who desires the hand of Arthur's elder daughter, Sarah. While Belasco makes life tough for Calvin, the time traveler introduces Katey to rollerblading and his own version of a Big Mac. Meanwhile, Sarah, who loves the weapons master Kane, tells Belasco her husband will be chosen by tournament victory. To gain the upper hand, Belasco has Katey kidnapped and blames Calvin. Sarah knows the truth, and Arthur is duly informed. He and Calvin don disguise, journey to Belasco's castle, and rescue Katey. At Camelot, Arthur opens the tournament to all free men. Thus Kane enters the lists. In the final joust, Belasco blinds Kane with a jewel in his helmet. Nevertheless, Kane is not completely unhorsed. Out of sight of the spectators, Calvin dons Kane's garb and bests Belasco. When Belasco attacks Calvin, the Black Knight intervenes and is revealed as Sarah. Arthur banishes Belasco to Cucamonga. After Calvin gives Arthur his Swiss army knife and takes leave of Katey, Merlin makes good on his promise. Calvin leaps into the well and finds himself back in the dugout—before he struck out. This time he hits a home run. Upon approaching home plate, he encounters Katey in his team's baseball uniform. In the stands a man like Arthur whittles a stick.

Review: "Sluggish and slow energy.... Everything that can look cheap does." (Caryn James, *New York Times*, August 11, 1995, p. C16)

Analysis: This film works for some generations but not for others. Quizzed separately, Michael and Courtney Holston, ages twelve and ten, respectively, were unanimous in their rating: four stars. For adults it's another matter: an uneasy mix of so-called comedy and Arthurian legend. It's unfocused, jumping from one locale to another. In contrast to previous versions, no one accuses Calvin of being a wizard. There are inconsistencies. For instance, Belasco chides his chief henchman for suggesting that he enter the tournament, then decides to do it. Of course, he's desperate. But how come he's so good? We see that

blinding jewel only in his final confrontation. Why can't the filmmakers give their time traveler more modern implements and knowledge to confound and amaze the Dark Ages inhabitants? There *are* a few good lines made better by the facial expressions: "Boogie. Boogie?" (Joss Ackland), "Cucamonga?" (Art Malik).

Conquest of the Planet of the Apes *see under* **Planet of the Apes**

Count Down, Son of Dracula *see* Son of Dracula (1974) *under* **Dracula**

Count Dracula and His Vampire Bride *see* The Satanic Rites of Dracula *under* **Dracula**

Count Yorga, Vampire
(AIP, 1970; 92 min.) **½

Produced by Michael Macready. Directed by Robert Kelljan. Screenplay, Robert Kelljan. Edited by Tony De Zarraga. Director of Photography, Arch Archambault. Color, Movielab. Music, William Marx. Set Decoration, Bob Wilder. Makeup, Mark Rogers, Master Dentalsmith. Special Effects, James Tanenbaum. Narration, George Macready.

Cast: Count Yorga (Robert Quarry), Dr. James Hayes (Roger Perry), Paul (Michael Murphy), Michael (Michael Macready), Donna (Donna Anders), Erica (Judy Lang), Brudah (Edward Walsh), Cleo (Julie Conners), Peter (Paul Hansen), Judy (Sybil Scotford), Vampiress (Deborah Darnell), Nurse (Erica Macready), Mother (Marsha Jordan), Narrator (George Macready).

Synopsis: A crate arrives at the Port of Los Angeles and is driven inland while a narrator discusses the possibility of vampirism. At a nighttime seance the Bulgarian-born Count Yorga puts Donna under his spell. After he leaves, Donna tells her friends Yorga was her late mother's lover and she doesn't understand why he didn't attend the funeral. Paul and Erica drive Yorga home in their Volkswagen bus. Leaving, they get stuck in the drive and during the night are attacked by Yorga. Next day Erica is attended by Dr. Jim Hayes, who advises her to eat lots of steaks to restore blood. He finds her neck punctures "fascinating." Later, Paul and Michael find her eating a cat. After a blood transfusion, Hayes runs a blood analysis and tells the men that Erica may have been bitten by a vampire. They are skeptical, but Hayes is willing to entertain any possibility. Erica is visited by Yorga and disappears. Paul drives to Yorga's and is killed by the servant Brudah. Hayes, Donna and Michael visit but fail to keep Yorga up till sunrise. Hayes and Michael plan to kill Yorga while he's in his coffin. They are unaware that Yorga calls Donna to him. Brudah rapes her on the way to the house and asks his master's forgiveness. Against their better judgment, Hayes and Michael arrive after dark. In the basement, Hayes is set upon and killed by Yorga's "brides," including Erica and Donna's mother. Michael disposes of Brudah, and in a hallway fight he thrusts a wooden stake into Yorga's chest. He takes Donna past the crumbling count, locks up Erica and another vampiress, but turns to find Donna leaping for his throat. The narrator asks, "Superstition?"

Review: "The film's principal virtues are the unusually fine production values ... and the careful photography of Arch Archambault. Its greatest weakness is the script.... Cast is sincere and straight ahead. Robert Quarry as the Count is properly insidious." (*Show*, September 17, 1970, p. 41)

Analysis: It's probably a good idea to move the vampire out of Transylvania, but some people, including one of this book's authors, didn't care for his modern destination. The low budget is evident only in certain scenes. Quarry is rather intimidating and haughty in his power. It's a tease insofar as skin goes, which is strange in this era of the R rating. On the other hand, a number of these actresses we wouldn't want to see au naturel.

The Return of Count Yorga
(1971; 97 min.) **½

Produced by Michael Macready. Directed by Bob Kelljan. Screenplay, Bob Kelljan and Yvonne Wilder. Based on characters created by Bob Kelljan. Edited by Fabien Tordjmann and Laurette Odney. Color, Movielab. Music, Bill Marx. Songs, Marilyn Lovell. Set Decoration, Vince Cresceman. Special Effects, Roger George.

Cast: Count Yorga (Robert Quarry), Cynthia Nelson (Mariette Hartley), Dr. David Baldwin (Roger Perry), Jennifer (Yvonne Wilder), Reverend Thomas (Tom Toner), Brudah (Edward Walsh), Lt. Madden (Rudy DeLuca), Tommy (Philip Frame), Bill Nelson (Walter Brooke), Professor Rightstat (George Macready), Sergeant O'Connor (Craig Nelson), Jason (David Lampson), Ellen (Karen Houston), Mrs. Nelson (Helen Baron), Mitzi (Jesse Wells), Joe (Mike Pataki), Witch (Corinne Conley), Michael Farmer (Allen Joseph), Claret Farmer (Peg Shirley), Laurie Greggs (Liz Rogers), Jonathan Greggs (Paul Hansen).

Synopsis: At the Westwood Orphanage Halloween party, Count Yorga introduces himself to teacher Cynthia Nelson. He tells her he just purchased the old Gateway mansion. That night, Yorga's female vampire minions invade the Nelson house, kill Cynthia's family, and cart Cynthia off to their master. Yorga uses his hypnotic powers to erase the memory of the event from the woman's mind. When she wakes, she believes she is recovering from an auto accident. Back at her house, the mute teacher Jennifer discovers the bodies, but when the police arrive, the bodies are gone. Jennifer is mystified by the disappearance and by a letter from Mr. Nelson indicating that they left to visit a critically ill relative. Young Tommy is no help; unknown to anyone, he has come under Yorga's spell. Next day Yorga's servant Brudah sinks the bodies of Cynthia's parents in a bog. In San Francisco, Cynthia's fiancé, David Baldwin, and his friend Jason discuss discrepancies in people's stories about the Nelson incident. David visits occult expert Dr. Rightstat, hoping to get his help, but the old man is senile. At night, Brudah opens Yorga's coffin. The vampire consults with a witch woman who advocates killing Cynthia. During dinner, Cynthia starts to recall the attack on her family. Afterward, Yorga takes his limo to town and kills Joe, the boyfriend of another orphanage teacher, Mitzi. He vampirizes the woman. Cynthia, meanwhile, explores Gateway. She hears voices and again remembers a scene of carnage. Tommy admits to Jason that he did go to Gateway and that Ellen is there. Following Tommy, Jason encounters the bloodsucker Ellen and her companions. He is killed by Yorga. In the drawing room, the count confesses his love for Cynthia: "Now you appear. The most fragile emotion ever known has entered my life and I must fear the most. It will surely threaten my ability to survive. You, Cynthia, have brought to my life a gentle pain which I can only define as love. Can you love me?" He kisses her and mesmerizes her a second time. The next evening, David, Reverend Thomas, Lieutenant Madden and Sergeant O'Connor go to Yorga's. David has the minister distract the count while the others snoop around. Yorga leads his guest into the bog while inside the police are killed by the female vampires — and Tommy. David finds Cynthia, and they get away from Brudah but are soon stymied by Yorga and his women. The vampire leaves with Cynthia as the women close in on their prey. But upstairs, Yorga hears David's angry yell. The pursued and the pursuer arrive on the roof where, coming out of her trance as the men fight, Cynthia plants an ax in Yorga's chest. David pushes him over the edge. In her fiancé's arms, Cynthia starts to scream as David bares his fangs.

Review: "Solid follow-up.... handsome-looking film.... two okay songs." (Murf., *Variety*, August 11, 1971, p. 28)

Analysis: Variety acknowledged this as a film succeeding on two levels, shock and satire. The "surprise" ending is pretty neat. There are unsettling moments, as when the Nelson clan suspects something's outside. There are in-jokes, e.g., Yorga watching Ingrid Pitt in a Spanish-dubbed version of *The Vampire Lovers* on TV. For some reason, audiences, ourselves included, roar when the police are running from the vampire women and the imperious Yorga glides by in her elevator. There is no explanation for Yorga's resurrection after his demise in the last film. Nor is Dr. Baldwin (Roger Perry) presented as a relation to the look-alike Dr. Hayes (Roger Perry) of the first film. Were the filmmakers hoping to disguise him with the beard and mustache? Years before *Poltergeist* and more years before his successful TV sitcom *Coach*, Craig Nelson provides a bit of comic relief as a disbelieving policeman.

The Creature from the Black Lagoon
(Universal-International, 1954; 79 min.) ***

Produced by William Alland. Directed by Jack Arnold. Underwater Sequences directed by James C. Havens. Screenplay, Harry Essex and Arthur Ross. Additional Script, Jack Arnold. Story, Maurice Zimm. Edited by Ted J. Kent. Director of Photography, William E. Snyder. 3-D. Underwater Photography, Charles S. Welbourne. Music, Hans J. Salter. Sound, Joe Lapis, Leslie I. Carey. Art Direction, Hilyard Brown, Bernard Herzbrun. Gill Man design, Bud Westmore, Millicent Patrick, William Alland, Jack Arnold, Jack Kevan, Chris Mueller, Bob Hickman.

Cast: David Reed (Richard Carlson), Kay Lawrence (Julia Adams), Mark Williams (Richard Denning), Creature out of water (Ben Chapman), Creature in water (Ricou Browning), Lucas (Nestor Paiva), Carl Maia (Antonio Moreno), Dr. Edwin Thompson (Whit Bissell), Zee (Bernie Gozier), Louis (Rodd Redwing), Chico (Henry Escalante), Tomas (Julio Lopez), Dr. Matos (Sydney Mason).

Synopsis: The discovery of a Devonian Age fossil — a webbed, taloned, yet startlingly manlike claw — sends an impromptu expedition of paleontologists into the primitive jungle setting aboard the fishing boat *Rita*, with her captain, Lucas, and his two-man crew. The scientists on board are Dr. David Reed; his assistant (and fiancée), Kay Lawrence; his employer, Mark Williams; and Drs. Maia and Thompson. A potential problem from the outset is the obvious jealousy felt by Williams over the relationship between Reed and Lawrence. Arriving at Dr. Maia's dig, the party finds the badly mangled bodies of Maia's native workers, victims (so the scientists think) of some jungle predator. Not discouraged, they set to work excavating the area in which the fossil was found, but have no luck discovering any more. They decide that their best bet is to look further downstream, in the area where fossils may have been swept by the current. This leads them into the legendary Black Lagoon, which Lucas describes as something of a paradise,

Poster art for *Creature from the Black Lagoon* (Universal-International, 1954).

but which they all find to be anything but that. Anchoring the *Rita* in the Black Lagoon, Reed and Williams don aqualungs and dive into the (surprisingly) lucent depths. Their descent is spied upon by the glassy, unblinking gaze of the very thing they seek: the missing link, the Gill Man. At first the monstrous amphibian skulks behind and beneath the surface dwellers, gliding through the kelp and submerged grasses as easily as any submarine creature, observing these strange intruders but making no overt moves against them. Later, when Kay steals a moment for a cooling swim in the lagoon, the creature likewise follows her every move, obviously mesmerized by this dazzling newcomer to its gloomy abode. Attempts to photograph the Gill Man prove fruitless, and after the beast kills one of Lucas's compatriots, Williams, ever impatient to add another notch to his professional totem, wounds the amphibian with a speargun bolt. Reed argues against this tactic, urging that capturing the beast would be preferable to killing it. Williams grudgingly concedes. Ultimately, the group has to subdue the creature with Rotenone, a drug used by the local natives to knock out fish. The narcotic does slow the creature enough for the scientists to entrap it in a nearby grotto, but not before another of Lucas's men falls under its talons. The capture is short-lived, however, and the creature breaks free, in the process gravely injuring Dr. Thompson. From this point on, it's the passengers of the *Rita* who are the hunted as the creature begins a cat-and-mouse pursuit of them, ultimately blocking their exit from the lagoon with a fallen tree. As Reed and Williams struggle underwater to attach a line to the obstacle so that it may be moved, the creature again attacks, enraged by another bolt from Williams's speargun, and drags the hapless victim to the bottom of the lagoon. Using the remaining Rotenone to keep the creature at bay, Richards finally manages to secure a line about the tree's trunk and Lucas is able to haul it clear, but not before the Gill Man climbs aboard the *Rita*'s stern. Grasping the fainting Kay, it leaps over the side before the others can react and disappears again into the depths. Reed pursues them underwater, coming to the surface in the aforementioned grotto. He ultimately finds Kay unconscious and revives her. Before they can escape, the creature appears, and Reed struggles with it briefly before shots ring out. Lucas and Carl Maia have arrived and fire a volley of rounds into the creature, apparently mortally wounding it.

Reviews: "If you approach it with your tongue in cheek and your 3-D glasses firmly planted you'll have a good scare and maybe even a laugh." (Philip T. Hartung, *Commonweal*, May 14, 1954, p. 145) ¶"The 3-D lensing adds to the eerie effects of the underwater footage. The below-water scraps ... will pop goose pimples on the

susceptible fan...." (Brog., *Variety*, February 10, 1954, p. 7)

Analysis: This film and its sequels began as after-dinner conversation between guests at a soirée hosted by Orson Welles in the early 1940s. William Alland, an associate of Welles from the *Citizen Kane* days, was one guest. Another was a South American filmmaker who entertained his host and fellow guests with the dubious tale of a strange race of semi-human fish people who frequented the remote banks of the Amazon. Alland dismissed the story as obvious fantasy but was nonetheless intrigued with the notion of a prehistoric survivor existing in the far reaches of an Amazonian backwater. Later, after serving in the Second World War and, returning to civilian life, working for several years at Universal Studios, Alland drafted a three-page story idea he called "The Sea Monster." Several rewrites (by Maurice Zimm and Arthur Ross) later under the title of "Black Lagoon," the story finally began to take on the shape of the B-movie classic we know today as *The Creature from the Black Lagoon*.

When *Creature* emerged in 1954, director Jack Arnold had already scored highly the previous year with *It Came from Outer Space*, also from Universal-International, and he would be involved — in one production or another — with most of UI's science fiction efforts throughout the decade. He would, in fact, become the director most identified with the science fiction movies of the decade. (Perhaps only England's Val Guest could make a similar claim.) Arnold enjoyed a great reputation from genre critics from the beginning, but *Creature from the Black Lagoon* put him in the position as something of a science fiction *auteur*. One scene from *Creature*, the one in which the Gill Man swims furtively beneath the unsuspecting Julie Adams, is always hailed as an example of Arnold's visual poetry. Likewise, co-stars Richard Carlson and Richard Denning were to be strongly identified with the genre, each appearing in a number of the decade's more celebrated (and some not-so-celebrated) fantastic films. Carlson, in particular, became the archetype of the scholarly scientist-hero so often depicted at the center of these science fiction films, with such roles as astronomer John Putnam in *It Came from Outer Space* and Dr. David Reed in *Creature*.

Most of *Creature* was shot on Universal's back lot; all underwater photography was done at Florida's Wakulla Springs. Ricou Browning, a college student at the time who also produced water shows at Weeki Wachi Springs and Rainbow Springs, had a chance meeting with cameraman Charles Welbourne, who was in Florida to scout locations for the film's underwater scenes. Welbourne shot some underwater test footage at Wakulla Springs, with Browning swimming ahead of him as a gauge of perspective and sizes. When director Jack Arnold saw this footage, he contacted Browning immediately and signed him to play the Gill Man in all the underwater scenes. Because of Ricou's relatively short stature, 6' 5" stuntman and actor Ben Chapman played the creature out of the water. Browning would be the man in the rubber suit (in the underwater shots, anyway) in each of the subsequent Gill Man films.

Whether or not *Creature from the Black Lagoon* is the *definitive* B-movie, as Douglas Brode has suggested in *The Films of the Fifties*, (p. 109), the Gill Man is very likely the definitive movie monster of the 1950s, with only perhaps Godzilla vying for that title. Despite its budgetary limitations (and these are quite on a par with other B-films of the era), *Creature* is a well-done and exciting adventure, well acted and unhampered by the plethora of subplots that usually accompany tales of this sort. But the main attraction of the film is the creature. At once scaly and reptilian, muscular and sensuous, the Gill Man invites the same kind of weird fascination that seems to go with all the classic monsters. Slow and clumsy out of the water, it can manage only a sloughing gate. In its natural watery haunts, however, it moves with an amazing grace and agility. Like King Kong, the Gill Man is the lord of his domain, and like the unlucky sovereign of that island, the Gill Man's undoing was also a Beauty-and-the-Beast tale. And like *King Kong*, *Creature from the Black Lagoon* scored with the theatergoing crowd, becoming one of

the big money-makers of 1954 (and 1954 was a very good year for movies).

It is worth noting that Steven Spielberg recognized *Creature from the Black Lagoon* in his 1975 smash, *Jaws* (see Peter Nichols, *The World of Fantastic Films*, p. 38). In the early 1980s, there was very nearly a remake of *Creature*, again to be directed by Arnold, with a script by Nigel Kneale. Considerable pre-production work was carried out on the project, with an early draft of a script done and locations scouted. Then, at the proverbial eleventh hour, the Powers That Be at Universal chose to go with *Jaws 3D* instead. (See Ted Newsom, "The Creature Remake that Never Got Made," *Filmfax* No. 37.) Rumors of a *Creature* remake have popped up since then — the latest one involving director John Carpenter — but there's been nothing substantial to date.

Revenge of the Creature
(Universal-International, 1955;
82 min.) **

Produced by William Alland. Directed by Jack Arnold. Screenplay, Martin Berkeley. Story, William Alland. Edited by Paul Weatherwax. Director of Photography, Charles S. Welbourne. Music, Herman Stein. Music Supervision, Joseph Gershenson. Sound, Leslie I. Carey, Jack Bolger. Art Direction, Alfred Sweeney, Alexander Golitzen. Makeup, Bud Westmore. Creature design, Millicent Patrick, Jack Arnold, William Alland, Chris Mueller, Jack Kevan, Bob Hickman.

Cast: Professor Clete Ferguson (John Agar), Helen Dobson (Lori Nelson), Joe Hayes (John Bromfield), Lucas (Nestor Paiva), Jackson Foster (Grandon Rhodes), Lou Gibson (Dave Willock), George Johnson (Robert B. Williams), Police captain (Charles Cane), Pete (Brett Halsey), Jennings (Clint Eastwood), Newscaster (Ned LeFevre), Miss Abbott (Diane DeLaire), Dr. McCuller (Robert Nelson), Joe (Robert Wehling), Announcer (Sydney Mason), Mac (Don C. Harvey), Skipper (Jack Gargan), Charlie (Robert Hoy), Bit (Don House), Policemen (Mike Doyle, Charles Gibb, Charles Victor).

Synopsis: A year after the Reed expedition into the Amazon, Florida's Ocean Harbor Oceanarium sends adventurers Hayes and Foster along the same route, hoping to find the alleged antediluvian survivor (or one of its kind, perhaps). Lucas

Ricou Browning, who played the gill man in the swimming scenes, emerges from the water in *Revenge of the Creature* (Universal-International, 1955).

again guides the North Americans (this time aboard the *Rita II*) upriver to the distant lagoon where the explorers find that the creature has not only survived the salvo of gunfire that closed its previous encounter with civilized man, but actually seems none the worse for the experience. In fact, it wastes no time at all in attacking and nearly doing in Joe Hayes, who has invaded his watery domain in an old-fashioned steel-helmeted diving suit. This expedition is loaded for bear, however, and round two sees them setting off under-water explosives which render the creature comatose. Arriving back in Ocean Harbor with their prize, the men deliver it to the oceanarium there. Hayes "walks" the senseless creature back to violent consciousness. Before it can do much damage, Hayes and attendants manage to subdue it and haul it into an enclosed portion of the tank, shackling it there with a heavy leg-iron and chain. At this point Professor Clete Ferguson and ichthyologist Helen Dobson set about testing the creature to learn its habits and the extent of its intelligence.

One "trick" they attempt to teach it is to obey the word *stop* — with an electrical shock incentive. This backfires later on when the electrical shocks so enrage the creature that it breaks free of its restraints, whereupon it runs amok, kills Joe Hayes, and, after scaring the bejesus out of the tourists at Ocean Harbor, disappears into the surf. After this rampage, the creature lies low for a bit, skulking about Helen Dobson's motel room and dispatching the German shepherd that's taken up with her, but otherwise keeping a low profile enough that the authorities figure it's either dead or headed back to the Amazon. This is apparently enough for Ferguson and Dobson who don't really seem to give their prehistoric subject any more thought. Before Ferguson has to leave Florida to return to California, the two take a day trip downriver to a coastal resort to "do some stepping," not knowing the Gill Man is following their progress underwater. That evening the creature makes its move, knocking Clete aside and abducting the fainting Helen off a crowded dance floor. Soon the whole countryside is scouting up and down the coast looking for some sign of the monster and its prey. Helen remains in a swoon, thus making it possible for the Gill Man to periodically deposit her on a secluded beach while it takes a "breather" in the surf. Ultimately, the unconscious Helen is spied by Clete and his party of rescuers who, fending off the creature by repeated cries of "stop," manage to pull the girl away from the creature so that, again, a volley of gunfire can send it to another presumed watery grave.

Reviews: "Expertly made up, [the Gill Man is] the only one who looks and acts believable." (Hift., *Variety*, March 16, 1955) ¶"Borrows too much from *King Kong* to stand very well on its own." (Tim Lucas, *Video Watchdog*, November/December 1993, p. 21)

Analysis: The Black Lagoon is the backdrop for only the initial setup, and that is probably the point where *Revenge of the Creature* goes wrong. Even though the first film's lagoon setting was only a backlot fabrication (and not an entirely convincing one, at that), the locale is sorely missed in the sequel. After its capture, the Gill Man is quickly removed to Florida's Ocean Harbor and put on display for the yokels. Between then and the time the creature makes its getaway, nothing much happens except for the dull competition between Ferguson and Hayes for the attentions of Helen Dobson (many Universal-International films seemed fond of depicting romantic triangles). Ferguson and Dobson seem to spend a rather callously small time grieving over Hayes' death; in fact, they go off on a carefree cruise upriver almost immediately.

Revenge of the Creature arouses very little of the kind of eerie tension that was present in much of its predecessor. The pathos generated by scenes of the Gill Man swimming desolately in that tank, leg tethered by stout chain, while the scientists go about their mundane tasks poking and prodding this Devonian relic, goes flat quickly and simply fails to evoke the ominous atmosphere of the original. Despite Jack Arnold's return as director, *Revenge* imparts no new insights into the creature's habits, and in fact most of its set pieces are merely variations on themes, or recreations of scenes, from the earlier film (for instance, the creature swimming below Lori Nelson as she and Agar take a dip). Like its predecessor, *Revenge* was filmed in 3-D, although it was most frequently shown "flat."

After what seemed a promising start in movies in the 1940s and a bid for major stardom fizzled out, John Agar seemed relegated to roles such as the one he has in *Revenge of the Creature* for the remainder of his career. Despite the fact that he appeared in more science fiction and horror films of the era than Richard Carlson and Kenneth Tobey combined, Agar's personality was somehow so bland that he never really made the impact that either of those two did. His work in *Revenge* is typical. Likewise, John Bromfield's film career never surmounted the type of role he had in *Revenge*, although he found steady work on television in the fifties, starring in "Sheriff of Cochise" and "U.S. Marshall" between 1956 and 1960. Similarly, Lori Nelson's career was limited to lightweight roles in the fifties. She also appeared in Roger Corman's *Day the World Ended*.

The Creature Walks Among Us
(Universal-International, 1956;
78 min.) **

Produced by William Alland. Directed by
John Sherwood. Screenplay, Arthur Ross.
Edited by Edward Curtiss. Director of Photography, Maury Gertsman. Special Photography, Clifford Stine. Music, Henry Mancini.
Sound, Robert Pritchard, Leslie I. Carey. Art
Direction, Robert E. Smith, Alexander Golitzen. Creature's New Face Design, Millicent
Patrick, Jack Kevan.

Cast: Dr. William Barton (Jeff Morrow),
Dr. Thomas Morgan (Rex Reason), Marcia
Barton (Leigh Snowden), Jed Grant (Gregg
Palmer), Creature (Ricou Browning), Creature after operation (Don Megowan), Dr. Borg
(Maurice Manson), Dr. Johnson (James Rawley), Captain Stanley (David McMahon),
Morteno (Paul Fierro), Mrs. Morteno (Lillian Molieri), State trooper (Larry Hudson),
Steward (Frank Chase).

Synopsis: Reports of attacks on a fisherman in the Florida Everglades by a monstrous manlike creature provoke a third expedition into those waterways in search of
the now-famous Gill Man. A year following
the events at Ocean Harbor, another group
of scientists, this time larger and better
equipped, follows the elusive amphibian
into a labyrinth of tributaries and waterways, finally confronting it. In the ensuing
struggle to subdue it, the creature is set
ablaze when it is doused in gasoline and attacked with a lighted flambeau. The combined effects of the burns and Rotenone
nearly kill the creature, but scientists Barton and Morgan and their guide Grant haul
it aboard their yacht (which has a fully
equipped operating room) and immediately
commence to "save" it by removing its gills
and laboring to inflate its dormant lungs.
The fire has also burned away most of the
creature's scaly exterior, leaving what appears to be skinlike tissue, to the amazement of the scientists on board. The scientists are divided on how to handle their
prize: Barton seems determined to carry
through with the forced metamorphosis
from amphibian to air-breathing animal.
Morgan, however, would prefer to see the
creature simply survive. Grant is less interested in the creature than he is in Barton's
shapely wife, Marcia. After a soirée in which

the liquor has brought out all sorts of repressed feelings from the Bartons, Grant
makes his move and begins pawing Marcia,
despite her muted protests. At this point,
the revived but sluggish creature emerges
from the locked operating room, tosses
aside the astonished Grant and leaps over
the side of the yacht. The noise has aroused
the entire crew, and Barton, knowing that
the now gill-less Gill Man will drown, leaps
overboard in pursuit, dragging an airline
with him. After a brief struggle, Barton subdues the weakened creature and returns it to
the surface, "feeding" it oxygen on the way.
The air-breathing creature, now wearing a
sail-cloth suit, is deposited at the Bartons'
estate, secluded not far from San Francisco.
It is hoped that a pastoral setting (albeit inside an enclosure protected by a heavy electrified fence) will assuage the creature's
more bestial instincts. Indeed, the picture
of tranquillity is augmented by a herd of
sheep incarcerated with the creature. It isn't
long before the complications first evident
aboard the yacht are again apparent; when
Barton spies Marcia and Grant taking a
moonlight swim together, he is outraged.
Later, he bursts in on Grant and fires him on
the spot, ordering him off the property.
Grant's unwise remarks as he's leaving push
Barton over the top, and he clubs the man
to death. Seeking to force the blame for
Grant's death on the Gill Man, Barton drags
the body into the cage with the creature
(who has witnessed the entire event). This
violent episode, however, rouses the creature from its torpor, and it reverts to its former fierce manner, ripping through the
fence and going after Barton, who seeks to
hide inside the house. The beast eventually
catches up to the desperately fleeing scientist and savages him, then lumbers off to the
beach, some miles distant.

Review: "Scripting ... is shadowy ... but
still holds together sufficiently in keeping
interest centered on the main character."
(Brog., *Variety,* March 14, 1956)

Analysis: This film unfortunately shares
the reputation of its immediate predecessor, but to its credit *The Creature Walks
Among Us* does attempt to take the series
in a new, though perhaps ill-advised, direction. The first third of the film has been

criticized for the amount of time spent pursuing the creature. Yet, it is precisely this part of the film that succeeds in capturing the eerie and claustrophobic atmosphere of the original film. Considerable tension is generated as the handful of scientists, in their frail motorboat away from the security of the yacht, pursue the wily creature through the winding mazes of the swamp. After the creature's near immolation and capture, however, things do slow down to a crawl, and the momentum is never recovered. Then, too, there is the matter of the creature's being *transformed* into the stout, shuffling Frankenstein monster–like being that it becomes in the film's second half. As Bill Warren correctly points out in *Keep Watching the Skies*, the thinking that led to this kind of plotting is unfathomable, destroying as it does the very *concept* of the creature and transforming it into something else altogether. Arthur Ross's script does tend to concentrate more on character relationships than the previous entries in the series (the typical romantic triangle is here extended to form a romantic rectangle), but this does nothing to distract us from the fact that the last of Universal's great monsters is denigrated into a semi-lobotomized brute with nothing of the alien magnetism of the earlier films.

Because *The Creature Walks Among Us* has never enjoyed a reputation as either a decent sequel or as very good entertainment on its own merits, director John Sherwood has likewise never garnered much in the way of a positive reputation. Unlike Jack Arnold, Sherwood's name never became associated with the genre (although he directed the generally superior *The Monolith Monsters* for Universal in 1957). Despite the shortcomings of the script, the director had a dependable cast to work with. Jeff Morrow, like Richard Carlson and Jon Agar, was something of a mainstay in science fiction films of the fifties (particularly those of Universal), appearing also in *This Island Earth*, *Kronos*, and (although he'd probably want to forget about it) *The Giant Claw*. Rex Reason (who co-starred in *This Island Earth* with Morrow) was apparently being groomed for Rock Hudson–style stardom in the mid-fifties; success with that eluded him, and his career barely endured the decade. Much the same can be said for Leigh Snowden, but Gregg Palmer maintained a Hollywood presence for a time and continued on in character roles into the early seventies.

The Creature Walks Among Us was the only one of the three Gill Man films to have an open ending, indicating that the studio sensed the strong possibility of a sequel. Mediocre box office receipts quashed that idea, although it's intriguing to imagine what a *fourth* creature film would have involved.

Notes of Interest: The Gill Man is celebrated as the last in a most distinguished line of monsters to come from Universal, at this point Universal-International. With the classic Frankenstein, Dracula, Wolf Man, and Mummy past their prime and (at least until the arrival of Hammer Studios a few years later) consigned to the monster hall of fame, this was the American studio's last entry in a justly prestigious lineup. Like his illustrious predecessors, though perhaps to a somewhat lesser extent, the Gill Man became a veritable horror icon for a short time in the mid–1950s, not only appearing in a trilogy of feature films, but popping up in such diverse other works as *The Seven Year Itch* and television as well. His likeness (if not his name) even turned up in the August 1954 issue of *Sub-Mariner*, when the prince of Atlantis locks horns with one humanoid sea-monster named Elmer, who in appearance was none other than our Gill Man.

Following the last appearance of the Gill Man in *The Creature Walks Among Us*, there were surprisingly few copies and rip-offs of the character. One, *The Monster of Piedras Blancas* (1958), had nothing of the Gill Man's magnetism nor the backing of a major studio, and was instantly forgettable, as were one or two Mexican-produced opuses that featured a most *Creature*-esque monster. As Bill Warren has rightly pointed out, the Gill Man costume was created with an undeniable logic; it was, indeed, almost impossible to imagine a design for a "man-fish" that *wouldn't* closely resemble Universal's Gill Man, surely a tribute to Westmore, Patrick, Arnold, et al.

Still, the influence is evident in such disparate examples as *Destination Inner Space* (1966) and *Humanoids from the Deep* (1982). The Gill Man did make a reappearance — of sorts — in the 1987 "homage" to the fifties movie monsters, *The Monster Squad*, which also featured the Frankenstein monster, the Mummy and the Wolf Man. (See this film listed under Frankenstein.) It is innocuous and forgettable, hardly an homage to the characters it seeks to honor.

There was to have been a remake of the original by John Carpenter.

The Creeping Unknown *see* **The Quatermass Xperiment**

Creepshow
(Warner Bros./United Film Distribution, 1982; 122 min.) **½

Produced by Richard P. Rubinstein. Directed by George A. Romero. Screenplay, Stephen King. Edited by Michael Spolan, Pasquale Buba, George A. Romero, Paul Hirsch. Director of Photography, Michael Gornick. Technicolor. Music, John Harrison. Dolby Stereo. Makeup Special Effects, Tom Savini. Roach Wranglers, David A. Brody, Raymond A. Mendez.

Cast: Henry (Hal Holbrook), Wilma (Adrienne Barbeau), Dexter Stanley (Fritz Weaver), Richard (Leslie Nielsen), Sylvia (Carrie Nye), Upson Pratt (E. G. Marshall), Aunt Bedelia (Viveca Lindfors), Hank (Ed Harris), Harry (Ted Danson), Jordy Verrill (Stephen King), Richard (Warner Shook), Charlie (Robert Harper), Cass (Elizabeth Regan), Becky (Gaylen Ross), Nathan Grantham (Jon Lormer), Mike the janitor (Don Keefer), Jordy's dad (Bingo O'Malley), Corpse (John Amplas), White (David Early), Mrs. Danvers (Nann Mogg), Billy's mom (Iva Jean Saraceni), Billy (Joe King), Tabitha (Christine Forrest), Richard Raymond (Chuck Aber), Host (Cletus Anderson), Maid (Katie Karlovitz), Yarbro (Peter Messer), Garbage men (Marty Schiff, Tom Savini).

Synopsis: Billy's dad tosses his son's *Creepshow* magazine in the trash. The pages flip open to **Father's Day:** Aunt Bedelia, who'd bludgeoned her nasty father with an ashtray on his birthday, returns to his home as she does every seven years.

While visiting the grave, she is strangled by Nathan Grantham's corpse, which then kills Hank before entering the house to get his cake. **The Lonesome Death of Jordy Verrill:** Hick Jordy Verrill finds a meteor which he intends to sell to the nearby college, but he is infected by the space invader and becomes host for its plant-producing essence. His house surrounded by greenery and he himself a veritable tree, he blows his head off with a shotgun. **Something to Tide You Over:** Richard devises a devilish scheme to make his adulterous wife Becky and her lover Harry pay. He makes Harry bury himself in the sand and watch a TV whose video hookup shows Becky in a similar predicament. Both die as the tide comes in, but their corpses rise and dish out the same punishment to Richard. **The Crate:** Mike, janitor at Anderson Hall, discovers a crate beneath the stairs. The stamped note indicates it was part of an Arctic expedition. The date: June 19, 1834. He brings this to the attention of Professor Stanley, but when they open it a gorilla-like beast reaches out and kills Mike. Stanley finds a student, but when they return to the lab, the crate is missing. They find it back under the stairs. When the student gets too close he too is killed and devoured. When Stanley's chess companion and fellow teacher Henry learns about the incident, he has a brainstorm. What better way to rid himself of his harridan of a wife than to have her meet the beast in the box? He cleans up the blood and suckers Wilma, who is indeed killed. Henry seals the crate and drops it in a quarry. He explains the situation to Stanley, who agrees to say nothing about the affair. Neither realize the box splits open in the water. The beast is free! **They're Creeping Up on You:** Ruthless businessman Pratt lives in a sterile skyscraper apartment. Obsessed with cleanliness, he wages war on dirt and bugs. A horde of roaches invades his sanctum and overwhelms him. Finally, in an epilogue, *Creepshow* is found by the garbage men, who glance at the voodoo doll ad. The order form is missing. Little Billy has sent for the doll and is pricking it to make his father suffer.

Review: "An unashamedly adolescent

spectacle." (David Ansen, *Newsweek*, November 22, 1982, p. 118)

Analysis: It's a grab bag of humorous and revolting vignettes. As *Newsweek's* Ansen pointed out, everything is *intentionally* "unsophisticated" and "one-dimensional." Many viewers remember with disgust the E. G. Marshall body disgorging and covered by roaches. "Bug wrangler" David Brody was interviewed on public radio and spoke of his journey to Trinidad to obtain some very large roaches in a bat cave. They joined some 20,000 of their kin in the film. Viewers who'd appreciated Adrienne Barbeau in the same year's *Swamp Thing* were disappointed by her henpecking character.

Creepshow 2
(New World, 1987; 92 min.) **½

Produced by David Ball. Directed by Michael Gornick. Screenplay, George A. Romero. Based on stories by Stephen King. Edited by Peter Weatherly. Directors of Photography, Richard Hart and Tom Hurwitz. Technicolor. Music, Les Reed. Makeup Effects, Howard Berger, Ed French. Makeup Effects Consultant, Tom Savini.

Cast: Ray Spruce (George Kennedy), Martha Spruce (Dorothy Lamour), Sam Whitemoon (Frank Salsedo), Annie Lansing (Lois Chiles), Hitch-hiker (Tom Wright), Creep (Tom Savini), Randy (Daniel Beer), Rachel (Page Hannah), Laverne (Jeremy Green), Truck driver (Stephen King).

Synopsis: Three tales. **Old Chief Woodenhead:** In the town of Dead River, Benjamin Whitemoon gives general store owner Ray Spruce valuable jewelry. If the tribe does not pay its debts in two autumns, Ray is to keep it. After Benjamin leaves, his nephew Sam and two punk friends rob the store and kill Ray and Martha. Revenge for this atrocity is taken by the wooden Indian on the porch. When Benjamin arrives next day and sees Sam's scalp in the statue's hand, he says, "Now, may your spirit rest, old warrior." **The Raft:** Randy and Rachel, Steve and Laverne drive to a rustic lake and swim to a moored raft. A disgusting mass surrounds the raft, and Rachel is sucked in when she touches it. Steve is pulled down by the ooze seeping through the cracks. Randy and Laverne

survive the night, but the woman is taken, and Randy desperately swims toward shore. He makes it, but the blob rises up and engulfs him. **The Hitch-Hiker:** After spending the afternoon with her lover in the city, Annie Lansing heads to her suburban home. On the way she loses control of the car and plows into a hitch-hiker. She leaves the scene but later stops to consider turning herself in. She thinks she sees a man in the road behind her; then the hitch-hiker she ran over appears at the window, crying, "Thanks for the ride, lady!" She drives away but can't shake the hitch-hiker. Finally, in the woods, he is knocked off the roof. Nevertheless, he reappears and Annie shoots him and rides over him again and again. He returns, crawling up over the hood. She crushes him against a tree and faints. When she awakes, there's no man, and she thinks everything was a dream — until she arrives home and the horribly mangled body of the hitch-hiker manifests himself and begins strangling her.

Review: "Episodes are marginally interesting, but each is a little too long." (Janet Maslin, *New York Times*, May 4, 1987, p. C17.)

Analysis: This is no-frills but interesting storytelling. In the *New York Times* review, Maslin comments that animated footage connecting the scenes appears to be intended for young viewers, while the rest of the film suggests an older audience. Filmed in Bangor, Brewer, and Dexter, Maine.

Critters
(New Line Cinema, 1986; 86 min.) **½

Produced by Rupert Harvey. Directed by Stephen Herek. Screenplay, Stephen Herek, Domonic Muir. Additional Scenes, Don Opper. Edited by Larry Bock. Directors of Photography, Tim Suhrstedt, Chris Tufty. Color, DeLuxe. Music, David Newman. Set Decoration, Anne Huntley.

Cast: Helen Brown (Dee Wallace Stone), Jay Brown (Billy Green Bush), Harv (M. Emmet Walsh), Brad Brown (Scott Grimes), April Brown (Nadine Van Der Velde), Bounty hunter (Terrence Mann), Charlie McFadden (Don Opper), Steve Elliot (Billy Zane), Jeff Barnes (Ethan Phillips), Preacher (Jeremy

Lawrence), Sally (Lin Shaye), Warden Zanti (Michael Lee Gogin), Ed (Art Frankel), Jake (Roger Hampton), Pool player (Chuck Lindsly).

Synopsis: Two intergalactic bounty hunters are sent after eight escaped prisoners from Prison Asteroid — Sector 17. The escapees look like tailless, snoutless porcupines. These "critters" land in Kansas and terrorize the Brown family farmstead. The Browns fight back, killing some with a shotgun, another with a firecracker. The bounty hunters kill more, but one critter grows to man size and drags April to its spaceship. Her brother pulls her out, and Charlie, who once had pretentions of becoming a major league baseball player, tosses a Molotov cocktail into the hatch. Brad's large, unlit firecracker had been left inside. It explodes, as does the alien craft, but it destroys the farmhouse. Next morning Brad receives a signal on his transmitter given him by the bounty hunters. He presses a button, and the house is rebuilt. But in the chicken coop are what appear to be alien eggs.

Reviews: "Dumb, but sometimes likable.... Cast is good, and ... Herek gives it some pizzazz and pace." (Michael Wilmington, *Los Angeles Times Calendar*, April 25, 1986, p. 8) ¶"Aims for little more than cheap thrills and sick jokes." (Joseph Gelmis, *Newsday*, April 11, 1986, Part III, p. 7)

Analysis: With a little more attention, this slightly unpolished *Gremlins*-inspired film might rate an unqualified three stars. There's an undercurrent of humor that frequently rises to the surface, as when two of the critters confronted by the bounty hunters cry, "Let's roll!" There are paeans to previous science fiction films, probably also a Clint Eastwood spaghetti western. Why didn't the producers or writers make one of the bounty hunters a female? A flaw: The bounty hunters don't seem to have any itinerary, any real plan for finding the critters once they land. Going to the bowling alley was just contrived to add yucks. The transformation of the bounty hunter is quite good: from a blank white face to skeleton to flesh. The critters themselves are not state-of-the art.

Critters 2
(New Line Cinema, 1988; 87 min.) **

Produced by Barry Opper. Directed by Mick Garris. Screenplay, D. T. Twohy and Mick Garris. Edited by Charles Bornstein. Music, Nicholas Pike. Ultra-Stereo. Director of Photography, Russell Carpenter. Color, DeLuxe. Set Decoration, Donna Stamps Scherer. Critters created by Chiodo Bros. Visual Effects, VCE/Peter Kuran. Special Effects and Pyrotechnics, Marty Bresin.

Cast: Bradley Brown (Scott Grimes), Megan Morgan (Liane Curtis), Charlie (Don Opper), Harv (Barry Corbin), Bounty hunter Ug (Terrence Mann), Lee (Roxanne Kernohan), Wesley (Tom Hodges), Mr. Morgan (Sam Anderson), Cindy Morgan (Lindsay Parker), Nana (Herta Ware), Sal Roos (Lin Shaye), Quigley (Doug Rowe), Reverend Fisher (Frank Birney), Sheriff Pritchett (David Ursin), Bus driver (Al Stevenson), Geek (Eddie Deezen).

Synopsis: The Council wants bounty hunters Charlie and Ug to return to Earth to check for residual critons. It's Easter time in Grover's Bend as Bradley Brown returns for a visit. Simultaneously, Wesley and Quigley remove strange, egg-shaped items from the Brown barn and take them to Quigley's antique barn. Quigley sells some of the eggs "from Europe" to an old lady, who places them in the church's Easter egg hunt. Meanwhile, eggs still at Quigley's hatch, and the critters inside devour him. An egg hatches in Megan's sister's room, but her father accidentally steps on it. Ug, Lee and Charlie land. Lee transforms into a duplicate of a *Playboy* centerfold. The three head for town. Church has become a sanctuary for the townsfolk. Lee is killed when she isn't careful and is surrounded by critters. Ug becomes depressed even though Charlie says he can't do it alone. "I'm back," says Harv as he returns with his six-shooters and blasts some critters. Bradley says if they lure the creatures to the Polar Ice Burger plant with the food as bait, they can blow all of them up. Ug becomes a critter to help. The ruse works, the plant is blown up, but a mass of critters forms a giant ball and heads for town. Charlie crashes the spacecraft into the ball. Ug becomes Charlie. Bradley goes to the bus and meets Ug/Charlie. Then the real Charlie arrives. He'd parachuted from the spacecraft the night before. A second craft arrives for Ug. Harv tosses Charlie his badge. *Review:* "Occasionally inspired *Gremlins* rip." (*Video Hound's Golden Movie Retriever 1994*, p. 237) *Analysis:* The mix of comedy and gut-gnawing monstrosities is unsettling. The ending is too long. At least they realized one of the bounty hunters should be a woman this time. And what a woman: the statuesque Roxanne Kernohan. What a shame they killed her off. *The Main Course* is supposed to be the subtitle, but it's not on the credits.

Critters 3

(New Line Cinema, 1991; 86 min.)

**½

Produced by Barry Opper and Rupert Harvey. Directed by Kristine Peterson. Screenplay, David J. Schow. Story, Rupert Harvey and Barry Opper. Edited by Terry Stokes. Director of Photography, Tom Callaway. Color, Foto-Kem. Music, David C. Williams. Critters created by Chiodo Bros.

Cast: Annie (Aimee Brooks), Josh (Leonard DiCaprio), Clifford (John Calvin), Charlie McFadden (Don Opper), Rosie (Diana Bellamy), Ug (Terrence Mann). With Katherine Cortez, Geoffrey Blake, William Dennis Hunt.

Synopsis: At a roadside rest, some teens and children encounter a strange-looking man when they chase a Frisbee into the woods. He relates the story of Grover's Bend, where aliens wreaked havoc in 1984. Unknown to anyone, some nearby critter eggs hatch and hitch a ride under Annie's father's truck. At their apartment house the critters enter the basement and kill superintendent Frank. Rosie is attacked, but Annie helps her get away. The landlord arrives with his stepson Josh and is devoured. Josh and tenant Marsha find Annie and the others upstairs. They flee to an attic crawlspace. "It's gotten too quiet out there. I don't like it," says Marsha, who works for the phone company. She attempts to reach the phone lines outside but falls. She is caught by a wire. Annie climbs down the elevator shaft and runs into some critters. She's saved by Charlie, who'd been called by one of the tenants. They retreat into the elevator and make their way back

to the others. Fighting off critters who follow, they gain the roof only to find that the building is on fire. One last critter arrives and charges Annie's brother, but Charlie intercepts it and both go over the roof. Charlie is saved by a flagpole and crashes through a trailer roof. Next day Charlie returns to the basement and finds two critter eggs. About to blow them away, he is radioed by Ug, who says a pod is being sent for these last critter eggs. "To be continued."

Review: "Not quite enough Critters action, but OK of its kind, with better characters than usual." (Leonard Maltin, ed., *Movie and Video Guide 1993*, p. 257) *Analysis:* Did they need the parent-child estrangement and rapprochement? Made for video.

Critters 4

(New Line Cinema, 1992; 94 min.) **

Produced by Barry Opper and Rupert Harvey. Directed by Rupert Harvey. Screenplay, Joseph Lyle and David J. Schow. Story, Rupert Harvey and Barry Opper. Edited by Terry Stokes. Director of Photography, Tom Callaway. Panavision. Color, Fotokem. Music, Peter Manning Robinson. Art Direction, Jeff Wallace. Critters created by Chiodo Bros. Photographic Visual Effects, Hollywood Optical Systems.

Cast: Charlie McFadden (Don Opper), Counselor Tetra/Ug (Terrence Mann), Captain Rick/Al Bert (Brad Dourif), Fran (Angela Bassett), Ethan (Paul Whitthorne), Nick (Anders Hove), Bernie (Eric Dare), Voice of Angela (Martine Beswicke), Dr. McCormick (Anne Elizabeth Ramsey).

Synopsis: "2045: Somewhere in Saturn Quadrant." Charlie receives a message from Ug to desist from killing the critters and to place the last two eggs in a special pod that will land soon. Charlie does as instructed but can't exit the pod before it takes off. A half-century later the pod is picked up by a salvage crew whose captain rashly opens the pod. Charlie is still alive. When Rick enters the pod he is attacked by the critters who've hatched the eggs. They escape into the space platform the salvage ship had landed on to wait for the pod's owners. By the time Ug's ship docks, Rick and one of his crew are dead. Ug's guards are killed by the critters. Ug, inexplicably nasty, kills another crew member and is shot by Charlie. Charlie escapes with two others in Ug's ship. Its nuclear pile unstable, the space platform explodes.

Review: "This time a strain of genetically engineered mutant critters (what's the difference?) wants to take over the universe." (*Video Hound's Golden Movie Retriever 1994*, p. 237)

Analysis: Continuity is maintained by the presence of Opper and Mann but the comedy-drama balance is bad: It's about 80 percent drama, 20 percent comedy. You've never seen so many hidden references to other science fiction films: *The Thing; It, The Terror from Beyond Space; Star Wars; Alien; The Terminator; Aliens.* There's too little planning, i.e., no one in their right mind would search for dangerous aliens on such a multi-level space platform.

The Curse

(Trans World Entertainment, 1987; 100 min.)**

Produced by Ovidio G. Assonitis. Directed by David Keith. Screenplay, David Chaskin. Edited by Claude Kutry. Director of Photography, Robert D. Forges. Color, Technicolor. Prints, Fuji. Music, John Debney. Dolby Stereo. Production Design, Frank Vanorio. Set Decoration, Arthur Fitzgerald. Makeup, Frank Russell. Visual Effects, Kevin Erham.

Cast: Nathan Hayes (Claude Akins), Zachary (Wil Wheaton), Frances (Kathleen Jordan Gregory), Dr. Alan Forbes (Cooper Huckabee), Mike (Steve Davis), Alice (Amy Wheaton), Cyrus (Malcolm Danare), Carl Willis (John Schneider), Esther Forbes (Hope North), Davidson (Steve Carlisle).

Synopsis: In Tellico Plains, Tennessee the family farm of Nathan Hayes is struck by what appears to be a meteorite. For fear the news will impede construction of a Tennessee Valley Authority reservoir in the vicinity, neighbor Dr. Forbes allows his real estate partner to convince him not to bring it to the attention of the authorities. The "meteor" disintegrates overnight, leaching into the soil. Crops begin growing profusely, but when Frances cuts open a head of lettuce she finds a core of disgusting liquid. The tomatoes have worms, as do the apples. Only Zachary understands that the water is polluted. Farm animals evince

changes. Frances contracts warts and slowly goes insane. Initially Nathan thinks it's God's punishment for his wife's adultery. Forbes suspects the water and has it analyzed. The lab reports molecular structure change. Forbes is too late to save the now infected Nathan, who kills him. Zachary is saved when the TVA man Carl Willis impales Nathan with a pitchfork. Zachary and Carl rescue young sister Alice upstairs as the house begins to collapse. Zachary locates his mother in the attic only to see her disintegrate into a blob. The house sinks into the earth as Carl, Zachary and Alice drive away.

Reviews: "The week's entry in suppuration stakes." (Walter Goodman, *New York Times*, September 11, 1987, p. C13) ¶"For a horror film, it's pretty inept, but it offers a fair amount of fun in a Saturday Night Schlock, campy way." (Kris Gilpin, *Deep Red*, March 1988, p. 60)

Analysis: One might compare this to H. G. Wells's *Food of the Gods*, but it bears closer kinship to H. P. Lovecraft's September 1927 *Amazing Stories* piece "The Color Out of Space," which was filmed previously as 1965's *Die, Monster, Die!* (g. v.), though its New England setting was transferred to England. *The Curse* was filmed in Tellico County, Tennessee, and commendably directed by actor David Keith. The prologue is unnecessary, however. Warning: Keep away from children. It's revolting and sad. "Fungi" films are disturbing to those of us who do not like to see humans degenerating slowly into mindless things. Cooper Huckabee would play the spy Harrison in 1993's *Gettysburg.*

Despite the "II" and "III" designations on the films that followed, nothing connects this "series" but the title. The first two are science fiction; the third is supernatural.

Curse II — The Bite

(Viva/Towa, 1988; 97 min.) **½

Directed by Fred Goodwin. Screenplay, Susan Zelouf and Federico Prosperi. Edited by Claude Cutry. Director of Photography, Roberto D'Ettore Piazzoli. Panavision. Technicolor. Music, Carlo Maria Cordio. Special Effects, Screaming Mad George.

Cast: Lisa (Jill Schoelen), Clark Newman (J. Eddie Peck), Harry Morton (Jamie Farr), Sheriff (Bo Swenson), Iris (Savina Gersak), Big Pig (Marianne Muellerleile), Gas station attendant (Al Fann), George (Sydney Lassick), Dr. Marder (Sandra Sexton).

Synopsis: While driving across the Southwest near the government's Yellow Sands nuclear testing site, Clark is bitten by a snake that apparently entered his jeep after he and Lisa ran over a bunch of reptiles on a desert roadway. A gas station attendant had warned them about nefarious experiments that were even confounding the animals. Although traveling salesman Harry Morton gives Clark an antivenin, Clark's hand becomes infected. Discovering that it was a bushmaster that bit Clark, Harry attempts to track him down and give him the proper antidote. Clark becomes increasingly manic and is hospitalized. His infected hand, now with the head of a snake, kills the doctor who believed a genetic mutation was at work. Clark hacks off his hand. Lisa finds him taking refuge with a religious couple, but his snake hand has grown back and his whole body is infested with the creatures, which pursue Lisa. Discovered at a construction project by the sheriff and Morton, Lisa is rescued while Harry shoots the giant snake erupting from Clark's body.

Review: "Insipid little fright picture with lousy special effects." (Mick Martin and Marsha Porter, *Video Movie Guide 1991*, p. 710)

Analysis: Even for those with no snake phobia, this will engender the creeps. It's illogical, revolting, but, dare we say it, scary? Or merely disgusting? Filmed in Las Cruces, New Mexico.

Curse III — Blood Sacrifice
(Epic Production/Blue Rock Films, 1990; 91 min.) ***

Produced by Christopher Coy. Directed by Sean Barton. Screenplay, John Hunt, Sean Barton. Original Story, Richard Haddon Haines. Edited by Micki Stroucken. Director of Photography, Phillip Grosvenor. Music, Julian Laxton and Patric Van Blerk. Dolby. Stunt Coordinator, Gavin Mey. Creature created by Chris Walas Inc. with Peter Greenwood.

Cast: Elizabeth Armstrong (Jenilee Harrison), Dr. Pearson (Christopher Lee), Geoff Armstrong (Andre Jacobs), Mletch (Henry Cele), Anthea Steed (Zoe Randall), Chloe Steed (Olivie Dyer), Cindy (Jennifer Steyn), Robert (Gavin Hood), Witch doctor (Dumi Shongwe).

Synopsis: East Africa, 1950: American Elizabeth Armstrong lives with farmer husband Geoff on a sugar cane tract. After her sister Cindy and Cindy's husband Robert interrupt a witch doctor sacrificing a goat, the witch doctor lays a curse on them, a curse involving a sea demon. Cindy and Robert are killed. Elizabeth, pregnant, suffers abdominal pains, and Dr. Pearson is summoned. His elixir helps her. Geoff, finding the bodies of Cindy and Robert, is chased back to the farm by someone or something. Elizabeth finds him dead in the pantry. Foreman Mletch is killed. Elizabeth flees to the home of a neighbor, Anthea Steed. Dr. Pearson arrives. Elizabeth thinks he's the perpetrator. The witch doctor is killed when the cane field is fired. Looking for an extra lamp in the shed, Elizabeth is set upon by a scaly humanoid creature. She spills gas on the floor, lights it up and escapes to the house.

Review: "Christopher Lee portrays a local doctor who may or may not have something to do with it. Too bad." (Mick Martin and Marsha Porter, *Video Movie Guide 1994*, p. 798)

Analysis: What a surprise! This is a quality film with good acting, excellent photography, tension, and a non-cop-out ending. In short, it's not another *Curucu, Beast of the Amazon*; there *is* a monster, but for most of the time the audience doesn't know that for sure, nor which of the humans is a bad guy. Is it Mletch? Dr. Pearson? Harrison and Steyn have nude scenes. A.k.a. *Panga*.

Notes of Interest: There is a *Curse IV: The Ultimate Sacrifice*, but it has a copyright of 1988 and was apparently a pickup of the Italian film *Catacombs* by Charles Band. If anyone's interested, we've seen it: It's boring and incoherent.

Curse of the Cat People *see under* **The Cat People**

The Curse of the Fly *see under* **The Fly**

The Curse of Frankenstein *see under* **Frankenstein**

The Curse of Michael Myers *see* Halloween: The Curse of Michael Myers *under* **Halloween**

The Curse of the Mummy's Tomb *see under* **The Mummy**

Daleks' Invasion Earth 2150 A.D. *see under* **Dr. Who and the Daleks**

Damien: Omen II *see under* **The Omen**

Darkman
(Universal, 1990; 120 min.) ** ½

Produced by Robert Tapert. Directed by Sam Raimi. Screenplay, Chuck Pfarrer, Sam Raimi, Ivan Raimi, Daniel Goldin, Joshua Goldin. Story, Sam Raimi. Edited by Bud Smith, Scott Smith. Director of Photography, Bill Pope. Color, DeLuxe. Music, Danny Elfman. Dolby. Makeup Effects, Tony Gardner, Larry Hamlin. Visual Effects, Introvision Systems International.

Cast: Peyton Westlake/Darkman (Liam Neeson), Louis Strack, Jr. (Colin Friels), Julie Hastings (Frances McDormand), Robert G. Durant (Larry Drake), Yakitito (Nelson Mashita), Eddie Black (Jesse Lawrence Ferguson), Rudy Guzman (Rafael H. Robledo), Rick (Theodore Raimi), Skip (Danny Hicks), Smiley (Dan Bell), Pauly (Nicholas Worth), Martin Katz (Aaron Lustig), Hung Fat (Arsenio "Sonny" Trinidad), Physician (John Landis), Bartender (John Cameron), Final shemp (Bruce Campbell), Doctor (Jenny Agutter).

Synopsis: Scientist Peyton Westlake is researching quasi-organic molecular polymers and the development of synthetic skin for use in primarily reconstructive surgery. Peyton and his assistant are stymied only by the miraculous polymer's time limit: after 99 minutes, lifelike prosthetics fashioned of the substance degenerate into a blubbery mass. Peyton's girlfriend, Julie Hastings, is an investigative newspaper reporter probing allegations of graft in the proposed multimillion-dollar urban construction project in the dilapidated dock district. Entrepreneur Louis Strack, Jr., is the construction mogul behind this mammoth project. When Julie unknowingly procures incriminating documents, Strack sends crime kingpin Robert Durant and his goons to retrieve them. They find the documents with Peyton, who, like Julie, is ignorant of their value. The mobsters trash the lab and immerse Peyton in a bubbling vat of prototype polymer. An explosion hurls the unconscious scientist through the window and into the bay some blocks away. When a badly burned body washes up days later, it is presumed to be that of a nameless vagrant. Unknown to any of the medical personnel, Peyton, though badly disfigured, has been vitalized by the experimental polymers in which Durant's men dunked him. Escaping from the hospital, he removes salvagable equipment from his ruined lab to an abandoned factory. He arduously puts things back in working order and resumes his experiments on synthetic skin in a bid to regain some semblance of his former appearance. Although heartbroken by Peyton's apparent death, Julie is won over by the charming Louis Strack. One of their outings is viewed surreptitiously by Peyton. When he sees Rick, one of the thugs who attacked him, Peyton drags the hapless lackey into a nearby sewer. Before throttling him, Peyton learns enough of Durant's operation to plan a caper against the crime boss. The caper is executed flawlessly, netting Peyton a tidy sum to live off of and finance further research. Utilizing his synthetic skin formula, Peyton is able to fashion a lifelike mask, which he uses to reveal himself to an overjoyed Julie. The unfortunate 99-minute limitation prevents any long-term involvement, and Peyton is hesitant to tell Julie the full truth about his discovery. With Peyton's reappearance, Julie resolves to break off her romance with Strack. In doing so she discovers the documents she'd thought destroyed in the lab fire to be in Strack's possession. Durant's men follow Julie to Peyton's lab. In the firefight that ensues, Durant's men are killed one by one. The crime boss himself is killed in a fiery helicopter crash as he duels the enraged Peyton. Disguised as Durant, Peyton then accompanies Strack to the top of an unfinished skyscraper. A trap using Julie as bait is revealed and is nearly successful in luring Peyton to his doom. Strack and Peyton battle each other across the skeletal girders high above the city streets. Ultimately, the entrepreneur plunges to his death, and Peyton rescues Julie. The future holds little allure for Peyton Westlake, however. Snatching bits of a "normal" life with Julie — 99 minutes at a time — is clearly not enough for him. He leaves her at the foot of the skyscraper, disappearing into the crowd.

Reviews: "Despite its torrid pace, the movie never really loses its sense of fun." (Michael Wilmington, *Los Angeles Times Calendar*, August 24, 1990, p. 10 "Sustains mild interest throughout, but it never takes off.... plenty of high action." (Caryn James, *New York Times*, August 24, 1990, p. C15) "Raimi isn't effective with his actors, and the dialogue lacks smart menace, but his canny visual sense carries many a scene." (Richard Corliss, *Time*, September 17, 1990, p. 71)

Analysis: Tim Burton's first *Batman* film has given rise to a number of similar dark, obsessive loner-heroes inspired by the comics. *The Punisher* (1989), an Australian quickie starring Dolph Lundgren, was one of the first of these; 1994's *The Crow*— at once the apex and the end of Brandon Lee's short-lived canon — one of the best. Somewhere between the extremes in this mini-genre is *Darkman*. Being Sam Raimi's first "A" film after a number of highly thought-of genre horror items, *Darkman* has many of the qualities that made Tim Burton's film distinctive, without the highly individual sense of stylism that distinguishes his work. Raimi's frankly tongue-in-cheek film vacillates between the high-gloss, highly polished world of high tech and the moldy damp of the abandoned vault, and handles both with a certain aplomb. If *Darkman* has a fault, it's that it goes over the top too often in its outbursts of *angst* and expressionist flashes — but then, that's part of the baggage, when one travels in the comics. Liam Neeson had few leading parts to his credit when he played the title character in *Darkman*, and he hasn't appeared often in *non*-leading roles since. He was nominated for an Academy Award for his performance in *Schlindler's List* in 1993.

Look for Raimi's ubiquitous favorite, Bruce Campbell, before fadeout, and yes, that's an unbilled Jenny Agutter appearing briefly as a doctor early on.

Darkman II: The Return of Durant
(Universal/Renaissance, 1995; 93 min.) *½

Produced by David Roessell. Directed by Bradford May. Screenplay, Steven McKay. Story, Robert Eisele and Lawrence Hertzog. Based upon characters created by Sam Raimi. Edited by Daniel Cahn. Director of Photography, Bradford May. Panavision. Color. Music, Randy Miller. Themes, Danny Elfman. Art Direction, Ian Brock. Set Decoration, Caroline Gee. Special Makeup Effects, Kurtzman, Nicotero and Berger EFT Group Inc.

Cast: Peyton Westlake/Darkman (Arnold Vosloo), Robert Durant (Larry Drake), Jill Randall (Kim Delaney), Laurie Brinkman (Renee O'Connor), Dr. Alfred Hathaway (Lawrence Dane), Eddie (David Ferry), Ivan (Rod Wilson), Dr. David Brinkman (Jesse Collins), Rollo (Jack Langedijk), Roy (Steve Mousseau), Whitey (Sten Eirik), Mr. Perkins (James Millington).

Synopsis: Unscrupulous master criminal Robert Durant survived his seemingly deadly encounter with Darkman, once known as Peyton Westlake, and now plans to make and sell specialty guns. He sends out his henchman to acquire the old Brinkman Electrical Company factory, which has the power necessary for weapons production. When money fails to persuade the young Dr. Brinkman to sell, they make threatening gestures until cowed by the unexpected intrusion of an intimidating man. After they leave, the man (Peyton Westlake) says he's familiar with Brinkman's biogenetics research and presents him with disks that contain his own discoveries. Peyton's goal is the creation of a stable polymer that will allow him to create a synthetic skin that will last longer than the 99 minutes he presently can achieve to hide his fire-damaged face and hands. To make his particle-beam weapons, Durant breaks Dr. Alfred Hathaway out of the Home for the Criminally Insane. The power source for the guns will be plutonium batteries smuggled out of the old

Soviet Union by Ivan, one of Durant's Russian minions. Durant has Brinkman killed. Peyton learns from investigative reporter Jill Randall that Durant is in fact the pending purchaser of the Brinkman property. Jill is killed in a car explosion after she begins an exposé of Durant on her TV show *Street Copy*. Peyton uses photos of Durant's men to create a duplicate mask of Eddie and infiltrates a meeting during which Laurie Brinkman decides to renege on the deal to sell her brother's property. Peyton can't get Laurie to safety and she's captured. Durant now knows that Westlake is alive and plans to use Laurie as bait. Peyton masquerades as Ivan but is found out. When right-wing extremist Millington arrives to buy his guns, Peyton uses his presence to scamper away and become Darkman. After Durant does away with Millington and his gang, Darkman does the same to Durant's crew and uses remote control to blow up Durant in his car.

Review: "Though decidedly brutal and occasionally nonsensical, this has a certain comic-book stylishness that keeps it from completely sinking." (Mick Martin and Marsha Porter, *Video Movie Guide 1997*, p. 253)

Analysis: Again, Darkman seems to exist in some nebulous near future, a world reminiscent of *RoboCop's* Detroit or *Batman's* Gotham. Frequent visions by Westlake tie his present adventure to the previous film. But there are many negatives to this sequel. Despite his half-maniacal cries for vengeance, Darkman doesn't kill his enemies when he has the opportunity. He gets himself captured. The henchmen cower when they have the guns and Darkman has none. There's no way Durant could plant a bomb in Jill Randall's car so fast, and the demise of this heinous crime lord is rather pedestrian: just another car explosion. *Darkman II* is listed in different publications as 1994 or 1995. *Darkman III* is another direct-to-video episode scheduled for 1996 release.

Daughter of Dr. Jekyll *see under* **Dr. Jekyll and Mr. Hyde**

Dawn of the Dead *see under* **Night of the Living Dead**

Day of the Dead *see under* **Night of the Living Dead**

A Dead Man Seeks His Murderer *see* The Brain *under* **The Lady and the Monster**

Die, Monster, Die!
(AIP, 1965; 80 min.) **½

Produced by Pat Green. Directed by Daniel Haller. Screenplay, Jerry Soho. Based on "The Color Out of Space" by H.P. Lovecraft. Edited by Alfred Cox. Director of Photography, Paul Beeson. Color. Music, Don Banks. Music Director, Philip Martell. Art Direction, Colin Southcott. Makeup, Jimmy Evans. Special Effects, Wally Veevers, Ernie Sullivan.

Cast: Nahum Witley (Boris Karloff), Stephen Reinhart (Nick Adams), Letitia Witley (Freda Jackson), Susan Witley (Suzan Farmer), Dr. Anderson (Patrick Magee), Mervyn (Terence De Marney). With Paul Farrell, Leslie Dwyer, Harold Goodwin, Sydney Bromley, Billy Milton, Sheila Raynor.

Synopsis: Graduate student Stephen Reinhart comes to the small English berg of Arkham to visit former schoolmate and girlfriend Susan Witley. Reinhart's arrival is greeted with anything but enthusiasm, with even the inhabitants of Arkham seeking to give him the bum's rush at his mere mention of the Witley name. En route to the Witley estate on foot, he passes through a fog-shrouded, blasted countryside largely devoid of either flora or fauna. Reinhart's welcome at the Witley estate is hardly any warmer than he'd received in the village, with the wheelchair-bound patriarch, Nahum, actually inviting the American to leave at once. The large Witley manor is now evidently occupied only by Witley, his wife and daughter, and Mervyn, the butler. Susan seems glad to see Stephen, however, as does her bedridden mother, Letitia Witley, who remains obscured by diaphanous hangings about her bed. Letitia actually wants the American to take her daughter with him back to the States. Despite Nahum's wishes, Reinhart settles in for a brief stay. The American has hardly got his bags unpacked when things take a decided turn for the bizarre. Ghoulish, unsettling howls are heard at all hours; Reinhart is attacked on the estate grounds by a shrouded, evidently deformed, figure; Mervyn collapses and dies of unspecified causes. Delving into the family history, Reinhart discovers that the Witleys have always had a reputation for the eccentric, and that rumors of ancestor Corbin Witley's devil-worship and dabbling into the occult are based on fact. It is revealed that, years before, a meteorite had been uncovered on the Witley property, and that Corbin had discovered that it possessed properties that affected the growth of vegetable life, accelerating it beyond belief. Unfortunately, the growth was uncontrolled and ultimately produced a corrupt fruit. It also had gross negative effects on the human residents of the Witley household, causing increasing dementia and deformity. Letitia finally succumbs to the meteorite's malign influence and becomes a murderous and misshapen figure, attacking Reinhart and Susan. Ultimately, Reinhart persuades Witley that the family is under the contaminating influence of the meteorite and not under any arcane curse associated with Corbin's occult pursuits. Witley concedes that this is the case and urges the young man to take his daughter and leave. When Nahum then attempts to destroy the meteorite (which is kept in a crypt beneath the manor), he is transformed into a powerful, glowing fiend, no longer bound to his wheelchair, and bent on murder.

Review: "Karloff is great." (*Video Hound's Golden Movie Retriever 1994*, p. 273)

Analysis: H. P. Lovecraft (1890–1937), while well known in literary circles high and low and much appreciated by aficionados of fantastic literature, was mostly unknown to the movie going public even in the 1960s. Although his work would seem a likely candidate for filming, it wasn't touched at all by filmmakers until the 1960s, and then it was usually with a result similar to *Die, Monster, Die!* While using the Lovecraft story as a premise, this film has the look and trappings of the Poe cycle Roger Corman was wrapping up for American International (*The Tomb of Ligeia*, the last of Corman's Poe adaptations, appeared the same year as *Die, Monster, Die!* and was also filmed in England): the old world setting,

the Gothic and occult trappings, and, of course, Boris Karloff. The resemblance to Corman's Poe isn't entirely coincidental, as director Haller had previously worked as art director with Corman on several productions (including the first Lovecraft adaptation, *The Haunted Palace*). Haller would return to Lovecraft again in 1969 as director of *The Dunwich Horror*, a more ambitious project, but similarly disappointing.

As a Lovecraft adaptation, *Die, Monster, Die!* is a typical disappointment, duplicating little of the tension of the original story and none of that inimitable Lovecraftian atmosphere, with its haunting New England locale and rustic eeriness. In its place is the stereotypical foggy Gothic estate, the *Jane Eyre*–style bromide of the crazy relative hidden away in the attic, and the hackneyed business of a family curse. Granted, Lovecraft can be a somewhat difficult writer to adapt to the screen, with his highly personal, stylized manner of writing. "The Color Out of Space" contains all of his typical fingerprints, being essentially a long, convoluted narrative told in the first person, with no important female characters and little in the way of dialogue. Such a work, particularly in the 1960s, would require much work in adapting it for the screen. This Samuel Arkoff/James Nicholson production accomplished the task in typical (for them) sleazy fashion, giving us a guy, a girl and a monster, and few surprises along the way.

In its defense, *Die, Monster, Die!* does deliver the goods, with an occasional shock here and there, and one or two moments of atmospheric effectiveness (mostly in the beginning). The principal actors, while hardly inspiring, go through the numbers with few problems beyond looking sincere. This Karloff was able to do in any film, and this film is more a Karloff vehicle than anything else. Confined to a wheelchair, he's able to convey little of the physical menace he projected during his prime, but is still able to project an appropriate threatening manner (the later scenes in the movie, with Nahum Witley stalking through the house, up and down stairs, smashing through doors, etc., were done by a stunt double). Nick Adams is clearly out of his element here, but he manages to get through the thing without disgracing himself. Veteran Patrick Magee has little more than a walk-on. John Stanley describes *Die, Monster, Die!* as "muddled and dull," which it is.

Aka *Monster of Terror* and *The House at the End of the World*.

The Curse
(Trans World Entertainment, 1987; 100 min.)***

This film was apparently also inspired by the Lovecraft story (uncredited); at any rate, like Die, Monster, Die! *it centers around a meteorite that leaches into the soil and causes excessive crop growth and significant family dysfunction. However,* The Curse *(or at least its title) was the progenitor for a series unrelated to the meteorite theme. For this reason, it has been placed as a main entry in the alphabetical listing, rather than as a subentry here.*

Deliver Us from Evil *see* Prom Night IV: Deliver Us from Evil *under* **Prom Night**

Dr. Jekyll and Mr. Hyde
(Paramount, 1932; 90 min.) ****

Produced and directed by Rouben Mamoulian. Screenplay, Samuel Hoffenstein and Percy Heath. Based on *The Strange Case of Dr. Jekyll and Mr. Hyde* by Robert Louis Stevenson. Edited by William Shea. Director of Photography, Karl Struss. Art Direction, Hans Dreier. Costumes, Travis Banton. Makeup, Wally Westmore.

Cast: Dr. Henry Jekyll/Mr. Hyde (Fredric March), Ivy Pierson (Miriam Hopkins), Muriel Carew (Rose Hobart), Dr. Lanyon (Holmes Herbert), Poole (Edgar Norton), Brigadier-General Carew (Halliwell Hobbes), Utterson (Arnold Lucy), Briggs (Eric Wilton), Mrs. Hawkins (Tempe Pigott), Hobson (Colonel MacDonnell), Doctor (Murdock MacQuarrie), Student (Douglas Walton), Waiter (John Rogers).

Synopsis: Young, handsome and accomplished, surgeon Dr. Henry Jekyll regales medical students with his theory of mankind's dual personality. How wonderful it would be if the evil self could be separated and banished. That evening he operates on

an elderly woman and arrives late at his fiancée Muriel's dinner party. Later he cannot budge General Carew: Marriage to his daughter must wait. Leaving, he and Dr. Lanyon break up an attack on one Ivy Pierson who lives in Diadem Court. While ministering to her, Jekyll is almost seduced. As he leaves, Jekyll argues with Lanyon about separating the two natures of man. In his laboratory, Jekyll mixes a potion. Before drinking, he leaves Muriel a note telling her that if he dies it was in the name of science but that he loves her eternally. He drinks the potion and gasps. When the room stops spinning, he finds a bestial face staring back from the mirror. "Free! Free at last!" he howls. He dresses to leave, but Poole knocks and this creature reverts to Jekyll. Jekyll goes to Muriel and asks her to marry. She says she'll try to convince her father to agree during their trip to Bath. Tiring of his existence without Muriel, Jekyll takes his mixture again and seeks out Ivy at the Variety Music Hall. Shocking all he meets, Hyde asks a waiter to bring Ivy over. "What a figure!" he cries, intimidating her. Later, at Ivy's, Hyde reads of Muriel's return and tells Ivy he's going away, but if Ivy thinks of fooling around, "I'll show you what horror means!" In his lab, Jekyll throws away the key to the back door and gives Poole an envelope and fifty pounds for Ivy. Jekyll meets Muriel and says he's trod a dangerous road and needs her help to find his way back. The general grudgingly gives his consent to the marriage, which will be announced at the next evening's dinner. Ivy comes to Jekyll to return the money and shows him her back, whipped by Hyde. She pleads for poison, but Jekyll promises she won't see Hyde again. Strolling through the park to Muriel's, Jekyll sees a cat kill a bird and becomes depressed, reciting a line: "Thou was not born for death." He is transformed without taking the elixir. He goes to Ivy and strangles her. With no key to the back door, Hyde goes to the front, but Poole denies admittance. In a bar, Hyde pens a note to Lanyon requesting he retrieve a vial from Jekyll's E cabinet that someone will pick up that evening. Hyde goes to Lanyon for the vial, but Lanyon pulls a gun and

Muriel (Rose Hobart), grieving over the strange behavior of fiancé Henry Jekyll (Fredric March), is unaware of the presence of her transformed beloved in *Dr. Jekyll and Mr. Hyde* (Paramount, 1932).

demands explanation. "I don't understand," says Lanyon after witnessing the transformation. Later Jekyll calls upon God, berating himself for going further than man should. He goes to Muriel, says he must give her up. "I'm in Hell.... I'm beyond the pale!" She flings herself on the piano when he leaves, but outside he becomes Hyde and returns. Muriel screams, and her father and the butler arrive. Jekyll beats them off and kills the General with his cane. Lanyon notes that the walking stick is Jekyll's. At his home, Hyde is transformed back to Jekyll and tries to convince the police Hyde left through the back. But before Lanyon and other police, Jekyll becomes Hyde, tries to escape but is shot by the police chief.

Reviews: "What with the audibility of the screen and the masterful photography, the new pictorial transcription of Stevenson's spine-chilling work ... emerges as a far more tense and shuddering affair than it was as John Barrymore's silent picture.... Mr. March's portrayal is something to arouse admiration, even taking into consideration the camera wizardry. As Dr. Jekyll he is a charming man, and as the fiend he is alert and sensual.... Miriam Hopkins does splendidly as the unfortunate Ivy. Rose Hobart is clever as the sympathetic Muriel." (Mordaunt Hall, *New York Times*, January 2, 1932, p. 14) ¶"March does an outstanding bit of theatrical acting. His Hyde make-up is a triumph of realized nightmare.... Miriam Hopkins plays Ivy, the London soiled dove, with a capital sense of comedy and coquetry.... Settings and lighting alone are worth seeing as models of atmospheric surroundings." (*Variety*)

Analysis: Because the Stevenson work is short, filmmakers throughout the twentieth century have sought to elaborate on the Jekyll and Hyde story, adding female characters and making Jekyll/Hyde the featured player even though in the original story he's mostly talked about and his letters read after his demise (by suicide). Mamoulian's film was a model in this regard, staying rather close to the book while fleshing out scenes effectively. Good examples of successful book-to-film translation are the variety hall scenes when Hyde intimidates everyone who looks upon him. Made before the Production Code restrictions were in place, it has more than a tinge of eroticism. A brilliant film from a brilliant director. March won a deserved Academy Award, sharing it with Wallace Beery, who won for MGM's *The Champ*. The tie was apparently a result of behind-the-scenes finagling by MGM head Louis B. Mayer.

Dr. Jekyll and Mr. Hyde
(MGM, 1941; 127 min.) ***

Produced by Victor Saville. Directed by Victor Fleming. Screenplay, John Lee Mahin. Based on *The Strange Case of Dr. Jekyll and Mr. Hyde* by Robert Louis Stevenson. Edited by Harold F. Kress. Director of Photography, Joseph Ruttenberg. Music, Franz Waxman. Art Direction, Cedric Gibbons, Daniel B. Cathcart. Set Decoration, Edwin B. Willis. Costumes, Adrian, Gile Steele. Makeup, Jack Dawn. Special Effects, Warren Newcombe and Peter Ballbasch.

Cast: Dr. Jekyll/Mr. Hyde (Spencer Tracy), Ivy Peterson (Ingrid Bergman), Beatrix Emery (Lana Turner), Dr. John Lanyon (Ian Hunter), Sir Charles Emery (Donald Crisp), Poole (Peter Godfrey), Bishop (C. Aubrey Smith), Sam Higgins (Barton MacLane), Mrs. Higgins (Sara Allgood), Dr. Heath (Frederic Worlock), Freddie (Dennis Green), Marcia (Frances Robinson), Mr. Weller (Billy Bevan), Old Prouty (Forrester Harvey), Dr. Courtland (Lawrence Grant), Colonel Weyworth (Lumsden Hare), Constable (John Barclay). With Alec Craig.

Synopsis: In 1888, Dr. Jekyll elucidates his theories about human transformation to skeptical, conservative guests at a dinner party. Even Sir Charles is aghast, and his daughter, Beatrix, is engaged to Jekyll. Sir Charles urges his future son-in-law to renounce his experiments and concentrate on building a good practice amongst the appropriate clientele. On their way home, Jekyll and Lanyon come to the aid of a barmaid who is being molested. Ivy is attracted to Jekyll and attempts a seduction, but Lanyon's arrival in her doorway breaks the clinch. At odds with the physician establishment, Jekyll concentrates on work in his home lab. Just when his experiments on animals suggest he's succeeded, the unbalanced man on whom he intended to try his formula dies. He drinks the elixir himself and is transformed, his more bestial side coming forth. During the transformation he sees both Beatrix and Ivy. He imagines himself driving a carriage and whipping two white horses, who become the women. "Mr. Hyde" seeks out Ivy, instigates a brawl where she works, and gets her fired. Outside, he offers her money and gains control over her, setting her up in a flat from which her friends cannot roust her until some convince her to see a doctor. The doctor they recommend is none other than Jekyll. She becomes half hysterical in

Ivy (Ingrid Bergman), the barmaid attacked by Mr. Hyde, reluctantly shows her wounds to Dr. Henry Jekyll (Spencer Tracy) in *Dr. Jekyll and Mr. Hyde* (MGM, 1941).

his presence, and he promises that Mr. Hyde will henceforth not bother her. However, Jekyll becomes Hyde while walking across the park to Bea's house to announce their official engagement. He goes to Ivy, recites words spoken by Jekyll, and strangles her. Fleeing other residents and police, he finds he lacks the key to the back entrance to Jekyll's home. He sends a note to Dr. Lanyon, directing him to ask Poole for admittance to Jekyll's lab, where he will find certain vials. Hyde accosts Lanyon at the latter's residence and attempts to leave with the vials. Lanyon pulls a gun and Hyde says he'll rue the day, but Hyde mixes the elixir and becomes Jekyll before the stunned onlooker. Jekyll goes to Bea to break the engagement but upon leaving is transformed again. Before he can hurt Bea, her father arrives. Hyde beats him to death with his cane and escapes. Lanyon arrives, realizes the cane is Jekyll's, and leads the police to his house. Hyde has become Jekyll, but Lanyon talks the police into remaining and they witness the reverse

transformation. Hyde goes on a rampage but is shot to death by Lanyon.

Review: "Extraordinary polished production.... a Grand Guignol chiller with delusions of grandeur.... Mr. Tracy's portrait of Hyde is not so much evil incarnate as it is the ham rampant." (T.S., *New York Times*, August 13, 1941, p. 13) ¶"Pretentious resurrection of Robert Louis Stevenson's ghoulish classic." (*Time*, September 1, 1941, p. 86) ¶"In the evident striving to make *Jekyll* a 'big' film ... some of the finer psychological points are dulled.... Nevertheless, it has its highly effective moments...." (*Variety*)

Analysis: It's given the handsome MGM treatment: sets, music, cast, director. Both Lana Turner and Ingrid Bergman are delicious, and the sequence in which Hyde whips them along erotically memorable. Ingrid in particular was never more bewitching. (The *New York Times*, *Time*, and *Variety* all singled her out for ringing praise.) Her scenes are the set pieces. While Fredric March was probably made over-ugly in the 1932 version, Tracy's makeup is rather underdone. But if he's out in public, he might as well look only half-crazed. Having Lanyon shoot Jekyll is the scriptwriter's invention. He takes poison in the novel. We wonder if MGM's Louis B. Mayer inserted the psalm spoken by Poole when his master is killed. Coming from conservative MGM is another reason for a less ugly Hyde. Note that during one chase scene, Hyde (a stuntman, no doubt) loses his hat but around the corner still has it. In *Me: Stories of My Life* (New York: Ballantine, 1992, pp. 254-55), Katharine Hepburn wrote that even before they met, Tracy envisioned her for the role of Ivy *and* the fiancee. Of the role itself, "He felt idiotic. He was so embarrassed by all this paraphernalia he used to drive down the lot in a limousine with the shades closed." He complained when she called it "very interesting": "Oh no—no—nothing—rotten.... I just can't do that sort of thing. It's like constructing a dummy and then trying to breathe life into it. I like to be the dummy myself, and then make people—force people—to believe that I'm whatever I want them to believe. Inside out—instead of outside in. No makeup."

Son of Dr. Jekyll
(Columbia, 1951; 77 min.) nv

Directed by Seymour Friedman. Screenplay, Edward Huebsch. Story, Mortimer Braus and Jack Pollexfen. Edited by Gene Havlick. Director of Photography, Henry Freulich. Music, Paul Sawtell. Art Direction, Walter Holscher. Set Decoration, William Kiernan.

Cast: Edward Jekyll (Louis Hayward), Lynn (Jody Lawrence), Dr. Kurt Lanyon (Alexander Knox), John Utterson (Lester Matthews), Richard Daniels (Gavin Muir), Inspector Stoddard (Paul Cavanagh), Michaels (Rhys Williams), Lottie Sarelle (Doris Lloyd), Hazel Sarelle (Claire Carleton), Joe Sarelle (Patrick O'Moore), Constables (James Logan, Leslie Denison), Willie Bennett (Robin Camp), Landlord (Pat Aherne), Inspector Grey (Matthew Boulton), Prosecutor (Olaf Hytten).

Synopsis: Hyde is killed. His son is hidden by Dr. Jekyll's friends. Edward Jekyll is not informed about his father's experiments

and their horrific outcome until he is thirty and about to marry. Edward intends to clear his father's name. However, Dr. Lanyon urges him to take up where his father faltered. Although Edward proves he is not guilty of present-day murders—committed by Lanyon under the influence of the original serum—he nevertheless dies in a fire.

Review: "Lightweight variation on the Jekyll and Hyde theme." (John Stanley, *The Creature Features Movie Guide*, p. 242)

Analysis: See *Daughter of Dr. Jekyll* for a companion piece from the same Jack Pollexfen.

Abbott and Costello Meet Dr. Jekyll and Mr. Hyde
(Universal, 1953; 77 min.) **

Produced by Howard Christie. Directed by Charles Lamont. Screenplay, Lee Loeb and John Grant. Based on stories by Sidney Fields and Grant Garrett. Edited by Russell Schoengarth. Director of Photography, George Robinson. Art Direction, Bernard Herzbrun, Eric Orbom. Set Decoration, Russell A. Gausman, John Austin. Makeup, Bud Westmore.

Cast: Slim (Bud Abbott), Tubby (Lou Costello), Dr. Henry Jekyll (Boris Karloff), Vicky Edwards (Helen Westcott), Bruce Adams (Craig Stevens), Inspector (Reginald Denny), Batley (John Dierkes), Mr. Hyde (Edwin Parker), Can-Can dancers (Patti McKaye, Betty Tyler, Lucille Lamarr), Japanese actor (Henry Corden), Javanese dancer (Carmen De Lavallade), Militant woman (Marjorie Bennett), Mrs. Penprase (Isabelle Dwan), Bartender (Arthur Gould), Drunks (Clyde Cook, John Rogers), Couple on bike (Gil Perkins, Judith Brian), Nursemaid (Hilda Plowright), Jailer (Keith Hitchcock), Suffragette (Betty Fairfax), Man (James Aubrey), Doorman (Wilson Benge), Girl (Susan Randall), Man with match (Harry Wilson), Juggler (Duke Johnson), Driver (Al Ferguson), Chimneysweep (Donald Kerr), Bobbies (Michael Hadlow, Tony Marshe, Clive Morgan).

Synopsis: While London experiences a wave of strange murders and suffragettes demonstrate for equal rights, two Americans, Slim and Tubby, are drummed out of the police force for incompetence. They hope to regain their jobs by catching the "monster" doing the killings. That monster is actually Dr. Henry Jekyll, who injects himself with a serum that changes him into a beast. His next mission is to kill newspaper reporter Bruce Adams, who has eyes for Jekyll's ward, Vicky Edwards. Slim and Tubby spot him climbing to the roof of the Jubilee Music Hall where Vicky performs. After a rooftop chase by Bruce, Slim and Tubby, Hyde descends into a wax museum. Tubby finds his way in and manages to trick the monster into a cell. But when he attracts Slim and the police, they find Dr. Jekyll. Jekyll invites Slim and Tubby to stay in his home that evening as bodyguards, but he intends to dispose of them. Tubby drinks one of Jekyll's formulas by mistake and turns into a mouse. When he changes back, he and Slim accompany Vicky and Bruce back to Jekyll's home. Jekyll shows them a wine cellar, not the laboratory that Slim and Tubby had seen. Bruce and Vicky tell Jekyll they'll marry. As they leave, Jekyll entices Vicky back inside and admits that he loves her. He turns into Hyde. Bruce hears a scream and breaks in. Tubby is pushed onto a hypodermic. Hyde breaks through the window. Tubby becomes another Hyde. The police chase both. Jekyll's Hyde returns to his house and grabs Vicky, but Bruce arrives and Jekyll climbs out the window but falls to his death. Slim brings the other Hyde to the police station, where the monster bites the chief before turning back to Tubby. When he looks up, the chief and his police have become monsters.

Review: "Funny, frolicking monster satire." (John Stanley, *The Creature Features Movie Guide*, p. 1)

Analysis: It's thin on plot. Some of the comedy is labored. Helen Westcott is pretty. Craig Stevens would achieve fame as TV's *Peter Gunn*.

Daughter of Dr. Jekyll
(Allied Artists, 1957; 71 min.) * ½

Produced by Jack Pollexfen. Directed by Edgar C. Ulmer. Screenplay, Jack Pollexfen. Edited by Holbrook N. Todd. Director of Photography, John F. Warren. Musical Direction, Melvyn Lenard. Art Direction, Theobold Holsopple.

Cast: George Hastings (John Agar), Janet

Smith (Gloria Talbott), Dr. Lomas (Arthur Shields), Jacob (John Dierkes), Mrs. Merchant (Martha Wentworth), Maggie (Molly McCart).

Synopsis: Janet Smith comes to England to claim her inheritance and learns from her guardian, Dr. Lomas, that her father was the infamous Dr. Jekyll. New murders occur and Janet seems the logical culprit. She even believes it till George Hastings solves the puzzle and reveals Lomas as an actual monster: a werewolf. Riled-up villagers invade his domain and impale him.

Review: "Ghastly." (Steven H. Scheuer, ed., *TV Key Movie Guide*, p. 79)

Analysis: The best thing about this film is John Agar's line: "Not *the* Dr. Jekyll?" Gloria Talbott, like Agar, was a fixture in fifties B-movies. Arthur Shields is the brother of famed character actor Barry Fitzgerald. Note that Pollexfen co-wrote 1951's *Son of Dr. Jekyll.*

The Two Faces of Dr. Jekyll
(Hammer, 1960; 88 min.)**½

Produced by Michael Carreras. Directed by Terence Fisher. Screenplay, Wolf Mankowitz. Based on *The Strange Case of Dr. Jekyll and Mr. Hyde* by Robert Louis Stevenson. Edited by Eric Boyd-Perkins. Director of Photography, Jack Asher. Music, David Heneker and Monty Norman. Art Direction, Don Mingaye.

Cast: Dr. Jekyll/Mr. Hyde (Paul Massie), Kitty Jekyll (Dawn Addams), Paul Allen (Christopher Lee), Litauer (David Kossoff), Inspector (Francis de Wolff), Jane (Janine Faye), Maria (Norma Marla), Sphinx girl (Magda Miller), Nanie (Helen Goss), Corinthia (Joe Robinson), Girl in gin shop (Pauline Shepherd), Coroner (Percy Cartwright), Cabby (Arthur Lovegrove), Barman (Oliver Reed).

Synopsis: London, 1874: Dr. Henry Jekyll is warned by Ernst Litauer that his research into the dual nature of man may prove dangerous. Meanwhile, Jekyll's neglected and pretty wife Kitty has entered into an affair with her husband's other friend, Paul Allen. After taking his drug and becoming young and handsome "Edward Hyde," Jekyll spies Kitty consorting with Paul at a nightclub. Later Hyde becomes friends with Paul, but he's rebuffed

Dr. Lomas (Arthur Shields) contemplates the reclining Janet Smith (Gloria Talbott), who has learned she is the *Daughter of Dr. Jekyll* (Allied Artists, 1957).

by Kitty when he seeks her as a mistress. Eventually Hyde comes to control Jekyll. Paul introduces Hyde to all the debauched sites in the city, yet Hyde becomes bored. He uses the snake dancer Maria's reptile to kill Paul and rapes Kitty. Upon finding Paul's body, Kitty becomes distraught and falls to her death. Hyde strangles Maria. Back at his house, Hyde shoots a workman and sets the laboratory afire. He tells the police Jekyll killed himself. The authorities rule, "Death by suicide." But while talking to Litauer in the hall, Hyde reverts to an aged, defeated Jekyll. "I have destroyed him," he utters as the police arrest him.

Review: "Lurid thriller.... takes many liberties with the original tale.... Paul Massie is excellent." (Philip Hartung, *Commonweal*, June 16, 1961, p. 306) ¶"Mr. Massie is frankly ridiculous. (Eugene Archer, *New York Times*, August 24, 1961, p. 25)

Analysis: Dawn Addams was a starlet, a leading lady, and, later, a cameo performer, e.g., *The Vampire Lovers*. Released

by Columbia in the U.K., by AIP in the U.S. Aka *House of Fright*.

The Nutty Professor
(Paramount, 1963; 107 min.) ***½

Produced by Ernest D. Glucksman. Directed by Jerry Lewis. Assistant Director, Ralph Axness. Screenplay, Jerry Lewis and Bill Richmond. Edited by John Woodcock. Director of Photography, W. Wallace Kelley. Technicolor. Music, Walter Scharf. Art Direction, Hal Pereira, Walter Tyler. Set Decoration, Sam Comer, Robert R. Benton. Costumes, Edith Head.

Cast: Professor Julius F. Kelp/Buddy Love (Jerry Lewis), Stella Purdy (Stella Stevens), Dr. Hamius R. Warfield (Del Moore), Millie Lemmon (Kathleen Freeman), Football players (Med Flory, Norman Alden, Skip Ward), Father Kelp (Howard Morris), Mother Kelp (Elvia Allman), Dr. Leevee (Milton Frome), Bartender (Buddy Lester), English boy (Marvin Kaplan), College students (David Landfield, Julie Parrish, Henry Gibson), Man in gym (Richard Kiel). With Les Brown and His Band of Renown.

Professor Julius Kelp (Jerry Lewis) ogles student Stella Purdy (Stella Stevens) in *The Nutty Professor* (Paramount, 1963).

Synopsis: Chemistry professor Julius Kelp receives a dressing-down by university president Warfield for his personal experiments and more or less promises to behave. In the classroom he forbids a student to skip class for football practice and is lifted bodily and thrust onto a shelf. This convinces him that he needs to build some muscles, and he goes to the Vic Tanny gym. However, he actually loses weight without gaining muscles. Browsing his physician's shelves, he finds a book that explains how the body can grow further through the use of chemicals. Using that and other books, Kelp creates a formula that turns him into the suave but brash, chain-smoking man of the world, Buddy Love. He devises the name when questioned by student Stella Purdy in the Purple Pit. Although she's turned off by this "egomaniac," she lets him drive her to a secluded spot. Strangely, he rushes away before their evening is over. Buddy had been reverting to Julius, who realizes he must increase the dosage to remain Buddy longer. He thinks heredity must account for some of the change and

recalls his wimpish father and overbearing mother. He mails a copy of the formula to his parents for safekeeping. As Buddy, he finds Stella in class and arranges a date. At the Purple Pit he arrives — lit up. The night of the prom arrives, and Buddy Love, who'd flattered Dr. Warfield, is one of the entertainers. But he begins transforming into Kelp. This time he stays and explains that you must remain true to yourself because you have to live with yourself all your life. Stella comforts Julius backstage. Later, Julius's parents show up while he's teaching. Father Kelp now has the upper hand and tries to sell the students his formula. Stella takes Julius into the hall. Unknown to him, she's got two bottles of the formula in her back pockets.

Reviews: "A very funny movie, with some brilliant visual gags and a stunning parody by Lewis of a Hollywood Rat Pack cad." (Jonathan Miller, *New Yorker*, August 10, 1963, p. 61) ¶"The Lewis film is his most painless romp in some time, and probably the most curiously imaginative one of his screen career...." (Howard Thompson,

New York Times, July 18, 1963, p. 15) ¶"Occasionally amusing hodgepodge.... The script asks us to believe that the girl [Stella Stevens] really prefers the former Jerry Lewis. Actually, so does Lewis." (Arthur Knight, *Saturday Review*, June 1, 1963, p. 16) ¶"Is half a funny movie.... But Lewis as the alter-ego maniac Buddy Love is a maudlin letdown." (*Time*, July 26, 1963, p. 80)

Analysis: It's Lewis's best film, with a terrific transformation spoof enhanced by the music. Who is Buddy Love? Evidently a parody of Lewis's old acting-singing partner, Dean Martin. He almost looks like Tony Curtis, too. Great scenes: Lewis on the floor under the collapsed door, sinking into the president's chair, making the president enact Hamlet. The Purple Pit and the prom seem like hangouts from the Stone age. As usual, all the "students" are too old.

The Mind Benders
(Anglo-Amalgamated/AIP, 1963; 99 min.) nv

Produced by Michael Relph. Directed by Basil Dearden. Screenplay, James Kennaway. Edited by John D. Guthridge. Director of Photography, Denys Coop. Music, Georges Auric. Musical Direction, Muir Mathieson. Art Direction, James Morahan. Costumes, Anthony Mendleson. Makeup, Harry Frampton.

Cast: Dr. Henry Longman (Dirk Bogarde), Major Hall (John Clements), Oonagh Longman (Mary Ure), Dr. Tate (Michael Bryant), Annabelle (Wendy Craig), Calder (Geoffrey Keen), Dr. Jean Bonvoulois (Roger Delgado), Aubrey (Norman Bird), Professor Sharpey (Harold Goldblatt), Norman (Terry Palmer), Coach (Terence Alexander), Persephone (Georgina Moon), Paul (Timothy Beaton), Penny (Teresa Van Hoorn), Peers (Christopher Ellis), Oxford student (Robin Hawdon), Porter (Edward Palmer), Father (Philip Ray), Mother (Pauline Winter).

Synopsis: Major Hall believes that the late Professor Sharpey, who worked for the British space agency, was a traitor, and says so to laboratory director Calder. There's no way to indict Sharpey. He committed suicide. When Sharpey's associate, Dr. Longman, hears of the charges, he is irate and says the sense deprivation experiments

Sharpy was involved with led to his death. In fact, Longman contends, Sharpey was brainwashed to divulge secrets. Longman aims to prove so by undergoing the same experiments. Immersed in a tank of water for hours, he emerges a nervous wreck. To help Longman prove his theory, Major Hall and Dr. Tate try to drive a wedge between Longman and his wife, Oonagh, through brainwashing. Eventually they succeed. Longman becomes infatuated with Annabelle. Concerned that they've gone too far, Hall plays for Longman the tape he and Tate made of the brainwashing session. Longman is seemingly unaffected and leaves with Annabelle. The pregnant Oonagh falls and begins labor. Only the birth of his son restores Longman to his senses.

Review: Smoothly machined drama, not entirely convincing but at least original." (Howard Thompson, *New York Times*, May 2, 1963, p. 40)

Analysis: At first glance, this is not a Jekyll and Hyde story, but parallels exist. In any case, it seems to have provided inspiration for *Altered States*.

I, Monster
(Amicus, 1970; 75 min.) nv

Directed by Stephen Weeks. Screenplay, Milton Subotsky. Director of Photography, Moray Grant. Eastmancolour. Music, Carl Davis. Art Direction, Tony Curtis.

Cast: Dr. Charles Marlowe/Blake (Christopher Lee), Utterson (Peter Cushing), Lanyon (Richard Hurndall), Diane (Susan Jameson), Poole (George Merritt), Enfield (Mike Raven), Deane (Kenneth J. Warren), Annie (Marjie Lawrence), Landlady (Aimee Delamain), Boy in alley (Michael Des Barres).

Synopsis: Upon imbibing his special elixir that divests him of inhibitions, Dr. Marlowe "becomes" Blake. Reliance on the serum turns Blake animalistic and he attempts to murder Utterson, his erstwhile friend. Utterson fends him off, a fire starts and Blake dies, turning back into Marlowe.

Reviews: "Production values are good in capturing the Victorian mood of London, but one wishes director Stephen Weeks had plugged up the script shortcomings." (John Stanley, *The Creature Features Movie Guide*, p. 124) ¶"Interesting minor work."

(Leslie Halliwell, *Halliwell's Film Guide*, 2nd ed., p. 356)
Analysis: Some of the characters use the names from the Robert Louis Stevenson novel; others do not!

Dr. Jekyll and Sister Hyde
(Hammer/AIP, 1971; 87 min.) ***

Produced by Albert Fennell, Brian Clemens. Directed by Roy Ward Baker. Screenplay, Brian Clemens. Edited by James Needs. Director of Photography, Norman Warwick. Music, David Whitaker. Musical Direction, Philip Martell. Art Direction, Robert Jones. Makeup, John Wilcox.

Cast: Dr. Jekyll (Ralph Bates), Sister Hyde (Martine Beswicke), Professor Robertson (Gerald Sim), Howard (Lewis Fiander), Mrs. Spencer (Dorothy Alison), Susan Spencer (Susan Brodrick), Sergeant Danvers (Paul Whitson-Jones), Burke (Ivor Dean), Hare (Tony Calvin), Byker (Philip Madoc), Julie (Anna Brett), Betsy (Virginia Wetherall), Yvonne (Irene Bradshaw), Town crier (Dan Meaden), Street singer (Julia Wright), Helen (Pat Brackenbury), Older policeman (Geoffrey Kenion), Petra (Petula Portell), Emma (Liz Romanoff), Margie (Rosemary Lord), Knife grinder (Roy Evans), Sailors (Derek Steen, John Lyons), Mine host (Will Stampe), Jill (Jeannette Wild), Apprentice (Bobby Parr).

Synopsis: After yet another brutal slaying of a prostitute in Whitechapel, Dr. Jekyll begins writing a testament. We flash back to when his predicament began the previous November. Susan Spencer, her brother Howard and her mother are moving into the flat above Jekyll's apartments. Professor Robertson visits Jekyll and, learning of his plans to cure this and that disease, comments upon how long it will take to develop anti-viruses. Taken aback, Jekyll charts a new course. In order to have time to complete his work, he will first create an elixir of life. After visiting a morgue, Jekyll returns to his lab with female hormones he injects into a fly. The insect lives much longer than its normal life span but as Robertson notes, it's become female! Finding the morgue out of suitable corpses for his experiments, Jekyll contracts with body snatchers Burke and Hare. When one of the bodies they provide is of a young lady Jekyll recently saw in a tavern, he

becomes suspicious, but he learns not to ask questions. Meanwhile, Susan Spencer introduces herself but can make no headway into Jekyll's world. Howard investigates a crash in Jekyll's apartment and sees a half-dressed and decidedly beautiful woman. Little does Howard know it's Jekyll, who drank his elixir and became, as he tells the man, "Mrs. Hyde," the widowed sister of Jekyll. When Robertson learns that Jekyll is having problems, he urges Jekyll to give up his work. Instead, Jekyll seeks out Burke and Hare but finds one hanging, the other tossed into a lime pit. Their neighbors had discovered their depredations. Jekyll must procure his own bodies — by murdering them himself. After all, when he obliquely speaks of the greater benefit for the greater number, Susan agrees that the means justifies the end. Jekyll knifes a prostitute in the fog. When found, the body is examined by Robertson, who terms it an expert mutilation. After a further murder, as Whitechapel is plastered with wanted posters, Robertson and a policeman stake out Jekyll's residence. But Jekyll realizes he's being watched and changes to Hyde. "Mrs. Hyde" knifes yet another prostitute. Robertson visits Jekyll and sees a dress. Later he meets Hyde, who gets herself invited to the professor's rooms and stabs him. Regretting his course of action, Jekyll rages through his lab but becomes Hyde and invites Howard in for a tête-à-tête. Later, as Jekyll, he warns Susan to stay away from "Mrs. Hyde." He and Susan plan an evening at the concert hall, but when he opens his closet and finds a dress, he reverts to Hyde. Hyde tracks Susan through the fog, but when her arm is raised to strike, Jekyll's will prevails. Instead, another prostitute is killed. Meanwhile, the blind man who realized he'd been in the vicinity of the murderer from time to time holds forth on the murders. A policeman overhears and has the beggar lead him to what turns out to be Jekyll's house. Inside, Jekyll is composing his testament. As the authorities break in, Jekyll flees. Unknown to him, his explanatory note has been smeared into illegibility by spilled ink. He climbs to the roof and jumps across an alley but finds himself holding a rain gutter for dear life. Finally, inching to a window, he feels Hyde's will exert itself. As the transformation begins, he falls to his death.

Reviews: "[Baker's] directorial reticence generally makes things bearable even when they aren't much fun." (Roger Greenspun, *New York Times*, May 18, 1972, p. 55) ¶"Baker has set a good pace, built tension nicely and played it straight.... He tops chills and gruesome murders with quite a lot of subtle fun." (Jock., *Variety*, October 27, 1971, p. 18)

Analysis: This is quite a good entry, mixing Stevenson's character with real-life body snatchers Burke and Hare, with a nod to Jack the Ripper. The sets are some of the foggiest ever. The audience knows about the gender reversal; not so the characters Jekyll/Hyde affects. This is where the humor comes in, and the viewer guffaws a lot. We can hardly imagine better casting than Bates and Beswicke. (*Variety* even noted a physical resemblance that helped make the transitions believable.) At a question-and-answer session during FANEX 8 in Baltimore (July 24, 1994), Beswicke said the studio wanted full frontal nudity. She balked and succeeded in toning it down. Paired with *Blood from the Mummy's Tomb*.

Dr. Black, Mr. Hyde
(Charles Walker-Manfred Bernhard Productions, 1975; 87 min.) nv

Produced by Charles Walker. Directed by William Crain. Screenplay, Larry LeBron. Edited by Jack Horger. Director of Photography, Tak Fujimoto. Color. Music, Johnny Pate. Special Makeup, Stan Winston.

Cast: Dr. Henry Pride (Bernie Casey), Dr. Billie Worth (Rosalind Cash), Linda Monte (Marie O'Henry), Lieutenant Jackson (Jitu Cumbuka), Lieutenant O'Connor (Milt Kogan), Silky (Stu Gilliam).

Synopsis: Los Angeles physician Dr. Henry Pride finds that the side effects of his cirrhosis of the liver experiments include skin pigmentation changes. While working at the free clinic with his lover, Billie, he injects a patient. Later he tests his drug on prostitute Linda, then upon himself. Not only does the serum turn him white, it also adversely affects his mind. He

kills Linda and her pimp, Silky. The police chase him to the Watts Tower. Shot, he falls to the street.

Review: "Unusual black exploitation picture.... All well intended but ultimately sleazy. A nice jazz score was obviously inspired by *Shaft*." (John Stanley, *The Creature Features Movie Guide*, p. 66)

Analysis: Bernie Casey should have had more leading roles. Ditto for Rosalind Cash, Charlton Heston's leading lady in *The Omega Man*. William Crain had directed *Blacula*. Check out the special makeup man: future famous creature maker (*Alien*) Stan Winston.

Dr. Heckyl and Mr. Hype
(Cannon, 1980; 99 min.) nv

Produced by Menahem Golan and Yoram Globus. Directed by Charles B. Griffith. Screenplay, Charles B. Griffith. Edited by Skip Schoolnik. Director of Photography, Robert Carras. Metrocolor. Music, Richard Band. Art Direction, Bob Ziembiki. Set Decoration, Maria Delia Javier.

Cast: Dr. Heckyl/Mr. Hype (Oliver Reed), Coral Careen (Sunny Johnson), Miss Finebum (Maia Danziger), Dr. Hinkle (Mel Welles), Lt. MacDruck "Il Topo" (Virgil Frye), Dr. Lew Hoo (Kedrick Wolfe), Sergeant Fleacollar (Jackie Coogan), Pizelle Puree (Corinne Calvet), Mrs. Quivel (Sharon Compton), Liza (Denise Hayes). With Charles Howerton, Dick Miller, Jack Warford, Lucretia Love, Ben Frommer.

Reviews: "Quite funny, right up there with Jerry Lewis's *The Nutty Professor*." (Mick Martin and Marsha Porter, *Video Movie Guide 1994*, p. 256) ¶"Out-and-out parody ... but the jokes aren't as funny as they might have been." (John Stanley, *The Creature Features Movie Guide*, p. 66)

Analysis: The director wrote the 1960 film *The Little Shop of Horrors*. Mel Welles was in that, too.

Altered States
(Warner Bros., 1980; 102 min.) ***

Produced by Howard Gottfried. Directed by Ken Russell. Assistant Directors, Gary Daigler, Peter Schindler. Screenplay, Sidney Aaron. Based on the novel by Paddy Chayefsky. Edited by Eric Jenkins. Director of Photography, Jordan Cronenweth. Technicolor.

Music, John Corigliano. Dolby Stereo. Costumes, Ruth Myers. Special Makeup, Dick Smith.

Cast: Edward Jessup (William Hurt), Emily Jessup (Blair Brown), Arthur Rosenberg (Bob Balaban), Mason Parrish (Charles Haid), Eccheverria (Thaao Penghlis), Primal man (Miguel Godreau), Hobart (Peter Brandon), Sylvia Rosenberg (Dori Brenner), the Brujo (Charles White Eagle), Margaret Jessup (Drew Barrymore), Grace Jessup (Megan Jefers), Hector Ortega (Jack Murdock), Obispo (Frank McCarthy), Schizophrenic patient (Deborah Baltzell), Young Rosenberg (Evan Richards), Endocrinology fellow (Hap Lawrence), Medical technician (John Walter Davis), Parrish's girl (Cynthia Burr), Eccheverria's girl (Susan Bredhoff), X-ray technician (John Larroquette), Dr. Wissenschaft (George Gaynes).

Synopsis: Professor Edward Jessup has had a lifelong interest in science, mysticism, the religious experience, and altered states of consciousness. Having access to a sensory-deprivation chamber at his university makes it possible for him to explore these situations in his students. Eventually, he enters the isolation chamber himself, finding the resultant near-transcendental states fascinating. A visit to an old Mexican hill tribe which uses a hallucinatory mushroom derivative in its religious ceremonies introduces Jessup to an arcane chemical substance that induces wildly accelerated and bizarre visions. Returning to his university, he continues his experiments inside the isolation chamber in conjunction with the drug. Despite his associate's objections that he might be doing himself untold damage with this unknown concoction, he persists until, during one experiment, he emerges from the chamber unable to talk, his mouth and throat covered with blood. X-rays show that he has undergone a temporary skeletal change, one that has altered the tracheal area. As this phase seems to be transient and he soon regains use of his vocal cords, Jessup ignores arguments from both his colleagues and his estranged wife, Emily, and continues his research. Later, he begins to manifest other, more bizarre transformations that indicate that the drug has altered his DNA structure and caused a process of *devolution*. When a worker is attacked by a diminutive, hairy creature one night, it is presumed that a lab animal is loose. Security people give chase, but it escapes into the streets, ultimately ending up at a nearby zoo, where it runs down and brains a goat. The unconscious Dr. Jessup is found beside the body of the partially eaten animal. Emily and Dr. Parrish recover the scientist from jail. He is shaken by his experience but is convinced that the Pandora's Box he has opened will not so easily be closed, that the physiological changes he has experienced will come again. Finally, when he is alone with Emily, the transformation begins again, this time the devolutionary process catapulting him to the state of a virtual primordial force, inexorable and uncontrollable. Emily rushes to him, screaming for him to fight it, that he can defeat it. When they make contact, the force infuses Emily, too, reducing her to a writhing, pulsating mass. Through force of will, Jessup drags himself to his wife, pounding the walls, the floor, each blow bringing on another phantasmagoric transformation. Reaching Emily, he cradles her luminous figure in his arms and there is one final, blinding burst. This time the contact between the fiery entities brings obvious release, and the two resume their normal forms, the devolutionary process spent.

Review: "Brilliant and terrifying vision of a human soul lost in infinity, a Faustian parable in which the Devil is man's scientific quest for knowledge of himself.... Where the film is weakest ... is in the screenplay.... in the end, a traditional love story." (Steve Vertlieb, *Cinemacabre* Number 4, pp. 35-36)

Analysis: Altered States was released with such advance hoopla that it nearly obscured the fact that this Ken Russell film was basically (yet) another manifestation of the hoary Jekyll and Hyde story, updated and embellished with much New Age drug culture jargon and high-tech visual effects. Still, it's an absorbing story, for the most part, and the production is generally first-rate. The performances by Hurt and Brown, along with those of Bob Balaban and Charles Haid, lend much to the narrative, although everyone speaks so much psycho-babble that frequently the dialogue is amusingly esoteric and surprisingly effective: Russell's vision of narco-plastic post-'60s academia is right on the mark. On the downside of things, once it's apparent that this *is* Jekyll and Hyde, there's no denying the disappointment of the discovery. What with all the talk of altered states of consciousness, New Age mysticism, religion, *d*evolution and all that, one has a right to expect more than just another man in an ape suit (however cleverly executed) running amok and making a public nuisance of himself.

Dr. Jekyll's Dungeon of Death
(New American/Rochelle, 1982; 88 min.) *

Produced and directed by James Wood. Arthur Weisberg Presents. Screenplay, James Mathers. Edited by James Wood. Director of Photography, James Wood. Color, Cinefex Color Lab. Music, Marty Allen. Makeup, Jan Feldman. Special Effects, Ripley Quinby III.

Cast: Dr. Henry Jekyll (James Mathers), Professor Atkinson (John Kearney), Julia Atkinson (Dawn Carver Kelly), Hilda Jekyll (Nadine Kalmes), Boris (Jake Pearson), Malo (Tom Nicholson), Officer Maloney (Peter R. Maloney).

Synopsis: In a confined room two black men engage in martial arts while the voice of Dr. Henry Jekyll muses on the serum he administered to them and on his great-grandfather Jekyll. He wants to discover the secret that will control the mind of man without using himself as a guinea pig. A newspaper headline reads, "KIDNAP CRIME WAVE CONTINUES." Professor Atkinson arrives. His daughter Julia had been a house guest but according to Jekyll suffered a fatal fall from her horse. He advises Atkinson to get a good night's sleep before viewing the body. Actually, the living Julia has been incarcerated in another room. While dining, Jekyll tells Atkinson that the strange woman in attendance is his sister Hilda, who has been "hopelessly insane since birth." Jekyll expounds on a pituitary stimulus serum he hopes to perfect. Later his shambling servant Boris brings two women to the house and Jekyll injects them. When they awake

they engage in martial arts, oblivious to the doctor's presence. Jekyll tells Hilda he hates her and that she resembles their mother; then he kisses her passionately. After learning that his daughter is alive and Jekyll's captive and after viewing one of Jekyll's martial arts demonstrations, Atkinson realizes that Jekyll is truly insane. When Jekyll finds a note that Atkinson gave Hilda to pass to whoever delivers the food, he sticks an ice pick in her arm. He also torments Boris. Boris hangs Hilda when he finds her trying to inject Julia with Jekyll's serum. Julia tries to stab Jekyll in his lab after he's shot her father. Jekyll disarms her, but Boris goes on the rampage and sticks a needle in Jekyll before falling mortally wounded. Under the influence of his own drug, Jekyll goes berserk and strangles Julia. Police sirens are heard outside.

Review: "Bizarre mixture of genres.… The one-man show is threadbare, stretched as thin as Mr. Wood himself." (John Stanley, *The Creature Features Movie Guide*, p. 67)

Analysis: This ill-lit film takes place in one house and the yard outside. It's a mess: incoherent, ridiculous, insufferable. There's no skin, and it's not funny enough to be camp. The video box cover shows skeletons and a man who are not in this movie! This has a claim to being the worst film featured in this book.

Jekyll and Hyde … Together Again
(Paramount, 1982; 87 min.) **½

Produced by Lawrence Gordon. Executive Producer, Joel Silver. Directed by Jerry Belson. Screenplay, Monica Johnson, Harvey Miller, Jerry Belson, Michael Lesson. Inspired by *The Strange Case of Dr. Jekyll and Mr. Hyde* by Robert Louis Stevenson. Edited by Billy Weber. Director of Photography, Philip Lathrop. Metrocolor. Music, Barry DeVorzon. Song: "Hyde's Got Nothing to Hide." Design, Peter Wooley. Costumes, Marilyn Kay Vance.

Cast: Dr. Jekyll (Mark Blankfield), Mary (Bess Armstrong), Ivy (Krista Errickson), Dr. Lanyon (Tim Thomerson), Dr. Carew (Michael McGuire), Queen (Neil Hunt), Busty Nurse (Cassandra Peterson), George

Chakiris (himself), Barbara (Jessica Nelson), Hubert (Peter Brocco), Students (Michael Kligher, Noelle North, David Murphy), Patient (Mary McCusker), Mrs. Larson (Liz Sheridan), Asian girl (Alison Hong), Elderly man (Walter Janowitz), Nurse Gonzales (Belita Moreno), Wong (Leland Sun), Injured man (George Wendy), Sushi chef (Glen Chin), Customer (Dan Barrows), Mme. WooWoo (Virginia Wing), Dutch (Jesse Goins), Baron (Jack Collins), Announcer (Michael Ensign), Macho kid (John Dennis Johnston), Brigham (David Ruprecht), Box boy (Clarke Coleman), Produce man (Sam Whipple), Mother (Nancy Lenehan), Child (Barret Oliver), Lawn jockeys (Tony Cox, Selwyn Emerson Miller), Clockman (Art LaFleur), Mrs. Simpson (Bernadette Birkett), Nurse (Lin Shaye), Helen (Madelyn Cates).

Synopsis: Dr. Jekyll is a surgeon at Our Lady of Pain and Suffering hospital. Believing that if he has time for pure research he can determine the ingredients of human survival instincts and therefore increase health and save lives, he plans to give up surgery. The hospital director, whose daughter Mary is Jekyll's enamorata, is aghast because he wants him to perform a total organ transplant on a wealthy patient. While working on his formula, Jekyll makes something that, once sniffed, turns him into a disco-, sex-crazed creature. He remembers Ivy, who had surgery to remove a foreign object (an Oriental man). He finds her singing at a local club. She takes him home. Hearing that he's won a $500,000 prize for medicine, he hitches a ride on the top of a plane to England and swings onto the stage. George Chakiris had been accepting in his place but steps aside. Pursued to the rooftops of London, Hyde is shot and falls, but revives as Jekyll and is helped off by Ivy and Mary, who want to share him.

Review: "Coarse, dopey update of the old story.... It does get slightly more bearable as it goes along." (Janet Maslin, *New York Times*, December 3, 1982, p. C30)

Analysis: If the *Airplane* and *Naked Gun* producers put together a Jekyll and Hyde spoof, it might look like this. This is a funny film that moves rapidly along. "Busty Nurse" is Cassandra Peterson, in short, future horror hostess and ultimate hot babe Elvira.

Dr. Jekyll and Ms. Hyde
(Savoy Pictures, 1995; 89 min.) *½

Produced by Robert Shapiro and Jerry Leider. Directed by David Price. Screenplay, Tim John, Oliver Butcher, William Davies, William Osborne. Story, David Price. Suggested by the novel *The Strange Case of Dr. Jekyll and Mr. Hyde* by Robert Louis Stevenson. Edited by Tony Lombardo. Director of Photography, Tom Priestley. Technicolor. Music, Mark McKenzie. Art Direction, Guy Lalande. Set Decoration, Francine Danis, Paul Hotte, Michele Nolet, Ginette Robitaille. Makeup Effects, Kevin Yagher. Visual Effects, Dream Quest Images.

Cast: Helen Hyde (Sean Young), Richard Jacks (Tim Daly), Sarah Carver (Lysette Anthony), Oliver Mintz (Stephen Tobolowsky), Yves DuBois (Harvey Fierstein), Pete (Jeremy Piven), Mrs. Unterveldt (Polly Bergen), Larry (Stephen Shellen), Valerie (Thea Vidale), Mrs. Mintz (Sheena Larkin).

Synopsis: Perfume chemist Richard Jacks inherits his great-grandfather's notebooks and discovers that his relative knew Dr. Jekyll in Edinburgh, Scotland. What's more, the notes provide a guide to human transformation as well as identification of the evil gene. Using his computer in the lab of Omage, Richard increases the estrogen in the formula, drinks it, and becomes—a woman, Helen Hyde. Helen uses her feminine wiles to ingratiate herself with Richard's superiors and in time decides to subvert Richard for good. When transformed back, Richard tries various ways to thwart his feminine alter ego, all to no avail. Finally he convinces his fiancée, Sarah, of his predicament, and she helps him make a concoction to break the genetic code. After securing him to a bed, Sarah is to inject the blue liquid after he turns into Helen. Sarah gets some of the serum into Helen, but Helen breaks free, accidentally starting a fire in the apartment. Sarah follows her to the launching party for Indulge, her new perfume, and manages to inject the rest of the serum into her leg. Helen becomes Richard on-stage. He collects himself and tells the audience he had to connect with his feminine side in order to create Indulge. At Mrs. Underveldt's urging, Richard's superior, Oliver Mintz, gives him a raise and his own lab. Richard plans a three-week honeymoon with Sarah first.

Review: "An ending worthy only of a 1960's sitcom.... There are actually a few bright spots. In particular, Tim Daly acquits himself nicely in his role.... The film's goofy humor would also be more welcome if presented in less clichéd a manner." (Kirby Tepper, *Magill's Cinema Annual 1996*, pp. 151-152)

Analysis: This seems to have been made a long time before its apparent one-week-in-a-theater-somewhere-then-on-to-video release. At no time does one laugh out loud, and the sulfuric acid and electrocution inflicted on Jeremy Piven are hardly riotous. This is at least the second Dr. Jekyll film set in the twentieth century in which a character believes Dr. Jekyll was a real human being and not the fictional creation of novelist Robert Louis Stevenson! (See *Daughter of Dr. Jekyll*.)

Donovan's Brain *see under* **The Lady and the Monster**

Dr. Black, Mr. Hyde *see under* **Dr. Jekyll and Mr. Hyde**

Dr. Heckyl and Mr. Hype *see under* **Dr. Jekyll and Mr. Hyde**

Dr. Jekyll and Ms. Hyde *see under* **Dr. Jekyll and Mr. Hyde**

Dr. Jekyll and Sister Hyde *see under* **Dr. Jekyll and Mr. Hyde**

Dr. Jekyll's Dungeon of Death *see under* **Dr. Jekyll and Mr. Hyde**

Dr. Phibes Rises Again *see under* **The Abominable Dr. Phibes**

Dr. Who and the Daleks
(Regal Films International/AARU Production, 1965; 85 min.) **½

Produced by Milton Subotsky and Max J. Rosenberg. Directed by Gordon Flemyng. Screenplay, Milton Subotsky. Based on the BBC TV serial by Terry Nation. Edited by Oswald Hafenrichter. Director of Photography, John Wilcox. Techniscope. Technicolor. Music, Malcolm Lockyer. Art Direction, Bill Constable. Set Decoration, Scott Slimon. Special Effects, Ted Samuels.

Cast: Dr. Who (Peter Cushing), Susan (Roberta Tovey), Barbara (Jennie Linden), Ian (Roy Castle), Alydon (Barrie Ingham), Temosus (Geoffrey Toone), Gamatus (Michael Coles), Elyon (Mark Peterson), Antodus (John Brown), Dyoni (Yvonne Antrobus).

Synopsis: Dr. Who shows his Tardis machine to Ian, who inadvertently throws a switch that sends himself, the doctor, Barbara and young Susan into the future. The planet they find shows signs of a holocaust and latent radiation. Discovering a city, they find it inhabited by the daleks, beings who shield themselves from the fallout in robotic machines. The daleks hope to use the humans to wipe out the human-like creatures — who are called something that sounds to us like "fauls" — and master the entire planet. Ian suggests that the daleks must have one weakness, which they determine is the fact that they must move on metal that has electricity necessary for their machines' movement. The humans escape by insulating a dalek from the floor. The Tardis won't go without the mercury element now in the possession of the daleks. The daleks plan to detonate a neutron bomb to destroy their enemies while at the same time they are attacked by the fauls and Who's crew. Barbara, Ian and two fauls enter the city from the rear after traversing a swamp, climbing a mountain, entering a tunnel and jumping a chasm. A battle in the control room leaves it wrecked, the bomb disabled, and daleks shooting each other. Dr. Who retrieves the mercury and the Tardis continues, but Ian opens the door and they discover they're in Roman times.

Reviews: "This juvenile science-fiction adventure should please youngsters." (Mick Martin and Marsha Porter, *Video Movie Guide 1991*, p. 928)

Analysis: Dr. Who was a British (and later U.S.) TV phenomenon. This film spin-off is set bound, fairly juvenile, but moderately entertaining.

Daleks' Invasion Earth 2150 A.D.
(British Lion/AARU Production, 1966; 84 min.) **½

Produced by Milton Subotsky and Max J. Rosenberg. Directed by Gordon Flemyng.

Screenplay, Milton Subotsky. Based on the BBC TV serial by Terry Nation. Edited by Ann Chegwidden. Director of Photography, John Wilcox. Techniscope. Technicolor. Music, Bill McGuffie. Art Direction, George Provis. Set Decoration, Maurice Pelling. Special Effects, Ted Samuels.

Cast: Dr. Who (Peter Cushing), Tom Campbell (Bernard Cribbins), Susan (Roberta Tovey), Louise (Jill Curzon), Wyler (Andrew Keir), David (Ray Brooks), Thompson (Eddie Powell), Wells (Roger Avon), Conway (Keith Marsh), Brockley (Philip Madoc), RoboMan (Geoffrey Cheshire), RoboMan leader (Steve Peters), Dorfmun (Godfrey Quigley), Man on bicycle (Tony Reynolds), Man with carrier bag (Bernard Spear), Dalek leader (Robert Jewell).

Synopsis: Dr. Who and his Tardis machine are on hand to pick up a policeman, Tom Campbell, who was trying to stop a robbery. They end up in London, 2150 A.D., where daleks are in control, having used cosmic rays and meteors to crush human resistance. Using "robomen," the daleks capture humans and turn them into slaves to work in a Bedfordshire mine. Why? To extract the earth's magnetic core, which will cause an explosion that will effectively turn the planet into a spaceship. Dr. Who and David, Tom and Louise, Wyler and Susan converge on the Watford mine from different directions. While the doctor diverts the daleks, Tom enters the mine shaft and redirects the bomb that the daleks drop to break into the earth's core. Instead, it detonates at the confluence of the earth's north and south magnetic poles. Magnetism being anathema to the daleks, they lose control of their suits and their spaceship and are destroyed. The Tardis returns to twentieth-century London a few minutes before it left so Tom can foil the robbery.

Review: "Fairly naive stuff decked out with impressive scientific jargon." (Rich., *Variety*, August 10, 1966)

Analysis: It's more adult than its predecessor, i.e., more bodies. *Variety* called the special effects "lively" and the Daleks "formidable heavies." Unlike the first of the series, this takes place outdoors for the most part. Intriguing plot device: three groups converging for the denouement. Aka *Invasion Earth 2150 A.D.*

Doctor X

(First National, 1932; 80 min.) ***½

Produced by Hal Wallis. Directed by Michael Curtiz. Screenplay, Earl Baldwin and Robert Tasker. Based on a play by Howard Warren Comstock and Allen C. Miller. Directors of Photography, Richard Tower, Ray Rennahan. Technicolor. Musical Direction, Leo Forbstein.

Cast: Dr. Xavier (Lionel Atwill), Lee Taylor (Lee Tracy), Dr. Wells (Preston Foster), Joanne Xavier (Fay Wray), Otto (George Rosener), Mamie (Leila Bennett), Dr. Rowitz (Arthur Edmund Carewe), Dr. Haines (John Wray), Dr. Duke (Harry Beresford), Stevens (Robert Warwick), O'Halloran (Willard Robertson), Editor (Thomas Jackson), Policeman (Harry Holman), Sheriff (Tom Dugan).

Synopsis: Reporter Lee Taylor discovers that Dr. Xavier, founder of the Academy of Surgical Research, is helping the police track down the "Moon Killer Murderer." While performing an autopsy on the latest victim, a scrubwoman, Xavier finds that she's been partially cannibalized. The police give Xavier 48 hours to conduct his own investigation of the scientists working at his institute, all of whom seem to have murderous motives. Xavier relocates to his residence at Blackstone Shoals, Long Island, to continue his investigation of his faculty via a psycho-neurological test involving thermal tubes and pulse pressure. Wells, absolved of any possible guilt due to his artificial left forearm, spins dials in an adjacent room. When the room becomes dark there is a scream and Dr. Rowitz is found dead. Reporter Taylor is found unconscious in a skeleton closet. Joanne, who'd found him sneaking around the Academy, takes him in tow. The police call and urge Xavier on. During a second test Otto the butler plays the part of the murderer, Joanne the victim. Xavier himself is strapped in with the other two scientists. In the adjacent lab, Wells removes his arm and replaces it with synthetic flesh. Smearing his face and head with goo, he is transformed into a monster who menaces Joanne. Speaking to the shackled scientists (he has killed Otto), he rages that his discovery will benefit other cripples. Taylor arrives and rushes upon Wells.

The superstrong Wells is not vanquished until Taylor breaks a lamp on him. Aflame, he is knocked through a window and falls screaming to the rocky coast below. Taylor wins Joanne.

Review: "Quite enough excitement to satisfy the most ardent admirer of murder mysteries." (Mordaunt Hall, *New York Times*, August 4, 1932, p. 17)

Analysis: Why? How? What property of synthetic flesh causes a man to become a monster? Why does the moon assist? It pays not to ask. Any explanation will have holes. There is much humor, not only the reporter's shenanigans (e.g., a hand buzzer), but lines like Xavier's: "Oh, will no one obey me anymore?" and the quirks of all his professors. "Necessity has no ethics, sir," says Rowitz. The *New York Times* called Atwill "master of his role" and Fay Wray "charming and capable." This is one of those films, like *The Mystery of the Wax Museum*, that for years remained unseen and acquired a considerable reputation. Some think it warranted, others do not. It does have atmosphere, something more contemporary horrors often lack.

The Return of Dr. X
(Warner Bros., 1939; 62 min.) **½

Associate Producer, Bryan Foy. Directed by Vincent Sherman. Assistant Director, Dick Mayberry. Screenplay, Lee Katz. Dialogue Director, John Langan. Based on the story "The Doctor's Secret" by William J. Makin. Edited by Thomas Pratt. Director of Photography, Sid Hickox. Music, Bernhard Kaun. Sound, Charles Lang. Technical Adviser, Leo Schulman. Art Direction, Esdras Hartley. Gowns, Milo Anderson. Makeup, Perc Westmore.

Cast: Walter "Wichita" Barnett/Garrett (Wayne Morris), Joan Vance (Rosemary Lane), Marshall Quesne (Humphrey Bogart), Dr. Michael Rhodes (Dennis Morgan), Dr. Francis Flegg (John Litel), Angela Merrova (Lya Lys), Pinky (Huntz Hall), Detective Ray Kincaid (Charles Wilson), Miss Sweetman (Vera Lewis), Chairman (Howard Hickman), Undertaker (Olin Howland), Guide (Arthur Aylesworth), Detective Sergeant Moran (Jack Mower), Hotel manager (Creighton Hale), Stanley Rodgers (John Ridgely), Editor (Joseph Crehan), Interns (Glenn Langan, William Hopper).

Synopsis: Morning Dispatch reporter "Wichita" Barnett goes to the Park Vista Hotel to interview actress Angela Merrova but finds her slain. When the police arrive there is no body. Then Merrova appears — alive, and Barnett is fired. Barnet consults with friend Dr. Michael Rhodes and mentions the knife wound he found near Merrova's heart and the pallor of the body. Dr. Francis Flegg performs a blood transfusion and talks about a coming age when man will control blood. Oddly, the original blood donor with Group #1 blood, Stanley Rodgers, is found dead. While Barnett observes through the window, Rhodes surprises Flegg with a blood sample from Rodgers' apartment that doesn't look human. Rhodes meets Flegg's assistant, Quesne [pronounced Cain], who has a pallor and a stripe of white through his hair. Merrova arrives at Flegg's after Rhodes leaves but not before Barnett spots her. Flegg gives Merrova a transfusion. The next day Barnett and Rhodes confront Merrova, who admits she was in fact attacked just before Barnett arrived the first time. She says she'll tell all the next morning. Quesne arrives. Merrova is found dead. Rhodes and Barnett look at her body in the funeral parlor. Going through the morgue files at the newspaper office, Barnett finds clippings on the execution for child murder of Dr. Maurice Xavier — with photos of Quesne! Rhodes and Barnett dig up Xavier's grave and find, as expected, an empty coffin. Confronted with this, Flegg admits that he resurrected Quesne, a man he considered a martyr to science. A combination of electrification and Flegg's special formula gave him new life, but he needs Group #1 blood to stay alive. Thus the deaths of Rodgers and Merrova. Flegg admits he hasn't succeeded with his synthetic blood. The magic element that gives life is missing. After Rhodes and Barnett leave, Quesne shoots Flegg and obtains his list of blood donors. He kidnaps Joan Vance and drives to an abandoned duck club outside Newark where the police corner him and shoot him off the roof. Dying, he says he'll have to postpone his talk with Rhodes about blood types. Barnett is rehired and given his own column.

Review: "A cheerful little picture."

(B.R.C., *New York Times*, November 23, 1939, p. 38)

Analysis: According to the *New York Times* review, restoring dead bodies to life had by 1939 become a "cinematic commonplace," but finding something interesting for the quickened corpses to do was always a problem. This somewhat large-scale B movie was one that Bogart would probably like to forget. Its only relation to the 1932 film comes in the use of the title character name and the word "synthetic" that is bandied about. It does move along quickly enough to maintain interest. The Wayne Morris character is often called Garrett, and that's what a newspaper headline calls him, too. However, the cast lists him as Walter Barnett. Note that Olin Howlin, who plays the undertaker, will be the first victim of *The Blob* in 1958.

Down to Earth *see under* **Here Comes Mr. Jordan**

Dracula
(Universal, 1931; 84 min.) ***

Produced by Carl Laemmle, Jr. Directed by Tod Browning. Screenplay, Garrett Fort. Based on the novel by Bram Stoker and the stage play by Hamilton Deane and John Balderston. Edited by Milton Carruth. Director of Photography, Karl Freund. Sound, C. Roy Hunter. Art Direction, Charles D. Hall.

Cast: Count Dracula (Bela Lugosi), John Harker (David Manners), Mina Seward (Helen Chandler), Professor Van Helsing (Edward Van Sloan), Renfield (Dwight Frye), Dr. Seward (Herbert Bunston), Lucy Weston (Frances Dade), Martin (Charles Gerrard), Maid (Joan Standing), Brigs (Moon Carroll), Innkeeper (Michael Visaroff), English nurse (Josephine Velez), Man in coach (Donald Murphy), Woman in coach (Daisy Belmore).

Synopsis: Arriving by coach at a Transylvanian inn on Walpurgisnacht, the Englishman Renfield is warned not to proceed to the Borgo Pass. He goes nonetheless and enters a carriage driven by a silent man dressed in black. When the coach runs hard, Renfield peers out the window and sees a large bat ahead of the horses. At Castle Dracula, Renfield meets Count Dracula. The nobleman is happy all is in order

for his imminent journey to Carfax Abbey in England. Renfield faints upon opening a window and observing a large bat. Three pale women approach his body, but Dracula enters and sinks down on the man. On the schooner *Vesta*, the obviously unbalanced Renfield implores his unseen master to let him have "little lives." The ship runs aground at Whitby, England. The crew is dead. Only Renfield lives, and he's incarcerated in Seward Sanitarium. Count Dracula, meanwhile, has arrived in London. He attends a concert and meets Dr. Seward, daughter Mina, John Harker, and Lucy Weston. That evening Dracula visits Lucy as she sleeps. She is next seen in an operating room suffering from an unnatural loss of blood. Doctors fail to save her. Professor Van Helsing tells Dr. Seward that a vampire is on the loose and interrogates Renfield. Mina dreams of little red eyes and of meeting Lucy. When new neighbor Dracula visits, Van Helsing notices that he casts no reflection in a small mirror. Shortly thereafter, he shows the mirror to Dracula, who knocks it to the floor. The count leaves after saying, "For one who has not lived even a single lifetime, you are a wise man, Van Helsing." Van Helsing endeavors to convince Harker and Seward of Dracula's heritage, occasionally interrupted by Renfield, who frequently escapes his cell. He speaks of hordes of rats promised him by his master. Although Van Helsing attempts to save Mina by strategically placing the wolf bane plant in her room, Dracula gains entrance and confronts the professor. Van Helsing, his will too strong to be overcome by Dracula's mental powers, shows his nemesis a crucifix, causing the vampire to fly. But Dracula has made Mina drink his blood and thus fall under his dominion. He takes her to Carfax Abbey. Renfield also makes his way there. Van Helsing and Harker follow, witnessing Renfield's death when the count believes he's led the men to his lair. Dracula carries Mina into the recesses of the abbey, but the sun's earliest rays force him to take refuge in his coffin. Van Helsing puts a stake in his heart, killing him and saving Mina.

Reviews: "What with Mr. Browning's imaginative direction and Mr. Lugosi's

Count Dracula (Bela Lugosi) points the way for Mina Seward (Helen Chandler) in *Dracula* (Universal, 1931).

make-up and weird gestures, this picture succeeds to some extent in its grand Guignol intentions." (Mordaunt Hall, *New York Times*, February 13, 1931, p. 21) ¶"Remarkably effective background of creepy atmosphere.... It is difficult to think of anybody who could quite match the performance in the vampire part of Bela Lugosi...." (*Variety*)

Analysis: Except for *Freaks*, director Tod Browning recently has taken plenty of knocks. He is lambasted for the staginess of *Dracula*, and there is much of that. The best scenes are those at the beginning: the Borgo Pass, the castle. Even in this version we find that Mina is Dr. Seward's daughter. She is *not* his daughter in the book. Renfield is Harker in the novel. Blame these changes on the filmmakers' decision to use the stage version as inspiration. Lon Chaney was to have played the Count, but he died, and Lugosi repeated his 1927 stage role. There is a Spanish version filmed coincidentally with the Lugosi film that gets high marks. It's available on video. At the

FANEX 6 convention in 1992, a panel discussed the greatest horror personality of all time, choosing between Lugosi, Karloff, Cushing and Lee. Consensus of panelists and audience was that Lugosi, familiar even to those who've not seen his films, is the hands-down winner. How many oft-recalled lines did he say in *Dracula*? "I am ... Dracula." "I bid you welcome." "Listen to them. Children of the night. What music they make." "I never drink ... wine." "To die. To be really dead. That must be glorious." "The blood is the life, Mr. Renfield."

Dracula's Daughter
(Universal, 1936; 70 min.) ***

Produced by E. M. Asher. Directed by Lambert Hillyer. Screenplay, Garrett Fort and John Balderston. Suggested by Oliver Jeffries. Based on a story by Bram Stoker. Edited by Milton Carruth. Director of Photography, George Robinson. Music, Heinz Roemheld. Art Direction, Albert D'Agostino. Gowns, Brymer. Special Cinematographer, John P. Fulton.

Cast: Countess Marya Zaleska (Gloria Holden), Dr. Jeffrey Garth (Otto Kruger), Professor Van Helsing (Edward Van Sloan), Sandor (Irving Pichel), Janet Blake (Marguerite Churchill), Sir Basil Humphrey (Gilbert Emery), Lady Esme Hammond (Hedda Hopper), Sir Aubrey Vail (Claud Assister), Lili (Nan Grey), Sergeant Clive (E. E. Clive), Albert (Billy Bevan), Constable Hawkins (Halliwell Hobbs), Miss Peabody (Eily Malyon), Hobbs, butler (Edgar Norton), Coachman (Christian Rub), Radio announcer (Guy Kingsford), Host (Gordon Hart), Motor bobby (David Dunbar), Dr. Beamish (Fred Walton), Dr. Graham (Joseph E. Tozer), Dr. Townsend (Douglas Wood), Innkeeper (Paul Weigel), Police officer (George Sorel), Policeman (William von Brincken), Attendant (Douglas Gordon), Butler (Eric Wilton), Groom (William Schramm), Friend (Owen Gorin), Bride (Agnes Anderson), Guests (Else Janssen, Bert Sprotte), Desk Sergeant (Clive Morgan), Wife (Hedwigg Reicher), Bobby (John Blood), Police official (John Power).

Synopsis: The police find a body with a stake through the heart and arrest Professor Van Helsing despite his protestations that the corpse is that of a vampire, Count Dracula. He hopes psychiatrist Jeffrey Garth, a former student, will defend him. The body of Dracula disappears from the police station after a woman in black mesmerizes policeman Albert. That woman is Countess Marya Zaleska, and she burns the body, which is her father. "Free. Free forever," she says to her manservant Sandor, who replies, "Perhaps." He is skeptical, and in fact, in London Marya mesmerizes a gentleman she meets on a foggy street. Doctors are mystified by the puncture wounds on his neck. After consulting with Van Helsing, Garth meets the countess at Lady Esme's party. Marya is interested in Garth's views, offering her opinion (straight out of *Hamlet*) that "possibly there are more things in heaven and earth than are dreamed of in your psychiatry, Mr. Garth." Later at her flat Garth urges her to confront her fears. She tries by agreeing to paint a portrait of Lily, a young woman Sandor brings to her studio. But before she can paint her, Marya is overcome by the spell of her ancestor. Lily is brought to the hospital, where Garth determines she is in a post-hypnotic trance.

Van Helsing tells Garth the marks on her throat were made by a vampire. Marya tells Garth she must leave London and wants him to accompany her. To make sure, she has his secretary Janet kidnapped and taken with her to Transylvania. Sir Basil Humphrey of Scotland Yard and Van Helsing follow Garth. At Marya's castle, Sandor is perturbed when he learns she wants to give Garth eternal life. When Garth arrives, Sandor shoots an arrow into Marya. Before he can get Garth, he is shot by a Transylvanian policeman. Sir Basil and Van Helsing find the body of Marya outside on the parapet, the wooden arrow shaft through her heart. Van Helsing agrees that "she was beautiful when she died — a hundred years ago."

Review: "Quite terrifying it all is.... Gloria Holden is a remarkably convincing bat-woman." (Frank S. Nugent, *New York Times*, May 18, 1936, p. 14)

Analysis: It's a literate sequel. It doesn't pay to investigate the time frame. It takes place immediately following Dracula's demise at Van Helsing's hands, but in this film there are airplanes. Carfax Abbey looks more like Frankenstein's watchtower. Gloria Holden is an imposing figure. Otto Kruger would become a very active character actor, sometimes villainous. Irving Pichel, who became a director, seems the model for late '50s and '60s Philadelphia and New York TV horror show host "Roland," aka Zacherle. Ironically, Halliwell Hobbes (here Hobbs) became one of filmdom's most familiar butlers. In this, Hobbs the butler is Edgar Norton.

Son of Dracula
(Universal, 1943; 78 min.) ***

Produced by Ford Beebe. Directed by Robert Siodmak. Screenplay, Eric Taylor. Based on a story by Robert Siodmak. Edited by Saul Goodkind. Director of Photography, George Robinson. Music, Hans Salter. Art Direction, John B. Goodman and Martin Obzina. Special Effects, John P. Fulton.

Cast: Count Alucard (Lon Chaney, Jr.), Katherine Caldwell (Louise Allbritton), Claire Caldwell (Evelyn Ankers), Frank Stanley (Robert Paige), Dr. Harry Brewster (Frank Craven), Professor Lazlo (J. Edward Bromberg), Judge Simmons (Samuel S. Hinds),

Queen Simba (Adeline Reynolds), Colonel Caldwell (George Irving), Sarah (Etta McDaniel), Jailer (Walter Sande), Sheriff (Patrick Moriarity), Coroner (Cyril Delevanti), Deputy Sheriff (Jack Rockwell), Steven (Jess Lee Brooks), Mrs. Land (Joan Blair), Andy (Sam McDaniel), Matthew (Charles Moore), Kirby (Robert Dudley), Tommy Land (Charles Bates), Servant (Emmett Smith).

Synopsis: In the railway station of a small town in the American South, Frank Stanley and Dr. Harry Brewster await the arrival of a Count Alucard, a European nobleman who is expected by the wealthy Caldwell family for an extended stay. Frank suspects that the unexpected guest will only aggravate the unnatural fascination that his fiancée, Katherine (Kay) Caldwell, has with the occult. The count's baggage arrives but he is nowhere to be seen. Brewster notes the unusual crest emblazoned upon one long rectangular box, and hides his alarm upon realizing that the count's name, spelled backwards, is *Dracula*. At a soiree that evening at the Caldwell home of Dark Oaks, Frank makes another fruitless attempt to convince Kay that her preoccupation with the supernatural is unhealthy. In fact, Kay had earlier received similar advice from an old-world savant, Queen Simba. But Kay is oblivious to Frank's request. A mysterious figure appears on the grounds, a figure that assumes the form of a large bat that disappears into the upstairs room of aged Colonel Caldwell. Presently, an alarmed crowd is drawn to the bedroom when smoke is seen billowing from the window. Colonel Caldwell is dead; a small fire had started near the window, caused evidently when the old man dropped his cigar. Dr. Brewster is alarmed both by the look of terror frozen on the dead man's features and by the curious bite marks on his throat. Later that night, Kay is drawn mysteriously to the adjacent marsh. She stares, transfixed, as a large, coffin-like box emerges from the depths of the bog. An eerie, luminous mist seeps from the coffin, a mist that solidifies into the form of a stately gentleman. He seems to glide across the surface of the watery fen. The two embrace; Kay swoons as the man's hungry mouth sinks toward her throat. Some time later, the local justice of the peace is awakened by the pair, who insist on a marriage ceremony. When Frank Stanley hears about this, he confronts his former fiancée and Alucard. Frank pulls a revolver and fires some shots. Alucard is apparently untouched by the shells, but Kay, standing behind him, slumps to the floor, mortally wounded. Frank flees to Dr. Brewster. Thinking the man merely hysterical, Brewster puts him to bed and drives to Dark Oaks. In the basement he discovers a coffin-like container partially filled with earth. He is interrupted by the count, who demands to know what is going on. Brewster explains that he is concerned about Kay's safety and health. The count responds that *he* is now master of Dark Oaks and that any comings and goings will be at his pleasure, as well as his wife's. However, to assuage the doctor's fears, he escorts the man to Kay's bedroom, where they find her, apparently unharmed. The count and Kay will conduct scientific research, comments the foreigner. During the day they will not be able to welcome guests. Next morning, Frank turns himself into the sheriff, who goes to Dark Oaks. He finds Kay's body in the crypt. Brewster is mortified, and the sheriff is highly suspicious of the doctor's story of having talked to the woman after Frank claims to have killed her. While Brewster consults Professor Lazlo, an expert in Carpathian lore, the count appears and attacks them. Only Lazlo's crucifix drives the vampire away. Asleep in his cell, Frank is visited by the now vampiric Kay. She explains that she still loves Frank and the two of them can kill Dracula. Humans can move about during the day, so she helps Frank escape. Confronting Dracula at Dark Oaks, Frank is nearly overcome until the vampire is distracted by smoke and flames. Tossing Frank aside, he investigates and finds to his horror his coffin engulfed in fire. Even as he helplessly watches, the sun creeps over the horizon and the vampire collapses and decomposes. The sheriff, Dr. Brewster and Professor Lazlo arrive to find only the skeletal remains of the count. Searching for Frank, they find him in the play room he and his beloved Katherine frequented as children. Kay's undead form had been secreted there, and that's where Frank turns her coffin into a pyre, immolating her and so freeing her spirit for eternal rest.

Review: "Often as unintentionally funny as it is chilling.... a pretty pallid offering." (A.W., *New York Times*, November 6, 1943, p. 16)

Analysis: *Son of Dracula* is a taut, well-paced and atmospheric little thriller, with good performances and the solid production values given most of the studio's efforts in that decade. Dismissed as the typical hokum that Universal had allowed its horror series to become in the forties, only slowly and relatively recently has it come to be viewed with anything like respect. Lon Chaney, Jr., may have been an actor of limited range, but one would never guess that from all the exposure he got in the 1940s. With his single outing as Count Dracula in *Son of Dracula*, Chaney held the remarkable status of being the single actor to have portrayed *all* the classic Universal monsters, from the Frankenstein monster in *Ghost of Frankenstein*, to the mummy Kharis in three films, to Lawrence Talbot *and* the Frankenstein monster in *Abbott and Costello Meet Frankenstein* (substituting for the ailing Glenn Strange in one scene). Despite the fact that, on the surface of things, Lon Chaney would hardly be thought of as adequate casting for the role of the Transylvanian count, he actually doesn't do bad by the part and in fact isn't that far from Bram Stoker's description of the character.

House of Frankenstein
(Universal, 1944; 70 min.) **½

Analysis: A "Parade of Monsters" film that features Dracula and the Wolf Man as well as Frankenstein's monster. See listing under *Frankenstein* for cast, credits, and discussion.

House of Dracula
(Universal, 1945; 67 min.) **½

Produced by Paul Malvern. Directed by Erle C. Kenton. Screenplay, Edward T. Lowe. Edited by Russell Schoengarth. Director of Photography, George Robinson. Special Photography, John P. Fulton. Music, Edgar Fairchild. Art Direction, John B. Goodman, Martin Obzina. Set Decoration, Russell A. Gausman, Arthur D. Leddy. Makeup, Jack P. Pierce.

Cast: Dracula/Baron Latoes (John Carradine), Lawrence Talbot (Lon Chaney, Jr.), Dr. Edelman (Onslow Stevens), Frankenstein monster (Glenn Strange), Inspector Holst (Lionel Atwill), Miliza Morell (Martha O'-Driscoll), Nina (Jane Adams), Steinmuhl (Skelton Knaggs), Brahms (Joseph E. Bernard), Siegfried (Ludwig Stossel), Johannes (Gregory Muradian), Gendarme (Fred Cordova), Villagers (Beatrice Gray, Dick Dickinson, Harry Lamont).

Synopsis: Count Dracula (traveling as Baron Latoes) ventures to the small village of Visaria to seek the help of Dr. Edelman. He seeks a cure, he explains to the medical man, to his vampirism. The pragmatic doctor is initially skeptical of the baron's request, doubtful that he is in fact the count of infamy. Nonetheless, he agrees to help the baron, taking a sample of his blood to study. As he leaves, Latoes encounters Miliza Morell, Edelman's pretty aide. Latoes and Miliza had known each other previously for a brief time. Had the young lady not left suddenly to take up work with Dr. Edelman, she would undoubtedly have become one of the vampire's undead retinue. At the same time, Lawrence Talbot has appeared at the doctor's door, pleading for a cure for the lycanthropy that has made a horror of his life. Stung by Edelman's incredulity, Talbot flees to nearby Visaria, entreating the local constabulary to lock him in a cell in time for the coming of the full moon. At a loss as to how to deal with this evident lunatic, Inspector Holtz sends for the doctor. Edelman and Miliza arrive precisely at the time of Talbot's transformation into the Wolf Man. The monster hurls itself about the confines of the cell until it presently collapses into a swoon. Convinced that Talbot does indeed have peculiar needs that require his attention, Dr. Edelman has the man removed to his home, where he performs a series of tests that indicate that there might be hope for his recovery. X-rays reveal that certain cranial pressures are exerted upon Talbot's brain, pressures that in conjunction with hysteria and self-hypnosis cause a surge of hormones to be released that effect his lycanthropic change. Using a certain bone-softening fungus that he has produced in the herbarium of his laboratory, the doctor expresses his belief that the structure of Talbot's skull can be altered in such a fashion as to relieve these pressures. It's a risky procedure, and the lycanthrope is unconvinced. In a frenzy of despair, he throws himself from the cliffs outside the doctor's estate. The surf below forces Talbot through a concealed entrance to a labyrinth of caves that wormhole beneath the manor. That night (under the full moon) Edelman has himself lowered to the cave entrance and goes in search of Talbot. Under the lunar influence, Talbot is now the lycanthrope. In this form he attacks the doctor, easily overpowering him. Before he can throttle his would-be rescuer, however, the cursed moment passes, and the Wolf Man transforms back into Lawrence Talbot. Edelman calms the fatalistic Talbot, urging him to at least give the possible cure a chance. As the two are making their way back to the surface, they happen across a body and a skeleton that have been revealed by a subterranean mud-flow. The skeletal remains are those of Dr. Niemann, who had revived the Frankenstein monster years earlier and launched a short-lived reign of terror against the terrified locals. Forced to retreat from an angry mob into a nearby swamp, man and monster were sucked into the depths of the bog. Niemann succumbed, but the indestructible monster has merely lain dormant these many years. Edelman and Talbot wrest the monster's body from the mire and trundle it into the doctor's laboratory far above. The real reason behind Count Dracula's appearance on the scene is revealed when he casts his nefarious spell over Miliza Morrell. Not the least interested in any "cure" for his vampirism, the count has only used this as a pretext to gain access to Edelman's assistant. The doctor has discovered a parasite in Latoes' blood that he believes accounts for the nobleman's sanguinary obsession. He then devises an antitoxin which he introduces into his own blood which, when transfused into Dracula, will eventually rid the count's system of the parasite. While Edelman is in a swoon after transfusing Dracula, the other mischievously reverses the flow of blood, introducing his own tainted fluid into the veins of the doctor. When he has recovered his senses the next morning, Edelman searches out Dracula in his coffin, drags the opened box into the deadly rays of the morning sun, and the undead lord withers and disappears into thin air. However, under the malign influence of the vampire's blood, Dr. Edelman begins to change, transforming into a sinister nocturnal character with murderous vampire-like tendencies of his own. When he kills a villager, it is Lawrence Talbot who is at first suspected of the deed. But, since Talbot is barely ambulatory following the treatments he has received from Edelman, these suspicions are allayed. Somewhat later, when he's recovered enough to walk into the moonlit garden while Edelman and Miliza gaze on, Talbot is overjoyed to discover that the doctor's treatments have been successful: the full moon no longer brings on his transformation into the Wolf Man. When evidence is found linking the doctor with the recent murder, the townspeople descend upon his manor. There they find that the deranged Edelman has revived the Frankenstein monster, who lurches into the crowd, tossing the hapless policemen aside easily. As the scientific equipment explodes, a blaze erupts. Edelman, in a murderous frenzy, advances upon Talbot and Miliza. The former lycanthrope retrieves the pistol dropped by disabled Inspector Holtz and fires at the fiend that was once the benevolent doctor. As Edelman collapses, Talbot and Miliza retreat from the burning manor, even as blazing timbers fall upon the raging Frankenstein monster.

Reviews: "As a result of being visited in one evening by Count Dracula, the Wolf Man and the Frankenstein monster, a sympathetic doctor goes on the rampage. Mind-boggling finale to the first Universal monster cycle.... has to be seen to be believed." (Leslie Halliwell, *Halliwell's Film Guide*, 7th ed., pp. 484–85) ¶"Frankenstein's little boy doesn't die easily. And, unfortunately, neither does this type of cinematic nightmare." (Thomas Pryor, *New York Times*, December 22, 1945, p. 16)

Analysis: *House of Dracula* might well have been titled *House of Edelman* if that character had any significance with the public at all, since the film really belongs to Onslow Stevens. His portrayal of Dr. Edelman is certainly the most significant part of the story. Neither John Carradine's Dracula nor Lon Chaney's Wolf Man dominates the story, and the Frankenstein monster's virtual cameo appearance seems needless. While the depths to which Universal had allowed its own classic bogeyman to descend are to be regretted, *House of Dracula* is nonetheless an entertaining grade-B programmer, containing as it does nearly every horror movie icon that had been introduced by Universal (and others) over the preceding decade and a half. Monsters galore, a mad doctor, weird science, a damsel in distress, a hunchback assistant (Jane Adams), an angry mob, a simmering burgomaster (well, in this case, police inspector). It has castles, tunnels, sepulchers and coffins; foggy nights, chases through swamps and leaps from cliffs. It has Lon Chaney, Jr., John Carradine, Onslow Stevens and Lionel Atwill. That it packs all this into a barely coherent story told in little over an hour, and has the Frankenstein monster again trapped in a blazing structure, has Dracula again going discorporeal with the rising of the sun, and has the mad doctor come to his own chaotic end … well, to paraphrase Leslie Halliwell, the film has to be *experienced* to be believed. Almost lost in the finale's hysteria is the fact that this yarn has a happy ending for the Wolf Man: Dr. Edelman's unlikely "cure" has indeed provided a release for Lawrence Talbot, as he and his nurse paramour leave to live, evidently, happily ever after. In fact, however, Larry's lycanthropy lies in remission for a mere three years: He turns up again, baying at the moon and growing long in the tooth, in *Abbott and Costello Meet Frankenstein.*

Horror purists will probably always lament that the triumphs of the 1930s were — rather literally it seems, considering all the locales with swamp settings —

dragged through the mud in the final several minor titles with which Universal wrapped up its genre series in the mid-1940s. After the initial entries, driven by the talents of Karloff and Lugosi, James Whale, Tod Browning and Karl Freund, the Frankenstein monster, Dracula, the Mummy, and even the late-entry Wolf Man were themselves sucked dry by the vampire of repetitious sequelization. With *House of Dracula* Universal was through with its monsters (except for the ignominy of using them as foils for Abbott and Costello) for a while. The next batch of Universal monsters would arrive early in the next decade from outer space, the depths of the sea, and dank lagoons far up the Amazon. Meanwhile, Dracula, the Mummy and Frankenstein's monster would return, this time from across the Atlantic from an obscure outfit known as Hammer Studios.

Abbott and Costello Meet Frankenstein
(Universal, 1948; 92 min.) ***

Analysis: Another monster parade, this time with Abbott and Costello thrown in! Dracula, Frankenstein's monster, and the Wolf Man all appear. See listing under Frankenstein for cast, credits, and discussion.

Horror of Dracula
(Hammer/Universal, 1958; 82 min.)
***½

Produced by Anthony Hinds. Executive Producer, Michael Carreras. Associate Producer, Anthony Nelson-Keys. Directed by Terence Fisher. Assistant Director, Robert Lynn. Screenplay, Jimmy Sangster. Based on the novel *Dracula* by Bram Stoker. Edited by Bill Lenny and James Needs. Director of Photography, Jack Asher. Technicolor. Music, James Bernard. Musical Director, John Hollingsworth. Art Direction, Bernard Robinson. Makeup, Phil Leakey. Special Effects, Sydney Pearson.

Cast: Count Dracula (Christopher Lee), Dr. Van Helsing (Peter Cushing), Mina Holmwood (Melissa Stribling), Arthur Holmwood (Michael Gough), Vampiress (Valerie Gaunt), Lucy Holmwood (Carol Marsh), Jonathan Harker (John Van Eyssen), Marx, undertaker (Miles Malleson), Tania

(Janine Faye), Gerda (Olga Dickie), Dr. Seward (Charles Lloyd Pack), Porter (Geoffrey Bayldon), Landlord (George Woodbridge), Inga (Barbara Archer), Frontier official (George Benson).

Synopsis: The 3rd of May, 1885: the diary of Jonathan Harker. Harker has arrived at Castle Dracula, ostensibly to index books but in reality to put an end to the count's reign of terror. His mission gets off to a rocky start as a beautiful woman pleads for his help, then attacks him. Set upon herself by Dracula, she and Harker are throttled. When Harker wakes, he discovers two puncture wounds in his neck. Hoping to accomplish his mission before he too becomes a monster, he locates the crypt and puts a wooden stake into the heart of the woman, who turns to a hag. He is too late to destroy Dracula, who arises as the sun goes down. At a village inn a stranger asks about his friend Harker. Only Inga will speak to this Dr. Van Helsing. She gives him Harker's diary, found at the crossroads. As Van Helsing arrives at Dracula's castle, a horse-drawn hearse flies across the bridge. Van Helsing enters the castle and finds Harker's picture frame minus his photographs of fiancée Lucy. In the crypt Van Helsing finds Harker's body. He too has become a vampire and must be destroyed. Later, at the Holmwood residence, Van Helsing tells Arthur and his wife, Mina, of Harker's death. They do not tell Lucy, who's abed in the house possibly suffering anemia. When Van Helsing examines Lucy he finds neck punctures and urges Mina to place garlic flowers in the room and keep the windows closed. But maid Gerda complies with Lucy's entreaties, removes the plants and opens the window. Next morning Lucy is dead. Van Helsing leaves Harker's diary with the angry Arthur. Gerda's child says she's seen Aunt Lucy, and Van Helsing finds this to be true. Lucy is an undead. With Arthur's help, they put Lucy to peaceful rest. While discussing vampirism, Van Helsing tells Arthur it's a fallacy that vampires can turn into animals. However, Dracula could be 500 to 600 years old! Van Helsing and Arthur travel to the frontier to learn where Dracula's hearse was headed. Back home, Mina receives a message to meet Arthur.

When Van Helsing and Arthur locate the undertaker who was Dracula's destination, they find the coffin gone. At home, Mina faints when Arthur places a crucifix in her hand. It leaves a mark. A transfusion revives Mina. How did Dracula find her? Where is his resting place? From Gerda, Van Helsing learns that there's something strange in the basement. He finds a coffin just as Dracula returns. The vampire flees with Mina. Arthur and Van Helsing pursue him to his castle where Arthur saves his wife and Van Helsing chases the monster inside. Realizing his strength is no match for Dracula's, Van Helsing nevertheless sees a chance to destroy the fiend. He leaps onto curtains keeping out the morning sun. When the light enters, Dracula writhes in agony and turns to dust. Only his ring remains.

Reviews: "A throwback to the good old bloodcurdling days when Boris Karloff and the late Bela Lugosi were in their prime.... in many ways a model screen adaptation of a literary horror classic.... acted with perfect conviction and matter-of-factness by an excellent British cast...." (*America*, June 21, 1958, p. 358) ¶"Horribly gory but cleverly realistic chiller thriller which carries far more terrifying conviction than is usual with this type of film." (F. Maurice Speed, ed., *Film Review 1958-59*, p. 84) ¶"Heart-staking episodes are spattered through this Technicolor film, and they are every bit as messy as you'd suppose.... The cast play their roles straight and capably, giving the impression that they believe every line of this extravagant nonsense." (G.G., *New York Herald Tribune*, May 29, 1958) ¶"Peter Cushing is impressive.... Christopher Lee is thoroughly gruesome." (Gilb., *Variety*, May 7, 1958)

Analysis: While this is a seminal vampire movie and we suspect that most fans rate this their favorite Dracula film, it is no closer to the Stoker novel than other film versions. Though not so blatantly as in the 1979 version, events and characters are compressed. There's no London, although a number of characters are obviously English. This Harker knows what he's getting into before arriving at Castle Dracula. The castle is spanking clean and

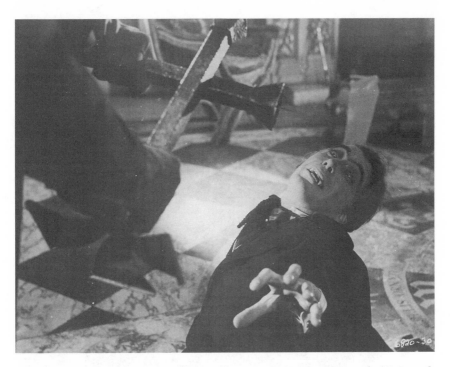

Christopher Lee as Dracula recoils from the cross in *Horror of Dracula* (Universal, 1931).

apparently has no cobwebs. Could the blather about the vampire's inability to transform into a bat or other animal be a way of justifying the absence of special effects that Hammer couldn't afford? On the plus side, James Bernard's score is pulse-pounding. This most satisfying ending in a Hammer Dracula film features a chase through Castle Dracula and the confrontation between Van Helsing and his vampire prey, culminating in a sunlight disintegration of the Count that still packs a wallop. Teenage audiences loved the heart-staking that transformed vixen to hag. Both Carol Marsh and Melissa Stribling convey through facial contortions the ambivalence of wanting yet dreading the vampire's kiss. Although Cushing would play Van Helsing again in 1960's *The Brides of Dracula*, Lee was busy in such Hammer vehicles as *The Man Who Could Cheat Death* and *The Mummy* and didn't play Dracula again till *Dracula, Prince of Darkness* in 1966. Under the British film rating

system, *Horror of Dracula* got an X certificate.

The Return of Dracula
(United Artists/Gramercy, 1958; 77 min.) ***

Produced by Jules V. Levy and Arthur Gardner. Directed by Paul Landres. Story and screenplay, Pat Fielder. Edited by Sherman Rose. Music, Gerald Fried. Art Direction, James D. Vance.

Cast: Bellac Goudal/Count Dracula (Francis Lederer), Rachel Mayberry (Norma Eberhardt), Cora Mayberry (Greta Granstedt), Tim (Ray Stricklyn), Mr. Meyerman (John Wengraff), Micky Mayberry (Jimmy Baird), Sheriff Bicknell (John McNamara), Reverend (Gage Clark), Bellac Goudal (Norbert Schiller), Doctor (Robert Lynn), Cornelia (Hope Summers), Jenny (Virginia Vincent), County Clerk (Dan Gachman), Porter (Mel Allen), Station master (Harry Harvey, Sr.).

Synopsis: A group of para-governmental European vampire hunters led by Meyerman think they have found the coffin of

The vampire Bellac Goudal meets his end in *The Return of Dracula* (United Artists, 1958).

the dreaded Dracula — but it's empty. On a German train, Bellac Goudal, an artist planning to visit relatives in America, is attacked. No one is seen debarking the train in Carleton, California, but a man appears, saying he is Bellac Goudal. The Mayberrys, his American relatives, take him home. Bellac says he must have his freedom, he's been confined. Mickey finds his cat killed in a cave where, unknown to him, Bellac spends his days in a coffin. A blind woman, Jenny, is attacked and becomes a vampiress. A large white dog kills a man who questions the Mayberry family about any strangers. Meyerman, who's tracked Dracula to this vicinity, convinces the authorities and the reverend to let him disinter Jenny. The coffin is empty. They wait for her return and impale her. Bellac lures Rachel to his cave. Her boyfriend finds her there and during a fight with Bellac, manages to push the vampire into a pit, where, impaled, he turns into a skeleton.

Review: "Wonderful horror romp.... manages to blend nostalgia for the small-town innocence of the 1950s with the gothic horror suspense ... needed to make horror involving." (Gary J. Svehla, *Midnight Marquee*, Summer 1991, p. 43) ¶"A well-made little picture but it is somewhat short on its most marketable quantity — horror." (Powe., *Variety*, April 16, 1958)

Analysis: Though buried at its release by the competition of Hammer's *Horror of Dracula* (released the same year), this B-film is rather good, rather scary in parts. The music theme seems classical. Were they thinking of the *Swan Lake* music used in Lugosi's *Dracula*? There are little in-jokes and humorous patches, like Bellac saying he'd been "confined." Francis Lederer had been a European-type leading man in '30s-'40s Hollywood. He went on to play the Dr. Moreau–like character in 1959's *Terror Is a Man*.

The Brides of Dracula
(Hammer/Universal, 1960; 85 min.)
***

Produced by Anthony Hinds. Directed by Terence Fisher. Screenplay, Jimmy Sangster, Peter Bryan, and Edward Percy. Edited by Alfred Cox. Director of Photography, Jack Asher. Technicolor. Music, Malcolm Williamson. Sound, James Groom and Jock May. Art Direction, Bernard Robinson, Thomas Goswell. Special Effects, Sydney Pearson.

Cast: Dr. Van Helsing (Peter Cushing), Baron Meinster (David Peel), Marianne (Yvonne Monlaur), Baroness Meinster (Martita Hunt), Greta (Freda Jackson), Dr. Tobler (Miles Malleson), Herr Lang (Henry Oscar), Frau Lang (Mona Washbourne), Gina (Andree Melly), Hans (Victor Brooks), Cure (Fred Johnson), Coachman (Michael Ripper), Village girl (Marie Devereux), Severin (Harold Scott).

Synopsis: At the end of the nineteenth century, Count Dracula may be dead, but his disciples live on. From Paris, Marianne comes to Transylvania to be a student teacher. But before arriving at Herr Lang's School for Young Girls, she is stuck at an inn and accepts an invitation from Baroness Meinster to spend the night at her chateau. The baroness explains that the young man Marianne spies from her balcony is her ill son. When Marianne inquires about his happiness, the baroness replies, "Are madmen happy?" That evening Marianne observes the man, who she believes is about to jump. She rushes to his apartments and finds that he could not leap; his left leg is chained to the wall. She retrieves the key from the baroness's drawer and frees the prisoner, who tells her to dress. When she finishes she finds servant Greta laughing maniacally and the baron gone. Marianne flees the castle and is found the next day unconscious in the woods by Dr. Van Helsing. Back at the inn, Van Helsing observes the body of a young girl who died the previous night. He tells Marianne he's studying the cult of the undead prevalent in Transylvania and the lower Danube. He accompanies her to Herr Lang's school before returning to the inn to discuss the dead girl with the village priest. Van Helsing tells the cleric that vampirism is a holdover from an ancient pagan religion and explains that vampires have no reflection, can sometimes become a bat, need a human servant to assist their depredations, and can be killed by burning or stakes in the heart. Observing the grave of the young girl, Van Helsing sees Greta imploring the corpse to arise. The dead body does leave the grave and escapes Van Helsing, who is attacked by a large bat. At the Meinster chateau, Van Helsing confronts the baron and baroness. While the baron escapes, Van Helsing indicates he can help the mother find peace. The baron goes to the Lang school and asks Marianne to be his wife. He vampirizes Gina, the other student treacher. Van Helsing, meanwhile, puts a stake in the baroness's heart. Later he examines Gina's body and discovers puncture wounds in her neck. After he leaves, Gina rises and tries to seduce Marianne, but Van Helsing returns and she runs off. Marianne tells Van Helsing the baron is at the mill. There Van Helsing finds the Meinster coffin, but Greta grabs

Marianne (Yvonne Monlaur) is horrified by the effect of holy water on the baron (David Peel) in *Brides of Dracula* (Hammer, 1960).

his crucifix and Meinster overpowers him and bites his neck. Van Helsing wakes, feels his wound and cauterizes it with a sizzling iron and holy water. When the baron arrives with Marianne he has his face dashed with that same holy water. He flees into the courtyard after knocking over the brazier and setting the mill on fire. Van Helsing and Marianne escape via an upstairs room and ladder. On the way, Van Helsing leaps to the mill's sails and creates the shadow of a cross, which destroys the baron.

Reviews: "Blood-and-thunder mish-mash.... Not one new thrill has been added to the original *Dracula* film." (Judith Crist, *New York Herald Tribune*, September 6, 1960) ¶"Nothing new or imaginative about it." (Bosley Crowther, *New York Times*, September 6, 1960, p. 41) ¶"Technically well-made film.... However, if the true aficionado of the horror cult is seeking a real eerie experience, he'll be disappointed." (Holl., *Variety*, May 18, 1960)

Analysis: Van Helsing's opinions have changed: He now posits the possibility that vampires *can* become animals. Van Helsing's cauterization was traumatic for many audience members. Contemporary critics failed to discern undertones of incest. This had a rather risque paperback tie-in.

Dracula, Prince of Darkness
(Hammer/20th Century–Fox, 1966; 90 min.) ***

Produced by Anthony Nelson Keys. Executive Producer, Anthony Hinds. Directed by Terence Fisher. Assistant Director, Bert Batt. Screenplay, John Sansom. Based on an idea by John Elder [Anthony Hinds]. Edited by Chris Barnes. Supervising Editor, James Needs. Director of Photography, Michael Reed. Technicolor. Music, James Bernard. Musical Supervision, Philip Martell. Art Direction, Don Mingaye. Makeup, Roy Ashton. Special Effects, Bowie Films.

Cast: Count Dracula (Christopher Lee), Helen Kent (Barbara Shelley), Father Sandor

(Andrew Keir), Charles Kent (Francis Matthews), Diana Kent (Suzan Farmer), Alan Kent (Charles Tingwell), Ludwig (Thorley Walters), Klove (Philip Latham), Brother Mark (Walter Brown), Landlord (George Woodbridge), Brother Peter (Jack Lambert), Priest (Philip Ray), Mother (Joyce Hemson), Coach driver (John Maxim).

Synopsis: Traveling through the forests about a Carpathian village, Father Sandor crosses the path of a burial party whose members he has to admonish for their festooning of the deceased with numerous artifacts intended to ward off the undead: crucifixes, sprays of garlic, etc. Has not the infamous Count Dracula been dead these many years, and has not the land known a peace from his fiendish reign of terror? The peasants grudgingly accept the priest's censure. When he arrives at the village inn, Sandor meets two English couples: Charles Kent and wife Helen, and Alan Kent (Charles's younger brother) and wife Diana. The foursome are venturing to the more out-of-the-way spots and ask the priest about their proposed next stop: Castle Dracula. Sandor warns them in no uncertain terms to stay away from that foul place. When they travel on the next day, it is obvious that they intend to heed the priest's warning, but when they are stranded by a surly coachman at a crossroads near the castle, they are in a quandary as to how to proceed. The arrival of a mysterious, driverless coach seems to be the solution to their problem until, despite the attempts of younger brother Alan to direct the horses, the steeds turn and hurry the coach and its helpless occupants to Castle Dracula. The couples at first believe the tower to be deserted, although in an excellent state of repair and evidently recently lived-in. They are surprised by the sudden appearance of Klove, the steward of the castle, who claims to keep the place in such a fine state at the bequest of his late employer, the master of the castle. Being impressed with Klove's polished, if reserved and distant, manner, the travelers spend the night, despite Helen's nervous premonition that things are not right here. A noise in the night arouses Charles, who goes out into the dark corridors to investigate, despite Helen's desperate pleas that

he stay with her. As Charles moves quietly through the hallways into a candlelit chamber far below, Klove approaches furtively and deals him a lethal blow. Dragging his victim into a secluded room in the center of which sits a stone crypt, the murderer uses block and tackle to hoist his victim head downward over the open bier. Taking up a small cask, Klove empties its contents, a fine powdery ash, into the cairn. Then, taking his knife, he slits the throat of Charles, allowing the blood to gush downwards, inundating the ash. From the commingling of blood and ash a gaseous, swirling mass appears, slowly congealing into the form of a man. Some time later, a knock brings the frightened Helen to her door; Klove informs her that her husband has had an accident. Following the manservant into the chamber below, Helen is terrified at the sight of her dead husband and even more so at seeing the vampire about to strike: Count Dracula descends upon her. The next morning Alan and Diana are unnerved to find no trace of their companions and spend the day searching for them. With the coming of dusk, Dracula appears, along with Helen, who is no longer the timid, nervous little wife of Charles, but now a vivacious and ravenous bride of Dracula. The pair, aided by Klove, attack Alan and Diana. Braining the vampire's servant and fending off the undead with crucifixes, they flee in Klove's carriage. They are found by Father Sandor, who takes them to his monastery, where the injured Diana is treated by the monks. Their respite is brief, as Klove arrives in a coach containing Dracula's coffin. That night, with the aid of Ludwig, a depraved inmate of the monastery, Dracula gains egress into the sanctum sanctorum, casts a spell over Diana and carries her off. With his master in one coffin, Diana in a second, Klove drives his steeds madly back towards Castle Dracula, with Alan and Father Sandor in hot pursuit. At dusk, the wagon wrecks just before reaching its destination, hurling the coffin containing Dracula down onto the frozen moat surrounding the castle. While Sandor retrieves the dazed Diana, Alan scrambles down, stake and mallet in hand, to deal the death blow to the Count. Before he can do the deed, the sun descends below the horizon; the coffin lid flies open and the prince of darkness leaps out and overpowers Alan. As Diana and Sandor look on, the woman fires a desperate shot in the direction of the struggling pair. The shot misses its mark, but Sandor notes that Dracula reacts with alarm to the water that gushes from the hole the projectile makes in the ice. Snatching the rifle from Diana, the priest fires repeatedly into the ice, breaking it at key points until Dracula, separated now from Alan, is stranded upon an exceedingly unsteady cake of frozen surface. As the lord of the undead strains to keep his balance and avoid the rushing water, the sheet upends, sending the vampire to a watery grave.

Reviews: "After a slowish start some climate of eeriness is evoked but more shadows, suspense and suggestion would have helped." (Rich., *Variety*, January 19, 1966) ¶ "None of it is any creepier than a fun-fair ghost-train, and even Christopher Lee of the silver-green skin has little to do but smile and show the sort of teeth we used to make out of orange skin." (Isabel Quigly, *Spectator*, January 7, 1966, p. 13)

Analysis: Hammer Films was not slow to realize what a money-maker its revival of the Universal horror characters could be. The Frankenstein films took off immediately, and within ten years of the appearance of *The Curse of Frankenstein*, Mary Shelley's misanthropic doctor was featured in no fewer than three sequels, culminating in *Frankenstein Must Be Destroyed* in 1969. In each of these films, Hammer spun its own version of the Frankenstein myths in linear fashion, centering the events on Dr. Frankenstein rather than on his misshapen creature. The Dracula series got off to a much slower start primarily because of (1) the titular character being killed off quite definitively in the first film, and (2) the star's reluctance to continue the role and risk being typecast in the part. The first sequel to 1958's *Horror of Dracula*, *The Brides of Dracula* (1960), had the same Carpathian setting and Dr. Van Helsing and his bag full of wooden stakes, but Dracula is evident nowhere except in the title. The year 1964 saw Hammer's *Kiss of the Vampire*, which concerned late-nineteenth-century travelers coming upon a virtual coven of vampires in the Carpathians, but is otherwise unrelated to the Dracula series. *Dracula, Prince of Darkness* is a direct sequel to *Horror of Dracula*, and, indeed, the pre-credits sequence is a scene-for-scene synopsis of that film's final moments, complete with the vampire's disintegration by sunlight. Immediately noticeable is the absence of Dr. Van Helsing, his place being taken by Andrew Keir's Father Sandor, who performs the role of vampire hunter with even more ruthless determination than his Prussian predecessor. Christopher Lee has not a word of dialogue in this film, imposing his will through gesture and threatening visage alone (a choice negatively commented upon by some critics). The film maintains interest throughout, mainly through the tense atmosphere established from the beginning, as well as from interesting performances by some of the main players. Barbara Shelley, in particular, stands out in what is virtually a dual performance as the mousy Helen Kent whose timid demeanor is transformed into ravenous voluptuousness after her seduction by the vampire Count. Also interesting here is the method of Dracula's death: being overcome by running water, one of the more esoteric vampire banes. Klove will appear again in *Scars of Dracula*.

Billy the Kid vs. Dracula
(Embassy, 1966; 72 min.) *

Produced by Carroll Case. Assistant to the Producer, Howard W. Koch, Jr. Directed by William Beaudine. Screenplay, Carl K. Hittleman. Director of Photography, Lothrop Worth. Pathé Color. Music, Raoul Kraushaar. Sound Effects, Delmore Harris. Art Direction, Paul Sylos. Set Decoration, Harry Reif. Photographic Effects, Cinema Research Corporation. Makeup, Ted Goodley.

Cast: Dracula (John Carradine), Billy (Chuck Courtney), Betty Bentley (Melinda Plowman), Franz Oster (Walter Janovitz), Eva Oster (Virginia Christine), Dr. Henrietta Hull (Olive Carey), Lila Oster (Hanie Landman), Mrs. Ann Bentley (Marjorie Bennett), Ben (Harry Carey, Jr.), Red Thorpe (Bing

Russell), Joe Flake (George Cisar), James Underhill (William Forrest), Nana (Charlita), Yancy (Lennie Geer), Marshal Griffin (Roy Barcroft). With Richard Reeves, Max Kleven, Jack Williams, William Challee.

Synopsis: Dracula goes West, feasting on settlers and impersonating a ranch owner to get at perky Betty. Billy the Kid, going straight, is the ranch foreman and in love with this virgin desired by Dracula. Dracula prepares a nearby cave as a hideout, takes Betty there but is found out. Billy fires his six-shooter uselessly at the vampire, who wrestles him to the ground. The sheriff arrives and empties his pistol into the monster. Billy grabs the sheriff's gun and throws it into Dracula's face, felling him. He takes a spike and puts it through his heart. Dracula disintegrates, and Betty revives.

Review: "Western abomination." (John Stanley, *The Creature Features Movie Guide*, p. 21)

Analysis: While Hammer was turning out respectable Dracula sequels in England, in the U.S. the mid-1960s was a transitional period for bad science fiction and horror. Color started becoming *de rigueur*, and here both color and sound are good. That's all that's good. It doesn't "rise" to the level of ***Bomb because it's not worth more than one viewing. It's a mite disappointing to find Dracula incapacitated by a pistol (silver barreled?) to the kisser. The ad read, "The West's Deadliest Gun-Fighter! The World's Most Diabolical Killer!"

Dracula Has Risen from the Grave

(Hammer/Warner Bros.–Seven Arts, 1968; 92 min.) **½

Produced by Aida Young. Directed by Freddie Francis. Screenplay, John Elder [Anthony Hinds]. Based on the character created by Bram Stoker. Edited by James Needs and Spencer Reeve. Director of Photography, Arthur Grant. Technicolor. Music, James Bernard. Art Direction, Bernard Robinson. Makeup, Heather Nurse, Rosemarie McDonald-Peattie. Matte Artist, Peter Melrose. Special Effects, Frank George.

Cast: Count Dracula (Christopher Lee), Monsignor (Rupert Davies), Maria (Veronica Carlson), Paul (Barry Andrews), Priest (Ewan Hooper), Zena (Barbara Ewing), Anna (Marion Mathie), Max (Michael Ripper), Landlord (George A. Cooper), Boy (Norman Bacon), Student (John D. Collins), Farmer (Chris Cunningham), First victim (Carrie Baker).

Synopsis: A village priest finds a dead woman in the church and realizes that the previous year's terror has not been exorcised. When the monsignor arrives, he learns that no one now attends services. He takes the crucifix from the altar and, with the priest, trudges to the castle, where he places the crucifix on the door. Unknown to the monsignor, the priest, whose courage failed and who has remained some distance behind, stumbles and falls onto an ice-covered stream. Beneath the ice is Count Dracula, who awakes when blood from the priest's cut revives him. He puts the priest under his spell, finds that the monsignor has desecrated his castle entrance and seeks revenge. He goes to the monsignor's town and kills the barmaid and attempts to seduce the monsignor's niece, Maria. Dracula puts his spell on waitress Zena but is initially foiled in his attempt to seduce Maria by the efforts of her atheist boyfriend, Paul. Later he kidnaps her but is pursued to the castle. Dracula orders Maria to remove the crucifix from the door. Paul arrives and manages to push the vampire over the rocks onto the crucifix.

Reviews: "Has snap and style. Its story hurtles from shock to shock with such momentum that it almost manages to skip over some gaping plot holes ... The excellent cast doesn't seem bothered by unanswered questions.... They go about their business with impressive deadpan seriousness." (Margaret Ronan, *Senior Scholastic*, January 31, 1969, p. 29) ¶"The story's slight, the horror and the bloodcurdling essential to these pix is minimal and even Dracula himself appears bored at being resurrected yet again." (Rich., *Variety*, November 20, 1968, p. 34)

Analysis: Awakening the count from the ice follows directly from the previous film, *Dracula, Prince of Darkness*, in which he was drowned by running water. Barry Andrews informed us in 1992 that he had a

Two alumni of *Dracula Has Risen from the Grave* (Hammer/Warner Bros.–Seven Arts, 1968)— female lead Veronica Carlson (left) and composer James Bernard (second from left)— sit with Hammer director Val Guest (far right) and his wife, Yolanda Donlan Guest, at FANEX 8 in Towson, Maryland, July 1994.

great time working with Veronica Carlson, whom he termed "a real sweetie — a talented artist as well. She did a portrait of me which I still treasure." Carlson lives in the States and has shown her beautiful self at several FANEX conventions in the Baltimore area. Filmed at Pinewood Studios.

Blood of Dracula's Castle
(Paragon International/Crown International, 1969; 84 min.)
***Bomb

Produced by Al Adamson and Rex Carlton. Directed by Al Adamson. Screenplay, Rex Carlton. Edited by Peter Perry. Director of Photography, Leslie Kovacs. Pathé Color. Music, Lincoln Mayorage. Song sung by Gil Bernal. Makeup, Jean Hewitt. Special Makeup, Kent Osborne.

Cast: George (John Carradine), Countess Townsend (Paula Raymond), Count Townsend (Alex D'Arcy), Johnny (Robert Dix), Glen Cannon (Gene Shane), Liz Arden (Barbara Bishop), Ann (Vicki Volante), Mango (Ray Young). With John Cardos, Kent Osborne.

Synopsis: Glen Cannon and his fiancée, Liz, arrive at Falcon Rock Castle, which Glen has inherited from his uncle. The current residents are Count and Countess Townsend, butler George and an ugly servant, Mango. Next morning, Glen and Liz discover women chained to a basement wall. One of the victims, Ann, reveals that the Townsends are none other than Count and Countess Dracula. That evening Glen and Liz observe the sacrifice of a woman to the "Great God Luna." After Mango and George are dispatched, the vampires are killed by sunlight. Freeing the other women, Glen and Liz leave.

Review: "Grainy, out-of-focus horror cheapie tries to drain a few laughs from the vampire formula, but the results are lifeless." (John Stanley, *The Creature Features Movie Guide,* p. 25)

Analysis: Another interloper among the Hammer entries, this is a pretty funny film. The best line belongs to John Carradine as butler George: "Screams. What screams? I didn't hear any screams." The ad when it was paired with *Nightmare in Wax*: "Superhorrorama. All-New! All-Shock! All-Color! Horror Beyond Belief ... Lies Waiting For All Who Dare Enter The Vampire's Dungeon! Count Dracula and His Coffin-Mate Countess Dracula Need Young Girls To Stay Alive ... Another 300 Years!" Both Paula Raymond and Alex d'Arcy had major movies and some leading roles behind them.

Taste the Blood of Dracula
(Hammer/Warner Bros., 1970; 95 min.) ***

Produced by Aida Young. Directed by Peter Sasdy. Assistant Director, Derek Whitehurst. Screenplay, John Elder (Anthony Hinds). Edited by Chris Barnes. Director of Photography, Arthur Grant. Technicolor. Music, James Bernard. Musical Supervisor, Philip Martell. Sound, Roy Hyde. Sound Re-recording, Denis Whitlock. Art Direction, Scott MacGregor. Makeup, Gerry Fletcher. Special Effects, Brian Johnson.

Cast: Count Dracula (Christopher Lee), William Hargood (Geoffrey Keen), Lord Courtley (Ralph Bates), Alice Hargood (Linda Hayden), Martha Hargood (Gwen Watford), Lucy Paxton (Isla Blair), Samuel Paxton (Peter Sallis), Jonathan Secker (John Carson), Jeremy Secker (Martin Jarvis), Paul Paxton (Anthony Corian), Weller (Roy Kinnear), Cobb (Michael Ripper), Dolly (Maddy/Madeline Smith), Felix (Russell Hunter), Hargood's maid (Shirley Jaffe), Father (Keith Marsh), Son (Peter May), Vicar (Reginald Barratt), Chinese girl (Lai Ling), Snake girl (Malaika Martin).

Synopsis: Occultist Lord Courtley lures three respectable middle-aged men to an abandoned church, where he begins a black mass. Dropping dried blood into goblets, he asks them to drink. They refuse, but Courtley drinks, only to fall to the floor in agony. The men kick him away as he clutches at them. After they leave, wind covers the body with dust, which hardens and then splits open, revealing— Dracula. "They have destroyed my servant. They shall be destroyed," states the vampire after his reincarnation from Courtley's body. He locates the Hargoods and

gains control over Alice, who kills her father with a shovel. Alice lures Lucy to the church, where Dracula vampirizes her. Hargood's chums Secker and Samuel Paxton return to the church to see if Courtley's body is there. They find Lucy in a coffin. Lucy's father wounds Secker and drives him from the church. Lucy arises when he decides the best move is to drive a stake into her heart. Lucy and Alice impale him instead. When Lucy asks Dracula if she pleases him, he tells her she's served her purpose and kills her. Paul Saxton reads a letter from Jonathan, who's been killed by his vampire son, Jeremy. It advises him to arm himself with knowledge, for Alice may yet be saved. Paul goes to the church and finds Lucy's body in a stream nearby. In the church, he places a crucifix at the door and prepares the altar for a Christian ceremony. Dracula cannot escape; he falls onto the altar and disintegrates. Paul and Alice leave.

Reviews: "Excellent blend of Satanism/vampirism backed by one of the best, most literate Hammer scripts in a very long time." (*Castle of Frankenstein* 16, July 1970, p. 62) ¶"Smart special effects, excellent Arthur Grant Technicolor lensing, and liberal use of blood.... Christopher Lee can now play Dracula in his sleep and ... looks occasionally as if he is doing so." (*Variety*, May 20, 1970, p. 26)

Analysis: This could be the second-best Chris Lee Dracula film. There is enough movement between the town and church to give audiences a feeling of space. The killing of parents by their offspring is subversive and disturbing.

Scars of Dracula
(Hammer/American Continental, 1971; 94 min.) **

Produced by Aida Young. Directed by Roy Ward Baker. Screenplay, John Elder [Anthony Hinds]. Edited by James Needs. Director of Photography, Moray Grant. Technicolor. Music, James Bernard. Musical Supervision, Philip Martell. Art Direction, Scott MacGregor. Special Effects, Roger Dicken.

Cast: Dracula (Christopher Lee), Sarah Framsen (Jenny Hanley), Simon (Dennis Waterman), Paul Carlson (Christopher Matthews),

Protected by a strategically located crucifix, Sarah (Jenny Hanley) comes to no harm in *Scars of Dracula* (Hammer, 1971). Photo courtesy of the National Film Archives, London.

Tania (Anoushka Hempel), Klove (Patrick Troughton), Priest (Michael Gwynn), Julie (Wendy Hamilton), Innkeeper (Michael Ripper), Alice (Delia Lindsay), Burgomaster (Bob Todd), First officer (David Lealand), Second officer (Richard Durden), Farmer (Morris Bush), Wagonmaster (Toke Townley), Landlord's wife (Margot Boht).

Synopsis: A bat drips blood on the cloak and remains of Dracula, causing the resurrection of the vampire. Enraged by the ensuing murder of a young girl, villagers rush to Castle Dracula, brush servant Klove aside, and set the castle afire. Meanwhile, bats kill their wives and children in the church. Weeks later, in Kleinenburg, Sarah Framsen is celebrating her birthday. Late for the affair is Paul, who dallied with Alice and is now on the run from her burgomaster father. Turned out of another village's inn, Paul discovers a coach and falls asleep inside. Upon awaking, he finds himself in an old castle across the frontier. He meets Dracula, the castle's owner, and

stays the night — with the lovely Tania. But in the morning he finds the count stabbing the woman and himself no match for his host's superhuman strength. Later, he makes a ladder of bed curtains and descends to another window. But Klove pulls the bedclothes up, and Paul finds himself incarcerated in the room containing Dracula's coffin. Meanwhile, Sarah and Paul's brother Simon track Paul to the castle. Dracula denies having met Paul and offers Sarah and Simon refuge for the night. Dracula is foiled in his attempt to vampirize the sleeping Sarah by the crucifix about her neck and by Klove's refusal to remove it. Next day Simon learns that Paul had been in the castle. He and Sarah flee to the town, where the priest allows them to take refuge in the church. At dawn, Simon and the priest set out for the castle, but the clergyman loses faith and returns to the village. With a wooden stake, Simon descends to Dracula's resting place, but like

Paul, he is marooned there by Klove; worse, the vampire's spell prevents him from impaling the body. He falls unconscious. Awakened by a storm, he finds his brother's body and is taunted by Dracula. Meanwhile, bats have killed the priest and driven Sarah from the church. Sarah rushes to the castle. Again refusing to help Dracula harm the lovely young woman, Klove lowers a rope to Simon and attempts to stab his master, only to be thrown from the battlements. Simon is astonished to see Dracula remove the metal fence spike he thrust into his chest. About to hurl it back, Dracula is struck by a lightening bolt. In flames, he careens from the parapets.

Review: "An attempt to lift the series, in plot and style, above some of its current handicaps.... an attempt at returning to form.... Roy Ward Baker's direction is not as atmospheric as it was in, say, *The Vampire Lovers*, and the film suffers from cheap set design and the obvious low budget." (John R. Duvoli, *Cinefantastique*, Fall 1971, p. 29)

Analysis: It sounds much better than it is. Even though there are some good things here — Dracula climbing the castle wall, lightning striking the vampire — the dearth of different sets suggest a low budget. Confoundingly in this era of the R rating for female flesh, the lovely Jenny Hanley does not disrobe. Delia Lindsay does show her fanny. Some sources give it a 1970 U.S. release.

Dracula vs. Frankenstein
(Independent-International, 1971; 90 min.) ***Bomb

Produced by Al Adamson and John Van Horn. Directed by Al Adamson. Story and screenplay, William Pugsley and Samuel M. Sherman. Edited by Irwin Cadden. Directors of Photography, Gary Graver, Paul Glickman. Color, DeLuxe. Music, William Lava. Art Direction, Ray Markham. Electronic Special Effects, Ken Strickfaden.

Cast: Dr. Durea (J. Carrol Naish), Groton (Lon Chaney, Jr.), Judith Fontain (Regina Carrol), Mike (Anthony Eisley), Count Dracula (Zandor Vorkov), Frankenstein monster (John Bloom), Grazbo (Angelo Rossito), Sergeant Martin (Jim Davis), Rico (Russ Tamblyn), Dr. Beaumont (Forrest J. Ackerman), Samantha (Anne Morell), Strange (Greydon Clark), Joanie (Maria Lease), Beach girl (Connie Nelson), Beach boy (Gary Kent), Hippie (Lu Dorn), Creature (Shelly Weiss), Bikers (William Bonner, Bruce Kimball), Policemen (Albert Cole, Irv Saunders).

Synopsis: While Count Dracula is disinterring the Frankenstein monster from the Oakmoor Cemetery, the paraplegic Dr. Durea sends out the mentally disturbed Groton to behead a comely lass. Using a Los Angeles beachfront house of fright as a cover for his laboratory experiments, Durea reattaches the woman's head and with his serum keeps her alive. Count Dracula visits and reveals that he knows Durea is the last of the Frankensteins. Together they can assist each other. The return of a comet helps Dracula revive the monster, which he sends to murder Durea's one-time rival, Dr. Beaumont. Meanwhile, Las Vegas singer Judith Fontain arrives in town looking for her missing sister Joanie — the woman Groton "killed." She falls in with Mike. Together they search for Joanie and visit Durea's emporium. Suspicious, they return, only to confront a gun-toting Durea, the mad Groton, the dwarf barker, and Dracula. In the running fight, the dwarf falls on an ax blade, Durea is decapitated and Sergeant Martin shoots Groton off the roof. But Dracula fries Mike with a blast from his ring and takes Judith to an old house. The monster won't allow Dracula to feast on the woman, and the supernatural beings fight outside until the vampire tears off the monster's arms and head. But the sun rises before Dracula can return to his coffin. After breaking her bonds, Judith discovers his decayed body.

Review: "This pathetic pairing of horrordom's erstwhile greats is good for a few masochistic laughs." (Phantom of the Movies, *The Phantom's Ultimate Video Guide*, p. 519).

Analysis: America interrupts the Hammer canon again. Naish, one of Hollywood's most versatile character actors, is trapped here in a script that provides incomprehensible reasoning for his actions. What, exactly, does his serum do? What's it made of? What is the ultimate goal? Apparently the scriptwriters didn't know.

Christopher Lee is *Dracula A.D. 1972* (Hammer/Warner Bros., 1972).

Forrest Ackerman is the guru of fantasy, horror and science fiction fans and collectors. It's hard to believe that only a decade before this opus, Russ Tamblyn, a biker "guest star" here, received a Best Supporting Actor Academy Award nomination for *West Side Story*. Jim Davis had a few moments in the sun in B westerns and would recover from this film to star as family patriarch in TV's *Dallas*.

Dracula A.D. 1972
(Hammer/Warner Bros., 1972;
100 min.) **½

Produced by Josephine Douglas. Directed by Alan Gibson. Assistant Director, Robert Lynn. Screenplay, Don Houghton. Edited by James Needs. Director of Photography, Dick Bush. Eastman Color. Music, Michael Vickers. Songs: "Alligator Man," Sal Valentino; "You Better Come Through," Tim Barnes. Performed by Stoneground. Sound, Roy Baker, Bill Rowe, A.W. Lumkin. Makeup, Jill Carpenter. Special Effects, Les Bowie.

Cast: Van Helsing (Peter Cushing), Count Dracula (Christopher Lee), Jessica Van Helsing (Stephanie Beacham), Laura Bellows (Caroline Munro), Johnny Alucard (Christopher Neame), Inspector Murray (Michael Coles), Anna Bryant (Janet Key), Gaynor (Marsha Hunt), Bob Tarrant (Philip Miller), Joe Mitchum (William Ellis), Detective Sergeant (David Andrews), Greg (Michael Kitchen), Matron (Lally Bowers), Hippy girl (Penny Brahms), Rock group (Stoneground).

Synopsis: 1872: Count Dracula wrestles with Lawrence Van Helsing atop a runaway carriage, which crashes into a tree, throwing Van Helsing to the ground. He arises and finds that Dracula is impaled on the broken spokes of a carriage wheel. He helps push the wood in further, and the vampire disintegrates. Van Helsing collapses. A young man on horseback arrives, puts some of the vampire's ashes into a vial and makes off with two items: the stake that was in Dracula's chest, and the creature's ring. Later, during Van Helsing's funeral, this young man places the stake and ashes in a nearby hole. 1972: After crashing a London party, Johnny Alucard proposes to his gang (which includes Jessica Van Helsing) that they meet at the soon-to-be-demolished St. Bartolph's church and perform a black mass. Johnny returns to his home and collects a vial and a ring. Jessica is hesitant but arrives at the church with her boyfriend and finds a gravestone with her great-grandfather's name on it. He died on that very date in September 1872. She wonders why the tombstone says, "Rest in Final Peace." Meanwhile, Jessica's grandfather inspects portraits of Dracula and his father. During the ceremony in the church, Laura asks to be the sacrificial victim and is carried to the altar. Johnny has her hold a chalice into which he pours ashes and then drips blood from his arm. The goblet overflows onto Laura's cheek and neck. She screams and can't make herself leave when the others rush off. Outside, Johnny pulls a stake from the ground and Dracula appears. "I summoned you," says Johnny. "It was my will," states Dracula, who goes inside and feasts on Laura. Learning that Jessica Van Helsing knew Laura, Inspector Murray visits her grandfather to see if he can again help the police with his knowledge of ritual murder. Van Helsing explains that he's really an expert in the occult and is very concerned because the facts of Laura's murder suggest vampirism. That evening Dracula, who tells Johnny that his family's mission has been to track down the Van Helsings, gives his acolyte "the power." Johnny converts Bob as well, and they capture Jessica. Van Helsing goes to Johnny's pad, the two battle and Alucard, smitten by sunlight, falls into a bathtub and accidentally turns on the running water. Dying, he rages that Jessica is lost. Van Helsing prepares for the confrontation he knows is imminent. That night he finds Jessica in St. Bartolph's. The count appears, chiding Van Helsing: "You would play your brains against mine? Against me, who has commanded nations?" Van Helsing lures him to the choir loft and stabs him with a silver knife. The vampire falls, but Jessica removes the knife. Van Helsing runs outside, pursued by his nemesis. Tossing holy water on him causes Dracula to slip into the pit and onto the stake Van Helsing had prepared. The man uses the shovel to drive the monster deeper onto the stake. He disintegrates while Van Helsing comforts his granddaughter.

Reviews: "The novice ... sets into motion a complex chain of forbidden rituals designed to display Stephanie Beacham's cleavage to the greatest possible advantage. This isn't a terrific rationale for another horror flick but ... it will have to do." (Roger Ebert, *Chicago Sun-Times*, December 13, 1972) ¶"Stephanie Beacham is a delectable potential victim." (Donald J. Mayerson, *Cue*, December 2, 1972) ¶"Should be avoided by all horror fans who expect at least a halfway interesting product for their time and money." (Anitra Earle, *San Francisco Chronicle*, November 3, 1972) ¶"Slow in starting ... but once away builds along the horror lines expected ... Gibson's direction is particularly effective in maintaining mood and spirit." (Whit., *Variety*, October 25, 1972, p. 22) ¶"What a wonderful try! ... Despite the rock music, the plot is at least interesting, pitting Scotland Yard against the supernatural. Van Helsing's explanations are priceless! ... Don't expect brilliance, but do expect plenty of fang." (*Vampire Quarterly*, February 1986, p. 20)

Analysis: The final battle between Van Helsing and Dracula is mighty good, covering downstairs, upstairs, and outside. Some dialogue is virtually straight from Stoker's novel, in which the vampire says "And so you, like the others, would play your brains against mine.... Whilst they played wits against me — against me who commanded nations." One wonders why this film has received generally unfavorable reviews by aficionados. Although we believe that the best settings for horror films are nineteenth-century England or twentieth-century New England, we cannot condemn Hammer for trying something different. During first-run theatrical release a three-minute film featured an actor dressed as Dracula who urged the audience to join the Dracula Society.

The Satanic Rites of Dracula
(Hammer/Dynamite, 1973; 88 min.)
**1/2

Produced by Roy Skeggs. Directed by Alan Gibson. Screenplay, Don Houghton. Edited by Chris Barnes. Director of Photography, Brian Probyn. Technicolor. Music, John Cacavas.

Musical Supervision, Philip Martell. Art Direction, Lionel Couch.

Cast: Professor Lorimer Van Helsing (Peter Cushing), Count Dracula (Christopher Lee), Inspector Murray (Michael Coles), Jessica Van Helsing (Joanna Lumley), Torrence (William Franklyn), Professor Julian Keeley (Freddie Jones), Mathews (Richard Vernon), Lord Carradine (Patrick Barr), Porter (Richard Mathews), Chin Yang (Barbara Yu Ling), Freeborne (Lockwood West), Jane (Valerie Van Ost), Doctor (Peter Adair), Hanson (Maurice O'Connell), Mod C (Marc Zuber), Vampire girls (Maggie Fitzgerald, Mia Martin, Pauline Heart, Finnuala O'Shannon).

Synopsis: In modern England, a government organization investigates the pagan cult at Pelham House on Croxton Heath. Why? An operative escaped with some pictures showing important personages involved in what appeared to be human sacrifice. Murray of Scotland Yard is called in, and Professor Helsing is asked for his advice. He provides background on rituals and visits one of the men involved, an old school chum, the biologist Keeley. The nervous Keeley reveals that some culture dishes contain a new strain of plague — bacilli exposed to radiation. Van Helsing wonders what pleasure Count Dracula would derive from a world without people and theorizes that the vampire wants to take everyone with him in some sort of Götterdämerung. A man from Croxton Heath wounds Van Helsing, who comes to and finds Keeley hanging from the ceiling. Meanwhile Dracula has captured Jane, who works at Scotland Yard. Inspector Murray visits Pelham House, finds Jane vampirized and kills her. He escapes along with Jessica Van Helsing, who'd also been mucking about. Van Helsing says his family has fought vampires for centuries. He realizes that Dracula, whom he'd disposed of two years ago in the churchyard of St. Bartolph's Church, is back, perhaps in the building on that spot — the Denham Group of Companies. He knows that the 23rd of the month is coming and a great sabbat will be held. While reconnoitering Pelham House again, Murray and Jessica are captured. Van Helsing is caught after finding Dracula in the Denham building, and he is taken to Pelham House. Dracula's minions protest his plans to use the bacilli. A tube breaks in one man's hand and he goes into convulsions. Murray, who started a fire, gets Jessica away, and Van Helsing is followed into the woods by Dracula. Realizing that there are hawthorn bushes about, Van Helsing waits behind one, drawing Dracula to him. Caught, Dracula falls, and Van Helsing drives a fence stake into his heart. The vampire disintegrates.

Review: "Christopher Lee is … now surrounded by a cheap devil cult and is allowed to speak — an insipid device which destroys the mystique Lee established in earlier films." (John Stanley, *The Creature Features Movie Guide*, p. 44)

Analysis: Michael Coles again plays Inspector Murray. Van Helsing's granddaughter Jessica is no longer Stephanie Beacham but Joanna Lumley. Again, this is a quite acceptable entry undeservedly panned by many genre fans. Did they see it when it came out? Aka *Count Dracula and His Vampire Bride.*

The Legend of the 7 Golden Vampires

(Hammer/ Shaw Bros./Warner Bros., 1973; 110 min.) ✦✦✦

Produced by Don Houghton and Vee King Shaw. Directed by Roy Ward Baker. Screenplay, Don Houghton. Edited by Chris Barnes. Director of Photography, John Wilcox and Roy Ford. Music, James Bernard. Musical Supervision, Philip Martell. Special Effects, Les Bowie.

Cast: Dr. Van Helsing (Peter Cushing), Vannessa Buren (Julie Ege), Count Dracula (John Forbes-Robertson), Hsi Ching (David Chiang), Leyland Van Helsing (Robin Stewart), Mai Kwei (Shih Szu), Kah (Chan Shen), British Consul (Robert Hanna).

Synopsis: Transylvania, 1804: Kah arrives at Dracula's castle and begs its owner to restore his own power over the seven golden vampires of China. But Dracula takes Kah's form and himself journeys to the East. A century later, Dr. Van Helsing lectures to faculty at Chungking University. They reject his theories of vampirism. But Hsi Ching knows them to be true; his grandfather had killed one of the golden vampires. He asks Van Helsing to accompany him and his brothers to their ancestral village deep in the interior. With his assistance, they know they can defeat the seven golden vampires. The widow Vanessa Buren agrees to finance the expedition as long as they take her along. Not long after setting out, they are ambushed by men loyal to the Chinese man spurned by Van Helsing's son Leyland and Vanessa. Hsi, his sister Mai and their brothers prove their martial arts skill and annihilate their attackers. Continuing on, they approach their destination, and Van Helsing feels their arrival is foreseen. In a cave three bats become golden vampires and attack the party but are destroyed. Van Helsing expresses his confidence they will succeed. At the village, they prepare traps for the nighttime confrontation they expect. The three remaining vampires ride upon the village, leading their undead minions. Three of the brothers are killed while two of the vampires meet their doom. Vanessa is bitten and must be destroyed. The remaining vampire kidnaps Mai and takes her on horseback to the temple. Leyland rides after them, followed by Van Helsing and Hsi. The vampire is dispatched, but when only Van Helsing remains, Kah appears and shows himself as Dracula. In the fight, Van Helsing impales his nemesis once again.

Reviews: "One of the best martial arts movies ever filmed.... James Bernard's score is a real pulse-pounder and makes the film's already fast pace seem even brisker." ("Hallenbeck's Guilty Pleasures," p. 16) ¶"Pretty unique." (Phantom of the Movies, *The Phantom's Ultimate Video Guide*, p. 198) ¶"Whenever fight scenes are called for, there's always pop mayhem in kung fu battles and other unorthodox Chinese martial arts techniques." (Cano., *Variety*, June 4, 1975, p. 19.)

Analysis: Shades of *The Magnificent Seven!* The people who dislike this film probably don't like the concept, but they have a better argument complaining about the absence of Christopher Lee, who that year declared his intention of never playing Dracula again. "I'm increasingly disenchanted with the way he has been presented," Lee told a *Variety* reporter. "Bram Stoker's book has never been done in its entirety on the screen. They write stories into which they fit the character, and that simply doesn't work." (Peter Besas, "Surface Has Only Been Scratched in 'Fantastic' Film Field: Chris Lee," *Variety*, July 4, 1973, p. 33) All the same, we agree with Michael *The Psychotronic Encyclopedia of Film* Weldon, who called *The Legend of the 7 Golden Vampires* "better than any of the last Hammer Dracula movies and an exciting martial-arts adventure." Some of the fight scenes could be trimmed; the villains take too long to be killed. The main *Horror of Dracula* theme is used and is complemented by excellent new James Bernard music. Julie Ege had been in Hammer's *Creatures the World Forgot*. Aka *The Seven Brothers Meet Dracula*.

The Hammer films mostly seem to come down, in the end, to Dracula's being impaled in some manner, with a stake of some sort through his heart. This ending is most bothersome with *The Legend of the 7 Golden Vampires*, in which Van Helsing, after listening to the vampire's usual climactic teeth-clenched epithet, simply impales his ancient fiend—for the umpteenth time—and watches him wither away yet again.

It would have been intriguing to see the Christopher Lee Dracula turn up in a futuristic setting, maybe even on another planet (say a lunar or Mars colony). How would Drac get along in deep space, do you suppose? Would he be confined to a coffin of his native soil if he were so far from the sun that it was just another star in the firmament? Maybe he could migrate to a planet that had one hemisphere in perpetual darkness where he could reign supreme forever. Conversely, such a planet would hardly be likely to evolve any kind of human(oid) life that could sustain the vampire, so it's a moot point. Just speculation.

Son of Dracula

(Cinemation, 1974; 90 min.) nv

Produced by Ringo Starr. Directed by Freddie Francis. Screenplay, Jay Fairbanks. Director of Photography, Norman Warwick. Music, Harry Nilsson.

Cast: Count Down (Harry Nilsson), Merlin (Ringo Starr), Van Helsing (Dennis Price),

Count Frankenstein (Freddie Jones), Girl (Susanna Leigh), Amber (Rosanna Lee). With Peter Frampton, Keith Moon, Skip Martin, John Bonham.

Synopsis: Frankenstein kills Count Dracula, but the vampire's son, Count Down, escapes and is raised by Van Helsing. Grown, Count Down uses Merlin's help to track down his father's murderer.

Review: "Horror-comedy flop." (Michael Weldon, *The Psychotronic Encyclopedia of Film*, p. 645)

Analysis: U.K. Aka *Count Down — Son of Dracula*, and *Young Dracula*.

Old Dracula
(AIP, 1975; 89 min.) nv

Produced by Jack H. Wiener. Directed by Clive Donner. Screenplay, Jeremy Lloyd. Edited by Bill Butler. Director of Photography, Tony Richmond. Movielab Color. Music, David Whitaker. Theme Song "Vampira," Anthony Newley. Music Performed by the Majestics. Song "When You Look for a Dream" composed and performed by John and Rosalind. Art Direction, Philip Harrison.

Cast: Count Dracula (David Niven), Vampira (Teresa Graves), Maltravers (Peter Bayliss), Marc (Nicky Henson), Angela (Jennie Linden), Helga (Linda Hayden), Ritva (Veronica Carlson), Pottinger (Bernard Bresslaw), Gilmore (Freddie Jones), Hotel room couple (Patrick Newell, Aimi MacDonald), Playboy bunnies (Penny Irving, Nicola Austine, Hoima McDonald), Rose (Minah Bird), Eve (Andrea Allan), Mr. King (Frank Thornton), Milton (Christopher Sandford), Nancy (Cathy Shirriff).

Synopsis: Too feeble to go far abroad, Dracula turns his castle into a resort in order to attract victims. *Playboy* magazine rents the castle for a photo shoot. As the bunnies sleep, Dracula "examines" them for the blood type he needs to revive his mate. He gives his dead wife, Countess Vampira, a blood transfusion, and she lives again — but as a lovely black woman. Dracula follows the bunnies to London to try to find an antidote for the darkness which is becoming his shade as well.

Review: "Graceful use of the moving camera, expressive comic timing, and skeptical sexual attitude make the film watchable." (Mack., *Variety*, November 12, 1975, p. 24)

Analysis: Note the people who've been in previous Dracula films: Veronica Carlson, Linda Hayden. Penny Irving was a former model, the star of *House of Whipcord* and a regular on British TV's *Are You Being Served? Variety* found Niven's performance "stylish" but the plot "inane." U.K. title *Vampira*. U.S. release 1975.

Love at First Bite
(AIP, 1979; 96 min.) ***

Produced by Joel Freeman. Executive Producers, Robert Kaufman, George Hamilton. Directed by Stan Dragoti. Screenplay, Robert Kaufman. Story, Robert Kaufman and Mark Gindes. Edited by Allan Jacobs and Mort Fallick. Director of Photography, Edward Rosson. Panavision. CFI Color. Music, Charles Bernstein. Song "I Love the Nightlife" performed by Alicia Bridges. Set Decoration, Ethel Richards. Choreography, Alex Romero. Makeup, William Tuttle.

Cast: Count Dracula (George Hamilton), Cindy Sondheim (Susan St. James), Dr. Jeff Rosenberg (Richard Benjamin), Renfield (Arte Johnson), Lt. Ferguson (Dick Shawn), Judge (Isabel Sanford), Reverend Mike (Sherman Hemsley), Russell (Eric Laneuville), Flashlight vendor (Barry Gordon), Mobster (Michael Pataki), Gay man in elevator (Ronnie Schell), TV repairman (Bob Basso), Priest (Bryan O'Byrne), Lady in elevator (Beverly Sanders), Desk clerk (Basil Hoffman), Cab driver (Stanley Brock), Billy (Danny Dayton), W. V. Man (Robert Ellenstein), Customs inspector (David Ketchum), Woman in subway (Arlene Golonka).

Synopsis: When he is informed by the government that he must leave or share his castle with young athletes, Count Dracula uses the opportunity to seek out Cindy Sondheim, a fashion model and cover girl he believes is his true love. With servant Renfield, Dracula travels to New York's Plaza Hotel. He locates Cindy at a fashion shoot and, at a disco, professes his love. At her apartment he bites her for the first time. When Cindy's psychiatrist, Jeffrey Rosenberg, learns of this, he recalls that his grandfather was Fritz Von Helsing — Dracula's nemesis. He also remembers that if a vampire bites a victim three times, that victim will become an undead. He confronts Dracula and attempts to destroy him but fails and is locked up as a madman.

Finally convincing Lt. Ferguson that there is a vampire in the city, they pursue Dracula and Cindy to the airport but fail to prevent their flight — as bats.

Reviews: "A coarse, delightful little movie.... contains both good jokes and awful jokes but is never slow." (*New York Times*, April 13, 1979, p. C10) ¶ "A flatness about Stan Dragoti's direction ... prevents the film from realizing all its comic potential. But the performances are uniformly jolly ... and [the] social commentary deliciously off the wall." (Richard Schickel, *Time*, May 14, 1979, p. 76)

Analysis: "Children of the night, shut up!" are Hamilton's first words in this sparkling spoof. Each viewer will have his or her favorite scene: the black church where Dracula emerges from the coffin, the hypnosis duel between Hamilton and Benjamin, Dracula's revelation that only three women had nervous breakdowns in the fourteenth century. Hamilton went the spoof route again in the underrated *Zorro, The Gay Blade*. Benjamin is excellent as the butt of several hilarious jabs at psychiatry. Arte Johnson's Renfield has his predecessor Dwight Frye's maniacal laugh down pat.

Dracula
(Universal, 1979; 109 min.) ***

Produced by Walter Mirisch. Directed by John Badham. Screenplay, W. D. Richter. Based on the play by Hamilton Deane and John L. Balderston from Bram Stoker's novel. Edited by John Bloom. Director of Photography, Gilbert Taylor. Panavision. Technicolor. Music, John Williams. Dolby Stereo. Art Direction, Brian Ackland-Snow.

Cast: Dracula (Frank Langella), Lucy Seward (Kate Nelligan), Dr. Van Helsing (Laurence Olivier), Dr. Seward (Donald Pleasence), Jonathan Harker (Trevor Eve), Mina Van Helsing (Jan Francis), Renfield (Tony Haygarth), Annie (Janine Duvitski), Swales (Teddy Turner), Scarborough sailor (Ted Carroll), Mrs. Galloway (Kristine Howarth), Tom Hindley (Joe Belcher), Harbormaster (Frank Birch), Priest (Peter Wallis), Demeter Captain (Gabor Vernon), Demeter sailor (Frank Henson).

Synopsis: During a raging storm, sailors unsuccessfully attempt to toss a crate overboard. A hairy arm emerges and grabs a crew member. When the vessel is shipwrecked at Whitby, England, near Dr. Seward's sanitarium, the visiting Mina rushes to the shore. Following what appears to be a large dog or wolf into a cave, she instead finds a man, Count Dracula. The Romanian nobleman is the only survivor of the wreck. He was bound for nearby Carfax Abbey. While hauling Dracula's crates into the abbey, Renfield is attacked by a large bat. Dracula has dinner at Dr. Seward's, where he indicates a desire to revel in London's humanity. When Mina swoons, Dracula assists, but later, he enters her bedroom. Lucy Seward doesn't notice Mina's pale complexion till next morning. Mina begins choking, and Dr. Seward can do nothing to prevent her demise. Seward sends a cable to her father, the esteemed Dr. Van Helsing. Meanwhile, solicitor Jonathan Harker takes Dracula his key and the original deed. Driving away, Harker is beset by Renfield, who demands help. He's admitted to the sanitarium. After Mina's funeral, Lucy dines at Carfax, where, through gentle kisses, her host makes his interests known. Lucy is not averse to his attentions. While this transpires, a train arrives with Van Helsing. At the sanitarium, the baby of an inmate is murdered. The mother says Mina Van Helsing did it. Van Helsing finds puncture marks on the child. After reading about vampirism, Van Helsing and Seward examine Mina's grave. There is no body, but there is a hole leading into the mines beneath Whitby. While Van Helsing journeys thither, Lucy is visited by Dracula, who binds her to him by forcing her to drink his blood. Underground, Van Helsing meets his living dead daughter. She attacks him, but Seward discomfits her with a crucifix and her father impales her. Back inside, they find Jonathan concerned about Lucy's comatose state. A blood transfusion is in order. After removing Mina's heart — the only way to keep her dead — Van Helsing is visited by Dracula. In short order he realizes the man is an undead but manages to ward him off with garlic. Lucy tries to go to Carfax, but Jonathan, Van Helsing and her father prevent her. At Carfax, Jonathan and Van Helsing meet Dracula, who locks them in

Frank Langella essays the famous count in *Dracula* (Universal, 1979).

a room and, as a bat, attacks Jonathan. Van Helsing causes a beam to fall, letting sunlight into the room and causing the bat to catch fire briefly and fly off. Nevertheless, Dracula kills Renfield in the sanitarium and takes Lucy from the cell where it was thought best to keep her. They are pursued to the coast and onto a ship bound for the Continent. Below decks, Jonathan and Van Helsing have another go at Dracula, who impales his nemesis and endeavors to strangle Jonathan. But the dying Van Helsing manages to shove a hook into the monster's back. Jonathan starts the winch that pulls Dracula through the deck and to the mast, where the sun destroys him. Or does it? A half-smile crosses Lucy's face as she watches his cape flap away.

Reviews: "Howling dog of a movie ... is often incoherent.... cheesy on a grand scale." (David Denby, *New York*, July 30, 1979, p. 61) ¶"It is as if someone decreed that this was to be a *Dracula* for adults, forgetting that the story has always been for

adults regressing to adolescence." (Richard Schickel, *Time*, July 23, 1979, p. 80) ¶"Puts the male vamp back in vampire.... More humanly seductive, [Langella is] terrific with the ladies." (*Variety*)

Analysis: Upon viewing this during its initial 1979 release, we were disappointed. A more recent viewing causes us to revise our opinion upward. Our initial negative reaction was obviously prompted by the disconcerting character switch: Lucy is normally the main female victim. In this instance it's Mina, who's now a Van Helsing! Chalk these distressing events up to the stage-play basis. One supposes they wanted to play against type, but Donald Pleasence should have played Renfield, not the doctor. What are we to make of the fact that he's constantly eating? Female audience members are — not surprisingly — taken by suave, handsome Frank Langella. And males have the under appreciated Kate Nelligan, whom *Time*'s critic called "superbly spirited." Langella's vampire does get to scale a wall from the top down, which is a scene in the novel (although it takes place in Transylvania there; Chris Lee climbed down a wall in *Scars of Dracula*). The movie is opulent, and Carfax Abbey is visually outstanding.

Dracula's Widow
(De Laurentiis Entertainment Group/HBO Home Video, 1988; 92 min.) **

Produced by Stephen Traxler. Directed by Christopher Coppola. Screenplay, Kathryn Ann Thomas and Tom Bloomquist. Edited by Tom Siter. Director of Photography, Giuseppe Macari. Technicolor. Music, James Campbell. Ultra-Stereo. Special Effects, Joe Quinlivan and Tex X. Special Effects created by Sirius Effects. Special Makeup, Dean Gates.

Cast: Vanessa (Sylvia Kristel), Lt. Hap Lannon (Josef Sommer), Raymond Everett (Lenny Von Dohlen), Helsing (Stefan Schnabel), Brad (Marc Coppola), Jenny Harker (Rachel Jones), Bart (Duke Ernsberger), Victim (Candice Sims).

Synopsis: Crates begin arriving at Raymond Everett's Hollywood House of Wax. That evening, a striking woman picks up a man at the Blue Angel Club and savagely kills him as well as a thief breaking into the museum. She informs Raymond that he will do her bidding, which includes transporting her back to her husband in Romania. He says her husband, Dracula, died. Who killed him? Van Helsing, he answers. An old man reads a book indicating that Dracula's wife, Vanessa, survived him. She's a changeling, a feaster on flesh. Each evening Vanessa kills again, on one occasion annihilating a coven of would-be devil worshippers. Lt. Hap Lannon, investigating the series of grisly murders, interviews Raymond, who feigns ignorance. Helsing, the man who read the ancient tome on vampires — and the grandson of the Van Helsing who put an end to Dracula — tells the detective a vampire is the culprit. Lannon begins to believe when a stake hammered into a corpse causes the apparently dead person to cry out in anguish. Raymond gives his girlfriend, Jenny, a cross to wear. Angry, Vanessa sucks more of Raymond's blood and turns Van Helsing into an undead who must be killed by Lannon.

Raymond is arrested and questioned. Vanessa comes for him. He escapes, but as a bat she flies after him and kills his guards. In female form, she unsuccessfully attempts to ward off Lannon's stake.

Review: Here's another film that never gets a proper, i.e., analytical, review. It gets two stars from Mick Martin and Marsha Porter in *Video Movie Guide 1994* p. 808).

Analysis: There's a fairly novel plot. It's gruesome and slightly tongue-in-cheek. The fact that Dracula's wife doesn't get out of her coffin until modern-day Los Angeles suggests that she's been in transit for a hundred years! Dutch-born Sylvia Kristel may be a cult star on the strength of her appearances in the earlier soft core *Emmanuelle* movies and such exploitation films as the Linda Blair *Red Heat*. In *Dracula's Widow* she goes in for Max *Nosferatu* Schreck hand gestures.

The Monster Squad
(Tri-Star/Taft Entertainment Pictures, 1988; 81 min.) **½

Analysis: This Parade-of-Monsters entry features Dracula, Frankenstein's monster, Wolf Man, the Gill Man, and the Mummy! See listing under *Frankenstein* for cast, credits, and discussion.

Bram Stoker's Dracula
(Columbia, 1992) ***½

Produced by Francis Ford Coppola, Fred Fuchs and Charles Mulvehill. Co-Producer, James V. Hart. Directed by Francis Ford Coppola. Screenplay, James V. Hart. Based on the novel *Dracula* by Bram Stoker. Edited by Nicholas C. Smith, Glen Scantlebury, Anne Goursaud. Director of Photography, Michael Ballhaus. Technicolor. Music, Wojciech Kilar. "Love Song for a Vampire" written and performed by Annie Lennox. Dolby Stereo. Art Direction, Andrew Precht. Set Decoration, Garrett Lewis. Costumes, Eiko Ishioka. Special Makeup Effects, Greg Cannom. Special Effects, Roman Coppola and Wojciech Kilar. Special Visual Effects, Fantasy II Film Effects. Additional Visual Effects, VCE Inc./Pete Kuran, Kevin O'Neill. Movement for the Brides, Michael Smuin. Project Conceptualist, Jim Steranko.

Cast: Count Dracula (Gary Oldman), Wilhelmina Murray (Winona Ryder), Lucy

Westerna (Sadie Frost), Van Helsing (Anthony Hopkins), Dr. Seward (Richard E. Grant), Jonathan Harker (Keanu Reeves), Holmwood (Cary Elwes), Renfield (Tom Waits), Quincy (Bill Campbell), Brides (Monica Bellucci, Michaela Bercu, Florina Kendrick), Mr. Hawkins (Jay Robinson), Hobbs (I. M. Hobson).

Synopsis: In the mid-fifteenth century the Turks capture Constantinople and forge their way north through the Balkans. One of the Christian princes who stands against them is the Transylvanian Dracula. He is victorious on the battlefield and impales the defeated, but a Turkish saying that he has been killed causes his bride to throw herself from the parapets of his castle. Told that her soul is damned, Dracula rages and thrusts his sword into the chapel cross, which gushes blood. In the waning years of the nineteenth century, solicitor's agent Renfield inhabits a lunatic asylum after having returned from Transylvania. Next to be sent to the castle of Count Dracula is Jonathan Harker, his coach traveling through a shield of blue flames to a rotting castle on a forbidding crag. An aged nobleman — Count Dracula — asks him to write letters home saying he will stay a month to help his client with English manners and language. Dracula notes the photograph of Mina Murray, Harker's betrothed. She seems much like his dead bride! Harker witnesses strange sights during his stay, such as his host climbing the castle wall — going down head first. Back in England, Mina and her vivacious, flirtatious friend Lucy discuss Jonathan and Lucy's various suitors, including Holmwood, the Texan Quincy, and Dr. Seward. At Castle Dracula, Harker is drawn to a room wherein he is accosted by three lovely ladies. Dracula appears and throws them aside, giving them a baby instead to quench their bloodlust. Later Harker observes Dracula's gypsy minions shoveling dirt into crates before the count leaves for England. His ship, the *Demeter*, runs aground on the English coast, its crew dead. In London, now a youthful-looking gallant, Dracula finds Mina, who at first reluctantly gives this strange but intriguing foreigner a tour. By night Lucy is visited by Dracula as werewolf. Mina sees them copulating in the garden maze. Lucy falls ill. Dr. Seward calls in his mentor, Van Helsing, who comes to realize that he has the chance to battle a demon from hell, a vampyre, nosferatu — the undead. Harker finally escapes the brides of Dracula, and Mina speeds to marry him. Dracula knows and ravages Lucy. Van Helsing, called in by Seward, convinces his former pupil and Lucy's fiancé, Holmwood, that Lucy is undead. Investigating her tomb, they find it empty. But she returns with a child. Holmwood is convinced he must pound home the stake through her heart. Van Helsing decapitates her to induce final peace. Returned to London, Mina is once more accosted by Dracula, who almost against his will induces her to taste of his blood so she can become one with him. Van Helsing destroys his boxes of earth, and Dracula kills Renfield before taking ship for his homeland. Van Helsing, Quincy, Holmwood, Harker, Mina and Seward pursue overland. They fail to find Dracula as expected at the Black Sea port of Varna. Heading north, they chase his carriage to the castle where Van Helsing and Mina have preceded them. Quincy is killed by a gypsy, but Dracula, risen from his crate as the sun sinks, receives a throat wound and is stabbed in the heart. He takes Mina into the castle, where he calls upon her to put him to rest. She presses the knife home and decapitates him so both can be freed from the satanic spell.

Reviews: "To the director, the count is a restless spirit who has been condemned for too many years to internment in cruddy movies. This luscious film restores the creature's nobility and gives him peace." (Richard Corliss, *Time*, November 23, 1992, p. 71) ¶"Deliriously imaginative piece of work.... The movie's overall Victorian point of view and weird erotic fancies really belong to its women." (Julie Salamon, *Wall Street Journal*, November 12, 1992, p. A12) ¶"Not the least bit frightening. Despite buckets of blood, it's not even horrifying.... Coppola takes a new tack with Drac — he makes him a tragic figure in a centuries-old romance.... a unique and artful entry in the crowded vampire movie catalog." (Jack Garner, *Wilmington*

News Journal 55 Hours, November 13-15, 1992, p. 7)

Analysis: This is probably as close as we're likely to get to an epic treatment of Stoker's undying character. Just about every element of the novel is put into one film. In the final analysis, though, it's evident that this Dracula *really* doesn't offer very much more than its predecessors. After all, we've seen his pale brides feast on the innocent; we've seen their dark lord slither up and down walls and trot lupine through the countryside. Sure, the hothouse eroticism is emphasized in Coppola's film, but hardly any more than in Hammer's later efforts or in a host of independent productions, even back to Universal's in the 1930s. There are, however, many fine moments: the *Demeter,* crewless, forging toward the coast; the Count's brides rising from the sheets; the spooky shadows cast by Dracula. Hopkins is an excellent choice as Van Helsing. Cary Elwes (*The Princess Bride*) is always agreeable in a period piece, but he and the other suitors should have been fleshed out. They never really emerge as separate characters or assume any real identity. Suffice it to say that Gary Oldman will never be identified with this role, and Winona Ryder? We guess she's as appropriate for the role of Mina Harker as Mary Elizabeth Mastrantonio was for that of Maid Marian. Certainly no less. Yet Bram Stoker's Count didn't leave Transylvania for a reincarnated love, and why would this one leave the voluptuous brides for an innocent Briton? This centuries-old romance angle is a bit much — and not in the book. Was this "Love Never Dies" theme done in part to attract a female audience? Winona Ryder is too young, too immature and not radiant enough to make this Mina memorable. We presume she got the part because she was the driving force behind this project and interested Coppola in Jim Hart's script. Is Keanu Reeves a Ryder crony? He is really miscast. Wouldn't it have been nice to have some veterans of other Dracula movies play the brides? How about Veronica Carlson, Caroline Munro, Ingrid Pitt? How come there was no ruckus raised over the "Love Song for a Vampire" sung by Annie Lennox over the end titles? Recall the stink critics made over "Strange Love" in *Lust for a Vampire.* Academy Awards for Costumes, Sound Effects Editing, Makeup.

Notes of Interest: Once you've read Bram Stoker's 1897 novel *Dracula,* you are hard-pressed to give an unqualified four-star rating to any of the film versions — not Bela Lugosi's, Christopher Lee's or even director Francis Ford Coppola's. Either the makers can't afford epic treatment — and the 400-page novel *is* epic — or, as in Coppola's case, the screenplay distorts the Transylvanian Count's character. (He is *not* a swain seeking a reincarnated princess.)

A little cinematic history: *Nosferatu* was a silent (1922) German version with Max Schreck in makeup never surpassed for horror. (Germany's Werner Herzog remade it in 1978 with Klaus Kinski.) In Monogram's 1941 film *Spooks Run Wild* Bela Lugosi plays a magician who masquerades as Dracula. In MGM's *Mark of the Vampire* (1935) Bela pretends to be a Dracula-like vampire. In 1943's *Return of the Vampire* for Columbia he's Armand Tesla, a Dracula figure in World War II London. Not all of Christopher Lee's impersonations took place in English-language films; see Italy's *Uncle Was a Vampire* (1959). In 1967 Ferdy [later Ferdinand] Mayne played a Dracula clone in Roman Polanski's *The Fearless Vampire Killers.* Paul Morrissey directed *Andy Warhol's Dracula* (a.k.a. *Blood for Dracula,* 1974), an Italian-French co-production with Udo Kier as the Count and Roman Polanski as a villager. *Dracula Sucks* was a 1979 porno film. On television, Jack Palance starred in a 1974 TV movie directed by Dan Curtis. Louis Jourdan was the Count in the excellent 1978 British mini-series shown on American public TV's "Great Performances."

Countess Dracula (1972)sounds like a Dracula spin-off, but it's not; in that film, Ingrid Pitt played the real-life noblewoman Elisabeth Bathory. *Lemora: A Child's Tale of the Supernatural* (1973) is sometimes titled *Lady Dracula,* but title character Lesley Gilb never says she is related to the Transylvanian noble. *Blood of Dracula*

(1957) had nothing whatsoever to do with the count or his blood; it was one of AIP's teen-monster flicks.

There are some films that feature Count Dracula's relatives and pets. A few we've not been able to find. These include *The House of Dracula's Daughter* (First Leisure/ Ellman Enterprises, 1972), *Dracula's Dog*, Crown, 1977), and *Nocturna, Granddaughter of Dracula* (Compass International, 1979).

Dracula, Prince of Darkness *see under* **Dracula**

Dracula A.D. 1972 *see under* **Dracula**

Dracula Has Risen from the Grave *see under* **Dracula**

Dracula — The Love Story *see* **To Die For**

Dracula's Daughter *see under* **Dracula**

Dracula's Widow *see under* **Dracula**

The Dream Child *see* A Nightmare on Elm Street: The Dream Child *under* **A Nightmare on Elm Street**

The Dream Master *see* A Nightmare on Elm Street 4: The Dream Master *under* **A Nightmare on Elm Street**

Dream Warriors *see* A Nightmare on Elm Street 3: Dream Warriors *under* **A Nightmare on Elm Street**

The Empire Strikes Back *see under* **Star Wars**

Enemy from Space *see* Quatermass II *under* **The Quatermass Xperiment**

Escape from the Planet of the Apes *see under* **Planet of the Apes**

Escape to Witch Mountain
(Buena Vista, 1975; 97 min.) ***

Produced by Jerome Courtland. Executive Producer, Ron Miller. Directed by John Hough. Assistant Directors, Fred Brost, Jerry

Ballew. Screenplay, Robert Malcolm Young. Based on the book by Alexander Key. Edited by Robert Stafford. Director of Photography, Frank Phillips. Technicolor. Music, Johnny Mandel. Art Direction, John B. Mansbridge, Al Roelofs. Costumes, Chuck Keehne, Emily Sundby.

Cast: Tia (Kim Richards), Tony (Ike Eisenmann), Jason O'Day (Eddie Albert), Aristotle Bolt (Ray Milland), Deranian (Donald Pleasence), Sheriff Purdy (Walter Barnes), Mrs. Grindley (Reta Shaw), Uncle Bene (Denver Pyle), Astrologer (Alfred Ryder), Ubermann (Lawrence Montaigne), Biff Jenkins (Terry Wilson), Grocer (George Chandler), Truck (Dermott Downs), Guru (Shepherd Sanders), Gasoline attendant (Don Brodie), Sergeant Foss (Paul Sorenson), Policeman #3 (Alfred Rossi), Lorko (Tiger Joe Marsh), Captain Malone (Harry Holcombe), Mate (Sam Edwards), Psychic (Dan Seymour), Deputy (Al Dunlap), Cort (Eugene Daniels), Hunters (Rex Holman, Tony Giorgio).

Synopsis: Their foster parents — the Malones — dead, Tia and Tony find themselves at the Pine Woods Child Welfare Development center. During a trip to town to see the movie *Snow White and the Seven Dwarfs*, they foresee an accident and warn a man across the street. That man, Deranian, realizes that these children have a gift — a gift his employer, millionaire Alexander Bolt, is seeking. Forging documents that indicate he is the children's Uncle Lucas, Deranian takes them to live at the Bolt coastal estate, Xanthus. They have all they could desire, but Tia frequently recalls bits from their past, especially a sea wreck and Uncle Bene. Tony thinks they can find the answer when they figure out the map on Tia's star case purse. Hearing that they are about to be taken to Bolt's chateau, Tia and Tony use the cat Winkie and horse Thunderhead to escape. Hiding in the Winnebago camper of Jason O'Day, they convince him to take them to Stony Creek. Although Deranian and the police track them, Tia and Tony manage to escape the former, only to be incarcerated by the sheriff until Tony employs his telepathic and harmonic powers to bewilder him. Finding Jason, they drive to the mysteriously unpeopled Stony Creek Misty Valley Cooperative. Tia and Tony hear a voice with a plan to discourage their pursuers.

The Winnebago flies into the air over Deranian's car and Bolt's helicopter is turned upside down. Landing, Jason, Tia and Tony are greeted by Uncle Bene, who takes the children into a flying saucer. 'Tis proof that they came from not another place, but another world.

Review: "Mildly ingenious story frittered away by poor scripting and special effects. A stimulating change in children's films, however." (Leslie Halliwell, *Halliwell's Film Guide*, p. 321)

Analysis: Richards and Eisenmann are engaging. Pleasence and Milland, ostensible villains, have gray shadings. You'll howl with laughter when the broom, coat and hat team up to terrorize the sheriff.

Return from Witch Mountain
(Buena Vista, 1978; 93 min.) ***

Produced by Ron Miller, Jerome Courtland. Associate Producer, Kevin Corcoran. Directed by John Hough. Screenplay, Malcolm Marmorstein. Based on characters created by Alexander Key. Edited by Bob Bring. Director of Photography, Frank Phillips. Technicolor. Music, Lalo Schifrin. Art Direction, John B. Mansbridge, Jack Senter.

Cast: Tia (Kim Richards), Tony (Ike Eisenmann), Letha Wedge (Bette Davis), Victor Gannon (Christopher Lee), Mr. Yokomoto (Jack Soo), Dazzler (Christian Juttner), Eddie (Dick Bakalyan), Uncle Bene (Denver Pyle), Crusher (Poindexter), Sickle (Anthony James), Mr. Clearcole (Ward Costello), Muscles (Brad Savage), Rocky (Jeffrey Jacquet).

Synopsis: A flying saucer leaves the mountains and lands in Pasadena's empty Rose Bowl. Uncle Bene gives Tia and Tony instructions for their visit. While being driven into town in a taxi, Tony foresees an accident. He leaves the cab and uses his energization capabilities to save Sickle, who'd fallen from a building after the mind control device of Victor Gannon was broken. Gannon and his sister Letha kidnap Tony. Gannon realizes that Tony is capable of "molecular mobilization." While looking for Tony, Tia befriends the youthful members of the "Earthquake Gang," who promise to help her find her brother. Gannon says, "My experiments are more important than the law" to his sister's protestations that they'll go to jail for kidnapping. But if Tony can help them make money, she'll comply with Victor's wishes. Letha and Sickle take Tony to a museum to steal a gold exhibit. Tia finds them there but in the chaos can't rescue Tony. Victor arrives and in a high-speed chase eludes Tia, her friends and Mr. Yokomoto, the truant officer. Gannon agrees to use Tony to make some money. They infiltrate an underground plutonium plant. Tony's powers are used to shut down the furnace room's cooling system. Gannon tells the authorities he wants $5 million. Tia arrives and uses her powers against Gannon and Tony. Finally Gannon's control device is damaged and Tony comes out of his trance. He and Tia capture Gannon, Letha and Sickle. Later they fix Yokomoto's van and bid adieu to the Earthquake Gang, rejoining Uncle Bene and returning to their hinterland home.

Review: "Principals are serviceable, but not nearly as lively as some of their costars...." (Janet Maslin, *New York Times*, July 14, 1978, p. C14) ¶"Basically a chase caper." (Variety)

Analysis: It's logical, perhaps, to move this to an urban setting, but this is a flaw, as it was for the remake of *Invasion of the Body Snatchers* and any number of films. The story could have been better. Nevertheless, it holds the interest and deserves a "good" rating.

The Evil Dead
(New Line Cinema/Renaissance Pictures, 1983; 90 min.) ***

Produced by Robert G. Tapert. Executive Producers, Robert G. Tapert, Bruce Campbell, Samuel M. Raimi. Directed by Samuel M. Raimi. Screenplay, Samuel M. Raimi. Edited by Edna Ruth Paul. Directors of Photography, Tim Philo, Joshua M. Becker. Color. Music, Joe LoDuca. Special Makeup Effects, Tom Sullivan. Photographic Special Effects, Bart Pierce.

Cast: Ash (Bruce Campbell), Cheryl (Ellen Sandweiss), Linda (Betsy Baker), Scott (Hal Delrich), Shelly (Sarah York).

Synopsis: Three women and two men drive south to a secluded Tennessee cabin whose basement contains a tape recorder and an archaic book with drawings of skulls and the like. Listening to the tape, they hear a professor speak about ancient Sumerian rites and demons. Cheryl is disturbed and, thinking something is in the forest, walks out into the night. Vines, roots and tendrils bind her, and she is raped by the forest itself. Escaping to the cabin, she demands that Ash drive her back to town immediately. He can't do so because the bridge has been destroyed. Shortly thereafter, Cheryl changes into a hideous being who attacks Linda and jams a pencil into her ankle. Ash and Scott force Cheryl into the basement. Shelly is attacked when she's alone in another room and returns as a possessed being who must be impaled and her limbs severed. Ash and Scott bury the parts, and Scott attempts to leave on his own but staggers back, injured. Linda, apparently infected by the pencil, becomes a giggling hag whom Ash impales and decapitates. Back in the cabin, he is attacked by the now demonic Scott and by Cheryl, who's broken out of the basement. Ash realizes he can save himself only by throwing the arcane book of demon worship into the fireplace. When he does, the two nemeses cease moving and begin decaying. Morning comes and Ash prepares to leave, but something rushes through the cabin and out the front door at him. He turns and screams.

Review: "Just mechanical mayhem in scene after scene." (David Sterritt, *Christian Science Monitor*, May 5, 1983, p. 16) ¶"Probably the grisliest well-made movie ever." (Kevin Thomas, *Los Angeles Times Calendar*, May 26, 1983, p. 4) ¶"Although the screeching possessees here recall Dario Argento, and their messy, startling fates evoke the dread Lucio Fulci, *The Evil Dead* is more successful than its Italian precursors.... enjoyable, catch-all rollercoaster ride through the splatter genre." (Kim Newman, *Monthly Film Bulletin*, November 1982, p. 264) ¶"While injecting considerable black humor,... Raimi maintains suspense and a nightmarish mood." (*Variety*, February 9, 1983, p. 19) ¶"The movie's palette is richer than you'd expect in a sleazoid horror film." (Elliott Stein, *Village Voice*, May 3, 1983, p. 54)

Analysis: Filmed in Morristown, Tennessee, and Detroit, Michigan, in 16mm,

this cult film apparently got a U.S. distributor after achieving success in England. It's increasingly revolting and keeps you on edge despite characters who break all the rules of common sense. You wouldn't think, in 1983, a director of something other than a *Friday the 13th* film would allow his characters to walk into the threatening nighttime woods, neglect to shutter the window, or fail to stick together. In a 1993 TV interview, Raimi intimated that he would not include the rape scene if he had it to do over again and lamented the special effects that suffered from a low budget. Nevertheless, *Variety* called the camerawork "powerful" for its ability to suggest the presence of evil in the woods. There's one brief topless scene involving the comely Ms. York.

Evil Dead II
(Rosebud Releasing/Renaissance Pictures, 1987; 85 min.) **½

Produced by Robert G. Tapert. Directed by Sam Raimi. Screenplay, Sam Raimi and Scott Spiegel. Edited by Kaye Davis. Director of Photography, Peter Deming. Night Photography, Eugene Shlugleit. Technicolor. Music, Joseph LoDuca. Sound, Tom Morison. Art Direction, Philip Duffin, Randy Bennett. Set Decoration, Elizabeth Moore. Special Makeup, Mark Shostrom. Animated Dance Sequence, Doug Beswick. Choreography, Susan Labatt, Andrea Brown, Tam G. Warner. Special Effects, Vern Hyde, Dale Johnson, Dave Thiry.

Cast: Ash (Bruce Campbell), Annie (Sarah Berry), Jake (Dan Hicks), Bobby Joe (Kassie Wesley), Possessed Henrietta (Theodore Raimi), Linda (Denise Bixler), Ed (Richard Domeier), Professor Knowby (John Peaks), Henrietta (Lou Hancock), Voice (William Preston Robertson).

Synopsis: Ash brings girlfriend Linda to a secluded cabin. He discovers a tape player and listens to a recording made by a scientist who discovered the "Book of the Dead" in a Canda dig. Ash hears a crash and discovers that Linda is missing. She reappears as a hag after his soul. He decapitates her with a shovel but later watches her body regain its head out in the woods. Other spirits are also at work, picking Ash up and hurling him through the forest. His right hand takes on a life of its own and beats and batters him until he cuts it off. Meanwhile, Annie, the scientist's daughter, makes her way to the cabin with a male friend and two locals who carry her trunk and guide the way. She has pages from the ancient Canda book. The other woman is attacked by the woods, and Ash himself turns demonic at night, but by day he regains his composure and equips himself with a shotgun and a chainsaw. The pages from the ancient book having been tossed into the basement, he must recover them by battling a "witch" claiming to be Annie's mother. He retrieves the pages, "kills" the witch, and Annie recites the spell to return the demons to their world. Ash is sucked into the vortex as well and finds himself amongst medieval-looking knights. When he kills a flying demon with his gun, the knights hail him as their leader.

Review: "A flashy good-natured display of special effects and scare tactics so extreme they can only be taken for laughs." (Jagr., *Variety*, March 18, 1987)

Analysis: Tongue securely in cheek and accompanied by better cinematography than its predecessor, *Evil Dead II* deserves a fair to good rating despite some irrational behavior from the main character, Ash. Why would he return to this creepy, deadly cabin? And bring a new girlfriend? Wasn't he set upon by the main Candarian demon at the conclusion of *Evil Dead*? There are funny scenes, e.g., all the punishment Ash takes before coming back swinging, the chainsaw attached to his stump, the novel *A Farewell to Arms*, the footlocker Annie brought with her. This is the kind of film our parents wouldn't, couldn't comprehend. *Dead by Dawn* was not on the print we saw. There was no subtitle.

Army of Darkness
(Universal, 1993; 81 min.) ***½

Produced by Robert Tapert. Directed by Sam Raimi. Screenplay, Sam Raimi and Ivan Raimi. Edited by Bob Murawski and R.O.C. Sanstorm. Director of Photography, Bill Pope. Color, DeLuxe. Music, Joseph LoDuca. Dolby Stereo. Art Direction, Aram Allan. Set Decoration, Michele Poulik. Visual Effects, Introvision International, Inc. Stop-Motion Supervision, Peter Kleinow. Special Makeup Effects, Kurtzman, Nicotero and Berger EFX Group. Swordmaster, Dan Speaker.

Cast: Ash (Bruce Campbell), Sheila (Embeth Davidtz), Blacksmith (Timothy Patrick Quill), Duke Henry (Richard Grove), Possessed witch (Patricia Tallman), Linda (Bridget Fonda).

Synopsis: After being sucked into a vortex in the twentieth-century North American woods, Ash guesses his new time is A.D. 1300. Believed to be a soldier of their enemy Duke Henry, knights take Ash to a castle and thrust him into "the pits." A wise man tosses him his chainsaw, and he defeats the monstrous humanoid within. Climbing out, he intimidates the crowd with the shotgun he calls a "boom stick" and sets Duke Henry free. The wise man tells him that in order to return home, he must retrieve the *Necronomicon*. Before proceeding to the cemetery where that dread book is located, Ash creates an artificial hand for his right stump. Pursued to a windmill by an unseen force and pestered by mini-duplicates of himself, Ash swallows one of the little people. A duplicate, full-sized replica of himself emerges. Ash shoots his double, carves it up, and buries it. At the cemetery he finds not one but three books. One sucks him in, but he pulls himself out. The second bites him. It must be the third he wants, but he can't remember the "N-word" in the incantation he must recite before taking it. He stumbles through "Klaatu birada nikto" and leaves, but because he didn't do it right, skeletons emerge from the ground and the duplicate Ash revives. Demon Ash plans to attack the castle and get the *Necronomicon* back. A flying demon abducts Sheila from the castle courtyard. Using his own knowledge and the chemistry book in the trunk of his car, Ash instructs the knights and inhabitants in techniques of martial arts and twentieth-century warfare. When the castle is besieged, the defenders are ready. With explosive charges affixed to arrows and catapults, they wreak havoc on the army of the dead. His car fixed and modified for destruction, Ash makes mincemeat of the skeletons before crashing. He knocks the possessed Sheila into the foul pit. Duke Henry's forces arrive.

Demon Ash confronts his human counterpart and temporarily acquires the *Necronomicon* but by a catapult is hurled into the sky and explodes. "Let's get outta here!" cries a skeleton. Sheila is restored, but Ash takes his leave, drinking a special potion and properly reciting, "Klaatu birada nikto." Back at S-Mart in Housewares, Ash finishes his tale. He is momentarily interrupted by a witch woman, whom he blows away with a repeating rifle obtained from the sports department.

Review: "Blood-spewing, amputation-happy, sadistic and chaotic.... seems to last three hours." (Ralph Novak, *People Weekly*, March 15, 1993, pp. 17-18)

Analysis: Despite the title, this is a direct sequel to *Evil Dead II*, even though we don't see Ash blowing that flying demon out of the sky to start it off. Nor did Bridget Fonda play Linda in the first film. Such minor inconsistencies aside, this is a helluva film. It mixes all sorts of excellent special effects, moves at a fast clip, and produces a goodly share of chuckles and guffaws. It's a comic book on film. Bruce Campbell finally demonstrates actual acting ability.

The Evil of Frankenstein *see under* **Frankenstein**

The Exorcist
(Warner Bros., 1973; 121 min.) ****

Produced by William Peter Blatty. Directed by William Friedkin. Screenplay, William Peter Blatty. Based on the novel by William Peter Blatty. Edited by Jordan Leondopoulos, Evan Lottman, Norman Gay, Bud Smith. Directors of Photography, Owen Roizman, Billy Williams. Panavision. Metrocolor. Music, Jack Nitzsche. "Tubular Bells" by Mike Oldfield. Set Decoration, Jerry Wunderlich. Makeup, Dick Smith. Special Effects, Marcel Vercoutere.

Cast: Chris MacNeil (Ellen Burstyn), Father Lancaster Merrin (Max Von Sydow), Regan MacNeil (Linda Blair), Father Karras (Jason Miller), Lt. William Kinderman (Lee J. Cobb), Sharon (Kitty Winn), Burke Dennings (Jack MacGowran), Father Dyer (Rev. William O'Malley), Karras's mother (Vasiliki Maliaros), Karras's uncle (Titos Vandis), Bishop (Wallace Rooney), Assistant director (Ron Faber), University president (Rev. T. Bermingham), Voice of demon (Mercedes McCambridge).

Synopsis: In northern Iraq, near the ancient city of Nineveh, Father Merrin unearths the statue of a demon. In the Washington, D.C., suburb of Georgetown, film actress Chris MacNeil rents a home while starring in the movie *Crash Course* for director Burke Dennings. In the house are her twelve-year-old daughter, Regan; housekeeper, Sharon; a cook and the handyman. Nearby is the seminary where Father Damien Karras uses his psychiatry background to help those in need. He himself is distressed by his mother, who won't leave her New York slum neighborhood and who dies in an institution before he can get there. Karras tells Father Dyer he's lost his faith. One morning a priest finds a desecrated statue. At a party at Chris's house, Regan comes downstairs and wets herself in front of the guests. Later Chris is stunned to see Regan's bed shaking. A doctor thinks there is a lesion in Regan's temporal lobe that is causing a seizure disorder, but a brain scan reveals nothing. The doctor visits the increasingly violent Regan, who urges him, "Fuck me!" Sedated, she undergoes another encephalogram. At wit's end, the physicians recommend a psychiatrist. Before that can take place, Dennings is killed on the steps adjacent to the MacNeil home. Police lieutenant Kinderman quizzes Karras on Dennings's death and reveals that the director's head had been turned completely around. Kinderman wonders if Dennings was murdered by the same person who desecrated the statue. Further, he suggests that Karras may know who's to blame. After a psychiatrist fails to help Regan, doctors tell Chris that perhaps an exorcism, a stylized ritual, is in order. The force of suggestion may be combated by same. Over coffee, Kinderman tells Chris he thinks Dennings was killed before being tossed down the steps. After Chris finds Regan masturbating with a crucifix and is knocked to the floor, she realizes she must take drastic action. She finds Father Karras. Regan vomits on the priest and mentions things about his life she couldn't know. During another visit,

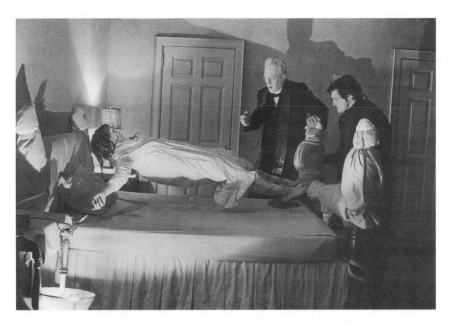

Regan (Linda Blair) is airborne as Father Merrin (Max Von Sydow, center) and Father Karras (Jason Miller) watch in *The Exorcist* (Warner Bros., 1973).

Regan says she killed Dennings. On an audio tape, Karras discovers that the girl spoke English in reverse. The name "Merrin" can be heard. Sharon calls Karras to the house and shows him the words "HELP ME" rising on Regan's abdomen. Convinced that Regan's condition meets the requirements for an exorcism, Karras seeks permission. Knowing that Father Merrin conducted an exorcism some dozen years previously in Africa, the church hierarchy contacts him in Woodstock, New York. When Merrin arrives before the MacNeil house, "Regan" knows. The rite of exorcism begins. Regan spits on Merrin and levitates. A cut appears on her leg. The priests see an image of the demon statue Merrin found in Nineveh. Regan appears to Karras as his mother. After a brief respite, Karras finds the slumped body of Merrin on the bed and tries unsuccessfully to revive him. Infuriated by the giggling Regan, he leaps upon her, crying out, "Take me! Come into me!" The spirit leaves Regan, but before he can be completely possessed, Karras leaps through the window, careening down the steps to the street

below. Later, when the MacNeils leave the house, Chris tells Father Dyer that Regan remembers nothing of the horror. Yet when Regan sees Dyer's clergyman's collar, she kisses him.

Reviews: "The trash bombshell of 1973, the aesthetic equivalent of being run over by a truck.... Ruthlessly manipulates the most primitive fears and prejudices of the audience." (Michael Dempsey, *Film Quarterly*, Summer 1974, pp. 61-62) ¶"Friedkin has a crass expertise with which he can keep the average moviegoer from laughing at these absurd goings-on, and he certainly gets great performances, not from his actors ... but from his special-effects and makeup men, who carry the film." (John Simon, *Esquire*, April 1974, p. 74) ¶"A chunk of elegant occultist claptrap." (Vincent Canby, *New York Times*, December 27, 1973, p. 46) ¶"Expert telling of a supernatural horror story.... spellbinding but never gratuitous, revolting but always compelling." (Murf., *Variety*, December 26, 1973, p. 12)

Analysis: Few films have raised more of a fuss than this high-class version of

William Peter Blatty's best-selling novel. The number-one grossing movie of its year, this is one of those films that almost everybody saw, discussed, and remembers vividly. Doubtless many people accurately could answer the question, "Where were you when *The Exorcist* came out?" People were both outraged and fascinated; many were appalled at what was done to Linda Blair, equally shocked by her filthy language and her use of a crucifix on her nether regions. Although it was filmed at Georgetown University and received some assistance from the Catholic Church, a number of clergy protested. They worried too many children under 16 would be admitted to this R-rated film. (*Esquire* cynically noted that the film would have been X-rated had Warner not sunk so much money into it.) Some Jews objected to the use of a personal devil. Actual litigation involved behind-the-scenes occurrences: Eileen Dietz wanted arbitration to prove that she doubled for Blair in a few scenes. Apparently Warner Bros. originally denied that there was a double. This followed Academy Award–winning actress Mercedes McCambridge's claims for more credit for providing the possessed Blair's voice. "Tubular Bells" became a hit 45rpm single. The ad for the film is one of the most famous of all time: Silhouetted by house lights is a man in a topcoat, wearing a hat and carrying a piece of luggage.

Lee J. Cobb died in 1976 and his Lt. Kinderman would be played by George C. Scott in the series' third installment. Linda Blair would star in the sequel and much later in the 1990 spoof *Repossessed*. She'd go on to become a cult actress of such execrable though entertaining entries as *Chained Heat* and *Savage Streets*. Nominated for Best Picture, Director, Actress (Burstyn), Supporting Actress (Blair), Supporting Actor (Miller), Cinematography, Art Direction-Set Decoration, Editing, it won Academy Awards for Best Screenplay and Best Sound.

Notes of Interest: Blatty explains the genesis of his novel and the making of the film in *William Peter Blatty on* The Exorcist: *From Novel to Film.*

Many cheapjack clones (rather than true

sequels) followed *The Exorcist*, including *House of Exorcism* and the Italian releases *Beyond the Door* (1975) and *Beyond the Door 2* (1979).

Exorcist II: The Heretic
(Warner Bros., 1977; 117 min.) **

Produced by John Boorman and Richard Lederer. Directed by John Boorman. Screenplay, William Goodheart. Edited by Tom Priestley. Director of Photography, William A. Fraker. Panavision. Technicolor. Music, Ennio Morricone. Art Direction, Jack Collis. Set Decoration, John Austin. Costumes, Robert de Mora. Special Makeup, Dick Smith. Special Visual Effects, Albert J. Whitlock and Van Der Veer Photo. Special Effects, Chuck Gaspar.

Cast: Regan (Linda Blair), Father Philip Lamont (Richard Burton), Dr. Gene Tuskin (Louise Fletcher), Father Merrin (Max Von Sydow), Sharon (Kitty Winn), Older Kokumo (James Earl Jones), Cardinal (Paul Henreid), Edwards (Ned Beatty), Liz (Belinda Beatty), Spanish girl (Rose Portillo), Mr. Phalor (Barbara Cason), Deaf girl (Tiffany Kinney), Young Kokumo (Joey Green), Young monk (Fiseha Dimetros), Abbot (Ken Renard), Conductor (Hank Garet), Accident victim (Lorry Goldman), Taxi driver (Bill Grant), Tuskin children (Shane Butterworth, Joely Adams).

Synopsis: Having witnessed a demonic possession in South America, Father Lamont has misgivings about being sent to the United States to investigate the death of Father Merrin. In New York he meets with Dr. Gene Tuskin, Regan's psychiatrist. Gene believes that mental illness, not evil, is responsible for Regan's disturbing dreams. Using a hypnotic synchronizer, Gene has Regan bring her into Regan's "tone," back to Georgetown, while Lamont questions the teenager. Gene becomes agitated; her heart fibrillates. Lamont takes the headgear and himself "travels" to Georgetown and sees the possessed Regan and Merrin. That night Regan dreams of Merrin and of locusts; she sleepwalks on her balcony. Lamont and Regan use the synchronizer again. Lamont sees Merrin exorcising an African youth and feels he must find the adult youth, Kokumo. In Africa, Lamont finally locates Kokumo in a village but fails the test of walking across spikes and wakes

in a doctor's office. The doctor is also Kokumo. He shows Lamont his experiments
with locusts. Back in New York, Lamont
and Regan take the synchronizer to Lamont's apartment, where Merrin's voice tells
Lamont to help Regan. She accompanies
Lamont to Washington. Gene and Sharon
fly down and arrive soon after Regan and
Lamont have entered the Georgetown
house where Regan was possessed and Merrin died. But the taxi carrying Gene and
Sharon crashes into the wall and the driver
is killed. Sharon is killed when she purposefully breaks a lamp which sets fire to
leaking gas. Inside, Lamont battles with the
image of a seductive Regan telling him to
kill the real girl. Locusts crash through the
window, the house begins crumbling, but
as he sinks into the rubble, Lamont succeeds in tearing the heart out of the demon.
Regan tames the locust horde and survives.

Reviews: "Twaddle.... The only synthe-
sis in the film is between the ludicrous and
the unintentionally comic." (Christopher
Porterfield, *Time*, July 4, 1977, p. 54) ¶"Beyond belief. It is the dumbest movie of the
year." (Richard A. Blake, *America*, August 6,
1977, p. 57) ¶"Not as good as *The Exorcist*.
It isn't even close." (*Variety*)

Analysis: Yes, Linda Blair gets top
billing. Director Boorman had turned
down directing the original. According to
him, "We will use practically every variation of special effects technique to make
it a film that leads the audience into the
unknown territory of the mind and into
strange worlds they have never before encountered." (Don Shay, "Zardoz Goes to
the Devil," *Cinefantastique*, Vol. 5, No. 3,
p. 32) This has the reputation of being one
of the all-time worst films. We don't know.
Certainly the synopsis makes it sound incoherent. The story is confusing, and Burton seems shell-shocked, but the most
ridiculous scenes involve Blair on the balcony of her high-rise apartment: There is
only a partial railing!

The Exorcist III

(20th Century–Fox, 1990; 109 min.)

**½

Produced by Carter De Haven. Directed by

William Peter Blatty. Screenplay, William
Peter Blatty. Based on the William Peter
Blatty novel *Legion*. Edited by Todd Ramsay
and Peter Lee-Thompson. Director of Pho-
tography, Gerry Fisher. DeLuxe Color. Mu-
sic, Barry DeVorzon. Dolby Stereo. Art Di-
rection, Robert Goldstein, Henry Shaffer. Set
Decoration, Hugh Scaife. Visual Effects, Abe
Milrad, Mat Beck. Mechanical Effects,
Michael Landi.

Cast: Lt. William Kinderman (George C.
Scott), Patient X/Karras (Jason Miller), Fa-
ther Joseph Dyer (Ed Flanders), Gemini killer
(Brad Dourif), Father Morning (Nicol Wil-
liamson), Dr. Temple (Scott Wilson), Nurse
Allerton (Nancy Fish), Stedman (George Di-
Cenzo), Sergeant Atkins (Grand L. Bush),
Ryan (Don Gordon), Mrs. Clelia (Mary Jack-
son), University president (Lee Richardson),
Nurse X (Viveca Lindfors), Dr. Freedman
(Ken Lerner), Mary Kinderman (Zohra Lam-
pert), Father Kanavan (Harry Carey, Jr.),
Nurse Amy Keating (Tracy Thorne), Shirley
(Barbara Baxley), Julie Kinderman (Sherrie
Wills), Patient A (Edward Lynch), Nurse
Merrin (Lois Foraker), Korner boy (Alex-
ander Zuckerman), Thomas Kintry (James
Burgess), Dr. Bruno (Clifford David), Nurse
Blaine (Tyra Ferrell), Altar boy (Kevin Cor-
rigan), Mrs. Kintry (Peggy Alston), Elderly
Jesuit (Father John Durkin), Nurse Bierce
(Bobby Deren), Alice (Jan Neuberger), Angel
of Death (Patrick Ewing), Larry King and C.
Everett Koop (themselves).

Synopsis: Georgetown 1990: Father Dyer
and Lt. Kinderman recall Damien Karras,
who fell to his death on a steep stairway
fifteen years before. Dyer and Kinderman
spend the afternoon at the movies watching *It's a Wonderful Life*. On this anniversary of Damien's death, Kinderman is
bothered by the recent decapitation — and
crucifixion — of a young black boy he knew.
Another gruesome death follows: Father
Kanavan is killed in the confessional. Dyer
goes into the hospital "for tests." But he's
found murdered, his body neatly drained
of all its blood. On the wall is a message
written in blood: "It's a Wonderful Life."
Inspecting the hospital's psycho ward,
Kinderman hears his name spoken, but
he's called away before he learns who said
it. He explains to the hospital administrator that someone knows the true modus
operandi of the deceased "Gemini killer."
Dr. Temple tells Kinderman about the man

in the isolation room. An amnesiac, he'd been picked up wandering the C&O Canal fifteen years previously. About six weeks ago he emerged from his catatonia, became violent, then said he was the Gemini killer. Upon visiting Cell 11, Kinderman is shocked. The man seems to be Damien Karras! The man admits to killing many people at random, and says he'll punish Kinderman if he doesn't tell the press the Gemini killer is back. Later, Kinderman reads the "Rite of Exorcism." In the hospital, Nurse Keating is gutted by a white-robed figure wielding surgical shears. Dr. Temple is found dead, a suicide. Kinderman interrogates the man in Cell 11 again and is once more told to tell the press. Additionally, Kinderman is told that he can be helped with his unbelief. A "nurse" heads for Kinderman's house, and, recalling warnings from the man in isolation, the lieutenant races to prevent a tragedy. But nothing's wrong when he gets there. Still, there is a nurse, and she asks Kinderman for help before pulling out shears, speaking in the prisoner's voice, and attempting to kill Kinderman's daughter. She fails because at that moment the Gemini killer/Karras is visited by Father Morning. An exorcism is begun. Kinderman arrives to find a Bible and Morning's body. Before Kinderman can shoot Gemini/Karras, he is pinned to the wall by an invisible force. Lightning-like bolts penetrate the cell and open a pit from which emerge, temporarily, the Gemini's victims and Karras. Father Morning is not quite dead and reaches out for his crucifix. He tells Damien to fight. Damien gains control of the body of Gemini. He urges Kinderman, "Shoot now! Kill me now!" and the policeman does.

Reviews: "This sequel's appeal is intellectual rather than visceral, which is a tough sell indeed.... intellectually stimulating." (Kevin Thomas, *Los Angeles Times Calendar*, August 20, 1990, p. 6) ¶"Seems muddled and the none-too-special effects are familiar." (Mike McGrady, *Newsday*, August 18, 1990, Part II, p. 17) ¶"I don't want to carp, but how about a little action here? A little suspense, a special effect or two?" (Jami Bernard, *New York Post*, August 18, 1990, p. 14) ¶"All mood and no meat." (*Variety*)

Analysis: It's interesting, but there's not much of a punch line. The "charm" of the original lay in revolting us by what was done to the innocent young girl. Without Regan, we are left with little to cheer for. What's the point of having Jason Miller alternate with Brad Dourif? Scott seems only to see Miller. We guess it's a way by which the viewer can visually know that Karras is possessed by another soul. In the final analysis, this is a lot of hooey, a premise carried, in Robert Castle's words, "a sequel too far." There is one really scary moment: the shears-wielding figure approaching Nurse Keating from the rear, observed by the helpless audience at long range. How come Kinderman didn't radio for police to guard his house when he suspected foul play approaching?

Repossessed
(New Line Cinema/Seven Arts, 1990; 84 min.) **

Produced by Steve Wizan. Directed by Bob Logan. Screenplay, Bob Logan. Edited by Jeff Freeman. Director of Photography, Michael D. Margulies. Panavision. CFI color. Music, Charles Fox. Ultra-Stereo. Art Direction, Gae Buckley. Set Decoration, Lee Cunningham. Costumes, Timothy D'Arcy. Special Visual Effects, Stargate Films.

Cast: Nancy Aglet (Linda Blair), Father Jedidiah Mayi (Leslie Nielsen), Ernest Weller (Ned Beatty), Father Luke Brophy (Anthony Starke), Braydon Aglet (Thom J. Sharp), Fanny Weller (Lana Schwab), Neg Aglet (Benj Thall), Frieda Aglet (Dove Dellos), Nancy's mother (Jacquelyn Masche), Announcer (Frazier Smith), the Pope (Eugene Graytak), Jake Steinfeld, Army Archerd, Jack LaLanne, Wally George, Jesse Ventura, Gene Okerlund (themselves).

Synopsis: Father Jedidiah Mayi lectures a class at the University of California at Chicago on an exorcism he conducted in 1973. The victim of possession was one Nancy, who is now a married housewife with two children. While watching the TV evangelists Ernest and Fanny Weller, Nancy is once again possessed by the devil. Dr. Hackett and other physicians are stumped by her condition. Young Father Luke Brophy takes on the case and seeks out Father Mayi. At the urging of Ernest and Fanny, the priest is given permission to conduct the exorcism on television. It is in the devil's best interests, as it turns out. The demon plans to enter the airwaves and possess the viewers. But Luke prevents that. When Father Mayi arrives, Nancy induces cardiac arrest. Revived, he watches as the devil spirit enters Luke, then Mayi, and finally returns to Nancy. When rock 'n' roll music is played, the demon spirit rises into the air while vowing to return. Nancy appears in Mayi's class to take questions.

Review: "Promising idea has too few gags, too many targets, and a poor finale." (Leonard Maltin, ed., *Movie and Video Guide 1993*, New York: Signet, 1992, p. 1020)

Analysis: It's in the style of *Airplane* and *The Naked Gun* but for some reason doesn't succeed half as well. Thank goodness it's not boring and moves at a fast clip. Leslie Nielsen has another field day in his late career choice of comedy, and Linda Blair shows a sense of humor. Although there is some risqué dialogue and nudity in a women's locker room scene and a student willingly exposes her breasts in Father Mayi's class, cult star Blair (*Chained Heat, Savage Streets*) sheds no attire. At least she could have sported sexy lingerie while awaiting and/or undergoing the exorcism. What were the producers thinking? Among the funniest scenes: Entering the chamber of the possessed Nancy, the young priest shuts off the cassette that had been supplying the ominous music; the Tammy Bakker character enters her closet to trade in her cat for a Chihuahua hanging in a harness next to many other small animals; Nielsen prepares à la Rocky to joust with the devil. The most evocative scene has Nielsen beating the devil to the punch and vomiting pea soup and eggs on Blair.

The Fall of the House of Usher

(AIP, 1960; 85 min.) ***

Produced and directed by Roger Corman. Executive Producer, James H. Nicholson. Screenplay, Richard Matheson. Based on the story by Edgar Allan Poe. Edited by Anthony Carras. Director of Photography, Floyd Crosby. CinemaScope. Eastman Color. Music, Les Baxter. Art Direction, Daniel Haller. Special Effects, Pat Dinga. Photographic Effects, Ray Mercer. Paintings, Burt Schoenberg.

Cast: Roderick Usher (Vincent Price), Madeline Usher (Myrna Fahey), Phillip Winthrop (Mark Damon), Bristol (Harry Ellerbe).

Synopsis: Phillip Winthrop rides across a blasted heath to the New England home of his fiancée, Madeline Usher. The butler Bristol requests that he exchange his boots for slippers. He learns why when he meets Madeline's older brother, Roderick. The Ushers, says Roderick, have a "morbid acuteness of the senses." Loud sounds, rough-textured clothing, and bright lights irritate them. As for food, "Any sort of food more exotic than the most pallid mash is unendurable to my tastebuds." Roderick cannot dissuade Phillip from seeing Madeline. Nor can he deter him from wanting to take her back to Boston as his wife, despite warnings that she's infected with the "plague of evil" that long ago crept over the land and infected the house. The house, in fact, is centuries old and was transported stone by stone from England. Roderick says Madeline must not bear children or she'll spread the cancer. Nevertheless, Phillip convinces Madeline to plan on leaving with him. That night Phillip hears Roderick and Madeline arguing. When he enters Madeline's room, he finds her devoid of life. During prayers in the crypt, Roderick notices Madeline's hand moving, but he closes the coffin. After they leave, Madeline's scream is heard. Phillip prepares to return to Boston, but Bristol inadvertently mentions catalepsy as an Usher malady. Racing to the crypt, Phillip finds an empty coffin and confronts Roderick, who swears his sister is dead now but won't reveal her whereabouts. Phillip has a nightmare of looking for Madeline and meeting her nefarious ancestors. A storm approaches and Roderick says the house will crumble. He admits to hearing Madeline in the coffin. Phillip finds a hidden crypt, but again, Madeline is gone. He pursues her through hidden passages. She attacks him, then Roderick, whom she strangles. Sparks from the fireplace start a conflagration that destroys the Ushers and the house. Only Phillip escapes.

Review: "Provides a fair degree of literacy at the cost of a patron's patience." (Eugene Archer, *New York Times*, September 15, 1960, p. 45)

Analysis: This film gave rise to a series of AIP movies based — sometimes loosely — on tales by Edgar Allan Poe. These well-regarded movies were directed by Roger Corman and usually starred Vincent Price. Most of the films are expansions of Poe short stories: "The Pit and the Pendulum," "Ligeia," "The Masque of the Red Death," "Hop-Frog," "The Fall of the House of Usher." In *Usher*, one wonders how they'll stretch the story to feature length, but they manage it. Making Madeline Phillip's fiancée is the screenwriter's invention. Its story bears comparison to the next in the series. How much is madness, how much supernatural? While the final conflagration is compelling, we would have liked to see the house collapse and sink into the adjacent tarn, as it does in Poe's tale.

The Pit and the Pendulum
(AIP, 1961; 85 min.) ***½

Produced and directed by Roger Corman. Screenplay, Richard Matheson. Based on the story by Edgar Allan Poe. Edited by Anthony Carras. Director of Photography, Floyd Crosby. Panavision. Color, Pathé. Music, Les Baxter. Art Direction, Daniel Haller. Set Decoration, Harry Reif. Special Effects, Pat Dinga.

Cast: Nicholas Medina (Vincent Price), Francis Barnard (John Kerr), Elizabeth Barnard Medina (Barbara Steele), Catherine Medina (Luana Anders), Dr. Charles Leon (Anthony Carbone), Maximillian (Patrick Westwood), Maria (Lynne Bernay), Isabella (Mary Menzies), Bartolome (Charles Victor), Nicholas as a child (Larry Turner).

Synopsis: In 1546, Englishman Francis Barnard arrives at the Spanish coastal castle of Nicholas Medina. He hopes to learn the cause of his sister Elizabeth Barnard Medina's death. Nicholas tells Francis his sister succumbed to a blood malady, but this does not satisfy the visitor. In private, Nicholas's sister Catherine explains that as a child her brother witnessed the murder of his uncle Bartolome and the torture and death of his mother Isabella. Their murderer was Nicholas's father, Sebastian, an infamous inquisitor who accused brother

and wife of adultery. Nicholas reveals that he may have buried Elizabeth alive after she found the torture chamber, became infected with the castle's poisonous miasma, and eventually collapsed. Hearing strange noises, Nicholas believes he can only find peace if he knows for certain that he did not inter Elizabeth alive. The vault is opened, and it is obvious that the now-dead Elizabeth had struggled to get out. Dr. Leon argues that it was not Nicholas's fault, that he himself verified the death. Later Nicholas hears Elizabeth's voice calling him to her tomb. The vault opens, a bloody hand emerges, then a woman's figure masked by shadow. Nicholas becomes unhinged and collapses in the torture chamber. In this state he hears Elizabeth speak with Dr. Leon of their conspiracy to drive him mad. Nicholas rises up and castigates the two. He believes he is his father, Sebastian; Elizabeth is Isabella; and Dr. Leon is Bartolome. Trying to escape, Leon falls to his death in an adjacent chamber. Nicholas mistakes Francis for Leon/Bartolome and straps him beneath a giant pendulum. Only the timely arrival of Catherine and servant Maximillian prevent Francis's death. Nicholas topples to his doom next to Leon. As the survivors leave the torture chambers, Catherine says, "No one will ever enter this room again." Staring at them from an Iron Maiden are the horrified eyes of the still-living but gagged Elizabeth. End title: "The agony of my soul found vent in one loud, long, and final scream of despair.— Poe"

Reviews: "No match for the surprising excellence of its predecessor.... simply a proficient but finally distasteful exercise in horror for its own sake." (Moira Walsh, *America*, September 2, 1961, p. 693) ¶"Roger Corman, who is not too successful with his actors, is much better at creating a creepy atmosphere, and he is greatly helped by some stunning color photography.... Poe fans may not be happy with this, but perhaps Poe himself would have found its jumpy suspense and sinister trappings quite passable." (Philip T. Hartung, *Commonweal*, September 22, 1961, p. 518)

Analysis: This disguised supernatural tale — it's really madness — made a big impression on its youthful audience, which had nightmares about Barbara Steele in that iron maiden at fadeout. The matte castle exterior is impressive. Price does a fine job of descending into madness. In his *Danse Macabre*, Stephen King makes a keen observation about the "corpse" Price finds and realizes was buried alive: "Following the Hammer films, this becomes, I think, the most important moment in the post–1960 horror film, signaling a return to an all-out effort to terrify the audience — and a willingness to use any means at hand to do it" (p. 135).

Tales of Terror
(AIP, 1962; 90 min.) ***

Produced and directed by Roger Corman. Screenplay, Richard Matheson. Based on stories by Edgar Allan Poe. Edited by Anthony Carras. Director of Photography, Floyd Crosby. Panavision. Color, Pathé. Music, Les Baxter. Art Direction, Daniel Haller. Set Decoration, Harry Reif. Special Effects, Pat Dinga. Photographic Effects, Butler-Glouner, Inc.

Cast: "Morella": Locke (Vincent Price), Morella (Leona Gage), Lenora (Maggie Pierce), Driver (Ed Cobb); "The Black Cat": Fortunato (Vincent Price), Montresor Herringbone (Peter Lorre), Annabel Herringbone (Joyce Jameson), Bartender (Wally Campo), Chairman (Alan Dewit), Policemen (Lenny Weinrib, John Hackett); "The Case of M. Valdemar": Ernest Valdemar (Vincent Price), Carmichael (Basil Rathbone), Helene (Debra Paget), Dr. Eliot James (David Frankham), Servant (Scotty Brown).

Synopsis: "Morella": Locke receives an unexpected and unwanted visit from his daughter Lenora, who's been separated from him for 26 years. "Morella, my beloved wife. Your murderer has returned," he says to his late wife's portrait. Lenora discovers the corpse of Morella. Lenora herself is dying. Locke tells her of her mother's death and how he couldn't bury her underground. Morella's spirit strangles Lenora, who seems dead, then alive. Locke visits Morella's corpse and finds it Lenora. Morella attacks Locke. A fire starts from a dropped candelabra. Locke's body is seen covered by Lenora. Morella's corpse smirks. "The Black Cat": The alcoholic, jobless Montresor stumbles into the Wine Merchants Convention, where he engages in a

wine-tasting contest with the expert Fortunato. Fortunato escorts Montresor home and is much taken with his comely wife, Annabel. Montresor learns of their adulterous affair, plies Fortunato with wine and walls up both him and the dead Annabel in the basement. Ill luck is Montresor's, for his nemesis, a black cat, has also been imprisoned and its meow is heard by the police. "The Case of M. Valdemar": Through mesmerism, Mr. Carmichael eases the pain of the dying Ernest Valdemar and convinces him that a radical experiment should be conducted. Valdemar agrees to be hypnotized at the point of death. Dr. James and Valdemar's wife Helene are against it. "Perhaps he asks for nothing because he desires everything — including you," says James to Helene. He's right. After mesmerizing Valdemar, Carmichael informs Helene that he will have her. And although Valdemar had told Helene to marry James after his own death, the horrible voice that now comes from his body tells her to wed Carmichael. She agrees as long as Carmichael releases Valdemar from the netherland he inhabits. Carmichael doesn't make deals, and his rage against Helene causes Valdemar's body to rise up and stalk the mesmerist. Dr. James breaks in and carries Helene away from the dead Carmichael and the liquid putrescence covering the corpse.

Review: "Tolerable short story compendium, rather short on subtlety and style." (Leslie Halliwell, *Halliwell's Film Guide*, 7th ed., p. 989)

Analysis: "The Black Cat" segment is really Poe's "The Cask of Amontillado." Price has a welcome license to be broad in this one. A wine connoisseur himself, he is a riot in the tasting scene. The best segment is the last. Who can forget the melting Valdemar? Egads!

The Premature Burial
(AIP, 1962; 81 min.) **½

Produced and directed by Roger Corman. Screenplay, Charles Beaumont and Ray Russell. Based on the story by Edgar Allan Poe. Edited by Ronald Sinclair. Director of Photography, Floyd Crosby. Panavision. Eastmancolor. Music, Ronald Stein. Art Direction, Daniel Haller. Set Decoration, Harry

Reif. Costumes, Marge Corso. Special Effects, Pat Dinga.
Cast: Guy Carrell (Ray Milland), Emily Gault (Hazel Court), Miles Archer (Richard Ney), Dr. Gideon Gault (Alan Napier), Kate Carrell (Heather Angel), Sweeney (John Dierkes), Mole (Richard Miller), Minister (Brendan Dillon).

Synopsis: Afraid that he, like his father, will inherit the family's malady of catalepsy, Guy Carrell decides not to marry fiancée Emily Gault. He leaves London with his sister Kate for a country house surrounded by bleak moors and takes up painting. Emily visits and convinces him their marriage will work. Still, he has dreams of being buried alive and cries, "Don't humor me! I'm not mad. I saw them as clearly as I'm seeing you." He builds a burial vault equipped with escape hatches — even poison — so that if he is entombed and recovers, he can escape. Miles Archer explains to Emily that catalepsy is not in fact inheritable but that Guy's state of mind could cause a seizure. Emily argues with Guy: "You don't fear burial alive because you are already buried alive. What is it you're afraid of, being locked in a tomb? You've been locked in a tomb for months. This tomb. And I've been your widow. And I don't like being your widow, Guy, and what's more, I'm not going to be much longer." Guy agrees to destroy the mausoleum. Perhaps this will stop the dreams in which all the escape devices fail and he is interred alive. Miles suggests that Guy open his father's grave to verify he was not prematurely buried. But the coffin reveals a skeleton in an unnatural position — trying to get out. Guy swoons, and Miles and Dr. Gault, Emily's father, pronounce him dead. Graverobbers open Guy's coffin after interment, but Guy emerges and kills them. He abducts Emily, binds and tosses her into a grave and begins shoveling dirt on her. Miles arrives, and as Guy is about to throttle him with a shovel, a gunshot from Kate brings her brother down. Kate reveals that she knew Emily was using Guy's fears to launch him on the road to madness.

Review: "Generally well acted — but being heavy-handed and slow, it comes out a Poe second." (*Newsweek,* April 2, 1962, p. 87)

Analysis: Whatever critical appreciation

ever existed for this has dissipated over time, and this Corman Poe film is reckoned dull. Even duller than *The Haunted Palace,* apparently, because *The Premature Burial* wasn't available for rent when we finished this book. Rarely is it telecast. Teenagers, like us, who saw it in a theater, were much taken with the concept. We put ourselves in Milland's place: What devices would we develop to help us out of the grave? The worms in the goblet made us cringe. We were sorry to see Hazel Court turn into the villain of the piece. She was almost justified. Her fiancé (Milland) was neglecting her to prepare for his impending catalepsy. Hazel told Kim Holston in a December 16, 1985, telephone conversation that she was indeed placed in that hole and covered with dirt. "That was me, too! It certainly was me! You know, in those days we did everything, we really did."

The Raven
(AIP, 1963; 86 min.) **½

Produced and directed by Roger Corman. Screenplay, Richard Matheson. Edited by Ronald Sinclair. Director of Photography, Floyd Crosby. Panavision. Color, Pathé. Music, Les Baxter. Art Direction, Daniel Haller. Set Decoration, Harry Reif. Raven trained by Moe DiSesso. Photographic Effects, Butler-Glouner, Inc. Special Effects, Pat Dinga.

Cast: Dr. Erasmus Craven (Vincent Price), Dr. Scarabus (Boris Karloff), Lenore Craven (Hazel Court), Dr. Bedlo (Peter Lorre), Rexford Bedlo (Jack Nicholson), Estelle Craven (Olive Sturgess), Grimes (William Baskin), Gort (Aaron Saxon), Maidservant (Connie Wallace).

Synopsis: Dr. Erasmus Craven receives an unexpected nighttime visit from a raven, which turns out to be Dr. Bedlo. His current condition was caused by grand master magician Dr. Scarabus. Craven restores Bedlo to human form via a potion that includes tongue of vulture and jellied spiders. One essential ingredient — dead man's hair — came from Craven's father, who when they opened his coffin urged his son to "beware!" Noticing a photo of Craven's late wife Lenore, Bedlo says he saw the woman at Scarabus's castle. Craven inspects Lenore's coffin and finds a body. Nevertheless, he fears Scarabus may have obtained a hold over Lenore's spirit and agrees to accompany Bedlo, his son Rexford, and his own daughter Estelle to the Scarabus manse. Scarabus seems glad to see them and acts the genial host, dismissing Craven's reminder that Scarabus was once a rival of Craven's father. Bedlo challenges Scarabus to a second magician's duel, during which Bedlo is struck by a bolt of lightning and apparently is destroyed. Staying the night, Erasmus thinks he sees Lenore in the window. It is indeed Lenore, and she consults with Scarabus, mentioning how she's stayed because of his wealth and power. Rexford finds his father, who says he merely pretended to disappear. They gather up Erasmus and Estelle, but escape is forestalled when Scarabus turns Erasmus into a statue. All the guests are bound. Lenore explains that it was another woman's body in her coffin. Claiming he would rather be a raven again than be tortured, Bedlo gets his wish. However, he returns and loosens Rexford's bonds. Confronted by a powerful Craven, Scarabus and his guest agree to a magician's duel. Erasmus wins. Lenore attempts to leave with him, but Scarabus pulls her into his lap as the ceiling falls. Later the two emerge none the worse for wear except for a coating of dust. At the Craven house Erasmus is told by the raven Bedlo that he will help him assume the grand master position in the magicians' brotherhood.

Reviews: "Has almost no relation to Poe. As a satire on thrillers, however, it may win some audiences." (Philip T. Hartung, *Commonweal,* February 15, 1963, p. 542) ¶The attribution of any of this to Edgar Allan Poe is outrageous, but there is a kind of low-grade fun which Lorre, Price, and especially Karloff maintain with irrelevant elegance throughout the pseudo-sinister proceedings." (*Newsweek,* February 4, 1963, pp. 78-79) ¶"Just a sappy little parody of a horror picture cutely calculated to make the children scream with terror while their parents scream with glee." (*Time,* February 1, 1963, p. 81)

Analysis: It's an interesting, occasionally amusing parody carried by its cast. The duel between Price and Karloff *is* a pleasure. Hazel Court doesn't appear till it's

half over. More's the shame. She's having a wickedly good time.

The Haunted Palace
(1963; 85 min.) ***

This film bears the title of a poem by Poe, which was first published in 1839 and later incorporated into "The Fall of the House of Usher." Beyond the title, however, the connection ends; the film is actually based on a story by H. P. Lovecraft, "The Case of Charles Dexter Ward." That story was later remade as *The Resurrected* (1991). Thus *The Haunted Palace* must be considered a progenitor film. For this reason, despite its association with the Corman Poe canon, we have listed *The Haunted Palace* as a main entry in the alphabetical listing, rather than as a sub-entry here.

The Masque of the Red Death
(AIP, 1964; 89 min.) ****

Produced and directed by Roger Corman. Associate Producer, George Willoughby. Assistant Director, Peter Price. Screenplay, Charles Beaumont and R. Wright Campbell. Based on the story by Edgar Allan Poe. Director of Photography, Nicholas Roeg. Panavision. Pathecolor. Music, David Lee. Choreography, Jack Carter.

Cast: Prince Prospero (Vincent Price), Juliana (Hazel Court), Francesca (Jane Asher), Gino (David Weston), Alfredo (Patrick Magee), Ludovico (Nigel Green), Hop-Toad (Skip Martin), Man in Red (John Westbrook), Anna-Marie (Doreen Dawn), Señora Escobar (Gay Brown), Señor Veronese (Julian Burton), Scarlatti (Paul Whitsun-Jones), Wife (Jean Lodge), Esmeralda (Verina Greenlaw), Lampredi (Brian Hewlett), Clistor (Harvey Hall), Guard (Robert Brown).

Synopsis: Angered by villagers, Prince Prospero aims to have two men killed, but Francesca, daughter of Ludovico and lover of Gino, begs for clemency. Prospero says she will choose one who may live, but the ordeal is postponed by screams from a hut. Investigation reveals a woman with plague — the Red Death. Prospero retires to his castle and sends messages to cohorts to come at once and take refuge from the pestilence. Francesca learns that Prospero worships Satan, whom he believes rules

Juliana (Hazel Court) "dreams" of sacrifice in *The Masque of the Red Death* (AIP, 1964).

this world of disease, misery, and death. She is horrified to see him use a crossbow bolt to kill a neighboring noble who offered Prospero his wife in order to gain entrance to the castle. Equally disturbing, but less intellectual, is Alfredo, who strikes a beautiful dwarfish dancer after she knocks over his goblet. Juliana, Prospero's consort, says she will undergo the final initiation into the satanic cult. Knowing she's jealous of Francesca, Prospero belittles her sincerity. Nevertheless, Juliana brands herself and recites hellish incantations. She confronts Francesca and gives her a key to the cell containing her father and Gino. Prospero discovers that Juliana betrayed him and recaptures the men. At dinner, Prospero offers them five daggers. One is poisoned. Each man cuts his arm. The fifth dagger is left. Ludovico takes it but is killed by Prospero's sword thrust as he attempts to stab the prince. Prospero sends Gino away, believing he will suffer the plague. Gino meets a man clothed in red, who gives him a sign and later tells him to wait on the castle battlements for Francesca. Meanwhile, Juliana undergoes another ritual during which she "dreams" of being sacrificed by demonic men from various historical epochs. When she awakes, she hears Prospero calling. She believes she is now wedded to Satan and more powerful than Prospero but in the main hall is attacked and killed by a raven. Prospero tells the gathering throng to bear no mind, for Juliana is at peace. The masque begins and Alfredo, dressed as a gorilla, is bound and set on fire by Hop-Toad, who intends fleeing with the dancer. Prospero spots a man in red, a color forbidden by his command. Confronting him, he thinks the figure a representative of the devil. Soon he is disabused of this notion. The man is an emissary of the Red Death. Only five people survive: Francesca and Gino, dwarf and dancer, and a villager.

Reviews: "Stylish excursion into demonology.... Small and sometimes amusing

Loyal butler Kenrick (Oliver Johnston) stands by with beverages as Verden Fell (Vincent Price) tends to Rowena (Elizabeth Shepherd) in *The Tomb of Ligeia* (AIP, 1965).

hints of depravity [suggest] unspeakably juicy violations of the natural order." (*Newsweek*, June 29, 1964, pp. 87-88) ¶"Vulgar, naive and highly amusing...." (Eugene Archer, *New York Times*, September 17, 1964, p. 52)

Analysis: Very disquieting, this movie might be part of a triple feature with *The Blood on Satan's Claw* and *The Wicker Man*. At one time this was reckoned the best of the Corman Poe outings. It had a larger budget, English sets, Nicholas Roeg on camera. Of late we detect equal fan and critical regard for *The Tomb of Ligeia* and *Pit and the Pendulum*. In truth, a case can be made for all three. Other than Prince Prospero, there are none of the film's specific human characters in Poe's story. Price is good, Jane Asher cute and appropriately innocent. Hazel Court's sacrifice scenes were originally excised by British censors. We can understand that. She's wearing a diaphanous gown and the scenes are sexually charged. The film is based not only on

the Poe story of the same name but also his "Hop-Frog."

The Tomb of Ligeia
(1965; 81 min.) ****

Produced and directed by Roger Corman. Screenplay, Robert Towne. Based on the story "Ligeia" by Edgar Allan Poe. Edited by Alfred Cox. Director of Photography, Arthur Grant. Music, Kenneth V. Jones, played by Sinfonia of London. Art Direction, Colin Southcott.

Cast: Verden Fell (Vincent Price), Rowena Trevanion/Ligeia Fell (Elizabeth Shepherd), Christopher Gough (John Westbrook), Kenrick (Oliver Johnston), Dr. Vivian (Richard Vernon), Lord Trevanion (Derek Francis), Parson (Ronald Adam). With Frank Thornton, Penelope Lee.

Synopsis: While Verden Fell buries wife Ligeia, a cat jumps on the coffin and the corpse's eyes open. Fell claims it's a nervous contraction. Years pass. During a fox chase, the Lady Rowena Trevanion discovers the Fell abbey and falls from her horse when a graveside cat spooks the animal. The black-spectacled Fell appears to compound Rowena's fright, but he carries her inside and wraps her ankle. Returning to the abbey with a message sent by mutual acquaintance Christopher Gough, Rowena is attacked by Fell, who desists when he realizes who she is. He tells her never to come unannounced. "Does she look like me?" she asks, and Fell explains Ligeia's will to live. The cat scratches Rowena's face as she and Verden embrace. He tells butler Kenrick to destroy the animal. Verden meets with Christopher and admits to fears of insanity. After all, the date of Ligeia's death is missing from her grave. Did he do it? Meanwhile, in an attempt to retrieve Verden's glasses which the cat has taken, Rowena finds herself trapped in the bell tower. Verden rescues her. They marry and honeymoon abroad. Returning to England, Verden informs Rowena that he and Christopher have been attempting to sell the estate so they can move and start life anew. That night Rowena hears a strange noise in her bedroom and finds dark hair in her brush. Next day Christopher tells Verden that Ligeia has no death certificate, thus the abbey's sale is jeopardized. Verden uses Rowena to demonstrate hypnotism for his guests. She remembers a song her mother sang. Suddenly, Rowena opens her eyes and in another's voice says, "I will always be your wife." That evening Rowena has a nightmare about a fox and a cat, a statue-filled candle-lit room, Verden and a black-tressed lady. She wakes with a fox on her chest. Next day she tells Christopher that she eats and sleeps alone. She says Ligeia is in the abbey. Christopher and two men exhume Ligeia. While this takes place, Rowena's door shakes and the cat appears. Rowena flees, the cat follows. A large mirror is broken, revealing stairs to a hidden room where Rowena finds Verden. Outside, Christopher finds a wax figure in Ligeia's coffin. Rowena discovers the perfectly preserved corpse of Ligeia and falls on it. Kenrick reveals that Ligeia's final words were that she wouldn't die and Verden must come to her. Rowena pretends to be Ligeia and to die. Fell consigns the corpse of Ligeia to the flames, then places

Rowena on the bed while knocking away the cat. He hears Rowena breathe. The cat gets up and Rowena relapses. Verden leaves, the curtain opens and a figure approaches — it's Ligeia! Verden strangles her. Christopher returns and reveals to Verden that he's been gripping Rowena. Christopher takes Rowena as Verden pursues the cat. During the chase, a hearth fire spreads. Verden strangles the cat but in the conflagration is killed and lies with — Ligeia. Outside, Rowena lives.

Reviews: "May not be the best of [Corman's Poe] series.... but it is the most far-out and, in the last half hour or so, his most concentrated piece of black magic." (*Newsweek*, March 1, 1965, p. 88) ¶"Opulently photographed.... offers meticulous decor, shrewd shock techniques, and an atmosphere of mounting terror that fails to deliver on its promise." (*Time*, May 21, 1965, p. 110)

Analysis: Also known as *Tomb of the Cat*, this may be Corman's most controlled Poe adaptation. It is the only one with extensive outdoor scenes, and the cinematography is outstanding, the English locales wonderful. The titles are artistically excellent. Vincent Price's performance is one of his best. Had the cinema audience had its say, the attractive and self-possessed Elizabeth Shepherd would have made more films. She's briefly in 1978's *Damien: Omen II*.

Farewell to the Flesh *see* Candyman: Farewell to the Flesh *under* **Candyman**

The Final Chapter *see* Friday the 13th: The Final Chapter *under* **Friday the 13th**

The Final Conflict *see under* **The Omen**

The Final Frontier *see* Star Trek V: The Final Frontier *under* **Star Trek — The Motion Picture**

The Final Nightmare *see* Freddy's Dead: The Final Nightmare *under* **A Nightmare on Elm Street**

Five Million Years to Earth *see* Quatermass III *under* **The Quatermass Xperiment**

Flash Gordon *see under* **Flesh Gordon**

Flesh Gordon

(Graffiti/Mammoth, 1974; 78 min.) nv

Produced by Howard Ziehm and Bill Osco. Associate Producer, Walter R. Cichy. Directed by Howard Ziehm and Michael Benveniste. Screenplay, Michael Benveniste. Edited by Abbas Amin. Director of Photography, Howard Ziehm. Color. Music, Ralph Ferraro. Art Direction, Donald Harris. Costumes, Ruth Glunt. Special Effects, Jim Danforth.

Cast: Flesh Gordon (Jason Williams), Dale (Suzanne Fields), Emperor Wang (William Hunt), Dr. Jerkoff (Joseph Hudgins), Professor Gordon (John Hoyt). With Mycle Brandy, Nora Wieternik, Candy Samples, Steven Grummette, Lance Larsen, Judy Ziehm, Donald Harris, Jack Rowe, Mark Fore, Maria Aranoff, Rick Lutze, Sally Alt, Linus Gator, Susan Moore.

Review: "Puerile is the word.... an expensive-looking mish-mash of obvious double entendres, idiotic characterizations and dull situations." (*Variety*)

Analysis: Chiefly notable for Jim Danforth's special effects, there are R- and X-rated versions.

Flash Gordon

(Universal, 1980; 110 min.) **

Produced by Dino De Laurentiis. Directed by Mike Hodges. Screenplay, Lorenzo Semple, Jr. Adaptation, Michael Allin. Based on characters created by Alex Raymond. Edited by Malcolm Cooke. Director of Photography, Gil Taylor. Technicolor. Todd-AO. Music, Howard Blake and Queen. Dolby Stereo. Art Direction, John Graysmark, Norman Dorme. Costumes and Sets designed by Danilo Donati. Special Effects, George Gibbs.

Cast: Flash Gordon (Sam Jones), Princess Aura (Ornella Muti), Dale Arden (Melody Anderson), Emperor Ming (Max von Sydow), Dr. Hans Zarkov (Topol), Prince Barin (Timothy Dalton), Prince Vultan (Brian Blessed), Klytus (Peter Wyngarde), Kala (Mariangela Melato), Arborian Priest (John Osborne), Fico (Richard O'Brien), Luro (John Hallam), Zogi, High Priest (Philip Stone), Serving girl (Suzanne Danielle), Hedonia (Bobie Brown), Biro (Ted Carroll), Munson (William Hootkins), Mongon doctor (Stanley Lebor), Airline pilots (John Morton, Burnell Tucker).

Synopsis: Maverick scientist Dr. Hans Zarkov is convinced that the sudden increase in torrential storms, earthquakes and puzzling celestial phenomena represents a deliberate attack on earth by some non-earthly agency. Flash Gordon, New York Jets quarterback, and traveling photojournalist Dale Arden are unfortunate enough to fall in with Zarkov as he rockets into space to investigate. A tractor beam pulls their craft through an energy portal to the planet Mongo, ruled by the iron-fisted Ming the Merciless, self-proclaimed Emperor of the Universe. Viewing earth as a threat, Ming intends to send its moon crashing into it. Ming has Zarkov hauled off to be lobotomized and "re-programmed" as an agent of his secret police. Dale is envisioned as a possible paramour and entrusted to the Royal Concubines. Flash has shown unforgivable disrespect by tossing Ming's guards and secret police about; the Merciless One orders him executed. Princess Aura, Ming's hot-blooded daughter, has other ideas about this stud, however, and conspires with the court physician to spirit Flash's merely sedated body out of the palace after the "execution." Aura rockets with Flash to Arboria, a thickly forested moon of Mongo, and deposits him into the care of Prince Barin, leader of the Tree People, who also happens to be Aura's betrothed. The Princess returns to Mongo, and Barin promptly has Flash imprisoned. Meanwhile, Dale has escaped from Ming's harem and found Dr. Zarkov, who has foiled the Emperor's mindwashing machine and retained his own intellect. Together, they steal a rocket cycle and escape the palace, only to be immediately captured by a patrol of flying warriors of King Vultan, liege of the Hawkmen. On Arboria, Flash escapes into the jungle, pursued by Barin. Both are captured by Hawkmen and taken to the floating Sky City of King Vultan. Back on Mongo, Princess Aura's treachery has been discovered by Klytus, Ming's chief lieutenant. Torturing her for information, Klytus boards a rocket bound for Arboria. Before King Vultan's assembled court, the winged monarch allows Barin and Flash to settle their differences in a duel. The contest ends with Flash's victory and his refusal to take Barin's life. The Prince swears allegiance to Gordon. Klytus arrives on the scene, but as he lunges toward Flash, the earth man tosses him onto the tournament dais, impaling him upon a number of spikes. Flash urges Barin and Vultan to cease their bickering and make a sneak attack upon the palace on Mongo, thereby achieving liberty for all Ming's subjugated minions. Before they can do much but argue further, Ming's own imperial vessel is seen approaching. Vultan and his Hawkmen make a discreet and hasty exit, leaving Flash, Barin, Zarkov and Dale to greet the Emperor. Ming is impressed with Gordon's obvious survival talents and offers him a position as a high-ranking imperial official; he sweetens the deal by offering to spare the earth and make it Flash's personal domain. When the earth man declines this offer, Ming nonchalantly leaves him in Sky City, taking the others with him as prisoners aboard his vessel, which then begins destroying the floating metropolis with explosive blasts. Flash manages to escape from the doomed Sky City on a rocket cycle. Joining Vultan, who has hidden his forces on Arboria, he then leads Vultan's men in the aforementioned sneak attack. Drawing the war rocket *Ajax* into a concealing cloud bank on a ruse, Gordon and Vultan's Hawkmen commandeer the vessel and launch an all-out assault upon Ming's palace on Mongo, even as the monarch is about to wed Dale Arden in an impromptu ceremony of great pomp. The Hawkmen overcome Ming's guards, and Flash drives the *Ajax* through the very dome of the palace, impaling the emperor upon the spire on the ship's prow. Vultan and Prince Barin's forces manage to stop the generators that are forcing earth's moon out of orbit. The world is saved.

Reviews: "Pure entertainment, a perfect escape.... awesome technical wizardry...." (Kevin Thomas, *Los Angeles Times Calendar*, November 30, 1980, p. 42) ¶ "It is clear that the entire cast is having a tough time keeping a straight face.... Curiously the special effects are considerably less spectacular than the costumes and sets." (Robert Asahina, *New Leader*, December 29, 1980, p. 18) ¶ "A lot more gaudy, and just as dumb, as the original series starring Buster Crabbe." (*Variety*, December 3, 1980, p. 22)

Analysis: Several years after trashing King Kong's good name with a bad sequel and a worse remake, Dino De Laurentiis managed to cash in on both the outer space and the superhero crazes that had been sparked by the Salkind brothers and George Lucas by reviving the original outer space superhero, Alex Raymond's Flash Gordon. Hoping to find gold in the vein already mined by Universal forty years earlier in a series of three thirteen-chapter serials, De Laurentiis only managed to produce a plastic, costume-jewelry bauble awash in day-glo colors that actually manages to pale beside the glorious black-and-white efforts of Ford Beebe. Newcomer Sam J. Jones is quite unremarkable as Flash, delivering his lines with a lack of enthusiasm that makes Buster Crabbe's essays in the role look like Great Acting, although the part did propel him into a career of B-movie fame. And Melody Anderson is hardly the eyeful that Jean Rogers was in 1936. Max Von Sydow's career in the (American film) genre of the fantastic began, more or less, with *The Exorcist*, and went pretty much downhill from there. Though *Variety* called his performance in *Flash Gordon* "adroit," his pinched, nasal drone makes us yearn for some of Charles Middleton's carpet-chewing rants. All in all, this one's a waste of time. De Laurentiis was to find (slightly) more promising material in Robert E. Howard's Cimmerian hero, Conan, within a couple of years.

Flesh Gordon Meets the Cosmic Cheerleaders

(Filmvest International/New Horizons, 1990; 100 min.) *

Produced by Maurice Smith. Directed by Howard T. Ziehm. Screenplay, Howard T. Ziehm and Doug Frisby. Edited by Joe Tornatore. Director of Photography, Danny Nowak. Color. Music, Paul Zaza. Visual Effects, FX Center. Creature Effects, Jim Towler. Stop-Motion Animation, Lauritz Larson.

Cast: Flesh Gordon (Vince Murdocco), Dale Ardor (Robyn Kelly), Dr. Jerkoff (Tony Travis), Robunda Hooters (Morgan Fox), Evil Presence/Emperor Wang (William Dennis Hunt), Master Bator (Bruce Scott), Babs (Stevie-Lyn Ray), Queen Frigid (Dee Luxe), Candy Love (Sharon Rowley), Bazonga Bomber (Melissa Mounds), Rocket girl #1 (Angelica Gordon), Rocket girl #2 (Liz Atkinson), Rocket girl #3 (Theresa Galbraith).

Synopsis: A strange planet approaches Earth as Flesh Gordon is making a movie for Hero Studios. He's kidnapped by outer space cheerleaders, who explain that a black-robed man used impotence radiation pollution on their men. The women have formed SCREW, the Society of Cheerleaders to Rehabilitate Erections Worldwide. After Flesh's girlfriend, Dale, and Dr. Jerkoff find him, Dale is frozen and kidnapped by the villain. Flesh and the scientist set off in pursuit, with the cheerleaders following them. The villain begins radiating Earth with his impotence ray. After meeting turd people, Flesh, Jerkoff and head cheerleader Rotunda Hooters take flight to an ice planet and find Dale about to be lowered into a well. Flesh gives himself up to save her. The other cheerleaders arrive and knock the mad scientist into the well. Flesh is rescued and told he must sleep with Queen Frigid and get her on his side. He does. The villain interrupts and is unmasked as Emperor Wang. He and Flesh fall into a giant spider web, but Flesh escapes, grabs a mysterious box from a leprechaun-like figure on the way out, and extracts what the mad scientist (who's pulled himself from the pit) says is a giant prophylactic. He drapes it over Wang's ray, and potency returns to Earth men. As the victors pair up, Wang skis by.

Review: No one seems to know about this turkey. We couldn't find a review.

Analysis: This video release is vulgar, scatological, terrible. Turd people, an "ass-teroid" belt, King Kong urinating from a skyscraper. For the most undiscriminating audiences. The prettiest woman is left behind on the movie set when Flesh heads into space.

Notes of Interest: Buster Crabbe starred as Flash in the Universal serials. Some of the serial episodes — e.g., *Flash Gordon's Trip to Mars* (1938) and *Flash Gordon Conquers the Universe* (1940) — were connected to create "movies."

Flesh Gordon Meets the Cosmic Cheerleaders *see under* **Flesh Gordon**

The Fly

(20th Century–Fox, 1958; 94 min.) ***

Produced and Directed by Kurt Neumann. Screenplay, James Clavell. Based on the story by George Langelaan. Edited by Merrill White. Director of Photography, Karl Struss. Color Consultant, Leonard Doss. Music, Paul Sawtell. Sound, Eugene Grossman, Harry M. Leonard. Art Direction, Theobold Holsopple, Lyle R. Wheeler. Wardrobe, Charles LeMaire. Hairstyles, Helen Turpin. Costumes, Adele Balkan. Makeup, Ben Nye and Dick Smith. Special Effects, L. B. Abbott.

Cast: Andre Delambre (Al [David] Hedison), Helene Delambre (Patricia Owens), François Delambre (Vincent Price), Inspector Charas (Herbert Marshall), Philippe Delambre (Charles Herbert), Emma (Kathleen Freeman), Dr. Ejoute (Eugene Borden), Nurse Andersone (Betty Lou Gerson), Gaston (Torben Meyer), Orderly (Harry Carter), Doctor (Charles Tannen), Police doctor (Franz Roehn), Waiter (Arthur Dulac).

Synopsis: At the Delambre electronics plant near Montreal, a woman runs from a machine press. The watchman discovers a dead man in the press. Helene Delambre calls her brother-in-law, François, and tells him she's killed her husband, Andre. François phones Inspector Charas. They visit Helene, who calmly talks about the death of her husband. During the visit she gets up and follows a fly around the room. Charas and François visit Andre's lab and find it a wreck. From her bed, Helene recalls the entire story, leading to a flashback: Andre's experiments have produced a disintegrator-integrator by which he can transport matter. When perfected, his machine will be of invaluable benefit to humankind. Surplus food could be instantaneously transported to starving people, for instance. But Andre doesn't succeed with Dandalo, the cat; the animal disappears, its atoms presumably scattered about the universe. Andre perfects the machine, but Helene finds a mysterious note under the door when she visits the lab. It says Andre has had an accident and asks Helene to bring a cup of milk laced with rum. When she returns, Andre, whose head is draped in a black cloth, writes a note directing her to find a white-headed fly. She recalls telling son Philippe to release the strange fly he caught. The search is fruitless. Back in the lab, she sees Andre's hairy right arm. He explains that he used the machine but that a fly was in it and their atoms mixed. Andre indicates he must kill himself if the fly isn't found. Helene urges him to try the disintegrator-integrator without the fly. But it doesn't work, as she learns to her horror when she removes the cloth covering Andre's head. He has the head of a fly! When Helene wakes from her faint, she finds Andre burning his records. She follows him to the factory, where he sets the press and places himself in it. Helene starts the press but has second thoughts and unsuccessfully tries to pull him free. His fly arm is not crushed, and she resets the press. In private, Charas tells François he believes Madame Delambre to be insane and that she must be incarcerated. Next day he arrives with an ambulance and a warrant, but François hears from Philippe that he's seen the white-headed fly. Charas and François locate the spider web, where they see a fly with the head of Andre. Charas crushes the fly as a large spider attacks it, and François argues that if Helene murdered, so did Charas. Time passes, and in the garden, Philippe asks his uncle why his father died. François tells him Andre died searching for the truth, the most important search of all.

Reviews: "The movie is a good one.... achieves the plausible air of good science fiction by sugar-coating its bizarre thesis with the correct proportion of homely everyday details and reasonable-sounding scientific explanation." (*America*, August 23, 1958, pp. 537-38) ¶"The special effects department have their big moment during the transmitting scenes, but perhaps because *The Fly* is done so simply, the horror when it comes is all the more terrifying." (Philip T. Hartung, *Commonweal*, August 8, 1958, p. 472) ¶"Above-average science fiction thriller.... Terribly gripping." (F. Maurice Speed, ed., *Film Review, 1959-1960*, p. 86)
Analysis: This was *the* shock film of

1958. There are three supreme thrills: the man with a fly head, the squashing of the man-fly in a press, and the spider about to kill the fly with a man's head. Of course it's nutty — why would a fly face and head affect a man's brain, and why would the man's head on the fly be small? Besides the horror, it's a moral and thought-provoking film, with Price's speech about truth quite compelling. Note the major behind-the-scenes first-string Fox crew. Patricia Owens was a Fox contract star (*No Down Payment*) who appeared in major films for various studios, e.g., *Sayonara* at Warner Bros. Hedison's most notable moments would come on TV's *Voyage to the Bottom of the Sea*. The film belongs to Hedison and Owens. Price appears infrequently.

Return of the Fly
(20th Century–Fox, 1959; 78 min.)
**½

Produced by Bernard Glasser. Directed by Edward L. Bernds. Assistant Director, Byron Roberts. Screenplay, Edward L. Bernds. Based on characters from the story "The Fly" by George Langelaan. Edited by Richard C. Meyer. Director of Photography, Brydon Baker. CinemaScope. Music, Paul Sawtell and Bert Shefter. Sound Effects, Arthur J. Cornell. Art Direction, John Mansbridge, Lyle R. Wheeler. Set Decoration, Joseph Kish, Walter M. Scott. Makeup, Hal Lierley.
Cast: François Delambre (Vincent Price), Philippe Delambre (Brett Halsey), Alan Hinds (David Frankham), Inspector Beachamp (John Sutton), Cecile Bonnard (Danielle de Metz), Max Berthold (Dan Seymour), Nun (Florence Strom), Madame Bonnard (Janine Grandel), Sergeant Dubois (Richard Flato), Detective Evans (Pat O'Hara), Lieutenant Maclish (Barry Bernard), Granville (Jack Daly), Gaston (Michael Mark), Priest (Francisco Villalobas), Fly creature (Ed Wolff), Nurse (Joan Cotton), Policemen (Gregg Martell, Rick Turner, Courtland Shepard).
Synopsis: After his mother passes away, Philippe Delambre asks his uncle François to fully explain the details of his father's death years before. François takes Philippe to the old Delambre plant and shows him Andre's laboratory. Against his better judgment, he describes the disintegrator-integrator experiment that left Andre with the head and arm of a fly. Philippe vows to

Cecile Bonnard (Danielle de Metz) evinces terror at the sight of the human-become-fly in *Return of the Fly* (Twentieth Century–Fox, 1959).

carry on his father's work, and with the reluctantly given financing of François and the help of Alan Hinds, he builds a laboratory in the basement of his inherited home. Neither François nor Philippe is aware that Hinds is wanted by the British police and that he plans to steal the plans for the disintegrator-integrator. Hinds kills a policeman on his trail, and when Philippe accosts him he knocks Philippe unconscious and places him in the machine.

He adds a fly, and once again, a Delambre is transformed. Philippe's body has the head, arm and foot of a fly. Wounded by Hinds and hospitalized, François calls for Inspector Beauchamp, who'd worked with Inspector Charas on Andre Delambre's case. Beauchamp says he understands and helps François to prepare the laboratory for the hoped-for return of Philippe. Beauchamp catches the fly with Philippe's head. Meanwhile, Philippe has tracked and killed

Hinds and his cohort in crime, Max Ber-thold. Returning, he is assisted into the disintegrator and transformed back to fully human form.

Review: "Underrated sequel.... nice low budget film." (John Stanley, *The Creature Features Movie Guide*, p. 218)

Analysis: One supposes that the bandying about of the term "gigantism" covers the implausibility of the transformation, not only the large fly/tiny human heads but also the policeman who ends up with the enlarged hands and feet of a rabbit. It's interesting, though, with veteran actors like John Sutton taking their parts seriously and lending credibility.

The Curse of the Fly
(20th Century–Fox, 1965; 86 min.) **

Produced by Robert L. Lippert and Jack Parsons. Directed by Don Sharp. Screenplay, Harry Spalding. Inspired by the story "The Fly" by George Langelaan. Director of Photography, Basil Emmott.

Cast: Henry Delambre (Brian Donlevy), Patricia Stanley (Carole Gray), Martin Delambre (George Baker), Albert Delambre (Michael Graham), Inspector Ronet (Jeremy Wilkins), Inspector Charas (Charles Carson), Tai (Bert Kwouk), Wan (Yvette Rees), Madame Fournier (Rachel Kempson), Judith (Mary Manson), Hotel manager (Warren Stanhope), Porter (Arnold Bell), Creature (Stan Simmons).

Synopsis: Escaping from the Fournier Mental Hospital near Toronto, Patricia Stanley hitches a ride from Martin Delambre. She conceals the fact that she is recovering from a mental breakdown occasioned by her mother's death. For his part, Delambre is reticent to talk about his circumstances, mentioning only that he is involved in "research." In fact, this *research* has involved several generations of Delambres who have tried to perfect the process of teleportation. Most experiments ended tragically. For this reason, the family is viewed with suspicion by the authorities. Even as Martin works at home in Canada, his father and brother, Henry and Albert, are experimenting in England; they have sent inanimate objects from one location to the other successfully. Animate matter is a different matter, and failures have cost

lives. Both Martin and his father, in fact, have been adversely affected by the experiments: Henry has received severe radiation burns, while Martin has developed a peculiar condition of dramatically accelerated aging. Martin and Patricia's relationship turns romantic, and they marry. They arrive at the Delambre mansion, where Martin receives an urgent message from his father in England. Officials there suspect that Henry is without proper passport. To forestall an investigation that would reveal the nature of their work, Henry has Martin set up his machine as a receiver, and Henry arrives without incident. Henry becomes alarmed when Police Inspector Ronet and Madame Fournier arrive. Patricia Stanley, after all, is a fugitive from a mental institution. No laws have been broken, however, and the new Mrs. Delambre seems fully rational. Unsatisfied, Ronet pursues his investigation by contacting the invalid Inspector Charas, who had been involved in the earlier case involving Martin's grandfather. Charas relates how the elder Delambre had inadvertently merged his own atoms with that of a common housefly, resulting in a monstrous mutation. Investigating further, Ronet learns that two research assistants of the Delambres have been missing. While exploring the grounds, Patricia discovers a secluded outbuilding. Opening a small eye-level trap in a door, she is horrified to find herself face-to-face with a deformed visage. She runs screaming to Martin and Henry. What she saw is a disfigured animal, the unfortunate result of an experiment, Henry explains. That evening Patricia comes upon a disfigured woman playing the piano. Martin tries to convince her that she was dreaming. In truth, the maimed figure is that of Martin's first wife, Judith, who confronts the new wife but is killed by the housekeeper, Wan. To keep Ronet at bay, Henry decides to teleport the "animals" in the outbuildings to England. In reality, these animals are the mutated research assistants. Martin is hesitant to teleport Patricia and himself but helps Henry with the "animals." In England, Andrew is disgusted by the writhing mass that appears. Henry radios Andrew, announcing his intention to teleport himself to Britain. Andrew is cut off before he can tell his father he wrecked his reintegrator. Martin is oblivious to the fact that when he pulls the switch, his father is permanently disintegrated. He trundles the unconscious Patricia onto the device when Inspector Ronet appears. Patricia resumes consciousness and escapes just as Martin is struck by one of his fits of aging. Without access to his serum, the scientist ages fantastically in a matter of moments, and the detective finds only a smoldering pile of bones in Martin's car.

Review: "Pacing is slow, action too infrequent." (John Stanley, *The Creature Features Movie Guide*, p. 49)

Analysis: With its tenuous connections to the preceding two films documenting the exploits of the Delambre family, the British Lippert's *Curse of the Fly* went practically unnoticed at the time of its release and remains obscure to this day. Lacking the more fantastic elements and monstrous makeup effects of the previous films, *Curse* is a science fiction melodrama whose plot involving Martin's secretly sequestered first wife derives more from Alfred Hitchcock's *Rebecca* (and *Wuthering Heights*) than from the American films based upon George Langelaan's short story. Director Don Sharp keeps the film's focus on Patricia Stanley and her predicament at the Delambre mansion rather than on either of the scientists, although it can't be said that the film really suffers from this. In fact, *Curse of the Fly*'s reputation as the worst and most forgettable of the three original Fly films is probably unwarranted and worthy of reconsideration. Brian Donlevy brings the same sort of bullying surliness to the role of Henry Delambre that he brought to the character of Bernard Quatermass in the first two Hammer films involving Nigel Kneale's scientist hero. Henry Delambre is more akin to Victor Frankenstein than Quatermass, however, in his zeal to perfect his creations and his demonstrated disregard for human life.

The Fly

(20th Century–Fox, 1986; 95 min.)
****

Produced by Stuart Cornfield. Directed by David Cronenberg. Screenplay, Charles Edward Pogue and David Cronenberg. Based on the story by George Langelaan. Edited by Ronald Sanders. Director of Photography, Mark Irwin. Color, DeLuxe. Music, Howard Shore. Sound, Bryan Day, Michael Lacroix. Sound Effects, Jane Tattersall. Art Direction, Rolf Harvey. Set Decoration, Elinor Rose Galbraith, James McAteer. Costumes, Denise Cronenberg. Special Effects, Louis Craig, Ted Ross. Computer/Video Effects, Lee Wilson. Fly created and designed by Chris Walas, Inc.

Cast: Seth Brundle (Jeff Goldblum), Veronica Quaife (Geena Davis), Stathis Borans (John Getz), Tawny (Joy Boushel), Dr. Cheevers (Les Carlson), Marky (George Chubalo), Man in bar (Michael Copeman), Gynecologist (David Cronenberg), Nurse (Carol Lazare), Clerk (Shawn Hewitt), Brundle stunt double (Brent Meyers), Gymnastic doubles (Doron Kernerman, Romuald Vervin).

Synopsis: Seth Brundle takes journalist Veronica Quaife to his private laboratory and explains that the large objects she labels "designer phonebooths" are telepods. He demonstrates by transporting her stocking from one to another — through the air, as it were. Although Bartok Industries funds his work, only he knows the progress that has been made. The "fly" in the ointment is the fact that he cannot teleport animate objects — yet. Veronica takes him up on his proposal to write an entire book about the project, concluding when he transports himself. He fails with a baboon, which is apparently turned inside out. After he and Veronica make love, he transports steak, but it's inedible. He determines that the computer needs to be taught to go crazy after "flesh," and the next baboon he transports comes through okay. While Veronica is away, Seth transports himself. He fails to notice a fly in his telepod. The experience seems to go smoothly, and he tells Veronica. Shortly thereafter he finds he can do handstands, catch flies in his hands and maintain his sexual potency indefinitely. Veronica discovers coarse hairs growing on his back, and when Seth demands that she be teleported in order to become like him, she knows something has gone wrong. Seth picks up a girl in a bar after winning her in an arm wrestling contest — by shattering the other man's forearm. He and Tawny have sex, but Veronica arrives and tells Seth she had the hairs from his back analyzed. They are insect. Seth kicks her out but soon realizes she may be right. His fingernails come off. Reviewing his computer records, he is told that a secondary object was in the telepod when he was transported: "Secondary Element is — Not Brundle." He and a fly have been fused at the molecular-genetic level! Four weeks pass before he phones Veronica for assistance. When she arrives she discovers that he uses canes. An ear falls off while she's there. She tells her editor, Stathis Borans, who says he'll believe when he sees Seth. At the laboratory, Veronica finds Seth walking on the ceiling. He says the disease has a purpose. He's becoming Brundle Fly. Veronica shows Borans a videotape of Seth eating. Veronica finds that she's pregnant. Meanwhile, Seth asks the computer how to reduce the fly in Brundle Fly. Another human is needed, he learns. Veronica visits, but Seth tells her to leave and not come back. She tells Borans she wants an abortion immediately, but Seth breaks in and carries her from the hospital. He urges her to have the baby. Borans arrives at the lab with a shotgun but is beset by the now hideous Seth, who dissolves his hand and foot. Brundle Fly asks Veronica to help him be more human by merging with him via telepod. Though in agony, Borans reaches his gun and fires a shot that severs the cable connecting Veronica's telepod to the others. Before Brundle Fly can exit its pod, the process begins and it merges with the machine itself, falling from the third telepod a misshapen thing. It welcomes an end to its misery by shotgun in the hands of an anguished Veronica.

Reviews: "Cronenberg always hits below the belt…. This would not be a Cronenberg film if sex did not mean, mainly, big trouble." (Thomas Doherty, *Film Quarterly*, Spring 1987, p. 38) ¶"Sensitive script…. wonderful performances by Goldblum and Davis." (Patrick Goldstein, *Los Angeles Times Calendar*, August 14, 1986, p. 1) ¶"Cronenberg's work … belongs … within more extreme Gothic traditions in which the human body becomes the external site of an internal struggle between ego and id, 'good' and 'bad' psychic forces." (Pam Cook, *Monthly Film Bulletin*, February 1987, p. 45)

Analysis: This is one of the best examples of a movie whose mission is entered into without rigamarole. It is realized after the finale that one's muscles have been progressively tightening. One viewer came in late and hardly knew it was a science fiction film. This is how good the romance is, a love story that goes awry. Audiences feel supreme sympathy for the characters and the bind into which they've gotten. Even Stathis Borans undergoes a transformation from schmuck to savior. Academy Award winner for Makeup. There was talk of Jeff Goldblum getting an Academy Award nomination for Best Actor. It didn't happen, although Sigourney Weaver had a Best Actress nomination that year for *Aliens*. Like *Aliens* — another Twentieth Century–Fox release — it attracted a large mainstream audience.

The Fly II
(20th Century–Fox, 1989; 105 min.)
**

Produced by Steven-Charles Jaffe. Directed by Chris Walas. Screenplay, Mick Garris, Jim and Ken Wheat, Frank Darabont. Story, Mick Garris. Edited by Sean Barton. Director of Photography, Robin Vidgeon. Panavision. Color, DeLuxe. Music, Christopher Young. Dolby Stereo. Art Direction, Sandy Cochrane. Set Decoration, Rose Marie McSherry. Stunts, John Wardlow. Effects created and designed by Chris Walas. Creature Effects Supervisor, Jon Berg. Special Effects Makeup Supervision, Stephan Dupuis.

Cast: Martin Brundle (Eric Stoltz), Beth Logan (Daphne Zuniga), Anton Bartok (Lee Richardson), Stathis Borans (John Getz), Dr. Shepard (Frank Turner), Dr. Jainway (Ann Marie Lee), Scorby (Gary Chalk), Ronnie (Saffron Henderson), Ten-year-old Martin (Harley Cross), Four-year-old Martin (Matthew Moore), Baby Martin (Sterling Cottingham), 1½-year-old Martin (Rodney Clough, Jr.), Wiley (Rob Roy), Hargis (Andrew Rhodes), Mackenzie (Pat Bermel), Obstetrician (Duncan Fraser), Dr. Trimble (William Taylor), Simms (Jerry Wasserman), Nurse (Janet Hodgkinson), Perinatologist (Sean O'Byrne), Neonatologist (Mike Winlaw), Guards (Allan Lysell, Suzanne Ristic, Danny Virtue), Marla (Kimelly Anne Warren), Linder (Ken Camroux), Technician

(Bruce Harwood), Woman (Lorena Gale), Flywalker (David Mylrea).
Synopsis: Martin, Seth Brundle's son, grows at an accelerated pace at Bartok Industries. On his fifth birthday, when he looks about eighteen, Martin gets his own pad and an invitation from Anton Bartok to continue his father's work on teleportation. After watching videos of his father, Martin begins experimenting and successfully transports a telephone. But he doesn't succeed with the cactus belonging to his new friend, Beth Logan. He does succeed with a kitten. The aberrant chromosomes in his body begin to take a toll. He finds the video of his father turning into a fly. He runs, finds Beth, and they drive to the country home of Stathis Borans, a man who knew his father and who tells Martin his only cure lies in the pods. But Martin knows that the gene-swapping procedure involves taking another's life. Captured by Bartok's guards, Martin begins "cocooning." Breaking out as a monstrous fly, he kills Dr. Jainway and makes his way to Bay 17. He's wounded but manages to drag Bartok into one of the teleporter chambers. Beth activates the procedure and Martin is restored to normality. Not so Bartok, who is a writhing, disgusting creature relegated to the cell where once a similarly deformed golden retriever was put out of its misery by Martin.
Reviews: "Faintly silly in its dead-seriousness.... Its makers had better be braced for unintended laughter." (Kevin Thomas, *Los Angeles Times Calendar*, February 11, 1989, p. 3) ¶"Constructed with a refreshing intricacy and visual panache.... has an unexpected integrity...." (Philip Strick, *Monthly Film Bulletin*, October 1989, p. 300)
Analysis: The Bartok Industries security force *and* the scientists in general are too inconsiderate. Bartok himself didn't deserve the fate in store for him. We're expected to believe his deformed self would be incarcerated in that awful cell? Compare this big science with the homegrown labs of many '50s scientists. It strains credulity at the far-too-drawn-out finale, when we can see everything coming. This should have been a 90-minute movie. Stoltz was in his horrendous makeup phase. There are two really gross images: the guard whose head is crushed by an elevator, and another security person whose face disintegrates when the fly spits on him.

Food of the Gods
(AIP, 1976; 88 min.) **

Produced and directed by Bert I. Gordon. Executive Producer, Samuel Z. Arkoff. Screenplay, Bert I. Gordon. Based on the novel by H. G. Wells. Edited by Corky Ehlers. Director of Photography, Reg Morris. Movielab Color. Music, Elliot Kaplan. Art Direction, Graeme Murray. Set Decoration, John Stark. Special Effects, Tom Fisher, John Thomas, Keith Wardlow.
Cast: Morgan (Marjoe Gortner), Lorna Scott (Pamela Franklin), Mrs. Skinner (Ida Lupino), Bensington (Ralph Meeker), Brian (Jon Cypher), Rita (Belinda Balaski), Thomas (Tom Stovall).
Synopsis: Mrs. Skinner waits in her island farmhouse while her husband drives to the mainland to interest Bensington in what Skinner calls "F.O.T.G." (Food of the Gods), a milky fluid that erupts from his farmyard. He mixed it with grain and fed it to the chickens. The babies grew huge and killed the adults. Morgan, a football player, and his agent, Brian, visit the island to investigate the death of a friend killed by bees. Mr. Skinner never makes it home. Stopping to fix a flat, he is attacked by rats the size of ponies. Morgan and Brian arrive at the farmhouse, where Bensington is making a nuisance of himself. Morgan shoots some huge wasps, then burns up their giant nest. He and Brian electrify the fence that runs across the island, but after initial success the rats fell a tree and cross. Brian is killed. Back at the farm, a young couple, Rita and Tom, arrive from their camper, which was overrun by the rats. Intent on saving some F.O.T.G., Bensington is killed by the rodents. Taking refuge in the house, Morgan makes some bombs out of shotgun pellets. He and Tom break through the rats and blow up a dam. Racing back to the house, they, Lorna and Rita climb onto a second-floor balcony and watch as the rats, too heavy to swim, drown. Morgan kills their leader, a white

rat. Later, as two bottles of F.O.T.G. are washed into the river and past some cows, Morgan's voice is heard wondering if they destroyed all of the growth food, or will nature strike back again? *Review:* "Rather flat Bert I. Gordon film.... Technical credits are standard, and pic is a tax shelter job." (Murf., *Variety*, June 9, 1976, p. 23) *Analysis:* This "could have been" film is irreparably flawed by mostly lousy special effects — a Bert Gordon trademark — although a couple of process shots are above average. More compromising are the stupid characters. Only Marjoe Gortner's is resourceful. The film moves at a fairly fast pace although the camera lingers on rat packs a bit longer than necessary. The setting at least is attractive, i.e., suitably spooky. The Great North woods make for fright. These are on Bowen Island, British Columbia. Astoundingly, the film won Grand Prize at the Sixth Paris International Fantastic and Science Fiction Film Festival in March 1977.

Food of the Gods Part 2
(Concorde/Centauri, 1989; 90 min.) *

Produced by David Mitchell and Damian Lee. Directed by Damian Lee. Screenplay, Richard Bennett and E. Kim Brewster. Story, Richard Bennett. Edited by David Mitchell. Director of Photography, Curtis Petersen. Color. Music, Steve Parsons and Dennis Haines. Creature Designs, David B. Miller. Visual Effects, Ted Rae.

Cast: Neil Hamilton (Paul Coufos), Alex Reed (Lisa Schrage), Professor Edmund Delhurst (Colin Fox), Jacques (Frank Moore), Mark (Real Andrews), Lt. Weisel (Michael Copeman), Dean White (David B. Nichols), Dr. Kate Treger (Jackie Burroughs), Al (Stuart Hughes), Mary Anne (Kimberly Dickson), Joshua (Frank Pellegrino), Angie (Karen Hines), Bobby (Sean Mitchell).

Synopsis: Plant researcher Neil Hamilton receives an urgent phone call from Dr. Kate Treger. When he visits the home where she is living, he finds that one Bobby, a boy of approximately twelve years, is as tall as the ceiling. Treger explains that she injected him with the growth hormone "192" but certainly didn't expect this outcome. Hamilton returns to his lab to analyze the hormone and attempt to develop

an antidote. When his tomatoes increase in size, Hamilton's assistant says, "This is the food of the gods." It could end world hunger. However, animal rights protesters break into the lab and accidentally release the rapidly growing rat into which 192 has been injected. The other rodents escape as well, and because they've eaten the tomatoes, they start to grow. Police investigate the death of one of the protesters, but the dean's response is merely to call in exterminators. Hamilton, meanwhile, develops an antidote. More people are killed, including Hamilton's assistant and Professor Delhurst, who decays as a result of accidentally infecting a cut with 192. Hamilton and his girlfriend, Alex, implement a plan to attract the monster rodents using his white female rat. The giant rats enter the swimming pool of the new sports complex and savage the synchonized swimming team as well as spectators before being gunned down outside. But far away, the giant Bobby kills Kate and escapes. *Review:* "Disgusting sequel." (Mick Martin and Marsha Porter, *Video Movie Guide 1994*, p. 1016) *Analysis:* Whatever charm *Food of the Gods* had lay in its rustic setting and sense of isolation. With the sequel's college-campus milieu, the story is distinctly urban. But that's not the chief problem of this Canadian production. It's boring. The characters are really stupid. (Ditto whoever decided a Rottweiler is a tracking dog.) The filmmakers seem to have changed gears midway through — or maybe during the editing stage — and decided to produce what becomes a disconcerting semi-spoof. The rat effects were better in the first film.

Frankenstein
(Universal, 1931; 71 min.) ****

Directed by James Whale. Screenplay, Garrett Fort and Francis Edwards Faragoh. Adapted by John L. Balderston from the play by Peggy Webling. Based on the novel by Mary Wollstonecraft Shelley. Edited by Clarence Kolster. Director of Photography, Arthur Edeson. Art Director, Charles D. Hall. Special Electrical Effects, Frank Graves, Kenneth Strickfadden, Raymond Lindsay. Technical Assistant, Dr. Cecil Reynolds. Sound, C. Roy Hunter.

Cast: Henry Frankenstein (Colin Clive), the Monster (Boris Karloff), Elizabeth (Mae Clarke), Doctor Waldman (Edward Van Sloan), Fritz (Dwight Frye), Victor Moritz (John Boles), Baron Frankenstein (Frederick Kerr), Ludwig (Michael Mark), Vogel, the burgomaster (Lionel Belmore), Little Maria (Marilyn Harris), Bridesmaids (Arletta Duncan, Pauline Moore), Lecture extra/wounded villager (Francis Ford).

Synopsis: After robbing a grave, Henry Frankenstein and his hunchback assistant, Fritz, inspect a body hanging from a gibbet — but it's not good. The neck is broken, the brain useless. Fritz breaks into the Goldstadt medical center and steals an abnormal brain after dropping the good brain. Concerned about Henry's health, his fiancée, Elizabeth, and friend Victor Moritz approach Dr. Waldman for help. Waldman says Frankenstein was a brilliant but erratic student whose specialties were chemical galvanism and electro-biology. Waldman agrees to accompany them to the old watchtower Henry uses. There Henry and Fritz prepare for a major experiment while a storm rages without. Against his better judgment, Henry allows his unwanted guests to witness his work. "I have discovered the great ray which first brought life into the world," he says and sends a sewn-together body up to the heavens to receive the power of lightning. The arm moves, and Henry is ecstatic. Waldman calls the creature a fiend and tells Henry it has a criminal brain stolen from his lab. Henry seems perturbed but says, "Oh well, it's only a piece of dead tissue." Later the creature appears in the doorway. Henry makes it sit and opens a skylight. It reaches for the light. Fritz comes in and torments the creature with a flaming brand and later, a whip. Upstairs, Henry and Waldman hear sickening screams. Rushing downstairs, they find Fritz hanging from the ceiling. The monster is locked in, but they know it will break the door down soon. Henry lures the creature out and Waldman injects it in the back with a hypodermic. The injured, worn-out Henry is taken away by his father and Elizabeth. Waldman plans to dissect the monster, but it wakes and strangles him. Frankenstein's wedding day dawns while by a lake the monster confronts a little girl. They play with flowers, but when the monster's are gone, it tosses the girl in. She drowns, and her father brings the body to town. The monster arrives, too, terrorizing Elizabeth. Henry, the burgomaster and the villagers track the fiend by night. In the mountains the monster overcomes Henry and carries him off to a windmill. The monster tosses his creator onto a circling arm of the mill. The villagers recover Henry and set the mill afire. A beam crashes down on the frantic creature. Back in town, Henry and Elizabeth seem destined for marriage.

Reviews: "An artistically conceived work…. far and away the most effective thing of its kind. Beside it *Dracula* is tame." (Mordaunt Hall, *New York Times,* December 5, 1931, p. 21) ¶"*Frankenstein* looks like a *Dracula* plus, touching a new peak in horror plays and handled in production with supreme craftsmanship." (*Variety*)

Analysis: Like *Dracula,* this was a big success during the Great Depression. And later, what teenager could forget the first time this was presented on TV's *Shock Theater* in the late fifties? Weren't the visages of Frankenstein and Fritz peering into the graveyard thrilling? Mary Shelley's novel has the monster's maker track it into the frozen north; none of that trip is in this — or many other — Frankenstein films. Boris Karloff's performance here and in *Bride of Frankenstein* deserved an award, but "monster movies" weren't critically respectable back then. Like Kong two years hence, this creature reaching for the light is to be pitied. The restored version, which is available on video, includes the previously excised scene where the monster tosses the girl into the lake.

Bride of Frankenstein
(Universal, 1935; 80 min.) ****

Produced by Carl Laemmle, Jr. Directed by James Whale. Screenplay, William Hurlbut. Based on characters in the novel *Frankenstein* by Mary Wollstonecraft Shelley's. Adapted by William Hurlbut and John L. Balderston. Edited by Ted Kent. Editorial Supervisor, Maurice Pivar. Director of Photography, John J. Mescall. Photographic Effects, John P.

Fulton. Music, Franz Waxman. Art Direction, Charles D. Hall. Makeup, Jack Pierce. *Cast:* Henry Frankenstein (Colin Clive), the Monster (Boris Karloff), Dr. Pretorious (Ernest Thesiger), Elizabeth (Valerie Hobson), Bride/Mary Shelley (Elsa Lanchester), Karl (Dwight Frye), Hermit (O. P. Heggie), Ludwig (Ted Billings), Burgomaster (E. E. Clive), Minnie (Una O'Connor), Shepherdess (Anne Darling), Percy Shelley (Douglas Walton), Lord Byron (Gavin Gordon), Rudy (Neil Fitzgerald), Hans (Reginald Barlow), Hans's wife (Mary Gordon), Uncle Glutz (Gunnis Davis), Albert (Lucien Prival), Aunt Glutz (Tempe Pigott), Hunters (John Carradine, Frank Terry, Robert Adair), Marta (Sarah Schwartz), Coroner (Edwin Mordant), Neighbors (Rollo Lloyd, Walter Brennan, Mary Stewart), Baby (Billy Barty), Priest (Lucio Villegas), Mother (Brenda Fowler), Little Archbishop (Norman Ainsley), Little Queen (Joan Woodbury), Mermaid (Josephine McKim), Ballerina (Kensas DeForrest), Communion girl (Helen Parrish), Villagers (Ed Peil, Sr., Anders Van Haden, John George).

Synopsis: During a raging thunderstorm, Mary Shelley recites for Percy Shelley and Lord Byron the sequel to her tale, *Frankenstein:* Villagers leave the wreckage of the mill wherein they thought Frankenstein's heinous creation had burned to death. The injured Henry Frankenstein is taken home. Hans, meanwhile, wants to see the blackened bones of the monster that killed his child. He falls into the water-filled cavity beneath the mill, only to be drowned by the still-living monster. The creature climbs out and sends Hans's wife careening down to her husband. At his home, Henry recovers under the care of his fiancée, Elizabeth. He wonders if he is destined to know the secret of eternal life. Elizabeth thinks not. A gaunt man — Dr. Pretorious — is admitted to the house. The former professor of philosophy wants to collaborate with Henry and intimates that Frankenstein is actually responsible for the recent murders. Pretorious invites Henry to his abode. There the older man proposes a toast, "To a new world, of gods and monsters!" He brings forth a chest of glass canisters filled with miniature people: a queen, a king, an archbishop, the devil, a ballerina, a mermaid. Pretorious says he grew his creatures from cultures. With Henry's help, he can achieve size. They may

make a mate for Henry's original creation. In the surrounding environs, the monster roams, frightening a shepherdess and taking a bullet in the arm from a hunter. The burgomaster is contacted, and the citizens track the monster. Bound to a post, it is brought to the old dungeon and chained. No sooner is this accomplished than the monster uses its strength to break free and scatter a newly frightened populace. In the forest, it stumbles upon a cabin. A hermit is there, playing the violin. The monster understands the blind hermit, who is grateful to have a friend. He teaches the monster some words: "good," "friend," "alone," "fire." Two lost hunters ruin the idyllic scene, a fire is started, and the monster is on the prowl again. In a cemetery, it finds a passage beneath a monument and enters the crypt. Dr. Pretorious arrives to exhume a body and makes the acquaintance of the monster. Pleased to learn the doctor will make a woman, the monster says, "Woman. Friend. Wife." Pretorious visits Henry and congratulates him and Elizabeth on their marriage. When Elizabeth leaves the room, Pretorious says he's created a perfect brain. Henry is as yet unwilling to collaborate, so Pretorious opens the door. There stands the monster, now capable of speech. Nevertheless, Henry refuses to promise assistance, and the monster kidnaps Elizabeth. To get her back, Henry agrees to help Pretorious, and they go to Frankenstein's castle laboratory. To keep the monster amenable and out of the way, Pretorious slips it a mickey. A storm approaches, and kites are sent aloft to capture the life-giving lightning. The wrapped body is raised to the roof and imbued with animation. It is not keen on its intended mate, however, and Henry's male creation is disturbed and distraught. Discovering a lever that can blow the place to smithereens, the monster urges Henry and Elizabeth to leave, Pretorious to remain: "Yes. Go. You live. Go. You stay. We belong dead." Explosions rend the castle.

Reviews: "In background, atmosphere, dramatic invention, *The Bride of Frankenstein* will stand up as one of the best of the year." (Otis Ferguson, *New Republic,* May 29, 1935, p. 75) ¶"Mr. Karloff is so

The monster (Boris Karloff) finds solace in the company of the hermit (O. P. Heggie) in *The Bride of Frankenstein* (Universal, 1935).

splendid in the role that all one can say is 'he is the Monster'.... a first-rate horror film." (Frank S. Nugent, *New York Times*, May 11, 1935, p. 21) ¶"Karloff manages to invest the character with some subtleties of emotion that are surprisingly real and touching. Especially is this true in the scene where he meets a blind man." (*Variety*)

Analysis: Frankenstein is a classic, but *Bride* is a better film, a masterpiece of the cinema, matching shock with humor and pathos. The monster is perhaps more brutal. Witness his killing of the man and wife at the burned mill, and the boulder he dumps on two men. The hermit scene alone should have gotten Karloff an Academy Award nomination. (It's well parodied in Mel Brooks's *Young Frankenstein*.) The interior sets are reminiscent of the silent German expressionist cinema, notably *The Cabinet of Caligari*. Check out the Christ imagery when the monster is tied to the post, raised up and tipped into the cart. It may be subversive, or merely ironic, as is

the scene when the hermit is thankful for a friend he cannot see who is wolfing down his soup and bread like a beast. We wonder why the monster let his maker go at the end. Perhaps he felt sorry for Elizabeth. Dwight Frye, Frankenstein's hunchback assistant killed in the previous film, returns as a graverobber only to be tossed from the castle tower. Franz Waxman's music is also a screen milestone. Note that the end credits ask the audience to guess the identity of the actress playing the monster's mate.

Son of Frankenstein
(Universal, 1939; 94 min.) ***

Produced and directed by Rowland Lee. Assistant Director, Fred Frank. Screenplay, Willis Cooper. Edited by Ted Kent. Director of Photography, George Robinson. Music, Frank Skinner. Musical Director, Charles Previn. Set Decorations, R. A. Gausman. Art Director, Jack Otterson. Gowns, Vera West. Makeup, Jack Pierce.

Cast: Baron Wolf von Frankenstein (Basil

Inspector Krogh (Lionel Atwill) is confronted by his own right arm in the hand of the monster (Boris Karloff); Peter (Donnie Dunagan) is under the monster's foot in *Son of Frankenstein* (Universal, 1939).

Rathbone), Inspector Krogh (Lionel Atwill), Ygor (Bela Lugosi), Elsa von Frankenstein (Josephine Hutchinson), Peter (Donnie Dunagan), Burgomeister (Lawrence Grant), Butler Thomas Benson (Edgar Norton), Mrs. Neumuller (Caroline Cook), Amelia (Emma Dunn), Lang (Lionel Belmore), Fritz (Perry Ivins), Oswald Neumuller (Michael Mark), Burghers (Gustav von Seyffertitz, Tom Ricketts, Lorimer Johnson). With Dwight Frye, Ward Bond.

Synopsis: Baron Wolf von Frankenstein returns by train to claim his inheritance in the village of Frankenstein. He knows something of his father's work, blaming a stupid assistant for whatever went wrong. At their new home Wolf exclaims, "It's medieval. Exciting, exhilarating!" Inspector Krogh of the District Police visits and promises protection if the townsfolk threaten harm. Wolf inspects the laboratory and meets Ygor, a man with a broken neck. He was hanged but not killed. Ygor oversees the "monster," which lies comatose with

two bullets in its heart. Frankenstein attempts to revive it with electricity but seemingly fails. However, his child Peter speaks of visits by a giant. Wolf returns to the lab and learns that the monster is in fact mobile. It loves Ygor, who spurns Wolf's desire to make the monster better: "He is well enough for me and you no touch him again!" Ygor sends the creature out to kill those council members who voted to hang him years before. Wolf shoots and kills Ygor when the monster is absent. Discovering Ygor's body, the monster kidnaps Peter. Inspector Krogh arrives and fires at the monster with little effect. Wolf swings down on a rope and topples his father's creation into the sulfur pit. Wolf deeds his estate to the village and leaves.

Review: "If ... *Son of Frankenstein* isn't the silliest picture ever made, it's a sequel to the silliest picture ever made.... But the silliness is deliberate..., perpetrated by a good director in the best traditions of cinematic horror." (B. R. Crisler, *New York Times*, January 30, 1939, p. 9)

Analysis: The sets are the thing, and that sulfur spring is fascinating. Based on the 1816 story by Mary Shelley, how can Wolf be so young, still alive? Obviously the first *Frankenstein* didn't start in 1816, right? Atwill's role is the inspiration for Kenneth Mars in *Young Frankenstein*. Lugosi has one of his best roles as Ygor, which he would reprise in the next entry.

The Ghost of Frankenstein
(Universal, 1942; 67 min.) **½

Produced by George Waggner. Directed by Erle C. Kenton. Screenplay, W. Scott Darling. Story, Eric Taylor. Edited by Ted Kent. Directors of Photography, Milton Krasner, Elwood Bredell. Music, Hans J. Salter. Art Direction, Jack Otterson. Set Decoration, R. A. Gausman. Makeup, Jack Pierce.

Cast: Frankenstein monster (Lon Chaney, Jr.), Dr. Ludwig Frankenstein (Sir Cedric Hardwicke), Dr. Theodore Bohmer (Lionel Atwill), Erik Ernst (Ralph Bellamy), Ygor (Bela Lugosi), Elsa (Evelyn Ankers), Cloestine (Janet Ann Gellow), Dr. Kettering (Barton Yarborough), Martha (Doris Lloyd), Chief constable (Leyland Hodgson), Hussman (Olaf Hytten), Magistrate (Holmes Herbert). With Dwight Frye.

Synopsis: Townsfolk blow up Frankenstein's castle, but Ygor escapes below and discovers the monster sticking out of the now solidified sulfur. Breaking the creature free and leading it outside, Ygor finds it empowered by a bolt of lightning. He leads the monster into Visaria to find Dr. Ludwig Frankenstein, Henry Frankenstein's second son. In town, the monster befriends a child, Cloestine Hussman, but is subdued and incarcerated by the police. Ygor confronts Ludwig, who believes the monster has been a curse on the family. Ygor threatens to tell the entire family about its history. Ludwig examines his father's diary. The monster is put on trial but breaks free and threatens bodily harm to Ludwig until Ygor's horn calls it to him. They drive off in a cart. While reading Henry Frankenstein's diary, Ludwig's daughter Elsa sees the monster at the window. When the deadly duo break in, Ludwig gases them into unconsciousness and

extracts Elsa. In the laboratory, Ludwig finds that his assistant Dr. Bohmer won't help him dissect a living being. Ludwig sees his father's apparition, which urges his son to give the monster a healthy brain. Ygor convinces Bohmer to transplant his brain into the monster, not that of a dead assistant, Kettering. While Erik and the police search the premises, the monster seeks Cloestine. Again, Ygor recalls his friend with his horn. The monster shows the child to Ludwig, indicating that it wants her unspoiled, innocent brain. But Ludwig manages to turn Cloestine over to Elsa. Unknown to Ludwig, Bohmer removes Ygor's brain, which is then placed into the skull of the monster. Two weeks pass. Cloestine's father thinks his daughter is alive, and he and the townsmen head for the Frankenstein manor. Erik confronts Ludwig concerning the missing Kettering. Ludwig takes Erik to the "patient" and is astounded to hear the creature speak with Ygor's voice. The townsfolk break in. Bohner turns on the gas, but it's too late. The monster loses its sight, the result of different blood types between Ygor's brain and its new housing. Bohner is electrocuted. The house is set afire, and the monster and Ludwig perish. Erik and Elsa escape and ascend a hill, silhouetted by the sun.

Reviews: "Several captivating scenes.... The cast is one of the finest ever assembled by Universal.... Chaney is good as the monster.... script is rich in action and pathos. Unfortunately, Erle C. Kenton's bland direction and the shared cinematography duties fail to interpret the script in any consistent or artistic way." (Tim Lucas, *Video Watchdog*, November/December 1993, pp. 10-11)

Analysis: It's a logical progression down the ladder. The monster ends with Ygor's brain and voice. This poses interesting questions about its real identity in ensuing entries. Is that why it only grunts from here on? Check out Dwight Frye as an irate villager. It's not the first time the Frankenstein monster has entered a village, but the crispness of this film may militate against mystery and atmosphere. According to Bosley Crowther in the *New York Times*, the scariest thing about the picture is that the monster (with Chaney's body and Lugosi's voice) might return for another picture.

Frankenstein Meets the Wolf Man
(Universal, 1943; 72 min.) **½

Produced by George Waggner. Directed by Roy William Neill. Screenplay, Curt Siodmak. Edited by Edward Curtiss. Director of Photography, George Robinson. Music, Hans J. Salter.

Cast: Lawrence Talbot (Lon Chaney, Jr.), Frankenstein monster (Bela Lugosi/Eddie Parker), Dr. Frank Mannering (Patric Knowles), Elsa Frankenstein (Ilona Massey), Mayor (Lionel Atwill), Maleva (Maria Ouspenskaya), Inspector Owen (Dennis Hoey), Rudi (Dwight Frye), Bruno (Harry Stubbs), Vazec (Rex Evans), Francis (Don Barclay), Hospital nurse (Doris Lloyd), Villagers (Adia Kuynetzoff, Beatrice Roberts), Little girl (Martha Vickers). With Jeff Corey, Torben Meyer.

Synopsis: Two graverobbers enter the Talbot mausoleum intent on stealing valuables left on the corpse of Lawrence Talbot. A full moon illuminates the body beneath the wolf bane, and a hand reaches out and grabs one of the men. The other flees. Later an unconscious man with a head injury is found by the police and taken to Queen's Hospital in Cardiff. There Dr. Mannering learns that his patient claims to be Lawrence Talbot and a werewolf. That night the moon shines again and a policeman is killed. Although no one believes the lycanthropy story, Talbot is straitjacketed. Nevertheless, he escapes and tracks down the gypsy woman Maleva on the Continent. "Maleva, here I still carry the sign of the Pentagram, the mark of the werewolf. I kill people. When the moon is full I turn into a wolf." She agrees to watch over him. They begin a journey to the town where lives Dr. Frankenstein, a scientist Maleva believes can help Talbot find the peace of death. However, the innkeeper tells them that the execrable Frankenstein is dead. He points out the castle near the dam. Talbot is distraught and in the wagon sees the full moon. He leaps off and runs into the woods. He discovers the body of the Frankenstein monster frozen in cave ice and cuts it out. At a village festival Talbot hears a tune he dislikes and he rants, "Stop that!

Stop this! Quit that singing! Will you? Eternally! I don't want to live eternally! Why did you say that to me?! Get away from me! Stay away! Go away! All of you! Let me alone! Stay away!" Mannering and Elsa Frankenstein find the book of Dr. Frankenstein and restore the laboratory. While Dr. Mannering is supposed to be drawing out the force from Talbot, he changes his mind and decides to make the monster stronger than before. The monster breaks free. Talbot turns into a werewolf and attacks the monster, who is carrying off Elsa. The woman and Mannering leave. The dam bursts from the explosive charge set by villagers, and the raging floodwaters carry away the castle and its strange inhabitants.

Review: "Too bad. Not very horrible. Universal will have to try again." (Bosley Crowther, *New York Times*, March 6, 1943, p. 8) ¶"Eerie atmosphere generates right at start.... creepy affair in grand style." (*Variety*)

Analysis: Teenagers seeing this for the first time on TV's *Shock Theater* in the late fifties thought it was quite good. Viewing it as a young adult, one found it less than classic. A middle-aged person can find faults and good elements. The beginning is excellent — for some, the best opening of any Universal movie. Bela Lugosi is unnecessary. His voice is his fortune and he can't use it here, but he should have been able to do so. After all, the monster ended its previous outing with Ygor's (Lugosi's) voice. We are perplexed: How did Larry Talbot, a modern-day monster in *The Wolf Man*, end up resurrected in the Frankenstein era?

House of Frankenstein
(Universal, 1944; 70 min.) **½

Produced by Paul Malvern. Directed by Erle C. Kenton. Screenplay, Edward T. Lowe. Based on a story by Curt Siodmak. Edited by Philip Cahn. Director of Photography, George Robinson. Music, Hans J. Salter. Art Direction, John B. Goodman, Martin Obzina. Set Decoration, Russell A. Gausman, R. J. Gilmore. Makeup, Jack Pierce. Special Photography, John P. Fulton.

Cast: Dr. Gustav Niemann (Boris Karloff), Larry Talbot (Lon Chaney, Jr.), Count Dracula (John Carradine), Daniel (J. Carrol Naish),

Poster art for *House of Frankenstein* (Universal, 1944).

Frankenstein monster (Glenn Strange), Professor Lampini (George Zucco), Rita Hussman (Anne Gwynne), Ilonka (Elena Verdugo), Inspector Arnz (Lionel Atwill), Carl (Peter Coe), Burgomaster Hussman (Sig Ruman), Fejos (William Edmunds), Villagers (Olaf Hytten, Brandon Hurst), Muller (Julius Tannen), Strauss (Michael Mark), Ullman (Frank Reicher), Man at horror show (Gino Corrado), Muller (Phillip Van Zandt).

Synopsis: Escaping from Neustadt Prison during a lightning storm, Dr. Niemann and the hunchback Daniel kill Bruno Lampini and take over his traveling show which includes a coffin purported to contain the skeleton of the infamous Count Dracula. In Reigelberg, Niemann removes the stake from the skeleton and to his surprise finds Dracula in corporeal form. He makes a deal: Niemann will protect the soil if Dracula will assist him. Calling himself Baron Latoes, Dracula kills Burgomaster Hussman and calls Rita Hussman to him. But the police are hot on his trail. To avoid their own capture, Niemann orders Daniel to thrust Dracula's coffin into the roadway. The sun

rises before Dracula can incarcerate himself. The police find only a skeleton grasping the coffin. Near the village of Frankenstein, Niemann finds the ruins of Castle Frankenstein and the ruined dam and torrent that washed away the monster and the Wolf Man. At a gypsy encampment, Daniel falls in love with the dancer Ilonka. She accompanies them to the ruins, where Niemann hopes at least to find Frankenstein's records. First, he finds the frozen forms of the Wolf Man and the monster. Thawed out, the werewolf becomes Lawrence Talbot. Niemann says he can help Talbot really die if they find Frankenstein's records. They discover Henry Frankenstein's notes in a hidden recess and leave for Visaria and Niemann's estate. Niemann abducts his old enemies, Strauss and Ullman. During the full moon, Talbot becomes the Wolf Man. A man is found dead and the people cry werewolf. To Daniel's consternation, Ilonka comforts the human Larry. Talbot threatens Niemann. Villagers see light in Niemann's house as the "scientist" charges the monster. The moon rises and Talbot changes into the lycanthrope. He attacks Ilonka, but she shoots him with the silver bullet she made. They die in each other's arms. Daniel carries Ilonka inside and attacks Niemann, but the monster breaks free and tosses Daniel through a window to the feet of the villagers. The monster carries the injured Niemann into the swamp, heedless of the man's warnings about quicksand. Both sink into a bog.

Review: "It's like a baseball team with nine Babe Ruths.... a truly remarkable script...." (A.W., *New York Times*, December 16, 1944, p. 19)

Analysis: It's certainly not classic, but it's a good deal of fun. This contains John Carradine's first outing as Count Dracula, as well as Glenn Strange's first as the Frankenstein monster. Over the years, Carradine's count has gained in stature. There is some animation used when the count turns into a bat. We do wonder why he could cross running water, as he does while driving the wagon. Perhaps the stream was placid and he only became giddy. There is more atmosphere here than in *The Ghost of Frankenstein.*

House of Dracula
(Universal, 1945; 67 min.)**½

Analysis: A "Parade of Monsters" film that features Frankenstein's monster, the Wolf Man, and Dracula. See listing under *Dracula* for cast, credits, and discussion.

Abbott and Costello Meet Frankenstein
(Universal, 1948; 92 min.) ***

Produced by Robert Arthur. Directed by Charles T. Barton. Screenplay, Robert Lees, Frederic I. Rinaldo, John Grant. Edited by Frank Gross. Director of Photography, Charles Van Enger. Music, Frank Skinner. Art Direction, Bernard Herzbrun, Hilyard Brown. Set Decoration, R. A. Gausman, Oliver Emert.

Cast: Chick Young (Bud Abbott), Wilbur Gray (Lou Costello), Dracula (Bela Lugosi), Lawrence Talbot (Lon Chaney, Jr.), Frankenstein monster (Glenn Strange), Sandra Mornay (Lenore Aubert), Joan Raymond (Jane Randolph), Mr. McDougal (Frank Ferguson), Professor Stevens (Charles Bradstreet), Mr. Harris (Howard Negley), Man in armor (Clarence Straight), Photographer (Harry Brown), Woman at baggage counter (Helen Spring), Sergeant (Paul Stader), Invisible man's voice (Vincent Price). With Joe Kirk.

Synopsis: London. A man makes a call to Florida and tries to keep porters Chick Young and Wilbur Gray from delivering two crates to Mr. McDougal's House of Horrors until he arrives. During the call the man turns into a werewolf. In Florida, McDougal arrives with a bill of lading. He tells Sandra Mornay, Wilbur's girlfriend, he's got the remains of the original Dracula as well as the Frankenstein monster in the crates. Chick dismisses his buddy's fears about the coffin in one. While Chick is outside, Dracula emerges and mesmerizes Wilbur, then uses his ring to impart a charge to the Frankenstein monster's electrodes. The creature utters, "Master," and, dragging the coffin, follows Dracula. A bat flies to an island castle, observes the lab in which Professor Stevens is working, and, transforming into Dracula, meets Sandra. He tells her he must be called Lahoes. Sandra and Dracula discuss reviving the monster properly. Sandra knows where to get a viable brain. Lawrence Talbot, the man who made the call from England, arrives and tells Wilbur and Chick he followed Dracula to destroy him before he revives Dr. Frankenstein's creation. Wilbur accedes to Talbot's request to lock him in his room that night. Shippers Insurance investigator Joan Raymond arranges bail for Wilbur and Chick, jailed by McDougal for allegedly stealing the contents of his crates. Joan pretends she's interested in Wilbur, and they plan to attend the masquerade ball. Wilbur, Chick and Joan go the island to pick up Sandra. While Joan is freshening up, Wilbur and Chick case the joint. Wilbur happens on Dracula and the monster, but a swinging door conceals the nemeses from Chick. Meanwhile Joan finds *The Secrets of Life and Death* by Dr. Frankenstein. "Baron Lahoes" appears. Dracula vampirizes Sandra when she doesn't fulfill his wishes fast enough. At the masquerade party, Talbot accosts "Lahoes." Sandra invites Wilbur back to the island. Joan disappears. Talbot transforms and chases Wilbur. Escaping the werewolf, Wilbur and

Dracula (Bela Lugosi) regards a boxed monster (Glenn Strange) in *Abbott and Costello Meet Frankenstein* (Universal, 1948).

Joan are taken to the island, where Sandra prepares to transfer Wilbur's brain into the monster. Chick and Talbot interrupt the proceedings. Finally everyone makes it to the boat, but they realize they must rescue Joan. Talbot, now a werewolf again, pursues Dracula and catches him as he becomes a bat. Both fall to the breakers far below. The monster chases Chick and Wilbur, who jump into a boat. The revived Professor Stevens sets the dock on fire and the monster burns up. Wilbur and Chick think they're safe until a cigarette is lighted — by the invisible man.

Review: "Most of the comic invention … is embraced in the idea and the title." (Bosley Crowther, *New York Times*, July 29, 1948, p. 17)

Analysis: It may be that *Abbott and Costello Meet Frankenstein* is not as funny as we found it as kids, but it moves along quite nicely. This is only the second time Bela Lugosi played Count Dracula. Both Jane Randolph (*Cat People*) and Lenore Aubert are lovely companions for good and

evil, respectively. Why is that scene in which Bud and Lou barricade the door that opens outward so funny? Big mistake: Dracula's reflection in a mirror!

This movie resurrected the career of Abbott and Costello, and at the same time caused a decade-long death knell for supernatural horror films. One can't blame it entirely for putting the kibosh on horror. Other forces were at play, like supposed UFO sightings and the threat of radiation and all that stuff scientists were doing.

When the resurrection of the supernatural horror genre did occur, the Frankenstein monster, like his colleague Dracula, first came back to life on the other side of the Atlantic. England's Hammer Studios had been around for a while but had made few waves. In 1956 the release of *The Quatermass Xperiment* (*The Creeping Unknown*) had brought it some measure of international success. When its producers turned to gothic horror, Hammer skyrocketed to fame and some degree of fortune, and its string of Frankenstein films earned a place in horror history.

The Curse of Frankenstein
(Hammer/Warner Bros., 1957; 83 min.) ***

Produced by Anthony Hinds. Executive Producer, Michael Carreras. Associate Producer, Anthony Nelson-Keys. Directed by Terence Fisher. Screenplay, Jimmy Sangster. Based on the novel *Frankenstein* by Mary Wollstonecraft Shelley. Edited by James Needs. Director of Photography, Jack Asher. Eastmancolor. Music, James Bernard. Musical Supervision, John Hollingsworth. Sound, W. H. May. Art Direction, Ted Marshall. Production Manager, Donald Weeks. Makeup, Phil Leakey. Hairdresser, Henry Montsash. Wardrobe, Molly Arbuthnot.

Cast: Baron Victor Frankenstein (Peter Cushing), Monster (Christopher Lee), Elizabeth (Hazel Court), Paul Krempe (Robert Urquhart), Justine (Valerie Gaunt), Aunt Sophie (Noel Hood), Mother (Marjorie Hume), Victor as a youth (Melvyn Hayes), Elizabeth as a child (Sally Walsh), Professor Bernstein (Paul Hardtmuth), Grandfather (Fred Johnson), Burgomaster (Hugh Dempster), Small boy (Claude Kingston), Schoolmaster (Henry Caine), Werner (Michael Mulcaster), Kurt (Patrick Troughton), Fritz (Joseph Behrman), Burgomaster's wife (Anne Blake), Father Felix (Raymond Rollett), Priest (Alex Gallier), Undertaker (Ernest Jay), Uncle (J. Trevor Davis), Tramp (Bartlett Mullins), Second priest (Eugene Leahy).

Synopsis: In prison about to be executed, Baron Victor Frankenstein tells a priest his life story. As a youth he inherited his mother's estate and hired Paul Krempe to be his tutor. As Victor grows to manhood, Paul becomes his collaborator in scientific experiments. They actually manage to bring a puppy back to life in Victor's laboratory. To experiment on humans it is necessary to take bodies from the gibbet. When cousin Elizabeth comes to visit and to marry Victor, Paul warns her to leave because of the dangerous experiments taking place. Little do they know that Victor has been consorting with the maid, Justine. In order to obtain a brilliant mind for his work, Victor pushes the visiting Professor Bernstein from a second floor landing. He uses Bernstein's brain, but it's damaged when

Paul tries to physically prevent Victor from continuing the experiment. Without Paul, Victor transplants the brain into a lifeless body. Thinking he still needs help, he asks Paul to return to the laboratory, but when they arrive, the new "man" is up and about — and tries to strangle Victor. Paul helps subdue it and argues that it must be destroyed. Victor says he'll operate next day. The creature escapes and kills a blind hiker before Paul shoots it in the head. They bury the monster, and Paul leaves Victor's house. Victor goes to his lab, where he has brought the monster with the intention of restoring its life once again. Justine, angry that Victor is to marry Elizabeth, threatens to divulge his secrets. Victor locks her in with the now living monster. Paul returns on the wedding day, and Victor shows him the chained creature, to which he has taught some commands. He blames Paul for shooting the creature — thus the poor brain. Paul says he's going to the authorities. While Victor argues with him outside, Elizabeth enters the lab. The two men spy the monster on the roof. Paul runs for town, and Victor races into the house. His gunshot accidentally hits Elizabeth. A lamp tossed at the monster sets it afire and it falls through a skylight into a vat of acid. Later, Paul and Elizabeth go to the prison, but Paul refuses to tell anyone about a monster. He merely mentions that Victor killed Justine. Victor is escorted toward the guillotine.

Reviews: "Everything that happens ... has happened the same way in previous films.... may titillate the blissful youngsters." (Bosley Crowther, *New York Times*, August 8, 1957, p. 15) ¶ "Not as good as *Horror of Dracula*, but entertaining enough." (Phantom of the Movies, *The Phantom's Ultimate Video Guide*, p. 148)

Analysis: This is the film that put Hammer Studios on the international map, the one that along with the following year's *Horror of Dracula* caused a resurgence in supernatural horror, which had been dormant or subservient to postwar science fiction movies. Filmed in color and imbued with eroticism, they attracted a large audience. It's an increasingly interesting show, with a fairly nice balance of interiors and

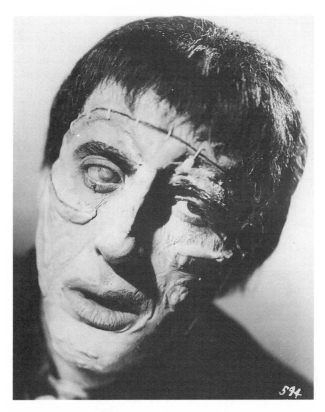

Christopher Lee is the monster in *The Curse of Frankenstein* (Hammer, 1952).

exterior woods. This Frankenstein is definitely amoral, sometimes criminal in his pursuit of scientific knowledge. As for the monster, the *New York Times* review complained that he was more "cantankerous" than gruesome. Peter Cushing and Christopher Lee would be a team for years to come, and Hazel Court found a new home in the horror genre, working at Hammer and AIP. The stuntman who took the fall for Professor Bernstein must be commended. He seems to land on his head. (Do the British let felons do this sort of thing in return for a reduced sentence?)

I Was a Teenage Frankenstein

(AIP, 1957; 74 min.) ***Bomb

Produced by Herman Cohen. Directed by Herbert L. Strock. Screenplay, Kenneth Langtry [Aben Kandel]. Edited by Jerry Young. Director of Photography, Lothrop

Worth. Music, Paul Dunlap. Art Direction, Leslie Thomas. Set Decoration, Tom Oliphant. Makeup, Philip Scheer.

Cast: Professor Frankenstein (Whit Bissell), Teenage monster and Bob (Gary Conway), Margaret (Phyllis Coates), Dr. Carlton (Robert Burton), Sergeant Burns (George Lynn), Sergeant McAfee (John Cliff), Dr. Randolph (Marshall Bradford), Arlene's mother (Claudia Bryar), Beautiful girl (Angela Blake), Woman in corridor (Gretchen Thomas), Dr. Elwood (Russ Whiteman), Jeweler (Charles Steel), Man at crash (Paul Keast), Arlene (Joy Stoner), Young man (Larry Carr), Policeman (Pat Miller).

Synopsis: The Englishman Professor Frankenstein, living descendant of the infamous ancestor, lectures American scientists about limb transplants. Dr. Randolph labels Frankenstein's pet theory "preposterous." In his rented house, Frankenstein tells his associate Dr. Carlton that Randolph has forced his hand. He will begin assembling a human from young body parts and animate it. "I'll point the way to perfection in the human race," says the professor. Conveniently, cars crash outside, and Frankenstein and Carlton abscond with one of the dead victims. At a party in his honor, Frankenstein notices that nurse Margaret is depressed. He asks her to be his assistant, duties to include typing and screening calls. He also proposes marriage — but not until his monumental experiment is completed. Frankenstein and Carlton begin their grisly business, amputating mangled limbs and tossing them to the alligator in the basement. Needed now are two hands and a right leg. These are procured from the Fallbrook Cemetery after they read the newspaper headline, "MASS FUNERAL FOR TEENAGE VICTIMS," which referred to the Plymouth track team killed in a plane crash. Later, Frankenstein finds Margaret sulking. He agrees to take a ride, and they park on lover's lane. Back in his lab, the doctors observe the new body, its head swathed in bandages, only one eye visible. Frankenstein thinks it's ready: "Good morning, my boy. Come, come, my boy. Say good morning to your creator. Speak, you've got a civil tongue in your head. I know you have because I sewed it back myself." The doctors are amazed when it speaks, more so when it cries: a sensitive teenager! When Margaret tries to discuss wedding plans, Frankenstein brushes her off. When she angrily says she could find out what he's experimenting with, he slaps her. When he and Carlton are away purchasing supplies, she has a key made and enters the lab. When she opens a vault, the monster sits up; she screams and flees. Margaret doesn't tell her fiancée anything, and he continues teaching the creature and allowing it to exercise. When the monster complains about not being able to go among normal folk, Frankenstein cuts off his bandages and shows it its horrible visage in a mirror. But he leaves the door open, and the monster explores the neighborhood. When a comely blonde in a slip observes it observing her, she screams. The monster breaks in. "CRAZED MAN KILLS YOUNG WOMAN" is next day's

newspaper headline. Frankenstein realizes his creation committed the crime and makes it promise to obey him in future. When Frankenstein finds a jeweler showing Margaret wedding rings, he becomes furious. Margaret confronts him, saying she knows he's hiding something. What's more, she admits to having seen the monster. Frankenstein agrees to tell her everything soon. In the lab, he tells the monster that he was going to start on his new face next day but for a meddling woman who threatens to contact the authorities. Later, Frankenstein brings Margaret downstairs, leaves her "feeding" his creation and locks the door, letting the monster do its dirty work. The doctor and his creation take a drive to select someone with a suitable face. The handsome Bob, found smooching in a car, is strangled. When Dr. Carlton returns from a purchasing expedition, Frankenstein tells him that Margaret up and ran off. Carlton is amazed by the monster's new face. Because it might be recognized in this vicinity, Frankenstein informs his associate that they will dismantle the creature, pack it in suitcases with false bottoms, and transport it to England, where it will be restored. When the monster suspects something's amiss, it goes on a rampage and tosses its maker to the alligator. Carlton calls in the police, and when they arrive, the monster backs up and accidentally electrocutes itself.

Reviews: "Arrived ... at a time when the city's newspapers were carrying banner accounts of the deepening crisis brought on by teen-age violence. It is difficult to disassociate what was happening on the screen from the day's occurrences in the real world." (Richard W. Nason, *New York Times*, January 30, 1958, p. 19) ¶"In less time than it takes an ordinary doctor to take a temperature, they have built themselves a real live teen-age monster (Gary Conway) and fed the leftovers to a crocodile that is kept around as a sort of garbage-disposal unit." (*Time*, March 10, 1958, p. 95)

Analysis: AIP broke into the Hammer sequence with a movie that can't really be critiqued on purely cinematic grounds. *I Was a Teenage Frankenstein*, like *I Was a*

Teenage Werewolf, is a historical record of late 1950s attitudes. There's something to be learned here about the battle of the generations during the onslaught of rock and roll and hot rods. After his role in *I Was a Teenage Werewolf*, Whit Bissell, disparaged by Robert Castle as the typical (read "bland" or, perhaps, podlike?) twentieth-century American, here consolidates his position as one of the screen's wonderful mad scientists. Of course it's crazy: Where'd the alligator come from? Who built the vaults? Why doesn't Frankenstein have a British accent? But it is entertaining; Bissell is actually excellent — if schizophrenic — and within its nutty world it makes sense. The amputated limbs created a stir amongst the generally youthful audience. The original color sequences during the electrocution are on the video release, which is *Teenage Frankenstein* — the British title.

The Revenge of Frankenstein
(Hammer/Columbia, 1958; 89 min.)
***

Produced by Anthony Hinds. Executive Producer, Michael Carreras. Associate Producer, Anthony Nelson-Keys. Directed by Terence Fisher. Screenplay, Jimmy Sangster. Additional Dialogue, Hurford Janes. Edited by Alfred Cox. Supervising Editor, James Needs. Director of Photography, Jack Asher. Color. Camera Operator, Len Harris. Music, Leonard Salzedo. Music Director, Muir Matheson. Makeup, Phil Leakey. Wardrobe, Rosemary Burrows. Hairstyles, Henry Montsash.

Cast: Dr. Frankenstein (Peter Cushing), Dr. Hans Kleve (Francis Matthews), Karl before operation (Oscar Quitak), Karl after operation (Michael Gwynn), Margaret Konrad (Eunice Gayson), Janitor patient (Richard Wordsworth), Bergman (John Welsh), Fritz (Lionel Jeffries), Kurt (Michael Ripper), Medical Council president (Charles Lloyd Pack), Inspector (John Stuart), Molke (Arnold Diamond), Countess Barscynska (Margery Gresley), Vera Barscynska (Anna Walmsley), Murderous janitor (George Woodbridge), Gerda (Avril Lewslie), Boy (Ivan Whittaker).

Synopsis: Aided by the cripple Karl, to whom he has promised a new body, Dr. Frankenstein escapes the guillotine. Three years later in Carlsbruck, the Medical Council discusses the case of a Dr. Stein, a

physician ministering to the poor who refuses to join their group. Dr. Kleve goes to Stein and relates the story of Frankenstein. He knows "Stein" is Frankenstein but volunteers to learn from him. Stein shows him a brain, a hand and eyes, which work via wires connected to their separate vats. All Stein needs for a perfect man is a brain. Karl volunteers to provide that. Margaret Conrad comes to work at Stein's hospital and meets Dr. Kleve and Karl. Stein informs Kleve that the chimpanzee Otto has an orangutan brain; that's why the ape now eats meat. Stein and Kleve perform the operation on Karl. Later Margaret is led to Karl's room by a patient who works in the clinic. Impatient to be out and perturbed when he learns from Kleve that Stein wants him to talk to scientists from all over the world, Karl dresses and leaves. At the lab he burns his old body, but the janitor hears, and they fight. Karl kills his tormentor and flees. Margaret finds him in her stable and fetches Kleve. Meanwhile Karl, his limp and crooked hand become manifest in his new body, runs off. He breaks into a recital at Margaret's and calls out "Frankenstein" before collapsing in the doctor's arms. The Medical Council investigates. Stein goes to the council and says he is indeed a Frankenstein, but not *the* infamous maniac. Nevertheless, the grave of Frankenstein is opened and a priest's garb found. At the clinic the patients attack Stein. Kleve arrives and takes the torn body to the laboratory. Frankenstein tells him he knows what to do. The operation is performed. A door opens; "Dr. Franck" appears.

Reviews: "A high grade horror film, gory enough to give adults a squeamish second thought...." (Powe., *Variety*, June 18, 1958) ¶"Not too serious addition to the 1958 horror cycle...." (F. Maurice Speed, ed., *Film Review 1959-60*, p. 96)

Analysis: Are there goofs here? How come Dr. Franck, except for the mustache, looks like Stein/Frankenstein when Kleve removed the brain of the doctor but presumably put it in the body in the case? The police examined the dead Frankenstein. Did Kleve take the head later on? Then why take the brain out? Anyway, this has a good reputation — and deserves it. Whereas there

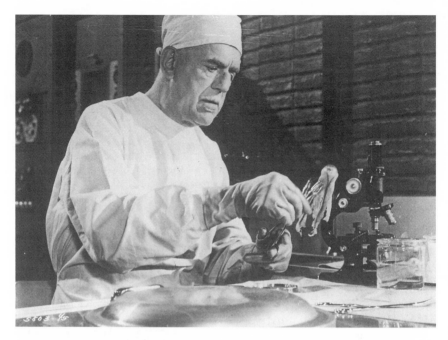

Baron Victor von Frankenstein (Boris Karloff) is looking for a few good body parts in *Frankenstein—1970* (Allied Artists, 1958).

is no hideous monster and thus teenage viewers were disappointed upon initial release, adults see that this is an intelligent film. Cushing is excellent. He *is* Doctor Frankenstein, misguided perhaps, but often admirable.

Frankenstein—1970
(Allied Artists, 1958; 83 min.) **

Produced by Aubrey Schenck. Directed by Howard W. Koch. Screenplay, Richard Landau and George Worthing Yates. Story, Aubrey Schenck and Charles A. Moses. Edited by John A. Bushelman. Director of Photography, Carl E. Guthrie. CinemaScope. Music, Paul A. Dunlap. Set Decoration, Jerry Welch. Makeup Supervision, Gordon Bau. Makeup, George Bau.

Cast: Baron Victor von Frankenstein (Boris Karloff), Douglas Row (Donald Barry), Carolyn Hayes (Jana Lund), Judy Stevens (Charlotte Austin), Wilhelm Gottfried (Rudolph Anders), Mike Shaw (Tom Duggan), Shuter (Norbert Schiller), Morgan Haley (John Dennis), Inspector Raab (Irwin Berke), Hans/Monster (Mike Lane), Assistant cam-

eraman (Jack Kenney), Cab driver (Franz Roehn), Station porter (Joe Ploski).

Synopsis: A damsel is pursued into a mist-shrouded lake by a monster. But it's just a movie set, and the film is to be a documentary about the Frankenstein family. During the shoot, the crew stays at the castle of Baron Victor von Frankenstein. During the war, torture caused his disfigured face and deformed body. He permits the filming and even plays a part himself. But later, he enters his secret laboratory. His butler, Shuter, accidentally finds him there and is hypnotized. The baron will use his heart and brain for the human he, like his ancestor, is creating. Using an atomic reactor, the baron brings the still-eyeless creature to life. The monster mistakenly kills Judy Stevens instead of director Douglas Row, then the cameraman, then the inquisitive Gottfried, whose eyes are suitable. Frankenstein hypnotizes Mike Shaw and has him lead the film's star, Carolyn, downstairs. When Carolyn realizes that Shuter, who was fond of her, is the beast carrying her, she urges him not to harm her. The monster enters the lab and begins smashing the equipment. Later, men in radiation suits investigate the ruins and find the bodies of Frankenstein and the monster.

Review: "Chiller-diller with the bad old Baron creating a monster in an atomic reactor and then having it turn on him." (F. Maurice Speed, ed., *Film Review 1959-1960*, p. 86)

Analysis: No Hammer horror here. We went to this film with high hopes, only to be disappointed after the promising but "fake" Gothic opening. Donald, once "Red," Barry had been a B western star. Jana Lund, like Yvonne Lime, with whom she co-starred this same year in *High School Hellcats*, was perky and a prime sweater girl. Charlotte Austin had a number of films to her credit.

Frankenstein's Daughter
(Astor, 1958; 85 min.) ***Bomb

Produced by Marc Frederic. Directed by Richard E. Cunha. Screenplay, H. E. Barrie. Edited by Everett Dodd. Director of Photography, Meredith Nicholson. Edited by Everett Dodd. Music, Nicholas Carras. Art Direction, Sham Unlimited. Set Decoration, Harry Reif. Sound, Robert Post. Sound Effects Editor, Harold E. Wooley. Makeup, Harry Thomas and Paul Stanhope. Special Effects, Ira Anderson.

Cast: Oliver Frank[enstein] (Donald Murphy), Trudy Morton (Sandra Knight), Carter Morton (Felix Locher), Elsu (Wolfe Barzell), Johnny Bruder (John Ashley), Suzie Lawler (Sally Todd), Don (Harold Lloyd, Jr.), Lieutenant Boyle (John Zaremba), Detective Dillon (Robert Dix), Mr. Rockwell (Voltaire Perkins), Monster (Harry Wilson), Warehousemen (Bill Coontz, George Barrows). With Charlotte Portney, Page Cavanaugh and His Trio.

Synopsis: The elderly Carter Morton and his assistant, Oliver Frank, experiment with a new drug in Carter's household laboratory. Oliver is skeptical of his boss's ability to develop a drug to wipe out disease and secretly administers his own serum to Carter's niece Trudy, who becomes a hideous, blue-hued female and runs amok. She thinks it was a dream when she awakes. The gardener, Elsu, works for Oliver and

knows his last name is not Frank but Frankenstein. His grandfather was the original genius. To facilitate his experiments, Carter knows he needs Digenarol from his old employer, Rockwell Laboratories. He steals the chemical. Sally visits Trudy, accusing her of being after all the guys. Oliver introduces himself to Sally and makes a date. He gets rough, she slaps him, and when she scampers off down the highway he runs her down. Now he has the head and brain he's been looking for. With Elsu's help, he grafts it to the body in the wine cellar off Carter's lab. While Oliver and Elsu are engaged elsewhere, the creature arises and leaves, killing a warehouseman before returning. Trudy faints when she sees it, but Oliver convinces her she has been under stress; there was no monster. Lt. Boyle arrives and questions Carter and Oliver. He takes Carter downtown. Oliver admits to Trudy that he's a Frankenstein and shows her the monster, which he orders to kill Elsu. Trudy flees to the police and learns that her uncle has died of a heart attack. The police return to the Carter residence and question Oliver. Detective Dillon is strangled by the monster. Johnny and Trudy arrive and are cornered by the monster and Oliver. But Johnny tosses a jar of acid at the monster that hits Oliver. While examining its master's body, Lt. Boyle arrives, and the monster catches fire. Trudy and Johnny recover from their shocks and take a swim.

Review: "Papa was no lily and neither is *Frankenstein's Daughter*.... claptrap." (Howard Thompson, *New York Times*, November 17, 1958, p. 37)

Analysis: Here's another late-50s teen-oriented oddity. It's got a monster, a poolside party, crew cuts, hip music like "Daddy-Bird" (with bongos). The story goes that the makeup person didn't know he was supposed to create a woman's head for the monster; that's why it's squared off and hideous. Most of the action takes place in the Carter house. It's cheap, but never boring. We *are* expected to accept untenable situations. Carter didn't know the bookcase in his lab concealed a wine cellar and stairs to hidden rooms? Some pretty good lines: "A monster in a bathing suit?"

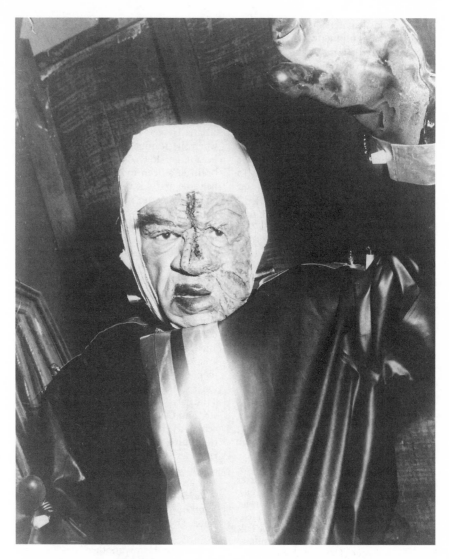

Harry Wilson is the monster in *Frankenstein's Daughter* (Astor, 1958).

(Robert Dix). "But now we're aware that the female brain is conditioned to a man's world. Therefore it takes orders where the other ones didn't." (Murphy) Robert Murphy reminds us of William Shatner. Sandra Knight's other "important" part was in Roger Corman's 1963 film *The Terror*. John Ashley had more of these films in his repertoire. "And Introducing Harold Lloyd, Jr."! Paired with *Missile to the Moon*. The

current video is introduced by Elvira and features a riotous epilogue in which she pretends the soundtrack is available.

The Evil of Frankenstein
(Hammer/Universal, 1964; 98 min.)
**½

Produced by Anthony Hinds. Directed by Freddie Francis. Assistant Directors, Bill

Cartlidge and Hugh Harlow. Story and Screenplay, John Elder [Anthony Hinds]. Director of Photography, John Wilcox. Eastman Color. Music, Don Banks. Musical Supervision, Philip Martell. Makeup, Roy Ashton. Special Effects, Les Bowie.

Cast: Baron Frankenstein (Peter Cushing), Zoltan (Peter Woodthorpe), Hans (Sandor Eles), Police chief (Duncan Lamont), Rena (Katy Wild), Burgomaster (David Hutcheson), Burgomaster's wife (Caron Gardner), Body snatcher (Tony Arpino), Priest (James Maxwell), Landlord (Alistair Williamson), Dr. Sergado (Steve Geray), Manservant (Frank Forsyth), Rena's father (William Phipps), Rena's mother (Maria Palmer), Little girl (Michele Scott), Rena as a child (Tracy Stratford), (Kenneth Cove), Drunk (Howard Goorney), Policeman (Anthony Blackshaw, David Conville), David Carrell (Patrick Horgan), Hypnotized man (Timothy Bateson), Creature (Kiwi Kingston). With Derek Martin, Robert Flynn, Anthony Poole, James Garfield.

Synopsis: After a ten-year exile, Baron Frankenstein returns to Karlstadt with his aide, Hans, intent on continuing his research in artificially created life. The baron tells his associate about his earlier experiments in which he succeeded in piecing together a human form from diverse lifeless parts, and bringing this being to life using the forces harnessed in a fierce thunderstorm. Later, the creature escaped; after killing some sheep, it was hunted by frightened townsfolk. Hiding in the mountains, it was shot and fell to its death in a deep crevice. Afterwards, the baron had to flee for his freedom. Hans worries that the townspeople will remember the baron, but Frankenstein assures him that these peasants have short memories. Plus, a festival is taking place and it will be possible to walk about masked. Besides, everything they might require for their experiments will be found at the baron's former manor. They find the manor mostly in a ruinous state. It is a disheartened Frankenstein who returns to the village. Dismay turns to outrage when he spies his own ring decorating the finger of the village burgomaster. Frankenstein and Hans are ejected from the inn when they make a row. That night, the baron invades the burgomaster's home and discovers that the house is filled with

his own furniture. Another loud verbal barrage attracts the police. Knowing he has revealed his true identity, Frankenstein makes a hasty exit over the balcony. On one of the narrow paths in the low mountains above Karlstadt, Frankenstein and Hans are met by the mute girl, Rena, who remembers them from town. She leads them to a cave where they can shelter for the night. Awaking in the wee hours, Frankenstein explores an interior chamber and discovers, frozen in an ice floe, his monster. He, Hans and Rena build a fire to free the monster and carry his limp form to the manor. Setting up his laboratory as best he can, Frankenstein makes every attempt to electrically inject life into his creation. Finally, with the aid of a traveling hypnotist, Zoltan, the monster is restored to action, although it is evident that the creature is only aware of, and obedient to, Zoltan. While Frankenstein and Hans go about their work, Zoltan plots revenge against the burgomaster and chief of police, who expelled him from town as a charlatan. Frankenstein learns of Zoltan's larceny and the murder of the burgomaster and casts the man from his house. Zoltan returns with the monster, who, in the ensuing scuffle, impales the hypnotist. The police chief arrives and arrests Frankenstein. While the baron languishes in jail, Rena tends the creature. When it shows signs of an excruciating pain in the head, she tries to remedy this with a flagon of brandy. Finding more and more of the intoxicant, the monster goes into a drunken rage. The baron, having escaped from jail, bursts in with the police and townspeople not far behind. When a raging fire breaks out in the laboratory, Hans is just able to pull Rena away, even as the blaze spreads to the rest of the manor. The baron and his raging creation are trapped within.

Review: "Picture begins to say something about superstition and hypocrisy. Then it simply goes hog-wild (monster gets drunk) and heads for the ash heap." (Howard Thompson, *New York Times*, June 18, 1964, p. 29)

Analysis: Of all the films in the Hammer Frankenstein cycle, *The Evil of Frankenstein* comes closest in plot and style to

Poster art for *The Evil of Frankenstein* (Hammer, 1964).

the hoary old Universal films of the forties, even to the Baron's unlikely, but serendipitous, discovery of his monster frozen in an ice floe (shades of *Frankenstein Meets the Wolf Man* and *House of Frankenstein*) and the monster's resemblance to the Karloff version. Roy Ashton's modeling on Jack Pierce's classic makeup is unfortunate, for the mimicry is clumsy and amateurish in the extreme (although Kiwi Kingston's mime as the monster is a suitable foil for the makeup). *The Evil of Frankenstein* stands quite apart from the rest of Hammer's Frankenstein cycle, despite

Peter Cushing's continued portrayal of the obsessed Baron. The first two films in the series, *The Curse of Frankenstein* (1957) and *The Revenge of Frankenstein* (1958), both directed by Terence Fisher, came in rapid succession and actually form a continuous narrative. In the six years that elapsed before the third film appeared, Fisher directed the commercial flop *The Phantom of the Opera*. Perhaps because of this, Freddie Francis was assigned the directorial chores of the third film. Overall, Francis's direction is efficient but unremarkable, and the absence of Fisher's style of heavy gothicism is greatly missed. Ultimately, it's the plot that proves most fatal to this maverick Hammer Frankenstein, by shifting the focus from Cushing's sometimes sympathetic, sometimes overbearing Baron Frankenstein onto an ungainly brute of a monster. Some scenes were added to the American version (the rendition sold to television) that featured the mute girl, Rena, as a child encountering the monster.

Jesse James Meets Frankenstein's Daughter
(Circle Productions, 1966; 82 min.)
***Bomb

Produced by Carroll Case. Assistant to the Producer, Howard Koch, Jr. Directed by William Beaudine. Screenplay, Carl K. Hittleman. Director of Photography, Lothrop Worth. Color. Music, Raoul Kraushaar. Sound Effects, John Hall. Art Direction, Paul Sylos. Set Decoration, Harry Reif. Makeup, Ted Goodley. Photographic Effects, Cinema Research Corporation.

Cast: Jesse James (John Lupton), Maria Frankenstein (Narda Onyx), Hank (Cal Bolder), Juanita (Estelita), Marshall McFee (Jim Davis), Rudolph Frankenstein (Steven Geray). With Nestor Paiva, Rayford Barnes, Roger Creed, Rosa Turich, Felipe Turich, Dan White, Page Slattery.

Synopsis: Jesse James's gang has been decimated at Northfield, so James and his friend Hank head for New Mexico to join the "Wild Bunch." After an abortive stagecoach hold-up during which Hank is wounded, they take refuge at the abandoned mission now inhabited by Central European expatriates Maria Frankenstein and her brother. Unbeknownst to Jesse, Count Frankenstein's granddaughter has been experimenting on ailing local Hispanics, who usually die after her ministrations. After removing the bullet from Hank, Maria transplants one of her grandfather's "artificial" brains into his skull and communicates with him telepathically via helmets fitted with electrodes. Maria makes a play for Jesse, but he's become enamored of Juanita. Jesse rides into town for some medication, not realizing the note he carries tells the shopkeeper his customer is a notorious outlaw. The shopkeeper informs the law, and Jesse must gun down

the lawman. He reads the note, learns of Maria's perfidy, and heads back to the hacienda. He meets Juanita on the way. She warns him not to go, for Hank is not himself. Jesse goes anyway. Rejecting Maria again, he is knocked unconscious by Hank and strapped to an operating table. The marshall arrives, but he too is incapacitated by Hank. But when Maria orders Hank to kill Juanita, he turns on Maria and strangles her. Hank then attacks Jesse, and Juanita must shoot him. After praying over Hank's grave, Jesse bids farewell to Juanita and rides off with the Marshall.

Review: "Unmitigated disaster.... abomination." (John Stanley, *The Creature Features Movie Guide*, p. 136)

Analysis: It would not win a contest for worst most entertaining horror film of the decade, but it deserves to be nominated. There is an impressive backdrop at the end of the village street that shows a hill and the abandoned mission in which the Frankensteins live. It is acceptable at a distance, but at one point a character at the end of the avenue turns to look up the "hill" and the camera shows us his view: a painting. Narda Onyx is a healthy woman. It's a shame she didn't appear in more of these. John Lupton, who's main claim to fame was the Tom Jeffords character on the TV series *Broken Arrow*, is pretty bad as Jesse. Like its co-feature, *Billy the Kid Versus Dracula*, this has decent color and sound. Get a load of the yellow, red and green helmets Ms. Frankenstein has at her disposal.

Frankenstein Created Woman
(Seven Arts-Hammer/Fox, 1967; 92 min.) ***

Produced by Anthony Nelson Keys. Directed by Terence Fisher. Screenplay, John Elder [Anthony Hinds]. Edited by James Needs. Director of Photography, Arthur Grant. Color, DeLuxe. Music, James Bernard. Musical Supervision, Philip Martell. Art Direction, Don Mingaye. Makeup, George Partleton. Special Effects, Les Bowie.

Cast: Baron Frankenstein (Peter Cushing), Christina (Susan Denberg), Dr. Hertz (Thorley Walters), Hans (Robert Morris), Anton (Peter Blythe), Karl (Barry Warren), Hans's father (Duncan Lamont), Johann (Derek

Hank (Cal Bolder) puts an end to Maria Frankenstein (Narda Onyx) in *Jesse James Meets Frankenstein's Daughter* (Circle/Embassy, 1966).

Fowlds), Police chief (Peter Madden), Mayor (Philip Ray), Kleve (Alan MacNaughtan), Priest (Colin Jeavons), Jailer (Kevin Flood), Spokesman (Alec Mango), New landlord (Ivan Beavis), Bystander (Bartlett Mullins), Police sergeant (John Maxim), Hans as a boy (Stuart Middleton).

Synopsis: The child Hans sees his father guillotined for murder. As an adult, Hans assists Dr. Hertz and Baron Frankenstein. The baron's latest experiment involves freezing himself. After one hour he's still alive. He was dead but his soul remained. Why? Hans is sent to the tavern for champagne and trades a coat for it. He flirts with the landlord's daughter, Christina, who walks with a limp and has a half-scarred face. Three swains — Anton, Johann and Carl — enter the tavern and tease Christina, causing a brawl with Hans. The police arrive but do not charge Hans. The baron and Hertz arrive for dinner. Hans

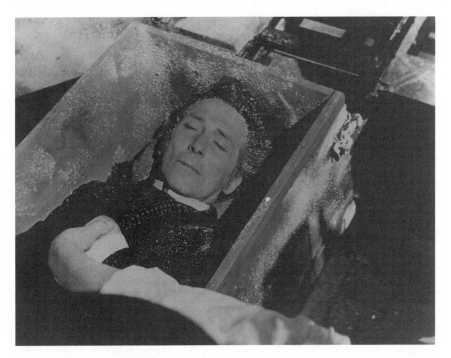

Peter Cushing as Baron Frankenstein subjects himself to an experiment in cryogenics in *Frankenstein Created Woman* (Seven Arts–Hammer/Fox, 1967).

sneaks into Christina's room. She talks about seeing a new doctor. Hans admits his love for her, and she turns down the light. In the lab, the baron shows Hertz an important source of energy in his rocky vault. "Everything we don't understand is magic until we understand it." After Christina's father leaves the restaurant, the swains gain access, but the father misses his key and returns. The trio beat him to death, but the blame falls on Hans because the coat he'd traded for champagne is found on the body. In the laboratory, the baron creates a shield of indestructible matter that he says will give life after death. If he can take a soul from a damaged or dead body and replace it, he will have conquered death. Hans is convicted because he won't tell the court that he was in Christina's bed, and she doesn't know his predicament because she's left to visit a doctor. This is a not entirely unwelcome development for the baron. He can take Hans's soul if he gets the body for an hour

after the execution. "Bodies are easy to come by, souls are not." Christina witnesses Hans's execution from her coach and leaps to her death from a bridge. Hertz gets Hans's body. Christina's body is pulled from the river and taken to Hertz. The baron captures Hans's soul, which looks like a round, white, floating cloud. The baron directs Hertz's hands in an operation that eliminates the blood clot that caused Christina's deformities. Hans's soul is given to her. "Please, who am I?" she asks upon waking. The baron won't let her go out, but Hertz explains a little, saying Frankenstein "is a wonderful man." Frankenstein takes Christina to see the guillotine. Her reaction is, "Pa-pa!" It becomes evident that Hans's soul *is* in Christina's body, but not all the time. Hans/Christina accosts Anton, who is later found dead. Carl and Johann wonder if it was retribution for their act. Christina uses a cleaver on Carl. A mob accosts Frankenstein. He suggests they open Hans's grave. They do, and find a headless body. Christina has the head. Johann tries to leave the town, but a beautiful blonde is in the coach he takes. While picnicking, he is stabbed and decapitated. Frankenstein was too late to stop Christina, as he is from preventing her leap into the river.

Review: "The good doctor ... doesn't really create woman, he just makes a few important changes in the design. Considering the result is beautiful blonde Susan Denberg, most film fans would like to see the doctor get a grant from the Ford Foundation, or even the CIA." (*Variety*)

Analysis: The soul part is very interesting. Pair it with *The Asphyx*? Susan Denberg was Miss August 1966 in *Playboy*.

Frankenstein Must Be Destroyed
(Hammer, 1969; 97 min.) ***

Produced by Anthony Nelson Keys. Directed by Terence Fisher. Screenplay, Bert Batt. From an original story by Anthony Nelson Keys and Bert Batt. Edited by Gordon Hales. Director of Photography, Arthur Grant. Technicolor. Music, James Bernard. Musical Director, Philip Martell. Art Direction, Bernard Robinson. Makeup, Eddie Knight. Special Effects, Studio Locations Limited.

Cast: Baron Frankenstein (Peter Cushing), Anna Spengler (Veronica Carlson), Dr. Richter (Freddie Jones), Dr. Karl Holst (Simon Ward), Inspector Frisch (Thorley Walters), Ella Brandt (Maxine Audley), Dr. Frederick Brandt (George Pravda), Police doctor (Geoffrey Bayldon), Mad woman (Colette O'Neal), Burglar (Harold Goodwin), Third guest (Frank Middlemass), Dr. Heidecke (Jim Collier).

Synopsis: Returning to his laboratory after decapitating a physician with a scythe, a murderer accosts a burglar. The thief escapes, and the killer disposes of a body and other incriminating evidence through a trapdoor. The police investigate and realize a doctor must have been responsible for the burglar's fright and the murdered physician. Using the name "Fenner," the murderer takes up residence in the boarding house of Anna Spengler. In the drawing room he listens to men discuss the insane Dr. Brandt's theories of brain transplantation. They recall a like mind: Frankenstein.

Anna is visited by Karl Holst, who works at the asylum. Karl sells drugs to assist Anna's mother. But he's dropped his package of cocaine, and Fenner finds it. He blackmails Karl and Anna. For their help in his experiments, he won't turn them in to the narcotics bureau. Anna ousts her boarders so Fenner can establish his lab. Anna refuses to leave Karl when he tells her about the night watchman he murdered when helping Fenner steal medical supplies. Fenner tells them his real identity: Frankenstein. He plans to abduct and cure the insane Brandt. He will then learn from Brandt how to freeze brains for future use. Frankenstein's goal is to preserve the brains of great men when they die. Frankenstein and Karl kidnap Brandt. During their flight, Brandt has a heart attack. Frankenstein realizes Brandt will die soon and that he must transplant Brandt's brain into someone else, like Professor Richter. When Karl is at the asylum, Frankenstein's human urges get the better of him, and he rapes Anna. The operation takes place. Brandt's body is buried. Police search houses, including Anna's. The sergeant recognizes Karl, who says he's painting to help out his fiancée. He's actually obscuring the door to the basement lab. At Anna's, the water main in the garden bursts, and Brandt's body is unearthed. She drags the body into the bushes before anyone can see. Ella Brandt, having recognized Frankenstein on the street, confronts him at Anna's. Frankenstein takes her downstairs. He says her husband must rest for a week; then she can take him away to start a new life. But when she leaves, Frankenstein turns to Karl and says, "Pack! We're leaving!" When Ella returns, no one is there, and she goes to the police. They find "Brandt" under the shed. In an abandoned house, Karl tells Anna they must leave before Frankenstein abandons them. Frankenstein spies Karl harnessing the horses. They fight, and Karl is knocked out. Brandt, stabbed by a frightened Anna, staggers upstairs. Frankenstein finds Anna, learns she injured Brandt, and stabs her. Karl finds her body. Brandt survives and goes to his home. He knows Frankenstein will follow, and when he does, sets a trap. Frankenstein initially escapes the burning building but is waylaid outside by Karl. Brandt knocks Karl aside and carries Frankenstein back inside to his doom.

Reviews: "A good-enough example of its low-key type, with artwork rather better than usual (less obvious backcloths, etc.), a minimum of artless dialog, good lensing by Arthur Grant and a solid all round cast." (*Variety*)

Analysis: There is food for thought and analysis in this surprisingly grim film. Almost everyone dies. Frankenstein becomes unsympathetic. This has achieved modern classic status with some (most?) aficionados. Much have they commented upon the Veronica Carlson rape scene. At the FANEX 8 convention in July 1994, Ms. Carlson told the audience that the producers wanted Cushing to rip open her blouse and expose her breasts. She would have none of it, and director Fisher yelled, "Cut!" as the scene in question arose. At FANEX, Ms. Carlson received a best actress award for this role from the Horror and Fantasy Film Society. Note that Thorley Walters, Dr. Hertz in 1967's *Frankenstein Created Woman*, is here a police inspector.

The Horror of Frankenstein
(Hammer/American Continental, 1970; 95 min.) **½

Produced and directed by Jimmy Sangster. Assistant Director, Derek Whitehurst. Screenplay, Jimmy Sangster and Jeremy Burnham. Based on characters crated by Mary Shelley. Edited by Chris Barnes. Director of Photography, Moray Grant. Technicolor. Music, James Bernard. Art Direction, Scott MacGregor. Makeup, Tom Smith.

Cast: Victor Frankenstein (Ralph Bates), Alys (Kate O'Mara), Elizabeth (Veronica Carlson), Graverobber (Dennis Price), Graverobber's wife (Joan Rice), Wilhelm (Graham James), Elizabeth's father (Bernard Archer), Monster (David Prowse). With Jon Finch.

Synopsis: For his father's unwillingness to send him to Vienna University, Victor Frankenstein has the baron killed. But Victor is bored at university and returns to his castle with Wilhelm. There he puts in motion his plan to create new life from body parts supplied by graverobbers. Wilhelm doesn't support all this and is electrocuted

and thrust into a vat of acid. After killing a professor, Victor gives refuge to the man's daughter, Elizabeth, a woman who has known and loved him since childhood. Because the male graverobber drops the professor's brain, Victor tosses him into the acid. With lightning, Victor brings his creation to life, but it knocks him down, takes to the woods, and frightens the locals. Victor captures it. Alys, the housekeeper jealous of Elizabeth, and the graverobber's wife are disposed of by Victor's monster when they threaten to expose the doctor for the murderer and arcane scientist that he is. A little girl who saw the monster brings the police to the castle. Victor is saved from imprisonment when the girl turns on spigots which release acid into the vat wherein the monster is hidden. With no evidence of a monster, Victor is free to start over again.

Review: "In a complete departure from their earlier entries, this new film is laced with thinly veiled humor and penetrating self-satire while maintaining a mock seriousness to keep up appearances as the horror film it is supposed to be.... We should regard it as an innovative and fascinating experiment, and one that has met with very pleasing success." (Frederick S. Clarke, *Cinetantastique*, Fall 1971, pp. 30-31)

Analysis: As you can see from the synopsis, *The Horror of Frankenstein* can be viewed as a black comedy. The monster (David Prowse, who would supply the body of Darth Vader in the *Star Wars* trilogy) doesn't make us forget Karloff, Christopher Lee or even Glenn Strange, but he's a secondary character. It's Ralph Bates's show, and he makes the most of it. Joan Rice once was a leading lady; see the 1954 Burt Lancaster film *His Majesty O'Keefe*.

Dracula vs. Frankenstein
(Independent-International, 1971; 90 min.) ***Bomb

Analysis: See cast, credits, and discussion in this film's listing under *Dracula*.

Lady Frankenstein
(New World, 1972; 84 min.) **½

Produced and directed by Mel Welles.

Story and screenplay, Edward DiLorenzo. Original Story, Dick Randall. Edited by Cleo Converse. Director of Photography, Richard Pallotin. Color. Music by Alessandro Alessandroni. Art Direction, Francis Mellon. Costumes, Maurice Nichols. Makeup, Timothy Parson. Special Effects, CIPA. Animation, Charles Ramboldt.

Cast: Baron Frankenstein (Joseph Cotten), Tanya Frankenstein (Sara Bey), Dr. Charles Marshall (Paul Muller), Captain Harris (Mickey Hargitay). With Herbert Fux, Peter Whiteman, Renata Cash, Adam Welles.

Synopsis: Tanya Frankenstein returns home from university, having graduated as a licensed surgeon. She wants to help her father, the baron, with his "animal transplants" and admits that as a child she spied on his laboratory. She knows he wants to create life in a dead human. He tells her to have patience. With the assistance of Dr. Marshall, he transplants the vital parts of a recently hanged man into another cadaver. Using lightning to provide the spark of life, they succeed, but only the face catches fire, and the hypothalamus had been previously damaged. The hideous brute kills the baron and escapes. Tanya convinces Marshall to continue her father's experiments. His status must be accorded renown. Marshall reluctantly agrees, partly because he's in love with Tanya. She says they must create a second creature with the power of the first, thus to do in the brute. She says she could love Marshall if his brain were in the dimwit Thomas's beautiful body. Marshall smothers Thomas while Tanya copulates with the unfortunate man. Tanya transplants Marshall's brain into Thomas's body, and the new being battles the baron's original creation, which has returned to the castle. Marshall/Thomas and Tanya manage to destroy the monster, but Marshall/Thomas strangles Tanya during intercourse as the castle is set afire by the villagers.

Review: "Sorry mess." (John Stanley, *The Creature Features Movie Guide*, p. 146) ¶ "A fully clothed Mickey Hargitay investigates." (Phantom of the Movies, *The Phantom's Ultimate Video Guide*, p. 196)

Analysis: When is a "foreign" film not one? This has an American producer-director, an American actor in the lead, and unless their names have been anglicized, many American or British people behind the scenes. It was filmed in Italy, and according to Michael Weldon in *The Psychotronic Encyclopedia of Film*, Sara Bey is really Rosalba Neri. Funding may have been Italian, but who knows? Let's call it an international co-production, and not bad for a B film. It's not boring, there's a bit more scientific explanation than usual, and Sara Bey is sympathetic — and sexy in her two nude lovemaking scenes. She deserved a better fate than death during sex. Joseph Cotten was taking the Ray Milland route from notable Hollywood leading man to low-budget horror film star. Body builder Mickey Hargitay had been Jayne Mansfield's husband.

Frankenstein and the Monster from Hell
(Hammer, 1973; 93 min.) **

Produced by Roy Skeggs. Directed by Terence Fisher. Assistant Director, Derek Whitehurst. Screenplay, John Elder [Anthony Hinds]. Edited by James Needs. Director of Photography, Brian Probyn. Technicolor. Music, James Bernard. Sound, Maurice Askew, Les Hammond. Art Direction, Scott MacGregor.

Cast: Dr. Karl Victor, aka Frankenstein (Peter Cushing), Dr. Simon Helder (Shane Briant), Sarah/Angel (Madeline Smith), Monster (David Prowse), Asylum Director (John Stratton), Tarmud (Bernard Lee), Muller (Sydney Bromley), Body snatcher (Patrick Troughton).

Synopsis: In the sense that the institutionalized Dr. Frankenstein has blackmailed the director into letting him have a lab and come and go at will, the lunatics are running the asylum. A young doctor, Simon, is brought there for the crime of graverobbing for experimentation. Frankenstein, his hands having been burned, realizes he can use Simon to assist in surgery. Also helping "Dr. Victor" is Sarah, known as "Angel" to the inmates. They replace one man's brain with that of "the Professor," his hands with those of a craftsman. Victor believes a mating of the new creature with Sarah will produce a wonderfully gifted human being. The monster runs amok before that can happen, and the inmates gang up and destroy it.

David Prowse is the eponymous monster in *Frankenstein and the Monster from Hell* (Hammer, 1973).

Review: "That the results look more like a miniature King Kong in drag is not fatal to the film's mild impact. Overall it's a good tight little dual bill item...." (Murf., *Variety*, June 26, 1974, p. 20)

Analysis: Disappointing. Here's another film rated R for some gore, nothing else: neither language nor nudity — and Madeline Smith was not loath to disrobe in 1970's *The Vampire Lovers*. A peek at her fleshly charms would have enlivened this opus. Some think this Frankenstein is completely insane. Looked at in that respect, the film is not without interest. *Variety* says this was originally a 1972 release. Terence Fisher, the director who started Hammer Studios on its path to greatness with 1957's *The Curse of Frankenstein*, died after completing this film.

Blackenstein: The Black Frankenstein

(Exclusive International, 1973;
93 min.) *

Produced by Frank R. Saletri. Directed by

William A. Levey. Screenplay, Frank R. Saletri. Edited by Bill Levey. Director of Photography, Robert Caramico. Color, DeLuxe. Music, Cardella DeMilo and Lou Frohman. Prosthetic Devices, Bill Munns.

Cast: Dr. Stein (John Hart), Monster (Joe DeSue), Dr. Winifred Walker (Ivory Stone), Malcomb (Roosevelt Jackson), Eleanor (Andrea King), Woman in bed (Liz Renay), Lt. Jackson (James Cousar), Cardella DeMilo (Herself), Bruno (Nick Bolin), Hospital attendant (Bob Brophy), Captain (Don Brodie). With Andy C.

Synopsis: Dr. Winifred Walker asks Dr. Stein to help her fiancé Eddie Turner, who lost all his limbs in a land mine explosion in Vietnam. An expert in restoring amputated and severed extremities as well as a Nobel Peace Prize [sic] winner for solving the DNA genetic code, Dr. Stein agrees. But Stein's valet, Malcomb, becomes infatuated with Winifred and doctors the DNA that Stein injects into Eddie. Stein and Winifred are mystified when Eddie's facial structure begins changing. Although they confine him to a secure cell, Eddie leaves at night and kills people, including the veterans hospital orderly who had taunted and abused him. Returning one night to find Malcomb forcing himself on Winifred, Eddie kills him as well as patients Eleanor and Bruno, and finally Stein himself. Leaving the building, Eddie chases a woman into an abandoned factory where Dobermans corner and kill him. Lt. Jackson comforts Winifred.

Review: "Tasteless and grotesque entry in the subgenre of blaxploitation horror films." (Mick Martin and Marsha Porter, *Video Movie Guide 1994*, p. 784)

Analysis: Don't compare this with *Blacula*. It's like apples and oranges. We do fear, however, that someone will analyze it on the basis of race, disabilities, and Vietnam. We wonder a theatrical showing didn't cause (1) a riot or (2) death by laughter. It's a travesty of poor acting, overwrought 1950s-type music, padding. How many times must we see the outside of the building and the lab gizmos? Its science isn't half baked; it never made it into the oven. We were unaware that the Nobel Peace Prize could be won for medical developments. Lt. Jackson is called Sergeant Jackson and the captain has become a lieutenant in the credits! Prefiguring Linda Hamilton's revenge in *Terminator 2* is the monster's return to the hospital to attack the nasty orderly. The monster has the swankiest shoes of any of the Frankenstein creations.

Young Frankenstein
(20th Century–Fox, 1974; 108 min.)
****

Produced by Michael Gruskoff. Directed by Mel Brooks. Screenplay, Gene Wilder and Mel Brooks. Based on characters the novel *Frankenstein* by Mary Wollstonecraft Shelley. Edited by John Howard. Director of Photography, Gerald Hirschfeld. Prints, DeLuxe. Music, John Morris. Violin Solo, Gerald Vinci. Set Decoration, Bob De Vestal. Costumes, Dorothy Jeakins. Makeup created by William Tuttle. Special Effects, Henry Millar, Jr., Hal Millar. Special thanks to Kenneth Strickfadden for original Frankenstein laboratory equipment.

Cast: Dr. Frankenstein (Gene Wilder), Monster (Peter Boyle), Inga (Teri Garr), Elizabeth (Madeline Kahn), Igor (Marty Feldman), Frau Blucher (Cloris Leachman), Inspector Kemp (Kenneth Mars), Herr Gerhard Falkstein (Richard Haydn), Mr. Hilltop (Liam Dunn), Herr Waldman (Leon Askin), Medical student (Danny Goldman), Sadistic jailer (Oscar Beregi), Frightened villager (Lou Cutell), Village elder (Arthur Malet), Inspector Kemp's aide (Richard Roth), Gravediggers (Monte Landis, Rusty Blitz), Little girl (Anne Beesley), First villager (Terrence Pushman), Second villager (Ian Abercrombie), Third villager (Randolph Dobbs), Blind man (Gene Hackman).

Synopsis: Gerhard Falkstein presents Baron Von Frankenstein's will to the grandson, Dr. Frankenstein. Bidding adieu to his fiancée, Elizabeth, Frankenstein takes a train to Transylvania. The bug-eyed, hunchback Igor (pronounced Eyegor) meets him at the station. The comely blonde Inga accompanies them to the ancestral castle, where Frau Blucher welcomes them. During the night, Frankenstein and Inga discover a secret passage to a hidden laboratory. Igor also makes his way there via the dumbwaiter. They find a still warm violin and a smoldering cigar. To his great delight, Frankenstein finds his grandfather's book, *How I Did It*. Stealing a body from a grave, and using a brain procured by Igor, Frankenstein brings life to the creature. When the doctor is attacked by his creation, Frankenstein learns that Igor provided him with an abnormal brain. Frau Blucher pacifies the monster by playing the violin, but accidentally receiving an electric shock, the monster runs off. In the forest he finds the blind hermit Harold, who offers him succor, but when the monster is consistently scalded and burned by his unseeing host, he leaves. Frankenstein captures his creation and convinces it of its own inherent goodness. At the Bucharest Academy of Science, he takes it on stage. But when the creature is frightened by a broken lightbulb, the audience pelts it with fruit and vegetables. He goes on the rampage and is jailed. Elizabeth makes an unexpected visit. The monster escapes, and Inspector Kemp leads the villagers in pursuit. The monster carries off Elizabeth, and his sexual prowess intoxicates her. Hearing the strains of Frankenstein's violin, he returns to the castle. Frankenstein prepares

Dr. Frankenstein (Gene Wilder) and assistant Inga (Teri Garr) contemplate the monster (Peter Boyle) in *Young Frankenstein* (Twentieth Century–Fox, 1974).

for a transference between himself and the monster. Kemp and the villagers break in before the procedure is completed, but the monster speaks, ordering the rabble to put Frankenstein down. He explains how Frankenstein gave him life and risked his own to provide him with a calmer brain and a better way of expressing himself. Kemp offers his friendship. Frankenstein marries Inga, and the monster weds Elizabeth.

Reviews: "Miracles still happen: Mel Brooks has made a funny movie.... The horror film is absurd by definition.... It can absorb any number of excesses and still cannot be desecrated.... [Brooks] has a real histrionic find in Marty Feldman." (John Simon, *Esquire,* April 1975, p. 54) ¶"A silly, zizzy picture.... It's what used to be called a crazy comedy, and there hasn't been this kind of craziness on the screen in years." (Pauline Kael, *New Yorker,* December 30, 1974, p. 58) ¶"Mel Brooks's funniest, most cohesive comedy to date.... The anarchy is controlled.... has an affectionate look to it." (Vincent Canby, *New York Times,* December 16, 1974, p. 48)

Analysis: This is Mel Brooks's best film — because it's structured on *Frankenstein* and the standard Frankenstein film clichés. Hackman is great as the hermit. Looniest scene: The monster gets booed by the audience because he can't sing and dance "Puttin' on the Ritz" to their satisfaction. Leachman's Frau Blucher is wonderful, carrying the unlit candelabra and advising Wilder, "Stay close to the candles. The staircase can be — treacherous." Not to mention her revelation about Victor Frankenstein: "Yes, yes! Say it! He vas — *my boyfriend!*"

Frankenstein Island
(Chriswar Productions, 1981; 89 min.)
***Bomb

Produced and directed by Jerry Warren. Screenplay, Jacques Lacouter. Director of Photography, Murray De Ately. Color. Musical Director, Erich Bromberg.

Cast: Dr. Hadley (Robert Clarke), Jocko (Steve Brodie), Jayson (Cameron Mitchell), Dr. Frankenstein (John Carradine), Colonel (Andrew Duggan), Melvin the dog (Himself).

With Robert Christopher, Tain Bodkin, Patrick O'Neil, Kathrin Victor.
Synopsis: Their balloon damaged and blown off course, a dog and four men paddle a rubber raft to a strange island inhabited by a tribe of women wearing leopard-skin bikinis and a lady who claims descent from Dr. Frankenstein. She tells them her invalid husband is being used as a channel by Frankenstein. Occasionally a person sees the visage of Frankenstein and hears him speaking about the "power" he will grant. Dr. Hadley agrees to help with transfusions and an implant for the invalid. It is learned that Dr. Frankenstein's creation was chained and tossed into the watery grotto the shipwrecked men passed on their way inland. Things go awry when the humanoid "mutants" guarding the laboratory go on the rampage. The monster is called forth and lends his strength until the channeling brain in the lab is put out of commission and Frankenstein's power dissipated. With the help of the leopard women, the four men escape on a raft and inform an American colonel about the island. Returning, they find nothing, and the colonel thinks they hallucinated. After he leaves the men find their dog, Melvin, and the amulet given him by one of the leopard women.
Review: "Absolutely unmitigated failure.... Sex and sadism won't rescue this picture." (John Stanley, *The Creature Features Movie Guide*, p. 92)
Analysis: Filmed in California, Baja, and Colossal Cave in Tucson, Arizona, this is total nonsense. It may well be the last American film to emulate (intentionally?) those all-time worst (but funny) science fiction films of the late '50s and early '60s, e.g., *The Astounding She-Monster*, *The Slime People*, *The Horror of Party Beach*. It's got everything: mad scientists, scantily clad women, pseudo-mutants, and a Frankenstein monster who must have modeled his arm movements on Glenn Strange's. The synopsis above is only part of the story, really. Steve Brodie — second billed — merely stumbles around and laughs. Cameron Mitchell recites Poe from his prison cell. John Carradine is shown only from the chest up. (He was probably filmed at

his home.) It's a howling mess, an embarrassment for most of the actors involved. A *Scarlet Street* (Fall 1993, p. 15) letter to the editor by Joe Jaworsky contends that *Frankenstein Island* is a remake of Jerry Warren's own *Teenage Zombies* (1957; released 1960). That film also features Katherine (Kathrin) Victor, but has no Frankenstein, apparently.

The Bride
(Columbia, 1985; 119 min.) ***

Produced by Victor Drai. Directed by Franc Roddam. Screenplay, Lloyd Fonvielle. Edited by Michael Ellis. Director of Photography, Stephen H. Burum. Color. Music, Maurice Jarre. Dolby Stereo. Supervising Art Direction, Bryan Graves. Art Director (France), Damien Lanfranchi. Set Decoration, Tessa Davies. Stunt Coordinator, Gerry Crampton.
Cast: Charles Frankenstein (Sting), Eva (Jennifer Beals), Clerval (Anthony Higgins), Viktor (Clancy Brown), Mrs. Bauman (Geraldine Page), Rinaldo (David Rappaport), Magar (Alexei Sayle), Bela (Phil Daniels), Countess (Veruschka), Dr. Zalhus (Quentin Crisp), Josef (Cary Elwes), Paulus (Tom Spaull), Pedler (Ken Campbell), Count (Guy Rolfe), Priest (Andrew de la Tour), Tavern keeper (Tony Haygarth).
Synopsis: During a storm, Frankenstein's female creation is imbued with life by lightning. His male creation wants her; thwarted, in his rage he causes an explosion that virtually destroys the laboratory. Frankenstein makes the new woman rest while his first creation wanders toward a village and takes up with a dwarf, Rinaldo, on his way to Budapest. Frankenstein entertains Dr. Clerval, telling him about his house guest, whom he pawns off as a woman struck by lightning, who with the proper instruction might become as independent as a man. He asks his housekeeper, Mrs. Bauman, to instruct "Eva" in the ways of polite society. Rinaldo is doing the same for his new friend and learning about him: "I always say you don't know a man until you know what his dream is." There are times during the journey when the "monster" feels odd. These are the moments when Eva is doing something, like spinning. Rinaldo gives his friend a name:

Viktor, for "he will win." They obtain employment with a circus, where Viktor drives tent pegs. Eva, in the meantime, is learning perhaps too much. She wonders about her heritage. Frankenstein promises her a life here and now and "presents" her to the Countess as his ward. Except for screeching at a cat she thought was a tiny lion, she acquits herself well and catches the eye of Josef. At the circus, Bela puts a slice in Rinaldo's rope, and he crashes into the seats. Before he succumbs, Rinaldo gives Viktor his amulet and urges him to find his dream. Back at Frankenstein's castle, Eva too feels the grief. Viktor takes the money Rinaldo had hidden and prepares to leave the circus. Overhearing Bela talking about cutting the rope, Viktor overturns the wagon and kills him, then flees. One day Eva meets Viktor in the forest and gives him something for luck. He, in turn, gives her Rinaldo's amulet; later, meeting a gypsy, he purchases some "jewels" for a lady. But after climbing the walls of the Frankenstein castle and observing Mrs. Bauman placing a real necklace about Eva's throat, he tosses his baubles into the river. The circus comes to town; learning that Viktor has been seen, the circus owner rousts the officials, and Viktor is jailed. Frankenstein is upset when he finds Eva being seduced by Josef. She wants explanations. Goaded into it, he tells her how he sewed together her body from corpses. She doesn't believe it, so he shows her his journals. In his cell, Viktor senses Eva's scream. Frankenstein tells Eva his first creation perished in the tower fire. Viktor breaks his shackles and the cell door and takes a horse, interrupting his creator as he forces himself on Eva. Frankenstein chases Viktor with a flaming brand into the old tower lab but falls to his death. Viktor returns to Eva, and they plan to journey.

Reviews: "An odd and engrossing release.... Director Franc Roddam concocts a new creation by stitching together bits and pieces of old material that once had lives of their own: themes and story devices from *Pygmalion* and *The Bride of Frankenstein*, spiced with folksy humor and a primitive sort of feminism." (David Sterritt, *Christian Science Monitor*, August 16,

1985, p. 23) ¶"Brings to mind the candlelit *Barry Lyndon*. But too often, for all its elegance and tenderness, it seems like a series of still life paintings." (Kevin Thomas, *Los Angeles Times Calendar*, August 16, 1985, p. 18) ¶"Bears no relation to the marvelous original — and, more unfortunately, lacks any of the sharp wit and sense of wonder which characterized James Whale's film." (Steve Jenkins, *Monthly Film Bulletin*, November 1985, p. 336)

Analysis: Much attention was given to this production, evidenced by having Academy Award–winning composer Maurice Jarre compose the score and getting renowned actress Geraldine Page for a supporting role. No Frankenstein movie has such sunlit scenes or plethora of European locations (France), from palaces and castles to bridges and statuary-filled parks. As Viktor (with as much or more screen time than Sting), Clancy Brown steals the show. Check out Cary *Robin Hood: Men in Tights* Elwes in one of his first period roles as the young officer with an eye for Beals. Also catch Guy *Puppet Master* Rolfe in a small role as a nobleman. The fall that Frankenstein takes from the tower is one of the best we've ever seen. We see him (a dummy, no doubt) hit and bounce. This film puts the lie to the axiom that circus people look out for each other. Well, maybe *Circus of Horrors* (1960) did it, too.

The Monster Squad
(Tri-Star/Taft Entertainment Pictures, 1988; 81 min.) **½

Produced by Jonathan A. Zimbert. Directed by Fred Dekker. Screenplay, Shane Black and Fred Dekker. Edited by James Mitchell. Director of Photography, Bradford May. Panavision. Metrocolor. Art Direction, David M. Haber. Set Decoration, Garrett Lewis. Costumes, Michael Hoffman. Makeup, Zoltan and Katalin Elek. Visual Effects, Richard Edlund. Special Effects, Phil Cory.

Cast: Sean (Andre Gower), Patrick (Robby Kiger), Del (Stephen Macht), Count Dracula (Duncan Regehr), Frankenstein (Tom Noonan), Horace (Brent Chalem), Rudy (Ryan Lambert), Phoebe (Ashley Bank), Eugene (Michael Faustino), Emily (Mary Ellen Trainor), Wolf Man (Carl Thibault), Gill Man (Tom Woodruff Jr.), Van Helsing (Jack

Gwillim), Derek (Adam Carl), Mummy (Michael Mackay), Scary German Guy (Leonardo Cimino), Detective Sapir (Stan Shaw), Desperate man (Jonathan Gries), Patrick's sister (Lisa Fuller), E. J. (Jason Hervey), Peasant girl (Sonia Curtis), Vampire bride (Charly Morgan), Vampires (Mary Albee, Joan-Carroll Baron, Julie Merrill), Mrs. Carlson (Marianne De Camp).

Synopsis: At the end of the nineteenth century, Abraham Van Helsing fails to rid the world of Dracula and his minions. In the late twentieth century, Dracula makes his way to the United States in search of a magic amulet. Young Sean realizes there's something wrong in his community and turns his club into "The Monster Squad." Getting a German-born resident to translate Van Helsing's diary, they learn that the amulet is pure good and that only once every hundred years are good and evil in balance. At midnight the amulet can be shattered and evil triumph. But a ceremony can open a hole into limbo to swallow the forces of evil. Tomorrow is that date! Dracula sends the Frankenstein monster to kill the children, but the pathetic beast becomes their ally. The squad obtains the amulet at 666 Shadowbrook Road and flees to the church in the center of town. On the way they unravel the mummy. The wolf man is dynamited, but his parts flow back together until Rudy shoots him with a silver bullet he'd made in shop. Horace guns down the Gill Man with a rifle. Little Phoebe recites the incantation that begins sucking the monsters into limbo. Before disappearing, the Frankenstein monster impales Dracula on a fence. The fiend escapes and grabs Sean, intending to drag him into the void. Sean extracts himself from Dracula as Van Helsing appears in the maelstrom and grabs the undead.

Reviews: "Delightfully rambunctious and affectionate homage to *The Little Rascals* and the vintage Universal monster movies of old…. Dekker makes the Monster Squad kids natural and believable enough to win audience affection and sympathy." (Taylor White, *Cinefantastique*, March 1988, p. 113) ¶"Is such fun, it makes you wish you were a kid again." (Kevin Thomas, *Los Angeles Times Calendar*, August 14, 1987, p. 20) ¶"Enjoyable kiddies'

horror pic … monsters recalls Universal creature features of the '40s…." (Nigel Floyd, *Monthly Film Bulletin*, July 1988, p. 205) ¶"Takes itself too seriously. It has trouble going for laughs when it is so clearly impressed with its own special effects." (Jami Bernard, *New York Post*, August 14, 1987, p. 25) ¶"The visual effects (by four-time Oscar-winner Richard Edlund) are high-tech. The script is low-grade comedy, an anything-for-a-laugh condescending vision of childhood." (Joseph Gelmis, *Newsday*, August 14, 1987, Part III, p. 5)

Analysis: It's cute but not saccharine. The effects are excellent, as they should be from Richard Edlund. Would that they had pondered a bit to come up with something to make it longer. Of course it's just silly to have the New World Gill Man around for this trip. They just wanted to get in all the seminal Universal monsters, we guess.

Roger Corman's Frankenstein Unbound
(20th Century–Fox, 1990; 85 min.)
**½

Produced by Roger Corman, Thom Mount, and Kabi Jaeger. Directed by Roger Corman. Screenplay, Roger Corman, F.X. Feeney, and Ed Neumeier. Based on the novel *Frankenstein Unbound* by Brian W. Aldiss. Edited by Jay Cassidy and Mary Bauer. Director of Photography, Armando Nanuzzi, Michael Scott. Color, Deluxe. Music, Carl Davis. Ultra-Stereo. Art Direction, Enrico Tovagliei. Set Decoration, Enio Michettoni. Costumes, Franca Zuchelli. Special Visual Effects, Illusion Arts, Syd Dutton, Bill Taylor. Special Makeup Effects and Monster Design, Nick Dudman. Second Unit Director, Thierry Notz.

Cast: Dr. Joe Buchanan (John Hurt), Dr. Frankenstein (Raul Julia), Mary Godwin (Bridget Fonda), Elizabeth (Catherine Rabett), Monster (Nick Brimble), Lord Byron (Jason Patric), Percy Shelley (Michael Hutchence), Justine (Catherine Corman), General (Mickey Knox), Voice of car (Terri Treas).

Synopsis: In New Los Angeles, 2031, Dr. Joe Buchanan invents an implosion device that has an unwanted side effect: a strange cloud that sucks in Buchanan and his car and transports them to Geneva, Switzerland, in the early nineteenth century. Buchanan

meets Dr. Victor Frankenstein, who is be-
mused when he hears that the newcomer
knows about his work. Frankenstein has
already created his "monster," which roams
the woods. In town, Buchanan attends the
trial of Justine Moritz, a young woman accused of murdering Frankenstein's young
brother. In the forest, Buchanan observes
the monster urging his maker to create a
mate. It says it will kill Frankenstein's
fiancée, Elizabeth, if he doesn't. After failing to convince Elizabeth to save Justine,
Buchanan meets Lord Byron, Percy Bysshe
Shelley and Mary Godwin. He tries on his
own to save Justine but fails and is tossed
into the lake. He wakes with Mary at his
side. To her he reveals some of her future.
The monster captures and kills Elizabeth.
With Buchanan's car's electricity, Frankenstein restores his fiancée to life. As Buchanan had directed, his car starts the implosion device. The time slip opens, and
Buchanan finds himself in a ruin amidst a
wilderness of snow. When Frankenstein
attempts to shoot the monster, "Elizabeth"
directs the pistol at herself and is killed for
the second time. The monster breaks his
maker's back. Buchanan pursues the monster, finding it in an underground laboratory. He disables it with lasers, yet it says
it can't be destroyed. Outside, Buchanan
heads toward a strange city.

Reviews: "At his most authoritative,
Corman directs with an appealing preci-
sion.... At his less confident, Corman's
staging is no better than functional."
(Philip Strick, *Monthly Film Bulletin*, January 1991, p. 4) ¶"Inspired, over-the-top
performances from both John Hurt and
Raul Julia.... The movie manages to entertain because of its wildly fabricated scenario..., its marvelous special effects...,
and its energetic direction...." (Gary J.
Svehla, *Midnight Marquee*, Summer 1991,
p. 41)

Analysis: It's Corman and Aldiss, not a
remake. It's a shame the sense of wonder
inherent in the time slip can't be sustained.
And the philosophical message is wasted —
or unnecessary? We're hanging at the end.
Did Bridget Fonda get the Mary Godwin
part because she was the daughter of Peter
Fonda, star of Corman's 1966 film *The Wild

Angels? Filmed in Milan, Bergamo and
Bellagio, Italy.

Frankenhooker

(Shapiro Glickenhaus, 1990; 90 min.)
***

Produced by Edgar Ievins. Directed by
Frank Henenlotter. Screenplay, Robert Mar-
tin and Frank Henenlotter. Edited by Kevin
Tent. Director of Photography, Robert M.
Baldwin. Color, T.V.C. Music, Joe Renzetti.
Art Direction, Artemus Pizarro, Pat Jacoby.
Special Makeup Effects, Gabe Bartalos. Spe-
cial Visual Effects, Al Magliochetti.

Cast: Jeffrey Franken (James Lorinz), Eliz-
abeth (Patty Mullen), Honey (Charlotte
Helmkamp), Spike (Shirley Stoler), Jeffrey's
mother (Louise Lasser), Zorro (Joseph Gon-
zalez), Crystal (Lia Chang), Angel (Jennifer
Delora), Sugar (Vicki Darnell), Monkey
(Sandy Colisimo), Amber (Kimberly Taylor),
Chartreuse (Heather Hunter), Anise (Ste-
phanie Ryan), Goldie (Paul Felix Montez).
With John Zacherle.

Synopsis: Jeffrey Franken works for New
Jersey Gas and Electric in Hohokus. When
his girlfriend, Elizabeth, is ground up and
killed by a remote control mower, he decides to restore her to life. He obtains her
head and a few other body parts and keeps
them in his estrogen-based blood serum
tank. To provide her with a perfect body,
he crosses the river to Manhattan and examines a number of prostitutes who work
for pimp Zorro. With his super crack mixture, Jeffrey causes the whores to explode.
Thus he has an assortment of body parts
with which to resurrect Elizabeth. Sorry he
had to kill them, he promises to put them
back together after he has Elizabeth back.
He succeeds in restoring Elizabeth, but
she has the morals of the prostitutes and
returns to the street. Jeffrey finds her, but
Zorro follows them home and decapitates
Jeffrey. The excess body parts in Jeffrey's
tank kill Zorro. Elizabeth puts Jeffrey's
head on female body parts. He doesn't like
it.

Review: "Takes the director deeper down
the urban alleyway of soft-core sexism and
perversity.... mistakes fraternity high jinks
and gross-out lavatory humor for creativ-
ity, cleverness, and wit." (Gary J. Svehla,
Midnight Marquee, Summer 1991, p. 41.)

Analysis: Henenlotter's urban sleaze milieu of *Basket Case* is captured again in this blackest of black humor. It's not totally satisfying. Note the TV weather man: beloved TV horror show host John Zacherle, who began his hosting chores as Roland on *Shock Theater* in Philadelphia in the late 1950s. How did Zorro know about the explosion? Were there body parts left behind? Pair it with *Bride of Re-Animator*.

Mary Shelley's Frankenstein
(Columbia/TriStar, 1994; 123 min.)
**½

Produced by Francis Ford Coppola, James V. Hart, John Veith. Directed by Kenneth Branagh. Screenplay, Steph Lady and Frank Darabont. Edited by Andrew Marcus. Director of Photography, Roger Pratt. Panavision. Technicolor. Music, Patrick Doyle. Art Direction, John Fenner, Desmond Crowe. Creature Makeup and Effects, Daniel Parker.

Cast: Victor Frankenstein (Kenneth Branagh), Monster (Robert De Niro), Elizabeth (Helena Bonham Carter), Victor's father (Ian Holm), Professor Waldman (John Cleese), Henry (Tom Hulce), Justine (Trevyn McDowell), Caroline Frankenstein (Cherie Lunghi), Captain Robert Walton (Aidan Quinn), Mrs. Moritz (Celia Imrie), Professor (Robert Hardy), Grandfather (Richard Briers).

Synopsis: "Arctic Sea 1794": Preparing to leave his icebound ship for an overland attempt on the North Pole, Captain Robert Walton and his crew encounter a strange man, Victor Frankenstein. The exhausted wayfarer tells Walton of his background, beginning in 1773 in Geneva, Switzerland: Into his household comes the orphaned Elizabeth, with whom Victor forms a lasting bond. When Victor is still a youth, his beloved mother, Caroline, dies in childbirth. "No one need ever die," he vows. At the Ingolstadt medical school in 1793 under the tutelage of one Professor Waldman, he charts unknown waters, hoping to restore, maintain, or create life. When Waldman is stabbed to death by a pegleg man he was trying to inoculate, Victor merges the professor's brain with the killer's body. Using electricity from generators, chemicals and electric eels, Victor imparts life to his creation. However, it seems mentally defective, and when some

equipment falls on it, Victor presumes it dead again. He decides to give up his experiments and destroy the creature. Before he can do that, it escapes. After fleeing a mob, the monster takes refuge in a secluded cabin and reads his maker's journal, which it finds in its coat. Although the monster helps a blind man's family, when seen by the son, it is driven off. Finishing the journal, the creature vows revenge, goes to Geneva, and kills Victor's young brother, pinning the blame (via a locket) on governess Justine. A mob lynches the governess. The creature then accosts Victor and invites him to a meeting in the mountains on the "sea of ice." Victor aims to kill his creation but is subdued and told to create a female companion. Instead, Victor marries Elizabeth and leaves the estate. But on their wedding night, the creature finds them and rips out Elizabeth's heart. Victor rushes back to his estate and puts Elizabeth's head and hands on Justine's body. His original monster appears to take possession of the "bride," but she immolates herself. On his ship, Captain Walton listens patiently to the fantastic story. Victor, exhausted by his pursuit of the monster, succumbs. The monster comes aboard and grieves because "he was my father." During a burial, the ice breaks, and Walton and his men return to their ship. Urged to come with them, Frankenstein's creation says, "I am done with man," and swims to the ice floe, where he conducts fiery last rites for his maker and himself.

Reviews: "Dehorrorized, desensitized $45 million costume epic.... Branagh lets himself overact at a fever pitch.... This movie shamelessly lifts the *Bride* scene in which the monster meets a kindly old blind man in a cabin — the one Mel Brooks, Gene Hackman and Peter Boyle parodied so artfully in 1974's *Young Frankenstein*." (Ralph Novak, *People*, November 17, 1994, p. 19) ¶ "Unfortunately, the good stuff here isn't so good. Branagh doesn't evoke terror, only repulsion.... The most authentically bizarre thing about the film is that John Cleese appears as a heavy and does a very nice job." (Richard Schickel, *Time*, November 7, 1994, p. 73)

Analysis: As in *Bram Stoker's Dracula*,

the set decoration and art direction are superb. The arctic scenes of the book usually omitted from Frankenstein films are installed here. Novel here as well are scenes of the monster using his super strength to toss men hither and yon. Robert De Niro's monster *is* an ugly sight, but there's nothing of the haunting alienness of Karloff's monster, or of the empty loneliness reflected in that hollow gaze. Much is done to imbue the monster with a kind of sad humanity, but that's so obvious that it belabors the point. The film has no glaring flaws until the monster is created. Why does Frankenstein give up on his creation so quickly? It doesn't make sense considering his life goals. Ensuing events happen too fast. The monster escapes without so much as a thumb of the nose. Why was the mob so intent on lynching Justine? Why were Elizabeth's hands as well as head attached to Justine's body? That involved more work, and time should have been of the essence for Frankenstein. Did Victor want the wedding ring that badly? It is disturbing to find that this and *Bram Stoker's Dracula*, both with lavish budgets, still can't be made in the complete spirit of their literary bases. Do the filmmakers plunge ahead so fast because they know we've seen the basic story before? On the plus side, Patrick Doyle's score is a highlight. The end credits segued from rich romanticism into a rousing, pounding allegro that would have done any adventure or superhero fantasy epic proud.

Notes of Interest: Mary Wollstonecraft Shelley wrote *Frankenstein* in 1816. The 1910 Thomas A. Edison silent film version prints no longer exist. *Frankenstein Meets the Space Monster* (1965) concerns a robot, although Robert Reilly plays Colonel Frank Saunders/Frankenstein. *Frankenstein Conquers the World* is a 1966 Japanese entry. In 1973 NBC-TV presented a two-part miniseries, *Frankenstein: The True Story*, starring James Mason, David McCallum and Michael Sarrazin. The 1993 TV version with Patrick Bergin and Randy Quaid had good photography, costumes and sets — and no style whatever.

Frankenhooker *see under* **Frankenstein**

Frankenstein and the Monster *see under* **Frankenstein**

Frankenstein Created Woman *see under* **Frankenstein**

Frankenstein Island *see under* **Frankenstein**

Frankenstein Meets the Wolf Man *see under* **Frankenstein**

Frankenstein Must Be Destroyed *see under* **Frankenstein**

Frankenstein — 1970 *see under* **Frankenstein**

Frankenstein's Daughter *see under* **Frankenstein**

The Freaks *see* Howling VI: The Freaks *under* **The Howling**

Freddy's Dead: The Final Nightmare *see under* **A Nightmare on Elm Street**

Freddy's Revenge *see* A Nightmare on Elm Street Part 2: Freddy's Revenge *under* **A Nightmare on Elm Street**

Friday the 13th
(Paramount/Georgetown Films, 1980; 95 min.) **

Produced and directed by Sean S. Cunningham. Associate Producer, Stephen Miner. Assistant Directors, Cindy Veazey, Stephen Ross. Screenplay, Victor Miller. Edited by Bill Freda. Director of Photography, Barry Abrams. Panavision. Color. Music, Harry Manfredini. Art Direction, Virginia Field. Special Makeup Effects, Tom Savini.

Cast: Alice (Adrienne King), Mrs. Voorhees (Betsy Palmer), Bill (Harry Crosby), Brenda (Laurie Bartram), Ned (Mark Nelson), Marcie (Jeannine Taylor), Annie (Robbi Morgan), Jack (Kevin Bacon), Steve (Peter Brouwer), Truck driver (Rex Everhart), Sergeant Tierney (Ronn Carroll), Dorf (Ron Millkie), Crazy Ralph (Walt Gorney), Barry (Willie

Adams), Claudette (Debra S. Hayes), Trudy (Dorothy Kobs), Sandy (Sally Anne Golden), Operator (Mary Rocco), Doctor (Ken L. Parker), Jason (Ari Lehman).

Synopsis: "Camp Crystal Lake, 1958": Two teenage camp counselors making love in a loft are killed. "Friday, June 13, The Present": Annie gets a lift from a truck driver who warns her not to accept the job of summer camp counselor. She'd also heard an admonition from small-town coot Ralph, who mentioned a death curse. The driver tells her about a jinx on the camp and a boy drowning there in 1957, two counselors killed in 1958, and bad water in 1962. Annie is dropped off by the Moravian Cemetery to make her way on foot to the lake. Meanwhile, at the camp, Alice tells Steve she'll give it a week before deciding on whether to stay on for the duration. Other counselors arrive and begin fixing the camp up. When Steve goes to town they take a break and swim. Annie is picked up by the unseen driver of a jeep. She leaps out when the driver refuses to stop at the road to the lake. Fleeing, she is caught and her throat slashed. Brutal murders begin at "Camp Blood." Finally only Alice is left to confront the killer: Mrs. Voorhees, who talks about her son Jason drowning on this day, Friday the 13th, years before while counselors engaged in hanky-panky and left him unattended. Alice incapacitates her nemesis several times, only to be pursued to the lake front. Alice and Mrs. Voorhees struggle, but Alice picks up a machete and decapitates the maniac. In the morning the police find Alice adrift in a canoe. Before she can be rescued she is pulled into the water by a rotting young boy. In the hospital the police greet with skepticism her comments about the lad. They did not see one. She says he must still be there.

Reviews: "Should be judged on its own merits apart from the flock of imitators which hurriedly followed…. Sean Cunningham's direction is fairly inspired…. effective ambiance of confusion and terror maintained throughout the movie." (Charles Baun, *The Connoisseur's Guide to the Contemporary Horror Film*, Albany NY: Fantaco Books, 1992, p. 29) ¶"Appears to be a quite bare-faced duplication of John Carpenter's *Halloween*…. implausibly and uninventively worked out, and the result is shoddily dependent on simulating its gory murders with maximum relish." (Tim Pulleine, *Monthly Film Bulletin*, July 1980, p. 132) ¶"The unending quest for suspense has seldom produced a bloodier mess." (Archer Winsten, *New York Post*, May 9, 1980, p. 33) ¶"The plot of the movie is almost non-existent." (Bill Kaufman, *Newsday*, May 10, 1980, Part II, p. 22) ¶"Only in unveiling the killer, a semifamous, semi-retired Broadway actress who seems to have been training with Bruno Sammartino in New Jersey, does the director invite derisive whoops of laughter." (Tom Allen, *Village Voice*, May 19, 1980, p. 50)

Analysis: There is no supernatural explanation for what to the audience is patently supernatural! Can we make sense of the senseless? Jason is deformed, sort of rotted. Can he see from only one eye? Obviously the police did not recover his body. When the cop said they'd pulled Alice from the lake, did he mean she was *in* the water? If she was in the lake, Jason probably put her there. If so, she wasn't dreaming. So, if Jason was real and alive, how did he live underwater, or did he swim out from the shore? When Mrs. Voorhees speaks as a child, is she possessed or merely psychotic? If Jason is alive, she's a nut. If not, she's possessed. Does Mrs. Voorhees pretend she was the cook in lieu of Annie?

Frankly, we shouldn't ask too many logic-related questions about this film or any of its sequels, as though they're *supposed* to make some kind of sense. All they're really doing is presenting a scenario: a gang of horny, doofus teens being victimized by an unstoppable force. The filmmakers, we think, were basically intrigued by the success of *Halloween* (and that film's obvious progenitors). The premise of each film bears no closer scrutiny than do the fireside horror stories that are frequently included therein. The plots for these horror stories are stripped down to the bare essentials of horny teens, stupid adults, isolated boondocks and mad slasher. These ingredients are put together in a *reasonably* plausible formula with nighttime rural settings and some degree of atmosphere (which is a plus), and the audience is treated, usually, to the sight of naked and semi-naked nymphets prior to their ritual sacrifice. One must — for the sake of the story — have at least the willingness to witness the slaughter of the young and the beautiful to even sit through this trash. And make no mistake, this stuff is the trash of the horror movie genre. It doesn't have the benefit of a reasonably inventive script (*Re-Animator*, for instance), even though the budget is on the respectable side of low. In fact, these flicks seem to have a certain contempt for plot, as though the "loophole" is part and parcel of this sort of film.

Betsy Palmer had been on Broadway and appeared on TV game shows. Adrienne King does a nice job of screaming and whimpering. Harry Manfredini's music is effective and at the end, ironically lyrical, perhaps as a counterpoint to what will emerge from the lake depths.

Friday the 13th, Part II
(Paramount, 1981; 87 min.) *½

Produced by Steve Miner and Dennis Murphy. Directed by Steve Miner. Screenplay, Ron Kurz. Based on characters created by Victor Miller. Edited by Susan E. Cunningham. Director of Photography, Peter Stein. DeLuxe Color. Music, Harry Manfredini. Costumes, Ellen Lutter. Makeup, Cecilia Verardi. Special Makeup Effects, Carl Fullerton. Special Effects, Steve Kirshoff.

Cast: Ginny (Amy Steel), Paul (John Furey), Alice (Adrienne King), Terry (Kirsten Baker), Ted (Stu Charno), Jason (Warrington Gillette), Crazy Ralph (Walt Gorney), Sandra (Marta Kober), Mark (Tom McBride), Cop (Jack Marks), Jeff (Bill Randolph), Vickie (Lauren-Marie Taylor), Scott (Russell Todd), Mrs. Voorhees (Betsy Palmer), Max (Cliff Cudney), Prowler (Jerry Wallace), Jason Stunt Double (Steve Daskawisz), Counselors (David Band, Jaime Perry, Tom Shea, China Chen, Carolyn Loudon, Jill Voight).

Synopsis: Alice lives alone, taking a breather after her gruesome days at Camp Crystal Lake. She talks to her mother on the phone, then thinks something's amiss. She's right. An intruder puts an ice pick in her temple. Five years later, at a lodge near Camp Crystal Lake, counselors take a retraining session. The semi-codger and nearby town crazy, Ralph, warns the people again. Paul Holt, who is running the camp, pooh-poohs rumors that Jason Voorhees is roaming the area. A policeman finds corpses in an outhouse at Camp Crystal Lake but is killed himself. While most of the counselors visit a bar, Terry and Scott are killed. Sandra and Jeff are impaled while making love. Next to meet their doom are the wheelchair-bound Mark and Vickie. Jason, who wears a cloth bag over his head with one eye hole, attacks Paul and Ginny. Ginny flees and discovers the head of Mrs. Voorhees in a candle-lit shrine. She dons the woman's ratty sweater and pretends to be Jason's mother. He believes her at first, but Paul arrives, and during the struggle Ginny puts a machete into Jason's back and shoulder. He collapses but reappears later, crashing through the window of the main building and grabbing Ginny. Next day an ambulance carries Ginny off as she asks Paul's whereabouts.

Reviews: "Life, we all know, isn't fair, but what is even more annoying is when movies cheat — and this one really does." (Linda Gross, *Los Angeles Times Calendar*, May 4, 1981, p. 2) ¶"Rather more polished than its predecessor, *Part 2* is no less feeble in plot and dialogue." (Tim Pulleine, *Monthly Film Bulletin*, July 1981, p. 138) ¶"Does have a continuous stream of taut and suspenseful moments, only because you never know when some atrocity will take place.... mindless gore and carnage." (Bill Kaufman, *Newsday*, May 2, 1981, Part II, p. 26)

Analysis: It was patently gratuitous to kill off the Adrienne King character. How did Jason recover his mother's head? How did he get to the town where Alice lived? Was that town near the lake? We thought she was from California. How did this end, exactly? Ginny was attacked through the window by Jason, then taken to the hospital. What happened to her boyfriend? To Jason?

Friday the 13th, Part III
(Paramount, 1982; 96 min.) **

Produced by Frank Mancuso, Jr. Directed by Steve Miner. Screenplay, Martin Kitrosser

Ginny (Amy Steel) bravely holds off her attacker in *Friday the 13th, Part II* (Paramount, 1981).

and Carol Watson. Based on characters created by Victor Miller and Ron Kurz. Edited by George Hively. Director of Photography, Gerald Feil. 3-D Supervisor, Martin Jay Sadoff. Music, Harry Manfredini. Art Direction, Rob Wilson King. Set Decoration, Dee Suddleson. Makeup, Cheri Minns. Special Effects, Martin Becker. Special Visual Makeup Effects, Make-Up Effects Labs, Douglas J. White, Allan Apone, Frank Carrisosa. Stunt Coordinator, John Sherrod.

Cast: Chris Higgins (Dana Kimmell), Rick (Paul Kratka), Debbie (Tracie Savage), Andy (Jeffrey Rogers), Vera (Catherine Parks), Chili (Rachel Howard), Shelly (Larry Zerner), Jason

Voorhees (Richard Broker), Chuck (David Katims), Fox (Gloria Charles), Ali (Nick Savage), Loco (Kevin O'Brien), Cashier (Annie Gaybis), Edna (Cheri Maugans), Newscaster (Steve Miner), Newswoman (Gianni Standaart), Mrs. Sanchez (Perla Walter), Harold (Steve Susskind), Abel (David Wiley), State Troopers (Terry Ballard, Charlie Messenger, Terence McCorry).

Synopsis: While the radio station announces numerous deaths at a Crystal Lake resort, the perpetrator continues his butchery at a nearby grocery, putting meat cleaver to Harold and impaling his wife through a door. The next day Chris Higgins picks up her pals and they head for Higgins Haven on Crystal Lake. On the way they pass the grocery and shortly thereafter stop for a man lying in the road. He warns them of danger and brandishes an eyeball. Shelly and Vera go to the store and are harassed by two bikers and their moll. The gang follows the duo back to the camp, and while preparing to fire the barn, Fox and Loco are pitchforked, Ali cudgeled. Chris explains to one-time boyfriend Rick that she's come back to prove she's strong and relates a past fight with her parents and afterward when she sat in the woods and was attacked by a hideous man. She blacked out and woke in her own bed. Wading in the lake that night to retrieve a wallet, Vera is speargunned in the left eye by a man in a hockey mask. Andy is split by a machete from the same fellow, and Debbie is knifed in the back from beneath her hammock while reading *Fangoria*. Shelly reappears, collapsing from a neck wound. Chuck is electrocuted, and Chili gets a hot poker to the midsection. Returning to the darkened camp, Rick has his head squished by the killer and his eyeball squirts out. Chris stabs the killer in the leg and escapes out the second floor window. Waiting on the porch, she batters him with a piece of firewood. He chases her into the barn, where she clobbers him with a shovel, then hangs him from the loft. When she goes outside, she is amazed to see the killer pull himself out of the noose. A momentary respite comes when the resuscitated Ali appears, but he has his hand chopped off and is killed. During that fight, Chris plants an ax in the head of the killer, who when briefly unmasked seems to be the man who assaulted her two years before. She gets in a boat and drifts on the lake during the night. Next morning she sees the hideous visage in the upstairs window. The killer rushes out the door, but when Chris looks back, he's not there. A worm-infested body rises from the lake and drags Chris into the water. The police arrive and talk about the young woman who's gibbering about her experience and the lady in the lake. Chris is taken away in a police car. The killer stands in the barn doorway.

Reviews: "Ironically, *Friday the 13th Part 3*

is so terrible that *Friday the 13th Part 1* and *Friday the 13th Part 2* don't seem so bad." (Linda Gross, *Los Angeles Times Calendar*, August 16, 1982, p. 6) ¶"Considering the unabashed sideshow aspects of the previous *Friday the 13th* installments, the adoption by this one of gimmick-laden 3-D seems to represent a logical next step...." (Tim Pulleine, *Monthly Film Bulletin*, May 1983, p. 131) ¶"The same butcher's delight." (Archer Winsten, *New York Post*, August 13, 1982, p. 41) ¶"Plot is a rehash.... The performances ... cohorts — are no improvement over the beach blanket bingo days of Annette and Frankie." (Joseph Gelmis, *Newsday*, August 13, 1982, Part II, p. 12)

Analysis: There is some continuity with Part II; the end of that is shown. Jason gets the hockey mask in this one. The negatives: the actors are irrational — e.g., Debbie is standoffish at one moment, the next she's eager for a sexual liaison with Andy; the lines are often terrible; it's predictable; the film is almost boring until the final quarter hour. On the positive side, the final confrontations between Chris and Jason are slam-bang, rapid-fire, and Chris shows resourcefulness in her attempts to escape and to kill her nemesis. But who was the lady in the lake referred to by police? Mrs. Voorhees?

Friday the 13th: The Final Chapter

(Paramount, 1984; 90 min.) *½

Produced by Frank Mancuso, Jr. Directed by Joseph Zito. Screenplay, Barney Cohen. Story, Bruce Hidemi Sakow. Based on characters created by Victor Miller, Ron Kurz, Martin Kitrosser, and Carol Watson. Edited by Joel Goodman. Director of Photography, Joao Fernandes. Panavision. Color, Movielab. Music, Harry Manfredini. Art Direction, Joe Hoffman. Set Decoration, Debra Steagall. Special Effects Makeup, Tom Savini, Alex Gillis, Kevin Yagher, Jill Rockow, Jim Kagel, Larry Carr, Mike Maddi. Stunt Coordinator, John Sherrod. Special Effects, Martin Becker, Reel EFX Inc., Frank Inez, John Hartigan, Dave Walton, John Godfroy.

Cast: Trish Jarvis (Kimberly Beck), Tommy Jarvis (Corey Feldman), Rob (E. Erich Anderson), Mrs. Jarvis (Joan Freeman), Sara

(Barbara Howard), Doug (Peter Barton), Jimmy (Crispin Glover), Ted (Lawrence Monoson), Vincent (Antony Ponzini), Lainie (Frankie Hill), Axel (Bruce Mahler), Nurse Morgan (Lisa Freeman), Paul (Alan Hayes), Samantha (Judie Aranson), Fat girl (Bonnie Hellman), Tina (Camilla More), Terri (Carey More), Doctor (Paul Lukather), Jason (Ted White).

Synopsis: Over a campfire, a head counselor relates the story of Jason. Later an ambulance arrives at the camp. Among the bodies of some counselors is the body of Jason, found in the barn. Taken to the Wessex County Medical Center morgue, he comes to life, cuts an orderly's throat with a hacksaw and guts a nurse. He stabs a hitchhiking girl on his return to the lake. At Crystal Point six young folk rent a house next to the Jarvis residence. During a nighttime swim a girl is stabbed, and when Paul investigates, he is skewered by a speargun. Rob, ostensibly bear hunting but actually after Jason, hears the screams but can't locate the murderer. As the night proceeds, the renters, their twin girl guests, and Mrs. Jarvis are killed. In the renter's basement, Rob is killed. Trish runs back to her house and brother Tommy. Jason throws Rob through the window and grabs Tommy, but Trish puts a claw hammer in Jason's neck. She and Tommy run upstairs. Jason recovers and breaks into their house. Trish smashes a TV onto his head and runs back to the other house, jumps through a window and falls to the ground. She returns to her house, where Tommy has made himself up as the young Jason. This confuses the real Jason, and Trish knocks off his mask, revealing a repugnant visage. Tommy puts a machete in Jason's head. There's a strange look in Tommy's face when he hugs his sister.

Reviews: "Seems an act of irresponsibility right down the line from producer to distributor to exhibitor, and most of all the MPAA, which gave it an R rating. If this film doesn't rate an X for violence, then you have to wonder what film does." (Kevin Thomas, *Los Angeles Times Calendar*, April 16, 1984, p. 5) ¶"While *Friday the 13th* and its ilk appeal to an audience's sexism, hooking it with lavish displays of T&A, they also function as a gruesome

corrective to a culture that relentlessly exploits sex without ever comprehending it." (David Edelstein, *Village Voice*, April 24, 1984, p. 57)

Analysis: Strange cast: the still attractive Joan Freeman was Elvis Presley's leading lady in 1964's *Roustabout*. Thank goodness for small favors: she's killed, but we don't see her stabbed or maimed and never see the body. Paul Lukather (look fast) was the compassionate surgeon in 1962's *Hands of a Stranger*. It's a poor trick ending to suggest that Tommy is somehow "possessed" by Jason. The murders are grisly — and revolting; there's more nudity than usual; and the promise of the title turned out to be a lie.

Friday the 13th: A New Beginning
(Paramount, 1985; 92 min.) *½

Produced by Timothy Silver. Directed by Danny Steinmann. Screenplay, Martin Kitrosser, David Cohen, Danny Steinmann. Story, Martin Kitrosser and David Cohen. Edited by Bruce Green. Director of Photography, Stephen L. Posey. Metrocolor. Music, Harry Manfredini. Set Decoration, Pamela Warner. Makeup, Kathryn Miles Logan. Special Makeup Effects, Martin Becker. Special Effects, Reel EFX Inc. Stunt Coordinator, Richard Warlock.

Cast: Tommy Jarvis (John Shepherd), Tommy at 12 (Corey Feldman), Pam Roberts (Melanie Kinnaman), Reggie (Shavar Ross), Dr. Peters (Richard Young), Violet (Tiffany Helm), George (Vernon Washington), Jake (Jerry Pavlon), Tina (Debisue Voorhees), Robin (Juliette Cummins), Ethel (Carol Locatell), Eddie (Robert Dixon), Victor (Mark Venturini), Joey (Dominic Brascia), Carl Dodd (Richard Lineback), Sheriff Tucker (Marco St. John), Junior (Ron Sloan), Duke Johnson (Caskey Swain), Roy (Dick Wiend), Raymond (Sonny Shields), Male nurse (Bob De Simone), Vinnie (Anthony Barille), Lana (Rebecca Wood-Sharke), Mayor Cobb (Ric Mancini), Les (Curtis Conaway), Neil (Todd Bryant), Demon (Miguel A. Nunez, Jr.), Anita (Jere Fields), Nurse Yates (Susanne Bateman).

Synopsis: Tommy Jarvis wakes from a dream in which as a twelve-year-old he sees two teenagers open Jason Voorhees's grave on a stormy night. Jason kills them and advances upon Tommy. Awake, Tommy finds himself being driven from the Unger Institute of Mental Health to Pinehurst, a more relaxed facility for disturbed teens. Almost immediately the camp is disturbed by the murder of Joey by Vic. More murders follow: rustic neighbor Ethel and her son, two young men whose car stalls on a country road, Reggie's older brother and his girlfriend. Eventually the killings take place at Pinehurst, reaching their conclusion on another stormy night when the hockey-masked Jason Voorhees pursues counselor Pam and Reggie into the barn. Tommy arrives and confronts his nemesis, who slashes him with his machete. Tommy stabs Jason in the leg and climbs to the loft with Pam and Reggie. In a free-for-all Jason is pushed from the loft and impaled on some old farm equipment. His mask has come off, and it turns out he is paramedic Roy. The police surmise that Roy went bonkers after finding that his son Joey was killed by Vic. In the hospital, Tommy dreams of stabbing Pam. Awake, he hallucinates that Jason is in the room. The image disappears. From his bedstead drawer Tommy extracts a hockey mask, and when Pam enters the room he sneaks up behind her with a knife upraised.

Reviews: "Danny Steinmann and his co-writers have done the smart thing and sent everything up." (Kevin Thomas, *Los Angeles Times Calendar*, March 25, 1985, p. 6) ¶"If anyone tries to tell you that *Friday the 13th — A New Beginning* … is the dirtiest, most murderous, foulest in language and most suspensefully nonsensical of this endless and popular series, believe him." (Archer Winsten, *New York Post*, March 23, 1985, p. 10)

Analysis: It's a no-frills Jason. His weapon of choice is the machete. Still, he employs a couple other implements of destruction. Perhaps the hedge clipper used in the eyes of Tina (Debisue Voorhees!) is a paean to Michael Gough's spike-loaded binoculars in *Horrors of the Black Museum*. The filmmakers seem not to have known how to end the film. It's confusing. Is Jason really in this movie? Roy acted as Jason, but was Jason guilty of some of the murders? Why did Tommy have the hockey

mask in his hospital room? We can only assume that when he donned the mask and raised the knife behind Pam he was mentally disturbed. Evidently he did not stab her because in the ensuing series entry he's not in jail. And Tommy's not tall enough for us to believe he's responsible for other murders in the film that we see committed by "Jason." But recall its immediate predecessor: The 12-year-old Tommy *may* have been possessed.

Friday the 13th, Part VI: Jason Lives

(Paramount, 1986; 85 min.) **

Produced by Don Behrns. Directed by Tom McLoughlin. Screenplay, Tom McLoughlin. Edited by Bruce Green. Director of Photography, Jon Kranhouse. Color, Metrocolor. Music, Harry Manfredini. Ultra-Stereo. Songs, Alice Cooper. Art Direction, Pat Tagliaferro. Set Decoration, Jerie Kelter. Stunts, Michael Nomad. Special Effects, Martin Becker. Special Effects Makeup, Chris Swift, Brian Wade. Special Mechanical Effects, David Wells, Ken Sher.

Cast: Tommy Jarvis (Thom Mathews), Megan (Jennifer Cooke), Jason (C. J. Graham), Sheriff Garvis (David Kagen), Sissy (Renee Jones), Paula (Kerry Noonan), Deputy Rick Cologne (Vincent Guastaferro), Cort (Tom Fridley), Nikki (Darcy Demoss), Darren (Tony Goldwyn), Lizbeth (Nancy McLoughlin), Allen Hawes (Ron Palillo), Stan (Matthew Faison), Larry (Alan Blumenfeld), Katie (Ann Ryerson), Roy (Whitney Rydbeck), Nancy (Courtney Vickery), Officer Pappas (Michael Swan), Martin (Bob Larkin), Thornton (Michael Nomad), Burt (Wallack Merck), Steven (Roger Rose), Annette (Cynthia Kania), Tyen (Tommy Nowell), Billy (Justin Nowell), Bus monitor (Sheri Levinsky). With Temi Epstein, Taras O'Har.

Synopsis: "Jason belongs in hell," says Tommy Jarvis as he and a companion prepare to disinter Jason Voorhees. Tommy intends spilling gas on the ghoul, but after they impale the maggot-covered body with a metal fence rod, a storm comes up and lightning strikes the rod twice. Jason is revived and kills Tommy's companion. Tommy flees to the Forest Green County police station. While he unsuccessfully tries to convince the sheriff that Jason is back, Jason kills two camp counselors in a

Volkswagen, four survivalists, the cemetery caretaker, two lovers, and two more counselors copulating in a motor home. Tommy, escorted to the county line, returns with books on the occult and enlists the help of the sheriff's daughter, Megan. Meanwhile, Jason arrives at his old home, Camp Crystal Lake, where he uses his machete and hands on the female counselors, then the police. Finally Tommy lures him into the lake and manages to shackle him to a boulder. Megan swims out to rescue Tommy, is grabbed by Jason but starts the boat's motor; the blades put a large nick into the monster. But at fadeout we see Jason's eye open.

Reviews: "The humor is welcome, some of the camera work inventive. And the young actors ... are cute or lively." (Michael Wilmington, *Los Angeles Times Calendar*, August 4, 1986, p. 1) ¶"What distinguishes *Friday the 13th, Part VI* is its humor." (Stephen M. Silverman, *New York Post*, August 2, 1986, p. 13)

Analysis: What is the real title of this film, anyway? *Jason Lives: Friday the 13th Part VI* appears on the screen at the beginning. *Friday the 13th Part VI: Jason Lives* appears at the end. To quibble further, we wonder about the location shooting in Georgia woods. The camp cabins have no screens. What, no mosquitoes? These complaints aside, this is a rather entertaining, frequently tongue-in-cheek entry with a witty credits sequence in which Jason crosses the screen à la James Bond, turns and slashes the viewer's eyeball. To be expected: hacking, mutilation, decapitation. There are ten corpses in the first half-hour. Just as gratuitous is the beetle squashed by a cop.

Friday the 13th, Part VII — The New Blood

(Paramount, 1988; 90 min.) **

Produced by Ian Paterson. Directed by John Carl Buechler. Screenplay, Daryl Haney and Manuel Fidello. Edited by Barry Zetlin, Maureen O'Conartin, Jay Sadoff. Director of Photography, Paul Elliott. Technicolor. Music, Harry Manfredini and Fred Mollin. Ultra-stereo. Stunts, Kane Hodder. Special Makeup Effects, Magical Media Industries.

Special Mechanical Effects, Image Engineering, Inc. *Cast:* Tina (Lar Park Lincoln), Nick (Kevin Blair), Jason Voorhees (Kane Hodder), Mrs. Shepard (Susan Blu), Dr. Crews (Terry Kiser), Melissa (Jennifer Sullivan), Sandra (Heidi Kozak), Eddie (Jeff Bennett), David (Jon Renfield), Robin (Elizabeth Kaitan), Maddy (Diana Barrows), Russell (Lary Cox), Ben (Craig Thomas), Mr. Shepard (John Otrin), Kate (Diane Almedia), Michael (William Clarke Butler), Jane (Staci Greason), Young Tina (Jennifer Banko). With Michael Schroeder, Debora Kessler.

Synopsis: A narrator tells us that there's a death curse on Crystal Lake. At the lake a young girl, angry with her father for arguing with her mother, takes out a rowboat and causes the wharf to collapse and kill her father. Years later that girl is the disturbed teen Tina, brought to the lake by her mother and Dr. Crews, who seems more intent on observing her telekinetic powers than on curing her. Next door are many teenagers who've prepared their house for a surprise birthday party. The guest of honor and his girlfriend never arrive because Jason kills them when their car breaks down. Jason had been resurrected by Tina when she stared into the lake and thought of her father. Jason's cable broke and he rose to the surface. Now he's on the warpath and returns to kill everyone, including Tina's mother and Dr. Crews. Jason interrupts coitus in several instances. Tina strives to deter Jason and does — temporarily, through electrocution and by causing a porch to fall on him. Finally he corners her in a basement, but she sets him on fire. She escapes with Nick and the house explodes. She and Nick are taken away in an ambulance.

Reviews: "There is a lot less blood, less screaming, less energy in this installment, as if Jason has become rather bored with his job.... leads to a rather dull final showdown...." (Caryn James, *New York Times*, May 15, 1988, p. 56) ¶"A carefully developed anxiety is needed to compensate for the reduced quota of entrails, but John Buechler's direction provokes yawns instead." (*Cinefantastique* January 1989, p. 112)

Analysis: Jason's demise in the previous

film is recapped. There are good touches. The audience knows Tina's telekinetic powers may prove his match. Naturally many of the teens are stupid. Jason uses several items to kill: a long-handled circular saw, metal tent spikes, machete. Jason in the form of Kane Hodder is an imposing figure, and when he removes his hockey mask the skull beneath is truly ugly. Filmed in Alabama, evidently in fall or winter; the vegetation is sparse. (There is truly no need for bug-proof screens this time around.) The funniest moments: when Tina "throws" a potted plant with a head in it at Jason; the circular saw. Yes, there is some nudity, thus the R rating. They wouldn't give it just for violence, would they?

Friday the 13th, Part VIII: Jason Takes Manhattan

(Paramount, 1989; 100 min.) **

Produced by Randolph Chevaldave. Directed by Rob Hedden. Screenplay, Rob Hedden. Edited by Steve Mirkovich. Director of Photography, Bryan England. Technicolor. Music, Fred Mollin. Ultra-Stereo. Special Makeup Effects, Jamie Brown. Special Effects, Martin Becker. Stunts, Ken Kirzinger.

Cast: Jason (Kane Hodder), Rennie Wickham (Jensen Daggett), Sean Robertson (Scott Reeves), Charles McCulloch (Peter Mark Richman), Colleen Van Deusen (Barbara Bingham), Julius Gaw (V. C. Dupree), Tamara Mason (Sharlene Martin), Wayne Webber (Martin Cummins), Young Jason (Timothy Burr), Young Rennie (Amber Pawlick).

Synopsis: Jason Voorhees is resurrected by the electrical charge generated when an underwater power line is broken by a falling boat anchor. The two teens who indulge in ill-advised fornication on the cabin cruiser above are Jason's first victims. Fresh victims appear on a cruise ship that's taking soon-to-be-graduates of Lakeview High on a class trip to New York City. The party's complement includes Rennie McCulloch, talented fledgling writer whose gifts are seemingly appreciated only by her boyfriend, Sean Robertson, and her teacher, Colleen Van Deusen. Rennie's been raised by her overbearing, bullying uncle, Charles McCulloch, after her parents died in an auto accident. Likewise,

Sean is a disappointment to his father, Admiral Robertson, who sees little chance for his dreams of a son who carries on the family maritime tradition. Jason climbs aboard the *Lazarus* as the ship gets underway. During the voyage, Jason systematically disposes of the passengers until Rennie, Sean, McCulloch, Colleen Van Deusen and Julius take to a lifeboat. The five disembark at a deserted New York wharf and fail to notice that Jason climbs ashore after them. Muggers accost the newcomers and kidnap Rennie, but Jason makes short work of the criminals, as well as a policeman. Colleen is killed when the police car explodes. Jason finishes off Julius and McCulloch and pursues Rennie and Sean into a diner on Broadway, then into the subway. Jason is electrocuted but lurches to his feet and follows them into the sewer drains. Rennie entices Jason and tosses a bucket of "toxic waste" into his face. He screeches and writhes in agony. His goalie mask falls off, revealing a monstrous countenance, perversely reminiscent of the boy Jason who drowned in Crystal Lake decades earlier. Rennie returns to Sean and they find a ladder. But a wire grate prevents their escape and Jason arrives at the foot of the ladder. As the enraged monster claws at Rennie, the tunnel fills with onrushing toxic waste. Jason catches the full brunt of the poison deluge, and his body disappears in the noxious mass. When the noisome brew subsides, at the foot of the ladder is the spotless body of a lifeless boy, Jason Voorhees.

Reviews: "It seems like just about anyone who's taken a film school class or two can get a shot at doing one of these." (Chris Willman, *Los Angeles Times Calendar,* July 31, 1989, p. 4) ¶ "The commercials are a scam. *Part VIII* is nearly over before it delivers the scenes used in the TV spots." (Terry Kelleher, *Newsday,* July 29, 1989, Part II, p. 15)

Analysis: Removing Jason from his Crystal Lake setting might seem like taking the Creature out of the Black Lagoon, but in fact, after seven films set in that cursed camp, Jason was ready for a vacation. *Jason Takes Manhattan* does manage to open up the series in a way the other films did not, restricted as they were to the Camp Crystal Lake environs. Not that it matters very much: Master Voorhees goes about his grisly business as usual, sending his victims to the promised land in short order, whether in the woods around the camp, in the bowels of the *Lazarus*, or roaming the alleys, sewers, or rooftops of the Big Apple. As had been the case with the previous film or two, this eighth installment "lightens" the mood at times with instances of dark humor, in this case mostly aimed at the churlish inhabitants of New York City. Otherwise, the cast of "high school kids" introduced in the first quarter-hour of the movie is dispatched one by one in turn, each in his or her unique fashion, until only the heroine and her boyfriend (and their dog) are left. This is, of course, the formula of each film in this series.

By the time of *Jason Takes Manhattan*, the production quality of the *Friday the 13th* series had taken on a slickness that was quite absent in the original outings lensed grainily by Sean Cunningham. This hardly represents any improvement in the minds of most of the series' critics — and that includes just about everybody. *Friday the 13th* and its progeny represent everything that is wrong with the post–*Psycho* horror film, and was in effect the equivalent of a modern geek show. Dressing up the show in a higher-quality production did nothing to improve the product. Curiously, the *Friday the 13th* films became something of an institution of the 1980s, something like the James Bond films in the sixties, perhaps. Cunningham's *Friday the 13th* appeared in 1980 as one of numerous *Halloween* clones, complete with a Michael Myers look-a-like who ushers a host of horny teens into early graves. The irony is that Cunningham, who showed little of John Carpenter's visual ingenuity, narrative gifts, or fondness for the genre, should have inspired a series that for a long time looked as unstoppable as Jason himself.

For some time, the word was that this eighth chapter of the Jason saga would be his last. But fans of the series, whoever *they* might be, evidently proved forceful enough at the box office that, once again, the eyes behind that dirty goalie's mask popped open, and we heard that *next* time … *Jason Goes to Hell*!

We never knew Crystal Lake wasn't landlocked! This "Manhattan" film was shot in Vancouver! Remember when it was just Mark, not Peter Mark Richman?

Jason Goes to Hell: The Final Friday
(New Line Cinema, 1993; 88 min.)
*½

Produced by Sean S. Cunningham. Directed by Adam Marcus. Screenplay, Dean Lorey and Jay Huguely. Story, Jay Huguely and Adam Marcus. Edited by David Handman. Director of Photography, William Dill. Color, DeLuxe. Music, Harry Manfredini. Dolby Stereo. Set Decoration, Natalie K. Pope. Stunt Coordinator, Kane Hodder. Special Makeup Effects, Kurtzman, Nicotero and Berger EFX Group. Special Visual Effects, Al Magliochetti.

Cast: Steven Freeman (John D. LeMay), Jessica Kimble (Kari Keegan), Jason Voorhees (Kane Hodder), Creighton Duke (Steven Williams), Coroner Phil (Richard Gant), Diana Kimble (Erin Gray), Sheriff Landis (Billy Green Bush), Alexis, blonde camper (Kathryn Atwood), Vicki (Allison Smith), Shelby (Leslie Jordan), Robert Campbell (Steven Culp), Deborah, brunette camper (Michelle Clunie), Luke, boy camper (Michael Silver), Elizabeth Marcus, F.B.I. (Julie Michaels).

Synopsis: A young woman is chased into the woods by a hulking maniac. Lights illuminate the clearing, and the monster, Jason Voorhees, is ripped to pieces by bullets and other explosives. At the federal morgue in Youngstown, Ohio, coroner Phil finds that the maniac's deformed, extra large heart contains a "black, viscous fluid." Unable to control himself, he starts eating it. Light nodes emanate from the corpse and enter Phil's body. On the TV series "American Case File," reporter Robert recounts the story of Jason Voorhees, responsible for 83 confirmed murders, perhaps scores more, including a coroner and two security guards. Creighton Duke tells the newsman that Jason only wears flesh as a suit and that he will get rid of him once and for all — for $500,000. At Crystal Lake, Duke tells waitress Diana that Jason is coming for her. At Camp Crystal Lake, three hikers are savaged by Phil, who then kills a woman and "infects" a policeman. The cop kills Diana, and Steven impales him. But the body disappears and Steven is arrested. In a jail cell next to Duke, Steven hears that Jason killed Diana and that he needs Jessica to truly be reborn. Breaking out of jail, Steven cases the old Voorhees place. While hiding in a closet, he watches as the policeman he'd impaled passes on his awful infection to Robert before disintegrating. Robert attacks Jessica, but Steven rescues her. Still, she can't accept his explanation and drives to the police. At the police station, Steven saves Jessica again from a rampaging Robert. They flee to the restaurant, where Robert is again dispatched. But Jessica's baby has been taken to the Voorhees house by Duke. Jessica arrives, and Duke tosses her a knife that changes shape as she catches it. Duke tells her only a Voorhees can kill a Voorhees and send Jason to hell. A demonic crawling creature comes out of the body of the young cop. It enters Diana's body, but the rebirth is short-lived, and Jason is pulled into the earth. His hockey mask remains above ground till a clawed glove reaches up and pulls it below.

Review: "Offers a little humor.... Unfortunately, first-time director Adam Marcus and writers Dean Lorey and Jay Hugely also have a story to tell. And it's a confusing mess ... [with] substandard sound and lighting." (Terry Kelleher/*Newsday*, *Philadelphia Inquirer*, August 16, 1993, p. E6)

Analysis: There's gore, nudity, sex, even a young woman peeing in the woods. (Is this really necessary?) The woman running through the forest at the beginning is sometimes shod, sometimes barefoot. Maybe it was planned. It's tongue-in-cheek but lacks the proper mix that was demonstrated in *Return of the Living Dead*. Cinematic in-jokes: the crate from the Horlicks Arctic Expedition (*Creepshow*); the Freddy Krueger–style hand that reaches from the earth at the end (*A Nightmare on Elm Street*). How can Jason's visage be in the mirror when the body he inhabits is someone else? Ours is not to reason why, or how. It does not follow directly from the preceding entry. The title promises something special

(Jason literally in hell from the git-go), but the movie does not deliver, and as the end approaches, we can't wait for it to be over.

Fright Night
(Columbia/Vistar, 1985; 105 min.)
***½

Produced by Herb Jaffe. Directed by Tom Holland. Screenplay, Tom Holland. Edited by Kent Beyda. Director of Photography, Jan Kiesser. Panavision. Metrocolor. Music, Brad Fiedel. Sound, Don Rush. Dolby Stereo. Choreographer, Dorain Grusman. Costumes, Bettylee Balsam. Creatures, Randall William Cook and Steve Johnson. Makeup, Ken Diaz. Visual Effects, Richard Edlund. Special Effects, Michael Lantieri.

Cast: Jerry Dandridge (Chris Sarandon), Charley Brewster (William Ragsdale), Peter Vincent (Roddy McDowall), Amy Peterson (Amanda Bearse), "Evil" Ed (Stephen Geoffreys), Billy Cole (Jonathan Stark), Judy Brewster (Dorothy Fielding), Detective Lennox (Art J. Evans), Cook (Stewart Stern), Jonathan (Robert Corff), Miss Nina (Pamela Brown). With Nick Savage, Ernie Holmes, Heidi Sorenson, Irina Irvine, Chris Hendrie, Prince A. Hughes.

Synopsis: Charley Brewster can't convince his mother or the police that a vampire and his male attendant have moved in next door and are responsible for the recent killings in town. Friend "Evil" Ed, though skeptical, tells Charley how to ward off the undead. However, Charley's mother invites in Jerry Dandridge, the new neighbor. That evening Dandridge calls on Charley and asks him to forget about what he's seen. Charley stabs a pencil through his visitor's hand, initiating a hideous transformation, but Charley's mother wakes and Dandridge leaves, promising to return next evening. Charley fails to enlist the assistance of horror show host Peter Vincent, but Charley's girlfriend, Amy, and Ed promise the recently fired Vincent $500 to play along with Charley. Vincent calls Dandridge, and they agree that Vincent will give Dandridge regular water disguised as holy water to prove he's human. At Dandridge's, the vampire gives Amy the eye and drinks the water. On the way out Vincent notices that Dandridge has no reflection in his compact mirror. Vampirized on the way home by Dandridge, Ed attacks Vincent, but the latter burns the outline of a crucifix in Ed's head. Dandridge pursues Charley and Amy to a disco. While Charley phones for help, Dandridge mesmerizes Amy. When Charley returns and attempts to rescue her, bouncers confront Dandridge, who tosses them around. In the ruckus Charley is separated from Amy. Charley seeks Vincent while Amy is vampirized at Dandridge's. Charley and Vincent enter the house only to face a blasé Dandridge who tosses Charley over the banister. Vincent flees to Charley's house, finds Ed has become a wolf and impales him. Returning to Dandridge's, he finds Charley with the comatose and quite monstrous Amy. They shoot and impale Billy, Dandridge's daytime surrogate, and he disintegrates. Dandridge commands Amy to kill the intruders, but the clocks stop at 6 A.M. Dandridge becomes a huge bat, attacks Vincent but is warded off by Charley, and flies down the hall. Charley and Vincent pursue the bat into the basement. Charley battles the now horrific Amy while Vincent locates Dandridge's coffin and puts a stake into his chest. Nevertheless, Dandridge rises up, extracts the stake and prepares to kill his nemeses. Charley and Vincent break the windows, letting in the sunlight, which destroys Dandridge, who turns to a skeleton of a human-size bat creature. Amy is reborn, Vincent gets his job back, but does Charley see red eyes in the dark in the Dandridge house?

Reviews: "Staged ... in such a stodgy, turgid fashion that you'd think no one had ever seen Bela Lugosi bare his teeth on late-night TV before." (Patrick Goldstein, *Los Angeles Times Calendar*, August 1, 1985, p. 8) ¶ "Holland has evidently learned enough to put together an efficient first film as director. Elegantly photographed...." (Philip Strick, *Monthly Film Bulletin*, April 1986, p. 108) ¶ "Picks up a couple of good marks by tempering the emetic with the erotic, notably in the unlikely context of a disco." (John Coleman, *New Statesman*, April 11, 1986, p. 27)

Analysis: This is a progressively excellent, consistently entertaining vampire film, with horrific scenes leavened with welcome humor, e.g., Sarandon humming "Strangers in the Night." The bat-like skeleton that Sarandon transforms into at the end is great. One of the movies Charley watches on TV is *Scars of Dracula*. Bearse went on to co-star in the successful TV sitcom "Married with Children."

Fright Night Part 2

(New Century/Vista, 1989; 101 min.)
**1/2

Produced by Herb Jaffe and Mort Engelberg. Directed by Tommy Lee Wallace. Screenplay, Tim Metcalfe, Miguel Tejada-Flores, and Tommy Lee Wallace. Based on characters created by Tom Holland. Edited by Jay Lash Cassidy. Director of Photography, Mark Irwin. Panavision. Color, DeLuxe. Music, Brad Fiedel. Art Direction, Randy Moore. Set Decoration, Michele Starbuck. Costumes, Joseph Porro. Special Effects, Rick Josephson. Special Visual Effects, Gene Warren, Jr., and Fantasy II Film Effects.

Cast: Peter Vincent (Roddy McDowall), Charley Brewster (William Ragsdale), Alexandra Goode (Traci Lin), Regine Dandridge (Julie Carmen), Belle (Russell Clark), Bozworth (Brian Thompson), Louis (Jonathan Gries), Dr. Harrison (Ernie Sabella), Richie (Merritt Butrick).

Synopsis: After three years of therapy, Charley Brewster is convinced that he and Peter Vincent never did fight vampires. But while he and his new girlfriend, Alexandra, visit Peter, Charley observes large crates being delivered to the hotel next door. A coed is killed, and Alexandra is next on the murderer's list. Charley is visited by the svelte Regine, who comes on to him. Or was it a dream? What about Richie whom he thinks he sees savaged through a hotel window? But when he and Peter investigate, they discover a party and Richie in fine fettle. Regine turns out to be a "performance artist," but when Peter notices she has no reflection in his mirror, he knows she's more than that. Regine tells Peter that the late Jerry Dandridge was her brother and that he and Charley will pay for his death. Regine drains some of Charley's blood while he sleeps. She takes over Peter's horror show. Peter can't convince Charley or Alexandra that Regine is a vampire until Richie is found dead. Charley discovers coffins in the hotel basement and tries to hammer a stake into the body of Regine. But her eyes open, and he can't do it. He's under her spell. Still, he does rescue Alexandra from Regine's minion, Louis. Peter, too, is unsuccessful in staking Regine. Regine bails Charley out of jail. Peter is sent to a mental hospital, but Alexandra pretends to be a psychiatrist and gets him out. They obtain holy water, communion wafers, and stakes and climb the hotel to the room where Charley awaits a vampiric transformation — so Regine can torture him forever. Peter and Alex kill Richie with holy water and Louis with a stake. Regine and another minion try to make Charley bite Alex. But the other female vampire's nails are pulled into the male monster, and he dies. A religious cloak is tossed over the woman, and she disintegrates. Regine is trapped in an elevator. Charley and Alex race downstairs and fill her coffin with communion wafers. As a hideous bat creature, Regine breaks out of the elevator and flies to the coffin. As Regine, she entreats Charley. In the elevator shaft, Peter uses a piece of broken mirror to reflect the sun's rays onto the vampire. Regine goes up in flames.

Review: "Like its predecessor ... takes a fang-in-cheek attitude toward horror flicks, but it isn't the certifiable spoof the original was." (Mick Martin and Marsha Porter, *Video Movie Guide 1994*, p. 815)

Analysis: This is yet another film that eschews a relatively intimate — and thus more terrifying — locale for a populated center, in this case a hotel. There are too many people about. It's hardly a "haunted house." The special effects are fine, and some of the humor is welcome, e.g., when Alexandra unknowingly slams down the window and cuts off the nails of the beast trying to get in. But the comedy is ladled on too thick in the railroad scene when the vampire keeps blabbing after being staked by Alex. Why does Charley end up in the calaboose after the library incident with vampire Richie? Was he jailed for destroying property?

Future Cop *see* **Trancers**

Futureworld *see under* **Westworld**

The Gate
(New Century/Medusa/Vista, 1987; 92 min.) ***

Produced by John Kemeny. Directed by Tibor Takacs. Screenplay, Michael Nankin. Edited by Rit Wallis. Director of Photography, Thomas Vamos. Color, Medallion Film Laboratories. Music, Michael Hoenig and J. Peter Robinson. Dolby Stereo. Set Decoration, Jeff Cutler, Marlene Graham. Makeup, Craig Rearson. Special Effects, Randall William Cook.

Cast: Glen (Stephen Dorff), Terry (Louis Tripp), Alexandra (Christa Denton), Lori Lee (Kelly Rowan), Linda Lee (Jennifer Irwin), Mom (Deborah Grover), Dad (Scot Denton), Paula (Ingrid Veninger), Eric (Sean Fagan).

Synopsis: After Glen's treehouse is destroyed by lightning and the tree cut and carted away, a hole is uncovered. Glen's pal Terry says the egg-like rocks they find inside are valuable geodes. Glen and his teenage sister, Alexandra, (Al) are left alone for the weekend by their parents. During the party Al throws, Glen is levitated. That night, while Terry sleeps over, he sees his dead mother's image. Glen, meanwhile, sees his bedroom wall moving. Glen's dog, Angus, dies. At his house, Terry reads *The Dark Book*, which tells of a gate into this world for the old gods. Back at Glen's, they are surprised to find that the hole they'd covered is now open. Terry says they've got demons. That night Glen's window is broken, and when Al comes into the room, she's grabbed by goblin-like arms from beneath the bed. Escaping the multitude of little demons, Terry, Glen and Al hurry to the basement rec room for *The Dark Book*, which has spells to exorcise the old gods. But it goes up in flames. They take the Bible instead and go to the hole. Reciting passages seems to work, but Terry falls in and is attacked by little gremlins. Pulled out, he tosses the Bible in, and the hole closes. Back at the house, a cadaver comes out of the wall and grabs Terry and Al. A hole has opened in the living room floor, and Glen witnesses the arrival of an immense demon, who implants an eye in the boy's palm. Rushing to his window, Glen sees a rush of smoke into the atmosphere. Knowing the old demons are entering his world, he stabs his hand-eye and then finds one of his toy rockets under the bed. He launches it into the great demon, which is destroyed. At sunrise, Terry, Al *and* Angus reappear.

Reviews: "Sort of an *Evil Dead* for preteen nerds, *The Gate* boasts some fine effects and monsters, but is ultimately hampered by the singularly obnoxious nature of the two male leads.... The last 40-odd minutes are above average for this type of material." (Stefan Jaworzyn, *Shock Xpress,* Summer 1987, p. 18) ¶"Well written and directed, with excellent special effects and sympathetic performances, *The Gate* is a winner in the horror genre." (Jay., *Variety,* May 20, 1987)

Analysis: This is an often frightening Canadian production with welcome humor to relieve the tension. The gibbering little demons are truly horrible. This would agreeably be paired with *Poltergeist.* By the way, the male leads are *not* obnoxious, no matter what *Shock Xpress* thinks.

Gate II
(Vision International/Alliance Entertainment, 1992; 95 min.) **

Produced by Andras Hamori. Directed by Tibor Takacs. Written by Michael Nankin. Edited by Ronald Sanders. Director of Photography, Bryan England. Color. Music, George Blondheim. Ultra-Stereo. Special Makeup, Craig Rearson. Special Visual Effects Design, Randall William Cook. Special Effects, Frank Carere.

Cast: Terrence Chandler (Louis Tripp), Moe (Simon Reynolds), Liz (Pamela Segall), John (James Villemaire), Art (Neil Munro), Mr. Chandler (James Kidnie), Minion (Andrea Ladanyi), Doctor (Elva Mai Hoover).

Synopsis: The now teenage Terry enters the abandoned home of his boyhood friend Glen and conducts a ritual. Using the other worldly power he and Glen once unleashed, Terry hopes to get his father a job. Terry is interrupted by Liz, Moe and John. Explaining how demonology is not Satanism, he enlists their aid. They end up with a "minion," a foot-tall gremlin. John shoots it, but after they leave Terry picks it up and takes it home. Next day his father says he's going to a job interview. Could this be the result of Terry's spell? John tells Moe he wished to be king of the world. Moe, in

turn, wants a healthy heart. The minion comes back to life, but Terry recaptures it. Liz comes over, and to Terry's surprise, her little ritual gets results: a red Corvette. But next day the car disintegrates. Terry realizes the wishes only work for a short time. Mr. Chandler is injured in an airline accident. Terry decides to sent the minion back. John and Moe, however, steal the minion and conduct their own ritual to get cash. But the minion bites John, and he slowly turns into a demon. Moe leads Liz and Terry to the warehouse where John is hiding. Moe has a heart attack and falls, but the demon John carries him off. Terry realizes the demons are coming from inside, not the visible gate. He finds the minion and places it in the ritual box. Liz is kidnapped, and Terry falls in the hole and emerges in a strange, barren land. He ascends to a peak, where Liz is about to be sacrificed. Liz hurls the box into the pit. Back in the real world, Liz can't revive Terry, but at his funeral he breaks out of the coffin. After he, his father and Liz leave, Moe and John also emerge from the coffin.

Review: "Idiotic horror film boasting good monster effects." (Lawrence Cohn, *Variety,* March 9, 1992)

Analysis: Some of the incidents and explanations border on nonsense. The audience's suspension of disbelief is strained. There's a chronological mistake when Terry says "Last year after my mom died." That was years before. All in all, though, it's entertaining.

Generations *see* Star Trek: Generations *under* **Star Trek**

The Ghost Breakers
(Paramount, 1940; 85 min.) ***

Produced by Arthur Hornblow, Jr. Directed by George Marshall. Screenplay, Walter De Leon. Based on a play by Paul Dickey and Charles W. Goddard. Edited by Ellsworth Hoagland. Director of Photography, Charles Lang. Process Photography, Farciot Edouart. Music, Ernest Toch. Art Direction, Hans Dreier, Robert Usher. Costumes, Edith Head.

Cast: Larry Lawrence (Bob Hope), Mary Carter (Paulette Goddard), Alex (Willie Best), Geoff Montgomery (Richard Carlson), Ramon

Mederos/Francisco Mederos (Anthony Quinn), Parada (Paul Lukas), Havez (Pedro De Cordoba), Raspy Kelly (Tom Dugan), Frenchy Duvall (Paul Fix), Zombie (Noble Johnson), Martin (Lloyd Corrigan), Mother zombie (Virginia Brissac), Hotel porter (James Flavin), Lt. Murray (Robert Elliott), Interns (Douglas Kennedy, Robert Ryan).

Synopsis: While New Yorker Mary Carter consults with Mr. Havez of the Cuban consulate and Mr. Parada concerning Cuba's Black Island and castle, radio commentator Larry Lawrence and his retainer Alex prepare for a vacation. Mary is phoned by a Ramon Mederos with a strange warning about her inheritance. Called to the hotel by mobster Frenchy Duvall, Lawrence thinks he's being shot at by a man in the hall — Mederos. Larry closes his eyes and fires. The man falls dead, but Larry doesn't see that it was Parada who did him in. Larry hides in Mary's steamer trunk during the police search and ends up in Mary's stateroom. Although a newspaper reveals Mederos was shot with a .38, not Larry's .32, Larry spies the note Mary had received — "Death Waits For You On Black Island!" — and decides to help. Parada also takes ship and tells Mary about her remote ancestors, the spirit of Don Santiago, and voodoo. Lawrence tells Parada he's a "ghost breaker" who explains mysteries and ghosts in closets. Someone drops a flower pot that just misses Larry and Mary. Before disembarking in Cuba, Mary finds a knife and voodoo charm in her door. Geoff Montgomery, whom Mary had met in New York, appears and explains the charm. He says Parada can't be trusted. At dinner Mary sees a man who looks like Ramon Mederos. It's his twin brother, Francisco, who wants to know who killed Ramon. Larry and Alex row to Black Island during the night and observe the zombie and its mother who live in a shack on stilts. In the castle they find a portrait of Maria Ysobel Sebastian that is strikingly like Mary. Both witness an apparition leaving a chest and returning. Opening it, Larry finds a skeleton. A second boat approaches the island, and a woman swims to shore. It's Mary. Inside the castle she is observed by Parada, who is grabbed from behind and disappears. The zombie enters and fights Larry

and Alex. When it sees Mary in the gown of her ancestor, the zombie is cowed and Larry and Alex lock it in an anteroom. Geoff appears. Mary and Larry find an inscription on a wall about a key to unlock the castle's secret. Their search is interrupted by Parada, who's been stabbed. Before he succumbs he mentions a fortune under the castle and the words, "Music, marching men." Mary finds musical notes on the wall and plays them on the organ. A column swings aside and they find railway tracks. It's a mine. Francisco confronts them with a gun, but Geoff shoots it out of his hand. But it is Geoff who's the bad guy. He intends to shoot them and gain control of the silver mine. But he falls to his doom when Alex accidentally pushes a button that makes the floor collapse. On the boat leaving the island, Francisco tells them that the apparition of Don Santiago was a real ghost.

Review: "Occasionally ghosts, zombies, moldy coffins, and sliding panels make a bid for chills, but they haven't a chance against Hope's comic exorcism and the clowning of Willie Best...." (*Newsweek,* June 24, 1940, p. 51) ¶"Not many pictures can make your goose-pimpled sides shake with laughter, but this one does — or should." (Bosley Crowther, *New York Times,* July 4, 1940, p. 12)

Analysis: Based on the vision we see and Anthony Quinn's opinion, the only truly supernatural element in this film is the ghost of Don Santiago. It's a good mystery, however. You don't know the villain until the end. Spunky and beautiful Paulette Goddard makes an Edith Head fashion statement in lingerie, dresses, antique gown, swimsuit, and casual evening wear. Goddard and Hope had clicked the previous year in *The Cat and the Canary.* While Willie Best has become a symbol of subservience, he's a most suitable sidekick for Hope and hardly less frightened than his employer. This had been filmed as a silent in 1925.

Scared Stiff

(Paramount, 1953; 108 min.) **½

Produced by Hal Wallis. Directed by George Marshall. Screenplay, Herbert Baker and Walter De Leon. Additional Dialogue, Ed Simmons and Norman Lear. Based on a play by Paul Dickey and Charles W. Goddard. Edited by Warren Low. Director of Photography, Ernest Laszlo. Music, Leith Stevens. Musical numbers staged by Billy Daniel. New Songs, Mack David and Jerry Livingston. Art Direction, Hal Pereira, Franz Bachelin. Set Decoration, Sam Comer, Ross Dowd. Costumes, Edith Head. Special Photographic Effects, Gordon Jennings, Paul Lerpae. Process Photography, Farciot Edouart.

Cast: Larry Todd (Dean Martin), Myron Myron Mertz (Jerry Lewis), Mary Carroll (Lizabeth Scott), Carmelita Castinha (Carmen Miranda), Mr. Cortega (George Dolenz), Tony Warren (William Ching), Rosie (Dorothy Malone), Carriso Twins (Paul Marion), Zombie (Jack Lambert), Police lieutenant (Tom Powers), Trigger (Tony Barr), Shorty (Leonard Strong), Pierre (Henry Brandon), Cop (Hugh Sanders), Elevator boy (Earl Holliman), Man in hall (Percy Helton), Drunk on dock (Frank Fontaine).

Synopsis: After learning that waiter Pierre got into hot water with gangster Shorty due to his involvement with chorus girl Rosie, Chit Chat Club busboy Myron Mertz attempts to help singer Larry Todd, who is also on Rosie's date list. Myron goes to Shorty's apartment and acts tough. Larry learns what Myron is up to and goes to the hotel with a pistol. Meanwhile, Mary Carroll is preparing to leave for Black Castle on Lost Island in the Antilles. A strange phone call warns her not to sell the island to Mr. Cortega. A man appears in the hall, and Cortega shoots him. Larry thinks he's being shot at and fires blindly. He sees a man fall, thinks he did it and hides in Mary's apartment. In her steamer trunk he is taken to the dock, where Myron finds him. Myron ends up in the trunk when one of Shorty's men is spotted. The trunk is hauled onto the ship. Larry follows. Mary is surprised to find that Cortega is also taking ship, more surprised to receive a note that reads "Death waits for you on Lost Island." Although Myron learns from the paper that a .38 caliber was involved in the hotel murder, not Larry's .32, Larry decides to accompany Mary to Cuba and tells Cortega, "I'm a ghost buster." Also on board is Carmelita Castinha, who thanks Myron for once getting her fired. Now she's

lead singer with the Brazilian Revue. Larry and Myron perform a bongo number with her. Arriving in Cuba and venturing to Lost Island, Larry and Myron thwart a zombie when it thinks Mary is the woman in a portrait. Mary deciphers a cryptic message leading to underground tunnels and the fortune all the blackguards are seeking. Myron saves the day by almost inadvertently dropping the latest gun-toting villain into a pit. Was there a ghost on Lost Island? Well, there *was* that specter that emerged from a casket in the great hall.

Reviews: "Revised script that fails to be either chilling or particularly chipper." (*Newsweek*, July 20, 1953, p. 97) ¶"Scratchily put-together ... disappointing...." (Bosley Crowther, *New York Times*, July 3, 1953, p. 10) ¶"Shrill blend of spooks and slapstick." (*Time*, June 29, 1953, p. 95)

Analysis: It's not as good as the original, although it's an appropriate vehicle for Martin and Lewis. But Martin playing Hope is embarrassing. It's interesting how they switch Lewis around. In *The Ghost Breakers*, Hope is the only one in the steamer trunk. In this one Martin hides there first, then Lewis. Lewis has the Willie Best part. Best scene: Lewis pretending to be a ventriloquist's dummy in front of the drunk Frank Fontaine, who here is performing the shtick he perfected on the Jackie Gleason TV show in the sixties. Why isn't this film in color? Could Paramount have been thinking of the haunted house atmosphere rather than the costumery of the inimitable Carmen Miranda? Note the holdovers from *The Ghost Breakers*: director Marshall, costumer Head, process photographer Edouart.

The Ghost of Frankenstein *see under* **Frankenstein**

Ghostbusters

(Columbia, 1984; 107 min.) ***

Produced by Ivan Reitman. Directed by Ivan Reitman. Screenplay, Dan Aykroyd and Harold Ramis. Edited by Sheldon Kahn and David Blewitt. Director of Photography, Laszlo Kovacs. Panavision. Metrocolor. Music, Elmer Bernstein. Song, Ray Parker, Jr. Dolby Stereo. Art Direction, John DeCuir, Jr. Costumes, Theoni V. Aldredge. Visual Effects,

Richard Edlund. Special Effects, Chuck Gaspar and Joe Day.
Cast: Dr. Peter Venkman (Bill Murray), Dr. Raymond Stantz (Dan Aykroyd), Dr. Egon Spengler (Harold Ramis), Dana Barrett (Sigourney Weaver), Louis Tully (Rick Moranis), Winston Zeddmore (Ernie Hudson), Janine Melnitz (Annie Potts), Walter Peck (William Atherton), Mayor (David Margulies), Students (Steven Tash, Jennifer Runyon), Gozer (Slavitza Jovan), Hotel manager (Michael Ensign), Librarian (Alice Drummond), Dean Yeager (Jordan Charney), Library administrator (John Rothman), Violinist (Timothy Carhart), Roger Grimsby (Himself), Larry King, (Himself), Joe Franklin (Himself), Casey Kasem (Himself), Fire commissioner (Norman Matlock), Police captain (Joe Cirillo), Police sergeant (Joe Schmieg), Jail guard (Reggie Vel Johnson), Real estate woman (Rhoda Gemignani), Man at elevator (Murray Rubin), Doorman (Lenny Del Genio), Mayor's aide (Tommy Hollis), Hot dog vendor (Sam Moses), Con Edison man (Larry Dilg), Coachman (Danny Stone), Chambermaid (Frances E. Nealy), Woman at party (Patty Dworkin), TV reporter (Christopher Wynkoop), Cop at apartment (Ric Mancini), Businessman in taxi (Winston May), Louis's neighbor (Eda Reiss Merin), Mrs. Van Hoffman (Kathryn Janssen), Ted Fleming (Paul Trafas), Annette Fleming (Cheryl Birchfield), Library ghost (Ruth Oliver), Dream ghost (Kym Herrin).

Synopsis: In New York City, three researchers of the paranormal, Peter Venkman, Raymond Stantz, and Egon Spengler, form their own company after continued academic funding is revoked and they actually encounter a spirit in a public library. Luckily, they find a client in the form of the beautiful Dana, who's seen a demonic form in her Central Park West apartment refrigerator. Venkman, whom Dana terms more of a game show host than a scientist, investigates but finds nothing. Called to a hotel, the "Ghostbusters" capture a green spirit in a ballroom by using their positron guns. Said spirit is incarcerated in a special holding tank in the old fire hall they've rented. A flurry of spectral activity in the Northeast gives the Ghostbusters business and notoriety. The Environmental Protection Agency, however, suspects that the arcane company is fomenting bogus spirits or at the very least storing hazardous substances. Obtaining a warrant, the EPA shuts down the holding tank, which explodes and releases the spirits. Venkman convinces the mayor that only the Ghostbusters, who now include driver Winston, can put a stop to increasing spirit activity. Having examined the architect's plans for Dana's building, they realize it is a conduit into the spirit world. Meanwhile, Dana and nerdy neighbor Louis Tully have been possessed by the spirit of Zool, an ancient Hittite/Mesopotamian/Sumerian deity. Dana is the gatekeeper, Louis the key master. The Ghostbusters make their way to the 22nd floor and Dana's apartment, now a shambles. They encounter a powerful female demon — Gozer — and a gate to the spirit dimension. A voice asks them to name a creature that will wreak havoc. Ray can't keep his mind blank and thinks of the Stay-Puft marshmallow boy. A giant version appears, stomping through the city streets. The Ghostbusters take a chance and cross their beams into the gate, reversing the flow and sucking back the spirits. Dana and Louis are freed from their gargoyle-like encasements. The throng applauds their success when the Ghostbusters reach the street.

Reviews: "Everyone connected with it has hit the right tone — art direction, photography, sound track, the music." (Sheila Benson, *Los Angeles Times Calendar*, June 8, 1984, p. 1) ¶"A movie of, by and for Yuppies." (Andrew Kopkind, *Nation*, July 21, 1984, pp. 61) ¶"The great thing about *Ghostbusters*, a convulsively funny mock horror film ... is how loose and shaggy it is. This is one of the most elaborate comedies ever made." (David Denby, *New York*, June 11, 1984, p. 66) ¶"Praise is due to everyone connected with *Ghostbusters* for thinking on a grandly comic scale and delivering the goofy goods, neatly timed and perfectly packaged." (Richard Schickel, *Time*, June 11, 1984, p. 83) ¶"Bill Murray is the most serenely corrupt comic actor since W. C. Fields." (David Edelstein, *Village Voice*, June 12, 1984, p. 52)

Analysis: It was a monster hit (the top grosser of year), and "He slimed me!" caught on, but nothing Bill Murray says in this is as funny as lines he had on TV's *Saturday*

Night Live or in his movies *Meatballs* or *Stripes*. Of course it's all ridiculous, but there should have been a greater attempt to build plausibility, to create a believable universe. The New York scene is too real, too contemporary, to make us suspend *our* disbelief. How come the city so readily accepts as gospel all this spirit activity and the Ghostbusters? And what exactly are those positron guns? What's in them? Who made them? Is this one of those films people *think* they like? It has a big cast, a catchy title song, excellent special effects, but for those who've put childish things aside, it's not worth a second look. Academy Award nominations for song and visual effects.

Ghostbusters II
(Columbia, 1989; 102 min.) ***

Produced by Ivan Reitman. Directed by Ivan Reitman. Screenplay, Harold Ramis and Dan Aykroyd. Edited by Sheldon Kahn and Donn Cambern. Director of Photography, Michael Chapman. Panavision. Deluxe Color. Music, Randy Edelman. Theme, Ray Parker, Jr. Dolby Stereo. Art Direction, Tom Duffield. Visual Effects Supervisor, Dennis Muren. Special Visual Effects, Industrial Light & Magic. Creature and Makeup Design, Tim Lawrence. Costumes, Gloria Gresham.

Cast: Dr. Peter Venkman (Bill Murray), Dr. Raymond Stantz (Dan Aykroyd), Dr. Egon Spengler (Harold Ramis), Winston Zeddemore (Ernie Hudson), Dana Barrett (Sigourney Weaver), Louis Tully (Rick Moranis), Janine Melnitz (Annie Potts), Janosz Poha (Peter MacNichol), Judge (Harris Yulin), Mayor (David Margulies), Vigo (Wilhelm Von Homburg), Hardemeyer (Kurt Fuller), Prosecutor (Janet Margolin), Baby Oscar (William T. Deutschendorf, Henry J. Deutschendorf, II), Frank (Michael P. Moran), Meter maid (Olivia Ward), Man with ticket (Mordecai Lawner), Woman on crutches (Susan Boehm), Brownstone mother (Mary Ellen Trainor), Brownstone boys (Christopher Villasenor, Jason Reitman), Norman (Aaron Lustig), Spengler's assistant (Page Leong), Rudy (Walter Flanagan), Plaza Hotel man (Douglas Seale), Police commissioner (Phillip Baker Hall), Fire commissioner (Erik Holland), Psychiatrist (Brian Doyle Murray).

Synopsis: Having rid the city of Gozer, Zool and a host of ghosts, the Ghostbusters are out of work as well as saddled with bills for destruction of city property. Peter has a TV show about psychic phenomena, while Ray and Winston hire themselves and their proton packs out to children's parties. Egon at least is conducting "legitimate" scientific research. When Dana's baby carriage seems to maneuver through traffic on its own, she goes to Egon. He and Ray examine her apartment and her baby, Oscar. Dana is already divorced, and Peter is happy about that. Inspecting the street where Dana's carriage stopped, Ray and Egon discover paranormal activity. In the guise of construction workers, they drill and find the old Pneumatic Transit tunnels. What's more, there's a river of slime roiling away. Discovering that they are unauthorized to dig up city streets, the police arrest the Ghostbusters. Louis Tully is engaged as their counsel, but he's worse than useless. Just as the Ghostbusters are about to be sentenced to jail, the slime sample in evidence becomes agitated and explodes, releasing the Scolari Brothers, executed on the recommendation of the current judge. He asks the Ghostbusters for help, and with their proton packs, they contain the spirits and gain their own freedom. They're back! And there's more spook activity to engage their attention. Meanwhile, in the museum where Dana helps restore paintings, her instructor, Janosz Poha, comes under the spell of a large painting of Vigo, a seventeenth-century European nobleman of decidedly dangerous mien. Janosz promises Vigo Dana's child as long as he gets the woman. Entering the abandoned subway system, Ray, Egon and Winston find a ghost train. When sounding the slime river, Winston is pulled in. Ray and Egon follow, and when the three emerge, they soon realize the slime has given them an attitude. They remove their coveralls and return to their normal selves. Oscar is kidnapped by Janosz and taken to the museum, which is the ultimate destination of the slime. After Dana tracks Oscar there, the slime surrounds the building. The Ghostbusters spray good slime on the Statue of Liberty and play funky music. The monolith takes on a life of its own and transports them to the museum, where it breaks the skylight. The Ghostbusters enter, incapacitate Janosz and, after a time, force Vigo back into the painting and a nether realm. Outside, Tully, who's donned Ghostbusters attire, thinks he's responsible for melting away the slime.

Reviews: "The makers of *Ghostbusters II* have worked hard to keep their movie's edge sharp." (Sheila Benson, *Los Angeles Times Calendar*, June 16, 1984, p. 1) ¶"*Ghostbusters II* is a flirtatiously self-conscious sequel, a movie playing happily with the spectacle of its own inconsequence." (David Denby, *New York*, July 17, 1989, p. 46) ¶"Pleasantly ramshackle comedy — relaxed and goosey, with consistent stretches of laughs." (David Edelstein, *New York Post*, June 16, 1989, p. 23)

Analysis: The story is essentially the same. Exchange the skyscraper for the museum, the Stay-Puft boy for the Statue of Liberty, and Vigo for Zool. Everybody else is back, and that's good. But Peter MacNichol has the funniest scenes and lines. Why so many facial close-ups? Was director Reitman watching a Sergio Leone movie before starting this?

Ghoulies

(Empire/Vestron, 1985; 88 min.) **

Produced by Jefery Levy. Directed by Luca Bercovici. Screenplay, Luca Bercovici and Jefery Levy. Edited by Ted Nicolaou. Director of Photography, Mac Ahlberg. Color, Movielab. Music, Richard Band and Shirley Walker. Art Direction, Karen Kornbau, Cindi Sowder. Special Effects Makeup and Ghoulies Design, John Carl Buechler. Sets Special Effects, Roger Kelton.

Cast: Jonathan Graves (Peter Liapis), Rebecca (Lisa Pelikan), Malcolm Grave (Michael Des Barres), Wolfgang (Jack Nance), Grizzel (Peter Risch), Mark (Ralph Seymour), Greedigut (Tamara De Treaux), Mike (Scott Thomson), Dick (Keith Joe Dick), Donna (Mariska Hargitay), Eddie (David Dayan), Anastasia (Victoria Catlin), Robin (Charlene Cathleen), Temptress (Bobbi Bresee).

Synopsis: Malcolm Graves leads a coven of devil worshippers, but the baby he wants to sacrifice — his son Jonathan — is saved. Years later Jonathan and girlfriend Becky inherit the Graves estate. While cleaning up, Jonathan discovers a grave, cryptic runes, raiment and a book of spells. At a

party, Jonathan tries to conjure up a spirit, but the spell doesn't seem to work. Unbeknownst to Jonathan, an ugly small demon appears after the group leaves the room. Jonathan discovers more devices: a robe and a dagger. He draws symbols on the floor and makes a talisman to protect Becky. Conducting a ritual in private, he draws forth little demons and tells them they may roam the grounds as long as they obey him and remain invisible. Unreceptive to Jonathan's plea that his explorations might reveal more about his parents, Becky leaves. During Jonathan's next ritual two dwarves appear: Grizzel and Greedigut. Grizzel agrees that Jonathan may find knowledge and power but must be careful and that the necessary ritual will require the full moon and seven others. When Becky returns, Jonathan explains his mysterious green eyes and makes her stay. After a dinner party, Jonathan recites his incantation, and from the grave outside rises Malcolm Graves, who informs the little demons that their true master has returned. The demons attack the dinner party guests. Malcolm tells Jonathan what should have happened twenty-five years before will transpire now. He will have Jonathan's youth — but caretaker Wolfgang, who had been one of Malcolm's coven, intervenes and fends off the demonic father. Jonathan's friends awake none the worse for wear and they, Jonathan and Becky drive pell-mell from the estate. All seems well till the ghoulies appear in the back of the jeep.

Reviews: "The toilet is exactly where *Ghoulies* belongs." (Michael Wilmington, *Los Angeles Times Calendar*, January 21, 1985, p. 2) ¶"Witty characterizations and an inventive scenario...." (Kim Newman, *Monthly Film Bulletin*, April 1985, p. 114)

Analysis: Unlike the title characters in *Gremlins*, these nasties are not prime movers, but rather minions of a stronger power. It might more properly be termed a demon worshipper tale. There is some humor, e.g., "Rebecca, you're home early," says a slightly mortified Jonathan as Becky catches him in his odd gear. There's at least one technical faux pas: we see an overhead microphone entering the basement set.

Ghoulies II
(Empire Pictures/Vestron Video, 1987; 89 min.) **

Produced and directed by Albert Band. Screenplay, Dennis Paoli. Story, Charlie Dolan. Edited by Barry Zetlin. Director of Photography, Sergio Salvati. Music, Fuzzbee Morse. Ultra-Stereo. Ghoulies, John Buechler.

Cast: Larry (Damon Martin), Uncle Ned Prentiss (Royal Dano), Nigel (Phil Fondacaro), Hardin (J. Downing), Nicole (Kerry Remsen), Dixie (Dale Wyatt), Teddy (Sasha Jenson).

Synopsis: Satan's Den is a house of horrors that deploys at a carnival in Greenville. Little do Uncle Ned and his nephew Larry realize that they're infested with nasty, deadly little critters who boarded their van when it stopped at a garage. While Ned resuscitates his "Great Fausto" magic act he sees the monstrosities and believes he's conjured them up. But when he finds that they kill patrons, he tries to send them back to hell. They turn on him. Next day Nigel sees the creatures and warns Larry. With Nicole's help, Nigel recovers Ned's book of spells and brings forth a large demon to eat all the little ones — except the one that hid in a toilet and kills the carnival's despicable new owner, Hardin.

Review: "Creatures by John Carl Buechler are not very convincing hand puppets, augmented with some stop-motion for long shots. Most of the film's dark humor ... falls flat." (Dan Scapperotti, *Cinefantastique*, January 1989, p. 117)

Analysis: This went directly to video after Empire Pictures' demise. We congratulate the producers on casting veteran Lincolnesque character actor Royal Dano. Again, the puppets are not especially convincing this time out. Again, we see an overhead microphone boom intruding on one scene. The excellent color and clarity actually work against atmosphere and dissipate the impact of the huge demon at the end. The pace needed to pick up at the finale. The two-star rating may be kind, but we award it for this ho-hum but not entirely execrable outing. Filmed at Empire's Rome studio.

Ghoulies Go to College
(Lightning /Vestron Video, 1990; 94 min.) *

Produced by Ian Paterson. Directed by John Carl Buechler. Screenplay, Brent Olson. Based on characters created by Luca Bercovici and Jefery Levy. Edited by Adam Bernardi. Director of Photography, Ronn Schmidt. Color, Foto-Kem. Music, Michael Lloyd and Reg Powell. Ghoulie and Makeup Effects, John Carl Buechler and Magical Media Industries. Set Decoration, Maggie Martin, Miranda Amador.

Cast: Professor Quentin Ragnar (Kevin McCarthy), Skip Carter (Evan Mackenzie), Erin Riddle (Eva La Rue), Jeremy Heilman (John Johnston), Veronica (Hope Marie Carlton), Mookey (Patrick Labyorteaux), Miss Boggs (Marcia Wallace), Wesley (Billy Morrisette), Barcus (Stephen Lee), Kyle (Jason Scott Lee).

Synopsis: "21 Years Ago": A toilet sculpted with grotesque faces disgorged ghoulies who caused a boatload of trouble before being forced back into their realm. "Glazier College: The Present": While rival fraternities led by Skip and Jeremy battle for the prank week crown, Wesley finds a copy of *Ghoulish Tales* hidden in the bathroom wall. It is taken from him in class by Professor Ragnar, who that night reads from it and releases three ghoulies from the cursed toilet. They stuff Wes into the hopper before appearing at Ragnar's residence. The professor uses the comic to control the monstrosities and sends them off to start a frat war. They succeed in making each fraternity think the other is breaking the rules, strangle Miss Boggs with her own tongue and use a plunger on Veronica in the shower. Ragnar tells them to kill Skip. Conveniently, Skip and Erin visit Ragnar to reveal that Jeremy, not Skip, destroyed the professor's desk. They find Miss Boggs's body. Jeremy's boys begin to throttle Skip; Erin goes for help but encounters Ragnar and his minions. Skip breaks free, finds Erin and temporarily constrains the monsters with his glue gun. Getting possession of the comic, he sics the ghoulies on Ragnar. From a molten yellow mess, Ragnar returns with increased power, but when Skip puts the comic in the toilet, super-Ragnar is sucked in. Back with his frat brothers,

Skip says, "Let's party!" A grotesque hand lifts a beer can from the toilet.

Review: "The stiff, not-always convincing ghoulies were designed by John Carl Buechler, who also directed what amounts to a series of PORKY-like sequences." (John Stanley, *John Stanley's Creature Features Movie Guide Strikes Again*, p. 161)

Analysis: It's a comedy, but a rather mean-spirited one; look at what happens to Marcia Wallace and Hope Marie Carlton. There are time-wasting scenes and lame in-jokes. McCarthy, one of our favorite cinema heroes (the original *Invasion of the Body Snatchers*), has changed little over the years. It's a shame he has to suffer through this.

Ghoulies IV

(CineTel Films, 1993; 84 min.) *½

Produced by Gary Schmoeller. Directed by Jim Wynorski. Screenplay, Mark Sevi. Edited by Richard Gentner. Director of Photography, J. E. Bash. Panavision. Color, Foto-Kem. Music, Chuck Cirino. Set Decoration, Cindy E. Downes. Special Creature and Makeup Effects, Magical Media Industries.

Cast: Detective Jonathan Graves (Pete Liapis), Captain Kate Farr (Barbara Alyn Woods), Alexandra (Stacie Randall), Scotty Mancuso (Bobby DiCicco), Jeanine (Raquel Krelle), Monica (Peggy Trentini), Ghoulie Lite (Arturo Gil), Ghoulie Dark (Tony Cox), Dr. Rochelle (Ace Mask).

Synopsis: A woman in black leather uses her considerable physical strength as well as a strange pistol to kill warehouse guards whom she drags into a pentagram. A hooded figure arises and asks for the gem Alexandra has found there. But the jewel is lost when she steps into the pentagram. The hooded figure also disappears. Two small, ugly creatures appear in his stead. The warehouse "robbery" is investigated by Jonathan Graves and his ex-lover, now police captain Kate Farr. Alexandra kills two sewer workers and resurrects the hooded man again. His name is Faust, and he wants the companion jewel—which is worn by Jonathan. In the warehouse, the two little creatures observe the detective and recall a scene from their world where he wielded magical powers. At home, he is briefly possessed in front of his mirror. While he

sleeps, his hooker girlfriend Jeanine tries on his necklace. Alexandra uses Jonathan's buddy Scotty to lure him back to the warehouse. Because Jonathan no longer has the jewel, Scotty is ordered to kill Jonathan. During the fight the two ghoulies antagonize Alexandra and Scotty disappears. Outside, Alexandra drags a bum into a pentagram to locate Faust again. He wants a sacrifice, and Alexandra captures Jeanine for that purpose. In pursuit, Jonathan tells Kate of the ritualistic stuff he used to engage in with Alexandra, who must have escaped the Hochstatter Mental Hospital. When she uses the jewel to make Faust real Jonathan will fade away. On the Hochstatter lawn, Jeanine is prepared for the sacrifice and Faust appears. Jonathan gets there ahead of Kate, but she shows up in time to stop Jonathan, who's turning into Faust, from stabbing Jeanine. The ghoulies steal the jewel from Jeanine's neck and toss it to Kate, who uses it to blast Alexandra and Faust. The real Jonathan and Scotty reappear. The ghoulies find the jewel in the garden.

Review: "This series ... got real old even before the first chapter came out." (Mick Martin and Marsha Porter, *Video Movie Guide 1997*, p. 416)

Analysis: An uneasy mixture of comedy and killing, it does feature what director Wynorski knows best: attractive female leads. The two new ghoulies are played by people. The old ghoulies are present in one flashback, as is Pete Liapis from the first in the series playing the same character. That at least provides some continuity. How could the ghoulies find the jewel in the garden after they'd already returned to their world?

Ghoulies Go to College *see under* **Ghoulies**

The Glass Slipper

(MGM, 1955; 94 min.) ***

Produced by Edwin H. Knopf. Directed by Charles Walters. Screenplay, Ballet Librettos, and Lyrics, Helen Deutsch. Edited by Ferris Webster. Director of Photography, Arthur E. Arling. Eastman Color. Music, Bronislau Kaper. Ballets, Roland Petit. Costumes, Helen

Rose and Walter Plunkett. Art Direction, Cedric Gibbons, Daniel B. Cathcart. Set Decoration, Edwin B. Willis, Richard Pefferle. Makeup, William Tuttle. Special Effects, Warren Newcombe.

Cast: Ella (Leslie Caron), Prince Charles (Michael Wilding), Mrs. Toquet (Estelle Winwood), Kovin (Keenan Wynn), Widow Sonder (Elsa Lanchester), Duke (Barry Jones), Birdena (Amanda Blake), Serafina (Lisa Daniels), Cousin Loulou (Lurene Tuttle), Tehara (Liliane Montevecchi and Ballet De Paris).

Synopsis: In a happy European principality, young Ella is not so sanguine. Dirty from cinders she sweeps up for the Widow Sonder and her two daughters, "Cinderella" is a virtual town pariah. She finds solitude in a hidden dell not far from the palace of the Duke. There she meets and confides in the seemingly eccentric Mrs. Toquet. After arriving home from university, Prince Charles introduces his companion, Kovin, to the very same glade and recalls a young child who had a tragic, sad face. Ella finds the two and, during an altercation, pushes Charles into the pool. Charles sends Kovin to investigate. Later, Ella returns for her shoes, and Charles, whom she thinks a mere cook at the palace, gives her an invitation to the ball and teaches her to dance. Mrs. Toquet provides her with a beautiful gown and a coach but tells her to leave by midnight. Ella is the hit of the ball, though she remains mute until Charles appears and reveals that he is not a chef. She flees at midnight, losing one slipper in the process. At the palace next day, a rumor circulates that the strange girl is an Egyptian princess. Ella thinks that the Prince is to marry a foreigner and plans to run away, but Charles arrives with the missing slipper and takes her to the palace.

Review: "Cinderella has turned up in the movies under such a variety of circumstances and names that it is thoroughly disarming and refreshing to see her played frankly by the girl of *Lili*, little Leslie Caron.... This is strictly the story of Cinderella — mythical country, Prince Charming and all. In candy-land costumes and color, it makes a happy, ingenuous show.... Helen Deutsch ... has touched it up ever so lightly with those modern psychological

overtones.... not just for the tots." (Bosley Crowther, *New York Times*, March 25, 1955, p. 19)

Analysis: The narrator sounds like Walter Pidgeon, and if it wasn't for his closing remarks and the fading away of Estelle Winwood, one would be hard pressed to detect any supernatural element in this version. It's a hybrid. There's dancing but no singing — and it could have used more of the former. Yet the classic MGM treatment is evident. Estelle Winwood is excellent as Mrs. Toquet, the nominal fairy godmother. She had the look for such films. See her in *The Magic Sword* (1962). Caron is of course the definitive waif and looks lovely. She was in the midst of many excellent MGM vehicles: *An American in Paris* (1951), *Lili* (1953), *Gigi* (1958).

Cinderfella
(Paramount, 1960; 91 min.) **½

Produced by Jerry Lewis. Directed by Frank Tashlin. Screenplay, Frank Tashlin. Edited by Arthur P. Schmidt. Director of Photography, Haskell Boggs. Technicolor. Music, Walter Scharf. Songs, Harry Warren and Jack Brooks. Choreography, Nick Castle. Art Direction, Hal Pereira, Henry Bumstead. Set Decoration, Sam Comer, Robert Benton. Costumes, Edith Head. Special Photographic Effects, John P. Fulton. Process Photography, Farciot Edouart.

Cast: Fella (Jerry Lewis), Fairy Godfather (Ed Wynn), Emily/Wicked Stepmother (Judith Anderson), Princess Charmein (Anna Maria Alberghetti), Maximilian (Henry Silva), Rupert (Robert Hutton), Count Basie (Himself), Cinderella (Nola Thorpe), Del Moore (Himself).

Synopsis: After his father dies, Fella is relegated to the kitchen and garage by his stepmother. She and her two sons, Maximilian and Rupert, hope that one day they will find the money Fella's father hid on the estate. They hope one of the dreams Fella has of his father will reveal the loot's whereabouts. Hedging their bets, they host Princess Charmein of Merovia on her stateside tour. Emily knows that if Rupert can make her his bride, they'll be set for life. Little do they know that Fella has been visited by his Fairy Godfather, who foresees the Princess in his future. Smartly attired in a bright red jacket, Fella attends the ball and entrances the Princess. But he must leave at midnight. She finds a black shoe left behind. Back home, Fella is accosted by Maximilian, who thinks that because his stepbrother had that fancy suit, he must have money. Fella says he's always known where the money was and pulls a branch. Coins spray from the tree onto Max, knocking him unconscious. Next day Fella tells his stepmother she can stay if she wants to and says they can have the money. Outside, he meets the Princess and initially rejects her protestations of love. But he returns, and they dance.

Review: "Jerry is quite appealing at times.... [He] knows when to stop clowning to turn on the poignant act. But ... Frank Tashlin ... didn't take a firm enough hand with his star.... The good cast ... isn't used enough." (Philip T. Hartung, *Commonweal*, December 23, 1960, pp. 341–342)

Analysis: If the ball was somewhere else — and Fella *was* driven home — how could he and Alberghetti end up dancing on the same patio at the conclusion? What will feminists make of Ed Wynn's analysis of the Cinderella story? "Women are strange, Fella. They're like the Russians. They want credit for inventing everything." He says that if an average Joe like Fella wins the Princess' hand, centuries of abuse by women will be broken, and men and women will learn to be satisfied with each other. Some of this movie prefigures *The Nutty Professor*, Lewis's 1963 Jekyll and Hyde film. In his ball attire and manner, he even prepares for his outing as Buddy Love in that film. Michael Jackson might have learned a step or two from the plastic Lewis's footwork when he descends the steps at the ball. The songs make little impression.

The Slipper and the Rose: The Story of Cinderella
(Paradine, 1976; 146 min.) ***

Produced by Stuart Lyons. Directed by Bryan Forbes. Screenplay, Bryan Forbes, Richard M. Sherman, Robert B. Sherman. Edited by Timothy Gee. Director of Photography, Tony Imi. Color. Music and Lyrics, Richard M. Sherman and Robert B. Sherman. Choreogaphy, Marc Breaux.

Cast: Prince Edward (Richard Chamberlain), Cinderella (Gemma Craven), Lord Chamberlain (Kenneth More), Fairy Godmother (Annette Crosbie), King (Michael Hordern), Stepmother (Margaret Lockwood), John (Christopher Gable), Dowager Queen (Edith Evans), Queen (Lally Bowers). With Andre Morell, Gerald Sim, Geoffrey Bayldon, Bryan Forbes.

Synopsis: While Prince Edward arrives home unbetrothed, a subject of the kingdom, Cinderella, is relegated to the kitchen by her stepmother. Cinderella's father has died, and the stepmother will run the house for the benefit of her two daughters from a previous marriage. At the palace, the Lord Chamberlain proposes a ball to which all eligible princesses will be invited. Prince Edward is outraged but agrees to the "cattle show." Cinderella is visited for the second time by her Fairy Godmother, who creates a beautiful gown and provides an ornate coach for "Princess Incognito." The Prince is enthralled, but as the clock begins striking midnight, Cinderella rushes off. Three months later Sir John observes a girl in a field dancing about with the glass slipper Edward had angrily thrown from castle window. Edward rides out and is reunited with his love. However, there is no precedent for the marriage of noble and commoner, and the kingdom needs a powerful alliance to stave off aggressive neighbors. The Lord Chamberlain convinces Cinderella to go into exile. Angrily, Edward tells his father to select any bride. He will marry, but sire no offspring. The Fairy Godmother appears before her charge, irritated that Cinderella is not at the palace on Edward's wedding day. She gets Cinderella there and solves the alliance problem by proposing that the King's cousin marry Edward's fiancee. After all, those two love each other.

Review: "Tired musical version.... An air of desperation prevails throughout." (Steven H. Scheuer, ed., *Movies on TV: 1982–1983 Edition*, p. 609)

Analysis: Like *The Glass Slipper*, this is an opulent production. Unlike *Slipper*, it uses many real castles. There is dancing *and* singing this time. The acceptable but not memorable songs are by Disney Studio veterans, the Sherman Bros. (*Mary Poppins*,

Bedknobs and Broomsticks, The Jungle Book). Choreographer Breaux did the big 1968 roadshow *Chitty Chitty Bang Bang.* Like that, it's out of time for a musical. The 1950s golden age of MGM musicals is past; there are no more three-hour roadshows, musical or otherwise. A couple of minutes could have been cut from the ball dancing to tighten this rather long film. The casting is fine. Our favorite character is the delightfully witty Annette Crosbie, who in some respects is similar to Estelle Winwood in *The Glass Slipper.* Margaret Lockwood was Britain's most popular leading lady for a number of years in the 1930s and 1940s. Director Bryan Forbes is a former actor who appears briefly as a herald in this.

Notes of Interest: The most famous film version of the ancient Cinderella story is Walt Disney's 1950 animated movie. There is a 1964 TV version featuring Lesley Ann Warren and the music of Rodgers & Hammerstein.

The Glob *see* **The Blob**

Glump *see* Please Don't Eat My Mother *under* **The Little Shop of Horrors**

The Golden Voyage of Sinbad *see under* **The 7th Voyage of Sinbad**

Graveyard Shift
(Cinema Ventures/Lightshow Communications, 1987; 88 min.) ***

Produced by Michael Bockner. Directed by Gerard Ciccoritti. Screenplay, Gerard Ciccoritti. Edited by Robert Bergman and Norman Smith. Director of Photography, Robert Bergman. Color.

Cast: Stephen Tsepes (Silvio Oliviero), Michelle Hayden (Helen Papas), Eric Hayden (Cliff Stoker), Gilda (Dorin Ferber), Robert Kopple (Dan Rose), Detective Winsome (John Haslett Cuff), Detective Smith (Don James), Mario Bava (Frank Procopio), Coroner (Martin Bockner).

Synopsis: Black Cat Taxi Number 237 driver Steve is a vampire who falls in love with Michelle, a director of videos who has a philandering husband. Despite his affliction — and perhaps because she has a

terminal illness — Michelle returns Steve's love. Steve yearns to die himself. He's lived too long. Michelle helps him, but he relapses and attacks a female visitor to Michelle's house; then, at the mock graveyard site for a video, he is impaled by Michelle's husband. The husband's cohort is killed by women previously vampirized by Steve, and Michelle is attacked by one of the vampire women. The vampires are killed when the husband opens the door and light streams in. While preparing to put a stake into Michelle, the husband is shot by one of the policemen who'd been investigating the savage murders. Later a man needs a taxi. The driver is Michelle.

Review: Do any reviews of this exist? We haven't found any. Usually there is a one or two-sentence synopsis. The "turkey" symbol is appended in Mick Martin and Marsha Porter, *Video Movie Guide 1994* p. 818.

Analysis: Slightly primitive, occasionally incoherent but nevertheless compelling, this is definitely worth a look. Note the character named Mario Bava in tribute, no doubt, to the Italian horror film director of that name. Aka *Central Park Driver.*

The Understudy: Graveyard Shift II
(Cinema Ventures, 1988; 88 min.)
***

Produced by Stephen R. Flaks and Arnold H. Bruck. Directed by Gerard Ciccoritti. Screenplay, Gerard Ciccoritti. Edited by Neil Grieve. Director of Photography, Barry Stone. Color. Music, Philip Stern.

Cast: Camilla Turner/Patti Venus (Wendy Gazelle), Baissez (Silvio Oliviero), Matthew (Mark Soper), Ash (Ilse Von Glatz), Duke/Lenny (Tim Kelleher), Martina (Lesley Kelly), Ramon/Apache (Carl Alacchi), Alan (Paul Amato).

Synopsis: A vampire movie is being made in an old warehouse. Up-and-coming star Camilla is the female lead. Self-important, experienced Ramon plays the male vampire, but he's killed by Camilla when she comes under the spell of the dark and mysterious Baissez, a true vampire. She stabs herself, hoping to become like him and also to help him regain his power. He seduces makeup mistress Ash and later sucks her dry. Camilla's fiancé, Matthew, the editor, finally figures out what's going on and stabs Baissez with a broken pool cue. Baissez removes the cue, but Camilla tells Matthew to tear down the curtains. He does so, and Baissez is destroyed by the sunlight. But because Camilla remains under the spell of the vampire, Matthew wishes to join her. Later, under the nom de plume Patti Venus, Camilla hustles a pool shark.

Review: Again, existing "reviews" consist of brief synopses that cast doubt on whether the reviewers actually saw it. Mick Martin and Marsha Porter give it two stars in *Video Movie Guide 1994* p. 869.

Analysis: Like the first in this series, it's a diamond in the rough. It's at least as incoherent as the progenitor and not quite as compelling, but there's some sort of enticing undercurrent — eroticism maybe?

Notes of Interest: Stephen King's Graveyard Shift (Paramount, 1990) is not related to these two films.

Gremlins

(Warner Bros., 1984; 111 min.) **½

Produced by Michael Finnell. Executive Producers, Steven Spielberg, Frank Marshall, Kathleen Kennedy. Directed by Joe Dante. Screenplay, Chris Columbus. Edited by Tina Hirsch. Director of Photography, John Hora. Technicolor. Music, Jerry Goldsmith. Dolby Stereo. Set Decoration, Jackie Carr. Gremlins created by Chris Walas.

Cast: Billy Peltzer (Zach Galligan), Kate (Phoebe Cates), Randall Peltzer (Hoyt Axton), Lynn (Frances Lee McCain), Mrs. Deagle (Polly Holliday), Grandfather (Keye Luke), Chinese boy (John Louie), Mr. Futterman (Dick Miller), Mrs. Futterman (Jackie Joseph), Sheriff (Scott Brady), Anderson (Harry Carey, Jr.), Rockin' Ricky Rialto (Don Steele), Pete (Corey Feldman), Pete's father (Arnie Moore), Roy Hanson (Glynn Turman), Mrs. Yarris (Belinda Balaski), Gerald (Judge Reinhold), Deputy (Jonathan Banks), Santa (Joe Brooks), Corben (Edward Andrews), Jones (Chuck Jones), Dorry (Kenny Davis), Lew (Jim McKrell), Gas station attendant (Kenneth Tobey), Barney the dog (Mushroom).

Synopsis: In Chinatown at Christmas time, inventor Rand Peltzer buys a "mogwai," a cute, small, furry creature, for his son. He is warned not to expose it to sunlight or water and never to feed it after midnight. Arriving home in Kingston Falls, Rand gives the mogwai to Billy, who names it Gizmo. Young Pete visits and spills water on it. Fur balls pop off and rapidly become other mogwai. When Rand finds out, he suggests that the "Peltzer Pet" could be a big hit across the nation. But Billy discerns a different temperament in these offspring. The mogwai that Billy takes to the school's science teacher, Mr. Hanson, eats a leftover sandwich after midnight. At the Peltzers' next morning, Billy finds all the mogwai but Gizmo encased in cocoons. He realizes his clock was broken and he fed them after midnight. Later, Gizmo watches with trepidation as the cocoons split open, revealing ugly — and mean — gremlins. Billy finds Hanson dead. His killer enters the ductwork. At the Peltzers', Gizmo is harassed by the nasty creatures. Billy phones and warns his mom. She has a fight on her hands but disposes of one in a mixer, another by stabbing, yet another in a microwave. One gremlin knocks the Christmas tree on her, but Billy arrives in the nick of time. This gremlin leader escapes through the window. Billy and Gizmo track it in the snow to the Y.M.C.A. However, it jumps into the pool, and Billy rushes to the police. Having spawned a horde, the leader gremlin leads its offspring through the streets and begins terrorizing — and killing — the citizenry. In the tavern, Kate discovers how matches and camera flashes can deter the monsters before she's rescued by Billy. As dawn approaches, the gremlins hole up in the movie theater and watch *Snow White and the Seven Dwarfs*. Billy and Kate start a fire in the boiler room. But "Stripe," the leader, is across the street getting candy when the building goes up. Billy chases it through the store, and Kate turns on the lights while Gizmo lets in sunlight that destroys the menace. The media considers mass hysteria the cause of the havoc. The Chinese man whose grandson sold Gizmo retrieves the creature from the Peltzers.

Reviews: "The visual and satirical thrust of *Gremlins* is manifestly mean-spirited in the tradition of Robert Altman, but made worse here because *Gremlins'* patrons, like Custer's men, thought they were invited to dinner, not for it." (Harlan Jacobson, *Film Comment*, July-August 1984, p. 50) ¶"Its wacky sense of comic horror, its all-American mix of malicious mischief, is uniquely its own." (David Ansen, *Newsweek*, June 18, 1984, p. 99)

Analysis: Another film in which the characters accept the eminently strange and unfamiliar with nary a question asked. Logic could be dispensed with, we guess, because scriptwriter Chris *Home Alone* Columbus has another agenda: bemoaning family disintegration. If gremlins emerged from mogwais, how did more gremlins emerge from gremlins? In-jokes: Billy Peltzer greeting "Dr. Moreau," Robby the Robot and the time machine at an inventor's convention. This was the fourth highest grossing film of 1984.

Gremlins II: The New Batch
(Warner Bros., 1990; 106 min.) **½

Produced by Michael Finnell. Executive Producers, Steven Spielberg, Kathleen Kennedy, Frank Marshall. Directed by Joe Dante. Screenplay, Charlie Haas. Edited by Kent Beyda. Director of Photography, John Hora. Technicolor. Music, Jerry Goldsmith. Dolby Stereo. Sound Effects, Mark Mangini and David Stone. Effects Supervisor, Rick Baker. Visual Effects Supervisor, Denis Michelson.

Cast: Billy Peltzer (Zach Galligan), Kate Beringer (Phoebe Cates), Daniel Clamp (John Glover), Dr. Catheter (Christopher Lee), Mr. Wing (Keye Luke), Sheila Futterman (Jackie Joseph), Murray Futterman (Dick Miller), Grandpa Fred (Robert Prosky), Forster (Robert Picardo), Marla Bloodstone (Haviland Morris), Katsuji (Gedde Watanabe), Microwave Marge (Kathleen Freeman), Martin (Don Stanton), Lewis (Dan Stanton), Wally (Shawn Nelson), Movie theater mom (Belinda Balaski), Projectionist (Kenneth Tobey), Janitor (John Astin), Fired employee (Henry Gibson), Hulk Hogan (Himself), Dick Butkus (Himself), Bubba Smith (Himself). Voices: Brain gremlin (Tony Randall), Gizmo (Howie Mandel), Mohawk gremlin (Frank Welker), Gremlins (Kirk Thatcher, Mark Dodson), Announcer (Neil Ross), Bugs Bunny and Daffy Duck (Jeff Bergman).

Synopsis: The aged owner of an Oriental bric-a-brac shop dies, and Clamp Industries

demolishes the store in order to add to its own building. A mogwai is put out on the street, picked up by a human and deposited in Dr. Catheter's laboratory. Meanwhile, the mogwai's friend Billy Peltzer and his girl Kate Beringer begin jobs at the Clamp building. Billy finds Gizmo, the mogwai, but gremlins capture and imprison him. Catheter's experiments go awry and the gremlins proliferate, imbibing any number of substances. One speaks. Gizmo breaks out, trains à la Rambo and "becomes war," using a fire arrow to destroy a spiderlike gremlin preying on Kate and Marla. The Clamp building is evacuated, and Zach convinces Daniel Clamp that they can destroy the nasty critters by moving the clocks ahead three hours to 7:30 P.M. and raising a fake nighttime sky backdrop outside. When the gremlins exit to wreak havoc on the city, they will be annihilated. However, that scheme fails, so Zach uses a fire hose to wet down the gremlins in the lobby, then uses electricity to zap and melt them.

Reviews: "The only postmodern picture to sneak into mainstream theaters this summer." (David Sterritt, *Christian Science Monitor*, July 6, 1990, p. 12) ¶"It's an infernally funny mass entertainment: the Dream Machine snapping at its own tail." (Michael Wilmington, *Los Angeles Calendar*, June 15, 1990, p. 1)

Analysis: A beginning that promises little gives way to some fun and games that make this film at least as entertaining as the first. Having the lead gremlin speak with Tony Randall's voice is also a plus. What's the funniest in-joke? A "Dr. Quatermass" office sign. Besides Chris Lee, other 50s s-f/fantasy personages are back from the first film. But hey, we thought the Jackie Joseph and Dick Miller characters were killed in the last picture!

A Guy Named Joe
(MGM, 1943; 118 min.) **

Produced by Everett Riskin. Directed by Victor Fleming. Screenplay, Dalton Trumbo. Adaptation, Frederick Hazlitt Brennan. Story, Chandler Sprague and David Boehm. Edited by Frank Sullivan. Directors of Photography, George Folsey, Karl Freund. Music, Herbert

Stothart. Song "I'll Get By (As Long as I Have You)," Roy Turk and Fred Ahlert. Art Direction, Cedric Gibbons. Set Decoration, Edwin B. Willis. Special Effects, Arnold Gillespie, Donald Jahraus, Warren Newcombe.

Cast: Major Pete Sandidge (Spencer Tracy), Dorinda Durston (Irene Dunne), Ted Randall (Van Johnson), Al Yackey (Ward Bond), Colonel "Nails" Kilpatrick (James Gleason), General (Lionel Barrymore), Dick Rumney (Barry Nelson), Colonel Hendricks (Henry O'Neill), "Powerhouse" O'Rourke (Don Defore), Major Corbett (Addison Richards), Sanderson (Charles Smith), Dance hall girl (Mary Elliott), Captain Robertson (Maurice Murphy), Colonel Sykes (Earl Schenck), Powerhouse girl (Eve Whitney), Ellen Bright (Esther Williams), Officers in heaven (John Whitney, Kirk Alyn), Orderly (James Millican), Bartender (Gibson Gowland), Girl at bar (Kay Williams), Majors (Frank Faylen, Philip Van Zandt), Fliers (Marshall Reed, Blake Edwards), Helen (Jacqueline White), George (Edward Hardwicke), Cyril (Raymond Severn), Elizabeth (Yvonne Severn), Peter (Christopher Severn), Mess sergeant (Walter Sande), Sergeant Hanson (Peter Cookson), Lieutenant Ridley (John Frederick), Lieutenant Hunter (Matt Willis).

Synopsis: Major Pete Sandidge returns to England from a bombing mission over the Continent. The fact that his plane is filled with holes indicates to Colonel "Nails" Kilpatrick that Pete was flying too low. He tells Pete that a squadron leader must not be a lone wolf. Pete is transferred to Scotland for reconnaissance duty. When his girlfriend Dorinda arrives, she has the feeling his time is up. Although she convinces him to return to the States to be an instructor, he's called away by a reported sighting of a German aircraft carrier. Fighters and flak disable his B-25, the crew bails out, but Pete buzzes the carrier and puts it out of commission with his bombs before crashing into the ocean. Al Yackey tells Dorinda about Pete. Pete finds himself walking across a cloud field. He meets Dick Rumney, another downed flyer, who informs Pete that he's dead. But there's work to do, and he is led to the General. The General informs Pete that all flyers get help from those that went before and that Pete will have his chance to assist a young pilot. At a training base near San Francisco, Pete and Dick take charge of Ted Randall and

"Powerhouse" O'Rourke, respectively. The young flyers gain confidence under the spirits' tutelage and are assigned to a P-38 squadron in the Pacific, the base where now Colonel Yackey and Brigadier Kilpatrick are in command. And Dorinda flies in. Ted is struck by her, and she notices that he plucks his eyebrows like Pete did. When he gets promoted to captain and proposes marriage, she agrees. During a training flight for new pilots, Pete urges Ted to hotshot. Kilpatrick admonishes him afterward but gives him the opportunity to bomb a Japanese ammunition dump. Meanwhile, Pete is called to the General, who explains how everyone must work together for a free future. Dorinda has second thoughts and says she can't marry Ted; she still loves Pete. When she finds out that Ted has a dangerous mission, she commandeers his plane and makes the run herself, or so she thinks. Pete is aboard, and when he cannot dissuade her, he urges her on. She destroys the base and survives. On the way back, Pete tells her what a great life she'll have. She lands and clinches with Ted.

Reviews: "As a war film, it combines excellent intentions and superb aerial combat shots with too much talk and an overcharge of sentiment." (*Newsweek*, January 10, 1944, p. 82) ¶"A sincere wartime homily on some of the nobler aspects of death, tradition, bereavement. It would succeed more thoroughly if Miss Dunne's grief and her scenes with Van Johnson were not—apparently for Pete's sake and the audience's—so smoothly soft pedaled." (*Time*, January 10, 1944, pp. 92, 94)

Analysis: Its strength is an excellent cast and a good mix of miniature and actual planes, but it's overlong and drags. There's entirely too much blabbing. It could be the only film in which Spencer Tracy plays an irritating character. It might be the only major Hollywood film made during the war that features the twin-engine P-38 Lightning fighter. The plot must have caused airmen to laugh. Irene Dunne knew where the largest Japanese ammo dump was? She could commandeer a plane? How come it wasn't bombed into oblivion earlier? No one fighter plane could do the damage this one does. Preview audiences are said to have disliked the original ending in which Irene Dunne's character meets a hero's death and joins Spencer Tracy in the clouds. You can tell where they changed it: the ammo dump scene. *Here Comes Mr. Jordan*, which also featured James Gleason, is similar — and better.

Always
(Universal/United Artists, 1989; 125 min.) **

Produced by Steven Spielberg, Frank Marshall, Kathleen Kennedy. Directed by Steven Spielberg. Screenplay, Jerry Belson. Based on *A Guy Named Joe* (Screenplay, Dalton Trumbo; Adaptation, Frederick Hazlitt Brennan; Story, Chandler Sprague, David Boehm). Edited by Michael Kahn. Director of Photography, Mikael Salomon. Panavision. Color, DeLuxe. Music, John Williams. Dolby Stereo. Art Direction, Chris Burian-Mohr. Set Decoration, Jackie Carr. Special Effects, Industrial Light and Magic.

Cast: Pete Sandich (Richard Dreyfuss), Dorinda Durston (Holly Hunter), Ted Baker (Brad Johnson), Al Yackey (John Goodman), Dave (Roberts Blossom), Hap (Audrey Hepburn), Powerhouse (Keith David), Nails (Ed Van Nuys), Rachel (Marg Helgenberger), Alex (Brian Haley), Fire Boss (Dale Dye), Charlie (James Lashly), Grey (Michael Steve Jones), Bus driver (Doug McGrath), Mechanic #1 (Joseph McCrossin), Singer (J. D. Souther), Carl (Gerry Rothschild), Bartender (Loren Smothers), Girl in bar (Taleena Ottwell).

Synopsis: Pilot Pete Sandich irritates Dorinda Durston with his antics as they battle forest fires. She offers a deal: She'll ground herself in Flatrock, Colorado, where he can teach pilots. Otherwise, she'll continue to fly. She has a feeling his time is up. Al Yackey phones Pete for help fighting a fire on the South Ring. Al's plane catches fire but, flying above it, Pete unloads his water and quenches it. However, his own plane catches fire and explodes. In the forest, Pete meets Hap and learns he's dead. But he can inspire living novice pilots. In San Diego, Al meets Dorinda, now a standby flight controller, and takes her to Flatrock, where he's teaching young pilots. Pete is instructing Ted Baker at Flatrock. Ted has eyes for Dorinda, and Pete can

hardly stand it, begging Hap to take him away. She says she also sent him back to Earth to say a proper good-bye. A severe fire surrounds some smokejumpers, and Pete convinces Ted to go up. But when Dorinda learns of this from Al, she steals Ted's plane and with her load, clears a path to the river for the stranded men. Pete, who's aboard, "tells" Dorinda she'll have a wonderful life. The oil pressure falls and the plane crashes in a lake. Dorinda sees Pete, who pulls her to the surface.

Reviews: "*Always* is a bore — the most tedious and washed-out picture this energetic filmmaker has ever done." (Davis Sterritt, *Christian Science Monitor*, January 23, 1990, p. 11) ¶"*Always* can best be enjoyed as a series of shimmering, borderline-outrageous images. Spielberg … charges up the frame in a way that no other director can match." (David Denby, *New York*, January 8, 1990, p. 58) ¶"Depending on your weakness for this kind of corn, you'll love it or hate it. I actually loved it — well, parts of it (and this is no Spielberg fan talking.)" (Georgia Brown, *Village Voice*, December 26, 1989, p. 102)

Analysis: Why couldn't someone write an *original* romantic screenplay about smoke jumpers and their women? This is maybe the third major studio film about forest fires. Only *The Forest Rangers* (1942) and *Red Skies of Montana* (1952) spring to mind as predecessors. The visuals and sound are superb, but like its inspiration, the film is too long.

Halloween
(Compass International, 1978; 93 min.) ***½

Produced by Debra Hill. Executive Producer, Irwin Yablans. Directed by John Carpenter. Screenplay, John Carpenter and Debra Hill. Edited by Tommy Wallace and Charles Bornstein. Director of Photography, Dean Cundey. Panavision. Metrocolor. Music, John Carpenter. Set Decoration, Craig Stearns. Stunt, Jim Windburn.

Cast: Laurie Strode (Jamie Lee Curtis), Sam Loomis (Donald Pleasence), Annie (Nancy Loomis), Lynda (P. J. Soles), Leigh Brackett (Charles Cyphers), The Shape (Nick Castle), Lindsey (Kyle Richards), Tommy

(Brian Andrews), Bob (John Michael Graham), Richie (Mickey Yablans), Marion (Nancy Stephens), Graveyard keeper (Arthur Malet), Dr. Wynn (Robert Phalen), Michael at 23 (Tony Moran), Michael at 6 (Will Sandin), Lonnie (Brent LePage), Keith (Adam Hollander), Judith (Sandy Johnson), Boyfriend (David Kyle), Laurie's father (Peter Griffith).

Synopsis: Halloween night, Haddonfield, Illinois, 1963: The young Michael Myers stabs his sister Judith to death after she's "fooled around" with her boyfriend. Smith's Grove, Illinois, May 1, 1964: At a mental institution, Dr. Sam Loomis, who's observed Michael four hours a day for six months, fails to convince a board to place the patient in a maximum security institution. Loomis considers the boy the most dangerous case he's ever seen. "He's waiting," he tells the doctors. But for what, even Loomis doesn't know. Smith's Grove, October 30, 1978: Loomis and a nurse drive to the Illinois State Hospital to take Michael to a judge. Loomis tells the nurse to give Michael thorazine so he won't be too conscious. As their station wagon approaches the hospital gate, they observe patients wandering the grounds. When Loomis gets out and goes to a phone, a patient scares the nurse and commandeers the car. "The evil is gone!" cries Loomis. Haddonfield, October 31: Tommy greets baby-sitter Laurie on her way to drop off a key at the abandoned Myers house, which has a prospective buyer. Laurie leaves the key on the porch and fails to see the form watching from inside. Loomis inspects Myers's room at the hospital and finds "SISTER" scrawled on the back of the door. Loomis knows where Myers went: Haddonfield, 150 miles away. In school, Laurie notices a parked station wagon across the street. At his school, Tommy is harassed by bigger kids who tease him about the bogeyman. The station wagon follows him briefly. On the way to Haddonfield, Loomis finds an abandoned pickup truck and a matchbox from his own car that verifies his hunch that Myers is headed for Haddonfield. Loomis doesn't see the dead body in the weeds. In Haddonfield, Laurie gets a phone call, but no one speaks. Someone breaks into the hardware store and steals

masks and rope. Loomis arrives and convinces Sheriff Brackett that something bad is about to happen to his community. In the old Myers house they find a dead dog. Tommy tells Laurie he saw the bogeyman. Both watch *The Thing* on television. Annie is strangled in her garage across the street. In the house after making love, Lynda's boyfriend Bob is knifed and Lynda strangled with a telephone cord. Laurie finds the bodies and Judith Myers's tombstone on a bed. A masked figure stabs her in the arm, and she falls down the stairs. She flees to her house. The phone is dead. Her attacker gets in, and she stabs him in the neck with a sewing needle. Tommy says, "You can't kill the bogeyman." He's right; the monster reappears. Thrusting at him with a clothes hanger from her crouching position in the closet, Laurie incapacitates the creature for a second time. Nevertheless, the monster sits up and comes at her again. But Loomis heard the commotion from outside, runs upstairs and shoots Michael Myers off the balcony. When he walks over to look, the body is missing. A still frightened Laurie asks, "Was — the bogey man?" Loomis replies, "As a matter of fact, that was."

Reviews: "Succeeds in being really scary .... well made, titillating, minor masterpiece." (Charles Balun, *The Connoisseur's Guide to the Contemporary Horror Film*, p. 32) ¶"A superb exercise in the art of suspense, and it has no socially redeeming value whatsoever." (Bill Ansen, *Newsweek*, December 4, 1978, p. 116) ¶"The first 10 minutes are a blatant rip-off of the shower scene in *Psycho*, and the entire movie is studded with fancy camera angles and obtrusive tracking dolly shots.... 'Sex kills' seems to be *Halloween*'s message." (Robert Asahina, *New Leader*, December 18, 1978, p. 17)

Analysis: This watershed film works in no small degree due to the music and the absence of studio shots. There's a wee bit of welcome comic relief, as when Donald Pleasence hiding in the bushes urges trick or treaters to get away from the Myers house: "Hey Lonnie, get your ass away from there." His character provides what little justification there is for Michael Myers' actions. That is, the audience must come to believe he's supernatural even if most of the film's characters don't realize it. How come the sight or knowledge of sex sets off so many killing sprees in this type of film? Introducing Jamie Lee Curtis, daughter of famous film folk Janet Leigh and Tony Curtis. The mask Michael wears is supposed to be the face of William Shatner. Sam Loomis, the character played by Donald Pleasence, is the name of the character played by John Gavin in *Psycho*.

Halloween II
(Universal, 1981; 92 min.) **

Produced by Debra Hill and John Carpenter. Executive Producers, Irwin Yablans and Joseph Wolf. Directed by Rick Rosenthal. Screenplay, John Carpenter and Debra Hill. Edited by Mark Goldblat and Skip Schoolnik. Director of Photography, Dean Cundey. Panavision. Color, MGM. Music, John Carpenter, with Alan Howarth. Dolby Stereo. Set Decoration, Peg Cummings. Makeup, Michael Germain and John F. Chambers. Masks, Don Post. Special Effects, Frank Munoz. Special Effects Supervisor, Larry Cavanaugh. Stunt Coordinator, Dick Warlock.

Cast: Laurie Strode (Jamie Lee Curtis), Sam Loomis (Donald Pleasence), Leigh Brackett (Charles Cyphers), Karen (Pamela Susan Shoop), Graham (Jeffrey Kramer), Jimmy (Lance Guest), Gary Hunt (Hunter Von Leer), Shape/Patrolman #3 (Dick Warlock), Mr. Garrett (Cliff Emmich), Jill (Tawny Moyer), Alice (Anne Bruner), Janet (Ana Alicia), Budd (Leo Rossi), Mrs. Alves (Gloria Gifford), Dr. Mixter (Ford Rainey), Marion (Nancy Stephens), Marshal (John Zenda), Producer (Catherine Bergstrom), Announcer (Alan Haufrect), Mrs. Elrod (Lucille Bensen), Assistant (Dana Carvey).

Synopsis: While Dr. Loomis searches for missing maniac Michael Myers, Laurie Strode is taken to the Haddonfield Memorial Hospital. Michael learns of Laurie's whereabouts. At the hospital, Michael kills the security guard, nurses and orderlies, including Karen, drowned and scalded in a Jacuzzi. Waking from sedation, Laurie senses that something is amiss and leaves her room. In the hospital hall, Laurie encounters Michael, who chases her. Outside, she hides in a car until Loomis, his associate and a state trooper arrive. Loomis had been told of a secret file revealing that

Laurie Strode is Michael Myers's sister. She was born two years before he was committed to an institution. When her parents died, she was adopted by the Strodes. Loomis shoots Michael down, but he gets up, kills the trooper, and chases Loomis and Laurie into an operating room. There he stabs Loomis in the stomach. Laurie blinds the maniac with shots to the head. Recovering from his wound but waiting for Laurie to get away, Loomis turns on ether and oxygen and snaps his cigarette lighter. The explosion sets Michael on fire, and he collapses in the hall. Next day Laurie is taken away in an ambulance.

Reviews: "The killings are varied, judicious touches of humor added: value is, in a sense, given for money. But what it all adds up to is a dispassionately executed episode in a successful serial...." (John Pym, *Monthly Film Bulletin*, March 1982, p. 43) ¶"Of course, ... the whole thing is as ridiculous as a nightmare. Even movie madmen don't walk through 12 point-blank bullets, then two more in the eyes, and still walk burning out of an explosion." (Archer Winsten, *New York Post*, October 30, 1981, p. 47) ¶"Director Rick Rosenthal knows the conventions of the craft — the uses of subjective camera, of ambiguous shadow, and so forth." (Alex Keneas, *Newsday*, October 30, 1981, Part II, p. 7) ¶"Quite scary, more than a little silly and immediately forgettable." (David Ansen, *Newsweek*, November 16, 1981, p. 117) ¶"What's not here? Motivation. Causality. Conscience." (Carrie Rickey, *Village Voice*, November 4-10, 1981, p. 50)

Analysis: Dare we say it: The only worthwhile thing in this needless, plot-thin sequel is the gratuitous Jacuzzi scene involving Pamela Susan Shoop? A leading lady and co-star of films (*Empire of the Ants*, *The One Man Army*) and TV, Ms. Shoop deserved better than her ensuing annihilation. (Maybe she got it. She married a priest in 1987.) Even though Donald Pleasence rants about his quarry's inhuman qualities, some critics still thought Myers was merely a madman. Most suspenseful scenes: Michael trying to get Laurie as she climbs through a window and as she waits for the elevator door to close.

Halloween III: Season of the Witch

(Universal, 1982; 96 min.) ***

Produced by Debra Hill and John Carpenter. Executive Producer, Irwin Yablans and Joseph Wolf. Directed by Tommy Lee Wallace. Screenplay, Tommy Lee Wallace. Edited by Millie Moore. Director of Photography, Dean Cundey. Music, John Carpenter and Alan Howarth. Set Decoration, Linda Spheeris. Animation, Bakshi Productions. Illustrator, Carl Aldana. Special Makeup Effects, Tom Burman. Halloween Masks, Don Post. Special Effects, Jon G. Belyeu. Stunt Coordinator, Dick Warlock. Animal Coordinator, Clint Rowe. Silver Shamrock Commercial, Sam Nicholson.

Cast: Dr. Daniel Challis (Tom Atkins), Ellie Grimbridge (Stacey Nelkin), Conal Cochran (Dan O'Herlihy), Buddy Kupfer (Ralph Strait), Rafferty (Michael Currie), Betty Kupfer (Jadeen Barbor), Little Buddy (Bradley Schachter), Marge (Garn Stephens), Starker (Jon Terry), Technician (Patrick Pankhurst), Harry Grimbridge (Al Berry).

Synopsis: Nighttime, Saturday, October 23. In a northern California hospital a half-crazed man sees a TV ad for Silver Shamrock Novelties' glow-in-the-dark masks and cries out, "They're coming!" Later that evening Dr. Daniel Challis chases a man who's killed the patient. The killer sets himself afire in his car. On Sunday the 24th Ellie Grimbridge comes to the hospital to identify her dead father. On the 27th, Challis asks an associate to perform an autopsy on the man in the car. On Friday the 29th Ellie takes Challis to her father's general store. Checking his records, she believes he ran into trouble between the store and the town of Santa Mira, where Silver Shamrock is located. It's an Irish community, and Silver Shamrock is run by one Conal Cochran. Challis and Ellie drive up and take a room at the Rose of Shannon motel. Challis reads the register and finds that Mr. Grimbridge had checked in on the 20th. Loudspeakers announce a 6 P.M. curfew. A derelict who spoke with Challis has his head torn off, and a saleswoman in the motel has her face blistered by a ray from the Silver Shamrock insignia that had fallen from a mask. On the 30th a family is given a tour of Cochran's plant. The father had sold more masks than any other

of Cochran's outlets. Challis and Ellie accompany the family. During the tour, the father tells Challis that Cochran was once the master of the practical joke. Outside after the tour, Ellie spots her father's car in a warehouse. That evening she is kidnapped. So is Challis when he tries to find her. Sunday the 31st dawns, and Challis is shown the stone block Cochran had stolen from Stonehenge. Cochran reveals his ancestry, his belief in magic and sacrifice. The insignia on his masks will be activated that evening and children all over the country will be killed. Challis witnesses a demonstration in Test Room A, where the family of the previous day is killed. Challis is incarcerated but manages to break his bonds and crawl through an air duct. Rescuing Ellie, he ascends with her to a catwalk, and they drop scores of the insignia to the floor amongst the computers near the Stonehenge block. The automatons are incapacitated, and Cochran applauds his adversary's victory. Beams strike out from the computer circle and the block and destroy him. Challis and Ellie ride away from the burning plant, but this Ellie is a robot that attacks Challis. On foot, he arrives at the same gas station where Mr. Grimbridge took refuge. Calling TV stations, he convinces them to curtail the broadcast of the Silver Shamrock commercial.

Reviews: "Plot doesn't bear close scrutiny but proceeds briskly with nightmare logic under the taut direction of Tommy Lee Wallace.... a slick, assured effort." (Kevin Thomas, *Los Angeles Times Calendar*, October 27, 1982, p. 4) ¶"The plot is ingenious, and the film remains highly enjoyable thanks chiefly to Dean Cundey's camerawork." (Tom Milne, *Monthly Film Bulletin*, June 1983, p. 158) ¶"I've had worse scares from my goldfish bowl." (Rex Reed, *New York Post*, October 22, 1982, p. 43) ¶"More imagination than the lame violence-against-nurses terror of the sequel." (Carrie Rickey, *Village Voice*, November 2, 1982, p. 46)

Analysis: The only content connection with the original is a TV ad promoting the broadcast of *Halloween*. In short, Michael Myers is not in it. Not to worry: It's a solid fright film with a novel premise. Still, how come bugs and snakes emanate from the victims' pulverized faces? Santa Mira is the community from *Invasion of the Body Snatchers*. Is Tom Atkins any relation to Christopher Stone? Good effects. The visage of Cochran when struck by the beams is excellent. TV sections often give this a single-star rating. We suspect they either have not seen it or have no truck with the genre. Nigel *Quatermass Xperiment* Kneale worked on the original script but had his name removed from the credits!

Halloween 4: The Return of Michael Myers

(Galaxy International/Trancas International, 1988; 88 min.) **½

Produced by Paul Freeman. Executive Producer, Moustapha Akkad. Directed by Dwight H. Little. Screenplay, Alan B. McElroy. Story, Dhani Lipsius, Larry Rattner, Benjamin Ruffner, Alan B. McElroy. Edited by Curtiss Clayton. Director of Photography, Peter Lyons Collister. Panavision. Color. Music, Alan Howarth. Theme, John Carpenter. Ultra-Stereo. Sound, Mark McNabb. Art Direction, Roger S. Crandall. Set Decoration, Nickie Lauritzen. Makeup Design, John Buechler. Stunts, Fred Lerner. Special Effects, Larry Fioritto.

Cast: Dr. Loomis (Donald Pleasence), Rachel Carruthers (Ellie Cornell), Jamie Lloyd (Danielle Harris), Michael Myers (George P. Wilbur), Dr. Hoffman (Michael Pataki), Sheriff Meeker (Beau Starr), Kelly (Kathleen Kinmont), Brady (Sasha Jenson), Earl (Gene Ross), Jack Sayer (Carmen Filpi), Richard Carruthers (Jeff Olson), Wade (Richard Stay), Darlene Carruthers (Karen Alston), Tommy (Danny Ray), Kyle (Jordan Bradley), Deputy Pierce (Michael Flynn), Logan (George Sullivan), Justin (Morgan B. White), Unger (Walt Logan Field), Big Al (Michael Ruud), Orrin (Eric Hart).

Synopsis: On the stormy night of October 30, 1988, Michael Myers's transfer from Ridgemont Federal Sanitarium to the Smith's Grove facility is begun. Jamie Lloyd, the daughter of the late Laurie Strode, dreams that her maniac uncle, Michael Myers, is in her room. Haddonfield, Illinois, October 31: Rachel Carruthers, with whom Jamie lives, learns that she'll have to baby-sit that evening and tells Jamie they'll trick-or-treat. Dr. Sam Loomis accosts Dr. Hoffman about Myers, whom

Loomis calls "evil on two legs." When the ambulance that was transporting Myers is found upside-down in a creek, Loomis knows Myers escaped. He heads for Haddonfield, four hours away, stopping at a truck stop where Myers has already killed the mechanic and a waitress. Spotting Michael, Loomis tells him to leave those people in Haddonfield in peace and fires his gun. But Myers escapes in a pickup. That evening, Rachel and Jamie trick-or-treat while Michael examines photos of Laurie and Jamie in his old house. Loomis, who hitchhiked with a "reverend," finds that Sheriff Brackett retired. Sheriff Meeker is initially skeptical that Myers is about, but the doctor's suggestion that they look for Jamie is acted upon. TV announcements tell businesses to close. In the Carruthers house, Loomis and Meeker find the photos and a dead dog. A power plant man is electrocuted at the substation, and the town goes dark. Searching for Jamie, Rachel sees a strange figure. Frightened, she runs, scaling fences, until she finds Jamie. Loomis and the sheriff find them and take them to the police station, which is a shambles. Myers has obviously done his thing. Rachel and Jamie are ensconced in Meeker's house, but Myers has already gotten in and kills Deputy Logan, Meeker's daughter and Brady. Rachel and Jamie retire to the attic and climb out onto the roof. Rachel falls while lowering Jamie, who runs off. Loomis finds Jamie, and they seek refuge in the school. Myers throws Loomis through a window. Revived, Rachel uses a fire extinguisher on Myers and extracts Jamie. Bartender Earl and his cronies drive Rachel and Jamie out of town, but Myers climbs into the truck and disposes of the men before Rachel takes the wheel, jams on the brakes and sends him flying. She rams him and he flies into an old cemetery where the police blast him. He falls into a hole. In Haddonfield, Loomis says, "Michael Myers is in hell." Jamie, apparently unbalanced, is seen with the scissors she must have used on her foster mother a moment before.

Reviews: "Turns into a series of special effects, including an exploding gas station and an electrocution. Does Michael Myers need all this high tech help? Isn't it enough to be a homicidal maniac?" (Caryn James, *New York Times*, October 22, 1988, p. 12) ¶"Uninteresting screenplay … okay twist ending … Makeup effects are good...." (Lor., *Variety*, October 26, 1988)

Analysis: This is a sequel to *Halloween II.* Although Loomis has some facial scars, we would have expected him to sport more evidence of the fire he obviously lived through in that episode. There is an excellent rooftop chase scene. Would children really taunt Jamie about her maniac uncle? It appears that some critics didn't recognize the supernatural aspect till this entry.

Halloween 5

(Galaxy International/Trancas International, 1989; 96 min.) **½

Produced by Ramsey Thomas. Directed by Dominique Othenin-Girard. Screenplay, Michael Jacobs, Dominique Othenin-Girard, Shem Bitterman. Edited by Charles Tetoni. Director of Photography, Robert Draper. CFI Color. Music, Alan Howarth and John Carpenter. Theme, John Carpenter. Ultra-Stereo. Stunt Coordinator, Don Pie. Costumes by Simon Tuke.

Cast: Dr. Loomis (Donald Pleasence), Rachel (Ellie Cornell), Jamie (Danielle Harris), Michael Myers (Donald L. Shanks), Mountain man (Harper Roisman), Stepmother (Karen Alston), Nurse Patsey (Betty Carvalho), Dr. Hart (Max Robinson), Tina (Wendy Kaplan), Billy (Jeffrey Landman), Deputy Nick (Frank Como), Deputy Tom (David Ursin), Samantha (Tamara Glynn), Mike (Jonathan Chapin), Young policeman (Stanton Davis), Gardener (Jack North), Spitz (Matthew Walker), Announcer (Russ McGinn), Little girl (Angela Montoya), Policemen (Jon Richard Platten, Steve Anderson, Tom Jacobsen), Tall policeman (Jay Bernard), Mole man (Patrick White), Charlie (Troy Evans), Eddy (Fenton Quinn), Troopers (Frank Kanig, Donre Sampson), Fat sniper (John Gilbert).

Synopsis: Michael Myers is pursued to a graveyard, where he is shot and falls into an old well or mine shaft which leads to a stream. "Halloween Eve, One Year Later": At the Haddonfield, Illinois, Children's Clinic Jamie has nightmares but is mute through her convulsions. Apparently she "sees" what her murderous uncle, Michael

Myers, is up to. Dr. Loomis says, "She has something to tell us." He talks to a policeman about the killings twelve years ago. A bus arrives in town carrying a man wearing steel-toed shoes. Meanwhile, Myers has returned to town and starts killing. This time he gets Rachel Carruthers. He "attends" a party on the outskirts of town and kills two copulating teens in a barn. Jamie arrives and is chased into the woods. Myers wrecks his car following her. "Michael, go home. Go home!" yells Loomis into the woods. In the old house, Jamie, Loomis and a cop battle Michael until Loomis catches him in a net, shoots him and bashes him with a board. "Die, die, die!" Loomis cries as he suffers a stroke. At the police station, Jamie is told Michael will be taken to a maximum security facility for the rest of his life. "He'll never die," says Jamie. While she's outside, gunshots are heard. Returning, Jamie finds that Michael has been busted out of jail—by the steel-toed stranger.

Reviews: "[Pushes] the series' subjective camera strategy to hand-held, quasi-Polanski extremes." (Michael Wilmington, *Los Angeles Times Calendar*, October 16, 1989, p. 5) ¶"The special effects are routine as these things go.... The acting is adequate at best; and the direction … is of the paint-by-numbers variety." (V.A. Musetto, *New York Post*, October 14, 1989, p. 15)

Analysis: The subtitle (not on screen) is *The Revenge of Michael Myers.* Why hasn't he gone to New York yet? More pointedly, why do the teens of this town persist in partying on Halloween and copulating in dark barns? Because they're brain dead. (A comedian once said they call the Midwest the heartland because the brain's somewhere else.) Who is the steel-toed stranger, a mad scientist? We presume that Jamie is in the clinic and not a prison only because she's a juvenile. Didn't she kill her foster mother in the previous entry?

Halloween: The Curse of Michael Myers

(Dimension/Nightfall, 1995; 88 min.) *½

Produced by Paul Freeman. Executive Producer, Moustapha Akkad. Directed by Joe

Michael Myers (Donald L. Shanks) is ready for some grim reaping in *Halloween 5* (Galaxy International/Trancas, 1989).

Chappelle. Screenplay, Daniel Farrands. Based on characters created by John Carpenter and Debra Hill. Edited by Randolph K. Bricker. Director of Photography, Billy Dickson. Panavision. Color, Consolidated Film Industries. Art Direction, T. K. Kirkpatrick. Special Makeup Effects, John Carl Buechler and Magical Media Industries.

Cast: Dr. Sam Loomis (Donald Pleasence), Tommy Doyle (Paul Stephen Rudd), Kara Strode (Marianne Hagan), Dr. Wynn (Mitchell Ryan), Debra Strode (Kim Darby), John Strode (Bradford English), Tim Strode (Keith Bogart), Beth (Mariah O'Brien), Barry Simms

(Leo Geter), Jamie Lloyd (J. C. Brandy), Danny (Devin Gardner), Mary (Susan Swift), Mrs. Blankenship (Janice Knickrehm), The Shape (George P. Wilbur).

Synopsis: For her efforts in helping Jamie Lloyd and her baby boy escape from the hospital, a woman doctor is thrust into a spike on the wall by a masked figure. That figure pursues Jamie. It's Halloween in Haddonfield, Illinois, again. There is much radio talk about the maniac Michael Myers. Tommy says to himself that he'll be ready this year. Dr. Wynn visits the retired

Dr. Loomis, hoping to lure him back to work. Meanwhile, the fleeing Jamie eludes her pursuer at a bus depot, takes the truck again but is driven off the road. Cornered in a barn, she is impaled. The murderer returns to the truck and finds — no baby. At the Strode house in Haddonfield the boorish father antagonizes his daughter Kara and her "bastard," Danny. When Jamie's body is found, Loomis and Wynn are informed. "He's come home," says Loomis. Tommy discovers Jamie's baby in the bus depot. He goes to Loomis and says he's the Tommy who Laurie baby-sat for on that terrible Halloween years before. In the Myers house, where the Strodes are living, Debra is informed by Loomis that she'd best get her family away. She packs up but is axed in the backyard. Tommy uses his computer to try to explain Michael Myers's existence to Kara and Danny. Apparently Druids had something to do with his evil. Coming home, Debra's husband John is stabbed and electrocuted by Myers, who shortly thereafter kills radio DJ Barry. Back at the Myers house, he cuts Tim Strode's throat and repeatedly stabs girlfriend Beth. Kara follows Danny over there and trips Myers on the stairs. Nevertheless, he arises in a few minutes to take up the pursuit. At Tommy's house, Tommy, Loomis and Kara discover that Dr. Wynn is in charge of the Druids. Kara, who jumps out the window, is captured and taken to the Smiths Grove, Warren County, Sanitarium. Loomis rebuffs Wynn's offer to join his project. Tommy rescues Kara from her cell and eludes Myers, who goes into the operating room and kills everyone. Afterward Tommy and Kara batter him with a pipe and stab him with multiple hypodermics before leaving Loomis behind to do whatever he has to.

Review: "Easily the most inept episode of the *Halloween* series.... It has forgotten how to be suspenseful." (Stephen Holden, *New York Times*, September 30, 1995, p. 115)

Analysis: Although we hoped it would recapture some of the magic, this sixth entry in the *Halloween* series is a disappointment. The low rating is not so much for technique or acting as for a story that's the same as the others. Why go into more

depth about Michael's behavior at this point? *Druids?* Having Mitchell Ryan revealed as the man in black (minus the steel-toed shoes of the previous entry) is a letdown. It's like Michael Gough being uncovered as the essence of evil in *The Legend of Hell House* (1973). Gough was too familiar then, Ryan too familiar an actor now. The film is dedicated to the late Donald Pleasence, who looks aged and tired. Except for the operating room massacre, there's no big finale; it just fizzles out. Previews on other videotapes indicate that this was to have been titled *Halloween: The Origin of Michael Myers. Curse* does sound better.

The Hands of Orlac *see under* **Mad Love**

Hands of a Stranger *see under* **Mad Love**

Hands of the Strangler *see* The Hands of Orlac *under* **Mad Love**

The Haunting of Hamilton High *see* Hello Mary Lou: Prom Night II *under* **Prom Night**

Heaven Can Wait *see under* **Here Comes Mr. Jordan**

Hell on Earth *see* Hellraiser III: Hell on Earth *under* **Hellraiser**

Hellbound: Hellraiser II *see under* **Hellraiser**

Hello Mary Lou: Prom Night II *see under* **Prom Night**

The Haunted Palace
(AIP, 1963; 85 min.) ***

Produced and directed by Roger Corman. Screenplay, Charles Beaumont. From the poem by Edgar Allan Poe and a story ["The Case of Charles Dexter Ward"] by H. P. Lovecraft. Edited by Ronald Sinclair. Director of Photography, Floyd Crosby. Panavision. Pathé Color. Music, Ronald Stein. Art Direction, Daniel Haller. Titles, Armand Acosta. *Cast:* Joseph Curwen/Charles Dexter Ward

(Vincent Price), Simon Orne (Lon Chaney, Jr.), Ann Ward (Debra Paget), Dr. Willet (Frank Maxwell), Ezra/Edgar Weeden (Leo Gordon), Micah Smith (Elisha Cook, Jr.), West (John Dierkes), Jabez Hutchinson (Milton Parsons), Hester Tillinghast (Cathy Merchant), Mrs. Weeden (Barboura Morris), Minister (Harry Ellerbe), Bartender (Bruno De Vota), Leach (Guy Wilkerson), Victim (Darlene Lucht). With Stanford Jolley.

Synopsis: When Joseph Curwen is burned for a warlock, he vows revenge on the New England community of Arkham. A hundred and ten years later a stagecoach brings Charles Dexter Ward and his wife Ann to Arkham, where only Dr. Willet will direct them to Ward's inheritance: the "palace" of Joseph Curwen, Ward's great-great grandfather. On their way there they see a girl with no eyes. In the house they find a portrait of Curwen that's a dead ringer for Ward. They meet Simon the caretaker. At Edgar Weeden's, the descendant of Ezra Weeden hands a piece of raw meat to a growling creature in a locked room. The Curwen portrait begins to affect Ward. Dr. Willet explains the curse and history of the palace. Curwen supposedly obtained the dreadful book the *Necronomicon*, which held the key to the Dark Ones, the Elder Gods — Cthulhu, Yog-Sothoth. Curwen was trying to make a new race and restore these gods to this world. More rapidly now, the spirit of Curwen invades Ward. Simon produces the *Necronomicon*. Curwen/Ward, Simon and Jabez disinter Hester Tillinghast, once Curwen's mistress. Curwen/Ward releases the mutant in Edgar's house, and it kills him. Curwen/Ward sets Micah on fire. Curwen/Ward tries to force himself on Ann. Dr. Willet takes Ann to town, where they see the charred body of Gideon. Back at the palace, Curwen/Ward restores Hester to life. Willet and Ann find the secret panel allowing access to the underground chamber. Confronted by Curwen/Ward, Ann is prepared for sexual sacrifice to what appears to be a demon in a pit. A mob from town arrives and sets the house on fire. When they burn the portrait of Curwen, Ward is released from the curse. Willett leads Ann outside and returns for Ward. But once outside, Ward seems not himself.

Review: "A well-made horror film.... The perverse and yet persistent interest of the public in necromancy ... raises a competent work to inadvertent moments of lyricism." (*Newsweek*, September 16, 1963, p. 86)

Analysis: AIP borrowed a title from a poem by Edgar Allan Poe in order to pass this film off as part of the Corman-directed Poe series, but the plot was strictly Lovecraft. Many fantasy film aficionados seem to frown on this film. Are they disappointed that we don't get to see Yog-Sothoth? It's a pleasure nonetheless to hear those wonderful Lovecraftian names. Eugene Archer in the *New York Times* (January 30, 1964) found only the color photography worthy of comment. Perhaps some audiences dislike the film's set-bound nature, and nobody likes Lon Chaney, Jr., anymore. Veteran character actor John Dierkes' (*The Thing, Abbott and Costello Meet Dr. Jekyll and Mr. Hyde, Shane*) name is misspelled as Dierkies. This was Debra Paget's second Corman "Poe" film. She'd been a Twentieth Century–Fox contract star in the fifties (e.g., *Stars and Stripes Forever*, 1952). Another fantastic film credit for her was *Most Dangerous Man Alive* (1961). Ronald Stein's theme is ominous but perhaps overused in the course of the film.

The Resurrected
(Scotti Brothers Pictures, 1991; 108 min.)

Produced by Mark Borde and Kenneth Raich. Directed by Dan O'Bannon. Screenplay, Brent V. Friedman. Inspired by "The Case of Charles Dexter Ward" by H. P. Lovecraft. Edited by Russell Livingstone. Director of Photography, Irv Goodnoff. Music, Richard Band. Special Visual Effects, Todd Masters.

Cast: John March (John Terry), Claire Ward (Jane Sibbett), Charles Dexter Ward/Joseph Curwen (Chris Sarandon), Lonny Beck (Robert Romanus), Holly Tender (Laurie Briscoe). With Ken Camroux, Patrick Pon, Bernard Cuffling, J. B. Bivens, Roberd Sidley, Des Smiley, Eric Newton.

Synopsis: Providence, Rhode Island: The distraught, newly wedded Mrs. Ward procures the services of March Investigations,

Inc., to shed some light on the guarded activities of her husband, Charles. Ward has sequestered himself in a remote country estate formerly occupied by his "five-times great grandfather," Ezra Ward. Not only are the nights full of howls, screams and assorted disturbances, the whole area has become permeated by the most noisome stench. March investigates and finds that Ward himself has taken on an unsavory appearance, as well as the affectation of antiquated speech. March and Claire soon connect a number of baffling and gruesome murders in the vicinity with Charles' bizarre activities, making it obvious that "intervention" is necessary. But even when Ward is strait-jacketed and locked behind padded walls at a local asylum, the weird killings continue. Investigating further, March discovers a diary of Ward's ancestor, Ezra, which outlines how the seventeenth-century wizard, Joseph Curwen, had been discovered dabbling in the Black Arts by the community fathers. A midnight raid by the outraged citizenry brought an end to the wizard's activities as well as his life, and the diary concludes by telling how Ezra wed Curwen's widow, only to learn that she was pregnant with the necromancer's child, which explains how Charles Dexter Ward comes to so uncannily resemble this contemporary of his five-times great grandfather. March and Claire conclude that Charles has indeed continued his ancestor's experiments in animating the dead and that one or more of his "experiments" are paying murderous nocturnal visits on the locals. To keep Claire's name out of the tabloids, she and March, accompanied by March's associate, Lonny Beck, venture to the house and discover an underground labyrinth which leads to the wizard's lair of both Joseph Curwen and Charles Ward. Perusing a number of ancient and crumbling tomes, March reads how the dead can be reanimated, provided their remains are intact, and pockets a vial of "Reflux," the elixir Curwen used for the resurrection process. Unfortunately, the trio stumbles onto one of Charles's more unhappy, less anatomically complete experiments, and Lonny becomes its victim. March and Claire barely manage to escape

and detonate a sufficient amount of explosives to blow the Curwen house to smithereens and collapse the tunnels beneath. Returning to the asylum, March confronts Charles Ward with the truth: that Ward is really the resurrected Joseph Curwen, who killed Charles Dexter Ward and assumed his identity. As proof, March produces a suitcase with the skeletal remains of Charles Ward. Faced with this, and no longer able to contain his insatiable appetite for flesh, Curwen rips free of his restraints with preternatural strength, decapitates a hospital orderly, and prepares to "strip the flesh from [March's] bones like a suckling pig." The beleaguered March throws a vial of Reflux onto the pile of bones of Charles Ward. These immediately spring to life in a spectacular display of pyrotechnics and set upon Curwen, literally ripping the flesh from his bones. Both skeleton and madman disappear in a supernal conflagration.

Review: "O'Bannon brings ... a measured pace and obvious reverence for Lovecraft.... Structure is a drawback to viewer involvement." (Lawrence Cohn, *Variety*, April 13, 1992))

Analysis: While *The Haunted Palace* placed the Lovecraft novella into Corman's Poe canon, Dan O'Bannon and scenarist Brent Friedman update "The Case of Charles Dexter Ward" to the present day and give it an even more topical spin by having the tale narrated in flashback form by a harried gumshoe, in the time-honored tradition of many a classic *film noir*. It's an approach that works quite well; *The Resurrected* may be the best in a respectably lengthy line of H. P. Lovecraft adaptations, adaptations that have always seemed to go wanting for one reason or another. O'Bannon strikes an almost ideal balance between story and atmosphere, and he gives us characters that, while never departing much from genre convention, still exert enough presence to maintain our interest through to the end. John Terry delivers a credible performance as the capable John March, who is probably more at home lurking outside hotels and keyholes than working as private ghostbuster, and Jane Sibbett is appropriately sultry and vulnerable as the harried

Mrs. Ward. But *The Resurrected* obviously belongs to Chris Sarandon, who brings admirable conviction to both his dual roles as the doomed Charles Dexter Ward and the corrupt Joseph Curwin.

Notes of Interest: H. P. Lovecraft wrote "The Case of Charles Dexter Ward" in 1927–28, but it was not published in its entirety until 1943, after his death.

Hellraiser
(New World, 1987; 90 min.) ****

Produced by Christopher Figg. Directed by Clive Barker. Screenplay, Clive Barker. Based on his novel *The Hellbound Heart*. Edited by Richard Marden. Director of Photography, Robin Vidgeon. Panavision. Technicolor. Music, Christopher Young. Dolby Stereo. Sound, John Midgely. Art Direction, Jocelyn James. Special Makeup Effects Designer, Bob Keen. Stunts, Jim Dowdall.

Cast: Larry Cotton (Andrew Robinson), Julia Cotton (Clare Higgins), Kirsty (Ashley Laurence), Frank Cotton (Sean Chapman), Pinhead (Doug Bradley), Frank the Monster (Oliver Smith), Steve (Robert Hines), First victim (Antony Allen). With Leon Davis, Michael Cassidy, Frank Baker, Kenneth Nelson, Gay Barnes, Niall Buggy.

Synopsis: American Frank Cotton buys an intriguing, mysteriously inscribed box at a bazaar and disappears while unlocking it. In a dimly lit room, a strange man with pins covering his head examines body parts and pieces a face together. Larry Cotton moves into Frank's house in Britain, his second wife Julia's native land. Julia discovers some pornographic pictures of Frank and other women and remembers an affair she had with Frank. Frank left, telling her it's never enough. Julia is frigid — with Larry. Kirsty, Larry's daughter by his first wife, comes to visit and find a job. While moving in, Larry catches his hand on a nail and bleeds profusely on the floor of an upstairs room. The floor sucks up the blood and Frank — in a netherworld — is "reborn" but needs more blood to become whole. He confronts Julia and she agrees to help, enticing men to the house and killing them. One day Kirsty arrives, hears screams, and investigates. She is confronted by her Uncle Frank, not as yet wholly human. Laying hands on the demonic box, she tosses it through the window and, escaping outside, retrieves it. She collapses and is taken to a hospital. Fiddling with the box, she is confronted by the pinhead and other grotesqueries. She is horrified to discover that they think she's called them. They initially brook no objections to her coming with them, but she makes a deal: In return for leading them to Frank, she *might* be left alone. At the Cotton house, Kirsty hears her father say he and Julia have done away with Frank. She demands to see the body and enters the upstairs room, where she sees the life-drained corpse and finds herself once more in the presence of the Cenobites. They want the man who did this thing, and Kirsty realizes that the corpse is not Frank, but her father. Frank had killed Larry and taken her father's face. Frank attempts to stab Kirsty but impales Julia instead. While Kirsty retreats upstairs, Frank takes advantage of the situation to drain Julia of her lifeforce. Unaware that the Cenobites are on his trail, Frank corners Kirsty. The demons appear, and once again his flesh is rent and torn by hooks and barbs. Kirsty frantically reassembles the magic box to escape a Cenobite in the stairwell. Tossing the box into a fire outside, she is shocked to see a vagrant place his hand into the fire. He is set aflame but turns into a flying demon. The box is returned to the bazaar.

Reviews: "Creaky, suspensless, yet refreshingly literate shocker...." (Dean Lamanna, *Cinefantastique*, March 1988, pp. 108, 123) ¶"Unique and original.... The cinematography is perfectly dark and moody, the acting more than sufficient." (Dennis Daniel, *Deep Red*, March, 1988, p. 64) ¶"Well made, well acted, and the visual effects are generally handled with skill." (Besa., *Variety*, May 20, 1987)

Analysis: Clive Barker is the Stephen King of Britain, and his work on this film obviously helped make *Hellraiser* the scary, grisly, and superior movie it is. A number of scenes stick with you: pinhead's vault with the chains and body parts, the blood dripping on the floor, the resurrection of Larry. We feel sorry for Julia. She's not all bad even if she does become a murderess.

The monstrous Frank (Oliver Smith) confronts Julia (Clare Higgins) in *Hellraiser* (New World, 1987).

Some humor ameliorates the situation and releases tension, especially Kirsty's take-charge attitude when her boyfriend tries to be helpful with the box. She yells, tears it out of his hands and gives him a nasty look. There are excellent production values: music, sound, cinematography. "Introducing Ashley Laurence."

Hellbound: Hellraiser II
(New World, 1988; 97 min.) ***½

Produced by Christopher Figg. Executive Producers, Christopher Webster, Clive Barker. Directed by Tony Randel. Screenplay, Peter Atkins. Edited by Richard Marden. Director of Photography, Robin Vidgeon. Panavision. Technicolor. Music, Christopher Young. Dolby Stereo. Sound, John Midgeley. Art Direction, Andrew Harris. Special Effects, Graham Longhurst. Special Makeup Effects, Bob Keen. Flying Effects, Geoff Portass, Bob Keen. Stunts, Bronco McLoughlin.

Cast: Julia (Clare Higgins) Kirsty (Ashley Laurence), Dr. Channard (Kenneth Cranham), Tiffany (Imogen Boorman), Frank (Sean Chapman), Kyle (William Hope), Pinhead

(Doug Bradley), Cenobite (Barbie Wilde), Butterball (Simon Bamford), Chatterer (Nicholas Vince), Browning (Oliver Smith), Ronson (Angus McInnes), "Skinless" Julia (Deborah Joel), Cortez (James Tillitt), Kucich (Bradley Lavelle), Patient (Edwin Craig), Workmen (Ron Travis, Oliver Parker), Mother (Catherine Chevalier).

Synopsis: A British soldier overseas solves a puzzle box, but his reward is capture by hooks and barbs. Scene shift: Kirsty Cotton awakes in a hospital to be questioned by police and psychiatrists. Alone, she sees a bloody human figure in the corner. It writes, "I am in hell. Help me." She believes it is her father. Kyle, an associate of brain surgeon Dr. Channard, volunteers to help Kirsty after he overhears Channard on the phone and then, spying in his house, discovers the bloody mattress on which Julia Cotton had died. Channard brings a lunatic into the room, sits him on the mattress and gives him a scalpel. The lunatic believes he is covered with maggots and uses the scalpel to cut them off. The mattress once more blood-soaked, arms

and legs sprout from it, enfolding the lunatic. It's Julia. Channard resurrects her
completely via other crazed people she
drains of their lifeforce. Kyle and Kirsty investigate, but Kyle is killed. Before Julia can
kill Kirsty, Channard brings in Tiffany, a
mute girl trying to decipher the puzzle. She
cracks it and brings forth the Cenobites,
whose pinhead leader understands that it
was not this innocent but someone else's
desire that called them. They retreat. Tiffany explores the strange passages, as does
Kirsty, who picks up the box Tiffany left.
Kirsty encounters the Cenobites, but they
say they have eternity to explore her flesh,
therefore she is free to roam. Meanwhile,
Julia conducts Channard to a grid, above
which is a giant revolving, pointed puzzle
much like the one Tiffany and Kirsty hold.
Julia explains that it is her god, the god of
flesh, hunger and desire, the god of the
labyrinth. Too late Channard discovers that
Julia was chosen to bring him here. Channard is imprisoned, tubes and needles
pierce his body, the door closes and the box
sinks out of sight. Kirsty finds Uncle Frank
in his private hell. It was he who appeared
to her in the hospital. He aims to possess
Kirsty but is foiled, first by his niece, then
by Julia, who plucks out his heart. Tiffany
and Kirsty encounter Julia, who gets possession of the puzzle but loses her skin and
is sucked into a maelstrom. Finding the
Cenobites, Kirsty produces the picture she'd
taken from Channard's study — a picture of
pinhead when he was human. He and his
cohorts attempt to protect the women
when Channard arrives, now a Cenobite
with a tentacle attached to his head. They
are "killed." He floats out into his hospital
and eviscerates and mauls his lunatics before returning to the labyrinth to pursue
Tiffany. Tiffany solves the small puzzle in
time, and Channard's head is ripped off by
the tentacle. The two women rush back
through the labyrinth and squeeze into the
real world before the entrance closes. Moving men clean out Channard's house and
one touches a bloody mattress and is sucked
in. A second mover watches in amazement
as a column arises from the mattress bearing faces, a baby, a mini-skeleton. A face
asks, "What is your pleasure, sir?"

Review: "Campy, gore-soaked horror
tale with technically first-rate effects...."
(Rich., *Variety*, September 14, 1988)
Analysis: What's going on here? American policemen investigate the Cotton
house we thought was in England. Dr.
Channard is obviously British, Kyle obviously American. It's difficult to describe
but nonetheless riveting, actually epic
when the labyrinth is entered. For the cinema, this is an original — and disturbing —
conception. Perplex your friends by asking what would happen to you if you'd
been imprisoned in the Cenobite world,
returned to this earth and got your skin
back, then died. Barring accident, are
Cenobites immortal?

Hellraiser III : Hell on Earth
(Miramax, 1992; 93 min.) ***

Produced by Lawrence Mortoff. Executive
Producer, Clive Barker. Directed by Anthony
Hickox. Screenplay, Peter Atkins. Story,
Peter Atkins and Tony Randel. Based on
characters created by Clive Barker. Edited by
James D. R. Hickox. Director of Photogra-
phy, Gerry Lively. Color, Foto-Kem. Music,
Randy Miller. Ultra-Stereo. Art Direction,
Tim Eckel. Set Decoration, David Allen Ko-
neff. Special Effects, Bob Keen.

Cast: Elliott/Pinhead (Doug Bradley), Joey
Summerskill (Terry Farrell), Terri (Paula
Marshall), J. P. Monroe (Kevin Bernhardt),
Doc/Camerahead (Ken Carpenter), Kirsty
(Ashley Laurence).

Synopsis: At the Pyramid Gallery, J. P.
Monroe buys a unique piece of statuary
which sucks the skin off of J. P.'s one-night
stand before ingesting the body. A pin-
headed face tells J. P. he can indulge the
man's tastes. Meanwhile, reporter Joey
Summerskill has been investigating a
strange death by questioning one of J. P.'s
girlfriends, Terri. They find the Pyramid
Gallery and files from the Channard Institute. Joey obtains a videotape of Kirsty
Cotton trying to explain a mysterious box
and the demons it disgorges. Periodically
Joey dreams of her father who was killed in
Vietnam, sometimes of World War I
trenches. Terri fights with J. P. and pushes
him to the statue, which grapples with him.
Pinhead emerges whole at last. Joey has a
dream, then "wakes" and sees a Quonset

hut outside her window. She enters and proceeds through another door. She meets Captain Elliot Spencer, who tells her hell has come to earth and they are going to stop it. He reveals that after World War I he was disillusioned and opened the demonic box. Kirsty freed him, but what he was is still in Joey's world — Pinhead. They must keep the demon from destroying the box and must lure him to this realm where Elliot has the power. Pinhead can't take the box, Elliot reveals, for it must be *given* to him. Beware of his duplicity. At J. P.'s Boiler Room club, Pinhead wreaks havoc. Joey arrives and finds more bodies and flees Pinhead. She is chased through the streets and trapped at a building construction site. She opens the box, and it sucks in all of the demons but Pinhead. She finds herself in a field with her father. But it's Pinhead in disguise, and he now has the box. But the "dream" changes; they're in Elliot's dimension. He says Pinhead came into his world through Joey's mind. Elliot and Pinhead become one. "Joey, send me to Hell!" it cries. She stabs it with the pointed end of the box and finds herself back at the construction site. She sinks the box in cement. Later, the lobby of the building over it looks like the box.

Review: "Faithful to Barker's themes.... Genre fans will appreciate the blood flow and the gore, and director Anthony Hickox keeps things moving so that there's never a dull moment — or dull blade. Consider Hell raised." (Richard Harrington/Washington Post, *Philadelphia Inquirer*, September 14, 1992, p. F2)

Analysis: It's harder to explain than the others and not as good. It drags when Joey and Terri yammer about things. There aren't as many interesting and forceful characters as the preceding entries featured. Still and all, it's imaginative.

Herbie Goes Bananas *see under* **The Love Bug**

Herbie Goes to Monte Carlo *see under* **The Love Bug**

Herbie Rides Again *see under* **The Love Bug**

Here Comes Mr. Jordan
(Columbia, 1941; 93 min.) ***½

Produced by Everett Riskin. Directed by Alexander Hall. Screenplay, Sidney Buchman and Seton I. Miller. Based on the *Heaven Can Wait* play by Harry Segall. Edited by Viola Lawrence. Director of Photography, Joseph Walker. Music, Frederick Hollander. Art Direction, Lionel Banks. Gowns, Edith Head.

Cast: Joe Pendleton/Bruce Farnsworth/K.O. Murdock (Robert Montgomery), Bette Logan (Evelyn Keyes), Mr. Jordan (Claude Rains), Julia Farnsworth (Rita Johnson), Messenger 7013 (Edward Everett Horton), Max Corkle (James Gleason), Tony Abbott (John Emery), Butler (Halliwell Hobbes), Inspector Williams (Donald McBride), Lefty (Don Costello), Plane #22 Pilot (Lloyd Bridges), Bugs (Benny Rubin).

Synopsis: In Pleasant Valley, "where all is peace ... and harmony ... and love ... and where two men are beating each other's brains out," Joe Pendleton trains under Max Corkle's tutelage for a shot at the boxing title held by Ralph K.O. Murdock. Pendleton, who is nicknamed "The Flying Pug," takes his plane to New York but crashes en route. Not realizing he's dead, Joe is escorted by Messenger 7013 across a cloud field to a passenger plane. He meets Mr. Jordan, who finds that Joe is not on the list. Messenger 7013 made a mistake by taking Joe from his body before his plane hit the earth. This means that they must return to earth and resuscitate Joe. However, they find that the body has been cremated. Jordan promises Joe another body. After traveling the world, Joe picks banker Bruce Farnsworth after Farnsworth is drowned in the bathtub by his private secretary, Tony Abbott, and wife, Rita. Part of his reason is to help Bette Logan, a beautiful young woman who needs Farnsworth's help to get her father out of jail. Farnsworth shocks Julia and Tony by reappearing. He clears Bette's father of securities fraud and decides to stay in Farnsworth's body, which he can train to be "in the pink" for a shot at Murdock. He calls in Corkle, convinces him that Farnsworth is in fact Joe, and gets Corkle to schedule a bout with Murdock. Jordan returns and warns Joe to leave

Farnsworth's body: "You cannot change the course of your destiny." But Joe/Farnsworth won't believe it. He's shot by Tony. Corkle goes to the missing persons bureau and the police. Joe and Jordan observe a police interrogation at the Farnsworth house. Corkle turns on the radio to the Murdock-Gilbert fight. When Murdock is knocked down, Joe learns from Jordan that Murdock was shot by mobsters. Joe takes up Jordan on his offer to become Murdock, knock out Gilbert, and become the champion. Joe/Murdock hires Corkle as his new manager. Leaving the auditorium, Joe/Murdock bumps into Bette. During their conversation she recalls what Farnsworth told her about meeting a fighter someday and sees in Murdock's eyes a special something. They leave together. "So long, champ!" says Jordan, who's worked it so that Murdock has no memory of Joe.

Review: "A delightful and totally disarming joke at heaven's expense.... rollicking entertainment." (Theodore Strauss, *New York Times*, August 8, 1941, pp. 8, 13)

Analysis: It's cute, it's charming. It's somewhat odd casting to have one of the screen's handsomest men playing a pugilist, but Montgomery does a nice job. Few audiences have forgotten his lucky saxophone. The *New York Times* review praised Rains for his "kindly authority," and James Gleason is, well, the inimitable James Gleason, character actor par excellence. Donald McBride contributes yet another harassed police investigator. How about this? Farnsworth goes after his secretary, Tony Abbott, calling out, "Hey Abbott!" Is this a coincidence? Abbott and Costello debuted on film in the previous year's *One Night in the Tropics*, but they'd been on radio for years. Would Columbia plug Universal? Unlikely.

Down to Earth
(Columbia, 1947; 101 min.) **½

Produced by Don Hartman. Directed by Alexander Hall. Screenplay, Edwin Blum and Don Hartman. Based on characters created by Harry Segall in the play *Heaven Can Wait*. Edited by Viola Lawrence. Director of Photography, Rudolph Mate. Technicolor. Music, George Duning, Mario Castelnuovo-Tedesco, Heinz Roemheld. Songs, Doris Fisher and Allan Roberts. Choreography, Jack Cole. Art Direction, Stephen Gooson, Rudolph Sternad. Set Decoration, William Kiernan. Costumes, Jean Louis.

Cast: Terpsichore/Kitty Pendleton (Rita Hayworth), Danny Miller (Larry Parks), Mr. Jordan (Roland Culver), Max Corkle (James Gleason), Joe Mannion (George Macready), Messenger 7013 (Edward Everett Horton), Georgie Evans (Adele Jergens), Eddie (Marc Platt), Police lieutenant (William Frawley), Kelly (James Burke), Dolly (Kathleen O'-Malley), Betty (Jean Donahue), Spike (William Haade), Orchestra leader (Fred Sears), Sloan (Myron Healey), Muses (Lynn Merrick, Dusty Anderson, Doris Houck, Shirley Molohon, Peggy Maley, Dorothy Brady, Jo Rattigan, Lucille Casey, Virginia Hunter), Escort 3082 (Lucien Littlefield).

Synopsis: Terpsichore, Greek goddess of the dance, returns to Earth with Mr. Jordan's blessing. Masquerading as a showgirl, she aims to prevent producer Danny Miller from putting on the play *Swinging the Muses*, which pokes fun at the muses and uses swing music, no less. She tries to convince Miller to use classical Greek dancing. But Miller works his magic on her, and she performs in a modern jazz rendition. Mr. Jordan refuses her request to remain on Earth but shows her the future—when Danny will join her in the clouds.

Review: "One more genial interference by the gentleman in *Down to Earth* ... gets a pretty good musical under way." (Bosley Crowther, *New York Times*, September 12, 1947, p. 18)

Analysis: Larry Parks was on top of the world after his outing as the famed song-and-dance man Al Jolson in *The Jolson Story* (1946). Blacklisting in a few years would stymie his career. Hayworth was in her prime. (Her singing was dubbed by Anita Ellis. Kay Starr dubbed Adele Jergens.) Repeating their roles from *Here Comes Mr. Jordan* were James Gleason and Edward Everett Horton. *Xanadu* (1980) is considered a *Down to Earth* remake by some.

Heaven Can Wait

(Paramount, 1978; 101 min.) ***

Produced by Warren Beatty. Directed by Warren Beatty and Buck Henry. Assistant Directors, Howard W. Koch, Jr., Craig Huston. Screenplay, Elaine May and Warren Beatty. Based on the play by Harry Segall. Edited by Robert C. Jones and Don Zimmerman. Director of Photography, William A. Fraker. Panavision. Movielab Color. Music, Dave Grusin. Art Direction, Edwin O'Donovan. Set Decoration, George Gaines. Costumes, Theodora Van Runkle and Richard Bruno. Special Effects, Robert MacDonald.

Cast: Joe Pendleton/Leo Farnsworth/Tom Jarrett (Warren Beatty), Betty Logan (Julie Christie), Mr. Jordan (James Mason), Max Corkle (Jack Warden), Tony Abbott (Charles Grodin), Julia Farnsworth (Dyan Cannon), Escort (Buck Henry), Krim (Vincent Gardenia), Sisk (Joseph Maher), Bentley (Hamilton Camp), Everett (Arthur Malet), Corinne (Stephanie Faracy), Lavinia (Jeanie Linero), Gardener (Harry D. K. Wong), Security guard (George J. Manos), Peters (Larry Block), Conway (Frank Campanella), Tomarken (Bill Sorrells), TV interviewer (Dick Enberg), Coach (Dolph Sweet), General Manager (R. G. Armstrong), Trainer (Ed V. Peck), Former owner (John Randolph), Oppenheim (Keene Curtis), Renfield (William Larsen), Nuclear reporter (William Sylvester), TV commentators (Curt Gowdy, Al DeRogatis).

Synopsis: While bicycling through a tunnel, Los Angeles Rams quarterback Joe Pendleton is struck and killed by a truck. Or so it seems. In what he thinks is a dream, Joe discovers that a heavenly "Escort" plucked him from earthly life too soon. Mr. Jordan finds that Joe isn't expected to visit his way station until 2025. They must find a new body. They can't use the old; it's been cremated. After searching the world, Joe accepts the body of financier Leo Farnsworth, who was drugged and drowned by his wife, Julia, and her lover, the confidential secretary Tony Abbott. Joe does this in order to assist Betty Logan. Ms. Logan wants him to relocate a refinery that will displace 1,673 persons in England. After boning up on his company's record, Joe, now Leo, attends a board meeting where he uses a football analogy and agrees to relocate the refinery. Considering him crazy, Julia and Tony plan a second murder. Joe convinces his old trainer Max

Corkle that he is in fact Joe in Farnsworth's body. Max agrees to train him for a shot at quarterbacking the Rams in the forthcoming Super Bowl championship game. Joe/Leo buys the team and does well in a scrimmage, but Jordan warns him that he must leave Farnsworth's body. Tony's bullet finds its mark, and Farnsworth falls into a well. Joe leaves with Jordan. While the police under Krim investigate the murder, Joe and Jordan attend the Super Bowl. Quarterback Tom Jarrett is killed. Joe takes his place and leads the team to victory. Meanwhile, Corkle and Krim uncover the murderers, and the caretaker discovers Farnsworth's body. Jordan tells Joe he is Jarrett now and won't remember Joe or Leo. Leaving the stadium, Jarrett meets Betty. Remembering Leo's prediction about meeting a football player and the importance of his eyes, she agrees to take a walk with Jarrett.

Reviews: "Already exercises a weaker hold on my memory than the grubby black-and-white, relentlessly studio-made original version.... Much of the humor misfires." (John Simon, *National Review*, August 4, 1978, pp. 970-71) ¶"A hybrid of no great style but of a good deal of charm and with a marvelous cast." (Vincent Canby, *New York Times*, June 28, 1978, p. C17)

Analysis: We wonder what possessed the modern screenwriters to change the lucky sax to a clarinet, or why Bruce Farnsworth changed his name to Leo. There's something a smidgen tacky about the production values, which is odd for such an A production. Several highly amusing moments grace the film, e.g., Max Corkle's admonition, "Joe, don't you understand? You're playing football with a bunch of butlers!" The casting is excellent. Charles Grodin and Dyan Cannon are a scene-stealing tandem.

The Heretic *see* Exorcist II *under* **The Exorcist**

Highlander

(20th Century–Fox, 1986; 111 min.)
**½

Produced by Peter S. Davis and William N.

Panzer. Directed by Russell Mulcahy. Screenplay, Gregory Widen, Peter Bellwood, Larry Ferguson. Story, Gregory Widen. Edited by Peter Honess. Director of Photography, Gerry Fisher. Technicolor. Music, Michael Kamen. Songs and Additional Music, Queen. Dolby Stereo. Art Direction, Tim Hutchinson, Martin Atkinson, Mark Raggett. Set Decoration, Ian Whittaker. Costumes, Jim Acheson, Gilly Hebden. Special Effects, Martin Gutteridge, Graham Longhurst, Garth Inns, Bert Luxford. Makeup Effects, Bob Keen, Alix Harwood, Robert Verner Gresty, John Schoonraad. Stunts, Peter Diamond.

Cast: Connor MacLeod (Christopher Lambert), Brenda Wyatt (Roxanne Hart), Kurgen (Clancy Brown), Juan Villa-Lobos Ramirez (Sean Connery), Heather (Beatie Edney), Lieutenant Moran (Alan North), Rachel (Sheila Gish), Det. Bedsoe (Jon Polito), Sunda (Jugh Quarshie), Kirk (Christopher Malcolm), Fasil (Peter Diamond), Dugal (Billy Hartman), Angus (James Cosmo), Kate (Celia Imrie), Chief Murdoch (Alistair Findley), Garfield (Edward Wiley), Father Rainey (James McKenna), Kenny (John Cassady), Bassett (Ian Reddington), Hotchkiss (Sion Tudor Owen), Tony (Damien Leake), Dr. Kenderly (Gordon Sterne), Erik (Ron Berglas).

Synopsis: Connor MacLeod leads his people against a rival Highlands clan in sixteenth-century Scotland. During the battle, Connor is opposed by a seven-foot-tall Goliath garbed in black and bedecked in an outlandish helm. The Scotsman is run through, but before the giant can deliver a decapitating *coup de grace*, the MacLeod clan piles upon him. As the fray turns against the foe, the colossus disappears. Connor apparently dies of his wounds that night, but, miraculously, seems to revive by morning and shows no signs of a wound. Fearing diabolism, MacLeod's clansmen and other villagers of Glen Fennen banish Connor. He takes up his exile in an isolated keep in the company of a woman, Heather. Connor's idyll with Heather is interrupted by the arrival of an exotically costumed cavalier, Juan Ramirez, former armorer to the King of Spain. Not a Spaniard, the newcomer explains that he is actually an Egyptian, born in that faraway place some 2,437 years earlier, and that he is one of a number of unique immortals. Connor is likewise an immortal, says Ramirez, who adds he has come to instruct him in the skills necessary for survival. Because, he concludes, in the end, only *one* can survive. The Scotsman has already met a fellow immortal, the dark giant on the fields at Glen Fennen. This was one of the Kurgen, an evil sect of Russians who threaten to plunge humanity into "an eternity of darkness." Ramirez begins training Connor. His main weapon will be the sword, the chosen weapon of these immortals, for the only way to *permanently* kill one is by beheading. One evening while Connor is away, the Kurgen appears, and after a tremendous sword battle in which the giant welds his broadsword against Ramirez's Samurai sword, Connor's teacher is beheaded. Heather is raped. Returning, Connor collects Heather and the Samurai sword and moves. They spend the rest of their days in a rustic, but peaceful, existence. Connor learns of the true heartache of immortality: He may never grow old and die, but his beloved will. As Heather's time comes and she dies quietly in his arms, he knows that to fall in love is one experience he must deny himself from now on. Connor moves to the New World, living under various guises, pretending to die after a time and picking up a new identity. In 1985 he is known as Russell Nash, an antique dealer in New York City. He encounters a fellow immortal in a parking garage, and the two square off in a sword fight that ends with the stranger's decapitation. Nash conceals his Samurai sword in the garage rafters before being apprehended by the police. Unable to connect him with the murder, the authorities release him. Forensics expert Brenda Wyatt is intrigued by both the valuable antique Spanish sword carried by the dead man and the metal shards she finds in the body. Investigating, she finds that the metal is incredibly old but was fashioned using more recent techniques. She follows Nash one evening, and both are accosted by the giant Kurgen. The confrontation is prematurely ended by a police helicopter, and the Russian disappears into the night. Ultimately, Brenda discovers the secret of Russell Nash, and the two fall in love. When the Kurgen kidnaps Brenda, Nash pursues. In a hugely conflagratory duel, the swordsmen come to death grips until the Scotsman's greater skill carries the day. The Russian's head topples off his shoulders. In the dazzling and explosive display of protoplasmic energy that follows, Russell Nash-Connor MacLeod absorbs the collected essences of all the previous departed immortals, the ethereal voice of his old friend Ramirez telling him that he will now have the power to know the thoughts of men's minds, that he has power beyond his wildest dreams. "Use it well," the voice intones. Now mortal, Nash returns to the Highlands, where he and Brenda will have children and grow old together.

Reviews: "In spite of a sturdy cast and dazzling production design, *Highlander* is stultifyingly, jaw-droppingly, achingly awful." (Sheila Benson, *Los Angeles Times Calendar*, March 11, 1986, p. 5) ¶"On the surface ... *Highlander* periodically manages to be quite exhilarating." (Tim Pulleine, *Monthly Film Bulletin*, August, 1986, p. 236)

Analysis: At one point in *Highlander*, Ramirez says to his Scottish friend, "You have the manners of a goat, and you smell like dung heap, and you've no knowledge whatsoever of your potential." This was also the view of most of the film's critics about the movie itself, who found its style too reminiscent of director Mulcahy's numerous rock videos. Perhaps they were put off by the film's frequent jumps between the sixteenth century and the twentieth; the above synopsis relates the narrative in linear fashion, but the movie's account is told through constant, and frequently jarring, flashback. Mulcahy's video roots constantly show through, too, in the inclusion of Queen's rock-music background in the most anachronistic places, like that sixteenth-century highlands setting. Still, *Highlander* is glossy and entertaining, with (predictably) first-rate performances by Sean Connery as Juan Villa-Lobos Ramirez and Clancy Brown as the evil Kurgen. Brown plays the villain very broadly, in almost comic manner in the twentieth-century scenes, and is a welcome foil to Christopher Lambert's decidedly wooden MacLeod/Nash.

Highlander 2: The Quickening

(InterStar, 1991; 91 min.) *

Produced by Peter S. Davis, William Panzer. Directed by Russell Mulcahy. Screenplay, Peter Bellwood. Story, Brian Clemens, William Panzer. Based on characters created by Gregory Widen. Edited by Hubert de la Bouillerie, Anthony Redman. Director of Photography, Phil Meheux. CinemaScope. Color. Music, Stewart Copeland. Dolby Stereo. Costumes, Deborah Everton. Special Effects, John Richardson.

Cast: Connor MacLeod (Christopher Lambert), Juan Villa-Lobos Ramirez (Sean Connery), Louise Marcus (Virginia Madsen), General Katana (Michael Ironside), Blake (John C. McGinley), Alan Neyman (Allan Rich), Reno (Peter Buccossi), Bartender (Eddie Trucco), Trout (Peter Antico), Cabbie (Phil Brock), Drunk in cafe (Rusty Schwimmer), Usher (Max Berlinger), Holt (Edwardo Sapag), Doctor (Jeff Altman).

Synopsis: In 1999, the earth's weakened ozone layer is virtually gone, allowing lethal doses of ultraviolet radiation to wreak havoc on the world's population. Connor MacLeod and Alan Neyman devise the mammoth project that will construct a protective energy field about the planet. In the quarter-century that passes after the installation of the energy field, the world becomes a crime-ridden, impoverished ghetto, with the monolithic Earth Screen Company virtually dominating even the world governments. Connor, now mortal, is an aged, world-weary tycoon who seeks refuge in drink and spends his nights dozing through grand opera. His troubled dreams are of his home planet of Zeist, whence he and his mentor, Ramirez, were exiled five hundred years earlier for crimes against the totalitarian leadership there. On earth, the Zeistian expatriates are immortal and forced to stay on the earth until all but one remains; that one can then return to Zeist. On that distant planet, General Katana, hated enemy of MacLeod, sends two assassins to murder the highlander. They fail, and MacLeod is reinvigorated by their life-force. He cries out the name of his old friend, Ramirez, and that immortal materializes on stage during a performance of *Hamlet* in Scotland. MacLeod falls in with Louise Marcus, a former ESC employee. Louise was discharged and labeled an eco-terrorist when she began to suspect that all was not as it seemed with this supposedly world-minded company. She and her fellows have learned that the ozone layer has repaired itself and that ESC has perpetuated the myth of ozone depletion to insure its continued existence. MacLeod verifies this in a visit to Neyman, who is still with the ESC. Unfortunately, Blake sees Neyman with MacLeod and condemns him to "Max," the maximum security penal facility beneath ESC headquarters. When the highlander learns of this, he and the recently arrived Ramirez make plans for an assault on the fortress-like headquarters. Infuriated by his incompetent henchmen, General Katana comes to earth and informs Blake that he has a new partner. As the general's announcement is accompanied by the throttling of Blake's associates, Blake begrudgingly accepts the situation. The two are alert to the entrance of MacLeod and Ramirez and fill their car with bullets. Louise Marcus emerges from the car's trunk, claiming to be a hitchhiker. Taken for dead, the two men are taken to the dispensary. Springing into action and overcoming the medical and security personnel, MacLeod, Ramirez and Marcus move quickly to the maximum security area and find the tortured and dying Neyman. Reuniting, the three promptly find themselves trapped in a chamber into which huge blades are descending from above. Ramirez sacrifices himself so that the other two can escape. Connor and Louise enter the interior of the facility, where the energy beam that powers the earth shield is generated. While Louise holds the plant guards at bay with her atomic weapons, MacLeod and Katana fight to the death with swords. Ultimately the highlander's skill is uppermost and the general's head is sent flying. Amidst the swirling protoplasmic vapors, Connor steps into the dazzling shaft of energy jetting skyward. This added influx of power overloads the system, causing a tremendous surge to flare upward to the satellite receiving dish orbiting the earth. With the destruction of the satellite, the earth shield vanishes, allowing starlight and the night sky to be seen from the earth for the first time in a quarter-century.

Reviews: "Blithely rewrites the history and logic of the original.... The actors obviously were thinking about mortgage payments and a holiday in Argentina, where this was filmed." (Betsy Pickle, Scripps Howard News Service, *Daily Local News*, West Chester, PA, November 7, 1991, D3) ¶"This movie has to be seen to be believed.... almost awesome in its badness." (Roger Ebert, *Movie Home Companion, 1993*, pp. 294-295) ¶"Samuel Johnson once sneered to James Boswell that the only good thing that ever came out of Scotland was the road to England, and no one who sees this sequel will give him an argument." (*Philadelphia Inquirer*, November 8, 1991, p. 6)

Analysis: Somehow, the earlier film's premise — that the immortals like MacLeod and Ramirez are merely *different* humans, afflicted with the peculiar curse of immortality but indigenous to our own world — is discarded, and in this sequel we're told that MacLeod and company are fugitives from distant Zeist. All this seems unnecessary, because the first film got by quite nicely without it, and also because the interplanetary angle adds nothing at all to the story except to allow for some unnecessary slapstick, as when General Katana catapults himself to earth and lands with a crash and a thud into the interior of a moving subway train. Obviously influenced by the success of Tim Burton's *Batman*, this sequel to *Highlander* offers a very similar *noir*-ish, Gotham-like cityscape of shadowy, rain-drenched streets and alleyways winding around brooding statuary and grim, monolithic buildings. Certain visuals and character types also allude to David Lynch's *Dune*, in the nasty-boy assassination team that General Katana sends to terminate Connor MacLeod. Visual flair is indeed about the only thing one can praise in *Highlander 2*, which has even more sequences that look like extended moments from music videos than its predecessor. Christopher Lambert is only occasionally able to bring any real energy to his character, even after he is "rejuvenated" by the failed assassination attempt. Connery, almost always a saving grace to a film, mostly enjoys what could be called an extended cameo in this film, and is really here only to get the title character out of a tight spot. Even the usually excellent Michael Ironside is reduced to empty burlesque here, playing Katana in too-broad, camp fashion, wearing a constant smirk and mouthing inane one-liners. Many lines and elements are incongruous: Why in the world would this alien being make a comment about the proceedings looking like something out of a high school reunion?

Honey I Blew Up the Kid *see under* **Honey, I Shrunk the Kids**

Honey, I Shrunk the Kids
(Buena Vista/Walt Disney Productions, 1989; 93 min.) ***

Produced by Penney Finkelman Cox. Directed by Joe Johnston. Screenplay, Ed Naha, Tom Schalman. Story, Stuart Gordon, Brian Yuzna, Ed Naha. Edited by Michael A. Stevenson. Director of Photography, Hiro Narita. Panavision. Metrocolor. Music, James Horner. Art Direction, Gregg Fonseca. Dolby Stereo. Sound, Wylie Stateman. Art Direction, John Iacovelli, Dorree Cooper. Stunts, Mike Cassidy. Mechanical Effects Coordinator, Peter M. Chesney. Visual Effects Coordinator, Michael Muscal. Creatures and Miniatures Supervisor, David Sosalla.

Cast: Wayne Szalinski (Rick Moranis), Diane Szalinski (Marcia Strassman), Big Russ Thompson (Matt Frewer), Mae Thompson (Kristine Sutherland), Little Russ Thompson (Thomas Brown), Ron Thompson (Jared Rushton), Amy Szalinski (Amy O'Neill), Nick Szalinski (Robert Oliveri), Tommy Pervis (Carl Steven), Don Forrester (Mark L. Taylor), Gloria Forrester (Kimmy Robertson), Dr. Brainard (Lou Cutell), Police (Laura Waterbury, Trevor Galtress), Harold Boorstein (Martin Aylett), Lauren Boorstein (Janet Sunderland).

Synopsis: While inventor Wayne Szalinski unsuccessfully tries to interest a conference of scientists in his almost-perfected size reduction machine, his son Nick, daughter Amy and neighbor kids Little Russ and Ron Thompson are shrunken when they enter the attic lab. They were looking for the baseball Ron had hit through the window. That ball had bounced on the computer keyboard and into the machinery and caused the machine to do what Wayne wanted. But when he returns home disappointed, he smashes the machine. The kids can't make themselves heard. When Wayne cleans up the glass, they are swept into the trash. Cutting open the bag, they find themselves at the far end of the yard, a yard become an obstacle-course jungle. After finding a miniature couch and chair, Wayne finally realizes his machine works — and the kids are shrunk! He realizes the kids may be in the yard and begins the search. The kids are having a tough time: fighting off a scorpion with the aid of an ant, escaping a "flood" and a lawnmower. Finally they find their dog Cork. On his fur they make it inside the house, but Nick falls into Wayne's cereal and is almost eaten. Cork bites Wayne's ankle, and Wayne spots Nick. In the attic, with Big Russ Thompson's help, Wayne uses the machine to restore the children to normal size.

Reviews: "A Nintendo game brought to life, at about the same level of character development, but without as many challenging situations." (Randy Pitman, *Library Journal*, February 15, 1990, pp. 226-27) ¶"A little toy balloon of a TV sitcom episode pumped up to zeppelin proportions." (Michael Wilmington, *Los Angeles Times Calendar*, June 23, 1989, p. 12) ¶"Essentially a pleasant return to such vintage Disney items as *The Absent-Minded Professor* and *The Love Bug*." (Kim Newman, *Monthly Film Bulletin*, February 1990, p. 41) ¶"In the best tradition of Disney and even better than that because it is not so juvenile that adults won't be thoroughly entertained." (*Variety*, 1989) ¶"Why the tired adherence to gender clichés?" (Manohla Dargis, *Village Voice*, June 27, 1989, p. 75)

Analysis: This was an unforeseen financial bonanza that challenged *Batman* for top grosser of the summer. The sound and effects are excellent. Distressingly, the kids act pretty dumb for a while. But then, so does Marcia Strassman when she worries about daughter Amy spending a night in the vicinity of teenager Russ. The laugh-producing scenes are those with Rick Moranis searching the yard and explaining to

Strassman what happened to the children. There is more adventure to be accomplished with shrunken people, but the Disney studio elected to follow this up with a giant toddler — a major miscalculation from an aesthetic point of view.

Honey I Blew Up the Kid
(Buena Vista/Walt Disney Productions, 1992; 89 min.) **

Produced by Dawn Steel and Edward Feldman. Directed by Randal Kleiser. Screenplay, Thom Eberhardt, Peter Elbling and Garry Goodrow. Story, Garry Goodrow. Edited by Michael Stevenson and Harry Hitner. Director of Photography, John Hora. Technicolor. Music, Bruce Broughton. Art Direction, Ed Verreaux. Set Decoration, Dorree Cooper. Baby Adam Special Makeup Effects, Kevin Yagher. Mechanical Effects Design, Peter Chesney.

Cast: Wayne Szalinski (Rick Moranis), Diane Szalinski (Marcia Strassman), Dr. Sterling (Lloyd Bridges), Adam Szalinski (Daniel and Joshua Shalikar), Nick Szalinski (Robert Oliveri), Dr. Charles Hendricksen (John Shea), Mandy (Keri Russell), Amy Szalinski (Amy O'Neill), Security guard Smitty (Kenneth Tobey). With Gregory Sierra.

Synopsis: The Szalinskis have moved to Vista Del Mar, Nevada, where Wayne works for Sterling Laboratories. When wife Diane takes daughter Amy off to college, Wayne and teenage son Nick are left babysitting the youngest son, Adam. The three go into the lab on a Saturday. Wayne aims the laser cannon at a toy rabbit, but Adam runs over and is also struck by the ray. At home he grows to room size, aided by electrical sources like the microwave. Hoping they can reverse the ray and shrink Adam back to normal size, Wayne and Nick return to the lab. But Dr. Charles Hendricksen is there, and Wayne must leave. Hendricksen tries to figure out what caused the power failure that morning. Diane arrives home and faints when she sees Adam. While Adam naps, Wayne and Diane try to locate Wayne's old shrinking machine in a warehouse. Wayne convinces Mr. Sterling it will restore his son to his normal size. Sterling fires Charles, who nevertheless uses his influence with the military to chase Adam. Adam has grown to giant size

because electricity from high voltage lines struck the truck in which he was being transported. Headed toward Las Vegas, Adam carries Nick and baby-sitter Mandy in his pocket. In the city, the neon causes Adam to grow even taller. Diane convinces Wayne to turn his machine on her. Adam will respond to a mother larger than he. Giant Diane grabs the helicopter in which Hendricksen intends to stun Adam. Wayne reduces both to normal size but in so doing shrinks Nick and Mandy. They are located, however, and will be enlarged after Nick has had a few moments alone with the girl.

Review: "Subpar sequel…. By expanding the action … director Randal Kleiser … spoils the back-yard-as-universe fun of *Shrunk*." (Joe DeChick, *Wilmington News Journal 55 Hours*, July 17-19, 1992, p. 7.)

Analysis: The premise *is* indeed weak, but the public bought it with some élan. It's hard to believe they gave Marcia Strassman those clichéd lines. Although she has a job, her character is frequently a caricature of a sitcom mom-at-home. Symptomatic of public distrust, authority is presented as practically all powerful — and easily manipulated by lab director Hendricksen. It's stupid, semi-lame, but not entirely boring. Funniest scene: two scientists watching a blurred computer screen of toy rabbit and child and thinking it's a three-eyed mutant. Can we draw any parallels with *The Amazing Colossal Man*? It also took place in Las Vegas.

Horror of Dracula *see under* **Dracula**

The Horror of Frankenstein *see under* **Frankenstein**

The Horror Show *see under* **House**

House
(New World, 1986; 93 min.) ***

Produced by Sean S. Cunningham. Directed by Steve Miner. Screenplay, Ethan Wiley. Story, Fred Dekker. Edited by Michael N. Knue. Director of Photography, Mac Ahlberg. Metrocolor. Prints, Technicolor. Music, Harry Manfredini. Art Direction, John Reinhart. Set Decoration, Anne Huntley. Stunt Coordinator, Kane Hodder. Creature Effects,

Backwood Film, James Cummins. Special Effects, Tassilo Baur, Joe Viskocil, Dream-Quest Images.

Cast: Roger Cobb (William Katt), Harold Gorton (George Wendt), Big Ben (Richard Moll), Sandy Sinclair (Kay Lenz), Tanya (Mary Stavin), Chet Parker (Michael Ensign), Jimmy (Erik Silver and Mark Silver), Aunt Elizabeth (Susan French), Police (Alan Autry, Steven Williams), Grocery boy (Jim Calvert), Cheesy stud (Jayson Kane), Priest (Billy Beck), Frank McGraw (Steve Susskind), Lieutenant (Dwier Brown), Fitzsimons (Joey Green), Scott (Stephen Nichols), Robert (Robert Joseph), Witch (Peter Pitofsky), Little Critter (Elizabeth Barrington, Jerry Marin, Felix Silla).

Synopsis: Separated from his actress wife Sandy and unable to locate his missing son Jimmy, depressed author Roger Cobb decides to reside in his Aunt Elizabeth's Victorian home in Marin County. He grew up there after his parents died. Aunt Elizabeth recently committed suicide — or so it seemed. To his surprise, Roger encounters her upstairs, where she says the house tricked her and will trick him. Roger begins writing about his Vietnam war experiences but hears a voice like his son's. Opening a closet at midnight, he finds a monstrous creature reaching out for him. He forces the door closed, then sets up a battery of cameras. But neighbor Harold Gorton interrupts. Hearing Roger's incredible story, Harold surreptitiously takes Roger's personal telephone directory and calls Sandy. When she says she can't come because of a morning filming, Harold volunteers to watch out for Roger. Roger finds his uncle's trophy marlin twitching and tools in the shed flying at him. Worst of all, Sandy shows up, then becomes a hideous hag he must shoot with a shotgun. But the body turns back to Sandy on the porch. He hides it under the stairs as the police arrive. When they are gone, Roger can't locate the body. Then, as the hag, it says his son is dead. He opens the bathroom door and the tools fly out, impaling and decapitating the demon. Roger buries its various parts in the yard. Continuing with his book after interruption by neighbor Tanya, Roger recalls the death of his pal Ben. Tanya's small son Robert is grabbed by two creatures, but Roger gets him

back. After Tanya takes Robert away, Roger has Harold over, hands him a harpoon gun and opens the closet door. The monster is indeed there, and although Harold manages to shoot it, Roger gets entangled in the line and is dragged into a jungle. It's Vietnam, and he finds the dying Ben, whom he cannot bear to kill. Viet Cong soldiers drag Ben off while Roger makes for a lighted doorway and finds himself back in Aunt Elizabeth's house. In a strange painting, Roger sees his son's face screaming in a medicine cabinet mirror. In the bathroom, he smashes the real mirror and fends off several demons in that entrance to a netherworld. Equipping himself with a flashlight, shotgun and rope, Roger descends into the darkness. A winged demon wrests the shotgun from his hands and severs the rope. Roger falls into water, coming up in the jungle again. He finds Jimmy in a cage, breaks him free, and they flee back to the water and emerge in the pool next to Aunt Elizabeth's house. All is not well, however, for at the house Roger and Jimmy are confronted by the rotted, skeletal Ben. Roger and Ben fight it out throughout the house until Roger pulls Ben over a precipice. Still, Ben reappears inside and threatens to slit Jimmy's throat. He slashes at Roger's hand, but all of a sudden Roger realizes he controls this situation. He pulls Jimmy from Ben's clutches, sticks a grenade into the monster's gut and runs off as the monster explodes. He and Jimmy meet Sandy outside.

Reviews: "An unexpectedly ambitious, refreshingly unpredictable horror comedy with some serious undertones." (Kevin Thomas, *Los Angeles Times Calendar*, February 28, 1986, p. 15) ¶"I found it repetitiously boring, laboriously horrible, and a waste of enormous make-up effort." (Archer Winsten, *New York Post*, February 28, 1986, p. 23)

Analysis: The ghost/demon character doing the prime moving is excellent. Is it sometimes Richard Moll or stunt coordinator Kane Hodder? Hodder is one of the more daunting Jasons in the *Friday the 13th* series. An early dream sequence features an arm bursting from the ground in front of a child. This could be an in-joke reference to Katt's appearance in *Carrie* (1976). The mix of suspense, horror and humor is fine. We might wish for Katt to spend more time searching for Jimmy in that netherworld, but then, we have more *House* films on tap. Thank goodness the Sandy who appeared at the end was the real woman, not a trick-ending monster.

House II: The Second Story
(New World, 1987; 88 min.) *½

Produced by Sean S. Cunningham. Directed by Ethan Wiley. Screenplay, Ethan Wiley. Edited by Marty Nicholson. Director of Photography, Mac Ahlberg. Metrocolor. Prints, Technicolor. Music, Harry Manfredini. Art Direction, Larry Fulton, Don Diers. Set Decoration, Dorree Cooper. Makeup and Creature Effects, Chris Walas. Visual Effects, DreamQuest Images.

Cast: Jesse McLaughlin (Arye Gross), Charlie (Jonathan Stark), Gramps (Royal Dano), John (Bill Maher), Bill Towner (John Ratzenberger), Kate (Lar Park Lincoln), Lana (Amy Yasbeck), Rochelle (Jayne Modean), Sheriff (Gregory Walcott), Slim (Dean Cleverdon).

Synopsis: After a man and wife send their baby away, they are visited by a strange figure who demands "the skull." They claim ignorance and are shot. Twenty-five years later Jesse McLaughlin and Kate take up residence in the house. Jesse is the baby who was sent away. Examining an album, he is fascinated by the photos of his great-great grandfather holding a crystal skull. He and pal Charlie dig up the ancestor's grave in which they hope to find the skull and treasure. Instead, they find "Gramps," come back to life. When he finds out that Jesse is his kin, he becomes friendly and urges him to protect the house and the skull from the forces of evil. During a Halloween party, the skull begins to glow. A brute enters the room and steals it. Jesse and Charlie follow and find themselves in a prehistoric jungle. They find the skull, but it's torn from their hands by a flying reptile and dropped into its nest. Jesse climbs up to retrieve it, but he and the reptile's baby fall back into the contemporary house. The skull is stolen again, apparently by Aztecs who use it in their human sacrifice. With the help of electrician Bill Towner, Jesse and Charlie rescue a sacrificial maiden and

retrieve the skull. At dinner, Slim, Gramps's former nemesis, rises from the main course, draws and shoots Gramps. He grabs the girl and the skull and is chased by Charlie. Gramps gives his six-shooter to Jesse. Jesse finds Slim in a western town where the girl and Charlie are the ghost's prisoner. Wounded, Jesse is chased back to his world, where he finally gets a bead on Slim with a rifle and blows his head off. Arriving because of the gunfire, the police blaze away at the headless body as Jesse carries Gramps away. Burying Gramps in the Old West he once lived in, Jesse places the skull on the grave and, with the maiden and Charlie, heads out in a wagon.

Reviews: "Utterly worthless 'sequel' to the largely enjoyable *House* appears to have been conceived by people whose perceptions are permanently distorted.... sluggish, nonsensical and a generally pointless venture." (Stefan Jaworzyn, *Shock Xpress,* Summer 1987, p. 18)

Analysis: Except for the same producer, cinematographer, and composer, there's hardly any connection with the first *House.* Although it provides similar egress to other worlds, it's not the same building or even the same neighborhood. There are a few humorous moments: the Gross-Stark Indiana Jones or Bill and Ted–type adventures, the venerable Royal Dano as a 170-year-old man, John Ratzenberger (Cliff of TV's *Cheers*) as "Bill Towner, Electrician and Adventurer." But there's not much rhyme or reason in the story. What power does the skull have anyway? Was Kate married to Jesse? Kate is played by Lar Park Lincoln, the heroine of *Friday the 13th, Part VII.* Amy Yasbeck will have an important leading role or two, e.g., *Robin Hood, Men in Tights* (1993). Jayne Modean (*Spring Break,* 1983) is wasted. Initially obnoxious, Jonathan Stark quickly becomes likable.

The Horror Show
(United Artists, 1989; 94 min.) *½

Produced by Sean S. Cunningham. Directed by James Isaac. Screenplay, Alan Smithee and Leslie Bohem. Edited by Edward Anton. Director of Photography, Mac Ahlberg.

Metrocolor. Prints, DeLuxe. Music, Harry Manfredini. Dolby Stereo. Set Decoration, Diane Campbell. Stunt Coordinator, Kane Hodder. Special Makeup Effects, Kurtzman, Nicotero, Berger EFX Group.

Cast: Detective Lucas McCarthy (Lance Henriksen), Donna McCarthy (Rita Taggart), Max Jenke (Brion James), Bonnie McCarthy (Dedee Pfeiffer), Scott McCarthy (Aron Eisenberg), Dr. Tower (Matt Clark), Vinnie (David Oliver), Peter Campbell (Thom Bray), Lt. Miller (Lewis Arquette), Casey (Terry Alexander), Warden (Laurence Tierney), Chili salesman (Alvy Moore), Little girl (Meshell Dillon).

Synopsis: After capturing mass murderer Max Jenke, believed responsible for about 110 deaths, Lucas has nightmares. He hopes viewing Jenke's execution at Turner State Penitentiary will exorcise the dreams and thus let psychiatrist Dr. Tower sign the papers permitting Lucas back on the beat. It takes 50,000 volts and many minutes to kill Jenke, who rises to his feet and, before collapsing, warns Lucas he'll be back. As Professor Peter Campbell examines the corpse in the morgue, a ghostly, maniacally laughing apparition leaves the body and enters the furnace of the McCarthy home. In the basement, Jenke hacks up Vinnie, Bonnie McCarthy's boyfriend, and taunts Lucas by phone and by what Lucas initially thinks are hallucinations. Lucas cases Jenke's apartment and finds photos of his own family. Professor Campbell tells Lucas that Jenke is pure evil. There is a homemade electric chair in the apartment which indicates Jenke built up his resistance to electrocution. Campbell argues that if they can locate Jenke and send enough juice into him, they can bring him back and then blow him away. When Lucas returns home, he finds the police there. Bonnie found Vinnie's body. Everyone suspects Lucas and they take him downtown. Jenke appears in his apartment and kills Campbell. Internal Affairs wants to try Lucas for two murders. Lucas knows Jenke is terrorizing his family and escapes. Jenke uses all his tricks to mystify Lucas, who finds himself in the power plant but with Donna's help manages to electrocute the monster. Lucas then finds himself and Jenke in Jenke's apartment. Campbell was right. Lucas blows him

away. The terror over, the McCarthys prepare to move.

Review: "Henriksen gives typically strong performance…. Confused, silly and boring." (Leonard Maltin, ed., *Movie and Video Guide 1993*, p. 557)

Analysis: Again, the connection to the first *House* lies in the title and behind-the-scenes personnel. This time the residence is a veritable chalet. One wonders how they'll extend this to feature length. It's nice to see Lance Henriksen in leading roles. He seems to have acquired a cult following. Brion James follows in the footsteps of such imposing screen villains as Robert Tessier (*The Glory Stompers*, 1968). Note the scriptwriter named Alan Smithee. This is a bogus name used over the years by directors and writers who don't want observable credit. Aka *House III*.

House IV
(Sean S. Cunningham Films, 1992; 100 min.) *½

Produced by Sean S. Cunningham. Directed by Lewis Abernathy. Screenplay, Geoff Miller and Deirdre Higgins. Story, Geoff Miller, Deirdre Higgins, Jim Wynorski, R. J. Robertson. Edited by Seth Gavin. Director of Photography, James Mathers. Music, Harry Manfredini. Set Decoration, Ildiki Toth.

Cast: Kelly Cobb (Terri Treas), Roger Cobb (William Katt), Verna (Denny Dillon), Grandfather (Dabbs Greer), Ezra (Ned Romero). With Melissa Clayton, Scott Burkholder, Mark Gash, Ned Bellamy, Paul Keith.

Synopsis: Roger Cobb declines to sell his grandfather's old house to his stepbrother but is killed when the family's car has a blowout and crashes. His widow Kelly and daughter intend living in the house. Ezra, a native American, tells her about the sacred spring beneath the house. The stepbrother wants the house so the nearby chemical company can store its toxic waste on the grounds. He uses his thugs to terrorize Kelly and the now paralyzed daughter. Roger's spirit helps Kelly, and it is revealed to her that the reason the car crashed was that the thugs shot the tire. The thugs set the house on fire, but the sacred spring erupts and douses it. The stepbrother unintentionally confesses his nefarious intentions to the FBI and is carted off.

Review: "Slow, overlong, thrill-less, this lurches from comedy to horror without rhyme or reason." (Leonard Maltin, ed., *Movie and Video Guide 1993*, p. 562.)

Analysis: Nothing much happens in the first half-hour but it's not boring. At about the 45-minute mark the gears switch to virtual slapstick, and the reason the brother wants to buy the house — as a toxic waste storage facility for the chemical plant run by a midget — becomes totally ludicrous. Producer Cunningham directed *Friday the 13th.*

The House at the End of the World *see* **Die, Monster, Die!**

House of Dark Shadows
(MGM, 1970; 97 min.) ***

Produced and directed by Dan Curtis. Screenplay, Sam Hall and Gordon Russell. Edited by Arline Garson. Director of Photography, Arthur J. Ornitz. Metrocolor. Music, Robert Cobert. Set Decoration, Ken Fitzpatrick. Special Makeup, Dick Smith. Stunt Coordinator, Alex Stevens.

Cast: Barnabas Collins (Jonathan Frid), Maggie Evans (Kathryn Leigh Scott), Elizabeth Collins Stoddard (Joan Bennett), Dr. Julia Hoffman (Grayson Hall), Jeff Clark (Roger Davis), Carolyn Stoddard (Nancy Barrett), Professor T. Eliot Stokes (Thayer David), Willie Loomis (John Karlen), Roger Collins (Louis Edmonds), Todd Jennings (Donald Briscoe), David Collins (David Henesy), Sheriff George Patterson (Dennis Patrick), Daphne Rudd (Lisa Richards), Minister (Jerry Lacy), Mrs. Johnson (Barbara Cason), Old man (Paul Michael), Dr. Forbes (Humbert Astredo), Todd's nurse (Terry Crawford), Pallbearer (Michael Stroka), Deputy (Philip Larson).

Synopsis: Upon opening a coffin in the old Collins crypt, handyman Willie Loomis finds himself gripped by a powerful hand. At the front gate, Daphne Rudd is attacked. When she is found, her neck is bloodied. During all this, Maggie Evans has been locked in an old room while looking for young David Collins. Carolyn Stoddard speaks with Willie in a restaurant and finds him a quite different person from the chip-on-his-shoulder fellow she knew. Barnabas Collins arrives at Collinwood, saying he is an English cousin. He is a dead ringer for the Barnabas Collins of the eighteenth century. He presents Elizabeth with a magnificent necklace the family thought lost. Barnabas takes up residence in the old manor with Willie as his caretaker. After Carolyn pays a visit, Barnabas reciprocates — appearing in her room with bared fangs. At a ball, Barnabas sees Maggie across a crowded room and introduces himself. He says her dress was once worn by Josette Dupree. "Josette. Josette, you have come back to me," Barnabas says to himself. He offers some of his story to Willie. When the curse was placed upon him, Josette would not become like him and jumped from a cliff. Barnabas was chained in the coffin by his father. A jealous Carolyn interrupts and says she'll tell Maggie everything. Barnabas attacks her and orders Willie to take her away. He helps her back to Collinwood, where she's found dead. Examining the blood of the victims, Doctor Julia Hoffman discovers an unusual cell. Professor T. Eliot Stokes strongly suggests the attacker is a vampire. Julia thinks she could cure anyone so afflicted, but Stokes says vampirism is not a disease. While playing in an abandoned swimming pool, the child David falls and is knocked unconscious. He wakes when it's dark and encounters his dead sister Carolyn. He runs home with the tale. Only Stokes is compassionate, and he urges the family to consider the possibility that Carolyn is a vampire. Roger and Elizabeth are skeptical, to say the least. Todd, though himself doubtful, goes to the vault and is bitten by the specter. Barnabas warns Carolyn to stay clear of all residents of Collinwood. When Barnabas visits Collinwood, Julia discovers that Barnabas casts no reflection in a mirror. Returning to his estate, Barnabas discovers that Carolyn overcame Willie. As Carolyn approaches Collinwood, Todd wakes, knocks out a policeman and meets Carolyn in an nearby loft. Police find them, surround Carolyn with crosses and subdue her while Stokes pounds a wooden stake through her heart. Julia goes to Barnabas's house. While keeping him at

Barnabas Collins (Jonathan Frid) escorts Maggie Evans (Kathryn Leigh Scott) around Collinwood in *House of Dark Shadows* (MGM, 1970)

bay with a small crucifix, she argues that she can turn him into a normal person. He lets her take blood samples. When Barnabas learns that Willie has urged Maggie to leave Collinwood, Barnabas throws his servant down the stairs and clubs him with his cane. Stokes warns Julia that if anything happens to Maggie, he'll hold her responsible. He maintains that Barnabas is interested in Maggie, not her. When Barnabas tells Julia he's going to ask Maggie to marry him, Julia injects him improperly, and he becomes a hideous old man. He strangles Julia and bites Maggie before leaving. Stokes and Roger Collins delve into Collins family history and realize that Maggie resembles Josette Dupree. Stokes is convinced that Barnabas will attempt to make Maggie his bride on the anniversary of the day he was supposed to wed Josette. The aged Barnabas enters Maggie's room via a hidden panel, overcomes a policeman and sucks more of Maggie's blood. He regains his "normal" appearance and abducts his beloved. Jeff Clark, Maggie's old boyfriend,

is lured into the woods by the now-vampirized Stokes. Jeff fills Stokes full of silver bullets. Jeff impales Roger in the old house and finds a crossbow. But he's knocked insensible by Willie, who guides Maggie to the chapel. Jeff wakes and, from a balcony, looses a dart at Barnabas. But it hits Willie in the back as he himself tries to stop the unholy wedding. Barnabas calls Jeff to him and makes him watch, but as he leans over Maggie, he is impaled from behind by the still living Willie. His trance broken, Jeff forces the dart through the vampire's torso. He lifts Maggie into his arms.

Review: "Really has no subject except its special effects (which aren't very good) and its various shock sequences." (Roger Greenspun, *New York Times*, October 29, 1970, p. 58)

Analysis: This film and its sequel were inspired by the popular afternoon soap opera of 1966-1971, "Dark Shadows." Most of the TV cast showed up in one or both films. Question: What's with the bat flying away during the end titles? Does it mean

Barnabas was not killed? Were they thinking sequel with Frid? We've never seen police so readily accept the existence of vampires — or so many silver bullets. Audiences laugh loudly when Barnabas enters his house yelling, "Willie!" after hearing that his handyman had warned Maggie. Kathryn Leigh Scott gets worked up right off the bat, screaming her head off every time a door opens. Well she should, in a spooky old place like that. We guess Barnabas wasn't a proponent of free love, else he wouldn't have risked his demise by conducting the wedding ceremony. The transformation of Barnabas from old to young is not state-of-the-art. Nor are the gunshots. The *New York Times* complained of a "pallid" approach to the sexuality that usually infuses a vampire film. Oddly enough, with all these defects, we find the film more than passable. Filmed in Tarrytown, New York, and Norwalk, Connecticut.

Night of Dark Shadows
(MGM, 1971; 97 min.) **½

Produced and directed by Dan Curtis. Assistant Director, Stanley Penesoff. Screenplay, Sam Hall. Story, Sam Hall and Dan Curtis. Edited by Charles Goldsmith. Director of Photography, Richard Shore. Panavision. Metrocolor. Music, Robert Cobert. Art Direction, Trevor Williams.

Cast: Angelique (Lara Parker), Quentin/Charles (David Selby), Tracy (Kate Jackson), Carlotta Drake (Grayson Hall), Alex Jenkins (John Karlen), Claire Jenkins (Nancy Barrett), Gerard (James Storm), Laura Collins (Diana Millay), Gabriel (Christopher Pennock), Reverend Strack (Thayer David), Sarah Castle (Monica Rich), Mrs. Castle (Clarisse Blackburn).

Synopsis: Quentin Collins inherits the family estate and moves there with his bride, Tracy. Housekeeper Carlotta offers a brief history of the house, built in the late 1600s. Quentin is entranced by a portrait of Angelique Collins, who died in 1810. Looking outside, he seems to see a human figure hanging from a tree limb. That night he hears voices and "sees" a man on horseback trampling another man under foot. Next day he takes a horseback ride and comes across the funeral of Angelique Collins.

When Alex and Claire visit, Quentin confides in Alex that he's imagining things. In the tower room Quentin decides to use as his studio, he finds another, unfinished picture with Angelique. He seems to see her with Charles, his look-a-like. Walking outside, he sees a girl screaming in a window. Carlotta reveals more of the estate's history before Quentin imagines he's gone back in time, meeting Angelique and fighting with Charles's brother Gabriel. When brought around by Tracy, he finds himself battering Gerard, the handyman. Alex observes a white-garbed figure entering a dilapidated greenhouse. Upon entering, he is almost injured by falling roof panels. Quentin decides to leave the tower room. Carlotta indicates that the girl Quentin saw in the window was Sarah Castle, who lived there over one hundred and fifty years ago. She, Carlotta, is the reincarnated Sarah. As Sarah, she witnessed Angelique's hanging — for being a witch who seduced Charles while married to his brother. Sarah's love kept Angelique alive. Carlotta tells Quentin he will come to believe this, at which time there will be no room for Tracy. Tracy finds Quentin a changed person who rants, "You make me sick. I can't stand the sight of you anymore!" Later, she finds the previously unfinished picture of Angelique. Two figures have been added: Charles/Quentin carrying the unconscious body of Tracy. Alex and Claire return from a city gallery with a portrait of ancestor Charles Collins: a dead ringer for Quentin but for a facial scar. Alex hopes this will snap Quentin out of his spell. That night, though, Alex is almost killed by Angelique's ghost. Simultaneously, a possessed Quentin tries to drown Tracy in the old indoor pool. Alex and Claire save her, and Alex warns Quentin to leave the cursed house. Gerard follows Alex in his pickup and forces his car into a tree. Although wounded by Claire, Gerard kidnaps Tracy. But he fails to run down Quentin, and the two fight on a bridge. Although Gerard's knife cuts Quentin's face, Tracy smacks her husband's adversary with a board and he falls to his death. Quentin realizes Carlotta is keeping the spirit of Angelique alive. Alex confronts Carlotta on the roof, and she steps off to her death. With Carlotta's demise, Tracy is freed from Angelique, who'd attacked her in the underground recesses of the mansion she and Quentin were exploring. Quentin puts the house up for sale but returns for his canvasses. When he fails to come out, Tracy enters and finds him with a limp and a scar, the scar his forebear Charles had. Compounding events, Angelique appears on the stairway. Tracy screams and screams and screams. A UPI news bulletin reports that Alex and Claire Jenkins were killed in a car accident. Strangely, said passersby, their car filled with a white smoke before the crash.

Review: "Requires considerable imagination by the audience to figure out what's happening." (Whit., *Variety*, August 11, 1971, p. 16)

Analysis: Variety called the film's setting its "most outstanding feature." Like *House of Dark Shadows*, it was filmed on the Tarrytown, New York, estate of railroad magnate and robber baron Jay Gould (died 1892). It's well photographed, but some close-ups smack of Dan Curtis's television background. David Selby's face is suitable for expressing a descent into madness. Actress Grayson Hall, here playing a different character than the one she essayed in *House of Dark Shadows*, is scriptwriter Sam Hall's wife. Thayer David, Nancy Barrett, and John Karlen also return from the first film in different roles. Lara Parker might be the most beautiful cinematic witch ever. "And introducing Kate Jackson as Tracy."

House of Dracula *see under* **Dracula**

House of Frankenstein *see under* **Frankenstein**

House of Fright *see* The Two Faces of Dr. Jekyll *under* **Dr. Jekyll and Mr. Hyde**

The Howling

(Avco Embassy/International Film Investors, 1981; 91 min) ****

Produced by Michael Finnell and Jack Conrad. Directed by Joe Dante. Assistant Director, Jack Cummins. Screenplay, John Sayles and Terence H. Winkless. Based on the novel by Gary Brandner. Edited by Mark Goldblatt and Joe Dante. Director of Photography, John Hora. Color. Music by Pino Donaggio. Art Direction, Robert A. Burns. Set Decoration, Steve Legler. Special Effects, Roger George.

Cast: Karen White (Dee Wallace), Dr. George Waggner (Patrick Macnee), Chris (Dennis Dugan), Bill Neill (Christopher Stone), Terry Fisher (Belinda Balaski), Fred (Kevin McCarthy), Earle Kenton (John Carradine), Sam (Slim Pickens), Marsha (Elizabeth Brooks), Eddie Quist (Robert Picardo), Donna (Margie Impert), Policeman (Kenneth Tobey), Bookstore owner (Dick Miller), Man in phone booth (Roger Corman), Bookstore customer (Forrest J Ackerman). With Noble Willingham, James Murtaugh, Jim McKrell, Don McLeod, Dick Miller, Steve Nevil, Herb Braha, Joe Bratcher.

Synopsis: Channel 6 news anchor Karen White tracks down an obscene phone caller who may also be a murderer. He corners her in an adult book and movie store, but the police arrive and shoot him. His name is Eddie Quist. Karen is traumatized by the events, so Dr. George Waggner recommends that she and her husband, Bill, go up the coast to "The Colony," where she can relax and engage in some group therapy. It's not as peaceful as she expected. Sexy Marsha makes a play for Bill. There are howls in the night, and some cattle are found mutilated. Back in the city, Terry and Chris find Eddie Quist's apartment and some artwork, most of it horrible portraits. They buy books on lycanthropy and the occult. Meanwhile, Bill is attacked in the dark and bitten. He visits Marsha and they make love. Both transform into werewolves. Terry drives up to the Colony. Visiting Marsha's cabin, she's assaulted, but severs the arm of her attacker. The hairy arm turns into a human hand. Terry returns to Dr. Waggner's office, calls Chris but is killed by a werewolf after a valiant defense. Karen is also attacked — by Eddie Quist — but throws acid into his face and escapes. Chris arrives bearing a rifle. Eddie takes Chris's gun but gives it back, not knowing there are silver bullets inside. Chris kills him. Karen is taken to a barn and learns that all of the people at the Colony are werewolves with the exception

Reporter Terry Fisher (Belinda Balaski) meets a werewolf in *The Howling* (Avco Embassy, 1981).

of Dr. Waggner, who hoped to keep them under control. They turn on him. Chris rescues Karen, shoots some of the monsters, including the sheriff, and sets the barn on fire. More attack the car and Karen is bitten but she and Chris make it to the city. She goes on the news and warns the audience about the hidden evil in mankind's midst. She transforms and Chris shoots her. Some viewers believe what they've seen, some don't. Marsha is shown in a bar.

Reviews: "The first half is dull ... and the second half is sparked mainly by some technically brilliant (and bloody and brutal) special effects." (David Sterritt, *Christian Science Monitor*, April 16, 1981, p. 18) ¶"The most refreshing horror film to brighten theater screens in years.... Dante's affection for his subject is evident in every frame." (Steve Vertlieb, *Cinemacabre*, no. 4, pp. 46–47) ¶"A suitably lurid horror-comic homage to the schlock-meisters of two generations." (Paul Taylor, *Monthly Film Bulletin*, June 1981, p. 114) ¶"What makes *The Howling* newsworthy is its exceptional monsters.... extraordinary transformation scenes." (Joseph Gelmis,

Newsday, March 13, 1981, Part II, p. 7) ¶"Fuels itself on a combination of perverse sexuality and genre send-up. The film is both comic and scary." (J. Hoberman, *Village Voice*, March 11–17, 1981, p. 48)

Analysis: The Howling was released in the same year as *An American Werewolf in London.* Although *American* had Jenny Agutter and terrific werewolf transformation, *The Howling* was more coherent and more responsive to werewolf cinema history. Note uncredited performances by director Roger Corman; fan, collector and publisher Forrest J Ackerman; and actor Dick Miller. Patrick Macnee and John Carradine played characters named George Waggner and Earle Kenton — real producer-directors of '40s Universal horror films. There are excellent spooky forest scenes. A feisty character, Belinda Balaski can't survive. Too bad. (Revolting chicken guts were sprinkled on Belinda to simulate deadly wounds.) At least there's no trick ending. Evil was quashed for the nonce, even if the Marsha character reappears. We already knew some werewolves survived the Colony's incineration.

Howling II ... Your Sister Is a Werewolf

(Hemdale/Thorn EMI/Granite Productions, 1986; 90 min.) **

Produced by Steven Lane. Directed by Philippe Mora. Screenplay, Robert Sarno, Gary Brandner. Based on the novel *Howling II* by Gary Brandner. Edited by Charles Bornstein. Director of Photography, Geoffrey Stephenson. Color. Music, Steve Parsons. Set Decoration, Milos Preclik. Special Effects Makeup, Jack Bricker.

Cast: Stefan Crosscoe (Christopher Lee), Stirba (Sybil Danning), Ben White (Reb Brown), Jenny Templeton (Annie McEnroe), Mariana (Marsha A. Hunt), Vlad (Judd Omen), Karen White (Hana Ludvikova), Erle (Ferdinand Mayne), Father Florin (Ladislav Krecmer), Vasile (Jiri Krytmar), Punk group (Babel).

Synopsis: "Los Angeles, California, U.S.A. City of the Angels." After the funeral of Karen White, occult investigator Stefan Crosscoe tries to convince the woman's skeptical brother Ben and Jenny Templeton that Karen was a werewolf and that there are more of them. Titanium stakes, not silver bullets, will destroy them, according to Stefan. He says their leader is a woman named Stirba and that the tenth millennium of her birth approaches. All werewolves will reveal themselves. Ben is convinced only upon finding werewolves near Karen's crypt, and he and Jenny agree to accompany Stefan to the "Dark Country," Transylvania. Stefan knows that if they follow Mariana, they will find Stirba. In her castle, the aged Stirba restores her youth by sucking the life from a young woman, then watches the mating of Mariana and a male werewolf. Jenny is captured and used as a lure for Stefan — Stirba's brother. Stirba knows Stefan is approaching and interrupts the castle revelry to dispatch her minions. They are beaten off, however, and Jenny is rescued. Stefan stabs Stirba with a titanium shaft and both go up in flames. Ben and Jenny leave the country.

Review: "Ridiculous sequel.... Attempt at sending up the genre falls flat." (Leonard Maltin, ed., *Movie and Video Guide 1993*, p. 567)

Analysis: The subtitle promises a tongue-in-cheek outing, but it's mostly serious and does follow directly from the first. Not that it's any good. The best things are the firefights at the cemetery and in the Transylvanian forest. Transformations are not fully shown. How can Stefan be the ancient Stirba's brother? Is he supernatural, too? Yes, Sybil Danning displays her ample breasts. Partially filmed in Czechoslovakia.

The Howling III

(Bancannia Entertainment/Square Pictures/Vista Home Video, 1987; 95 min.) **½

Produced by Charles Waterstreet and Philippe Mora. Directed by Philippe Mora. Story and screenplay by Philippe Mora. Based on the book *The Howling III* by Gary Brandner. Edited by Lee Smith. Director of Photography, Louis Irving. Panavision. Music, Allan Zavod. Dolby. Set Decoration, Brian Edmonds. Special Effects, Bob McCarron.

Cast: Professor Harry Beckmeyer (Barry Otto), Jerboa (Imogen Annesley), Professor Sharp (Ralph Cotterill), President of the United States (Michael Pate), Jack Citron (Frank Thring), Olga Gorki (Dasha Blahora), Thylo (Max Fairchild), Donny Martin (Leigh Biolos), Kendi (Burnham Burnham). With Barry Humphries.

Synopsis: Professor Beckmeyer shows his class a film made in Cape York, Australia, in 1905. Natives circle what one takes to be a woman in a wolf mask tied to a tree. Meanwhile, the U.S. National Intelligence Agency intercepts a KGB message about werewolves. Beckmeyer tells the president that werewolves do exist, in the Soviet Union and in Australia. Meanwhile, down under, the beauteous Jerboa leaves her people in the backwater village of Flow for life in the big city. Donny Martin employs her in Jack Citron's horror movie, *Shape Shifters, Part 8*. During a cast party, the flashing lights cause a transformation of Jerboa, who runs into the street and is hit by a car. In the hospital, doctors learn of her secret: she's a pregnant marsupial with a pouch for raising her young. Before the physicians can do anything, three werewolves dressed as nuns invade the hospital and carry Jerboa back to her "tribe." Having come to Australia, Beckmeyer and scientist Sharp observe a ballet rehearsal only to find the prima ballerina Olga Gorki turning into a werewolf. Donny follows the two scientists as they track her. In Flow, Jerboa gives birth to her half-human, half-wolf child. Olga arrives, attracted by the tribe's leader, Thylo. Donny locates Jerboa and they elude the army, which captures Thylo, Olga and the rest of the tribe. Beckmeyer hypnotizes Olga, who says she came from the snow. Thylo is quizzed, but flashing lights cause him to change and break loose until subdued by Sharp's tranquilizer gun. Later Thylo reveals that the last of the Tasmanian devils made his spirit enter those who became werewolves. Beckmeyer agrees to help Olga escape and with her and Thylo "goes bush." Before dying, Kendi kills the trackers of Jerboa and Donny. Thylo changes into a monstrous werewolf and kills two soldiers, though he dies himself. Sharp urges the president to stop the killing of this alien race. In the bush, Beckmeyer and Olga produce a girl child while Jerboa and Donny raise their son. One day Donny and Jerboa leave, planning to assume new identities in the big city. Years pass and Sharp finds Beckmeyer, telling him the president has endorsed the Pope's contention that we're all God's children. In Hollywood, Jerboa, aka actress Loretta Carson, and Donny have been making films. Beckmeyer, now teaching at the University of San Andreas, is approached by the grown son of Jerboa and Donny. Jerboa wins an acting award, but when the flashes of the photographers go off, she begins changing.

Reviews: "Assertively boring film…. bypasses every potentially original avenue." (Bill Kelley, *Cinefantastique*, May 1988, p. 52) ¶"Campy recycling of familiar fangoria that is fitfully entertaining." (Kevin Thomas, *Los Angeles Times Calendar*, November 13, 1987, p. 12) ¶"A tongue-in-cheek parody of the genre, handled with lots of verve and affection by Philippe Mora." (Strat., *Variety*, May 20, 1987)

Analysis: Made in Australia, it's mostly set there, but they ask us to believe Michael Pate is the president of the United States. Australian-born Pate was one of the great purveyors of American Indian mayhem in '50s and '60s Hollywood westerns. (See *Hondo* and *Major Dundee* in particular.) He was also the vampire gunslinger in *Curse of the Undead*. Frank Thring, now, is another interesting fellow. Here he's playing a pseudo–Hitchcock character — and even looks like the late director. Remember Aella, the wicked king in *The Vikings* (1958)? Pontius Pilate in *Ben-Hur* (1959)? Herod in *King of Kings* (1961)? The evil lord of Valencia in *El Cid* (1961)? That's Thring. As for *Howling III*, it doesn't know when to end. If it did, one might be tempted to raise the rating a half star. Imogen Annesley is one of the most attractive of cinema werewolves. Photography is good. Werewolf transformations are acceptable but not state-of-the-art. This can be viewed as a straight film or taken tongue-in-cheek. It manages to straddle the line, providing some chills and not a few smirks. Aka *The Marsupials*. This could be paired with 1982's *Cat People*.

Howling IV: The Original Nightmare
(Allied Entertainment, 1988; 94 min.) **

Produced by Harry Alan Towers. Co-Producer, Clive Turner. Directed by John Hough. Story, Clive Turner. Based on the books *The Howling I, II, III* by Gary Brandner. Director of Photography, Godfrey Godar. Music, David George. Sound Editing, Sound Busters.

Cast: Marie Adams (Romy Windsor), Richard (Michael T. Weiss), Janice (Susanne Sevareid), Tom Billings (Antony Hamilton).

Synopsis: When her doctor tells writer Marie she can dispel her nightmares by taking a rest, friend Tom drives her to a cabin near the quiet town of Drago. There she meets her husband, Richard, but continues having nightmares. Her dog disappears into what she perceives as sinister woods. Janice, a former nun, visits and mentions Sister Ruth, who heard howling like Marie. Two hikers are killed in a stream by a werewolf-like thing. Richard, meanwhile, has become enamored of a town shopkeeper and mates with her. Marie shoots at a "wolf." Richard is attacked by the shopkeeper turned werewolf.

The next day the doctor says Richard merely fell, and Richard himself denies the attack. Tom arrives and is struck by Richard for making a pass at Marie. Tom finds Janice at the Twin Forks Hotel and learns that Sister Ruth was the daughter of the couple who lived in the cabin. Obviously the townsfolk are hiding something. Tom is attacked. Richard disintegrates but is restored as a werewolf. All the townsfolk become werewolves. When Janice rings the bell and summons the monsters to the church, Marie sets the building on fire.

Review: "A turkey in wolf's clothing." (Leonard Maltin, ed., *Movie and Video Guide 1993*, p. 568)

Analysis: It's a mite plodding and while not entirely bad, you wouldn't care to see it twice. Our "fair" rating is generous.

Howling V: The Rebirth
(Allied Vision, 1989; 99 min.) **

Produced by Clive Turner. Directed by Neal Sundstrom. Original Story, Clive Turner. Screenplay, Clive Turner and Freddie Rowe. Based on the books *The Howling I, II, III* by Gary Brandner. Edited by Claudia Finkle and Bill Swenson. Director of Photography, Arledge Armenaki. Music, The Factory. Production Designer, Nigel Triffitt.

Cast: The Count (Philip Davis), Marylou Summers (Elizabeth She), David (Ben Cole), Richard (William Shockley), Anna (Mary Stavin), Ray (Clive Turner), Gail (Stephanie Faulkner), Dr. Catherine (Victoria Catlin).

Synopsis: Budapest, 1489: In a castle, a prince kills his wife and himself after all the dinner guests have been murdered. Hearing the cry of a baby he thought dead, he cries that all was in vain. Budapest, 1989: Four men and four women from various parts of the world gather at the Ramada Grand Hotel. They include writers, a professional U.S. tennis player, a British photographer, a Scandinavian film actress, and an American waitress who aspires to be an actress. They have won a contest to be present at the opening of a castle closed for 500 years. A count is their guide. At the castle a ninth member, a professor, investigates old rooms and is assaulted. Gail is next. The rest form search parties through labyrinthine passages. Fears of a set-up concern some members. The count finally admits that a werewolf is responsible, and he discloses that all of them are related to the castle's original inhabitants, who'd become werewolves. The surviving baby of 1489 passed on his satanic inheritance. One of the guests is a true werewolf who must be destroyed. Seemingly convinced that the count is the monster, the apparently brainless Marylou ("The devil was a werewolf. Wow, that's incredible!") shoots him. Comforted by the only remaining member of the group, she smiles knowingly at the camera as the full moon emerges from cloud cover.

Review: "Much better than II or IV.... some suspense, OK performances, and a genuine surprise at the end." (Leonard Maltin, ed., *Movie and Video Guide 1993*, p. 568)

Analysis: An initially well-mounted, interesting castle film seems dumber upon reflection. Except for the Budapest scenes at the beginning, little expense was lavished on the production, most of which takes place in dark rooms and passages. The guests are stupid, running off in all directions instead of sticking together. If they all have the mark, how come only one is a werewolf? What was Marylou doing back in the States? There are no transformations, needless to say, since we are not allowed to know the monster until the final minute — although we can identify the culprit about ten minutes before fade-out.

Howling VI: The Freaks
(Allied Vision/Lane Pringle, 1990)
**½

Produced by Robert Pringle. Directed by Hope Rebello. Screenplay by Kevin Rock. Based upon the series of books, *The Howling I, II, III* by Gary Brandner. Edited by Adam Wolfe. Director of Photography, Edward Pei. Color, Foto-Kem. Music, Patrick Gleeson. Ultra-Stereo. Harker and Winston Effects, Steve Johnson. Special Makeup Effects, Todd Masters Company. Special Effects Coordinator, John P. Cazin.

Cast: Ian Richards (Brendan Hughes), Lizzie (Michele Matheson),Harker (Bruce Martyn Payne), Winston (Sean Gregory Sullivan), Sheriff Faller (Carlos Cervantes), Bellamey (Antonio Fargas), Miss Eddington

(Carol Lynley), Mary Lou (Elizabeth She). With Jered Barclay.

Synopsis: Englishman Ian Richards arrives in the small western town of Canton Bluff and helps spruce up the church. Arriving soon after is Harker's Worlds of Wonder carnival, which counts among its members a three-armed midget; a half-man, half-woman; a geek; and Winston, the scaly-necked "Alligator Boy." Harker, the strange carny owner, thinks he remembers Ian from some time past. Discovering that Ian can be transformed into a werewolf under the full moon through incantation, he captures and adds him to the freak show. Escaping, Ian is finally cornered. Still, the citizens are loath to shoot him, which prompts Harker to lose his composure and turn into a vampire beast. He pursues the human Ian through the carny grounds and exhibits. Winston helps Ian transform and fight off his nemesis. After driving a metal stake into the vampire, Ian pulls down a portion of the tent to let in the rising sun's rays. The vampire disintegrates. Ian and Winston leave town together.

Review: "Intelligently written ... but pretentious.... Awkward and confusing...." (Leonard Maltin, ed., *Movie and Video Guide 1993*, p. 568)

Analysis: Not bad, not bad at all. The vampire is an imposing beast, truly terrifying. Rising from his lair in a trailer to attack the mayor, he reminds us of the vampire popping out of the grave onto Thalmus Rasulala in *Blacula*. His demise is excellent. There are good werewolf transformations as well. The werewolf's face is more human than wolfish. Oftentimes we prefer this. (What we really object to are werewolves that run on all fours. This usually translates into the use of German shepherds.) The end credits list Elizabeth She as Mary Lou (sic), the actress and character from *Howling V*, but where was she in this film? Did we miss something? Carol Lynley's part is negligible.

Hungry Pets *see* Please Don't Eat My Mother *under* **The Little Shop of Horrors**

I, Monster *see under* **Dr. Jekyll and Mr. Hyde**

I Was a Teenage Frankenstein *see under* **Frankenstein**

I Was a Teenage Werewolf
(1957; 76 min.) ***

Produced by Herman Cohen. Directed by Gene Fowler Jr. Screenplay, Ralph Thornton. Edited by George Gittens. Director of Photography, Joseph LaShelle. Music, Paul Dunlap. Art Direction, Leslie Thomas. Set Decoration, Morris Hoffman.

Cast: Tony Rivers (Michael Landon), Dr. Alfred Brandon (Whit Bissell), Arlene (Yvonne Lime), Charles (Malcolm Atterbury), Pepi (Vladimir Sokoloff), Miss Ferguson (Louise Lewis), Doyle (Eddie Marr), Jimmy (Tony Marshall), Vic (Ken Miller), Chris Stanley (Guy Williams), Police Chief Baker (Robert Griffin), Bill (S. John Launer), Theresa (Dawn Richards), Detective Donovan (Barney Phillips), Dr. Hugo Wagner (Joseph Mell), Pearl (Cindy Robbins), Mary (Dorothy Crehan), Frank (Michael Rougas).

Synopsis: Rebellious teenager Tony, a student at Rockdale High School, is sent to Dr. Alfred Brandon, but the psychiatrist realizes Tony is a prime candidate to test his evolutionary theories: "Through hypnosis I'm gonna regress this boy back, back into the primitive past that lurks within him. I'm gonna transform him and unleash the savage instincts that lie hidden within." Later, "Then I'll be judged the benefactor. Mankind is on the verge of destroying itself. The only hope for the human race is to hurl it back into its primitive dawn, to start all over again. What's one life compared to such a triumph?" The day after Tony is hypnotized, he turns into a werewolf, killing a boy in the woods and a girl practicing on the parallel bars in the school gym. Chased, he kills a dog, turns back into Tony, then seeks safe haven at Dr. Brandon's. Although he has a premonition of being killed, he implores Brandon not to let them find him in his lycanthropic state. The doctor is hardly moved. Hypnotized again, Tony becomes the monster and kills Brandon and his assistant. The police arrive, and Tony is killed.

Review: "Though rarely dignified with newspaper or magazine reviews, the programs whipped up by AIP are welcome news to box offices. The accent is on youth, the beat is rock and roll, the tempo is violent.... The low budget special effects are woeful.... The picture ... will do well. Long-sideburns and the fangs: it's an unbeatable combo." (Charles Shapiro, *New Republic*, August 26, 1957, p. 22)

Analysis: Before his stint as Little Joe on TV's *Bonanza*, Michael Landon had some "important" movie roles. His role as a werewolf is, of course, well known to a generation of science fiction movie fans. (The following year he'd play an albino in *God's Little Acre*.) Whit Bissell, master pipe smoker, is a mad scientist with fantastic lines. Of this and *I Was a Teenage Frankenstein*, Bissell said to Marty Rybicki ("Interview: Whit Bissell," *Bits n Pieces*, Summer 1990, p. 24), "I don't think I have a favorite between those two. I'm just amazed that they're still showing them. When I did them I just thought of it as a job, you know? We never had any idea that they were going to turn out to be cult classics.... Some of the lines kill me!" The most famous scene has to be the confrontation between the leotard-clad gymnast and the slavering werewolf. This is the science fiction version of the James Dean classic *Rebel Without a Cause* (1955). Paired with *Invasion of the Saucermen*.

Teen Wolf
(Atlantic, 1985; 91 min.) ***

Produced by Mark Levinson and Scott M. Rosenfelt. Directed by Rod Daniel. Screenplay, Joseph Loeb III and Matthew Weisman. Edited by Lois Freeman-Fox. Director of Photography, Tim Suhrstedt. Panavision. Color, United Color Lab. Music, Miles Goodman. Original song lyrics, Douglas Brayfield. Art Direction, Chester Kaczenski. Set Decoration, Rosemary Brandenberg. Special Makeup Effects, The Burman Studios.

Cast: Scott Howard (Michael J. Fox), Harold Howard (James Hampton), Lisa "Boof" Marconi (Susan Ursitti), Rupert "Stiles" Stilinsky (Jerry Levine), Lewis Erikson (Matt Adler), Pamela Wells (Lorie Griffin), Russell Thorne (James MacKrell), Mick McAllister (Mark Arnold), Chubby (Mark Holton), Coach Finstock (Jay Tarses), Kirk Lolley (Scott Paulin).

Synopsis: The Beavers high school basketball team loses its first game of the season 71-12. Scott Howard doesn't like the score or the town and doesn't want to end up working in his father's hardware store the rest of his life. Complicating matters, he can hear dog whistles, and his hands sprout excessive hair. In front of his bathroom mirror he becomes a werewolf. When he opens the door, he finds that his father, too, is a werewolf. His dad says he hoped this had skipped a generation. Scott is not amused. He demonstrates his "ability" to Stiles, who though initially shocked quickly realizes they can turn this into something "monstrous." During a basketball game, Scott transforms. He takes the ball and continues playing, scoring at will and gaining the attention of the desirable Pamela — to Boof's annoyance. Scott becomes the school's idol and gets a big head. Pamela seduces him in the dressing room after play rehearsal. After they go bowling together, Scott learns that Pamela spreads her attentions around. The team becomes irritated with Scott's penchant for hogging the ball. Scott's father tells him he's making a fool of himself, then relates how he turned into a werewolf in front of now vice principal Thorne when they were students. He urges Scott to control his power. Scott refuses Boof's plea to attend the dance as himself. At the dance, Boof convinces Scott to change back to human form for a half hour. When Pamela's boyfriend Mick slugs him, Scott changes and rips Mick's shirt. In the hall, Thorne tells Scott he'll be kicked out. Scott's father appears and solves that situation. When Scott decides to do his part in the play as himself, the director says wolf only. Scott decides to drop off the team before the championship game. Stiles tells him to do the right thing, which Scott says is all he wants to do. He dresses for the game as Scott and gives the team a pep talk. Chubby makes a long basket and gets a rebound on the other end. The team fights back and wins, 52-51. Scott hugs Boof.

Reviews: "Essentially a moral tale, *Teen Wolf* is not so much an up-date of *I Was a Teenage Werewolf* as a reworking of the Jekyll and Hyde story or, more pertinently, *The Nutty Professor*." (Anne Billson, *Monthly Film Bulletin*, February 1986, p. 50) ¶"Fox, a talented young actor ... is perfect as the teen wolf, playing the part with youthful vigor." (Bill Kaufman, *Newsday*, August 23, 1985, Part III, p. 3) *Analysis:* It is *not* a horror story, nor even a horror comedy. It is about growing up and learning to be true to yourself. Scott is probably a lycanthrope because the writers thought a werewolf would be quick. The music, both vocal and instrumental, is good. The final basketball game is as well done and as realistic as we can remember in any movie. Fox is the right choice for his role. Cute Susan Ursitti is delightfully spunky. Why haven't we seen more of her? There was a *Teen Wolf* TV cartoon series for a couple of seasons.

Teen Wolf Too
(Atlantic, 1987; 99 min.) **

Produced by Kent Bateman. Directed by Christopher Leitch. Assistant Director, Tana Maners. Screenplay, R. Timothy Kring. Story, Joseph Loeb III and Matthew Weisman. Based on characters created by Joseph Loeb III and Matthew Weisman. Edited by Steven Polivka, Kim Secrist, Harvey Rosenstock, Raja Gosnell. Director of Photography, Jules Brenner. Color, Consolidated Film Industries. Music, Mark Goldenberg. Dolby Stereo. Art Direction, Peg McClellan. Set Decoration, Cynthia McCormac. Wolf Makeup, John Logan, Michael Smithson.

Cast: Todd Howard (Jason Bateman), Professor Tonya Brooks (Kim Darby), Dean Dunn (John Astin), Coach Finstock (Paul Sand), Uncle Howard (James Hampton), Chubby (Mark Holton), Nicki (Estee Chandler), Stiles (Stuart Fratkin), Emily (Rachel Sharp), Lisa (Beth Ann Miller), Gustavson (Robert Neary), Admissions lady (Kathleen Freeman).

Synopsis: Dean Dunn plans to bring glory back to Hamilton State University. Phase one is a winning boxing team. Coach Finstock recruits Todd Howard, cousin of Scott Howard. Uncle Howard drives Todd to college. Todd is told to keep his possibilities open. He rooms with Scott's pal Stiles and meets another of Scott's chums, Chubby. Intimidated by an administrator when he wants to change the classes Stiles signed him up for, Todd's eyes blaze and his voice deepens. He gets the changes and also gets into Professor Tonya Brooks's class. He wants to be a vet-

erinarian and needs her class. She is also his advisor. Todd tells Coach Finstock he's not like Scott. He's urged to show up for boxing at least once; that way he'll get his scholarship. During a scholarship student reception, Todd gets riled and for the first time turns into a werewolf. Stiles is elated but students harass Todd. Professor Brooks offers her help, and classmate Nicki consoles him. During his first boxing match, Todd turns into a werewolf and wins. That evening at a bash Todd the wolf sings and dances. Fame goes to his head. Professor Brooks tells Todd he must use his gift wisely. When both Nicki and Stiles reject him, Todd seeks assistance from Uncle Howard, who gives him advice and shows him some boxing moves. Nicki helps him study for the makeup biology exam. Professor Brooks succeeds in making Dean Dunn lay off Todd by starting her own transformation into a wolf.

Reviews: "Lame jokes.... another howlingly bad comedy-fantasy: a dog in wolf's clothing." (Michael Wilmington, *Los Angeles Times Calendar*, November 20, 1987, p. 14) ¶"Provides more than a few wacky moments." (Bill Kaufman, *Newsday*, November 20, 1987, Part III, p. 5) ¶"What we have here is a failure of imagination." (Roger Ebert, *New York Post*, November 20, 1987, p. 40)

Analysis: No new roads are taken. In short, it might as well be a remake as a sequel. The boxing matches are not as authentic as the basketball game in the first film. Weight class is ignored, the referee permits illegal punches, cheerleaders urge the fighters on, and there's a card girl (though far be it from us to complain about the lissome Rachel Sharp). Returning from the *Teen Wolf* cast are James Hampton and Mark Holton.

Indiana Jones and the Last Crusade *see under* **Raiders of the Lost Ark**

Indiana Jones and the Temple of Doom *see under* **Raiders of the Lost Ark**

Island of Dr. Moreau *see under* **Island of Lost Souls**

The Innocents

(20th Century–Fox/Achilles Film, 1961; 99 min.) ***

Produced and directed by Jack Clayton. Screenplay, William Archibald and Truman Capote. Additional Material, John Mortimer. Based on the novel *The Turn of the Screw* by Henry James and the play *The Innocents* by William Archibald. Edited by James Clark. Director of Photography, Freddie Francis. CinemaScope. Music, Georges Auric. Song: "O Willow Waly," Georges Auric and Paul Dehn. Art Direction, Wilfred Shingleton. Set Dresser, Peter James. Costumes, Sophie Devine. Costume Design, Motley. Makeup, Harold Fletcher.

Cast: Miss Giddens (Deborah Kerr), Flora (Pamela Franklin), Miles (Martin Stephens), Mrs. Grose (Megs Jenkins), Uncle (Michael Redgrave), Peter Quint (Peter Wyngarde), Anne (Isla Cameron), Miss Mary Jessel (Clytie Jessop), Coachman (Eric Woodburn).

Synopsis: Hired by the uncle of Flora and Miles, Miss Giddens comes to Bly House to be the children's governess. Miss Giddens loves children and expects this, her first employment, to be splendid, even though the childrens' uncle wishes her to handle all affairs at Bly House without *ever* asking for his assistance or advice. Flora is a darling, but a letter preceding her brother says Miles is being expelled from school for corrupting his classmates. How can this be? Miles is perfectly adorable. Miss Giddens is next disturbed by a nameless man and woman she sees mucking about the grounds. To her horror, Miss Giddens is informed by Mrs. Grose, the housekeeper, that the images she describes match those of Peter Quint and Miss Jessel. Quint was the former valet of the childrens' late father and Miss Jessel their governess. Both Quint and Jessel are dead. The man had fallen; the grieving Miss Jessel drowned herself. Miss Giddens learns that they had consorted lewdly with each other — and worked their mischief in some way on the children. Miss Giddens believes the ghosts have returned to possess the children. Hoping to exorcise their power, she tries to make her charges speak of Quint and Jessel, but Flora becomes upset and Mrs. Grose takes her away. Alone with Miles, Miss Giddens urges him to admit Peter Quint's spirit roams Bly House. In the garden that night, Miss Giddens' efforts cause Miles to become frantic. He screams, "Quint!" To the governess's horror, the child falls dead.

Reviews: "Points up again the growing artistry of a new generation of film makers abroad.... Superbly effective, wholly evocative score supplied by Georges Auric ... puts the final polish to this perfect gem." (Arthur Knight, *Saturday Review*, December 23, 1961, p. 39) ¶"The main performances are most capably carried off.... Truman Capote and Playwright Archibald unhappily press hard, much harder than James did, for the psychiatric interpretation." (*Time*, January 5, 1962, p. 59)

Analysis: Arresting cinematography highlights an impeccable production that surprisingly did not earn Deborah Kerr yet another Academy Award nomination. The only problem with the film is that there may be no malevolent spirits at all, but merely figments of Miss Giddens's disturbed imagination. No ghosts? We realize there are some doubts about James's novel on this score, but we thought current opinion was that the supernatural entities *are* likely to inhabit Bly House. An excellent haunted house double feature would pair this with 1963's *The Haunting*. For a triple feature, add *The Legend of Hell House* (1974), starring the grown-up Pamela Franklin.

Notes of Interest: Henry James' novel *The Turn of the Screw* was published in 1898. William Archibald's play *The Innocents* opened in New York in 1950.

The Nightcomers

(Avco Embassy, 1972; 96 min.) ***

Produced and directed by Michael Winner. Screenplay, Michael Hastings. Based on characters from *The Turn of the Screw* by Henry James. Edited by Freddie Wilson. Director of Photography, Robert Paynter. Technicolor. Music, Jerry Fielding. Art Direction, Herbert Westbrook.

Cast: Peter Quint (Marlon Brando), Margaret Jessel (Stephanie Beacham), Mrs. Grose (Thora Hird), Flora (Verna Harvey), Miles (Christopher Ellis), Tutor (Harry Andrews), Governess (Anna Palk).

Synopsis: Their parents accidentally killed, Miles and Flora are left in the care

Miss Giddens (Deborah Kerr, left) tries to reason with Flora (Pamela Franklin) in *The Innocents* (Twentieth Century–Fox, 1961).

of nanny and instructor Miss Jessel and housekeeper Mrs. Grose. Once a valet, the rough-hewn Peter Quint is now instructed to make himself useful in the garden and at whatever else might need attention. Flora and Miles get some insight into life from Quint. He, in fact, is the only adult to tell them of their parents' death. He says there is no Heaven or Hell for the dead. Miles observes Quint in Miss Jessel's room, where Quint ties her up and incorporates pain into their lovemaking. After Mrs. Grose discovers dolls Quint made for the children — hers has pins stuck in it — she forbids him entrance to the house. The children plan a rendezvous for Quint and Jessel. This time Jessel is the aggressor, but when she answers his request to stay with him by commenting on his pigsty, he slaps her. Next day Mrs. Grose notices the nanny's bruises. They hear the children fighting. They are acting out the parts of Quint and Jessel. Later Quint tells them that if you really love someone, you really

want to kill them. Miss Jessel prepares to leave for good, but the children tell her Quint is waiting for her on the pond's island. Miles had put holes in the rowboat, and Jessel, who can't swim, drowns. Flora observes and says, "We don't want you to go." Next day Quint finds Jessel's body on the shore. Grief-stricken, he stumbles off until Miles shoots two arrows into him and shoves the body into the marsh. He and Flora believe the spirits of Quint and Jessel will meet. A new governess arrives at Bly House.

Reviews: "A film that rightly savors the neglected technique of dissolves.... The structure, too, is neat — one might almost call it an aptly old-fashioned example of the 'well-made' screenplay, especially when scenes on a boating lake and at archery practice are developed shrewdly for the hair-raising climax." (Gordon Gow, *Films and Filming*, May 1972, p. 49).

Analysis: While there are no supernatural elements here, this prequel sets the stage for the ghosts of the future. There *are* horrifying moments, especially Quint's discovery of Miss Jessel's drowned corpse. The countryside of Cambridgeshire is totally appropriate. Marlon Brando was in the cinematic doldrums when he made this, but would soon enter a new and important phase as *The Godfather*. Stephanie Beacham was the female lead in *Dracula A.D. 1972* the same year.

Invaders from Mars
(20th Century–Fox/Edward L. Alperson, 1953; 78 min.) ***½

Produced by Edward L. Alperson. Directed by William Cameron Menzies. Assistant Directors, Ben Chapman, Leonard Kunody, Wesley Barry. Screenplay, Richard Blake, John Tucker Battle, William Cameron Menzies. Edited by Arthur Roberts. Director of Photography, John F. Seitz. Color. Music, Raoul Kraushaar. Music Editor, Richard Harris. Sound, Earl Crane, Sr. Art Direction, Boris Leven. Set Decoration, Eddie Boyle. Production Manager, Ben Chapman. Special Mechanical Effects and Miniatures, Theodore Lydecker. Opticals and Mattes, Jack Rabin and Irving Block. Special Costumes, Norma Koch. Makeup, Gene Hibbs and Steve Drum. Special Makeup for Martian in Globe, Anatole Robbins.

Cast: Dr. Pat Blake (Helena Carter), Dr. Stuart Kelston (Arthur Franz), David MacLean (Jimmy Hunt), George MacLean (Leif Erickson), Mary MacLean (Hillary Brooke), Colonel Fielding (Morris Ankrum), Sergeant Rinaldi (Max Wagner), Captain Roth (Milburn Stone), Major Cleary (Bill Phipps), Officer Blaine (Charles Kane), Chief Barrows (Bert Freed), Sergeant Finley (Walter Sande), Dr. William Wilson (Robert Shayne), Kathy Wilson (Janine Perreau), Officer Jackson (Douglas Kennedy), Brainard (Peter Brocco), Secretary (Barbara Billingsley), General Mayberry (William Forrest), Chief of staff (Frank Wilcox), Sentry Regan (Richard Deacon), Martian in globe (Luce Potter), Mu-tants (Max Palmer, Lock Martin), Stand-ins and doubles (Billy Curtis, Harry Monty, Paul Klatt, Tommy Cotonaro, George Spotts, Buster Resmukndi).

Synopsis: Waking during the night, young David MacLean spots a flying saucer. His father, George, goes out to investigate and returns in a surly mood,

backhanding David when questioned too much. David notices something on the back of his father's neck. The two policemen who went looking for George return and act strangely. Later George takes his wife, Mary, to the sand pit. Meanwhile, David, who'd seen little Kathy disappear into the ground, tries to convince her mother of the fact. But Kathy shows up at the door. She too has a strange device on her neck. David tries to make the police understand what's happening, but it becomes obvious Chief Barrows has been seduced by the aliens. However, psychologist Dr. Pat Blake takes David in tow and refuses to turn him over to his parents, suggesting that he might have been exposed to polio. Pat and David visit astronomer Dr. Stuart Kelston. He listens attentively and discusses the possibility of life in outer space. Perhaps there are advanced life forms, possibly mu-tants to do the bidding of higher powers. Kelston calls the military and speaks with Colonel Fielding. The military are not unresponsive, and Fielding calls in tanks and infantry to surround the sand pits. His aide, Sergeant Rinaldi, investigates and falls into the underground chamber. Fielding's sappers blow their own entrance. The army enters and wages war with tall, large-eyed mu-tants who have captured Pat and David. Just in time, the psychologist is saved from a neck implant. The controlling alien — a tentacled head in a globe — directs a strategic retreat. Next evening David wakes again and sees — a flying saucer!

Reviews: "Suspenseful story.... maximum physical values from what appears to be a medium budget." (Gilb., *Variety*, April 8, 1953) ¶"Will probably frighten witless a lot of small children." (O.A.G., *New York Times*, May 30, 1953, p. 7)

Analysis: This film gives some people stomach aches. It probably has to do with the bug-eyed Martians with zippers up their backs. Yet if one views it as a dream, which it is, all of this nonsense makes sense. There are a number of fascinating moments: the tentacled Martian leader's head in a ball, the nape of Helena Carter's neck toward which the implant is directed,

Luce Potter is the alien in *Invaders from Mars* (Twentieth Century–Fox, 1953).

the music accompanying the people's disappearance into the sand, and Carter's line, "Moo-tants. What would they want here?" Beautiful Carter's character is an innocent — but a quick study. Arthur Franz's pipe-smoking astronomer is a veritable savant. William Cameron Menzies had worked on *Gone with the Wind*. His production design gives the film a unique look. A flaw: too much tinted stock footage of military hardware.

Invaders from Mars
(Cannon, 1986, 94 min.) **½

Produced by Menahem Golan and Yoram Globus. Associate Producers, Edward L. Alperson, Jr., Wade H. Williams III. Directed by Tobe Hooper. Screenplay, Dan O'Bannon and Don Jakoby. Based on a screenplay by Richard Blake. Edited by Alain Jakubowicz. Director of Photography, Daniel Pearl. Color. Music, Christopher Young. Additional Music, David Storrs. Art Direction, Craig Stearns.

Set Decoration, Randy Moore, Cricket Rowland, Portia Iversen. Special Visual Effects, John Dykstra. Invader Creatures, Stan Winston. Special Effects, Robert Shepherd and Phil Corey. Special Martian Vocal Effects, Ron Bartlett, Jim Cushinery, Craig Bodkin, Tony Campisi.

Cast: David Gardner (Hunter Carson), Linda (Karen Black), George Gardner (Timothy Bottoms), Ellen Gardner (Laraine Newman), General Wilson (James Karen), NASA scientist (Bud Cort), Mrs. McKeltch (Louise Fletcher), Sergeant Rinaldi (Eric Pierpoint), Captain Curtis (Christopher Allport), Scientists (Donald Hotton, William Bassett), Chief (Jimmy Hunt), Heather (Virginia Keehne), Officer Kenney (Kenneth Kimmins), Mr. Cross (Charlie Dell), Kevin (Chris Hebert), Doug (Mason Nupuf), Ed (William Frankfather), M.P.s (Joseph Brutsman, Eric Norris), Johnson (Mark Giardino), Corporal Walker (Debra Berger), Hollis (Eddy Donno), Classmates (Daryl Bartley, Roy Mansano, Shonda Whipple, Amy Fitzpatrick, Shawn Campbell, Brett Johnson).

Synopsis: After David Gardner and his

Mrs. McKeltch (Louise Fletcher) attempts to stop David (Hunter Carson) from fleeing the Martians in *Invaders from Mars* (Cannon, 1986).

father, George, watch shooting stars one night, David sees a spacecraft that lands over the hill in a sand pit. His father investigates. Next morning George acts strange, and David notices a wound in the back of his neck. His mother begins acting strange next morning, serving black bacon. He notices that his teacher, Mrs. McKeltch, has a neck device, and he catches her swallowing a large frog whole. Nurse Linda befriends him. He follows Mrs. McKeltch into a tunnel near the sand pit and discovers Martians. Escaping, he finds Linda. They get to the NASA base where David's father works and try to convince General Wilson of their story. When two men with strange metal cylinders are foiled in their attempt to assassinate the general, the officer begins to believe David. He's convinced when a tank truck rams the missile due to send a satellite to investigate Mars. As some scientists suggest, perhaps under the Martian surface are beings that do not want visitors. Wilson orders out the troops and they invade the sand pit, killing the Martian drones and forcing their master to retreat. David is rescued, as is Linda, who'd been sucked into the pit. David's father and mother survive when the pit is blown up

and the Martian spacecraft destroyed during its takeoff. Yet David awakes again and sees a craft landing over the hill.

Reviews: "Except for Menzies' superb production design, everything in the remake is better: the acting, the camera work, definitely the Martians." (Michael Wilmington, *Los Angeles Times Calendar*, June 5, 1986, p. 1) ¶"Incredibly, Tobe Hooper and scriptwriters Dan O'Bannon and Don Jakoby ... are so faithful to their course that they reproduce all [the original's] faults along with some of its virtues." (Kim Newman, *Monthly Film Bulletin*, September 1986, p. 274)

Analysis: With all the behind-the-scenes talent involved, one would hope for an experience to equal the original. Not so. There are too many daylight shots. It becomes rather tongue-in-cheek near the end; witness Karen's lines like "Marines have no qualms about killing Martians." This was another here-today, gone-tomorrow film. Nobody cared.

Invasion Earth 2150 A.D. *see* Daleks' Invasion Earth 2150 A.D. *under* **Dr. Who and the Daleks**

Invasion of the Body Snatchers

(Allied Artists, 1956; 80 min.) ****

Produced by Walter Wanger. Directed by Don Siegel. Screenplay, Daniel Geoffrey Homes Mainwaring. Based on the *Collier's* magazine serial, later novel *The Body Snatchers*, by Jack Finney. Edited by Robert S. Eisen. Director of Photography, Ellsworth Fredericks. SuperScope. Music, Carmen Dragon. Art Direction, Ted Haworth. Set Decoration, Joseph Kish. Makeup, Emile La Vigne. Special Effects, Milt Rice.

Cast: Dr. Miles Bennell (Kevin McCarthy), Becky Driscoll (Dana Wynter), Dr. Dan Kaufman (Larry Gates), Theodora Belichec (Carolyn Jones), Jack Belichec (King Donovan), Sheriff Nick Grivett (Ralph Dumke), Nurse Sally (Jean Willes), Ira Lentz (Tom Fadden), Wilma Lentz (Virginia Christine), Grandma Grimaldi (Beatrice Maude), Jimmy Grimaldi (Bobby Clark), Grimaldi (Harry J. Vejar), Charlie Buckholtz (Sam Peckinpah), Dr. Harvey Bassett (Richard Deacon), Dr. Hill (Whit Bissell), Policeman (Guy Way), Mr. Driscoll (Kenneth Patterson), Aunt Eleda (Jean Andrew), Dr. Ed Pursey (Everett Blass), Mac (Dabbs Greer), Sam Janzek (Gay Way), Baggage man (Pat O'-Malley), Proprietor (Guy Rennie), Martha (Marie Selland). With Eileen Steens.

Synopsis: Called away from a physicians' convention by his nurse in Santa Mira, Dr. Bennell learns that his high school sweetheart Becky Driscoll is back in town. That's the good news. The bad news is that little Jimmy Grimaldi swears his mother isn't his mother, and Wilma Lentz believes her Uncle Ira isn't really her uncle; there's no emotion there. Psychiatrist Dan Kaufman tells Miles that it's a form of mass hysteria. Then Jack Belichec phones Miles and asks him to come out to their place. On Jack's pool table is a body. Is it dead? There are no fingerprints. Miles leaves, but Theodora sees the body open its eyes and notices its hand is bleeding where Jack had a cut. She and Jack go to Miles, who rushes to Becky's house and carries her away. When they return to Jack's house the body is gone. Miles calls Kaufman, and he and Jack go to Becky's to inspect the basement bin in which Miles said he saw a Becky duplicate. There's nothing there. The sheriff arrives and says the body on Jack's pool table was

found in a burning haystack. Kaufman tells Miles he's in the grip of the mass hysteria. But back at Miles's house, while he, Becky and the Belichecs barbecue, they hear something strange in the greenhouse and discover four pods splitting open to reveal their own likenesses. Miles attempts to call the authorities but can't get through; obviously the lines are controlled by the aliens. Jack and Theodora leave while Miles and Becky go to Sally's. Through the window Miles sees that his nurse, too, has been replaced by a pod person. He fights off the sheriff, and he and Becky flee to his office. From the window on the square they observe trucks of pods distributed to "people" who will spread them to their relatives in other communities. They hear voices, one of which is Jack's. But when they let him in they learn that he's not Jack anymore. Kaufman insists that Miles and Becky will soon realize that this human life of fear and pain should be eschewed in favor of the alien life they now have no choice but to welcome. Left alone, Miles prepares hypodermic needles and injects Jack and Dan. Becky does the same to the sheriff. They pretend to be converted when outside, but Becky betrays her humanness by crying out when a dog is almost hit by a truck. Miles and Becky are pursued by the townsfolk into the hills, where they hide in a mine until nightfall. Hearing singing, Miles investigates, only to learn that it's coming from a radio on a truck that's being filled with pods. When he returns to the cave, he finds that Becky has fallen asleep and is no longer human. He flees, finds the main highway, and attempts to make drivers listen to his fantastic story: "Look! You fools! You're in danger! Can't you see? They're after you! They're after all of us! Our wives, our children, everyone! They're here already! You're next! You're next! You're next! You're next! You're next!" At a hospital he is no more successful until a man injured in a traffic accident is brought in and the orderly says they had to pull him from beneath a bunch of pods. The psychiatrist calls the FBI.

Reviews: "The horrors and build-up of tension are extraordinarily well done…. Because the horrors are not senseless sensationalism but have a real value, the film

Miles (Kevin McCarthy) and Becky (Dana Wynter) hide from the pod people in *Invasion of the Body Snatchers* (Allied Artists, 1956).

will also give entertainment, and food for thought to audiences which cannot take the normal run of science shockers." (F.J., *Daily Film Reviewer* [London], August 23, 1956) ¶"Contains a great deal of solid emotion and suspense. The horror is intensified by being played against scenes that are seemingly matter of fact and commonplace." (Jack Moffitt, *Hollywood Reporter*, February 16, 1956) ¶"Wisely placed by Walter Wanger in a normal, everyday sort of town with normal everyday citizens as victims." (Sara Hamilton, *Los Angeles Examiner*, March 1, 1956, Section 2, p. 6.) ¶"Tense, offbeat piece of science-fiction.... builds to a strong climax." (Whit., *Variety*, February 29, 1956, p. 112)

Analysis: Released in the last great year of the golden age of science fiction, this is a cornerstone of that era. In McCarthy and Wynter, it has just about the most resourceful and intelligent protagonists in science fiction. (*Alien*'s Sigourney Weaver also comes to mind.) It doesn't matter that the beginning, with McCarthy narrating, and the end with Bissell calling the FBI were tacked on by the studio against producer and director wishes. Some think the film is anti-fascist, others anti-Communists. Director Siegel said, "I purposely had the prime spokesman for the pods be a pod psychiatrist. He speaks with authority, knowledge. He really believes that being a pod is preferable to being a frail, frightened human who cares. He has a strong case for being a pod. How marvelous it would be if you were a cow and all you had to do is munch a little grass and not worry about life. That's why there are so many of them." (In Stuart Kaminsky, *Don Siegel: Director*, p. 104) "Given the studio distributor interference, the tight budget, and a short shooting schedule, *Invasion of the Body Snatchers* is a dazzling success in almost every way," wrote Elizabeth McDermott in *Magill's Survey of Cinema, English Language Films*. What makes this better than the remake is the setting: a small town where everybody knows everybody. How many places are there to hide? From the novel: "This town lying out here in the darkness was filled with neighbors and friends. I knew them all, at least by sight, or to nod or speak to on the street. I'd grown up here; from boyhood I'd known every street, house, and path, most of the back yards, and every hill, field, and road for miles around."

Invasion of the Body Snatchers
(United Artists, 1978; 115 min.) ***½

Produced by Robert H. Solo. Directed by Philip Kaufman. Assistant Director, Jim Bloom. Screenplay, W. D. Richter. Based on the novel by Jack Finney. Edited by Douglas Stewart. Director of Photography, Michael Chapman. Technicolor. Music, Denny Zeitlin. Dolby Stereo. Design, Charles Rosen. Special Effects, Dell Rheume, Russ Hessey.

Cast: Matthew Bennell (Donald Sutherland), Elizabeth Driscoll (Brooke Adams), Dr. David Kibner (Leonard Nimoy), Nancy Bellicec (Veronica Cartwright), Jack Bellicec (Jeff Goldblum), Geoffrey (Art Hindle), Katherine (Lelia Goldoni), Running man (Kevin McCarthy).

Synopsis: San Francisco Board of Health officer Matthew Bennell is approached by associate Elizabeth Driscoll, who says her boyfriend Geoffrey has suddenly begun to act different, "alien," in some undefinable way. He takes Elizabeth to visit their mutual friend, the eminent psychologist Dr. David Kibner. Finding Kibner at a book party celebrating his most recent title, Elizabeth is alarmed when she overhears one of the other attendees telling a story almost identical to her own. Kibner assures Elizabeth that what she's experiencing is hardly an unusual delusion, especially in today's hectic and frequently emotionally abrasive world. He recommends rest and urges Matthew to take her home. Also at the party is Matthew's friend Jack Bellicec, who considers Kibner the dispenser of an irrelevant and banal pop psychology. He leaves and returns to the therapeutic mud baths owned by himself and his wife. He has hardly arrived at the Bellicec Baths when screams from Nancy startle him into breaking a glass (and cutting his hand). Finding Nancy, he sees upon one of the massage tables what is evidently a dead body. Closer inspection reveals some definite peculiarities

about the cadaver: it is covered with a quantity of gossamer-like webbing or threads, and it has an odd "unfinished" look about it; the face has no lines, no character. Most peculiar of all, perhaps, is the fact that the body bears an uncomfortable resemblance to Jack! Intrigued, Jack chooses to wait a bit before calling the police. Jack begins to doze. Nancy, who has continued to watch the body, is terrified when she notices that it has a bleeding cut on its hand identical to the one on her husband. When the corpse's eyes pop open, Nancy screams hysterically and runs to get Jack, who makes a quick call to Matthew. Bennell arrives, bringing with him Dr. Kibner. Flinging aside the curtain, they find the booth empty. With no sign of the body, Kibner is prepared to believe that Jack and Nancy are also victims of the mass hysteria. Matthew is not so sure. He hurries to Elizabeth's apartment and, to his horror, discovers a body alarmingly like Elizabeth lying in a herbarium. Unable to rouse the real Elizabeth upstairs, he carries her downstairs, again quietly past the living room where Geoffrey sits, and out to his car. With Elizabeth safe at his place, Matthew calls the police and meets them and Dr. Kibner back at Geoffrey's apartment. As with the body at the Bellicec Baths, Elizabeth's apparent double is missing. The police are irate over this seeming false alarm, but the inspector recognizes Kibner, and the doctor prevails upon him to forget the incident. Matthew tells Geoffrey that Elizabeth will be staying with him. In confidence, Kibner confesses to Matthew that he's really concerned that this delusion may be more serious than he'd first thought and might be something the Board of Health or some higher authority should investigate. Care must be taken, he warns, to see that a public panic doesn't begin. Frustrated at his inability to get anywhere at the mayor's office, Matthew returns to his apartment, settling into a lounge chair and a troubled sleep, oblivious to the rather large seed pods in his patio garden. Nancy Bellicec's screams bring Matthew out of his torpor, and he is horrified to see the source of Nancy's terror: the pods have burst open, producing a veritable nest of silently writhing humanoid forms. Matthew destroys the homunculi with a hoe, and he and the others make a hasty exit from the flat and the hissing denizens of the neighborhood. The humans decide to separate. Matthew and Elizabeth make it to Matthew's office and down amphetamines to stay awake. Jack arrives, but relief turns to dread when he leads in a party of men, including Kibner and the police inspector. The doctor tells Matthew and Elizabeth they will not be allowed to leave. Pods are brought in, and Kibner explains how these seed pods have drifted through the cosmos, alighting on worlds populated with accessible life forms that can be duplicated and eliminated. Resistance is useless, Kibner says; the best recourse for Matthew and Elizabeth is to relax and let it happen. Instead, Matthew drives a fistful of darts into the Jack-duplicate's neck, and Elizabeth brains Kibner with a laboratory flask. Matthew and Elizabeth head for the airport, but the suspicious cabby very nearly succeeds in turning them in to airport security. The nearly exhausted pair collapse some distance away in a vacant lot. Nearby music makes Matthew think that normal humans may be at hand; he investigates. Finding the music originating from the radio of a truck used to haul seed pods, the disappointed Matthew returns to the field and is dismayed to find Elizabeth nearly asleep. He tries to arouse her, but it is too late. As she lapses into total unconsciousness, her body withers and virtually implodes in his arms. Rising naked from the tall grass behind him is a newly formed pod Elizabeth. Matthew runs to a warehouse where alien pods are being sorted and stored. Climbing onto a catwalk, Matthew cuts electrical lines and causes a fire that quickly engulfs the facility. He barely escapes, a screeching mob of pod-beings at his heels, and seeks refuge in a nearby culvert. Some time later, Nancy Bellicec, who has somehow managed to survive, sees Matthew walking along the sidewalk on the way home after work. She calls his name furtively. He pauses and looks her way. She takes a step forward, smiling, when he raises a hand, glares strangely at her, and voices the shrill, piercing shriek of the pod duplicate spying its prey.

Reviews: "Not only matches the original in horrific tone and effect, but exceeds it in both conception and execution." (Poll., *Variety*, December 20, 1978) ¶"Marvelous fun.... I love Siegel's movie, but I think Kaufman's is more entertaining." (David Denby, *New York*, January 8, 1979, p. 71) ¶"On the whole, the San Francisco setting is a mistake.... Script ... is often laughably literal, and therefore incapable of establishing an air of mystery...." (Richard Schickel, *Time*, December 25, 1978, p. 27)

Analysis: Relocating the action of Jack Finney's classic to an already impersonal urban setting might seem more than a little perverse, but Philip Kaufman's remake of Don Siegel's 1956 classic has much to recommend it. A first-rate production with an able cast that delivers generally excellent performances, Kaufman's *Invasion of the Body Snatchers* is one of those thrillers that, while not unpredictable, is nonetheless fast-paced, gripping and entertaining. All this can be said for Siegel's film, too, of course. Classic though that earlier film is, however, it has had so much pseudo-intellectual blarney written about it, weaving the film into its period's paranoia or finding in it all manner of socio-political subtexts, that one ends up feeling rather guilty for enjoying it on the visceral level that was clearly the director's intention (something Siegel made plain in a number of interviews). Perhaps because it's a remake (and as such has been overlooked by the critical intelligentsia), the 1978 film has never acquired this conjectural baggage, and one is allowed simply to be entertained.

The appearance of Kaufman's *Invasion of the Body Snatchers* was something of a surprise, coming as it did in the closing years of the nineteen-seventies, a time when remakes of this sort were still few and far between (although *The Island of Dr. Moreau*, a worthy remake of *Island of Lost Souls*, had appeared the year before). In effect, Kaufman's film could be said to have kicked off the 1980s period that produced some outstanding (and some not-so-outstanding) remakes of classics.

Look for some interesting cameo appearances in this remake. Kevin McCarthy, pursued by a howling mob, accosts Sutherland

and Adams as they drive through downtown San Francisco: "They're coming … You're next!" he screams at them before reeling off down the street. And director Don Siegel is the suspicious cabby who takes the fleeing pair to the airport. A more enigmatic appearance is made by Robert Duvall, uncredited and unspeaking, as a priest on a swing in an early scene. The sequence with McCarthy has prompted some to suggest that Kaufman's film might be more properly termed a *sequel*, rather than a remake, although one would imagine that the writer(s) would have opted for a more novel approach for a sequel than a mere retelling of the original story.

Seedpeople (1992) is a variation.

Body Snatchers

(Warner Bros., 1993; 878 min.) **½

Produced by Robert H. Solo. Directed by Abel Ferrara. Screenplay, Stuart Gordon, Dennis Paoli, Nicholas St. John. Story, Raymond Cistheri, Larry Cohen. Edited by Anthony Redman. Director of Photography, Bojan Bazelli. Color. Music, Joe Delia.

Cast: Marti Malone (Gabrielle Anwar), Steve Malone (Terry Kinney), Carol Malone (Meg Tilly), Tim Young (Billy Wirth), Andy Malone (Reilly Murphy), Major Collins (Forrest Whitaker), Jenn Platt (Christine Elise), General Platt (R. Lee Ermey), Mrs. Platt (Kathleen Doyle).

Synopsis: Arriving at Fort Day, the family of Steve Malone, a field investigator for the Environmental Protection Agency, gradually settles into as normal an existence as transient life on a military facility will permit. Seventeen-year-old Marti is adjusting to her dad's new wife, Carol, and Carol's six-year-old son from a previous marriage, Andy. The boring existence Marti expects is shattered when she is accosted by a man who rasps to her that "they get you when you're asleep." But the man disappears and life settles down until Marti meets Jenn Platt, the ne'er-do-well daughter of the installation's commanding general. Jenn introduces Marti to the beer joints and pool halls. Meanwhile, young Andy doesn't find Fort Day's daycare much to his liking, especially when he discovers that, after completing finger-painting sessions, the other kids' paintings are all

entirely identical. And his teacher seems disconcertingly insistent that he take a nap. Andy leaves, bumps into helicopter pilot Tim Young, and strikes up a casual acquaintance. That evening, while Jenn takes Marti to a local tavern where they run into Tim, Andy witnesses the apparent implosion of his sleeping mother. But the closet door opens and out strides what appears to be Carol Malone, naked and staring coldly at her son, who runs screaming from the room. Andy's stepfather assures him he's only had a bad dream. Marti returns during the fracas, and Steve, seeing that she's with military men and smelling of beer, assumes the worst. Steve already has a lot on his mind. While out collecting soil samples, he is approached by an army doctor, Major Collins, who wonders if the chemical weapons stored at Fort Day could cause delusionary behavior. The next day Steve is perplexed during an examination of a torn protective suit; he finds components with which he is totally unfamiliar. That evening Marti dozes in a warm bath. Fingerlike tendrils descend upon her from above, entwining themselves about her. Only the increasing mass and weight of the pod-duplicate above her saves Marti, as it crashes into the bath, rousing the girl to terrified wakefulness. Marti flies to her parents' bedroom and wakes her dad. Steve readies his family to leave, but Carol coldly argues, "Where're you gonna go? Where're you gonna hide? Where're you gonna run to? There's no one like you … *left!*" Steve and the kids flee as Carol screeches a horrific cry that empties the houses all along the street of likewise racing, screeching imitation humans. The entire installation erupts with pod-duplicates frenziedly going after the few remaining humans. Major Collins also remains human, but when approached by General Platt and others, he commits suicide. Outside, Platt gives instructions for destinations to a convoy of trucks bearing alien seed pods: Fort Bliss, Texas; Fort Bragg, North Carolina. Marti and Andy find their father and they pile into a jeep, but Marti has suspicions and brings the jeep to a skidding halt. Tim Young, still human, races up as Marti insists that her father is not really her father anymore. To prove her point, she grabs Tim's automatic and fires a round into Steve, who collapses into a shrinking, melting heap. Marti and Andy are captured as Tim readies his chopper for their escape. Pretending to be a duplicate, Tim locates Marti. The two must run when Jenn realizes Marti is still human. Andy runs to the chopper and is pulled inside, whereupon he attacks Tim. Marti manages to pull him off and toss him to the camp far below. The next morning, armed with missiles and high-caliber machine guns, Tim's chopper attacks the convoy leaving Fort Day and then the installation itself, destroying it in a series of terrific explosions. Tim and Marti fly to a haven in Atlanta. Carol's words echo in Marti's mind: *Where're you gonna go? Where're you gonna hide? Where're you gonna run to? There's no one like you ... left!*

Review: "Impatience, rather than tension, is aroused, and the horror is diminished because it's strangers who are being replaced." (Leonard Maltin, ed., *Leonard Maltin's Movie and Video Guide 1995*, p. 142)

Analysis: Body Snatchers seems to have languished at the studio before its virtually unnoticed theatrical release, which, depending on the source, occurred in 1993 or 1994. This time only the basic theme and structure of the original remains, and an entirely new cast of characters is introduced into an entirely different setting. There is much to suggest that *Body Snatchers* is a sequel to the 1978 film, rather than a remake of the original. Or, maybe it is merely another variation on the Body Snatcher theme. Whatever, Abel Ferrara expends little time or energy on exposition in this fastest-paced version of the story to date (the first two films, which were hardly pikers, seem positively languid by comparison), perhaps because the director felt that everyone had seen the previous films and little was required in the way of explanation as to what the pods are or how they got here, or how they manage to duplicate human beings. Likewise, little effort is made to render any of the characters as anything beyond ciphers; what we have here to take the place of the harried individuals

in the earlier films is another dysfunctional family unit, one that's barely able to cope with the rigors of normal life, much less the horrendous experiences that confront them in *Body Snatchers*. Woefully lacking is the fact that we never sense any real *change* in people after they become victims of the pods. The pod "duplicates" are alien creatures, to be sure, but the human originals weren't much to begin with. Still, the idea of being somehow *taken over* and duplicated by a cold-blooded alien from the depths of space is a powerful theme, as horrifying now as it was in the 1950s. It would take a true lack of talent to utterly trash the idea (although that has happened, in fact, a number of times), and Abel Ferrara displays ample evidence of talent, mostly in the area of explosive visuals and hair-trigger editing. Nevertheless, when the smoke clears, nothing is done with this marvelous theme in *Body Snatchers* that hasn't been done before, and it's maybe a little ironic that, despite the obvious advances in cinematic state-of-the-art in the last forty years, Don Siegel's tidy little 1956 B-movie still makes the best case for Jack Finney's genuine science fiction classic.

The Invisible Man
(Universal, 1933; 71 min.) ***½

Produced by Carl Laemmle, Jr. Directed by James Whale. Screenplay, R. C. Sheriff and Philip Wylie. Based on the novel by H. G. Wells. Director of Photography, Arthur Edeson. Music, W. Frank Harling. Art Direction, Charles D. Hall. Special Effects, John P. Fulton.

Cast: Jack Griffin (Claude Rains), Flora Cranley (Gloria Stuart), Dr. Kemp (William Harrigan), Dr. Cranley (Henry Travers), Chief of police (Holmes Herbert), Jenny Hall (Una O'Connor), Jaffers (E. E. Clive), Chief of detectives (Dudley Digges), Reporter (Dwight Frye), Informer (John Carradine), Inspector Bird (Harry Stubbs), Inspector Lane (Donald Stuart), Boy (John Merivale), Milly (Merle Tottenham), Man with bicycle (Walter Brennan), Doctor (Jameson Thomas).

Synopsis: On a wintry night a strangely bedecked man with suitcase takes a room at The Lion's Head in the village of Iping. He asks landlady Mrs. Hall to have his trunks delivered next day. Weeks pass, and

Jack Griffin (Claude Rains) resists the pleas of Flora (Gloria Stuart), who wants him to abandon his experiments in *The Invisible Man* (Universal, 1933).

the stranger cannot pay his bill. That in addition to his surly, mysterious ways angers Mrs. Hall, who goads her husband into ousting the tenant. The tenant pleads, but Hall is adamant. The stranger rages and throws Hall out the door and down the stairs. The police are called in. The tenant refuses to be handcuffed, warns the police, then begins unwrapping his bandages. There's nothing beneath! One policeman surmises he's been all eaten up. The man removes all his clothes, "revealing" his invisibility, then escapes, wreaking havoc on his way through the village. Meanwhile, Flora Cranley expresses concern to her father and Dr. Kemp about their associate Jack Griffin, who's been missing for some time. "He meddled in things men should leave alone," Kemp says to Dr. Cranley. Cranley reveals that Griffin's experiments had involved the substance monocane, which was derived from an Indian flower. Besides bleaching things, it could cause madness. Kemp is then visited by the invisible Griffin, who aims to enlist his services.

Griffin talks of power and how it can be obtained by murdering rich and poor alike. When Griffin is sleeping, Kemp calls Dr. Cranley, who tells Flora. They go to Kemp, and Flora pleads with Griffin, who is kind toward her and at times talks of seeking a way back, but who evinces grotesque dreams of world conquest by whatever nation bids highest for his substance. The police arrive, called by Kemp, but they fail to capture Griffin, who ranges the environs, killing twenty of the men seeking him and wrecking a train. He's vowed to kill Kemp at 10:00 the next night and does so even though the police try to stop him. A hundred thousand men are pressed into service to find the madman. One day a farmer hears snoring in his barn and goes to the authorities. The police fire the barn, forcing Griffin out into the new fallen snow. Observing his footprints, they shoot him. In the hospital the mortally wounded Griffin asks for Flora. "I knew you would come to me, Flora. I wanted to come back to you. My darling, I failed. I meddled in things that man must leave alone." As he dies, Jack Griffin's visibility returns.

Review: "James Whale ... has taken a great deal of pains with something that is usually either reduced to a minimum or altogether ignored in these attempts to dramatize the more farfetched hypotheses of science — namely, setting.... Of Claude Rains's richly suggestive voice it is not too much to say that it is hardly less responsible than the direction for the peculiar quality of the picture as a whole.... Taken either as a technical exercise or as a sometimes profoundly moving retelling of the Frankenstein fable, *The Invisible Man* is one of the most rewarding of the recent films." (William Troy, *Nation*, December 13, 1933, p. 688)

Analysis: The beginning is very close to the Wells novel. Kemp is an amalgam of Wells's Kemp and the vagrant Marvel. The entrance of the invisible man into the Lion's Head Inn is perfect: Whale shoots from a low angle, and the visage in overcoat, hat, goggles, bandages and false nose *is* intimidating. This film made Claude Rains a star even though he is not seen until his character's death at the conclusion. His voice was his fortune.

The Invisible Man Returns
(1940, 81 min.) **½

Produced by Ken Goldsmith. Directed by Joe May. Screenplay, Kurt Siodmak, Lester Cole, Cedric Belfrage. Story, Joe May and Kurt Siodmak. "A Sequel to *The Invisible Man* by H. G. Wells." Edited by Frank Gross. Director of Photography, Milton Krasner. Music, H. J. Salter and Frank Skinner. Musical Director, Charles Previn. Art Direction, Jack Otterson. Set Decoration, R. A. Gausman. Special Photographic Effects, John P. Fulton.

Cast: Richard Cobb (Sir Cedric Hardwicke), Geoffrey Radcliffe (Vincent Price), Dr. Frank Griffin (John Sutton), Helen Manson (Nan Grey), Willie Spears (Alan Napier), Inspector Sampson (Cecil Kellaway), Governor (Edward Fielding), Ben Jenkins (Forrester Harvey), Shopworker (Harry Cording), Cotton (Ivan Simpson), Nurse (Frances Robinson), Constable Dukesbury (Harry Stubbs), Woman (Mary Field), Mineworker (Edmund MacDonald). With Billy Bevan.

Synopsis: About to be executed for the murder of his brother, Geoffrey Radcliffe is visited in prison by Dr. Frank Griffin. Griffin gives Geoffrey a dose of the substance that seven years before turned his brother Jack Griffin invisible — and insane. Frank hopes to find the antidote shortly. Geoffrey is hidden at a cottage by his fiancée Helen. The police find him nevertheless, and he flees. Meanwhile, Inspector Sampson of Scotland Yard is on the case. From the start he had the inkling that Geoffrey escaped prison through invisibility. Geoffrey, intent on clearing his name, learns from Radcliffe Collieries foreman Willie Spears that he'd seen mine manager Richard Cobb kill Geoffrey's brother. Geoffrey accosts Cobb, but the police intervene and protect Cobb, until one morning the invisible and progressively maniacal Geoffrey sneaks inside and forces Cobb at gunpoint to leave. Cobb breaks away, fleeing through the miners, but Geoffrey catches him on a coal chute. The police shoot and apparently hit Geoffrey, but Cobb falls into the slag heap. Dying, he tells Helen he killed Geoffrey's brother. Wounded, Geoffrey puts on a scarecrow's clothes and stumbles back to the colliery. Griffin gives him a blood transfusion and with Sampson's acquiescence, prepares to try the latest antidote. However, before it can be administered Geoffrey begins to appear. He is alive.

Review: "Fair measure of suspense and excitement and adequate enough performances." (Frank S. Nugent, *New York Times*, January 16, 1940, p. 19)

Analysis: As the *New York Times* review points out, the first installment was both more horrifying and more humorous. In the original the important ingredient was "monocane." In this one Cecil Kellaway seems to call it "juocane" while Sutton terms it "duocane." As teenagers watching this on TV for the first time, we loved the veins and muscles that appeared heralding Price's regeneration. Overall, this is a fair movie. It doesn't have a hard edge, although Hardwicke's death scene is somewhat grisly. Nan Grey is no actress.

Notes of Interest: This same year Universal released *The Invisible Woman* with John Barrymore and Virginia Bruce. Neither the story nor the characters have anything to do with the Griffin clan.

Invisible Agent
(1942; 84 min.) **½

Produced by George Waggner. Directed by Edwin L. Marin. Screenplay, Curt Siodmak. Edited by Edward Curtiss. Director of Photography, Les White. Music, Hans Salter. Art Direction, Jack Otterson. Set Decoration, Russell A. Gausman. Special Effects, John P. Fulton.

Cast: Maria Goodrich (Ilona Massey), Frank Griffin (Jon Hall), Baron Ikito (Peter Lorre), Conrad Stauffer (Sir Cedric Hardwicke), Karl Heiser (J. Edward Bromberg), John Gardiner (John Litel), Sir Alfred Spenser (Holmes Herbert), Surgeon (Keye Luke), Nazi assassin (Matt Willis), Brigadier general (Lee Shumway), German sentries (Duke York, Lane Chandler, Donald Curtis), German sergeant (Milburn Stone), Ship radioman (James Craven), Maid (Mabel Colcord), Killer (Marty Faust), Free Frenchman (Alberto Morin), Spenser's secretary (John Holland), Von Porten (Wolfgang Zilzer), Bartender (Ferdinand Munier), Storm trooper (Henry Guttman), General Chin Lee (Lee Tung-Fo), Stuntman (Eddie Parker).

Synopsis: Frank Griffin, grandson of the ill-fated Jack Griffin, calls himself Frank Raymond in New York, where he runs a print shop. Out of the blue come Conrad Stauffer and Baron Ikito, Axis partners seeking the Griffin invisibility formula. Although physically intimidated, Frank breaks free and escapes. The U.S. government also wants the formula, and after the Japanese attack Pearl Harbor, Frank agrees to turn it over with the proviso that he will take the drug. Dropped behind German lines, he finds Arnold Schmidt and is told to steal a list of Japanese spies operating in America. Stauffer, no less, has the list. Frank goes to Maria Sorenson, another Allied agent who's Stauffer's girlfriend. While Stauffer is away, Karl Heiser tries to worm his way into Maria's heart, only to be foiled by the invisible man. Although Stauffer returns and knows Frank is after the list, the invisible man gets it. On his way to Schmidt's, he visits Heiser in the cell where Stauffer had him imprisoned and makes him divulge the date Germany plans to attack New York. Frank is captured by Ikito when he arrives at Schmidt's shop. He and Maria are taken to the Japanese embassy. When Stauffer arrives and fights over them

with Ikito, they escape. Ikito stabs Stauffer, then commits hara-kiri. Maria and Frank steal a plane intended to take part in the New York bombing, drop its load on the airfield as they leave, and fly to England.

Reviews: "Sufficient levity to provide strong support entertainment." (Walt., *Variety*, August 5, 1942) ¶"John P. Fulton's Oscar-nominated special effects ... [are] less successful here than in previous efforts." (Tim Lucas, *Video Watchdog*, November/December 1993, p. 13)

Analysis: This is the sort of task an invisible man should be accomplishing: breaking spy rings and confounding the enemy. The supporting and character actor cast is wonderful. Some sources give the length as 79 minutes.

The Invisible Man's Revenge
(1944, 78 min.) **½

Directed by Ford Beebe. Screenplay, Bertram Millhauser. Based on characters created by H. G. Wells. Edited by Saul A. Goodkind. Director of Photography, Milton Krasner. Music, Hans J. Salter. Art Direction, John B. Goodman, Harold H. MacArthur. Set Decoration, Russell A. Gausman, Andrew J. Gilmore. Special Photographic Effects, John P. Fulton.

Cast: Robert Griffin (Jon Hall), Mark Foster (Alan Curtis), Julie Herrick (Evelyn Ankers), Herbert Higgens (Leon Errol), Dr. Peter Drury (John Carradine), Lady Irene Herrick (Gale Sondergaard), Sir Jasper Herrick (Lester Matthews), Cleghorn (Halliwell Hobbs), Jim Feeny (Ian Wolfe), Maude (Doris Lloyd), Al Parry (Skelton Knaggs), Sergeant Frederic Travers (Billy Bevan).

Synopsis: Robert Griffin escapes from a psycho ward in Capetown and accosts friends and business associates Sir Jasper and Irene Herrick. He accuses them of trying to kill him on an African safari when they were searching for diamonds. Kicked out, he meets Dr. Peter Drury, who has developed an invisibility formula. Although he'd only used it on animals so far, Drury gives it to Griffin, who terrorizes the Herricks but falls in love with their daughter after seeing her photo. He hopes to capture her affection by becoming visible again and learns from Drury that it may be possible to do so if he receives a blood transfusion.

Griffin knocks Drury out and takes his blood. Meeting Julie, he finds all is well until dinner when he starts to become invisible again. Capturing Julie's suitor Mark Foster, Griffin prepares to drain his blood but is killed by Drury's dog.

Review: "Reveals quite plainly that you don't see much when you see an 'Invisible Man.'" (Bosley Crowther, *New York Times*, June 10, 1944, p. 12)

Analysis: Except for the name Griffin, this bears no direct relation to the Griffin clan first made known to us by Claude Rains in *The Invisible Man.* Thus it must be categorized with *The Invisible Woman.* That is, it's a series entry only by being a product of Universal studios.

Abbott and Costello Meet Frankenstein *see under* **Frankenstein**

Abbott and Costello Meet the Invisible Man
(1951; 82 min.) ***

Produced by Howard Christie. Directed by Charles Lamont. Screenplay, Robert Lees, Frederic I. Rinaldo, John Grant. Based on a story by Hugh Wedlock, Jr., and Howard Snyder. Suggested by H. G. Wells's *The Invisible Man.* Edited by Virgil Vogel. Director of Photography, George Robinson. Special Photography, David S. Horsley. Music supervision, Joseph Gershenson. Art Direction, Bernard Herzbrun, Richard Riedel. Set Decoration, Russell A. Gausman, John Austin.

Cast: Bud Alexander (Bud Abbott), Lou Francis (Lou Costello), Tommy Nelson (Arthur Franz), Morgan (Sheldon Leonard), Helen Gray (Nancy Guild), Detective Roberts (William Frawley), Boots Marsden (Adele Jergens), Radio announcer (Sam Balter), Dr. Philip Gray (Gavin Muir), Waiter (Syd Saylor), Rooney (Billy Wayne), Rocky Hanlon (John Day), Torpedo (George J. Lewis), Sneaky (Bobby Barber), Lou's handler (Carl Sklover), Rocky's handler (Charles Petter), Referee (Frankie Van), Dr. James C. Turner (Paul Maxey), Newspapermen (Russ Conway, Billy Snyder), Milt (Ed Gargan), Stillwell (Herb Vigran).

Synopsis: Bud Alexander and Lou Francis are part of Dugan's Detective Training Graduation Class 1951 and report to a real detective agency to get experience. On the night shift, they are visited by Tommy Nelson, a boxer wanted by the police for murdering his manager. He hires Bud and Lou to help him find the real killer. They go to the 823 Maple address of Dr. Philip Gray. He's been experimenting with John Griffin's invisibility formula but is loath to administer it to Tommy for fear it will affect his mind as it affected John's. When the police arrive and Philip and Helen Gray are distracted, Tommy injects himself with the serum and disappears in front of Lou. Later Helen gives Lou and Bud a $500 dollar retainer from Tommy. She says her Uncle Philip is working on the reagent. Bud and Lou deliver a grip with clothes and goggles to Tommy. At the gym, Tommy tells Bud and Lou that he wouldn't take a fall in a fight with Rocky Hanlon; that's why his manager was killed. Tommy overhears gangster Morgan's scheme. Lou pretends to be a boxer while the invisible Tommy makes the punching bag move. Tommy hatches a plan to entice Morgan to make a deal with Lou and Bud. Morgan uses a go-between — moll Boots Marsden. Although Lou records her proposition to take a dive, he breaks the record. Meanwhile, Tommy seems affected by the serum. He is getting power crazy. In the bout between Lou and Rocky Hanlon, the invisible Tommy KOs Rocky. Morgan and his torpedo attempt to murder Lou and Bud, but Tommy prevents the mayhem, though he himself is wounded by a knife. In the hospital, he receives a blood transfusion from Lou plus Dr. Gray's reagent. He becomes visible while Lou becomes invisible for a short time.

Review: "The boys try hard, and ... appear to have recaptured a good deal of their old spunk." (Thomas M. Pryor, *New York Times*, April 13, 1951, p. 18)

Analysis: There are quite a few hilarious scenes (the punching bag is number one) and a couple of notable lines delivered by Lou and such sterling character actors as William Frawley ("I saw two men carrying no man"). A portrait of John Griffin (Claude Rains) and Gray's explanation about the serum that made Gray a maniac and was willed to him connect this with the first film in Universal's series. Arthur

Franz would soon become a mainstay lead-ing man of science fiction films like *In-vaders from Mars*.

The Invisible Man Returns *see under*
  The Invisible Man

The Invisible Man's Revenge *see under*
  The Invisible Man

Island of Lost Souls
(Paramount, 1933; 72 min.) ****

Directed by Erle C. Kenton. Screenplay, Waldemar Young and Philip Wylie. Based on the novel *The Island of Dr. Moreau* by H. G. Wells. Director of Photography, Karl Struss. Special Effects, Gordon Jennings. Makeup, Wally Westmore.

Cast: Dr. Moreau (Charles Laughton), Ed-ward Parker (Richard Arlen), Sayer of the Law (Bela Lugosi), Montgomery (Arthur Hohl), Ruth Thomas (Leila Hyams), Lota the panther woman (Kathleen Burke), Ouran (Hans Steinke), Captain Davies (Stanley Fields), Hogan (Robert Kortman), M'Ling (Tetsu Komai), Gola (Harry Ekezian), Sa-moan girl (Rosemary Grimes), Captain Don-ahue (Paul Hurst), American consul (George Irving).

Synopsis: In the Pacific, the freighter *Covena* out of San Francisco picks up the shipwrecked Edward Parker, who tele-graphs his fiancée, Ruth, on the island of Apia. She is disappointed when the ship docks and Parker is found to have been left on an unnamed island. Parker had been knocked unconscious by Captain Davies in retaliation for a punch that laid him out earlier. Parker had been angered to see Da-vies harass M'Ling, a strange creature as-sisting Mongomery. Montgomery was in charge of various big game which Parker finds delivered to one Dr. Moreau, an Eng-lish-born scientist working in secret on the island. It soon becomes apparent that Mo-reau is engaged in questionable surgery. He's trying to transform animals into peo-ple, and in the case of Lota, has virtually succeeded. "Mr. Parker, do you know what it means to feel like God?" he asks. All that remains to prove his technique is the mat-ing of a human — Parker — with Lota and

the production of human offspring. There are many examples of Moreau's failed at-tempts at accelerated evolution on the is-land. These "men" live in a village presided over by the Sayer of the Law, who guides them in answering Moreau's question, "What is the Law?" with admonitions not to go on all fours, not to eat meat, not to spill blood. Moreau's plans go awry when Ruth and Captain Donahue locate the is-land. Moreau sees a chance to have Ruth mate with his beast-man Ouran, but first Donahue must be killed. Moreau directs Ouran to do the deed. Ouran brings the body to the village, and the beast-men re-alize that if this man could be killed, Moreau too is mortal. Remembering the "House of Pain" where they were turned into not-men and not-beasts, they rise up, capture Moreau and perform grisly work on his body. To protect Parker, Lota kills Ouran but is herself killed. Parker, Ruth and Montgomery escape.

Reviews: "Although the attempt to hor-rify is not accomplished with any marked degree of subtlety, ... some of the scenes are ... interesting. The general effect ... is enhanced greatly by Mr. Laughton's ur-bane impersonation." (Mordaunt Hall, *New York Times*, January 13, 1933, p. 19) ¶"Some horror sequences ... are unri-valed.... good picturization." (*Variety*) ¶"Touches a nerve that no other horror film — with the possible exception of Tod Browning's *Freaks* (also '32) — comes near.... Laughton ... is unforgettable." (Tim Lucas, *Video Watchdog*, November/December 1993, pp. 13-14)

Analysis: Like *The Mystery of the Wax Museum* and *Doctor X*, in the sixties this was one of those "lost" films. Now it can be seen on the American Movie Classics cable channel. Wonder of wonders, its reputation is deserved. (The novel is ab-solutely one of the most frightening you will ever read.) Laughton is a definitive mad scientist, the foggy island is spooky, several of the animal-men are hideous. There is no Ruth Thomas character in the book. Parker *does* arrive on the island in the way Wells describes. In the ensuing films the character drifts ashore in a long-boat.

Montgomery (Arthur Hohl, center, in safari hat) and Dr. Moreau (Charles Laughton) square off as Edward Parker (Richard Arlen, far right) approaches; they are surrounded by Moreau's strange creations in *Island of Lost Souls* (Paramount, 1933).

Terror Is a Man
(Valiant, 1959; 89 min.) ***

Lynn-Romero Production. Produced by Kane W. Lynn and Eddie F. Romero. Directed by Gerry De Leon. Screenplay, Harry Paul Harber. Edited by Gervasio Santos. Director of Photography, Emmanuel I. Rojas. Music, Ariston Auelino. Sound Recording, Pedro Nicolas. Art Direction, Vicente Bonus. Production Coordinator, Artemio B. Tecson. Special Effects, Hilario Santos.

Cast: Dr. Girard (Francis Lederer), Frances Girard (Greta Thyssen), William Fitzgerald (Richard Derr), Walter (Oscar Keesee), Selene (Lilia Duran), Tiago (Peyton Keesee), The Man (Flory Carlos).

Synopsis: A lifeboat from the *Pedro Queen* washes up on a remote island a thousand miles from the coast of Peru. One half-dead man is aboard: William Fitzgerald, the *Pedro Queen*'s engineer, who learns from Dr. Girard that he is the only survivor. Furthermore, he finds that Girard has no radio or boat and that ships rarely stop. Outside, Girard is confronted by his wife, Frances,

who speaks of the tormented thing out in the forest. He can't agree with her that they should leave. While she sleeps, something watches through the window before moving off to a village where it kills two inhabitants. Next day most of the populace flee the island in their outriggers. Fitzgerald explores the abandoned village before encountering Girard and meeting Frances for the first time. Girard and Walter are covering a pit in which they hope to catch something. Over dinner, Girard tells Fitzgerald he left his practice in New York to conduct research here. Shots are heard outside and, pistol in hand, Girard leaves to investigate. Frances tells Fitzgerald a "panther" escaped the night before. She says she's a nurse but doesn't think she can help her husband anymore. She asks Fitzgerald for help. Girard and Walter arrive with the animal. Fitzgerald decides to do some exploring and observes the Girards in the lab. More than that, he sees a bandaged, human-like figure that the doctor will be operating upon and hears Frances say to it, "I'm sorry." Next day Fitzgerald quizzes the sunbathing Frances about the animal and the deaths it caused in the village. When Fitzgerald kisses her, she gently brushes him off and says, "I'm not lonely, I'm frightened." That evening over cocktails, Walter rants about the stinking island and the doctor. Fitzgerald peruses the books in Girard's library till the doctor comes in and begins to explain his work: to modify a species so that it takes on the basic characteristics of another species. "It's no more unnatural than evolution. It *is* evolution." Of course, the real changes must be in the brain. He can alter the brain's size and cellular structure via new chemicals. He invites Fitzgerald to observe the operation in the morning. That evening Frances enters Fitzgerald's room. Next day Fitzgerald accompanies Girard downstairs and helps him and Walter with the surgical preparations. After the operation, when Frances goes down to help clean up, Walter says her husband is crazy and that he really wants to help her. When he makes a play for her, the beast gets one arm free, and Walter must shackle it. When Frances leaves, Walter beats the creature with a board. In the afternoon, Fitzgerald tells Girard he saw a soul in the creature's eyes. Girard says the animal will father a new race of men with complete objectivity, a perfect man. Why wait for natural laws, argues the scientist. He shows Fitzgerald sketches tracing the evolution of the creature. That evening Girard teaches the creature to say "man." It becomes agitated upon seeing Walter and breaks free, wrecking the lab. Walter sets the creature on fire with his torch. Girard and Frances put it out. Frances threatens to leave. Girard returns to the lab, and Walter follows with a gun. When the lights flicker, the beast savages Walter. When Fitzgerald and Frances go into the hall, they are confronted by the beast, its facial bandages off. Girard appears, says Walter is dead, and follows the creature with the reluctant help of Fitzgerald. While they are gone, the beast attacks Selene and enters the house. It pursues Frances, and the men hear her scream. But she's not there when they arrive. They venture out again, Girard to find the creature,

Fitzgerald to find Frances. At the top of a cliff, Girard confronts the beast, which puts Frances down only to claw Girard and toss him from the cliff. Fitzgerald puts a bullet into the monster, which stumbles off. Selene's young brother Tiago helps it into a longboat. Fitzgerald and Frances stare out over the ocean. Followed by the man, Frances walks off down the beach.

Review: "Quiet, sensibly restrained and quite terrifying." (Howard Thompson, *New York Times*, July 14, 1960, p. 23)

Analysis: Before the credits we see this admonition: "Warning. The picture you are about to see has a scene so shocking that it is necessary to forewarn you. We suggest that the squeamish and faint-hearted close their eyes at the sound of the bell and reopen them when the bell rings again. The Management." The warning bell — which sounds like a telephone ringing — goes off as Lederer uses his scalpel on the creature's neck. The *New York Times* review found the warning bell as hair-raising as the scene itself. This has the reputation as the best U.S.–Filipino co-production, and it *is* atmospheric and spooky. Francis Lederer, who'd played the vampire in the previous year's *The Return of Dracula*, had had a Hollywood career, including *Confessions of a Nazi Spy* (1939), *Midnight* (1939), and *The Man I Married* (1940). Any teenage boy seeing this was much impressed by the gorgeous Greta Thyssen, the Danish beauty queen who made several English-language films, including *The Beast of Budapest*, *Journey to the 7th Planet*, and *Three Blondes in His Life*. Typical of the time, she wears heels while traipsing about the jungle compound or assisting in the lab. Atypically, her character has a mind of her own, and though she gives in to sexual longing one night, the next day she spurns her lover. At the end, she heads down the beach, Fitzgerald bringing up the rear.

The Island of Dr. Moreau
(AIP/Filmways, 1977; 98 min.) ***

Produced by John Temple-Smith and Skip Steloff. Directed by Don Taylor. Screenplay, John Herman Shaner and Al Ramrus. Based on the novel by H. G. Wells. Edited by Marion Rothman. Director of Photography, Gerry

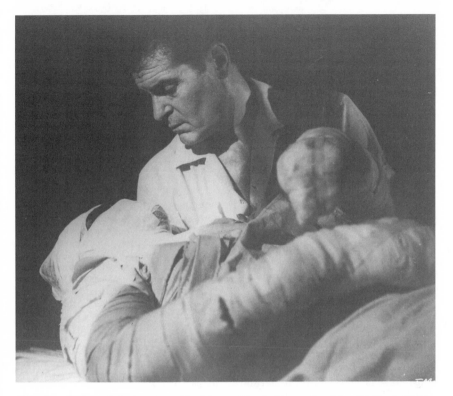

Dr. Girard (Francis Lederer) cradles his creation in *Terror Is a Man* (Valiant, 1959).

Fisher. Music by Laurence Rosenthal. Art Direction, Philip Jefferies. Set Decoration, James Berkey. Creative Makeup, John Chambers, Dan Striepeke, Tom Burman. Animals, Enchanted Village, Inc. Animal Stunt Coordinator, Ralph D. Helfer. Special Effects, Cliff Wenger.

Cast: Dr. Moreau (Burt Lancaster), Andrew Braddock (Michael York), Maria (Barbara Carrera), Sayer of the Law (Richard Basehart), Montgomery (Nigel Davenport), M'Ling (Nick Cravat), Boarman (the Great John L.), Bullman (Bob Ozman), Hyenaman (Fumio Demura), Bearman (David Cass), Tigerman (John Gillespie).

Synopsis: Engineering officer Andrew Braddock escapes in a lifeboat from the shipwreck of the *Lady Vain* and lands on a strange island. Fleeing from dimly seen figures in the jungle, he falls into an animal trap before a palisaded residence. The American Dr. Moreau owns the plantation, managed by mercenary Montgomery. Braddock explores the forest from which

hideous growls and howls have been heard and enters a cave where he encounters humanoid creatures. One attacks him, but Moreau arrives and makes the leader of this group recite "the law": "not to spill blood, not to eat flesh." Back at the plantation Braddock learns that Moreau has been operating on animals, attempting to transform them into humans in the laboratory his pitiful creations call "the house of pain." Moreau explains: "I have proved — *almost* proved — the existence of a cell particle that controls the living organism. This cell, this particle, controls the shape of life. This is the second stage of treatment for this creature. This serum contains the distillation of the biological code message, a new set of instructions erasing the natural instincts of the animal. Some surgery, implants to various organs and he should grow to resemble any creature we please, in this case a human being." Braddock is aghast. After a pursuit of one of Moreau's creatures during which Braddock shoots the creature to put it out of its misery, Moreau incarcerates Braddock and begins experiments designed to cause his prisoner's reversion to pure animal. Montgomery protests but is shot by Moreau. The creatures outside the stockade learn that Moreau himself spilled blood; they attack their persecutor. Braddock and Maria escape the compound while the animal people ransack it, setting fires and releasing the big cats Moreau intended to operate on. Some of those kill the animal people. One of Moreau's creations tracks Braddock to his boat but is killed. On the open sea, Braddock and Maria sight a freighter.

Reviews: "Handsome, well-acted, and involving.... York gives one of his best performances." (*Variety*, July 13, 1977) ¶"Answers all the questions too soon and then has nowhere to go.... Brutish humanoids ... cease to be creatures of the viewer's imagination and become exhibits of the make-up man's craft." (Christopher Porterfield, *Time*, July 18, 1977, p. 87) ¶"Quite tame.... An air of embarrassed self-consciousness makes the whole movie too foolish to be taken seriously but not silly enough to be fun." (Janet Maslin, *Newsweek*, July 25, 1977, p. 57C)

Analysis: Filmed in the U.S. Virgin Islands, this story is photographed in daylight and color—a risky proposition, but for the most part it's a success and may be the best movie former actor Don Taylor ever directed. Casting is good. Makeup is good. The finale when the "manimals" invade Moreau's abode, start fires, then release and battle the animals is an exceptional action sequence. The ending is perfunctory. Although this was never established in the film, a shot suggests that Maria may have transformed into an animal—but she doesn't. Did they delete the scene? How come?

Notes of Interest: H. G. Wells's thought-provoking and truly frightening novel *The Island of Dr. Moreau* was published in 1896. Imagine yourself stranded on an eight-square-mile desert island with a mad doctor, a drunk, and three score "Beast Men"! The several films based on it are decent translations, but the book contains no love interest—neither animal woman or fiancée left behind—for the island's unexpected visitor Prendick, who is called Parker, Fitzgerald and Braddock in the respective movies.

Island of The Alive *see* It's Alive III: Island of the Alive *under* **It's Alive**

It Lives Again *see under* **It's Alive**

It's Alive

(Warner Bros., 1974; 91 min.) **½

Produced and directed by Larry Cohen. Screenplay, Larry Cohen. Edited by Peter Honess. Director of Photography, Fenton Hamilton. Panavision. Technicolor. Music, Bernard Herrmann. Makeup, Rick Baker.

Cast: Frank Davis (John Ryan), Lenore Davis (Sharon Farrell), Detective Lieutenant Perkins (James Dixon), Captain (Michael Ansara), Dr. Perry (Andrew Duggan), Clayton (Guy Stockwell), Charlie (William Wellman, Jr.), Executive (Robert Emhardt), Doctor (Samus Locke), Nurse (Mary Nancy Burnett), Secretary (Diana Hale), Boy (Daniel Holzman), Expectant fathers (Patrick Macallister, Gerald York, Gwill Richards, Jerry Taft, W. Allen York).

Synopsis: Frank and Lenore Davis arrive at the hospital in the pre-dawn hours excited about the imminent birth of their second child. Frank's exhilaration turns to confusion and horror when screams from the operating room send him rushing in to find his wife in hysterics and the delivery team the victims of a very grisly murder. Most appalling is the fact that the killer seems to have been the Davises' newborn son. A search proves fruitless and the authorities are baffled, but the most obvious conclusion is that the Davises' infant is some sort of homicidal mutation, equipped with lethal teeth and claws and capable of moving with great quickness. Even before the hapless couple have left the hospital, the news media have gotten hold of the story. The ensuing notoriety causes Frank to lose his public relations job. A number of gruesome murders occur in the vicinity. The police grow more persistent in their investigation. Relations between Frank and Lenore become even more strained when the media and police connect the murders

Burt Lancaster is H. G. Wells's famous doctor in *The Island of Dr. Moreau* (AIP/Filmways, 1977).

to the couple's vicious offspring. When Frank discovers quantities of milk and raw meat missing from the refrigerator, he concludes that the nocturnal noises that he's noticed of late are not merely a matter of overwrought nerves. He begins carrying a loaded revolver, having determined to put this horror out of his life the first time he spies it. It is Lenore who actually discovers the child late one night. It makes no vicious move toward its mother, and Lenore finds her fear of it disappearing, to be replaced with a very real concern for its safety. She hides it in the basement, barring access to it when Frank appears. He brushes her aside. Firing his pistol at the small form that moves quickly behind the basement clutter, Frank wounds the child, which is nevertheless able to make a hasty exit, killing neighbor Charlie in the process. The police arrive and follow a bloody trail to a storm drain, which they conclude has been used by the child to move about under the city. Frank joins the manhunt into the labyrinth and finds the mewling infant at the end of a dark corridor. His resolve to kill it is overcome at the last second by his own sense of paternalism. Scooping up the infant, he evades the other searchers until he emerges from the sewer. There, the police surround him. The wriggling newborn gets away from Frank, and the police open fire. As he sits in a police cruiser returning him to his home, a message over the radio informs the inspector that "another one has just been born in Seattle."

Reviews: "Unlike *The Exorcist*, it does *not* reimpose repression at the end.... And unlike *Rosemary's Baby* and *The Omen*, it does *not* present the birth as the inevitable outcome of ancient prophecy, its consequences beyond anyone's control." (Robin Wood, *Film Comment*, September 1978, p. 23) ¶"Stomach-churning little film.... Some gut-level power ... a deadening assault on the human spirit." (Mack., *Variety,* October 16, 1974, p. 16)

Analysis: *It's Alive* is a slowly paced, somber little film that would be too depressing if it weren't for the occasional flashes of dark humor that informs it. Writer-producer-director Cohen rounded up a small host of veterans including Guy Stockwell, Andrew Duggan, Michael Ansara and Robert Emhardt for significant cameo appearances to support his main players, but possibly the major accomplishment of this film is that it marked the return of composer Bernard Herrmann to American films after a hiatus of nearly a decade. (After his unfortunate rift with Alfred Hitchcock regarding the composer's score for that director's *Torn Curtain* in 1965, and the industry's swing toward more popular, rock-oriented scores, Herrmann left the U.S. to make his home in England.) Cohen's dour little B-movie may have made for a seemingly inauspicious return for a composer who had worked with Orson Welles, William Dieterle, Robert Wise, Hitchcock, and other luminaries, but a return it did mark. Shortly, Herrmann would provide much-heralded scores for Brian De Palma (*Sisters, Obsession*) and Martin Scorsese (*Taxi Driver*) before an early, and quite unexpected, death claimed him in 1975. As for Herrmann's eerie and atmospheric score for *It's Alive*, it was sufficiently successful that

Cohen used it (as re-orchestrated and adapted by Herrmann's associate, Laurie Johnson) in both of the film's subsequent sequels.

It Lives Again
(Warner Bros., 1978; 91 min.) **½

Produced and directed by Larry Cohen. Associate Producer, William Wellman, Jr. Screenplay, Larry Cohen. Based on characters in the film *It's Alive*. Edited by Curt Burch, Louis Friedman, Carol O'Blath. Director of Photography, Fenton Hamilton. Technicolor. Music, Bernard Herrmann.

Cast: Eugene Scott (Frederic Forrest), Judy Scott (Kathleen Lloyd), Frank Davis (John P. Ryan), Mallory (John Marley), Dr. Perry (Andrew Duggan), Dr. Forest (Eddie Constantine), Detective Perkins (James Dixon).

Synopsis: Frank Davis tells Eugene and Judy Scott the story of the mutant baby gunned down by police several years earlier. Frank has come to feel that no one has the right to prevent the birth of such babies, as he knows a secret government agency is now attempting to do. Rather, he feels that they should be isolated, studied, and helped. To that purpose he has joined a secret network of people who feel the same way, a group which tries to intervene in cases where mutant births may be imminent. Thwarting Mallory, the head of the government group implementing the termination, Judy has her baby and takes up residence in a secluded country estate. Two mutant children are already securely caged in the basement, their care overseen by Dr. Perry. Eventually, Mallory and the police locate the site. Their raid coincides with the escape of the two slightly older mutant infants, who run amok, kill Perry and his staff and injure Eugene. Frank Davis manages to escape, carrying the Scott infant. The child, startled by a security guard, kills the man and crawls off into the underbrush. Mallory uses the Scotts as bait to draw their baby back. The government man reveals to the couple that his wife, too, had given birth to a mutant infant, and that the child slaughtered its mother. Having seen the killer instincts of these creatures at first hand, the Scotts are now more than willing to go along with Mallory's plan. After several evenings pass, their fanged and taloned son crashes into their bedroom. Their parental instincts prove stronger than their fears, and they are both drawn to it. Alerted by the Scotts' open bedroom window, the police flood the house with toxic gas. Mallory bursts in, attacks and is attacked by the child. The man goes down, even as the police fire round after round into the mutant child. Some time later, Eugene Scott is in San Francisco. He has his eye on a couple crossing the street; the woman is obviously pregnant. He goes to speak to them.

Review: "One of the richest horror movies of the Seventies and a decisive confirmation (if any were still needed) of Cohen's intelligence, consistency, and capacity for significant development." (Robin Wood, Richard Lippe, Andrew Britton, *Film Comment*, September 1978, p. 25)

Analysis: Containing more action than its predecessor, and probably more properly termed a *horror* film than *It's Alive*, this second essay into the child-mutant category by writer-producer-director Larry Cohen again tends to focus more on those being affected by the horror than on the horror itself. With the inclusion of the governmental conspiracy angle, Cohen adds an element of paranoia that was absent in the first film, and one that he would expand upon somewhat in the third installment. Also, as director, Cohen is canny enough to keep his plastic and unconvincing mutant infants mostly off camera, directing his lens towards the reaction of his actors more often than not, and the occasional point-of-view shot from the infants themselves. *It Lives Again* is a minor effort, to be sure, but one worth a look.

It's Alive III: Island of the Alive
(Warner Bros., 1987; 91 min.)**½

Produced by Paul Strader. Executive Producer, Larry Cohen. Directed by Larry Cohen. Screenplay, Larry Cohen. Edited by David Kern. Director of Photography, Daniel Pearl. Color. Music, Laurie Johnson. Theme, Bernard Herrmann. Creature Design, Rick Baker.

Cast: Steve Jarvis (Michael Moriarty), Ellen Jarvis (Karen Black), Sally (Laurene Landon), Ralston (Gerrit Graham), Lt. Perkins (James Dixon), Dr. Brewster (Neal Isreal), Judge Milton Watson (Macdonald Carey), Dr. Swenson (Art Lund), Dr. Morrell (Ann Dane), Robbins (Patch Mackenzie), Tony (Rick Garcia), Cabot (William Watson), TV host (Bobby Ramsen).

Synopsis: Stephen and Ellen Jarvis are the parents of another of the monstrously mutated infants that are routinely searched for by government execution squads. The experience itself was enough to destroy the Jarvis's marriage; Ellen leaves for Florida while Stephen remains in New York, petitioning the court to have his child spared. The hideous infant, present in a steel cage at the hearing, escapes and leaps at the judge. The child heeds its father's admonishments and stops short of harming the judge, who is touched by Stephen's plea and rules in his favor. The children will be removed to an uninhabited Caribbean island where they can perhaps be studied. Stephen attempts a reconciliation with Ellen, but she wants to put the entire episode behind her. After the children have been on the island for a time, a quartet of hunters appear. They are executives of a pharmaceutical firm which has marketed a certain drug speculated to be linked with the monstrous births. To prevent anyone from verifying this, they intend killing the children. But they fail to appreciate the quickness or viciousness of the now nearly full-grown monsters, and none leave the island alive. Four years later, the still troubled Stephen Jarvis is approached by Lt. Perkins, who had been involved with these monster children since the first one born to Mrs. Davis years earlier. Perkins informs Stephen of the death of Judge Watson. There will be a policy change, now, Perkins says, and the revisionist Dr. Swenson intends to go to the island to study the children. Perkins is going, owing to his experience, and he wants Jarvis to come along as well. Drawn by curiosity and a desire to protect the children, Stephen agrees to go. The party's sojourn upon the island is death to all except Stephen. Two males and a female mutation board his yacht and force him to accompany them. Feeding off the corpses of the former scientific party and sailing crew, the mutants force Stephen to pilot the ship until one of them mysteriously forces him onto a makeshift raft. Stephen is picked up by a Cuban patrol boat and makes his way to Florida. By chance, he comes ashore near the restaurant where his ex-wife Ellen works. Nearby also are the mutated creatures, one of whom kills one of Ellen's unwanted suitors. She sees the bloodied corpse and flees, pursued by the shambling mutant. Stephen climbs to her side on the rooftops. There, they see that two of the mutants are huddled together, one, the female, cuddling an infant of her own. Stephen and Ellen realize that this is their own grandchild. The older mutants seem to be dying, naturally perhaps, maybe of "old age." The two humans are touched and take their soon-to-be-orphaned child for their own. Police, alerted by the clamor, have the third mutant cornered. In the confusion, Stephen and Ellen steal a car. They're penniless fugitives, with a monster for a grandchild. For the time being, however, they have each other again.

Review: "Various types of satire blend satisfyingly.... remains interesting throughout." (Lor., *Variety*, May 20, 1987)

Analysis: It's Alive III is rich with the same uncomfortable brand of dark humor that made the first two entries in this series so unique, and is easily the slickest of the three. These films are not conventional thrillers and they are hardly gory enough to satisfy the demands of the slasher genre. Furthermore, the special effects remain crude by the standards of the late 80s. Cohen continues to prefer to make his viewer squirm through his choice of subject matter, which concentrates on thorny issues rather than customary chills; *It's Alive* and its sequels are not for all tastes. Michael Moriarty is ideal as Stephen Jarvis. James Dixon recreates his role of Lt. Perkins from the previous two films.

It's About Time *see* Amityville 92: It's About Time *under* **The Amityville Horror**

Jack of Swords *see* Trancers 4: Jack of Swords *under* **Trancers**

Jason Goes to Hell: The Final Friday *see under* **Friday the 13th**

Jason Lives *see* Friday the 13th, Part VI: Jason Lives *see under* **Friday the 13th**

Jason Takes Manhattan *see* Friday the 13th, Part VIII: Jason Takes Manhattan *see under* **Friday the 13th**

Jesse James Meets Frankenstein's Daughter *see under* **Frankenstein**

Judgment Day *see* Terminator 2: Judgment Day *under* **The Terminator**

Jungle Woman *see under* **Captive Wild Woman**

A Kid in King Arthur's Court *see under* **A Connecticut Yankee**

Killer Tomatoes Strike Back! *see* **Attack of the Killer Tomatoes**

King Kong
(RKO, 1933; 100 min.) ****

Executive Producer, David O. Selznick. Directed by Ernest B. Schoedsack and Merian C. Cooper. Screenplay, James Creelman, Ruth Rose and Merian C. Cooper. Story, Edgar Wallace and Merian C. Cooper. Edited by Ted Cheeseman. Directors of Photography, Edward Linden, Vernon L. Walker, J. O. Taylor. Music, Max Steiner. Sound, E. A. Wolcott. Sound Effects, Murray Spivak. Art Direction, Carroll Clark, Al Heman. Special Effects, Willis O'Brien. Technical Staff, E. B. Gibson, Marcel Delgado, Fred Reefe, Orville Goldner, Carol Shepphird. Production Assistants, Archie S. Marshek, Walter Daniels. Art Technicians, Mario Larrinaga, Byron L. Crabbe.

Cast: Carl Denham (Robert Armstrong), Jack Driscoll (Bruce Cabot), Ann Darrow (Fay Wray), Captain Engelhorn (Frank Reicher), Native chief (Noble Johnson), Second Mate Briggs (James Flavin), Witchdoctor (Steve Clemento), Charlie (Victor Wong), Weston (Sam Hardy), Mate (Ethan Laidlaw), Sailors (Dick Curtis, Charlie Sullivan), Theater patrons (Vera Lewis, LeRoy Mason), Apple vendor (Paul Porcasi), Reporters (Lynton Brent, Frank Mills).

Synopsis: Famous for his films made in

The giant ape menaces Carl Denham's crew in *King Kong* (RKO, 1933).

exotic locales, Carl Denham desperately seeks a leading lady for a new production before the authorities impound his explosive-laden ship, the *Venture*. Searching New York City, he convinces Ann Darrow that she'll have a swell time if she accompanies him. They set sail to a previously uncharted island on which an ancient manmade wall separates the inhabited portion from forbidding mountain and jungle. Landing, the party stumbles on a tribal ritual, seemingly the sacrifice of a young woman. Finding that they are observed, the natives express much interest in the blonde Miss Darrow. Captain Engelhorn parlays with the chief and promises to return the next day. That night Ann is kidnapped and taken through the massive gate, and tied between two pillars. Atop the wall a gong is struck. Meanwhile Denham and most of his crew have discovered that Ann is missing and go ashore. At the gate they see a giant gorilla carrying Ann into the jungle. Kong! Leaving some men at the gate, Denham and Driscoll and some others chase Kong and his captive into a primeval world. Encountering a prehistoric stegosaurus, they kill it without casualties. This is not the case with a brontosaurus which upsets their raft and chases them inland. Hearing the ruckus, Kong places Ann in a tree and investigates. At a chasm Kong shakes the log bridge and most of the men fall to their deaths. Driscoll climbs into a cave, fending off Kong's hand with his knife. Hearing Ann's screams, Kong returns to her and fights a tyrannosaurus to the death. Driscoll yells across the chasm to Denham that he will track Kong while Denham returns for help. Kong secretes Ann in his mountain cave but must kill a lizard before resting on a precipice. Hearing Driscoll, Kong goes inside. Ann crawls to the edge of the precipice but is grabbed by a pterodactyl. Kong rushes back and grasps the creature before it can get away. While Kong busies himself with the flying reptile, Driscoll and Ann descend on a vine. Kong notices and begins hauling them back up. They let go and fall into a lake. Reaching the wall, they find Kong on their heels. He breaks through the gate and kills many of the natives before being stopped on the shore by a gas bomb. Denham promises to share the fame and fortune with everyone once they get Kong back to New York. In the city Kong is put on display but breaks his chains when he thinks the reporters' flashbulbs are harming Ann. He rages through the city, destroys an elevated train and kidnaps Ann for the second time. He carries her to the top of the Empire State Building, where biplanes machine-gun him. Mortally wounded, he picks up Ann one last time and, after placing her down, releases his hold and falls to his death.

Reviews: "Decidedly compelling.... enough thrills for any devotee of such tales." (Mordaunt Hall, *New York Times*, March 3, 1933, p. 12) ¶"Highly imaginative and super-goofy.... technical excellence." (Bige., *Variety*, March 7, 1933)

Analysis: Kong is the daddy of sound-film giant creatures, and the film has never been eclipsed for sheer adventure and special effects. The *New York Times* review praised the camera tricks that propelled the narrative forward: multiple exposures, process shots, tricky camera angles. Max Steiner's music is the first truly great film symphonic score. There is the proper amount of suspense-building (the first half-hour) before we are introduced to the fantastic and dangerous primordial creatures on the island where a giant gorilla is lord. Fay Wray was a great screamer, of course, ranking right there with Miriam Hopkins and Susan Hayward. She's also lovely and sexy as her clothes get torn to shreds during her trials. Willis O'Brien's dinosaurs are larger than the real ones, but then, Kong is much larger than a real gorilla. Kong, in reality an armatured automaton of various heights, displays the emotions of a human. For many of us, his death on the Empire State Building is the saddest moment in film history. Some of the sets were used in RKO's *The Most Dangerous Game* (1932). There are innumerable memorable scenes, and not just the usually noted ones of the Empire State Building and the fight with the tyrannosaurus. For instance: Kong and Ann on the precipice with the wall and the *Venture* moored offshore in the distance; their rush through the jungle as Steiner's thumping notes heighten the tension. For decades *King Kong* was seen minus several scenes. Janus Films restored them in the early 70s: Kong fiddling with Ann's dress, Kong stomping and chewing on natives. Apparently never found was the footage with giant spiders from which stills exist. Unbelievably, as late as 1986's *King Kong Lives*, some critics believed that a man in a monster suit played the original Kong.

Son of Kong
(RKO, 1933; 70 min.) ***

Directed by Ernest B. Schoedsack. Story, Ruth Rose. Edited by Ted Cheeseman. Directors of Photography, Eddie Linden, Vernon Walker, J. O. Taylor. Sound, Earl Colcott.

Cast: Carl Denham (Robert Armstrong), Hilda Peterson (Helen Mack), Captain Engelhorn (Frank Reicher), Charlie (Victor Wong), Helstrom (John Marston), Mickey

(Lee Kohlmar), Red (Ed Brady), Peterson (Clarence Wilson), Native chief (Noble Johnson), Witchdoctor (Steve Clemento), Chinese trader (James L. Leong), Process server (Frank O'Connor), Mrs. Hudson (Katharine Ward), Girl reporter (Gertrude Short), Servant girl (Gertrude Sutton).

Synopsis: Pursued by creditors and sued for damages caused by the giant ape Kong when he escaped in New York, Carl Denham takes Captain Engelhorn up on his offer to return to the South Seas where they can make a decent living hauling goods between the islands. At Dakang they meet Hilda Peterson, whose father dies after a fire destroys their rinky-dink carny show. They take her and Helstrom aboard for a return trip to Kong's island 1,753 miles away. They've heard there is a treasure there. Upon landing, Denham and Hilda are separated from the other three, who are attacked and cornered by a triceratops-like dinosaur. Denham and Hilda rescue a twelve-foot white ape from quicksand, and it repays their kindness by driving off a monstrous bear and later a dragon-like reptile. Helstrom is killed by a marine lizard. An earthquake tears down the whole island, but little Kong saves Denham, holding him above the water till Engelhorn, Charlie and Hilda row over. They will use the diamonds they found in a temple to start a new life.

Review: "Low melodrama with a number of laughs ... although the comical intent of the producers is open to argument." (A.D.S., *New York Times*, December 30, 1933, p. 9)

Analysis: It's too fast, too cute and thus disappointing. The effects are, of course, great, and Kong's island is a masterpiece of mystery and fantasy. It gives you the creeps. Why didn't Denham seem more worried?

King Kong
(Paramount, 1976; 134 min.) **

Produced by Dino De Laurentiis. Executive Producers, Federico De Laurentiis, Christian Fery. Directed by John Guillermin. Assistant Directors, David McGiffert, Kurt Neumann, Pat Kehoe. Screenplay, Lorenzo Semple, Jr. Edited by Ralph E. Winters. Director of Photography, Richard H. Kline.

Panavision. Color. Music, John Barry. Art Direction, Archie J. Bacon, David A. Constable, Robert Gundlach. Costumes, Moss Mabry. Choreography, Claude Thompson.

Cast: Jack Prescott (Jeff Bridges), Fred Wilson (Charles Grodin), Dwan (Jessica Lange), Captain Ross (John Randolph), Bagley (Rene Auberjonois), Joe Perko (Jack O' Halloran), Sunfish (Dennis Fimple), Carnahan (Ed Lauter), Garcia (Jorge Moreno), Timmons (Mario Gallo), Chinese cook (John Lone), City official (John Agar), General (Garry Halberg), Petrox Chairman (Sid Conrad), Helicopter pilot (George Whiteman), Air Force colonel (Wayne Heffley), Ape-masked man (Keny Long).

Synopsis: The *Petrox Explorer* leaves Indonesia seeking a mysterious South Pacific island which satellite photos show to be perpetually hidden behind dense mists. Unlike Fred Wilson, stowaway paleontologist Jack Prescott believes that rather than an immense oil reserve, there is a large, heretofore unknown life form on the island. En route to the island, a young woman named Dwan is plucked from a life raft. Arriving at the fog-shrouded island, the landing party is surprised to find a tribe of primitives who have apparently erected a huge wooden wall separating their portion of the island from the larger jungle and mountainous region beyond. When the natives pay unwelcome attention to the golden-haired Dwan, the oil men retreat to the *Explorer*. That night Dwan is kidnapped and taken to the village, where she is dressed in native attire and tied between pillars on an altar-like construction outside the walled village. The natives retreat behind their walls and raise a din soon answered by an approaching disturbance. Dwan looks up to see a gigantic ape above the treetops. Apparently mesmerized by the woman, it releases her bonds. Having discovered Dwan missing, a party led by Wilson and Prescott arrives in time to see Kong disappearing into the jungle with the unconscious girl. Jack leads a party after the gargantua while Wilson prepares a trap should the beast return. Next morning, after taking a closer look at his "sacrificial bride," Kong hears the sounds of the men, backtracks and dislodges a log which sends all but Jack to death in a crevice. Prescott follows the ape and snatches the girl, and the two flee back toward the village. Wilson has constructed a huge concealed pit filled with canisters of paralyzing gas. Capturing the giant, Wilson knows he's made a publicity coup and won't listen to Prescott's arguments that he's doing the natives a disservice and mocking the zoological find of the century. In New York, Kong is wheeled out of the ship's hold in chains, a Petrox crown upon his head. As the gala reaches its peak, with Dwan and Wilson mounting the nearby podium, Kong becomes agitated at the sight of the girl and breaks his shackles. Kong strides into the crowd, crushing the slowest of the gawkers. Jack Prescott arrives in time to whisk the frightened Dwan away; Fred Wilson isn't so lucky, going down beneath one of the ape's huge feet. Dwan's respite is short-lived, as the ape finds her and disappears into the night. Ultimately, Kong is drawn to the twin towers of the World Trade Center, similar as it is to a geological structure on his home island. Climbing to the top of the skyscraper with Dwan, the huge beast releases the girl safely before he is at last brought down by the combined firepower of a trio of helicopter gunships.

Reviews: "The 100 minutes of Kong I packed ten times more punch and poetry than the two and a quarter hours of Kong II.... positively phosphorescent with false sophistication." (Jack Kroll, *Newsweek*, December 20, 1976, pp. 102–103)

Analysis: Variety (December 15, 1976) found this remake "faithful" to the original and credited it with a neat balance of special effects and "dramatic credibility." And indeed, the film opens with some promise. In the fifty minutes it takes for Rick Baker to make his appearance in this Dino De Laurentiis production, one can almost get into the spirit of this 1976 remake of the Merian C. Cooper classic. However, once the painfully obvious man-in-the-ape-suit releases a screaming Jessica Lange from her perch atop the natives' sacrificial altar, the going is increasingly unpleasant and the scales tip incontrovertibly in favor of the earlier film. The 1933 film towers over the remake every bit as much as King Kong towered over Carl

Denham. Nowhere to be seen is the spectacular stop-motion animation that made the original film famous; likewise missing are the beautiful painted backgrounds that contributed so much to that one's sense of wonder. In place of the simple "beauty and the beast" parable of Edgar Wallace and Merian Cooper, we're given an all-too-hip potboiler that rants about big business, the oil companies, ecology, feminism, smarmy politics ... you name it. The only thing De Laurentiis's film has going for it is a handsome production and a first-rate cast, which are the only factors that account for the two-star rating. John Guillermin keeps things moving in the unimaginative and at times embarrassingly bad script, and John Barry provides a magisterial score that is totally wasted. Nominated for Academy Awards for cinematography and sound. Incredibly, it became the third highest grossing movie of the year and received a Special Achievement Academy Award for special effects. (The same award was given to *Logan's Run*.)

King Kong Lives
(De Laurentiis Entertainment Group, 1986; 105 min.) *½

Produced by Martha Schumacher. Directed by John Guillermin. Screenplay, Ronald Shusett and Steven Pressfield. Edited by Malcolm Cooke. Director of Photography, Alec Mills. Technicolor. Music, John Scott. Dolby Stereo. Art Direction, Fred Carter, Tony Reading, John Wood. Stunts, Bud Davis. Special Visual Effects, Barry Nolan. Creatures, Carlo Rambaldi. Special Effects Makeup, Dean Gates.

Cast: Amy Franklin (Linda Hamilton), Hank Mitchell (Brian Kerwin), King Kong (Peter Elliot), Lady Kong (George Yiasomi), Colonel Nevitt (John Ashton), Dr. Ingersoll (Peter Michael Goetz), Dr. Benson Hughes (Frank Maraden), Faculty doctor #1 (Alan Sader), Faculty doctor #2 (Lou Criscuolo), Crew chief (Marc Clement), Surgeon #1 (Natt Christian), Surgeon #2 (Mac Pirkle), Journalist (Larry Sprinkle), TV reporter (Rod Davis), Mazlansky (Robin Cahall), Security chief (Don Law), Wrangler #1 (Jack Maloney), Major Pete (Jimmie Ray Weeks), Radioman #1 (Jeff Benninghofen), Sergeant (Jim Grimshaw).

Synopsis: King Kong, the giant ape that

fell to his presumed death, is resuscitated by modern technological, not to say heroic, measures. Simultaneously, a giant female ape is discovered in Borneo and Kong taken to her. But it's no paradise for the giant apes. Hunters try to bury Kong with a landslide blast and torment him with fire. Kong breaks loose after tearing one hunter apart and eating another. Amy and Hank locate Kong by airplane and try to release the female from the underground prison in which the army has incarcerated her, but Kong accomplishes the deed. Kong kills an army captain and destroys his unit. The female has a baby, which sees its father before Kong is killed by army guns.

Review: "The problem with all the folk in *King Kong Lives* is that they're in a boring movie, and they know they're in a boring movie, and they just can't stir themselves to make an effort." (Roger Ebert, *New York Post*, December 22, 1986, p. 23) ¶"The battle scenes, for all their extravagance, are none too compelling." (Janice Berman, *Newsday*, December 20, 1986, Part II, p. 8)

Analysis: This is an odd film to be made at this stage of movie history. A big-time director, Carlo Rambaldi "effects," Linda Hamilton—but a B-movie plot. Not to mention the people in ape suits, which always makes us cringe. The she-ape and the baby live, because they are shown back in the jungle. But you don't exactly know how they got there. What happened to Amy and Hank?

The Lady and the Doctor *see* The Lady and the Monster

The Lady and the Monster
(Republic, 1944; 86 min.) nv

Produced and directed by George Sherman. Screenplay, Dane Lussier and Frederick Kohner. Based on the novel *Donovan's Brain* by Curt Siodmak. Director of Photography, John Alton. Music, Walter Scharf. Art Direction, Russell Kimball. Set Decoration, Otto Siegel. Special Effects, Theodore Lydecker.

Cast: Janice Farrell (Vera Hruba Ralston), Professor Franz Mueller (Erich von Stroheim), Patrick Cory (Richard Arlen), Eugene

Fulton (Sidney Blackmer), Chloe Donovan (Helen Vinson), Mrs. Fame (Mary Nash), Grimes (Charles Cane), Roger Collins (Bill Henry), G. Phipps, bank manager (Sam Flint), Ranger White (Lane Chandler), Dr. Martin (Harry Hayden), Mary Lou (Juanita Quigley), Receptionist (Maxine Doyle), Maning (Edward Keane), Bellhop (William Benedict), Warden (Wallis Chark), Mary Lou's grandmother (Josephine Dillon), Husky man (Tom London), Dancers (Lola Montes, Antonio Triano), Head waiter (Lee Phelps), Bank teller (Harry Depp), Cafe singer (Janet Mertin), Narrator (Frank Graham).

Synopsis: Professor Franz Mueller tries to keep alive the brain of mob financier Donovan. The brain takes control of his assistant, Patrick Cory, and makes him kill the mobster's enemies.

Review: "[The novel] *Donovan's Brain*, lost an intriguing title and a large portion of plausibility and pace...." (A.W., *New York Times*, April 8, 1944, p. 9)

Analysis: Erich von Stroheim had been a major silent film director and a star. Richard Arlen had been a leading man and co-starred with Charles Laughton in *Island of Lost Souls*. Czech-born champion ice skater Vera Hruba Ralston would become the wife of Republic's head Herbert Yates, who would put her in many films. Aka *The Lady and the Doctor*.

Donovan's Brain
(United Artists, 1953; 83 min.) ***

Produced by Tom Gries. Directed by Felix Feist. Screenplay, Felix Feist. Adaptation, Hugh Brooks. Based on the novel by Curt Siodmak. Edited by Herbert L. Strock. Director of Photography, Joseph Biroc. Music, Eddie Dunstedter. Special Effects, Harry Redmond, Jr.

Cast: Dr. Patrick J. Cory (Lew Ayres), Dr. Frank Schratt (Gene Evans), Janice Cory (Nancy Davis [Reagan]), Herbie Yocum (Steve Brodie), Chloe Donovan (Lisa K. Howard), Tom Donovan (Michael Colgan), Ranger Chief Tuttle (Kyle James), Advisor (Tom Powers), W. J. Higgins (Stapleton Kent), Mr. Webster (Peter Adams), Nathaniel Fuller (Victor Sutherland), Mr. MacNish (John Hamilton), Mr. Brooke (Harlan Warde), Mr. Smith (Paul Hoffman), Dr. Crane (William Cottrell), Receptionist (Faith Langley), Hotel desk clerk (Tony Merrill), Supply company clerk (Mark Lowell), Tailor (Shimen Ruskin).

Synopsis: Drs. Cory and Schratt are research scientists busily pursuing experiments that will lead to successful brain transplants, when word comes to them of a nearby plane crash. One of the victims is millionaire industrialist W. H. Donovan. Lacking nearby facilities, the rangers who rescue the victims bring the nearly dead Donovan to the home of Dr. Cory. The scientists are unable to save him, but Cory and Schratt manage to transfer his still-living brain to a tank of liquid nutrient. Miraculously, the organ not only lives, but seems to thrive and actually grow noticeably larger within its new confines. Not only that, it seems to exert at first a subtle, then a more malign influence over Cory. W. H. Donovan, the others learn, was a self-made millionaire, supremely independent of will, and intensely resentful of the taxes he has been forced to pay, a situation that had led to much trouble with the Internal Revenue Service. Within mere hours, Cory's personality begins to change, his features hardening, his manner becoming surly. He becomes left-handed, even as Donovan had been, and he begins to walk, as had the late millionaire, with a noticeable limp. Janice and Dr. Schratt notice the changes almost immediately, but are at first unable to make a connection between these oddities and the seemingly dormant brain floating in the tank in the lab. Herbie Yocum, a reporter who turns up shortly after the accident, gradually stumbles upon the truth and makes a demand for money. Cory, not entirely subsumed by the persona of ruthless Donovan, concedes to the blackmail, and Yocum leaves. Within a short time, the scientist's personality has been entirely repressed by the remorseless millionaire's will, and Cory becomes W. H. Donovan, assuming the role of the dead man's executor, going about the business of disinheriting Donovan's children. Plans are made to construct more permanent housing for the malicious brain. When Yocum appears at the lab sometime later, demanding more money, the brain, swollen and corpulent, exerts its will over his. Helpless to resist, the reporter staggers from the lab, gets into his car, and drives over a cliff. As the brain is focused

on Yocum, Cory's mind clears enough for him to make a recording that will be sent to Janice. Once more in full control of Dr. Cory, Donovan determines that Dr. Schratt and Janice both are too much of a threat and decides to kill them. Schratt, seeing the transformation that has been taking place with his friend Cory, decides to act on his own, forcing his way into the now secured lab and advancing upon the brain with a drawn gun to fire several shots ineffectively into the tank. However, he too is overcome by the force of the brain's will: He turns the gun upon himself and fires. Coming to see the cause of the shots, Janice is horrified, but her husband, cool and emotionless under the domination of the nearby brain, informs her that he has no further use for either Schratt or her, and proceeds to strangle her. Even at that moment, however, a thunderstorm is raging outside, and a lightning rod, which Janice has had installed after listening to the hastily recorded message from her husband, does its work. A lethal charge of electricity is routed from the rod through wiring leading to the tank housing the evil brain. W. H. Donovan dies a second time.

Review: "Limpid and artificial.... utterly silly." (Bosley Crowther, *New York Times,* January 21, 1954, p. 28)

Analysis: Donovan's Brain is a mild, leisurely paced little thriller that benefits mainly from the superb performance of Lew Ayres as Dr. Pat Cory. Eschewing special effects of almost any kind, this film achieves considerably more genuine effect by Ayres' convincing transformation from a gentle, dedicated man of science to the avaricious and ruthless W. H. Donovan. This transformation is made solely by Ayres' thespian talents, totally without photographic or lighting tricks, and without the application of makeup that usually accompanies such things. Gene Evans, a character actor usually noted for either his tough-guy or sinister portrayals, turns in a surprisingly sympathetic performance here as Dr. Schratt, Cory's good-natured, alcoholic assistant. Nancy Davis, later Nancy Reagan, provides the moral support all good wives and gal Fridays were expected to provide in science fiction films in the fifties. Lew Ayres had an auspicious career in the early 1930s, most notably as the star of the Academy Award–winning *All Quiet on the Western Front* (1930). He was the screen's Dr. Kildare, but his career suffered when, during World War II, he became a conscientious objector. One of his best postwar roles was as the empathetic doctor in *Johnny Belinda* (1947). Later (see *The Omen* in this book) he became a fine character actor.

The Brain
(Governor, 1962; 85 min.) nv

Produced by Raymond Stross. Directed by Freddie Francis. Screenplay, Robert Stewart and Phil Mackie. Edited by Oswald Hafenrichter. Director of Photography, Bob Huke. Music, Ken Jones. Art Direction, Arthur Lawson.

Cast: Dr. Peter Corrie (Peter Van Eyck), Anna Holt (Anne Heywood), Frank Shears (Bernard Lee), Stevenson (Cecil Parker), Marion Fane (Maxine Audley), Martin Holt (Jeremy Spenser), Furber (Jack MacGowran), Dr. Miller (Miles Malleson), Francis (Frank Forsyth), Gabler (George A. Cooper), Secretary (Ann Sears), Dr. Silva (Allan Cuthbertson), Mrs. Gabler (Irene Richmond), Ella (Ellen Schwiers), Inspector Pike (Alistair Williams), Martin (Siegfried Lowitz), Immerman (Hans Nielsen), Farmer (Victor Brooks), Newscaster (Kenneth Kendall), Miss Soong (Bandana Das Gupta), Parkin (Richard McNeff), Frederick (John Junkin), Priest (John Watson), Master of ceremonies (Brian Pringle), Dance hall girl (Patsy Rowlands).

Synopsis: Max Holt, survivor of an airplane accident, is taken to the lab of Dr. Peter Corrie and his assistant, Frank Shears. The body is past recovery, but Corrie keeps the brain alive in a special solution. The brain begins taking over Corrie. Corrie meets Holt's daughter, Anna, his son and lawyer at Holt's funeral. Suspecting that Holt was murdered, he searches for the killer. Corrie is framed for the murder of Holt's chauffeur Gable. Under Holt's influence, Corrie almost actually commits a murder, but Shears removes the brain from its tank in time to prevent the act. Later, Corrie learns that Anna caused the death of her father because he had monopolized a new drug.

Review: "Filmed twice before, but still effective as a suspenseful horror thriller." (Steven H. Scheuer, ed., *TV Key Movie Guide*, p. 42)

Analysis: A West German-British co-production with a fine cast. Other titles: *Vengeance* and *A Dead Man Seeks His Murderer*.

Notes of Interest: The TV/movie *Hauser's Memory* (1970) is another version of *Donovan's Brain*. Akin to this but not directly based on the Siodmak story is the 1962 Virginia Leith–starring film, *The Brain That Wouldn't Die*.

Lady Frankenstein *see under* **Frankenstein**

The Land That Time Forgot
(Amicus/AIP, 1975; 90 min.) **½

Produced by John Dark. Max J. Rosenberg and Milton Subotsky Production. Presented by Samuel Z. Arkoff. Directed by Kevin Connor. Screenplay, James Cawthorn and Michael Moorcock. Based on the novel by Edgar Rice Burroughs. Edited by John Ireland. Director of Photography, Alan Hume. Technicolor. Music, Douglas Gamley. Art Direction, Bert Davey. Set Decoration, Simon Wakefield.

Cast: Bowen Tyler (Doug McClure), Lisa Clayton (Susan Penhaligon), Captain Von Schoenvorts (John McEnery), Lt. Diets (Anthony Ainley), Bradley (Keith Barron), Borg (Godfrey James), Ahm (Bobby Farr), Olson (Declan Mulholland), Whiteley (Colin Farrell), Benson (Ben Howard), Sinclair (Andrew McCulloch), Deusett (Grahame Mallard), Schwartz (Brian Hall), Hindle (Peter Sproule), Jones (Ron Pember), Reuther (Andrew Lodge), Hiller (Stanley McGeagh), 1st Sto-Lu (Steve James).

Synopsis: A manuscript found in a bottle describes the strange adventure of American Bowen Tyler: On June 3, 1916, the ship he is traveling on is torpedoed by a German U-boat. Two longboats with Bowen, biologist Lisa, and some British crew members survive. When the submarine surfaces, Bowen's group surprises the Germans and commandeers the vessel. Trying to contact a British warship, they are fired on and submerge. After sailing six days south because Lt. Diets tampered with the compass, the Germans regain control, only to find Bowen using their torpedoes to sink their supply ship. Entering an ice field, the ship discovers what Captain Schoenvorts believes is the lost continent of Caprona. Finding a freshwater river flowing out of the coast through a tunnel, they take the sub down and emerge in a verdant world of prehistoric creatures and prehistoric men. Enlisting the aid of one of these, Ahm, they find crude oil they hope will run the sub until they can find a neutral port. While Bowen, Lisa and three men make the last trek to the oil deposits, a volcanic eruption occurs, and Diets takes control of the sub. But the river boils and the craft cannot escape to the outside world. Bowen and Lisa, having escaped the ape men's village, watch in horror and realize they are alone on Caprona with little hope of rescue.

Review: "The best Saturday matinee movie in much too long." (Jay Cocks, *Time*, April 14, 1975, pp. 65–66)

Analysis: Viewed as a B-movie, this is not bad. The dinosaurs are not state-of-the-art. In other words, there's no stop-motion animation; the dinosaurs are large mock-ups that are not flexible enough and do not, obviously, move fast enough to be believable. Are there men in the allosaurus suits? Why was the sub's cannon used on the triceratops-like creatures? That was gratuitous since they were not attacking. More could have been made of the overall situation: a longer trek, more creatures. It's difficult to fathom the biological basis tossed out as an explanation for the life forms. It has something to do with more advanced life in the molecules at the head of the spring.

The People That Time Forgot
(Amicus/AIP, 1977; 90 min.)**

Produced by John Dark. A Max J. Rosenberg Production. Executive Producer, Samuel Z. Arkoff. Directed by Kevin Connor. Assistant Director, Bryan Coates. Screenplay, Patrick Tilley. Based on the novel *The People That Time Forgot* by Edgar Rice Burroughs. Edited by John Ireland and Barry Peters. Director of Photography, Alan Hume. Movielab Color. Music, John Scott. Art Direction, Bert Davey, Fernando Gonzalez. Set Dresser, Simon

Wakefield. Costumes, Brenda Dabbs. Special Effects Supervisor — Spain, John Richardson. Special Effects Supervisor — United Kingdom, Ian Wingrove.

Cast: Major Ben McBride (Patrick Wayne), Lady Charlotte/Charly (Sarah Douglas), Dr. Edwin Norfolk (Thorley Walters), Bowen Tyler (Doug McClure), Ajor (Dana Gillespie), Sabbala (Milton Reid), Hogan (Shane Rimmer), Bolam the dwarf (Kiran Shah), Captain Lawton (Tony Britton), Executioner (Dave Prowse), Lieutenant Graham (Jimmy Ray), Telegraphist (Tony McHale). With John Hallam, Gaylord Reid, Richard Parmentier.

Synopsis: After finding Bowen Tyler's message about Caprona, a joint American-British expedition sponsored by the *Times* sails to the island aboard the *Polar Queen*. In a biplane, the *Amphibian*, Major Ben McBride, Lady Charlotte, Dr. Edwin Norfolk, and Hogan explore the interior. Attacked by a pterodactyl, they are forced down. Hogan is left to repair the plane while the others search for Tyler, an old friend of McBride. They meet a "cave girl," Ajor, who speaks some English and tells them Tyler taught her. She describes her flight from a savage stone age tribe and Tyler's capture. The three are themselves captured and staked out as a sacrifice to the prehistoric creatures that inhabit the island. Ajor cuts them free and they proceed to the land of a different tribe, one that worships a volcano. These people ride horses and are ruled over by Sabbala. Inside the Mountain of Skulls, McBride and Norfolk are incarcerated while the women are prepared for sacrifice to the volcano. Tyler makes his presence known and reveals that Lisa had been sacrificed. The three overcome their guards and confront Sabbala, who falls into the lava. Tyler uses the pistol Lady Charlotte produces from her camera bag to hold off pursuers until felled by an arrow. The others make it to the plane, lighten it to make it over the mountains, and rejoin the *Polar Queen* in time to escape the volcano's wrath.

Review: "What is really needed ... is a creative script, imaginative direction and acting and some levity...." (A.H. Weiler, *New York Times*, July 7, 1977, p. C18)

Analysis: It's for 10–12 year olds. How come that first pterodactyl wasn't grounded by two clips of machine gun bullets? Later the same fellow fells them from the sky with one shot from his rifle. The film does have excellent explosions and sound effects, and the Mountain of Skulls is an impressive set. The real scenery, which is the Canary Island of Santa Cruz de la Palma, is beautifully variegated. For most of the story, Sarah Douglas has buns on the side of her head; that same year, Princess Leia (Carrie Fisher) became famous for a similar coiffure in *Star Wars*.

The Last Kiss *see* Prom Night III: The Last Kiss *under* **Prom Night**

The Last Temptation of Toxie *see* The Toxic Avenger Part III: The Last Temptation of Toxie *under* **The Toxic Avenger**

The Legend of Boggy Creek

(Halco/Cinema Shares International/ Pierce-Ledwell Productions, 1975; 90 min.) **½

Produced and directed by Charles B. Pierce. Executive Producers, L. W. Ledwell, Charles Pierce. Screenplay, Earl E. Smith. Edited by Thomas F. Boutross. Director of Photography, Charles Pierce. Technicolor. Music, Jamie Mendoza-Nava.

Cast: Jim as a boy (Chuck Pierce), Jim as an adult (William Stumpp), Willie E. Smith (Himself), John P. Hixon (Himself), John W. Oates (Himself), James Crabtree (Buddy Crabtree), Herb Jones (Himself), Fred Crabtree (Jeff Crabtree). Narrated by Vern Stierman.

Synopsis: "This is a true story." A human-like hairy beast confounds the inhabitants of southwestern Arkansas, especially Foucke. Perhaps it is a sasquatch, an American Indian term for a lost tribe. Whatever, it periodically retreats to hidden lairs in the bottomlands. Originally it was only half seen. When it returned after an eight-year absence it made its presence felt by peering in windows. Occasionally it would kill a dog, cat or pig.

Reviews: "Often visually stunning and exciting because of the virgin Arkansas location sites.... lovely music score." (Goff., *Variety*, December 6, 1972, p. 20)

Analysis: An oddity, but *Variety* is on target. It's not boring, and the landscape *is* intriguing even if we can imagine only hermits wanting to live there. *Variety* suggested the movie's best chance of success was that its campy tone might inspire a cult following.

Return to Boggy Creek

(Samuel Goldwyn/Bob Gates Production, 1977; 87 min.) **

Produced by Bob Gates. Directed by Tom Moore. Screenplay, John David Woody. Story, Tom Moore. Edited by Jerry Caraway. Director of Photography, Robert E. Bethard. Panavision. Technicolor. Music, Darrell Deck. Song: "Return to Boggy Creek." Music composed and Sung by Winston Coulter. Lyrics, John David Woody. Set Decoration, Ken Kennedy. Monster designed by Terry Moore and June S. Grubb.

Cast: Jolene (Dawn Wells), Evie Jo (Dana Plato), John Paul (David Sobiesk), T Fish (Marcus Claudel), Grandpa (John Hofues), Uncle Bo (Jim Wilson), Crawfish Charlie (Ray Gaspard), Bruno (Richard Cusimano), Perkins (John Fiero), Monster (Louis Belaire).

Synopsis: At the market where youngsters Evie Jo, T Fish and John Paul are winning the fishing contest as usual, photographer Perkins mentions seeing something strange in the forest. Since there are no bears in this neck of the woods, the citizens recall "Big Bay Tie," the Boggy Creek monster. After being accosted but unharmed by the creature, Evie Jo, T Fish and John Paul follow Perkins when Bruno leads him in search of the monster. Hurricane Elsie hits the swamp and lightning strikes Bruno's boat. The children rescue the men and find refuge in a wrecked boat. They are dismayed to discover it's the monster's home, but the beast produces a smaller boat covered in a tarp with which he pulls and shoves the children and the unconscious men to safety. After he recovers, Perkins asks if there is a monster. Evie Jo says it's just a legend.

Review: "G-rated nonsense may intrigue young viewers." (Leonard Maltin, ed., *TV Movies and Video Guide 1989*, p. 877)

Analysis: It's tame enough to be broadcast on cable's Disney Channel, and that's how it should be reviewed: as a children's film. The "monster," after all, saves their lives. This is one of the few theatrical films of Dawn Wells, alumnus of TV's *Gilligan's Island*. Dana Plato has more screen time. Filmed in Louisiana. Louisiana *or* Arkansas, are there no bears there?

Boggy Creek II: And the Legend Continues ...

(Howco International Charles B. Pierce Pictures/Media Home Entertainment, 1983; 93 min.) *½

Produced and directed by Charles B. Pierce. Screenplay, Charles B. Pierce. Edited by Shirak Khojayan. Director of Photography, Shirak Khojayan. Color, Movielab. Music, Frank McKelvey. Makeup, Pam Pierce. Creature Costumes, Bill Khopler.

Cast: Dr. Lockhart (Charles B. Pierce), Tim Thornton (Chuck Pierce), Leslie Ann Walker (Cindy Butler), Tanya Yozzie (Serene Hedin), Old Man Crenshaw (Jimmy Clem), Deputy (Rick [Rock] Hildreth), Storekeeper (James Tennison), Otis Tucker (Don Atkins), W. L. Slogan (Charles Vanderburg), Oscar Culpotter (Charles Potter), Myrtle Culpotter (Pat Waggner), Girl at swimming hole (Pam Pierce), Big creature (Fabus Griffin), Little creature (Victor Williams).

Synopsis: "The swamps of southern Arkansas, stretching out for miles and miles," begins the narrator, who relates the tale of the boggy Creek monster, seen attacking a deer in the water. Following a report of new sightings, a University of Arkansas professor, a male and female student, and the coed's female friend drive to the Texarkana area and set up camp. An attack by a rabid dog frightens the quartet, but they continue their research, encountering a large, hairy humanoid several times and discovering a young one recently captured by old man Crenshaw. They take the little one back to the parent and return to civilization, content to let the monsters remain free.

Review: "Pseudo-documentary schlockmeister Charles B. Pierce is at it again.... Cut-rate production values abound." (Mick Martin and Marsha Porter, *Video Movie Guide 1994*, p. 788)

Analysis: Called "II" even though it's a third installment. The clarity of the cinematography is better than in the first film, but the documentary-like beginning is compromised by increasingly silly actions by the characters and by one unbelievable attribute of the monster: the ability to swim underwater for great lengths of time. Tasteless is a sequence with the rabid dog, which is wounded but not put out of its misery! Leonard Maltin says it was filmed in 1983, released in 1985. Aka *The Barbaric Beast of Boggy Creek, Part II*.

The Legend of the 7 Golden Vampires *see under* **Dracula**

The Little Shop of Horrors

(Filmgroup, 1960; 70 min.) **½

Produced and directed by Roger Corman. Assistant Director, Richard Dixon. Screenplay, Charles B. Griffith. Edited by Marshall Neilan, Jr. Director of Photography, Archie Dalzell. Music, Fred Katz. Art Direction, Daniel Haller. Sound, Phillip Mitchell. Makeup, Harry Thomas.

Cast: Seymour Krelboined (Jonathan Haze), Audrey Fulquard (Jackie Joseph), Gravis Mushnick (Mel Welles), Fouch (Dick Miller), Winifred Krelboined (Myrtle Vail), Mrs. Shiva (Leola Wendorff), Wilbur Force (Jack Nicholson), Dr. Phoebus Farb (John Shaner), Leonora Clyde (Meri Welles), Joe Fink (Wally Campo), Frank Stoolie (Jack Warford), Mrs. Fishtwanger (Lynn Storey), Teenage girls (Tammy Windsor, Toby Michaels), Kloy Haddock (Charles B. Griffith), Waitress (Dodie Drake), Drunk (Jack Griffith), Screaming patient (Charles B. Griffith), Voice of Audrey Junior (Charles B. Griffith).

Synopsis: At the skid row flower shop of Gravis Mushnick, the nerdy Seymour Krelboined is about to be fired. Just then, customer Fouch, a man who eats flowers, suggests to Mushnick that he look at Seymour's innovative plant. Seymour produces the strange item he grew from seeds given him by a Japanese gardener. He's named it Audrey, Jr., in honor of Audrey Fulquard, the love of his life. Alone with the plant, Seymour cuts his finger and discovers that the plant likes blood. It grows larger overnight. Customers flock to see it. The next evening it yells, "Feed me!" Seymour goes for a walk and accidentally causes a man to fall in front of a train. Seymour takes some of the body home and reluctantly feeds it to

Audrey, Jr. Mushnick observes in horror, but because his business is booming, he decides not to bring the plant to the attention of the police. Seymour reveals that the now giant plant is a cross between a butterwort and a venus flytrap. At the dentist's office, Seymour "duels" the dentist and incapacitates him. Then he must pretend to be the dentist for a masochistic Wilbur Force. Seymour takes the dead dentist home to the plant, which grows even larger. Mrs. Fishtwanger tells Seymour that the Society of Silent Flower Observers of Southern California will present him with a trophy. Audrey and Seymour have dinner at Seymour's mother's while Mushnick watches over the plant, which asks him to "Feed me!" To protect himself from a thief, Mushnick tells him the money is in the plant. Seymour's mother is not in favor of his marriage to Audrey. When Seymour and Audrey discuss matters in the shop, Audrey hears what she thinks is Seymour growling about food. When she leaves, the plant hypnotizes Seymour and sends him out for more food. He returns with a tart, Leonora Clyde. The sun sets on trophy day and buds open on Audrey, Jr., revealing the faces of the people the plant consumed. The police chase Seymour, but he escapes and returns to the shop. He takes a butcher knife and jumps into the plant. When Audrey and Seymour's mother and the police return, they observe Seymour's face in the newest bud.

Review: "Crowded with great gags and characters…. Not to be missed." (Michael Weldon, *The Psychotronic Encyclopedia of Film*, p. 425) ¶"Kind of one big sick joke, but it's essentially harmless and good-natured." (*Variety*)

Analysis: The quality of the film stock may suggest to the uninitiated that this was filmed in the thirties. Even at this early stage of his career, Jack Nicholson is a character on the edge. His scene is hardly germane to the story, however. Maybe they inserted it to lengthen the movie. Could this film contain the first media parody of TV's *Dragnet* series? Detectives Joe and Frank speak in the monotones of Jack Webb and Ben Alexander. We wonder if screenwriter Griffith gleaned any inspiration

from the "serious" 1959 British film *The Woman Eater*.

Please Don't Eat My Mother
(Boxoffice International, 1972; 95 min.) **

Produced and directed by Carl Monson. Director of Photography, Jack Beckett. Screenplay, Eric Norden. Movielab color. Sound by Dan Foly. Effects by Harry Wolman.

Cast: Henry Fudd (Buck Kartalian),Young widow (Rene Bond), Mother (Lyn Lundgren), Hooker (Alicia Friedland), Flower store owner (Dash Fremont), Young widow's husband (Ric Lutze). With Flora Wiesel or Wisel, Adam Blari, David Curtis.

Synopsis: Fortyish virgin bachelor Henry Fudd lives with his mother and during lunchtimes spies on couples making out. One day he buys a plant, and when he gets home, he discovers that it talks. It's also carnivorous and for sustenance needs bugs — then, as it grows, cats and dogs, finally humans. One evening Henry observes an altercation between a husband and wife during which the wife shoots her spouse. Henry offers to dispose of the body. In return, the widow prepares to divest Henry of his virginity. However, she backs into the plant and is eaten while Henry is undressing. Distraught, Henry prepares to destroy the plant but is mollified when he discovers it has had babies by a recently purchased male plant. He gives them away from a streetside stand, and as the camera recedes from the city, the audience hears the sound of plants munching.

Review: "May well trigger an entire new cycle of motion picture spoof…. Kartalian serves up as engrossing a performance in the genre as has appeared in many, many years." (*Boxoffice*, May 15, 1972)

Analysis: Boxoffice had this "exploitip" for theater owners: "Contact the more imaginative columnists and broad-casting opinion-makers for spoof commentary. Invite a venturesome lady patron to sit through a midnight screening alone, the performance to be covered by the press." Hey, it's not that good. It's primitive and unbelievable, e.g., the vantage points from which Kartalian spies on lovers in cars and parks would not give him the views we see. Nevertheless, the plant is good even if they cut corners at feeding time (cutting away as Kartalian steps up to drop in a dog or human). Best of all is porn cult star Rene Bond, whom *Boxoffice* called "lithesome." She was one of the first flesh stars when skinflicks were even covered in *Screen World*—before they left theaters for the videocassette. Be warned: Rene does not appear till the last quarter-hour, but the wait is worth it. Yes, there's full-frontal nudity, possibly coitus. The working title was *Glump*. When re-released in 1974 it became *Hungry Pets*.

Little Shop of Horrors
(Warner Bros., 1986; 93 min.) **½

Produced by David Geffen. Directed by Frank Oz. Screenplay, Howard Ashman. Based on the stage play by Howard Ashman and Alan Menken. Edited by John Jympson. Director of Photography, Robert Paynter. Panavision. Technicolor. Music, Miles Goodman. Choreography, Pat Garrett. Dolby Stereo. Songs: Music, Alan Menken; Lyrics, Howard Ashman. Art Direction, Stephen Spence, John Fenner. Set Decoration, Tessa Davies. Special Visual Effects, Brian Ferren. Animatronics Design, Neal Scanlan, Christian Ostwald. Special Effects, Christine Overs, Tim Willis. "Audrey II" designed and created by Lyle Conway.

Cast: Seymour Krelborn (Rick Moranis), Audrey (Ellen Greene), Mushnik (Vincent Gardenia), Orin Scrivello, D.D.S. (Steve Martin), Crystal (Tichina Arnold), Chifon (Tisha Campbell), Ronette (Michelle Weeks), Patrick Martin (James Belushi), Wink Wilkinson (John Candy), First customer (Christopher Guest), Arthur Denton (Bill Murray), Narrator (Stanley Jones), "Downtown" old woman (Bertice Reading), "Downtown" bums (Ed Wiley, Alan Tilvern, John Scott Martin), Chinese florist (Vincent Wong), Doo-wop street singers (Mak Wilson, Danny Cunningham, Danny John-Jules, Gary Palmer, Paul Swaby), Second customer (Mildred Shay), Third customer (Melissa Wiltsie), Fourth customer (Kevin Scott), Fifth customer (Barbara Rosenblat), Children (Kelly Huntley, Paul Reynolds), Radio station assistant (Adeen Fogle), Dental nurse (Miriam Margolyes), Voice of "Audrey II" (Levi Stubbs).

Synopsis: During the Kennedy presidency an unexpected eclipse occurs. At first no one knows its effect on the strange plant Seymour Krelborn nursed in the basement of Mushnik's flower shop on skid row. But once it tastes blood from Seymour's cut, it grows. Customers flock to see it and buy other plants. Seymour promotes it and the shop on Wink Wilkinson's radio show. When the plant, now named "Audrey II" in honor of the shop worker Seymour loves, needs more than Seymour can give, it convinces him that Audrey's abusive dentist boyfriend Orin Scrivello is the appropriate candidate for its digestive tract. But before Seymour can shoot the dentist, Scrivello dies from an overdose of laughing gas. Mushnik observes Seymour cutting up the dentist's body but is eaten before he can get to the police. Seymour and Audrey realize they love one another. Seymour rescues Audrey from Audrey II. Patrick Martin, licensing and marketing, World Botanical Enterprises, offers to take leaf cuttings to sell on a worldwide basis. But Seymour realizes the plant is out of hand and tries to kill it. It pulls down the ceiling on him, but he grabs an electric cable and destroys it. However, in a hedge in front of the house the newly married Seymour and Audrey have purchased, another man-eating plant is growing.

Reviews: "Grandly loony, full-bodied and explosively funny." (Michael Wilmington, *Los Angeles Times Calendar*, December 19, 1986, p. 1) ¶"A mess ... but not unenjoyable in its Muppety way." (David Denby, *New York*, January 27, 1987, p. 5) ¶"Sneaks up on you." (Richard Corliss, *Time*, December 29, 1986, p. 71)

Analysis: Differences from the original film: Seymour has no mother, he doesn't die, and Mushnik is eaten. The songs are okay, but Ashman and Menken would do better shortly with the Disney animated movies *The Little Mermaid* and *Beauty and the Beast*.

Lord of the Dead *see* Phantasm III: Lord of the Dead *under* **Phantasm**

Love at First Bite *see under* **Dracula**

Lost Horizon
(Columbia, 1937; 125 min.) ***½

Produced and directed by Frank Capra.

Assistant Director, C. C. Coleman. Screenplay, Robert Riskin. Based on the novel by James Hilton. Edited by Gene Havlick and Gene Milford. Director of Photography, Joseph Walker. Aerial Photography, Elmer Dyer. Music, Dimitri Tiomkin. Musical Direction, Max Steiner. Voices, Hall Johnson Choir. Art Direction, Stephen Goosson. Interior Decoration, Babs Johnstone. Costumes, Ernst Dryden. Technical Advisor, Harrison Forman. Special Camera Effects, E. Roy Davidson and Ganahl Carson.

Cast: Robert Conway (Ronald Colman), Sondra (Jane Wyatt), Alexander P. Lovett (Edward Everett Horton), George Conway (John Howard), Henry Barnard (Thomas Mitchell), Gloria Stone (Isabel Jewell), Chang (H. B. Warner), High Lama (Sam Jaffe), Maria (Margo), Lord Gainsford (Hugh Buckler), Carstairs (John Miltern), First man (Lawrence Grant), Wynant (John Burton), Meeker (John T. Murray), Seiveking (Max Rabinowitz), Bandit leaders (Willie Fung, Victor Wong), Missionary (Wyrley Birch), Missionary (Carl Stockdale), Montaigne (John Tettener), Assistant Foreign Secretary (Boyd Irwin, Sr.), Foreign Secretary (Leonard Mudie), Steward (David Clyde), Radio operators (Neil Fitzgerald, Darby Clark), Talu (Val Durand), Missionaries (Ruth Robinson, Margaret McWade), Porter leader (Noble Johnson), Aviator (Dennis D'Auburn), Fenner (Milton Owen), Passengers (Beatrice Curtis, Mary Lou Dix, Beatrice Blinn, Arthur Rankin), Chinese priest (George Chan), Englishman (Eric Wilton), Porter (Chief Big Tree), Shanghai Airport official (Richard Loo).

Synopsis: March 10, 1935: Robert Conway, soldier, diplomat and public hero, the "Man of the East" and prospective British foreign secretary, assists ninety refugees fleeing war-ravaged Baskul, China. On the last plane, he is accompanied by his brother George, Henry Barnard, Gloria Stone, and Alexander P. Lovett. At dawn they discover they are flying west, not east to Shanghai. The pilot turns out to be an Asian. After stopping for fuel, they enter the mountains and crash. The pilot is killed. Just as Robert prepares to start an overland hike, they are found by a party of men led by one Chang. He leads them to the secluded Valley of the Blue Moon. Over the course of the ensuing weeks, Robert learns that the valley was discovered in 1713 by a Belgian priest, Father Perrot. The 2,000-odd people who live there base their

lives on moderation. Because there is gold in abundance, they can pay for the infrequent shipments of books and other items from the outside world. When Robert meets the High Lama, he realizes he is in the presence of Father Perrot, kept alive by this strange valley. The High Lama explains how he had a vision of doom in the outside world, so he gathered all he could of beauty here in the place called Shangri-La. When brutality perishes, Shangri-La will be ready to help humankind. The basic rule will be: Be kind. Robert meets Sondra, like himself a Caucasian. Her parents were explorers. She had read Robert's books and suggested he be brought here. The High Lama says that Robert will replace him when he dies. Robert accepts the charge until his brother George convinces him that it's all a hoax, that Father Perrot is insane, and that Maria, with whom George is smitten, was not brought here in 1888. (Robert had warned him that if Maria were taken out of the valley, she'd grow old.) His faith shaken, Robert accompanies his brother and Maria as they begin a journey back to modern civilization. Chang observes the departure and assures Sondra that Robert will return. When Maria ages and dies, Robert knows the High Lama and Chang were telling the truth. George dies in a fall, and Robert is found by some villagers. British newspapers report he has been seen in a Chinese prison. Lord Gainsford is sent to retrieve him, but when he recovers from some memory loss, Robert jumps ship and leads Gainsford on a 10-month chase. Robert disappears over the mountains. His efforts are rewarded when he sees the entrance to Shangri-La.

Reviews: "Grand adventure film, magnificently staged, beautifully photographed and capitally played." (Frank S. Nugent, *New York Times*, March 4, 1937)

Analysis: It pays to appreciate the time this was made, when Japan was savaging China and rumblings of war were heard in Europe. Capra's populism comes through early on. Just when modern audiences might be prepared to condemn the rescue of the 90 whites at the expense of the peasants, the Robert Conway character expresses regret that no one will care about the annihilation of the 10,000 left behind. And no one will write about that. The restored version includes stills to fill in gaps. The soundtrack was not lost and is played over the stills. Academy Awards for editing and interior decoration. Nominated for supporting actor (H. B. Warner) and picture.

Lost Horizon
(Columbia, 1973; 150 min.) *

Produced by Ross Hunter. Directed by Charles Jarrott. Second Unit Director, Russ Saunders. Screenplay, Larry Kramer. Based on the novel by James Hilton. Edited by Maury Winetrobe. Director of Photography, Robert Surtees. Panavision. Metrocolor. Music, Burt Bacharach. Lyrics, Hal David. Musical Numbers staged by Hermes Pan. Title Song sung by Shawn Phillips. Costumes, Jean Louis.

Cast: Richard Conway (Peter Finch), Catherine (Liv Ullman), George Conway (Michael York), Sam Cornelius (George Kennedy), Sally Hughes (Sally Kellerman), Maria (Olivia Hussey), Harry Lovett (Bobby Van), Brother To-Linn (James Shigeta), High Lama (Charles Boyer), Chang (John Gielgud), Dr. Virdon (John Van Dreelan), Mr. Ferguson (Kent Smith).

Synopsis: Statesman Richard Conway and an assorted group of Westerners escape rioting Asians in some remote country, but their plane crashes in the Himalayas. The mysterious Chang and his men rescue them and take them from the beautiful but barren snowfields to a land of milk and honey: Shangri-La. As Richard learns from Chang and the High Lama, Shangri-La preserves the wisdom of the world, keeping it safe for the day the outside world will require it — after some holocaust of man's making. Richard has been selected to replace the High Lama. Each of Richard's companions — embezzling businessman Sam Cornelius, misguided woman of the world Sally Hughes, nightclub entertainer Harry Lovett — finds peace in the valley. But Richard's brother George, although he falls in love with Maria, longs to leave. Even though Richard is in love with the teacher Catherine, he lets George convince him that Shangri-La is a fake. Richard accompanies George out

of the valley, but Maria begins to age, and a maddened George falls to his death. Richard heads back to what he now realizes is a true sanctuary for the human spirit.

Reviews: "A filmed operetta in three acts, superbly mounted…. Script is serviceable, as are the … songs…." (Murf., *Variety*, March 7, 1973, p. 18) ¶"The leads are pitilessly miscast…. Jarrott's version lacks visual contrasts, the narrative has no energy." (Pauline Kael, *New Yorker*, March 17, 1973, pp. 119–21)

Analysis: How bad is it? Well, your authors saw it at a big theater in London's Leicester Square when it premiered as a reserved-seat roadshow. We recall exiting the theater with nothing much to say. We realized it was a waste of our precious time off from the United States Army. In no way did it eclipse the original. The color and the cheery but unmemorable songs destroy any mystery. And mystery is just about all the story has when it comes down to it. There's little action. The cast of the first film made you forget that.

The Love Bug
(Buena Vista, 1968; 108 min.) ***

Produced by Bill Walsh. Directed by Robert Stevenson. Assistant Director, Christopher Hibler. Screenplay, Bill Walsh and Don Da Gradi. Based on a story by Gordon Buford. Director of Photography, Edward Colman. Technicolor. Music, George Bruns. Costumes, Bill Thomas.

Cast: Jim (Dean Jones), Carole (Michele Lee), Thorndyke (David Tomlinson), Tennessee Steinmetz (Buddy Hackett), Havershaw (Joe Flynn), Mr. Wu (Benson Fong), Detective (Joe E. Ross), Police sergeant (Barry Kelley), Carhop (Iris Adrian). With Ned Glass, Robert Foulk, Gary Owens, Pedro Gonzalez Gonzalez, Alan Fordney, Gil Lamb, P. L. Renoudet, Andy Granatelli, Nicole Jaffe, Russ Caldwell, Wally Boag, Brian Fong, Stan Duke, Max Balchowsky, Chick Hearn.

Synopsis: Down-on-his-luck race driver Jim Douglas needs cheap transportation to a race track and purchases a Volkswagen from the Thorndyke dealership. The transaction was not without rancor, however. Unbeknownst to Jim, the car originally had followed him to his home overlooking San Francisco Bay, and the police thought he

Driver Jim Douglas (Dean Jones) is all set to race in Herbie the Love Bug; mechanic Tennessee Steinmetz (Buddy Hackett) stands by in *The Love Bug* (Buena Vista, 1968).

stole it. Sometimes the car seems to have a life of its own, which Jim proves to sales gal Carole. Jim's mechanic partner Tennessee Steinmetz says he foresaw this day—when machines would take on human attributes. Jim, on the other hand, believes Herbie is one of those very few machine-made items that is just better than its kin. Jim begins to race Herbie, #53, and wins, and finally realizes that Herbie is sentient. Jim and Tennessee take great pleasure in beating Thorndyke in a lengthy cross-country race.

Review: "Rates as one of the better entries of the Disney organization." (Whit., *Variety*, December 11, 1968)

Analysis: This was a big hit for the Disney studios, praised by *Variety* for "inventiveness" and "charm." It's very, very entertaining. There is good teamwork by Jones, Lee and Hackett.

Herbie Rides Again

(Buena Vista, 1974; 88 min.) **
Produced by Bill Walsh. Directed by Robert

Stevenson. Assistant Directors, Ronald R. Grow, Dorothy Kieffer. Screenplay, Bill Walsh. Based on a story by Gordon Buford. Edited by Cotton Warburton. Director of Photography, Frank Phillips. Technicolor. Music, George Bruns. Art Direction, John B. Mansbridge, Walter Tyler. Set Decoration, Hal Gausman. Costumes, Chuck Keehne and Emily Sundby.

Cast: Mrs. Steinmetz (Helen Hayes), Willoughby Whitfield (Ken Berry), Nicole Harris (Stefanie Powers), Mr. Judson (John McIntire), Alonzo Hawk (Keenan Wynn), Judge (Huntz Hall), Taxi driver (Vito Scotti), Chauffeur (Ivor Barry), Lawyer (Raymond Bailey), Doctor (Liam Dunn), Traffic commissioner (Richard X. Slattery), Lostgarten (Chuck McCann), Lawyer (Dan Tobin), Secretary Millicent (Elaine Devry), Red Knight (Rob McCary), Sir Lancelot (Hank Jones).

Synopsis: Mrs. Steinmetz lives in the San Francisco firehouse once inhabited by her nephew Tennessee Steinmetz, who is visiting his guru in Tibet. She now owns Herbie, the Volkswagen with a life of its own. Its previous driver, Jim, is off racing on the European circuit. Alonzo Hawk plans to demolish the firehouse in order to put up yet another skyscraper, but Mrs. Steinmetz won't budge. Not realizing that his uncle Alonzo is a greedy, corrupt person, new lawyer Willoughby Whitfield tries to get Mrs. Steinmetz to move. However, he falls in love with Nicole Harris, Mrs. Steinmetz's companion. Nicole reveals the "human" nature of Herbie. Various attempts to demolish the house are foiled till Hawk brings a fleet of earthmovers and bulldozers one night. But Herbie gathers a host of Volkswagens and, along with rancher Judson, drives the machines and Hawk off. The police, already irritated with Hawk's activities, haul him away. Mrs. Steinmetz get to keep her home, and Willoughby and Nicole get married.

Reviews: "Simply not very good." (Vincent Canby, *New York Times*, June 7, 1974, p. 23)

Analysis: This is not as good as the first or third in the series, and setting-wise, not as good as the fourth, which moves from locale to locale. The main problem: not enough plot. Secondly, the "real" incidents strain credulity. There *is* a funny dream sequence when Keenan Wynn has a nightmare in which he's chased by Indian headdress–equipped Volkswagens tossing tomahawks, and flying, oil-squirting cars circling him on top of the Empire State Building. Wynn plays the same character he'd played in 1961's *The Absent Minded Professor* and 1963's *Son of Flubber*. His secretary, Elaine Devry, had had some important supporting roles, noticeably in 1967's *A Guide for the Married Man* and 1970's *The Cheyenne Social Club*, and a couple of leading roles, like *The Boy Who Cried Werewolf* (1973).

Herbie Goes to Monte Carlo
(Buena Vista, 1977; 105 min.) ***

Produced by Ron Miller. Directed by Vincent McEveety. Assistant Directors, Paul "Tiny" Nichols, Win Phelps. Screenplay, Arthur Alsberg and Don Nelson. Based on characters created by Gordon Buford. Edited by Cotton Warburton. Director of Photography, Leonard J. South. Technicolor. Music, Frank DeVol. Art Direction, John B. Mansbridge, Perry Ferguson. Costumes, Chuck Keehne and Emily Sundby.

Cast: Jim Douglas (Dean Jones), Diane Darcy (Julie Sommars), Wheely Applegate (Don Knotts), Quincey (Roy Kinnear), Bruno von Stickel (Eric Braeden), Duval (Laurie Main), Max (Bernard Fox), Emile (Alan Caillou), Inspector Bouchet (Jacques Marin), Detective Fontenory (Zavier Saint Macary), Monsieur Ribeaux (Françoise Lalande), Claude (Mike Kulcsar), Taxi driver (Stanley Brock), Waiter (Gerard Jugnot). With Tom McCorrey, Jean-Jacques Moreau, Lloyd Nelson, Yveline Briere, Madeleine Damien, Raoul Delfosse, Sebastian Floche, Ed Marcus, Alain Janey.

Synopsis: Twelve years after Herbie's last race, Jim Douglas and new mechanic Wheely Applegate decide to enter #53 in a French cross-country race from Paris to Monte Carlo. They are sneered at by drivers like Von Stickel. To make matters worse, Herbie falls for the Lancia driven by Diane and disrupts initial qualifying rounds for both cars. Diane thinks Jim doesn't want women to race. Further complications arise when jewel thieves hide a large diamond in Herbie's fuel tank. Finally the race to the south is begun, with jewel thieves pursuing and Von Stickel making life difficult. On the final leg, Herbie pulls the Lancia out of a river, the thieves are brushed aside, and Douglas and Applegate beat Von Stickel when Herbie passes him upside down in a tunnel. The Parisian police chief who instigated the jewel theft tries to get the diamond, but Herbie squashes that, too.

Reviews: "(Herbie's) assortment of tricks ... possesses a somewhat limited power to captivate." (Lawrence Van Gelder, *New York Times*, August 4, 1977, p. C14) ¶"Often slapstick and mirthful effect." (*Variety*)

Analysis: This is a solid, entertaining entry in the series. This supporting role fits Don Knotts to a T.

Herbie Goes Bananas
(Buena Vista, 1980; 100 min.) **½

Produced by Ron Miller. Directed by Vincent McEveety. Screenplay, Don Tait. Based on characters created by Gordon Buford. Edited by Gordon D. Brenner. Director of Photography, Frank Phillips. Technicolor. Music, Frank DeVol. Songs: "Look at Me" and "I Found a New Friend," Frank DeVol. Art Direction, John B. Mansbridge, Rodger Maus. Special Effects, Art Cruikshank and Danny Lee.

Cast: Paco (Joaquin Garay III), Aunt Louise (Cloris Leachman), Pete Sanchez (Stephan W. Burns), D. J. (Charles Martin Smith), Prindle (John Vernon), Captain Elythe (Harvey Korman), Melissa (Elyssa Davalos), Shepard (Richard Jaeckel), Quinn (Alex Rocco), Chief steward (Fritz Feld), Armando (Vito Scotti). With Jose Gonzalez Gonzalez, Rubin Moreno, Allan Hunt, Tina Menard, Jorge Moreno, Tom Scott, Iris Adrian, Patricia Van Patten, Henry Slate, Ceil Cabot, Hector Morales, Jack Perkins.

Synopsis: In Puerto Vallarta, Mexico, Pete Sanchez and D. J. take possession of the race car Pete's uncle left to him: a beat-up Volkswagen they hardly believe won the Monte Carlo Grand Prix. Meanwhile, Prindle and Quinn meet with Shepard, who has apparently discovered a pre–Colombian Inca site from which they hope to reap a fortune by not informing the government. Paco, a streetwise urchin, steals the wallets of Pete and Shepard and hides in Herbie. Herbie is loaded aboard the *Sun Princess*, his destination Rio. On board, Louise and Melissa have dinner with Pete and D. J. while Herbie raises havoc in the hold. Later he disrupts the captain's party and is dropped overboard. He "swims" through the Panama Canal, however, and is reunited with Paco. Prindle, who realized who stole Shepard's wallet with the film, captures Paco. But Paco transferred the film into Pete's wallet. Prindle sets in motion a chase into the interior. After wowing the crowd by his bullfighting prowess ("They got voodoo down here, you know that?" states observer Quinn), Herbie evades Prindle. But Paco is captured and taken on board Shepard's plane. They locate the Inca treasure, steal some of it but are caught by the police after Herbie wrecks Shepard's plane. Back on the *Sun Princess*, Herbie is lodged in a stateroom, and Paco gets a race-driving outfit.

Reviews: "An agreeable enough piffle...." (Sheila Benson, *Los Angeles Times*, August 6, 1980, Part VI, p. 5) ¶"Makes a good case for scrapping Herbie and the series." (Joseph Gelmis, *Newsday*, September 12, 1980, Part II, p. 8)

Analysis: This doesn't really deserve the poor rating it gets in weekly TV listings. It's fairly entertaining, with a couple of amusing voodoo lines from Alex Rocco. Recalling that Herbie needed fill-ups in *The Love Bug*, Michael Holston, age 8, observed halfway through this entry that "he should be running out of gas by now."

Lust for a Vampire *see under* **The Vampire Lovers**

Mad About Men *see under* **Miranda**

Mad Love
(MGM, 1935; 70 min.) ***½

Produced by John W. Considine, Jr. Directed by Karl Freund. Adaptation, Guy Endore, from Maurice Renard's novel *Les Mains D'Orlas*. Screenplay by P. J. Wolfson and John L. Balderston. Edited by Hugh Wynn. Director of Photography, Chester Lyons, Gregg Toland. Music, Dimitri Tiomkin.

Cast: Dr. Gogol (Peter Lorre), Madame Yvonne Orlac (Frances Drake), Steven Orlac (Colin Clive), Reagan (Ted Healy), Marie (Sarah Haden), Rollo (Edward Brophy), Prefect Rosset (Henry Kolker), Dr. Wong (Keye Luke), Françoise (May Beatty).

Synopsis: French surgeon Dr. Gogol spends evenings at a "theater of horrors," viewing tableaux, especially one featuring the beautiful Madame Orlac. He is saddened to learn that she's leaving to spend full time with her husband, the pianist Orlac. She rejects Gogol's romantic overtures. "You are cruel — but only to be kind," he responds. When Orlac has his hands crushed in a train crash, Madame Orlac asks Gogol to help her husband. He realizes the hands must be amputated, but he has a brainstorm: Replace them with the hands of the executed murderer Rollo. He does so without telling Orlac. Later Orlac finds his hands have a will of their own and like to throw knives. Gogol thinks he can drive Orlac insane. He dresses as Rollo and tries to convince Orlac that he put Rollo's head back on after the guillotining. He kills the stepfather, and Orlac is arrested. Madame Orlac goes to Gogol's house, discovers the waxwork of herself, knocks it over and, when Gogol appears, pretends to be the statue. She screams, however, when a bird comes near her, and Gogol realizes she is the real Yvonne, not a Galatea. Obviously insane now, Gogol says to himself, "Each man kills the thing he loves." But Madame Orlac is rescued because the police, aided by an American newspaper man, have realized something fishy has been going on. Orlac throws a knife into Gogol's back as he tries to strangle Yvonne with her own braids.

Review: "Mr. Lorre cuts deeply into the darkness of the morbid brain.... frequently excellent." (Andre Sennwald, *New York Times*, August 5, 1935)

Analysis: This definitive *Grand Guignol* movie must be the film that gave impressionists and cartoons the Peter Lorre mannerisms and laugh—though that laugh is pretty subdued here. It was Lorre's first American film. This was a remake of the silent 1924 Austrian film, *Orlacs Haende* (*The Hands of Orlac*).

The Hands of Orlac
(1961; 95 min.) *½

Produced by Steven Pallos and Donald Taylor. Directed by Edmond T. Greville. Screenplay, John Baines and Edmond T. Greville. Edited by Oswald Hafenrichter. Director of Photography, Desmond Dickinson. Music, Claude Bolling. Art Direction, John Blezard. Choreography, Hazel Gee.

Cast: Stephen Orlac (Mel Ferrer), Louise (Lucile Saint-Simon), Nero (Christopher Lee), Li-Lang/Regina (Dany Carrell), Professor Volcheff (Donald Wolfit), Dr. Francis Cochrane (Felix Aylmer), Siedelman (Basil Sydney), Child (Janine Faye), Coates (Donald Pleasence). With David Peel.

Synopsis: In France, concert pianist Stephen Orlac survives a plane crash, but his hands are burned. Simultaneously, Louis Vasseur is executed. Six months after his operation, Stephen is still disturbed and asks his fiancée, Louise, to help him. But on holiday he almost strangles her. He drives off and checks in at a hotel. Nero, a two-bit magician, tells his associate, Li-Lang, to ingratiate herself with Stephen so they can blackmail him. When Louise locates Stephen, Nero overhears her talking about hands that might not be his. Approaching Stephen, Nero pretends he knew

Louis Vasseur and asks to shake *his* hand. Stephen runs out, finds Louise, and returns to the concert stage. Just as he is about to perform he receives a note with gloves with "L. Vasseur" imprinted on them. While performing, he imagines the gloves on his hand, begins making mistakes, and leaves the stage. Dr. Cochrane, Louise's uncle, advises a checkup and good night's rest. Stephen receives a call asking for Vasseur. In London, Li-Lang poses as Vasseur's widow and tells Louise her late husband wants back what's his. After more of Nero's machinations fail to produce quite the desired effect, he skewers Li-Lang in the course of his magic show. He fights with Stephen in the dressing room, and the police arrive. Stephen is shown a letter from the Sûreté in Paris to the effect that Louis Vasseur was innocent. "My hands are innocent," states Stephen. He appears in concert.

Review: "Reportedly film was butchered for American audiences and is not as effective as original." (John Stanley, *The Creature Features Movie Guide*, p. 108)

Analysis: It's a British-French film and the mess that often results from international co-production. One version exists in French. The video we watched featured neither Donald Pleasence nor David Peel, and only Donald Wolfit's eyes are visible as he operates. We never know until the end if he really grafted the executed man's hands onto Ferrer. This should have had a hard edge, but it's just plain irritating and stupid. The "beat" music intrudes and destroys scenes. Aka *Hands of the Stranger.*

Hands of a Stranger
(Allied Artists, 1962; 86 min.) **½

Produced by Newton Arnold and Michael DuPont. Written and directed by Newton Arnold. Edited by Bert Honey. Director of Photography, Henry Cronjager. Music, Richard Lasalle. Art Direction, Ted Holsopple. Set Decoration, John Sturdevant. Makeup, Charles Gemora. Special Photographic Effects, Howard A. Anderson Company.

Cast: Dr. Gil Harding (Paul Lukather), Dina Paris (Joan Harvey), Vernon Paris (James Stapleton), Dr. Russ Compson (Ted Otis), Holly (Irish McCalla), Dr. Ken Fry (Michael DuPont), George Britton (Michael

Rye), Lt. Syms (Larry Haddon), Sue (Sally Kellerman), Eileen Hunter (Elaine Martone), Skeet (Barry Gordon), Taxi driver (George Sawaya), Carnival barker (David Kramer).

Synopsis: On a dark street a man is shot and surgeon Gil Harding cannot save his life. He notes the powerful but sensitive hands. Meanwhile, pianist Vernon Paris's concert is a triumph. Sister Dina and business manager George assure a brilliant career, but Paris's taxi has an accident, and his hands are severely damaged and must be amputated. There is one possibility: give Paris the hands of the murdered man. Dina calls it ego, but Harding wins his case. At least mental defects, if the murdered man had any, do not translate to extremities, Harding assures Dina. Paris can't believe the calamity happened to him. "Why?" "Because it is!" retorts Harding. Paris calls on Eileen, and during their confrontation she knocks over a lamp that sets her dress on fire. Paris visits the taxi driver's house and attempts to play piano with his son Skeet, but his new hands are clumsy. He grabs Skeet's hands, crushing them, and kills the boy when he hurls him to the floor. Accompanying Harding and Dina to the carnival, Paris is rattled by his inability to hit anything with baseballs, and he attacks a barker. Paris appears at Dr. Fry's apartment. Fry and his fiancée, Sue, are found dead. After murdering another doctor who participated in the original operation, Paris confronts his sister and Harding on a theater stage. Paris tries to strangle Harding, but Lt. Syms shoots him. "What is past is prologue" appears on the screen.

Review: "Mild suspense.... Its theme is ... novel ... but much of the unfoldment is sloppy...." (Whit., *Variety*, September 26, 1962)

Analysis: This is a true '50s B movie released in that early 60s transitional period: black and white, simple sets, non-star or future star (Sally Kellermann) cast, some stiff performers (Michael Rye might be a cyborg), head-and-shoulder shots. Lukather is not a mad doctor. He's sincere, and it's interesting to hear his prescient predictions for the future of medicine. We are happy he survives to continue serving

mankind. James Stapleton also has some profound lines, e.g., "The only real enemies the world has are the enemies of beauty." The film introduces Barry Gordon.

Mad Max
(Filmways/AIP, 1979; 90 min.) ***

Produced by Byron Kennedy. Associate Producer, Bill Miller. Directed by George Miller. Assistant Director, Ian Goddard. Screenplay, James McCausland and George Miller. Edited by Tony Paterson. Director of Photography, David Eggby. Movielab Color. Music, Brian May. Art Direction, Jon Dowding. Costumes, Clare Griffin.

Cast: Max Rockatansky (Mel Gibson), Toecutter (Hugh Keays-Byrne), Jessie (Joanne Samuel), Jim Goose (Steve Bisley), Johnny (Tim Burns), Fifi Macaffee (Roger Ward), Bubba Zanetti (Geoff Parry), Nightrider (Vince Gil), Station master (Reg Evans).

Synopsis: "A few years from now...": On Highway 9, Sector 6, the Main Force Patrol is foiled by the speeding Nightrider until Max Rockatansky puts the heat on and his prey crashes into a truck and dies. Nightrider's motorcycle chums vow vengeance. They attack a man and his girlfriend. Max and Jim Goose are called in. They capture gang member Johnny, who is released from the Halls of Justice on a technicality. Goose is attacked and though he lives, he is burned beyond recognition. Fifi tells Max to take a few weeks off. Max takes his wife Jessie and young son to the coast, where Jessie is harassed by Toecutter's gang while Max is having a tire fixed. Later, while Max is again separated from her, she and his child are run down and killed. Max goes on the warpath, annihilating gang members as he comes upon them. Finally Johnny trips him up and he's shot in the leg. But he blows away Bubba with his sawed-off shotgun and, pursuing Toecutter, causes him to smash headlong into an oncoming tractor trailer. Finding Johnny, Max cuffs him to an overturned car and gives him a hacksaw after setting a flame next to leaking gasoline. He tells Johnny it will take ten minutes to cut through the steel — or 5 minutes to sever his ankle. As Max rides away, an explosion occurs.

Reviews: "Ugly and incoherent." (Tom Buckley, *New York Times*, June 14, 1980, p. 13) ¶"An all-stops-out, fast-moving exploitation pic." (*Variety*, May 16, 1979, p. 38)

Analysis: It has some energy, but also some boring interludes between Max and wife. The *New York Times* found it rife with sadism and "homosexual overtones." The sound is substandard and the music intrusive. Except for a couple of instances— e.g., the severed hand or Toecutter smashing into the truck—the violence is relatively subdued, certainly more than it would be in an American film with this plot made at this time. For instance, when Max shoots Bubba, we see no blood. Nor does the camera examine his body. The villains are not so intimidating as they will become. It *is* an interesting choice Max gives Johnny at the end. According to *Variety*, the film works because of the cinematic understanding of first-time feature director George Miller, as well as his cameraman and stuntman; despite good work by the leads, "it's not an actor's piece."

Mad Max II

(aka *The Road Warrior*; Warner Bros./Kennedy Miller Entertainment, 1982; 94 min.) ***

Produced by Byron Kennedy. Directed by George Miller. Screenplay, Terry Hayes, George Miller, Brian Hannant. Edited by David Stiven, Tim Wellburn, Michael Chirgwin, Michael Balson. Director of Photography, Dean Semler and Andrew Lesnie. Panavision. Color. Music, Brian May. Sound, Lloyd Carrick. Sound Effects, Bruce Lemshed. Art Direction, Graham Walker. Costumes, Norma Moriceau. Makeup Special Effects, Bob McCarron. Special Effects Supervisor, Jeffrey Clifford. Animal Handler, Dale Aspin.

Cast: Max Rockatansky (Mel Gibson), Gyro Captain (Bruce Spence), Wez (Veron Wells), Feral kid (Emil Minty), Humungus (Kjell Nilsson) Pappagallo (Mike Preston), Quiet man (David Slingsby), Big Rebecca (Moira Claux), Warrior Woman (Virginia Hey), Lusty girl (Arkie Whiteley), Curmudgeon (Syd Heylen), Farmer (William Zappa), Toadie (Max Phipps), Mechanic (Steve J. Spears), Golden youth (Jimmy Brown), Wounded man (David Downer), Defiant victim (Tyler Coppin), Broken victim (Max

Fairchild), Mechanic's assistant (Kristoffer Greaves), Tent lovers (Anne Jones, James McCardell), Mohawk biker with bearclaw (Guy Norris), Mohawk biker (Tony Deary), Narrator (Harold Baigent).

Synopsis: In the post-apocalyptic world inhabited by semi-barbarous humans, Max foils a "tribe" of miscreants and discovers a mid-desert refinery. He needs gas for his car but must wait till the nasties are beaten off with arrows and flame-throwers. He watches from his high cliff as the scurvy crew rapes and kills some refinery people who attempt a getaway. Once inside, he makes a deal. In return for gas, he will bring in a big rig to the refinery so the people can fill it up and trek north a couple thousand miles to a perceived land of milk and honey. He leaves by night on foot with gas cans, fills the tanker and drives back, breaking through the ring of thieves. Leaving in his car, he is bushwhacked and his dog is killed. He is thought dead but returns to the refinery with the help of a young boy. Although injured, he volunteers to drive the tanker during the breakout. In the ensuing chase the leader of the refinery people is killed, as are the woman and man riding shotgun on the tanker. The gyro captain lends his services, dropping homemade bombs. Finally the leader of the nasties and his top henchman are killed in a head-on collision. The tanker, Max discovers, is filled with sand. The refinery people secreted the gas on their other vehicles. A narrator says it was the last they saw of the road warrior as he stood there on the freeway.

Reviews: "The habit of judging movies by style alone has become ingrained, at the expense of every other element. And pictures like *The Road Warrior* reap the benefit." (David Sterritt, *Christian Science Monitor*, September 2, 1982, p. 18) ¶"A rare example of the sequel that is better than its predecessor." (David McGillivray, *Monthly Film Bulletin*, May 1982, p. 87) ¶"This is a movie with lots of faces and bodies but no real characters—costuming has been substituted for characterization." (David Denby, *New York*, August 30, 1982, p. 61)

Analysis: There's not much plot but plenty of bloodshed, some of which can be termed gratuitous: the killing of the dog and the woman on the tanker. Having two major — and frightening — villains (the leader in the hockey mask and his Mohawk-coiffed henchman) is a definite plus. Stunts are superior to those in *Mad Max*, as are all production values.

Mad Max: Beyond Thunderdome
(Kennedy/Miller/Warner Bros., 1985; 106 min.) ***

Produced by George Miller. Directed by George Miller and George Ogilvie. Screenplay, Terry Hayes and George Miller. Edited by Richard Francis-Bruce. Director of Photography, Dean Semler. Panavision. Color-film. Music, Maurice Jarre. Dolby Stereo. "We Don't Need Another Hero (Thunderdome)" performed by Tina Turner. Costumes, Norma Moriceau. Key Stunts, Glen Boswell. Special Effects, Mike Wood, Steve Curtley and Brian Cox. Special Visual Effects, Universal City Studios Matte Department.

Cast: Mad Max (Mel Gibson), Aunty Entity (Tina Turner), Jedediah (Bruce Spence), Jedediah, Jr. (Adam Cockburn), The Collector (Frank Thring), The Master (Angelo Rossitto), The Blaster (Paul Larsson), Ironbar (Angry Anderson), Pigkiller (Robert Grubb), Blackfinger (George Spartels), Dr. Dealgood (Edwin Hodgeman), Ton Ton Tattoo (Andrew Oh), Waterseller (Bob Horery), Savannah Nix (Helen Buday), Mr. Skyfish (Mark Spain), Gekko (Mark Kounnas), Scrooloose (Rod Zuanic), Anna Goanna (Justine Clarke), Eddie (Shane Tickner), Cusha (Toni Allaylis), Tubba Tintye (James Wingrove), Finn McCoo (Adam Scougall), Slake (Tom Jennings), Mr. Scratch (Adam Willits).

Synopsis: Max Rockatansky's camel-driven wagon is stolen by Jedediah the pilot, and he must walk into Bartertown across the steaming wastes. Taken to Aunty Entity, he agrees to kill a man in return for his camels. She shows him an underworld of pigs. The methane from their excrement powers Bartertown. Max is to dispose of the helmeted Blaster, the man upon whom rides the diminutive Master. To case the joint, Max gets a job shoveling shit. Max learns that the Blaster is extremely sensitive to high-frequency sound. Topside, he solidifies the deal with Aunty Entity. He must now engage in a "fair" battle with Master-Blaster and picks a fight over his vehicle. The conflict is to be a gladiatorial combat undertaken at Thunderdome. Using his high-pitched whistle, Max disables his adversary but can't bring himself to kill him when he discovers an innocent's face beneath the helmet. Aunty Entity is not pleased and forces Max to face the "wheel." It spins and comes up "Gulag." Max is placed upon a horse and sent into the desert. The convict Pigkiller sends a message and canteen with Max's monkey to its owner. But it's not enough to keep him going for long. Help arrives in the form of a woman who drags him to a verdant abode beyond the desert. Nursed back to health, his hair cut by these "Walkers," Max is informed he's the man they've waited for: "Captain Walker." They want him to lead them home, to a world of cities with "highscapers" and videos. He tells them that world is gone. The tribe leads Max to the half-buried jetliner they've kept stocked and ready, but he turns and walks away. Although Max argues against it, Savannah starts to leave. Max takes a rifle and tries to "persuade" her to stay. That failing, he knocks her out. But she and her cohorts escape, and Max follows with three children. They catch up near Bartertown, which they enter via air ducts. Max was right, it seems, and the Walkers realize they must return to their haven. Pigkiller starts up the jury-rigged train engine and punches through to the sunlight while destroying much that was Bartertown. Aunty Entity says Bartertown will rebuild. But first, they must take revenge. In their jalopies, they set out across the desert. After a running fight, the train comes to end of track. Providentially, Jedediah, Jr., appears and inadvertently leads the way to his father's underground hideout and aircraft. With all these passengers, the aircraft can't get off the ground. Max takes a truck and charges into Aunty Entity's oncoming phalanx. "Well, ain't we a pair, raggedy man," says Aunty Entity to Max before leaving him alone amongst the burned out vehicle hulks. Meanwhile, the plane passes over a ruined city (Sydney). Later, Savannah tells the tale of the past and of the man who "finded" us. Someday he and other men out there will see a distant light and come home.

Reviews: "Great action sequences crop up frequently today, but great action movies are always few and far between. *Beyond Thunderdome is* one...." (Michael Wilmington, *Los Angeles Times Calendar,* July 10, 1985, p. 1) ¶"Opens strong.... Gibson impressively fleshes out Max, Tina Turner is striking in her role as Aunty." (*Variety,* June 26, 1985, p. 18)

Analysis: One feared this larger-budget Max saga would be overloaded and sink. But it succeeds. Nor does the obviously imposing Tina Turner dominate the action. Subterranean scenes are balanced with outdoor shots. The hard edge is mitigated by humorous episodes, too much so during the finale when Ironbar *keeps* coming back from certain deaths. The composer of the music for *Lawrence of Araba* (1962), Maurice Jarre, gets to score another film in which a child is sucked into desert quicksand.

The Mad Max films, especially the second and third installments, are the cinema's best rendition of the post-apocalyptic world frequently evoked in science fiction novels. Although each episode is self-contained, there is a cohesiveness to the series, and a progression, showing Max transforming into an ever lonelier — and hairier — fellow. This is that rare series that improves with each entry.

The Main Course *see* Critters 2: The Main Course *under* **Critters**

The Man Who Could Cheat Death *see under* **The Man in Half Moon Street**

The Man in Half Moon Street
(Paramount, 1944; 91 min.) ***

Produced by Walter MacEwen. Directed by Ralph Murphy. Screenplay, Charles Kenyon. Adaptation, Garrett Fort. Based on the play by Barre Lyndon. Edited by Tom Neff. Director of Photography, Henry Sharp. Music, Miklos Rozsa. Art Direction, Hans Dreier, Walter Tyler. Set Decoration, Sam Comer. Makeup, Wally Westmore.

Cast: Dr. Julian Karell (Nils Asther), Eve Brandon (Helen Walker), Professor Kurt Van Bruecken (Reinhold Schunzel), Allen Guthrie (Morton Lowry), Dr. Henry Latimer (Paul Cavanagh), Inspector Garth (Matthew Boulton), Mr. Taper (Reginald Sheffield), Sir Humphrey Brandon (Edmond Breon), Harris (Forrester Harvey), Dr. Vishanoff (Konstantin Shayne), Colonel Ashley (Edward Fielding), Simpson (Brandon Hurst), Sir John Aldergate (Arthur Mulliner), Lady Minerva Aldergate (Aminata Dyne), Inspector Lawson (Eustace Wyatt).

Synopsis: At the unveiling of Eve Brandon's portrait by Dr. Julian Karell, Lady Minerva Aldergate notes how Julian resembles his grandfather, and he recollects in great detail incidents from her life he says were told to him. Before the portrait can be unveiled, Julian is called home to Half Moon Street. His butler Simpson hands him a message from Professor Van Bruecken: "Departure Delayed. Should Symptoms Appear Before I Arrive Use Prescribed Remedy With Utmost Caution." In his study, Julian examines his hand with a magnifying glass and from a safe extracts a glowing liquid. That night, Julian sees a man trying to drown himself. He pulls the man from the river and takes him home. When Julian turns on the light, the man — a medical student — recognizes him from the university. He shows the man a Van Bruecken letter about transplanting glands to lengthen life. The student is reborn and agrees to work with his rescuer under the name "Waters." Surgeon and endocrinologist Van Bruecken arrives. After meeting Eve, he warns Julian, "Men like us must always walk alone," and urges him to reveal his secret to the world. After all, sixty years have passed and nothing new has been learned about their discovery. Julian argues that one more operation will be necessary; then he will go on and on. To Julian's dismay, he learns that Van Bruecken can't operate because of a stroke that weakens his hands. He only came to help find someone who could perform the operation. Julian's hands have a faint glow. Time is of the essence. Julian is turned down by the once respected but now discredited Vishanoff. He is equally unsuccessful at a hospital. Eve tells Julian his eyes look strange. Dr. Latimer also finds Julian queer. He and Eve's father go to Scotland Yard but can't get the police to do anything. Julian is licensed and associates himself with the respected Van Bruecken. Julian finds Waters reading his notes and becoming disturbed by the dates. Pretending he's come to meet Van Bruecken, Latimer arrives and drops his walking stick. Julian picks it up. At Scotland Yard, the fingerprints Julian left on the cane are examined. Could it be the man in Half Moon Street is over 90 — and a murderer? Eve's portrait is taken to Scotland Yard to be compared with a painting done fifty years before. When a letter from a French surgeon reports that he cannot enter England, Van Bruecken suggests that they approach Latimer. When Julian rejects the idea and refuses to publish their findings, Van Bruecken tells him he's no longer working for science. Julian tries to dissuade Eve from spending any more time with him, but upon learning of his goals, she only loves him the more. Waters dies from the medicines Julian has been administering. Van Bruecken breaks the glass containing the life-giving elixir. Julian is visited by Inspector Garth, who is shown the doctor's lab. Police search the house for the missing medical student Allen Guthrie. Julian says he knew him as Waters but that he'd gone. Garth tells Julian his fingerprints match those of a murderer who killed six people at ten-year intervals. Julian mails a letter to Latimer, and gets in a car whose passenger seat contains the dead Allen Guthrie. Later, sailors accidentally haul his body from the river. The police intend to arrest Karell. Julian phones Van Bruecken and tells him to meet him at Victoria Station. Van Bruecken burns records as the police break in. Meanwhile, the portraits are found to have been done by the same man. Eve joins Julian, intending to accompany him to Paris. Without his "medicine," Julian weakens on the train and begins aging. Realizing something of Julian's predicament, Eve vows that he'll always be in her heart. When the train stops, an old man exits the compartment and stumbles down the platform to fall dead.

Reviews: "Much better than average settings.... occasionally succeeds in establishing a measure of ominous tension." (Thomas M. Pryor, *New York Times*, January 20, 1945, p. 16) ¶ "Well set up tale of its type.... Plot has a few new twists." (Walt., *Variety*, October 18, 1944)

Analysis: Though the *New York Times* review complained that the story was "old stuff," this is a solid piece of work, atmospheric, consistently interesting. Paramount was capable of this, as it had proven a decade earlier in *Island of Lost Souls*. Nils Asther, once thought to be matinee idol material, does a splendid job. Even though we know he's a murderer, we are anxious for him to pull the wool over the eyes of the authorities. Years later — in the 1959 remake — the protagonist would go out as a grotesquerie. In this more civilized time, we do not see his aged, decaying body on the train platform. In the remake, Christopher Lee plays the Paul Cavanagh part and does in fact perform an operation. Here that option is merely discussed. Talk about mixed signals: The Helen Walker character walks triumphantly into the future, oblivious to the fact that Julian was a serial killer. A nice retrospective double feature would pair this with *The Picture of Dorian Gray*.

The Man Who Could Cheat Death
(Hammer/Paramount, 1959; 83 min.)
***

Produced by Michael Carreras. Directed by Terence Fisher. Screenplay, Jimmy Sangster. Based on the play *The Man in Half Moon Street* by Barre Lyndon. Edited by John Dunsford. Supervising Editor, James Needs. Director of Photography, Jack Asher. Color, Technicolor. Music, Richard Bennett. Musical Supervision, John Hollingsworth. Art Direction, Bernard Robinson. Makeup, Roy Ashton.

Cast: Dr. Georges Bonner (Anton Diffring), Janine Dubois (Hazel Court), Dr. Pierre Gerrard (Christopher Lee), Dr. Ludwig Weiss (Arnold Marle), Inspector Legris (Francis de Wolff), Margo Philippe (Delphi Lawrence). With Charles Lloyd-Pack.

Synopsis: While awaiting the overdue arrival of his onetime associate Ludwig Weiss, Paris physician Georges Bonner shows selected guests his latest sculpture of Margo Philippe at his home at 13 Rue Noire, next to the Clinique de Paris Central. Unexpectedly, Bonner's former lover Janine Dubois arrives in the company of

Dr. Ludwig Weiss (Arnold Marle, left) and Dr. Georges Bonner (Anton Diffring) regard the age-retarding elixir in *The Man Who Could Cheat Death* (Hammer, 1959).

Dr. Gerrard. Watching his time, Bonner asks everyone to leave, retires to his quarters and opens a vault. He's interrupted by Margo, who refuses to leave. Too late she finds Bonner undergoing some sort of transformation. He knocks her down and drinks a strange potion. Finally Ludwig arrives, but he's had a stroke and cannot perform the operation on Bonner that is needed every decade. Bonner and Weiss are of the same generation, although Bonner looks 35 and Weiss is 89. Actually, they've discovered that replacement of a certain parathyroid gland can grant immortality. The elixir can retard the aging process for four weeks, but a new thyroid is needed by Bonner. Weiss argues that it may be time for Bonner to give up the ghost. Bonner is adamant. He does not want to undergo the ravages of disease that would overcome his 104-year-old body should he fail to have the surgery. He convinces Weiss to ask Gerrard to do the operation. Weiss reluctantly agrees. Bonner has plans to perform a similar operation on Janine so that he will not be alone any longer. When Weiss learns that Bonner has killed people to acquire the needed gland, he breaks the beaker of precious, life-giving liquid. They fight and Weiss is killed. Gerrard, told that Weiss had to leave, refuses to perform the surgery until Bonner reveals that he's imprisoned Janine. After the surgery, Bonner goes to his love with a gland he's taken from a prostitute. He explains his state. Gerrard and Inspector Legris locate Bonner's warehouse in time to rescue Janine. Bonner has begun aging — Gerrard only made an incision and did not replace the gland. Margo, half crazed, tosses a lamp onto Bonner, setting him afire.

Review: "Good Technicolor ... well-acted and intelligently conceived. But invention and embellishment [sic] in this field appear to have been exhausted...." (Powe., *Variety*, June 24, 1959)

Analysis: Although the film offers minimal sets, cast, and physical excitement, the Hammer style comes to the rescue, and the story on its own is intriguing enough to make it worthwhile. Hazel Court, a sculptress in real life, is radiant. Anton Diffring is properly haunted. Christopher Lee is properly restrained. Some medical mysteries: Why would a parathyroid gland be placed in one's side? What were the components of the elixir? *Would* sudden aging at 104 include the ravages of diseases not borne? If they were not borne, would they exist?

Maniac Cop

(Shapiro Glickenhaus Entertainment/Trans World Entertainment, 1988; 92 min.) **½

Produced by Larry Cohen. Directed by William Lustig. Screenplay, Larry Cohen. Edited by David Kern. Director of Photography, Vincent J. Rabe. Medallion color. Music, Jay Chattaway. Ultra-Stereo. Art Direction, Jonathon Hodges. Special Effects Makeup, More Than Skin Deep. Stunt Coordinator, Spiro Razatos. Special Effects, Hollywood Special Effects.

Cast: Detective Frank McCrae (Tom Atkins), Jack Forrest (Bruce Campbell), Theresa Mallory (Laurene Landon), Matthew Cordell (Robert Z'Dar), Commissioner Pike (Richard Roundtree), Captain Ripley (William Smith), Sally Noland (Sheree North), Ellen Forrest (Victoria Catlin), Dr. Gruber (Erik Holland).

Synopsis: A very large policeman breaks the neck of a young woman fleeing two muggers. Detective McCrae investigates. Another killing takes place. Again, a cop is incriminated. A third victim, a musician, is found face down in what was wet cement. McCrae realizes the murderer is, as his newswoman friend suggests, a "maniac cop." He gives her a file. Hearing the report on TV, a woman shoots an innocent cop when he approaches her car. Captain Ripley tells Commissioner Pike he'll get the maniac cop. Officer Jack Forrest goes on night duty, and his wife Ellen receives a call indicating that he's the murderer. She takes her gun and follows him to a motel, where she finds him in bed with a blonde. Next day her lifeless, mutilated body is found in Jack's motel room. Captain Ripley reads Jack his rights. McCrae sits in with Ripley

during the interrogation and realizes Jack is covering someone. Jack later admits to McCrae that Officer Theresa Mallory was the woman he'd shacked up with. Working the beat as a hooker, Theresa is accosted by a hulking cop. He grabs her throat, but she manages to put some slugs into him, as does McCrae, who is tossed aside. The cop disappears. Theresa doesn't understand how even a guy in a bulletproof vest could have survived. McCrae follows the crippled policewoman Sally Noland to the docks and spots her talking to a large cop. She calls him "Matt" and urges him to kill only those who deserve it. Back at the station, McCrae digs up newspaper clippings about Matt Cordell, a trigger-happy cop who was indicted and sent to Sing Sing. At Pier 14, the maniac cop thinks back on his days in prison and how inmates killed him and carved up his face. McCrae tells Jack he's going up to Sing Sing to talk to the medical examiner about Cordell. Before he can leave, Sally and he are killed by the maniac cop, McCrae thrown to his death from a window. Finding the station a killing ground, Theresa and Jack run into the night. Jack keeps McCrae's appointment at Sing Sing and quizzes Dr. Gruber about Cordell. They learn that Cordell's body was claimed by Sally Noland. Gruber grudgingly admits resuscitating him. He says they couldn't put him back in prison. Anyway, he had brain damage and was legally dead. Theresa goes to Commissioner Pike with this revelation, but Pike and Ripley are skeptical. In the hall, Cordell knifes Pike and the captain and kills the cop handcuffed to Teresa. She finally unlocks the cuffs and evades Cordell by climbing out a window. Simultaneously, Jack is captured and tossed into the back of a police van. Cordell takes the wheel. Theresa and another cop pursue the speeding van to Pier 14. Jack leaps on Cordell and tries to pull him out. A beam impales Cordell, who loses control and crashes into the river. When the truck is pulled out, there is no body—but a hand reaches from the water onto a pylon.

Reviews: "Too many opportunities to mull over gaps in exposition, especially the 'back-from-the-dead' Cordell's unexplained invincibility…. still sufficient wackiness to raise a few ghoulish grins." (Paul Taylor, *Monthly Film Bulletin*, February 1989, p. 53)

Analysis: It's an interesting concept but, we contend, not as compelling as it might have been. Note the Cast: Richard Roundtree was *Shaft*, dancer Sheree North had starring roles in the fifties (ironically, her leg is in a brace here), William Smith was king of movie bikers, Bruce Campbell was starring in the *Evil Dead* series (and continuing his human punching bag impression in this film). You'll witness one of the most dangerous stunts ever as the police van exits the pier into the river and a man jumps clear. Much planning must have gone into that, but how could they be sure the van would roll right while the man would be propelled far enough left?

Maniac Cop 2
(Movie House Sales Co., Ltd./Fadd Enterprises, 1990; 88 min.) ***

Produced by Larry Cohen. Directed by William Lustig. Screenplay, Larry Cohen. Edited by David Kern. Director of Photography, James Lemmo. Color, Foto-Kem. Panavision. Music, Jay Chattaway. Dolby Stereo. Electronic Music performed by Pete Levin. Set Decoration, Ann Job, Andrew Ness. Makeup, Dean Gates. Hair Stylist, Gladys Rieva. Stunt Coordinator, Spiro Razatos. Production Designers, Gene Abel, Charles Lagola.

Cast: Susan Riley (Claudia Christian), Detective Sean McKinney (Robert Davi), Jack Forrest (Bruce Campbell), Matt Cordell (Robert Z'Dar), Edward Doyle (Michael Lerner), Teresa Mallory (Laurene Landon), Blum (Clarence Williams III), Lew Brady (Charles Napier), Turkell (Leo Rossi), Detective Lovejoy (Lou Bonacki).

Synopsis: After a grocery store robbery and murder, a policeman and a policewoman believe that Matt Cordell is back and wreaking havoc on city streets. Eventually the police therapist Susan Riley is convinced, especially after a harrowing experience when a strange policeman handcuffs her to the wheel of a car and sets it in motion. The strange cop is indeed Matt Cordell, who finds habitation with Turkell, a psycho who likes to kill strippers. Cordell and Turkell break back into Sing Sing,

whereupon Cordell takes revenge on those inmates who'd savaged him during his incarceration. The police offer Cordell a retrial, but he is "killed" falling through a window. When the onlookers leave his gravesite, a hand bursts through the coffin and retrieves his badge that Detective McKinney had tossed there.

Review: "A few flashes of producer-writer Larry Cohen's wit…. the film still suffers from the stodgy direction of William Lustig, with the result that some of the best-conceived action sequences fall flat." (Kim Newman, *Monthly Film Bulletin*, January 1991, p. 22)

Analysis: It's a thoroughly likable revenge movie. Claudia Christian makes a good heroine, and the scene where she's handcuffed to the steering wheel — from the outside — is hair-raising. We don't recall seeing this trick on screen before.

Maniac Cop 3: Badge of Silence
(NEO/First Look Pictures, 1993) **½

Produced by Joel Soisson and Michael Leah. Directed by William Lustig and Joel Soisson. Screenplay, Larry Cohen. Edited by David Kern and Michael Eliot. Director of Photography, Jacques Haitkin. Color, Foto-Kem. Music, Joel Goldsmith. Set Decoration, Michele Spadaro. Fire Coordinator, Ken Bates.

Cast: Sean McKinney (Robert Davi), Matt Cordell (Robert Z'Dar), Dr. Fowler (Caitlin Dulany), Kate Sullivan (Gretchen Becker), Hank (Paul Gleason). With Jackie Earle Haley, Julius Harris, Grand Bush, Doug Savant, Bobby DiCicco, Frank Pesce.

Synopsis: A black man prays and inserts a knife in a bodyless head. The coffin of Matt Cordell breaks open from within and a hand reaches out for the badge on the top. Called to a murder scene, Sean McKinney discovers a headless body with a double triangle symbol on the pavement. It smacks of the occult practice of Santoría. Meanwhile a pharmacy is held up by the drug-crazed Jessup, who wounds several police until Kate arrives and seriously wounds him. But the young lady he'd held hostage shoots Kate. It was an inside job, but the two men videotaping the action edit their tape, which leads one to assume police brutality was at work. A hulking policeman — Matt Cordell — swinging a nightstick enters the abandoned St. Godard's church and meets the black man responsible for his resurrection. Cordell remembers prison and falling on fire onto a bus. Outside the hospital where Kate is in intensive care, Cordell shoots a taunter. McKinney visits Jessup and Kate. She dreams of a church and a wedding. Dr. Meyerson, a bit too flip for Cordell's tastes, is electrocuted by the cop. Dr. Fowler tells McKinney Cordell went into the basement. McKinney traverses the tunnels and comes out in St. Godard's. The black man talks of resurrection. In the hospital, a doctor is asked about terminating Kate's life support system. That doctor is killed via X-ray. Next Cordell finds and kills the videotapers and puts the undoctored tape on McKinney's car seat. He enters Jessup's room and unlocks the cuffs. Jessup and his cronies escape. Cordell takes Kate to the church. McKinney terminates Jessup in the ladies' room and Fowler joins McKinney in searching for Kate. When she and her guardian are found, McKinney tells Cordell not to condemn Kate to his fate. Cordell advises the black man to "Finish it," but is told Kate will not allow her soul to be resurrected. Cordell shoots him. In the ensuing melee Cordell and Kate catch fire. McKinney and Fowler escape into an ambulance chased by the flaming Cordell. McKinney tosses a gas canister into Cordell's car and it explodes. When the charred bodies are taken to the hospital, Cordell's hand reaches out and touches Kate's.

Review: "Unfortunately for the supporting cast, [Matt Cordell] seems to be rather inexact in his methods (to be expected from a moldering corpse, we suppose)." (Mick Martin and Marsha Porter, *Video Movie Guide 1994*, p. 834)

Analysis: It's another solid action film with good production values. Best scene: McKinney lights a cigarette with Cordell's smoking, severed hand.

Mannequin
(20th Century–Fox/Gladden Entertainment, 1987; 90 min.) **½

Produced by Art Levinson. Directed by Michael Gottlieb. Screenplay, Edward Rugoff

and Michael Gottlieb. Edited by Richard Halsey. Director of Photography, Tim Suhrstedt. Color, Du Art. Prints, DeLuxe. Music, Sylvester Levay. Song "Nothing's Gonna Stop Us Now" performed by Starship. Dolby Stereo. Art Direction, Richard Amend. Set Decoration, Elise "Cricket" Rowland. Special Effects, Phil Cory.

Cast: Jonathan Switcher (Andrew McCarthy), Emmy (Kim Cattrall), Claire Timkin (Estelle Getty), Richards (James Spader), Roxie (Carole Davis), Felix (G. W. Bailey), B. J. Wert (Stephen Vinovich), Armand (Christopher Maher), Hollywood (Meshach Taylor), Emmy's mother (Phyllis Newman), Mannequin factory boss (Phil Rubenstein).

Synopsis: Choosing not to marry a camel dung salesman in ancient Egypt, an inquisitive young woman wishes for a different life and finds her wishes answered: She floats through time and chooses a department store mannequin at Philadelphia's Prince and Company as her new incarnation. She — Emmy — reveals her corporeal self to Jonathan Switcher, who made the dummy. The two work together to create innovative window displays that entice customers back to the financially ailing retailer. Because Emmy will not let any other person see her alive, her mannequin self is easily stolen by employees of the Wert company, an organization out to acquire Prince. Jonathan's former girlfriend Foxie, a Wert employee, sends the mannequin toward certain doom in a trash compactor, but Jonathan rescues it just in time. Emmy finds herself coming alive to be seen by all. She and Jonathan can have a normal married life, it appears.

Reviews: "The movie stars Andrew McCarthy and Kim Cattrall, actors I have admired before and will, no doubt, admire again. In years to come, they will look back on this project with a rueful smile and a shrug, much as Paul Newman remembers *The Silver Chalice*." (Roger Ebert, *New York Post*, February 13, 1987, p. 28) ¶"Kim Cattrall and Andrew McCarthy have the right trendy, rock 'n' roll sparkle as the dummy and her protégé, assuring the film the youth cult audience at which it's aimed." (Rob Baker, *Women's Wear Daily*, February 12, 1987, p. 22)

Analysis: An ingratiating Andrew McCarthy, a lovely and unusually vibrant Kim

Cattrall, and a funny Meshach Taylor almost save a script that telegraphs every incident. As Michael Wilmington pointed out in the *Los Angeles Times Calendar* (February 13, 1987, p. 6), the funniest aspect of the story — that Jonathan is so careful to hide an "affair" with a presumably inanimate object — is somehow never used to best effect. Filmed in Philadelphia, specifically in the famous John Wanamaker department store.

Mannequin: On the Move
(20th Century–Fox, 1991; 95 min.) **

Produced by Edward Rugoff. Directed by Stewart Raffill. Screenplay, Edward Rugoff, David Isaacs, Ken Levine, and Betty Israel. Edited by John Rosenberg, Joan Chapman. Director of Photography, Larry Pizer. Color, Du Art. Music, David McHugh. Dolby Stereo. Art Direction, Norman B. Dodge, Jr. Set Decoration, Scott Jacobson. Special Effects, Joey Di Gaetano.

Cast: Jessie (Kristy Swanson), Jason Williamson/Prince William (William Ragsdale), Hollywood Montrose (Meshach Taylor), Count Spretzle (Terry Kiser), Mom/Queen (Cynthia Harris), Mr. James (Stuart Pankin), Andy Ackerman (Andrew Hill Newman).

Synopsis: In the medieval kingdom of Hauptmann-Koenig, the queen denies her son Prince William the right to marry Jessie and turns the peasant girl into a statue. The queen says the charmed necklace cannot be removed for a thousand years and the girl/statue meets a true love from another land. A millennium passes, and the statue and jewels from Hauptmann-Koenig are removed to the United States for display in Philadelphia's Prince and Company department store. The van transporting the valuables has an accident on a bridge. New Prince employee Jason Williamson, working for window dresser "Hollywood" Montrose, leaps into the river to rescue what he thinks is a woman. Jessie does comes alive in the store. He recalls the legend, then shows Jessie the town while Hauptmann-Koenig's Count Spretzle arrives, ostensibly to oversee the exhibition but actually to abscond with its jewels. Jason is aghast when Jessie turns back to a mannequin and initially fails to realize it occurred when the necklace was replaced

on her neck. Hollywood is responsible for bringing Jessie back to life but is frozen himself until Spretzle and his goons remove the necklace. Hollywood tells Jason the mannequin-come-to-life has happened before. Spretzle realizes Jason is the reincarnated Prince William and aims to eliminate him. Jason survives a duel and chases Spretzle to the roof and a hot-air balloon. Jason climbs aboard, and with Jessie's help, Spretzle comes under the necklace's spell, turns to a dummy and crashes to the street. Jason and Jessie start a new life together.

Reviews: Insipid in the extreme." (Kevin Thomas, *Los Angeles Times Calendar*, May 20, 1991, p. 6) ¶"Nearly every joke and setpiece is signaled well in advance." (Julian Stringer, *Sight and Sound*, November 1991, p. 48)

Analysis: It's not as intolerable as you might expect. Just broader, and perhaps for a teeny-bopper audience. Again, Philadelphia is the location, and there is some advantage taken of the environs, not just center city. William Ragsdale had been in *Fright Night*, and Kristy Swanson would be starring as *Buffy the Vampire Slayer*, while Terry Kiser would gain some notoriety as the corpse in *Weekend at Bernie's* and *Weekend at Bernie's II*. Starship reprises its hit tune "Nothing's Gonna Stop Us Now" over the end credits.

March of the Wooden Soldiers *see* **Babes in Toyland**

Mary Shelley's Frankenstein *see under* **Frankenstein**

The Marsupials *see* The Howling III *under* **The Howling**

The Masque of the Red Death *see under* **The Fall of the House of Usher**

The Mind Benders *see under* **Dr. Jekyll and Mr. Hyde**

Miracle on 34th Street
(20th Century-Fox, 1947; 96 min.)
***½

Produced by William Perlberg. Directed by

George Seaton. Screenplay, George Seaton. Story, Valentine Davies. Edited by Robert Simpson. Director of Photography, Charles Clarke, Lloyd Ahern. Music, Cyril Mockridge. Art Direction, Richard Day, Richard Irvine. Set Decoration, Thomas Little, Ernest Lansing. Special Effects, Fred Sersen.

Cast: Doris Walker (Maureen O'Hara), Fred Gailey (John Payne), Kris Kringle (Edmund Gwenn), Susan Walker (Natalie Wood), Judge Henry X. Harper (Gene Lockhart), Mr. Sawyer (Porter Hall), Charles Halloran (William Frawley), D. A. Thomas Mara (Jerome Cowan), Mr. Shellhammer (Philip Tonge), Doctor Pierce (James Seay), Mr. Macy (Harry Antrim), Peter's mother (Thelma Ritter), Girl's mother (Mary Field), Cleo (Theresa Harris), Peter (Anthony Sydes), Alfred (Alvin Greenman), Mrs. Mara (Anne Staunton), Thomas Mara, Jr. (Robert Hyatt), Reporters (Richard Irving, Jeff Corey), Santa Claus (Percy Helton), Dr. Rogers (William Forrest), Sawyer's Secretary (Anne O'Neal), Mrs. Shellhammer (Lela Bliss), Bailiff (Joseph McInerney), Drum majorette (Ida McGuire), Post office employee (Jack Albertson), Mail-bearing court officer (Snub Pollard).

Synopsis: Doris Walker hires Kris Kringle to replace a drunken Santa Claus in the annual Macy's department store holiday parade. Kris is such a hit he's hired for the season. At her house for dinner, he meets Doris's daughter, Susan, and fiancée, Fred, an attorney. Susan tells Kris she doesn't believe in Santa, but a series of events causes her to doubt her conviction. For instance, when Kris meets a little girl who only speaks Dutch, he easily converses with her in her native tongue. Although Mr. Macy had welcomed Kris enthusiastically, Mr. Sawyer demotes him. During an argument, Kris bops Sawyer on the head with his cane. Fred agrees to represent Kris in court and try to keep him from being institutionalized. Prosecuting district attorney Thomas Mara argues that Kris has not a shred of evidence to prove he's Santa. During a recess, political boss Charlie Halloran warns the judge that a verdict against Santa will rile women voters. When a post office employee decides to clean out the dead letter office, Fred asks the judge if he'll accept the U.S. Post Office as arbiter in the case. When the judge agrees, bags and bags of mail addressed to Santa are brought in. Kris is termed the real Santa. After the trial

Doris, Susan and Fred drive through a housing development. Susan urges them to stop at a newly built house that looks just like the house of her dreams, which she has seen in a picture. Inside what they realize will become their home, they notice Kris's cane.

Review: "It is largely because this job isn't loaded to the hubs with all the commercial gimmicks that it is such a delightful picture." (Bosley Crowther, *New York Times*, June 5, 1947, p. 32)

Analysis: It's a holiday favorite and deservedly so. All are perfectly cast. For his delightful portrayal of an opinionated, persnickety Santa, the great character actor Edmund Gwenn won a Best Supporting Actor Academy Award.

Miracle on 34th Street
(20th Century–Fox, 1994; 114 min.)
***

Produced by John Hughes. Directed by Les Mayfield. Screenplay, George Seaton and John Hughes. Based on the 1947 motion picture screenplay by George Seaton. Story, Valentine Davies. Edited by Raja Gosnell. Director of Photography, Julio Macat. Color, DeLuxe. Music, Bruce Broughton. Art Direction, Steve Arnold. Set Decoration, Leslie Rollins.

Cast: Kriss Kringle (Richard Attenborough), Dorey Walker (Elizabeth Perkins), Susan Walker (Mara Wilson), Bryan Bedford (Dylan McDermott), Ed Collins (J. T. Walsh), Jack Duff (James Remar), Judge Henry Harper (Robert Prosky), Alberta Leonard (Jane Leeves), C. F. Cole (William Windom), Shellhammer (Simon Jones), Tony Falacchi (Jack McGee), Bailiff (Joe Pentangelo), Doorman (Alvin Greenman), Victor (Joss Ackland).

Synopsis: Dorey Walker replaces Tony, an inebriated Santa, with an elderly gentleman named Kriss Kringle for C. F. Cole & Company's annual New York Thanksgiving Day Parade. Even Victor, president of rival department store chain Shopper's Express, admits that this new Santa plays his role expertly. Dorey hires Kriss for the season. Although he tells children and their moms where to find certain toys cheaper, his company prospers. Moms love him. C. F. Cole's Christmas motto becomes, "If We Don't Have It, We'll Find It

For You." Even though Dorey's daughter Susan has been informed there is no Santa, the child comes to suspect that Kriss may have special powers. Kriss decides to use Dorey as a test case: If he can convince her he's the genuine article, he can continue what he's been doing for ages. When Kriss babysits Susan, she shows him a newspaper picture of a house she wants. Susan feels that if she can have that and a father, Kriss is for real. That evening, attorney Bryan Bedford presents Dorey with an engagement ring, but she refuses it, and he gives it to Kriss to do with as he sees fit. Tony, Cole's original Santa, is hired by Shopper's Express troubleshooters Jack Duff and Alberta Leonard to harass Kriss. Kriss is made to seem dangerous when he raises his cane and strikes at Tony. Incarcerated in Bellevue Hospital pending a competency hearing, he is downcast, telling Bryan he's exceeded the rules of propriety. But Bryan argues that it was a set-up. Meanwhile Dorey convinces her employer to support Kriss. At the first day's hearing Bryan makes points in his client's favor, but next day, prosecutor Ed Collins gains the upper hand. Judge Harper wishes he had a way out and the following day finds it in the form of a Christmas card from Susan. With the card is a dollar bill with "In God We Trust" circled. He explains that if the government of the people of the U.S. can place its faith in an unseen entity, Kriss Kringle can indeed be Santa Claus. Case dismissed. As it is Christmas eve, Kriss indicates that he'll be very busy. Both Bryan and Dorey receive cards requesting their presence at St. Francis. When they arrive at the church they discover that the priest has the engagement ring Bryan had given to Kriss. To her delight, on Christmas morning Susan discovers that she's gained a dad. On the pretext of taking pictures of C. F. Cole's catalog house, the three are driven to the suburbs, whereupon they discover that Dorey's Christmas bonus will help them buy this dwelling. Kriss has obviously been at work.

Review: "Offers us a Santa Claus cut along classic lines — round, twinkly and played with a nice, comforting restraint by the redoubtable Richard Attenborough."

(Richard Schickel, *Time*, November 28, 1994, p. 80)

Analysis: Surprisingly palatable, this remake has several affecting scenes, including Attenborough's use of sign language to communicate with a deaf child and his dressing in his Santa attire. Mara Wilson plays the slightly precocious Susan well. Some of the impact is lessened for those who've seen the original. We know from the outset that Kriss *is* Santa. Perhaps they eschewed the mail bags denouement to surprise those audiences, but the "In God We Trust" dollar bill explanation lacks visual panache. This must be the only film in which notable heavy James Remar (*48 Hrs.*) wears a suit.

Miranda
(GFD/Gainsborough, 1947; 80 min.)
**½

Produced by Betty Box. Directed by Ken Annakin. Screenplay, Peter Blackmore, Denis Waldock. Based on the play by Peter Blackmore. Director of Photography, Ray Elton.

Cast: Miranda (Glynis Johns), Dr. Paul Marten (Griffith Jones), Nurse Cary (Margaret Rutherford), With Googie Withers, John McCallum, David Tomlinson, Sonia Holm, Yvonne Owen, Brian Oulton, Maurice Denham, Zena Marshall, Charles Penrose, Lyn Evans, Anthony Drake, Stringer Davis, Hal Osmond, Charles Rolfe, Charles Paton, Frank Webster, Toni McMillan, Thelma Rea, Joan Ingram, Gerald Campion.

Synopsis: While vacationing in Cornwall, Dr. Paul Marten is captured in a cave by the mermaid Miranda. She promises to release him if he'll show her London. To hide her tail, Miranda acts the invalid. Her condition and natural buoyancy attract a host of admirers, but she keeps her true identity known from all but Nurse Cary. After savoring the sights of the human world, Miranda drops into the Thames via the Embankment and returns to her natural habitat.

Review: "We weren't sorry when the mermaid finally slithered into the Thames.... It had become pretty much of a bore." (Bosley Crowther, *New York Times*, April 25, 1949, p. 20)

Analysis: The underrated (some can't

brook her voice) Glynis Johns is so appropriate as the mermaid. The *New York Times*, despite its dissatisfaction with the mermaid, called Ms. Johns "bewitching." U.S. release is 1949.

Mad About Men
(GFD/Group Films, 1954; 90 min.)
**

Produced by Betty Box. Directed by Ralph Thomas. Screenplay, Peter Blackmore. Director of Photography, Ernest Steward. Technicolor.

Cast: Caroline/Miranda (Glynis Johns), Nurse Cary (Margaret Rutherford), Jeff (Donald Sinden), Barbara (Anne Crawford), Berengaria (Dora Bryan), Barclay (Nicholas Phipps), Ronald (Peter Martyn), Old Salt (Noel Purcell), Madame Blanche (Irene Handl), Mrs. Forster (Joan Hickson), Viola (Judith Furse), Mantalini (David Hurst), Dr. Fergus (Martin Miller), Editor (Deryck Guyler), Pawnbroker (Anthony Oliver), Symes (Harry Welchman). With Meredith Edwards, Marianne Stone, Douglas Ives, George Woodbridge, Lawrence Ward, Dandy Nichols Martin Boddey, Ken Richmond, Stringer Davis, Henry Langhurst, John Horsley.

Synopsis: Caroline is accosted by the mermaid Miranda, who looks like her! Miranda convinces the human to take a bicycle trip while she substitutes for her — in a wheelchair to hide her tail. For the second time in her life, she is assisted by Nurse Cary. A magnet for men due to her charm and apparent naiveté, Miranda/Caroline also attracts the ire of jealous women, especially Barbara. Although Barbara learns of Caroline/Miranda's secret, the real Caroline returns to foil the revelation.

Review: "Of all the films that ever were produced, *Miranda* ... seemed the least likely to have a sequel.... There is neither sufficient continuity in the story nor humor in the lines to carry the film along." (*Times* [London], October 28, 1954, p. 5)

Analysis: Betty Box and Ralph Thomas were responsible for any number of British comedies, some quite good, some, like this, merely passable. Johns and Rutherford reprise their roles.

Missile to the Moon *see under* **Catwomen of the Moon**

The Molten Meteor *see* **The Blob**

Monster of Terror *see* **Die, Monster, Die!**

The Monster Squad *see under* **Frankenstein**

The Mouse on the Moon *see under* **The Mouse That Roared**

The Mouse That Roared
(Columbia/Highroad, 1959; 83 min.)
***

Produced by Walter Shenson. Directed by Jack Arnold. Screenplay, Roger MacDougall and Stanley Mann. Based on the novel by Leonard Wibberley. Eastman Color. Music, Edwin Astley. Costumes, Anthony Mendleson.

Cast: Grand Duchess Gloriana/Tully Bascombe/Prime Minister Count Mountjoy (Peter Sellers), Helen Kokintz (Jean Seberg), Professor Kokintz (David Kossoff), Will (William Hartnell), Roger (Timothy Bateson), Cobbley (Monty Landis), Pedro (Harold Krasket), Benter (Leo McKern), BBC announcer (Colin Gordon), Snippet (MacDonald Parke), U.S. Secretary of Defense (Austin Willis), O'Hara (George Margo), Mulligan (Richard Gatehouse), Ticket collector (Jacques Cey), Cunard captain (Stuart Sanders), Second Officer (Ken Stanley).

Synopsis: In the French Alps lies the smallest nation on earth, the Grand Duchy of Fenwick. Settled by the British, it is the only English-speaking nation on the European continent. Its prime export is Grand Fenwick wine, most of which goes to the United States. Problems arise when a California winery produces "Grand Enwick" and drives its competitor out of the market. What to do? Fenwick's prime minister hatches a scheme whereby war will be declared on the U.S. and game warden and field marshal Tully will take Fenwick's twenty-man army to New York. Naturally they will be taken prisoner. The war over, Fenwick will enjoy the fruits of defeat by America: foreign aid. Tully does as instructed but locates Dr. Kokintz, who has created the football-size Q(uodium) bomb. Instead of surrendering, Tully kidnaps Kokintz and his lovely daughter Helen as well as a general and four New York policemen, returns to Fenwick and reports on his victory. Aghast, the prime minister plans to help daughter and father retrieve the bomb and leave. World powers send representatives hoping to form an alliance with Fenwick and take charge of the bomb. Eventually the U.S. representative signs a peace accord. Tully gets Helen. The bomb falls to floor but conks out. Apparently it's a dud. They leave it there in the dungeon, swearing not to tell anyone else. After they leave, a mouse climbs from the bomb, and it begins making noise again.

Reviews: "Rambunctious satiric comedy.... cheerful nonsense." (Bosley Crowther, *New York Times*, October 27, 1959, p. 40) ¶"Fairly witty example of a rare film form: political burlesque." (*Time*, November 9, 1959, p. 84)

Analysis: This is a cute, sometimes irresistible satire whose budget could have been larger and thus avoided the rear projection scenes. Nevertheless, it's a tale with many funny moments, e.g., the general eating off a Geneva Convention–mandated tin plate while buxom girls serve the captive police on the finest china. It's a tale that one likes to tell other people.

The Mouse on the Moon

(United Artists, 1963; 82 min.) **

Produced by Walter Shenson. Directed by Richard Lester. Screenplay, Michael Pertwee. Inspired by the novel *The Mouse That Roared* by Leonard Wibberley. Edited by Bill Lenny. Director of Photography, Wilkie Cooper. Eastman Color. Music, Ron Grainer. Animation, Trevor Bond.

Cast: Grand Duchess Gloriana XIII (Margaret Rutherford), Prime Minister Mountjoy (Ron Moody), Vincent (Bernard Cribbins), Cynthia (June Ritchie), Kokintz (David Kossoff), Spender (Terry-Thomas), Dave Benter (Roddy McMillan), British delegate (John LeMesurier), British aide (Michael Trubshawe), Bracewell (John Phillips), Plumber (Hugh Lloyd), Russian delegate (Peter Sallis), Russian aide (Jan Conrad), Wendover (Tom Aldredge), Mario (Mario Fabrizi), Peasant girl (Coral Morphew), American civilian (Frank Lieberman), Sergeant (Stuart Saunders), Bandleader (Bruce Lacey), Ladies-in-waiting (Lucy Griffiths, Carol Dowell), First councilor (Stringer Davis), June (Carolyn

Pertwee), April (Sandra Hampton), U.S. general (Archie Duncan).

Synopsis: Wine, the Grand Duchy of Fenwick's prime export, has an unfortunate propensity to explode. Prime Minister Mountjoy is more concerned with raising money to fix the castle plumbing. Approaching the United States for financial aid supposedly for building a moon rocket, the Duchy finds itself receiving money from the Americans and an old rocket from the Russians while the British spy on the unusual proceedings. Professor Kokintz discovers that the country's wine can serve as rocket fuel. Fueled by the wine, a rocket is launched, quickly followed by American and Russian spacecraft. The Fenwick ship lands on the moon first, and the professor says it's a nice place to visit but he wouldn't like to live there. The American and Russian ships sink into the moon's surface. Their crews obtain safe passage when the Fenwick ship returns to Earth. Fenwick rejoices.

Review: "Blithely outrageous spoof." (Bosley Crowther, *New York Times*, June 18, 1963, p. 32)

Analysis: It's not up to the ingratiating silliness of its predecessor. Partly this is due to the absence of Peter Sellers. Still, there are amusing moments, like the female mannequin shooting past an airplane, garbage dumped into space, and the cooking of Irish stew aboard the spacecraft. The *New York Times* review actually felt the "erratic" direction and "frightful" photography contributed to the overall fun. Ron Moody's day would come in 1968's *Oliver!* when he played Fagin. Although unfamiliar to American audiences, June Ritchie made some significant British films, e.g., *A Kind of Loving*. Margaret Rutherford was, of course, a grand dame of U.K. films.

The Mummy

(Universal, 1932; 72 min.) ***½

Produced by Carl Laemmle, Jr. Directed by Karl Freund. Screenplay, John L. Balderston. Based on a story by Nina Wilcox Putnam and Richard Schayer. Edited by Milton Carruth. Director of Photography, Charles Stumar. Art Direction, Willy Pogany. Makeup, Jack P. Pierce. Special Effects, John P. Fulton.

Left to right: Bramwell Fletcher (Ralph Norton), the mummy of Im-ho-tep (Boris Karloff), Dr. Muller (Edward Van Sloan), and Sir Joseph Whemple (Arthur Bryon) in *The Mummy* (Universal, 1932).

Cast: Im-ho-tep/Ardath Bey (Boris Karloff), Dr. Muller (Edward Van Sloan), Helen Grosvenor/Princess Ankh-es-en-Amon (Zita Johann), Frank Whemple (David Manners), Sir Joseph Whemple (Arthur Byron), Ralph Norton (Bramwell Fletcher), Professor Pearson (Leonard Mudie), The Nubian (Noble Johnson), Dr. Le Baron (Eddie Kane), Frau Muller (Kathryn Byron), Warrior (Henry Victor), Pharaoh (James Crane), Knight (Arnold Grey), Police Inspector (Tony Marlow).

Synopsis: On the British Museum's 1921 Egyptian field expedition, Dr. Muller of Vienna advises Sir Joseph Whemple against opening a small casket that might contain the Scroll of Thoth. While Muller and Whemple discuss the find, which includes a well-preserved mummy they believe to have been a priest of the Temple of the Sun at Karnak, Ralph Norton opens the casket and begins deciphering the hieroglyphs. When a bandaged hand reaches out for the scroll, Norton screams. The now

mad Norton tells Whemple, "He went for a little walk!" In 1932 Frank Whemple is on a similar expedition and meets Ardath Bey, who advises them to dig in a certain place for a princess buried 3,700 years before. Sure enough, her vault and casket are found. The artifacts are taken to the Cairo Museum, where Dr. Muller and his patient, Helen Grosvenor, are visiting. Ardath Bey realizes that Helen is a reincarnated princess and attempts to reclaim her as his love. He uses his mysterious pool to show her their deaths eons before. When she died he — the priest Im-ho-tep — attempted to raise her from the dead using the Scroll of Thoth. Muller comes to realize that Ardath is the mummy Sir Joseph Whemple found in 1921. "Call her! He has called her back to ancient Egypt. Her love for you may bridge the centuries," Dr. Muller urges Frank. Im-ho-tep tells Helen, "No man ever suffered as I did for you. But the rest, you may not know. Not until you are about to pass through the great night of terror and triumph. Until you are ready to face moments of horror for an eternity of love." Before the altar of Anubis, Imhotep plans to kill and resurrect Helen, now garbed in ancient attire. Dr. Muller and Frank arrive but cannot face Im-ho-tep's stare and spell. Helen fears for her life and soul and implores Isis, whose statue raises its right arm and destroys Im-ho-tep.

Review: "For purposes of terror there are two scenes ... that are weird enough in all conscience. In the first the mummy comes alive.... In the second Im-Ho-Tep is embalmed alive." (Andre Sennwald, *New York Times*, January 7, 1933, p. 11)

Analysis: When we first saw this on the late night *Shock Theater* in the late 1950s, we were disappointed. Expecting the usual bandaged, shambling creature from the pharaoh's tomb, we didn't much care for the Karloffian interpretation. He was only bandaged at the beginning. But seeing this as an adult provides a different perspective. It is an atmospheric classic with the oft-commented upon fright scene at the beginning, when the young archaeologist sees the mummy's hand reach for the scroll. What would you do?

The Mummy's Hand
(Universal, 1940; 67 min.) ***

Produced by Ben Pivar. Directed by Christy Cabanne. Screenplay, Griffith Jay and Maxwell Shane. Story, Griffith Jay. Edited by Phil Cahn. Director of Photography, Elwood Bredell. Musical Director, Hans J. Salter. Art Direction, Jack Otterson. Set Decoration, R. A. Gausman. Costumes, Vera West.

Cast: Steve Banning (Dick Foran), Marta Solvani (Peggy Moran), Professor Andoheb (George Zucco), Babe Jenson (Wallace Ford), Kharis (Tom Tyler), High Priest (Eduardo Ciannelli), The Great Solvani (Cecil Kellaway), Professor Petrie (Charles Trowbridge), Beggar (Sig Arno), Bazaar owner (Michael Mark), Bartender (Harry Stubbs), Girl (Mara Tartar), Egyptian (Eddie Foster).

Synopsis: In Egypt, two expatriate American archaeologists, Steve Banning and Babe Jenson, happen across some broken pottery that contains a large part of a map to the hidden tomb of the legendary Princess Ananka. Excited by their find, they deliver the fragments to Andoheb, the curator of a local museum. Unknown to the Americans, Andoheb is the son of the late High Priest of Ananka. Before his death, the High Priest charged Andoheb with protecting Ananka's tomb. The legend of Kharis unfolds before us: Ananka is the third daughter of a royal monarch. Kharis is a prince of the royal house who is in love with Ananka, despite the chastity of her station. When Ananka unexpectedly dies, the grief-stricken Kharis refuses to accept her death. After the burial ceremony, he steals into the crypt and pilfers the forbidden Tana leaves, the magical properties of which will restore life to the dead. Discovered committing this blasphemy, Kharis is taken by the priests of Ra, who impose a terrible penalty: the living death as a mummy buried with the remains of Ananka. Back at the museum, Andoheb pooh-poohs Banning and Jenson's find, saying that it is merely a clever forgery, the kind he sees periodically as museum curate. Dr. Petrie, Andoheb's associate, is not so sure, and supports Banning and Jenson in an expedition into the desert. Also throwing in with the expedition are the Great Solvani, a Brooklyn magician touring the Middle East, and his daughter Marta. When the expedition uncovers Ananka's tomb, the first discovery is not the princess, but the mummified remains of Kharis. Alarmed at the violation of the tomb, Andoheb appears and, brewing a potion of nine Tana leaves, brings Kharis to life. At the curate's command, Kharis throttles Dr. Petrie. Roaming the explorer's camp at night, the mummy is about to perform the same function on Solvani, but stops dead in his tracks upon seeing Marta, whom he takes to be the reincarnation of his beloved lost Ananka. Grasping the young woman to him, Kharis makes his shambling way back to the tomb. Marta's screams arouse the camp. Finding Solvani unconscious in his tent, Banning tears off in pursuit of the monster, while Jenson is accosted by Andoheb, who has every intention of killing him. Andoheb doesn't reckon with the Yank's quick trigger-finger, however, and he is presently lying at the foot of the tomb, evidently dead. Inside, Banning finds Marta trussed up on an altar slab prior to Kharis's treating her with a Tana leaf potion that will reduce her to a mummified existence. As Banning is freeing her, Kharis reappears. Banning and the mummy struggle briefly. During the fight, the precious Tana potion is knocked to the floor and drains away; Kharis lurches forward to salvage some if he can. Banning takes advantage of the respite to send a torch Kharis's way, engulfing the mummy in flames. Afterwards, Banning proposes to Marta, and a cablegram arrives to announce that Banning, because of his find, has been rewarded with the directorship of the Scripps Museum in Massachusetts.

Review: "Once or twice Miss Moran makes a grimace … and screams. Otherwise everyone seems remarkably casual." (T.S., *New York Times*, September 20, 1940, p. 27)

The Mummy's Tomb
(Universal, 1942; 61 min.) **

Produced by Ben Pivar. Directed by Harold Young. Screenplay, Griffith Jay and Henry Sucher. Based on a story by Neil P. Varnick. Edited by Milton Carruth. Director of Photography, George Robinson. Musical Direction, Hans J. Salter. Art Direction, Jack Otterson. Set Decoration, R. A. Gausman. Makeup, Jack Pierce.

Cast: Kharis (Lon Chaney, Jr.), High Priest Mehemet Bey (Turhan Bey), Steve Banning (Dick Foran), Isobel Evans (Elyse Knox), John Banning (John Hubbard), Jane Banning (Mary Gordon), Mrs. Evans (Virginia Brissac), Babe Hanson (Wallace Ford), Professor Norman (Frank Reicher), Jim (Paul E. Burns), Andoheb (George Zucco), Coroner (Emmett Vogan), Girl in car (Janet Shaw), Sheriff (Cliff Clark), Stunts (Eddie Parker). With Glenn Strange, Grace Cunard.

Synopsis: Thirty years after discovering the legendary tomb of the Egyptian princess Ananka, Professor Stephen A. Banning is now the retired director of the Scripps Museum in Mapleton, Massachusetts. Enjoying a visit from his son John and Isobel Evans, John's fiancée, Stephen recounts the discovery of Ananka's tomb and the subsequent appearance of the living mummy

Kharis, Ananka's guardian through the ages, and how the party of archaeologists managed to defeat the monster. After that episode, the Banning party returned to America with the remains of Ananka. Stephen married Marta Solvani and assumed the directorship of the Scripps. Now, with Marta gone (she passed away some years ago), Stephen is resigned to a life of retirement, respected and admired for his accomplishments as an archaeologist and director of a prestigious museum. Unknown to the Bannings, however, the high priest Andoheb was not killed, nor was Kharis destroyed in the fiery struggle that concluded the adventure. Now a wizened old man, Andoheb recruits Mehemet Bey, an acolyte of the Ananka cult, to journey to America, locate surviving members of the Banning expedition and kill them, and return with Ananka's remains. Arriving in the United States with the bulky sarcophagus containing Kharis, Bey takes up residence in Mapleton as the caretaker of the local cemetery. He sets to work almost immediately, brewing Tana leaves and administering the potion that will render Kharis ambulatory. The mummy commences its grisly mission at once, with Stephen Banning as his first victim. Hearing of the misfortune befalling his old friend's family, Banning's old friend Babe comes to Mapleton. Learning details of the murder that has authorities baffled, Babe is convinced that Kharis has somehow returned and is pursuing a vendetta against the survivors of the original expedition. It's Babe's bad luck that he's the monster's next victim; cornered alone by the mummy in a blind alley, the elderly Babe makes easy prey. Mehemet Bey's mission is complicated, and ultimately undone, by his chance spying of Isobel, with whom he becomes infatuated. He has Kharis abduct her from her bed in the dead of night, an act which rouses the already nearly hysterical townspeople to action. Suspecting Bey from the start (he is the only "foreigner" in the community), the angry mob descends upon the cemetery before the Egyptian can administer the Tana potion to the bound woman. Wary of the rabble, and determined not to be caught red-handed

The mummy Kharis (Lon Chaney, Jr.— or stuntman Eddie Parker) in a publicity shot with Isobel (Elyse Knox) for *The Mummy's Tomb* (Universal, 1942).

with the captive, Bey has Kharis remove her through a rear exit. An unwise move with a revolver proves to be Bey's undoing; when he pulls one on John Banning, the sheriff pulls his and shoots the acolyte dead. Someone spies the mummy and his burden, and the mob pursues the monster to the Banning house. John rescues Isobel while members of the impromptu posse fight the mummy off with torches. In a moment the entire house is engulfed in flames, and Kharis disappears in the inferno.

Reviews: "Somehow the spell of belief has been broken." (Theodore Strauss, *New York Times*, October 26, 1942, p. 19) ¶ "Full of messy carpentry and indelible, enchanting images." (Tim Lucas, *Video Watchdog*, November/December 1993, p. 19)

The Mummy's Ghost
(Universal, 1944; 60 min.) **

Produced by Ben Pivar. Directed by Reginald LeBorg. Screenplay, Griffith Jay, Henry Sucher, Brenda Weisberg. Based on a story by Griffith Jay and Henry Sucher. Edited by Saul Goodkind. Director of Photography, William Sickner. Musical Director, Hans J. Salter. Art Direction, John B. Goodman, Abraham Grossman. Costumes, Vera West. Makeup, Jack Pierce.

Cast: Kharis (Lon Chaney, Jr.), Youssef Bey (John Carradine), Amina Monsouri/Ananka (Ramsay Ames), High Priest (George Zucco), Tommy Harvey (Robert Lowery), Inspector Walgreen (Barton MacLane), Mrs. Ellen Norman(Claire Whitney), Professor Norman (Frank Reicher), Sheriff Elwood (Harry Shannon), Sheriff's associate (Anthony Warde), Scripps Museum guide (Ivan Triesault), Students (Martha Vickers, Don Barclay), Coroner (Emmitt Vogan), Dr. Ayab (Lester Sharpe), Nightwatchman (Oscar O'Shea), Mrs. Martha Evans (Mira McKinney), Mrs. Ada Blake (Dorothy Vaughan), Ben Evans (Eddy Waller), Mapleton woman (Bess Flowers).

Synopsis: Andoheb, high priest of Antar, sends Youssef Bey, another acolyte of the faith, to America to retrieve the remains of both Kharis and Princess Ananka. Arriving in Mapleton, Youssef Bey awaits the first moonlit night and brews the potion of nine Tana leaves, summoning the shambling mummy Kharis. The mummified remains of Ananka crumble to dust at the first touch of Kharis; the spirit of the princess flees and takes refuge in the body of Amina Monsouri, a college student of Egyptian descent who resides nearby. Amina is given to spells of moodiness and feelings of isolation. As the spirit of Ananka becomes stronger in her, these spells become more frequent and of longer duration, a condition her boyfriend Tom Harvey notices. He determines to remedy the situation by insisting that they leave immediately for his family home in New York, where they'll be married. Their plans are complicated when murders begin again in Mapleton, murders with an alarming similarity to the ones several years earlier that were committed by Kharis on his rampage to wipe out all surviving members of the Banning expedition. When Professor Norton is strangled by Kharis, Amina is implicated by her presence at the scene. Inspector Walgreen admits that Amina lacks the means or motive for committing the crime, but as she's the only lead he has, he insists that the lovers "stick around." In the meantime, Youssef Bey catches sight of the lovely Amina. Just as predecessor Mehemet Bey had fallen for the charms of Isobel Evans, this new acolyte becomes smitten and determines to have Amina for his own. Having Kharis abduct the woman, Bey prepares the Tana solution that will give her eternal life. Enraged at yet another act of sacrilege, the mummy attacks and kills the priest, even as a mob descends on the isolated mill the priest and monster have used as a hideout. Picking up the unconscious Amina, the mummy lurches into a nearby swamp. As he staggers deeper into the bog, Amina undergoes a strange metamorphosis, her hair turning white and her limbs growing wizened. Her possession by the spirit of Ananka is now complete. Kharis disappears into the quicksand, clutching the mummified princess to him.

Reviews: "Eventually Kharis carries her off and they sink blissfully beneath a swamp…. Oh! please, Universal, do not disturb their rest." (Thomas M. Pryor, *New York Times*, July 1, 1944, p. 10) ¶ "Brisker-than-usual pace… builds to a surprisingly pessimistic finale." (Tim Lucas, *Video Watchdog*, November/December 1993, p. 19)

The Mummy's Curse
(Universal, 1945; 60 min.) **

Produced by Oliver Drake. Directed by Leslie Goodwins. Screenplay, Bernard Schubert. Story, Leon Abrams and Dwight V. Babcock. Edited by Fred R. Feitshans. Director of Photography, Virgil Miller. Musical Director, Paul Sawtell. Art Direction, John B. Goodman. Makeup, Jack Pierce.

Cast: Kharis (Lon Chaney, Jr.), Ananka (Virginia Christine), Dr. Ilzor Zardad (Peter Coe), Betty Walsh (Kay Harding), Dr. James Halsey (Dennis Moore), Raghab (Martin Kosleck), Major Pat Walsh (Addison Richards), Dr. Cooper (Holmes Herbert), Michael (William Farnum), Cajun Joe (Kurt Katch), Tante Berthe (Ann Codee), Skilles (Charles Stevens), Goobie (Napoleon Simpson). With Claire Whitney.

Synopsis: To the backwater community where the mummy Kharis and Princess Ananka sank into a murky grave twenty-five years earlier comes Dr. James Halsey from the Scripps Museum. With Halsey is the Egyptian, Dr. Zardad; the two are searching for Kharis and Ananka for the museum. Unknown to Halsey, however, Zardad is really an agent for the priests of Zarkon, and his interest is in restoring the living relics to their original station, the Tomb of Ananka in Egypt. Introducing themselves to Major Pat Walsh, foreman of the engineering project that is attempting to drain the swamp in a land management venture, they are greeted with impatient but generally good-natured surliness. The major is intent on getting on with his project and doesn't relish these archaeologists getting in the way. However, at the urging of his secretary (and niece) Betty, he gives in and provides free access to the area. Kharis's remains are unearthed by one of the workers; Raghab, Zardad's local confederate, kills the man and absconds with the mummy to the ruins of an ancient monastery in a remote part of the swamp. Shortly afterwards, earth-moving equipment uncovers Ananka. Upon exposure to the sun's rays, she regains the appearance she had as a living person three thousand years earlier, although her memory of those times is cloudy and unfocused. Cajun Joe finds her wandering aimlessly in the swamp and takes her to Tante Berthe, the proprietress of a local tavern. Berthe puts the swooning girl to bed while Joe leaves to fetch a doctor. During his absence, Kharis, sensing the presence of the reincarnated princess, bursts in and strangles Berthe. During the struggle, Ananka revives enough to make an escape. She is shortly found by Dr. Halsey, whom she impresses with her knowledge of things antiquarian and Egyptian. He puts her to work immediately as his assistant. Zardad, too, is impressed; he recognizes her as the reincarnated Ananka, and sets to work (via Tana leaves and Kharis) to reclaim her. The mummy appears at Ananka's tent one night, and she flees to the tent of Dr. Cooper. Kharis follows and attempts to take the unsuspecting princess by force;

Cooper tries to defend her but is killed. Ananka escapes into the swamp. The next morning, Major Walsh is outraged by yet another murder and connects these with the presence of Halsey and his party, threatening to revoke the grant that gives them permission to dig in the swamp. Halsey and Cajun Joe search the swamp, convinced that the mummy Kharis is responsible for the killings. Joe's search is all too successful; he comes upon the creature at night and is throttled forthwith. Meanwhile, Ananka stumbles into the tent of Betty Walsh, who gives the frightened and confused woman shelter for the night. Their slumber is disturbed by Kharis, who lurches in and snatches up the fainting Ananka, disappearing immediately into the swamp, returning to the secluded monastery. There, Zardad administers to her the Tana potion that renders her mummified in preparation for her return to her Egyptian tomb. Emerging from the shambles of her wrecked tent, Betty encounters Raghab. The man feigns surprise at her account of the mummy and offers to take her to Halsey. He takes her instead to the monastery, intent on expressing his lecherous yearnings for her. He is interrupted by Zardad, who denounces him as an infidel and defiler of his sacred trust. Pulling a knife, Raghab stabs the priest to death. Halsey appears and leaps upon the murderer. In their struggle, Halsey is knocked unconscious. Before Raghab can act, Kharis emerges from the shadows and pursues the terrified murderer into an unstable wing of the monastery. Their fray causes the dilapidated roof to collapse, burying them together.

Review: "A wretched little shocker.... as dull as Uncle Henry's old jack-knife." (Bosley Crowther, *New York Times*, March 31, 1945, p. 16)

Abbott and Costello Meet the Mummy
(1955; 79 min.) *½

Produced by Howard Christie. Directed by Charles Lamont. Screenplay, John Grant. Story, Lee Loeb. Edited by Russell Schoengarth. Director of Photography, George Robinson. Special Photography, Clifford Stine.

Musical Supervision, Joseph Gershenson. Art Direction, Alexander Golitzen, Bill Newberry. Set Decoration, Russell A. Gausman, James M. Walters. Makeup, Bud Westmore.

Cast: Freddie Franklin (Lou Costello), Pete Patterson (Bud Abbott), Semu (Richard Deacon), Madame Rontru (Marie Windsor), Charlie (Michael Ansara), Josef (Dan Seymour), Dr. Gustav Zoomer (Kurt Katch), Hetsut (Richard Karlan), Klaris (Eddie Parker), Iben (Mel Welles). With Peggy King, Mazone-Abbott Dancers, and Chandra Kaly Dancers.

Synopsis: Dr. Gustav Zoomer has found the mummy Klaris, but others covet it: Madame Rontru and her "associates," and the mummy's rightful owners led by Semu. Semu's people bring him the mummy but have not located the all-important sacred medallion. Freddie and Pete are incriminated in the murder of Dr. Zoomer. Freddie finds the medallion, and Semu learns of that fact. So does Rontru, who offers to buy it and meets Freddie at the cafe. Freddie mistakenly eats the medallion in his hamburger. Made prisoners by Rontru, Freddie and Pete are captured, Freddie x-rayed. Everyone learns that they must go to the temple. Semu is taken prisoner by Rontru, who bandages Charlie as a mummy. Charlie knocks out Klaris, but Pete knocks out Charlie and dons bandages himself. Rontru uses a metal detector in the temple but doesn't find the treasure. When Klaris is destroyed by dynamite, the tomb of the princess is revealed. But the explosion was so devastating, Semu thinks his people have only a legend left. Pete proposes that the legend be profitably propagated, and Cafe Klaris is opened.

Review: "Marie Windsor as a harem girl cannot resurrect a dead script." (John Stanley, *The Creature Features Movie Guide,* p. 1)

Analysis: This will put you to sleep if you watch from a reclining position. Sloppiness is evident: Despite playing Pete and Freddie, late in the film Bud calls Lou "Lou" and "Costello." Bud says, "Let's get outta here!" three times and Lou once. Semu's minions are fine fellows at fadeout. The audience forgot they killed Dr. Zoomer with a blowgun. Why exactly was everyone disguising himself as Klaris? Peggy King sings "You Came a Long Way from St. Louis."

Notes of Interest: For those who felt that Karloff's appearance as the mummy Imho-tep was altogether too brief, the Kharis films were either a welcome offering or an embarrassment of riches. Although not specifically intended as sequels to Im-ho-tep's outing, the Kharis series owes much to the Karloff vehicle by way of both a nearly identical storyline and extensive use of stock footage, both from that film and from James Whale's *Green Hell* (1940). Veteran of countless B westerns of the '30s and '40s, Tom Tyler was surprisingly effective as the unhappy Kharis, the Egyptian prince whose blasphemous yearnings for the Princess Ananka precipitated his downfall. After *The Mummy's Hand,* the role of Kharis was played by Lon Chaney, Jr., for the remainder of the series. With Karloff pursuing more character roles and Lugosi clearly out of the running for such a part, Chaney, whom Universal was promoting as their current "king of horror" (for some reason), got the role more or less by default. In any event, swathed as he was under a mile of wrappings and Jack Pierce's superior makeup, Chaney was virtually unrecognizable, and certainly indistinguishable from stuntman Eddie Parker, who substituted for Chaney in most of the action footage. The Kharis films abound in Universal contract players (as did virtually all of that studio's genre efforts during the 1940s): Dick Foran, Wallace Ford, George Zucco (who appeared in three of the four films), etc.

One of the more unusual aspects of the Kharis series is the trick it plays with the space-time continuum. *The Mummy's Hand* is set, presumably, in contemporary Egypt, circa 1940. Its sequels, *The Mummy's Tomb* and *The Mummy's Ghost,* take place some thirty years and more afterwards, which would logically place the action in the 1970s. And yet the setting is still obviously the 1940s! The last film, *The Mummy's Curse,* takes place (we are told) some twenty-five years after the events of *The Mummy's Ghost,* which would set the calendar in the late 1990s! And, still, things look quite unchanged from the 1940s. Not only that, but Kharis and the reincarnated Ananka sank into a swamp in Massachusetts at the end of *Ghost*, only to emerge somehow from a swamp in the Louisiana bayou in *Curse!*

Universal's Kharis series never garnered much critical acclaim, although it did well enough at the box office to generate four rather mediocre films, barely long enough to qualify as "features". Kharis seemed to borrow in equal measure qualities of two other Universal monsters of the time: the great strength and shambling gait of the Frankenstein monster, and the penchant for operating under moonlight from the Wolf Man, Lon Chaney's other major horror character for the studio. Operating costs were obviously a consideration, too, in removing the setting from the exotic Egyptian locales (albeit still backlots) to fictitious, mundane Mapleton as well as bayou country. It would be difficult, too, to find any series of any genre that borrowed so heavily from previous films in terms of stock footage; the first Kharis opus borrows much from Karloff's film, and subsequent entries borrow from those two. This makes viewing any two in tandem a decidedly wearisome affair. Adding to the tedium is the fact that the stories themselves are repetitious in the extreme. Each of the three sequels to *The Mummy's Hand* tells virtually the same story of some ill-advised acolyte of Antara journeying to America to procure the lost remains of Kharis and Ananka. One time around would have been plenty.

Seen today, the Kharis films have more of an arthritic camp charm than any genuine chills. The Mummy, seen lurching under pale moonlight with its one groping hand outstretched, might generate a shock or two in one film. It's a stretch indeed to think that this awkward menace could produce enough terror to populate four feature films.

Nevertheless, when killed off at last by Abbott and Costello (whose appearance on the scene always represented the true death knell for a Universal horror figure), the mummy was resurrected yet again for three films by Hammer, who based their first mummy screenplay on John Balderston's 1932 work for Universal. By this time a mummy outing was the most predictable of all horror films: An expedition, usually

around 1920, finds an Egyptian tomb, opens it and learns of a curse. The mummy, revived, begins to kill off desecraters. Although the second two films in the Hammer series used to be lambasted — when mentioned at all — lately there seems to have been some turnabout. *The Curse of the Mummy's Tomb* and *The Mummy's Shroud* are getting some recognition as acceptable programmers. See Richard Klemensen's "Hammer Films Unearth the Mummy" in *A Tribute to Hammer Films* (Baltimore: *Midnight Marquee*, Summer 1994), pp. 74–87.

The Mummy
(Hammer, 1959; 88 min.) ***

Produced by Michael Carreras. Directed by Terence Fisher. Screenplay, Jimmy Sangster. Based on John L. Balderston's 1932 screenplay based on the story by Nina Wilcox Putnam and Richard Schayer. Edited by James Needs and Alfred Cox. Director of Photography, Jack Asher. Technicolor. Music, Frank Reizenstein. Art Direction, Bernard Robinson. Special Effects, Bill Warrington, Les Bowie.

Cast: John Banning (Peter Cushing), Kharis (Christopher Lee), Isobel Banning/Ananka (Yvonne Furneaux), Inspector Mulrooney (Eddie Byrne), Mehemet (George Pastell), Stephen Banning (Felix Aylmer), Joseph Whemple (Raymond Huntley), Coroner (Jon Stuart), Poacher (Michael Ripper), Pat (Harold Goodwin), Mike (Dennis Shaw).

Synopsis: Egypt, 1895: The badge of the Karnak gods is found at a British dig. For twenty years Stephen Banning and Joseph Whemple have been searching for the tomb of Ananka. Stephen's son John has broken his leg and can't enter the tomb. "I don't understand," says Stephen when the Egyptian Mehemet warns, "He who robs the graves of Egypt dies." Stephen and Joseph enter the tomb, which is intact. Leaving later, Joseph returns when he hears a scream. Stephen has collapsed. There's an aura of menace about the tomb, says John. The party uses explosives to cover the tomb entrance when they are finished. Mehemet prays to Karnak and promises to reenter the tomb to locate the instrument of his revenge. England, 1898: In a home for the mentally disturbed, Stephen tells

The mummy Kharis (Christopher Lee) brushes off John Banning (Peter Cushing) to attack Joseph Whemple (Raymond Huntley) in *The Mummy* (Hammer, 1959).

his son he brought forth a mummy when he read the Scroll of Life. "Someone has found the scroll, the mummy is released again." A crate of "relics" bound for a house near the nursing home falls off a wagon into a bog. The police dredge, but they don't think the crate can be recovered. Mehemet says its contents were "Egyptian relics, nothing more." At night, Mehemet calls on Karnak and reads from the scroll. A mummy emerges from the bog. Mehemet tells it to destroy those who desecrated the tomb. It breaks into Stephen's padded cell and strangles him. The authorities believe a homicidal maniac was responsible. Whemple mentions that Egyptian fellow to John, who recalls 2,000 B.C. and the Princess Ananka. She died on a journey, and the priest Kharis made her tomb there rather than in the coastal plain where she'd ruled. But Kharis entered the tomb and attempted to revive his beloved princess. Discovered in his blasphemy, he had his tongue cut out, then was swathed in bandages and buried alive in the tomb as Ananka's guardian. Back in the present, Mehemet sends Kharis to kill Whemple, which he does despite being shot by John. Attacked in turn, John is saved by his wife, who to Kharis looks like Ananka. Kharis leaves. John visits Mehemet and they discuss archaeology, which Mehemet finds loathsome when graves are "robbed." He sends Kharis out again. John runs Kharis through with a poker to no avail. Again, Isobel saves him, and when Mehemet urges Kharis to kill her, the mummy revolts, breaks Mehemet's back and carries Isobel into the swamp. Isobel awakens and tells Kharis to put her down. When she moves to the side, the locals fire away. In deeper water, the mummy sinks as it holds the Scroll of Life aloft.

Review: "Should have been better.... just lumbers." (Howard Thompson, *New York Times*, December 17, 1959, p. 51)

Analysis: It may be hard now to remember how pleased kids were to anticipate and then see this in '59. Like dinosaurs, mummies were inherently fascinating. This is a remake of all Universal mummy films as it includes the standard tomb desecration theme and resurrected princess from the 1932 version as well as the mummy's "mentor" from the follow-ups. Best scenes: the mummy breaking into Stephen's cell, the gun blasts that merely rend its wrappings, and Cushing's athleticism in battling his adversary. Released in the U.S. by Universal.

The Curse of the Mummy's Tomb
(Hammer/Columbia, 1964; 81 min.)
**

Produced and directed by Michael Carreras. Screenplay, Henry Younger. Edited by Eric Boyd Perkins. Supervising Editor, James Needs. Director of Photography, Otto Heller. Techniscope. Technicolor. Music,

Carlo Martelli. Musical Supervision, Philip Martell. Makeup Artist, Roy Ashton. Introducing Jeanne Roland.

Cast: John Bray (Ronald Howard), Annette Dubois (Jeanne Roland), Adam Beauchamp (Terence Morgan), Alexander King (Fred Clark), Sir Giles Dalrymple (Jack Gwillim), Hashmi Bey (George Pastell), Professor Dubois (Bernard Rebel), mummy (Dickie Owens). With Harold Goodwin, Michael Ripper.

Synopsis: Egypt in the year 1900: Professor Dubois, archaeologist, is killed by desert nomads, leaving the expedition under the command of John Bray, Sir Giles, and Dubois's daughter Annette. They've discovered a mummy's tomb. They receive the expedition's backer, the American Alexander King, with some dismay when he proposes to feature the discoveries in roadshow arrangements across the United States. On the ship to England Adam Beauchamp introduces himself and invites John and Annette to stay at his lodgings. Beauchamp knows something himself about ancient Egypt: the story of Ra, the nomad chief killed by assassins. King exhibits the mummy. Beauchamp notices Annette's medallion, which he says is 2,000 years older than the tomb. The mummy disappears. King is killed by it as he walks the streets. John goes to Hashmi. Sir Giles is killed. Beauchamp speaks to the mummy. Hashmi asks to be killed for spoiling the tomb. Adam is the other son of Rameses the eighth. Now he can die and intends to spend eternity with Annette — but the mummy refuses to kill her. Instead the mummy kills Adam, then brings down the sewer roof on himself. Annette is rescued.

Review: "One of Michael Carreras' best-directed pictures.... played in the slightly overripe style it deserves, and the production values are modest but colorful.... Any movie which features the ubiquitous Michael Ripper as an Arab is not to be missed." (Bruce Hallenbeck, "Hallenbeck's Guilty Pleasures," p. 15)

Analysis: George Pastell makes a return appearance as an Egyptian. He'd been killed in *The Mummy* when he'd played Mehemet. Evidence of cheapness: no squibs when Sir Giles shoots at mummy. Reminiscent of original *Mummy*, with Im-ho-tep wanting to kill the modern girl who will

The mummy Prem (Eddie Powell) attacks Sir Basil Walden (Andre Morell) as Haiti (Catherine Lacy) looks on in *The Mummy's Shroud* (Hammer–Seven Arts/Warner Bros., 1967).

then spend eternity with him. The Beauchamp character is a Dorian Gray, but more could have been made of it, perhaps. A disintegration? That's up in the next entry.

The Mummy's Shroud
(Hammer-Seven Arts/Warner Bros., 1967; 90 min.) *½

Produced by Anthony Nelson Keys. Directed by John Gilling. Screenplay, John Gilling. From an original story by John Elder. Edited by Chris Barnes. Supervising Editor, James Needs. Director of Photography, Arthur Grant. Color, DeLuxe. Music, Don Banks. Musical Supervision, Philip Martell. Sound Editor, Roy Hyde. Production Supervisor, Bernard Robinson. Makeup, George Partleton. Special Effects, Bowie Films Ltd.

Cast: Sir Basil Walden (Andre Morell),

David Buck (Paul Preston), Claire (Maggie Kimberley), Stanley Preston (John Phillips), Barbara Preston (Elizabeth Sellars), Haiti (Catherine Lacey), Longbarrow (Michael Ripper), Prem, the Mummy (Eddie Powell), Prem (Dickie Owen), Inspector Barrani (Richard Warner), Hasmid Ali (Roger Delgado), Pharaoh (Bruno Barnabe), Pharaoh's wife (Toni Gilpin), Curator (Andreas Malandrinos), Kahto-Bey (Toolsie Persaud), Harry Newton (Tim Barrett).

Synopsis: 2,000 B.C.: A son is born to Pharaoh, but his younger brother foments revolt and Pharaoh is killed, his son escaping into the desert with slave bodyguard Prem. The boy dies after giving Prem the royal seal. In 1920 an expedition locates the makeshift tomb. Sir Basil is bitten by a snake but seems to recover. Stanley Preston arrives and tries to take credit for everything. The actual tomb is opened. Claire, a language expert, becomes distraught and refuses to translate the inscription near the body of the prince buried in the sand. Back in the city, Basil is consigned to an asylum by Preston, who wants the glory of the discovery for himself. Preston's son Paul accuses his father of sending Basil to the asylum. Basil escapes. Hasmid, whose family has protected the tomb for centuries, revives Prem, the mummy, who crushes Basil's head. Claire wants to examine Harry's photos of the shroud. Harry is killed by the mummy. Then, before he can book passage to England, Preston meets his doom, as does his assistant, Longbarrow. Finally David and Claire cause Prem to disintegrate by reciting words on the shawl.

Review: "Totally uninspired Hammer mummy flick, following every 'walking dead' cliché established since Karloff played Im-Ho-Tep in 1932." (John Stanley, *The Creature Features Movie Guide*, p. 176)

Analysis: It's lousy but the disintegration is good: the bandages fall, revealing first the skull and ribcage and finally naught but dust. This was the last Hammer film made at Bray Studios. Distributed by Twentieth Century–Fox.

Notes of Interest: Hammer released one more mummy film, *Blood from the Mummy's Tomb*, in 1970. However, that film sprang from a different source; it was based

on Bram Stoker's novel *The Jewel of the Seven Stars*, which was later filmed as *The Awakening* by EMI/Orion/Warner Bros. (1980). Thus we consider *Blood from the Mummy's Tomb* not only an independent entry (unrelated to the other mummy films) but a progenitor feature as well. It is listed as a main entry in the alphabetical sequence.

The Mummy puts in a cameo appearance in *The Monster Squad* (Tri-Star/Taft Entertainment Pictures, 1988; 81 min.) See that film's listing under *Frankenstein* for cast, credits, and discussion.

The Mummy's Curse *see under* **The Mummy**

The Mummy's Ghost *see under* **The Mummy**

The Mummy's Hand *see under* **The Mummy**

The Mummy's Shroud *see under* **The Mummy**

The Mummy's Tomb *see under* **The Mummy**

The Muppet Christmas Carol *see under* **Scrooge**

Mysterious Island *see under* **20,000 Leagues Under the Sea**

The New Batch *see* Gremlins II: The New Batch *under* **Gremlins**

A New Beginning *see* Friday the 13th: A New Beginning *under* **Friday the 13th**

A New Generation *see* Amityville: A New Generation *under* **The Amityville Horror**

The New Order *see* Scanners II: The New Order *under* **Scanners**

Night of the Living Dead
(Walter Reade/Continental, 1968; 98 min.) ****

Produced by Russell W. Streiner and Karl

Left to right: Barbra (Judith O'Dea), Ben (Duane Jones), and Tom (Keith Wayne) face the horror of the *Night of the Living Dead* (Walter Reade/Continental, 1968).

Hardman. Directed by George A. Romero. Screenplay, John A. Russo and George A. Romero. Sound, Gary Streiner. Director of Photography, George A. Romero, The Latent Image. Makeup, Hardman Associates. Special Effects, Regis Survinski and Tony Pantanello.

Cast: Ben (Duane Jones), Barbra (Judith O'Dea), Johnny (Russell Streiner), Harry (Karl Hardman), Tom (Keith Wayne), Judy (Judith Ridley), Helen (Marilyn Eastman), Karen (Kyra Schon), Judy (Judith Ridley). With Charles Craig, Bill Heinzman, Mark Ricci, George Kosana, R. J. Ricci, Bill "Chilly Billy" Cardille, Frank Doak, Jack Givens, Samuel R. Solito, A. C. McDonald.

Synopsis: After placing a marker on their father's grave in a rural cemetery outside Pittsburgh, Johnny and Barbra are attacked by a pasty-faced elderly man. Barbra flees to an isolated farmhouse. Locking herself in, she is joined at dusk by Ben, who carries a tire iron and tells her how he encountered scores of the "things." He says fire deters them and begins boarding up doors and windows. Barbra irrationally cries that they must go out and find Johnny,

to which Ben replies, "This is no Sunday school picnic!" After she slaps him, he knocks her unconscious. The radio reports that there is an outbreak of mass homicide by "assassins" all over the eastern U.S., murderers who devour the flesh of their victims. Ben and Barbra are surprised when two men appear from the basement where they've been hiding with a child and two women. Finding a television, Ben locates an emergency station that suggests a returning Venus Explorer satellite spewing forth great amounts of radiation *may* be responsible for bringing back to life the recently deceased. Police and posses are shown shooting ghoulombies in the brain — just about the only way to stop their depredations. Ben hatches a plan to get gas and escape in the pick-up, but the truck catches fire and explodes, killing Judy and Tom. Ben makes it back to the house and shoots Harry, who refused to let him in. The zombies make a concerted effort and break in, dragging off Barbra. In the basement, Ben must re-kill Harry and his wife Helen, who'd been turned to a zombie by daughter Karen. The night passes and Ben hears shots and sirens. Thinking he's saved, he leaves the cellar, peers through the window and is mistakenly shot as a zombie. The posse prepares to drag him to the bonfire.

Reviews: "Putrid, with indistinct, amateurish photography, bad acting and needlessly gruesome bloodletting." (*Castle of Frankenstein* 16, July 1970, p. 60) ¶"Casts serious aspersions on the integrity and social responsibility of its Pittsburgh-based makers, distrib Walter Reade, the film industry as a whole and exhibs who book the pic." (*Variety*, October 16, 1968, pp. 6, 26)

Analysis: Except for *White Zombie* (1932) and Val Lewton's *I Walked with a Zombie* (1943), zombie movies were dull until George Romero's vision hit paydirt. Initial reviews, whether fanzine or mainstream, were not prescient for what became a watershed horror film. Camera angles, the play of light and shadow give a sense of nightmare. What can be made of the freeze frame images at the end, when the zombie hunters are seen with hooks to impale and drag to the bonfire the black man they took for a ghoul? Made on a shoestring in the Pittsburgh area, this groundbreaking film built a cult following and led to the increasingly plotless but just as gross splatter films of the seventies and eighties. Drive-ins were playing it two years later, and it became a favorite midnight film. It's for strong stomachs, needless to say. For fans thus equipped, it's something of a masterpiece. It was a shame to see the resourceful Ben killed, but if he hadn't been, the finale would not have provided as much food for thought. *Mutant* may be a hidden remake/sequel. *Raiders of the Living Dead* has zombies.

Dawn of the Dead
(United Film Distributors/Laurel Group, 1979; 125 min.) ****

Produced by Richard P. Rubinstein. Written, edited and directed by George A. Romero. Director of Photography, Michael Gornick. Technicolor. Music, The Goblins with Dario Argento. Makeup and Cosmetic Special Effects, Tom Savini. Costumes, Josie Caruso. Hairstyles, Hairtique. Wardrobe,

Michelle Martin. Still Photography, Katherine Kolbert. Weapons Coordinator, Clayton Hill. Stuntmen, Tom Savini, Taso Stavrakis.

Cast: Peter (Ken Foree), Francine (Gaylen Ross), Stephen (David Emge), Roger (Scott H. Reiniger), Dr. Foster (David Crawford), Mr. Berman (David Early), Scientist (Richard France), TV commentator (Howard Smith), Pasquale Buba (Tom Savini), Tony Buba (Marty Schiff), Lead zombies (Sharon Ceccatti, Pam Chatfield, Mike Christopher, Clayton Hill, Jay Stover)

Synopsis: Philadelphia. Police and national guard troops seek and destroy hosts of the risen dead while TV and radio stations inform the living of safe havens. TV station employee Francine, her helicopter pilot boyfriend Stephen, and policemen Peter and Roger decide to use the copter to escape the carnage. Proceeding west, they land on the roof of an abandoned shopping mall. Blocking the entrances with tractor trailers, they kill the zombies inside. Roger becomes infected from a zombie bite and must be killed permanently by Peter. Just in case they have to leave, the pregnant Francine learns how to fly the chopper. When all seems well a motorcycle gang descends on the mall but is turned back by Peter and Stephen, who use zombies and their own arsenal to deny the gang permanent residence. Stephen, however, is bitten and becomes an undead. He leads zombies to the hideout of Peter and Francine. Francine revs up the chopper. Dispelling his gloom, Peter battles his way to Francine and they fly north.

Reviews: "Violence becomes increasingly less shocking — and less scary — as the tongue in Romero's cheek becomes progressively pronounced." (David Ansen, *Newsweek*, May 7, 1979, p. 90) ¶"Romero's script is banal when not incoherent.... Michael Gornick's photography warrants a special nod." (*Variety*)

Analysis: The 11-year gap between this sequel and 1968's *Night of the Living Dead* was worth it. *Dawn of the Dead* is a bloody, funny, and exciting film, and one of the few cinematic instances where the characters, afeared for their lives, do logical things to preserve themselves. Even the motorcycle hoodlums, whom one would expect to capture the pregnant

Left to right: Roger (Scott H. Reiniger), Francine (Gaylen Ross), Stephen (David Emge), and Peter (Ken Foree) are armed and ready to fight the zombies in *Dawn of the Dead* (United Film Distributors, 1979).

Francine, do not. Francine makes her presence known, demanding a say in the proceedings and instruction in operating a chopper. Most surprising scene: a zombie crumples to the ground as the very top of its head is sliced off. By what? The still revolving helicopter blade. The Monroeville Mall was the location, and served as the site for the Night of the Living Dead 25th Anniversary Reunion & Horror Exposition on August 27–29, 1992.

Notes of Interest: A Tom Savini–made severed arm from this film could be had for a mere $600.00 in 1992.

Day of the Dead
(United Film Distribution Company, 1985; 102 min.) **

Produced by Richard P. Rubinstein. Laurel Production. Directed by George Romero. Screenplay, George A. Romero. Director of Photography, Michael Gornick. Edited by Pasquale Buba. Music, John Harrison. Art Direction, Bruce Miller. Set Decoration, Jan Pascale. Costumes, Barbara Anderson. Special Makeup, Tom Savini. Special Effects, Steve Kirshoff, Mark Mann.

Cast: Sarah (Lori Cardille), John (Terry Alexander), Captain Rhodes (Joseph Pilato), McDermott (Jarlath Conroy), Miguel (Antone DiLeo), Steel (G. Howard Klar), Dr. Logan (Richard Liberty), "Bub" (Howard Sherman). With Ralph Marrero, John Amplas, Phillip G. Kellams, Taso N. Stavrakis, Gregory Nicotero, William Cameron, Don Brockett, Deborah Carter, Winnie Flynn, Debra Gordon, Jeff Hogan, Barbara Holmes, David Kindlon, Bruce Kirkpatrick, William Andrew Laczko, Susan Martinelli, Barbara Russell, Kim Maxwell, Gene A. Saraceni, John Schwartz, Mark Tierno, Michael Trcic, John Vulich.

Synopsis: From a 14-mile-long underground government storage cavern in Florida, a group of military men and a civilian helicopter pilot try to locate other living humans while a small scientific team tries to understand the zombie plague that has overtaken the country. Dr. Logan attempts to teach captured zombies how to behave civilly, while Sarah tries to figure out how they became flesh-eating fiends. John, the pilot, theorizes that the Creator is teaching humankind a lesson. Logan has some success teaching a zombie he calls "Bub," but Captain Rhodes kills Logan after he learns that the doctor has been rewarding his subject with the flesh of dead soldiers. Rhodes determines to leave the compound and attempts to intimidate John into flying him and the remaining soldiers to safety. John escapes, then tracks Sarah and his radioman in the zombie-infested tunnel to which they were consigned. Meanwhile, Miguel, his arm severed by Sarah after he was bitten by a zombie, takes the elevator topside, opens the gate and lets in a host of the undead. They pursue the soldiers through the caverns. Rhodes is shot by "Bub" but before dying has the misfortune to be torn apart by a roomful of zombies. Sarah, John and the radioman escape to an island.

Review: "Sheer gruesomeness overwhelms [Romero's] ideas and even his dynamic visuals." (Kevin Thomas, *Los Angeles Times Calendar*, October 4, 1985, p. 4) ¶"An unsatisfying part three.... Acting here is unimpressive." (*Variety*, July 3, 1985, p. 16)

Analysis: This is a "confined spaces" movie that doesn't work because most of the characters are incredibly irritating. The military characters are too loud, too vulgar and uncouth, and hardly disciplined. "Submoronic" best describes them. There's too much talk. All of the characters state that they can't waste ammunition, yet half the time they are blazing away fruitlessly at midsections or using more than the one necessary head shot. The music is inappropriate. As for the effects, sure, they're revoltingly well done.

The Return of the Living Dead
(Orion/Hemdale, 1985; 91 min.)
***½

Produced by Tom Fox. Directed by Dan O'Bannon. Screenplay, Dan O'Bannon. Story, Rudy Ricci, John Russo, Russell Streiner. Edited by Robert Gordon. Director of Photography, Jules Brenner. CFI Color and DeLuxe Prints. Music, Matt Clifford. Art Direction,

Robert Howland. Set Decoration, Robert Lucas. Special Visual Effects, Fantasy & Film Effects.

Cast: Burt (Clu Gulager), Frank (James Karen), Freddy (Thom Mathews), Tina (Beverly Randolph), Chuck (John Philbin), Casey (Jewel Shepard), Scuz (Brian Peck), Trash (Linnea Quigley), Suicide (Mark Venturini), Spider (Miguel Nunez), Colonel Glove (Jonathan Terry), Mrs. Glover (Cathleen Cordell), Paramedics (Drew Deighan, James Dalesandro), Radio corps (John Durbin, David Bond), Riot cops (John Stuart West, Michael Crabtree, Ed Krieger), Dispatcher (Leigh Drake). With Derrick Brice, Terrence M. Houlihan, Robert Benett, Allan Trautman, Jerome Daniels Coleman, Cherry Davis.

Synopsis: On July 3, 1984, at UNEEDA Medical Supply in Louisville, Kentucky, Frank shows Freddy the facility, including canisters in the basement that contain "zombies" the army mistakenly shipped there after an outbreak back in Pittsburgh in 1969. Frank thumps a canister, which begins leaking the 245 Trioxin gas. Both men are rendered unconscious. Trioxin enters the air vents and brings to life a cadaver. Recovering, Frank phones boss Burt. Recalling that the Pittsburgh zombies could be killed only by destroying their brains, they pickax this one. However, it continues to writhe. The three men take the body across the street to the Resurrection Funeral Home, whose owner allows them to incinerate it in return for a future favor. Meanwhile, the friends of Freddy who've killed time in the nearby cemetery are set upon by corpses rising from the grave. The Trioxin fumes from the burnt cadaver have escaped the chimney and the rain washed them into the ground. Soon Burt and his people realize that there is a zombie outbreak. Paramedics called to assist Frank and Freddy (who've been poisoned by the Trioxin) are attacked. Police arrive but are also overpowered. Frank and Freddy become zombies, but Frank incinerates himself before he can hurt anyone. Freddy's girlfriend Tina and the undertaker take refuge in the attic while Burt and one of Freddy's friends commandeer a police car. They can't get far and take refuge back at UNEEDA with more of Freddy's friends. The only phone they can get to is in the basement, as is the

Burt (Clu Gulager) wields an axe against the encroaching zombies in *Return of the Living Dead* (Orion/Hemdale, 1985).

first zombie to escape from the canister. Burt whacks off its head with a baseball bat, phones the number on the side of the canister and is transferred to Colonel Glover in San Diego. He's been trying to find the canisters for years. Back at UN-EEDA, Burt hears something strange. POW! An atomic cannon has sent its charge into Louisville, destroying a 20-square block area.

Reviews: "The carnage becomes a setup for the gags.... The writing makes it." (Michael Wilmington, *Los Angeles Times Calendar*, August 16, 1985, p. 14) ¶"Rather threadbare production." (*Variety*, June 19, 1985, p. 25)

Analysis: Just slightly tongue-in-cheek and scary as all get out, this film features zombies who evince fast thinking *and* locomotion in a police car convoy ambush. *Variety* called the first 30 minutes "terrifically funny," and there is a neat, black comedic ending, making it definitely worth seeing. Linnea Quigley, a B-video favorite, bares considerable skin. A frightening thought: The female zombie, her lower limbs severed, her head and torso

confined, explains that the dead need to eat the brains of the living to reduce their pain. Although Dan O'Bannon, not George Romero, directed, there are strong tie-ins with *Night of the Living Dead*, in particular the mention of the 1969 Pittsburgh zombie outbreak. Of course, it was the whole eastern third of the nation that was affected, and all of the folks in this movie should have remembered *that*.

Return of the Living Dead Part II
(Lorimar/Greenfox, 1988; 89 min.)
**

Produced by Tom Fox. Directed by Ken Wiederhorn. Screenplay, Ken Wiederhorn. Edited by Charles Bornstein. Director of Photography, Robert Elswit. Metrocolor. Music, J. Peter Robinson. Ultra-Stereo. Art Direction, Dale Allan Pelton. Special Makeup, Kenny Myers Stunts, Gary Davis. Visual Consultant, Raymond G. Storey.

Cast: Jesse Wilson (Michael Kenworthy), Billy (Thor Van Lingen), Ed (James Karen), Brenda (Suzanne Snyder), Joey (Thom Matthews), Lucy Wilson (Marsha Dietlein), Aerobics instructor (Suzan Stadner), Colonel

(Jonathon Terry), Tarman (Allan Traut-man), Billy's mother (Sally Smythe), Billy's father (Don Maxwell), Tom Essex (Dana Ashbrook), Soldier (Reynold Cindrich), Frank (Terrence Riggins), Officer (James McIntire), Les (Arturo Bonilla), Zombies (Forrest Ackerman, Douglas Benson, David Eby, Nicholas Hernandez, Derek Loughran, Annie Marshall, Richard Moore, Steve Neuvenheim, Brian Peck).

Synopsis: An army convoy passing through a small community late on a stormy evening encounters some rough road. In the back of one of the trucks, a sealed cylinder breaks free and tumbles into the road, rolling down a hill and into a watery culvert. The next day young Jessie Wilson is chased by schoolmates Billy and Johnny into the culvert. After locking Jessie in an adjacent cemetery's crypt, Billy and Johnny return to the culvert and open the canister. A noxious gas jets forth, sending the boys coughing and reeling. Moments later a bug-eyed zombie crawls from the cylinder even as the gas coils out across the creek and to the cemetery. That evening Jessie sneaks back to the culvert and is attacked by the zombie, who wants to eat his brain. The boy escapes to home, but his sister and cable company man Tom Essex have no idea his wild story has any basis in truth. In the cemetery, corpses come alive and chase prospective graverobbers Ed and Joey. The foiled robbers end up at the Wilson home, where they are beset by a host of zombies. Ed and Joey break into the Wilsons' in their attempt to escape. Once inside, the zombies are momentarily mesmerized by one of Lucy Wilson's exercise videos. The Wilsons, Ed and Joey, Essex and Joey's girlfriend Brenda flee to the home of a local doctor and take his convertible toward town. The town is deserted, even the police station and the hospital. Both Ed and Joey look bad, having whiffed the noxious gas. When Lucy, Tom, Jessie and Doc try to escape town, they are forced back by the military and realize the authorities thinks everyone in town is a zombie. Hitting on a plan, they drive to the electric power plant, luring a parade of zombies with brains they'd taken from the mortuary. One of the zombies is Billy, who attacks Jessie but is dispatched when Doc

tosses him onto a transformer. Throwing a switch, Jessie and Doc fry the zombies standing in puddles about the power plant.

Reviews: "It's not scary. It's not funny. It's got some of the cheesiest zombie makeup seen in a long time." (Judith P. Harris, *Cinefantastique*, May 1988, pp. 53–54) ¶"Intentionally hilarious." (Kevin Thomas, *Los Angeles Times Calendar*, January 16, 1988, p. 5) ¶"Even the essential gross-out effects are fumbled." (Kim Newman, *Monthly Film Bulletin*, March 1989, p. 85)

Analysis: Obviously the intention here was to capture the over-the-top kind of comedy-terror that *Return of the Living Dead* also only partly accomplished. *Part II* likewise fails to pull the thing off, despite some effective sequences. Performances are perfunctory, as is the production as a whole. If anything could have put living dead movies in a well-deserved grave, it would have been films such as this one. However, both a remake of the original and another sequel followed.

Night of the Living Dead
(Columbia/Twenty-First Century Film Corporation, 1990; 96 min.) ***

Produced by John A. Russo and Russ Streiner. Executive Producers, Menahem Golan and George A. Romero. Directed by Tom Savini. Screenplay, George A. Romero. Based on the original screenplay by John A. Russo and George A. Romero. Edited by Tom Dubensky. Director of Photography, Frank Prinzi. Color, TVC. Music, Paul McCollough. Ultra-Stereo. Special Makeup Effects, John Vulich, Everett Burrell. Costumes, Barbara Anderson. Designer, Cletus R. Anderson.

Cast: Ben (Tony Todd), Barbara (Patricia Tallman), Harry (Tom Towles), Helen (McKee Anderson), Sarah (Heather Mazur), Tom (William Butler), Judy Rose (Katie Finneran), Johnnie (Bill Mosley), Hondo (David Butler), Bulldog (Zachary Mott), The Mourner (Pat Reese), Newsman (William Cameron), Uncle Rege (Pat Logan), Flaming Zombie (Berle Ellis), TV interviewer (Bill "Chilly Billy" Cardille). With Greg Funk, Tim Carrier, John Hamilton, Dyrk Ashton, Jordan Berlant, Albert Shellhammer, Jay McDowell, Walter Berry, Kendal Kraft, David Grace, Stacie Foster, Charles Crawley.

Synopsis: Barbara and her brother are visiting the mother's grave in a rural area when they are attacked by strange people. The brother is knocked unconscious and possibly killed. Without car keys, Barbara can only coast backwards away from two tormentors. Wrecking the car, she flees to a farmhouse, discovering another strange man bent on attacking her. She kills him with a poker to the head. Ben pulls up in a truck running out of gas and tries to explain what little he knows. They discover five other normal people in the basement. They board up the windows. Eventually they think they've found the keys to the gas pump, but the keys are the wrong ones. A shotgun blast to the lock only ignites the gas and the car and pump explode. Only Ben, of the three who set out, makes it back to the house, where Harry is battling Barbara for possession of the rifle. Harry wounds Ben and hides in the attic when his daughter dies and becomes a zombie. Ben secretes himself in the basement, and Barbara runs for help. She finds some good old boys shooting zombies. Returning to the farmhouse, she finds that Ben has become a zombie. The men shoot him. Harry appears and Barbara kills him, pretending he's a zombie. She watches as a bonfire is built of the recently resurrected.

Review: "The impact of the new *Night* is allegorical rather than visceral, its blood and guts patently phony no matter how skillfully designed.... A well-sustained entertainment." (Kevin Thomas, *Sunday News Journal* [Wilmington, DE], October 21, 1990, p. H4)

Analysis: Basically a recap of the original, it moves rather fast and it has hardly any impact. The *Sunday News Journal* review claimed this version had "more character development," but there is also more pretension this time out, e.g., when Barbara says the zombies and real humans are one and the same while she watches the latter taunting and killing the former. This makes it less a horror film than a plea for tolerance. "Hidden" pleas this blatant always harm a film.

Return of the Living Dead III
(Trimark, 1993; 97 min.) **½

Produced by Brian Yuzna and Gary Schmoeller. Directed by Brian Yuzna. Screenplay, John Penney. Edited by Christopher Roth. Director of Photography, Gerry Lively. Color, Foto-Kem. Music, Barry Goldberg. Special Effects Makeup, Steve Johnson.

Cast: Julie Walker (Mindy Clarke), Curtis Reynolds (J. Trevor Edmond), Colonel John Reynolds (Kent McCord), Riverman (Basil Wallace), Lt. Colonel Sinclair (Sarah Douglas), Colonel Peck (James T. Callahan), Chief Scientist (Jill Andre), Mindy (Abigail Lenz). With Mike Moroff, Sal Lopez, Fabio Urena, Pia Reyes, Dana Lee.

Synopsis: Julie and Curtis Reynolds sneak into a laboratory and observe Curt's father, Colonel Reynolds, overseeing revolting experiments which appear to bring the dead back to life. The goal is creation of bioweapons: zombies resuscitated by the chemical Trioxin and controlled by paralysis bullets and meat batteries. When an experiment goes awry, Colonel Reynolds is reassigned. Curt refuses to go and, with Julie, speeds away on his motorcycle. Julie is killed when she's thrown from the cycle. Curt takes her back to the lab and revives her with Trioxin. But she's cold and incredibly hungry. Normal food fails to satisfy her, and she begins eating the corpse of a grocery store owner. She attempts to destroy herself by falling from a bridge. It doesn't work, and she and Curtis take refuge in the sewers with a derelict calling himself Riverman. The perpetrators of the grocery burglary are in pursuit because Julie had bitten one of them and caused increasing agony. Julie savages them and they become the living dead. She even attacks Riverman. Colonel Reynolds arrives and uses the paralysis gun to subdue the zombies and rescue Curt. Later Curt finds Julie imprisoned in the lab, Specimen 32. He releases her. Other zombies escape, including deformed ones who've been in Trioxin containers for years. Curt is bitten. Knowing his fate, he takes Julie to the incinerator, where both are consumed.

Review: "A very different approach ... results in a serious thriller ... but it doesn't know when to quit." (Leonard Maltin, ed., *Movie and Video Guide 1995 Edition*, New York: Signet, 1994, p. 1076)

Analysis: All the living dead films put the viewer on edge because one knows any scratch inflicted by a zombie results in death and zombieism for the injured. This one adds a grim, no-win romance. Evidently makeup and special zombie effects used up the budget because the cast is rather small and there are few sets — and no hat for Kent McCord. Continuity with its predecessors lies in references to 1969 and the canisters of Trioxin. We get an explanation for why the zombies crave brains: electricity from neurons. This seems to have gone direct to video.

The Nightcomers *see under* **The Innocents**

A Nightmare on Elm Street
(New Line Cinema, 1984; 91 min.)
***

Produced by Robert Shaye. Directed by Wes Craven. Screenplay, Wes Craven. Edited by Rick Shaine. Director of Photography, Jacques Haitkin. Color, DeLuxe. Music, Charles Bernstein. Set Decoration, Anne Huntley. Special Effects, Jim Doyle. Special Makeup Effects, David Miller.

Cast: Freddy Krueger (Robert Englund), Lt. Thompson (John Saxon), Marge (Ronee Blakley), Nancy (Heather Langenkamp), Tina (Amanda Wyss), Rod (Nick Corri), Glen (Johnny Depp), Sergeant Parker (Joseph Whipp), Dr. King (Charles Fleischer), Teacher (Lin Shaye).

Synopsis: Tina is mysteriously, horrifyingly murdered, and her boyfriend is thought guilty. Friend Nancy, who's had disturbing dreams about a character named Fred Krueger, realizes something's wrong. She takes pills to stay awake because in her dreams she is accosted by the murderous Krueger, who's fashioned a claw hand to savage people. *He* obviously killed Tina. Nancy learns from her mother that Fred Krueger was a child molester and murderer who got off on a technicality. Her mother and other townsfolk banded together and set fire to Krueger's house. Now his "ghost" infects the teenagers' dreams. Nancy hatches a plan to bring Krueger back into the real world, where she hopes her policeman father will be able to destroy him. Falling asleep on purpose, she finds Krueger in his boiler room and makes him

chase her into the waking world. The traps she set beforehand slow but do not stop him. Nancy sets Krueger on fire. When Nancy's father does arrive, he sees footprints burned into the carpet leading to his wife's bedroom. Breaking in, he and Nancy see a disgusting, incinerated figure on the bed. When her dad leaves, Nancy is confronted by Krueger. But now she knows what to do: Deny him. She turns her back, and he disappears trying to throttle her. Next morning Nancy gets in the car with the friends she thought were dead and waves to her mom on the front step. The car seems to have a mind of its own, locks them in and drives off. As she recedes from her home, Nancy watches her mother pulled from the porch through the door's small window.

Reviews: "Well crafted when some flat performances don't get in the way, and it's refreshing to see a young woman win a few in a horror picture for a change." (David Sterritt, *Christian Science Monitor*, November 28, 1984, p. 34) ¶"A superior example of an over-worked genre, thanks to Craven's skill at organizing individual shock scenes and getting neat performances out of his mostly young cast." (Kim Newman, *Monthly Film Bulletin*, September 1985, p. 283) ¶"Last-minute cop-out.... Certainly it's most refreshing to see a chiller in which the strongest character, by far, is female." (Francis Wheen, *New Statesman*, September 6, 1985, p. 33)

Analysis: Subdued compared to later entries, it is nevertheless better. Langenkamp makes an intelligent, feisty heroine. Freddy Krueger is unique. But is he compelling? The metal clawed glove the child molester made and uses in nightmares is a vestige of the human, technological world, which to some of us compromises this character's monstrousness. Quibbling over looks aside, this film gave rise to a very consistent series whose developments follow "logically" from the original premise. In that respect it is manifestly superior to the "Jason" (*Friday the 13th*) and "Michael Myers" (*Halloween*) series. Effects are state-of-the-art.

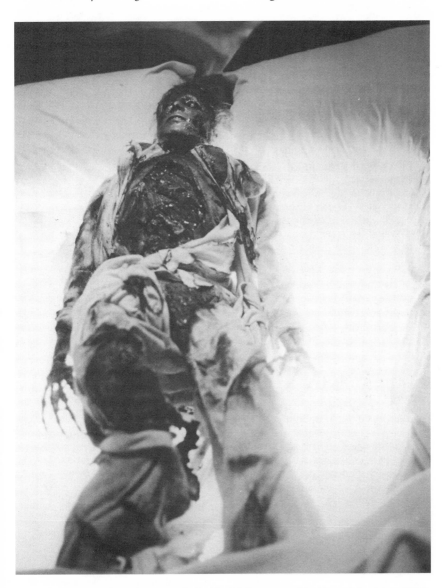

A disgusting figure has taken over the bed in *Nightmare on Elm Street* (New Line, 1984).

A Nightmare on Elm Street
Part 2: Freddy's Revenge
(New Line Cinema, 1985; 85 min.)
***

Produced by Robert Shaye. Directed by Jack Sholder. Screenplay, David Chaskin. Edited by Bob Brady. Director of Photography, Jacques Haitkin. Color, DeLuxe. Prints, Technicolor. Music, Christopher Young. Set Decoration, Pamela Warner. Freddy Krueger's Makeup, Kevin Yagher. Special Effects, A & A Special Effects/Dick Albain. Transformation Effects, Mark Shostrom.

Cast: Freddy Krueger (Robert Englund), Jesse Walsh (Mark Patton), Lisa (Kim Myers), Ron Grady (Robert Rusler), Mr. Walsh (Clu Gulager), Cheryl Walsh (Hope Lange), Coach

Schneider (Marshall Bell), Mrs. Webber (Melinda O. Fee), Mr. Webber (Thom McFadden), Kerry (Sydney Walsh), Policeman (Steve Eastin), Teacher (Hart Sprager), Angela (Christie Clark).

Synopsis: A Springwood High School bus drives into a desert and the earth caves in, leaving it precariously balanced on a spire. It's a dream by new kid in town Jesse Walsh. He learns from classmate Ron Grady that the house he's residing in, 1428 Elm, has a history. A mother went crazy there, and her daughter watched her boyfriend get butchered across the street. Jesse observes a strange man at the basement furnace. The ugly man tells Jesse he needs him. Was *this* a dream? Lisa finds Nancy Thompson's diary in Jesse's closet. There are references to a murderous individual named Fred. That night Fred asks Jesse to kill for him. Coach Schneider is first, stripped and scourged in the boys shower. When the police find Jesse wandering the streets naked, his father thinks he's on drugs. Lisa and Jesse explore the old power plant where Fred Krueger worked — and killed twenty kids. Jesse begins taking Sta-Up pills but falls asleep at Ron's, and Freddy emerges from his body and kills Ron. Jesse returns to Lisa's pool party. Lisa examines the diary again and reads that living people give Freddy the energy to return. She urges Jesse to fight Freddy, but he becomes the monster and chases her. From within Freddy, Jesse asks her to kill him. She stabs him, but Freddy laughs and jumps through the glass door, raiding the poolside revelers and starting fires before disappearing through a wall. Lisa drives to the power plant and is attacked by Freddy but again hears Jesse's voice. Fires start, and Freddy burns up on a catwalk. Jesse emerges and Lisa embraces him. Everything is hunky dory on the clear day when Jesse sits next to Lisa on the school bus. But the bus speeds into the desert again.

Review: "As stomach-turning as might be expected, but … has a lot going for it…." (Janet Maslin, *New York Times*, November 1, 1985, p. C10)

Analysis: Among this film's good points, the *New York Times* review cites the special effects — good and judiciously employed — as well as the lead performance and even

the chattiness of the villain. Excellent is the emergence of Freddy from Jesse. Why won't Jesse confide in his sympathetic mother? Do the pool party guests see Freddy or Jesse? Freddy, we guess, since Jesse wasn't jailed. Or he could have been jailed, because the ending we see might be another dream. The funniest line comes after a scream from upstairs. Sis, at the breakfast table, asks, "Mommy, why can't Jesse wake up like everybody else?"

A Nightmare on Elm Street 3: Dream Warriors
(New Line Cinema, 1987; 97 min.)
***

Produced by Robert Shaye. Executive Producers, Wes Craven, Stephen Diener. Line Producer, Rachel Talalay. Directed by Chuck Russell. Screenplay, Wes Craven, Bruce Wagner, Chuck Russell, Frank Darabont. Story, Wes Craven and Bruce Wagner. Edited by Terry Stokes. Director of Photography, Roy Wagner. Color. Music, Angelo Badalamenti. Song, Dokken. Art Direction, Mick Strawn, C. J. Strawn. Set Decoration, James R. Barrows. Freddy Krueger Makeup, Kevin Yagher. Makeup Effects, Peter Chesney. Special Visual Effects, Dream Quest Images.

Cast: Nancy Thompson (Heather Langenkamp), Freddy Krueger (Robert Englund), Kristen Parker (Patricia Arquette), Dr. Neil Goldman (Craig Wasson), Lt. Thompson (John Saxon), Max (Larry Fishburne), Dr. Elizabeth Simms (Priscilla Pointer), Elaine Parker (Brooke Bundy), Joey (Rodney Eastman), Phillip (Bradley Gregg), Will (Ira Heiden), Kincaid (Ken Sagoes), Jennifer (Penelope Sudrow), Lorenzo (Clayton Landey), Taryn (Jennifer Rubin), Sister Mary Helena (Nan Martin), Marcie (Stacey Alden), Little girl (Kristin Clayton), Nurse #1 (Sally Piper), Nurse #2 (Rozlyn Sorrell). With Dick Cavett, Zsa Zsa Gabor.

Synopsis: Kristen Parker dreams of trying to rescue a little girl from a basement. Upon waking, she is slashed in the bathroom while a strange man watches from the mirror. Kristen is only the latest teenager thought to be suicidal. Now an intern, Nancy Thompson gives solace to Kristen and consults with Dr. Goldman. Later Nancy dreams of being in a nightmare with Kristen and next day questions Kristen about the model house that looks like Nancy's old home on Elm Street. Nancy tell Kristen the man in her dream is real. After the deaths of Phillip and Jennifer and a recommendation from Sister Mary Helena that the unquiet spirit must be laid to rest, Dr. Goldman allows Nancy to conduct a group therapy session. She tells the teens how six years earlier Freddy killed her friends. These teens are the last offspring of the Elm Street adults who torched Freddy. Nancy says Kristen is the key to destroying the monster. Goldman finds the nun, who explains how in the 1940s Amanda Krueger was accidentally locked in an asylum and raped by the inmates. She bore "the bastard son of a hundred maniacs"—Freddy Krueger—who must be buried in hallowed ground. In the hospital, as Nancy sits by the comatose Joey, "Come And Get Him Bitch" is carved in his chest. Nancy and Goldman locate Nancy's father, who takes Goldman to the Penny Bros. Auto Salvage. In the middle of the car graveyard they find the Cadillac whose trunk contains Krueger's skeleton. Meanwhile, Nancy, Kristen, Kincaid and Taryn enter the dream world to find Joey. They encounter Freddy, who emerges into the real world when his bones are disturbed. His skeleton kills Nancy's father and knocks Goldman into the grave before returning to the dream world. Although mortally wounded, Nancy manages to twist Freddy's lethal fingers into himself. Topside, Goldman comes to and sprinkles holy water on Krueger's bones. Holes appear in Freddy and he disappears. At Nancy's funeral, Goldman finds the 1968 grave of Mary Helena Craven. The nun was Freddy's ravaged mother. That night while Goldman sleeps, a light comes on in Kristen's model house.

Reviews: "Freddy Krueger is the most talkative of slashers, and also the most creative.... The film's dream sequences are ingenious." (Janet Maslin, *New York Times*, February 27, 1987, p. C15) ¶"Cannily conceived follow-up ... which unfortunately tips the balance heavily towards the special effects department, leaving the human side of the equation deficient." (Lor., *Variety*, February 25, 1987)

Analysis: This is a solid entry with imaginative strokes like the Krueger-designed wheelchair and the hypodermic needle fingers. Continuity is maintained and more of Freddy's past revealed.

A Nightmare on Elm Street 4: The Dream Master
(New Line Cinema, 1988; 93 min.)***

Produced by Robert Shaye and Rachel Talalay. Directed by Renny Harlin. Screenplay, Brian Helgeland and Scott Pierce. Story, William Kotzwinkle and Brian Helgeland. Edited by Michael N. Knue and Chuck Weiss. Director of Photography, Steven Fierberg. Metrocolor. Music, Craig Safan. Dolby Stereo. Art Direction, Thomas A. O'Conor. Set Decoration, James R. Barrows. Makeup Effects, Steve Johnson, Magical Media Industries Inc., Screaming Mad George, R. Christopher Biggs. Freddy Krueger Makeup, Kevin Yagher. Mechanical Effects, Image Engineering. Special Visual Effects, Dream Quest Images.

Cast: Alice (Lisa Wilcox), Freddy Krueger (Robert Englund), Joey (Rodney Eastman), Kristen (Tuesday Knight), Dan Jordan (Danny Hassel), Rick (Andras Jones), Sheila (Toy Newkirk), Kincaid (Ken Sagoes), Debbie (Brooke Theiss), Elaine (Brooke Bundy), Paramedic (Jeff Levine), Jonson (Nicholas Mele), Pin Up Girl (Hope Marie Carlton). With Jake the Dog.

Synopsis: Kristen calls Kincaid and Joey into her dream, where they argue that Freddy Krueger is history. But Kincaid dreams of an auto salvage yard where his dog unearths Freddy's bones, which reattach themselves and grow flesh. Kincaid crushes his nemesis beneath a wrecked car to no avail, and Freddy stabs him. Joey is next, drowned in his waterbed. Alice tells Kristen nightmares can be controlled by thinking about something good: Remember, as the dream master, you're in control. Alice's brother Rick explains to Dan the Freddy Krueger legend: If he kills you in a dream, you're dead in real life. Kristen's mother slips her a sleeping pill. Dreaming of the boiler room and confronting Freddy, Kristen is tossed into the furnace, but not before warning Alice. When Sheila is killed, Alice realizes she has become Freddy's conduit to the real world.

Robert Englund is Freddy Krueger in *A Nightmare on Elm Street 4: The Dream Master* (New Line, 1958).

Alice knows that Kristen was the last of the kids of the parents who killed Freddy. He needs a new way to get to new kids. After Rick is killed, Alice finds herself changing. She knows how to use Rick's numchuks. In the Rialto movie theater she finds herself sucked into the picture, and in a restaurant Freddy says, "Bring me more," while dining on miniature human heads in a pizza. Waking, Alice and Dan try to warn Debbie but find themselves repeating the scene over and over. Meanwhile, Debbie is turned into a giant roach, then squished. Dan is injured in a car wreck. Taking pills, Alice prepares for a martial arts contest. Alice confronts the demon, who says, "I am eternal," but is perturbed when he sees evil in the piece of stained glass Alice shines in his face. "Let them out, Krueger!" demands Alice, and the souls of the victims he contains erupt from his torso and rend his head and body. "Rest in Hell," says Alice. Walking in the park, Alice tells Dan she has been able to sleep two to three hours at a time. But she sees what appears to be Freddy's reflection in the fountain.

Reviews: "Better than #2 but not as good as #3.... The nightmare/reality switch is done so often that the audience is no longer taken by surprise. Still, this delivers the nightmare imagery and Krueger mayhem that its audience expects." (Dennis K. Fisher, *Cinefantastique*, January 1989, p. 118) ¶"Streamlined approach here emphasizes the elaborate physical, visual and makeup effects ... plus the black humor of monster Freddy Krueger's funny 1-liners." (Lor., *Variety*, August 17, 1988)

Analysis: New *York Times* reviewer Caryn James complained (August 19, 1988, p. C8) that *Elm Street* and its sequels were failing to take advantage of "the most intelligent premise" in genre moviemaking. Nevertheless, this installment has its moments. The resuscitation of Freddy is among the best of its kind. His crushing beneath a wrecked car just afterward is lovely. *Variety* liked the "spectacular climax." Lisa Wilcox is an engaging heroine. Kristen was played by Patricia Arquette in the previous entry. Finnish director Renny Harlin would go on to direct the swashbuckling critical flop *Cutthroat Island*.

A Nightmare on Elm Street: The Dream Child
(New Line Cinema, 1989; 90 min.)
***

Produced by Robert Shaye, Rupert Harvey. Directed by Stephen Hopkins. Screenplay, Leslie Bohem. Story by John Skip, Craig Spector, Leslie Bohem. Based on characters created by Wes Craven. Edited by Chuck Weiss, Brent Schoenfeld. Director of Photography, Peter Levy. Metrocolor. Music, Jay Ferguson. Dolby Stereo. Art Direction, Timothy Gray. Set Decoration, John Jockinsen. Freddy Krueger Makeup/Baby Freddy Creator, David Miller. Visual Effects, Alan Munro.

Cast: Alice (Lisa Wilcox), Freddy Krueger (Robert Englund), Dan Jordan (Danny Hassel), Jacob (Whitby Hertford), Yvonne (Kelly Jo Minter), Greta (Erika Anderson), Mark (Joe Seely), Alice's father (Nick Mele), Amanda Krueger (Beatrice Boepple), Dan's father (Burr DeBenning), Dan's mother (Valorie Armstrong), Racine Gibson (Pat Surges), Mark's father (Clarence Felder), Delivery doctor (E. R. Davies), Jock (Matt Borlenghi), Truck driver (Bill Dunna), Anne (Beth Depatie), Coach Ostrow (Don Maxwell), Guest (Cameron Perry), Girl in locker (Stacey Elliott), Thirty something (Marc Siegler), Orderly #1 (Andre Ellington), Dr. Moore (Steven Grives), Alice body doubles (Cherie Romans, Crisstyn Dante).

Synopsis: During the Springwood High School graduation, Alice tells Dan she had a dream in which she felt out of control. That night she follows a nun and witnesses Amanda Krueger's breech delivery of a hideous offspring. Alice follows the "baby" into the church where Freddy Krueger was presumably destroyed. "No, not again," Alice cries, but Freddy's reborn. Amanda appears and says she must destroy him and tells Alice they must meet, but the door closes on her as Freddy says, "We'll see, bitch." He causes Dan's death in a motorcycle accident. Alice finds she's pregnant and in the hospital meets a mysterious young boy named Jacob. Alice explains to three friends how she brings Freddy victims. But she wasn't asleep when Dan was killed, they inform her. Freddy must have found another way. Freddy kills Greta. As Mark falls asleep, Alice observes his figure in his drawing of Freddy's house. She quickly draws a female stick figure, labels it "Alice," and enters Mark's dream. She almost rescues Mark, but he falls through the floor, and she meets Jacob, who she realizes is her child. She finds Mark and asks herself the rhetorical question, "Do babies dream?" Using ultrasound to examine her fetus, Alice sees Freddy. There is no body in Amanda Krueger's grave. Perhaps that is because she apparently killed herself. Alice must find where she died and release her soul. While searching, Alice rescues Yvonne and closes a door on Freddy. Alice realizes he's afraid to enter because of Amanda's spirit. Mark reads the *Nightmare from Hell* comic and is sucked in, becoming his own comic creation, the Phantom Prowler. He guns Freddy down, but "Super Freddy" arises and shreds the paper Mark. Alice awakes and tells Yvonne to go to the old asylum to find Amanda. While she's there, Alice dreams of tracking Freddy. She impales Freddy on his lethal wheelchair, and he's pushed into the basement of the asylum. The lunatics dismember him, but he reappears with Jacob. Jacob tells Alice that Freddy hides out inside her. When Freddy appears, Jacob pretends to be his pal until Krueger is attacked by his recent victims. The Krueger babe and Alice's baby appear. Amanda pulls the Krueger baby into herself and "fights" with the evil spirit. Later, Alice walks in the park with her baby.

Review: "A genre film that won't totally insult your intelligence or your eyes." (Caryn James, *New York Times*, August 11, 1989, p. C10)

Analysis: Has anyone analyzed these as tales of friendship? The *New York Times* review said this one emphasized motherhood. The reviewer also found "hints" of some deeper "psychological intrigue," but nothing beyond the hints. Almost as if this was real, Lisa Wilcox looks harder and older in this 1989 outing than in the 1988 film. Sometimes she looks like a different person. Did she really need a body double? Perhaps she's modest. There are a number of pungent lines, e.g., Freddy's admonition to Dan not to dream and drive. Good stuff: Mark's Phantom Prowler impersonation and subsequent shredding by Freddy. Another tack that could have been taken: Mark could have finished the comic book's blank frames to end the story they way he wanted it.

Freddy's Dead: The Final Nightmare

(New Line Cinema, 1991; 96 min.)

**½

Produced by Robert Shaye and Aron Warner. Directed by Rachel Talalay. Screenplay, Michael DeLuca. Story, Rachel Talalay. Based on characters created by Wes Craven. Edited by Janice Hampton. Director of Photography, Declan Quinn. Color. Music, Brian May. Dolby Stereo. Freddy Krueger's Makeup Design, David B. Miller. Special Makeup Effects, Magical Media Industries Inc. 3-D Supervision and Special Visual Effects, The Chandler Group. Special Visual Effects, Dream Quest Images.

Cast: Freddy Krueger (Robert Englund), Maggie Burroughs (Lisa Zane), Doc (Yaphet Kotto), John (Shon Greenblatt), Tracy (Lezlie Deane), Carlos (Ricky Dean Logan), Spencer (Breckin Meyer), Childless couple (Tom Arnold, Roseanne Arnold), Orphanage woman (Elinor Donahue), Little Maggie (Cassandra Rachel Friel), Teen on TV (Oprah Noodlemantra), Kelly (David Dunard), Maggie's mother (Marilyn Rockafellow), Woman on plane (Virginia Peters), Carlos's mother (Angelina Estrada), Tracy's father (Peter Spellos), Teen Freddy (Tobe Sexton), Young Freddy (Chason Schirmer), Spencer's father (Michael McNab), Public Service Announcer (Johnny Depp), Freddy's father (Alice Cooper).

Synopsis: Ten years pass, and no teenagers or children remain alive in Springwood except John, who's fleeing town in a plane. He falls through the fuselage and ends up confronting Freddy Krueger on a bus. Then he wakes up by the side of the road. Found by police, the amnesiac "John Doe" is taken to a recovery center where Maggie Burroughs works with troubled adolescents. Maggie has dreams similar to John's. Doc recommends dream therapy. An old newspaper headline reminds Maggie of something and she drives her charges — John, Spencer, Tracy, and Carlos — to Springwood, visits a fair and a school where she hears that Freddy Krueger had a child. At Freddy's house, Carlos is killed. Spencer is next. Maggie and Tracy find Freddy's adoptive mother, then in a dream Maggie learns that she is Freddy's child, Katharine. Doc dreams that the Dream People gave Freddy his "job" and concocts a plan to pull him into the waking world. Maggie enters the dream world, observes Freddy's tormented youth, and drags him into the real world. There he is destroyed with various knives and a small pipe bomb. Freddy's past as a serial killer and the aid rendered him by dream demons is recounted.

Review: "Disappointingly ho-hum, without the spectacular — and often very funny — special effects that have become the hallmark of this series…. The joke is on the filmmakers: By taking the finality out of death, they've already robbed the horror genre of its giddy sting." (*Entertainment Weekly*, September 27, 1991, p. 46.)

¶"Here we are asked to believe that a monster who has survived myriad deaths and been resurrected countless times could be disposed of with sticks of dynamite. This laziness is equally evident in the visually poor 3-D sequence…." (Philip Kemp, *Sight and Sound*, February 1992, p. 45)

Analysis: We'd like to give this an unqualified three-star rating, but we can't. The series is in decline.

Wes Craven's New Nightmare
(New Line Cinema, 1994; 112 min.)
**

Produced by Marianne Maddalena. Directed by Wes Craven. Screenplay, Wes Craven. Edited by Patrick Lussier. Director of Photography, Mark Irwin. Color, Foto-Kem/Fototronics. Music, J. Peter Robinson. Visual Effects, Flash Film Works. Mechanical Effects created by Lou Carlucci. Special Makeup Effects, Kurtzman, Nicotero and Berger EFX Group. Freddy Krueger Makeup, David Miller Creations.

Cast: Robert Englund/Freddy Krueger (Robert Englund), Heather Langenkamp (Herself), Dylan (Miko Hughes), Chuck (Matt Winston), Terry (Rob LaBelle), Chase Porter (David Newsom), Wes Craven (Himself), Julie (Tracy Middendorf), Dr. Heffner (Fran Bennett), John Saxon (Himself), Marianne Maddalena (Herself), Sara Risher (Herself), Robert Shaye (Himself), Patrice Englund (Tamara Mark).

Synopsis: Following her appearances in two *Nightmare on Elm Street* movies, Heather Langenkamp has had the routine existence of the journeyman actress, appearing in the occasional film and television show. A series of peculiar incidents accompany the announcement of a new Freddy Krueger film: Special effects technicians are injured in weird accidents, and Heather receives frightening telephone calls. Then, a grisly traffic accident kills husband Chase, leaving her a widow with a five-year-old son. As plans proceed with the development of the new Freddy Krueger vehicle, Heather experiences terrifying visions that involve the razor-fingered demon. These visions invade both her dreaming and waking moments. Worse still, her son Dylan begins to sleepwalk and enter trance-like states while awake. During these episodes, he chants the kind of sing-song nursery rhyme references similar to ones used by the school kids in the early *Elm Street* films. Heather seeks advice from her friends. Most, like former co-star John Saxon, consider these occurrences nothing more than unfortunate coincidences. Desperately, she visits writer-director Wes Craven and tells him of her recent woes. He is well into writing the latest installment of the series and has determined that Krueger is much more than he'd originally

speculated. Freddy is actually the manifestation of a much more ancient and powerful entity. This being lives for the slaughter of innocents. As powerful as it is, it can sometimes be "captured" by storytellers who incorporate it in their tales, as Craven himself has done. The *Nightmare* series has "kept the genie in the bottle," so to speak; now that the series is finished, Freddy is free to make the transition into the real world. Craven believes his only recourse is to finish the screenplay and produce another film, killing off Freddy definitively. Heather reluctantly agrees to resurrect her role as "Nancy" to help defeat the demon. Meanwhile, Dylan's condition worsens, and Heather and babysitter Julie rush him to a clinic, where Dr. Heffner cautiously diagnoses his behavior as the early stages of schizophrenia. Heffner insists on keeping Dylan overnight in the clinic and, worse, sedating him to give him the sleep she feels he desperately needs. As Dylan fights futilely to stay awake, Krueger appears and kills Julie. In the chaos, Dylan flees for home. His mother frantically pursues him. On his bed she tumbles through a dimensional rift into a Dante-esque world of nightmare, a burning charnel ruin where Freddy rules supreme. The demon chases both, literally trying to consume young Dylan, until confined in a blazing trap. As Freddy is consumed in the fires of his own hell, Heather and Dylan are propelled back into the real world of Dylan's bedroom.

Review: "An ingenious, cathartic exercise in illusion and fear." (Janet Maslin, *New York Times*, October 14, 1994, p. C8)

Analysis: Despite the bold initiative of taking the charter members of *Nightmare on Elm Street* out of their fictional context and into the "real" world, this film quickly finds itself trudging down the tried-and-true slasher ruts. Placing a host of real characters in the story is a novelty that quickly wears thin. Rather than fleshing out the characters or pursuing the story in any innovative way, *Wes Craven's New Nightmare* merely puts them all through the same tired paces once again, with another series of grisly killings, more time wasted by the terrified as they try to convince the disbelieving authorities, and there's another hysterical, predictable pursuit through a dimly lit hell. Making Freddy Krueger a centuries-old demon is hardly a startling revelation, and the particular hell whence he originates is clearly less phantasmagoric than in previous outings. Still, diehard *Elm Street* fans probably won't be terribly disappointed. There is enough creepy atmosphere and credible performances to make *Wes Craven's New Nightmare* watchable. This is a slickly produced series wrap-up that is disappointing only in its redundancy. We can only hope that Freddy is dead for good this time.

1984
(Associated British–Pathé, 1955; 91 min.) ***

Produced by N. Peter Rathvon. Directed by Michael Anderson. Screenplay, William P. Templeton and Ralph Gilbert Bettinson. Based on the novel by George Orwell. Edited by Bill Lewthwaite. Director of Photography, C. Pennington-Richards. Music, Malcolm Arnold. Art Direction, Terence Verity.

Cast: Winston Smith (Edmond O'Brien), Julia (Jan Sterling),O'Connor (Michael Redgrave),Mr. Charrington (David Kossoff), Jones (Mervyn Johns), Parsons (Donald Pleasence), Selina Parsons (Carol Wolveridge), Announcer (Ernest Clark), Rutherford (Ronan O'Casey), Prisoner (Kenneth Griffith). With Michael Ripper, Ewen Solon, Patrick Allen.

Synopsis: Big Brother rules London in Oceania, one of three world powers. Big Brother observes all. Love is outlawed, but Winston Smith, who works in the Ministry of Truth, receives a note from another worker, Julia, which says she loves him. They rendezvous in the slums with the help of a junk man, not knowing he is one of the Thought Police. Nor are they aware that O'Connor, the man who gets them to join an underground party against Big Brother, is a high level Inner Party official. A hidden camera observes their lovemaking. Confronted with their "crimes," Winston is tortured and breaks when confronted with rats, his worst fear. He condemns Julia. Later they meet and she admits she also betrayed him. Now soulless tools of the state, they part. At a rally, Winston

adds his "Long live Big Brother!" to the massed chant.

Reviews: "Stark, sober and thoughtful, if not altogether persuasive...." (A.H. Weiler, *New York Times*, October 1, 1956, p. 31) ¶"Grim, depressing picture.... little entertainment value...." (Myro., *Variety*, March 14, 1956)

Analysis: At one time this had a good reputation. The *New York Times* found O'Brien sympathetic, Jan Sterling competent, and Michael Redgrave "fine." Most every reviewer who writes it up now has major complaints. Apparently the original English ending has the lovers gunned down.

Nineteen Eighty-Four
(Atlantic, 1985; 117 min.) ***

Produced by Simon Perry. Directed by Michael Radford. Assistant Director, Chris Rose. Screenplay, Michael Radford. Based on the novel by George Orwell. Edited by Tom Priestley. Director of Photography, Roger Deakins. Eastmancolor. Music, Dominic Muldowney and the Eurythmics. Sound, Bruce White. Art Direction, Martin Herbert, Grant Hicks. Costumes, Emma Porteous.

Cast: Winston Smith (John Hurt), O'Brien (Richard Burton), Julia (Suzanna Hamilton), Charrington (Cyril Cusack), Parsons (Gregor Fisher), Syme (James Walker), Tillotson (Andrew Wilde), Tillotson's friend (David Trevena), Martin (David Cann), Jones (Anthony Benson), Rutherford (Peter Frye), Waiter (Roger Lloyd Pack), Winston as a boy (Rubert Baderman), Winston's mother (Corinna Seddon), Winston's sister (Martha Parsey), Mrs. Parsons (Merelina Kendall), Susan Parsons (Lynne Radford), William Parsons (P. J. Nicholas), Inner Party speaker (Pip Donaghy), Whore (Shirley Stelfox), Instructress (Janey Key), Aaronson (Joscik Barbarossa), ARTSEM lecturer (Hugh Walters), Telescreen announcer (Phyllis Logan), Washerwoman (Pam Gems), Goldstein (John Boswall), Big Brother (Bob Flag).

Synopsis: While working for the monolothic, ever-watchful INGSOC during the war between Oceania and Eurasia, Winston Smith keeps a hidden diary in which he writes that the Proletariat would not have to conspire if they were conscious of their own strength. On occasion Smith enters the Prols' territory to buy a razor blade or a bauble, and, after he meets Julia, to rent a bedroom for their rendezvous. Their affair must be kept secret because it is the goal of INGSOC and ARTSEM to wipe out orgasms and create a new race of beings. On the way to work one day, Smith is approached by O'Brien, who tells him to stop by and pick up the latest edition of the *Dictionary of Newspeak*. Between its pages Smith finds Emmanuel Goldstein's subversive book, which he reads in bed to Julia. Their idyll is interrupted when a picture falls from the wall and a Big Brother screen appears. Charrington, who rented them the room, turns out to be one of the Thought Police. O'Brien tortures Smith and tells his captive that *he* co-authored the Goldstein book. Triumph and self-abasement are the goals of society, says O'Brien. When Smith is about to be tortured by his lifelong fear — rats — he breaks and tells O'Brien to use them on Julia. At a cafe where Smith plays chess against himself, Julia enters and says she informed on him. He admits condemning her for sex and thought crimes. When she leaves, the telescreen announces a victory over Eurasian forces in Africa.

Review: "Poetic intensity…. Burton … is splendid." (Japa., *Variety*, October 10, 1984)

Analysis: It's as grim as grim can be and as such, suitable for only special tastes. Cyril Cusack had prepped for this in *Fahrenheit 451* (1966), when he supervised the burning of books. This was Richard Burton's last film and it's dedicated to him, "with love and admiration."

Notes of Interest: George Orwell's grim, futuristic satire was published in 1949. While it is a socialist's attack on Stalinism and fascism, it is also Orwell's assault on Britain, which underwent rationing after World War II. The changing allegiances are based on fact: the Western democracies' rapprochement with Russia during World War II and the about-face immediately afterward.

Not of This Earth
(Allied Artists, 1956; 67 min.) ***
Produced and directed by Roger Corman.

Screenplay, Charles B. Griffith and Mark Hanna. Edited by Charles Gross. Director of Photography, John Mescall. Music by Ronald Stein. Sound, Paul Mitchell. Special Effects by Paul Blaisdell.

Cast: Mr. Johnson (Paul Birch), Nadine Storey (Beverly Garland), Officer Harry Sherbourne (Morgan Jones), Dr. Frederick W. Rochelle (William Roerick), Jeremy Perrin (Jonathan Haze), Joe Piper (Dick Miller), Joanna Oxford (Tamar Cooper), Woman from Davanna (Ann Carrol), Sergeant Walton (Roy Engel), Teenagers (Gail Ganley, Ralph Reed), Oriental specimen (Harold Fong), Officer Simmons (Pat Flynn).

Synopsis: The mysterious Mr. Johnson, who habitually wears sunglasses, hires nurse Nadine Storey to help him with the blood transfusions he requires. Johnson uses mental telepathy to keep Dr. Rochelle from revealing the startling fact that Johnson's blood is drying up. Johnson is an alien from the planet Davanna who has come to Earth to see if human blood can be used by the warring Davannans. Johnson periodically kills people by blasting them with his eyes and sends their blood to his home planet via a matter-transmitter. A female Davannan who arrives to inform Johnson that the wars go badly dies when Johnson accidentally injects her with rabid dog blood. Dr. Rochelle speaks of the dead woman to Nadine and Johnson finds out. He chases and hypnotizes Nadine, intending to transport her to Davanna. Nadine's boyfriend, the motorcycle cop Harry Sherbourne, interrupts and pursues Johnson. The wailing of the police siren causes the sound-sensitive alien to drive off a cliff. After Johnson's burial, which Harry and Nadine attend, a second man dressed like Johnson walks up.

Review: "Handy entry for exploitation playdates … rather gory…." (Brog., *Variety*, March 27, 1957)

Analysis: Is this a cult movie? Probably. Beverly Garland, whom the *Variety* review called "attractive and competent," is a genre cult star, and Paul Birch frequently appeared in '50s science fiction films, e.g., *Day the World Ended*. This is the role of his career, and he makes the most of it. *Variety* also credited the photography and score for keeping up the pace of the film. As Bill Warren points out in *Keep Watching the*

Skies! the characters in this film are transmitting matter through space a year before Delambre in *The Fly*.

Not of This Earth
(Concorde, 1988; 80 min.) **

Produced by Jim Wynorski and Murray Miller. Directed by Jim Wynorski. Screenplay, R. J. Robertson and Jim Wynorski. Based on a screenplay by Charles B. Griffith and Mark Hanna. Director of Photography, Zoran Hochstatter. Foto-Kem color. Art Direction, Hayden Yates. Special Effects, Jim Stewart, Linda Obalil. Stunts, Patrick Statham.

Cast: Nadine Story (Traci Lords), Alien/ Mr. Jonson (Arthur Roberts), Dr. Frederick Rochelle (Ace Mask), Harry (Roger Lodge), Jeremy (Lenny Juliano), Davanna woman (Rebecca Perle), Vacuum cleaner salesman (Michael Delano), Stripper (Becky LeBeau), Bag lady (Monique Gabrielle), Hookers (Roxanne Kernohan, Ava Cadell, Cynthia Thompson), Nurse Osford (Kelli Maroney). With Belina Grant, Ed Morgan, John Branagan, John Dresden, Shawn Klugman, Paul Shaver.

Synopsis: A mysterious Mr. Jonson appears at the office of Dr. Frederick Rochelle, demanding a blood transfusion. Telepathic commands from the enigmatic dark-suited stranger, his eyes hidden by sunglasses, override Rochelle's inclination to ask for a blood test beforehand. Upon leaving, Jonson procures the help of nurse Nadine Story. Nadine moves into Jonson's impressive residence to administer the daily transfusions Jonson requires. Nadine finds that Jonson has curious habits (such as never being seen eating), and takes an instant dislike to his chauffeur, the leering and wisecracking Jeremy. Nadine's boyfriend, police officer Harry Sherbourne, is acquainted with Jeremy through a string of two-bit larcenies the young man has served time for. Jonson *is* a strange man, and not unconnected with the bizarre deaths occurring in the community. In fact, Jonson is an extraterrestrial from the planet Davanna. This planet is undergoing political turmoil and warfare to such an extent that the blood of native Davannans has become weakened and diseased. The blood of earthlings is rich and invigorating. Jonson's nocturnal depredations allow him to send samples of blood back to Davanna via teleporter. Jonson's second mission is to teleport a human for "vivisectional research." Ultimately, if appropriate, the earth is to be conquered. The alien's victims, among others, include a teenage couple he finds necking at a nearby lover's lane, a door-to-door vacuum cleaner salesman, a trio of streetwalkers, and a nearsighted strip-o-gram girl. When a female Davannan teleports into his living room, weak for want of blood, Jonson inadvertently gives her the blood of a rabies victim, a transfusion which results in the woman running on a murderous rage through the streets. Eventually, Nadine tumbles to Jonson's unusual doings and alerts her boyfriend. When Jonson discovers Nadine's knowledge, he attempts to overcome her and teleport her to Davanna. Harry intercedes, and during a high-speed chase through the countryside, the alien loses control of his car and is killed. Harry and Nadine pay their last respects at Mr. Jonson's gravesite. They fail to notice, as they leave, the approach of a stranger dressed in black, wearing dark glasses.

Review: "What's wrong here is the flick's campy, soulless film-nerd script and direction — ingredients that utterly destroy what fragile charm the original pic possessed." (Phantom of the Movies, *The Phantom's Ultimate Video Guide*, p. 324)

Analysis: This 1988 remake is largely a scene-for-scene replay of the 1956 Roger Corman original, being primarily a vehicle by which teenage porn star Lords makes her "legitimate" screen debut. Ms. Lords gets to strut her stuff in a variety of skimpy outfits (and less) to make it easy enough to see where her assets lie insofar as the adult film industry is concerned. Beyond that, her credentials as a thespian have yet to be established. *Not of This Earth* is too low on suspense, too short on action, and too shy of laughs to be considered more than a passable diversion. Hardly a must-see.

The Nutty Professor *see under* **Dr. Jekyll and Mr. Hyde**

Oh, God!
(Warner Bros., 1977; 97 min.) ***
Produced by Jerry Weintraub. Directed by

Carl Reiner. Assistant Directors, Bob Birnbaum, Victor Hsu, David Nicksay. Screenplay, Larry Gelbart. Based on the novel by
Avery Corman. Edited by Bud Molin. Director of Photography, Victor Kemper. Technicolor. Music, Jack Elliott. Art Direction, Jack
Senter. Set Decoration, Stuart Reiss.

Cast: Jerry Landers (John Denver), God
(George Burns), Bobbie Landers (Teri Garr),
Dr. Harmon (Donald Pleasence), Sam Raven
(Ralph Bellamy), George Summers (William
Daniels), Judge Baker (Barnard Hughes),
Reverend Willie Williams (Paul Sorvino),
Priest (Barry Sullivan), Dinah (Dinah Shore),
Rabbi (Jeff Corey), Briggs (George Furth),
Mr. McCarthy (David Ogden Stiers), Greek
bishop (Titos Vandis), Adam (Moosie Drier),
Becky (Rachel Longaker), Court clerk (Won-
derful Smith).

Synopsis: Jerry Landers, an assistant
manager at Food World in Burbank, California, receives a letter asking him to come
to Room 2700 on the twenty-seventh floor
of 1600 N. Hope Street. He's to have an interview with God. Jerry thinks it's a practical joke until he learns that there is no
twenty-seventh floor and the voice he
heard in the room speaks to him from the
car radio. The voice tells Jerry to act as a
messenger from the almighty and to rein-
force the idea that humankind can work.
Jerry's wife Bobbie is skeptical. Finally God
appears to Jerry as an old man in sneakers,
windbreaker and ball cap. "Why me?" asks
Jerry. "Why not you?" answers God. He
tells Jerry that he gave people a world but
that all the choices are theirs. Jerry is initially brushed off by the religious editor of
the *L.A. Times* but he persists and even gets
on Dinah Shore's TV show. A group of eminent theologians makes him an offer. He
agrees to be sequestered in a hotel room
with a list of 50 questions only God could
answer. God visits Jerry and provides answers, directing Jerry to go to Reverend
Willie Williams and tell him to shut up
and sell shoes. Williams sues Jerry, but
God appears, playing a card trick on the
judge and making himself invisible. In
chambers, Judge Baker dismisses the slan-
der charges against Jerry. Jerry loses his job
but meets God on the street and is com-
plimented on getting the word out. God
says he's going to visit the animals for a
while.

Review: "An uneasy amalgam of incon-
sistent attitudes.... questionable premise."
(Janet Maslin, *New York Times*, October 8,
1977, p. 13)

Analysis: It attempts to answer a host of
great questions, but we certainly aren't
going to cite screenwriter Larry Gelbart or
novelist Corman for ultimate answers, are
we? It's most telling portions are the parody of evangelists and the easily duped. In
the first instance, Paul Sorvino gives a great
performance as Reverend Willie Williams.
In the second, we get a cross-section of
nutty religiosi of all persuasions flocking to
Denver's house, some to give advice, others to touch him or, if possible, mate with
him. Barnard Hughes's line, "Nobody erases
tapes anymore," comes a couple of years
after Richard Nixon got into hot water
over audio tapes. Overall, it's amusing and
cute, and don't we wish George Burns *were*
God?

Oh, God! Book II
(Warner Bros., 1980; 94 min.) ***

Produced and directed by Gilbert Cates.
Screenplay, Josh Greenfeld, Hal Goldman,
Fred S. Fox, Seama Jacobs, Melissa Miller.
Story, Josh Greenfeld. Edited by Peter E.
Berger. Director of Photography, Ralph Wool-
sey. Panavision. Technicolor. Music, Charles
Fox. Set Decoration, Chris Westlund.

Cast: God (George Burns), Paula Richards
(Suzanne Pleshette), Don Richards (David
Birney), Tracy Richards (Louanne), Shingo
(John Louie), Mr. Benson (Conrad Janis),
Dr. Jerome Newell (Anthony Holland), News-
caster (Hugh Downs), Dr. Joyce Brothers
(Herself), Rosa (Alma Beltran), Dr. Barnes
(Hans Conried), Judge Miller (Wilfrid Hyde-
White), Dr. Benjamin Whitley (Howard
Duff), Joan (Denise Galik), Harriet (Marian
Mercer), Miss Hudson (Mari Gorman).

Synopsis: While having lunch with her
father Don, Tracy finds two fortune cookie
notes: "Meet me in the lounge. God," and
"I mean you — Tracy. God." In the lounge
she hears a voice which identifies itself as
God. God explains that she interests him
because of what she said about believing
in things you can't see. God appears to her
on the way home. He says he's still not in
people's thoughts enough. They have to be
reminded he's still around. When Tracy

says he should perform some miracles, he responds that people remember the miracle, not why he did it. They agree that she should come up with a slogan. When God reappears she has several, like "How do you spell relief: G-O-D," "God is bullish on humanity," and "You're in good hands with God." God gives her one more week to come up with a better slogan and says her next-door pal Shingo can help. When Shingo says they have to go home, they'll think God tomorrow, Tracy says they've got it: "Think God." God approves. Tracy tries to get her classmates to promote the phrase, and they put up signs and write it all over town. Tracy tells her mother she sees and speaks with God. Her father suggests to Tracy that maybe she imagines God. When Mr. Benson the principal finds the school covered with "Think God" signs, he calls in the school psychologist and Tracy's parents. Tracy agrees to call off the sign-making — after she gets permission from God. Tracy is suspended, but Shingo and the other students aim to help. Dr. Newell theorizes that Tracy has created a father figure to substitute for the father she only sees on weekends. He conducts a battery of physical and mental tests and finds a real psychosis. He thinks she should be institutionalized for observation. Shingo tells Tracy she can stay with his grandparents. Her father finds out and, warned, Tracy goes to Union Station, but God convinces her that running away is not the answer. He takes her home in a motorcycle sidecar. On TV, Hugh Downs describes the phenomenon started by Tracy. Dr. Joyce Brothers says that Tracy may indeed have met God. A court case begins. The judge wants a panel of top psychiatrists to examine Tracy before he'll make a decision. The panel votes for institutionalization. But God enters as "Dr. Stevens," and during his presentation on behalf of Tracy, he makes the chandelier disappear and turns day into night. Tracy's parents realize Dr. Stevens is God and take Tracy home. Paula and Don reconcile. God visits Tracy one more time and thanks her for the wonderful job she and the other children did.

Review: "An unusually happy sequel.... a very pleasant 94 minutes of Christian

fantasy and family re-unitedness." (Archer Winsten, *New York Post*, October 3, 1980, p. 51)

Analysis: Louanne is very natural. Burns has amusing, sometimes pertinent lines, like "'Bananas.' I hate that expression. I make a beautiful fruit and people use it for 'crazy.'" Why did Suzanne Pleshette wear such unflattering, severe hairdos in this period?

Oh, God! You Devil
(Warner Bros., 1984; 96 min.) ***

Produced by Robert M. Sherman. Directed by Paul Bogart. Screenplay, Andrew Bergman. Edited by Randy Roberts, Andy Zall. Director of Photography, King Baggot. Panavision. Technicolor. Music, David Shire. Set Decoration, Gary Moreno. Special Effects, Ray Klein.

Cast: God/Harry O. Tophet (George Burns), Bobby Shelton (Ted Wass), Wendy Shelton (Roxanne Hart), Charlie Gray (Eugene Roche), Gary Frantz (Ron Silver), Arthur Shelton (John Doolittle), Bea Shelton (Julie Lloyd), Young Bobby (Ian Giatti), Mrs. K (Janet Brandt), Joey Vega (Danny Ponce), Mrs. Vega (Belita Moreno), Hotel manager (Jason Wingreen), Bellhop (Danny Mora), Widow (Jane Dulo), Louise (Susan Peretz), Waiter (Steven Dunaway), Billy Wayne (Robert Desiderio), Cap (Anthony Sgueglia), Receptionist (Cynthia Tarr), Joe Ortiz (Robert Picardo), Groupie (Christie Mellor), Houseman (Arthur Malet), Priest (James Cromwell), Shamus (Martin Garner), Preacher (Arnold Johnson), Reporter (Patricia Springer), Stage manager (Buddy Powell), Doctor (Jim Hodge), Restaurant couple (Tracy Bogart, Crawford Binion).

Synopsis: In New York City, 1960, God answers the prayers of Bobby Shelton's father, who is concerned about his son's fever. In Los Angeles, 1984, Bobby is a struggling musician married to caseworker Wendy. When he says to himself he'd sell his soul to get a break, one Harry Tophet appears and offers to be his new agent. In Cleveland, rock star Billy Wayne's seven-year contract with the devil expires. Bobby signs what he believes is a trial contract with Tophet and becomes Billy Wayne. Wayne, meanwhile, becomes Bobby. Wendy doesn't know anything's amiss. Bobby as Billy achieves incredible success. He has it all: fame, money, women. But while visiting L.A., Bobby/Billy sees Wendy. She's pregnant, and he learns that it's his child. Although Tophet told Bobby that God is disillusioned and doesn't visit much anymore, Bobby/Billy seeks the almighty in a church, then a synagogue. Finally he hears a black preacher on the street say he'll find God in the desert. In a Vegas hotel, he pages and gets a call back from "The Lord." God appears at the gaming table where Tophet is gambling. They agree to a card game for Bobby's soul—and millions of others if God loses. God bluffs and wins. Bobby becomes his old self and is visited by God, who says he looked in on him when he was ill in 1960. Bobby returns to his wife. Five years later Bobby sings to his feverish daughter what his father sang to him: "Can Do." He hears God singing along.

Reviews: "Consistently amusing, buoyant comedy.... satisfying finish." (Kevin Thomas, *Los Angeles Times Calendar*, November 9, 1984, p. 1) ¶"Frequently delightful comedy-fantasy." (Archer Winsten, *New York Post*, November 9, 1984, p. 19) ¶"Has a shopping-mall message. Don't do drugs or dream of fame; go home, be ordinary." (Richard Corliss, *Time*, December 3, 1984, p. 79)

Analysis: It's not great and might have that hidden message critic the *Time* reviewer described (Corliss mourned the absence of Gracie Allen, who he felt would have injected a note of class), but it's solid and entertaining. It's relatively subdued, however, and we wish Burns as God appeared sooner and had more of a tussle with his alter ego.

Old Dracula *see under* Dracula

The Omen
(1976; 111 min.) ****

Produced by Harvey Bernhard. Directed by Richard Donner. Assistant Director, David Tomblin. Screenplay, David Seltzer. Edited by Stuart Baird. Director of Photography, Gilbert Taylor. Panavision. Color, DeLuxe. Music, Jerry Goldsmith. Art Direction, Carmen Dillon. Special Effects, John Richardson.

Cast: Robert Thorn (Gregory Peck), Katherine Thorn (Lee Remick), Keith Jennings (David Warner), Mrs. Baylock (Billie Whitelaw), Archaeologist Buchenhagen (Leo McKern), Father Brennan (Patrick Troughton), Father Spiletto (Martin Benson), Dr. Becker (Anthony Nicholls), Young nanny (Holly Palance), Psychiatrist (Jon Stride), House staff (Robert MacLeod, Sheila Raynor), Damien (Harvey Stevens).

Synopsis: At a Rome hospital, American diplomat Robert Thorn learns that his wife's child died at birth. A priest tells him a woman has died in childbirth; why not take her baby as his own and not tell his Katherine? It's a sign. Thorn mulls it over and agrees. They name the child Damien. Shortly thereafter Thorn is appointed ambassador to the Court of St. James in London. Several years pass. At a party Damien's young governess, having seen a strange dog, hangs herself from the roof of the house in full view of the partygoers after calling out that she's doing this for Damien. At Robert's office Father Brennan warns of calamity if he does not take daily communion and drink the blood of the Lord. At the Thorns' a new governess appears in the form of Mrs. Baylock, who informs them that she's been sent by the agency. Damien has a fit when his parents try to take him to church for a wedding. That night Robert wonders why his son has never been sick. At the Windsor Safari Park, baboons attack the car containing Katherine and Damien. Father Brennan again approaches Thorn and tells him Katherine is pregnant and that Damien will kill the child, then Katherine, and finally Robert. Brennan meets his doom during a strange storm when a staff atop his church topples and impales him. Katherine reveals her pregnancy to Robert but says she wants an abortion. In the newspaper Robert sees the photo of the dead priest. Katherine's doctor tells Robert his wife thinks Damien is not her child. Robert says he will fight to save the unborn child, but Katherine falls over a second-floor railing when Damien runs into her with his tricycle. In the hospital, Katherine says, "Don't let him kill me. Don't let him kill me." Photographer Keith Jennings shows Thorn photos revealing a ghostly line aimed at people who are now dead — and at Jennings. Jennings reveals that Father

Brennan had a birthmark, "666," on his inner thigh. That's the mark of the devil. They visit Brennan's cell, its walls covered with pages from the Bible, its door containing over two score crucifixes. They examine a diary and newspaper clippings and learn that a strange comet appeared five years ago on June 6 at 6 A.M.—the date of Damien's birth. Jennings and Thorn fly to Rome and learn that the hospital where Damien was born burned down. All the records were destroyed. At a monastery they locate Father Spiletto, scarred and mute from the hospital fire. He does manage to scrawl the name of a cemetery. Thorn and Jennings find an animal skeleton in the grave where they expected to find Damien's mother. In the next grave they do find a baby's skeleton, its skull crushed. Thorn realizes his child was murdered. Dogs attack and chase them away. In London, Katherine is pushed through a hospital window to her death by Mrs. Baylock. Thorn and Jennings proceed to the Megiddo archaeological dig, and Thorn learns from archaeologist Buchenhagen how to kill Damien with special daggers. He's not convinced until Jennings is decapitated by plate glass from a runaway truck and, back home, he finds "666" on Damien's head. Baylock tries to stop him but is killed. The police pursue Thorn's speeding car to a church and shoot him as he's about to stab the child. At the funeral of Robert and Katherine, Damien stands near the president of the United States.

Reviews: "The audience suspends its disbelief of the demonic forces long before the central characters do.... The film seems targeted to appeal to the current American mood, for we are now in a political campaign in which the clearest message the American people seems able to give is that we don't want to choose a President at all." (Gerald Forshey, *Christian Century*, August 4-11, 1976, pp. 689–691) ¶"The unnerving thing about all this is that the producers are apparently correct in supposing that you can mix biblical prophecy and this sort of jejune carrying-on, and get the public to buy it.... The film is a disquieting reflection of the vocabulary and preoccupations of contemporary pop Christianity, and the evangelical church is not without guilt here." (Thomas Howard, *Christianity Today*, August 6, 1976, pp. 1121–1122) ¶"One of the classiest big-budget horror films of all time." (Charles Balun, *The Connoisseur's Guide to the Contemporary Horror Film*, pp. 44–45) ¶"Gregory Peck ... looks better-dressed, and sounds more sonorous, than ever." (Penelope Gilliatt, *New Yorker*, July 5, 1976, p. 63) ¶"Donner's direction is taut. Performances and players are all strong, and the violence, utilized with discretion and economy, is properly motivated...." (Murf., *Variety*, June 9, 1976, p. 23)

Analysis: The Omen is a quality horror film apparently spawned by the success of 1968's *Rosemary's Baby* and 1973's *The Exorcist*. *The Omen* came to pass when a market survey revealed that women were turned off by too much violence and that older people were not interested. (Was this a big surprise?) "In a subliminal way the ad denoted quality—but scariness. The unknown, yes. Blood and gore, no." ("The Devil As Soap," *Forbes*, December 15, 1976, p. 73) Nevertheless, there are some horrifying scenes: the nanny who hangs herself, the photographer's decapitation. We are a little perturbed by the ending. It permitted evil to win, which was typical of films at that time. And it was doubtless contrived to bring forth sequels. Gregory Peck made a sort of comeback and said, "The script held my interest like a good pulp thriller. Sure, it had some loopholes, but ... Hitchcock's films always have holes you could drive a truck through. If you try to patch up every hole with conventional logic, you get into expository scenes that nobody wants to hear. So instead, you try to keep going at such a breakneck pace that most people won't apply any careful analysis to the logic of what's going on." (In Don Shay, "Filming *The Omen*," *Cinefantastique*, Vol. 5, No. 3, p. 40.) In 1978 *The Omen* was condemned by the Medveds, who unaccountably ranked it one of the 50 worst films of all time. *Now* we know that it was the satanic subject matter that flummoxed them, not the production's inherent quality. Leo McKern plays the Megiddo archaeologist (Buchenhagen) but is uncredited. Academy Award for Best Original Music Score.

Robert Thorn (Gregory Peck, right) refuses to heed the warning of Father Brennan (Patrick Troughton), who says that tragedy threatens Thorn's family in *The Omen* (Twentieth Century–Fox, 1976).

Damien: Omen II
(1978; 110 min.) **½

Produced by Harvey Bernhard. Directed by Don Taylor. Assistant Directors, Al Nicholson, Jerry Balle, Richard Luke Rothschild. Screenplay, Stanley Mann and Michael Hodges. Story, Harvey Bernhard. Based on characters created by David Seltzer. Edited by Robert Brown, Jr. Director of Photography, Bill Butler. Israeli Sequence, Gil Taylor. Miniatures photographed by Stanley Cortez. Panavision. Color, DeLuxe. Music, Jerry Goldsmith. Set Decoration, Robert de Vestel. Special Effects, Ira Anderson, Jr.

Cast: Richard Thorn (William Holden), Ann Thorn (Lee Grant), Damien Thorn (Jonathan Scott-Taylor), Paul Buher (Robert Foxworth), Charles Warren (Nicholas Pryor), Bill Atherton (Lew Ayres), Aunt Marion (Sylvia Sidney), Sergeant Neff (Lance Henriksen), Joan Hart (Elizabeth Shepherd), Mark

Thorn (Lucas Donat), Pasarian (Alan Arbus), Dr. Kane (Meshach Taylor), Archaeologist (Leo McKern), Butler (John Charles Burns), Murray (Fritz Ford), Teddy (John J. Newcombe), Colonel (Paul Cook), Jane (Diane Daniels), Teacher (Robert E. Ingham), Minister (William B. Fosser), Greenhouse technician (Corney Morgan), Maid (Judith Dowd), Truck driver (Russell P. Delia), Sergeant (Thomas O. Erhart), Pasarian's assistant (Anthony Hawkins), Guide (Robert J. Jones, Jr.), Girl (Cornelia Sanders), Jim (Rusdi Lane), Priest (Charles Mountain), Dr. Fiedler (Felix Shuman), Byron (Owen Sullivan), Guard (William J. Whelehan), Technician (James Spinks).

Synopsis: In Israel, archaeologists unearth ancient relics, including depictions of the whore of Babylon and the antichrist: a child's face that may be that of Damien Thorn. Nine years have passed since his father's death, and Damien is being raised by his uncle Richard Thorn and his wife, Ann. Both Damien and Richard's natural son, Mark, who is Damien's age, attend a U.S. military academy. There the new sergeant, Neff, advises Damien to read the Book of Revelation. Damien does so and finds that the number 666 is in fact carved on his scalp. While Damien learns of his destiny, many deaths occur: Aunt Marion, who advised Richard to separate Mark from Damien; Joan Hart, the reporter who endeavored to convince Richard that his brother believed Damien was the antichrist; Bill Atherton, a Thorn company executive who disagreed with Paul Buher about buying land in developing countries and, in Atherton's view, blackmailing starving masses; a doctor who discovered that Damien's blood was akin to a jackal's. Dr. Warren receives a package of daggers and a note. He also tries to warn Richard. Richard suspects something is seriously wrong after Mark dies — apparently of a brain hemorrhage but actually at the hands of Damien when Mark refused to cast his lot with him. While Richard inspects the piece of wall with Damien's face, Warren is crushed. Convinced at last of Damien's identity, Richard takes Ann to the museum, where he intends to kill Damien with the daggers. Ann protests, then stabs Richard with two of the daggers, revealing that she's always been on Damien's side. Having overheard everything from the hall, Damien

causes the boiler to explode, setting fire to Ann.

Reviews: "Apart from William Holden's worried features and Sylvia Sidney's distinguished aging beauty ... everyone's face seems to have been ironed." (*New Yorker*, June 19, 1978, pp. 85–86) ¶"There s one genuinely poignant moment when Damien discovers his identity and tries to flee from it.... unable to appropriate the moral vision of the original, but it provides numerous thrills." (*Christian Century*, August 30-September 6, 1978, p. 803)

Analysis: The early scenes have a slapdash look. Continuity with the progenitor is good. Lew Ayres's death under the ice *is* disturbing. Elizabeth Shepherd! See *The Tomb of Ligeia*. It's an unbilled Leo McKern again as an archaeologist in the beginning.

The Final Conflict
(1981; 108 min.) **

Produced by Harvey Bernhard. Directed by Graham Baker. Screenplay, Andrew Birkin. Directors of Photography, Robert Paynter, Phil Meheux. Panavision. Color, DeLuxe. Music, Jerry Goldsmith. Art Direction, Martin Atkinson.

Cast: Damien Thorn (Sam Neill), Father DeCarlo (Rossano Brazzi), Kate Reynolds (Lisa Harrow), Harvey Dean (Don Gordon), President (Mason Adams), Peter Reynolds (Barnaby Holm), Ambassador (Robert Arden), Brother Matteus (Tommy Duggan), Barbara (Leueen Willoughby), Brother Martin (Milos Kirek), Brother Paulo (Louis Mahoney), Brother Simeon (Richard Oldfield), Brother Antonio (Tony Vogel), Dr. Philmore (Norman Bird), Carol (Arwen Holm), Manservant (Hugh Moxey), Vicar (Richard Williams), Astronomer (Arnold Diamond), Diplomats (William Fox, John Baskcomb), Astronomer's assistant (Eric Richard), Press officer (Marc Smith), Stigwell (Stephen Turner), Workman (Al Matthews), Orators (Larry Martyn, Harry Littlewood, Frank Coda), Woman at hunt (Hazel Court).

Synopsis: A dagger is found at a Chicago construction site. It and six others are auctioned off and make their way to Father DeCarlo in Subiaco, Italy. Back in the U.S., at age 32, Damien Thorn plans on becoming ambassador to Britain and with that in mind makes the current ambassador kill himself with a shotgun. While discussing the destruction of the Aswan Dam (obviously done by Thorn's henchmen) the president appoints Thorn ambassador as well as president of the U.N. Youth Council. Meanwhile, at a British observatory a forthcoming March 24 Trinity alignment of stars means something important. In Subiaco seven priests are given the daggers to kill Damien, son of Satan. The mission must be accomplished before the stellar alignment, they believe. One priest is killed during an assassination attempt in a TV station, causing the others to forestall more attempts until they find the birthplace of a holy child who is to be born at the time of the alignment. Thorn prays to his father and a statue of Christ. He fails to notice the blood that runs from the crown of thorns. Another ambush is unsuccessful and three priests are killed, one when he is mistaken for Damien. Two others are killed — by a fall off a bridge and by dogs at a fox hunt. Damien tells his Disciples of the Watch to kill all male children born at the time of the alignment: "Slay the Nazarene." Father DeCarlo seeks out Kate after seeing her TV report on baby deaths. Kate's son Peter tells Damien of DeCarlo's visit and is told to follow him. DeCarlo visits Harvey's wife. She confronts Harvey. Kate and Damien take a country walk. She falls in the river but is rescued by Damien. That night they mate. "Beauty is pain," says Damien. Waking alone, Kate finds Damien in his room with the Christ statue and discovers the mark of the devil — the number 666 behind his right ear. Damien tells Harvey to kill his newborn son. Harvey's wife, possessed, kills the baby and Harvey. DeCarlo confronts Kate and tells her of Peter and Damien. DeCarlo stabs Peter by mistake when Kate leads Damien to a ruin. Kate stabs Damien in the back as he searches for the Nazarene. He stumbles off and sees the figure of the adult Christ. Dying, he says, "Nazarene, you have won nothing." Biblical passages appear on the screen to the effect that this Second Coming is by the adult Christ.

Review: "Not only the silliest chapter in the Omen trilogy, it's the dullest and most inept." (David Ansen, *Newsweek*, March 30, 1981, p. 83)

Analysis: Why seven swords if one will do? How did Damien make that one priest look like him? Still and all, it's not as boring as the mere mention of a third film and its setting would indicate. Look for Hazel Court at the fox hunt, but look fast. She's standing and lifting a goblet to a rider. Is the "Nazarene, you have won nothing" line in case there would be a sequel? Filmed in Cornwall and Yorkshire.

On the Move *see* Mannequin: On the Move *under* **Mannequin**

One Million B.C.
(Hal Roach/United Artists, 1940; 80 min.) **

Produced by Hal Roach. Directed by Hal Roach and Hal Roach, Jr. Screenplay, Mickell Novak, George Baker, Joseph Frickert. Edited by Ray Snyder. Director of Photography, Norbert Brodine. Music, Werner R. Heymann. Art Direction, Charles D. Hall. Set Decoration, W. L. Stevens. Photographic Effects, Roy Seawright. Descriptive Narrator, Grover Jones.

Cast: Tumak (Victor Mature), Loana (Carole Landis), Akhoba (Lon Chaney, Jr.), Ohtao (John Hubbard), Nupondi (Mamo Clark), Peytow (Nigel De Brulier), Wandi (Mary Gale Fisher), Shakana (Edgar Edwards), Tohana (Inez Palange), Ataf (Jacqueline Dalya), Narrator (Conad Nagel).

Synopsis: European hikers take refuge from a storm in a cave, the recesses of which are temporarily inhabited by a scholar studying the carvings of ancient man. He volunteers to relate a possible ancient scenario: The Rock tribe is truly barbaric, its leader Akhoba ruling by strength alone. When his son Tumak refuses to hand over food, he is exiled. Pursued by a mastodon, he falls into a river and floats downstream. Rescued by the Shell tribe and mentored by Loana, he slowly learns to share his food as well as how to use a spear, with which he kills a threatening dinosaur. Meanwhile, Akhoba is gored by a bison, and true to the nature of the tribe, left to fend for himself. Back at the Shell tribe, Tumak steals another man's spear and is outlawed. Loana accompanies him, and they encounter various dinosaurs on their way to Tumak's tribe. Loana takes pity on Akhoba and reinstalls him in the elder's seat. She demonstrates how to share and grow fruit, but a volcanic eruption separates her from Tumak. Later a man from the Shell tribe arrives with dire news. The Rock tribe, including Tumak and Akhoba, follow the messenger and discover a dinosaur threatening Loana and her people. After unsuccessfully trying to dislodge it, Akhoba suggests causing a landslide. The dinosaur is buried. Tumak and Loana are reunited and walk with a child into the sunset.

Review: "The most delightfully amusing tableau from a museum of unnatural history in the history of the cinema." (B.R. Crisler, *New York Times*, April 27, 1940, p. 9)

Analysis: This curio is embarrassing, almost painful, to watch. Forget the mammoths and dinosaurs; mankind could not have survived if it lived in the dog-eat-dog fashion of these Rock people. Leonard Maltin wrote that the special effects were excellent. He must have meant the process shots, not the prehistoric creatures: a man in a mini-tyrannosaurus suit? modern-day lizards enlarged photographically? elephants with rugs? The music score is Wagnerian.

One Million Years B.C.
(Hammer/Seven Arts/Fox, 1967; 91 min.) ***

Produced by Michael Carreras. Associate Producers, Hal E. Roach, Sr., and Aida Young. Directed by Don Chaffey. Assistant Director, Denis Bertera. Screenplay, Don Chaffey. Adapted from an original screenplay by Mickell Novak, George Baker, and Joseph Frickert. Edited by Tom Simpson. Director of Photography, Wilkie Cooper. Color, DeLuxe. Music and Special Musical Effects, Mario Nascimbene. Art Direction, Robert Jones. Costumes, Carl Toms. Special Effects, George Blackwell. Special Visual Effects, Ray Harryhausen.

Cast: Loana (Raquel Welch), Tumak (John Richardson), Akhoba (Robert Brown), Nupondi (Martine Beswick), Sakana (Percy Herbert), Ahot (Jean Wladon), Ullah (Yvonne Horner), Tohana (Malya Nappil), Payto (William Lyon Brown), Sura (Lisa Thomas), Young

Rock man (Richard James), First Rock man (Frank Hayden), First Shell man (Terence Maidment), First Shell girl (Micky De-Rauch), Narrator (Robert Beatty).

Synopsis: Ages ago Tumak, son of Akhoba, was ousted from the tribe when he and his father fought over a shank of meat. Tumak journeys to the sea and finds a fair-skinned tribe that fishes with spears, not the blunt staves of his tribe. Tumak is made welcome by Loana and kills an allosaurus, but when he steals a spear and fights with its owner, he is again made an outcast. However, he is given a spear, and Loana accompanies him. He retraces his steps, not knowing that his perfidious brother Sakana has taken control of the tribe after causing his father to fall and become a cripple. Tumak and Loana escape from a triceratops when a ceratosaurus attacks the plant eater. The humans enter the cave of some anthropoids and escape by climbing a tree to an exit hole. Eventually they find Tumak's tribe, and Tumak wounds Sakana with his spear. Loana herself must fight Nupondi, but having learned compassion from the Shell tribe, Tumak tosses aside the rock his people give Loana to crush Nupondi's skull. While bathing in a nearby pond, Loana is carried off by a pteranodon which, unknown to Tumak, is itself attacked by another flying reptile. The pteranodon drops Loana into the sea. She swims to shore, finds her tribe, and leads them to Tumak. Meanwhile, Sakana has regained power. With the aid of Loana's people, Tumak takes it back. In the fight he kills Sakana. A volcanic explosion and earthquake kills many, and the survivors, including Tumak and Loana, trudge off across a forbidding landscape.

Review: "Good humored full-of-action commercial nonsense...." (Rich., *Variety*, December 28, 1966, p. 18)

Analysis: The theme and much of the plot is a scene-for-scene remake of the 1940 film. Additions are Ray Harryhausen's state-of-the-art dinosaurs, although he inserted a few process shots of modern iguanas. What was he thinking? (See his *Film Fantasy Scrapbook*, third edition, for unconvincing justification.) The allosaurus battle with the humans is very well done.

All of a sudden you realize this can't be real — but it certainly looks it. Normally a brunette, Raquel Welch, whose first "big" film this was, is a blonde — to fit in with the Shell tribe and to counter the dark Martine Beswicke (here Beswick). It's a sweaty movie, one that makes the viewer feel grubby. It was filmed on the island of Lanzarote.

One Million Years B.C. *see under* **One Million B.C.**

The Origin of Michael Myers *see* Halloween: The Curse of Michael Myers *under* **Halloween**

The Original Nightmare *see* Howling IV: The Original Nightmare *under* **The Howling**

The Other Side *see* Poltergeist II: The Other Side *under* **Poltergeist**

Panga *see* Curse III *under* **The Curse**

The People That Time Forgot *see under* **The Land That Time Forgot**

Pet Sematary
(Paramount, 1989; 105 min.) ***

Produced by Richard P. Rubinstein. Directed by Mary Lambert. Screenplay, Stephen King, based on his novel. Edited by Michael Hill and Daniel Hanley. Director of Photography, Peter Stein. Panavision. Technicolor. Music, Elliot Goldenthal. Dolby Stereo. "Pet Sematary" performed by the Ramones. Art Direction, Dins Danielson. Set Decoration, Katharine Briggs. Costumes, M. Stewart. Special Makeup, Lance Anderson. Special Visual Effects, Fantasy II Film Effects.

Cast: Dr. Louis Creed (Dale Midkiff), Jud Crandall (Fred Gwynne), Rachel Creed (Denise Crosby), Victor Pascow (Brad Greenquist), Irwin Goldman (Michael Lombard), Ellie Creed (Blaze Berdhal), Gage Creed (Miko Hughes), Missy Dandridge (Susan Blommaert), Minister (Stephen King).

Synopsis: Dr. Louis Creed, his wife Rachel, young daughter Ellie and younger son Gage arrive at their new Maine home. Creed will work at the local university hospital. Neighbor Jud Crandall warns the family of the tank trucks that speed by and shows them the path to the "Pet Sematary" where many victims of those trucks rest in peace. At the hospital, Creed unsuccessfully tries to revive Victor Pascow, a young man hit by a truck. Having given up, Creed is shocked when Pascow speaks to him and that evening appears in his house. Pascow's spirit leads Creed to the pet cemetery and warns him not to trespass on the land beyond. Creed wakes in his bed but finds his feet muddy. Was it a dream after all? At Thanksgiving, Rachel and the children visit her parents in Chicago. Louis decided not to go because Rachel's father doesn't like him. While they are gone, Ellie's cat Church is found dead by the side of the road. Crandall leads Creed past the pet cemetery to an old Indian burial ground. Creed buries Church, then finds him alive back at the house. Crandall convinces him that he did not bury the cat alive; it's been resurrected. Time passes. Picnicking in the field, the Creeds and Crandall watch Gage fly a kite, but Louis is too slow to retrieve his son from the path of an oncoming truck. While Rachel and Ellie are away, Louis, against Jud's protestations, raises Gage from the dead. The spirit of Victor Pascow warns Rachel to return, but she's too late and is killed by the maniacal Gage, who uses his father's scalpel on her as he had on Jud. Louis awakes and realizes something's wrong, goes to the Crandall home, and re-kills Church and Gage. Louis sets the house on fire and carries the body of his wife to the burial ground. He believes that since she's not been dead long, she'll be okay when she's resurrected. A battered, bloody Rachel returns, embraces Louis but grabs a knife from the table. As the screen goes dark, Louis screams.

Reviews: "Americana at its most Gothic.... The actors ... couldn't be more aptly cast." (Kevin Thomas, *Los Angeles Times Calendar*, April 24, 1989, p. 5) ¶"Mary Lambert falls on King's story with an enjoyable ferocity.... conveys some surprisingly genuine anguish from time to time." (Philip Strick, *Monthly Film Bulletin*, November 1989, p. 341) ¶"Breaks no new ground in the horror thriller realm."

(Bill Kaufman, *Newsday*, April 22, 1989, Part II, p. 15)

Analysis: If you can stomach the deaths of children and animals, you'll find this a quality film, well photographed and acted, suspenseful, and with a good central premise. The *L. A. Times*'s Kevin Thomas pointed out that King's work tends to compel and repel at the same time but that director Mary Lambert has worked effectively with that contradiction. Is it the first theatrical film in which a child of these tender years is so murderous and put out of his misery so vividly — with a hypodermic to the neck? He's younger than Patty McCormack in *The Bad Seed*. He's like a real live Chucky. What, we wonder, lies near the burial ground that makes the resurrected so bloodthirsty? The Pascow spirit provides some welcome humor.

Pet Sematary II
(Paramount, 1992; 106 min.) ***

Produced by Ralph S. Singleton. Directed by Mary Lambert. Screenplay, Richard Outten. Inspired by the novel *Pet Sematary* by Stephen King. Edited by Tom Finan. Director of Photography, Russell Carpenter. Panavision. Color, Du Art. Prints, DeLuxe. Music, Mark Governor. Art Direction, Karen Steward. Set Decoration, Susan Benjamin. Makeup, Jeanine Greville-Morris. Special Effects Coordinator, Dean W. Miller. Special Effects Mechanical, Design FX Company. Special Effects Designer, Peter M. Chesney.

Cast: Chase Matthews (Anthony Edwards), Jeff Matthews (Edward Furlong), Sheriff Gus Gilbert (Clancy Brown), Drew Gilbert (Jason McGuire), Renee Hallow (Darlanne Fluegel), Amanda Gilbert (Lisa Waltz), Clyde Parker (Jared Rushton), Marjorie Hargrove (Sarah Trigger), Quentin Yolander (Jim Peck).

Synopsis: In a freak accident while making the film *Castle of Terror*, actress Renee Hallow is electrocuted. Her veterinarian ex-husband Chase takes teenage son Jeff, who witnessed the tragedy, to Maine. Jeff insists that all of his mother's clothes be placed in the attic. Sheriff Gus Gilbert brings his stepson Drew and his dog to the animal hospital. Gus says he was once Renee's sweetheart —"the whole nine yards." At school Jeff is harassed by toughs who steal his kitten. Jeff chases them on his bike

through the abandoned Creed residence to a path leading to a pet cemetery. After a fight which Clyde wins, Jeff heads down the path and finds "Tiger" safe in a bird cage. Drew Gilbert arrives and makes friends. Later Drew's dog Zowie is shot by Gus as it tries to get in the rabbit hutch. Drew and Jeff take Zowie to the "Pet Sematary," but Drew knows a better place beyond the timber bulwark to bury his pet: an ancient Indian burial ground. Maybe Zowie will come back. That night Mrs. Gilbert thinks she hears Zowie, and she's right. Chase takes the dog in for observation. Jeff dreams of his mother. Three days pass. Chase can't detect a heartbeat in Zowie, so he extracts blood and sends it to a lab. Halloween comes. At the Pet Sematary, boys and girls listen to horrible stories related by Clyde. Gus, angry that Drew went trick-or-treating against his wishes, breaks up the session. Zowie kills Gus, and Drew and Jeff bury him in the Indian burial ground. A slightly tipsy, increasingly uncouth Gus reappears and forces himself upon his wife. But Drew tells Jeff that Gus is friendlier — it's like a real family. Chase learns from the lab that Zowie's blood cells show deterioration. So how come the dog is still alive? Visiting the former vet who is now a taxidermist, Chase hears of the Creed tragedy. Chase dreams of Renee, who says, "I can come back, Chase." Zowie attacks him while Jeff is attacked by Clyde. Gus intervenes, tells Jeff to go home, then accidentally kills Clyde. Fleeing the house, Drew and his mother are killed in a truck crash. Gus takes Clyde to the burial ground. Jeff fiddles with his mother's clothes and tells his dad about the place in the woods. A phone call upsets Chase: Gus was seen with Renee's corpse. Jeff sneaks out on housesitter Marjorie and finds Gus, who tells him, "Ya bury your own." Attacked by Zowie, Chase shoots and chases her. He stops Gus with a bullet to the brain. In the attic, Renee kills Marjorie, dressed in one of Renee's gowns. Jeff and Chase arrive. The resurrected, ax-wielding Clyde is electrocuted. Renee sets the attic on fire, but she melts and flames out after pleading with Jeff to stay with her. Jeff realizes that his father must be attended to. Next day Chase and Jeff leave town.

Review: "Expresses and attempts to resolve in bold mythological terms the anxieties of being 13." (Kevin Thomas, *Philadelphia Inquirer*, August 31, 1992, p. C7)

Analysis: While it may not be as scary as the first, this is a solid film from the same director. The *Philadelphia Inquirer* reviewer found the film too horrifying for young children and too silly for high schoolers — perfect, he said, for junior high filmgoers. Edward Furlong is better than he was in *Terminator II*. In this he's "normal": neither tough and streetwise nor innocent and naive. There is humor; e.g., after burying Gus, Drew says, "Nothing happened, Mom, we just ditched Gus, that's all." There *are* inconsistencies. Why bring back Gus? It's not really evident that the Renee Hallow character is buried in Maine. Until her resurrection, we were wondering how with any sense of plausibility they'd get her corpse there. Although the setting is Maine, it was filmed in Georgia. The suspicion that it's not New England arises when we see and hear Lisa Waltz and Sarah Trigger, neither of whom sounds anything like a Yankee.

Phantasm

(Avco Embassy, 1979; 90 min.) **½

Produced by D. A. Coscarelli. Directed by Don Coscarelli. Co-producer, Paul Pepperman. Screenplay, Don Coscarelli. Edited by Don Coscarelli. Director of Photography, Don Coscarelli. Panavision. Technicolor. Music, Fred Myrow and Malcolm Seagrave. Art Direction, David Gavin Brown. Special Effects, Paul Pepperman. Silver Sphere, Willard Green.

Cast: Jody (Bill Thornbury), Mike (Michael Baldwin), Reggie (Reggie Bannister), The Tall Man (Angus Scrimm), Lady in Lavender (Kathy Lester), Granddaughter (Terrie Kalbus), Caretaker (Ken Jones), Girlfriend (Susan Harper), Sally (Lynn Eastman), Toby (David Arntzen), Bartender (Ralph Richmond), Tommy (Bill Cone), Double Lavender (Laura Mann), Fortune teller (Mary Ellen Shaw), Maid (Myrtle Scotton).

Synopsis: During intercourse in the Morningside Cemetery, a woman knifes her lover, Tommy. Her face changes to that of a man. Jody and Reggie, Tommy's friends, can't believe he's dead. Jody's younger brother Mike spots a tall man from the funeral parlor lifting Tommy's coffin all by himself and putting it into the hearse. After visiting a psychic, Mike follows his brother and a bar pickup into the cemetery. Hearing something behind him, he rushes off screaming. Jody follows him, then returns for his girl but can't find her. Mike has a bad dream before being attacked by something in the garage. Returning to the funeral parlor, he is grabbed by a caretaker, but a flying metal sphere with spikes misses him and impales the man. The Tall Man appears, but Mike cuts off one of his fingers and escapes. He shows Jody the *living* finger. Opening the box a second time, they are attacked by a giant bee, which they finally manage to jam into the garbage disposal. Jody breaks into the funeral parlor and is attacked by a small, hooded figure which he must shoot. Mike rescues Jody and in the ensuing high-speed chase, the hearse crashes. The skewered driver is Tommy! Reggie says they must tackle the Tall Man. Mike finds Reggie's ice cream truck overturned; then he, Sally and Suzie are attacked by dwarves and Mike is thrown through the back window of the car. He follows Jody to the funeral parlor, and together they find Reggie and discover a room with barrels of dwarves. Mike is half-sucked into another dimension but is pulled out by Jody and Reggie. Mike saw "slaves," which explains the dwarves: In that other world the gravity demands short people. The lights go out, and the three are attacked by dwarves and separated. When the lights come back on, Reggie places his hands over the two pylons bounding the gate to the other world and shorts the process. Outside, Reggie is stabbed by the blonde/Tall Man. Jody and Mike drive away, planning to attract the Tall Man to an abandoned 1,000-foot mine shaft. The plan doesn't go precisely as formulated, but the Tall Man does fall in, and Jody caps the shaft with a boulder. Later Reggie tells Mike all of this was a dream, that Jody died in a car wreck. In his room, Mike is grabbed by the Tall Man in his mirror.

Review: "Thoroughly silly and endearing."

(Vincent Canby, *New York Times*, June 1, 1979, p. C12)

Analysis: For a one-man show lacking much rhyme or reason, this is pretty good. It won't pay to ask many questions, like why the police don't investigate, why the Tall Man can appear at will but can't seem to render his human antagonists incapable of further pursuit (perhaps he likes the game), or what the devil the mechanical, flying spheres are or where they hail from. There's some humor, e.g., "No warning shots. Warning shots are bullshit." The brief scenes of the other world are disquieting: a serpentine line of black-robed dwarves trudging across a windswept alien plain.

Phantasm II
(Universal, 1988; 100 min.) **½

Produced by Roberto A. Quezada. Directed by Don Coscarelli. Screenplay, Don Coscarelli. Edited by Peter Teschner. Director of Photography, Daryn Okada. Foto-Kem Color. Music, Fred Myrow, Christopher L. Stone. Sound, Izak en-Meir, Alan Howarth. Dolby Stereo. Art Direction, Byrnadette di Santo. Set Decoration, Dominic Wymark. Costumes, Carla Gibbons. Special Makeup, Mark Shostrom. Special Effects, Wayne Beauchamp. Special Visual Effects, Dream Quest Images. Sphere, Steven Patino.

Cast: Mike (James Le Gros), Reggie (Reggie Bannister), Elizabeth (Paula Irvine), Tall Man (Angus Scrimm), Alchemy (Samantha Phillips), Father Meyers (Kenneth Tigar), Grandma (Ruth C. Engel), Jeri (Stacey Travis), Mortician (Mark Anthony Major), Grandpa (Rubin Kushner), Psychologist (J. Patrick McNamara), Young Mike (Michael Baldwin). With Amanda Gray, Elizabeth Quezada, Lauren Gray, June Jordan, Megan Gibbons, Craig Murkey, Amanda Gibbons, Troy Fromin, Georgeana Valdez, Guy Alford, Irene Korman, Ricky Murkey, Katie Carlin, Delia Ortega, Lee Craig, Ramona Ortega, Richard F. Berry, Patrick W. Allen.

Synopsis: Elizabeth (Liz) knows the story of Mike and the unearthly Tall Man, who is plundering earth's graveyards for slaves. Mike is released from the Morningside Psychiatric Clinic. He knows Liz needs him. First, he takes a pickax to the cemetery where Reggie finds him. There are no bodies in the graves. Reggie realizes they must find the Tall Man, and the two track the monster into the northwest, passing through small towns with desecrated cemeteries. They find "Liz," but it's really a Tall Man minion who says, "You play a good game, boy. Come East if you dare." They torch it and head for Perigord, Oregon, population 891. Liz is in fact in Perigord at her grandfather's funeral and encounters the Tall Man. Reggie and Mike pick up a girl hitchhiker named Alchemy. In the funeral parlor Liz observes a man replacing a cadaver's blood with some yellow liquid. Liz flees the house after being confronted by the Tall Man and a dwarf grandmother. She finds Mike, and they return to the abandoned house where Mike, Reggie and Alchemy are planning. Liz is kidnapped by Tall Man and taken to the crematorium but escapes and finds Mike again. Mike manages to get one of the silver spheres, which Mike turns on the Tall Man with limited effectiveness. However, during the struggle Liz stabs him with the embalming hose leading to the yellow fluid Reggie had mixed with hydrochloric acid. The Tall Man is eaten up. Alchemy drives up and whisks them away, but she's not what she seems. Reggie is tossed out of the front seat. Mike thinks, "It's only a dream." The Tall Man says, "No, it's not."

Reviews: "Some well set-up suspense sequences, but primarily it takes the original and gives you more of the same.... It's efficient but not progressive." (Dennis Fischer, *Cinefantastique*, January 1989, p. 118) ¶"Utterly unredeeming, full-gore sequel." (Daws., *Variety*, July 13, 1988)

Analysis: A bit more polished than the first, its story starts making more sense. With a bigger budget, this could have been epic adventure for "real ghostbusters": the pursuit over time and topography of a demon. Disturbing scenes: the cemeteries with tombstones but no coffins or bodies. Why did Reggie throw away his shotgun after one blast? Disposing of or losing weapons is almost a film cliché. By now audiences realize it's a plot contrivance supposedly to create tension.

Phantasm III: Lord of the Dead
(Starway International/Universal, 1993; 91 min.) *½

Produced and directed by Don Coscarelli. Screenplay, Don Coscarelli. Edited by Norman Buckley. Director of Photography, Chris Chomyn. Color, Foto-Kem. Music, Fredric Myrow, Christopher L. Stone. Dolby Stereo. Art Direction, Wendy Guidery, Candi Guterres. Set Decoration, Charley Cabrera. Sphere Effects created by D. Kerry Prior. Special Makeup Effects, Mark Shostrom, Dean Gates.

Cast: Reggie (Reggie Bannister), Mike (A. Michael Baldwin), Tall Man (Angus Scrimm), Tim (Kevin Connors), Rocky (Gloria Lynne Henry), Jody (Bill Thornbury), Edna (Cindy Ambuehl), Henry (John [David] Chandler), Rufus (Brooks Gardner).

Synopsis: Mike recalls Jodie's death and the Tall Man's meltdown. "But somehow he keeps coming back." For sure. As Reggie pulls Mike from a car wreck and fights off those damned dwarves, the Tall Man reappears. When Reggie pulls the pin on a grenade, the Tall Man says he doesn't want Mike in pieces and leaves. In the hospital, a sphere emerges from the head of an attendant, inspects Mike, and flies away. Upon leaving, Reggie and Mike meet Jodie, dead but temporarily in physical form. He becomes a sphere and tries unsuccessfully to protect Mike from the Tall Man. Reggie takes Jodie's now dormant sphere and drives to Holtsville. He's waylaid by a woman and two unsavory men, stashed in a car trunk but released by young Tim, who has killed the three hoods. He explains how the Tall Man took his family and joins Reggie. At the Holtsville Cemetery mausoleum they destroy a sphere and are joined by Rocky. Rocky says her family vanished. The three head east and enter the ghost town of Boulton. Jodie's sphere regains mobility and Jodie's form helps Reggie find Mike. On the road, the three people Tim killed give chase. Reggie and company head for the big mortuary. It's the last place the Tall Man would look. Mike realizes that the Tall Man doesn't like cold and uses Jodie's sphere to learn more: the Tall Man tampers with the corpse brains and compacts the bodies into the drone dwarves. While Reggie, Tim and Rocky confront the three criminals once again,

the Tall Man subdues Mike. Rocky stabs the Tall Man with a pike and forces him into the freezer. But a sphere emerges from his head and breaks out, chasing Tim. Mike finds a sphere implanted in his head. Jodie urges Reg to be patient with the distraught Mike. Inside, Tim finds that the cryogenic vat in which they'd dunked the Tall Man's sphere has been overturned. "It's all over!" cries Reggie as a multitude of spheres subdue him. "It's never all over," says the Tall Man, and Tim is grabbed from behind.

Analysis: Apparently this entry went direct to video. Too much happens too fast, too soon. To prevent us from finding the story holes? Does Reggie have an inkling of a plan? Nothing seems to stop the Tall Man for any length of time. Reggie's comic relief is occasionally irritating. Why does he question the new implausibilities? Was it necessary to turn Cindy Ambuehl into a hag so soon? This was supposed to conclude the series, but the filmmakers again leave the door open. Without more logic, we don't want a fourth installment.

The Picture of Dorian Gray
(MGM, 1945; 107 min.) ***½

Produced by Pandro S. Berman. Directed by Albert Lewin. Screenplay, Albert Lewin. Based on the novel by Oscar Wilde. Edited by Ferris Webster. Director of Photography, Harry Stradling. Color sequences, Technicolor. Music, Herbert Stothart. Musical Direction, Mario Castelnuovo-Tedesco, Franz Waxman. Art Direction, Cedric Gibbons, Hans Peters. Makeup, Jack Dawn.

Cast: Dorian Gray (Hurd Hatfield), Lord Henry Wotton (George Sanders), Gladys Hallward (Donna Reed), Sibyl Vane (Angela Lansbury), Basil Hallward (Lowell Gilmore), Allen Campbell (Douglas Walton), James Vane (Richard Fraser), David Stone (Peter Lawford), Sir Robert Bentley (Miles Mander), Lady Agatha (Mary Forbes), Mrs. Vane (Lydia Bilbrook), Adrian Singleton (Morton Lowry), narrator (Cedric Hardwicke). With Devi Dja and Her Balinese Dancers.

Synopsis: London—1886: As young gentleman Dorian Gray poses for artist Basil Hallward's full-size portrait, Lord Henry Wotton advises Dorian to live life to the full, for he'll never look like this again. Dorian says he would give all, even his soul, to stay like the portrait. Wotton warns him that his wish may come true. There's an Egyptian cat statue, a god, that may grant it. Taking Wotton's advice, Dorian explores life, visiting the seamier side of London. In the Two Turtles pub he becomes infatuated with Sibyl Vane, songstress, whose signature tune is "Yellow Bird." Dorian arranges to meet Sibyl, and shortly thereafter they fall in love. He plans to marry, but Wotton suggests he make a scene: When it's time for her to return home, test her by asking her to stay. If she insists on leaving, tell her to let herself out. Dorian scoffs, but when the time comes he does what Wotton advised. Sibyl starts to leave but, with tears in her eyes, returns. Convinced that Sibyl is not as virtuous as she seemed, Dorian abandons her. He notices that his portrait's face has some lines of cruelty about the mouth — or is it his imagination? Before he can make it up to Sibyl, Wotton arrives and informs him that she's apparently committed suicide. Dorian decides to become indifferent and tells Basil he doesn't want to be at the mercy of his emotions. Basil recommends a book about Buddha. Fearing that someone might see the changes in his portrait, Dorian has it moved upstairs to his old schoolroom. Only he has the key. Years pass and people marvel at Dorian's agelessness, but there are rumors of his "visits to the abyss." Gladys Hallward, Basil's niece, grows to womanhood. She yearns to marry Dorian, but he says that would be a great wickedness. On the eve of Dorian's 38th birthday he meets Basil, who says he and Gladys are going to Paris for a couple months. Before departing, Basil mentions the rumors about Dorian — and certain letters believed to incriminate him. Basil says he would have to see Dorian's soul to believe them. Dorian takes Basil to the schoolroom. After he views the portrait, which now shows the effects of moral leprosy, Basil asks, "Do you know how to pray, Dorian?" Realizing that Gladys must never hear of this, and overcome by panic, Dorian stabs Basil and blackmails Allen Campbell into disposing of the body. Dorian asks Gladys to marry him, and she accepts. At Bluegate Field, Sibyl Vane's

brother James, on leave from his seafaring, seeks "Sir Tristam," the name his sister used for the man he knows was responsible for her death. By chance, Dorian appears and is called "Sir Tristam," but when James threatens him he finds that Dorian could not be the proper age. However, when Dorian leaves, James is informed that "Sir Tristam" has looked twenty-two for the past twenty years. James follows Dorian to his Mayfair-Selby estate but is accidentally shot and killed during a hunt. Dorian bids farewell to Gladys. David Stone arrives and informs Gladys that he secured entrance to Dorian's rooms and discovered a portrait of a debauched "uncle." Gladys reads the farewell note Dorian left her. At his house, Dorian notices that his good deed of leaving Gladys shows in the eyes of the portrait. There is hope, he thinks, and he supposes it best to destroy the portrait. But when he stabs it with a knife he falls dead. His portrait regains his unsullied youth while Dorian's corpse turns vile.

Reviews: "The elaborately mystical treatment which Metro has given the tale is matched in egregious absurdity by the visual affectations of the film. And the whole thing … makes little or no intelligible sense." (Bosley Crowther, *New York Times*, May 2, 1945, p. 15) ¶"Follows closely enough the pattern of the original, and an extremely difficult task is accomplished with no little skill and dexterity.... Helped by some interior decorating which understands the period, the atmosphere of the book finds a true enough reflection." (*Times* [London], May 2, 1945, p. 6) ¶"Represents an interesting experiment by Metro.... Hurd Hatfield is a pretty-boy Gray. He plays it with little feeling, as apparently intended...." (*Variety*)

Analysis: This is a very compelling film version of Wilde's only novel. One can easily imagine the consternation one would feel if only one's portrait aged. This has a good reputation, much of it based on D'Agostino's art direction. It reeks of atmosphere. The color sequences involve the portrait. George Sanders — the only performer the *New York Times* saw fit to praise — fits to a tee the role of world-weary raconteur.

Donna Reed never looked prettier and is in fact radiant in her evening gowns, but her character is not in the book, nor is Peter Lawford's. In the novel the Angela Lansbury character is an actress, not a dance hall singer. The film did nothing for Hurd Hatfield's film career. The next time we notice him is in 1961's *El Cid*. It sounds like Arthur Shields as the minister haranguing the slum crowd, but we see only his back. Academy Award for Cinematography. Best Supporting Actress Academy Award nomination for Angela Lansbury. A comprehensive forties film retrospective would pair this with *The Man in Half Moon Street*.

The Secret of Dorian Gray
(AIP/Commonwealth United, 1970; 93 min.) *

Produced by Harry Alan Towers. Directed by Massimo Dallamano. Screenplay, Marcello Coscia and Massimo Dallamano. Based on the novel by Oscar Wilde. Edited by Nicholas Wentworth. Director of Photography, Otello Spila. Color, Movielab. Music, Peppino DeLuca and Carlo Pes. Art Direction, Mario Ambrosino.

Cast: Dorian Gray (Helmut Berger), Basil (Richard Todd), Sybil (Marie Liljedahl), Henry Wotton (Herbert Lom), Gwendolyn (Margaret Lee), Mrs. Patricia Ruxton (Isa Miranda), Alice (Maria Rohm), Adrienne (Beryl Cunningham), Esther (Eleonora Rossi Drago), Dr. Alan Campbell (Renato Romano), James Vane (Stewart Black).

Synopsis: A man washes blood from his hands, returns to a room with a dead body and burns the man's belongings. We flash back as he remembers: After leaving a pub, Dorian Gray stops off at a small theater, where he observes a lovely young woman rehearsing the part of Juliet. Her name is Sybil Vane, and she finds him attractive. They have dinner, then mate on the stage bed. Dorian continues posing for artist Basil and meets Henry Wotton, who is much impressed by the portrait. When Basil finishes it, Dorian says, "I would give my soul to stay like that." Sybil senses that Dorian has been changed by the portrait. At Henry's party, Dorian has an idea and takes the attendees to *Romeo and Juliet*. But his hopes of having Sybil impress them

are dashed when she gives an amateurish performance. She later explains that she does not need to act anymore; she's living a life of feelings and love. But Dorian rejects her and takes up with Gwendolyn Wotton. Dorian notices changes in his portrait, but a lab analysis reveals no decomposition of the chemicals. He sends an apology to Sybil, but Henry brings the news that she's thrown herself in front of traffic and is dead. After Dorian sells some property to Mrs. Patricia Ruxton and makes love to her in the stable, he observes more distressing changes in the portrait and hides it in the attic. Years pass. Dorian needs more experiences and enters the world of the pornographic cinema. He seduces friend Alan Campbell's wife. Running into Basil before the latter leaves for Paris, Dorian perversely shows him the portrait, then stabs him. The portrait's hands now have blood on them. Back to the present: Dorian blackmails chemist Alan into destroying the body. In a club, Sybil's brother James hears Dorian called "Sir Galahad" and accosts him. But in the light, Dorian looks too young to be the man who caused Sybil's death. Later he learns the truth. Following Dorian to his estate at Selby, Vane is accidentally shot by sportsmen. Alan dies by a sleeping pill overdose. Dorian finds his portrait disgusting and stabs himself. His body ages, his portrait is restored.

Review: "Has nothing to compare with the rich, decadent '45 version." (*Castle of Frankenstein* 16, July 1970, p. 62)

Analysis: This West German–Italian–British co-production is a dreadful, often laughable updating of the famous novel. The filmmakers here have the nerve to include a line of dialogue about the "epigrams of Oscar Wilde." What were they thinking when they had Berger stab himself rather than the portrait? Best scene: the veteran character and supporting actor Herbert Lom entering the shower with Berger. That's a riot! Berger's claim to fame was the previous year's critically acclaimed Italian production *The Damned*. We'd like to see a version from directors Martin Scorsese or James Ivory. Or even a better "exploitation" version.

The Pit and the Pendulum *see under*
The Fall of the House of Usher

Planet of the Apes
(20th Century–Fox, 1968; 112 min.)
****

Produced by Arthur P. Jacobs. Associate Producer, Mort Abrahams. Directed by Franklin Schaffner. Assistant Director, William Kissel. Screenplay, Michael Wilson and Rod Serling. Based on the novel *Monkey Planet* by Pierre Boulle. Director of Photography, Leon Shamroy. Color, DeLuxe. Panavision. Music, Jerry Goldsmith. Costumes, Morton Haack.

Cast: George Taylor (Charlton Heston), Zira (Kim Hunter), Nova (Linda Harrison), Cornelius (Roddy McDowall), Dr. Zaius (Maurice Evans), Dodge (Jeff Burton), President of the Assembly (James Whitmore), Maximus (Woodrow Parfrey), Julius (Buck Kartalian), Lucius (Lou Wagner), Honorius (James Daly), Hunt leader (Norman Burton), Dr. Galen (Wright King), Minister (Paul Lambert).

Synopsis: On a spacecraft many light-years from Earth, NASA astronaut George Taylor makes final verbal reports to his home planet. Before injecting himself with a drug and entering a hibernation compartment, he ponders the possibility of a better planet than Earth. Three other astronauts — Landon, Dodge and the woman Stewart — are already in deep sleep. The spacecraft crash-lands in a lake surrounded by desolate mountains and deserts. It's 3950 A.D. Taylor and the two men awake and make it to shore with their raft and some supplies. Stewart, now a corpse, was killed by an air leak. The men have only a three day's supply of water, but they find some plants and a stream. While bathing, their clothes are stolen. Pursuing the thieves, they find humanoids, nay, humans like themselves, only mute. Taylor theorizes that if this is the best of the bunch, he and his pals will be running the planet in a week. The natives hear a noise in the surrounding woods and rush off. The earthmen do likewise and find that the pursuers are apes — on horseback, firing rifles. Taylor is wounded in the neck and cannot tell his captors that he's come from a distant world. Eventually he regains his voice and receives help from scientist apes Zira and

Cornelius. However, Dr. Zaius wants Taylor gelded. There is a hearing. Taylor cannot convince his interrogators of his birthplace. He escapes with the woman Nova, Zira and Cornelius. Pursued by Zaius, they enter the Forbidden Zone. Capturing Zaius, Taylor wrests the concession that he and Nova be allowed to proceed. Zaius tells Taylor he may not like what he finds. Up the coast, Taylor dismounts from his horse, looking with surprise at some large structure he finally realizes is the Statue of Liberty. He's back on Earth, which ages ago — while he was in space — blew itself up.

Reviews: "Interesting in a boring sort of way. The central situation is attractive and the physical details are ingenious, but the story development is unaspiring and the dialogue stultifying." (Robert Hatch, *Nation*, March 11, 1968, p. 356) ¶ "A very entertaining movie.... At times, it has the primitive force of old *King Kong*. It isn't a difficult or subtle movie; you can just sit back and enjoy it." (Pauline Kael, *New Yorker*, February 17, 1968, p. 108) ¶ "On the screen the story has been reduced from Swiftian satire to self-parody.... The best thing about the film results from Producer Arthur P. Jacobs' decision to allocate $1,000,000 for masks and costumes." (*Time*, February 23, 1968, p. 95)

Analysis: This was a huge hit and deservedly so, but the best part is the first half-hour when the audience doesn't know exactly what awaits the three astronauts trudging over eerie and beautiful terrain. (The filmmakers must be credited with finding western locales that were unfamiliar to most viewers.) The ending was a shocker — unless you waited too long to see it and heard about it from friends or classmates. In truth, the filmmakers wanted it both ways: adventure and allegory. The many "hip" lines and attitudes label this a definitive sixties movie. For instance, the "trust no one over 30" motto is run out. Its Academy Award for makeup should have gone to *2001: A Space Odyssey*.

Beneath the Planet of the Apes
(20th Century–Fox, 1970; 95 min.)
**½

Directed by Ted Post. Screenplay, Paul

Scientists Zira (Kim Hunter, left foreground) and Cornelius (Roddy McDowall, right foreground) observe George Taylor (Charlton Heston), the human specimen brought before them in *Planet of the Apes* (Twentieth Century–Fox, 1968).

Dehn. Based on a story by Paul Dehn and Mort Abrahams from characters created by Pierre Boulle. Edited by Marion Rothman. Director of Photography, Milton Krasner. Color, DeLuxe. Music, Leonard Rosenman. Sound, Stephen Bass, David Dockendorf. Art Direction, Jack Martin Smith, William Creber. Set Decoration, Walter M. Scott, Sven Wickman. Wardrobe, Morton Haack. Makeup, John Chambers and Dan Striepeke.

Cast: Brent (James Franciscus), Taylor (Charlton Heston), Nova (Linda Harrison), Dr. Zaius (Maurice Evans), Mendez (Paul Richards), Fat man (Victor Buono), Ursus (James Gregory), Albina (Natalie Trundy), Caspay (Jeff Corey), Minister (Thomas Gomez), Cornelius (David Watson), Negro (Don Pedro Colley), Skipper (Tod Andrews), Verger (Gregory Sierra), Gorilla sergeant (Eldon Burke), Lucius (Lou Wagner).

Synopsis: During the opening credits the ending of *Planet of the Apes* is recapped, with Taylor discovering the wrecked Statue of Liberty. Then he and Nova proceed on

horseback further into the Forbidden Zone. Scene shift to another wrecked spaceship. Its captain dies, leaving Brent to figure out his location. They'd followed Taylor's trajectory and gone through a bend in time. It's now 3955 A.D. After burying the captain, Brent sees a woman on a horse. It's Nova. Brent recognizes Taylor's dogtags. She takes him to observe a city. "My God, it's, it's a city of apes." The ape general is making a speech about invading and conquering the Forbidden Zone. When she hears that "the only good human is a dead human," Zira is aghast. Nova leads Brent to the home of Cornelius and Zira, who give them food and warn Brent to wear the skins of the planet's indigenous humans or else he'll be dissected and killed. On their way back to the interior, Brent and Nova are captured, but Zira manages to unlock their cage. The duo discover a cave that leads to ruins of the twentieth century's

Queensborough Plaza subway stop in New York City. "My God, did we finally do it?" asks Brent. Back at ape city, the young demonstrate for peace, but the invasion begins. Brent and Nova explore the tunnel, finding the remains of the New York Public Library, Radio City Music Hall and a cathedral at 51st Street. They are watched by a species of human different from Nova's. These use telepathic powers to communicate. They think that Brent can tell them about the ape plans. They make him attempt to drown, then strangle Nova. Brent learns that these people's god is a still-armed missile, which they call a holy weapon of peace. The apes advance, and the telepathics prepare to destroy them with "holy fallout." Brent is put in a cell with Taylor. One of the telepathics uses his power to make them fight each other, but Nova hears and interrupts and Taylor kills their nemesis. The apes enter the tunnels. Nova is killed. Taylor and Brent try to prevent detonation of the missile, but the dying Taylor's hand depresses the detonator. A voice says the third insignificant planet from the sun is now dead.

Reviews: "Lots of favorite mid-50's SF clichés in somewhat hasty sequel to slightly overrated *Apes* original.... Brisk direction by Ted Post compensates for plot familiarity, but not for telltale signs of production cost-cutting. Some fine visuals, nevertheless." (*Castle of Frankenstein* 16, July 1970, p. 53) ¶"Blown-up matinee serial, that blows up (literally), but really blew it by not deepening the concept of the original." (*Show*, July 9, 1970, p. 43)

Analysis: Sequels compromise originals. Edges are lost. This is not about the future, rather about the era in which the film was made — e.g., anti–Vietnam war and anti-nuclear protests, young vs. old. Withal, it moves quickly and is quite entertaining. Natalie Trundy is Albina. In *Escape from the Planet of the Apes* she will play Dr. Branton. In *Conquest of the Planet of the Apes* and *Battle for the Planet of the Apes* she'll be Lisa. Trundy was producer Jacobs's wife.

Escape from the Planet of the Apes

(20th Century–Fox, 1971; 98 min.) **

Arthur P. Jacobs Production. Associate

Producer, Frank Capra, Jr. Directed by Don Taylor. Screenplay, Paul Dehn. Based on characters created by Pierre Boulle. Edited by Marion Rothman. Director of Photography, Joseph Biroc. Panavision. Color, DeLuxe. Music, Jerry Goldsmith. Art Direction, Jack Martin Smith, William Creber. Set Decoration, Walter M. Scott, Stuart A. Reiss. Creative Makeup Design, John Chambers. Makeup Supervision, Dan Striepeke. Makeup Artist, Jack Barron. Special Photographic Effects, Howard A. Anderson.

Cast: Cornelius (Roddy McDowall), Zira (Kim Hunter), Dr. Lewis Dixon (Bradford Dillman), Armando (Ricardo Montalban), Dr. Stephanie Branton (Natalie Trundy), Dr. Otto Hasslein (Eric Braeden), President (William Windom), Milo (Sal Mineo), E-1 (Albert Salmi), E-2 (Jason Evers), Chairman (John Randolph), General Brody (Steve Roberts), Aide-Captain (M. Emmet Walsh), Cardinal (Peter Forster), Lawyer (Roy E. Glenn, Sr.). With James Sikking.

Synopsis: A spacecraft is found floating off the southern California coast, but the three astronauts are apes! Taken to the Los Angeles Zoo infirmary, they converse with each other but not the humans. Dr. Milo believes they have traveled 2,000 years into the past and urges his companions to remain silent about earth's destruction. Dr. Dixon, a psychologist and veterinarian, is astounded by the female ape's intelligence. Finally Zira blurts out that she hates bananas. After Milo is strangled by the gorilla in the next cage, Zira and Cornelius decide Dixon and his associate Dr. Stephanie Branton can be trusted. The president convenes a commission of inquiry in Los Angeles. Zira tells them, "We came from your future" and convinces Cornelius to talk of Taylor, the astronaut they'd befriended. Cornelius admits, "We saw the earth destroyed." Panelist and presidential science advisor Dr. Otto Hasslein gives his opinion of the apes' story on TV. He explains how time is a freeway with an infinite number of lanes. If man changes lanes, he can change the future. Become celebrities, the apes are given a suite at the Beverly Wilshire and begin speaking engagements and tours. Cornelius finds a prizefight barbaric. At the Los Angeles County Museum of Natural History, Zira faints and tells Hasslein she's pregnant. Back at the hotel, she sips "Grapejuice+" (wine) and tells Hasslein more about the future war and the white light and "tornado" in space they witnessed from their spacecraft. Hasslein talks to the president about 3955 A.D. and requests permission to execute the apes. The president only agrees to have the commission secretly interrogate the apes at Camp 11. Cornelius thinks a manmade weapon was responsible for the earth's destruction. He relates a story of ape prehistory, when a plague killed all dogs and cats, thus depriving man of pets. Men took apes as pet surrogates. After two centuries the apes could perform services. Then came Aldo, who articulated "No" to slavery. Zira admits under sodium pentothal that she dissected humans and performed brain surgery (lobotomies) to stimulate atrophied speech centers. The tape of her remarks is sent to the president. The result: Zira's pregnancy is to be terminated and she and Cornelius sterilized. Cornelius and Zira escape. Dixon, who'd helped deliver babies for him, has no problem getting Armando of Armando's Circus to hide the apes. While another chimp and baby watch, Zira delivers and calls her baby Milo. Hasslein orders searches of zoos, menageries and circuses. Armando gives his St. Francis medal to Milo. Eventually the apes are supposed to leave the circus in the Everglades, where they can found a colony. Cornelius asks Dixon for a gun so they can kill themselves if found. Zira's suitcase is found, and Hasslein spots Cornelius at a dockside refinery area. On a derelict ship, Hasslein shoots the baby and mortally wounds Zira but is himself killed by Cornelius, who in turn is shot by the police. Zira tosses the baby overboard, then collapses on the body of Cornelius. At the circus, Armando talks to a baby chimp wearing the St. Francis medal. The baby says, "Mama."

Review: "I cannot think of any fantasy film *series* that has evolved as dynamically or as inventively as these three films while maintaining so convincingly a continuous and consistent storyline.... Don Taylor has directed the screenplay's very difficult turnabout in mood, from comedy to tragedy, smoothly and with a gradual ease

that evens out the harsh contrasts yet deepens the impact of the concluding portion...." (Frederick S. Clarke, *Cinefantastique*, Fall 1971, p. 28)

Analysis: It holds the interest and there are some thought-provoking concepts here, and Hasslein, though we find him pernicious, has the ability to question himself. In real life none of this would happen, of course. That is, any intelligent apes that came from outer space wouldn't be summarily dismissed and plans made for their sterilization. Imagine the scientists, ACLU lawyers, and media members who'd be pounding on the gates. Truly asinine is the goal of releasing the apes in the Everglades to found a colony.

Conquest of the Planet of the Apes
(20th Century–Fox, 1972; 87 min.)
*½

Produced by Arthur P. Jacobs. Directed by J. Lee Thompson. Assistant Director, David "Buck" Hall. Screenplay, Paul Dehn. Based on characters created by Pierre Boulle. Edited by Marjorie Fowler and Allan Jaggs. Director of Photography, Bruce Surtees. Color, De-Luxe. Music, Tom Scott. Sound, Herman Lewis, Don Bassman. Art Direction, Philip Jefferies. Set Decoration, Norman Rockett.

Cast: Caesar (Roddy McDowall), Governor Breck (Don Murray), Armando (Ricardo Montalban), Lisa (Natalie Trundy), MacDonald (Hari Rhodes), Kolp (Severn Darden), Bus boy (Lou Wagner), Hoskyns (H. M. Wynant).

Synopsis: "North America—1991": Armando of Armando's Old-Time Circus arrives in the city by helicopter to promote his entertainment. In tow is the ape Caesar, who can speak but does not for fear he will be killed. He observes with horror the apes made slaves of a gestapo-like state. As the offspring of Cornelius and Zira, Caesar poses a threat to the future of humankind, and Governor Breck is only too eager to change that future. Under suspicion and interrogated, Armando tries to break free and falls to his death through a window. Breck discovers Caesar's ancestry and believes he has him executed by electrocution, but MacDonald secretly turned off the power. Caesar rouses the ape slaves, who attack and rout the police and capture

Breck. Caesar warns him of the coming storm: "Tonight we have seen the birth of the planet of the apes!"
Review: "Handsomely produced ... deftly directed ... and well-written...." (Murf., *Variety*, June 14, 1972, p. 18)
Analysis: Some thought this was a solid entry in the series while others, including your authors, rated it stinko when we first saw it at the Coleman Barracks theater in Sandhofen, West Germany. Ricardo Montalban as Armando? Don Murray is the last angry man: "This will be the end of civilization and the world will belong to a planet of apes!" It is all too obvious to even the most undiscriminating viewer that the "hordes" of apes battling humans are no more than scores or perhaps a couple hundred. We sneered at ads proclaiming the epic scope of this production. Night scenes hide the dearth of promised multitudes. All this said, a second viewing causes us to revise our opinion. It's not a bomb. The *Variety* review pointed out that the scriptwriter was careful to match the violence with the "gross injustices" wrought against the apes. We like Roddy McDowall's character. Why is his name Caesar, not Milo—for protection? It's only twenty years after Zira and Cornelius died and their child was born. What about the two centuries that were to pass after the dog and cat plague during which time the apes learned to perform services and Aldo to speak? (Perhaps that's an alternate future.)

Battle for the Planet of the Apes
(20th Century–Fox, 1973; 86 min.)
*½

Produced by Arthur P. Jacobs. Associate Producer, Frank Capra, Jr. Directed by J. Lee Thompson. Screenplay, John William Corrington, Joyce Hooper Corrington. Story, Paul Dehn. Based on characters created by Pierre Boulle. Edited by Allan L. Jaggs, John C. Horger. Director of Photography, Richard H. Kline. Panavision. DeLuxe Color. Music, Leonard Rosenman. Art Direction, Dale Hennesy.
Cast: Caesar (Roddy McDowall), General Aldo (Claude Akins), Lawgiver (John Huston), Lisa (Natalie Trundy), Kolp (Severn Darden), Mandemus (Lew Ayres), Virgil (Paul Williams), MacDonald (Austin Stoker),

Teacher (Noah Keen), Mutant captain (Richard Eastham), Alma (France Nuyen), Mendez (Paul Stevens), Doctor (Heather Lowe), Cornelius (Bobby Porter), Jake (Michael Stearns), Soldier (Cal Wilson), Young chimp (Pat Cardi), Jake's friend (John Landis), Motorcycle mutant (Andy Knight).
Synopsis: In North America, 2670 A.D., the Lawgiver ape speaks of the past: In the twentieth century an atomic holocaust reduced mankind's numbers and relegated him to a primitive state, working with but subservient to the apes they so recently mastered. The ape Caesar wonders if he can learn something of the future by visiting the archives in the ruined city of Los Angeles. He, orangutan Virgil and human MacDonald arm themselves and make the trek. They find the tape of the presidential commission that interrogated Caesar's parents, but they also find surviving, semimutated humans, including Kolp, now the "mayor." He tries to capture the trio, but they escape. Kolp organizes his "army" for pursuit. Back in "ape city," General Aldo, a gorilla, urges his kin to prepare for war. Overhearing the campfire conversation, Caesar's son Cornelius is discovered. Aldo cuts the branch he is on, and the child is mortally injured in the fall. Before Caesar can investigate properly, the humans attack. The battle seems to favor the humans until a ruse is used and they are captured. Aldo's band kills the fleeing Kolp. Shortly thereafter it is learned that Aldo was responsible for Cornelius's death, and since apes must not and have never killed another ape, he is ostracized. Pursued by Caesar up a tree, in the resulting confrontation Aldo falls to his death. MacDonald tells Caesar that humans and apes can live in peace as equals. Caesar complains about bad humans, but Virgil reminds him that Aldo was a bad ape. The weapons are reclaimed, but Mandemus, who's spent 27 years guarding them, says he's had enough. Nevertheless, Caesar believes they can't destroy them just yet. Flash forward 600 years in the future to the Lawgiver. He lectures to ape and human children before a statue of Caesar, which seems to shed a tear.
Review: "Characters this time out are formula-sketched.... sluggish tone." (Murf., *Variety*, May 23, 1973, p. 28)

Analysis: The dates are very confusing. The final battle ranks right down there with the worst in cinema history. As it begins, anyone can see that the apes outnumber the ramshackle and half-mutated attacking humans. As the battle winds down the human attackers outnumber the defenders! Strangely, this does not make the entire film execrable. Would that we saw more of the melted city. *Variety* (June 27, 1973, p. 9) had a full-page ad: "America Goes Ape!" and the film is said to have made $2,274,334 at 306 engagements.

The Premature Burial *see under* **The Fall of the House of Usher**

Poltergeist
(MGM/United Artists, 1982; 115 min.) ****

Produced by Steven Spielberg and Frank Marshall. Directed by Tobe Hooper. Screenplay, Steven Spielberg, Michael Grais, Mark Victor. Story, Steven Spielberg. Edited by Michael Kahn. Director of Photography, Matthew F. Leonetti. Metrocolor. Music, Jerry Goldsmith. Dolby Stereo. Set Decoration, Cheryal Kearney. Visual Effects Supervision, Richard Edlund. Special Visual Effects, Industrial Light & Magic.

Cast: Steve Freeling (Craig T. Nelson), Diane Freeling (JoBeth Williams), Dr. Lesh (Beatrice Straight), Dana (Dominique Dunne), Robbie (Oliver Robins), Carol Anne (Heather O'Rourke), Tangina (Zelda Rubinstein), Marty (Martin Casella), Ryan (Richard Lawson), Mrs. Tuthill (Virginia Kiser), Tuthill (Michael McManus), Teague (James Karen).

Synopsis: Developer Steve Freeling lives in Cuesta Verde, one of his employer's new housing tracts. Daughter Carol Anne begins talking to the television. "They're here," she says and soon disappears. Her family hears her voice but cannot locate her. Paranormal investigators are called in and record demon-like specters. The investigators in turn bring in psychic Tangina, who radiates confidence. She offers to enter Carol Anne's bedroom — a maelstrom of moving furniture and toys — but Diane convinces her that since neither has had this experience, she as the mother should enter. "You're right! You go!" shouts Tangina. Secured tenuously by a rope, Diane

enters the other dimension, finds her daughter and is pulled *down* into the living room, covered with slime. While preparing to leave for another residence, Diane is closed out of her own house as a storm approaches. She slips into the water-filled hole that was to become a swimming pool. Mud-covered skeletons and coffins spurt to the surface beside her. Diane finally crawls free and with Steve's help rescues their family before the house implodes. Steve had learned that his boss Teague had built Cuesta Verde over a cemetery. The Freelings enter a motel room. A few seconds later the television is sent careening onto the balcony.

Reviews: "The filmmakers work on us, scaring us over and over, yet most of the visual effects are startling, and some are shockingly beautiful.... The movie is scary but not sadistic, violent but not bloody (except for one short scene).... A hokey 'serious' idea is churning around under all the thrills." (David Denby, *New York*, June 7, 1982, p. 71) ¶"Marvelously spooky ghost story...." (Vincent Canby, *New York Times*, June 4, 1982, p. C16) ¶"A riveting demonstration of the movies' power to scare the sophistication out of any viewer.... creates honest thrills...." (Richard Corliss, *Time*, May 31, 1982, p. 56)

Analysis: Could the 1962 *Twilight Zone* episode "Little Girl Lost" have inspired this humorous, thrilling and chilling film? The effects are topnotch. Why does this movie have a warm feel to it? Because evil doesn't win? Because there's no trick ending? The *New York Times* review found it "witty" in a way Hitchcock might have liked. It's a perfect film to see on the big screen with a big audience. Academy Award nominations for music score, sound editing and visual effects.

Poltergeist II: The Other Side
(MGM/United Artists, 1986; 92 min.) **½

Produced by Mark Victor. Directed by Brian Gibson. Screenplay, Mark Victor and Michael Grais. Edited by Thom Noble. Director of Photography, Andrew Laszlo. Panavision. Metrocolor. Music, Jerry Goldsmith. Dolby Stereo. Special Sound Effects Design,

Frank Serafine. Set Decoration, George R. Nelson. Visual Effects, Richard Edlund. Special Effects, Michael Lantieri, Clay Pinney, Doug DeGrazzie, Bill Aldridge, Albert Delgado. Creatures, Steve Johnson, Randall William Cook. Conceptual Artist, H. R. Giger. Paranormal Research, Terri Barrile. Paranormal Phenomena Advisor, Kevin Ryerson. Psychic Advisor, Jill Cook.

Cast: Diane Freeling (JoBeth Williams), Steve Freeling (Craig T. Nelson), Carol Anne Freeling (Heather O'Rourke), Robbie Freeling (Oliver Robins), Tangina Barrons (Zelda Rubinstein), Taylor (Will Sampson), Kane (Julian Beck), Gramma Jess (Geraldine Fitzgerald), Old Indian (John P. Whitecloud), Vomit creature (Noble Craig), Daughter (Susan Peretz), Mother (Helen Boll), Young Jess (Kelly Jean Peters), Young Diane (Jaclyn Bernstein).

Synopsis: After losing their house, the Freelings experience financial difficulties. For one thing, they can't collect insurance on a house that just disappeared. Meanwhile, the native American sage Taylor arrives in Cuesta Verde. Tangina takes him underneath the Freeling swimming pool where there are skeletons — and a presence. At a mall, Carol Anne sees a man dressed in black through whom other people walk and through whom he can walk. He seems pleasant enough, however, and sings a song to her. At home, she gets a phone call from Gramma. She learns next morning that her grandmother died. As a strange cloud approaches the house, Diane dreams of being pulled underground. Carol Anne's toys begin moving. Steve and Diane rush to her room and find her in the corner. "They're back," says she. Taylor introduces himself to the Freelings and informs Steve that he can make a difference, that he can control the forces arrayed against his family, that he too can be a warrior and defeat Kane. Tangina tells Diane that Carol Anne is truly clairvoyant, as was her grandmother and as is Diane. She shows her photos of Kane and his followers and explains how all died underground when Kane said the end of the world was coming. Kane is now a beast. The human manifestation of Kane has almost fooled Steve into letting him into the house. Taylor informs Steve that they can only defeat the beast by surprising him: Return to Cuesta Verde. When

his current house is invaded by spirits, Steve is convinced, and they jump in the station wagon and light out. Tangina awaits them and guides them into the pit. Horrified at the skeletons of those who died needlessly, Diane sees Kane's remains, and she and Carol Anne are whisked into his dimension. Steve hears Taylor chanting and takes his directions to jump with Robbie into his fire. The family is reunited, but Carol Anne is grabbed by the demon. Taylor sends Steve a lance with which he impales it. But Carol Anne spins away and Taylor thinks he's lost her. Yet she reappears, framed by the image of Gramma. The Freelings find themselves back in the excavation. When topside, Taylor asks for Steve's car, which the latter gladly gives him.

Reviews: "Never has the hardness or urgency of the first." (Michael Wilmington, *Los Angeles Times Calendar,* May 23, 1986, p. 1) ¶"Based on an old Hollywood credo: 'When you hit on a money-making proposition, drive it into the ground until nobody can stand it anymore.'" (Rex Reed, *New York Post,* May 23, 1986, p. 21)

Analysis: With the principals back, it's a shame they couldn't engage in a compelling story. Perhaps they try to explain too much and that's why this has such little impact. The final confrontation in the other dimension isn't long enough. Was Kane really defeated, or did the filmmakers know there would be a third series entry? Were the Freelings really down and out? They were shopping at a swank mall.

Poltergeist III
(MGM, 1988; 97 min.) **

Produced by Barry Bernardi. Executive Producer, Gary Sherman. Directed by Gary Sherman. Screenplay, Gary Sherman and Brian Taggert. Edited by Ross Albert. Director of Photography, Alex Nepomniaschy. Technicolor. Music, Joe Renzetti. Dolby Stereo. Art Direction, Steve Graham. Set Decoration, Linda Lee Sutton. Stunts, Ben R. Scott. Special Makeup Design, John Caglione, Jr., Doug Drexler. Special Effects Makeup, Dick Smith. Visual Effects Design, Gary Sherman.

Cast: Bruce Gardner (Tom Skerritt), Patricia Gardner (Nancy Allen), Carol Anne Freeling

(Heather O'Rourke),Tangina Barrons (Zelda Rubinstein), Donna Gardner (Lara Flynn Boyle), Scott (Kip Wentz), Dr. Seaton (Richard Fire), Kane (Nathan Davis), Burt (Roger May), Martin (Paul Graham), Sandy (Meg Weldon), Jeff (Joey Garfield), Melissa (Stacy Gilchrist), Dusty (Chris Murphy), Nathan (Roy Hytower), Deborah (Meg Thalken), Takamitsu (Dean Tokuno), Marcie (Catherine Gatz), Helen (Paty Lombard), Mary (E. J. Murray), Mrs. Seaton (Sherry Narens), Bill (Phil Locker), Old woman (Maureen Steindler). With Alan Wilder, Brent Shaphren, Mindy Bell, Maureen Mueller, Conrad Allen, John Rusk, Sam Sanders, Laurie V. Logan, Jerry Birn, Jane Alderman.

Synopsis: Carol Anne Freeling is having an extended visit with uncle Bruce and Aunt Pat in the new Chicago skyscraper whose operations are managed by Bruce. She attends a school for very bright children with developmental or emotional problems. The therapist Seaton believes that Carol Anne might be able to induce mass hypnosis but pooh-poohs the notion that she's ever encountered truly extraordinary events. Carol Anne begins seeing apparitions. Back in California, psychic Tangina realizes that the spirit Kane has once more found Carol Anne. He appears to the girl and implores her to bring him and his followers into the light. Carol Anne, cousin Donna and her boyfriend Scott are sucked into a pool of water in the parking garage. Scott reappears in the swimming pool and tries to convince Bruce and a skeptical Dr. Seaton that something weird is happening. Bruce and Pat begin to believe when Tangina arrives and explains how Kane needs the innocence of Carol Anne to give him strength and bring him into the light. She says Kane cannot succeed as long as someone on this side loves Carol Anne. Tangina "disappears" during a battle with Kane's forces only to reappear and give her necklace to Pat. After setting fire to the ice-bound cars controlled by Kane in the garage, Bruce and Pat think they're home free, but they find the dead Dr. Seaton, killed by the false Donna. Bruce chases who he thinks is Carol Anne. He remembers Tangina's admonition of "outside in" and with Pat uses a window cleaning scaffold to break into Carol Anne's room. Pat brandishes the necklace

against the dark powers. Kane appears, as does Tangina, who tells the spirit *she* will lead him into the light.

Review: "Visually drab, perfunctory sequel.... You've never seen so many close-ups and hammy performances." (Bill Kelley, *Cinefantastique*, January 1989, p. 118) ¶"Routine spook show." (Bill Kaufman, *Newsday*, June 10, 1988, Part III, p. 5)

Analysis: This sequel is unnecessary but not unwatchable — for the first half. It's almost a "confined spaces" movie, most of the action taking place in the skyscraper. There's *House* and *Ghostbusters*, of course, and the shopping mall in *Dawn of the Dead*, but we think someone could come up with a *Die Hard* movie in which the Bruce Willis character does battle with ghosts and demons in a high-rise. There is good continuity with its predecessors. *Poltergeist III* sinks in the second half. Skerritt and Allen seem to take the demonic forces in stride, in this way reminiscent of Grade B '50s sci-fi and horror films in which the characters aren't worried enough. Nancy Allen's character undergoes unmotivated (unreasonable) character changes. Both Skerritt and Allen inexplicably believe they've won after blowing up the cars — and they make plans for a night of passion. But Carol Anne's not back yet, and their daughter (who's really a demonic duplicate) is in a state of shock. While we could accept Tangina's insights in episode one, in this her views seem empty balderdash. What, exactly, is the light into which Tangina leads Kane? It's best not to ask too many questions.

The Possession *see* Amityville II: The Possession *under* **The Amityville Horror**

Predator
(20th Century–Fox, 1987; 107 min.)
****

Produced by Lawrence Gordon. Directed by John McTiernan. Assistant Directors, Beau E. L. Marks, J. Tom Archuleta, K. C. Colwell, Jose Luis Ortega. Screenplay, Jim Thomas and John Thomas. Edited by John F. Link and Mark Helfrich. Director of Photography,

Donald McAlpine. Color, DeLuxe. Music, Alan Silvestri. Dolby Stereo. "Long Tall Sally" by R. Penniman, E. Johnson, R. Blackwell. Art Direction, Frank Richwood, Jorge Saenz, John K. Reinhart, Jr. Set Decoration, Enrique Estevez. Makeup Design, Scott Eddo. Special Effects, Al DiSarro, Laurencio "Chob" Cordero. Special Visual Effects, R/Greenberg. Creature created by Stan Winston. Stunts, Craig R. Baxley.

Cast: "Dutch" (Arnold Schwarzenegger), Dillon (Carl Weathers), Mac (Bill Duke), Anna (Elpidia Carrillo), Blain (Jesse Ventura), Billy (Sonny Landham), Poncho (Richard Chaves), Hawkins (Shane Black), General Phillips (R. G. Armstrong), Predator (Kevin Peter Hall).

Synopsis: Dutch and his mercenaries arrive in Central America at the behest of General Phillips. As it transpires, they have also been called by Dillon, CIA, a former pal. They are supposed to fly a helicopter across the border and rescue a cabinet minister. The raid on the guerrilla encampment is successful, but there's no cabinet minister. Dutch realizes Dillon has used them. In any event, they have to escape with one woman guerrilla in tow. Heading into a valley that will take them to a chopper pick-up site, Billy, the American Indian member of the team, stares into the forest, knowing there's something hiding in the trees. Not long thereafter their numbers begin to be depleted by an unknown terror that camouflages itself in the jungle. "There's something out there waiting for us and it ain't no man. We're all gonna die," says Billy matter-of-factly. "If it bleeds we can kill it," says Dutch. But all attempts fail till only Dutch and the woman remain. Urging her to escape and find the helicopter, he leads the alien a merry chase and is saved only by the fact that he ends up covered in mud. The creature, now visible in its body armor, fails to detect Dutch's body heat. Dutch creates traps and makes a bow and arrow. He cries into the night, arousing the creature, who seeks its escaped quarry. In a one-on-one confrontation without weapons, the creature still has the advantage, but Dutch finally kills it in a deadfall. However, with its dying breath it activates a self-destruct mechanism. Dutch flees the resulting eruption and is picked up by General Phillips and the woman.

Reviews: "Production is high tech and the script, and its values and mentality, are Stone Age." (Michael Wilmington, *Los Angeles Times Calendar,* June 12, 1987, p. 6) ¶"*Predator*'s one claim to fame, finally, is in contributing to the process whereby a Schwarzenegger (or a Stallone) can come to embody the common man...." (Adam Barker, *Monthly Film Bulletin,* January 1988, p. 19) ¶"Ultimately, a stomach-turning fairy tale inside a monstrous, enchanted forest." (Leo Seligsohn, *Newsday,* June 12, 1987, Part III, p. 5) ¶"*Predator* moves at a breakneck pace, it has strong and simple characterizations, it has good location photography and terrific special effects, and it supplies what it claims to supply: An effective action movie." (Roger Ebert, *New York Post,* June 12, 1987, p. 27)

Analysis: We are perhaps the only two people alive who consider this one of our favorite movies, a film we could watch with enjoyment every few months. There is excellent cinematography, exciting action scenes, tension, the proper locale, and a smidgen of humor (Arnold's "Stick around" to a stabbed victim) making this a worthy *Alien* clone and a film to be enjoyed again and again. Filmed in Mexico.

Predator 2
(20th Century–Fox, 1990; 108 min.)
⋆⋆½

Produced by Joel Silver, Lawrence Gordon and John Davis. Directed by Stephen Hopkins. Screenplay, James and John Thomas. Edited by Mark Goldblatt. Director of Photography, Peter Levy. Color. Music, Alan Silvestri. Art Direction, Geoff Hubbard. Special Effects, Ken Pepiot. Visual Effects, R/Greenberg Associates, J. W. Kompare. Creature created by Stan Winston.

Cast: Mike Harrigan (Danny Glover), Predator (Kevin Peter Hall), Peter Keyes (Gary Busey), Leona Cantrell (Maria Conchita Alonso), Danny Archuleta (Ruben Blades), Jerry Lambert (Bill Paxton), Captain Pilgrim (Kent McCord), Garber (Adam Baldwin), Colombian girl (Teri Weigel).

Synopsis: In the near future, L.A. gangs battle it out in the streets with state-of-the-art weaponry. The police mop up but find strangely ravaged bodies. Policeman Mike Harrigan investigates. Peter Keyes

Kevin Peter Hall reprises his monstrous predator role in *Predator 2* (Twentieth Century–Fox, 1990)

seems to know something but has secrets, like a special unit prepared to capture the murderer. Harrigan discovers that an alien caused the deaths. Keyes's unit attempts to capture the creature in a warehouse but is unsuccessful. Keyes himself is killed. Harrigan gives the creature a run for its money. They battle on a rooftop and Harrigan chops off one of its hands with its own weapon. However, the hand regenerates. Harrigan falls into a tunnel, discovers a spaceship and kills the monster. The alien crew materialize but allow Harrigan to live because he proved himself a worthy opponent. Harrigan races out of the tunnel and away from the ship as it blasts off.

Review: "Predator 2 is high of tech and low of brow.... The special effects are imaginative, but ... squandered on an essentially mindless enterprise." (Desmond Ryan, *Philadelphia Inquirer*, November 23, 1990, p. 5)

Analysis: Predator 2 is worthy; it's a good action film, well acted, tautly paced, and generally quite enjoyable. Unlike *Aliens*, however, which took its precursor as its point of departure and went on from there, *Predator 2* only puts its feet down in the tracks left by the first film and never really tries to go off in its own direction. This lack of innovation puts it in the category of those sequels that were really unnecessary.

Second impression: The film raises more questions than it answers. A sequel should *answer* some questions, not just ask the same ones over again. Take the scene in the cemetery. Was it there just to suggest that our Predator had taken a special interest in cop Danny Glover, and was out to taunt him with one of Reuben Blades' possessions? To the point of following him to the cemetery? And how did it manage to get from there to the subway scene with Bill Paxton and Maria Conchita Alonso in what seems to be mere moments? For that matter, how did it manage to single out the subway train Paxton and Alonso were on, or was this all just a coincidence? The preceding would seem to suggest that there was perhaps more than one Predator stalking these guys, yet we know this is not the case. Confused (or confusing) editing is more than likely the answer.

The Progeny *see* Basket Case 3 *under* Basket Case

Prom Night

(Avco Embassy, 1980; 91 min.) **

Produced by Peter Simpson. Directed by Paul Lynch. Screenplay, William Gray. Based on a story by Robert Guza, Jr. Edited by Brian Ravok. Director of Photography, Robert New. Color. Music, Carl Zittrer and Paul Zaza. Art Direction, Reuben Freed. Special Effects, Allan Cotter.

Cast: Kim Hammond (Jamie Lee Curtis), Mr. Hammond (Leslie Nielsen), Nick (Casey Stevens), Wendy (Eddie Benton), Mrs. Hammond (Antoinette Bower), Alex Hammond (Michael Tough), Sykes (Robert Silverman), Vicki (Pita Oliver), Drew (Jeff Wincott), Lou (David Mucci), Kelly (Marybeth Rubins), McBride (George Touliatos), Henri-Anne (Melanie Morse MacQuarrie), Fairchild (David Gardner), Jude (Joy Thompson).

Synopsis: Playing hide and seek in an abandoned school in 1968, a boy and three girls chase and frighten Robin Hammond, who falls to her death. The four responsible swear not to tell they caused the calamity. Six years later it's prom day at Alexander Hamilton Senior High School. The four responsible for Robin's death — Wendy, Nick, Kelly and Vicki — receive "obscene" phone calls. At the police station an officer reads the file on Leonard Murch, institutionalized as a schizophrenic six years previously. He's escaped and might be heading back to town. Meanwhile, Wendy is miffed that Nick is going to be prom king and escort her rival, Kim Hammond, who is queen. Wendy plans revenge. As the festivities proceed, a ski-masked man tracks and kills Kelly and Vicki, and after a long chase through empty school corridors, labs and shops, murders Wendy. He fails to get Nick, and Kim uses his own ax to bring him low. Removing the mask, she finds her brother Alex, who dies in her arms. He had witnessed his sister Robin's death and seen those responsible.

Reviews: "Efficient rather than stylish...." (Kevin Thomas, *Los Angeles Times*, August 18, 1980, Part VI, p. 4) ¶"Strictly for illiterates of the Third Kind, submoronic, that is." (Archer Winsten, *New York Post*, August 16, 1980, p. 9) ¶"Has got to be the sorriest rip-off of the year.... tediously demystifies the plot of *Halloween* by turning loose a very real madman among horny teenagers." (Tom Allen, *Village Voice*, August 27-September 2, 1980, p. 40)

Analysis: Prom Night is not supernatural, but its sequels are. *Prom Night* is simply a bald-faced clone of *Carrie* and *Halloween* complete with the latter's Jamie Lee Curtis. But would Ms. Curtis really be prom queen? Why is cute Vicki presented as a girl who can't get a date? Disco didn't start in 1974, did it? Andrea True was singing the top ten hit "More, More, More" in 1976, and *Saturday Night Fever* was 1977. The murderer's pursuit of Wendy *is* good, and there are enough red herrings to keep you guessing the murderer's identity. Leslie Nielsen and Antoinette Bower have little to do. Nielsen, captain of the space cruiser in 1956's *Forbidden Planet*, would make a greater impression this year in the spoof, *Airplane.*

Hello Mary Lou: Prom Night II
(Samuel Goldwyn/Simcom, 1986; 87 min.) **

Produced by Peter Simpson. Directed by Bruce Pittman. Screenplay, Ron Oliver. Edited by Nick Rotundo. Director of Photography, John Herzog. Color. Music, Paul Zaza. Art Direction, Sandy Kybartas.

Cast: Bill Nordham (Michael Ironside), Vicki Carpenter (Wendy Lyon), Craig Nordham (Justin Louis), Mary Lou Maloney (Lisa Schrage), Father Cooper (Richard Monette), Kelly Hennenlotter (Terri Hawkes), Beverly Hendry (Monica Waters). With Brock Simpson, Beth Gondek, Wendel Smith, Judy Mahbay.

Synopsis: The tragic highlight of Hamilton High's 1957 senior prom is a fire that kills class vamp Mary Lou Maloney, a fire caused by Mary Lou's scorned date, Billy Nordham after he catches her in a tryst with classmate Buck Cooper. Three decades later, Bill Nordham is principal at Hamilton High, where his son Craig is about to graduate. Craig is dating Vicki Carpenter, who has aspirations of becoming prom queen. Because her conservative mother isn't willing to spring for a new dress for the occasion, Vicki prowls through the school's overloaded prop room, where she stumbles across a locked trunk. Forcing the lock (an act occasioned by flashing lights and shattered glass upstairs), she discovers the gown and costume jewelry that were to be used at the ill-fated 1957 prom. Vicki carries the items to the art department. Strange events begin to occur almost immediately: One of the senior girls is killed by a malevolent, unseen force (a death that is taken for a suicide at the time). Both Buck Cooper, now Father Cooper, and Bill Nordham experience violent flashbacks of

their time with Mary Lou Maloney. More importantly, similar visions come to Vicki Carpenter, and she begins to show signs of a decided character change, becoming moody, prone to bursts of temper and growing increasingly intolerant of her parents' authority. Following her obscene outburst at Father Cooper, the priest suspects the true cause and conducts an ineffective ritual exorcism at Mary Lou's gravesite. The principal rejects his advice to take communion as a protective act. Vicki, now totally controlled by the malign spirit, kills the priest. Finding the priest's body in Mary Lou's grave erases Nordham's skepticism. He procures a loaded revolver and makes his way to the senior prom. Through her diabolical facilities, Vicki/Mary Lou is pronounced queen of the prom, at which moment Nordham unloads his pistol into her. From her collapsed form arises the grotesque, disfigured form of Mary Lou, who launches a furious telekinetic attack on all assembled. Bill Nordham she hauls down from his perch on the catwalk, slamming him with crippling force to the floor below. When she is attacked by Craig Nordham, she repels him easily, pursuing him with deliberate ease downstairs to the prop room. Just as she is about to deliver the *coup de grace*, the elder Nordham appears with the prom queen crown that would have been Mary Lou's in 1957. They embrace. When he places the crown upon her head, the two disappear in a flash. Craig struggles to his feet and finds the miraculously revived Vicki in the trunk that contained the relics from the earlier prom. As the two emerge from the shambles of the gym, they are greeted by Bill Nordham, now seeming none the worse for wear, and he hurries them to his car. The wicked leer he turns on them, and the fact that his formerly brown eyes are now a very Mary Lou blue, indicates that the worst is hardly over.

Review: "Essentially a remake of *Carrie* ... peppered with interesting hallucination sequences, heavily influenced by the *Nightmare on Elm Street* series, which elevates it beyond the usual dumb teenage possession film." (Judith P. Harris, *Cinefantastique*, March 1988, p. 117)

Analysis: While *Prom Night* was essentially one of the legion of *Halloween* clones to appear in the wake of John Carpenter's film, with a dash of *Carrie* thrown in during the senior prom, *Hello, Mary Lou: Prom Night II* tips its hat not only to those two films, but also to Craven's *Nightmare on Elm Street* in a number of dream/hallucination sequences, to *The Exorcist* for the scenes in the church with Father Cooper, to *Poltergeist* in the sequence in Vicki's bedroom, even to *Alien* in the way that Mary Lou's horribly disfigured form arises from the body of Vicki. That this Canadian production actually manages to derive from so many sources while maintaining some identity of its own is a fair enough compliment. That it also manages to hold its own as a worthy horror opus is an added accolade. Director Bruce Pittman manages to make the most of what could have been an unwieldy melange of elements. True, we've seen most of this stuff before, but *Prom Night II* manages to hold our attention through to its pyrotechnic, if unsurprising, finale. Wendy Lyon projects the appropriate degree of scrubbed blonde innocent, Vicki Carpenter, in the film's first half, while portraying the fleshy evil incarnate she becomes when possessed by the spirit of Mary Lou in the second. Michael Ironside, who is the only really familiar face in this production, delivers his usual solid, dependable performance as the alternately guilty and obsessed Bill Nordham. The third most notable presence in the film is that of Lisa Schrage, who brings the proper demonic spirit to the proceedings.

Prom Night III: The Last Kiss
(Norstar Entertainment/Comweb, 1989; 90 min.) *½

Produced by Ray Sager and Peter Simpson. Directed by Ron Oliver and Peter Simpson. Screenplay, Ron Oliver. Edited by Nick Rotundo. Director of Photography, Rhett Morita. Color. Music, Paul Zaza. Set Decoration, Brendan Smith. Special Effects, Light and Motion Corporation.

Cast: Alex Gray (Tim Conlon), Sarah (Cyndy Preston), Mary Lou Maloney (Courtney Taylor), Shane (David Stratton), Leonard (Jeremy Ratchford), Andrew (Dylan Neal), Mr. Weatherall (Roger Dunn), Mr. Walker (George Chuvalo), Miss Richards (Lesley Kelly), Leah (Juno Mills Cockell). With Terry Doyle, Robert Collins, Nicole Evans, Sabrina Boudot.

Synopsis: Hamilton High School's dead (1957) prom queen Mary Lou Maloney is attracted to living average high school student Alex Gray and makes life exciting for him by inserting As on his papers, helping him score touchdowns in football, and killing teachers and friends who get in her way. Alex appreciates the attention but already has a girlfriend, Sarah, whom Mary Lou tries to kill at the latest prom. Alex makes a bargain: He will accompany Mary Lou to the underworld if she leaves Sarah alone. However, Sarah follows Alex, and the duo fight their way to what they think is safety, only to discover that they've not yet left 1957. Sarah is killed.

Review: "Done with some style and humor." (Mick Martin and Marsha Porter, *Video Movie Guide 1994*, p. 847)

Analysis: Once you realize this Toronto-lensed film is a spoof — about five minutes into it — it's bearable. There are some amusing double entendres and in-jokes, but mostly it's cheap thrills and shoddy verisimilitude, e.g., the football field without yard lines. The first two films of this series were "straight" horror thrillers obviously indebted to *Halloween*, *Carrie* and a number of other precedents. This third installment is one of those tongue-in-cheek affairs that try hard to provide a giggle for every shiver, giving the viewer one or the other every minute. While competently put together, it fails to score very highly in either direction. For movies of this type to work at all, of course, depends largely upon whether one takes his horror straight or with laughs. Comedy thrillers stretch back to *The Old Dark House* and the Bob Hope/Paulette Goddard *The Ghost Breakers*, and the success of the *Ghostbusters* films provides ample evidence that the public still has an appetite for the genre. *Prom Night III* is a minor entry in a very minor series. Its level of competence is only moderate and its inspiration decidedly low.

Prom Night IV: Deliver Us from Evil
(Norstar Entertainment, 1991; 95 min.) *½

Produced by Ray Sager. Directed by Clay Borris. Screenplay, Richard Beattie. Edited by Stan Cole. Director of Photography, Rick Wincenty. Color, Kodak/Medallion. Music, Paul J. Zaza. Art Direction, Jasna Stefanovic. Set Decoration, Caroline Gee.

Cast: Meagan (Nikki de Boer), Mark (Alden Kane), Laura (Joy Tanner), Jeff (Alle Ghadban), Father Jonas (James Carver), Father Jaeger (Ken McGregor), Father Colin (Brock Simpson), Jennifer (Deni Delroy).

Synopsis: Prologue: A young priest prays for help to save whores. Then, at Hamilton High School's 1957 prom, Father Jonas kills lovers in a car. Fr. Jonas is discovered with the murder weapon — a metal crucifix — while flagellating himself. His hands begin to bleed. At St. George Church in 1991, Father Colin is assigned to care for Fr. Jonas, who has been strapped to a bed in an underground chamber since 1957. He is ordered never to reveal the existence of Jonas, who is possessed and must be contained. Colin decides to stop sedating his charge but pays with his life when Jonas breaks loose and strangles him. Two couples, Meagan and Mark, Laura and Jeff, forego the prom and are dropped off at a summer house that was once a monastery. Their weekend lovemaking is curtailed by the arrival of Jonas, who kills Jeff, Laura and Mark before Meagan sets him on fire in the woodshed. Next day, Meagan's eyes snap open just as those of the charred corpse open in another ambulance.

Review: "Okay ... despite wafer thin credibility." (Doch., *Variety*, May 27, 1991)

Analysis: While some of its heritage can be traced to *The Exorcist*, it's mostly the hoary every-woman's-a-slut tale. In that sense, it's indebted to *Psycho*, *Halloween*, *Prom Night*, ad infinitum. It has very little connection with its predecessors. There's no Mary Lou Maloney, for instance. It must be the same prom, though. Just think, in 1957 Hamilton High harbored a murderer, and at the nearby seminary demonic possession was at work. Is any audience not bored by observing at length the victims through the eyes of the victimizer? Placing the young Father Colin in charge of the possessed Jonas without an in-depth briefing is unreasonable. *Prom Night IV* is not primitive, but it's relatively low budget: few sets, few actors. What the sam hill are we supposed to make of the eye openings at the end? That Meagan's possessed by Jonas? That she knows he's still "alive"? Filmed in Ontario, Canada.

Puppet Master
(Full Moon/Paramount, 1989; 90 min.) **

Produced by Hope Perrello. Directed by David Schmoeller. Screenplay, Joseph G. Collodni. Story, Charles Band and Kenneth J. Hall. Director of Photography, Sergio Salvati. Music, Richard Band. Puppet Effects, David Allen Productions. Production Design, John Myhre.

Cast: Alex Whittaker (Paul LeMat), Dana Hadley (Irene Miracle), Frank Forrester (Matt Roe), Carissa Stamford (Kathryn O'Reilly), Theresa (Merrya Small), Neil Gallagher (Jimmie Skaggs), Megan Gallagher (Robin Frankes), Andre Toulon (William Hickey).

Synopsis: Prologue: Puppeteer Andre Toulon has managed to unearth ancient Egyptian methods of giving life to inanimate objects. The objects in question here are Toulon's troupe of grotesque puppets. Toulon has fallen afoul of certain foreign elements, whose hired assassins have tracked him to his refuge at the Bodega Bay Inn resort on the California coast. After secreting his beloved puppets in the walls of his room, Toulon thwarts his would-be assassins by committing a hasty suicide. Fifty years later, psychic Neil Gallagher locates the old puppet master's hiding place and recruits former associates Alex Whittaker, Dana Hadley, Carissa Stamford and Frank Forrester to come to the location to help him sort out the late Mr. Toulon's secrets. Upon arrival, they find themselves greeted by Megan Gallagher, Neil's young widow; it seems that the psychic killed himself shortly before his associates arrived. The first night of their stay at Bodega Bay Inn proves to also be the last for Dana, Frank and Carissa, who are visited by Toulon's puppets one by one and who meet grisly ends. Alex and Megan stumble upon Toulon's diary barely in time to learn their jeopardy and are about to escape from the inn when Neil Gallagher suddenly appears and stops them. He confesses that he has been responsible for all the murders and that he did, in fact, commit suicide in order to "live forever" utilizing old Toulon's discoveries. As the others had all been aides to his uncovering the lost secrets of Andre Toulon, Gallagher feels it necessary to do away with anyone who might also want to partake of this questionable "immortality." It is Gallagher's insufferable ego and disdain for Toulon's beloved (and quite deadly) puppets that prove to be his undoing, as the little marionettes turn on him and perform some gruesome mutilations.

Review: "The human characters ... are totally forgettable.... all sizzle and no steak." (Randy Pitman, *Library Journal*, November 15, 1989, p. 128)

Analysis: As is the case with so many horror films of the eighties, *Puppet Master* can't boast of having a genuine protagonist. Paul LeMat ostensibly fills the bill here, but the poor guy is totally overwhelmed by his circumstances. For most of the film he's seen aimlessly wandering the halls of the Bodega Bay Inn looking tired and bewildered. Irene Miracle does too well at being the "top mother bitch" to be at all likable, and her relentless bitchiness only earns her a well-deserved dispatching halfway through the film. Likewise, Roe and O'Reilly amuse themselves with constant fornication while their own death is woven about them. Having such a paucity of identifiable characters in a film only succeeds in lessening any impact the film would otherwise have. It simply makes all the actors fall into one of two types: victims or victimizers. In this particular case, all the characters are victims.

As a production, *Puppet Master* stands a notch or two above its material. The shots of the Bodega Bay Inn are well staged, particularly the ones in the film's prologue. Afterwards, with the inn being largely deserted, and most of the action being confined to the guests' separate rooms, the effect is somewhat lessened. This is unfortunate,

as there was ample opportunity to open things up in the agoraphobic manner of Stanley Kubrick's *The Shining*.

The puppet effects by David Allen Productions are adequate, but nothing compared to the virtuoso effects we've seen from similar films involving malicious homunculi (*Child's Play*, for example). Stop-motion effects are used sparsely; most of the time the puppets' movements are being achieved by the unseen hand of the effects man.

The puppets themselves are an assorted lot. The leader, so to speak, is a skeletal, white-faced chap with knives and hooks for hands and tiny spikes that emerge from shadowed eye-sockets whenever its interest is aroused. In his retinue is a rather malformed little fellow with longshoreman tags and a peanut-sized head, a ballerina/hooker puppet who discharges leeches from her mouth, and a rather forlorn-looking jester who doesn't seem to have much to do in the film other than sit and stare abjectly. Considering all the mayhem its more active cohorts inflict, the abject look is perhaps not terribly surprising.

Puppet Master II
(Full Moon, 1990; 90 min.) **

Produced by David DeCoteau and John Schoweiler. Executive Producer, Charles Band. Directed by David Allen. Screenplay, David Pabian. Story, Charles Band. Director of Photography, Thomas F. Denoue. Music, Richard Band. Production Design, Kathleen Coates. Puppet Effects, David Allen Productions.

Cast: Carolyn Bramwell/Elsa (Elizabeth Maclellan), Michael Kenney (Collin Bernsen), Patrick Bramwell (Gregory Webb), Wanda (Charlie Spradling), Andre Toulon/Eriquee Charnee (Steve Welles), Lance (Jeff Weston), Marge (Sage Allen), Cairo merchant (Ivan J. Rado), Matthew (George "Buck" Flower), Camille Kenney (Nita Talbot).

Synopsis: Strange goings-on in the small cemetery behind Bodega Bay Inn late one night: Small hands pour a noxious green potion into the open grave with the headstone marked "Andre Toulon." Spindly arms reach skyward. Shortly thereafter, a van bearing the logo "Paranormal Research" and a federal emblem pulls up to the inn. Lance and Wand, Patrick Bramwell and his sister Carolyn disembark and set up equipment to find what "drove Alex Whittaker out of his mind." The skeptical Patrick thinks Alex was insane to begin with but helps measure the walls and panels and looks for the hidden passageways constructed by the inn's builder, "an eccentric old woman who fancied herself a mystic." Odd things happen: A bird figure falls from its pedestal, there are flapping noises. The fifth member of the team, psychic columnist Camille Kenney, arrives late because she'd taken a wrong turn and ended up at the farm of Marge and Matthew, who were erecting an electric barbed-wire fence to stop the animal mutilations. They warn Camille about the inn. Carolyn explains that the previous inn owner, Megan Gallagher, was mysteriously killed and died intestate. The state took control of the inn. Next day Patrick finds Toulon's open grave and snaps a picture. Over dinner that night Camille is told that the inn's previous owner was found dead "with her brain extracted." Alex Whittaker is now a raving lunatic. Next morning Patrick tells Carolyn about the Toulon grave. Camille screams upstairs, saying she's seen little demons in her room. Carolyn suggests puppets. Packing to leave, Camille is attacked and dragged away. Patrick is killed that night by Toulon's drill-headed puppet. The others incapacitate it and find gears and wheels inside. But what fuels its movements? Eriquee Charnee (pronounced Eric Charnay) arrives, a strange figure whose face and hands are swathed in gauze, his eyes covered with smoked goggles, his hands in gloved black leather, wide-brimmed floppy hat and black cloak embracing him. He says he has been the inn's sole occupant for decades and is actually its owner but has no documents to prove it. No one suspects that Charnee is Toulon. Michael Kenney arrives looking for his mother. That night Matthew and Marge are killed by marionettes. Toulon needed more brain matter to restore himself properly and to insure a continued existence for his puppet retinue. Toulon is struck by Carolyn's resemblance to his wife Elsa, murdered by Nazis in the 1930s. In a flashback sequence, we see how in 1912 Cairo, a mysterious Egyptian introduced

them to sorcery. Toulon now orders his puppets to take care of all save Carolyn. Lance and Wanda are killed. Carolyn investigates the house and finds evidence that Charnee is Toulon. Toulon captures her and plans to use the elixir on her. He has two life-sized mannequins which will contain their respective essences. The puppets, not wanting to become rotting wood, overcome Toulon in his new body. Michael and Carolyn leave the inn. Miles away on a deserted stretch of California coast highway, a battered van pulls off the road. Driving the van is the life-sized mannequin that Toulon had prepared for Carolyn, only now it houses the essence of the dead Camille. Torch the puppet sits beside her studying a road map. Oops, they've missed their turn a few miles back. They'll backtrack and arrive at their new home — the Balderston Institute for Troubled Tots and Teens.

Review: "Less effective string pulling than in original." (*Video Hound's Golden Movie Retriever 1994*, p. 672)

Analysis: It's on about the same level as the first film in the series, in other words, fair.

Puppet Master III
(Full Moon, 1991; 86 min.) *½

Produced by John Schouweiler and David DeCoteau. Directed by David DeCoteau. Screenplay, C. Courtney Joyner. Edited by Carol O'Blath. Director of Photography, Adolfo Bartoli. Music, Richard Band. Color, DeLuxe. Ultra Stereo. Art Direction, Jonathan Bruce.

Cast: Andre Toulon (Guy Rolfe), Major Kraus (Richard Lynch), Dr. Hess (Ian Abercrombie), Lieutenant Eric Stein (Kristopher Logan), Peter Hertz (Aron Eisenberg), Elsa Toulon (Sarah Douglas), General Mueller (Walter Gotell), Lili (Michelle Bauer), Hertz (Matthew Faison), Prostitute (Jasmine Totschek).

Synopsis: During World War II some Nazis know that the puppet impresario Toulon has discovered a formula that rejuvenates the dead or brings the inanimate to life. They hope to use it for a super race of soldiers. The Gestapo major Kraus, on the other hand, wants to execute Toulon as soon as he's captured. Because his wife Elsa was murdered by the Nazis, Toulon vows vengeance and uses his puppets to kill them. Dr. Hess locates Toulon and asks about the secret of his puppets' life. Toulon replies that there's no strange secret or medicine. If the person truly wanted to live when he was dying, his spirit lived on. Thus the puppets. Hess tries to help Toulon but is killed by Kraus's men. Toulon escapes and kills Kraus.

Review: "Fine cast, but strictly for the followers." (*Video Hound's Golden Movie Retriever 1994,* p. 672)

Analysis: Increasingly asinine, this wastes the talents of old-line villain Rolfe (*King of the Khyber Rifles, Taras Bulba*) and contemporary bad guy Lynch (*Invasion U.S.A., The Sword and the Sorcerer*). Too many shots are eye level, meaning they skimped on sets. It's patently stupid to expect us to believe the few leeches could act so fast to drain blood or that the victims would hang around to let them plop onto them from the mouth of the Elsa doll. Puppet effects are good.

Puppet Master IV
(Full Moon Entertainment/New City Releasing, 1993; 80 min.) *½

Produced by Charles Band. Directed by Jeff Burr. Screenplay, Todd Henschell, Steven E. Carr, Jo Duffy, Doug Aarniokoski, Keith Payson. Edited by Mark Manos and Margaret-Anne Smith. Director of Photography, Adolfo Bartoli. Color. Music, Richard Band. Special Makeup and Mechanical Effects, AlchemyFX, Michael S. Deak. Puppet Effects, David Allen.

Cast: Rich Meyers (Gordon Currie), Susie (Chandra West), Cameron (Jason Adams), Lauren (Teresa Hill), Dr. Carl Baker (Felton Perry), Dr. Leslie Piper (Stacie Randall), Andre Toulon (Guy Rolfe).

Synopsis: Biotech Industries scientists Drs. Baker and Piper are stalked and attacked by a pair of grotesque, eighteen-inch-tall puppets delivered by a mysterious stranger. After rendering them immobile, the bizarre mannequins absorb their spiritual essences and send them to a subterranean dimension ruled by homunculi of a similar frightful aspect. Biotech's goal has been to bridge the gap between artificial and human intelligence through advanced

robotics. Baker and Piper have been downloading the innovative programming data provided by Rick Meyers, computer wunderkind. Rick is also the caretaker for the Bodega Bay Inn, finding its off-season isolation conducive to his work. One evening, Rick's girlfriend Susie arrives for an overnight stay with friends Lauren and Cameron in tow. Cameron is also employed at Biotech and can barely conceal his jealousy when he finds out that the relatively routine programming procedures he accomplishes are based upon Rick's data. After dinner, the couples discover an old trunk in a storage room. Opening it, they find the papers of Andre Toulon, which reveal his troubles with the Nazis and their interest in his puppets. The trunk also contains several vials of Toulon's animation serum, with which Rick injects a number of the odd puppets in the storage room. The puppets slowly come to life, although Cameron suspects some sort of trick. Rick, however, sees obvious ramifications for Biotech. Later, while Rick studies the puppets' peculiar movements, Cameron and Lauren play around with a Ouija board. Lauren inadvertently opens a dimensional portal which allows the murderous dolls that killed Baker and Piper to enter the room. Fleeing, Cameron is killed in his car, and Lauren rushes back inside to warn Rick and Susie. The young people spend a terrifying night fending off the attacking marionettes, but the scales are tipped in the humans' favor by Toulon's puppets, who counterattack and defend Rick and Susie. The appearance of Andre Toulon's spirit provides the puppet "Decapitron," which summarily defeats the last of the killer dolls, and the ones from the subterranean dimension as well. Toulon's shade declares that Rick, with his knowledge of the original puppet master's formula, in addition to his skill in computer science, is the new puppet master.

Analysis: After a promising beginning, with the evil puppets (which in form are shameless rip-offs of H. R. Giger's *Alien*) attacking the scientists in their high-tech computer lab, *Puppet Master IV* soon settles into its old formula. Again we have a handful of terrified and largely ineffectual humans being harassed by a gang of killer puppets through the maze of suites and corridors in a darkened Bodega Bay Inn. The most terrifying thing about this sequel is the implication at the end that there will be further entries in the Puppet Master series.

Puppet Master 5
(Paramount/Full Moon Entertainment, 1994; 81 min.) **1/2

Produced by Charles Band. Directed by Jeff Burr. Screenplay, Steven E. Carr, Jo Duffy, Todd Henschell, Doug Aarniokoski, Keith Payson. Edited by Margaret-Anne Smith. Director of Photography, Adolfo Bartoli. Color, Foto-Kem. Original Puppet Master Music, Richard Band. Music adapted and edited by Michael Wetherwax. Art Direction, Arlan Jay Vetter. Set Decoration, Nicki Roberts. Special Effects Makeup, AlchemyFX, Michael S. Deak.

Cast: Rick Myers (Gordon Currie), Susie (Chandra West), Dr. Lawrence Jennings (Ian Ogilvy), Hendy (Nicholas Guest), Toulon (Guy Rolfe), Lauren (Teresa Hill), Jason (Willard Pugh), Scott (Duane Whitaker), Attorney (Diane McBain), Man #1 (Clu Gulager), Man #2 (Kaz Garas), Nurse (Harri James), Detective (Ron O'Neal), Policeman (Chuck Williams).

Synopsis: Rick Myers is interrogated by the police concerning the deaths of Doctors Baker and Piper at the Robotics Division of Omega's Biotech. Before being released on bail, Rick is also questioned by Dr. Lawrence Jennings of Omega. Unknown to Rick, the skull-faced, dark-garbed, knife-wielding puppet originally made and given life by Andre Toulon has been found and entered into evidence. Also unknown to Rick and his girlfriend Susie is the fact that the puppet has cut itself out of its plastic bag and is hiding in Rick's pack. Nor does anyone realize that a netherworld demon plans to acquire Toulon's secrets via resurrection of yet another, smaller demon, a process that causes bad dreams and spasms for the hospital-bound Lauren, recovering from her previous experiences with Toulon's creations. At Rick's place the puppet emerges from his sack. Rick is glad to see it, and they head back to the Bodega Bay Inn to gather up the other puppets. Along with three cohorts, Dr. Jennings precedes

them. In his old room, Rick reads "HELP ME" on his computer screen. The netherworld's creation emerges into the "upworld" and kills two of Jennings's men while Toulon's Pinhead incapacitates another. Susie shows up and meets Pinhead. The cowboy puppet and his fellow with the flaming hand deter the demon — for the moment. Jennings finds Rick, Rick finds Susie. The door slams and on the computer is Toulon's formula as well as the message, "Help Me Kill Beast." Rick types back, "Is this Toulon?" The answer, "Lauren." The Jester puppet beckons and shows them the inanimate Decapitron. Meanwhile, Pinhead is attacked by the demon, but Skullface intervenes and the demon flies up and away. When Decapitron is activated, Toulon's face appears on it and tells Rick he and the puppets will take care of the demon. Jennings wants to take just one puppet with him and knocks Rick senseless. However, the puppets force him to his death in an empty elevator shaft. While Rick and Susie flee, the puppets battle the demon. Realizing he cannot defeat them all, the demon summons the portal to the netherworld, but Decapitron causes an explosion that destroys the monster. Later Rick repairs the stunned and battered puppets. Toulon reappears to say that the future and the magic are Rick's. Rick understands that there is more evil to combat and he'll have to help fight it.

Review: "New and inventive ways of killing people have been devised in order to show what the puppets do best." (Mick Martin and Marsha Porter, *Video Movie Guide 1997*, p. 862)

Analysis: The generally wild premise and grotesque puppets count for something, and these proceedings are not boring. Just as people had their favorite member of the Village People, audiences will embrace a particular puppet. Some will find the netherworld demon either reminiscent of a Power Rangers adversary, or fairly frightening. Several actors appear in what can only be called cameos: Ron *Superfly* O'Neal, Diane *Claudelle Inglish* McBain, Clu *Return of the Living Dead* Gulager. Some books add the subtitle *The Final Chapter*, but that's not on screen.

The Quatermass Xperiment (The Creeping Unknown)
(Hammer/United Artists, 1956; 82 min.) ***½

Produced by Anthony Hinds. Directed by Val Guest. Assistant Director, Bill Shorr. Screenplay, Richard Landau and Val Guest. Based on Nigel Kneale's BBC TV serial. Edited by James Needs. Director of Photography, Jimmy Harvey. Music, James Bernard. Music conducted by John Hollingsworth. Sound Recording, H. C. Pearson. Art Direction, J. Elder Wills. Makeup, Phil Leakey. Hairdresser, Monica Hasler. Wardrobe, Molly Arbuthnot. Special Effects, Les Bowie.

Cast: Professor Bernard Quatermass (Brian Donlevy), Inspector Lomax (Jack Warner), Victor Carroon (Richard Wordsworth), Julia Carroon (Margia Dean), Dr. Gordon Briscoe (David King Wood), Christie (Harold Lang), Blake (Lionel Jeffries), Rosie (Thora Hird), Television producer (Gordon Jackson), Marsh (Maurice Kaufman), Little girl (Jane Asher), Charles Green (Gron Davies), Reichenheim (Stanley Van Beers).

Synopsis: Sighted at 9:15 P.M., a rocket plunges into the English soil. Arriving on the scene, Professor Quatermass says he sent it 1500 miles into space. Blake of the Ministry of Defense is angry about the unauthorized mission. Finally the portal opens, one man falls out. "Help," is all that space traveler Victor Carroon can utter. In the ship are space suits but no Green, no Reichenheim. Quatermass visits Inspector Lomax to complain about the police interrogation of Carroon. In the laboratory it is noted that Carroon's shoulder is laced with strange lines and his facial structure is slightly changed. Quatermass talks about the uncharted world out in space and how Carroon's been there, he has the map. When Inspector Lomax shows Quatermass the inhuman finger prints they've taken from Carroon, the professor asks, "Is this a joke?" Inspecting the rocket, Quatermass and his team find a strange goo between the outer and inner hulls. They tentatively conclude that this may be the remains of the other two men. "There's no room for personal feelings in science, Julia," says Quatermass when Carroon's wife berates him. Quatermass, Gordon Briscoe and Lomax view the film from the mission. It shows the three crewmen falling prey to something invisible. Julia sends a man to retrieve her husband from the clinic but Carroon, who has plunged his hand into a cactus, kills his visitor. Judith screams when Victor displays his hideous right arm, and he runs into the night. The dead man seems to have had the life drained from him. Could it be that the invisible space life the rocket passed through was a form of pure energy that can unite plant and animal and multiply? Carroon kills a pharmacist and hides out in a barge on the waterfront. Next morning a little girl finds him. Spurning her friendship, he runs off. Next day Quatermass and Lomax are called in to examine dead animals in the zoo: a lion, a leopard, some antelope. The life's been drained from their bodies. In the lab, Briscoe and Quatermass find mice are absorbed by the viscous substance they found on the zoo grounds. Troops are called out to prevent the spread of the monstrous stuff. "The Restoration of Westminster Abbey" is a TV production being broadcast that night. A workman is found dead, having fallen from the scaffolding. Cameras spots a monstrous jelly-like creature, twenty feet across, high in the abbey. Quatermass warns that it must be killed before it can spread its spores. Electricity from all over London is diverted to Westminster, and the creature is electrocuted. Quatermass leaves to plan the next flight into space. A rocket blasts off.

Review: "Competently made.... Guest's direction brings out the maximum suspense factors." (Holl., *Variety*, June 27, 1956)

Analysis: The Quatermass films are amongst the most widely respected science fiction films of the 1950s and 1960s, yet they remain obscure to all but aficionados of the genre, at least in the United States. Each film is based upon a series of very popular 1950s television serials authored by Nigel Kneale. *The Quatermass Experiment* aired in six 40-minute installments during the summer of 1953, with Reginald Tate appearing in the titular role. The serial's popularity prompted Hammer Studios to pick up the property and release a film version in 1956. (*The Quatermass*

Victor Carroon (Richard Wordsworth) is a frightening figure after a mysterious outer space encounter in *The Quatermass Xperiment* (Hammer/United Artists, 1956).

Xperiment was on British ads — a ploy to lure audiences as it played off the rating code's "X.") Val Guest directed, although he admitted in July 1994 at the FANEX 8 convention that unlike everyone else in Britain, he never watched the TV series. Following the custom of the time and because American companies frequently provided funding for the property, Hammer signed American Brian Donlevy as the rocket group leader. Kneale never made any pretense of liking either the actor chosen by Hammer to play his professor or the film itself. In fact, he stated his displeasure a number of times for the record. The author's disapproval is somewhat understandable in light of the reduction his teleplay had to undergo for its transition to the big screen: Fully half the material had to be scrapped in order to fit the eighty-minute time limit.

Donlevy's Quatermass is brusque, even surly, accustomed to snapping out instructions in short bursts. Always impatient with slow-moving subordinates, bureaucrats and any other potential hindrance, his Quatermass is obviously a leader accustomed to having his orders carried out without question. In the eyes of many a theatergoer, Donlevy's Quatermass was characterized by a refreshing realism, and his performance would be the most memorable in the film, if it weren't for the one by Richard Wordsworth, who plays the unfortunate surviving astronaut, Victor Carroon.

Wordsworth, an otherwise obscure British utility actor (he appeared in minor roles in one or two other genre films), delivers a performance that has most often been compared to Boris Karloff's as the Frankenstein monster of the '30s. Apart from a single word of (whispered) dialogue, Wordsworth's delivery is managed entirely through agonized facial expressions and distorted mannerisms that convey with painful acuity the torment that a man in his slowly metamorphosing state would have felt.

Val Guest's direction is tense and atmospheric, with some superb moments (especially in the zoo sequence) reminiscent of the Val Lewton thrillers of the 1940s. In this film (and even more in the sequel), Guest manages to produce images whose almost Orwellian grayness is most appropriate to the material.

Quatermass II
(Enemy from Space)
(Hammer/United Artists, 1957; 85 min.) ***½

Produced by Anthony Hinds. Executive Producer, Michael Carreras. Directed by Val Guest. Assistant Director, Don Weeks. Screenplay, Nigel Kneale and Val Guest. Based on Kneale's BBC TV serial. Edited by James Needs. Director of Photography, Gerald Gibbs. Music, James Bernard. Sound, Cliff Sanders. Art Direction, Bernard Robinson. Makeup, Phil Leakey. Special Effects, Bill Warrington, Henry Harris, Frank George.

Cast: Quatermass (Brian Donlevy), Inspector Lomax (John Longden), Jimmy Hall (Sidney James), Marsh (Bryan Forbes), Tom Brand (William Franklyn), Paddy Gorman (Percy Herbert), Dawson (Charles Lloyd Pack), Vincent Broadhead (Tom Chatto), Sheila (Vera Day), Public relations man (John Van Eyssen), Ernie (Michael Ripper), E. J. McLeod (John Rae), Secretary (Marianne Stone), Young man (Ronald Wilson), Mrs. McLeod (Jane Aird), Kelly (Betty Impey), Inspector (Lloyd Lamble), Commissioner (John Stuart), Banker (Gilbert Davies), Woman M.P. (Joyce Adams), Peterson (Edwin Richfield), Lab assistants (Philip Baird, Robert Raikes), Intern (John Fabin), Superintendent (George Merritt), Constable (Arthur Blake), Harry (Michael Balfour), Young girl (Jan Holden).

Synopsis: Returning one evening from an unhappy meeting with government officials, Professor Bernard Quatermass is nearly run off the twisting country road by an oncoming car. Both cars come to a jarring halt. Investigating, Quatermass finds the other car occupied by a young couple. The man has been injured before this incident, his face bearing a peculiar scar or burn. The nearly hysterical young woman informs the professor that her friend was hurt when he handled one of many odd objects found in the vicinity of nearby Wynerton Flats, where they'd been picnicking. A short time later, Quatermass arrives at his laboratory and finds that his

assistants, Brand and Marsh, have been monitoring some unusual activity on their radar screen, meteors perhaps. The professor is hardly inclined to show an interest in this; his day hasn't been a good one, having been highlighted by a decidedly unfavorable meeting with the aforementioned government people, who have shown little interest in either Quatermass's atomic rocket or the moon project. Only when Brand points out that the unusual meteoric activity is taking place around Wynerton Flats is Quatermass's curiosity piqued. He notes with interest the trajectories of these "meteors" and remarks that their movement hardly seems consistent with natural phenomena. The next morning Quatermass and Marsh drive to the somewhat desolate and isolated area of Wynerton Flats. Topping a hill, they are astonished to see a near replica of their moon project habitat, complete with towers and sealed domes, sprawling across the valley below. Marsh notices that the ground where they stand is pocked and littered with debris, small objects that seem identical to the shell-like projectiles described by the girl Quatermass had aided the night before. Picking up one of the undamaged ones, Marsh barely has time to remark that it is warm and that he feels something like a slight vibration, when it emits a puff of gas and breaks open in his hand. By the time the professor scrambles to his aid, Marsh is barely conscious and showing an ugly burn-like scar on his face. A truckload of guards from the facility below arrives and begins scanning the ground with metal detectors. These guards have little to say, but then put the now senseless Marsh onto a stretcher. When Quatermass attempts to join his companion, he is swatted with a rifle butt, hustled into his own car and told to leave. The appalled professor seeks help in the civic center of a nearby community, but once the citizens there learn that he and Marsh were near the plant at Wynerton Flats, they fall silent and send him on his way. The local constabulary also seem disinclined to involve themselves in the affair. Sensing that whatever is wrong here is beyond the scope or wish of local authorities to investigate,

Val Guest, director of *The Quatermass Xperiment* and *Quatermass II*, at FANEX 8 convention in Towson, Maryland, July 1994.

Quatermass seeks out his old acquaintance at Scotland Yard, Inspector Lomax. When he hears Quatermass's story, Lomax, too, is initially hesitant to lend his direct support, but he does inform the scientist that Wynerton Flats is a classified government project. The inspector introduces Professor Quatermass to Vincent Broadhead, a member of Parliament who has been investigating the goings-on at Wynerton Flats. Far from suspecting that this secret project is in any way nefarious — the official line is that the facility is manufacturing synthetic food — Broadhead is mainly concerned about misspent tax moneys. Quatermass tells his story to Broadhead, who invites him on a tour he has secured for himself and others that very day. Before the trip, Quatermass learns from Brand that radar has discovered a mysterious large mass in orbit "on the dark side of the earth." Quatermass deduces a connection between this object and the meteors. At Wynerton Flats, Quatermass, Broadhead and party are escorted by a stiffly formal guide, ultimately to a structure leading into one of the domes. Broadhead disappears. The guide shows some alarm at this and moves to the exit, throwing a switch which causes the sealing doors to slowly close. Quatermass impulsively slips through an exit and wanders the compound, calling for Broadhead. As he approaches one of the domes, there is the loud clang of a metal door being thrown open and a piercing scream from above. Staggering down the curving gangway from the summit of the dome is Vincent Broadhead, his skin and clothing charred and smoking. Barely coherent, he falls at Quatermass's feet. He'd gone off on his own, he's barely able to explain, climbed to the top of the dome, and fallen in. The tarry black stuff that clings to him is the food, he exclaims before he dies. Alarms sound and Quatermass dashes to a car and smashes through a gate amid a hail of automatic weapons fire. At Scotland Yard, he convinces Lomax that Wynerton Flats conceals something sinister, that what is really being carried out is "the mass destruction of men's minds." Lomax seeks the advice of a superior but notices the telltale burn-like mark on the official's wrist, evidence that the infected and "possessed" have moved into high places. Feeling they must alert the news media, Quatermass, Lomax and reporter Jimmy Hall return to the village near Wynerton Flats. On the way, they stop at the lab to give Hall a first-hand look at the "official" moon project. Quatermass instructs Brand to prepare their rocket for immediate launch, with coordinates set for the mysterious mass circling the earth. In the village, they try to convince the skeptical townsfolk of the true nature of the plant at Wynerton Flats. Only the timely falling of more "meteorites" convinces the villagers. Armed and gas-masked guards from the plant arrive and machine-gun Hall as he tries to phone in his story. Quatermass and Lomax dash off. After inadvertently running down a guard, Quatermass dons the dead man's uniform while Lomax goes for help. In the plant, Quatermass accompanies an entourage who feed the contents of the fallen objects to the contents of the dome: a pulsating mass of steaming ooze, the deadly, burning "food" that was the death of Vincent Broadhead. Lomax finds himself carried along with the town mob, which crashes the plant gate. At Quatermass's lab, Brand is confronted by Marsh, now totally under alien control, but before being gunned down he falls on the launch control and sends the QM2 into space. In the plant, Lomax and some townsfolk hole up in a control building, replete with weapons. Quatermass determines that decreasing the amount of ammonia and methane in the domes while increasing oxygen will damage the life forms within. Two men give themselves up, but moments later blood is seen dripping from the pipes sending oxygen into the domes: the facility people are blocking the pipes "with human pulp!" One of the victim's mates fires a rocket grenade into one of the domes, causing a conflagration from which erupt the hugely grotesque figures. In a chain reaction, neighboring domes erupt, their malevolent contents shambling forth blindly, crushing everything in their path. Quatermass and company flee the control room and pile into a nearby car, making a hasty exit from the fiery complex. From the top of a hill, they scan the plant, now a blazing ruin, the gigantic alien creatures rising and falling as if in great pain. The oxygen, Quatermass explains, is as painful to them as the ammonia-methane compound had been to the dying Vincent Broadhead. Even as he speaks, there is a blinding light from above: the atomic rocket launched by Brand has collided with the mysterious satellite. There is a sympathetic shudder from the valley below as the alien giants stumble and collapse, imploding in on themselves.

Review: "All characters are stodgy.... Special effects ... are imaginative." (Whit., *Variety*, September 4, 1957)

Analysis: A heady film, its gritty production values give it a creaky look that is almost antique by even the standards of the 1950s. These (relatively) early Hammer films *look* almost a decade older than they actually are. It's rather amazing to think that *Quatermass II* is only five years away from the production of *Dr. No!* And somehow this rococo look adds so much that's eerie and otherworldly to the first two

Professor Bernard Quatermass (Brian Donlevy, center) is unceremoniously escorted out of Wynerton Flats in *Quatermass II (Enemy from Space)* (Hammer/United Artists, 1957).

Quatermass films, and it is a sorely missed quality in *Quatermass III (Five Million Years to Earth)*. Another quality one hates to lose in the next installment is the presence of Brian Donlevy. One might wonder why an obvious American is heading a British space program, but he otherwise brings an undeniable authority to the role and gives it his own stamp.

Enemy from Space would be the lost jewel in the crown of British science fiction film if Nigel Kneale had had his way. As with *The Quatermass Experiment*, this sequel suffered considerable trimming when it came time to adapt the three-and-a-half hour television serial to feature film dimensions. The 1955 serial starred John Robinson as Professor Quatermass; Hammer's *Quatermass II* runs a bare eighty-five minutes, and Brian Donlevy reappears as the title character. Kneale was even less happy with this film than with the first, despite the fact that he co-authored the script with director Guest. When the rights reverted to him in 1965 he withdrew it from

circulation. Between then and the early 1980s the film went virtually unseen, and many considered it permanently lost. Only with the rise of video and the eventual appearance of all manner of "lost" classics did *Quatermass II/Enemy from Space* make a comeback. Unlike a number of films whose reputation is only enhanced by rareness or inaccessibility, *Enemy from Space* is every bit the classic that its proponents have always claimed it to be.

The narrative of the television serial and Hammer's *Quatermass II* are virtually identical, with the main departure at the end of the story. In the serial, Quatermass rockets into space and travels to the mysterious planetoid that orbits the earth, there detonating the atomic device that ends the menace. The feature, of course, has the rocket remotely controlled, while Quatermass remains earthbound to confront the alien spoor on Wynerton Flats.

Brian Donlevy brings the same brusque manner to his portrayal of Bernard Quatermass: He's still as impatient and arrogant as ever. Rumors circulated concerning Donlevy's drunkenness, that he couldn't remember his dialogue or had to be prevented from knocking over furniture or walking into walls when he concluded a scene. At FANEX 8 in July 1994, Val Guest said Donlevy never drank while working. His performance is professional and convincing, and while a British actor (any of those who essayed the role on television, for instance) could no doubt have carried the part, Donlevy nevertheless acquits himself nicely. Two other characters — Marsh, the professor's assistant, and Scotland Yard's Inspector Lomax — make a return appearance, although this time they are played by different actors. William Franklyn is effective as the sincere Brand, the hapless assistant of Quatermass who is gunned down as he launches the Q2, and Tom Chatto is memorable as the feisty MP, Vinnie Broadhead.

With its obvious parallels to Don Siegel's *Invasion of the Body Snatchers* (1956), *Quatermass II* is universally regarded as the best British science-fiction film of the 1950s. While many would argue that *Five Million Years to Earth* (*Quatermass III*) boasts a superior plot, few would deny that *Quatermass II* is the more consistently satisfying production. Val Guest again effectively directs the film in a crisp documentary style, relying more on atmosphere than on special effects. As Guest indicated at FANEX 8, there really was no budget for special effects, and Les Bowie had to make do. (Guest said the interior of the rocket in *The Quatermass Experiment* was the interior of a modest shack constructed outside the Bray house in an area normally reserved for parking.) In *Quatermass II* the effects are quite convincing in the cataclysmic finale. (The huge and shambling aliens that burst forth from the containment domes at Wynerton Flats, however, bear an amusingly — and surely coincidentally — close resemblance to the comic monster *The Heap* of E. C. Comics fame.) Nigel Kneale's opinion to the contrary, *Quatermass II* is gripping entertainment and excellent science fiction.

Quatermass III
(*Five Million Years to Earth*)
(Hammer/20th Century–Fox/Seven Arts, 1967; 98 min.) ***

Produced by Anthony Nelson Keys. Directed by Roy Ward Baker. Assistant Director, Bert Batt. Story and screenplay, Nigel Kneale. Edited by Spencer Reeve. Supervising Editor, James Needs. Director of Photography, Arthur Grant. DeLuxe Color. Music, Tristram Cary. Musical Supervision, Philip Martell. Sound Recording, Sash Fisher. Sound Editor, Roy Hyde. Makeup, Michael Morris. Special Effects, Bowie Films.

Cast: Quatermass (Andrew Keir), Dr. Roney (James Donald), Barbara Judd (Barbara Shelley), Colonel Breen (Julian Glover), Sladden (Duncan Lamont), Captain Potter (Bryan Marshall), Howell (Peter Copley), Minister (Edwin Richfield), Police Sergeant Ellis (Grant Taylor), Sergeant Cleghorn (Maurice Good), Watson (Robert Morris), Journalist (Sheila Steafel), Sapper West (Hugh Futcher), Elderly journalist (Hugh Morton), Pub customer (Hugh Manning), Blonde (June Ellis), Vicar (Thomas Heathcote), Joonson (Keith Marsh), Corporal Gibson (James Culliford), Abbey librarian (Noel Howlett), Miss Dobson (Bee Duffell), Electrician (Roger Avon), Technical officer (Brian Peck), Inspector (John Graham), News vendor (Charles Lamb).

Synopsis: At London's Hobbs End Underground station workmen uncover ancient humanoid skeletons dubbed by the tabloids as "Underground Ape Men." Also unearthed is what appears to be an unexploded German bomb of World War II vintage. Colonel Breen and his men determine that it is not, however. Professor Quatermass, now working in concert with Breen, assists Dr. Roney and his assistant Barbara Judd in determining that the vessel may be of extraterrestrial origin. It resists heat of 3,000 degrees and has a Pentacke — an ancient cabalistic sign — on it. Quatermass and Judd find references to goblins in the area in a 1927 newspaper and also in 1763. In the Westminster Abbey archives they learn of strange sightings as early as 1341. When they notice that the station was once called Hob's Lane, Barbara recalls that hob was a word for the devil. Finally the interior of the vessel is reached and inside are large, long-deceased, locust-like creatures. Quatermass

Poster art for *Quatermass III (Five Million Years to Earth)* (Hammer/Twentieth Century–Fox/Seven Arts, 1967).

suggests that the gargoyle statues around the world may have been inspired by these creatures. Roney finds a 30,000-year-old cave painting of similar beings. "Was this really a Martian?" asks Quatermass. Did they leave a dying planet and colonize by proxy? Perhaps mankind owes its condition to the intervention of "insects"? Perhaps they came to earth and took the apes to Mars where they altered them. Breen is nonplussed and says it may be a German propaganda weapon. Sladden, the civilian operating the drill, is set upon by a wind and forced out of the Underground and through the city. He's "seen" the Martians. Roney volunteers to undergo an experiment, attaching a device to his head so that his unconscious visions might be picked up on a monitor. Donning the device, Quatermass duplicates Sladden's drilling inside the capsule, and while the vibrations and levitations occur, nothing registers on the screen. However, Barbara can "see" the Martians and takes the headset. Quatermass shows the film to Breen and the government officials, telling them that it shows a ritual purging of the Martian populace, a purging they obviously intended to continue in their human mutants. Breen and the officials remain skeptical. Perhaps Barbara was hallucinating. They open the Underground to the public to prove that it's safe. Quatermass tries to dissuade them but fails. The television cables add power to the capsule, which begins to glow. The spectators scatter, buildings begin collapsing, Quatermass is possessed but Roney calms him. A giant image of a Martian is projected above the rooftops. Roney suggests that mass into energy is the key and that if they can project iron into the image, it will be dissipated into the earth. Otherwise the people who are now possessed by the Martians' purging instincts will continue killing and the city will be destroyed. The possessed Barbara attempts to stop them, but Quatermass subdues her while Roney ascends a crane which he shifts into the frightful image, sacrificing himself as his theory is proven correct.

Review: "Pseudo-scientific talk seemed to short-circuit the audience's interest...." (Vincent Canby, *New York Times*, May 30, 1968, p. 21)

Analysis: Quatermass and the Pit was the title of both the 1958 BBC teleplay and this film. U.S. release, 1968.

How lackluster is the execution of this third Quatermass film. It's true that this one has the most intriguing plot of the series, but Roy Ward Baker really miscalculated with this one. Every scene (except at the very end) is so evenly, flatly lighted, and so unimaginatively shot, that there was no mood or atmosphere whatsoever. We wonder how this or that scene would have looked if it had been staged by Val Guest or even Terence Fisher. Also missed was the music of James Bernard, a film composer whose personal style seemed ideally matched to the Hammer method. These shortcomings really hurt a film that, based on its script qualities, could have been the best in the series.

As Bill Warren suggests in *Keep Watching the Skies!*, *X the Unknown* is an imitation Quatermass film. Also, Tobe Hooper's *Lifeforce* is virtually a Quatermass film in that it has a curmudgeon professor spearheading an investigation of an invasion by aliens who "possess" human beings and who are tied into our history by events happening epochs ago.

The first two Hammer Quatermass films appeared in rapid succession a year or two after the television serials upon which they were based. Nigel Kneale's third Quatermass story, appearing on the BBC as *Quatermass and the Pit*, aired in 1958. A feature from Hammer was announced at the time, and as with Ray Bradbury's *The Martian Chronicles*, rumors abounded for years of a film project that never seemed to materialize. The success of the British studio's gothic horror melodramas (beginning with 1957's *The Curse of Frankenstein*) caused the venture to be postponed several times. When *Five Million Years to Earth* (the American title) did appear in 1967 (1968 in the U.S.), the grainy gray "documentary" style of Val Guest, favored by Hammer in numerous films of the mid-1950s, had long since given way to the more colorful (even lurid), less expensive manner of Hammer's horror artists, like Terence Fisher and Roy Ward Baker, who was in fact the director of *Five Million Years to*

Earth. The long lapse between segments two and three of the trilogy of Quatermass films accounts for the stylistic differences between them, and it was precisely the slick 1960s look that seemed to garner the most censure, at least from genre critics who otherwise agreed that the script was the most intriguing of the three films. *Five Million Years to Earth* gives us the first British Professor Quatermass, as portrayed by Andrew Keir, whose performance seems more informed by Brian Donlevy's brusque precedence than by his predecessors from the BBC serials. Keir's Professor Q is likewise inclined to be impatient when dealing with the pedantries of either the British political or military sects. This time, however, a number of other British stalwarts join Keir in supporting roles. Julian Glover is Colonel Breen, the stiff-upper-lip type whose adherence to by-the-book militarism proves to be his undoing (and nearly the undoing of the world). Barbara Shelley, who made a career as the femme fatale of many a Hammer horror film, is seen here as the more subdued Miss Judd, Doctor Roney's secretary and assistant. Matthew Roney is played by the excellent James Donald. The part of Roney is somewhat less emphasized than in the teleplay, but it is still of prime importance (Donald, in fact, receives billing above Andrew Keir in the credits). Special effects are a notch above what they'd been in the previous Quatermass films, but still a far cry from what was state-of-the-art in the late '60s. Tristram Cary's music lacks the piercing eeriness of Hammer's laureate composer, James Bernard, but is more than adequate, bearing a passing resemblance to American Leonard Rosenman's.

The original BBC broadcast of *Quatermass and the Pit* was released on video in America in the early 1990s. To those bemoaning the departure taken by Hammer from the black-and-white style of Val Guest, this three-hour video is highly recommended. Essentially, the storyline is identical to the Hammer feature, albeit unfolded at a considerably more deliberate pace and with even less emphasis upon special effects (although the special effects are surprisingly good for a production with

a reputed minuscule budget). This production — produced (and presumably directed) by Rudolph Cartier — does, in fact, provide a good basis for speculating upon just what a Hammer effort made in the late '50s would have looked like.

In 1979, the BBC brought the Quatermass series to a conclusion by the appropriately named, *Quatermass Conclusion*, a television series starring Sir John Mills as a rather exhausted, world-weary Bernard Quatermass. The story is set in a near-future, near-apocalyptic England where large expanses of urban area are given over to gang-warfare and barbarism. In this setting, a worldwide youth cult has emerged, convinced that the world's salvation lies in the coming of extraterrestrials. At the telepathic bidding of these aliens, huge multitudes of young people congregate at certain locales, to be "beamed up" to some otherworldly paradise. The curious powdery substance that Professor Quatermass discovers as the residue of this teleportation turns out to be *human* ash: the extraterrestrials are using young humanity for food! When the professor learns that his own granddaughter is among a mass of youngsters soon to be "teleported," he destroys the aliens, and himself, by detonating an atomic device at the moment the beam illuminates the area.

Quatermass and the Pit *see* Quatermass III *under* **The Quatermass Xperiment**

The Quest for Peace *see* Superman IV: The Quest for Peace *under* **Superman and the Mole Men**

The Quickening *see* Highlander 2: The Quickening *under* **Highlander**

Raiders of the Lost Ark
(Paramount, 1981; 115 min.) ****

Produced by Frank Marshall. Executive Producers, George Lucas, Howard Kazanjian. Directed by Steven Spielberg. Screenplay, Lawrence Kasdan. Story, George Lucas and Philip Kaufman. Edited by Michael Kahn. Director of Photography, Douglas Slocombe. Panavision. Metrocolor. Music, John Williams. Dolby Stereo. Sound Effects Editing,

Indiana Jones (Harrison Ford) faces a roomful of his worst fear — snakes — in *Raiders of the Lost Ark* (Paramount, 1981).

Benjamin Burtt, Richard L. Anderson. Art Direction, Leslie Dilley. Set Decoration, Michael Ford. Costumes, Deborah Nadoolman. Stunt Coordinator, Glenn Randall. Visual Effects Supervision, Richard Edlund.

Cast: Henry "Indiana" Jones (Harrison Ford), Marion (Karen Allen), Belloq (Paul Freeman), Toht (Ronald Lacy), Sallah (John Rhys-Davies), Marcus Brody (Denholm Elliott), Dietrich (Wolf Kahler), Gobler (Anthony Higgins), Satipo (Alfred Molina), Barranca (Vic Tablian), Colonel Musgrove (Don Fellows), Jock (Fred Sorenson), Major Eaton (William Hootkins), Bureaucrat (Bill Reimbold), Australian climber (Patrick Durkin), Second Nazi (Matthew Scurfield), Ratty Nepalese (Malcom Weaver), Mean Mongolian (Sonny Caldinez), Mohan (Anthony Chinn), Otto (Christopher Frederick), Imam (Tutte Lemkow), Giant Sherpa (Pat Roach), Omar (Ishaq Bux), Abu (Kiran Shah), Fayah (Souad Messaoudi), Monkey Man (Vic Tablian), Swordsman (Terry Richards), German Agent (Steve Hanson), Katanga (George Harris), Sergeant (John Rees), First mechanic (Pat Roach), Pilot (Frank Marshall), Young soldier (Martin Kreidt), Messenger pirate (Eddie Tagoe), Tall captain (Tony Vogel), Peruvian porter (Ted Grossman), Stand-in (Jack Dearlove).

Synopsis: With a ratty old map, a gringo locates a cave in a South American jungle. Evading the booby traps placed there centuries ago, he and his guide discover a golden idol upon a pedestal. Replacing the priceless find with a bag of sand fails to deceive the temple's makers, and the place begins to crumble. Leaping a moat, scooting under a descending rock door, and outrunning a giant boulder, the man — one Professor Indiana Jones — encounters an old nemesis, the renegade French archaeologist Belloq. Relieved of the idol, Indiana makes a run for it, pursued by Belloq's "guides"— poison arrow–shooting savages. He escapes by reaching the seaplane piloted by Jock. Back in the United States, Professor Jones lectures on archaeology. After class, he informs administrator Marcus Brody that he can still retrieve the idol. But unexpected United States Army visitors give him another assignment: Find the ancient Hebrew Ark of the Covenant, something the Nazis — with Belloq's help — are trying to unearth outside Cairo. Indy realizes the key to discovering the Ark is the medallion, or headdress, in the Staff of Ra. His former lover, Marion, has it. Indy finds her running a bar in Nepal. The Nazis also find her, but after a gun battle and fire that ruins the bar, Indy and Marion escape — with the medallion still in their possession. In Cairo they are apprised of the Nazi dig by Sallah. After Marion is kidnapped and then presumably killed in a truck explosion, Indy meets Belloq. The Frenchman says the Ark is a radio for speaking to God. Avoiding capture himself, Indy and Sallah discuss events and realize that Belloq is digging in the wrong place. They dress as Egyptians and descend into the well, where Indy uses the Staff of Ra to pinpoint the true site of the Ark. Equally pleasant is the discovery that Marion is still alive. But he must leave her imprisoned for the moment. With Sallah's men, Indy gains entrance to the underground room wherein lies the Ark. First, however, he and Sallah must run a gauntlet in the form of a floor full of snakes. But the Ark is there, and it's hauled up. However, Belloq spies the unusual activity and tosses Marion in with Indy before blocking the entrance. Toppling a statue, Indy breaks through a wall and, with Marion's almost accidental help, wreaks havoc on the German camp. In a race to Cairo, Indy outfights and outwits the Nazis and regains the Ark. It's boarded on a cargo ship, but a German submarine intercepts it. Marion is again captured, but Indy is nowhere to be found. He's swum to the sub and is hiding topside while it proceeds into the Aegean Sea to a small island. Following the Germans, Belloq, and Marion inland, he threatens to blow up the Ark with an anti-tank gun but is dissuaded by Belloq, who rhetorically asks how Indy could destroy a priceless artifact. Tied to a post with Marion, Indy realizes that if they look upon the Ark when it is opened, they may die. He is correct. Spirits arise from the relic and destroy Belloq and the Nazis before returning to their rest. Back in the States, Indy is informed that "top men" are examining the Ark. Irritated, he leaves for a drink with Marion. In a huge warehouse, a man is seen storing the "Top Secret" crated Ark amongst a zillion other boxes.

Reviews: "What makes this movie good — what makes it a lot better than *Superman II* — is that Indiana is completely at the mercy of forces beyond his control." (Colin L. Westerbeck, Jr., *Commonweal*, August 28, 1981, pp. 470–71) ¶"Nothing in *Raiders of the Lost Ark* quite so becomes it as its very beginning." (Richard Combs, *Monthly Film Bulletin*, August 1981, p. 159) ¶"You keep expecting things to sag, *Raiders* to run out of tricks, but that never happens." (David Ansen, *Newsweek*, June 15, 1981, p. 58) ¶"A two-hour roller coaster ride.... What Spielberg is after is a cinema of pure sensation, a visceral experience for the eye and the gut operating independently of the brain." (Howard Kissel, *Women's Wear Daily*, June 8, 1981, p. 10)

Analysis: Raiders of the Lost Ark was the brainchild of George Lucas and Steven Spielberg, an obvious labor of love for these baby-boomers who had grown up on pulp fiction and Saturday matinee movies. Rich with that sense of wonder that seems to suffuse this particular corner of the adventure film genre, *Raiders* was an immediate success that gave birth to a number of cheap imitations. This first Indiana Jones adventure has just the right amount of heroic daring-do, exotic atmosphere, and outlandish action, along with the inevitable stereotypical characterization, to satisfy any lover of the action film genre. Innumerable action films before *Raiders* obviously owed much to the Saturday afternoon cliffhangers of the 1930s and 1940s, but none recaptured the rousing, headlong spirit of those efforts with quite the panache of this first Lucas-Spielberg opus. Accounts vary as to the casting of Harrison Ford as Indiana Jones. The most common is that Tom Selleck was strongly considered for the role but lost the opportunity because of his television commitments. George Lucas, on the other hand, has stated that Harrison Ford (whom he'd used as far back as *American Graffiti*) was his choice from the beginning. Whatever the case, the fact that Ford's somewhat wooden, rather taciturn manner is nicely offset by his affinity for violent action made him an immediate success in the part of the far-ranging archaeologist. Along with his portrayal of Han Solo in Lucas's *Star Wars* films, the Indiana Jones character paved the way for roles far outreaching his efforts in the genre of the science fiction action-adventure film. The other roles in *Raiders* are effectively filled out by Karen Allen, John Rhys-Davies, Paul Freeman and the late Denholm Elliott. *Raiders of the Lost Ark* gave birth to both a sequel *and* a prequel. Both of the subsequent films abound in the same elements that made *Raiders* a real accomplishment, but neither really inspired the same wild *frisson* that the original seemed to arouse so naturally. Academy Awards for Editing, Visual Effects, Art Direction, Sound. Special Achievement Award for Sound Effects Editing. Academy Award nominations were received for picture and director, music score and cinematography. *Raiders* made over a hundred million dollars to become the year's top grosser.

Indiana Jones and the Temple of Doom
(Paramount, 1984; 118 min.) ***

Produced by Robert Watts. Directed by Steven Spielberg. Screenplay, Willard Huyck and Gloria Katz. Story, George Lucas. Edited by Michael Kahn. Director of Photography, Douglas Slocombe. Panavision. Color, DeLuxe. Music, John Williams. Dolby Stereo. Sound Design, Ben Burtt. Choreography, Danny Daniels. Art Direction, Alan Cassie, Roger Cain. Set Decoration, Peter Howitt. Stunt Arrangers, Vic Armstrong, Glenn Randall. Visual Effects, Dennis Muren.

Cast: Indiana Jones (Harrison Ford),Willie Scott (Kate Capshaw), Short Round (Ke Huy Quan), Mola Ram (Amrish Puri), Chattar Lal (Roshan Seth), Captain Blumburtt (Philip Stone), Lao Che (Roy Chiao), Wu Han (David Yip), Kao Kan (Ric Young), Chen (Chua Kah Joo), Maitre d' (Rex Ngui), Chief henchman (Philip Tann), Weber (Dan Aykroyd), Chinese pilot (Akio Mitamura), Chinese co-pilot (Michael Yama), Shaman (D. R. Nanayakkara), Chieftan (Dharmadasa Kuruppu), Sajnu (Stany De Silva), Little Maharajah (Raj Singh), Merchants (Frank Olegario, Ahmed El-Shenawi), Eel eater (Art Repola), Sacrifice victim (Nizwar Karanj), Chief guard (Pat Roach), Guards (Moti Makan, Mellan Mitchell, Bhasker Patel), Cell boys (Arjun Pandher, Zia Gelani).

Synopsis: In Shanghai, China, in 1935, Indiana Jones tries to conclude a deal with Lao Che only to find himself poisoned.

Happily, chanteuse Willie Scott obtains the vial of antidote before she and Indy crash through the window and fall through awnings to the car driven by the child Short Round, Indy's pal. Racing to the airport, they fail to realize they're boarding one of Lao Che's planes. Over mountains far to the west, the pilots bail out. To save themselves when the fuel runs out, Indy, Willie and Short Round use an inflatable raft to fall to the snowfields, thence downhill and over a cliff into a river. Soon they find themselves in India at a village from which a sacred stone — and the children — have been taken to a restored palace. The villagers believe Shiva sent Indy to restore the stone and their offspring. Indy, Willie and Short Round take the proffered elephants and journey to the palace, where they find themselves wined and dined along with a British officer. Over dinner Indy learns that the palace was once site of Kali worship. Worse: Thugee human sacrifice. During the night, Indy is assaulted. Using his whip to advantage, he escapes. In Willie's room he discovers a hidden entrance to tunnels leading to the site of a Thugee ceremony. The man conducting the ritual is Mola Ram. He pulls a man's heart from his chest. The man still lives — until lowered into a flaming pit and incinerated. Three sacred stones are brought forth and placed in a skull wall relief. After the ceremony, Indy slips down and places the stones in his sack. He discovers the child labor gangs but is captured and placed in a cage with Short Round. Another child tells him of the blood-drinking ritual that turns men into the living dead. After informing Indy that the children are digging for the last two sacred stones that will give the Thugees unlimited power, Mola Ram forces Indy to drink the tainted blood. He goes into convulsions, then does Mola Ram's bidding, which involves shackling Willie to the sacrificial cage. But Short Round escapes from the mines, and his pleas break the spell on Indy, who rescues Willie and then begins releasing the children. Fighting off Mola Ram's chief henchman and racing pell-mell through the mines, Indy, Willie and Short Round find themselves confronting Mola Ram on a rope bridge.

After warning his friends, Indy cuts the rope and they smash against the chasm wall. Willie and Short Round climb to safety as Indy and Mola Ram fight. The latter eventually falls to his death in the crocodile-infested river. Indian army troops arrive to drive off Mola Ram's Thugee minions. Indy, Willie and Short Round return the last remaining sacred stone to the village, which is also joyful to find its children returning.

Reviews: "Any adventure film worth its salt should break a few rules — either of the genre or of the bubble you live in — and *Indiana Jones* breaks none." (Harlan Jacobson, *Film Comment*, July-August 1984, pp. 50–51) ¶ "Pure cinematic energy encumbered with as little soul food as possible." (Jack Kroll, *Newsweek*, June 4, 1984, p. 78) ¶ "The movie is a triumph and, at another level, a disaster." (David Denby, *New York*, June 4, 1984, p. 72) ¶ "A sequel that is even better than the original. It's unpretentious and totally entertaining." (Rex Reed, *New York Post*, May 23, 1984, p. 30) ¶ "Inordinately racist and sexist, even by Hollywood standards." (J. Hoberman, *Village Voice*, June 5, 1984, p. 1)

Analysis: If *Indiana Jones and the Temple of Doom* has one overriding problem, it's the fact that two-thirds of the action takes place in a dark and claustrophobic subterranean temple, eschewing the colorful world-hopping of the first film. Another disappointment is the element of excess that seems to frequently creep into films of this type. The slithering mass of snakes that made our skin crawl in *Raiders* is replaced here with a multitude of creepie-crawlies, a mass of six-legged insectoid horrors exotic enough to make Yoda on faraway Dagobah roll his eyes in exasperation. Then, too, there's Willie Scott's grating and incessant screaming that becomes annoying far too early and continues far too long; most viewers clearly preferred Karen Allen's Marion Ravenwood in *Raiders* to this squealing sissy. Despite these shortcomings, though, *Temple of Doom* has enough thrills to make a respectable sequel to *Raiders of the Lost Ark*. Actually, any sequel to that one-of-a-kind experience was largely doomed to some degree of failure anyway, as comparisons with it would almost invariably be negative. At least Lucas and Spielberg (and writers Huyck and Katz) opted to take Indiana Jones in a somewhat different direction in this prequel to their earlier hit. In this respect, the film does rate some real points and somehow seems a more genuinely creative effort than the follow-up *Indiana Jones and the Last Crusade*, which reverted to the assured formula of *Raiders*. In any event, *Temple* was hardly a failure in any way other than by comparison, as the film remains the tenth most (financially) successful film on record. Academy Award for special effects. Nominated for music score.

Indiana Jones and the Last Crusade
(Paramount, 1989; 127 min.) ***

Produced by Robert Watts. Executive Producers, George Lucas, Frank Marshall. Directed by Steven Spielberg. Screenplay, Jeffrey Boam. Story, George Lucas and Menno Meyjes. Director of Photography, Douglas Slocombe. Panavision. Rank/DeLuxe Color. Aerial Photography, Peter Allwork. Music, John Williams. Dolby Stereo. Sound, Ben Burtt, Willie Burton. Art Direction, Stephen Scott. Set Decoration, Peter Howitt. Costumes, Anthony Powell, Joanna Johnston. Visual Effects, Industrial Light and Magic. Visual Effects Supervisor, Michael J. McAlister. Mechanical Effects Supervisor, George Gibbs. Stunt Coordinator, Vic Armstrong.

Cast: Indiana Jones (Harrison Ford), Professor Henry Jones (Sean Connery), Marcus Brody (Denholm Elliott), Dr. Elsa Schneider (Alison Doody), Sallah (John Rhys-Davies), Walter Donovan (Julian Glover), Young Indy (River Phoenix), Vogel (Michael Byrne), Kazim (Kevork Malikyan), Grail knight (Robert Eddison), Fedora (Richard Young), Sultan (Alexei Sayle), Young Henry (Alex Hyde-White), Panama Hat (Paul Maxwell), Butler (Vernon Dobtcheff), Mrs. Donovan (Mrs. Glover), Herman (J. J. Hardy), Roscoe (Bradley Gregg), Half Breed (Jeff O'Haco), Rough Rider (Vince Deadrick), Sheriff (Marc Miles), Deputy Sheriff (Ted Grossman), Young Panama Hat (Tim Hiser), Scout master (Larry Sanders), Scouts (Will Miles, David Murray), World War I ace (Frederick Jaeger), Professor Stanton (Jerry Harte), Dr. Mulbray (Billy J. Mitchell), Man at Hitler rally (Martin Gordon), German officer at Hitler rally (Paul

Humpoletz), Hatay soldier in temple (Tom Branch), Zeppelin crewman (Graeme Crowther), Principal SS officer at castle (Luke Hanson), Officers (Chris Jenkinson, Nicola Scott, Louis Sheldon), Hatay tank gunner (Stefan Kalipha), Film director (Suzane Roquette), Irene (Julie Eccles), Flower girl (Nina Almond), G-man (Eugene Lipinski), Gestapo (Pat Roach), Hatay tank driver (Peter Pacey).

Synopsis: Utah, 1912: Teenage scouts discover men who've uncovered the Cross of Coronado, a priceless crucifix young Henry Jones, Jr., knows belongs in a museum. He grabs the cross and, after a rather unusual chase involving a circus train, gains his home. The sheriff arrives and takes the cross for a man in white, telling Henry that the men from whom he stole it won't press charges. The man in charge of the robbers tells Henry he lost — but doesn't have to like it — and gives him his hat. In 1938: Henry "Indiana" Jones is aboard a ship off the Portuguese coast, fighting to regain possession of the Cross of Coronado from the man in white. Leaping into the sea just as the ship is racked by explosion and fire, Indy watches as the *Coronado* sinks. Back in the states, Jones shows the cross to Marcus Brody. In his office, he discovers a packet mailed from Venice. Before he can open it, he is "invited" to the home of college benefactor Walter Donovan. The man shows Indy a partial slab from Ankara, bearing an inscription that mentions the Canyon of the Crescent Moon. Donovan and Indy go over the legend of Christ's Holy Grail and the Crusader knights who obtained it. Donovan believes it grants eternal life. How to find it — especially when the project leader already embarked on the mission has disappeared? Indy takes on the project when he learns that the missing man is none other than his father, Henry Jones, Sr. Finally remembering to open his package, he discovers his father's "Grail Diary." He and Marcus take plane to Venice, where they are met by Elsa Schneider. She takes them to the church-become-library where Henry, Sr., was last seen. Using the diary, Indy locates a hidden tomb under the floor. What's more, one of the crusader knights is found. On his shield is inscribed more of the information they need to locate the

Grail. Indy makes a rubbing just before the men who've followed them set fire to the oily water. Indy and Elsa escape in the sewers but upon emerging must commandeer a speedboat. Finally Indy gets the drop on the leader of his pursuers and learns that the man, Kassim, is part of a holy order entailed with protecting the location of the Grail. Indy says that all he wants is his father. He is told his father is incarcerated in a castle on the German-Austrian border. Indy and Elsa drive to the castle just north of Salzburg, sneak inside and find Henry, Sr. But Elsa turns out to be a Nazi herself. And Donovan appears, a traitor. Donovan notices missing pages in the diary. Indy says Marcus has them and a head start. Indy and his dad escape and go to Berlin to retrieve the diary from Elsa. Then, taking a zeppelin and a biplane, the two are forced down by German fighters but eventually make their way to the Republic of Hatay, where Donovan, who has captured Marcus, has bargained with the ruler for guides to the interior. As Indy and Sallah observe the convoy, Kassim's men ambush it. They are beaten off and Henry, Sr., is again captured, but Indy rescues him and escapes with his own life as the German tank on which he was fighting goes over a cliff. Indy, his father, Sallah and Marcus take horses and find the ancient entrance they've been seeking — but Donovan and Elsa have preceded them. Donovan shoots Indy's father as a way of forcing the son to run the terror-filled gauntlet to the Grail. Only the Grail can keep Henry, Sr., from dying. Using his brain and his heart, Indy reaches the chamber wherein the third Crusader knight guards the Grail. The knight believes Indy has come to take on the burden of guardianship and warns him that the Grail cannot go past the seal on the floor in the other chamber. But which Grail of the many is it? "He chose poorly," says the knight after Donovan selects the wrong Grail from which to drink and turns to dust. Indy selects a common-looking vessel, the sort a carpenter would have. "You have chosen wisely," says the knight. But Elsa tries to take it past the seal, causing the floor to open. She falls into the chasm. Indy himself tries to retrieve it from a ledge until his father, his wound miraculously healed, convinces him to let it be. Indy, Henry, Sr., Marcus and Sallah leave after watching the knight lift his hand in farewell.

Reviews: "Seems reasonably fresh and energetic much of the way, although it bogs down in a silly chase (on a military tank) just when it needs a shot of real inventiveness." (David Sterritt, *Christian Science Monitor*, June 13, 1989, p. 11) ¶"Only a determined grouch could deny that *The Last Crusade* is a lot of fun." (David Ansen, *Newsweek*, May 29, 1989, p. 69) ¶"Infuses vitality into the action adventure, a movie staple whose ravenous popularity and endless, predictable permutations have nearly exhausted it." (Richard Corliss, *Time*, May 29, 1989, p. 82)

Analysis: After the relative disappointment that greeted *Indiana Jones and the Temple of Doom* , George Lucas decided to play it safe in this film, one he and director Spielberg touted as definitely the final chapter in the exploits of their archaeologist adventurer. *Indiana Jones and the Last Crusade* returns — and adheres — to the *Raiders of the Lost Ark* formula almost to the point of being as much a remake of the 1981 film as a sequel. Again we see Indiana Jones racing against a refined and urbane villain who teams with Third Reich scum to acquire a priceless holy relic in the deserts of the Middle East. The blueprint worked for *Raiders*, and it works generally here, too, except that now these deeds don't seem nearly as fresh and thrilling as they did the first time around. Some of the film's big set pieces simply ring hollow. The Joneses' motorcycle chase through the forest should have been some sort of high point, but isn't (consider the merry chase on which Steve McQueen led his Nazi pursuers in *The Great Escape*, for instance). And the sequence involving Indy's rescue of his dad and Brody from Vogel in the tank ... this one goes on way too long. Still, *Indiana Jones and the Last Crusade* is a pleasant and generally exciting wrap-up of the Lucas-Spielberg Indiana Jones trilogy. There's definite chemistry between Harrison Ford and Sean Connery, even if there is *none* between Ford and newcomer Alison Doody. It's nice to see Denholm Elliott and John Rhys-Davies return to recreate the roles they had in the first feature. It would have been nice, though, if Karen Allen had returned at least for a cameo appearance as Marion Ravenwood. Explained here are the origin of Indy's hat, whip and aversion to snakes. Academy Award for sound effects editing.

The Raven *see under* **The Fall of the House of Usher**

Re-Animator
(Empire, 1985; 86 min.) ***

Produced by Brian Yuzna. Directed by Stuart Gordon. Screenplay, Dennis Paoli, William J. Norris, Stuart Gordon. Based on the story "Herbert West — Re-animator" by H. P. Lovecraft." Edited by Lee Percy. Director of Photography, Mac Ahlberg. Color, DeLuxe. Music, Richard Band. Art Direction, Robert A. Burns. Set Decoration, Becky Block. Special Effects and Special Makeup Effects, Anthony Doublin, John Naulin. Makeup Supervisor, John Carl Buechler.

Cast: Herbert West (Jeffrey Combs) Dan Cain (Bruce Abbott), Megan Halsey (Barbara Crampton), Dr. Carl Hill (David Gale), Dean Halsey (Robert Sampson), Mace (Gerry Black), Dr. Harrod (Carolyn Purdy-Gordon), Melvin (Peter Kent), Nurse (Barbara Pieters), Dr. Gruber (Al Berry).

Synopsis: After an unfortunate experience with the now deceased Dr. Gruber in Zurich, Herbert West returns to the U.S. and begins a third year of internship at Miskatonic Medical School in Arkham, Massachusetts. He insults renowned brain surgeon Dr. Carl Hill but sets up his own lab in the basement of the building he shares with Dr. Dan Cain. Cain's fiancée, Megan Halsey, daughter of the hospital's Dean Halsey, discovers the body of Dan's cat Rufus in West's refrigerator. West says he was going to tell them later how it suffocated when it got its head stuck in a jar. That night, a bloodcurdling scream wakes Dan. In the basement he finds his cat clawing at the back of West. They kill it, but in order to convince Cain it was dead earlier, West uses his reagent to restore its life a second time. Cain can't convince Dean Halsey of any of this and has his loan revoked. Halsey adds that West will no longer be attending Miskatonic. When Halsey interrupts West and Cain in the hospital morgue, the corpse they've re-animated kills him. West injects Halsey and in seventeen seconds he responds, trying to strangle the two doctors before cowering in the corner from Megan. Megan gives Dr. Hill permission to do exploratory surgery, not realizing Hill is going to lobotomize her father. Cain tells Megan her father is dead, not insane. When Hill demands his secret, West decapitates the blackmailer with a coal shovel, then injects his reagent. But the body knocks him out and absconds with head and reagent. Megan's father takes her to the morgue, where Hill straps her down and removes her clothes preparatory to performing oral sex on her. West and Cain interrupt but are beset by Hill's lobotomized, reanimated minions. Finally Megan makes her father understand her plight, and he crushes Hill's head. West stabs two hypodermics in the body, which spouts tentacles and grabs him. Megan is strangled by a reanimated corpse and Cain can't revive her. When the emergency room attendants leave, he fishes out some reagent. As the screen goes black, a woman's scream is heard.

Review: "Fast pace and a good deal of grisly vitality." (Janet Maslin, *New York Times*, October 18, 1985, p. C6)

Analysis: Although generally overlooked in favor of Poe as a source for cinematic chills for many years, the fiction of H. P. Lovecraft apparently came into its own by the 1980s, when a number of his stories came to the big screen. Previous attempts to film Lovecraft met with varying degrees of success, probably because of the uncinematic nature of the man's fiction, with its long, frequently rambling narratives, its lack of characterization, its conspicuous absence of any meaningful female characters, and its general avoidance of anything even remotely resembling a romantic relationship. When all of these elements were interjected *post facto* by screenwriters, the result was invariably ersatz Lovecraft. Then, too, Lovecraft frequently employed a pantheon of cosmic monstrosities that

would have severely taxed the special effects department of any studio attempting to film his work in the days before the advent of today's computer-generated technologies and other highly advanced FX methods. These techniques now make it possible to put virtually *anything* on screen, so Lovecraft's writhing, oozing, pulsating and exploding horrors are just an everyday challenge to the effects team. Otherwise, what we see most of the time is still ersatz Lovecraft to a large degree, with today's relaxed restrictions on sex and nudity allowing scenes that would have sent the author reeling.

Re-Animator was among the first, and best, of the late-century Lovecraft adaptations, being drawn from a minor cycle of short stories (*Herbert West—Reanimator*) that appeared in a quasi-amateur publication in the early 1920s. Writer Robert M. Price calls *Re-Animator* "by far the most faithful rendering of a Lovecraft tale to date." (Robert M. Price, "Lovecraft on Screen," *Scarlet Street*, Winter 1994, p. 75.) Stuart Gordon's direction is atmospheric and spirited, obviously influenced by George Romero. Jeffrey Combs makes a convincing Lovecraftian protagonist, while David Gale should certainly be considered if a film biography of Lovecraft himself is ever undertaken. Combs has the distinction of appearing in more Lovecraft adaptations than any other actor; following *Re-Animator* he had roles in *From Beyond* (1986, along with his *Re-Animator* co-star Barbara Crampton), *Lurking Fear* (date unknown), and *Necronomicon* (1993, as Lovecraft).

The most unheralded "reanimation" to be found in *Re-Animator* is Richard Band's probably unauthorized refashioning of Bernard Herrmann's classic *Psycho* score. This most assuredly would have the late Bernie Herrmann gyrating in his grave not unlike Herbert West's reanimated creations.

Re-Animator was much anticipated in the trade press, but its theatrical release was distinctly limited. Besides the gore, there is one scene that might have turned off exhibitors: the heroine being stripped by a headless corpse, then licked by the disembodied head. How was this presented to Barbara Crampton?

Bride of Re-Animator
(50th Street Films/Wildstreet Pictures, 1991; 97 min.) **

Produced and directed by Brian Yuzna. Screenplay, Woody Keith and Rick Fry. Story, Brian Yuzna, Woody Keith, Rick Fry. Based on the H. P. Lovecraft story "Herbert West — Re-Animator." Edited by Peter Teschner. Director of Photography, Rick Fichter. Foto-Kem color. Music, Richard Band. Ultra-Stereo. Art Direction, Joseph Ressa. Set Decoration, Simon Dobbin. Special Makeup and Visual Effects, Screaming Mad George, David Allen.

Cast: Herbert West (Jeffrey Combs), Dan Cain (Bruce Abbott), Lt. Chapman (Claude Earl Jones), Francesca (Fabiana Udenio), Dr. Hill (David Gale), Gloria/The Bride (Kathleen Kinmont), Dr. Wilbur Graves (Mel Stewart), Nurse (Irene Forrest).

Synopsis: After giving of their time and expertise during a Peruvian civil war, Doctors West and Cain return to Miskatonic Hospital in Arkham, Massachusetts — eight months after the "Miskatonic Massacre." West intends to create new life. Police Lieutenant Chapman brings the head of the late Dr. Hill to Dr. Graves. Graves shows the bagged remains of the massacre to Chapman. Strangely, the body parts evince no deterioration. Later, West takes one of the body parts surreptitiously but notices Hill's head and speaks to it, saying it is now proven that consciousness resides in all cells. In West's basement lab he shows Cain the late Megan Halsey's heart. Dr. Graves restores Dr. Hill's head with a strange reagent. Hill says he has unfinished business. Francesca, whom West and Cain met in Peru, arrives in town. Lt. Chapman questions her and shows her three seemingly lunatic humans, including Chapman's wife, who were victims of the massacre. West and Cain prepare a body into whose chest cavity West places Megan's heart and into which he plans to inject the reagent. Lt. Chapman enters the basement. West kills, then reanimates him. In the ensuing fight, Chapman's right hand is severed and he kills Francesca's dog. Later West puts the human limb on the dog and

reanimates it. At the hospital the terminally ill patient Gloria dies and West takes her head. Meanwhile, Chapman secures Hill's head. The West-Cain operation proceeds, but a knock on the door takes West upstairs. Outside on the doorstep is a crate. When West opens it, out flies Hill's head, now equipped with bat wings. In the basement Gloria/Megan revives. Success is compromised by the lunatics and Chapman, who attack the house. Francesca arrives and helps build a barricade. While this transpires, Cain realizes he can't quite love the new Gloria/Megan, who then rips out her heart and offers it to him. Gloria/Megan fights Francesca but is electrocuted and shortly thereafter falls apart. West tries to exit via his tunnel through the mausoleum next door but is captured by his "rejects." The roof collapses and only Cain and Francesca emerge.

Review: "Strong stuff.... wait till you see the crawling eyeball! ... [not] nearly as successful as the original *Re-Animator*." (Leonard Maltin, ed., *Movie and Video Guide 1993*, p. 151)

Analysis: There's plenty of gore and some fun, e.g., West's "My God, they're using tools!" When you see something like this, you realize how good Hammer Studios was at casting superlatively beautiful women in its horror films.

The Rebirth *see* Howling V: The Rebirth *under* **The Howling**

Repossessed *see under* **The Exorcist**

The Resurrected *see under* **The Haunted Palace**

Return of Count Yorga *see under* **County Yorga, Vampire**

The Return of Dr. X *see under* **Dr. X**

The Return of Dracula *see under* **Dracula**

The Return of Durant *see* Darkman II: The Return of Durant *under* **Darkman**

The Return of Michael Meyers *see* Halloween 4: The Return of Michael Meyers *under* **Halloween**

Return of the Fly *see under* **The Fly**

Return of the Jedi *see under* **Star Wars**

Return of the Living Dead *see under* **Night of the Living Dead**

Return of the Living Dead Part II *see under* **Night of the Living Dead**

Return of the Living Dead Part III *see under* **Night of the Living Dead**

The Return of Swamp Thing *see under* **Swamp Thing**

Return to Boggy Creek *see under* **The Legend of Boggy Creek**

Return to Witch Mountain *see under* **Escape to Witch Mountain**

Revenge of the Boogeyman *see* Boogeymen II *under* **The Boogey Man**

Revenge of the Creature *see under* **The Creature from the Black Lagoon**

The Revenge of Frankenstein *see under* **Frankenstein**

The Revenge of Michael Meyers *see* Halloween 5 *under* **Halloween**

The Road Warrior *see* Mad Max II *under* **Mad Max**

Robocop
(Orion, 1987; 103 min.) ***½

Produced by Arne Schmidt. Directed by Paul Verhoeven. Screenplay, Edward Neumeier, Michael Miner. Edited by Frank J. Urioste. Director of Photography, Jost Vacano. DeLuxe Color. Music, Basil Poledouris. Song "Show Me Your Spine," P.T.P. Sound, Robert Wald. Dolby Stereo. Surround Sound.

Art Direction, Gayle Simon. Set Decoration, Robert Gould. Stunts, Gary Combs. Special Effects, Dale Martin. Special Photographic Effects, Peter Kuran and Visual Concept Engineering. Robomovement, Moni Yakim. Special Effects, Bill Purcell, Keith Richins, Lawrence Aeschlimann. Robocop Design and Creation, Rob Bottin. ED-209 Sequences, Phil Tippett. ED-209 Design and Creation, Craig Davies, Peter Ronzana. Visual Effects, Harry Walton. Animation, Randy Dutra.

Cast: Murphy/Robocop (Peter Weller), Anne Lewis (Nancy Allen), Old Man (Dan O' Herlihy), Dick Jones (Ronny Cox), Clarence Boddicker (Kurtwood Smith), Morton (Miguel Ferrer), Sergeant Reed (Robert DoQui), Leon (Ray Wise), Johnson (Felton Perry), Emil (Paul McCrane), Joe (Jesse Goins), Kaplan (Del Zamora), Minh (Calvin Jung), Walker (Rick Lieberman), Sal (Lee DeBroux), Miller (Mark Carlton), Manson (Edward Edwards), Lt. Hedgecock (Michael Gregory), Bobby (Fred Hice), Dougy (Neil Summers), Prisoner (Gene Wolande), Slimy lawyer (Gregory Poudevigne), Bail bondsman (Charles Carroll), Kinney (Ken Page), Startweather (Tyress Allen), Chessman (John Davies), Cecil (Laird Stuart).

Synopsis: Detroit, in the near future, is a typical urban nightmare of crumbling neighborhoods bordering glass and steel high-rises. The beleaguered police departments are barely able to hold their own against the burgeoning crime rate, and private companies take a larger hand in what seems to be the losing battle of crime control. Omni Computer Products (OCP) is the foremost of those companies providing sophisticated computerized weaponry and robotized law enforcement automatons. At OCP, vice president Dick Jones is promoting the tank-like ED-209 series, while Morton, up and coming junior executive, eagerly pushes his own cyborg "Robocop" line. Meanwhile, police officer Alex Murphy has transferred into Detroit's Metro West division and is teamed with the female officer Lewis. Lured into an abandoned steel mill after a freeway firefight, Murphy is ambushed by felons led by Clarence Boddicker. Lewis arrives and finds Murphy more dead than alive, his body virtually blown apart by the fusillade. When Morton's people at OCP hear about what has happened, the patrolman's brain and facial features are transferred into a powerful metallic humanoid fabrication. After weeks of preparation, OCP's Robocop is released to serve a tour of duty at Metro West. Robocop's arrival causes a popular sensation, as the cyborg collars violent criminals of all descriptions. His creators had failed to reckon with resurgent memories, however, and nightmare visions of Boddicker's gang alternate with less unpleasant flashbacks of Murphy's former happy family life. Robocop captures Boddicker, who confesses that he is on the payroll of Dick Jones. When he attempts to arrest Jones, the cyborg cop is stricken with a sudden weakness, barely able to maintain consciousness. Jones reveals that Robocop's programming contains "Directive Four": an encoded protection against attacking upper-level OCP executives. Robocop barely escapes an attacking ED-209 and finds himself facing a phalanx of heavily armed OCP security and Detroit police, whom Jones summoned on the pretext that Robocop has gone berserk. The man-android escapes only with the help of Officer Lewis, who has come to realize that this Robocop is her former partner, Murphy. Jones pulls the strings necessary to have Boddicker and his gang released from jail. Armed with lightweight armor-piercing cannon, Boddicker and his men launch an all-out assault on Robocop and Lewis at the steel mill. The cyborg eliminates the gangsters one by one but is very nearly done in himself by Boddicker. The scales are tipped by Lewis, however, and Robocop triumphs. Returning to OCP headquarters, the cyborg enters the boardroom and delivers incontrovertible evidence of Jones's crimes but states that he is unable to make an arrest, prevented by Directive Four. The vice president pulls a gun and grabs the Old Man for a hostage. The wily old exec promptly fires his junior officer, clearing the way for Robocop to carry out his duty, and Jones meets his fate as the cyborg's gun blazes away.

Reviews: "Assembled with ferocious, gleeful expertise...." (Michael Wilmington, *Los Angeles Times Calendar*, July 17, 1987, p. 1) ¶"One must applaud Dutch-born director Paul Verhoeven for maintaining a balance between man and machine.

Edward Neumeier and Michael Miner have written a script rising miles above the action-adventure category." (Mike McGrady, *Newsday*, July 17, 1987, Part III, p. 3) ¶"Uses the brutal future as a mere convention, a way of upping the level of violence." (David Denby, *New York Post*, July 27, 1987, p. 58)

Analysis: While at first glance appearing to be something along the lines of a *Terminator* clone, *Robocop* plainly has its own hard-edged agenda. Though clearly very much a part of the sci-fi action-adventure crowd that was given impetus (more or less) by 1982's *The Road Warrior* (*Mad Max II*), *Robocop* is set in an almost dystopian near future that would seem all too grim and bitter, even ugly, if it weren't relieved with touches of broad, almost slapstick, humor that takes its stabs at the medical profession, yuppie snots, politics and, of course, the kind of corrupt big business that Omni Computer Products represents. Dutch director Paul Verhoeven made his American debut here, having been active in the foreign art film market (*The Fourth Man* and *Flesh + Blood* in 1983 and 1985, respectively). He handles *Robocop* with great esprit and command of technique. Verhoeven went on to direct the Schwarzenegger opus *Total Recall*, another sci-fi actioner that delights in bloodying the nose of big business. Peter Weller's rather mannequin-like good looks are certainly appropriate to the role of Alex Murphy/Robocop, and his stiff, robotic movements as the cyborg seem quite natural. Nancy Allen, while usually projecting rather too girlish an image to be entirely believable in a role seemingly intended more for the likes of a Sigourney Weaver, doesn't do badly either, and Ronny Cox (as Dick Jones), formerly seen in more likable, homespun roles, was just beginning his Slimy Villain phase (he turned up, too, in *Total Recall*, playing a similar corporate creep). *Robocop*'s action heavy is Kurtwood Smith, whose cold features and harsh, cutting voice make him perfect for such roles. Special effects are to this kind of movie what big skies are to westerns, and the cyborg effects by Rob Bottin, Phil Tippett, et al., make *Robocop* the exciting blend of

action and satire that it is. The ED-209 sequences, in particular, stand out; the makers obviously had a riot in creating these
scenes, and ED very nearly steals the show.

Robocop 2
(Orion, 1990; 118 min.) ***

Produced by Jon Davison. Directed by Ir-
vin Kershner. Assistant Director, Tom Davies.
Screenplay, Frank Miller and Walon Green.
Story, Frank Miller. Based on characters cre-
ated by Edward Neumeier and Michael
Miner. Edited by William Anderson. Director
of Photography, Mark Irwin. DeLuxe Color.
Music, Leonard Rosenman. Dolby Stereo. De-
sign, Peter Jamison. Costumes, Rosana Nor-
ton. Stunts, Conrad E. Palmisano. Special
Effects Supervision, Dale Martin, William
Greg Curtis. Robocop Design/Creation, Rob
Bottin. Robocop Animation, Phil Tippett.

Cast: Robocop (Peter Weller), Anne Lewis
(Nancy Allen), Donald Johnson (Felton
Perry), Sergeant Reed (Robert DoQui), Cain
(Tom Noonan), Mayor Kuzak (Willard Pugh),
Dr. Juliette Faxx (Belinda Bauer), Hob (Gab-
riel Damon), Angie (Galyn Gorg), Old Man
(Dan O'Herlihy), Duffy (Stephen Lee), Whit-
taker (Roger Aaron Brown), Lab Technician
Garcia (Patricia Charbonneau), Holzgang
(Jeff McCarthy), Estevez (Waanda De Jesus),
Schenk (John Doolittle), Delaney (Ken Ler-
ner), Tak Akita (Tzi Ma), Sunblock woman
(Fabiana Udenio), Magnavolt salesman (John
Glover), Casey Wong (Mario Machado), Gil-
lette (George Cheung), Catzo (Michael Me-
deiros), Leeza Gibbons (Jess Perkins), Sur-
geon General (John Ingle), Stef (Mark
Rolston), Poulos (Phil Rubenstein).

Synopsis: Crime in Detroit has gone
from bad to worse, especially with the police strike now occurring. Not only is crime
enervating the authorities, but the city is
about to suffer foreclosure by its biggest
financier, Omni Consumer Products. One
of the few non-striking officers is Robocop.
His main target is the crime lord known as
Cain. This criminal has been manufacturing and distributing a new and fashionable
designer drug, a euphoric called Nuke. Invading Cain's plant, Robocop finds that
he's entered a carefully planned ambush.
Using heavy machinery, the crooks largely
disassemble the cyborg. At first Omni Consumer Products is reluctant to fund the
multi-million dollar repair, but Dr. Juliette
Faxx prompts OCP's Old Man to rebuild

Robocop because (1) the company's "Robocop 2" project has been a costly failure,
and (2) it would be a public relations coup.
The go-ahead is given, and Robocop is
soon back on the job with his partner,
Lewis. Lewis and the other officers learn
that Robocop's original directives have
been augmented with thousands of others
of every legally, psychologically and po-
litically correct stripe imaginable. Hearing
a suggestion that these directives might be
eliminated by an infusion of electricity,
Robocop finds an electrical substation and
emerges as originally designed. He and his
inspired fellow police raid Cain's sludge
plant hideaway. Robocop pursues the drug
lord through the streets of Detroit before
a crash nearly kills Cain. Meanwhile, Juliette Faxx has concluded that Robocop 2
might succeed if a fiercely determined
criminal brain is installed. The gravely injured Cain seems an ideal choice. The
monstrous automaton's first mission is to
disrupt a meeting between the mayor and
the remnants of Cain's own gang. The
mayor barely manages to escape. Later, at
a gala for the news media at OCP headquarters, the Old Man presents both his
ambitious views for New Detroit, now that
his corporation "owns" the city, and the
new law enforcement entity that will make
the streets safe: Robocop 2. But when the
Old Man says they will eliminate Nuke, the
addicted Cain cyborg runs amok, his fiery
guns spitting death in all directions. Robocop appears, and in the ensuing battle,
much of the building is demolished. Lewis
commandeers an armored personnel carrier and rams the larger automaton, giving
Robocop a short breather. Then, as Lewis
distracts Robocop 2 with a canister of
Nuke, Robocop leaps on the back of his
larger foe and tears into the monster's
metal cowling. Extracting the living brain,
Robocop smashes it to a pulp. Robocop 2
collapses in a smoky heap.

Reviews: "The sequel as unmitigated
disaster." (David Sterritt, *Christian Science
Monitor*, July 6, 1990, p. 12)

Analysis: This sequel to 1987's *Robocop*
didn't fare altogether well at the box office,
although the returns were enough to generate interest in a third film concerning the

postmortem exploits of Officer Alex Murphy, the Robocop. Critics, too, were ungenerous with *Robocop 2*, most of them maligning it as merely a retread of the original. Peter Ranier in the *Los Angeles Times Calendar* (June 22, 1990, p. 1) claimed that director Kershner was hamstrung by a script that gave him no chance to express his "usual range." In fact, however, *Robocop 2* has much to recommend it. One finds the same sort of biting dark humor in this second look at Detroit's supposed dystopian future; where else would one likely encounter a mess of felonious Little Leaguers maniacally trashing a sporting goods store, while their gun-toting coach held off the police in a firefight outside? Where else would one find the action put on hold while a California babe pitches the thick, blue "Sunblock 5000" that protects her delicate hide from the deadly ultraviolet that is no longer deflected by an atmosphere that is ozone-depleted? Where else would one find a foul-mouthed, machine gun–wielding twelve-year-old raising such a murderous ruckus (other than, unfortunately, on the streets of just about every big city in America today)? The Robocop films escalate urban decay and disintegration to the level of high-tech art in their level of mayhem. Although short on subtleties, *Robocop 2* delivers the goods in terms of action and effects, something one should not find surprising coming from the director of *The Empire Strikes Back*. Peter Weller returns in the title role, bringing his own kind of nuance to the part. Also returning are Nancy Allen, Dan O'Herlihy, Felton Perry and Robert DoQui in the roles they had in the earlier film. As with the first film, naturally, the real stars of *Robocop 2* are the special effects and robotic design work of Mssrs. Bottin, Tippett, et al., without whose inspired and lunatic creations films like this couldn't exist.

Robocop 3
(Orion, 1993; 105 min.) **½

Produced by Patrick Crowley. Directed by Fred Dekker. Screenplay, Frank Miller and Fred Dekker. Story, Frank Miller. Based on characters created by Edward Neumeier and Michael Miner. Director of Photography, Gary B. Kibbe. Music, Basil Poledouris. Stop-Motion Animation, Phil Tippett.

Cast: Robocop (Robert John Burke), Anne Lewis (Nancy Allen), Nikko (Remy Ryan), Dr. Marie Lazarus (Jill Hennessy), CEO (Rip Torn), Bertha (CCH Pounder), Paul McDaggett (John Castle).

Synopsis: Detroit continues to go downhill as gangs of thugs similar to the west side's Spatterpunks make life miserable for urban poor and beleaguered police alike. Omni Consumer Products has been taken over by the giant Japanese Konomitsu Corporation, and plans for OCP's long-anticipated Delta City proceed at full speed. Only the inhabitants of Cadillac Heights, the site of the proposed megalopolis, stand in the way. OCP's newly organized Urban Rehabilitation Officers, headed by "incident commander" Paul McDaggett, sweep the Heights, rounding up homeless and lawful residents alike, sending them to relocation centers. An organized underground resists the Rehab teams. Robocop Murphy and Officer Anne Lewis intercede on behalf of the resisters. Lewis is gunned down by McDaggett, and Robocop is damaged by a grenade. The indigents hold off McDaggett's men until the downed cyborg can be dragged into the church behind bolted doors. Later, with the help of Dr. Marie Lazarus, the mechanical man is repaired. Lazarus throws in with the urban guerrillas. During his "recuperation" the cyborg cop develops an almost fatherly fondness for the precocious twelve-year-old computer savant, Nikko. With the "Murphy" side of his personality becoming stronger with the murder of Anne Lewis, Robocop tracks McDaggett down. The Rehab man manages to escape. Later, an armed Rehab team invades the guerrilla hideout and Robocop is attacked by a samurai sword–wielding ninja sent by Konomitsu. After the cyborg has his hand lopped off, he manages to snare a rocket launcher. The resulting explosion reveals that the ninja is a robot, now destroyed. Next day at the police station, McDaggett demands that Sergeant Reed hand over fifty of his men to aid the Rehab team's sweep through Cadillac Heights. Reed refuses and tosses his shield to the floor. His action is followed by his men. The embittered sergeant and his troop go to the Heights and join the guerrillas. The crafty Mc-Daggett augments his forces with Splatterpunk recruits and makes things bad for the defenders of the Heights. The timely appearance of a flying Robocop, equipped with an energizing jetpack designed by Dr. Lazarus, turns the tide. Smashing into OCP headquarters, Robocop is beset by a pair of the robot ninjas, who would easily outmatch him if not for the ingenuity of young Nikko, who reprograms the androids into attacking and destroying each other. Their demise triggers an automatic self-destruct device in the OCP command center. Robocop scoops up Lazarus and Nikko and jets them to safety as the top of the skyscraper, McDaggett included, vaporizes behind them.

Reviews: "About as deadly a case of the third-chapter blues as I've encountered since *Poltergeist III*.... Script appears to have been Scotch-taped together from half a dozen discarded ideas...." (Owen Gleiberman, *Entertainment Weekly*, November 5, 1993, p. 51) ¶"Nothing charming — or even remotely engaging." (Marshall Fine, *News Journal 55 Hours*, Wilmington, DE, November 5-7, 1993, p. 7) ¶"It's still hard to get very involved with Robocop; rooting for him is like cheering for an electric can opener." (Ralph Novak, *People Weekly*, November 8, 1993, p. 19) ¶"A tad more coherent than the ultraviolet second installment.... Weller had an ironic pucker that his stolid substitute, Robert John Burke, sorely lacks." (Carrie Rickey, *Philadelphia Inquirer*, November 5, 1993, p. 4)

Analysis: Less nasty, not as vicious as the earlier films, this slickest sequel benefits from nice performances by its principals, although John Castle packs not the nasty punch of Robo's earlier villains, and Peter Weller is sorely missed in the title role. Robert Burke has the sculpted features for the part, but his movements are less stylishly "mechanical" than his predecessor's, a derogatory comment on any movie but this.

Rocket to the Moon *see* **Cat-Women of the Moon**

Roger Corman's Frankenstein Unbound *see under* **Frankenstein**

The Satanic Rites of Dracula *see under* **Dracula**

Scanner Cop *see under* **Scanners**

Scanners
(Avco Embassy/Filmplan International, 1981; 103 min.) ***

Produced by Claude Heroux. Directed by David Cronenberg. Screenplay, David Cronenberg. Edited by Ron Sanders. Director of Photography, Mark Irwin. Color. Panavision. Music, Howard Shore. Art Direction, Carol Spier. Special Effects, Gary Zeller. Makeup, Brigitte McCaughry. Consultant for Special Makeup Effects, Dick Smith.

Cast: Cameron Vale (Stephen Lack), Kim Obrist (Jennifer O'Neill), Dr. Paul Ruth (Patrick McGoohan), Braedon Keller (Lawrence Dane), Darryl Revok (Michael Ironside), Gaudi (Charles Shamata), Crostic (Adam Ludwig), Dr. Gafineau (Victor Desy), Trevellyan (Mavor Moore), Benjamin Pierce (Robert Silverman).

Synopsis: Cameron Vale is picked up by Dr. Paul Ruth, who works for Con Sec, an international security business. Ruth hopes to use scanners — special people with telepathic powers — to benefit mankind. First, however, he must enlist scanners like Vale to infiltrate a scanner underground headed by the vicious Darryl Revok. Ruth explains that the scanning ability may have been caused by radiation or disease. The drug ephemerol stops the flow of telepathy and grants scanners a modicum of peace. Braedon Keller is in charge of Con Sec's internal security, but he betrays the organization to Revok. Vale finds Benjamin Pierce, scanner and artist, but Pierce is assassinated. With his dying breath, he gives Vale some clues. Vale finds Kim Obrist and some other independent scanners. Another assassination team kills Obrist's friends. Only she and Vale escape. They go to Ruth. Vale tells Ruth that Biocarbon Amalgamate Company, apparently headed by Revok, is sending batches of ephemerol across the country. Ruth, whose company Biocarbon originally was, tells Vale to merge his nervous system with the computer system to find the list of doctors

Darryl Revok (Michael Ironside, left) is locked in combat with a fellow scanner in *Scanners* (Avco Embassy/Filmplan, 1981).

receiving the shipments of ephemerol. Keller kills Ruth. Vale and Kim escape. Using the telephone, Vale enters the computer system. Keller learns about it and shuts the system down. Far from being destroyed by this move, Vale blows up the computers, killing Keller. He and Kim visit Dr. Frane, and when Kim is scanned by an unborn baby, they realize the ephemerol is being administered to pregnant women to create a scanner race. Revok captures Kim and Vale and reveals that Ruth was his father and that Vale is his brother. Vale refuses to work with his brother, and they have a scan war. Vale is set on fire, but when Kim enters the room she finds that the charred body on the floor, while that of Vale, does not contain Vale's mind. It's in Revok's. They've won.

Reviews: "David Cronenberg's *Scanners* is easily his finest film to date. Its engrossing plot ... and its many fine individual scenes hold one's interest in a way that the Canadian writer-director's earlier works, such as *Rabid* and *The Brood*, never could.... There isn't the deliberate effort to disgust." (Bruce McClelland, *Cinemacabre* Number 4, p. 50) ¶"This is a picture that can provide

you with gigantic goose pimples of horror if you don't close your eyes. Kids in search of a movie thrill will be delighted." (Archer Winsten, *New York Post*, January 14, 1981, p. 17) ¶"The writer/director is as involved with social affects as he is with special effects: he supplements his terror with philosophy." (Carrie Rickey, *Village Voice*, January 28-February 3, 1981, p. 46)

Analysis: Notwithstanding director David Cronenberg's reputation, we found the sequel as good or better than this admittedly fascinating progenitor. It may be that Cronenberg's characters are not all that likable or that the audience knows early on that they are headed for oblivion. Michael Ironside, the ostensible villain of this piece, is the most compelling character. It's fairly subdued after an early scene in which a man's head explodes.

Scanners II: The New Order
(Triton Pictures/Image Organization/ Malofilm Group, 1991; 105 min.)
***½

Produced by Rene Malo. Directed by Christian Duguay. Screenplay, B. J. Nelson.

Based on original characters created by David Cronenberg. Edited by Yves Langlois. Director of Photography, Rodney Gibbons. Color. Music, Marty Simon. Special Makeup, Mike Smithson.

Cast: David Kellum (David Hewlett), Julie Vale (Deborah Raffin), Commander John Forrester (Yvan Ponton), Alice Leonardo (Isabele Mejias), Peter Drak (Raoul Trujillo), Dr. Morse (Tom Butler), Mayor (Dorothee Berryman), Walter (Stephan Zarou), Lieutenant Gelson (Vlasta Vrana), George Kellum (Murray Westgate), Susan Kellum (Doris Petrie).

Synopsis: Police Commander John Forrester and Dr. Morse realize that Peter Drak, a man who destroyed a video parlor, is a scanner with telepathic powers. Drak is captured and sedated with other scanners in the Morse Neurological Research Institute. Meanwhile, David Kellum, studying at the Sir Rodwick Gibbons Veterinary School, is befriended by fellow student Alice Leonardo. David foils a grocery store robbery, and as the video camera indicates, he is obviously the clean, virgin scanner that the fascistic Forrester is seeking to help him destroy crime. Dr. Morse tells David his condition is probably the result of his mother taking a drug in the 1950s that caused his "birth defect." Peter Drak, now more amenable, is brought in as a test. David helps Forrester identify the man guilty of poisoning milk. Peter, meanwhile, makes the chief of police commit suicide. At Forrester's urging, David makes the mayor appoint Forrester interim chief. Peter tells David about Forrester's ultimate goals, and David goes to the Morse Institute and scans Forrester before fleeing to his home. He tells his parents of the problem and they reveal that his real parents, Kim and Cameron, were scanners. Lt. Gelson and Drak arrive, wound David's adoptive father and kill his mother. David returns from his walk and saves his father's life. His father tells him he has an older sister, Julie Vale, living up north. David finds Julie, who reveals that Forrester killed their father. She tells him it's useless to fight or go back, but he says he loves Alice and must go. David tells the mayor about scanners, but Lt. Gelson shoots her through the window. David flees. Julie arrives and

explains a trick that allows them to get into Lt. Gelson's mind. Manipulating Gelson, they see inside the Institute and kill Morse. Drak realizes Gelson *is* David and explodes the lieutenant's head. Julie and David crash the gate. Inside, Julie is wounded by a sedation bullet and David battles Drak. He is aided by the incarcerated scanners, including Julie's old boyfriend, Walter. Forrester arrives but so does the press, obviously called by Alice. David scans Forrester to make him confess. When he grabs a gun, Julie and David deform him. "We mean you no harm," says David to the press and other police. Julie comforts Walter.

Review: "Aside from Mejias, thesps are well cast.... Tech credits and special effects are excellent." (Suze., *Variety*, May 6, 1991)

Analysis: This is a fascinating, exciting, tense and engrossing sequel. Nice touch: a comment about not wanting any scan wars in the warehouse. O-o-h, sounds dangerous, exciting, forbidden. Highly recommended.

Scanners III: The Takeover
(Malofilm Group, 1992; 101 min.) ***

Produced by Rene Malo. Directed by Christian Duguay. Screenplay, B. J. Nelson, Julie Richard, David Preston. Based on characters created by David Cronenberg. Edited by Yves Langlois. Director of Photography, Hugues De Haeck. Music, Marty Simon. Special Makeup, Mike Maddi.

Cast: Helena Monet (Liliana Komorowska), Alex Monet (Steve Parrish), Joyce (Valerie Valois), Michael (Daniel Pilon). With Claire Celluci, Collin Fox, Harry Hill.

Synopsis: A preface indicates that in the 1940s the drug ephemerol caused "Scanner Syndrome" in the offspring of some women who'd taken the drug during pregnancy. Urged on by a friend, the adult Alex Monet uses his telepathic powers to propel a friend across the room — but he loses control and the friend falls to his death from the balcony. Alex leaves to find peace in a Thai monastery. His sister Helena suffers from severe migraines. Her father says a new drug may help but he doesn't want to test it on her. She remembers terrible ordeals as a youth at the hands of the "perverted" Dr. Baumann. She finds her adoptive father's briefcase full of sample patches, puts one behind her ear and experiences relief. Yet it changes her personality. She locates Dr. Baumann and explodes his head and releases the scanners upon which he'd been experimenting. She kills her father and takes over the Monet Pharmaceutical Company. Michael, executor of her father's will, finds Alex but is killed by scanners controlled by Helena. Alex is told by his Thai mentor that he must seek out and destroy evil. Helena learns from scientist Joyce, Alex's old girlfriend, that the drug created by her father is inert and has no properties that would give Helena the relief she experiences. Helena watches videos made by her father and finds that the missing ingredient is a secretion in scanners themselves. Returning to his home, Alex is set upon by Helena's henchmen but escapes. Learning that she can project her scanning powers via television, Helena attempts to convert an estimated 75,000,000 viewers into her slaves. Alex disposes of her cohorts and in a battle of wills causes Helena's drug patch to fall to the floor. She realizes what she's become and electrocutes herself. Her essence enters the cable and the video camera — dissipated or latent?

Review: "Tech credits are excellent and thesps do as much as possible...." (Susan Ayscough, *Variety*, February 10, 1992)

Analysis: It's a good movie but has serious flaws, namely Helena's scanner minions who dress like the Blues Brothers and act like larger-than-life villains from *Batman*. They interject unwanted, unexpected humor, and their marksmanship is poor. *Variety* noted that the violence was not so graphic and more interesting this time.

Scanner Cop

(Republic/Image, 1993; 94 min.) ***

Produced and directed by Pierre David. Screenplay, George Saunders and John Bryant. Based on original characters created by David Cronenberg. Edited by Julian Semilian. Director of Photography, Jacques Haitkin. Color, Foto-Kem. Music, Louis Febre. Special Makeup and Creature Effects, John Carl Buechler and Magical Media Industries. **Cast:** Samuel Staziak (Daniel Quinn), Dr.

Joan Alden (Darlanne Fluegel), Commander Peter Harrigan (Richard Grove), Glock (Richard Lynch), Lt. Brown (Mark Rolston), Zena (Hilary Shepard), Damon Pratt (Gary Hudson), Melvin Jones (James Horan), Dr. Krench (Luca Bercovici), Riley (Christopher Kriesa), Margaret Harrigan (Savannah Smith Boucher), Rick Kopek (Ben Reed) Sara Kopek (Cyndi Pass), Young Samuel (Elan Rothschild), Dr. Hampton (Brion James).

Synopsis: Young Sam Staziak's father goes berserk after four days without ephemerol and is killed by his landlord. Pete Harrigan, a policeman whom the son has saved from his demented father, takes Sam into his home. "15 Years Later": Samuel Staziak becomes a police officer. While he and his family celebrate, two police officers are unaccountably shot by a diner counter man, and at a newsstand a man perceives a cop as an attacker and beats him. Is it a coincidence? A gaudy woman shows a newspaper headline to a man who resides behind the walls of a psychic parlor. He says they'll have to tease the police next time. After hospital intern Damon Pratt stabs a cop he is diagnosed as catatonic. Sam refuses now-commander Pete Harrigan's request to use his special powers to help the investigation. But when janitor Melvin Jones kills Sam's partner in the station's locker room, he decides to interrogate Pratt. Lt. Brown is skeptical (but Pete is not) when Sam says he sees the hallucinations Pratt saw. When they're out of the room, Pratt kills himself by thrusting his head through a pane of glass. That night Sam uses his scanning powers to stop a mugging and decides to stop taking ephemerol until this case is closed. Dr. Joan Alden, a psychiatrist, discovers a puncture mark on Pratt's head. He'd been injected with something. The lady in black kidnaps Sara Kopek, who stabs and kills her policeman husband whom she thinks is a giant insect. Sam scans her and sees the street she was on during her abduction. Because Sara begins to hemorrhage at the ears, Dr. Alden stops the process before Sam can see the face of the man who brainwashed her. With one more day to solve the case before he'll agree to go back on ephemerol, Sam cruises the city looking for the intersection Sara saw. He enters a psychic's shop and during the session scans the woman in black, Zena. When he leaves, he looks back through the window and sees a man. He recreates the man's face on a computer and learns that it's Glock, a neurosurgeon who lost his license, then indoctrinated teenagers with his hairbrained ideas and drugs. Pete had shot him some years before, necessitating the placement of a metal plate in his head. Glock had gained the confidence of a doctor at the Chatsworth Mental Institute, then stabbed a pen into his ear and escaped. The police raid Zena's shop but find neither her, Glock nor the secret door. Lt. Brown is kidnapped, and from the detective's files Glock learns that Sam is a scanner *and* Pete's son. Brown wounds Pete before being shot. At the hospital Sam senses the presence of Zena. He finds her outside but she's run into by an ambulance. As she dies, Sam scans her and enters a hell-like realm where he must explode her head in order to escape himself. Returning to the psychic parlor, Sam is captured by Glock but uses his powers to start an electrical fire. Glock rushes out, crying that he'll get Pete himself. Sam breaks his bonds and races after the lunatic. Glock incapacitates the chief surgeon and takes his place, but before he can put his scalpel to horrific use Sam arrives and tries to scan him. It works a little, but the titanium plate in Glock's head prevents total control. Again, Sam must use manmade devices to foil the madman. He teleports electric heart paddles from their machine to Glock. Yet Glock is only down, not out, and comes at Sam with a scalpel. Grabbing his arm, Sam summons all his powers and causes the plate to eject from Glock's head. The insane murderer collapses. Later, in the station locker room, Sam takes his "vitamins" and welcomes a new patrolman partner.

Review: "Good effects, suspense and a honed script." (John Stanley, *John Stanley's Creature Features Movie Guide Strikes Again*, p. 335)

Analysis: At least twice a phone call or radio message would have stopped the mayhem. Such flaws aside, this is an engrossing film. The Scanners films may be the most consistently entertaining modern

science fiction film series. Daniel Quinn makes an ingratiating hero.

Scanners 4: The Showdown
(Republic/Image, 1994; 95 min.) ***

Produced by Pierre David. Directed by Steve Barnett. Screenplay, Mark Sevi. Based on the original characters created by David Cronenberg. Edited by Patrick Rand. Director of Photography, Thomas Jewett. Color, Foto-Kem. Music, Richard Bowers. Set Decoration, Susanna Bernstein. Special Makeup Effects, John Carl Buechler and Magical Media Industries. Special Effects, S.P.F.X., Ltd.

Cast: Samuel Staziak (Daniel Quinn), Karl Volkin (Patrick Kilpatrick), Carrie Goodart (Khrystyne Haje), Jim Mullins (Stephen Mendel), Glory Avionis (Brenda Swanson), Detective Jack Bitters (Robert Forster), Sheriff (Jerry Potter), Nurse (Jewel Shepard), Rachel Staziak (Barbara Tarbuck), Doctor Tom (Allan Kolman), Denise (Lisa Comshaw), Dr. Gordon (Aaron Lustig), J. J. (Evan Mackenzie), Pickpocket Jones (Tony Fasce), Kidnapper #1 (Kane Hodder).

Synopsis: A rowdy drifter picked up by rural police is revealed as a scanner who may not be taking his ephemerol. In order to escape custody, the scanner uses his special mental powers to make the deputy kill an examining physician and prevents the sheriff from firing his gun. Scanners are the subject of research at the Trans-Neural Resource Center in Los Angeles, where Detective Sam Staziak, a scanner himself, hopes scanner Carrie Goodart can locate his birth mother. The scanner who fled the police breaks into Trans-Neural and overcomes Carrie's forces and examines a computer screen of addresses. He discovers that he can suck the life force of a person but is prevented from killing Carrie when sirens herald the police. At Staziak's house the killer scanner tries to murder the detective with his own shotgun. A scanner duel takes place, but the criminal escapes. In an alley the mad scanner destroys another scanner, the pickpocket Jones. Not only does he kill him, he turns him to a blackened shell. Staziak uses his powers to make the unconscious Carrie draw a picture of her attacker: Karl Volkin. Staziak had caused Karl's brother's death during a robbery some time before. In the city, Karl continues his rampage, killing civilians and police alike in order to gain extra power to confront his nemesis Staziak. In a warehouse, Staziak is almost crushed and Karl gets away again. Learning the location of Staziak's mother, Karl proceeds to the St. Jude Retirement Home. Cornered on a balcony, Rachel Staziak jumps to her death rather than become a pawn in Karl's plan to kill her son. Staziak arrives and finds Karl a difficult opponent. Remembering Carrie's urging to create an illusion that will confound the increasingly demented Volkin, Staziak makes Karl use up his extra powers on two dead policemen looking like Sam. Then Staziak uses his will to explode Karl's head and torso.

Review: "Passable film." (Mick Martin and Marsha Porter, *Video Movie Guide 1997*, p. 940)

Analysis: This one is "4" even though *Scanner Cop* followed *Scanners III*. Admirably, they segue from the previous entry where Sam's mother was not in evidence. Her decision to leap to her death is logical and evidence of the filmmakers' decision to maintain a hard edge. The cinematography does not seem as polished as the first four. Lesser quality film stock?

Scared Stiff *see under* The Ghost Breakers

Scars of Dracula *see under* Dracula

Scrooge
(Twickenham, 1935; 78 min.) ***

Produced by Julius Hagen and Hans (John) Brahm. Directed by Henry Edwards. Screenplay, Seymour Hicks and H. Fowler Mear. Based on the novella *A Christmas Carol* by Charles Dickens. Directors of Photography, Sidney Blythe, William Luff. Music, W. Trytel.

Cast: Ebenezer Scrooge (Seymour Hicks), Cratchit (Donald Calthrop), Charwoman (Athene Seyler), Spirit of Christmas Present (Oscar Asche), Mrs. Cratchit (Barbara Everest), Poor man (Maurice Evans), Spirit of Christmas Future (C. V. France), Spirit of Christmas Past (Marie Ney), Tiny Tim (Philip Frost), Belle (Mary Glynne), Belle's husband (Garry Marsh), Poor man's wife (Mary Lawson), Poulterer (Morris Harvey), Fred (Robert Cochran), Fred's wife (Eve Grey), Scrooge's laundress (Margaret Yarde), Old Joe (Hugh E. Wright), Middlemark (Charles Carson), Undertaker (D. J. Williams), Worthington (Hubert Harben). With Peggy Church.

Synopsis: Charles Dickens's 1843 classic is so familiar and has been filmed and re-filmed so faithfully over the years, that we need summarize the plot only once: Accountant Ebenezer Scrooge is a London institution, a skinflint who runs the firm once owned by the Marleys. He makes life difficult for his bookkeepers, including Bob Cratchit. As Christmas approaches and Scrooge dines alone, he is visited by the ghost of his late partner Jacob Marley as well as the ghosts of Christmas Past, Present and Yet to Be. He is shown his childhood, the current state of affairs including the poor health of Cratchit's crippled son Tiny Tim, and a possibly bleak future. Scrooge realizes he can mend his ways and does so, contributing to the poor, buying a goose (or turkey) and presents for the Cratchits. It is then said of him that no one kept Christmas so well.

Review: "Faithful, tender and mellow...." (Frank S. Nugent, *New York Times*, December 14, 1935, p. 11)

Analysis: There are some epic moments here: the rooftops of London and St. Paul's Cathedral in the distance, the lord mayor's dinner party when the vast room resounds to the guests singing "God Save the Queen." The behind-the-scenes glimpse of Christmas celebrations by both rich and poor is an excellent touch. The special effects are more or less primitive (shadows, voices, cutaway and back to the ghostly embodiments) but acceptable. The *New York Times* review faulted the film for poor lighting and sound. This print looks like it could have been done in 1843.

A Christmas Carol
(MGM, 1938; 69 min.) **

Produced by Joseph L. Mankiewicz. Directed by Edwin L. Marin. Screenplay, Hugo Butler. Edited by George Boemler. Director of Photography, Sidney Wagner. Music, Franz Waxman. Art Direction, Cedric Gibbons. Set Decoration, Edwin B. Willis. Character Makeup, Jack Dawn.

Cast: Ebenezer Scrooge (Reginald Owen), Bob Cratchit (Gene Lockhart), Mrs. Cratchit (Kathleen Lockhart), Tiny Tim (Terry Kilburn), Fred (Barry Mackay), Marley's ghost (Leo G. Carroll), Bess (Lynne Carver), Young Scrooge (Ronald Sinclair), Spirit of Christmas Present (Lionel Braham), Spirit of Christmas Past (Ann Rutherford), Spirit of Christmas Yet to Come (D'Arcy Corrigan). With June Lockhart.

Review: "Good Dickens, good cinema and good for the soul." (Frank S. Nugent, *New York Times*, December 23, 1938, p. 16)

Analysis: If there were no other versions, this might seem acceptable. The *New York Times* review praised Metro's restraint and lack of embellishment, but still, the MGM gloss and polish work against it. It's too light and cheery and not scary. Bob Cratchit's home is comfy. Ann Rutherford's headpiece is goofy. There are too many segments without Scrooge, and his transformation is too abrupt. Many liberties are taken, and we suspect conservative, family-oriented studio head Louis Mayer is to blame. At first glance, we were surprised to see Scrooge buying a turkey rather than a goose on Christmas morning. But a look into the book finds that it was indeed a turkey.

A Christmas Carol
(Renown, 1951; 86 min.) ****

Produced and directed by Brian Desmond-Hurst. Screenplay, Noel Langley. Edited by Clive Donner. Director of Photography, C. Pennington-Richards. Music, Richard Addinsell. Conducted by Muir Matheson. Art Direction, Ralph Brinton. Makeup, Eric Carter.

Cast: Scrooge (Alastair Sim), Bob Cratchit (Mervyn Johns), Mrs. Dilber (Kathleen Harrison), Young Scrooge (George Cole), Mr. Jorkins (Jack Warner), Jacob Marley (Michael Hordern), Mrs. Cratchit (Hermione Baddeley), Old Joe (Miles Malleson), Peter Cratchit (John Charlesworth), Tiny Tim (Glyn Dearman), Alice (Rona Anderson), Mrs. Wilkins (Clifford Malleson), Young Marley (Patrick Macnee), Fan (Carol Marsh), Undertaker (Ernest Thesiger). With Roddy Hughes, Michael Dolan, Eliot Makeham, Louise Hampton, Noel Howlett, Fred Johnson, Douglas Muir, Henry Hewitt, Hugh Dempster, Francis de Wolff, Olga Edwards, Peter Bull, Brian Worth, Hattie Jacques.

Review: "Should prove a most popular entertainment.... an accurate comprehension of the agony of a shabby soul." (Bosley Crowther, *New York Times*, November 29, 1951, p. 41)

Analysis: Also sometimes known as *Scrooge*, this is the critical favorite and the version public television favors at Christmastime. As the *New York Times* review noted, it is less cheery, more "spooky and somber" than the previous version. Sim is both mean and darkly funny, making both aspects of the character believable. A great cinema moment occurs when the regenerated Scrooge decides to take nephew Fred up on the invitation to a dinner party. Scrooge enters the foyer, hands the maid his coat and hat, but then hesitates to enter the parlor. The audience knows he's wondering if it is appropriate. Complementing the scene is the haunting ballad "Barbara Allen" emanating from the parlor. Scrooge finally opens the doors and enters. The singers stop; Fred's wife turns and utters an exclamation of surprise. Fred welcomes his uncle, who approaches Fred's wife and asks her forgiveness for being a pigheaded old fool. She busses his cheek twice. This wonderful sequence brings tears to the eyes. The Spirit of Christmas Present looks like that same spirit in the 1970 version. Perhaps the dark-robed Spirit of Christmas Yet To Be is not up to snuff—we can sometimes see the human face through the gown. Better to be blank or ghoulish. Michael Hordern has some wonderful screeches as Marley. Note Patrick Macnee, future star of famed *Avengers* TV series, as Young Marley. Recall Ernest Thesiger as Dr. Pretorius in 1935's *Bride of Frankenstein*.

Scrooge
(National General, 1970; 115 min.) ***

Produced by Robert H. Solo. Executive Producer, Leslie Bricusse. Directed by Ronald Neame. Assistant Director, Ted Sturgis. Screenplay, Leslie Bricusse. Edited by Peter Weatherley. Director of Photography, Oswald Morris. Panavision. Technicolor. Music conducted and supervised by Ian Fraser. Musical Sequences staged by Paddy Stone. Music

Editor, Kenneth Runyon. Songs, by Leslie Bricusse: "A Christmas Carol," "Christmas Children," "I Hate People," Father Chris'mas," "See the Phantoms," "December the Twenty-Fifth," "Happiness," "You ... You," "I Like Life," "The Beautiful Day," "Thank You Very Much," "I'll Begin Again." Art Direction, Bob Cartwright. Set Decoration, Pamela Cornell. Costume Design, Margaret Furse. Makeup, George Frost. Hairstyles, Bobbie Smith. Special Effects, Wally Veevers. Special Effects Photography, Jack Mills. Main Titles, Ronald Searle.

Cast: Scrooge (Albert Finney), Marley's ghost (Alec Guinness), Ghost of Christmas Past (Edith Evans), Ghost of Christmas Present (Kenneth More), Ghost of Christmas Yet to Come (Paddy Stone), Fezziwig (Laurence Naismith), Nephew (Michael Medwin), Bob Cratchit (David Collings), Mrs. Cratchit (Frances Cuka), Isabel (Suzanne Neve), Tom Jenkins (Anton Rodgers), Mrs. Fezziwig (Kay Walsh), Nephew's friend (Gordon Jackson), Women debtors (Molly Weir, Helena Gloag), Portly gentlemen (Roy Kinnear, Derek Francis), Tiny Tim (Richard Beaumont), Toy shop owner (Geoffrey Bayldon), Punch and Judy man (Reg Lever), Well wisher (Keith Marsh), Party guest (Marianne Stone). With Philip Da Costa, Raymond Hoskins, Gaynor Hodgson, Nicholas Locise, Peter Lock, Joy Leigh, Sara Gibson, Clive Moss, John O'Brien, David Peacock, Michael Reardon, Karen Scargill, Terry Winter, Stephen Garlick.

Reviews: "Tremendously beautiful, opulent British made production.... a future screen classic." (*Castle of Frankenstein* 16, July 1970, p. 62) ¶"The horribly-wrought knocker on the door of Scrooge's house.... is the first agreeable technical feat of a movie that abounds in rich old ruses.... Since this is a musical, I'd have like more actual singing rather than the preponderance of *Sprechgesang*. Still, the look of thing is never excessively twee, and the Cratchit family is kept sensibly to heel — and the nightmare-prone will probably be able to judge for themselves when to shut their eyes and put cotton wool in their ears." (Gordon Gow, *Films and Filming*, January 1971, p. 48)

Analysis: Though neither a critical nor a commercial success and bearing unfavorable comparison with another Dickens screen translation — 1968's *Oliver!* — this film looks better on subsequent viewings.

There are acceptable songs, in particular "Thank You Very Much" and "I Like Life." Albert Finney's portrayal cannot be faulted. Warning: TV versions often truncate Scrooge's descent into hell.

Scrooged
(Paramount, 1988; 115 min.) **½

Produced by Richard Donner and Art Linson. Directed by Richard Donner. Screenplay, Mitch Glazer and Michael O'Donoghue. Suggested by "A Christmas Carol" by Charles Dickens. Edited by Frederick Steinkamp and William Steinkamp. Director of Photography, Michael Chapman. Panavision. Technicolor. Music, Danny Elfman. Dolby Stereo. Art Direction, Virginia L. Randolph. Set Decoration, Linda DeScenna. Special Makeup Effects created and designed by Thomas R. Burman and Bari-Dreiband Burman. Special Visual Effects by Dream Quest Images.

Cast: Frank Cross (Bill Murray), Claire Phillips (Karen Allen), Lew Hayward (John Forsythe), Brice Cummings (John Glover), Ghost of Christmas Past (David Johansen), Ghost of Christmas Present (Carol Kane), Preston Rhinelander (Robert Mitchum), John Houseman (Himself), Lee Majors (Himself), Eliot Loudermilk (Bobcat Goldthwait), Robert Goulet (Himself), Grace (Alfre Woodard), Earl (Brian Doyle Murray), Calvin (Nicholas Phillips), Jacob Marley (Jamie Farr), TV Ghost of Christmas Present (Pat McCormick), Mary Lou Retton (Herself), Herman (Michael J. Pollard).

Reviews: "Begins well, but then veers entirely out of hand...." (Sheila Benson, *Los Angeles Times Calendar*, November 23, 1988, p. 1) ¶"Murray gives a weirdly ambivalent performance, as if torn between sincerity and contempt, and the film is so violently misdirected that, for the first time, he flounders." (David Edelstein, *New York Post*, November 23, 1988, p. 31) ¶"Works in fits and starts." (Vincent Canby, *New York Times*, November 23, 1988)

Analysis: In this updated version of Dickens' classic, Bill Murray plays an American TV network president visited by the traditional ghosts whose goal is to make him into a generous, caring human being. The effects are excellent and there are numerous amusing scenes although it fits into the "bloated comedy" era of Murray's career (between *Stripes* and *Groundhog*

Two Scrooges: Alastair Sim at top in *A Christmas Carol* (Renown, 1951); Albert Finney at bottom in *Scrooge* (National General, 1970).

Day). The surrounding cast is fine. We could hardly understand what advice Carol Kane was offering, but she's always a treat, and it was mostly visual anyway. IBC network holiday promos are funny: *Bob Goulet's Old Fashioned Cajun Christmas, Father Loves Beaver*, the John Houseman-hosted *Scrooge*.

The Muppet Christmas Carol
(Walt Disney/Jim Henson Productions, 1992; 89 min.) ***

Produced by Brian Henson and Martin G. Baker. Directed by Brian Henson. Screenplay, Jerry Juhl. Edited by Michael Jablow. Director of Photography, John Fenner. Color. Music, Miles Goodman. Songs, Paul Williams. Dolby Stereo.

Review: "Takes proven material and brings out its greatest strengths, even while fitting it with that unique Muppet sensibility of both mischievous fun and unabashed sentiment…. Story is faithfully retold…. a version that could easily become a holiday perennial." (Marshall Fine, *Wilmington News Journal 55 Hours*, December 11-13, 1992, p. 7)

Analysis: The songs are pleasant. Michael Caine is a perfect choice for Scrooge. The grim reaper-like ghost of Christmas Yet to Be is imposing and scary — yet sympathetic.

Scrooged *see under* **Scrooge**

The Search for Spock *see* Star Trek III: The Search for Spock *under* **Star Trek — The Motion Picture**

Season of the Witch *see* Halloween III: Season of the Witch *under* **Halloween**

The Second Story *see* House II: The Second Story *under* **House**

The Secret of Dorian Gray *see under* **The Picture of Dorian Gray**

The Secret of the Ooze *see* Teenage Mutant Ninja Turtles II: The Secret of the Ooze *under* **Teenage Mutant Ninja Turtles**

The Seven Brothers Meet Dracula *see* The Legend of the 7 Golden Vampires *under* **Dracula**

The 7th Voyage of Sinbad
(Columbia, 1959; 87 min.) ****

Produced by Charles H. Schneer. Morningside Production. Directed by Nathan Juran. Assistant Directors, Eugenio Martin, Pedro de Juan. Screenplay, Kenneth Kolb. Music, Bernard Herrmann. Dynamation. Technicolor. Special Effects, Ray Harryhausen. Main Titles, Bob Gill. Fencing Instructor, Enzo Musumeci-Greco.

Cast: Sinbad (Kerwin Mathews), Princess Parisa (Kathryn Grant), Genie Barani (Richard Eyer), Sokura (Torin Thatcher), Caliph (Alec Mango), Karim (Danny Green), Sultan (Harold Kasket), Harufa (Alfred Brown), Sadi (Nana de Herrera), Gaunt sailor (Nino Falanga), Crewman (Luis Guedes), Ali (Virgilio Teixeira).

Synopsis: Captain Sinbad escorts a sultan's daughter, the Princess Parisa, to the caliph in Baghdad, where a marriage will cement good relations. Stopping for food and water at an uncharted island, they are accosted by a giant cyclops pursuing a man with a lamp. Rubbing the lamp and reciting, "From the land beyond beyond, from the world past hope and fear, I bid you genie now appear," the man asks the boy genie who appears to produce a wall to separate them from the cyclops. The genie complies, creating an invisible force field. However, the cyclops tosses a boulder over the wall, and the wave it creates tosses all the men out of the longboat and the lamp sinks. The cyclops wades out and retrieves it. Sokura — the magician — is bereft, but Sinbad will not return. In Baghdad, Sokura demonstrates his magic for the caliph and the sultan but by night turns the princess into a miniature. Sinbad asks him to restore the princess to her proper size and Sokura informs him that part of the potion necessary is a fragment of the egg of the giant two-headed roc, a bird which lives on the island of the colossi — in short, the island of the cyclops. Sinbad gathers a crew of reliables and prisoners to return to the island. The ex-prisoners mutiny, but Sokura, Sinbad and his trusty men, knowing

Sinbad (Kerwin Mathews) grapples with an animate skeleton in *The 7th Voyage of Sinbad* (Columbia, 1959).

that the ship is headed for an island where sirens call, stuff their ears with cloth and regain control of the ship. On the island of the colossi, Sokura and Sinbad separate, hoping to meet that night at the end of a valley. A cyclops appears and imprisons Sinbad and his party, but the princess releases the latch on their cage. Sokura finds the magic lamp in the cyclops's treasure horde. Sinbad blinds the monster with a flaming brand and lures it to a cliff from which it falls. Sinbad allows Parisa to enter the magic lamp to speak with the genie, who is but a boy, Barani. He agrees to give Parisa the secret of the lamp in return for her help in making him a real boy: "From the land beyond beyond, from the world past hope and fear, I bid you genie now appear." While Parisa relays this information to Sinbad, a two-headed roc attacks Sinbad and his men, carrying Sinbad to its eyrie before leaving. Awaking, Sinbad climbs down, realizing that Sokura has taken Parisa to his abode inside the mountain. A dragon blocks his way. Barani tells him to tighten the chain that attaches the

monster to the wall. Sinbad passes safely and finds Sokura, who returns Parisa to normal size. Sinbad agrees to give up the lamp once they are back at his ship, but Sokura uses his magic to bring a skeleton to life. It and Sinbad duel until the man knocks the skeleton from a height and it is smashed. Sokura unleashes the dragon, which must first battle another cyclops. The cyclops killed, Sokura urges the dragon to kill Sinbad and his men. They have rigged a giant crossbow and impale the creature, which falls on the magician. On board ship, Barani appears as Sinbad's cabin boy. All is well, and the ship sails off.

Review: "Briskly-paced.... more of a tribute to mechanics than to sheer acting artistry." (A.H. Weiler, *New York Times*; unpublished due to December 1958 strike)

Analysis: Seen by us now, Kerwin Mathews seems a bit stiff as Sinbad. But he was ill during much of the shooting in Spain. When we saw this as young teens, acting was of little import and the film remains one of our favorite movies, with special effects by the master, Ray Harryhausen. Interestingly, the cyclops design was changed during production because it was feared audiences might think they were men in monster suits. Apparently this was the first time stop-motion animation was used to bring mythological creatures to life on film. Main titles are excellent: The camera tracks over a painting featuring the creatures and incidents the audience will encounter. The music is by another master, Bernard Herrmann. The clarinet ditty he uses here can also be heard in his score for *Five Fingers*, a 1952 World War II espionage film set in Turkey.

The Golden Voyage of Sinbad
(1974; 105 min.) ***

Produced by Charles H. Schneer and Ray Harryhausen. Directed by Gordon Hessler. Assistant Director, Miguel A. Gil, Jr. Screenplay, Brian Clemens. Story, Brian Clemens and Ray Harryhausen. Edited by Roy Watts. Director of Photography, Ted Moore. Dynarama. Music, Miklos Rozsa. Art Direction, Fernando Gonzalez. Set Decoration, Julian Mateos. Designer, John Stoll. Special Masks, Colin Arthur. Costumes, Verena Coleman and Gabriella Falk. Special Effects, Ray Harryhausen.

Cast: Sinbad (John Phillip Law), Margiana (Caroline Munro), Koura (Tom Baker), Vizier (Douglas Wilmer), Rachid (Martin Shaw), Hakim (Gregoire Aslan), Haroun (Kurt Christian), Achmed (Takis Emmanuel), Abdul (John D. Garfield), Omar (Aldo Sambrell).

Synopsis: Sinbad comes into possession of a piece of worked gold dropped on deck by some strange flying creature. Rachid warns him about bad luck, but Sinbad scoffs. Ashore, Sinbad is accosted by a black-robed rider, Koura, who demands the gold. Sinbad escapes to the city, where the grand vizier apprises him of Koura's evil intentions and the secret of the gold: When all the pieces are placed together at the Fountain of Destiny, the supplicant will be granted youth, a cloak of invisibility and riches. Discovering a map, Sinbad and the vizier, along with Hakim's profligate son Haroun and the beautiful slave girl Margiana, set sail for the lost island of Lemuria. They realize they are racing Koura, who uses black magic to learn of their progress. Each time he invokes a spell, however, he ages, and his servant Achmed worries. On Lemuria, Sinbad discovers the Temple of the Oracle of All Knowledge. From a visage they hear riddles but understand that the Fountain of Destiny is not far off. Koura uses an explosive to seal them in, but they escape for a time, only to be captured by a barbaric tribe and confronted by a statue of Kali come to life. After causing it to fall and break, Sinbad and his men track Margiana into a pit where she's to be sacrificed to a one-eyed centaur. A griffin attacks the centaur, but Koura helps the centaur triumph. Sinbad leaps upon the centaur and kills it with knife thrusts. Nevertheless, Koura acquires all three gold pieces and arrives at the Fountain of Destiny first, using one piece to regain his youth, another to become invisible. He duels Sinbad, but Margiana sees his form in the center of the fountain and warns Sinbad, who dispatches Koura by a timely thrust. A crown found in the fountain is placed on the head of the vizier, whose mask is transformed, his human face restored. Sinbad is content to sail off with Margiana, refusing wealth and power. "I value freedom. A king is never truly free."

Reviews: "Children ... will probably find it a happy concoction.... Intellectually, *Sinbad* sails on shallow waters." (Lawrence Van Gelder, *New York Times*, April 6, 1974, p. 16)

Analysis: This is a good film with typically excellent Harryhausen creations: a gargoyle-like homunculus, a griffin, a centaur, the goddess Kali, a ship figurehead who comes alive. Tom Baker makes an imposing villain, John Phillip Law seems to enjoy his role as Sinbad. Caroline Munro is, as always, radiant. The story, however, is confusing. Where did the gold pieces come from? What riches will accrue to the bearer? Full-page ad in *Variety*, April 10, 1974, p. 21.

Sinbad and the Eye of the Tiger
(Columbia, 1977; 112 min.) **

Produced by Charles H. Schneer and Ray Harryhausen. Directed by Sam Wanamaker.

Margiana (Caroline Munro), the beautiful slave girl from *The Golden Voyage of Sinbad* (Columbia, 1974).

Assistant Director, Miguel A. Gil, Jr. Screenplay and story, Beverly Cross. Edited by Roy Watts. Director of Photography, Ted Moore. Metrocolor. Music, Roy Budd. Art Direction, Fernando Gonzalez, Fred Carter. Makeup, Colin Arthur. Costumes, Cynthia Tingey. Design, Geoffrey Drake. Special Effects, Ray Harryhausen.

Cast: Sinbad (Patrick Wayne), Farah (Jane Seymour), Dione (Taryn Power), Zenobia (Margaret Whiting), Melanthius (Patrick Troughton), Rafi (Kurt Christian), Hassan (Nadim Sawalha), Kassim (Damien Thomas), Maroof (Salami Coaker), Aboo-Seer (David Sterne), Balsora (Bruno Barnabe).

Synopsis: Sinbad drops anchor and prepares to trade his cargo. But Kassim's coronation is disrupted and the inner city gate barred — supposedly because of plague.

Sinbad accepts another trader's invitation for dinner, but a seaman drinks and becomes ill. Poison! Sinbad fights off assassins, but a dark-cloaked sorceress raises three bug-eyed, skeletal warriors from the fire. They pursue Sinbad through the encampment until they are crushed beneath falling logs. Farah, Kassim's sister and an acquaintance of Sinbad, accompanies him to the sea, where they leap in and swim to his ship. Next morning the sultan comes to the ship, telling Sinbad he will give him treasure to give Melanthius if he can find him and reverse the curse on Kassim. Zenobia, Farah's stepmother, arrives and claims what is done to Kassim is irreversible. Sinbad agrees to sail — for the hand of Farah. It transpires that the baboon taken aboard *is* Kassim. Sinbad arrives at the island of Melanthius, and inland they find the sage and his daughter Dione. Melanthius says Zenobia's drug must be a most powerful black magic. Reading ancient scrolls, Melanthius says they must travel into the frozen north, to Hyperborea, where they will find the Shrine of the Four Elements and the key to returning Kassim to his human form. Pursuing in her oared ship powered by her creation, the bull-headed Minaton, Zenobia drinks an elixir and turns to a gull. On Sinbad's ship she becomes a miniature Zenobia, is captured but escapes. But the elixir is running out and she retains a gull foot. Taking a sledge across the ice, Sinbad encounters a giant walrus before discovering Hyperborea and a large, club-wielding troglodyte — one of man's ancestors. Kassim the baboon communicates with it, and it leads them to the gate beyond which is the shrine. Unknown to them, Zenobia and Rafi have discovered the shortcut tunnel and arrive at the pyramid first. Using her powers and the Minaton, she breaks in and, in an ill-advised move, sets Rafi upon them. He's killed. In the blue beam of light, Sinbad lowers a cage containing the baboon, who emerges as Kassim. Zenobia transforms herself into the saber-tooth tiger statue and kills the troglodyte and Maroof. Sinbad impales her with a pike. Back at the palace, Kassim is crowned Caliph.

Review: "Technically adroit but childishly plotted...." (Mack., *Variety*, May 25, 1977, p. 20)

Analysis: A lackluster, cheesy-looking start portends a lousy journey, but it picks up. Sometimes the battles between the marvelous Harryhausen creations go on too long. One supposes they wanted to give us *their* money's worth. Casting leaves something to be desired. Pat Wayne's voice lacks the timbre for he-man adventurer Sinbad. Jane Seymour and Taryn Power have a swim scene in which they are certainly nude, and while no Caroline Munro, Ms. Seymour actually shows a breast, which is odd for this "kids" film. It was filmed in Jordan, Spain, and Malta, but they must not have been able to afford transporting Wayne and Seymour to some of the locations because there are obvious — and disconcerting — process shots involving the leads. In long shots, stand-ins are used. Quite implausible is Rafi's lone attack on Sinbad's group. How was that going to succeed? Playing Rafi here, Kurt Christian had played Haroun in *The Golden Voyage of Sinbad*.

Notes of Interest: Among other Sinbad films, *Sinbad the Sailor* (1947) with Douglas Fairbanks, Jr. is entertaining but not supernatural. Guy Williams' *Captain Sindbad* is foreign. Sinbad is but one of many characters in the 1951 Columbia film, *The Thief of Damascus*.

The Shaggy Dog
(Buena Vista, 1959; 104 min.) ***

Produced by Walt Disney. Associate Producer, Bill Walsh. Directed by Charles Barton. Screenplay, Bill Walsh and Lillie Hayward. Suggested by *The Hound of Florence* by Felix Salten. Edited by James D. Ballas. Director of Photography, Edward Colman. Music, Paul Smith. Song, Gil George and Paul Smith. Art Direction, Carroll Clark. Set Decoration, Emile Kuri, Fred MacLean. Costumes, Chuck Keehne and Gertrude Casey.

Cast: Wilson Daniels (Fred MacMurray), Frieda Daniels (Jean Hagen), Wilby Daniels (Tommy Kirk), Allison D'Allessio (Annette Funicello), Buzz Miller (Tim Considine), Montgomery "Moochie" Daniels (Kevin Corcoran), Dr. Mikhail Andrassy (Alexander Scourby), Professor Plumcutt (Cecil Kellaway), Franceska Andrassy (Roberta Shore),

Officer Hanson (James Westerfield), Stefano (Jacques Aubuchon), Thurm (Strother Martin), Officer Kelly (Forrest Lewis). With Shaggy.

Synopsis: When his teenage son Wilby's missile interceptor rocket blasts a hole in the roof, Wilson Daniels makes him stop his experiments. Franceska Andrassy moves in across the street. Her Brataslavian sheepdog looks like one in a portrait of Lucrezia Borgia in the museum exhibit "The Age of Sorcery." Professor Plumcutt tells Wilby about shape shifting. At home, Wilby discovers a ring from the museum in the cuff of his pants. It has a Latin inscription, and when he recites it he becomes Franceska's dog. (That dog disappears.) Professor Plumcutt is not surprised and surmises that an act of heroism might bring Wilby back to his human form. He relates the tale of the "Hound of Florence" who became a man. Wilby's young brother "Moochie" discovers that Wilby is a dog, but his father who hates dogs, chases him with a shotgun. He goes to Franceska's, where he is locked in a closet, falls and is knocked out. He comes to as Wilby. At the country club dance, Wilby turns dog again. Back at Franceska's, Wilby observes the arrival of Thurm, who tells Franceska's father that he's been transferred and mentions Section 32 at the missile plant. It has something to do with an undersea hydrogen missile. Escaping next morning, Wilby tells Moochie about spies. When Moochie can't convince his father, Wilby decides on the shock treatment. Wilson faints but goes to the police when he wakes. Except for his knowledge of Section 32, they think he's crazy. Overhearing more secrets at the Andrassys, Wilby changes back to a boy and is captured. Thurm arrives with Section 32 and they leave for the dock. Wilby becomes a dog again and takes Buzz's car. The police chase him. At the dock, Wilby as dog pulls Franceska from the water as the boat speeds off. Wilby becomes human. The newspapers report the spy ring is broken and Wilson and the dog are heroes. Franceska returns to France but leaves her dog with Wilby.

Review: "Some of this skittish plot is very amusing thanks to the lively script and pleasing cast. Tommy Kirk is a delight."

(Philip J. Hartung, *Commonweal*, April 10, 1959, p. 59) ¶"Unhappily, Producer Walt Disney tells his shaggy-dog story so doggedly that he soon runs it into the pound." (*Time*, April 20, 1959, p. 78)

Analysis: Although this started Fred MacMurray's leading-man resurgence, Tommy Kirk is the real star, and it may be his best role at Disney or anywhere else. As the policemen, James Westerfield and Forrest Lewis have the funniest scenes. They would recap these roles in *The Absent Minded Professor* and *Son of Flubber*. Oddly, we never know if the spies got captured.

The Shaggy D.A.
(Buena Vista, 1976; 91 min.) **

Produced by Bill Anderson. Directed by Robert Stevenson. Screenplay, Don Tait. Suggested by *The Hound of Florence* by Felix Salten. Edited by Bob Bring, Norman Palmer. Director of Photography, Frank Phillips. Technicolor. Music, Buddy Baker. Title song sung by Dean Jones. Art Direction, John B. Mansbridge, Perry Ferguson. Set Decoration, Robert Benton.

Cast: Wilby Daniels (Dean Jones), Betty Daniels (Suzanne Pleshette), Tim (Tim Conway), John Slade (Keenan Wynn), Katrinka Muggelberg (Jo Anne Worley), Raymond (Dick Van Patten), Eddie Rorschak (Vic Tayback), Brian Daniels (Shane Sinutko), Admiral Brenner (John Myhers), Freddie (Dick Bakalyan), Dip (Warren Berlinger), TV director (Ronnie Schell), TV interviewer (Jonathan Daly), Howie Clemmings (John Fiedler), Professor Whatley (Hans Conried), Sheldon (Michael McGreevey), Desk Sergeant (Richard O'Brien), Roller rink announcer (Dick Lane), Waiter (Benny Rubin), Song chairman (Ruth Gillette), Policeman (Hank Jones), Manageress (Iris Adrian), Bartender (Pat McCormick), Taxi driver (Henry Slate).

Synopsis: A string of robberies in Medfield convinces now grown Wilby Daniels to run for district attorney against the corrupt John Slade. His chances are compromised when the ancient scarab ring is stolen from the local museum. Reciting its inscription turns Wilby into Elwood, a sheepdog belonging to ice cream truck driver Tim. Wilby tries to find the ring. When the thief tries to fence it, the police obtain it. Raymond, who works for Slade, gets the ring, and his boss turns Wilby back into the dog. But as the dog, Wilby records an incriminating conversation between Slade and mobster Rorshak. The pound dogs, who'd helped Wilby/Elwood escape, retrieve the ring for their friend.

Review: "Rather feeble sequel to *The Shaggy Dog*, with overtones of Watergate." (Leslie Halliwell, *Halliwell's Film Guide*, 7th ed., p. 906)

Analysis: It's plot-thin but mildly amusing. Credits are quite long. Jones is playing the character essayed in the original by Tommy Kirk. Medfield is the town from *The Absent Minded Professor*, which also featured Keenan Wynn. Here he plays a different character. Jones and Pleshette had paired previously in Disney's 1966 film *The Ugly Dachshund*. In 1987 there was the TV movie *The Return of the Shaggy Dog*.

She
(RKO, 1935; 89 min.) ***

Produced by Merian C. Cooper. Directed by Irving Pichel and Lansing C. Holden. Screenplay, Ruth Rose and Dudley Nichols. Based on the novel by H. Rider Haggard. Director of Photography, J. Roy Hunt. Edited by Ted Cheeseman. Music, Max Steiner. Art Direction, Van Nest Polglase.

Cast: She/Ayesha (Helen Gahagan), Leo Vincey (Randolph Scott), Holly (Nigel Bruce), Tanya Dugmore (Helen Mack), Billali (Gustav von Seyffertitz), Dugmore (Lumsden Hare), John Vincey (Samuel S. Hinds), Amahagger chief (Noble Johnson).

Synopsis: American Leo Vincey is summoned to London by his dying uncle, John Vincey, and is told the story of their sixteenth-century ancestor, an earlier John Vincey (to whose family portrait Leo bears an uncanny resemblance) who found the Flame of Eternal Life in a land of glacial volcanoes far to the north. His imagination fired, Leo proceeds, with his uncle's friend Horace Holly, to Siberia, where they take up with trader Dugmore and his adopted daughter, Tanya. The four travel as far as the fabled "Sugul Barrier," beyond which native bearers will not accompany them. The four find the frozen remains of the earlier Vincey party and the saber-tooth

tiger that killed them. John Vincey's body is not among the company. An avalanche takes Dugmore, but Leo, Holly and Tanya escape into caverns where they are accosted by primitive cave dwellers. Leo is wounded, but the explorers are saved by a band of soldiers from the land of Kor. Kor is a geographical anomaly: a lush and fertile jungle oasis in the midst of the frozen Arctic. Kor's ruler, Hascha-Mo-Tet (She Who Must Be Obeyed), also known as Ayesha, is staggered when she lays eyes on Leo. He is the living embodiment of her ancient lover, John Vincey. Ayesha, in a fit of jealousy, had killed Vincey five hundred years earlier, when he had chosen to remain faithful to his wife, who had escaped back to civilization. Determined to woo Leo to her side using both her considerable charms and the secret of life eternal, Ayesha escorts Leo to the crypts where the lifeless but undefiled body of John Vincey lies in state. Ayesha's lure is almost enough to sway him to join her. Because Ayesha recognizes that Tanya loves Leo, the mortal woman is scheduled for elimination. As the spectacular Ceremony of the Sacred Flame nears its deadly climax, Tanya is revealed as the intended sacrifice. Leo and Holly disrupt the ceremony and the trio escape through a narrow exit. Their route takes them past the flame, where they are met by Ayesha and the high priest Billali. Again, Ayesha entreats Leo to join her in the flame, to spend eternity with her in Kor, ageless and immortal. To demonstrate the power of the flame, the queen steps into its leaping fires several times. With each emergence, however, she ages, until ultimately it is a wizened crone who collapses and dies at the feet of the travelers. Holly guesses that the Flame, beneficial in a singular immersion, is deadly upon repeated exposures.

Review: "Gaudy, spectacular and generally fantastic.... likely to find its greatest favor with the younger generation." (Frank S. Nugent, *New York Times*, July 26, 1935, p. 18)

Analysis: Largely overlooked and infrequently aired, this film is usually neglected in favor of Merian C. Cooper's earlier triumph, *King Kong*. *Kong* is undoubtedly the more energetic and imaginative, but the opulence and exotic atmosphere of *She* earn it a secure place in Cooper's pantheon. (Cooper initially wanted Joel McCrea and Frances Dee to play Leo and Sally.) Sometimes actor Irving Pichel directed the actors; Holden, whose forté was architectural design, is credited with overseeing the visual elements. Max Steiner, whose music for *Kong* was one of film's earliest triumphs, produces a score no less splendid here. Several of the film's principals became famous outside the genre of fantastic cinema. Randolph Scott, of course, became one of moviedom's handful of immortal western heroes, second probably only to John Wayne in popularity. Nigel Bruce was soon to become famous as Dr. Watson in the Basil Rathbone *Sherlock Holmes* series. Helen Gahagan had married actor Melvyn Douglas in 1931. *She* was to be her only film. She went into politics and served in the U.S. Congress for two terms, in 1945 and 1949. Richard Nixon defeated her 1950 bid for a Senate seat.

Notes of Interest: H. Rider Haggard spent four years of his youth in South Africa. He drew on this experience for his fabulously successful adventure tales like *King Solomon's Mines* and *She*. The latter was published in 1887. There were several book sequels, including *She and Allan*. There were silent versions in 1908, 1911, 1916, and 1917.

She
(Hammer/MGM, 1965; 105 min.)
**½

Produced by Michael Carreras. Associate Producer, Aida Young. Directed by Robert Day. Screenplay, David Chantler. Based on the novel by H. Rider Haggard. Director of Photography, Harry Waxman. CinemaScope. Technicolor. Edited by Eric Boyd-Perkins. Supervising Editor, James Needs. Music, James Bernard. Musical Supervision, Philip Martell. Choreography, Christyne Lawson. Art Direction, Robert Jones, Don Mingaye. Costumes, Carl Toms, Roy Ashton. Special Effects, George Blackwell, Bowie Films.

Cast: Ayesha (Ursula Andress), Leo Vincey (John Richardson), Major Holly (Peter Cushing), Job (Bernard Cribbins), Billali (Christopher Lee), Ustane (Rosenda Monteros),

Haumeid (Andre Morell), Guard captain (John Maxim).

Synopsis: Palestine, 1918. World War I has ended. Holly wants some real experience to leaven his scholarship. Young Leo Vincey is game, but before they decide on a course of action, he is invited to a residence by the beautiful young Ustane. Knocked unconscious, he awakes to meet an exotic woman named Ayesha who says he must journey to her abode many leagues to the south. There he will gain all that he desires. Leo convinces Holly that they might find the lost city of Cuma. When some of their baggage is stolen and the party attacked by bedouins, Holly and former manservant Job have second thoughts. Not so Leo. He recalls Ayesha's charisma. The three trudge on and are finally succored by Ustane, who reveals that she was once a member of Ayesha's entourage but that a revolt left her previously influential father only in charge of the native inhabitants. They encounter some of those natives and shortly thereafter Haumeid, Ustane's father. He wonders how long he can check the desire for revenge of his subjects. Not long. They see that Leo looks like the long-dead Kallikrates and prepare to sacrifice him. Billali, Ayesha's chamberlain, appears with an escort dressed much like ancient Roman legionaries. The Europeans are saved and Ustane is permitted to accompany them to the city. Billali explains to Ayesha that Ustane helped doctor Leo, but later Ayesha observes Ustane kissing Leo. Although Ustane is saved by Holly's intervention from a fiery pit, knowing glances signify her imminent destruction. Her ashes are brought to her father, Haumeid, who leads an insurrection. Meanwhile, Ayesha has convinced Leo that he is the long-dead Kallikrates, her past lover and consort. They will rebuild their ancient city together once he accepts the immortality conferred by the sacred flame which periodically turns "cold." Ayesha and Leo enter the flame, but the queen begins to age. When she crumbles into dust, Holly explains to Leo the danger of twice being engulfed. Because he cannot live without his love, Leo says he'll await the next change in the now deadly flame.

Review: "Lacks style, sophistication, humor, sense and, above all, a reason for being...." (Bosley Crowther, *New York Times*, September 2, 1965, p. 36)

Analysis: Location scenes were filmed in Israel, and the film is at its best outside, with a jaunty camel-riding ditty that sticks with the viewer. When Cuma is reached, the sets are obvious, and there's one of those interminable native dancing scenes. Ursula Andress is a logical choice, but she may in fact be *too* exotic. A few years hence Ingrid Pitt would have been physically and facially ideal. (Would her Germanic accent have mattered?) Another what-if: Had Hammer waited, the R-rating would have permitted appropriate glimpses of the goddess's obviously extraordinary fleshly charms. Cushing has a couple of interesting monologues on immortality and lends authority to the film. Best fright scenes: (1) the natives roped together and thrown into the volcanic pit; (2) the aging Ayesha emerging from the flame, reaching for Leo with skinny, withering arms and bent body. When pressed at FANEX 8 in 1994 to name the film for which he composed his favorite score, James Bernard suggested this. It allowed him broad scope, from epic to intimately romantic. He said Christopher Lee, a master of several languages and a vocalist of some quality, made up some nonsense chant that was never used.

The Vengeance of She
(Hammer/Warner, 1968; 101 min.) **

Produced by Aida Young. Directed by Cliff Owen. Screenplay, Peter O'Donnell. Based on characters created by H. Rider Haggard. Edited by Raymond Poulton. Supervising Editor, James Needs. Director of Photography, Wolf Suschitzky. Color, DeLuxe. Music, Mario Nascimbene. Musical Supervision, Philip Martell. Saxophone Solo, Tubby Hayes. Makeup, Michael Morris. Hairstyles, Mervyn Medalie. Art Direction, Lionel Couch. Ritual Sequence Design, Andrew Low. Special Effects, Bob Cuff, Bowie Films.

Cast: Carol (Olinka Berova), Killikrates (John Richardson), Philip (Edward Judd), George (Colin Blakely), Sheila (Jill Melford), Harry (George Sewell), Kassim (Andre Morell), Za-Tor (Noel Willman), Men-Hari (Derek Godfrey), Sharna (Daniele Noel), The Seer (Gerald Lawson), Dancer (Christine Pockett), Lorry driver (Dervis Ward), No. 1 (Derick Sherwin), Magnus (William Lyon Brown), Servant (Charles O'Rourke), Putri (Zohra Segal).

Synopsis: A comely young blonde fends off a potential rapist and arrives at a Mediterranean beach, where she swims out to the yacht *Briseis*. She is found only after the yacht sails toward North Africa. She tells owner George she's Carol from Scandinavia. George's psychiatrist friend Philip speaks with her but she can't recall her past. She tells him of strange dreams. George dies of a heart attack after rescuing Carol, who'd jumped overboard. The yacht docks and Carol leaves, taking a bus inland. At Cuma, Killikrates says Ayesha is reborn and will return. Their ancient empire will once again be supreme. Kassim, an Arab adept at the forbidden arts, befriends Carol and offers his help. Philip and the yacht's captain, Harry, follow her. Kassim explains to Carol about an immortal man drawing her to him and says he will help break the spell. But he is killed when the Magi of Killikrates use their powers. Carol gives in and proceeds into the desert, where she's captured and sold by tribesmen. Phil and Harry rescue her but Harry is killed. Killikrates' adviser Men-Hari informs his master of Carol and the man accompanying her. She will arrive none too soon, for the proper star alignment is imminent. Men-Hari, who wants immortality, welcomes Carol and Phil. He uses his mental powers to convince Carol she is Ayesha. He tells her of the past, when Ayesha led her lover into the sacred flame; he became immortal, but because it was her second time, she perished. The Magi leader tells Phil that Men-Hari has Carol's mind in bondage. As the star alignment occurs, the slaves revolt. Phil tells Killikrates how Men-Hari found Carol and is using her to achieve his own immortality. Men-Hari stabs Za-Tor but is himself killed. The distressed Killikrates walks into the flame, ages and dies. Z-Tor rises and implores a spirit to destroy the city. Flame and earthquake oblige, but Phil and Carol escape.

Reviews: "A scriptwriter's mindless sequel." (Vincent Canby, *New York Times*, May 30, 1968, p. 21) ¶"Plastic confection...."

lacks thrills and punch." (Rich., *Variety*, April 10, 1968, p. 6)

Analysis: Variety called Berova a "looker" but found her unable to resuscitate a lifeless role. Location filming took place in Spain and France. Although the story requires it, the first half contemporary setting burdens the film, compromising mystery and exoticism. Paired with *Five Million Years to Earth* in the States.

Short Circuit
(Tri-Star, 1986; 99 min.) **½

Produced by David Foster and Lawrence Turman. Directed by John Badham. Screenplay, S. S. Wilson and Brent Maddock. Edited by Frank Morriss. Director of Photography, Nick McLean. Panavision. Metrocolor. Music, David Shire. Dolby Stereo. Visual Consultant, Philip Harrison. Robots, Syd Mead and Eric Allard. Robot Voices Synthesizer, Frank Serafine. Set Decoration, Garrett Lewis. Special Electrical Effects, Bob Jason, Larry "Big Mo" Keys, Walter Nichols.

Cast: Stephanie Speck (Ally Sheedy), Newton Crosby (Steve Guttenberg), Ben Jabituya (Fisher Stevens), Howard Marner (Austin Pendleton), Skroeder (G. W. Bailey), Frank (Brian McNamara), Voice of Number Five (Tim Blaney), Otis (John Garber), Duke (Marvin McIntyre), Mrs. Cepeda (Penny Santon), General Washburne (Vernon Weddle), Marner's aide (Tom Lawrence), Senator Mills (Barbara Tarbuck), Norman (Fred Slyter), Zack (Billy Ray Sharkey), Reporters (Robert Krantz, Jan Speck), Barmaid (Marguerite Hapy), Farmer (Howard Krick), Farmer's wife (Marjorie Huehes), Gate guard (Herb Smith).

Synopsis: Nova Laboratories demonstrates the military capabilities of its five new robots, which use lasers to disable tanks and other armored vehicles. After the demonstration, a lightning storm puts an extra charge into robot #5, which ends up on a garbage truck leaving the compound. Security and the robots' programmers, Newton Crosby and Ben Jabituya, give chase but lose it when it falls from a bridge, its parachute whisking it onto Stephanie Speck's lunch mobile. At her home she encounters #5, which she thinks is an alien. It demands input. She gives it the encyclopedia. After it squashes a grasshopper,

Stephanie explains that the insect cannot be resurrected. Number Five now thinks it has a soul itself and does not want to be reprogrammed. Stephanie convinces Newton of #5's sentience and they flee the base security. Cornered, the robot is blown up by a helicopter cannon. When the security forces leave, #5 emerges from the depths of the lunch wagon and reveals that the robot that was destroyed was one he made from spare parts.

Reviews: "The perfectly outrageous performance of Stevens boosts *Short Circuit* into the higher realms of juvenile fantasy." (Joseph Gelmis, *Newsday*, May 9, 1986, Part III, p. 5) ¶"The sight gags, the silly stuff, the 'isn't he cute' routines get boring. And there isn't any real imagination to [back them]." (Rex Reed, *New York Post*, May 9, 1986, p. 25)

Analysis: This made $17 million in domestic rentals, but it's fringe good. Fisher Stevens has the best lines, but there are some laughs from others, like Ally Sheedy when she first sees the robot and exclaims that she always knew "they" (aliens) would contact her. An irritating element of this and a number of other modern films is the paramilitary forces every business seems to employ, which run wild and are never questioned by the true authorities. (See like forces in the *Scanners* series and *Memoirs of an Invisible Man*.)

Short Circuit 2
(Tri-Star, 1988; 112 min.) **½

Produced by David Foster, Lawrence Turman and Gary Foster. Directed by Kenneth Johnson. Screenplay, S. S. Wilson and Brent Maddock. Edited by Conrad Buff. Director of Photography, John McPherson. Color, Medallion Laboratories. Prints, Technicolor. Music, Charles Fox. Dolby Stereo. Number Five Voice Design, Frank Serafine. Art Direction, Alicia Keywan. Set Decoration, Steve Shewchuk. Costumes, Larry Wells. Robot Supervisor, Eric Allard. Stunts, Ken Bates. Special Effects, Jeff Jarvis, Mike Edmonson. Special Visual Effects, Dream Quest Images.

Cast: Ben Jahrvi (Fisher Stevens), Fred Ritter (Michael McKean), Sandy Banatoni (Cynthia Gibb), Oscar Baldwin (Jack Weston), Saunders (Dee McCafferty), Jones (David Hemblen), Bones (Damon D'Oliveira), Zorro

(Tito Nunez), Lil Man (Jason Kuriloff), Voice of Johnny Five (Tim Blaney), Manic Mike (Don Lake), Spooky (Robert LaSardo), Priest (Gerry Parkes), Hans de Ruyter (Adam Ludwig), Dartmoor (Rex Hagon), Mr. Slater (Richard Comar), Bill (Jeremy Ratchford), Francis (Gary Robbins), Mr. Arnold (Kurt Reis), Russian taxi driver (Tony DeSantis). With Robert Mills, Gordon Robertson, Trish Leeper, Michael Sorensen.

Synopsis: Street vendor Fred Ritter helps Ben Jahrvi make a deal with Sandy Banatoni of Titanic Toys for a thousand small robots. Fred rents an abandoned building, but thieves who dig a tunnel from the basement to the bank nearby try to intimidate the toy makers. They smash what Ben had made, but a large crate is delivered containing #5, the full-size robot that had been living in Montana with Newton and Stephanie. He takes the name Johnny 5 and helps make the mini-robots. When he learns he's in a metropolis, he goes sightseeing, causing a problem when he enters a bookstore for more and more input. His security system foils the thieves, who attempt a second break-in. When Fred attempts to sell the robot, #5 backs through a window. His parasail allows him to land safely. But the police incarcerate #5 until Ben is summoned. Number 5 says he is sad people aren't treating him right, and Ben confides in him that he's having trouble expressing himself to Sandy. Number 5 helps him arrange a date. Oscar Baldwin, who works in the bank, is in league with the thieves and distracts #5 while his cohorts kidnap Fred and Ben and lock them in a freezer. Using a calculator and the electric lines, they manage to signal Sandy. Meanwhile, Oscar has convinced #5 to dig the tunnel into the bank. After getting the diamonds, Oscar's chums batter #5. Sandy and Ben are arrested when the police think they dug the tunnel. Fred finds #5 and, taking his instructions, makes repairs that turn him into a semblance of his old self. Number 5 tracks the criminals via their tire tracks and all three are caught. But #5 fails. A paramedic electric shock device restores his power. Both Ben and #5 obtain U.S. citizenship.

Reviews: "Not only lives up to its predecessor but in many ways outshines it.... Not a slapped together sequel, but a well thought out and cared for project." (Allen Malmquist, *Cinefantastique*, January 1989, p. 118)

Analysis: With his fractured English, Fisher Stevens is as funny as he was in the first film. The setting is supposed to be New York, but it was filmed in Toronto.

Sinbad and the Eye of the Tiger *see under* **The 7th Voyage of Sinbad**

The Slipper and the Rose *see under* **The Glass Slipper**

Son of Blob *see* Beware! The Blob *under* **The Blob**

Son of Darkness: To Die For 2 *see under* **To Die For**

Son of Dracula (1943) *see under* **Dracula**

Son of Dracula (1974) *see under* **Dracula**

Son of Dr. Jekyll *see under* **Dr. Jekyll and Mr. Hyde**

Son of Flubber *see under* **The Absent Minded Professor**

Son of Frankenstein *see under* **Frankenstein**

The Spaceman and King Arthur *see* Unidentified Flying Oddball *under* **A Connecticut Yankee**

A Spaceman in King Arthur's Court *see* Unidentified Flying Oddball *under* **A Connecticut Yankee**

Star Trek — The Motion Picture
(Paramount, 1979; 132 min.) ***

Produced by Gene Roddenberry. Directed by Robert Wise. Screenplay, Harold Livingston. Story, Alan Dean Foster. Based on the television series *Star Trek*, created by Gene Roddenberry. Edited by Todd Ramsay.

440   *Star Trek—The Motion Picture*

Director of Photography, Richard H. Kline. Panavision. Metrocolor. Music, Jerry Goldsmith. Dolby Stereo. Art Direction, Harold Michelson. Design, Harold Michelson. Special Effects, Douglas Trumbull.

Cast: Admiral James Kirk (William Shatner), Spock (Leonard Nimoy), Decker (Stephen Collins), Dr. McCoy (DeForest Kelley), Scotty (James Doohan), Uhura (Nichelle Nichols), Ilia (Persis Khambatta), Sulu (George Takei), Dr. Chapel (Majel Barrett), Chekov (Walter Koenig), Klingon Captain (Mark Lenard), Alien boy (Billy Van Zandt), Janice Rand (Grace Lee Whitney), Epsilon Technician (Roger Aaron Brown), Airlock Technician (Gary Faga), Cargo Deck Ensign (Howard Itzkowitz), Commander Branch (David Gautreaux), Rand's assistant (John D. Gowans), Chief DiFalco (Marcy Lafferty), Lt. Commander Sonak (Jon Rashad Kamal), Technician (Jeri McBride), Lieutenant (Michele Ameen Billy), Chief Ross (Terrence O'Connor), Lt. Cleary (Michael Rougas).

Synopsis: Long-range scans alert Federation outpost Epsilon Nine to the presence of a huge "cloud" of unknown substance and origin passing through the far reaches of Klingon space. Attacking Klingon starships are summarily destroyed as the puzzling mass proceeds upon its course — toward Earth. The United Federation of Planets sends Starfleet's most experienced officer, Admiral James Kirk, aboard the recently refitted *Enterprise* to investigate. This proves to be good news for Kirk's former shipmates — Chekov, Uhura, Sulu and Scott — who are among the crew members of the refurbished starship. Not so happy to see the admiral aboard is Captain Decker, whose first command *Enterprise* should have been. An irate Dr. McCoy is beamed aboard prior to leaving space dock; Kirk had arranged for him to be "drafted" for this mission. Also appearing aboard at the last minute is the ship's navigator, Lt. Ilia, a Deltan of striking beauty. Decker and Ilia had previously been in a relationship that had gone sour, and their meeting is cordial, but restrained. En route to the oncoming menace, the *Enterprise* is overtaken by a smaller craft bearing an unexpected passenger: an uncommonly taciturn Mr. Spock. Spock had left Starfleet after the conclusion of the *Enterprise*'s five-year mission, returning to his native planet to

undergo the Vulcan ritual of emotional purification, the *Kolinahr.* Prior to entering the final rites of this discipline, Spock had "sensed" the presence of the interstellar intruder. Aloof or not, Spock has valuable scientific knowledge, and he is welcomed with special fondness by his old comrades. When the *Enterprise* makes its rendezvous with the intruder, all are astounded at its size. Kirk chooses to avoid sensor scans, guessing that they would be construed as belligerent. Massive and gaseous, the cloud-like object dwarfs the starship and defies all attempts to visually penetrate its innumerable energy fields. The decision is made to guide the starship into the interior while Lt. Uhura radios messages of friendship in all known languages and dialects. The trek inside the cloud is uneventful until a brilliant column of light appears upon the *Enterprise* bridge. Spock ascertains that this is an alien probe. The dazzling pillar moves about unhindered until the crew realizes that the probe is "reading" the ship's databanks. The Vulcan smashes the computer console, at which time the probe turns its attention upon the humans. Spock and Decker are jolted by blasts of energy. Ilia is engulfed in a spiderweb of pulsating energy and disappears. The "Intruder Alert" klaxon signals an alien presence in Ilia's quarters. Kirk, Spock and McCoy take a security team and find what appears to be Lt. Ilia emerging from an electron shower-bath. This Ilia has a crimson jewel in her throat and speaks in a mechanical drone, claiming to be the "eyes of V'ger." Spock and McCoy rightly surmise that this figure is a quasi-cyborg. Kirk and company treat the Ilia clone with courtesy, answering direct questions obliquely while at the same time feverishly trying to determine exactly *what* this "V'ger" is. Considering Captain Decker's past relationship with Ilia, Kirk assigns the young officer to be the cyborg's guide. As they move throughout the ship, Decker discovers that this being is not entirely devoid of Ilia's memories and, he concludes, her feelings. Meanwhile, Spock surreptitiously commandeers a rocket-equipped space suit, exits the starship, and propels himself through a collapsing aperture into the innermost chamber of the huge craft that contains V'ger. There he traverses a huge panorama featuring scaled replicas of planets, moons and cities. Epsilon Nine is represented, and the destroyed Klingon starships. Ultimately he comes upon a mammoth likeness of Ilia. Spock deduces that this cyclopean chamber houses three-dimensional images of all that V'ger has experienced in its interstellar journey. When he attempts a Vulcan mind-meld with the intelligence he is overcome and lapses into unconsciousness. It is a profoundly changed Spock who awakens aboard the *Enterprise*. The aloofness that he formerly displayed has been replaced by a straightforward, even joyful, countenance. He informs Kirk and McCoy that his mind-meld has given him an impression of an immensely powerful child that is on a mission to seek its father, or its creator. The question posed by V'ger, Spock says, is the question all sentient beings pose themselves: Who am I? Why am I here? Uhura informs them that the V'ger craft has taken up a stationary orbit near Earth. *Enterprise* sensors determine that drone satellites possess the destructive power to eradicate all life. In a verbal joust with the Ilia clone, Kirk issues a flat ultimatum to Ilia/V'ger: there will be no dialogue with the creator as long as the death-dealing satellites orbit Earth. He also demands an "audience" with V'ger. The *Enterprise* is drawn into the central chamber of the V'ger cloud and an oxygen-nitrogen "envelope" permits Kirk, Decker, Spock, McCoy and the Ilia clone to journey the remaining meters to the very core of the huge cloudcraft. There they find the truth behind V'ger: It is in fact an early Earth space probe of the Voyager class that had been interdicted in deep space by a wholly mechanical civilization. This civilization gleaned only a portion of Voyager's original programming — to traverse the cosmos, gathering as much data as it can, for possible return to earth — and repaired the ancient probe, outfitting it with an immense power source and encasing it in the awesome vessel that surrounds it. Sent on its way through the galaxy with capabilities undreamed of by its human creators, Voyager, now V'ger, amassed so much data

that it became sentient and obsessed with the questions of its origin. V'ger has returned to Earth, to "join" with its creator, oblivious to the "biological infestations" it finds teeming about the planet. In the end, Decker and the Ilia clone merge with the intellect of V'ger — providing the "human element" that the machine intelligence finds so lacking in providing a fuller understanding of the universe. In effect, a new life-form is created, the next phase in human evolution. Kirk, Spock and McCoy return to the *Enterprise,* turning it toward deep space for a proper shakedown and a continuance of their earlier five-year mission.

Reviews: "The script is sub-zero science fiction.... I don't understand, given the ingenuity of the best SF novels, how scripts like this and *Star Wars* can be so widely accepted." (Stanley Kauffmann, *New Republic,* December 29, 1979, p. 20) ¶"A lot of talk. Much of it in impenetrable space flight jargon.... The special effects do not reflect the current state of the art.... nothing but a long day's journey into ennui." (R.S., *Time,* December 17, 1979, p. 61)

Analysis: Star Trek — The Motion Picture was one of the most highly anticipated features in the genre of science fiction cinema, due to the ongoing popularity of the television series which debuted in 1966, was canceled in 1969 after a marginally successful run, and went on in syndication to garner a huge following that still inspires "Trekkie" conventions every year. Ironically, this very anticipation worked very much against the film's initial success. For years after *Star Trek* left network television, rumors were rife concerning the show's returning in some way, in some altered format — perhaps in a made-for-TV movie or even as a mini-series. Network television, always a tepid purveyor of science fiction, was never really keen on the idea of bringing back an expensive-to-produce series merely to placate what was perceived as a small but noisy portion of its audience. George Lucas's blockbuster *Star Wars* in 1977, however, convinced Paramount that perhaps a feature revival of *Star Trek* would not be so much of a gamble, and *Star Trek — The Motion Picture* began filming in the waning days of 1977. It was not a trouble-free production, with script and special effects problems in abundance. Despite its seasoned cast, respectable budget, and celebrated director, reception of the film was mild, even amongst the Trekkies who had sung the gospel according to Gene Roddenberry for over a decade. Despite its impressive look, *Star Trek — The Motion Picture* was essentially a reworking of not one, but *three* episodes of the TV series. Everyone seemed wooden and awkward, the veteran ensemble stiff, even rather artificial. Box office receipts were, in the final analysis, more than respectable (the second highest grossing film that year behind *Kramer vs. Kramer*), but not outstanding for the closing year of a decade that had included Lucas's film, Ridley Scott's *Alien*, and the Salkind Brothers' *Superman — The Movie*. Even now, *Star Trek — The Motion Picture* is certainly the redheaded stepchild in the Star Trek film canon. In fact, this premier opus is often overlooked altogether when the *Star Trek* film series is discussed. While the film's critics are not entirely off the mark in their comments, this first *Star Trek* movie really isn't bad entertainment. True, the script borrows heavily from several episodes of the old series, but at least it borrows from some of the good ones (there surely were plenty of bad ones). And if the cast seemed a bit stiff, well, these roles had been in mothballs for ten years, and the awkwardness is understandable. On the other hand, it *is* an impressive production: the *Enterprise* never looked so good, either before or since. Robert Wise, hardly a member of the *Star Trek* stable in any event, provides admirable direction and does about as much with the material as anybody could have done. Admittedly, the film is somewhat shorter on the kind of action that fans had come to expect from their Starfleet stalwarts, but a level of tension is established early on and maintained pretty much throughout the length of the film. No other Star Trek film has the eerie magnificence of the best scenes in *Star Trek — The Motion Picture*. Trumbull's otherworldly fabrications of V'ger's interior are every bit as effective in their way as the bizarre visuals

of the Giger-inspired *Alien* or the similar "mother ship" sequence of Spielberg's *Close Encounters of the Third Kind*. Adding to this overall remarkable effect is the equally forceful score by Jerry Goldsmith, at turns majestic and lyrical, mystical and atmospheric. If *Star Trek — The Motion Picture* fails, it is, ironically enough, because it is not enough like the television series to really satisfy that show's fans, and at the same time, it's *too* much like the show to make happy those who never really liked it. Most everybody agrees that it was really, in many ways and despite its generally excellent production values, a poorly prepared first effort by a crew that really hadn't gotten its feature film legs yet. For better or worse, the series really hit its stylistic stride with the next film, *The Wrath of Khan*. Academy Award nominations for art direction-set decoration, visual effects and music score.

Star Trek II — The Wrath of Khan
(1982; 113 min.) ***½

Produced by Robert Sallin. Executive Producer, Harve Bennett. Directed by Nicholas Meyer. Screenplay, Jack B. Sowards. Story, Harve Bennett and Jack B. Sowards. Based on the television series *Star Trek*, created by Gene Roddenberry. Edited by William P. Dornisch. Director of Photography, Gayne Rescher. Panavision. Color, Movielab. Music, James Horner. Dolby Stereo. Art Direction, Michael Minor. Set Decoration, Charles M. Graffeo. Special Visual Effects, Industrial Light and Magic, Jim Veilleux, Ken Ralston.

Cast: Admiral James T. Kirk (William Shatner), Mr. Spock (Leonard Nimoy), Khan (Ricardo Montalban), Dr. Leonard (Bones) McCoy (DeForest Kelley), Chekhov (Walter Koenig), Sulu (George Takei), Chief Engineer Montgomery Scott (James Doohan), Commander Uhura (Nichelle Nichols), Dr. Carol Marcus (Bibi Besch), David (Merritt Butrick), Terrell (Paul Winfield), Lieutenant Saavik (Kirstie Alley), Preston (Ike Eisenmann).

Synopsis: In the twenty-third century, on his birthday, Admiral Kirk is depressed because he's merely conducting training missions for the likes of Lt. Saavik. McCoy urges him to get back into space. In space, Chekhov and Terrell beam down from the

Starship *Reliant* to what they think is Ceti Alpha VI. They need to determine if any life-forms exist there. If not, the planet can be used for the Genesis Project. The men are surprised to discover cargo carriers from the *Botany Bay*, and too late Chekhov realizes they've stumbled into the presence of the criminal Khan, a warlord from the late twentieth century who'd been in cryogenic freeze. He'd been marooned as punishment fifteen years earlier by the then Captain Kirk. He and his company explain to Chekhov and Terrell that they're really on Ceti Alpha V. Number VI had exploded. Only Khan's supreme intellect allowed his party to survive on V, which after the death of its sister planet had become desolate. To "worm" information out of his captors, Khan introduces beastly indigenous slugs into the men's ears. Chekhov contacts Dr. Carol Marcus, head of the Genesis Project, and provides a bogus story about the *Reliant* arriving at her space station — Regula I — to implement the project. Marcus, Kirk's ex-wife, contacts the admiral on a training mission aboard the *Enterprise*, but the transmission is garbled. At Starfleet's command, Kirk heads the *Enterprise* toward Regula I. On the way, Kirk, McCoy and Spock use their computers to learn of the Genesis Project. Encountering the *Reliant*, the *Enterprise* is unexpectedly hit by torpedoes. Khan appears on the screen, demanding information about the Genesis Project in return for Kirk's life. Kirk pretends he's retrieving the information while actually using his computers to obtain the *Reliant* code. When he does, he lowers its shields and fires his weapons. Damaged, *Reliant* withdraws and *Enterprise* proceeds to Regula I. Neither Dr. Marcus nor any of her scientific team — including her and Kirk's son David — is to be found. Suspecting governmental meddling, they'd beamed down to Ceti Alpha V. But Kirk, McCoy and Saavik find Chekhov and Terrell. They eventually get to the planet and find Marcus. Terrell and Chekhov turn out to be under Khan's control still. Terrell is told to kill Kirk but kills himself instead. Chekhov collapses. Khan beams up a Genesis cylinder, saying he's leaving Kirk "buried alive." *Reliant* can't find *Enterprise*. Kirk is

beamed up. He'd spoken to his crew via a crude code and fooled Khan into thinking he was stranded. "I don't believe in a no-win scenario," Kirk says. *Enterprise* heads for a nearby nebula where the fighting odds will be even. "Khan, I'm laughing at the superior intellect," Kirk broadcasts. Although severely wounded in the ensuing battle, Khan ignites the Genesis Project. In order to repair their nuclear reactor so they can speed from the area, Spock enters the reactor room. Warp speed is achieved as Genesis turns the nebula into a planet. Spock dies, and his encapsulated body is shipped to the new planet. "He's really not dead as long as we remember him," offers McCoy. David apologizes for being wrong about his father.

Reviews: "A brisk, handsomely designed film…." (Kevin Thomas, *Los Angeles Times Calendar*, June 3, 1982, p. 1) ¶ "Particularly enjoyable because it has a plot, and the characterizations are more important than the special effects." (Robert Asahina, *New Leader*, July 12-26, 1982, p. 20) ¶ "Better than the original." (Joseph Gelmis, *Newsday*, June 4, 1982, Part II, p. 7)

Analysis: Though the story has several threads, they do not overwhelm or complicate the main thrust: the confrontation between Kirk and Khan. Montalban is perfect, chewing scenery, mouthing seeming profundities, a beast about to pounce. Was DeForest Kelley's "Bones" always such a killjoy? Even miscalculations ("Amazing Grace" played on bagpipes at Spock's funeral) and obvious solutions not tried (beam the Genesis Project capsule into empty space) don't compromise our enjoyment. We are amazed at how well the spacecraft of this era take punishment. How quickly phaser holes self-seal! How long were Chekhov and Terrell supposed to look for pre-animate matter? Would they have spotted it if it were the size of, say, a biscuit? This entry, which is the tightest in the series and seems to have become the fans' favorite, segues nicely into the next.

Star Trek III:
The Search for Spock
(1984; 105 min.) ***
Produced by Harve Bennett. Directed by

Leonard Nimoy. Screenplay, Harve Bennett. Based on the television series *Star Trek* created by Gene Roddenberry. Edited by Robert F. Shugrue. Director of Photography, Charles Correll. Panavision. Movielab Color. Music, James Horner. Television Theme, Alexander Courage. Special Sound Effects, Alan Howarth, Frank Serafine. Dolby Stereo. Art Direction, John E. Chilberg II. Costumes, Robert Fletcher. Special Makeup, Burman Studio. Special Physical Effects, Bob Dawson. Visual Effects, Kenneth Ralston.

Cast: Admiral Kirk (William Shatner), Mr. Spock (Leonard Nimoy), McCoy (DeForest Kelley), Scotty (James Doohan), Sulu (George Takei), Chekov (Walter Koenig), Sarek (Mark Lenard), Uhura (Nichelle Nichols), Kruge (Christopher Lloyd), David (Merritt Butrick), High Priestess (Dame Judith Anderson), Captain Styles (James B. Sikking), Saavik (Robin Curtis), Alien at bar (Allan Miller), Commander Morrow (Robert Hooks), Lieutenant (Scott McGinnis), Valkris (Cathie Shirriff), Klingon Torg (Stephen Liska), Klingon Maltz (John Larroquette), Captain Esteban (Phillip Richard Allen), Spock at 9 (Carl Steven), Spock at 13 (Vadia Potenza), Spock at 17 (Stephen Manley), Spock at 25 (Joe W. Davis).

Synopsis: Still showing scars from its recent encounter in the Moltara sector, the *Enterprise* arrives back at Earth station. Admiral Kirk and his crew grieve for Captain Spock, who died in the battle with Khan and was "buried" on the newly formed Genesis planet. Kirk had hoped to have his ship repaired and return immediately to Genesis to join his son David Marcus and Lt. Saavik, already there aboard the USS *Grissom* to study the new world. However, Genesis has become a "galactic controversy" and further incursion is forbidden. On Earth, Vulcan ambassador Sarek, Spock's father, visits Kirk. He demands to know why the admiral hadn't returned his son's body to Vulcan. Surely Spock, knowing the moment of his death was at hand, must have mind-melded with Kirk, his closest friend. Kirk is mystified, knowing nothing of any such bonding. In any event, he tells Sarek that just prior to Spock's death the two were separated, preventing any such contact. Studying the ship's flight recorder, the two learn that Dr. McCoy was the recipient of Spock's telepathic implant. It is imperative, says Sarek, that both McCoy

and Spock's body be returned to Vulcan. Unknown to anyone on Earth, the Klingon Empire's Commander Kruge has learned about Genesis and directs his Bird of Prey to the new planet. Already orbiting the planet is the *Grissom.* Studying the world with long-range sensors, David and Saavik detect both Spock's burial tube and an unidentifiable life-form nearby. They beam down to a veritable Eden. All they find is the burial tube covered with bacteria. The cylinder that contained Spock is empty. Their tricorders indicate that the life-form they detected is some distance away. Proceeding, they are alarmed to find that Genesis is still very much in a state of flux. The "genesis wave" is causing unnaturally accelerated rates of planetary evolution. Later, amid seismic shudders and meteorological disturbances, their devices lead them to a naked boy, moaning and writhing in pain. Saavik comforts him and is astonished to discover that this is apparently a Vulcan youth. When confronted by Saavik, David confesses that he had used *proto-matter* in the matrix of Genesis, despite the established scientific community's abhorrence of that substance. It is this proto-matter that accounts for both Genesis's astonishing success and the instability and short-livedness of its creation. On Earth, Kirk has no luck convincing his superiors of the necessity of returning to Genesis to recover Spock's body. Taking matters into his own hands, he enlists his old crew. Rescuing Dr. McCoy from incarceration — the doctor had been apprehended for attempting to procure his own illegal transport to the forbidden Genesis — Kirk commandeers the dry-docked *Enterprise* and manages to elude the giant *Excelsior* and speed to distant Genesis. They arrive to find themselves in a Kruge-devised Klingon trap. *Grissom* has been destroyed, and Kruge and his lieutenants have captured David, Saavik and the young Vulcan. The *Enterprise* is severely damaged by the Klingon attack but manages to partially cripple the Bird of Prey. Kirk tricks the Klingons into boarding the *Enterprise* even as he triggers the countdown for his ship's self-destruct mechanism. The boarding Klingons are vaporized, while Kirk,

McCoy, Scott, Sulu and Chekov materialize on the planet's surface. They overpower the Klingon guards but find Kruge gone (beamed to his ship) and David dead. Via radio, Kruge demands Kirk's surrender and the secret of Genesis. As the others are beamed aboard the Bird of Prey, Kruge beams down to do battle hand-to-hand with Kirk. As the planet roars and crumbles, the two tear at each other until Kruge falls to his death in a crevice. Taking up the Klingon's communicator, Kirk issues a harsh command and is beamed up to the orbiting ship. He overpowers the transporter operator, takes his weapon and gains control of the Bird of Prey. Quickly deciphering the controls, Sulu and Scott activate its warp drive and make for Vulcan. There the youth, who had been aging at an accelerated rate, grows to manhood. It is obvious that this is indeed Spock, whose life has been restored by the Genesis wave. Away from that world, his metabolism has slowed to normal and, physically, he seems totally restored. However, his spirit and personality are still held within the mind of Dr. McCoy, and it is the Vulcan elders atop Mt. C'yleah who must utilize the ancient — and questionable — techniques that will restore Spock to his former self. The rite is performed and at the Vulcan dawn, Spock and McCoy both emerge.

Reviews: "Its innocence is downright endearing...." (Kevin Thomas, *Los Angeles Times Calendar*, June 1, 1984, p. 1) ¶ "Perhaps the first space opera to deserve that term in its grandest sense. The plot is as convoluted and improbable as ... Verdi.... the settings are positively Wagnerian.... The emotions of ... are as broad and as basic as ... *Rigoletto*." (Richard Schickel, *Time*, June 11, 1984, p. 83)

Analysis: Star Trek III: The Search for Spock is generally considered one of the high spots in the series. Leonard Nimoy's direction (his first of three in the series) follows nicely in the vein of Nicholas Meyer's previous entry. His handling of both action scenes and those more intimate ones between characters is well done, and the narrative pace is swift but unhurried. The special effects are quite good and

again are provided by Industrial Light and Magic. The ensemble acting is as dependable as ever (why shouldn't it be?) and William Shatner manages to look sincere through most of his scenes and deliver his lines with a noticeable absence of Shatneresque animation. Coming on the heels of Ricardo Montalban's performance as the villain of the previous *Trek* outing, Christopher Lloyd's Kruge is a miscalculation. Lloyd's first and most memorable character portrayal was that of "Reverend Jim" of CBS TV's *Taxi*, and it was a characterization nearly as indelible as Don Knott's Barney Fife or Art Carney's Ed Norton (or, for that matter, Leonard Nimoy's Mr. Spock). Visually, Lloyd is fine for a Klingon commander, but his voice dispels any notion that it's *not* Reverend Jim under all that greasepaint. Interestingly, also under much Klingon greasepaint is John Larroquette, whose stint as barrister Dan on TV's *Night Court* had not yet begun. One of the old TV show's most annoying plot devices was that of killing or nearly killing a major character three-quarters of the way through the episode, and then miraculously rescuing or resurrecting that character before the finish. This sort of *deus ex machina* is OK once, and might be excused twice, but it began to happen all too frequently during the show's three-season run. That, unfortunately, is the whole *raison d'être* behind *The Search for Spock*. Leonard Nimoy had carped for years that the Spock character, while it made him a household name, had become a millstone about his neck, and whenever talk of a *Star Trek* comeback popped up (as it did a number of times after the show's cancellation) the question was always, "Will Nimoy come back as Spock?" He did, of course, but when the opportunity appeared to lay the Spock character to rest in *The Wrath of Khan*, that opportunity was seized. In the interim between Treks *III* and *IV*, Nimoy evidently had time to reflect upon this decision and consider what life without *Star Trek* would be like. The choice to resurrect Spock, while it did represent a lapse into the easy-out thinking that had contributed to the shallowness of the television series, was ultimately a wise one — at least for Nimoy.

Getting his directorial feet wet with *The Search for Spock* and two subsequent films led to a number of choice directing assignments outside the genre of science fiction cinema.

Star Trek IV: The Voyage Home
(1986; 119 min.) ***

Produced by Harve Bennett. Directed by Leonard Nimoy. Assistant Directors, Patrick Kehoe, Douglas E. Wise, Frank Capra III. Screenplay, Steve Meerson, Peter Krikes, Harve Bennett, Nicholas Meyer. Based on the television series *Star Trek*, created by Gene Roddenberry. Executive Consultant, Gene Roddenberry. Director of Photography, Donald Peterman. Panavision. Technicolor. Music, Leonard Rosenman. Television Theme by Alexander Courage. Dolby Stereo. Sound, Gene S. Cantamessa. Sound Effects, Mark Mangini. Art Direction, Joe Aubel, Pete Smith. Set Decoration, Dan Gluck, James Bayliss, Richard Berger. Costumes, Robert Fletcher. Creature, Richard Snell Designs, Dale Brady, Craig Caton, Allen Feuerstein, Shannon Shea, Brian Wade, Nancy Nimoy. Special Effects, Michael Lantieri, Clay Pinney, Brian Tipton, Don Elliott, Robert Spurlock, Tim Moran. Visual Effects produced at Industrial Light & Magic.

Cast: Admiral Kirk (William Shatner), Mr. Spock (Leonard Nimoy), McCoy (DeForest Kelley), Scotty (James Doohan), Sulu (George Takei), Pavel Chekov (Walter Koenig), Uhura (Nichelle Nichols), Amanda (Jane Wyatt), Gillian (Catherine Hicks), Sarek (Mark Lenard), Lt. Saavik (Robin Curtis), Federation Council president (Robert Ellenstein), Admiral Cartwright (Brock Peters), Klingon Ambassador (John Schuck), Starfleet communications officer (Michael Snyder), Starfleet display officer (Michael Berryman), *Saratoga* science officer (Mike Brislane), Commander Rand (Grace Lee Whitney), Alien communications officer (Jane Wiedlin), Starship captain (Vijay Amritraj), Commander Chapel (Majel Barrett), *Saratoga* Helmsman (Nick Ramus), Controllers (Thaddeus Golas, Martin Pistone), Bob Briggs (Scott DeVenney), Joe (Richard Harder), Nichols (Alex Henteloff), FBI agent (Jeff Lester).

Synopsis: As the USS *Saratoga* tracks a probe headed toward the Terran solar system, in San Francisco the Vulcan ambassador Sarek counters Klingon accusations to the Federation that Admiral Kirk is a terrorist, that Genesis was a device to destroy the Klingon race. Star Date 8390—it's the third month of Kirk's Vulcan exile. The crew votes to return to Earth to face the music. In space, the strange probe renders inoperable all Federation and Klingon ships in its vicinity. Arriving in Earth orbit, it starts vaporizing the ocean and ionizing the atmosphere, creating a complete cloud cover. Speeding toward Earth, Kirk listens to Spock's suggestion that the probe's unusual transmission may be intended for some other inhabitant of the planet. Humpback whales make the noise, but they became extinct on Earth in the twenty-first century. Spock says they may have to find some humpbacks—via time warp—and he programs the ship for the late twentieth century. At San Francisco's Cetacean Institute, Kirk and Spock locate two humpback whales, George and Gracie. McCoy and Scotty visit Plexicorp while Uhura and Chekov locate an atomic pile aboard the U.S. aircraft carrier *Enterprise* in Alameda. Chekov is captured aboard the carrier, but Uhura is beamed back to ship with the necessary protons. Sulu brings the plastic by helicopter. Gillian, the twentieth century biologist who's been helping them, discovers that the whales are being transported to Alaska for release. Chekov, who'd fallen and suffered a severe injury, is located in a hospital. Curing and retrieving Chekov, his companions return to the ship and head for the Bering Sea. They discomfit a whaling ship before beaming up the whales. "Admiral, there be whales here!" cries Scotty. Heading forward into time, the ship loses power in the vicinity of the alien craft and crashes into San Francisco Bay. Through heroic efforts, Kirk manages to release the whales, which communicate with the alien. It ceases its transmissions and heads back into space. At a council meeting, all charges but one are dropped against Kirk and his officers. Due to the mitigating circumstances, he alone must suffer punishment: demotion to Starfleet captain. His ship, NCC 1701-A, is the *Enterprise.*

Reviews: "It's a Save the Whale movie." (David Ansen, *Newsweek*, December 1, 1986, p. 89) ¶"Feather-brained and looks like shit." (David Edelstein, *Village Voice*,

December 9, 1986, p. 72) ¶"Warmer, wittier, more socially relevant and truer to it TV origins than prior odysseys." (*Variety*, November 19, 1986, p. 16)

Analysis: Sure, it's a feel-good movie, but it's fun and often funny enough to make us chuckle. Going back in time was a way for the old TV show to avoid expense—and permit scriptwriters to pontificate—but this version has enough special space effects to mitigate the first failing. In short, we don't agree with critics who found the effects cheesy. With the collapse of the Soviet Union, this film's comments about nuclear arms development are already out of date. And wasn't whaling almost finished in 1986? Brock Peters will play Admiral Cartwright again in *VI*. Dedicated to the crew of the ill-fated NASA space shuttle *Challenger*. Filmed in Monterey, Long Beach and San Francisco. Academy Award nominations for cinematography, music score, sound and sound effects editing. It was number five amongst money-makers that year.

Star Trek V: The Final Frontier
(1989; 106 min.) **½

Produced by Harve Bennett. Executive Consultant, Gene Roddenberry. Directed by William Shatner. Screenplay, David Loughery. Story, William Shatner, Harve Bennett and David Loughery. Based on the television series *Star Trek*, created by Gene Roddenberry. Edited by Peter Berger. Director of Photography, Andrew Laszlo. Panavision. Technicolor. Music, Jerry Goldsmith. Dolby Stereo. Sound, David Ronne. Art Direction, Nilo Rodis-Jamero. Special Visual Effects, Brian Ferren. Special Effects Supervisor, Michael L. Wood. Special Makeup Design, Kenny Myers.

Cast: Captain James T. Kirk (William Shatner), Mr. Spock (Leonard Nimoy), Dr. Leonard "Bones" McCoy (DeForest Kelley), Montgomery Scott (James Doohan), Pavel Chekov (Walter Koenig), Commander Uhura (Nichelle Nichols), Sulu (George Takei), St. John Talbot (David Warner), Sybok (Laurence Luckinbill), Korrd (Charles Cooper), Caithlin Dar (Cynthia Gouw), Captain Klaa (Todd Bryant), Vixis (Spice Williams), J'onn (Rex Holman), "God" (George Murdock), Young Sarek (Jonathan Simpson), High priestess (Beverly Hart), Pitchman (Steve

Susskind), Starfleet chief of staff (Harve Bennett), Amanda (Cynthia Blaise), McCoy's father (Bill Quinn), Yeoman (Melanie Shatner).

Synopsis: The desert world of Nimbus III, also called the Planet of Peace, is the site of a tri-planetary experiment by the United Federation of Planets. Romulan and Klingon delegates hope to work in harmony. The experiment is only marginally successful, with just a few thousand lowlifes taking residence. The outcast Vulcan Sybok, who espouses a philosophy of "emotion over logic," appears on Nimbus III and acquires a militant following who help him take over the city of Paradise. Back on Earth, the Federation chief of staff asks Captain James Kirk, Captain Spock and Dr. McCoy to take the newly built starship *Enterprise* (NCC-1701-A) to Nimbus III to assess the situation and free Sybok's hostages: the respective Terran, Romulan and Klingon political envoys. The *Enterprise* arrives at Nimbus III with its transporters inoperative, making it necessary to use the shuttlecraft *Copernicus* to land a rescue party. This commando unit procures steeds from an outriding party of scouts and storms the city. When the "hostages" turn phasers upon their would-be rescuers, Kirk and Spock realize they've fallen into a trap. Spock is astonished to recognize Sybok as his long-lost half-brother. The renegade Vulcan forces Kirk to return to the *Enterprise* with armed minions who take over the starship. Sybok plans to take the vessel to the edge of the galaxy and penetrate the "galactic barrier" and find a fabled world. God has spoken to the Vulcan, he claims. Kirk thinks him quite mad but fails to recapture the ship. Sybok urges them to confront their inner "sources of pain." Kirk refuses to confront his personal *angst*, claiming that it is precisely from this that he derives whatever drive and passion that he has. Arriving at the galaxy's perimeter, the *Enterprise* proceeds through an energy barrier. Kirk and company are amazed to immediately view a mist-shrouded planet. While accompanying Sybok to the shuttle bay, Kirk urges engineer Scott to get the transporters operational. The planet has an earth-like atmosphere but a barren landscape. When Sybok raises his arms and

Captain Kirk (William Shatner, left) and Mr. Spock (Leonard Nimoy) in *Star Trek V: The Final Frontier* (Paramount, 1989).

proclaims his arrival, the sky grows dim and the ground trembles as huge carved stone monoliths drive upward, forming a curved partial enclosure. A large, spectral face appears, and from it come deep, booming words of welcome. When this godlike vision shows an unusual interest in their starship and a curious lack of omniscience, Kirk grows suspicious. When he asks what possible interest or use God could have for a starship, energy beams blaze forth from the entity's eyes, knocking the startled captain off his feet. When Spock utters similar words of doubt, he too is bowled over. Realizing that he has made a terrible mistake in taking this alien entity to be a god, Sybok rushes forward and throws himself into the being's countenance. In the huge burst of light and energy that follows, the three remaining men rush back to the shuttle as Kirk radios the *Enterprise* to fire a photon torpedo at the site of the disturbance.

Review: "It's full of big philosophical issues, all treated with a goofy irrationality that only Hollywood could dream up.... Characters are as wonderful as ever.... It's diverting, but forgettable." (David Sterritt,

Christian Science Monitor, June 18, 1989, p. 15) ¶"William Shatner, the muscular dentist who unaccountably wandered into acting, has now wandered into directing, and despite recourse to divine sanction, he mismanages the climax of what is mostly an amiable movie." (David Denby, *New York*, June 19, 1989, p. 68)

Analysis: Star Trek V: The Final Frontier is, by consensus, the weakest of the Star Trek films, with a flimsy script abetted by William Shatner's lackluster direction. Shatner also had a hand in the writing, and most critics consider the result something less than a spectacular notch on his creative guns. While generally true, this assessment is probably unnecessarily severe. The problem with the Star Trek films is that even the best of them really aren't as good as their partisan proponents suggest, just as the worst aren't as bad as the detractors would have you believe. Not to make excuses, but *The Final Frontier*, despite its faults, still has its moments and is not a total waste of time. While Shatner's direction lacks the finesse of Leonard Nimoy and Nicholas Meyer (to say nothing of Robert Wise), he does manage to keep things moving with a only a couple of lapses in momentum. As one of the co-writers, however, he was able to do no more than compile a rehash of previously used ideas. Yet again, we're given an *Enterprise* straight out of dry-dock that has badly or non-working parts (the seats squeak, the doors only half-open automatically, even the transporter system is down) sent off into a threatening situation. Again, there is the ship being taken over by hostile forces while an outraged Captain Kirk bellows his frustration. Again, there's a Klingon Bird of Prey that's snooping along at the heels of the *Enterprise*, this time used in a particularly well-timed (but then, aren't they all?) *deus ex machina*. And again, there is the crew of the *Enterprise* going off where no man has gone before, and finding some god or other who's neither all-powerful, all-knowing nor even very nice (and this one's not even as powerful or menacing as some of the ones they used to run into every other week on the old TV series). The Star Trek regulars are the longest-working ensemble in the medium (with the exception of James Bond's coterie of co-stars). *Variety* pointed out that it was a mistake to focus on the fanatical mission of someone who wasn't an *Enterprise* crew member. Characterization would be meaningless to discuss, at this point, beyond saying "James Doohan *is* Scotty" and letting things go at that. Laurence Luckinbill is both effective and refreshing as Sybok, a Vulcan who can and does emote on cue. The others are equally strong beneath their greasepaint, though the excellent David Warner curiously merits what is an essentially trivial role as St. John Talbot, the Terran representative on Nimbus III. Perhaps the producers noted this, too: Warner appears in a considerably meatier role in the next series entry. Production values on *Star Trek V* are a tad less impressive than previous Trek outings, with the computer-generated effects standing out quite noticeably in the live-action sequences. The desert setting is overused by making both Nimbus III and the strange planet (Shakaree?) desert worlds. Since Shakaree was supposedly the home of God, an Eden-like setting would have been preferable and would have provided a nice contrast to the previous settings.

Star Trek VI: The Undiscovered Country
(1991; 110 min.) ***½

Produced by Ralph Winter and Steven-Charles Jaffe. Directed by Nicholas Meyer. Screenplay, Nicholas Meyer and Denny Martin Flinn. Story, Leonard Nimoy, Lawrence Konner, Mark Rosenthal. Based on the television series *Star Trek*, created by Gene Roddenberry. Edited by Ronald Roose. Director of Photography, Hiro Narita. Panavision. Technicolor. Music, Cliff Eidelman. Dolby Stereo. Special Alien Makeup, Edward French. Costumes, Dodie Shepard. Special Effects, Industrial Light & Magic.

Cast: Captain James T. Kirk (William Shatner), Mr. Spock (Leonard Nimoy), Dr. Leonard "Bones" McCoy (DeForest Kelley), Chancellor Gorkon (David Warner), General Chang (Christopher Plummer), Lieutenant Valeris (Kim Cattrall), Montgomery Scott (James Doohan), Commander Pavel Chekov (Walter Koenig), Commander Uhura (Nichelle Nichols), Captain Hikaru Sulu (George Takei), Ambassador Sarek (Mark Lenard), *Excelsior* communications officer (Grace Lee Whitney), Admiral Cartwright (Brock Peters), Klingon ambassador (John Schuck), Chief in command (Leon Russom), Federation president (Kurtwood Smith), Azetbur (Rosana DeSoto), *Excelsior* ensign (Christian Slater), Martia (Iman), Behemoth alien (John Bloom), Klingon defense attorney (Michael Dorn), General Stex (Brett Porter), Martia as a child (Katie Jane Johnston), Colonel West (Rene Auberjonois).

Synopsis: When the Klingon moon Praxis explodes, the resulting space wave is so strong that the Klingon Empire's worlds will lose their oxygen within 50 Earth years. The Klingons propose a real peace with the Federation, which would mean permission to enter Federation space. Captain Kirk doesn't trust them but is assigned to bring the Klingon chancellor Gorkon to the Federation president. After the chancellor and *Enterprise* crew members enjoy a strained meal, the Klingon ship is hit by two torpedoes, apparently discharged from the Federation starship. Incredibly, the data bank registers a full complement of weapons. On board the Klingon ship, two helmeted beings in silver suits and metallic shoes shoot Chancellor Gorkon. Beamed aboard, Kirk and Doc fail to save his life and are imprisoned to stand trial for assassination. The Federation, fearing an all-out war if they try to rescue Kirk and McCoy, allow them to be sentenced to slave labor on a mining world. Meanwhile, Mr. Spock aboard *Enterprise*, and Sulu, now a Starfleet captain, feign mechanical problems and ignorance and remain in space, hoping to rescue Kirk. On the *Enterprise*, Spock and first officer Valeris search for magnetic boots, hoping to find the two assassins. They theorize that the Klingons themselves engineered the murder, firing torpedoes from a cloaked Bird of Prey. Like Kirk, who can't forgive the Klingons for killing his son, some Klingons want war with humans, Romulans, and Vulcans. Kirk and McCoy are approached by a "woman," a shape changer who promises to lead them to the surface in return for taking her with them when they beam aboard the rescue ship. It turns out to be a trick, but Kirk and McCoy are beamed aboard *Enterprise* before they can be shot. Spock and Kirk discover that Valeris was in cahoots with the Klingon Chang to disrupt the peace process. They also learn that Chang's Bird of Prey can fire when cloaked. They must try to prevent further assassinations. Off the planet, the Bird of Prey fires at the *Enterprise* and Sulu's ship, but the heat-seeking torpedo the *Enterprise* launches destroys Chang. Kirk and his people beam down and unmask the assassins and conspirators, including Admiral Cartwright. Later Kirk muses about this last mission before standing down.

Review: "The point is that peace is a scary business to a lot of people…. It wouldn't be the same without William Shatner, Leonard Nimoy, DeForest Kelley and the rest. As old as they get, they still have an insight into these characters that seems bred in their bones." (Marshall Fine, *Wilmington News Journal*, December 6-8, 1991, p. 6.)

Analysis: We recommend this on the grounds of suspense, mystery, action, good villains, and excellent effects.

Star Trek: Generations
(1994; 118 min.) **

Produced by Rick Berman. Directed by David Carson. Screenplay, Ronald D. More, Brannon Braga. Story, Rick Berman, Ronald D. Moore, Brannon Braga. Based on the television series *Star Trek*, created by Gene Roddenberry. Edited by Peter E. Berger. Director of Photography, John A. Alonzo. Panavision. Color, DeLuxe. Music, Dennis McCarthy. Special Visual Effects, Industrial Light and Magic, John Knoll.

Cast: Captain Jean-Luc Picard (Patrick Stewart), Admiral James T. Kirk (William Shatner), Commander William Riker (Jonathan Frakes), Lt. Commander Geordi La Forge (LeVar Burton), Lt. Commander Data (Brent Spiner), Montgomery Scott (James Doohan), Counselor Deana Troi (Marina Sirtis), Dr. Soran (Malcolm McDowell), Commander Pavel Chekov (Walter Koenig), Dr. Beverly Crusher (Gates McFadden), Lt. Commander Worf (Michael Dorn), Guinan (Whoopi Goldberg), Captain Harriman (Alan Ruck), Science Officer (Jenette Goldstein), Picard's wife (Kim Braden).

Synopsis: The newly commissioned *Enterprise NCC-1701-B* is on a maiden voyage mounted mainly as a public relations junket for journalists. Admiral James Kirk and his associates, Commanders Scott and Chekov, attend the event as guests. The *Enterprise* intercepts a distress call from a pair of vessels that are trapped within the vortices of an undulating energy ribbon. When the first vessel's hull collapses, killing 265 passengers, Kirk and his veteran companions hastily conceive a stratagem that allows for the recovery of over two score passengers of the remaining craft, the *Lacoul*. The cost of this action, unfortunately, is the life of Admiral Kirk. Seventy-eight years later, the crew of *Enterprise NCC-1701-D* investigates the wreckage of a devastated space observatory. One of the few survivors is Tolean Soran, who had likewise survived the destruction of the *Lacoul* three quarters of a century earlier. Soran approaches Picard, insisting that he be returned to the observatory to resume work on an important but undisclosed experiment. When Picard is slow to comply, Soran beams onto the observatory on his own and overpowers Geordi and Data. Firing a solar probe containing trilithium into the nearby star,

Soran initiates a concussive reaction that destroys the star and the observatory. The *Enterprise* warps to safety while Soran teleports with captive Geordi to a Klingon Bird of Prey cloaked nearby. Picard learns that Soran is really a 300-year-old Alorian whose family was killed by space marauders. He and other Alorians escaped their home world aboard the *Lacoul*, ultimately to become trapped in the energy ribbon that destroyed their companion vessel and nearly the *Enterprise-B*. Guinan informs Picard that Soran's obsession is with the energy ribbon, a gateway to something called the "Nexus." This Nexus is an immense cortex of cosmic neural energy capable of imparting to sentient beings a supreme sense of joy and contentment. Its seductiveness cannot be resisted by one who feel its power. Before being saved by Kirk's actions when aboard the *Lacoul*, Soran had felt this power. He will stop at nothing in order to experience it again. In the nearly 80 years that have passed since that encounter, Soran has perfected the trilithium probe that can stop the fusion process, causing whole stars to implode and drastically alter a stellar system's gravitational field. This way he plans to "attract" the energy ribbon phenomenon to him and thus gain access to the Nexus once again. That this action will cause the inevitable deaths of countless millions of life-forms in the wake of the chosen star system's collapse means nothing to Soran. While the *Enterprise* does battle with the Klingon ship in the system Soran has chosen as his guinea pig, Picard confronts Soran in an effort to dissuade him from launching a probe into this system's sun. As the two verbally joust, the space combat rages until the energy ribbon appears; the *Enterprise* gets the upper hand and destroys the Bird of Prey but is badly disabled. Herding crew and passengers into the ship's saucer-shaped section, Commander Riker skillfully pilots that portion to the planet below. Soran launches his trilithium missile toward the nearby sun and then fires an energy bolt at Picard precisely as the Nexus ribbon passes. Rather than being killed, Picard finds himself within the timeless continuum of the Nexus, where his path crosses that of fellow-traveler James T. Kirk. Again utilizing the nuances of the Nexus, Picard and Kirk return to the planet moments *prior* to the energy ribbon's appearance. Together they prevent Soran from launching the trilithium missile.

Reviews: "Over-hyped, underimagined walk-through that relies excessively on flashy fireworks effects and confusing leaps in time and space.... Since Shatner's acting style still comes in baked, boiled, spiced, deviled and chopped variations, he's no match for the Shakespearean-caliber Stewart." (Ralph Novak, *People*, December 5, 1994, pp. 18, 20) ¶"An archvillain (Malcolm McDowell) who is merely arch and not villainous. The moral of this slow but handsomely photographed film ... is that Enterprise captains come and go, but *Star Trek* is eternal." (C.R., *Philadelphia Inquirer*, March 5, 1995, p. G5)

Analysis: The *Star Trek* phenomenon was destined to outlive the charter members of Gene Roddenberry's original series. Network television's hesitancy to pick up the show, despite flirting with the idea for nearly two decades, ended only with the ball being dropped. The older show's relatively high cost was always a sticking point, and the idea of launching a new series, with the commensurate higher budgets that a more effects-conscious public would demand, remained sticky for conservative network executives. Not so with independent syndicated programmers. They picked up the ball and ran with it, all the way to the proverbial bank. Despite naysayers' predictions of an early demise, *Star Trek: The Next Generation* proved to be incredibly successful — the most successful syndicated series in TV history, in fact — and enjoyed a continuous run more than twice that of its NBC predecessor. So prodigious was the appeal that the series was able to "spin off" not one, but two new series in the mid–1990s: *Star Trek: Deep Space Nine* and *Star Trek: Voyager*. Cessation of small-screen production of *The Next Generation*, in fact, was more of a mutually agreed-upon creative decision than one dictated by demographics or Nielsen scores. With seven seasons' worth of material in the can (to generate even more lucrative returns in syndication), the cast and crew of *Star Trek: The Next Generation* was ready and willing to take the baton from the now long-in-the-tooth cast of the *Star Trek* feature films. *Star Trek: Generations* was the launching pad for *The Next Generation*'s crew. Unfortunately, *Generations* is not adequate either as a fitting swan song for the original cast — that function was better served in *Star Trek: The Undiscovered Country* — or as a theatrical debut for the *Next Generation* crew (one hopes that will be realized in the 1996 feature, *Star Trek: First Contact*). Instead, it plays more like a vanity piece for William Shatner, who manages to die heroically not once, but twice, and both times in woefully contrived situations. Otherwise, *Generations* is a rather routine *Star Trek* entry, long on sentimentality and fan appeal, but short on anything really new. Most noticeably, as a series, it seems to have lost sight of one of its earliest tenets, that of going where no man has gone before. Most of *Generations* has a been-there-done-that sense about it and plays very much like an expanded version of the television series. Still, the very idea of James T. Kirk dying *twice*, in a feature film made nearly thirty years after his original series died on television, demands a degree of respect for both the character and the series, regardless of whether one is a fan. Admittedly, fanhood helps.

Star Wars
(20th Century–Fox, 1977; 121 min.)
★★★★

Produced by Gary Kurtz. Written and directed by George Lucas. Assistant Directors, Tony Waye, Gerry Gavigan, Terry Madden. Edited by Paul Hirsch, Marcia Lucas, Richard Chew. Director of Photography, Gilbert Taylor. Panavision. Technicolor. Music, John Williams. Art Direction, Norman Reynolds, Leslie Dilley. Costumes, John Mollo. Special Photographic Effects, John Dykstra.

Cast: Luke Skywalker (Mark Hamill), Princess Leia Organa (Carrie Fisher), Han Solo (Harrison Ford), Darth Vader (David Prowse, voice of James Earl Jones), Obi Wan Kenobi (Alec Guinness), Grand Moff Tarkin (Peter Cushing), Chewbacca (Peter Mayhew), C-3PO (Anthony Daniels), R2-D2 (Kenny Baker), Uncle Owen Lars (Phil Brown), Aunt Beru Lars (Shelagh Fraser), Chief Jawa (Jack Purvis), General Dodonna (Alex McCrindle), General Willard (Eddie Byrne), Red Leader (Drewe Henley), Red Two/Wedge (Dennis Lawson), Red Three/Biggs (Garrick Hagon), Red Four/John D (Jack Klaff), Red Six/Porkins (William Hootkins), Gold Leader (Angus McInnis), Gold Two (Jeremy Sinden), Gold Five (Graham Ashley), General Taggi (Don Henderson), General Motti (Richard LeParmentier), Commander #1 (Leslie Schofield).

Synopsis: "A long time ago in a galaxy far, far away...." begins "Episode IV: A New Hope." After a battle in space, Darth Vader of the Galactic Empire captures Princess Leia of the Imperial Senate. She says she's headed for Alderan. He's looking for secret plans the rebels obtained of the Empire's Death Star. Meanwhile, on Tatooine, the robotic droids C-3PO and R2-D2 are purchased by the uncle of Luke Skywalker, a young man living on Tatooine. The droids had been jettisoned in a pod from the princess's ship and captured by small, hooded figures. R2-D2 has a message: a hologram of a young lady — the princess — imploring Obi Wan Kenobi for help. A hermit-like Ben Kenobi lives somewhere about, Luke recalls. Following R2-D2, he is captured by the sand people but rescued by a hooded figure revealed as Ben, or Obi Wan, Kenobi. He knew Luke's father; both were Jedi knights during the time of the Republic, before the Empire. He gives Luke his father's light saber. He tells Luke his pupil Darth Vader helped track down and destroy the Jedi knights. R2-D2 shows Ben the hologram. Princess Leia asks him to take the droid to Alderan, and Ben urges Luke to accompany him. After finding his aunt and uncle killed by Imperial storm troopers on the trail of the droids, Luke agrees. Han Solo is hired to pilot the *Millennium Falcon* to Alderan. Before he leaves, he shoots a bounty hunter who hopes to take Han to a certain Jabba. Escape is made under fire. Meanwhile, aboard the Death Star, Grand Moff Tarkin tricks Princess Leia into revealing the location of the rebel base and then destroys her home planet of Alderan. The *Millennium*

Falcon exits hyperspace amidst the wreckage of Alderan and is pulled by a tractor beam into the Death Star. Hiding in smuggling compartments, the crew sneaks out and takes over the area's control booth. Ben leaves Luke, who learns of Princess Leia's whereabouts and of the fact that she's about to be terminated. He, Han and Chewbacca find Leia, only to be trapped by storm troopers with no way of escape. Leia blasts a hole into the side of the tunnel and they drop into a garbage dump. A weird creature lives there and tries to drag Luke under. Why did it release him? Because it knew the walls would soon close in, crushing the contents. Luke contacts C-3PO, who instructs R2-D2 to shut down all garbage chutes. Ben confronts Darth Vader and the two engage in a duel with their light sabers. Seeing Luke and his companions heading for the *Millennium Falcon*, Ben allows himself to be killed. Yet his voice urges Luke on. Han's ship escapes the Death Star. But a homing device was planted aboard, and the Death Star follows the ship to the rebel base. With R2-D2's information about the Death Star, fighter pilots fly against it. Using the Jedi Force, Luke manages to drop torpedoes into its reactor. It is destroyed, but Vader, who has been flying a fighter, escapes. At a gala ceremony, Luke, Han and Chewbacca are presented medals of heroism by Princess Leia.

Reviews: "Belongs to the sub-basement, or interstellar comic-strip, school of science fiction; *Terry and the Pirates* with astro-drive.... I doubt that anyone will ever match it, though the imitations must already be on the drawing boards." (Robert Hatch, *Nation*, June 25, 1977, p. 794) ¶"Has nowhere near the romantic invention of, say, Edgar Rice Burroughs's Martian novels, featuring that dashing Virginia gentleman, John Carter, and the lovely shocking-pink princess, Dejah Thoris. Here it is all trite characters and paltry verbiage.... and then there is that distressing thing called the Force." (John Simon, *New York*, June 20, 1977, p. 71)

Analysis: After *American Graffiti* (1973) was a surprise hit, George Lucas's aim was to film a reprise of Alex Raymond's *Flash Gordon*. Unable to come to terms with the copyright holders, King Features Syndicate, Lucas decided to produce his own space opera more or less from scratch. Just about everything was tossed into Lucas's creative stew: traditional fairy tales, classic myths, American westerns, comic strips, World War II movies, even the James Bond films. He fashioned his movie, *Star Wars*, after the Saturday matinee serials he'd enjoyed as a boy, even scrolling an opening "synopsis" in the fashion of the old Universal serials with the banner proclaiming it as "Chapter IV," in the manner of an ongoing cliffhanger. Similarly, from the standpoint of story line, characterization and scientific accuracy, *Star Wars* is about on a par with those old chapterplays. As far as production values were concerned, however, Lucas's film had a technical polish far outstripping the accomplishments of its forerunners. In fact, *Star Wars* (and the subsequent chapters in the trilogy) set the standard for science fiction special effects after Kubrick's *2001: A Space Odyssey*.

Launching his planned space opera was no easy task for Lucas. His first film, a dystopian science fiction movie entitled *THX 1138* (1970), was a box-office flop despite being relatively well received by the critics within the fantasy film genre. Fantasy was replaced by nostalgia in *American Graffiti*, which was only his second movie and an enormous hit. Despite this success, Lucas's next project — his planned Flash Gordon–like space fantasy — promised to be both unusual and expensive to produce, and was rejected by more than one major studio (including Universal) before Twentieth Century–Fox's Alan Ladd, Jr., showed interest. Choosing a leading cast of three largely unknown young actors, Lucas balanced these neophytes with a number of veterans, including the splendid Alec Guinness and Hammer Studios' Peter Cushing. Behind the scenes, which is where a movie of this type is generally made or unmade, Lucas's choices were no less inspired: John Dykstra, whose computer-linked and -operated cameras generated the film's ground-breaking optical effects, teamed with John Stears, a mechanical-effects wizard whose work had been essential to many James Bond films; artist Peter

Ellenshaw provided the most breathtaking mattes seen in films in many a year; makeup artists Stuart Freeborn and Rick Baker (the latter of whom would later become famous for his sterling work in films like *An American Werewolf in London* and *The Howling*) produced outstanding "alien" visuals; composer John Williams provided a rousing score that would do much to make *Star Wars* an icon of science fiction cinema.

Production costs on *Star Wars* tripled from the anticipated $3.5 million to over $10 million during the period of its filming. Escalations like that usually signify an unsure hand on the tiller and, worse still, an approaching boondoggle. That was not to be the case with *Star Wars*, as it opened to packed houses in the late spring of 1977 and continued packing them in all through the summer and into the fall. *Star Wars* was the supernova success of the 1970s, quickly becoming the second most successful film in movie history (thus far topped only by *E. T.— The Extraterrestrial*). Suddenly, Lucas was hot stuff in Hollywood and everyone was beating a path to Lucasfilms, Ltd., to learn just when to expect a sequel to this sudden surprise hit, since it quite plainly ended on an open note. Brilliant producer-director and shrewd marketer that he was, George Lucas was unusually reticent when it came to doling out press conferences and interviews. *Star Wars*, he claimed, was actually only a small part of a vast and ongoing space opera that he hoped to be able to produce as not one, but a series of three separate trilogies. This first installment filmed was actually sequentially the fourth in what would eventually be nine films that would relate the rise and fall of a huge galactic empire. The only characters who would actually span this generations-long concept would be the two droids, C-3PO and R2-D2, that were introduced in the first film. Whatever the long-range plans for *Star Wars*, the immediate plans were for a sequel that would begin filming in the late seventies.

Unlike Kubrick's *2001: A Space Odyssey*, the first science fiction blockbuster which was far too *outré* to have any immediate successors, *Star Wars* flung open the doors—

for better or worse — to a huge number of clones and imitations. While the great majority of these were hastily produced and instantly forgettable, George Lucas had ushered in the biggest boom of science fiction movies since the 1950s.

On watching *Star Wars* again, we wondered why so little stop-motion miniature photography was used. It appears that George Lucas had his own ideas and didn't want Douglas Trumbull. Jim Danforth turned him down after hearing the lowdown.

Star Wars was the top grosser of 1977. Nominated for picture, supporting actor (Guinness), director, and original screenplay Academy Awards, it won for art direction-set decoration, sound, music score, editing, costumes, and visual effects.

The Empire Strikes Back
(1980; 124 min.) ****

Produced by Gary Kurtz. Executive Producer, George Lucas. Directed by Irvin Kershner. Screenplay, Leigh Brackett and Lawrence Kasdan. Story, George Lucas. Edited by Paul Hirsch. Director of Photography, Peter Suschitzky. Panavision. DeLuxe Color. Music, John Williams. Dolby Stereo. Art Direction, Leslie Dilley, Harry Lange, Alan Tomkins. Set Decoration, Michael Ford. Costumes, John Mollo.

Cast: Luke Skywalker (Mark Hamill), Princess Leia (Carrie Fisher), Han Solo (Harrison Ford), Lando Calrissian (Billy Dee Williams), Darth Vader (David Prowse, voice of James Earl Jones), Yoda (Kenny Baker), Chewbacca (Peter Mayhew), C-3PO (Anthony Daniels), R2-D2 (Kenny Baker), Ben "Obi Wan" Kenobi (Alec Guinness), Boba Fett (Jeremy Bulloch), Chief Ugnaught (Jack Purvis), Lando's Aide (John Hollis), Snow creature (Des Webb), Admiral Piett (Kenneth Colley), General Veers (Julian Glover), Admiral Ozzel (Michael Sheard), Captain Needa (Michael Culver), Officers (John Dicks, Milton Johns, Mark Jones, Oliver Maguire, Robin Scoby), General Rieekan (Bruce Boa), Zev (Christopher Malcolm), Hobbie (Richard Oldfield), Wedge (Dennis Lawson), Major Derlin (John Ratzenberger), Janson (Ian Liston), Dak (John Morton), Head controller (Jerry Harte), Deck lieutenant (Jack McKenzie), Officers (Noran Chancer, Norwich Duff, Ray Hassett, Brigitte Kahn, Burnell Tucker).

Rebel soldiers take aim at the Imperial "walkers" on the ice planet Hoth in *The Empire Strikes Back* (Twentieth Century–Fox, 1980).

Synopsis: The Empire sends droids throughout the galaxy to find the rebel alliance while on a frozen world the rebel leaders plan their next campaign. While scouting, Luke is attacked by a snow creature and dragged to its lair. Using his light sword, he wounds the creature, escapes and before freezing to death is rescued by Han. Han and Chewbacca investigate an alien presence near the base and destroy one of the spy droids. But they realize it signaled the Empire's fleet. Because of the force field that protects the alliance base from air attack, Darth Vader uses huge "walkers" to overrun it and destroy the energy generator. Most of the alliance escapes, Luke and R2-D2 to the planet Dagobah to which the image of Ben directed him. Luke seeks Yoda, another Jedi master. Han, Leia, Chewbacca, and C-3PO fly into an asteroid cluster, taking refuge in a huge cave only to discover that it's the gullet of a gigantic beast. They escape and make it to Lando Calrissian's mining planet. Han and Lando are old friends, but Vader preceded them and forces Lando to hand them over to him. After Vader tests a carbon freezing device on Han, a bounty hunter takes the body. Destination: Jabba the Hutt. Luke meanwhile has found Yoda and has undertaken a regimen of physical and mental activities designed to make him a full Jedi knight and possessor of the true power that will serve him well when he confronts Vader and the "dark side." Before his training is complete he leaves to rescue Leia and Han and proceeds to Lando's planet where he meets Vader. Vader tells Luke that he is his father, that they can depose the emperor and rule the galaxy together. Luke refuses the offer and Vader cuts off his hand. About to lose his hold, Luke is rescued by Lando and Leia in Han's *Millennium Falcon*. They plan to rescue Han from Jabba.

Reviews: "Good-natured hokum, got up in high cinematic style.... Rarely has high filmic art and Saturday-matinee excitement been so successfully combined." (David Sterritt, *Christian Science Monitor*,

May 21, 1980, p. 19) ¶"The special effects in
The Empire Strikes Back do not stand the
test of comparison very well.... (The film)
does have some enjoyable aspects." (Robert
Asahina, *New Leader*, June 2, 1980, p. 20)
¶"Appeals on only one level — as grandil-
oquent pop fantasy." (David Denby, *New
York*, May 26, 1980, p. 67)

Analysis: George Lucas has said that he
initially envisioned the *Star Wars* trilogy
as being structured like a three-act play,
with the central episode being the darkest,
most downbeat, of the three. And so it is
with *The Empire Strikes Back*, which features
a rallying Empire that retaliates harshly
against the insurrectionists. The freedom
fighters spearheaded by Luke Skywalker,
Han Solo and Princess Leia are on the retreat from the beginning of the film and
seem all but beaten by the end. By the conclusion (once again with an open ending),
Han Solo is encased in suspended animation inside a block of solidified carbon and
his body carted off as payment of his debt
to Jabba the Hutt; Luke has been maimed
and, worse, informed that the evil Darth
Vader is his *father*; and Leia is torn between
her feelings for Luke and Han. Despite its
generally darker tone, however, *The Empire
Strikes Back* was a hugely successful film
(the top money-maker in the U.S. in 1980,
in fact) and a worthy successor to *Star Wars*.

The Empire Strikes Back really opened up
the Star Wars mythos and nicely fleshed
out the characters introduced in that first
film. It also developed some interesting
complications with the Luke-Leia-Solo
triangle and the revelation about Darth
Vader being Luke's father. It has outstanding battle scenes on the ice world Hoth, stu-
pefying special-effects flying with Han Solo
piloting the *Millennium Falcon* through
that asteroid field, a dank, spooky Skull
Island of a world that was Yoda's planet in
the Dagobah system, and the fabulous "sky
city" of Lando Calrissian. It has one outstanding sword fight sequence in the best
Errol Flynn tradition. *The Empire Strikes
Back* captures that elusive sense of wonder
that epitomizes the best space-opera better
than any other film we can think of.

Irvin Kershner directs *Empire* accord-
ingly, giving full rein to spectacle while

handling the episodic nature of the narrative very well. It is this episodic nature that
makes *Empire* the more convoluted story
to tell, much more so than its more linear
predecessor. After the events on the ice
planet Hoth, the story line splits in two and
the director has to constantly shift between
Luke and Yoda on one hand, and Han and
Leia on the other. The result is an uneven
pace that some feel is to the film's detri-
ment. While the first film's raw energy and
narrative thrust is a definite plus, there's
no denying that *Empire* is the more polished and, ultimately, more gripping film.
Characterizations are fleshed out nicely (if
predictably), and the film's downbeat tone
does give the whole affair a weight that's
usually absent in cinema space opera. One
reason for the film's success in the space
opera genre is the fact that veteran science
fiction author and screenwriter Leigh Brackett was responsible for the script's first
draft. Brackett died after turning in the
first draft, and relative newcomer Lawrence Kasdan (who later scored his own
successes with *Body Heat* and *The Big
Chill*) carried through with revisions and
a final script.

In the years since its release, critics have
revised their opinions on *The Empire
Strikes Back*. While they concede its many
virtues — the astonishing set-pieces, the
sophisticated technical wizardry, etc.—
and the fact that it makes a nearly overwhelming good first impression, they find
the film's episodic quality taking its toll
after repeated viewing. Peter Nichols ar-
ticulates this argument in essence by stat-
ing that it lacks "the raw vigour of its
predecessor," and that, withal, there was
"something ever so slightly calculating
about it." (Peter Nichols, *The World of
Fantastic Films*, p. 95) Nichols, of course,
takes the position of many science fiction
purists who see space opera as an archaic
medium and certainly nothing *serious*. For
the most part, however, *The Empire Strikes
Back* is considered an excellent film, superior science fiction space opera, and ar-
guably the best of its class.

Academy Award for sound. Nominations for art direction-set decoration and
music score.

Return of the Jedi
(1983; 133 min.) ***½

Produced by Howard Kazanjian. Executive Producer, George Lucas. Directed by Richard Marquand. Screenplay, Lawrence Kasdan, George Lucas. Story, George Lucas. Edited by Sean Barton, Marcia Lucas, Duwayne Dunham. Director of Photography, Alan Hume. DeLuxe Color. Music, John Williams. Dolby Stereo. Art Direction, Joe Johnston, Fred Hole, James Schoppe. Costumes, Agie Guerard Rodgers, Nilo Rodis-Jamero. Makeup and creature design, Phil Tippett, Stuart Freeborn.

Cast: Luke Skywalker (Mark Hamill), Princess Leia (Carrie Fisher), Han Solo (Harrison Ford), Lando Calrissian (Billy Dee Williams), Darth Vader (David Prowse, voice of James Earl Jones), C-3PO (Anthony Daniels), Chewbacca (Peter Mayhew), Anakin Skywalker (Sebastian Shaw), Yoda (Frank Oz), Emperor (Ian McDiarmid), Ben "Obi Wan" Kenobi (Alec Guinness), R2-D2 (Kenny Baker), Mof Jererrod (Michael Pennington), Bib Fortna (Michael Carter), Admiral Piett (Kenneth Colley), Wedge (Dennis Lawson), Admiral Ackbar (Tim Rose), General Madine (Dermot Crowley), Mon Mothma (Caroline Blakiston), Wicket (Warwick Davis), Paploo (Kenny Baker), Boba Fett (Jeremy Bulloch), Sy Snotles (Michele Gruska), Fat dancer (Claire Davenport), Logray (Mike Edmonds), Chief Chirpa (Jane Busby), Nicki (Nicki Rade), Tebo (Jack Purvis), Oola (Femi Taylor).

Synopsis: Leia attempts to rescue Han Solo from gangster Jabba the Hutt on Luke's home world of Tatooine but is herself captured and made slave to the loathsome creature. After consulting with Yoda and realizing that he is indeed a Jedi knight who must confront Vader, Luke, along with Lando Calrissian, rescues Leia and Han, Chewbacca, C-3PO and R2-D2. In the fracas, Luke defeats a bantha beast, Han's bounty hunter falls into the maw of Sarnak, and Leia strangles Jabba. Meeting with Admiral Ackbar and other rebels, they plan an attack on the new Death Star undergoing final construction around the forest world of Endor. Meanwhile, Vader consults with the Emperor, who tells him they can convert young Luke to the dark side when he arrives — as they know he will. Luke, Leia and Solo land on Endor, hoping to destroy the reactor that controls

the force field protecting the Death Star. During a chase after troopers, Leia is knocked unconscious. She wakes to find herself confronting a small furry creature with a spear. This Ewok takes her to its tribe's treetop abodes, where later Solo, Chewbacca and Luke are brought as prisoners. There C-3PO is worshipped as a god, but Leia convinces him to make the Ewoks let her friends go. Luke informs her in private that he is her brother. Luke leaves, allowing himself to be captured so as to confront Vader. The emperor's walkers battle the rebels and Ewoks in the forest while Calrissian leads warships against the Death Star. Han, Leia and Chewbacca gain access to the generator controlling the force field and destroy it. On the Death Star, Luke wins Vader to the good side when the emperor tries to kill him. Vader tosses the emperor into the bowels of the Death Star. Upon request, Luke removes the helmet of his mortally wounded father so he can at last see his father's face. Lando dives his craft toward the innards of the Death Star and delivers the coup de grace. The Death Star explodes as he makes a fast getaway. On Endor all celebrate, including the "ghosts" of Obi Wan, Yoda and Vader.

Reviews: "On the down side, much of the action seems perfunctory.... The climax is a marvel of classical moviemaking." (David Sterritt, *Christian Science Monitor,* May 19, 1983, p. 16) ¶The special effects are indeed marvelous, if often improbable." (Lenny Rubenstein, *Cineaste,* Vol. XIII, No. 1 [1983], p. 60) ¶"One of the biggest cinematic cons of all time goes on its noisy, mindless way." (John Coleman, *New Statesman,* June 3, 1983, p. 27) ¶"The good news is that George Lucas & Co. have perfected the technical magic to a point where almost anything and everything — no matter how bizarre — is believable. The bad news is the human dramatic dimensions have been sorely sacrificed." (Har., *Variety,* May 18, 1983)

Analysis: Despite the fact that *Return of the Jedi* seems to tie up a multitude of loose ends and resolve all the conflicts created in *Star Wars* and *The Empire Strikes Back,* many fans of the series were disappointed. They felt that *Return* really broke no new

Han Solo (Harrison Ford, center) and other members of the rebel strike team are captured by storm troopers on Endor in *Return of the Jedi* (Twentieth Century–Fox, 1983).

ground and merely recycled the most popular ideas from the previous films, such as the alien-saloon sequence from *Star Wars* (in *Return*, the scene is only slightly modified to represent Jabba's dungeon rabble),

more breathtaking light-saber duels and outer space dogfights, and another kamikaze mission by space fighters against a seemingly impregnable Death Star that again has *one* nearly-impossible-to-get-at weak spot. But if there was about *Empire* the scent of the faintly calculated, much of *Return of the Jedi* seems clearly aimed toward the pre-teen audience which was probably the series's target all along. In this final film of the *Star Wars* cycle, potentially thorny complications are dismissed with barely a wave of the hand — for instance, the potentially sticky wicket of the Han-Luke-Leia triangle is instantly resolved when Luke and Leia turn out to be siblings — and the adventure is gotten on with. Many considered it unfortunate that George Lucas allowed the film to wallow in the truly banal, particularly with his introduction of the furry Ewoks. The forest battle between these cuddly teddy bears and the Imperial storm troopers is masterfully executed but is ultimately hamstrung by an unbelievable Ewok victory over the battle-hardened veterans (the carnage amongst the Ewoks is minimal, while the heavily armed and armored troops are practically obliterated). An ill-advised and totally anachronistic Ewok version of the Tarzan yell brings crashing to earth any disbelief that may have been suspended until that point.

The last quarter of *Return* is mostly equal amounts of the flashing light-sabers from the previous film (with another duel between Luke and Vader), and the Death Star–busting scene from *Star Wars*. *Return of the Jedi* is just a lazy sequel with a multi-million-dollar special effects budget to distract the audience. It has a feel-good ending that not only has everybody singing and dancing and slapping each other on the back, it includes protoplasmic images of the Dear Departed, apparently just so we don't have to worry about them, either. Everything's okay, the heroes are alive and happy — even the *dead* are alive and happy — and the evil ol' empire has gone up in smoke.

Whatever its shortcomings, however, *Return of the Jedi* was hardly an unsuccessful film. It became the big money-maker of 1983, eventually ranking third in the twenty-five top grossing films of all time (immediately behind *Star Wars* and ahead of the fifth-ranking *The Empire Strikes Back*). It is important to keep in mind that *Return of the Jedi*, like all of these films, is essentially a boy's fantasy, derived largely from westerns and Saturday matinee serials, all of which were violent, episodic, and populated by one-dimensional characters, and all of which dealt with the broadest of themes in the most simplistic manner. Issuing from such roots, it does not really merit much tortured romantic *angst* or explorations of the Oedipal myth, however closely these issues were skirted in *Empire*.

As one might expect, there are a number of interesting set-pieces in *Return of the Jedi*. The outstanding set-piece here takes the form of a high-speed special effects chase through a dense forest on low-flying speeders. The wizards at Industrial Light and Magic achieved this hyperkinetic tour de force by *walking* miniatures through a California redwood forest and then speeding up the action to lightning speed and jazzing things up with other high-tech pyrotechnics. The rousing battle scene set in the same forest between the Ewoks and Imperial storm troopers is no less exciting and spectacular (for all its banality), with the furry forest creatures using homemade techniques resembling those employed by the Robinson family against encroaching pirates in Disney's classic *Swiss Family Robinson*, and to greater effect. Space battles are also impressive as the vessels of the rebel alliance take on the massed fighters, cruisers and destroyers of the Imperial fleet. (Here, to quibble perhaps, there was some short-shrifting. One would expect that a space fleet of a *galactic* empire would number in the hundreds of thousands, at the very least; in this last onslaught, there probably aren't more than several dozen craft visible at any one time, even in the long shots. Still, the screen is quite full of ships, and all but the most jaundiced viewer is swept along with the action.)

Return of the Jedi was not the masterpiece most of its mature audience wanted it to be, but its earnings at the box office and on video made it the kind of failure we'd all find easy to live with. Curiously, of the three principals whose career was made by the *Star Wars* films, only Harrison Ford parlayed that success into superstardom, going on to do the Indiana Jones trilogy for Lucas and Steven Spielberg, and a host of acclaimed roles throughout the years. Mark Hamill spent some time on the stage after his Luke Skywalker days, returning to the screen in the late '80s to appear in a number of mostly B movies and direct-to-video releases. Carrie Fisher's work has mostly been limited to screenwriting. After Ford, the biggest success story to come out of *Star Wars* is that of George Lucas himself, who as the head of Lucasfilms and Industrial Light and Magic (which farms out special effects and opticals for many other studios), is a millionaire many times over.

Some years after finishing *Return of the Jedi*, George Lucas produced another epic fantasy, *Willow*. This was a more obvious paean to the heroic fantasy genre, more true to its fairy-tale roots than his space-opera trilogy had been. This time, however, the fantasy was more forced and the magic simply wasn't there. Despite an immense marketing effort that preceded the release of this handsomely produced opus, *Willow* was a huge disappointment and a box office disaster.

Jedi was nominated for Academy Awards for art direction-set decoration, music score, sound, and sound effects editing. It won a Special Academy Award for special visual effects.

Sudden Deth *see* Trancers 5: Sudden Deth *under* **Trancers**

Supergirl *see under* **Superman and the Mole Men**

Superman *see under* **Superman and the Mole Men**

Superman and the Mole Men
(Lippert, 1951; 67 min.) **½

Produced by Robert Maxwell and Barney A. Sarecky. Directed by Lee Sholem. Assistant Director, Arthur Hamond. Dialogue Director, Stephen Carr. Screenplay, Richard Fielding (aka Robert Maxwell) and Barney A. Sarecky. Edited by Al Joseph. Director of Photography, Clark Ramsey. Music, Darrell Calker. Sound Engineer, Harry Smith. Art Direction, Ernst Fegte. Special Effects, Ray Mercer. Wardrobe, Izzy Berne. Makeup, Harry Thomas.

Cast: Clark Kent/Superman (George Reeves), Lois Lane (Phyllis Coates), Luke Benson (Jeff Corey), Pop Sherman (J. Farrell MacDonald), Bill Corrigan (Walter Reed), Sheriff (Stanley Andrews), John Craig (Ray Walker), Weber (Hal K. Dawson), Hospital superintendent (Frank Reicher), Mrs. Benson (Margia Dean), Child (Beverly Washburn), Eddie (Stephen Carr), Doc Saunders (Paul Burns), Jeff Regan (Byron Foulger), Esther Pomfrey (Irene Martin), Matt (John Phillips), Deputy (John Baer), Nurse (Adriene Marden), Mole men (Jack Banbury, Billy Curtis, Jerry Marvin, Tony Barvis).

Synopsis: The small town of Silsby is the home of the world's deepest oil well, or so says the sign that welcomes Metropolis reporters Clark Kent and Lois Lane. They are greeted with diffidence by foreman Bill Corrigan, who is more intent on shutting the rig down and, rather curiously, burying some equipment used in the drilling. Kent and Lane try to pump Corrigan for some information, but are rewarded only by an increased skittishness. Later that night, the cap on the well springs open and out comes a trio of dwarfish "mole men." They spy on old Pop Sherman, who, when he sees them, promptly collapses with a fatal heart attack. The creatures scurry off as Clark and Lois arrive on the scene, ostensibly to snoop around for their story. Lois spies one of the little creatures, and soon an atmosphere of panic is spreading through the community. Before long, a number of sightings have been made, and panic mentality increases when it is learned that the creatures seem to emit a glowing phosphorescence that is suspected to be lethal radioactivity. A mob led by the bull-headed Luke Benson soon forms, and he incites the crowd to hunt the creatures down like animals. Superman appears and disperses the mob in town, but Benson and some cronies manage to catch a pair of the little men atop a local dam. The Man of Steel arrives too late to prevent one of them from being shot. When he takes the wounded creature to Silsby's hospital for treatment, the other races back to the oil well and disappears down the shaft. It returns some time later with two more of its kind; this time the trio carries a strange ray weapon. When they eventually corner Benson in an alley, bombarding him with bolt after bolt from the device, Superman appears, saves Benson's life and retrieves the wounded mole man from the hospital. He accompanies them back to the well site and bids them farewell as they descend again to their subterranean home. As soon as they've disappeared behind the closed well cap, they seal the opening permanently with their ray beam.

Review: "Juve idol makes okay impression.... Pic is a subtle plea for tolerance." (Gros., *Variety*, December 12, 1951)

Analysis: *Superman and the Mole Men*, a minor entry from a minor studio, nevertheless did represent a significant departure from the previous Superman efforts. Here was a film that strove, insofar as its meager budgetary limitations would permit, to present this comic book hero on something like an "adult" level. George Reeves's portrayal of the Man of Steel has nothing of Kirk Alyn's (or Bud Collier's) good humor, being a rather dour hero who views Luke Benson's lynch mob with the appropriate disdain. Despite extremely uneven distribution, *Superman and the Mole Men* was not unfamiliar to regular viewers of television series, as it appeared as a slightly edited two-part episode in the show's initial airing.

Superman
(Warner Bros., 1978; 143 min.) ****

Produced by Pierre Spengler. Executive Producer Ilya Salkind. Directed by Richard Donner. Assistant Directors, Vincent Winter, Michael Dryhurst, Allan James, Gareth Tandy. Screenplay, Mario Puzo, David Newman, Leslie Newman, Robert Benton. Based on characters created by Jerry Siegel and Joe Shuster. Edited by Stuart Baird. Director of Photography, Geoffrey Unsworth. Panavision. Technicolor. Music, John Williams. Dolby Stereo. Costumes, Yvonne Blake. Special Effects, Colin Chilvers. Dedicated to Geoffrey Unsworth.

Cast: Superman/Clark Kent (Christopher Reeve), Lois Lane (Margot Kidder), Lex Luthor (Gene Hackman), Otis (Ned Beatty), Perry White (Jackie Cooper), Jonathan Kent (Glenn Ford), Ma Kent (Phyllis Thaxter), Eve Teschmacher (Valerie Perrine), Jor-El (Marlon Brando), Lara (Susannah York), First elder (Trevor Howard), Second elder (Harry Andrews), General Zod (Terence Stamp), Non (Jack O'Halloran), Ursa (Sarah Douglas), Young Clark Kent (Jeff East), Vond-Ah (Maria Schell), Jimmy Olsen (Marc McClure). With Vass Anderson, John Hollis, James Garbutt, Michael Gover, John Ratzenberger, David Neal, William Russell, Penelope Lee, John Stuart, Alan Cullen, Lee Quigley, Aaron Smolinski, Diane Sherry, Jeff Atcheson, Brad Flock, Rex Reed, Matt Russo.

Synopsis: An issue of *Action Comics* opens. A young boy reads about the Metropolis newspaper the *Daily Planet* and the Great Depression. The credits begin. Then — the planet Krypton. Jor-El sums up the case of treason against the brute Non, the morally corrupt Ursa, and the once-trusted General Zod. The Council votes them guilty, and they are encased in a mirror-like prison and swept into space. A more momentous event is in the making: the destruction of Krypton by its nearby star within thirty days. But the Council can't believe Jor-El on this point. Vond-Ah says the planet is merely adjusting its orbit. Jor-El promises that neither he nor his wife Lara will leave Krypton. He did not mention his infant son, whom he places in a small, star-shaped space vessel for the long journey to Earth and safety. When Lara protests that the humans there are a thousand years behind him, Jor-El promises, "He will not be alone." As Krypton is rent by its sun, Jor-El's son shoots through the galaxies, learning much as his father's voice instructs him. Finally his craft crashes in a field near Smallville on Earth. The childless Kents discover the young boy in the crater and make him their own. He grows to manhood as Clark Kent, regretfully recalling his biological father's warning not to use his powers to affect human history. After his adoptive father dies, he inspects the remains of the space craft buried in the barn. He removes the crystals, bids his mother good-bye and treks north. In the arctic he hurls a crystal across the ice fields. In a short time a large crystalline habitation is formed. Clark enters and uses control crystals to materialize Jor-El's face. Jor-El speaks and reveals that he is Clark's true father. He explains Krypton's demise and why he sent his son to Earth: to serve humankind by example and leadership. Twelve years pass in instruction in the Fortress of Solitude before Clark leaves. Passing himself off as a well-meaning nerd from the heartland, he gets a job at the *Daily Planet* in Metropolis. Editor Perry White introduces him to reporter Lois Lane and junior photographer Jimmy Olsen as someone with a crisp writing style as well as the fastest typist he's ever seen. Escorting Lois outside at lunch, Clark is accosted by a mugger. In an alley, with Lois behind him and unable to see, he catches the bullet fired when the attacker falls. Meanwhile the police are tracking Otis into the subway, where he enters a hidden passage to the outlandish underground dwelling Lex Luthor shares with the voluptuous Eve Teschmacher. Lex sees a policeman on a monitor and caused him to fall in front of a subway engine. Lex is making plans for financial gain somehow to be caused by a U.S. missile program. That evening Lois boards a helicopter for a trip to the airport to greet the arrival of the president's Airforce 1. But the wind rips a rooftop cable loose, it hooks the chopper, and the craft crashes, dangling on the edge of the *Daily Planet* building. On the street, Clark finds Lois's hat. People are staring up. He rushes into a building and emerges in the blue and red suit of Superman, flies to catch Lois as she loses her grip, then with his other hand stops the falling helicopter. Placing his human and mechanical cargo safely on the roof, he prepares to leave. "Who are you?" asks Lois. "A friend." In the ensuing days, Superman foils a number of criminal schemes, then meets with Lois at her apartment to explain his origin and goals. "I'm here to fight for truth, for justice and the American way." He takes Lois on a flight, during which she wonders if he can read her mind. If so, she wants to be his friend. After he leaves, she realizes he's "Superman." Clark arrives and almost confides in Lois that he is Superman. Lex Luthor reads Lois's stories about Superman, learns that Krypton exploded in 1948, and theorizes some particles must have fallen to Earth. Lex realizes the radioactive content is lethal to Krypton's

residents, including Superman. Lex fakes an accident in order to halt a military convoy transporting a missile and change the missile's programming. Meanwhile, out west, Lois interviews a native American about land fraud. Lex uses a special frequency to contact Superman and warn him about a poison gas scheme, which Lex knows Superman will try to prevent. Drilling himself down into Lex's domain, Superman learns that the gas scheme is a fake, then hears of the arch criminal's plan to buy western land adjacent to California. Luthor changed those missile directions to cause a blast on the San Andreas Fault. The result: California will fall into the sea. The new coastline will belong to Lex. Superman is presented with the Kryptonite meteorite and pushed into Lex's pool. The second missile is headed for Hackensack, New Jersey. Even if Superman could get free, he couldn't stop both missiles. But Miss Teschmacher's mother lives in Hackensack, and she rescues Superman. He diverts the missile heading east, but the second one explodes on the San Andreas Fault. Superman dives into the fault and shores it up. Nevertheless, the quake has already caused damage. Superman helps mitigate it, rescuing Jimmy and blocking the river loosed when a dam cracked. But Lois's car goes off the roadway and is half buried. Superman hears her screams, but when he arrives she's succumbed. Superman can't accept her death and flies into space. He hears his father's voice forbid him to interfere in human affairs, but also Pa Kent's theory that he's there for a reason. Superman flies around the planet, reversing time. He returns to Lois, who's alive and having a hard time starting her car. When Superman leaves and Jimmy mentions Clark, Lois has a momentary thought that Clark is, might be.... Superman arrives at a prison with Lex and Otis.

Reviews: "No controlling vision.... The film rallies when Reeve takes over.... Yet after the first graceful feat, in which he saves Lois Lane.... the other miracles don't have enough tension to be memorable." (Pauline Kael, *New Yorker*, January 1, 1979, pp. 54–55) ¶ "Surprisingly infectious entertainment.... Christopher Reeve's entire

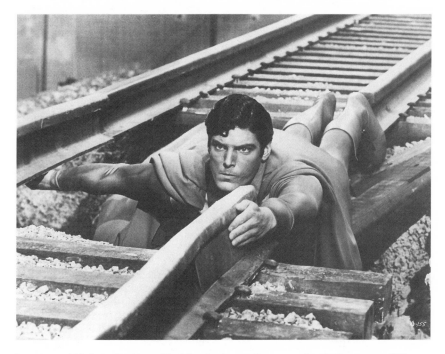

Superman (Christopher Reeve) holds a broken railway together in *Superman* (Warner Bros. 1978).

performance is a delight." (Jack Kroll, *Newsweek*, January 1, 1979, pp. 46–51)

Analysis: Almost as stunning as the previous year's *Star Wars*, this good-natured paean to the comics' Man of Steel has humor, action, and in Reeve, a facial and physical specimen to equal the mind's conception. As with *Star Wars*, John Williams provides an epic score (reusing the memorable TV theme) that gets everything off on the right foot and later on provides majesty — and a touch of sadness when Clark decides to leave Smallville. The movie's greatest scene — one that brought tears to the eyes in the theater — is Superman's rescue of Lois Lane from the crashed helicopter. Clark Kent can't use the modern, open-air telephone booth to change, so a revolving door must suffice. Lois falls, but Superman rises to catch her. Would that there was a being like him! And when he responds to her query about his identity with, "A friend," well, one wishes to be in Lois's place. As hackneyed as it sounds, the fighting for "truth, for justice and the

American way" ideal still can grab you. The Krypton venue at the beginning is impressive. Notwithstanding their undeniable ability to elicit yucks, Gene Hackman, Ned Beatty and Valerie Perrine are at odds with the rest of the film. Hackman's opulent residence and plans for power were disconcerting. But that's just quibbling. Director Donner had cut his teeth on 1976's *The Omen*. Note that when the jalopy passes the Kent farm, the car's radio is playing "Rock Around the Clock," which was made famous in Glenn Ford's 1955 film, *Blackboard Jungle*. Coincidence or an in-joke? *Superman* was the second highest grossing film of 1978 and received Academy Award nominations for sound, music score and editing.

Superman II
(Warner Bros., 1981; 127 min.) ★★★★

Produced by Pierre Spengler. Executive Producer, Ilya Salkind. Directed by Richard Lester. Screenplay, Mario Puzo, David Newman

Leslie Newman. Story, Mario Puzo. Based on characters created by Jerry Siegel and Joe Shuster. Edited by John Victor-Smith. Director of Photography, Geoffrey Unsworth, Bob Paynter. Panavision. Technicolor. Music, Ken Thorne. Dolby Stereo. Art Direction, Maurice Fowler. Set Decoration, Peter Young, Peter Howitt. Makeup, Stuart Freeborn. Costumes, Yvonne Blake, Susan Yelland. Production Design, John Barry, Peter Murton. Special Effects, Colin Chilvers.

Cast: Superman/Clark Kent (Christopher Reeve), Lois Lane (Margot Kidder), Lex Luthor (Gene Hackman), General Zod (Terence Stamp), Non (Jack O'Halloran), Ursa (Sarah Douglas), Perry White (Jackie Cooper), Eve Teschmacher (Valerie Perrine), Lara (Susannah York), Sheriff (Clifton James), President (E. G. Marshall), Jimmy Olsen (Marc McClure), Leueen (Leueen Willoughby), Alice (Robin Pappas), Spokesman (Roger Kemp), Terrorists (Roger Brierley, Anthony Milner, Richard Griffiths), Nun (Melissa Wiltsie), Gendarme (Alain DeHay), C.R.S. Man (Marc Boyle), Controllers (John Ratzenberger, Shane Rimmer), Cab driver (Alan Stuart), Boris (Jim Dowdell), Nate (John Morton), Warden (Angus McInnes), Bellboy (Anthony Sher), Mother (Elva May Hoover), Father (Todd Woodcroft), Jason (Hadley Kay), Krypton elder (John Hollis), Fisherman (Gordon Rollings), Deputy (Peter Whitman), Man at bar (Hal Galili), J. J. (Bill Bailey), Boog (Dinny Powell), Reporter (Richard Parmentier), General (Don Fellows), President's aide (Michael J. Shannon), Presidential impostor (Tony Sibbald), Diner owner (Tommy Duggan), Waitress (Pamela Mandell), News vendor (Eugene Lipinski), Rocky (Pepper Martin), Kids (Cleon Spencer, Carl Parris).

Synopsis: Clark Kent learns that Lois Lane is covering terrorists holding hostages on the Eiffel Tower. As Superman, he flies straightaway to Paris, saves Lois and pushes the atomic bomb the terrorists had into space. Unbeknownst to any on earth, the resulting explosion frees General Zod, Non and Ursa from their floating prison. Landing on the moon, they discover astronauts and cosmonauts and proceed to earth, which they believe is called the planet Houston. Back in the U.S., Clark and Lois delve into the honeymoon racket at Niagara Falls. Lois becomes suspicious when Superman saves a boy who falls over the falls while Clark is presumably out for hotdogs. She decides that Clark is in fact

Superman, and to test him, she jumps into the river. Clark manages to rescue her without becoming Superman, and Lois thinks she was wrong. But later, in their suite, Clark reaches into the fire and Lois sees that he has not been burned. He *is* Superman. Meanwhile, General Zod and his cohorts arrive on earth, and their depredations cannot be stopped by police or military. They make the president of the U.S. bow to them. Superman knows naught of this. He and Lois are at his fortress in the frozen north, where he gives up his super powers to become her husband. At the White House, Lex Luthor appears with news of the one who might challenge the aliens. Bored, Zod jumps at the chance for revenge against the son of Jor-El. Lex takes them to the *Daily Planet* and shows them Lois. He says Superman will come to her. Knowing he must destroy Zod, Clark has returned to his fortress to regain his powers. In the streets and air of New York, Superman, Zod, Ursa and Non wage super-war, but when he realizes his enemies will harm too many people, Superman flies away. Lex takes Zod to Superman's fortress. Using Lois as a bargaining chip, they force Superman to capitulate. Superman whispers to Lex that if they can get the three into a special chamber, they will lose their powers. Lex tells Zod, and Superman is forced into the chamber. Superman emerges and bows, but when Zod takes his hand Superman crushes it and then tosses him against the ice. He falls into the pit, as does Non when he attempts to fly and Ursa when Lois socks her. Lex figures it out: Superman was protected *in* the chamber; he'd reversed the transformation device so that Zod and *his* crew lost their powers. Back at the *Daily Planet*, Lois and Superman discuss problems inherent in their relationship. Clark kisses her, and she remembers nothing of his true identity. Clark returns to the diner where a bully previously had beaten him up. He puts the bully away and then as Superman returns the American flag to the White House. "I won't let you down again," he informs the president.

Reviews: "This film's fun comes from characters, dialogue and performances, not effects." (Sheila Benson, *Los Angeles Times Calendar*, June 18, 1981, p. 1) ¶"The key to Richard Lester's treatment of the Superman myth lies in his gleeful caricature of global events and politics." (Martyn Auty, *Monthly Film Bulletin*, April 1981, p. 79) ¶"Christopher Reeve makes his transitions from Clark Kent to Superman something more than a matter of fluffing up his cape; the man has a quiet sense of irony about him." (Richard Schickel, *Time*, June 8, 1981, p. 74) ¶"All in all, *Superman II* is a much more entertaining and intriguing film than its predecessor." (Howard Kissel, *Women's Wear Daily*, June 4, 1981, p. 10)

Analysis: Superman II is the equal of its predecessor. It's good to have alien villains as well as Hackman's human one. Hackman is undeniably funny, and Terence Stamp provides a good many droll touches. Director Lester is obviously partly responsible for the humor. Sarah Douglas is sexy. *Superman II* was the second highest grossing film of 1981.

Superman III

(Warner Bros., 1983; 123 min.) **½

Produced by Pierre Spengler. Executive Producer, Ilya Salkind. Directed by Richard Lester. Screenplay, David Newman, Leslie Newman. Based on characters created by Jerry Siegel and Joe Shuster. Edited by John Victor Smith. Director of Photography, Robert Paynter. Panavision. Color, Rank Film Laboratories. Music, Ken Thorne. Songs, Giorgio Moorder. Dolby Stereo. Art Direction, Brian Ackland-Snow, Charles Bishop, Terry Ackland-Snow. Set Decoration, Peter Young. Costumes, Evangeline Harrison. Director of Special Effects and Miniatures, Colin Chilvers.

Cast: Superman/Clark Kent (Christopher Reeve), Augustus "Gus" Gorman (Richard Pryor), Lana Lang (Annette O'Toole), Vera Webster (Annie Ross), Lorelei Ambrosia (Pamela Stephenson), Perry White (Jackie Cooper), Lois Lane (Margot Kidder), Ross Webster (Robert Vaughn), Brad Wilson (Gavan O'Herlihy), Ricky (Paul Kaethler), Captain of *British Reliance* (Robert Beatty).

Synopsis: Because Lois Lane is off on vacation, Clark Kent takes Jimmy Olsen to his Class of 1965 high school reunion in Smallville. On the way they encounter a factory fire. Jimmy is injured, but Clark as Superman puts out the fire with ice from a nearby lake. Meanwhile, Gus Gorman has discovered his talent as a computer hacker. At Webscoe Industries he's managed to route all the half-cents owed employees to himself. Ross Webster, head of the conglomerate, learns of Gus's infractions but realizes he can use the man's abilities. In Smallville, Clark finds himself attracted to his old high school chum, Lana Lang, and her son Ricky. In Metropolis, Webster sends Gus to Webscoe's Smallville subsidiary, from which he contacts the Vulcan weather satellite. Lasers are sent into the sky over Colombia, starting torrential rains and tornadoes. Webster's plan to corner the coffee crop seems to have worked. But Superman mitigates the disaster. Webster's "gal Friday," Lorelei Ambrosia, mentions that Superman can be destroyed by Kryptonite. Using the Vulcan satellite again, they discover and analyze debris from Krypton so Kryptonite can be recreated on Earth. A problem arises when .57 percent is "Unknown." Gus inserts "T.A.R." but when he, in the guise of a three-star general, presents Superman with a piece of high-tech green plastic, Superman is unaffected. Nevertheless, he soon feels weak, then forgets things. He straightens the Leaning Tower of Pisa. *Time* magazines features a cover story, "Goodness at the Crossroads." Superman creates an oil spill and takes up with Lorelei. Gus has Webster start the construction of a super computer in a western cave. Superman becomes a drunk. Visiting Metropolis, Ricky sees him and says he's just in a slump. In a car graveyard, Clark Kent separates from Superman but retains super powers. The two engage in an all-out battle for control of the man from Krypton. Clark wins, then cleans up the oil spill before flying to Webster's computer cave. Missiles distract him while Vera Webster prepares a beam of Kryptonite. Having second thoughts, Gus cuts the power, but the computer restores itself. Vera is taken into the machine and made a machine herself. Superman uses acid to destroy the computer. Superman urges Gus to get another job. Clark goes to Lana. She becomes Perry White's new secretary. Superman fixes the Leaning Tower of Pisa.

Reviews: "The variable special effects that have dogged the series are ever more in evidence than usual." (Kim Newman, *Monthly Film Bulletin*, August 1983, p. 221) ¶"And of all the summer trash we're drowning in, *Superman III* is the stupidest and the trashiest." (Rex Reed, *New York Post*, June 17, 1983, p. 43)

Analysis: It was the fifth highest grossing film of the year. That was due to the excellence of the previous entries, one supposes, because this has a middling story and so-so effects. With Richard *A Hard Day's Night/The Three Musketeers* Lester at the directorial helm, it should have been much better. And Richard Pryor, off screen a good deal of the time, is, like Robin Williams, a great comedian who frequently can't get untracked on the big screen. (He's done his best movie work co-starring with Gene Wilder.) Robert Vaughn takes a cue from Gene Hackman and plays his character broadly, too broadly for the era. Pamela Stephenson is as lush as Valerie Perrine, and we felt Superman should have advocated the law's mercy for her at the end. Annie Ross has another "sequels" role in the *Basket Case* series. Quite unbelievable is Gus's computer literacy, plus the capability of a satellite to cause weather with lasers and to locate debris from Krypton! A real faux pas occurs when Superman is encased in an invisible shield. His nemeses think he'll suffocate from lack of oxygen. So how does he fly through space? Filmed in Calgary, Alberta and, say the end credits, Italy. Yet the scenes featuring the toy towers of Pisa seem to have been photographed against a photo of the real Leaning Tower.

Supergirl
(Tri-Star/Thorn-EMI, 1984; 114 min.) **½

Produced by Timothy Burrill. Executive Producer, Ilya Salkind. Directed by Jeannot Szwarc. Screenplay, David Odell. Based on the Supergirl character appearing in DC Comics. Edited by Malcolm Cooke. Director of Photography, Alan Hume. Panavision. Color, Rank Laboratories. Music, Jerry Goldsmith. Dolby Stereo. Art Direction, Terry Ackland-Snow. Special Visual Effects, Derek Meddings.

Cast: Kara/Supergirl/Linda Lee (Helen Slater), Selena (Faye Dunaway), Zaltar (Peter O'Toole), Alura (Mia Farrow), Bianca (Brenda Vaccaro), Nigel (Peter Cook), Zor-El (Simon Ward), Jimmy (Marc McClure), Ethan (Hart Bochner), Lucy Lane (Maureen Teefy), Mr. Danvers (David Healy).

Synopsis: At Argo City, Superman's cousin Kara loses the Omega Hedron "borrowed" from the guardians by artist Zaltar. Kara takes Zaltar's "spacecraft" to retrieve the ball; if she fails, the city is doomed. The Omega Hedron lands in the picnic lunch of twentieth-century psychic and self-proclaimed witch Selena. Kara masquerades as private school girl "Linda Lee" while she searches for the device in America's heartland. Selena puts a love spell on the hunk Ethan, but the first person he sees when he wakes is Linda. Foiled at every turn, even when she sends a dark force against Linda, Selena obtains the help of her late lover and co-sorcerer Nigel. When Supergirl arrives at Selena's castle on a mountain, she is imprisoned in a glass pane and thrust into space. She lands on a desolate world where she meets Zaltar. He says they are in the Phantom Zone from which there is no escape. But Kara argues and finds that though they risk their lives, they may yet escape. Zaltar falls into the maelstrom, but Kara finds the exit and returns to Earth. Supergirl turns Selena's demon against her and, bidding adieu to Ethan, returns the Omega Hedron to Argo City under the sea — on Earth.

Reviews: "Feels as if it had no plot at all, only incidents that serve as excuses for cameo appearances.... Though Helen Slater makes a bad first impression, she's not a bad Supergirl by the end, being likably straightforward, guileless and sweet." (David Ansen, *Newsweek*, November 26, 1984, p. 119) ¶"Screenwriter David Odell and Director Jeannot Szwarc concentrate on strong, simple pleasures: Slater's easy grace and uncomplicated beauty; the bravura of (Obi-Wan) O'Toole...; and a hilarious wicked-witch turn by the delicious Dunaway." (Richard Corliss, *Time*, November 16, 1984, p. 105)

Analysis: If you have the feeling this will be unbearable, you're wrong. Except for some dull spots when the lunky Hart

Helen Slater is *Supergirl* (Tri-Star/Thorn-EMI, 1984).

Bochner character is around, it moves right along and is a worthy evocation of its comic book origins, with better effects than we expected. A radio broadcast is used to tell us why Superman is not around: He's on a peace mission to a galaxy several hundred trillion light years distant. Helen Slater is ingratiating. Dunaway and Vaccaro are funny. There are *some* implausibilities: Linda Lee/Supergirl need not enter the girls school to locate Selena. But it's supernatural versus superpower. Is it sensible to ask what would really happen?

Superman IV:
The Quest for Peace
(Warner Bros./Cannon, 1987; 90 min.) **

Produced by Menahem Golan and Yoram Globus. Directed by Sidney J. Furie. Screenplay, Lawrence Konner and Mark Rosenthal. Story, Christopher Reeve, Lawrence Konner, Mark Rosenthal. Based on characters created by Jerry Siegel and Joe Shuster. Edited by John Shirley. Director of Photography, Ernest Day. Color, Rank Film Laboratories. Music, John Williams. Music Adaptation, Alexander Courage. Additional Source Music, Paul Fishman. Song "A Whole Lotta Shakin' Goin' On," Jerry Lee Lewis. Dolby Stereo. Art Direction, Leslie Tomkins, John Fenner. Set Decoration, Peter Young. Costumes, John Bloomfield. Stunts, Alf Joint, John Lees. Flying Stunts, Mark Stewart. Special Effects, John Evans. Model Effects, Richard Conway. Visual Effects, Harrison Ellenshaw.

Cast: Superman/Clark Kent (Christopher Reeve), Lex Luthor (Gene Hackman), Perry White (Jackie Cooper), Jimmy Olsen (Marc McClure), Lenny (Jon Cryer), David Warfield (Sam Wanamaker), Nuclear Man #2 (Mark Pillow), Lacy Warfield (Mariel Hemingway), Lois Lane (Margot Kidder), Jeremy (Damian McLawhorn), Harry Howler (William Hootkins), Jean Pierre Dubois (Jim Broadbent), General Romoff (Stanley Lebor), Levon Hornsby (Don Fellows), President of the United States (Robert Beatty). With voice of Susannah York.

Synopsis: After rescuing a Soviet cosmonaut hit by a satellite, Superman becomes Clark Kent and visits his old Midwestern homestead. In the barn, he retrieves the last energy module and hears his mother's voice. Meanwhile, Lex Luthor's nephew helps his uncle escape from hard labor. In Metropolis, David Warfield takes over the *Daily Planet* and with his daughter Lacy aims to sensationalize news and build circulation. On TV, the president of the United States says the country must be second to none, therefore nuclear arms experiments will be continued. Stealing a strand of Superman's hair from a museum exhibit, Lex hopes to divine its genetic code and create

a super being subservient to him. The young boy Jeremy sends a letter to Superman imploring him to solve the nuclear arms dilemma. At his arctic base, Superman listens to the elders, who urge him not to interfere in Earth's activities. Back in Metropolis, Clark briefly reveals his true identity to Lois because she's the only one he can talk to. When he kisses her, she forgets. Superman goes to the United Nations and says he will do what Earth's nations cannot: Rid the world of nuclear weapons. He creates a cache of missiles in space which he flings into the sun. Lex attaches a box with Superman's genetic makeup to one of the missiles. In the sun, Nuclear Man is created. Lex controls him through sunlight. When it's dark, Nuclear Man has no power. Lex entices Superman to the Empire State Building, and he and Nuclear Man begin a fight that rages across Earth. Losing round one, Superman realizes that he must use his mother's module to win. He tricks his enemy into an elevator and flies it to the moon. But sunlight enters the container and Nuclear Man is restored to power. He pounds Superman into the soil. Back on Earth, this monster kidnaps Lacy. Superman rises from his grave and creates an eclipse. He throws the powerless Nuclear Man into a nuclear reactor. Perry White becomes the majority stockholder in the *Daily Planet*. Superman makes another address before the United Nations, saying Earth is still a young planet, there are inhabitants of other planets to be met, and when people want peace, it will occur. Capturing Lex and returning him to prison, Superman tells him that the world is as it always was: on the brink, with good fighting evil.

Reviews: "As the hero, Christopher Reeve oozes with sincerity in the world-peace scenes.... But he's also funny when he gets back to being klutzy Clark Kent, so the movie doesn't completely drown in its own good intentions." (David Sterritt, *Christian Science Monitor*, September 2, 1987, p. 21) ¶"Story ... suffers from a fatal lack of narrative structure." (Anne Billson, *Monthly Film Bulletin*, September 1987, p. 283) ¶"Aside from its cheesy visual effects and careless camera work, *Superman IV's* major problem is its script—or scripts." (Juliann Garey, *Village Voice*, August 11, 1987, p. 62)

Analysis: Color clarity is substandard. Ditto the sound. Worn out, that's what this movie is. Audiences unfamiliar with comics and pulp magazines might find the "birth" of Nuclear Man hard to believe.

Notes of Interest: Superman first appeared in *Action Comics* in the summer of 1938, the creation of Jerry Siegel and Joe Schuster. Their inspirations were numerous, but their primary source seems to have been Philip Wylie's *Gladiator* (1930). The Man of Steel had his own comic book in 1939. A successful radio series (utilizing the voice of Bud Collier as Superman) appeared in the early forties, as did a host of similar superheroes, the most successful being Fawcett's *Captain Marvel*. Negotiations with Republic Studios got off to a good start in 1940 to bring Superman to the silver screen in an action serial, but soon stalled when National Comics, the owner of the Superman copyright, demanded more control over the product than Herbert Yates was willing to concede. Nonetheless, a series of 17 outstanding Superman cartoons was produced by the team of Max and Dave Fleischer, again using the voice of Bud Collier and taking the icons of the Superman mythos (Metropolis, the *Daily Planet*, Perry White, Lois Lane, etc.) as established by the comic books. *Superman*, a 15-chapter Columbia serial, appeared in 1948, featuring Kirk Alyn in the (uncredited) role as Clark Kent/Superman, Noel Neil as Lois Lane, Tommy Bond as cub reporter Jimmy Olsen and Pierre Watkin as editor Perry White. A sequel, *Atom Man Vs. Superman*, appeared in 1950, reviving the same cast and bringing the Man of Steel's arch-enemy, Lex Luthor, to the screen for the first time in the persona of Lyle Talbot.

Swamp Thing
(Embassy, 1982; 92 min.) ***½

Produced by Benjamin Melniker and Michael Uslan. Directed by Wes Craven. Screenplay, Wes Craven. Edited by Richard Bracken. Director of Photography, Robin Goodwin.

Technicolor. Music, Harry Manfredini. Art Direction, David Nichols, Robb Wilson King. Set Design, Robb Wilson King. Set Coordinator, Mary Salter. Costumes, Patricia Bolomet, Bennett Choate, Paul A. Simmons. Evening Gown, Bennett Choate. Makeup, Tonga Knight. Special Makeup Effects, William Munns.

Cast: Alice Cable (Adrienne Barbeau), Dr. Arcane (Louis Jourdan), Dr. Alec Holland (Ray Wise), Swamp Thing (Dick Durock), Ferret (David Hess), Bruno (Nicholas Worth), Ritter (Don Knight), Arcane Monster (Ben Bates), Dr. Linda Holland (Nannette Brown), Jude (Reggie Batts), Messenger (Karen Price), Secretary (Mimi Meyer), Charlie (Al Ruban), Young agent (Bill Erickson), Commando (Dov Gottesfeld), Little Bruno (Tommy Madden).

Synopsis: Federal agent Alice Cable arrives via helicopter at a southern swamp where Dr. Alec Holland and his sister Linda have spent 10 weeks experimenting with recombinant DNA. Having created a plant cell with an animal nucleus, Holland's goal seems near: a plant-animal strain that ultimately will result in foodstuffs for an ever increasing humanity. Unknown to the scientists and their government protectors—except Ritter—the lab is about to be attacked by minions of one Dr. Arcane, thought dead. When the attack comes, Ritter is unmasked as Arcane. He shoots Linda, and Alec, set afire when he falls with the formula, leaps into the lake. When Ferret attempts to drown Alice the next morning, a green man-thing emerges from the water, kills some of Arcane's men, and bears the woman away. At his mansion, Arcane muses on Holland's notebooks. Intercepting a phone call Alice is making from a rural gas station run by the teenage Jude, Arcane sends Ferret and his men for her and the missing notebook. Alice is once again saved by the green humanoid. Arcane realizes that if he can get Alice and the notebook, he can capture this "swamp thing," which intuition tells him is an important cog in the scenario. Alice is captured but dives off Arcane's boat and finds temporary safety with the Swamp Thing, which kills Ferret. She discovers that this strange creature is Alec Holland. After a refreshing swim, Alice is confronted by Arcane. Swamp Thing rushes

The Swamp Thing (Dick Durock, left) and the Arcane Monster (Ben Bates) in a climactic battle in *Swamp Thing* (Embassy, 1982).

to her rescue but is captured in a net and taken to Arcane's mansion. At a celebratory banquet, Bruno unwittingly drinks the Holland mixture and is transformed into a misshapen dwarf. In the basement where Swamp Thing is chained, Arcane is told that Bruno became a small monstrosity because his original nature was small. Arcane begins to understand. He shackles Alice near Swamp Thing and retires upstairs. Drinking the serum he believes will increase his power, Arcane becomes a hideous swine-faced, fur-pelted humanoid. He takes a sword from the wall and heads for the basement. Meanwhile, Swamp Thing's arm that had been severed by Ferret grows back when the sunlight falls on his stump. His strength renewed, he breaks free and releases Alice. Little Bruno shows them how to escape via a pool from which they will emerge in the swamp. But Arcane follows. A sword thrust apparently kills Alice, but Swamp Thing restores her life with some moss from his body. A battered Arcane revives, but Swamp Thing kills him with the sword. Swamp Thing explains

that he cannot leave the swamp even though Alice says, "I'll be your hands." He tells Alice that she must tell their story and retires into the swamp.

Reviews: "There may be a couple of giggles for those who have already had it up to here with movie–comic book science." (Archer Winsten, *New York Post*, July 30, 1982, p. 41) ¶"About as scary as a chef's salad." (Alex Keneas, *Newsday*, July 30, 1982, Part II, p. 3) ¶"So-called performances … that make the posturing in TV's *Batman* look like profound thespian achievements by contrast." (Carrie Rickey, *Village Voice*, August 17, 1982, p. 48)

Analysis: The critics just didn't get it. Nor did the public at large. This cinematic evocation of DC pulp fiction was not appreciated for the exciting, funny and beautifully photographed movie it is. When interviewed in *Cinefantastique* (December, 1981, p. 16), director Wes Craven said, "We're going for a sort of stylistic approach…. Low angles, strange shadows, weird colors and fog. A comic book look, but in tandem with a very realistic human

Adrienne Barbeau and Dick Durock take a break on the set of *Swamp Thing* (Embassy, 1982).

way of approaching it. We're trying to keep the emotions very human. We're underplaying it a lot, and not trying for a camp look." A more resourceful heroine than Barbeau can hardly be imagined, she demonstrates martial arts and weapons expertise as well as a splendid figure in her verdant bathing scene. Louis Jourdan is appropriately hammy as an adherent of Nietzsche. It's even scary when he becomes what we'd imagine one of William Hope Hodgson's swine things from *The House on the Borderland* might look like.

The Return of Swamp Thing
(Millimeter Films/Lightyear Entertainment, 1989; 88 min.) *

Produced by Ben Melniker and Michael Uslan. Directed by Jim Wynorski. Screenplay, Derek Spenser and Grant Morris. Based on the characters in magazines published by DC Comics. Director of Photography, Zoran Hochstatter. Deluxe color. Music, Chuck Cirino. Sound, Blake Wilcox. Costume Designer, Vicki Graef. Makeup, Steve Neill. Swamp Thing created by Len Wein, Berni Wrightson. Filmed in Georgia.

Cast: Dr. Anton Arcane (Louis Jourdan), Swamp Thing/Dr. Holland (Dick Durock), Abigail (Heather Locklear), Dr. Lana Zurrell (Sarah Douglas), Dr. Rochelle (Ace Mask), Gunn (Joey Sagal), Miss Poinsettia (Monique Gabrielle), Darryl (Daniel Taylor), Leechman (Chris Doyle), Conklin (Tony Cecere), Clyde (Timothy Birch), Sheriff Beaumont (Ralph Pace), Dr. Rochelle mutation (Rex Pierson), Morty (Jim Grimshaw), Harry Dugan (Anthony Sears), Bob (J. Don Ferguson).

Synopsis: Government agents seeking a swamp still are attacked by a monster, which is in turn accosted by a more benevolent humanoid creature. Meanwhile, Dr. Anton Arcane works with Dr. Rochelle, seeking a rejuvenation formula. Arcane's stepdaughter Abigail visits his secluded mansion. Arcane thinks he can use Abigail's genetic material in his research. Outside, she meets and falls in love with "Swamp Thing." Suspicious that Dr. Rochelle was responsible for her mother's death, Abby finds she need take no revenge because Dr. Zurrell acts first. Then Arcane shoots Zurrell. The laboratory catches fire as he fights Swamp Thing. Escaping the inferno with Swamp Thing, Abigail observes a flower blossoming on her foot.

Reviews: "Enough to drive you back to the comic book stand. Or even the swamp." (Michael Wilmington, *Los Angeles Times Calendar*, May 12, 1989, p. 7) ¶ "A string of ill-motivated shoot-outs and conflagrations." (Verina Glaessner, *Monthly Film Bulletin*, February 1990, p. 48)

Analysis: Cut and dried cheap thrills. There is no character development and no justification for the "romance" between Swamp Thing and Abigail other than love at first sight, which is a little hard to believe. There is too much lame humor — comic relief from two kids in a film that is already too broad. There is no explanation for Arcane's existence — he was killed at the end of the first film — till a weak reason is supplied well into the movie.

The Takeover *see* Scanners III: The Takeover *under* Scanners

Tales of Terror *see under* The Fall of the House of Usher

Taste the Blood of Dracula *see under* Dracula

Teenage Mutant Ninja Turtles
(New Line Cinema/Golden Harvest, 1990; 93 min.) **½

Produced by Kim Dawson, Simon Fields, David Chan. Directed by Steve Barron. Screenplay, Todd W. Langen and Bobby Herbeck. Story, Bobby Herbeck. Based on characters created by Kevin Eastman and Peter Laird. Director of Photography, John Fenner. Technicolor. Prints, Deluxe. Music, John Du Prez. Dolby Stereo. Art Direction, Gary Wissner. Set Decoration, Brendan Smith and Barbara Kahn. Costumes, John M. Hay. Stunts/Martial Arts Choreography, Pat Johnson. Special Effects Supervisor, Joey Di Gaetano. Creatures designed by Jim Henson's Creature Shop.

Cast: April O'Neil (Judith Hoag), Casey Jones (Elias Koteas), Raphael/passenger in taxi (Josh Pais), Michaelangelo/pizza man (Michelan Sisti), Donatello/foot messenger (Leif Tilden), Leonardo/gang member (David

Forman), Danny Pennington (Michael Turney), Charles Pennington (Jay Patterson), Chief Sterns (Raymond Serra), Shredder (James Saito), Tatsu (Toshishiro Obata), Head thug (Sam Rockwell), June (Kitty Fitzgibbon), Cab driver (Louis Cantarini), Movie hoodlums (Joseph D'Onofrio, John D. Ward), Shinsho (Ju Wu), Technician (Mark Jeffrey Miller), New recruit (John Rogers), Talkative Foot #1 (Tae Pak), Talkative Foot #2 (Kenn Troum), Tall teenager (Robert Haskell), Beaten teenager (Joshua Bo Lozoff), Police officers (Winston Hemingway, Joe Inscoe). Voices: Raphael (Josh Pais), Michaelangelo (Robbie Rist), Splinter (Kevin Clash), Leonardo (Brian Tochi), Shredder (David McCharen), Tatsu (Michael McConnohie), Donatello (Corey Feldman).

Synopsis: Newswoman April O'Neil reports on a wave of urban theft involving juveniles. On her way home she stumbles on a robbery in progress but is rescued by unseen heroes. In the sewers those rescuers are revealed: four man-size turtles named Raphael, Michaelangelo, Donatello, and Leonardo. Experts in the martial arts, they owe their expertise to the giant, intelligent rat, Splinter. While watching TV, they see April speaking about unexplained crimes. Someone else watching orders her silenced. In the subway she is battered by masked ninjas but is rescued by Raphael. One of the masked villains follows. When April awakes she is shocked to find herself facing human-size turtles and a talking rat. Splinter explains the genesis of this strange group: radioactive waste dropped in the sewers. The turtles take April home and have some leftover pizza, but when they return to the sewer they find it a shambles and Splinter gone. The Turtles hole up at April's. April's boss, Charles Pennington, is called by the police chief about his son Danny. Danny tells his father he doesn't really know why he's stealing. In Shredder's lair, where Splinter is chained, boys like Danny find a home. Shredder, a helmeted ninja, says he is their father since they have been rejected by society. He inducts a new Foot ninja and says they have a new enemy, the Turtles. They sneak up on the good guys, who are helped by Casey Jones, the hockey stick–wielding guy who once bested Raphael in the park. After the fight, April takes the turtles and Casey to her old farmstead, where Raphael revives. Leonardo feels Splinter's presence and gathers the others around a campfire. Splinter appears and says they have learned the last thing they need: the power of the mind and love. They return to the city and find Danny hiding in the sewer. Casey follows him to Shredder's lair. Splinter tells Danny of his days in Japan, how he learned from his master, how his master and his lover were killed by another ninja, and how he himself had his ear sliced by that ninja's sword. Shredder confronts Danny and finds a picture of a turtle in his possession. He tells his second in command, Tatsu, to kill Splinter, but Casey and Danny rescue the rat. Shredder confronts the Turtles after his foot soldiers are disposed of. When Splinter appears, Shredder rushes at him but falls several stories into a garbage truck. Casey throws the switch to crush him. Danny is reunited with his father. Splinter proposes use of the exclamation "Cowabunga!"

Reviews: "Takes its slender joke too far…. Directed rather fuzzily." (Kim Newman, *Monthly Film Bulletin*, December 1990, p. 344) ¶"Despite Jim Henson's overzealous animatronics, the four turtles are basically lithe stuntmen wearing turtle costumes. Their dubbed voices sound like Bill & Ted on another, less excellent, adventure." (Jami Bernard, *New York Post*, March 30, 1990, p. 21) ¶"Tediously unamusing." (Richard Gehr, *Village Voice*, April 3, 1990, p. 68)

Analysis: The intriguingly named TV cartoon characters created by Kevin Eastman and Peter Laird swept the nation in the late 1980s. Toys, food and assorted merchandise followed, and this film was the first of three non-animated features. Perhaps if we were children again, we'd find this film entrancing. Instead, it's unbelievable. Not the talking, ninja amphibians, rather the Foot Clan and its leader Shredder. There are strange things in New York but this just seems ridiculous, perhaps to be compared with the spirits of *Ghostbusters*. The martial arts action is, however, very well choreographed. Funniest scene: waiting for Raphael to regain consciousness; he's face down in the bathtub.

In-joke of some interest: the Turtles go to see the movie *Critters*. Filmed in New York City and Wilmington, North Carolina.

Teenage Mutant Ninja Turtles II: The Secret of the Ooze
(1991; 88 min.) **½

Produced by Thomas K. Gray, Kim Dawson and David Chan. Directed by Michael Pressman. Screenplay, Todd W. Langen. Based on characters created by Kevin Eastman and Peter Laird. Edited by John Wright and Steve Mirkovich. Director of Photography, Shelly Johnson. Panavision. Technicolor. Music, John Du Prez. Dolby Stereo. Song "Ninja Rap," Vanilla Ice, Earthquake, Todd W. Langen. Performed by Vanilla Ice and Earthquake. Art Direction, Geoffrey S. Grimsman. Set Decoration, Brendan Smith. Stunt Coordinator and Martial Arts Choreographer, Pat Johnson. Animatronic Characters, Jim Henson's Creature Shop. "In Memory of Jim Henson."

Cast: April O'Neil (Paige Turco), Professor Jordan Perry (David Warner), Michaelangelo/Soho Man (Michelan Sisti), Donatello/Foot #3 (Leif Tilden), Raphael (Kenn Troum), Leonardo (Mark Caso), Splinter (Kevin Clash), Keno (Ernie Reyes Jr.), Shredder (François Chau), Tatsu (Toshishiro Obata), Chief Sterns (Raymond Serra), Rahzar (Mark Ginther), Supershredder (Kevin Nash), Tokka (Kurt Bryant), Freddy (Mark Doerr), Vanilla Ice (Himself), Disc jockey (Earthquake).

Synopsis: After helping pizza delivery boy Keno foil a shopping mall heist, the Turtles return to April O'Neil's apartment. The mess they make causes April to wonder if they've found a place to live yet. Splinter calms them down and tries to convince them they can never be part of the outside world, pizza excepted. They should focus on where they must go and leave the Shredder buried, argues Splinter. But Shredder rises from a trash heap and orders Tatsu to have April followed. The object: revenge on the Turtles. At a toxic waste cleanup site, April interviews Professor Jordan Perry of TGRI. While tailing April, one of Shredder's spies discovers extra-large dandelions and takes one to his master. That night, Splinter holds a conference and produces the canister that contains the ooze responsible for the Turtles'

size and appearance. The canister has "TGRI" printed on it. Tatsu steals the last such filled canister from Professor Perry's hands just before the Turtles arrive at his lab. Noticing the computer screen, they find that one canister of "ooze" remains active. Foot clan members attack as Tatsu flaunts the canister. The Turtles obtain it briefly before Tatsu throws a smoke bomb and disappears. Shredder gets the canister and Professor Perry. The Turtles decide to move so as not to put April in danger. Before they can leave, Keno discovers the Turtles and Splinter. They explain things and Keno informs them that word on the street is that the Foot are recruiting people with martial arts skills, especially teenagers. Keno's offer to infiltrate is turned down. While the Turtles set up shop in an abandoned subway complete with car, a giant snapping turtle and wolf are produced by Professor Perry. Yet they are too kind for Shredder. Still, their strength is a plus. Meanwhile, Keno and Raphael plan the former's induction into the Foot, but Raphael is captured. Keno escapes and finds April and the other Turtles. They enter the junkyard by night, but too easily. Hauled up in a net, they are rescued by Splinter. But Professor Perry's monstrosities — Tokka and Rahzar — are unleashed. The Turtles untie the professor and find a manhole down which they escape. Perry discusses the colloidal gel that is responsible for the Turtles current state. Next day, April is given a message for Splinter: Meet at the construction site or Tokka and Rahzar will be turned loose in Central Park. Perry mixes up an anti-mutagen that will work only if ingested by the monsters. At the construction site, the Turtles propose the ancient ritual of pre-fight donuts, but while munching, the monsters discover that there are cubes of some unknown substance inside. The Turtles are chased into a nightclub. Perry suggests that CO_2 will facilitate the anti-mutagen's effects, and the turtles use fire extinguishers on the monsters. Shredder enters, holding the last TGRI canister. Keno kicks the canister from his hand to Perry. Shredder tries to take a hostage, but he's blasted from the building when a speaker's volume is greatly amplified. Outside, the Turtles confront "Super Shredder," a result of Shredder's ingesting some of the ooze. Although he pulls pylons down on himself and the Turtles, the Turtles survive.

Review: "It doesn't have the quirky edge of the original film and the novelty's worn off, but kids may still get a bang out of this noisy, harmless adventure.... light and cartoonish." (*Daily Local News*, West Chester, PA, April 4, 1991, p. 4)

Analysis: When asked if the second was better than the original, the 6-year-old Michael Holston replied, "Nah." Nevertheless, we like this April O'Neil better than the original although her character has less to do than in the first film. The martial arts affairs are again excellent, and there are funny scenes, some of them perhaps lost on the younger crowd, e.g., the "wax on, wax off" parody of a painting scene in *The Karate Kid* and the Humphrey Bogart-Ingrid Bergman parting scene from *Casablanca*. Roger Ebert and Gene Siskel panned the vacuousness of the turtle characters on their TV show. Filmed in Wilmington, North Carolina, and New York City.

Teenage Mutant Ninja Turtles III
(1993; 95 min.) **

Produced by Thomas K. Gray, Kim Dawson, David Chan. Directed by Stuart Gillard. Screenplay, Stuart Gillard. Based on characters created by Kevin Eastman and Peter Laird. Edited by William D. Gordean and James R. Symons. Director of Photography, David Gurfinkel. Panavision. Technicolor. Music, John Du Prez. Dolby Stereo. Art Direction, Mayne Schuylerberke. Set Decoration, Ronald R. Reiss. Martial Arts Choreographer and Stunt Coordinator, Pat E. Johnson. Creature Effects, Eric Allard and Rick Stratton.

Cast: Leonardo (Mark Caso), Donatello (Jim Raposa), Michaelangelo (David Fraser), Raphael (Matt Hill), Splinter (James Murray), Casey Jones (Elias Koteas), April O'Neil (Paige Turco), Walker (Stuart Wilson), Kenshin (Henry Hayashi), Lord Norinaga (Sab Shimono), Mitsu (Vivian Wu), Yoshi (Travis A. Moon), Niles (John Aylward). Voices: Michaelangelo (Robbie Rist), Leonardo (Brian Tochi), Raphael (Tim Kelleher), Donatello (Corey Feldman).

Synopsis: Japan 1603: Lord Norinaga's son Kenshin is returned by force to his home. Late twentieth-century New York: April O'Neil plans a vacation in Japan. 1603: Norinaga Castle. The Englishman Walker is captain of three ships filled with firearms, and he hopes to sell the ships to Lord Norinaga. Not wanting to cause an unjust war, Kenshin finds art depicting man-size turtles and utters an incantation. April, who has an old Japanese scepter, is transferred to Japan, while Kenshin appears in America. Walker endeavors to convince Lord Norinaga that April is not a witch. Meanwhile, the Turtles figure out how to transfer themselves to feudal Japan. Casey Jones is filled in on the problem, which must be solved within sixty hours. The Turtles raise the scepter and are replaced by four of Lord Norinaga's honor guard. The Turtles find themselves in a battle on horseback. Michaelangelo's horse runs off and he's captured by the rebels. The other three find April in jail and rescue her and an English prisoner. They are attacked by the rebels until Mitsu, the female leader, realizes three of them are like Michaelangelo. As they approach the rebels' village, they find it under attack by the English. But the returning men, their woman leader and the Turtles rout them and save Michaelangelo from Walker's bullet. "Mikey" rushes into a blazing building to rescue Mitsu's young brother Yoshi. The question remains: What became of the scepter knocked out of Michaelangelo's hands in the woods? Back in New York, Norinaga's honor guard is mesmerized by ice hockey on TV, and Casey shows them the rudiments of the game. In Japan, Lord Norinaga agrees to pay Walker gold for guns. A blacksmith makes a new scepter based on the Turtles' drawing, but they drop and break it. The village learns of Walker's impending attack. Yoshi produces the scepter when Raphael visits. Walker takes Mitsu prisoner and obtains the scepter. The Turtles climb the castle while April distracts everyone. They release Mitsu and other prisoners, overcome Norinaga's soldiers and open the gate to the rebels. Walker holds April hostage, and his men enter the compound. The Turtles claim to be demons immune to bullets, and Walker's cannon only succeeds in blowing off the top of a bell. Walker falls from a parapet into the sea. The scepter is activated on both ends and the time transference made, although two of the Turtles regret leaving Japan.

Review: "The casting is uninspired.... The comic book and animated incarnations of the Turtles remain far funnier and more inventive." (Ralph Novak, *People Weekly*, April 5, 1993, pp. 14–15)

Analysis: One of the funny items that's all too brief is a Jerry Lewis imitation by one of the turtles. The manner in which Walker is thwarted at the end is bogus but in keeping with the children's nature of the series.

The Terminator

(Orion, 1984; 108 min.) ****

Produced by Gale Anne Hurd. Directed by James Cameron. Assistant Directors, Betsy Magruder, Thomas Irvine, Robert Roda. Screenplay, James Cameron and Gale Anne Hurd. Edited by Mark Goldblatt. Director of Photography, Adam Greenberg. DeLuxe Color. Art Direction, George Costello. Costumes, Hilary Wright. Special Effects, Stan Winston.

Cast: Terminator (Arnold Schwarzenegger), Sarah Connor (Linda Hamilton), Kyle Reese (Michael Biehn), Lt. Traxler (Paul Winfield), Vukovich (Lance Hendriksen), Ginger (Bess Motta), Dr. Silberman (Earl Boen), Matt (Rick Rossovich), Gun shop clerk (Dick Miller), Nancy (Shawn Schepps), Desk sergeant (Bruce M. Kerner), Future Terminator (Franco Columbo), Cop in alley (Ed Dogans), Punk leader (Bill Paxton), Punks (Brad Reardon, Brian Thompson), Policemen (William Wisher, Jr., Ken Fritz, Tom Oberhaus), TV anchorman (Joe Farago), Anchorwoman (Hettie Lynne Hurtes), Station attendant (Tony Mirelez), Derelict (Stan Yale), Mexican boys (Philip Gordon, Anthony R. Trujillo), Cleaning man (Norman Friedman), Ticket taker (Barbara Powers), Tanker driver (Wayne Stone), Tanker partner (David Pierce).

Synopsis: Los Angeles, 2029 A.D.: Man wages guerrilla war against monster tanks and airships conceived and developed by Skynet, the worldwide computer network that decided to eliminate humans after a late twentieth-century nuclear holocaust.

Los Angeles, 1984 A.D., 1:52 A.M.: Separately, a cyborg Terminator and a man arrive from the future. The cyborg's task is to find and kill Sarah Connor, mother of the unborn John Connor, who leads mankind against machines in the post-holocaust world. Kyle Reese, the man, has been assigned the task of protecting Sarah from the Terminator. The Terminator begins killing all women named Sarah Connor. The Terminator tracks the correct Sarah to a disco where Reese temporarily foils its deadly intent. After a car chase, the Terminator returns to a hotel room to repair its damaged arm and destroyed eye. Reese and Sarah are captured by the police. Reese is interrogated by a criminal psychologist. That evening the cyborg invades the station, but Reese and Sarah escape while their pursuer wreaks havoc. Reese and Sarah take refuge under an overpass, later finding a motel. Reese makes some homemade bombs and tells Sarah he's loved her since he saw her photo in the hands of her grown son in the next century. They make love. Found by the Terminator, they escape again and seemingly put the kibosh on the pursuer. Only injured, the monster commandeers a tank truck. Reese tosses one of his pipe bombs in a cylinder on the truck's side. It explodes. Sarah and Reese huddle amidst the wreckage, but the Terminator, now bereft of skin, rises from the ashes and chases them into a foundry, where Reese uses a bomb to blow the cyborg in half. Reese is killed, and the cyborg scrambles after Sarah, who crawls through a press and on the other side pushes the button that brings the press down on her tormentor: "You're terminated, fucker!" Months later at a gas station in Mexico, a young boy takes a Polaroid photo of a pregnant Sarah. She rides off, cognizant of the coming storm.

Reviews: "Crackling thriller full of all sorts of gory treats." (Patrick Goldstein, *Los Angeles Times Calendar*, October 26, 1984, p. 10) ¶"An exemplary piece of virtuoso, high-tech exploitation movie-making." (Julian Petley, *Monthly Film Bulletin*, February 1985, p. 58) ¶"Uses slow motion, pixilation and infra-red optics to make this the smartest looking L.A. nighttown

Arnold Schwarzenegger is *The Terminator* (Orion, 1984).

movie since *The Driver*." (Richard Corliss, *Time*, November 26, 1984, p. 105) ¶"A feral, cracker-jack B-movie, roiling with noisy, body-spattering shoot-outs and edited with samurai fleetness. It can also put a lump in your throat." (David Edelstein, *Village Voice*, November 13, 1984, p. 62)

Analysis: James Cameron's *The Terminator* was one of those rare star-making moments in cinema, bursting on the scene practically unheralded in 1984 and packing all the more wallop for that. Arnold Schwarzenegger had been something of a presence for a while, having had the title role in John Milius's *Conan the Barbarian* a couple of years earlier. That was an auspicious enough entry into the genre, but one that hardly prepared us for the emotionless, leather-jacketed killing machine he appeared as in Cameron's (relatively) modest B movie. Despite its fiscal limitations (which aren't all that apparent), *The Terminator* generates more white-knuckle thrills per minute than many an action-adventure film with several times the budget. From its dazzling, pyrotechnic opening in which the killer cyborg and (later) Kyle Reese materialize from the future, to the final fade-out when Sarah Connor drives off into the desert to meet her storm-shrouded destiny, the film hardly stops to catch its breath, maintaining its tension and excitement astonishingly well for its 108 minutes.

Schwarzenegger's career was not the only one to benefit from *The Terminator*. Co-star Linda Hamilton went on to a healthy run on TV's *Beauty and the Beast*, as well as a meatier role in *The Terminator*'s 1991 sequel. Michael Biehn continues to enjoy an active career in features, and was featured prominently in director Cameron's undersea opus, *The Abyss*. Biehn's character of Kyle Reese originally was slated to make a cameo appearance in *Terminator 2*, but that footage was dropped before the film's theatrical release (although this footage was restored in *T2*'s deluxe laser-disk release). Interestingly, before cast negotiations were finalized, actor Lance Hendriksen was to play the part of the murderous Terminator, while Reese was to have been played by Schwarzenegger. When Arnold opted for the Terminator's role, the part of Reese went to the more traditionally heroic-looking Biehn. Hendriksen's step-down to the less important role of police lieutenant Vulkovich notwithstanding, since appearing in *The Terminator* he has been more active than any half-dozen actors, landing roles in numerous genres, mostly action-adventure or crime oriented. He is featured prominently in Cameron's *Aliens* (as well as the ill-advised *Alien 3*). Like all movie hits, *The Terminator* spawned numerous clones. As might be expected, virtually all of these were made with an abundance of haste and cheap special effects, and a paucity of imagination and inspiration.

Terminator 2: Judgment Day
(Tri-Star, 1991; 135 min.) ****

Produced and directed by James Cameron. Screenplay, James Cameron and William Wisher. Edited by Conrad Buff, Mark Goldblatt, Richard A. Harris. Director of Photography, Adam Greenberg. CFI Color. Prints, Technicolor. Music, Brad Fiedel. Dolby Stereo. Costumes, Marlene Stewart. Art Direction, Joseph P. Lucky. Set Decoration, John M. Dwyer. Stunt Coordinators, Joel Kramer, Gary Davis. Special Makeup and Terminator Effects created by Stan Winston. Industrial Light & Magic Visual Effects Supervisor, Dennis Muren.

Cast: Terminator (Arnold Schwarzenegger), Sarah Connor (Linda Hamilton), John Conner (Edward Furlong), Evil Terminator/T-1000 (John Patrick), Miles Dyson (Joe Morton), Dr. Silberman (Earl Boen), Tarissa Dyson (S. Epatha Merkerson), Enrique Salceda (Castula Guerra), Tim (Danny Cooksey), Todd Voight (Xander Berkeley), Janelle Voight (Jenette Goldstein), Twin Sarah (Leslie Hamilton Gearren), Douglas (Ken Gibbel), Trucker (Shane Wilder), Old John Connor (Michael Edwards), Lewis (Don Stanton), Lloyd (Pete Schrum).

Synopsis: A new terminator, the T-1000, more dangerous than Cyberdyne Model 101, is sent back to the late twentieth century by the machines in 2029 A.D.. to kill the teenage John Connor. But the adult John sends a Model 101 to protect himself. Arriving in Los Angeles, the T-1000 kills a policeman and assumes his identity. The 101 finds John first, however, and they evade the assassin after a high-speed chase through the concrete drains of the Los Angeles River. Both Terminators converge at the Pescadero State Hospital, where John's mother, Sarah, is held in the psychiatric ward. Once again, the 101 and John escape the T-1000, taking Sarah with them to the Cyberdyne company scientist Dyson. They describe how his apparently harmless

Arnold Schwarzenegger in *Terminator 2: Judgment Day* (Orion, 1991).

efforts will lead to a worldwide holocaust and convince him to destroy his work. But at the lab, the police arrive and Dyson is killed. Still, his research goes with him. The T-1000 arrives and pursues its quarry to a smelting plant. Though apparently destroyed when liquid nitrogen freezes it and a bullet from 101's pistol shatters it, the robot reconstitutes itself and chases its prey into the bowels of the plant. In hand-to-hand combat, the T-1000 seemingly defeats the 101. Yet the virtually pulverized body of the latter reappears and fires a grenade that distorts the T-1000 and propels it into a vat of molten metal, where it is dissipated. The 101 itself has Sarah lower it into the vat so no evidence of these incidents will remain.

Reviews: "Jaw-dropping special effects and a pace that just might injure you.... Schwarzenegger is oddly endearing." (John Chambless, *Daily Local News*, West Chester, PA, July 4, 1991, p. D2) ¶"A kinder, gentler Terminator. What an affront.... It's Cameron's show; he's the reigning King of movie pow, with dark wit and a poet's eye for mayhem.... Still, the film's relentless pummeling grows wearying at 135 minutes. The first *Terminator*, a half-hour shorter, was leaner and meaner." (*Rolling Stone*, August 8, 1991, p. 78)

Analysis: Arnold Schwarzenegger spoke frequently about doing a sequel to his surprise 1984 hit, but the time — and financing — weren't right until 1991. In the interim, both he and director James Cameron became Big Names in Hollywood, each with a string of successes that propelled expectations for their next venture together. For the most part, these expectations were more than justly rewarded when *Terminator 2* finally saw the light of day seven years after the first film. While there were many who felt that the first film was superior in terms of innovation and technical ingenuity, not to mention the raw energy of its narrative, there is also no denying that the sequel is a mighty impressive achievement that keeps the viewer rooted to his or her seat for the duration of its 135-minute running time. For one thing, there apparently were no budgetary limitations on *Terminator 2*, coming in as it did at a rumored $95 million. For another, Cameron had previously experimented with a most successful special effects technique in his underwater opus, *The Abyss*, a computer-generated visual method known as morphing. Morphing allowed for the most convincing "liquid metal" optical effects ever seen in a film to be the basis for the murderous terminator's physiology, a physiology so fluid that it allowed that android to assume virtually any shape imaginable. The story itself is a mostly plausible science fiction action-adventure yarn, with not too much cumbersome social commentary. Unlike the first film, things do slow down for *Terminator 2* at about its third quarter, when the T-1000, John and Sarah are making their determined trek to kill Dyson and destroy that computer chip. Nor did the first film have anything like the saccharine moments of *Terminator 2*, as when John is attempting to educate his android protector in the ways of humankind.

Most of the essential cast of *The Terminator* returns for the sequel: Schwarzenegger, of course, this time as the "good" Terminator, whose mission is to protect John Connor from the sleeker, deadlier T-1000 model of killer android. Linda Hamilton is again Sarah, but this time a Sarah who has spent nearly a decade on the run, much of that time in places wildly dissimilar to the cafe she waitressed in the first time. Now she's a wild-eyed chain-smoker, paranoid and violently obsessive. Hamilton spent months in the gym and on a strict dietary regimen to prepare for this role. Needless to say, whatever girlish curves graced her slim form in the earlier film have been chiseled to hard, muscular lines in the sequel. Of the rest of the original cast, only Earl Boen, as the psychiatrist Dr. Silberman, returns in the sequel. Scenes that were filmed representing a hallucinatory visit by Kyle Reese (Michael Biehn) to Sarah, who languishes in the psychiatric ward, were deleted from the theatrical print prior to *Terminator 2*'s release (only to be reinserted, along with a considerable amount of other expunged material, with the release of the film's Special Edition in 1993).

Terror Is a Man *see under* **Island of Lost Souls**

The Terror Within
(Concorde/MGM-United Artists, 1988; 88 min.) *

Produced by Roger Corman. Directed by Thierry Notz. Screenplay, Thomas M. Cleaver. Edited by Brent Schoenfeld. Director of Photography, Ronn Schmidt. Color, Fotokem. Music, Rich Conrad. Art Direction, T. C. Chappelow. Set Decoration, Troy Myers. Creatures designed and created by Dean Jones.

Cast: David (Andrew Stevens), Linda (Terri Treas), Sue (Starr Andreeff), Hal (George Kennedy), Andre (John LaFayette), Neil (Tommy Hinchley), Butch the dog (Butch Stevens).

Synopsis: After a biological holocaust which annihilates about 99 percent of the world's population, only a few lucky humans survive. One group is located in the underground Mohave Laboratory. With food in short supply and mutant "gargoyles" roaming topside, David suggests that they leave for Rocky Mountain Lab, 1,800 miles away. Before his idea can be given much thought, a woman is brought in from outside. Linda examines her and finds that in addition to having an immunity to the plague, she's pregnant. To their horror, they find that her offspring will be a mutant. When Linda attempts an abortion, the monstrosity escapes. Andre and Neil are killed trying to track it down, and Sue is raped. She becomes pregnant and dies performing a self-abortion. Linda realizes that the almost invulnerable — and now man-size — gargoyle is not immune to David's high-frequency dog whistle, and a tape is made. The monster is trapped in a duct and falls into a fan. David, Linda and Butch the dog surface and head for Rocky Mountain Lab. Before leaving, they blow up their own lab as mutants inspect the entrance.

Review: "A cross between *Alien* and *The Day the World Ended*, with a routine, predictable plot." (Leonard Maltin, ed., *Movie and Video Guide 1993*, New York: Signet, 1992, p. 1244)

Analysis: This is incredibly irritating because even as an *Alien* clone, it could have been decent. Instead, the characters are stupid, not at all cautious, and oh so easily surprised. As soon as Terri Treas removed the whistle from around her neck, we knew she'd drop it. The only astounding thing in the film — and this we do applaud — is that her character survived. Butch the dog also lived, thank goodness. We gather that Butch is Andrew Stevens's actual pet. The "gargoyle" is better than those that appear in the next entry, and you can see it again in *Watchers II* (1990). Creature designer Dean Jones worked on both films.

The Terror Within II

(Concorde, 1991; 83 min.) *

Produced by Mike Elliott. Executive Producer, Roger Corman. Written and directed by Andrew Stevens. Based on characters created by Thomas M. Cleaver. Edited by Brent Schoenfeld. Director of Photography, Janusz Kaminski. Color, Foto-kem. Music, Terry Plumeri. Ultra-Stereo.

Cast: David Pennington (Andrew Stevens), Kara (Stella Stevens), Sharon (Barbara A. Woods), Ariel (Clair Hoax), Von Demming (R. Lee Ermey), Jamie (Larry Gilman), Elaba (Cindi Gossett), Mutant (Pete Koch), Kyle (Chick Vennera), Dewitt (Burton "Bubba" Gilliam), Robin (Renee Jones), Bo (Brad Blaisdell), Ernie (Lou Beatty, Jr.), Lusus (Brewster Gould), Butch the dog (Butch Stevens), Elabans (Scott Allen, The German Giant).

Synopsis: Pockets of humans survive a biological holocaust. Some are relatively unscathed, but others revert to tribalism. Still others are murderous mutants. To remain uninfected, a group of humans living in the Rocky Mountain Laboratory underground bunker periodically sends members topside to gather peyote. Its strychnine content is necessary for the antidote to the disease. Mutant humanoids make the peyote gathering difficult. On one mission David Pennington rescues the pregnant Ariel, but while he looks for peyote, she is made a sacrifice by less civilized humans led by a superstitious woman. Raped by a mutant, she gives birth in the laboratory to another, which grows to maturity in minutes and savages the humans. Most of the people are killed, but Pennington eventually manages to dispose of Ariel's hideous offspring. He, Ariel and two others survive.

Review: "Stevens ... fogs the cheap sets and shows a few good ideas, but his own absurd story sinks it all." (Leonard Maltin, ed., *Movie and Video Guide 1993*, p. 1244)

Analysis: Within minutes this turkey can be recognized as another *Thing/It/Alien* rip-off. Andrew Stevens obviously saw *Escape from New York*, since his character and performance seems modeled (not very successfully) on Kurt Russell's in that film. What lousy mutants, too. The humans are again as stupid as they come, separating to locate the hiding mutant, standing around and allowing themselves to be pummeled, preferring disintegration to flight. Whistles confounded the mutants, so why didn't the humans blow more? This post-apocalyptic clunker takes more of the glow from an intriguing science fiction subgenre. Actors have to act, but did R. Lee Ermey need this? It's hard to imagine that this was the same fellow who did such a bang-up job as the drill sergeant in Stanley Kubrick's *Full Metal Jacket.*

The Thing *see under* The Thing from Another World

The Thing from Another World

(RKO, 1951; 86 min.) ****

Produced by Howard Hawks. Directed by Christian Nyby. Assistant Directors, Arthur Siteman and Max Henry. Screenplay, Charles Lederer. Based on "Who Goes There?" by John W. Campbell, Jr. Edited by Roland Gross. Director of Photography, Russell Harlan. Music, Dimitri Tiomkin. Sound, Phil Brigandi and Clem Portman. Art Direction, John J. Hughes and Albert S. D'Agostino. Set Decoration, Darrell Silvera and William Stevens. Makeup, Lee Greenway. Special Effects, Donald Stewart. Special Effects Cinematography, Linwood Dunn.

Cast: Captain Hendry (Kenneth Tobey), Nikki Nicholson (Margaret Sheridan), Ned "Scotty" Scott (Douglas Spencer), Professor Carrington (Robert Cornthwaite), Lt. Eddie Dykes (James Young), Bob (Dewey Martin), Dr. Chapman (John Dierkes), Dr. Stern (Eduard Franz), Lt. Ken "Mac" MacPherson (Robert Nichols), Sergeant Barnes (William Self), Thing (James Arness), Thing disintegrating (Billy Curtis), Thing stunts (Tom Steele), Dr. Voorhees (Paul Frees), Mrs. Chapman (Sally Creighton), Dr. Redding (George Fenneman), Dr. Laurenz (Norbert Schiller), General Fogarty (David McMahon), Dr. Ambrose (Edmond Breon), Dr. Wilson (Everett Glass), Olson (William Neff), Cooks (Lee Tung Foo, Walter Ng), Captain Smith (Robert Stevenson), Corporal Hauser (Robert Gutknecht), Captain (Robert Bray), Lieutenants (Ted Cooper, Allan Ray), Ted Richards (Nicholas Byron).

Synopsis: From the Anchorage, Alaska, officers' club, Captain Hendry is called to General Fogarty's office and ordered to fly to Polar Expedition Six's site two thousand miles farther north. The scientific team there has picked up signs that a plane crashed nearby. With newsman Scotty in

tow, Captain Hendry and his crew land and learn from Professor Carrington that whatever crashed weighed twenty thousand tons. Flying to the sight of the crash, the military men, scientists and Scotty soon realize they've found a "flying saucer" beneath the ice. The thermite bombs used to thaw the craft accidentally start a fire and destroy it, but not its frozen occupant, who is chopped free in a block of ice and taken to the base. To no avail does Professor Carrington argue with Captain Hendry about examining the alien. Hendry has windows broken in the storeroom so the ice will remain frozen. He'll wait for instructions from General Fogarty. Scotty can't get permission to send out a story, either. Perturbed by the weird eyes he can see through the ice, Barnes covers the block with an electric blanket and forgets to turn if off. A shadow thrown across Barnes causes him to stand up, turn, and fire his .45 before fleeing the room. Rushing to the storeroom window, Hendry and his men see their captive running through the sled dogs, and when they go outside, they find a forearm torn from the alien. Examination of the tissue reveals that it is of vegetable matter. During an inside search for the alien, Professor Carrington notices some withered plants in the greenhouse. He and three fellow scientists find a dead sled dog in a bin. Obviously the visitor opened the outside door and secreted the dog. Carrington realizes the creature will return, and unknown to Captain Hendry, he sets up a watch. Hendry finds out when Dr. Stern collapses into the common room and gasps that the alien has killed two other scientists. Hendry opens the door only to find the alien staring him in the face. Its arm has been regenerated. It swings at Hendry. The men slam the door and portions of the flesh spray off. Bob fires his carbine into the door. The men block the outside door with metal drums and board up the inner entrance. Carrington realizes that the alien can live on blood, and he begins using plasma to grow his own aliens with "seeds" from the creature's severed arm. Nikki reveals what Carrington is doing, and Hendry has the experiments destroyed. Realizing that bullets

What to do about *The Thing from Another World* (RKO, 1951)? A group confers. Left to right, kneeling: Lt. Eddie Dykes (James Young), Bob (Dewey Martin), Dr. Redding (George Fenneman); Left to right, standing: Dr. Chapman (John Dierkes), "Scotty" Scott (Douglas Spencer), unidentified actor, "Mac" MacPherson (Robert Nichols), Professor Carrington (Robert Cornthwaite), Nikki Nicholson (Margaret Sheridan), and Captain Hendry (Kenneth Tobey).

only puncture the creature without doing real harm, the military men wonder out loud how to combat it. When Nikki says they can boil or stew it, an idea is formed. Just as they are readying kerosene, the Geiger counter picks up the alien's presence. It's out of the greenhouse. In fact, it breaks into the room with Hendry, Nikki, Scotty and some others. But they are ready for it. While one man splashes it with kerosene, another shoots a flare into it. Yet another douses it with a second can of kerosene. Ablaze, the monster leaps through the window and runs again into the blizzard. When Nikki notices Scotty's breath, they realize the fuel supply has been cut off. With no recourse but to hole up in the generator room and wait, the humans jury-rig an electric trap. When the alien approaches, Carrington rushes into the corridor and attempts to communicate with it but is

knocked unconscious. Carrying a beam in one hand, the creature advances. Hendry turns on the juice and the creature is caught between side wall and overhead currents. It slowly disintegrates. Scotty faints dead away, later reporting to the world on the earth's initial encounter with the decidedly deadly life force: "I bring you a warning. Every one of you listening to my voice. Tell the world. Tell this to everybody wherever they are. Watch the skies. Everywhere. Keep looking. Keep watching the skies!"

Reviews: "Good airplane take-offs and landings; wonderful shock effects (the plants that cry for human blood as human babies cry for milk); Kenneth Tobey's fine unpolished performance of a nice, clean, lecherous American Airforce officer; well-cast story, as raw and ferocious as Hawks's *Scarface*." (Manny Farber, *Nation*, January 5, 1952, p. 19) ¶"Its tongue just perceptible in its cheek, the picture goes about describing the arrival of the Martian on our native heath in a quite plausible manner.... For the cast of *The Thing*, I have nothing but admiration." (John McCarten, *New Yorker*, May 12, 1951, pp. 78–79) ¶"With all the comforts of home, including a comely, sweater-bulging secretary (Margaret Sheridan). Except for the Air Force captain (Kenneth Tobey), whom the script had fated for her, the men treat this cute tomato with vegetable-like indifference." (*Time*, May 14, 1951, p. 110)

Analysis: One of the great double features of all time would pair this with *The Day the Earth Stood Still*, which was released the same year. Here, however, the alien is murderous, not benevolent. The genesis of both may be traced to pilot Kenneth Arnold's report of an unidentified flying object on June 24, 1947. Both are also Cold War movies. (In *The Thing* the Russians are mentioned as being all over the North Pole.) This crew is about the best imaginable if one is to choose compatriots with whom to battle an extraterrestrial invader. For its time it's very shocking. Think of the severed arm, the alien's flesh spewing off when the door is shut on it, the creature on fire, the electric arc. Douglas Spencer has the role of his career and many wonderful lines in addition to the immortal warning, "Keep watching the skies." John Dierkes, the roughhewn, gaunt character actor (*The Red Badge of Courage, Shane*), is splendid as a scientist of more reasonable mien than Carrington. The film is frequently viewed as a battle between science and the military, but Dierkes's character is just one of several in the scientific team who question Carrington's goals. There is much repartee from the entire ensemble. Typical of director (here producer) Hawks, the dialogue is overlapping, naturalistic, snappy. Margaret Sheridan is also a typical Hawksian feisty heroine. There are memorable set-pieces: outlining the saucer and the thermite bomb, the confrontation at the greenhouse door, the alien set afire, the electrocution. Tiomkin's score is eerie and frightening. It is a mistake for any book to feature the close-up portrait of James Arness as the

monster. He looks ridiculous. Quite rightly, in the movie he's silhouetted, seen in the distance or outside in the storm, as a door opens and slams shut. For decades Christian Nyby's direction has been questioned. Didn't Hawks really direct? We recall an article in which Nyby asked what he was supposed to do with Hawks on the set: Disregard the master's advice? Beware of prints — even on cable's Disney Channel — that leave out the Tobey-Sheridan tête-à-tête.

The Thing
(Universal, 1982; 127 min.) ***½

Produced by David Foster and Lawrence Turman. Directed by John Carpenter. Assistant Director, Larry Franco. Screenplay, Bill Lancaster. Based on the story "Who Goes There?" by John W. Campbell, Jr. Edited by Todd Ramsay. Director of Photography, Dean Cundey. Technicolor. Panavision. Music, Ennio Morricone. Dolby Stereo. Special Makeup Effects, Rob Bottin. Art Direction, Henry Larrecq.

Cast: MacReady (Kurt Russell), Blair (A. Wilford Brimley), Nauls (T. K. Carter), Palmer (David Clennon), Childs (Keith David), Dr. Copper (Richard Dysart), Norris (Charles Hallahan), Bennings (Peter Maloney), Clark (Richard Masur), Garry (Donald Moffat), Fuchs (Joel Polis), Windows (Thomas Waites), Norwegian (Norbert Weisser), Passenger with rifle (Larry France), Helicopter pilot (Nate Irwin), Pilot (William Zeman).

Synopsis: An Antarctic United States scientific outpost is disturbed by the sudden appearance of a sled dog being fired upon by men in a helicopter. The dog seeks refuge in the American camp. In the melee that follows the chopper's landing, the chopper explodes, killing one of the occupants, and Mr. Garry kills a gun-wielding man as he stalks into the camp. Markings on the wreckage indicate that these men were from a Norwegian camp. Investigating, chopper pilot MacReady and Dr. Copper discover the Norwegian camp in ruins and all of its inhabitants dead — most by suicide. They note with interest a large, empty, crypt-like block of ice. They return to their camp with the partially burned remains of what appears to be a grotesquely deformed human being. Later, in the kennel, the sled dog undergoes a frightening metamorphosis, transforming into a raging tentacled thing that throws the other dogs into a howling panic. Investigating the disturbance, the men let loose a volley of small arms fire at the furious creature before subduing it with a flame thrower. More mystified than ever by this thing which seems to have been *absorbing* the dogs, the men decide that Blair should do a thorough examination of the remains. He is most disturbed by what he finds. Microscopic computer analysis indicates that they have a life-form that digests and imitates its victims on the cellular level. It is clear to Blair that if this creature should leave the camp, the entire world is at threat. Meanwhile, MacReady, Nauls and Norris fly to a sight indicated in the Norwegian records. There they find a large crevice, at the bottom of which is evidently a crashed alien spacecraft. Norris, the geologist, speculates that the craft had been buried for hundreds of thousands of years before natural forces brought it to the surface. A rectangular cube has been cut from the ice nearby, and the Americans speculate that this held the remains of the spacecraft's alien occupant. After MacReady and his comrades return to base, Blair's fear pushes him over the edge: He's convinced that this alien life-form will inevitably infect and take over all other life-forms with which it comes into contact. He disables the helicopter and other means of transportation as well as the radio, effectively isolating the camp from the rest of the world. Finally the others overpower him and lock him in a heated shack. Blair's fear proves well-founded, however, when MacReady and the others discover their blood supply has been sabotaged, thus preventing implementation of Dr. Copper's blood-serum test to reveal the presence of any infected individuals. Obviously someone else *is* infected. Over the next several hours Fuchs is lured outside and killed. Norris suffers an apparent heart attack. When Copper tries to administer electrocardiac shock, the geologist's entire chest cavity opens to reveal a fanged maw that fatally savages the doctor. Palmer, too, becomes a monstrous thing that kills Windows before MacReady can turn the flame thrower on him. Using his own variant of the blood-serum test, MacReady decides that Nauls, Childs and Garry are still human. When they check on Blair, they find he's gone. Beneath the floorboards of his hut a tunnel is discovered leading to a large chamber where they find some sort of flying craft. It is obvious that Blair, too, is now an alien creature, fabricating a craft to take him to a warmer clime — and an unsuspecting civilization. MacReady and his crew implement a scorched-earth campaign throughout the camp until only one structure stands. The alien, now huge, kills Nauls and Garry even as MacReady throws his last stick of dynamite, igniting the entire remaining compound and destroying the beast in the conflagration. He and Childs wait for death as the cold Antarctic night closes in.

Review: "Designer Rob Bottin's work is novel and unforgettable, but since it exists in a near vacuum emotionally, it becomes too domineering dramatically and something of an exercise in abstract art." (Richard Schickel, *Time*, June 28, 1982, p. 72) ¶"The most vividly gruesome monster ever to stalk the screen.... On all other levels, however, John Carpenter's remake ... comes as a letdown." (Cart., *Variety*, June 23, 1982)

Analysis: The Thing was John Carpenter's first *big* film for a major studio. His earliest films, *Assault on Precinct 13* and *Halloween*, were both made on the proverbial shoestring with much location shooting and casts of largely unknowns. They were all the better for that and achieved cult status almost immediately. Subsequent films (*The Fog* and *Escape from New York*) were built on incrementally larger budgets and fixed the young director's reputation as a master in the genre. With the coming of the eighties and the penchant for remakes that had begun with Phil Kaufman's remake of Don Siegel's *Invasion of the Body Snatchers*, a remake of Hawks's *The Thing from Another World* was pretty much a given. Carpenter never made a secret of the fact that Hawks's film was one of his personal favorites, and he even featured it prominently in the background of his own *Halloween*. Released during the summer of 1982 along with such blockbusters as *E.T., Star Trek III, Poltergeist, The Road Warrior, Conan the Barbarian* and others, John Carpenter's remake of the Howard Hawks classic was very nearly lost in the crowd. It was a box office disappointment and the critics were almost uniform in their disdain, finding it merely a celebration of the grotesque talents of Carpenter's special effects team. (The *Time* review cited "state-of-the-goo" makeup effects.) Those who saw Carpenter's film as nothing more than a showcase for gratuitous grotesquerie should read Campbell's "Who Goes There?" which describes in precise and colorful detail the many manifestations of an otherworldly creature not unlike the one depicted by Carpenter and his special effects crew. *The Thing*'s strong points include first-rate performances by a cast of actors who were (except for Kurt Russell) largely unknown, superior production values, an excellent score by Ennio Morricone, and a script that, in the main, remains faithful to the original Don A. Stuart (John Campbell) novella. Critics at the time complained loudly that Rick Baker's gross-out special effects pushed the limits of acceptability and reduced Carpenter's film to a geek show. However, the passage of time and a host of splatter films that have truly extended the envelope of what was considered "gross" have allowed us to view these in the proper light.

Through the Portal of Time *see* Beastmaster 2 *under* **The Beastmaster**

To Die For
(Skouras, 1989; 90 min.) **

Produced by Barin Kumar. Directed by Deren Sarafian. Screenplay, Leslie King. Director of Photography, David Boyd. Foto-Kem Color. Edited by Dennis Dolan. Ultra-Stereo. Sound, Robert Janiger. Art Direction, Greg Oehler. Costumes, Cynthia Bergstrom. Makeup, John Buechler. Special Effects, Eddie Surkin.

Cast: Vlad Tepish (Brendan Hughes), Kate Wooten (Sydney Walsh), Celia Kett (Amanda Wyss), Tom (Steve Bond), Martin Planting

(Scott Jacoby), Mike Dunn (Micah Grant), Jane (Remy O'Neill), Simon Little (Duane Jones), Lt. Williams (Al Fann), Rich (Lloyd Alan), Detective Bocco (Philip Granger), Paula Higgins (Julie Maddalena), Girl at party (Eloise Broady), Michelle (Cate Caplin), Franny (Ava Fabian), Ben (Dean Anthony), Bum (Fred Waugh), Dump truck driver (Bill Handy), Bartender (Richard Sarafian), Woman on yacht (Sharon Mullings).

Synopsis: At a Los Angeles boat party, a man makes a pass at real estate agent Kate Wooten, then mysteriously disappears. In the marina parking lot Rich is savagely killed. Kate finds she's been hired to find a house for one Vlad Tepish, who turns out to be the fellow who stood her up at the party. Ostensibly hired to decorate the palatial estate Kate found for Vlad, Kate's friend Celia finds herself vampirized. Another man watches: Tom. Outside, he and Vlad engage in a rather heated conversation about old times and another woman. Vlad warns Tom not to touch Kate. At Vlad's party, Kate meets Tom. Another guest, Martin, who loves Kate, finds a book about Vlad with illustrations, one being of Dracula's castle. He thinks he sees the dead Rich. Tom shows Kate a woman's portrait. Vlad interrupts, and Kate leaves the room. Tom says he'll make the bitch his. Vlad makes love to Kate. Celia observes and is enraged. Continuing his reading, Martin learns how to kill a vampire. Jane, one of Kate's associates, is found dead. Martin tries to convince Kate of Vlad's heritage. Celia "dies," but Martin and Celia's fiancée Mike determine to put a stake in her heart. Celia tries to attack Mike but becomes a disgusting corpse before disappearing. Kate refuses to leave Vlad and they mate again. He bites her neck; she cuts his chest and drinks his blood. Tom interrupts but in the ensuing battle of the vampires is impaled on the bedpost. Mike and Martin arrive and urge Vlad to let Kate alone. The sun rises and Vlad purposefully opens the door to the sun's rays, disintegrating as the police approach the house.

Review: "Dracula legend is updated ... the results are strictly second-rate." (Leonard Maltin, ed., *Movie and Video Guide 1993*, p. 1285)

Analysis: It's not bad, but there are many inconsistencies and implausibilities: There's no neck mark on one victim, there are shadows caused by blinds that aren't in the scene, the vampire history Martin finds just happens to be in English. There's one new weapon in the vampire's arsenal: a force of will that can levitate people and objects. Aka *Dracula: The Love Story.*

Son of Darkness: To Die For II
(Trimark Pictures, 1991; 95 min.)
**½

Produced by Richard Weinman. Directed by David F. Price. Screenplay, Leslie King. Edited by Barry Zetlin. Director of Photography, Gerry Lively. Color, Foto-Kem. Music, Mark McKenzie. "To Die For" Theme, Cliff Eidelman. Ultra-Stereo. Art Direction, James Vaughn. Set Decoration, Page Huyette. Stunt Coordinator, George Fisher. Special Effects Coordinator, Larry Fioritto. Special Makeup Effects, Magical Media Industries. Special Makeup Designer-Producer, John Carl Buechler.

Cast: Nina Black (Rosalind Allen), Tom (Steve Bond), Dr. Max Schreck/Vlad Tepish (Michael Praed), Martin Planting (Scott Jacoby), Danny (Jay Underwood), Celia (Amanda Wyss), Jane (Remy O'Neill), Tyler Black (Devin Corrie Sims), Detective (Vince Edwards).

Synopsis: A man with a horrendously bloodied chest dies in the emergency room. In a bar, Celia picks up Danny, but after a walk in the wood she disappears. The mysterious Tom tells her that he, not Max, would like to spend time with her. Celia goes to the hospital and receives some plasma from Max Schreck. Nina and brother Danny discuss the end of summer at their bed and breakfast. Martin Planting, who lost two friends the year before and is not allowed to see a traumatized Kate, hears about murders on television and takes time off from his bank job to investigate. When Nina's adopted baby won't stop crying, she takes him to the hospital, where he's examined by Dr. Schreck. Max's brother Tom interrupts to introduce himself. Martin arrives in town and in the bar spots Jane, a woman he'd thought dead. Tom tells Celia the west is his territory and he doesn't give a shit about depressed

Eastern Bloc countries. He and Celia kill a couple in a cabin. Martin can't convince the authorities that animals are not responsible. At Max's house for dinner, Nina learns of his Rumanian origins and takes a horseback ride made hazardous by Tom. Back home, they make love while Celia visits and vampirizes Danny. Martin describes to the police how blood and the remains of a murderer caused an explosion in a Los Angeles lab the year previously. Jane finds Martin in the bar and explains how she and Celia travel in flocks. She urges him to go home or help Nina. He shows Nina a picture of Vlad Tepish, who resembles Max Schreck, and tries unsuccessfully to apprise her of her danger. Max tells Steve there will be no more killing. Nina awakes in a circle of fire. An image of Max appears and tells her there is evil, yes, but some good in him. She begins reading the book Martin left behind. Working late at the marina, Nina is chased through the boat storage area by Tom until Max arrives. Realizing that Tom is right about being weak for not having eaten in ages, Max regretfully becomes a wolf and takes a woman. Jane attempts to help Martin, but Tom appears and chains her to a tree to face the rising sun. Max reveals to Nina that Tyler is his son. Tom barges in, grabs the child, and bites his wrist to "bring him in all the way." Max intervenes, but Tom forces him against the wall with a bureau. Downstairs, Danny attempts to stop Tom from taking the baby back but is decapitated by Tom's chain saw. Max appears; the two male vampires fight. Celia stabs Tom in the back, but before dying, he kills her. Max tries to convince Nina she must give him the baby or else other vampires will come and teach him to kill. He wants Nina with him, saying the darkness can be beautiful. Martin enters and, failing to impale Max, opens the curtains. The sunlight sets Max afire before he disappears. Outside, the baby has an unearthly gleam in its eyes.

Review: "One of those rare sequels that's much better written, directed and acted than its predecessor." (Ley., *Variety*, May 6, 1991)

Analysis: Son of Darkness: To Die For II, while a bit more focused and with more narrative thrust than its predecessor, still manages to lose itself in the last act and come down, as did the first film, to a slugfest between the two vampire brothers. The brawl is a little more prolonged than the first one, but the results are the same, and again we have Vlad Tepish coming to a fiery end with the dawn's early light. The coda, with the infant's glowing eyes, would seem to promise yet another sequel. There are no winners here. Max is sympathetic but on occasion reverts to a savage beast. Tom is funny but even more murderous. Nina loses her brother and must deal with a half-vampire baby. A number of familiar characters return from the first film. Max Schreck, of course, is the name of the actor who played *Nosferatu*. Nice touch: An upside-down Tom observes Max and Nina from the window. How did Tom get resurrected? The police are amenable to the possibility that coyotes or wolves killed people. Have they been living under a rock? Last we heard, there has never been a documented case of a wolf attacking a human being. An uncredited Vince Edwards gives another of his cantankerous cop portrayals.

The Tomb of Ligeia *see under* **The Fall of the House of Usher**

Topper
(MGM, 1937; 98 min.) ***

Produced by Hal Roach. Directed by Norman Z. McLeod. Screenplay, Jack Jevne, Eric Hatch, Eddie Moran. Based on a story by Thorne Smith. Edited by William Terhune. Director of Photography, Norbert Brodine. Music, Arthur Norton. Musical Director, Marvin Hatley. Song: "Old Man Moon" Music and Lyrics, Hoagy Carmichael. Set Decoration, W. L. Stevens. Gowns, Samuel M. Lange. Special Photographic Effects, Roy Seawright.

Cast: Cosmo Topper (Roland Young), Marion Kerby (Constance Bennett), George Kerby (Cary Grant), Clara Topper (Billie Burke), Wilkins (Alan Mowbray), Casey (Eugene Pallette), Mrs. Rutherford Stuyvesant (Hedda Hopper), Elevator boy/bellboy (Arthur Lake), Hotel manager (Theodore von Eltz), Policeman (J. Farrell MacDonald), Miss Johnson (Virginia Sale), Secretary (Elaine Shepard), Rustics (Doodles Weaver, Si Jenks), Three Hits and a Miss (Themselves), Hoagy (Hoagy Carmichael), Eddie (Ward Bond). With George Humbert.

Synopsis: George and Marion Kerby spend a night out at the Rainbow Room and other New York clubs before going to the National Security Bank for a board of directors meeting. George is the largest stockholder. Bank president Cosmo Topper chairs the meeting. Afterward, Marion tells the regimented, henpecked Topper that he shouldn't be a mummy, he should live a little. On the way home George and Marion crash into a tree. Their spirits leave the bodies and sit on a fallen tree. They realize they are spirits that may need to do a good deed in order to pass the Pearly Gates. After the Kerbys' funeral, Cosmo restores their car, takes a ride and runs off the road where the Kerbys did. They reveal themselves and have him take them to their penthouse. Cosmo becomes tipsy on booze and must be helped downstairs by the ghosts. After a fight with some taxi drivers he is hauled into court. The newspaper headline: "BANKER AND BABE IN BRAWL" confounds wife Clara, but to the neighbors it proves that the Toppers are not stuffed shirts, and they are invited to a party. Marion and Cosmo, meanwhile, have driven to the Sea Breeze Hotel. Casey, the house detective, becomes suspicious but can't prove Cosmo has a woman in his room. George shows up, angry that Marion is having such fun with Cosmo. All leave the hotel in an uproar. The car crashes again. Cosmo is injured but nursed by Clara, who has changed her stripes. George and Marion bid adieu.

Review: "Mr. Young and his fellow players are responsible for whatever success an otherwise completely irresponsible film enjoys." (B.R.C., *New York Times*, August 20, 1937, p. 21) ¶"Carefully made, excellently photographed, and adroitly employs mechanical illusions and trick sound effects.... Performances are usually good." (*Variety*)

Analysis: Roland Young received an Academy Award nomination—and deserved it. The film picks up steam in the middle, and you'll roll on the floor when the unconscious Topper, held up by the invisible Kerbys, takes the elevator and, arms akimbo, crosses the hotel lobby. Constance Bennett's liberated woman is most interesting. Her boldness with Young is refreshing.

Topper Takes a Trip
(United Artists/Hal Roach, 1939; 85 min.) ***

Produced by Milton H. Bren. Directed by Norman Z. McLeod. Screenplay, Jack Jevne, Corey For, Eddie Moran. Based on the novel *Topper Takes a Trip* by Thorne Smith. Director of Photography, Norbert Brodine. Music, Edward Powell, Hugo Friedhofer. Art Direction, Charles D. Hall. Set Decoration, W. L. Stevens. Gown for Constance Bennett by Irene, for Billie Burke by Omar Kiam. Special Effects, Roy Seawright.

Cast: Cosmo Topper (Roland Young), Marion Kerby (Constance Bennett), Clara Topper (Billie Burke), Wilkins (Alan Mowbray), Nancy Parkhurst (Verree Teasdale), Louis (Franklin Pangborn), Baron de Rossi (Alexander D'Arcy), Bartender (Paul Hurst), Jailer (Eddy Conrad), Prosecutor (Irving Pichel), Defender (Paul Everton), Gorgan (Duke York), Clerk (Armand Kaliz), "Mr. Atlas" ("Skippy").

Synopsis: During his divorce trial, Topper tells the odd tale of George and Marion Kerby, but the judge is incredulous. So astounding is the case — Marion has "reappeared" and come to the court with Atlas the terrier — that the decree is denied. The invisible Marion drags "Toppie" to a bar, where the bartender thinks he's going crazy as a martini glass levitates. Topper decides to pursue Clara and her friend Mrs. Parkhurst to Europe, and Marion tags along to the Hotel St. Pierre on the French Riviera, where Parkhurst instructs a "baron" to entertain Clara. The hotel manager, the baron's relative, tries to keep Cosmo out and thinks he can until Marion assists Cosmo at the casino. Glitches mar a reunion with Clara. Topper fights the baron and, with Marion's help, floors him. Clara is impressed, calling Cosmo "practically a cave man." Marion shows herself in front of the baron, incriminating him in an affair with herself. Cosmo is jailed after Marion tossed fruit through the hotel windows, so Marion breaks him out. Reunited with

Clara, he takes flight for the States. Marion and Atlas wave good-bye from the plane's wing.

Review: "The spirits are willing but the freshness is weak." (Frank S. Nugent, *New York Times*, December 30, 1938, p. 11)

Analysis: A count of camera tricks (Nugent of the *New York Times* called them "astonishing"), one-liners and expressions might verify that this is funnier than the original, even without Cary Grant. A flashback includes Grant. Could this be the first film with an invisible dog on a lead? Funniest scenes: Topper in the bar with an incredulous Paul Hurst, and dancing — quite well — by himself at the hotel. Once again, Constance Bennett is supremely appealing.

Topper Returns
(United Artists, 1941; 87 min.) **½

Produced by Hal Roach. Directed by Roy del Ruth. Screenplay, Jonathan Latimer, Gordon Douglas. Additional Dialogue, Paul Gerard Smith. Based on the fictional characters created by Thorne Smith. Edited by James Newcom. Director of Photography, Norbert Brodine. Music, Werner Heymann. Art Direction, Nicolai Remisoff. Set Decoration, W. L. Stevens. Special Photographic Effects, Roy Seawright.

Cast: Topper (Roland Young), Gail Richards (Joan Blondell), Chauffeur (Eddie "Rochester" Anderson), Ann Carrington (Carole Landis), Bob (Dennis O'Keefe), Mr. Carrington (H. B. Warner), Mrs. Topper (Billie Burke), Dr. Jeris (George Zucco), Sergeant Roberts (Donald McBride), Emily the maid (Patsy Kelly), Lillian (Rafaela Ottiano), Rama the butler (Trevor Bardette).

Synopsis: A cab carrying Gail Richards and Ann Carrington crashes near a cliff after being shot at by a sniper. Driving by, Cosmo Topper and his chauffeur Eddie give them a lift to Carrington Hall. Dr. Jeris tells Ann her father is not well. Ann is about to turn twenty-one and come into her inheritance. This will be the first time she's seen her dad. Dr. Jeris interrupts the father's tale of Ann's mother's death in a Sumatran tungsten mine. A chandelier falls, almost killing Ann. That night a cloaked figure enters Gail's room. She screams, he leaves, and a spirit rises from Gail's body and goes to Topper's house.

At Carrington Hall, Gail's stabbed body is found. The police arrive, headed by Sergeant Roberts. Meanwhile, Eddie sees three men with a body in a rowboat. Gail and Topper row out to a cabin cruiser and retrieve Gail's corporeal body. During an interrogating session, Gail gives Topper a note by Lillian and a sample of her handwriting. The lights go out. Lillian disappears and Ann is kidnapped by the man in black. Bob finds a tunnel and fights a masked man. Gail helps Bob and they find Ann. It turns out that the perpetrator of all the mayhem is Mr. Carrington, who tries to escape but whose car crashes. His ghost explains to Gail that he's not really Carrington. The real Carrington was killed in that mine cave-in.

Review: "Rather sluggish ghost-hunt." (T.S., *New York Times*, March 28, 1941, p. 26)

Analysis: This is a standard haunted house mystery. Donald McBride gives one of his patented "harried policeman" performances, possibly going a smidgen too far.

Topper Returns *see under* **Topper**

Topper Takes a Trip *see under* **Topper**

The Toxic Avenger
(Troma, 1985; 84 min.) *

Produced by Lloyd Kaufman and Michael Herz. Directed by Michael Herz and Samuel Weil. Screenplay, Joe Ritter. Story, Lloyd Kaufman. Edited by Richard W. Haines. Directors of Photography, James London and Lloyd Kaufman. Special Effects Makeup, Jennifer Aspinal.

Cast: Toxic Avenger (Mitchell Cohen), Sara (Andree Maranda), Melvin (Mark Torgl), Mayor Belgoody (Pat Ryan, Jr.), Wanda (Jennifer Babtist), Julie (Cindy Manion), Slug (Robert Prichard), Bozo (Gary Schneider), Officer O'Clancy (Dick Martinsen), Voice of Toxic Avenger (Kenneth Kessler).

Synopsis: Nerdy Melvin Fird is mop boy at the Tromaville Health Club in northern New Jersey where many toxic waste dumps are located. Melvin's mere presence distresses jock Bozo. Julie hatches a plan to humiliate Melvin. In the girls' locker room

Julie tells Melvin she wants to do "it" but he must wear a pink ballerina outfit. When he appears so attired and finds *everyone* waiting, Melvin jumps through a window and lands in an open can of radioactive waste on the back of a truck. Aflame, Melvin runs home, and in his bathtub a transformation occurs. That night a large, deformed human steps in to stop the beating of a cop. At a nearby dump, Melvin, now the Toxic Avenger, takes up residence. He foils a Mexican restaurant robbery and befriends a beautiful blonde blind girl, Sara. He beats up a pimp, saves some children, cuts off Julie's hair, and takes Bozo for a joyride. He and Sara take up residence in the dump, but after the Avenger loses his cool and kills a little old lady — who happened to be a criminal — they move to a pristine meadow. The corrupt mayor gets permission to use the National Guard to find the monster. He wants to kill it, but no one will. The Avenger is a local hero, and the mayor is discredited.

Review: "About half a joke more than in the intolerable *Class of Nuke 'em High....* Troma films represent the rock bottom, the absolute nadir of cinema.... Troma films are a disease. Don't support them." (Stefan Jaworzyn, *ShockXpress*, Summer 1987, p. 19)

Analysis: It's mostly awful, a turkey. The music is Mussorgsky's *Night on Bald Mountain.* There is much padding by use of footage already seen and minutes devoted to army tanks leaving the armory.

The Toxic Avenger, Part II
(Troma, 1989; 95 min.) *

Produced by Lloyd Kaufman and Michael Herz. Directed by Michael Herz and Lloyd Kaufman. Screenplay, Gay Partington Terry and Lloyd Kaufman. Story, Lloyd Kaufman. Edited by Michael Schweitzer. Director of Photography, James London. Music, Barrie Guard. Art Direction, Alexis Grey. Special Makeup Effects, Arthur Jolly, Joel Harlow, Kelly Gleason, William L. Decker. Special Effects, Pericles Lewnes.

Cast: Melvin/Toxic Avenger (Ron Fazio, John Altamura), Claire (Phoebe Legere), Apocalypse Inc. Chairman (Rick Collins), Malfaire (Lisa Gaye), Big Mac (Rikiya Yasuoka), Masami (Mayako Katsuragi), Announcer

(Tsutomu Sekine), Mrs. Junko (Jessica Dublin), Mr. Junko (Jack Cooper).

Synopsis: Melvin Junko, aka The Toxic Avenger, relates how he rid Tromaville of corruption and befriended the blind Claire. Now there are no criminals to fight and he's become concierge at the Tromaville Center for the Blind. A black limo pulls up and a host of thugs attack the Avenger after blowing up the building and putting up a sign, "Future Site of Apocalypse, Inc. Toxic Chemical Storage Area." In the battle, "Toxie" tears off arms, a head, ears. Apocalypse plans to destroy Toxie preparatory to taking over Tromaville preparatory to taking over New York. A flashback to the first film explains how Melvin Junko became the Avenger. A psychiatrist working for Apocalypse tells Toxie he must go to Japan to find his father. He wind surfs there, befriends a Japanese girl, battles and kills "Big Mac," who was presumably his father. He returns to the U.S., engages in a high-speed taxi and Hovercraft chase of an Apocalypse motorcycle, which blows up, and meets his real father, "Big Mac Junko." The man in Japan was "Big Mac Bunco."

Reviews: "Too silly to be funny." (Kevin Thomas, *Los Angeles Times Calendar*, March 31, 1989, p. 11) ¶"It's so bad it's just plain horrible." (Mike McGrady, *Newsday*, April 7, 1989, Part III, p. 5) ¶"Tired exploitation." (Jami Bernard, *New York Post*, April 7, 1989, p. 29)

Analysis: Why has Melvin Furd become Melvin Junko? Why has Sara become Claire? Scenes go on too long, especially the opening battle and the final chase. One funny scene: Toxie uses fish as numchuks.

The Toxic Avenger Part III: The Last Temptation of Toxie
(Troma, 1989; 89 min.) *½

Produced and directed by Lloyd Kaufman and Michael Herz. Screenplay, Gay Partington Terry and Lloyd Kaufman. Story, Lloyd Kaufman. Edited by Joseph McGirr. Director of Photography, James London. TVC Color. Music, Christopher DeMarco. Art Direction, Alexis Grey. Makeup, Kathy Mulshine. Special Makeup Effects, Arthur Jolly, Joel Harlow, Kelly Gleason, William L. Decker. Special Effects, Pericles Lewnes.

Cast: Toxic Avenger (Ron Fazio, John Altamura), Claire (Phoebe Legere), Chairman/Devil (Rick Collins), Malfaire (Lisa Gaye), Mrs. Junko (Jessica Dublin).

Synopsis: A flashback to 1984 recounts the saga of nerdy Melvin, who became the Toxic Avenger. Then his battle with Apocalypse Inc. in 1988 is reviewed. Now A.I.'s chairman talks the Avenger into a deal: Avenger will represent A.I. in return for $357,000 — the cost of an operation to restore Claire's sight. The operation is successful, but Claire is distraught to witness Tromaville's degeneration into a cesspool of dioxin controlled by Apocalypse Inc. She makes the Avenger realize that he must break his contract with A.I. The Avenger confronts the chairman, who turns into the devil and puts the Avenger through a real-life, "video game" test of five levels. The Avenger wins when a bolt from on high imbues him with renewed strength. He swings the devil around and around. With Tromaville rid of the pestilential Apocalypse Inc., the Avenger and Claire wed.

Reviews: "Best creative energies invested in the title alone.... Yet another case in which the agonizingly cretinous script seems to have been a bothersome afterthought to the brainstorming session for the name." (Chris Willman, *Los Angeles Times Calendar*, November 10, 1989, p. 8) ¶"Becomes sort of an absurd *Grand Guignol* played for laughs." (Bill Kaufman, *Newsday*, November 10, 1989, Part III, p. 9)

Analysis: It's better than part two, if that's saying much.

Trancers
(Empire Pictures, 1985; 85 min.) **½

Produced and directed by Charles Band. Screenplay, Danny Bilson and Paul De Meo. Director of Photography, Mac Ahlberg. Color, DeLuxe. Music, Mark Ryder and Phil Davies. Art Direction, Christopher Amy. Set Decoration, Gregory Melton. Makeup, Karen Kubeck.

Cast: Jack Deth (Tim Thomerson), Lena (Helen Hunt), Whistler (Michael Stefani), McNulty (Art La Fleur), Margaret Ashe (Anne Seymour), Spencer (Richard Herd), Engineer Raines (Telma Hopkins).

Synopsis: In the twenty-third century, the ruling Council is threatened by Whistler, a man who uses his mental powers to turn weak-minded people into murderous "trancers." Policeman Jack Deth thought he'd killed Whistler after his son was murdered by the maniac. Instead, Whistler is biding his time in the twentieth century till he can dispose of the Council and take power. Deth is sent back to deal with Whistler, who will make things difficult: He's in a detective's body. In L.A., December 1985, Deth makes friends with Lena and the two evade Whistler but can't save an ancestor of one of the Council members. They seek Ashby, aka derelict "Highball," another ancestor. Ashby, an ex-baseball player, uses his pitching arm to help capture Whistler. Because one of his vials is broken, Deth can only send one person to the twenty-third century. Because he likes Lena, he transports Whistler.

Review: "Low-budget *Blade Runner*." (*Video Hound's Golden Movie Retriever 1994*, p. 847)

Analysis: Not bad; its best scenes involve a watch that gives Deth an extra 10 seconds while his adversaries are "paralyzed" in real time. There's good pace. There's a scene of Los Angeles buildings half covered by the ocean, and an earthquake is mentioned as the cause. Someone should set a film in the upper stories of the structures. Aka *Future Cop*.

Trancers II
(Paramount/Full Moon Entertainment, 1991; 86 min.) **

Produced and directed by Charles Band. Screenplay, Jackson Barr. Director of Photography, Adolfo Bartoli. Color. Music, Mark Ryder and Phil Davies. Ultra-Stereo. Set Decoration, Lauren Gifford. Special Effects, Players Special Effects.

Cast: Jack Deth (Tim Thomerson), Lena (Helen Hunt), Alice (Megan Ward), Hap Ashby (Biff Manard), Dr. E. D. Wardo (Richard Lynch), McNulty (Alyson Croft and Art La Fleur), Nurse Trotter (Martine Beswicke), Raines (Telma Hopkins), Dr. Pyle (Jeffrey Combs), Wino #1 (John Chandler). With Barbara Crampton and Sonny Carl Davis.

Synopsis: Via the standard genetic line, McNulty is sent back to 1991 to find Jack Deth and another agent, Alice, who happens to have the mind of Jack's late wife. Deth will have a place on the Council when he returns. A special machine will be sent later in which Deth is to transport Dr. E. D. Wardo, the brother of trancer maker Whistler. Jack is now married to Lena and protects Hap Ashby, who became rich and lives in isolation. Although he doesn't know who she is, Wardo has Alice incarcerated at his complex where the mentally ill are transformed into trancers, their immediate goal the destruction of Ashby. When Alice escapes and finds Jack, Lena has a crisis. Jack can't tell Alice she'll die if she goes back to the future. Lena is captured by Wardo's trancers. Hap gets drunk. Jack and Alice rescue Lena and hide in the barn where the time machine is located. Wardo knew Jack would come and tries to burn him up, but Ashby and McNulty arrive in a fire engine while Jack, Alice and Lena blaze away and kill a number of Wardo's minions. Jack impales Wardo with a pitchfork. With only minutes remaining, Jack convinces Alice to use the machine. While Alice's body will be killed, this new Alice can start over. He'll stay with Lena.

Review: "Talkfest.... Extremely poor production values...." (Lor., *Variety*, June 10, 1991)

Analysis: It's not bad, but not up to the original. While some of the action scenes are above average, in particular the slo-mo shooting of three trancers at the nursery, the action denouement is rather perfunctory and badly choreographed. Unexplained: One of the hatches to the time travel machine came separately by accident, but no one was seen re-attaching it at the end. Catch one of the cinema's great punks, John Davis Chandler (here as John Chandler), as a wino. Recall him from *The Young Savages* (1961), *Major Dundee* (1965) and *Pat Garrett and Billy the Kid* (1973).

Trancers III
(Paramount/Full Moon Entertainment, 1992; 83 min.) **

Produced by Albert Band. Executive Producer, Charles Band. Directed by C. Courtney Joyner. Screenplay, C. Courtney Joyner. Edited by Lauren Schaffer and Margaret-Anne

Smith. Director of Photography, Adolfo Bartoli. Color, Foto-Kem. Music, Richard Band. Original Trancers Music, Mark Ryder and Phil Davies. Ultra-Stereo. Art Direction, Arlan Jay Vetter. Set Decoration, Miranda Amador. Special Makeup Effects, Kurtzman, Nicotero and Berger EFX Group.

Cast: Jack Deth (Tim Thomerson), R. J. Garrett (Melanie Smith), Colonel Muthuh (Andrew Robinson), Jason (Tony Pierce), Jana (Dawn Ann Billings), Lena (Helen Hunt), Alice Stillwell (Megan Ward), Harris (Stephen Macht), Commander Raines (Telma Hopkins), Matt (Randal Keith), Shark (R. A. Mihailoff), Stevens (Don Dowe), Senator McCoy (Hunter Von Leer).

Synopsis: It's 1992 and future cop Jack Deth is now a private detective whose affair with Lena seems about over. A hulking, ugly but verbal and intelligent humanoid known as Shark finds Deth at a motel stakeout, incapacitates him with a needle to the neck and takes him to the year 2352. Harris is in charge, Alice is a colonel. The Council is defunct, having been a casualty of resurgent and innumerable trancers. Jack is informed that only Lena knows who organized them — the Lena of 2005. Jack is sent to L.A. in 2005. There a prospective trancer loses control and must be destroyed. Another future trancer, Private Garrett, witnesses the carnage and leaves. Colonel Muthuh, the mastermind of these warriors, wants her returned. But Jack finds her when he finds Lena, now Lena Forest, newspaper columnist to whom Garrett has been revealing secrets. Jack and Garrett leave in his old Corvette, but they're captured by Colonel Muthuh's forces. Jack is given an injection. A senator visits and tells Colonel Muthuh he's got to be impressed if the funding is not to be cut off. Colonel Muthuh thinks of his troops as ridding the nation's streets of scum. Garrett helps Jack get free and they make a break, but Garrett has difficulty fighting off her trancer self. She asks Jack to kill her, which he does. Confronting Colonel Muthuh, Jack finds himself temporarily controlled and though wounded by the colonel, blows him away. Brought to the restored Council of Harris, Raines and Alice, Jack is informed that he's been made Peacekeeping Emissary of Time and Space.

Review: "Entertaining in a brutal, self-mocking sort of way." (Mick Martin and Marsha Porter, *Video Movie Guide 1994*, p. 1046)

Analysis: The few sets indicate that not much money was put into this, and it falls apart about a quarter-hour after it starts. One supposes they didn't care about mystery: We know that Colonel Muthuh is the criminal mastermind well before Jack. Andrew Robinson is a controlled over-the-top, but that's to be expected; this is a modern B movie. There's padding, e.g., shots of Jack's car backing up and roaring off, a needless martial arts fight between two trancers. We are mystified by Jack's reputation, seeing as how he gets captured so easily.

Trancers 4: Jack of Swords
(Full Moon Entertainment, 1993; 74 min.) **

Produced by Vlad Paunescu and Oana Paunescu. Executive Producer, Charles Band. Directed by David Nutter. Screenplay, Peter David. Edited by Lisa Bromwell. Director of Photography, Adolfo Bartoli. Color by Foto-Kem. Music, Gary Fry. Ultra-Stereo. Stunt Coordinator, Jeff Moldovan. Special Effects Makeup, AlchemyFX and Michael S. Deak.

Cast: Jack Deth (Tim Thomerson), Lyra (Stacie Randall), Prospero (Ty Miller), Caliban (Clabe Hartley), Lucius (Mark Arnold), Shafeen (Terri Ivens), Farr (Alan Oppenheimer), Sebastian (Lochlyn Munro), Harson (Jeff Moldovan), Harris (Stephen Macht).

Synopsis: In 2353, Jack Deth continues to travel up and down the time line to keep things in order. Shark, Jack's android companion, doesn't make it back from the last mission, and Jack is to be sent alone to investigate a time distortion in Kansas in 2160. Attacked in the time machine before he can start, he ends up who-knows-where during his tussle with the alien and discovers the medieval-like kingdom of Orpheus. Trancer "nobles" rule, periodically draining their subjects of a little or a lot of their life force to sustain themselves. After being captured by Lord Caliban, Jack is rescued by the rebels known as "tunnel rats." With the trancers on their trail, the humans know they must strike first and ambush their oppressors. During the fight,

Jack ascends a rocky outcropping and raises his pistol to the air. He temporarily disappears after being invested with a special force from the wizard Oberon's visage. Caliban rushes to the spot. Reappearing below, Jack shoots him, and Caliban disappears. Although Orpheus is rid of trancers, Jack is still stuck there.

Review: "New setting and swordplay breathe life into the series." (Mick Martin and Marshal Porter, *Video Movie Guide 1995*, p. 1085)

Analysis: The Romanian castle and forest outdoor locations give this a slight edge over the previous entry, but Jack still gets caught without much trouble. He's still got a big chip on his shoulder. (Thomerson wouldn't be tired of the character, would he?) Why didn't his special gun or time-stopping watch work properly in Orpheus? Worse, the trancers can be killed by arrows or deadfalls, yet this isn't done until the finale. So what did the humans need Jack for? *Trancers 4* is wide open for yet another B-video sequel.

Trancers 5: Sudden Deth
(Full Moon Entertainment, 1994; 73 min.) **

Produced by Vlad and Oana Paunescu. Executive Producer, Charles Band. Directed by David Nutter. Screenplay, Peter David. Edited by Lisa Bromwell. Director of Photography, Adolfo Bartoli. Color, Foto-Kem. Music, Gary Fry. Dolby. Art Direction—USA, Arlan Jay Vetter. Set Designer—USA, Milo. Special Effects Makeup, AlchemyFX, Michael S. Deak.

Cast: Jack Deth (Tim Thomerson), Lyra (Stacie Randall), Prospero (Ty Miller), Shaleen (Terri Ivens), Caliban (Clabe Hartley), Lucius (Mark Arnold), Farr (Alan Oppenheimer), Harson (Jeff Moldovan), Celia (Luana Stoica), Tessa (Rona Hartner), Angelo (Ion Haiduc), Defiant noble (Mihai Dinvale), Harris (Stephen Macht).

Synopsis: After a month of Tunnel Rat attacks, the Trancers are scattered and in hiding. Caliban, their leader, remains dead or missing due to that interloper from another dimension, Jack Deth. As Caliban's castle falls, Lucius takes the leader's portrait and flees. Caliban's son Prospero continues to help the humans although Jack is

suspect of his motives. Meantime, Caliban appears via his portrait. Deciphering runes, Prospero informs Jack that if he obtains a large jewel in the Castle of Unrelenting Terror, he may be able to return to his realm. While Prospero guides Jack, the sorcerer Farr appears to Jack's paramour Lyra and says it's time for her to use her gift. When he fades away she begins a charcoal drawing. In the Castle of Unrelenting Terror, Jack and Prospero are entertained by a host of dancing girls whose goal, they finally realize, is to keep them there forever. Back at Caliban's castle, Lyra continues to draw pictures of the respective castles as well as a "beyond" in the sky. Encountering his double, Jack remembers Lyra's remarks about reaching into his heart for what he treasures. He thrusts his hand into his double's chest and extracts the jewel. The dog that had saved Prospero's life from an assassin in the forest reappears and turns into Caliban! Knocking Jack aside, Caliban duels with his son. The lord wins, gets the jewel and locks up his two enemies. Using the magic of the jewel, Caliban returns to his castle. Jack and Prospero break free and ride swiftly back. The castle is besieged by trancers. Harson knocks Lucius onto Shaleen's sword. Caliban throws a knife into Jack's chest. Prospero cuts the cord around his father's neck, thus severing the jewel from him. Caliban retrieves it, but when he turns, he is impaled on his son's sword. When Jack shoots it with his gun, both he and Prospero disappear. Back in Jack's world, Lyra and Harris think Jack is lost forever, but Jack appears and Prospero decides he'd like to hang around. He no longer has a hunger for the life force of humans. Harris says he really loves Alice, and Jack wants to start clean with this Lyra.

Review: "This is hardly art, but Thomerson's unflappability and cynical humor, combined with a fast pace, make for an enjoyable romp through drive-in land." (Mick Martin and Marsha Porter, *Video Movie Guide 1997*, p. 1115)

Analysis: Nicely photographed in the forests and castles of Romania, it's not dull though there's no surfeit of action. The chip on Jack's shoulder wears a bit thin at times, however. The fact that Prospero doesn't revert to villainy is refreshing. How often in Hollywood films do the writers or producers contrive a bad guy just to add one more (usually unnecessary) wrinkle to an already fascinating film? See Donald Pleasence in *Fantastic Voyage* (1966) and Paul Reiser in *Aliens* (1986), for instance. Filmed at Buftea Studios, Bucharest, Romania.

Twins of Evil *see under* The Vampire Lovers

20,000 Leagues Under the Sea
(Buena Vista, 1954; 127 min.)****

Directed by Richard Fleischer. Screenplay, Earl Felton. Based on the novel by Jules Verne. Edited by Elmo Williams. Director of Photography, Franz Planer. Technicolor. Technicolor Color Consultant, Morgan Padelford. Cinemascope. Underwater Photography, Till Gabbani. Music, Paul Smith. Orchestration, Joseph S. Dubin. Diving Master, Fred Zendar. Special Processes, Ub Iwerks. Art Direction, John Meehan. Set Decoration, Emile Kuri. Matte Artist, Peter Ellenshaw. Costumes, Norman Martien. Special Effects, John Hench and Josh Meador. Effects Photographer, Ralph Hammeras.

Cast: Ned Land (Kirk Douglas), Captain Nemo (James Mason), Professor Aronnax (Paul Lucas), Conseil (Peter Lorre), Mate (Robert J. Wilke), John Howard (Carleton Young), Captain Farragut (Ted De Corsia), Diver (Percy Helton), Lincoln Mate (Ted Cooper), Casey Moore (Fred Graham), Shipping agent (Edward Marr), Billy (J. M. Kerrigan).

Synopsis: In 1868, oceanic expert Professor Aronnax and his apprentice, Conseil, accept the U.S. government's invitation to become passengers on a warship traversing the South Seas in search of a "monster" that has sunk several ships. For three and a half months the search is fruitless. Then a nearby ship is sunk and the warship fires on what appears to be a monster. It turns and rams its attacker, throwing Aronnax, Conseil and the harpooner Ned Land overboard. They climb onto the monster: a submarine. No one seems to be aboard. Through a port, the three observe men in diving suits burying a comrade. These men turn out to be Captain Nemo

and his crew; the submarine is the *Nautilus*. The professor declines his host's invitation to stay aboard and joins Conseil and Ned on the deck as the *Nautilus* begins to submerge. Nemo surfaces, telling Aronnax he wanted to find out if he would die for his fellow man. The *Nautilus* proceeds to the island of Crespo, where the crew "hunts" for its food under the sea. Ned and Conseil find treasure on a sunken ship and are saved from a shark by Nemo. He reveals to Ned that he has plenty of treasure, which he uses for ballast. Aronnax gets a concession from Ned that he won't start a one-man revolt — yet. Nemo shows Aronnax his source of power, a universal energy source that could destroy, or help, the world above. Nemo takes Aronnax to observe a slave labor camp where the inmates are mining nitrates and phosphates for purposes of war. He reveals that he was once a prisoner there. With other escapees, he built the *Nautilus* on the island of Volcania. He uses the *Nautilus* now to sink the ship leaving the prison colony. Aronnax protests. "You call that murder?... I am the avenger!" counters Nemo, who says his wife and young son were tortured to death. While Nemo supervises repairs, Ned and Conseil who also wants to escape search for charts and maps. Ned puts messages in bottles and tosses them overboard. While the *Nautilus* is stuck on a New Guinea reef, Ned and Conseil are allowed to go ashore, ostensibly to collect flora and fauna. Ned, however, takes a trail inland, disregarding Nemo's warnings about cannibals. He soon finds the captain was right and rushes back to the shore. He and Conseil row to the *Nautilus*, where Nemo electrifies the hull to dissuade the natives. Irate, Nemo has Ned incarcerated. A warship is spotted. The *Nautilus* breaks free as shells pepper the ocean. The propeller shaft is damaged, and the ship sinks further than man has ever been. The shaft is repaired and the submarine begins its ascent, but a giant squid attaches itself to the hull. Surfacing amidst a raging storm, Nemo and his men endeavor to dislodge the creature. Nemo is pulled under the water, but Ned, who has escaped his cabin, rescues him. Aronnax questions Nemo's

Captain Nemo (James Mason) meets a very large squid in *20,000 Leagues Under the Sea* (Buena Vista, 1954).

philosophy and finds that Nemo planned to use him as an emissary to the world. Now he's not so sure it would work and bring peace. They approach Volcania and find it surrounded by warships. Taking the *Nautilus* through the undersea tunnel to the lagoon, Nemo sets an explosive charge to his compound. He is wounded returning to the submarine. Dying, he intends this to be the *Nautiluss'* last dive. His crew agrees but Ned doesn't. He fights off the first mate and takes the submarine up to a reef. With Aronnax, Conseil and the seal Esmeralda, he rows away as a tremendous explosion destroys Volcania and the *Nautilus* sink into the depths.

Reviews: "As fabulous and fantastic as anything [Disney] has ever done in cartoons." (Bosley Crowther, *New York Times*, December 24, 1954, p. 7) ¶"A very special kind of picture making, combining photographic ingenuity, imaginative story telling and fiscal daring." (*Variety*, December 15, 1954) ¶"Long master shots, carefully, colorfully, and impeccably composed in Cinemascope, evoke a moody, intensely placid existence....The film is timeless, knowing no age, a natural for any time, and it deserves to be re-released every seven years from now to infinity." (Dale Winogura, *Cinefantastique*, Fall 1971, pp. 38–39 for reissue)

Analysis: The most aesthetically pleasing of all cinema vehicles, the majestic *Nautilus* is as much the star as the actors. The film should be seen in a theater, because it suffers mightily when seen on TV without letterboxing. It's a thoughtful as well as visually exciting show. The moral dilemma: stop war by killing its agents, noncombatants as well as soldiers? The film validates the concept of maintaining the period setting of the novel, a major flaw in the previous year's screen translation of H. G. Wells's *The War of the Worlds*. In 1959 James Mason would play another Verne hero in *Journey to the Center of the Earth*. Kirk Douglas's song "A Whale of a Tale" is remembered by a generation of moviegoers. Academy Award for special effects.

Mysterious Island

(Columbia, 1961; 101 min.) ***

Produced by Charles H. Schneer. Directed by Cy Endfield. Screenplay, John Prebble, Daniel Ullman, Crane Wilbur. Based on the novel by Jules Verne. Director of Photography, Wilkie Cooper. Eastman Color. Music, Bernard Herrmann. Special Effects, Ray Harryhausen. Superdynamation.

Cast: Captain Cyrus Harding (Michael Craig), Gideon Spilett (Gary Merrill), Herbert Brown (Michael Callan), Captain Nemo (Herbert Lom), Marquisa Maria Labrino (Joan Greenwood), Elena (Beth Rogan), Sergeant Pencroft (Percy Herbert), Neb (Dan Jackson), Tom (Nigel Green).

Synopsis: During the American Civil War, three Union soldiers escape from a Confederate prisoner of war camp in an observation balloon. Also aboard are newspaper correspondent Spilett and rebel soldier Pencroft. A storm blows the balloon across the continent and far into the Pacific. Landing on a desert isle, the men are soon joined by the shipwrecked Lady Mary and her niece, Elena. After exploring the island, they set up a base camp in a cave and begin building a boat. Their work is hampered by a giant crab and a giant, flightless bird. Finding a floating sea chest with weapons, books, a telescope and sextant from the *Nautilus*—believed to have been lost with all hands off the coast of Mexico eight years before—they attempt to fight off buccaneers. Just when the pirates' cannons find the range, an explosion rocks and sinks the ship. Meanwhile, Elena and Herbert have escaped from a giant beehive and discovered a submarine in a grotto. When the tide recedes they swim out to the beach. A strange-looking creature emerges from the surf, and Elena runs for help while Herbert waits, knife in hand. The creature removes headgear and reveals a man: Captain Nemo. When the others arrive, he admits that it was he who made the fire for the unconscious Captain Harding, he who floated the sea chest to them, he who brought down the bird with a shot, he who sank the pirate ship. Having demonstrated ingenuity and resourcefulness, they can help him raise the pirate craft. The *Nautilus* is incapable of moving, but escape is necessary due to the imminent eruption of the island's smoking volcano. Nemo recounts his experiments with living things, how he's created the giant plants and animals Harding and the castaways encountered. Whereas he once sought to destroy the weapons of war, by using his newfound knowledge he can stop war's causes: famine and want. The volcano begins erupting, and Nemo is resigned to death until Harding convinces him they can raise the pirate ship with their inflated balloon. This is accomplished after a battle with a many-tentacled undersea creature, but Nemo is trapped in the *Nautilus*. Harding and the others vow to continue his work for mankind.

Review: "Spirited direction...." (Eugene Archer, *New York Times*, December 21, 1961, p. 30) ¶"Will appeal to audiences seeking escape and easy diversion, and content to get along without dramatic nuance." (Tube., *Variety*, December 13, 1961)

Analysis: The Ray Harryhausen stop-motion creatures are not in Verne's 1870 novel—which is fine without them—but they are very welcome here. The mixing of real volcano eruptions with process shots is somewhat jarring. *Variety* praised both the underwater photography and the music score. Handsome Michael Craig is British but seems the complete Union officer. The *New York Times* found Joan Greenwood's vocal style "pleasantly distracting." We always wondered what happened to cute Beth Rogan. At the 1990 FANEX convention in Baltimore, Harryhausen told the authors she married a footwear magnate and retired from the screen.

Captain Nemo and the Underwater City

(MGM, 1969; 106 min.) **½

Produced by Bertram Ostrer. Directed by James Hill. Screenplay, Pip and Jane Baker. Inspired by the novel *20,000 Leagues Under the Sea* by Jules Verne. Edited by Bill Lewthwaite. Director of Photography, Alan Hume. Underwater Photography, Egil S. Woxholt. Panavision. Metrocolor. Music, Wally Stott. Art Direction, Bill Andrews. Costumes, Olga Lehmann. Special Effects, Jack Mills. Special Effects Photography, George Gibbs, Richard Conway.

Elena (Beth Rogan) and Herbert (Michael Callan) fight their way out of a giant bee-hive on *Mysterious Island* (Columbia, 1961).

Cast: Captain Nemo (Robert Ryan), Senator Robert Fraser (Chuck Connors), Mala (Luciana Paluzzi), Helena (Nanette Newman), Swallow (Kenneth Connor), Joab (John Turner), Barnaby (Bill Fraser), Lomax (Allan Cuthbertson), Engineer (Ralph Nosseck), Philip (Christopher Hartstone), Mate/Navigator (Vincent Harding), Sailors (Michael McGovern, Anthony Bailey, Alan Barry), Barmaids (Ann Patrice, Margot Ley, Patsy Snell).

Synopsis: A vessel sailing from New York to Bristol in the 1860s founders during a storm. A handful of passengers are tossed overboard, but their descending forms are intercepted by undersea swimmers, bedecked with light sources and self-contained breathing devices. The newcomers are taken aboard a large, swiftly moving submarine. Senator Robert Fraser awakens as one of the shipwreck survivors. The others are Helena and her son Philip, the engineer Lomax, and two brothers, the charlatans Barnaby and Swallow. These

survivors are introduced to their rescuer and host, Captain Nemo, who transports them in his ship, the *Nautilus*, to the underwater city of Templemere. This domed metropolis is the home of thousands who live and work on the ocean's floor, enjoying both the bounty of the sea and the advanced scientific knowledge of their leader, Nemo. Lomax finds Templemere oppressive and feels claustrophobic, so he tries to escape. His first attempt fails, and during the second, which nearly spells Templemere's destruction, he drowns. Barnaby and Swallow are stupefied to learn that the oxygen-generating machinery of Templemere produces huge volumes of solid gold as a by-product. Ultimately, Barnaby devises a plan to escape with as much gold as they can smuggle out. Fraser, who was originally bound for Europe on an important diplomatic assignment for the Civil War–torn United States, is desperate to leave. While in Templemere, he has fallen in love with Mala, who also happens to be the love object of Nemo's second-in-command, Joab. When Barnaby learns of the existence of the *Nautilus II*, he plants the idea in Joab's mind to help Fraser escape. With Joab's help, Fraser, Barnaby and Swallow leave Templemere in the *Nautilus II*, with Nemo in hot pursuit in his submarine. Barely managing to make it through the tight squeeze of a barrier reef, the *Nautilus II* is severely damaged, forcing Fraser and the brothers to don underwater breathing gear and abandon their ship. Barnaby, however, succumbs to his greed and replaces his breather with strands of jewels and gold — a fatal error. Fraser and Swallow swim to the surface as Nemo, resigned to letting the American regain his freedom, returns with Helena and Philip, who have chosen to remain in Templemere.

Review: "Robert Ryan is a solid Capt. Nemo.... Nemo's anti-war bent gives redeeming social value, special effects are good, only the somewhat formless story disappoints." (*Castle of Frankenstein* 16, July 1970, p. 53)

Analysis: Captain Nemo and the Underwater City is passable juvenile entertainment with handsome (though too slick) production values. It is too lightweight and unfocused for serious consideration, and has nothing to do with any of the writings of Jules Verne, but does make for a diversion. This is a handsome enough production that makes one wish that the producers had aimed for something rather heavier, rather than the decidedly dry, pacifist agenda that seems to inform it (a subplot that involves a gigantic mutated manta ray serves no purpose beyond providing for some contrived action by Connors' character). Certainly, the cast, while being asked to portray ciphers rather than realistically motivated characters, was capable of heavier stuff; Robert Ryan could have made a truly memorable Nemo, and Chuck Connors, at his physical peak at the time of this feature, could have provided better heroics than the manta ray fight. U.S. release was 1970.

Notes of Interest: Jules Verne's novel *20,000 Leagues Under the Sea* was published in 1870. Georges Méliès made a French film version in 1907. Another silent movie version appeared in 1916. The first *Mysterious Island* (1929) was silent except for 5 minutes of sound at the start. The characters in that version did not have the names of Verne's creations! Columbia produced a 15-episode serial in 1951 with Richard Crane.

2001: A Space Odyssey
(MGM, 1968; 141 min.) ****

Produced and directed by Stanley Kubrick. Screenplay, Stanley Kubrick and Arthur C. Clarke. Based on Clarke's short story "The Sentinel." Edited by Ray Lovejoy. Directors of Photography, Geoffrey Unsworth and John Alcott. Super Panavision. Metrocolor. Cinerama. Music: "Gayne Ballet Suite" by Aram Khachaturian, "Atmospheres," Lux Aeterna," "Requiem" by Gyorgy Ligeti, "The Blue Danube" by Johann Strauss, "Thus Spake Zarathustra" by Richard Strauss. Sound Supervision, A. W. Watkins. Sound Editor, Winston Ryder. Art Direction, John Hoesli. Makeup, Stuart Freeborn. Special Photographic Effects designed and directed by Stanley Kubrick. Special Photographic Effects Supervision, Wally Veevers, Douglas Trumbull, Con Pederson, Tom Howard. Special Photographic Effects Unit, Colin J. Cantwell, Bryan Loftus, Frederick Martin, Bruce Logan, David Osborne, John Jack Malick. Scientific Consultant, Frederick I. Ordway, III.

Cast: Dave Bowman (Keir Dullea), Frank Poole (Gary Lockwood), Dr. Heywood Floyd (William Sylvester), Moonwatcher (Daniel Richter), HAL 9000 (Douglas Rain), Smyslov (Leonard Rossiter), Elena (Margaret Tyzack), Halvorsen (Robert Beatty), Michaels (Sean Sullivan), Mission Controller (Frank Miller), Stewardess (Penny Brahms), Poole's father (Alan Gifford), Stewardess (Edwina Carroll), "Squirt" (Vivian Kubrick). With Edward Bishop, Mike Lovell, Peter Delman, Danny Grover, Brian Hawley, Glenn Beck, Ann Gillis, Heather Downham, John Ashley, Jimmy Bell, David Charkham, Simon Davis, Jonathan Daw, Peter Delmar, Terry Duggan, David Fleetwood, David Hines, Tony Jackson, John Jordan, Scott Mackee, Laurence Marchant, Darryl Pacs, Joe Refalo, Andy Wallace, Bob Wilyman, Richard Wood.

Synopsis: "The Dawn of Man": Ape-like creatures discover a rectangular black monolith, touch it, and begin using bones as

Astronaut Dave Bowman (Keir Dullea) re-enters the *Discovery* preparatory to disconnecting HAL in *2001: A Space Odyssey* (MGM, 1968).

weapons, first to kill animals for food, and then to kill another ape and drive off its kin from a water hole. The leader tosses his weapon into the sky, where it becomes a spaceship of the late twentieth century. Dr. Heywood Floyd journeys to the moon base at Clavius, from there to investigate the monolith discovered near Tycho crater. As Floyd and other scientists pose for a photo in front of the alien structure, an alignment of sun and earth takes place and an ear-splitting sound is heard. Eighteen months later, mankind launches the USS *Discovery* toward the solar system's largest planet, Jupiter. Crewmen Dave Bowman and Frank Poole are assisted by HAL 9000, an almost sentient computer. Although it gives no credence to reports of a strange item found on the moon, HAL begins having reservations about the mission. HAL tells the men that an element of the outside antenna will malfunction within seventy-two hours. Dave retrieves the device, but no flaw can be discovered. HAL says he is puzzled and suggests the device be reinstalled. When it does fail, they will know the answer. Dave and Frank consult in one of the pods. Both have misgivings about HAL. Frank wonders how HAL would react to being disconnected. Unknown to them, HAL is watching through the port and reading their lips. When Frank goes out to work on the antenna, HAL causes the pod to crash into him. Frank's oxygen line is disconnected, and he tumbles into

space. Dave tracks Frank in another pod. Inside the *Discovery*, HAL disrupts the life support systems of three hibernating astronauts. When Dave returns to the ship with Frank gripped in the pod's arms, HAL refuses to open the pod bay door and Dave, sans helmet, propels himself into the airlock. HAL argues with Dave but the man enters the Logic Memory Center and disconnects the now fearful computer: "Dave, stop. Stop, will you? Stop, Dave. Will you stop, Dave? Stop, Dave. I'm afraid. I'm afraid, Dave. Dave, my mind is going. I can feel it. I can feel it." As Dave completes the task, he receives a prerecorded video message about the mission from Dr. Floyd. Revealed is heretofore secret information, namely that a black monolith found on the moon sends a powerful signal to Jupiter. The monolith may be the key to other intelligent life in the universe. "Jupiter and Beyond the Infinite": Nearing the giant planet, Dave exits the *Discovery* and enters new dimensions, arriving at last in an earthlike, opulently furnished bedroom. He witnesses the stages of his life and watches a monolith from his deathbed. Reborn as a fetus, he floats above Earth.

Reviews: "[Kubrick's] potentially majestic myth ... dwindles into a whimsical space operetta.... The imagery is just obscure enough to be annoying, just precise enough to be banal." (Joseph Morgenstern, *Newsweek*, April 15, 1968, p. 97) ¶"Some sort of great film, and an unforgettable endeavor.... The film is not only hideously funny.... It is also a uniquely poetic piece of sci-fi...." (Penelope Gilliatt, *New Yorker*, April 13, 1968, p. 150) ¶"Somewhere between hypnotic and immensely boring." (Renata Adler, *New York Times*, April 4, 1968, p. 58) ¶"The ambiguous ending is at once appropriate and wrong. It guarantees that the film will arouse controversy, but it leaves doubt that the film makers themselves knew precisely what they were flying at." (*Time*, April 19, 1968, pp. 91–92) ¶"*2001* must ... be seen as a great step forward in film history. It deals with science fiction not on the level set by hundreds of Buck Rogers epics, nor in the vein of the flood of mediocrity since, but on a plane commensurate with the skill and depth of higher Man. Its creators have not condescended to the sci-fi film genre, they have uplifted it." (Michael Sargow, *Film Society Review*, January 1970, p. 26)

Analysis: 2001 was the controversial movie of 1968, a film about nothing — and everything. Some of us were content to enjoy without qualification this visual, visceral experience. *Time* had it right, pointing out that despite its problems, it was an excellent depiction of the "beauty and terror" of space. We were oblivious to any negative connotations about humanity, or technology. Many critics had to "understand" it. Many adults were bored. Because word of mouth made it a hit, like 1967's *Bonnie and Clyde*, many reviewers felt obliged to see it a second time and revise their original opinion. For those who want in-depth analysis and possible answers, Carolyn Geduld's *Filmguide to 2001: A Space Odyssey* (Bloomington, IN: Indiana University Press, 1973) provides a good starting point. This will present a reasonable analysis of the perplexing ending. Some of the audience wanted monsters, or at least visible aliens. But this was Kubrick, not *Alien*. Wasn't it disappointing to see the aliens in *Close Encounters of the Third Kind* a decade later? It's a conundrum. We want to see aliens, but we really have no idea what they are like and are inevitably disappointed. Arthur C. Clarke made a 15-city U.S. promotional tour for this film. Word of mouth was important. Confoundingly,

2001 did not receive a Best Picture Academy Award nomination. Those that did were *Oliver!* (winner), *Romeo and Juliet*, *The Lion in Winter, Funny Girl* and *Rachel, Rachel*. *2001* did win an Academy Award for state-of-the-art special visual effects. Kubrick was nominated for Best Director. It should have received an award for the ape makeup. The apes of *2001* are so convincing, one scratches one's head, wondering if these really are apes? (We can't believe the Academy distinguished between apeman and apes and thus gave *Planet of the Apes* the statuette.) Originally 160 minutes, *2001* was cut by Kubrick after its initial release.

2010
(MGM/United Artists, 1984; 114 min.) ***

Produced and directed by Peter Hyams. Screenplay, Peter Hyams. Based on a novel by Arthur C. Clarke. Edited by James Mitchell. Director of Photography, Peter Hyams. Panavision. Metrocolor. Music, David Shire. Dolby Stereo. Set Decoration, Rick Simpson. Visual Effects, Richard Edlund. Special Effects, Henry Millar. Stop-Motion, Randall William Cook.

Cast: Heywood Floyd (Roy Scheider), Walter Curnow (John Lithgow), Tanya Kirbuk (Helen Mirren), R. Chandra (Bob Balaban), Dave Bowman (Keir Dullea), HAL 9000 (Douglas Rain), Caroline Floyd (Madolyn Smith), Dimitri Moisevitch (Dana Elcar), Christopher Floyd (Taliesin Jaffe), Victor Milson (James McEachin), Betty Fernandez (Mary Jo Deschanel), Maxim Brailovsky (Elya Baskin), Vladimir Rudinko (Savely Kramarov), Vasali Oriov (Oleg Rudnik), Irina Yakuknina (Natasha Schneider), Yuri Svetlanov (Vladimir Skornarovsky), Mikolai Ternovsky (Victor Steinbach), Alexander Kovalev (Jan Triska), Jessie Bowman (Herta Ware).

Synopsis: Dimitri Moisevitch approaches Heywood Floyd with a bold proposition, namely that the U.S. and the Soviet Union collaborate on the forthcoming Jupiter mission to unlock the secrets of the USS *Discovery*. After all, the *Leonov* will be ready for launch before the American craft. Moisevitch reveals that the *Discovery's* orbit has changed and time is of the essence. Floyd tells his wife he'll be leaving in four months. Two days from Jupiter, Floyd is awakened from hibernation. When he doesn't receive the briefing he'd like, he learns that Cold War problems on Earth have made the Soviet crew close-mouthed. Nevertheless, the mission continues, and an unmanned probe is sent to investigate a possible life form on Jupiter's moon Europa. The probe is destroyed, which to Floyd is a warning. The *Leonov* "airbrakes" around Jupiter and takes an orbit around the moon Io near the *Discovery*. Dave Bowman's "My God, it's full of stars" haunts Floyd. Chandra and Curnow are awakened. Curnow and Maxim enter the *Discovery*, find breathable air, stop the ship's spinning, and turn on the reserve power. After connecting to the *Leonov*, Chandra enters HAL's logic area and begins to restore the computer's power. Distrusting HAL, Floyd gives Curnow a small explosive device to be detonated if necessary. The giant monolith floating in space is the next target. Although Floyd argues against it, Tanya sends Max to investigate, and his pod is sent careening into space. On Earth, Dave Bowman's visage appears to wife Betty. He tells her "something wonderful" will happen. Back in Jupiter space, Chandra explains how HAL was trapped into doing what he did by a National Security Council directive. HAL was told to lie. Nor did Bowman or Poole know about the monolith. Only the hibernating crew did. Due to an escalating Cold War crisis between the U.S. and USSR, a message from Earth orders the three Americans to stay on the *Discovery*. It seems to have enough power to return them to Earth. HAL tells Floyd he is receiving a message to leave Jupiter within two days. "I was David Bowman" says the image of the lost astronaut that now appears to Floyd. He says something wonderful will happen but that they must leave. Floyd convinces Tanya to use the *Discovery* as a booster. The monolith disappears. A dark spot on Jupiter becomes larger, and direct observation by HAL reveals 1,355,000, 1x4x9 monoliths in the circle, which seems to be growing and swallowing the planet. HAL is suspicious and wants to abort the firing of the *Discovery*'s engines but Chandra tells HAL

the truth, that after being used as a booster, the *Discovery* will be abandoned. "Dr. Chandra, will I dream?" asks HAL. After the U.S. ship uses up its fuel, the *Leonov* employs its own rockets to put more distance between itself and Jupiter. In the *Discovery*, Dave's voice asks HAL to point the ship's antenna toward Earth. This message is broadcast: "ALL THESE WORLDS ARE YOURS EXCEPT EUROPA ATTEMPT NO LANDING THERE USE THEM TOGETHER USE THEM IN PEACE." The *Leonov* is rocked by an expanding shock wave from Jupiter. A new sun has been created. Before going into hibernation, Floyd writes that he still doesn't know what the monolith is. But Earth has a new lease on life and a warning from the landlord. The new sun shines on Europa and a monolith standing in a primeval swamp.

Review: "The HAL mystery is the most satisfying substance of the film and handled the best.... audience can't really follow at all...." (Har., *Variety*, November 28, 1984)

Analysis: Hyams is trying to answer the unanswerable, but it's still an engrossing, tense piece of visually arresting space exploration. It's a tribute to Britisher Helen Mirren that she can be the Russian ship's skipper. (Why hasn't Mirren received more "big" movie roles?) The Cold War subplot is sometimes bothersome but does perhaps play a part in the alien entity's decision to cause "something wonderful" to happen.

2010 *see under* **2001: A Space Odyssey**

The Undiscovered Country *see* Star Trek VI: The Undiscovered Country *under* **Star Trek — The Motion Picture**

Unidentified Flying Oddball *see under* **A Connecticut Yankee**

Urban Harvest *see* Children of the Corn III: Urban Harvest *under* **Children of the Corn**

Vampira *see* Old Dracula *under* **Dracula**

The Vampire Lovers

(Hammer/AIP, 1970; 91 min.) ***½

Produced by Harry Fine and Michael Style. Directed by Roy Ward Baker. Assistant Director, Derek Whitehurst. Screenplay, Tudor Gates. Adaptation by Harry Fine. Based on the novella *Carmilla* by J. Sheridan Le Fanu. Edited by James Needs. Director of Photography, Moray Grant. Technicolor. Music, Harry Robinson. Musical Supervision, Philip Martell. Sound Editor, Roy Hyde. Art Direction, Scott MacGregor. Makeup, Tom Smith. Costumes, Brian Box.

Cast: Marcilla/Mircalla/Carmilla (Ingrid Pitt), Emma (Madeline Smith), Carl Ebbhardt (Jon Finch), General von Spielsdorf (Peter Cushing), Madame Perrodot (Kate O'Mara), Laura (Pippa Steele), Doctor (Ferdy Mayne), Countess (Dawn Addams), Baron Hartog (Douglas Wilmer), Morton (George Cole), Renton (Harvey Hall), Vampiress (Kirsten Betts), Man in black (John Forbes Robertson), Landlord (Charles Farrell), Gretchen (Janet Key).

Synopsis: Styria, 1794. Baron von Hartog attracts a beautiful female vampire by waving her stolen shroud; he then decapitates her, putting what he thinks is an end to the Karnsteins, a family of vampires responsible for his sister Isabella's death. Unbeknownst to Von Hartog, Mircalla Karnstein (1522-1546) has escaped. Masquerading as the daughter of a countess and using the *nom de plume* Marcilla, she insinuates herself into the home of General Spielsdorf, where she drains daughter Laura of her blood and life. Later, as Carmilla, she is welcomed into the home of visiting Briton Mr. Morton. She seduces Morton's daughter Emma and the governess, Madame Perrodot. Against Perrodot's wishes, Renton the butler calls in the doctor. Enraged and afraid that the physician will foil her plans, Carmilla trails and kills him. Returning from his business trip at the behest of Renton, Morton listens to the inn's landlord tell him of Baron Hartog and the terrible Karnsteins. Renton urges him to seek out General Spielsdorf. On his way to the Spielsdorf home, he encounters a coach carrying the General and Baron Hartog. Carl reveals the body of the doctor. While the rest head for Karnstein Castle, Carl rides to Emma. Having thought that Madame Perrodot

was responsible for Emma's deteriorating condition, Renton is unprepared for seduction and death at Carmilla's hands. Afterward she gathers up Emma, kills Perrodot and encounters Carl. Brushing aside his sword, she begins to strangle him but allows herself to be distracted by Emma. Carl pulls out his dagger, and Carmilla backs off from the sign of the cross and disappears into thin air. At Karnstein Castle, Spielsdorf, Harog and Morton search for Mircalla's coffin. Spying her, they follow her inside. Providentially, Morton notes a pendant on the floor. Removing the slab, they remove the coffin to the chapel, where Spielsdorf puts a stake into Carmilla's heart and beheads her. Emma is released from Carmilla's spell. Mircalla's portrait ages.

Reviews: "Smoothly and stylishly directed.... has a bevy of beautiful women, and some decent acting. But in sum, it's really the same old ritualistic stuff." (Donald J. Mayerson, *Cue*, February 20, 1971) ¶"First of a series of Lesbian vampire films to star the magnificently structured Ingrid Pitt.... There is really little impact left in the old LeFanu story." (Alan Dodd, *L'Incroyable Cinema: The Film Magazine of Fantasy & Imagination*, Spring 1971, p. 35) ¶"'Vampires are intelligent beings,' one authority remarks. They are also, in this film, gorgeous, as are their victims. Ingrid Pitt, Dawn Addams, Pippa Steele, Madeleine Smith and Kate O'Mara are absolutely yummy." (Judith Crist, *New York*, February 15, 1971, p. 56) ¶"Campy, literate, witty and dead-straight vampire movie. Luscious Ingrid Pitt plays a lesbian vampire who likes the blood of young maidens only. With Peter Cushing, Dawn Addams and countless beauties." (Joe Baltake, *Philadelphia Daily News*, November 27, 1970). ¶"One or two compensations, notably the bizarre appearances of Dawn Addams as a sort of vampires' Elsa Maxwell, making quite sure that her young ladies are on blood-sucking terms with all the right people." (*Times*, September 4, 1970, p. 11)

Analysis: As Kurt Brokaw wrote in *A Night in Transylvania*, this is probably the most beautifully photographed vampire movie. The creepiest and most evocative scene shows Carmilla gliding through the

Ingrid Pitt in *The Vampire Lovers* (Hammer/AIP, 1970).

mist to Karnstein Castle. Prudes and stuffed shirts had a conniption about this first Hammer film with nudity. Nevertheless, Hammer cannot be faulted for instituting something new. Screenwriter Tudor Gates said, "I went to see a number of Hammer films. While I enjoyed them, the one thing that struck me was that they were terribly outdated, at least for the modern cinema going public. That was the time over here when the floodgates of censorship opened. I felt that the thing to do was to bring Hammer Films up to the seventies. So I deliberately threw in the nudes and the lesbians and all the rest of it." (Bruce G. Hallenbeck, "Tudor Gates," *Little Shoppe of Horrors* No. 4 (May 1984) p. 43.) Pitt, whose first English-language starring role

Ingrid Pitt at FANEX 8 convention in Towson, Maryland, July 1994.

this was, had no objection to disrobing ("Now you don't want to do me out of my moment of glory, do you?") said she got the role the day after meeting Hammer Studios boss James Carreras at the *Alfred the Great* premiere: "I breezed into his office the next morning looking devastat- ing, clad in black maxi-gear and fetching grin. Brightly I announced that I was fit to kill and Jimmy asked if I wanted blood — so I became a vampire." (Kim Holston, "In Search of Ingrid Pitt," p. 2.) In *The Vampire Film*, Ursini and Silver posited the log- ical necessity for the vampiress's disrobe-ment before Emma. It was "the first in the pattern of sensual manipulation which the vampire practices throughout the film" (p. 112). Another spin was taken by David J. Hogan in *Dark Romance: Sexuality in the Horror Film*: "In essence, the film is a gleeful advertisement for the joys of lesbianism. That Hammer was able to get this past the censors is less a mark of the studio's ingenuity than an indictment of the review board's thickheadedness. The film's goings-on are outrageous, even offensive, if one is easily offended. But Hammer banked on the fact that horror films, a genre both despised and taken too lightly, would be able to get away with it. The studio was correct. *The Vampire Lovers'* parade of bare breasts, blood, and lesbian soul kissing would have been censored to ribbons if presented in a 'realistic' context" (pp. 155–56). Ironically, the most erotic scene in the film has no nudity: The governess is drawn inexorably to Marcilla's room. Inside, silhouetted against the moonlit window, Marcilla drops her nightdress. Madeline Smith is sometimes Madeleine. Ingrid Pitt became a cult star, following this with vampiric roles in *The House That Dripped Blood* and *Countess Dracula*. She lent a pathos to the role of Mircalla, as when she witnessed a passing funeral cortege: "You must die! Everybody must die!" Ingrid emerged from an upright coffin to introduce the three Karnstein films at the 1994 FANEX 8 convention in Baltimore hosted by the Horror and Fantasy Film Society. During one of the question-and-answer sessions that weekend, she reiterated that her Carmilla is not lesbian. She is a vampire, and vampires are asexual. Blood, not sex, is what they desire above all else. Therefore Carmilla's yearning and love for Emma is a pure love.

Notes of Interest: Like Bram Stoker, J. Sheridan Le Fanu was a master horror storyteller of the late nineteenth century and his 1871 novella *Carmilla* became, like Stoker's *Dracula*, a favored source for filmmakers. Roger Vadim's 1960 film *Blood and Roses* (French) was one manifestation. *Terror in the Crypt* was a 1963 Spanish version. One should mention that in *Captain Kronos, Vampire Hunter*, Wanda Ventham claims she's a "Karstein."

Lust for a Vampire
(Hammer/American-Continental/ MBM-EMI, 1971; 95 min.) ***

Produced by Harry Fine and Michael Style. Directed by Jimmy Sangster. Assistant Director, David Bracknell. Screenplay, Tudor Gates. Based on characters created by J. Sheridan Le Fanu. Edited by Spencer Reeve. Director of Photography, David Muir. Technicolor. Music, Harry Robinson. Musical Supervision, Philip Martell. Song "Strange Love" sung by Tracy. Lyrics, Frank Godwin. Art Direction, Don Mingaye. Makeup, George Blackler.

Cast: Mircalla (Yutte Stensgaard), Giles Barton (Ralph Bates), Richard Lestrange (Michael Johnson), Janet Playfair (Susanna Leigh), Countess Herritzen (Barbara Jefford), Susan Pelley (Pippa Steel), Count Karnstein (Mike Raven), Miss Simpson (Helen Christie), Pelley (David Healy), Landlord (Michael Brennan), Trudi (Luan Peters), Amanda (Judy Matheson), Coachman (Christopher Cunningham), Isabel (Caryl Little), Bishop (Jack Melford), Professor Hertz (Eric Chitty), Hans (Christopher Neame), Inspector Heinrich (Harvey Hall), Schoolgirls (Erica Beale, Christine Smith, Jackie Leapman, Melita Clarke, Patricia Warner, Vivienne Chandler, Sue Longhurst, Melinda Churcher).

Synopsis: Count and Countess Karnstein cut the throat of a comely maiden to resurrect their vampiric kin Mircalla. The countess takes Mircalla to a girls' school, where her beauty inflames the passions of novelist Richard Lestrange, instructor Giles Barton, and the female pupils. After the disappearance of Susan and the death of Barton, Lestrange suspects Mircalla's secret, and she responds, "It's quite simple. I *am* a Karnstein. Our family changed its name. If you've read the books you know why. That's why I look like Carmilla. And that's why my name is Mircalla. What else do you want to know? If I'm a vampire? Is that what you believe?" They make love. Instructor Janet informs the police of the dire doings at the school. Inspector Heinrich finds Susan's body in a well but is himself deposited there when a man cuts the rope on which he descended. Mircalla tries to seduce Janet, but the woman's cross pendant repels her. Susan's father arrives intent on solving the mystery of her disappearance. Though she loves Lestrange,

Yutte Stensgaard is the vampire Mircalla in *Lust for a Vampire* (Hammer/American-Continental/MBM-EMI, 1971).

Mircalla continues her depredations on the students, feasting on Amanda. The villagers obtain the help of the bishop, invade and set fire to Karnstein Castle. The vampires realize they cannot be harmed by the flames, but Mircalla, approaching Lestrange, is impaled by a falling beam.

Reviews: "Tepid horror film, more humorous than frightening.... generally stylish mounting." (*Variety*, September 15, 1971, p. 6)

Analysis: Contrary to most reviews — and critics who complained about the song "Strange Love" — this is a solid entry in the

Karnstein saga. Pippa Steele (Steel in the credits) is the first victim in this, too! Lovely Dane Yutte Stensgaard filled in for Ingrid Pitt, who was busy with bloodletting roles in *The House That Dripped Blood* and *Countess Dracula*. But Yutte is an ingenue vampire with none of the pathos or worldliness — or otherworldliness — of Pitt, and the film lacks the atmosphere of its predecessor. Harvey Hall is back as a different character and will be yet another one in *Twins of Evil*. Luan Peters and Judy Matheson will be resurrected from the dead in the next entry. Whereas Pitt's Karnstein finally was laid to rest in the nineteenth century, this Mircalla is supposed to have died the first time in 1710. Why did it take so long for her kin to resurrect her? Can a case be made that this is a prequel? That Pitt's vampiress is resurrected from Stensgaard's?

Twins of Evil
(Hammer/Universal, 1971; 87 min.)
***

Produced by Harry Fine and Michael Style. Directed by John Hough. Screenplay, Tudor Gates. Based on characters created by J. Sheridan Le Fanu. Edited by Spencer Reeve. Director of Photography, Dick Bush. Technicolor or Eastman Color. Music, Harry Robinson. Musical Supervision, Philip Martell. Art Direction, Roy Stannard. Makeup, George Blackler. Special Effects, Bert Luxford.

Cast: Frieda Gellhorn (Madelaine Collinson), Maria Gellhorn (Mary Collinson), Gustav Weil (Peter Cushing), Anton Hoffer (David Warbeck), Katy Weil (Kathleen Byron), Dietrich (Dennis Price), Count Karnstein (Damien Thomas), Gerta (Luan Peters), Franz (Harvey Hall), Ingrid Hoffer (Isobel Black), Hermann (Alex Scott), Countess Mircalla (Katya Wyeth), Joachim (Roy Stewart), Woodman (Inigo Jackson), Woodman's daughter (Judy Matheson), Aleta (Maggie Wright), Gaoler (Peter Thompson), Lady in coach (Sheelah Wilcox), Girl at stake (Kirsten Lindholm).

Synopsis: Central Europa. The Gellhorn sisters arrive at Uncle Gustav Weil's. A stern Puritan much addicted to witch burning, Weil frowns on their décolletage and frivolous behavior. Nevertheless, Frieda investigates Karnstein castle. Having been vampirized by his relation Mircalla, the decadent Count Karnstein finds Frieda a willing consort. "It is a test. One who is dedicated to the devil and his deeds will not die by a vampire's bite, but will become one of the undead, a vampire! The good and the innocent die!" Frieda attempts to seduce Anton while Maria is mistaken for Frieda. Anton fends off Frieda and convinces Weil of Maria's innocence, and she is saved from the pyre in the nick of time. Not so Frieda, who is decapitated by her uncle. Count Karnstein kills Weil but is himself impaled by Anton's well-aimed pike.

Reviews: "An above average Hammer horror entry.... good pace.... The Collinson twins are discoveries." ("Jack.," *Variety*, October 20, 1971, p. 14) ¶"If there really is a Hammer cult, and I don't believe a word of it, its followers should on no account miss *Twins of Evil*, which is pure Hammer, all throat-fanging and heart-staking and a very different kettle of fish from *Hands of the Ripper*, which is on the same bill." (David McGillivray, *Films and Filming*, January, 1972, pp. 61–62)

Analysis: This is a prequel, the story taking place before the doings in *The Vampire Lovers*. Mircalla has little to do. The Maltese-born Collinson twins were October 1970 *Playboy* centerspreads and apparently dubbed. The film is above average.

Vengeance *see* The Brain *under* **The Lady and the Monster**

The Vengeance of She *see under* **She**

Village of the Damned
(MGM, 1960; 78 min.) ***½

Produced by Ronald Kinnoch. Directed by Wolf Rilla. Screenplay, Stirling Silliphant, Wolf Rilla and George Barclay (Ronald Kinnoch). Based on the novel *The Midwich Cuckoos* by John Wyndham. Edited by Gordon Hales. Director of Photography, Geoffrey Faithfull. Music, Ron Goodwin. Art Direction, Ivan King. Makeup, Eric Aylott. Wardrobe, Eileen Sullivan. Hairstyles, Joan Johnstone. Photographic Effects, Ron Howard.

Cast: Gordon Zellaby (George Sanders), Anthea Zellaby (Barbara Shelley), David Zellaby (Martin Stephens), Alan Bernard (Michael

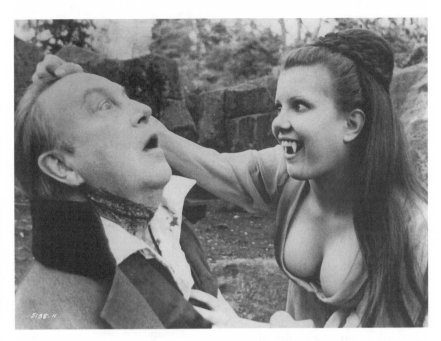

Dietrich (Dennis Price) is about to be the victim of the evil twin Frieda Gellhorn (Madelaine Collinson) in *Twins of Evil* (Hammer/Universal, 1971).

Gwynn), Mr. Willers (Laurence Naismith), Harrington (Richard Warner), Mrs. Harrington (Jenny Laird), Evelyn Harrington (Sarah Long), James Pawle (Thomas Heathcote), Janet Pawle (Charlotte Mitchell), Milly Hughes (Pamela Buck), Miss Ogle (Rosamund Greenwood), Mrs. Plumpton (Susan Richards), Vicar (Bernard Archard), Constable Gobby (Peter Vaughan), Normal children (Brian Smith, Paul Norman, John Bush, Janice Howley, Robert Marks, Billy Lawrence), Alien children (June Cowell, John Kelly, Lesley Scoble, Roger Malik, Theresa Scoble, Peter Taylor, Linda Bateson, Carlo Cura, Mark Mileham, Elizabeth Munden, Peter Priedel, Howard Knight), General Leighton (John Phillips), Sir Edgar Hargraves (Richard Vernon), Professor Smith (John Stuart), Dr. Carlisle (Keith Pyott), Coroner (Alexander Archdale), Nurse (Sheila Robins), Pilot (Tom Bowman), Lieutenant (Anthony Harrison), WRAC secretary (Diane Aubrey), Sapper (Gerald Paris) Bruno the dog (Himself).

Synopsis: One day, at 11:00 A.M., the entire population of Midwich falls unconscious. Major Alan Bernard helps cordon off the area. Whatever controls the area is static, invisible, non-metallic. Unexpectedly,

everyone wakes up. Two months later Anthea Zellaby, along with every other female of childbearing age, announces a pregnancy. When the births occur, all the children weigh over 10 pounds and have blonde hair. Their physical and mental growth is rapid. Gordon Zellaby attends a conference at which it is learned that similar births occurred in Australia and amongst the Eskimos but those children died or were killed. A surviving group lives in Russia and is being given accelerated education. Zellaby argues that he can control the strange children in Midwich and is given a year to prove it. The children won't answer when asked if their presence is proof of life on another planet. Zellaby is wrong; they can't be controlled. They use their mind control to kill a man who almost ran into them. Another is forced to shoot himself. Zellaby learns that a Russian army group west of the Urals fired an atomic cannon at the village where their alien children lived. David Zellaby says they must be left alone and wants his "father" Gordon to help them spread out so they can form new colonies. Gordon arrives at their school with a briefcase. Before they can invade his mind, his bomb explodes. Eyes seem to float away.

Reviews: "Director Wolf Rilla has handled [this] eerie tale so well that it seems as real as the most realistic of gangster thrillers. It is not for children or faint-hearted adults." (Philip T. Hartung, *Commonweal*, November 25, 1960, p. 232) ¶"One of the neatest little horror pictures produced since Peter Lorre went straight." (*Time*, December 5, 1960, p. 64) ¶"Tapers off from a taut beginning into soggy melodrama." (Rich., *Variety*, June 29, 1960, p. 8)

Analysis: This thoughtful movie was even a treat for teenagers who saw it first-run. An atomic cannon, wow, that's impressive. (A U.S. version is used in *The Return of the Living Dead*.) These children — are they the original Scanners?

Children of the Damned
(MGM, 1964; 90 min.) ***

Produced by Lawrence P. Bachmann. Associate Producer, Ben Arbeid. Directed by Anton M. Leader. Assistant Directors, Ted Sturgis, Terry Lens, Roger Simons. Screenplay, John Briley. Edited by Ernest Walter. Director of Photography, Davis Boulton. Music, Ron Goodwin. Art Direction, Elliot Scott.

Cast: Dr. Tom Lewellin (Ian Hendry), Dr. David Neville (Alan Badel), Susan Eliot (Barbara Ferris), Colin Webster (Alfred Burke), Diana Loran (Sheila Allen), Minister of Defense (Ralph Michael), Professor Gruber (Martin Miller), Harib (Harold Goldblatt), Mr. Davidson (Patrick White), Russian official (Andre Mikhelson), Mrs. Robbin (Bessie Love), Paul (Clive Powell), Mi Ling (Lee Yoke-Moon), Nina (Roberta Rex), Ago (Gerald Delsol), Rashid (Mahdu Mathen), Mark (Frank Summerscale).

Synopsis: Testing children for UNESCO in London, psychiatrist Tom Lewellin and geneticist David Neville realize Paul Loran is a prodigy. They learn that there are five others like him around the world, and plans are made to bring them all to London for further tests. Oddly, no fathers for the children can be found, and most of the mothers do not evince genius. In fact,

Paul's mother claims she was never with a man. Thinking there is a national security issue, the various governments attempt to interfere but Paul sneaks away and gathers the other children. They take up residence in an abandoned church and call Paul's aunt Susan to help them. When government agents arrive and kill the children's dog, the children make one agent shoot the other and then topple to his own death from the gallery. When the respective national representatives visit, Dr. Neville demonstrates how whatever each child learns, the others learn simultaneously. Susan tells the officials the children will live there; all they need is food. British troops are on guard outside, but four hired abductors sneak in. The children see them coming and use their minds and a self-made weapon partially composed of the church organ to render the men insensible. Government agent Colin Webster covers his ears with a scarf and, while shooting the instrument of destruction, accidentally kills Rashid. Learning that these children's blood cells are different from man's prompts Neville to theorize that they are not human and should be destroyed before they can breed and destroy humanity. Lewellin wants to give them a chance. Lewellin urges the children to return to their embassies as a token of good will. They do so but are frustrated by the uses to which they are to be put: building defensive weapons and the like. Paul causes the men interrogating him, including Webster, to kill one another. All governments agree to blow up the church and destroy the children. Professor Gruber suggests that perhaps their blood is man's a million years hence. Government representatives meet with the children once more outside the church, but a soldier drops a screwdriver against a button, which signals other soldiers to begin the bombardment. The children are killed as Lewellin and Susan and even Neville watch in horror. The camera focuses on the screwdriver.

Review: "Isn't nearly as good as its predecessor.... burdened with a 'message'...." (Tube., *Variety*, January 22, 1964)

Analysis: It's a Cold War story and one that demonstrates how mundane things — the screwdriver — can wreak havoc. It engages the attention. Likewise, Alan Badel *is* engaging, which is a shock to us who remember him as the ruthless dictator of 1969's *The Adventurers.* He and Hendry make a formidable pair until Badel goes hardline. Pert, perky Barbara Ferris had some leading roles later in the decade, e.g., *A Nice Girl Like Me.* There is no mention of Midwich. Was that covered up so well these characters had not heard of the outbreak only four years previously?

Village of the Damned

(Universal, 1995; 98 min.) **

Produced by Michael Preger and Sandy King. Directed by John Carpenter. Screenplay, David Hammerstein. Based on the book *The Midwich Cuckoos* by John Wyndham, and on the 1960 screenplay by Stirling Silliphant, Wolf Rilla, George Barclay. Edited by Edward A. Warschilka. Director of Photography, Gary B. Kribbe. Panavision. Eastman Color. Music, John Carpenter and Dave Davies. Art Direction, Christa Munro. Set Decoration, Ron De Fina, Rick Brown. Visual Effects Supervisor, Bruce Nicholson.

Cast: Alan Chaffee (Christopher Reeve), Dr. Susan Verner (Kirstie Alley), Reverend George (Mark Hamill), Jill McCowan (Linda Kozlowski), Frank McCowan (Michael Pare), Melanie Roberts (Meredith Salenger), David (Thomas Dekker), Ben Blum (Peter Jason), Callie Blum (Constance Forslund), Sarah (Pippa Pearthree), Barbara Chaffee (Karen Kahn), Mara (Lindsey Haun).

Synopsis: A mysterious force renders every living being unconscious one morning in the small West Coast village of Midwich. Later, all revive. Local authorities and the federal government are unable to find an explanation, but within a couple of months it is observed that every woman of childbearing age is pregnant. The mystery deepens when it becomes evident that they will all deliver simultaneously and that the moment of conception seems to coincide with the curious blackout. Further, many of these women are pregnant even in the absence of sexual activity. An initial potential hysteria is cut short when the federal government offers a sizable financial incentive for those families who decide to allow the pregnancies to come to term.

One family is that of the local doctor, Alan Chaffee, and his wife, Barbara. Another is Jill McGowan, who is pregnant and single, her husband Frank having been killed when he fell asleep at the wheel of his moving pickup truck during the blackout. Melanie Roberts, pregnant though still a virgin, also chooses to have her baby. Each delivery is made on the same night in a clinic erected to facilitate the births. These all go without complications, save that of Melanie, whose child is stillborn. Dr. Susan Verner, a government physician, quickly removes the dead infant for an autopsy. The surviving nine infants are all bright-eyed and fair-haired. *Very* early on they show signs of both incredibly accelerated intelligence and, when encountering a perceived threat, capable of exerting a terrible influence upon the source. Barbara Chaffee is an early victim. When she inadvertently serves daughter Mara some soup that is too hot, the mother is forced to immerse her hand in the pot. Later, Barbara commits suicide. Melanie Roberts, consumed by the guilt of her lost child, likewise kills herself. A rapport of sorts is established after a time between the widowed Dr. Chaffee and Jill McGowan's son, David. Both have lost someone: Alan, his beloved wife, and David, the stillborn daughter of Melanie. She was to have been his "other," he tells the puzzled Alan. Chaffee knows that the spate of suicides and accidents are connected to the children, and in his frustration and fear he approaches Dr. Verner. There have been other cases like Midwich, she tells him, with blackouts that resulted in the births of unusually "gifted" children. Several explanations are possible. Orthogenesis, unexpected mutation, is one. A secret governmental project artificially inseminating the women with "super-sperm" is another. Neither scenario would likely explain the widespread global occurrences, however. The third most likely explanation is xenogenesis, Verner says, with the human females being impregnated by extraterrestrial agencies. This hypothesis is given the most credibility when Verner shows the doctor the body of Melanie's stillborn infant: it appears quite alien. Whichever theory is correct, the children go on the offensive when the other colonies are destroyed. When he confronts his own daughter Mara, the child informs Alan that the Midwich group must disperse immediately to avoid a similar fate. Chaffee is now convinced that these beings will inevitably mature into a species that will dominate humanity. When he later finds Susan Verner's self-mutilated body at the clinic, he determines upon a desperate course of action. Secreting a supply of explosives in his briefcase, he enters a secluded barn where the children have taken shelter. The combined power of their super intellects is nearly able to penetrate the mental block the doctor has put over his thoughts, but not before the explosives detonate. Before the blast, however, Jill McGowan managed to escape with her son David, the one child who does show some sign of sympathy and humanity. Together, the two leave Midwich.

Review: "One scarifying trip down memory lane." (Janet Maslin, *New York Times*, April 28, 1995, p. C8)

Analysis: This isn't quite a scene-for-scene copy of the 1960 film, but the differences in the two are decidedly minor. Carpenter doesn't add much of his own other than a faddish suggestion that some sort of governmental conspiracy is operating behind the scenes. That's manifested in Kirstie Alley's character and the shadowy cabal she reports to. As it is, the government's clandestine purpose is so vague that it doesn't really add up to anything significant, although it seems to be a presence as malicious as the one behind the alien colony itself. The local Midwich residents, too, are all ciphers. We don't much give a hoot when they get charbroiled. The bright-eyed kids are a more malicious lot this time around. In the earlier film, the children did manage to gain some degree of sympathy, acting mostly in self-defense. In Carpenter's hands, they're murderous from day one and don't make any secret of their low opinion of their human cohabitants of this rural California community. The one unique angle that Carpenter introduces is the child David, who is the odd child of the group. The children are matched in male-female pairs, obviously

for later procreative purposes, and this odd little boy is all alone. His signs of normalcy and his empathy with the lonely Reeve could have been an interesting point of departure from the 1960 film. Curiously, Carpenter doesn't do a lot with this, and his film goes on its way aping the first film's plot. The plus side of Carpenter's remake is somewhat meager. It's a handsome production and the rural seacoast town of Midwich is effectively captured. The *New York Times* review called the opening scene among the "eeriest" in the history of horror. This was Christopher Reeve's last film before a horseback riding accident left him paralyzed. He delivers one of his stronger, effectively understated, performances.

Carpenter's earlier remake — of Howard Hawks's *The Thing*— departed strongly from the earlier film's premise (going instead with the literary version). Here, he adheres more closely to an earlier film, and the results are considerably less satisfying.

The Voyage Home *see* Star Trek IV: The Voyage Home *under* **Star Trek — The Motion Picture**

War of the Colossal Beast *see under* **The Amazing Colossal Man**

Warlock
(New World, 1991; 102 min.) ***

Produced and directed by Steve Miner. Screenplay, D. T. Twohy. Edited by David Finfer. Director of Photography, David Eggby. Color, DeLuxe. Prints, Technicolor. Music, Jerry Goldsmith. Art Direction, Gary Steele. Set Decoration, Jennifer Williams. Stunt Coordinator, David Ellis. Special Effects, Ken Pepiot. Additional Effects, Dream Quest Images.

Cast: Giles Redferne (Richard E. Grant), Warlock (Julian Sands), Kassandra (Lori Singer), Chas (Kevin O'Brien), Channeller (Mary Woronov), Mennonite (Richard Kuss).

Synopsis: Massachusetts, 1691: A warlock escapes execution only to find himself on the West Coast of the United States, late twentieth century. Pursued by his nemesis, Giles Redferne, he searches the country for pages to a legendary book containing the lost name for God. Once he recites that name backwards, creation will be reversed. In the company of Kassandra, a young lady upon whom the warlock has placed a curse of aging, Giles attempts to foil the warlock's mission and shadows him across the West. When Giles and Kassandra realize the last part of the book is located in Boston, they take a plane. So does the warlock — he's in the baggage compartment. The warlock and Giles fight over the magical book in an old cemetery until Kassandra saves the day by plunging her insulin syringes — now filled with salt water — into the warlock's neck. He goes up in flames, Giles disappears, and Kassandra buries the book beneath the surface of Utah's Bonneville Salt Flats.

Reviews: "Somewhat like *The Terminator*.... The variations are uninspired, lusterless." (Michael Wilmington, *Los Angeles Times Calendar*, January 17, 1991, p. 12) ¶"A horror film with large doses of action, necromancy, special effects and, surprisingly, humor." (Martin Burden, *New York Post*, March 30, 1991. p. 17)

Analysis: This is one of Steve Miner's best films: internally logical, tough, occasionally amusing. Julian Sands is appropriately menacing, but as one critic warned, after these two entries and *Boxing Helena*, he should choose less bizarre roles for fear of being typecast. On occasion, Lori Singer's wish to get out of this situation is perplexing. She's found time travelers! We suppose they don't impress valley girls.

Warlock: The Armageddon
(Trimark, 1993; 93 min.) ***

Produced by Peter Abrams and Robert L. Levy. Directed by Anthony Hickox. Screenplay, Kevin Rock and Sam Bernard. Story, Kevin Rock. Based on characters created by David Twohy. Edited by Christopher Cibelli and James D. R. Hickox. Director of Photography, Gerry Lively. Color, Image Transform. Music, Mark McKenzie. Dolby Stereo. Art Direction, John Chichester. Set Decoration, David Allen Koneff. Special Effects Makeup, Bob Keen. Visual Effects created by BB&J Visual Effects.

Cast: Warlock (Julian Sands), Kenny Travis (Chris Young), Samantha (Paula Marshall), Will Travis (Steve Kahan), Franks (R.

G. Armstrong), Reverend (Bruce Glover), Andy (Craig Hurley), Paula Dare (Joanna Pacula), Douglas (Zach Galligan).

Synopsis: Every several hundred years Satan has a chance to rise from his prison to cause untold horror on earth. But druids have always prevented this exit from the underworld. In the late twentieth century, as Satan's opportunity approaches, a warlock is sent to gather the magical gemstones that will facilitate his master's goal. However, two of the stones are guarded by druids in California, including Will Travis and Franks. Will informs his teenage son Kenny that he is a warrior druid and begins instructing him in his latent powers. So too is Samantha told of her heritage. When the warlock arrives — after acquiring the other stones by killing their owners — they fight to keep possession of their gems and thus to keep shut the entrance of Satan into this world. The warlock seems too strong for the duo, but they use their powers to switch on a truck's ignition. High beams striking the stones divest them of their power and Satan sinks back into the earth. The warlock tries to kill Kenny with a knife that may have components of the Holy Grail. With Sam's help, Kenny drives the knife into the warlock, who disintegrates yet manages to steal one of the stones.

Review: "Weak, jokey film has only Sands' sardonic performance and some good effects to recommend it." (Leonard Maltin, ed., *Movie and Video Guide 1995*, p. 1415)

Analysis: This is a solid fantasy with fine special effects. Juxtaposing the warlock's adventure with the druid-humans who want to stop him is good storytelling. Of course, the story doesn't bear close scrutiny. Why, for instance, did the Warlock take a taxi and car to California when he could have either used a plane's baggage compartment as in the original, or propelled his body through the air? In this entry, it's not noted that he needs broth of boy to fly.

Watchers
(Universal/Concorde/Centaur Films, 1988; 92 min.) ***

Produced by Damian Lee and David

Mitchell. Executive Producer, Roger Corman. Directed by Jon Hess. Screenplay, Bill Freed and Damian Lee. Based on the novel *Watchers* by Dean R. Koontz. Edited by Bill Freda, Rick Fields and Carolle Alain. Directors of Photography, Richard Leiterman, Curtis Petersen. Panavision. Filmhouse Color. Music, Rick Fields and Joel Goldsmith. Art Direction, Tom Duquette. Set Decoration, Marti Wright. Special Effects, Rory Culter, Scott Stofer, Ron Craig.

Cast: Travis (Corey Haim), Lem Johnson (Michael Ironside), Nora (Barbara Williams), Cliff (Blu Mankuma), Sheriff Gaines (Duncan Fraser), TV newscaster (Christopher Carey), Deputy Porter (Colleen Winton), Tracey (Lala), Bill Keeshan (Dale Wilson), Ted Hockney (Norman Browning), Teacher (Tong Lung), Oxcom (Phillip Wong). With Sandy the dog.

Synopsis: An explosion at a government laboratory leaves GH3, a golden retriever, on the loose and pursued by #7, an Oxcom (Outside Experimental Combat Animal). Lem Johnson and Cliff from the NSO (National Security Organization) are called in. Lem knows the Oxcom can track the dog telepathically. GH3 passes through a farmstead and jumps into the back of Travis's pickup truck. Only later does Travis learn that his girlfriend Tracey was attacked and her father killed. Travis only knows that "Furface" is extremely intelligent. Following him to school, it types "D ANG ER NSO" on the computer screen. Leaving a trail of destruction, the Oxcom tracks the dog. Sheriff Gaines demands an explanation from Lem, who tells him about the St. Francis Project that endeavored to create a beast that would track a dog to, say, a government's enemies, and eliminate them. It's too bad this went awry. This Oxcom's insane. Lem kills the sheriff and pokes out his eyes to make investigators think the Oxcom was responsible. Travis realizes that the thing killing all the people is after the dog. The Oxcom breaks into the house but he, his mother and the dog escape. Lem locates them at a motel, but while Nora stalls, Travis and the dog escape to the family cabin. Travis prepares to make a stand, buying weapons and setting up an alarm system. First to arrive are Lem, Cliff, Tracey and Nora. Using a homemade bomb, Travis distracts the NSO men and gets his

mother and Tracey inside. When Cliff argues with Lem for shooting at them, Lem tells him that he's the third experiment, the perfect killing machine. He shoots Cliff but is stabbed by Travis and gunned down by Nora. The Oxcom attacks but is driven off. Travis follows and kills it. Returning to the cabin, he finds that the dog is not dead but needs veterinary attention.

Review: "Tacky but effective." (*Video Hound's Golden Movie Retriever 1994*, p. 882)

Analysis: Based on Dean Koontz's 1987 science fiction/horror novel *Watchers*, this film and its successor are very entertaining, but we bemoan the fact that so much tampering was done in the screenplays. Characters are left out or much transformed. The dog in the book is Einstein, not Furface, and even more intelligent. The "monster" is called the Outsider, not an Oxcom. Would that there had been a budget and imagination for epic treatment that could follow the three sets of protagonists to the crashing conclusion.

Despite these complaints, this U.S.-Canadian production filmed in British Columbia is intriguing. Not only is it unusual to have such close collaboration between man and dog, but the mother-son collaboration is something of a novelty. (This is not part of Koontz's novel, where the rapport is between a grown man, a dog, and a reclusive young woman.) There are excellent chase and escape scenes. There are unexpected deaths. We were surprised when Michael Ironside (an actor we love to hate or hate to love) was revealed as the third genetic experiment. Compare his role in this with *Scanners*. (In the book *Watchers* the Ironside character is one Vince Nasco, a psychopathic hitman. The movie consolidates characters, unfortunately.) The music sets the appropriate moods. Who exactly blew up the lab at the beginning, an animal rights group? (In the book we're led to believe the Soviets were behind it.)

Watchers II
(Concorde/Centaur/New Horizon, 1990; 97 min.) ***

Produced by Roger Corman. Directed by

Thierry Notz. Screenplay, Henry Dominic. Based on the novel *Watchers* by Dean R. Koontz. Edited by Adam Wolfe, Diane Fingado. Director of Photography, Edward Pei. Color, Foto-kem. Music, Rick Conrad. Ultra-Stereo. Art Direction, Peter Flynn. Set Decoration, Michele Munoz. Outsider created by Dean Jones and William Starr Jones.

Cast: Paul Ferguson (Marc Singer), Barbara White (Tracy Scoggins), Outsider (Thomas W. Poster), Dr. Steve Maleno (Jonathan Farwell), Sarah Ferguson (Irene Miracle), Doctor (Mary Woronov). With Dalai as Einstein.

Synopsis: In California, after the genetically produced, mansize creature known as AE 74 kills two federal investigators, Dr. Steve Maleno is told that Project Aesop will be shut down. The lab animals will be killed, including AE 74. Maleno calls an animal rights organization. While they are setting the animals upstairs free, he prepares to abscond with AE 74. However, three of the people enter his lab and are killed. AE 74 escapes, but Maleno has a tracking device. He knows AE 74 is after the dog Einstein. A jeep taking Marine Paul Ferguson to the stockade for striking a senior officer runs off the road when Einstein gets in the way. One M.P. is thrown out and knocked unconscious. The other decides to investigate a strange form that ran past the jeep. His body rolls back into the roadway. The dog retrieves keys from the other M.P., and Paul drives off before a strange beast can savage him. He gets help from Sarah, his wife from whom he's separated. Although the police are suspicious and tail her, she manages to get Paul and the dog away. In his motel room, Paul is astounded when the dog makes him use the phone book to call Barbara White. In the meantime, Sarah is killed by AE 74, which tracks the dog to Paul's motel. But Paul has left to meet Barbara, who worked with Einstein on Project Aesop. A TV news report incriminates Paul in a series of murders, but to calm Barbara, Einstein types "Paul Nokilr" on the computer screen. Einstein then types "Outsidr" and "Kilr." The people begin to understand that they are pursued by a bloodthirsty thing. "It's coming," types Einstein. Meanwhile, Maleno has found AE 74 and is "treating" it.

When Barbara calls him, he dismisses her fears, saying the outsider stories are bogus. Maleno realizes AE 74 wants the dog. He wants the creature and the dog to work together, but AE 74 breaks free and injures him. When they arrive at Maleno's home, Paul and Barbara realize something's amiss and are chased by the monster. Einstein grabs Maleno's tracking device from his car before they flee. Having heard about Sarah's death on the TV, Paul plans to confront the monster and tracks it into the sewers near the Los Angeles River. It gets the upper hand, but it retreats when he blinds it with sunlight. Wounded by Paul, AE 74 discovers the tracking module in its skin and tears it out. It proceeds to Barbara's loft. Barbara shoots it on the fire escape just as Maleno arrives. He claims the fact that it tore out only *one* of his eyes demonstrates its compassionate nature toward him. But when he confronts it again, it impales him on a decorative but very real spear. Barbara and Einstein gain the roof, but so does AE 74. Arriving in the nick of time, Paul uses a knife and gun to end the rampage. As the creature lies dying, Einstein gives it the teddy bear toy it remembered when it was "born."

Review: "More a remake of than a sequel to *Watchers*, and a better movie, though still no world-beater." (Leonard Maltin, ed., *Movie and Video Guide 1993*, p. 1361)

Analysis: This U.S.-Canadian film is not a sequel, rather another version of the novel *Watchers*. The monster makeup may be better in this one. That is, we think its kisser is uglier. On the other hand, we feel sorrier for this one as he's dying. In the first, we empathized with Corey Haim's character and wanted vengeance for the creature's savaging of the dog. Without ladling it on too strong, there are nice homages to *The Thing from Another World* (1951)—when Dr. Maleno attempts to communicate with AE 74—and *Them* (1954) and *Alien* (1979)—when Paul tracks it in the Los Angeles sewer system. There's a wonderful scene when the injured Paul is about to be caught but falls into a drain pipe. In some ways, this film is closer to the novel. Singer is akin to the Travis Cornell character, the dog *is* called Einstein, and the "monster" goes by its book name, an Outsider.

Watchers III
(New Horizons, 1994; 80 min.) *½
Produced by Luis Llosa. Directed by Jeremy Stanford. Screenplay, Michael Palmer. Based on the novel *Watchers* by Dean R. Koontz. Edited by Gwyneth Gibby. Director of Photography, Juan Duran. Color, Foto-Kem. Music, Nigel Holton. Art Direction, Dan Goldstein. Special Makeup and Creature Effects created by Gabriel Z. Bartalos.
Cast: Major Ferguson (Wings Hauser), Bonetti (Gregory Scott Cummins), Einstein the dog (Alex), Gomez (Lolita Ronalds), Nat (Daryl Roach), Boy (Ider Cifuentes Martin), MacCready (John K. Linton), Stratton (Frank Novak), Outsider (Carlos Gonzalez, Christian Meier, Matt Singer).
Synopsis: Two Project Aesop "Medical Supplies" boxes are dropped over the Matagalpan Jungle in Central America. When a timer opens them, a monster hand reaches out. The equally ugly owner of the hand savages a guerrilla encampment, killing all but a young boy. A golden retriever appears to lend him comfort. Back at the Leavenworth Military Prison in Kansas, Major Ferguson is given an assignment that will result in his freedom: Retrieve sensitive documents from a secret jungle base. After landing in their helicopter and finding the wrecked camp, the four men and their female guide, Gomez, realize that something's amiss. One of their number, MacCready, is attacked and beheaded. The others find his body, the boy, and the dog Ferguson recognizes as Einstein. Ferguson tells the others about Project Aesop, which involved "recombinant engineering" to regulate aggression. The super-smart Einstein (AE 73) is the guide for AE 74, the "Outsider," a genetic mutation who can track the canine into enemy encampments and make the kill. Unknown to Ferguson's group, NSA Command in Nebraska is using a satellite to track Einstein, the Outsider and themselves. They are merely expendable pawns in the ongoing Project Aesop experiment. When Ferguson and company realize that the Outsider shuns the light of day, they follow Einstein, only to find the beast's cave unoccupied. They

prepare an ambush but are unsuccessful and Gomez, Nat and Bonetti are killed. Reaching the helicopter, Ferguson deactivates an NSA bomb, then returns to the boy's village to set a trap. Slowed by a net, the Outsider is driven into a pit and impaled on sharpened stakes. Ferguson lights a stream of gasoline that destroys the creature by fire and explosion. Knowing that the NSA can track the helicopter, he and the boy paddle toward a nebulous freedom.
Review: "Rips off *Predator* and the original *Watchers*." (Michael Weldon, *The Psychotronic Video Guide*, p. 610)
Analysis: If this were just a low-budget video adventure, it might rate two stars. But it's a blatant remake of *Predator* with the plot kernel from *Watchers* added for good measure. There is very little attempt made to lend pathos to the Outsider, which is slightly goofy looking. The film is not consistent. Bullets deter the monster sometimes, not others. Gregory Scott Cummins seems to have been inspired by the whining Bill Paxton character of *Aliens.* Why does it say "And Introducing Ider Cifuentes Martin"? He is one of the least charismatic child actors we've ever seen. Wings Hauser adds another role that makes him king of the contemporary B film.

Wes Craven's New Nightmare *see under* **Nightmare on Elm Street**

Westworld
(MGM, 1973; 88 min.) ***
Produced by Paul N. Lazarus III. Directed by Michael Crichton. Original Screenplay, Michael Crichton. Edited by David Bretherton. Director of Photography, Gene Polito. Panavision. Metrocolor. Music, Fred Karlin. Sound, Richard Church, Harry W. Tetrick. Art Direction, Herman Blumenthal. Set Decoration, John Austin. Makeup, Frank Griffin, Irving Pringle. Action Sequences, Dick Ziker. Special Effects, Charles Schulthies. Automated Image Processing, Information International, John Whitney, Jr.
Cast: Peter Martin (Richard Benjamin), John Blane (James Brolin), Gunslinger (Yul Brynner), Chief Supervisor (Alan Oppenheimer), Medieval knight (Norman Bartold), Queen (Victoria Shaw), Banker (Dick Van Patten), Daphne (Anne Randall), Arlette (Linda

Left to right at the bar in *Westworld* (MGM, 1973): John Blane (James Brolin), Peter Martin (Richard Benjamin), and the Gunslinger (Yul Brynner).

Scott), Technician (Steve Franken), Black Knight (Michael Mikler), Sheriff (Terry Wilson), Miss Carrie (Majel Barrett), Dungeon girl (Julie Marcus), TV announcer (Robert Hogan), Apache girl (Sharyn Wynters).

Synopsis: Martin and Blane take a Hovercraft across the desert to Delos, a vacationland comprising three parks: Westworld, Roman World, and Medieval World. For $1,000 per day they can live out their fantasies, in Westworld actually shooting Wild West gunslingers because said gunmen are robots. There is no danger of killing another human because the sixshooters have a heat-sensing device that prevents discharge at people. Unbeknownst to the two men, the robots — whether people or animals — have been experiencing an increasingly high failure rate, sometimes in their main components as well as their appendages. To correct the imperfections, Delos scientists agree to shut the parks for a time, but they will not oust the guests already there. Nevertheless, the scientists cannot halt what becomes a mass "rebellion" and the killing of the guests. The gunslinger twice "killed" by Martin

returns, running on stored power, and guns down Blane. Martin flees into the desert, pursued by the robot. He tries to shake him in Roman world, fails, but in the underground labs tosses acid in his face. Minutes later the gunslinger reappears, its sight hindered but not its hearing. Martin sets it on fire, but it comes back yet again before falling to the floor, losing its face, and fizzling out at last.

Review: "Combines solid entertainment, chilling topicality, and superbly intelligent serio-comic story values...." (Murf., *Variety*, August 15, 1973, p. 12)

Analysis: This interesting, basically well-executed concept is a *Jurassic Park* (1993) precursor. Did Michael Crichton base some of his ideas for the latter on this? Not only do we have that inspiration, we also have a *Terminator* inspiration. Yul Brynner's robot gunslinger — dressed in black, virtually impervious to acid and fire — is even said to be unstoppable. On the debit side, we'll quibble with the sparsely equipped robot operating room. The budget should have been larger. Are we to swallow the notion that the scientists died of asphyxiation? They had no air ducts into the control center? How are guests not supposed to be injured in fistfights or explosive jailbreaks? Anne Randall was *Playboy's* Miss May 1967.

Futureworld
(AIP, 1976; 107 min.) ***

Produced by Paul N. Lazarus III and James T. Aubrey. Executive Producer, Samuel Z. Arkoff. Directed by Richard T. Heffron. Screenplay, Mayo Simon and George Schenck. Edited by James Mitchell. Directors of Photography, Howard Schwartz, Gene Polito. Metrocolor. Music, Fred Carlin. Art Direction, Trevor Williams.

Cast: Chuck Browning (Peter Fonda), Tracy Ballard (Blythe Danner), Gunslinger (Yul Brynner), Duffy (Arthur Hill), Schneider (John Ryan), Harry (Stuart Margolin), Ron (Jim Antonio), Game show emcee (Allen Ludden), Mrs. Reed (Angela Greene), Mr. Reed (Robert Cornthwaite), Eric (Darrel Larson), Erica (Nancy Bell), Mr. Takaguchi (John Fujioka), General Karnovski (Burt Conroy), Mrs. Karnovski (Dorothy Konrad), KGB man (Alex Rodine), Maiden Fair (Joanna Hall).

Synopsis: Chuck Browning, the reporter who'd covered the bloody demise of the Delos vacation lands, receives a mysterious call from one "Frenchy." Frenchy is mortally wounded when Chuck meets him, and his dying word is "Delos." Chuck and TV newswoman Tracy Ballard are invited back to Delos by manager Duffy, who assures them the defects have been remedied. Duffy is himself assured of the complex's safety by Schneider. In Futureworld, Duffy takes Chuck and Tracy behind the scenes. Even the controllers are robots. On his own, Browning explores the remnants of Westworld. That evening both his and Tracy's dinners are drugged. Unconscious, they, a Russian general and a Japanese industrialist are taken to the labs, where their bodies are analyzed before being returned to their beds. Next day Chuck and Tracy use a tunnel map to continue their private explorations. In the research and development area they unwittingly release three samurai creations which chase them. Maintenance man Harry Croft helps them

escape and agrees to a forthcoming TV interview with Tracy. Chuck shows Tracy Frenchy's newspaper clippings of all the notable persons who'd visited Delos. Chuck quizzes Harry, who admits to having worked with Frenchy. He shows Chuck and Tracy the entrance to a secret area even he is not allowed to enter. With the face of an incapacitated robot as their key, they enter the room and find their own duplicates. Realizing that they are about to be killed, they plan to leave but are waylaid by Duffy. Tracy shoots him and they learn that he too is a robot. The duplicate Chuck kills Harry and chases his inspiration but eventually falls from a height. Tracy must outdraw her duplicate to survive. Chuck and Tracy pretend to be the duplicates and fool Schneider long enough to get to the subway taking visitors out of Delos. Chuck had already phoned the outside world with the story.

Review: "The most overt horrific variation as yet played on the Disney theme park theme.... Peter Fonda and Blythe Danner are both extremely attractive as the journalists.... Though production values in the film are admittedly modest, the location settings of the Houston Manned Space Center frequently achieve impressively epic effects." (Ross Care, *Cinefantastique*, Vol. 5, No. 3, p. 25)

Analysis: Here is virtual reality again, and before its time. It moves rapidly and is engrossing. The producers had the sense to skip a "trick" ending after Fonda's appropriate — and hilarious — arm gesture to Ryan. Yul Brynner's part is unfortunately negligible as he only appears in Tracy's dream. Blythe Danner is spunky as usual. Why hasn't she gotten tons of leading roles? Why is it that Futureworld in itself is lacking in luster? Compared to Westworld, Roman World, and Medieval World, it has little attraction. That's probably because we don't have a history of outer space and other worlds. It's also sterile and necessitates almost perpetual spacesuit garb.

Wild Jungle Captive *see* Jungle Captive *under* **Captive Wild Woman**

Willard

(Cinerama, 1971; 95 min.) ***

Produced by Mort Briskin. Directed by Daniel Mann. Assistant Director, Robert Goodstein. Screenplay, Gilbert A. Ralston. Based on Stephen Gilbert's novel *Ratman's Notebooks*. Edited by Warren Low. Director of Photography, Robert B. Hauser. Color, DeLuxe. Music, Alex North. Art Direction, Howard Hollander. Set Decoration, Ralph S. Hurst. Makeup, Gus Norin. Special Effects, Bud David. Socrates and Ben trained by Moe Di Sesso.

Cast: Willard Stiles (Bruce Davison), Al Martin (Ernest Borgnine), Henrietta Stiles (Elsa Lanchester), Joan (Sondra Locke), Brandt (Michael Dante), Charlotte Stassen (Jody Gilbert), Alice (Joan Shawlee), Mr. Barskin (William Hansen), Jonathan Farley (J. Pat O'Malley), Mr. Carlson (John Myhers), Mrs. Becker (Helen Spring), Ida Stassen (Pauline Drake), Carrie Smith (Almira Sessions), Mr. Walter Spencer (Alan Baxter).

Synopsis: Twenty-seven-year-old bachelor Willard Stiles lives with his semi-invalid mother and works in the office for Al Martin, a man generally thought to have stolen the company from Willard's late father. Willard makes friends with some yard rats, naming the white one Socrates and the black one Ben. He sics them and others on Martin's garden party. When his mother dies, Willard decides to keep the old house, although he soon learns that he must come up with $2,500 for taxes. He breaks into a client's house and steals some money. Martin fires temp Joan when she refuses to convince Willard to sell his house, and he gives Willard notice as well. His goal is to acquire the Stiles house and bulldoze it for apartments. When Socrates is discovered in the records storage room, Martin kills him. Willard couldn't bring himself to intervene, and Ben observed his human caretaker's cowardice. Willard retrieves Ben and that night drives a car full of rats back to the office where he turns them on Martin with the command, "Tear him up!" He leaves Ben there and at home drowns the remaining rats. But while entertaining Joan, he spots Ben. Sending Joan home, he tries to poison Ben, but the rat is too smart and calls his minions, who corner and kill Willard in the attic.

Review: "Fudges its real chance to deal with an unsettling theme in an intelligent and gripping manner.... Willard's four-legged friends are not as grotesque as the overdone adults who populate his world.... The ending is pure horror movie ritualism." (Robert L. Jerome, *Cinefantastique*, Fall 1971, p. 39)

Analysis: At first glance, this seems an odd movie to come from the director of *Come Back, Little Sheba* (1952) and *I'll Cry Tomorrow* (1955) and the composer of *Spartacus*. But Mann had done *Our Man Flint* (1966), and North's contemporary, Bernard Herrmann, wrote for the fantasy cinema. Bruce Davison's character, while put upon by mom and boss, is a disturbed human being and can only enlist a modicum of audience sympathy. Many of us roared in a combination of revulsion and delight when Ernest Borgnine flailed about and crashed through the window. In the final analysis, are regular-sized rats that frightening? According to *Variety*, with $8,200,000 in rentals, *Willard* placed eighth among top-grossing 1971 movies.

Ben

(Cinerama, 1972; 93 min.) **½

Produced by Mort Briskin. Directed by Phil Karlson. Screenplay, Gilbert A. Ralston. Based on characters created by Stephen Gilbert. Edited by Harry Gerstad. Director of Photography, Russell Metty. DeLuxe Color. Music, Walter Scharf. "Ben's Song" sung by Michael Jackson. Lyrics by Don Black. Art Direction, Rolland M. Brooks. Set Decoration, Antony Mondello. Animals trained by Moe DiSesso.

Cast: Danny Garrison (Lee Harcourt Montgomery), Cliff Kirtland (Joseph Campanella), Billy Hatfield (Arthur O'Connell), Beth Garrison (Rosemary Murphy), Eve Garrison (Meredith Baxter), Joe Greer (Kaz Garas), Kelly (Paul Carr), Reade (Richard Van Fleet), Engineer (Kenneth Tobey), Ed (James Luisi), Carey (Lee Paul), Policeman (Norman Alden), Henry Gray (Scott Garrett), Mrs. Gray (Arlen Stuart), George (Richard Drasin).

Synopsis: The community watches as the police take away Willard Stiles's body. Inside, a policeman is killed by rats. Exterminators are brought in. The rat Ben leads his kin down the street and is befriended by Danny, a young boy with a heart condition. To Danny, Ben and the rats are wonderful. He realizes they are hungry and doesn't really blame them for raiding a supermarket, a candy factory and a cheese shop. Ben shows Danny the nearby drain where he lives. One night Danny's sister Eve finds rats on his bed. Policeman Kirtland interrogates Danny, who won't divulge the rats' whereabouts. Drains are continually searched. Another man is killed. Danny enters the sewers and warns Ben about the coming holocaust of fire and flood. Eve finds Danny, and they climb to the surface while the rats battle humans. Ben survives, and Danny attends to the wounded creature.

Review: "Tension-packed sequel." (Whit., *Variety*, June 14, 1972, p. 24)

Analysis: Variety praised Karlson's direction for producing mounting excitement. We finally are treated to a rat horde, even if it's occasionally a special effect. People are too easily killed. The youthful Michael Jackson sings "Ben's Song" over the end credits. Note veteran '50s monster killer Kenneth Tobey as the sewer expert. Meredith Baxter would gain fame on TV's *Family Ties* and in numerous TV docudramas.

The Wizard of Oz
(MGM, 1939; 102 min.) ****

Produced by Mervyn LeRoy. Directed by Victor Fleming. Screenplay, Noel Langley, Florence Ryerson, and Edgar Allan Woolf. Adapted from *The Wonderful Wizard of Oz* by L. Frank Baum. Edited by Blanche Sewell. Director of Photography, Harold Rosson. Technicolor, with sepia opening and closing. Music, Herbert Stothart. Songs, E. Y. Harburg and Harold Arlen: "Over the Rainbow," "We're Off to See the Wizard," "Merry Old Land of Oz," "If I Were King," "Courage," "Welcome to Munchkin Land," "Ding Dong, the Witch is Dead," "If I Only Had a Heart." Musical numbers staged by Bobby Connolly. Orchestral and Vocal Arrangements, George Bassman, Murray Cutter, Paul Marquardt, Ken Darby. Art Direction, Cedric Gibbons, William A. Horning. Set Decoration, Edwin B. Willis. Character Makeup, Jack Dawn. Special Effects, Arnold Gillespie.

Cast: Dorothy (Judy Garland), Professor Marvel/Wizard (Frank Morgan), Hunk/Scarecrow (Ray Bolger), Hickory/Tin woodman (Jack Haley), Zeke/Cowardly lion (Bert Lahr), Miss Gulch/Witch (Margaret Hamilton), Glinda (Billie Burke), Uncle Henry (Charley Grapewin), Auntie Em (Clara Blandick), Nikko (Pat Walshe), Toto (Toto), Munchkin (Jerry Marenghi/Maren), Munchkins (Singer Midgets).

Synopsis: A tornado strikes the Kansas homestead of Dorothy and the house is swept into the whirlwind, crashing down in a strange land. "I have a feeling we're not in Kansas anymore," Dorothy tells her dog Toto. Her house lies atop someone the little inhabitants call a wicked witch. Dorothy obtains the witch's red shoes via good witch Glinda. Unless she removes them, Dorothy is immune to the fury of the wicked witch's sister. Glinda tells Dorothy she can return to Kansas through the efforts of the wizard who lives in the Emerald City of Oz. Following the Yellow Brick Road, Dorothy and dog Toto encounter a scarecrow who comes to life and who wants a brain, a tin woodsman who wants a heart, and a cowardly lion who wants courage. Although the wicked witch causes them to fall asleep in a field, Glinda causes a snowfall that wakes them. Entering the Emerald City, the group is brought before the intimidating presence of the wizard. He tells them he will help if they steal the wicked witch's broom. Before they can get very far, Dorothy and Toto are captured by the witch's flying monkeys. Her three friends masquerade as soldiers to gain entrance to the witch's castle. When the witch threatens to kill Toto, Dorothy spills water on her and she melts. When the victors return to the Emerald City, the wizard makes more demands, but Toto pulls a curtain aside and they discover the wizard is naught but a man manipulating various controls to simulate the giant visage. He may yet be of help and offers the services of his balloon. However, Dorothy and Toto fail to get aboard in time and it is swept away. Glinda tells a distressed Dorothy she always had the ability to return — by clicking her heels and saying "There's no place like home." She awakes in her bed in Kansas, surrounded by family and farmhands. Was it a dream? "But anyway, Toto, we're home. And this is my

The Wicked Witch of the West (Margaret Hamilton) watches from behind a tree as Dorothy (Judy Garland) encourages the scarecrow (Ray Bolger) in *The Wizard of Oz* (MGM, 1939).

room. And you're all here. And I'm not going to leave here ever, ever again because I love you all. Oh, Auntie Em, there's no place like home."

Reviews: "As for the light touch of fantasy, it weighs like a pound of fruitcake soaking wet.... many interesting gadgets.... It isn't that [Judy Garland] spoils the fantasy so much as that her thumping, overgrown gambols are characteristic of its treatment here: when she is merry the house shakes, and everybody gets wet when she is lorn." (Otis Ferguson, *New Republic,* September 20, 1939, p. 190) ¶"As long as *The Wizard of Oz* sticks to whimsy and magic, it floats in the same rare atmosphere of enchantment that distinguished Walt Disney's *Snow White and the Seven Dwarfs.* When it descends to earth it collapses like a scarecrow in a cloudburst." (*Time,* August 21, 1939, p. 41) ¶"Constructive dramatic values.... Judy Garland ... is an appealing figure...." (*Variety*)

Analysis: Can anything new be said

about this acknowledged classic, one of Hollywood's best, beloved and most enduring fantasies? It made Judy Garland a full-fledged star. Buddy Ebsen was to have played the tin man but became ill because of the makeup. Margaret Hamilton became a definitive screen witch. Children can still be frightened by the flying monkeys. The songs are uniformly excellent. Academy Awards for song "Over the Rainbow" and musical score. Some people cringe at Billie Burke's, "Toto, too!"

Notes of Interest: L. Frank Baum's *The Wonderful Wizard of Oz* (1900) and succeeding tales were the basis. There is a silent 1925 version.

The Wiz

(Motown/Universal, 1978; 133 min.)
***½

Produced by Rob Cohen. Directed by Sidney Lumet. Screenplay, Joel Schumacher. Based on the book *The Wonderful Wizard of*

Scarecrow (Michael Jackson) trades insults with some annoying crows in *The Wiz* (Motown/Universal, 1978).

Oz by L. Frank Baum and the musical *The Wiz*. Book, William F. Brown. Music and lyrics, Charalie Smalls. Choreography, Louis Johnson. Additional Music, Quincy Jones. Edited by Dede Allen. Director of Photography, Oswald Morris. Technicolor. Dolby Stereo. Art Direction, Philip Rosenberg. Set Decoration, Edward Stewart, Robert Drumheller. Costumes, Tony Walton. Special Makeup designed by Stan Winston. Visual Effects, Albert Whitlock.

Cast: Dorothy (Diana Ross), Scarecrow (Michael Jackson), Tinman (Nipsey Russell), Lion (Ted Ross), Evillene (Mabel King), Aunt Em (Theresa Merritt), Glinda the Good (Lena Horne), The Wiz (Richard Pryor), Miss One (Thelma Carpenter), Uncle Henry (Stanley Greene), Subway peddler (Clyde J. Barrett), Head Winkie (Carlton Johnson), Cheetah (Harry Madsen), Green lady (Vicki Baltimore), Rolls Royce lady (Glory Van Scott), Crows (Derrick Bell, Roderick Spencer Sibert, Kashka Banjoko, Ronald Smokey Stevens), Gold footmen (Tony Brealond, Joe Lynn), Green footman (Clinton Jackson, Charles Rodriguez), Munchkins (Ted Williams, Mabel Robinson, Damon Pearce, Donna Patrice Ingram).

Synopsis: Dorothy lives with Aunt Em at 433 Prospect Place, New York City. She's an elementary school teacher who Aunt Em surmises is afraid of the world below 125th Street. When Dorothy's dog Toto runs out into a snowstorm, Dorothy frantically follows and finds herself caught up in a twister. She crashes through a sign that lands on Evillene, a wicked witch according to the ecstatic graffiti-come-alive munchkins. They tell Dorothy to follow the Yellow Brick Road to get home. Outside, she encounters Scarecrow, harassed by crow-people. She and Toto drive them off and free the poor creature, who volunteers to accompany her to the Wiz. He might get some brains. At a defunct amusement park they find Tinman, who needs a heart. He, too, wants to accompany them. Passing a large building, they are accosted by Lion. He needs courage. Surviving an attack in the subway by pillars, trash receptacles and strange orange creatures — where Lion proves his courage — Dorothy and Lion are knocked out by a perfume. Tinman weeps, and his tears revive them. Spying the Yellow Brick Road spiraling into a great city, they cross a bridge. On the other side, a guardian observes Dorothy's slippers and welcomes her to the Emerald City. The voice of the Wiz requests that the one with the silver slippers be sent up. Dorothy refuses to come unless her friends accompany her. The Wiz relents. Though intimidated by the giant head from which emanate the Wiz's voice, light and fire, they make their requests. The Wiz demands that Dorothy kill Evillene, the wicked witch of the West. Leaving, they fail to see a normal human head appear in one of the statue's eyes. At the Emerald City Motel, Dorothy makes her decision: Find Evillene. She and her companions proceed beneath the city. In her sweat shop, Evillene summons her flying monkeys to capture Dorothy and accuses Dorothy of murdering her sister. When Dorothy refuses to give up the slippers, Evillene has Scarecrow sawed in half, Tinman compressed, and Lion raised to the rafters by his tail. When Evillene threatens to toss Toto into an oven, Dorothy relents. But Scarecrow brings the fire alarm to Dorothy's attention, and the sprinklers melt Evillene. The witch's former slaves help Dorothy restore her companions as a new day dawns. The flying monkeys escort them to the Wiz's rear entrance. Inside, they find a man on a simple cot. It's the Wiz, and he's a phony: Herman Smith, an incompetent politician from Atlantic City. He explains that while promoting his candidacy by balloon, he was carried to Oz where he set himself up as the all-powerful Wiz. Her friends are disconsolate, but Dorothy points out that they had brains, courage and heart all along. Otherwise, they wouldn't have found Evillene and triumphed. Glinda the Good appears and tells Dorothy home is knowing her own heart and mind. Dorothy urges Smith to leave his room, thanks her friends, thinks of home and clicks her heels three times. She finds herself in the snow and runs up to the front door.

Review: "It's the combination of Oswald Morris's cinematography, the special visual effects of Albert Whitlock and Tony Walton's production design and costumes that linger longest in the memory." (*Variety*)

Analysis: *Variety* called the cast "virtually flawless," and mighty impressive sets grace this big musical directed by Sidney Lumet, well known for more hard-boiled fare. The standard songs are "Ease on Down the Road" and "Brand New Day." "Bad News" and "Brand New Day" are exceptional production numbers worth several viewings. Michael Jackson puts in a smidgen of the moon walk he'd become famous for in a few years. *Variety* praised Diana Ross's suprisingly strong dance performance.

Return to Oz
(Buena Vista, 1985; 110 min.) ***

Produced by Paul Maslansky. Executive Producer, Gary Kurtz. Directed by Walter Murch. Screenplay, Walter Murch and Gill Dennis. Based on the books *The Land of Oz* and *Ozma of Oz* by L. Frank Baum. Edited by Leslie Hodgson. Director of Photography, David Watkin. Technicolor. Music, David Shire. Dolby Stereo. Art Direction, Fred Hole. Set Decoration, Michael Ford. Mime Movement, Pons Maar. Costumes, Raymond Hughes and William R. McPhail. Creature Design, Lyle Conway, Tim Rose. Special Effects, Ian Wingrove. Claymation, Will Vinton Productions.

Cast: Dorothy Gail (Fairuza Balk), Dr. Worley/Nome King (Nicol Williamson), Nurse Wilson/Princess Mombi (Jean Marsh), Aunt Em (Piper Laurie), Uncle Henry (Matt Clark), Tik Tok (Michael Sundin/Tim Rose), Voice (Sean Barrett), Billina (Mak Wilson), Jack Pumpkinhead (Brian Henson/Stewart Larange), Gump (Lyle Conway/Steve Norrington), Voice (Lyle Conway), Scarecrow (Justin Case), Cowardly Lion (John Alexander), Tin Man (Deep Roy), Ozma (Emma Ridley), Lead Wheeler/Nome Messenger (Pons Maar), Toto (Tansy).

Synopsis: Dorothy Gail can't sleep, and Aunt Em takes her to Dr. Worley in Cottonwood Falls. He has an electric machine that might be able to take away her strange recollections. But before it can be used, a young girl urges Dorothy to escape. They flee the house in a storm and fall into the river. Dorothy awakes with her hen Billina and finds herself in the Deadly Desert of Oz. Proceeding cautiously, they make it through the forest and shortly thereafter find Oz a ruined city with its people turned to stone. Chased by "wheelers," Dorothy uses the key she thinks the scarecrow sent to her via a shooting star to enter a room. She discovers Tik Tok, a metal soldier. When wound up, he helps her fight off the wheelers. They find Princess Mombi, who imprisons Dorothy, thinking to add her head to her large collection. Dorothy helps Jack Pumpkinhead recover his mobility and, with Tik Tok, hatches an escape plan. Dorothy gets Mombi's Powder of Life and sprinkles it on the mooselike gump head Jack attached to some sofas. They fly off toward the Nome King's mountain. Therein they hope to find the scarecrow and learn why the Emerald City is in ruins. After crashing on the mountain, Dorothy and her companions encounter the rocklike Nome King. He wears the red shoes and says the emeralds of the city were rightfully his. He makes a bargain with Dorothy. If she or her companions can guess which ornament the scarecrow has become, they can leave. If not, they become ornaments themselves. The others fail, but Dorothy selects a large emerald which turns into the scarecrow. The Nome King is irate and blames his predicament on Mombi, who has come into his presence. She is imprisoned, and he eats the sofa. He tries to eat Jack, but Billina's poison egg falls into his maw and he falls apart. Dorothy retrieves the red shoes and clicks them thrice. They are transported to the Emerald City, where Dorothy helps Ozma from the mirror. She looks like the little girl at Dr. Worley's. Dorothy awakes on the river bank and is discovered by Toto. She learns that Dr. Worley's clinic was burned to the ground after lightning struck it. Her own tornado-damaged house has almost been restored.

Reviews: "An appealing picture on its own terms, if you can overlook a couple of big miscalculations.... Early scenes are the best in the movie—tautly filmed, and extra scary because they're rooted in the real world." (David Sterritt, *Christian Science Monitor*, June 21, 1985, p. 24) ¶"Where the film ultimately falls short of *The Wizard of Oz* is in the charismatic quality of the leading characters. Fairuza Balk is good, if

no substitute for Garland." (Tom Milne, *Monthly Film Bulletin*, August 1985, p. 252) ¶"Though eleven-year-old Ms. Balk is a trouper, it is likely to be visual wonders that hang on in memory from this eclectic occasion." (John Coleman, *New Statesman*, July 12, 1985, p. 34)

Analysis: This was not a success, but it's consistently entertaining and imaginative. Did word of mouth say there was no music and keep people away? Fairuza Balk is fine. *Upstairs, Downstairs* alumnus Jean Marsh, who plays a wicked princess here, did a similar turn in *Willow*. Effects are excellent.

The Wolf Man
(Universal, 1941; 70 min.) ***

Produced and Directed by George Waggner. Screenplay, Curt Siodmak. Edited by Ted Kent. Director of Photography, Joseph Valentine. Music, Hans Salter and Frank Skinner. Musical Direction, Charles Previn. Art Direction, Jack Otterson. Set Decoration, R. A. Gausman. Makeup, Jack P. Pierce.

Cast: Lawrence Talbot (Lon Chaney, Jr.), Gwen Conliffe (Evelyn Ankers), Sir John Talbot (Claude Rains), Dr. Lloyd (Warren William), Captain Paul Montford (Ralph Bellamy), Maleva (Maria Ouspenskaya), Bela the gypsy (Bela Lugosi), Frank Andrews (Patric Knowles), Jenny Williams (Fay Helm), Twiddle (Forrester Harvey), Charles Conliffe (J. M. Kerrigan), Kendall (Leyland Hodgson), Mrs. Williams (Doris Lloyd), Wykes (Harry Gording), Reverend Norman (Harry Stubbs), Gypsy (Kurt Katch). With Martha Vickers, Margaret Fealy, Caroline Cooke, La Riana, Jessie Arnold, Connie Leon, Otola Nesmith, Eric Wilton, Olaf Hytten, Tom Stevenson, Ernie Stanton.

Synopsis: A hand opens a book to the term "Lycanthropy (werewolfism)," which is defined as a disease of the mind whereby a man thinks he's become a wolf. Larry Talbot returns to Talbot Castle in England after eighteen years in America. In his father's attic, converted into an observatory, he spies comely Gwen Conliffe through her window above her family's antique shop and later makes her acquaintance. He also buys a walking stick with a silver wolf head on the top. Gwen recites a poem: "Even a man who is pure in heart and says his prayers by night, may become a wolf when the wolfbane blooms and the autumn moon is bright." According to legend, each werewolf is marked with the sign of the pentagram and sees the same sign in the hand of its intended victim. Larry, Gwen and Jenny Williams visit the gypsy encampment where Jenny has her fortune told by Bela, who has a pentagram on his forehead hidden by a lock of hair. In the woods, Jenny is attacked by a wolf, which Larry kills with his cane. Bitten, he learns that Bela is dead, his skull crushed. Jenny has had her jugular severed. Strangely, Larry's wound has disappeared. Larry observes Bela's mother, Maleva, at her son's coffin. Later he meets Maleva, who says, "The wolf was Bela." She explains that only a silver bullet or knife — or a stick with a silver handle — can kill a werewolf. She gives him a pentagram charm to help him. He in turn gives it to Gwen. In his room, Larry finds hair growing profusely on his legs and feet. In the fog, a man-beast kills the gravedigger Richardson. Larry wakes in his bed with the pentagram sign appearing on his chest. He wipes out the muddy footprints in the room. When Larry tells Sir John and visitors that a werewolf is responsible for the murders, Dr. Lloyd advises Sir John to send his son away for a rest. That night Larry is caught in a trap but Maleva helps him. Larry goes to Gwen and says he's going away. He sees the sign of the pentagram in her palm and rushes out. Sir John hopes to convince his son that he's merely mentally disturbed and ties him to a chair before going into the woods to help with the hunt. Finding himself concerned about his son, he plans to return to the house when he finds Gwen attacked by the werewolf. He beats it with the silver-headed cane. To his horror and astonishment, he then observes Maleva reciting an incantation that turns the werewolf into his son. Captain Montford arrives and says that a wolf attacked Gwen and that Larry must have come to her rescue.

Reviews: "Has tried to make a little go a long way, and it has concealed most of that little in a deep layer of fog." (Theodore Strauss, *New York Times*, December 22, 1941, p. 24) ¶"Dazzlingly cast, moderately

well staged, but dramatically very disappointing…." (Leslie Halliwell, *Halliwell's Film Guide*, 7th ed., p. 1125)

Analysis: It's got atmosphere and a tremendous cast: the consummate supporting actor Claude Rains, thirties leading man Warren William (*Cleopatra, Imitation of Life*), accomplished actress Maria Ouspenskaya, lovely Universal heroine Evelyn Ankers, long-lived and respected Ralph Bellamy, and Bela Lugosi in one of his excellent supporting roles. Your authors, however, really prefer Henry Hull's makeup in *Werewolf of London* (1934) or Oliver Reed's in *The Curse of the Werewolf*, and the lycanthropes of *The Howling*. Here there is no transformation from man to wolf. Rather, we see it the other way around. Ankers, Rains and Fay Helm all get a chance to recite the infamous "Even a man…."

Notes of Interest: Whereas the wolf man (Larry Talbot) appeared in numerous Universal films, the lycanthrope played by Lon Chaney, Jr., did not himself generate a series. He appeared in series already underway. Because they were remaking most of the Universal films, Hammer's 1960 film *The Curse of the Werewolf* might be thought of as a remake, but on literal grounds must be dismissed. Its characters are not the same, and Oliver Reed does not become a werewolf via the bite of another one. He is the progeny of an imprisoned lunatic who ravishes a young woman. Huh?

Frankenstein Meets the Wolf Man
(Universal, 1943) **½

Analysis: It's a tough call, but since Frankenstein came first in Universal's horror series, we've classified this as a Frankenstein film. See listing under *Frankenstein* for cast, credits, and discussion.

House of Frankenstein
(Universal, 1944) **½

Analysis: A "Parade of Monsters" film featuring Dracula and the Wolf Man as well as the Frankenstein monster. See listing under *Frankenstein* for cast, credits, and discussion.

Lon Chaney, Jr., is *The Wolf Man* (Universal, 1941).

House of Dracula
(Universal, 1945) **½

Analysis: Another monster parade. See listing under *Dracula* for cast, credits, and discussion.

The Monster Squad
(Tri-Star/Taft Entertainment Pictures, 1988; 81 min.) **½

Analysis: This one adds the Gill Man to an already crowded roster of monsters. See listing under *Frankenstein* for cast, credits, and discussion.

The Wrath of Khan *see* Star Trek II — The Wrath of Khan *under* **Star Trek — The Motion Picture**

Young Dracula *see* Son of Dracula (1974) *under* **Dracula**

Young Frankenstein *see under* **Frankenstein**

Your Sister Is a Werewolf *see* Howling II ... Your Sister Is a Werewolf *under* **The Howling**

Zapped

(Embassy, 1982; 96 min.) **

Produced by Jeffrey D. Apple. Directed by Robert J. Rosenthal. Assistant Directors, Frank Capra III, K. C. Colwell, Stuart Neumann. Screenplay, Bruce Rubin and Robert J. Rosenthal. Edited by Robert Ferretti. Director of Photography, Daniel Pearl. Color. Music, Charles Fox. Lyrics, Steve Geyer. Art Direction, Boyd Willat. Special Visual Effects, Robert Blalack.

Cast: Barney Springboro (Scott Baio), Peyton Nichols (Willie Aames), Principal Walter Johnson (Robert Mandan), Bernadette (Felice Schachter), Jane Mitchell (Heather Thomas), Coach Dexter Jones (Scatman Crothers), Rose (Sue Ane Langdon), Mr. Springboro (Roger Bowen), Mrs. Springboro (Marya Small), Robert (Greg Bradford), Corrine (Hilary Beane), Roscoe (Hardy Keith), Art (Curt Ayers), Cary (Merritt Butrick), Melissa (Jennifer Chaplin), "Too Mean" (Irwin Keyes), Umpire (Henry Ford Robinson), Waiter (Dick Balduzzi), Croupier (Bennett Liss), Larry (Ron Deutsch), Sheldon (Ed Deezen), Father Murray (Bryan O'Byrne), Father Gallagher (Ed Bakey), Einstein (Jan Leighton), Mrs. Jones (Lawanda Page), Donna (Rosanne Katon), Amy (Sandy Serrano), Cindy (Corine Borher), Debby (Susan Ursitti).

Synopsis: In the Ralph Waldo Emerson High School science laboratory, baseball coach Dexter Jones spills plant food into another mixture and Peyton Nichols purposefully adds a bit of beer. None of this is known to senior Barney Springboro, who is conducting botanical and behavioral studies. He gives a mouse the mixture and it becomes telekinetic. Barney knocks over some equipment, there's an explosion, and when he awakes he finds he has the ability to transport things through the air. From this power, Peyton has plans to make money while class president Bernadette wants to publish a scientific paper. Interfering with the goals are cheerleader Jane, her college boyfriend, a baseball game, a trip to an amusement park, and the senior prom. At the prom, where Jane is queen and Peyton king, the latter makes Jane's boyfriend lose his cool when he shows him compromising photos of Jane. In the ruckus, Jane tosses a melon which hits Barney. He uses his power to strip off her clothes — and the clothes of practically everyone else. Barney is hit in the head a second time — by a water hose. Apparently losing his telekinetic power, he regains it outside and he and Bernadette are whisked into the air.

Reviews: "[Rosenthal and Rubin] have a genuine feeling for kids and capture some of the twinges of being different. However, the material is inherently mediocre...." (Linda Gross, *Los Angeles Times Calendar*, August 9, 1982, p. 3) ¶"Generally speaking, it's a one trick movie." (Archer Winsten, *New York Post*, August 27, 1982, p. 43) ¶"Cast is likable and competent." (Joseph Gelmis, *Newsday*, August 27, 1982, Part II, p. 9)

Analysis: Poking fun at teachers and parents and spoofing *The Exorcist* and *Carrie*, it is not raunchy enough to attract the adolescent crowd that lined up for *Animal House, Fast Times at Ridgemont High, Revenge of the Nerds* and *Porky's*. None of the scientific stuff makes any sense at all. (Can anyone explain the scene in which a model rocket ship is transported through an aquarium?) It's sporadically and mildly amusing. We surmise that Heather Thomas, while not loath to sport bikinis, was reluctant to expose more, and it was at her request that "A double was used for Miss Thomas in her nude scene and in the photograph" was added to the end credits.

Zapped Again

(ITC Entertainment Group, 1989) *½

Produced by Jeff Apple and Robert Rosenthal. Directed by Doug Campbell. Screenplay, Jack Morris, Vince Cheung and Ben Montanio. Based on characters created by Bruce Rubin and Robert Rosenthal. Edited by Michael Spence. Director of Photography, Tom Grubbs. Color, Foto-Kem. Music, Brian Bennett. Art Direction, Scott Herbertson.

Cast: Kevin W. Matthews (Todd Eric Andrews), Lucy (Kelli Williams), Wayne (Reed Rudy), Principal Rose Burnhart (Sue Ane Langdon), Miss Mitchell (Linda Blair), Substitute teacher (Karen Black), Coach Kirby (Lyle Alzado), Elliot (Ira Heiden). With Maria McCann, M. K. Harris, Ross Harris, Linda Larkin.

Synopsis: Kevin Matthews begins his first day at Ralph Waldo Emerson High

School with a fight over jock Wayne's girl Amanda. After school Kevin gets a job at a hot dog joint and meets Lucy, later joining her in Science Club. In a hole in the wall, club members discover Relaxo Prune Juice with the additional label, "Property of Barney Springboro," a former student they recall had something to do with people's clothes coming off at a prom. Key Club members Wayne and his cohort force Kevin to swallow some of the juice. When brought to his senses by Lucy, he has telekinetic powers. He opens girls' blouses, flips up teacher Mitchell's skirt, and transports bottles through the air. Lucy and he plan to analyze and market the elixir, but their plans are thwarted when the Key Club takes over the Science Club space. By winning the thirteenth annual Penguin Run at Homecoming, Science Club gets its room back. Principal Rose Burnhart expels Kevin after finding beer and panties that were planted by Wayne. Wayne makes a deal with Kevin: If Science Club works the social, he'll help Kevin remain in school. Science Club injects the hotdogs they are selling in Wayne's name with itching liquid. When Wayne readies the crowd to toss tomatoes at the tomato-allergic Kevin, the latter uses his powers to hurl them at Wayne instead. The itching starts. Kevin makes Wayne admit in front of the principal that he blackmailed Science Club. Key Club is suspended. Kevin propels Wayne across the compound above his tormenters.

Review: "Lame-brained sequel." (*Video Hound's Golden Movie Retriever 1994*, p. 920)

Analysis: The first half is not as bad as might be expected, but this film (video only?) is ultimately boring. When they are used at all, the telekinetic powers inherent in the "Prune Juice" are utilized for the most frivolous ends. This "high school" is like an Animal House college. Also unconvincing is an exotic — and not very curvaceous — Heather Thomas clone who is presented as the ultimate date. Is the Linda Blair character meant to be the adult Jane Mitchell of *Zapped*?

Zapped Again *see under* **Zapped**

Bibliography

Articles

Alpert, Hollis. "Comedy: The New King." *Saturday Review*, November 2, 1974, pp. 52–53.

Besas, Peter. "Surface Has Only Been Scratched in 'Fantastic' Film Field: Chris Lee." *Variety*, July 4, 1973. p. 33.

Biodrowski, Steve. "Coppola's Dracula." *Cinefantastique*, December 1992, pp. 24–26, 31, 35, 39, 43, 47, 51, 55.

_____. "The Many Faces of Ken Myers." *Cinefantastique*, May 1988, pp. 40–41, 57.

_____. Del Valle, David; and French, Lawrence. "Vincent Price: Looking Back on Forty Years as Horror's Crown Prince." *Cinefantastique*, January 1989, pp. 40–62, 67–84.

Bossone, Vincent. "Spotlighting Ed Parker, an Unknown Monster Star." *Castle of Frankenstein*, June 1975, pp. 17–21.

Clarens, Carlos. "Barbarians Now." *Film Comment*, May-June 1982, pp. 26–28.

DeChick, Joe. "*Alien* Flicks: Horror Mates with Mainstream." *News Journal* [Wilmington, DE], May 25, 1992. Includes "Bits and Pieces About *Alien* Trilogy."

Delson, James. "A Comprehensive Interview with Robert Wise, Still Making the Earth Stand Still with *Star Trek: The Movie*." *Fantastic Films*, September 1979, pp. 18–23, 38, 58–60, 62.

"Dietz Ducks Elaborate Arbitration, Says 'I've No Quarrel With Blair.'" *Variety*, March 13, 1974, p. 22.

Doense, Jan, and Robley, Les Paul. "H. R. Giger." *Cinefantastique*, May 1988, pp. 24–26, 29–31, 34–36, 39.

"*Exorcist* Arbitration 'Unavoidable.'" *Variety*, March 20, 1974, p. 26.

"*Exorcist*: Smash Hit Backlash; Catholic, Jewish Conservatives React; Recall Yiddish 'Dybbuk.'" *Variety*, March 13, 1974. p. 22.

Fox, Marion. "The Exorcist." *Castle of Frankenstein* 22, 1974, pp. 28–31.

Freese, Robert. "Belinda Balaski." *Film Ex*, Summer 1996, pp. 1–4.

French, Lawrence. "Price on Poe." *Cinefantastique*, January 1989, pp. 63–66, 119.

French, Todd. "Cocoon 2: The Return." *Cinefantastique*, January 1989, pp. 25, 120.

Gagne, Paul. "War of the Living Deads." *Cinefantastique* 13, June-July 1983, p. 12.

Gilmartin, Eric. "*Not of This Earth*." *Cinefantastique*, May 1988, p. 20.

Gingold, Michael. "History of Horror: The 1980's." *Fangoria*, March 1991, pp. 83–87.

Gold, Mike. "*Superman the Movie*: The Selling of the Man of Steel." *Fantastic Films*, April 1979, pp. 6–12, 26–27, 50.

Hallenbeck, Bruce. "Hallenbeck's Guilty Pleasures." *FANEX 8: Hammer Has Risen from the Grave* (Convention Program). Baltimore: 1994.

_____. "Tudor Gates." *Little Shoppe of Horrors*, No. 4, May 1984, pp. 42–45.

"Here Comes Superman!!!" *Time*, November 27, 1978, pp. 59–61.

Holston, Kim. "In Search of Ingrid Pitt: A Big Chapter in the History of Moviegoing." *Film Ex*, Summer 1992, pp. 1–3.

James, Clive. "*2001*: Kubrick vs. Clarke." *Film Society Review*, January 1970, pp. 27–34.

Johnson, Steven. "Dreams and the Human Material in *Night of the Living Dead*." *Delirious*, no. 1, 1992, pp. 9–16.

Jones, Stephen. "Prince of Peril." *Halls of Horror* 3, no. 4, 1984, pp. 14–18.

Jongeward, Steven. "*Fright Night 2*." *Cinefantastique*, May 1988. pp. 18, 57.

Karloff, Boris. "My Life As a Monster." *Castle of Frankenstein* 4, no. 2, 1969, pp. 14–16.

"The Karnstein Trilogy." *Little Shoppe of Horrors*, May 1984.

Klein, Andy. "Batman Returns! So Where Is He?" *WM*, July 13-26, 1992, pp. 9, 12.

_____. "The Evolution of Batman." *WM*, July 13-26, 1992, p. 12.

Kuehls, David. "Two Guys with a Lot of Nerve." *Fangoria*, December 1990, pp. 46–49, 64.

Landon, Brooks. "Giger: Sliming Technology." *Cinefantastique*, May 1988, pp. 27–28.

Larson, Randall D. "The Score/Christopher Young on *Hellraiser*." *Cinefantastique*, May 1988, pp. 22, 58–59.

Logan, Earl. "I Was a Teenage...." *Scarlet Street*, Summer 1993, pp. 36–38, 40–42.

Lowry, Brian. "Chris Columbus Dreaming Up *Gremlins*." *Starlog* 86, September 1984, pp. 51–53, 66.

Lucas, Tim. "History of Horror: The 1960s." *Fangoria*, March 1991, pp. 62–65, 78.

McDonough, Maitland. "History of Horror: The 1970s." *Fangoria*, March 1991, pp. 68–72.

McNichol, Tom. "*Batman* and His Maker." *USA Weekend*, June 12-14, 1992, pp. 4–6.

Marshall, Lorne. "Vampire Films of the Seventies." *Midnight Marquee*, Summer 1993, pp. 6–19.

Martin, Bob. "Alan Ormsby: From Live Productions in the Family Garage to Screenwriting Paul Schrader's *Cat People*!" *Fangoria* 17, pp. 10–11, 43, 65.

_____. "*Basket Case* Update." *Fangoria* 17, pp. 30, 64.

_____. "Part 3 — on the Set of *Swamp Thing*. Wes Craven! Also: Dinner with a Playmate." *Fangoria* 17, pp. 17–20.

Martin, R. H. "On the Set: *Day of the Dead*." *Fangoria* 46, pp. 34–36, 38, 67.

"Meanwhile, *Friday the 13th* at the Movies Lumbers On." *Cinefantastique*, May 1988, p. 42.

"Metro Flock to London's *2001* Preem; Criticism Mixed on Good Side." *Variety*, May 8, 1968, p. 17.

"Michael Ripper: The Unsung Hero of Hammer." *Fantastic Worlds*, no. 1 [no date], pp. 8–12.

Moss, Robert F. "Director Steven Spielberg: New Epic, Big Stakes." *Saturday Review*, June 1981, pp. 12–15.

Murphy, Kathleen. "The Last Temptation of Sigourney Weaver." *Film Comment*, July-August 1992, pp. 17–20.

Newson, Ted. "The Creature Remake That Never Got Made," *Filmfax* 37, Feb./Mar 1993, pp. 64–67, 82, 98.

_____. "The Ray Harryhausen Story: Part One: The Early Years, 1920-1958." *Cinefantastique*, December 1981, pp. 24–44.

Pirani, Adam. "David Tomblin: A.D. [assistant director] to Indy Jones." *Starlog* 86, September 1984, pp. 44–46, 58.

"*Planet of Apes* Draws 'Em Like It's Summer." *Variety*, May 8, 1968, p. 36.

Price, Robert M. "Lovecraft on Screen." *Scarlet Street*, Winter 1994, pp. 68–70, 73–76, 78–79.

Rebello, Stephen. "Jack Clayton's *The Innocents*." *Cinefantastique* 12, June-July 1983, pp. 51–55.

"Rocket to the Rue Morgue." *Famous Monsters of Filmland*, no. 122, January 1976, pp. 24–35.

Rose, Lloyd. "Dracula: The Monster in Evening Clothes: A Brief History." *Washington Post*, November 15, 1992, pp. G1, G5.

Ryan, Desmond. "It's a Scary Time for Horror Sequels." *Philadelphia Inquirer*, November 4, 1990. p. 2-G.

Rybicki, Marty. "Interview: Whit Bissell." *Bits n Pieces*, Summer 1990, pp. 23–27.

Senn, Bryan. "The Golden Age of Horror: *Island of Lost Souls, Mad Love.*" *Midnight Marquee*, Summer 1993, pp. 20–29.

Shapiro, Marc. "John Lafia Pulls Some Strings." *Fangoria*, December 1990, pp. 14–17.

_____. "*Predator 2* Stalks the Urban Jungle." *Fangoria*, December 1990, pp. 36–40, 64.

Shay, Don. "Filming *The Omen.*" *Cinefantastique* 5, no. 3, 1976, pp. 40–47.

Sheridan, Bob. "History of Hammer Part 8: *The Viking Queen* to *Dracula Has Risen from the Grave.*" *Halls of Horror* 3, no. 4, 1984, pp. 42–47.

Sragow, Michael. "*2001: A Space Odyssey.*" *Film Society Review*, January 1970, pp. 23–26.

"*Star Wars.*" *Screen Superstar*, no. 8, 1977.

Sunden, Ed, I. "Dan O'Bannon on *Alien.*" *Fantastic Films*, September 1979, pp. 7–17, 29–30.

Svehla, Susan. "Beauty and the Beast: Eroticism in the Horror Film." *Midnight Marquee*, Summer 1993, pp. 62–78.

Szebin, Frederick C. "George Romero: Monkeying with Horror." *Cinefantastique*, May 1988. pp. 21, 55.

Thomas, Michael R. "How to Make a Frankenstein Monster." *Scarlet Street*, Winter 1993, pp. 36–41.

Turnbull, Greg. "Ingrid Pitt." *Halls of Horror* 3, no. 4, 1984, pp. 36–40.

"*2001* Draws Repeat and Recant Notices, Also a Quasi-Hippie Public." *Variety*, May 15, 1968, p. 20.

"*2001* Gathers a Famous Fans File; Kubrick Reviews, Except in N.Y., Good." *Variety*, June 19, 1968, p. 28.

Valley, Richard. "Mornings with Peter Cushing." *Scarlet Street*, Winter 1993, pp. 58–63.

Warren, Bill. "History of Horror: The 1950s." *Fangoria*, March 1991, pp. 25–28, 98.

Watson, Elena. "A Brief History of Cinema Mermaids." *Film Ex*, Summer 1991, pp. 5–6.

Weaver, Tom. "History of Horror: The 1930s and 1940s." *Fangoria*, March 1991, pp. 6–11, 60.

Weinberg, Marc. "*The Bride.*" *Fangoria* 46, pp. 47–49.

White, Taylor L. "*Critters II.*" *Cinefantastique*, May 1988, pp. 15, 55.

Williams, Sharon. "*Poltergeist III.*" *Cinefantastique*, May 1988, pp. 17, 55.

Books and Monographs

Annan, David. *Movie Fantastic: Beyond the Dream Machine*. New York: Bounty, 1974.

Balun, Charles. *The Connoisseur's Guide to the Contemporary Horror Film*. Albany NY: Fantaco, 1992.

Baxter, John. *Science Fiction in the Cinema*. New York: Paperback Library, 1970.

Blatty, William Peter. *William Peter Blatty on* The Exorcist: *From Novel to Film*. New York: Bantam, 1974.

Bleiler, David, ed. *TLA Film and Video Guide 1996-1997*. Philadelphia: TLA, 1996.

Blum, Daniel, and Willis, John. *Screen World*. New York: Applause. 1949 — (annually).

Bojarski, Richard, and Beale, Kenneth. *The Films of Boris Karloff*. Secaucus NJ: Citadel, 1974.

Brode, Douglas. *The Films of the Fifties*. Secaucus NJ: Citadel, 1976.

Brosnan, John. *Future Tense: The Cinema of Science Fiction*. New York: St. Martin's, 1978.

_____. *The Horror People*. New York: St. Martin's, 1976.

Brunas, Michael; Brunas, John; and Weaver, Tom. *Universal Horrors: The Studio's Classic Films, 1931-1946*. Jefferson NC: McFarland, 1990.

Butler, Ivan. *Horror in the Cinema*. New York: Paperback Library, 1971.

Clarens, Carlos. *An Illustrated History of the Horror Film*. New York: Putnam, 1967.

Ebert, Roger, *Movie Home Companion*, 1993. Kansas City MO: Andrews, McMeel, 1992.

Eyles, Allen; Adkinson, Robert; and Fry, Nicholas. *The House of Horror: The Complete Story of Hammer Films*. 2d ed. London: Lorrimer, 1984.

Finney, Jack. *The Body Snatchers*. New York: Dell, 1961.

Flynn, John L. *Cinematic Vampires: The Living Dead on Film and Television, from* The Devil's Castle *(1896) to* Bram Stoker's Dracula *(1992)*. Jefferson NC: McFarland, 1992.

Frank, Alan G. *Horror Movies: Tales of Terror in the Cinema*. Secaucus NJ: Derbibooks, 1975.

Gifford, Denis. *Movie Monsters*. London: Studio Vista, 1969.

_____. *Science Fiction Film*. London: Studio Vista, 1971.

Greaves, Tim. *Madeline Smith: A Celluloid Retrospective*. Eastleigh, Hampshire, England: 1 Shot, 1993.

_____. *Veronica Carlson: An Illustrated Memento*. Eastleigh, Hampshire, England: 1 Shot, 1994.

_____. *Yutte Stensgaard: A Pictorial Souvenir*. Eastleigh, Hampshire, England: 1 Shot, 1992.

Haggard, H. Rider. *She*. New York: Hart, 1976.

Halliwell, Leslie. *Halliwell's Film Guide*. 2d ed. New York: Scribner's 1977.

_____. *Halliwell's Film Guide*. 7th ed. New York: Harper and Row, 1989.

_____. *Halliwell's Harvest: A Further Choice of Entertainment Movies from the Golden Age*. New York: Scribner's 1986.

Hardy, Phil, ed. *The Encyclopedia of Horror Movies*. New York: Harper and Row, 1986.

Hogan, David J. *Dark Romance: Sexuality in the Horror Film*. Jefferson NC: McFarland, 1986.

Hutchinson, Tom. *Horror and Fantasy in the Movies*. New York: Crescent, 1974.

Jackson, Frank. "A History of Horror — on the Screen!" In *Film Review 1959-1960*, ed. by F. Maurice Speed. London: Macdonald, 1959, pp. 27–30.

Johnson, William, ed. *Focus on the Science Fiction Film*. Englewood Cliffs NJ: Prentice-Hall, 1972.

Kaminsky, Stuart M. *Don Siegel: Director*. New York: Curtis, 1974.

King, Steven. *Danse Macabre*. New York: Berkley, 1983.

Koontz, Dean R. *Watchers*. New York: Berkley, 1988.

LaValley, Al, ed. *Invasion of the Body Snatchers/Don Siegel, Director*. New Brunswick NJ: Rutgers University Press, 1989.

Le Fanu, J. Sheridan. "Carmilla." in *Best Ghost Stories of J. Sheridan Le Fanu*. Reprint, New York: Dover. 1964.

Magill, Frank N. ed. *Magill's Survey of Cinema, English Language Films*. First series. Englewood Cliffs NJ: Salem, 1980.

Maltin, Leonard, ed. *Leonard Maltin's Movie and Video Guide 1995*. New York: Signet, 1994.

_____. *Movie and Video Guide 1993*. New York: Signet, 1992.

_____. *Video Movie Guide 1991*. New York: Signet, 1990.

Martin, Mick, and Porter, Marsha. *Video Movie Guide 1994*. New York: Ballantine, 1993.

_____ and _____. *Video Movie Guide 1995*. New York: Ballantine, 1994.

_____ and _____. *Video Movie Guide 1997*. New York: Ballantine, 1996.

Midnight Marquee. *A Tribute to Hammer Films*. Baltimore: 1994.

Murphy, Michael J. *The Celluloid Vampires: A History and Filmography, 1897-1979*. Ann Arbor MI: Pierian, 1979.

Nicholls, Peter. *The World of Fantastic Films*. New York: Dodd, Mead, 1984.

_____, and John Clute. *The Encyclopedia of Science Fiction*. New York: St. Martin's 1993.

Parish, James Robert, and Pitts, Michael R. *The Great Science Fiction Pictures II*. Metuchen NJ: Scarecrow, 1990.

Parish, James Robert, and Whitney, Steven. *Vincent Price Unmasked*. New York: Drake, 1974.

Pattison, Barrie. *The Seal of Dracula*. New York: Bounty, 1975.

Phantom of the Movies. *The Phantom's Ultimate Video Guide*. New York: Dell, 1989.

Pirie, David. *A Heritage of Horror: The English Gothic Cinema, 1946-1972*. New York: Avon, 1974.

_____. *The Vampire Cinema*. London: Hamlyn, 1977.

Poe, Edgar Allan. *Great Tales and Poems of Edgar Allan Poe*. New York: Pocket, 1959.

Rovin, Jeff. *The Fabulous Fantasy Films*. South Brunswick and New York: Barnes, 1977.

_____. *The Laserdisc Film Guide, 1993-1994 Edition*. New York: St. Martin's 1993.

Sackett, Susan. *The Hollywood Reporter Book of Box Office Hits*. New York: Billboard, 1990.

Scheur, Steven H., ed. *Movies on TV*. New York: Bantam, 1968.

_____. *Movies on TV: 1982-1983 Edition*. New York: Bantam, 1981.

_____. *TV Key Movie Guide*. New York: Bantam, 1966.

Silver, Alain, and Ursini, James. *The Vampire Film: From Nosferatu to Bram Stoker's Dracula*. Rev. ed. New York: Limelight, 1993.

Speed, F. Maurice, ed. *Film Review 1958-59*. London: Macdonald, 1958.

_____. *Film Review 1962-63*. London: Macdonald, 1962.

Stanley, John. *The Creature Features Movie Guide*. New York: Warner, 1984.

_____. *John Stanley's Creature Features Movie Guide Strikes Again*. Pacifica CA: Creatures at Large, 1994.

Steinbrunner, Chris, and Goldblatt, Burt. *Cinema of the Fantastic*. New York: Galahad, 1972.

Stevenson, Robert Louis. *Dr. Jekyll and Mr. Hyde*. 1886. Reprint, with an introduction by Vladimir Nabokov, New York: Signet, 1987.

Stoker, Bram. *Dracula*. New York: Signet, 1965.

Tepper, Kirby. *Magill's Cinema Annual 1996*. 15th ed. Detroit: Gale, 1996.

Ursini, James, and Silver, Alain. *The Vampire Film*. South Brunswick and New York: A. S. Barnes, 1975.

Video Hound's Golden Movie Retriever 1994. Detroit: Visible Ink, 1994.

Video Hound's Golden Movie Retriever 1997. Detroit: Visible Ink, 1996.

Warren, Bill. *Keep Watching the Skies! American Science Fiction Movies of the Fifties*. Vol. I: 1950-1957. Vol. II: 1958-1962. Jefferson NC: McFarland, 1982, 1986.

Weldon, Michael. *The Psychotronic Video Guide*. New York: St. Martin's, 1996.

Wells, H. G. *The Invisible Man*. 1897. Reprint, New York: Bantam, 1988.

_____. *The Island of Dr. Moreau*. 1896. Reprint, New York: Signet, 1988.

Wilde, Oscar. *The Picture of Dorian Gray*. 1891. Reprint, London: Everyman, 1992.

Index

A & A Special Effects 355
Aames, Willie 527
Aarniokoski, Doug 396, 397
Aaron, Sidney 122
Abbott, Bruce 413, 415
Abbott, Bud 116, 192, 293, 341
Abbott, L.B. 47, 177, 178
Abbott, Shepard 83
Abbott and Costello 135, 258, 342
Abbott and Costello Meet Dr. Jekyll and Mr. Hyde 116–117, 252
Abbott and Costello Meet Frankenstein 133, 135, 192–194
Abbott and Costello Meet the Invisible Man 293–294
Abbott and Costello Meet the Mummy 340–341
Abel, Gene 328
Aber, Chuck 102
Abercrombie, Ian 210, 395
Abernathy, Lewis 267
The Abominable Dr. Phibes 15–16
Abrahams, Mort 380, 381
Abrams, Barry 217
Abrams, Peter 91, 513
The Absent-Minded Professor 17–19, 20, 318, 434, 435
The Abyss 478, 480
Accomando, Beth 37
Acheson, Jim 260
Ackerman, Forrest J 147, 148, 271, 272, 352
Ackland, Joss 56, 91, 92, 331
Ackland-Snow, Brian 153, 465
Ackland-Snow, Terence 24, 47, 465, 466
Acosta, Armand 251

Acquanetta, Burnu 71
Act of Vengeance 60
Action Comics 469
Acuff, Eddie 72
Adair, Peter 150
Adair, Robert 186
Adam, Ronald 173
Adams, Brooke 286
Adams, Dallas 15
Adams, Ernie 72
Adams, Jane 133, 135
Adams, Jason 396
Adams, Joely 164
Adams, Joyce 400
Adams, Julia 94
Adams, Mason 370
Adams, Nick 110, 111
Adams, Peter 307
Adams, Willie 218
Adamson, Al 144, 147
Addams, Charles 20
Addams, Dawn 117, 118, 503
The Addams Family 20
Addams Family Values 20–21
Addinsell, Richard 426
Adler, Gil 79
Adler, Matt 277
Adrian 114
Adrian, Iris 316, 319, 434
Adu, Frank 83
The Adventurers 5
Aeschlimann, Lawrence 416
Agar, John 97, 99, 101, 117, 305
Agutter, Jenny 81, 82, 108, 109, 272
Ahern, Lloyd 331
Aherne, Pat 116
Ahlberg, Mac 235, 264, 266, 413, 491
Ahlert, Fred 243
Ahrens, Anne 63

Aiello, Danny, III 32
Aiken, Joseph E. 88
Ainley, Anthony 309
Ainsley, Norman 186
Aird, Jane 400
Airplane 125, 167, 391
Akins, Claude 106, 384
Akkad, Moustapha 248, 249
Alacchi, Carl 240
Alain, Carolle 514
Alan, Lloyd 486
Alaniz, Rico 30
Alarcon, Jose Maria 87
Albain, Dick 355
Albee, Mary 214
Alberghetti, Anna Maria 238
Albert, Eddie 158
Albert, Ross 386
Albertson, Frank 89
Albertson, Jack 19, 331
AlchemyFX 396, 397, 493, 494
Alcott, John 54, 499
Alda, Rutanya 32
Aldana, Carl 247
Alden, Norman 118, 519
Alden, Stacey 356
Alderman, Jane 387
Aldiss, Brian W. 214, 215
Aldredge, Theoni V. 232
Aldredge, Tom 334
Aldrich, Rhonda 67
Alessandroni, Alessandro 208
Alexander, Ben 313
Alexander, George 30
Alexander, John 523
Alexander, Roslyn 80
Alexander, Suzanne 77
Alexander, Terence 120
Alexander, Terry 267, 349
Alford, Guy 376

Alice in Wonderland (1931) 21

Alice in Wonderland (1933) 21–22

Alice in Wonderland (1951) 22

Alice's Adventures in Wonderland 22–23

Alice's Adventures in Wonderland (book) 23

Alicia, Ana 246

Alider, Nick 23

Alien 23–24, 106, 122, 285, 392, 396, 481, 501, 515

Alien 3 27–29, 478

Aliens 24–27, 106, 478, 495, 516

Alison, Dorothy 121

All Quiet on the Western Front 309

Allan, Andrea 152

Allan, Aram 161

Alland, William 94, 96, 97, 100

Allard, Eric 438, 475

Allaylis, Toni 323

Allbritton, Louise 131

Allen, Antony 254

Allen, Betty 77

Allen, Conrad 387

Allen, David 394, 396, 415

Allen, Dede 20, 522

Allen, Gracie 367

Allen, Karen 408, 410, 411, 413, 427

Allen, Marty 124

Allen, Mel 137

Allen, Nancy 386, 416, 417, 418, 419

Allen, Patrick W. (U.S. actor) 376

Allen, Patrick (British actor) 362

Allen, Phillip Richard 444

Allen, Rosalind 79, 487

Allen, Sage 394

Allen, Scott 481

Allen, Sheila 510

Allen, Tyress 416

Alley, Kirstie 442, 511, 512

Allgood, Sara 114

"Alligator Man" (song) 148

Allin, Michael 175

Allman, Elvia 118

Allport, Christopher 282

Allwork, Peter 411

Almedia, Diane 224

Almond, Nina 412

Almoney, Keith 61

Alonso, Maria Conchita 388, 390

Alonzo, John A. 450

Alperson, Edward L. 281

Alperson, Edward L., Jr. 282

Alsberg, Arthur 318

Alston, Karen 248, 249

Alston, Peggy 165

Alt, Sally 175

Altamura, John 490, 491

Altered States 120, 122–124

Altman, Jeff 261

Alton, John 307

Alvarez, Juanita 74

Always 244

Alyn, Kirk 243, 461, 469

Alzado, Lyle 527

Amador, Miranda 236, 493

Amato, Paul 240

The Amazing Colossal Man 30, 264

Ambrose, Roger 37

Ambrosino, Mario 379

Ambuehl, Cindy 377

Ameche, Don 84, 85

Amend, Richard 329

American Graffiti 409, 453

An American in Paris 238

An American Werewolf in London 82, 272, 454

Ames, Leon 17, 19

Ames, Ramsay 339

Amfitheatrof, Daniele 35

Amin, Abbas 175

Amityville: A New Generation 35

Amityville: The Evil Escapes (book) 34, 35

The Amityville Curse 35

Amityville 4: The Evil Escapes (TV movie) 35

The Amityville Horror 31–32

The Amityville Horror (book) 35

Amityville 92: It's About Time 34–35

Amityville 3-D 33–34

Amityville II: The Possession 32–33

Amos, John 54

Amplas, John 102, 349

Amritraj, Vijay 446

Amy, Christopher 491

Anastos, Peter 20

Anders, Donna 92

Anders, Luana 168

Anders, Rudolph 198

Anderson, Agnes 131

Anderson, Angry 323

Anderson, Barbara 349

Anderson, Bill 434

Anderson, Cletus R. 102, 352

Anderson, Dame Judith 444

Anderson, Dusty 258

Anderson, E. Erich 221

Anderson, Eddie "Rochester" 489

Anderson, Erika 359

Anderson, Howard A. 382

Anderson, Ira 77, 199

Anderson, Ira, Jr. 369

Anderson, Judith 238

Anderson, Lance 373

Anderson, McKee 352

Anderson, Max W. 78

Anderson, Melody 175

Anderson, Michael 362

Anderson, Milo 128

Anderson, Richard L. 408

Anderson, Robert J., Jr. 63

Anderson, Roland 89

Anderson, Rona 426

Anderson, Sam 104

Anderson, Steve 249

Anderson, Vass 461

Anderson, William 418

Andre, Jill 353

Andreeff, Starr 480

Andress, Ursula 436, 437

Andrew, Jean 284

Andrews, Barry 143

Andrews, Bill 497

Andrews, Brian 245

Andrews, David 148

Andrews, Edward 18, 19, 241

Andrews, Harry 66, 279, 461

Andrews, Real 184

Andrews, Stanley 65, 460

Andrews, Tod 381

Andrews, Todd Eric 527

Andrich, Stephen F. 37

Andy C. 209

Andy Warhol's Dracula 157

Angel, Heather 170

Angels in the Outfield (1951) 35–36

Angels in the Outfield (1994) 36

Animal House 527

Ankers, Evelyn 71, 131, 189, 292, 524

Ankrum, Morris 281

Annakin, Ken 332

Annesley, Imogen 273, 274

Ansara, Michael 298, 300, 341

Anselmo, Victor 54

Anson, Jay 31

Anthony, Dean 486

Anthony, Lysette 125

Antico, Peter 261
Anton, Edward 266
Antonio, Jim 518
Antrim, Harry 331
Antrobus, Yvonne 126
Anwar, Gabrielle 288
Apogee Inc. 80
Apone, Allan 220
Apple, Jeff 527
Aranoff, Maria 175
Aranson, Judie 222
Arbeid, Ben 510
Arbus, Alan 370
Arbuthnot, Molly 194, 398
Archambault, Arch 92
Archard, Bernard 509
Archdale, Alexander 509
Archer, Barbara 136
Archer, Bernard 207
Archerd, Army 166
Archibald, William 279
Archuleta, J. Tom 387
Arden, Robert 370
Are You Being Served? (TV series) 152
Argento, Dario 348
Arkoff, Samuel Z. 31, 32, 58, 111, 183, 309, 310, 518
Arlen, Harold 520
Arlen, Richard 294, 295, 307
Arling, Arthur E. 237
The Armageddon see *Warlock: The Armageddon*
Armenaki, Arledge 275
Armstrong, Bess 124
Armstrong, R.G. 78, 259, 388, 513
Armstrong, Robert 302, 304
Armstrong, Valorie 359
Armstrong, Vic 87, 410, 411
Army of Darkness 161–162
Arness, James 482, 484
Arno, Sig 336
Arnold, Jack 94, 96, 97, 101, 333
Arnold, Jessie 524
Arnold, Kenneth 484
Arnold, Malcolm 362
Arnold, Marilee 39
Arnold, Mark 277, 493, 494
Arnold, Melanie 39
Arnold, Newton 320
Arnold, Roseanne 360
Arnold, Steve 331
Arnold, Tichina 314
Arnold, Tom 360
Arntzen, David 375
Arpino, Tony 201
Arquette, Lewis 267

Arquette, Patricia 356, 359
Arthur, Colin 431, 432
Arthur, Robert 192
Asche, Oscar 425
Ashbrook, Dana 352
Asher, E.M. 130
Asher, Jack 117, 135, 139, 194, 197, 325, 342
Asher, Jane 171, 398
Ashley, Graham 452
Ashley, John (actor) 199, 200, 499
Ashman, Howard 314
Ashton, Dyrk 352
Ashton, John 306
Ashton, Roy 140, 201, 202, 325, 344, 436
Askew, Maurice 208
Askin, Leon 210
Aslan, Gregoire 431
The Asphalt Jungle 59
The Asphyx 206
Aspin, Dale 322
Aspinal, Jennifer 490
Assault on Precinct 13 485
Assister, Claud 131
Assonitis, Ovidio G. 106
Asther, Nils 324
Astin, John 20, 37, 38, 242, 278
Astley, Edwin 333
Astredo, Humbert 268
Atcheson, Jeff 461
Atencio, Xavier 39
Atherton, William 233
Atkins, Don 312
Atkins, Peter 255, 256
Atkins, Tom 247, 248, 327
Atkinson, Liz 177
Atkinson, Martin 260, 370
"Atmospheres" (musical composition) 499
Atom Man vs. Superman (serial) 469
Attack of the Killer Tomatoes 36–37
Attack of the Killer Tomatoes 3 see *Killer Tomatoes Strike Back!*
Attack of the Puppet People 31
Attenborough, Richard 331, 332
Atterbury, Malcolm 276
Atwill, Lionel 127, 128, 133, 135, 188, 189, 190, 191
Atwood, Kathryn 226
Aubel, Joe 446
Auberjonois, Rene 52, 305, 449

Aubert, Lenore 192
Aubrey, Diane 509
Aubrey, James T. (producer) 518
Aubrey, James (actor) 116
Aubuchon, Jacques 434
Audley, Maxine 206, 309
Auelino, Ariston 295
Auric, Georges 120, 279
Austin, Charlotte 198, 199
Austin, John 116, 164, 516, 293
Austine, Nicola 152
Avengers (TV series) 426
Avery, Val 31, 32
Avon, Roger 127, 404
The Awakening 64–65
Axness, Ralph 118
Axton, Hoyt 241
Ayers, Curt 527
Aykroyd, Dan 232, 233, 234, 410
Aylesworth, Arthur 128
Aylett, Martin 263
Aylmer, Felix 22, 320, 342
Aylott, Eric 508
Aylward, John 475
Ayres, Lew 307, 308, 309, 369, 370, 384
Ayres, Robert 75
Azcuy, Annette 57
Azito, Tony 20

Baar, Tim 61
Babbs, O.B. 36
Babcock, Dwight V. 72, 339
Babcock, Fay C. 76
Babel 273
Babes in Toyland (1934) 38–39
Babes in Toyland (1961) 39–40
Babtist, Jennifer 490
Bacharach, Burt 61
Bachelin, Franz 232
The Bachelor and the Bobby-Soxer 66
Bachmann, Lawrence P. 510
Back to the Future 40–42, 43
Back to the Future Part II 42–43
Back to the Future Part III 43–44
Backwood Film 265
Bacon, Archie J. 305
Bacon, Kevin 217
Bacon, Norman 143
"Bad News" (song) 523
The Bad Seed 374
Badalamenti, Angelo 356

Baddeley, Hermione 426
Badel, Alan 510, 511
Baderman, Rubert 362
Badge of Silence see *Maniac Cop 3: Badge of Silence*
Badham, John 153, 438
Baer, John 460
Baeza, Paloma 91
Baggot, King 366
Baigent, Harold 322
Bailey, Anthony 498
Bailey, G.W. 329, 438
Bailey, John 75
Bailey, Raymond 317
Bain, Frazier 56
Baines, John 320
Baio, Scott 527
Baird, Jimmy 137
Baird, Philip 4
Baird, Stuart 367, 461
Bakalyan, Dick 159, 434
Baker, Betsy 159
Baker, Brydon 178
Baker, Buddy 434
Baker, Carrie 143
Baker, Frank 254
Baker, George 180, 371, 372
Baker, Graham 370
Baker, Herbert 231
Baker, Kenny 452, 454, 457
Baker, Kirsten 219
Baker, Martin G. 429
Baker, Raymond 83
Baker, Rick 52, 84, 242, 298, 301, 306, 454, 486
Baker, Roy (sound man) 148
Baker, Roy Ward (director) 121, 145, 150, 404, 406, 503
Baker, Tom 431
Bakey, Ed 527
Bakshi Productions 247
Balaban, Bob 123, 501
Balaski, Belinda 183, 241, 242, 271, 272
Balchowsky, Max 316
Balderston, John L. 129, 130, 153, 184, 319, 334, 342
Balduzzi, Dick 527
Baldwin, Michael 375, 376, 377
Baldwin, Robert M. 45, 215
Balfour, Michael 48, 400
Balk, Fairuza 523, 524
Balkan, Adele 177
Ball, David 103
Ballard, Terry 220
Ballas, James D. 433
Ballbasch, Peter 114
Balle, Jerry 369
Ballet de Paris 238

Ballew, Jerry 158
Ballhaus, Michael 155
Balsam, Bettylee 227
Balson, Michael 322
Balter, Sam 293
Baltimore, Vicki 522
Baltzell, Deborah 123
Bamford, Simon 255
Banbury, Jack 460
Band, Albert 236, 492
Band, Charles 107, 393, 394, 396, 397, 491, 492, 493, 494
Band, David 219
Band, Richard 122, 235, 252, 394, 395, 397, 413, 493
Banjoko, Kashka 522
Bank, Ashley 213
Banko, Jennifer 224
Banks, Don 110, 201, 345
Banks, Harold 77
Banks, Jonathan 241
Banks, Lionel 257
Bannister, Reggie 375, 376, 377
Banton, Travis 112
Bara, Nina 77
Barajas, Fausto 76
Baranski, Christine 21
"Barbara Allen" (song) 426
Barbaric Beast of Boggy Creek, Part II see *Boggy Creek II: And the Legend Continues...*
Barbarossa, Joscik 362
Barbeau, Adrienne 102, 103, 469, 471, 472
Barber, Bobby 293
Barbi, Vince 61
Barboo, Luis 86
Barbor, Jadeen 247
Barclay, Don 190, 339
Barclay, George (Ronald Kinnoch) 508, 511
Barclay, Jered 276
Barclay, John 114
Barclay, William 46
Barcroft, Roy 143
Bardette, Trevor 489
Barille, Anthony 222
Barker, Clive 68, 69, 70, 254, 255, 256
Barlow, Reginald 186
Barnabe, Bruno 346, 432
Barnes, Chris 140, 145, 149, 150, 207, 345, 413
Barnes, Gay 254
Barnes, Rayford 203
Barnes, Tim 148
Barnes, Walter 158

Barnett, Steve 424
Barnett, Vince 71
Baron, Bob 46
Baron, Helen 93
Baron, Joan-Carroll 214
Barr, Jackson 492
Barr, Patrick 150
Barr, Tony 232
Barratt, Reginald 145
Barrett, Clyde J. 522
Barrett, Majel 440, 446, 517
Barrett, Nancy 268, 269, 270
Barrett, Sean 523
Barrett, Tim 346
Barrie, H.E. 77, 199
Barrile, Terri 386
Barrington, Elizabeth 265
Barron, Jack 382
Barron, Keith 309
Barron, Robert V. 56
Barron, Steve 472
Barrows, Diana 224
Barrows, George 199
Barrows, James R. 356, 357
Barry, Alan 498
Barry, Donald 198, 199
Barry, Ivor 317
Barry, John 22–23, 305
Barry, John (production designer) 464
Barry, Neill 33
Barry, Wesley 281
Barrymore, Drew 40, 52, 53, 123
Barrymore, John 291
Barrymore, Lionel 243
Bartalos, Gabe (Gabriel Z.) 45, 46, 215, 516
Barth, Eddie 31
Bartlett, Ron 282
Bartley, Daryl 282
Bartold, Norman 516
Bartoli, Adolfo 395, 396, 397, 492, 493, 494
Barton, Charles T. 192, 433
Barton, Peter 222
Barton, Sean 107, 182, 457
Bartram, Laurie 217
Barty, Billy 186
Barvis, Tony 460
Bary, Lindsey 42
Barzell, Wolfe 199
Basehart, Richard 297
Bash, J.E. 237
Basile, Pierluigi 86
Basinger, Kim 47
Baskcomb, John 370
Basket Case 44–45, 216, 466
Basket Case II 45

Basket Cast 3: The Progeny 45–47
Baskin, Elya 501
Baskin, William 170
Bass, Stephen 381
Bassett, Angela 105
Bassett, William 282
Bassman, Don 383
Bassman, George 520
Basso, Bob 152
Batchler, Janet Scott 52
Batchler, Lee 52
Bateman, Jason 278
Bateman, Kent 278
Bateman, Susanne 222
Bates, Ben 469, 470
Bates, Charles 132
Bates, Ken 328, 438
Bates, Ralph 121, 122, 145, 506
Bateson, Linda 509
Bateson, Timothy 201, 333
Batman (1966) 47
Batman (1989) 47–50, 109, 262, 263
The Batman 53
Batman Forever 52–54
Batman Returns 50–52
Batt, Bert 22, 140, 206, 404
Battle, John Tucker 281
Battle for the Planet of the Apes 382, 384–385
Batts, Reggie 469
Bau, Gordon 198
Bauer, Belinda 418
Bauer, Mary 214
Bauer, Michelle 395
Baum, L. Frank 520, 521, 523
Baur, Tassilo 265
Baxley, Barbara 165
Baxley, Craig R. 388
Baxter, Alan 519
Baxter, Les 167, 168, 169, 170
Baxter, Meredith 519, 520
Bayhi, Chester L. 47
Bayldon, Geoffrey 136, 206, 239, 427
Bayliss, James 446
Bayliss, Peter 152
BB&J Visual Effects 513
Beach Party 40
Beacham, Stephanie 148, 150, 279, 281
Beal, John 33, 34
Beale, Erica 506
Beals, Jennifer 212
Beane, Hilary 527
Bearse, Amanda 227, 228
The Beast of Budapest 296

The Beastmaster 54–55
Beastmaster 2: Through the Portal of Time 55
Beaton, Timothy 120
Beattie, Richard 393
Beatty, Belinda 164
Beatty, Lou, Jr. 481
Beatty, May 319
Beatty, Ned 164, 166, 461, 463
Beatty, Robert 90, 372, 465, 468, 499
Beatty, Warren 259
Beauchamp, Wayne 376
Beaudine, William 142, 203
Beaumont, Charles 169, 171, 251
Beaumont, Richard 437
"The Beautiful Day" (song) 427
Beauty and the Beast 314
Beauty and the Beast (TV series) 478
Beavis, Ivan 204
Beck, Billy 63, 265
Beck, Glenn 499
Beck, Julian 386
Beck, Kimberly 221
Beck, Mat 165
Beckel, Graham 83
Becker, Gretchen 328
Becker, Joshua M. 159
Becker, Martin 220, 221, 222, 223, 225
Beckett, Jack 313
Beckett, Scotty 65
Becwar, George 30
Bedford-Lloyd, John 83
Bedknobs and Broomsticks 240
Beebe, Ford 131, 176, 292
Beer, Daniel 103
Beery, Wallace 114
Beesley, Anne 210
Beeson, Paul 110
Beetlejuice 49
Begley, Ed, Jr. 52, 76
Behrman, Joseph 194
Behrns, Don 223
Belaire, Louis 311
Belcher, Joe 153
Belfrage, Cedric 291
Bell, Alexander Graham 91
Bell, Arnita 59
Bell, Arnold 180
Bell, Dan 108
Bell, Derrick 522
Bell, Jimmy 499
Bell, Marshall 356
Bell, Mindy 387

Bell, Nancy 518
Bellamy, Ned 267
Bellamy, Ralph 189, 365, 524
Bellucci, Monica 156
Bellwood, Peter 260, 261
Belmore, Daisy 129
Belmore, Lionel 185, 188
Beloin, Edmund 89
Belson, Jerry 124, 244
Beltran, Alma 365
Belushi, James 314
Belyeu, Jon G. 247
Ben 519–520
Ben-Hur 274
Bender, Jack 82
Bender, Russ 30
Bendix, William 89
Beneath the Planet of the Apes 380–382
Benedek, Tom 84
Benedict, Paul 20
Benedict, William 307
Benett, Robert 350
Benge, Wilson 116
Benjamin, Richard 152, 516, 517
Benjamin, Susan 374
Bennett, Brian 527
Bennett, Bruce 35
Bennett, Constance 488, 489
Bennett, Fran 361
Bennett, Harve 442, 443, 446, 447
Bennett, Hywell 22
Bennett, Leila 127
Bennett, Marjorie 116, 142
Bennett, Randy 160
Bennett, Richard 184, 325
Benninghofen, Jeff 306
"Ben's Song" (song) 519, 520
Bensen, Lucille 246
Benson, Anthony 362
Benson, Douglas 352
Benson, George 136
Benson, John 61
Benson, Martin 367
Bentley, Beverly 83
Benton, Eddie 390
Benton, Robert 461
Benton, Robert R. (set decorator) 118, 238, 434
Benveniste, Michael 175
Bercovici, Luca 235, 236, 423
Bercu, Michaela 156
Berdhal, Blaze 373
Beregi, Oscar 210
Berenson, Berry 76

Beresen, Meyer 21
Beresford, Harry 127
Berg, Jon 182
Bergen, Polly 125
Berger, Debra 282
Berger, Helmut 379
Berger, Howard 103
Berger, Peter E. 365, 447, 450
Berger, Richard 446
Bergin, Patrick 217
Berglas, Ron 260
Bergman, Andrew 366
Bergman, Harold 84
Bergman, Ingrid 114, 115, 475
Bergman, Jeff 242
Bergman, Robert 240
Bergman, Sandahl 86
Bergstrom, Catherine 246
Bergstrom, Cynthia 486
Berke, Irwin 198
Berkeley, Martin 97
Berkeley, Xander 68, 478
Berkey, James 297
Berlant, Jordan 352
Berlinger, Max 261
Berlinger, Warren 434
Berman, Pandro S. 377
Berman, Rick 450
Berman, Shelley 61
Bermel, Pat 182
Bermingham, The Rev. T. 162
Bernal, Gil 144
Bernard, Barry 178
Bernard, James 135, 137, 140, 143, 144, 145, 194, 203, 206, 207, 208, 398, 400, 406, 407, 436, 437
Bernard, Jay 249
Bernard, Joseph E. 133
Bernard, Sam 513
Bernardi, Adam 55, 236
Bernardi, Barry 386
Bernay, Lynne 168
Bernds, Edward L. 178
Berne, Izzy 460
Bernhard, Harvey 367, 369, 370
Bernhardt, Kevin 256
Bernota, George 45
Bernsen, Collin 394
Bernstein, Charles 152, 354
Bernstein, Elmer 76, 77, 232
Bernstein, Jaclyn 386
Bernstein, Susanna 424
Berova, Olinka 437, 438
Berry, Al 247, 413
Berry, Ken 317

Berry, Richard F. 376
Berry, Sarah 160
Berry, Walter 352
Berryman, Dorothee 422
Berryman, Michael 446
Bertera, Denis 372
Besch, Bibi 442
Best, Willie 230, 231
Beswick, Doug 160
Beswick, Martine 372, 373; see also Beswicke, Martine
Beswicke, Martine 105, 121, 122, 492
Bethard, Robert E. 311
Bethune, Ivy 40
Bettinson, Ralph Gilbert 362
Betts, Kirsten 503
Bevan, Billy 114, 131, 291, 292
The Beverly Hillbillies 63
Beware! The Blob 61–63
Bewes, Rodney 90
Bey, Sara 208
Bey, Turhan 337
Beyda, Kent 227, 242
Beyond Thunderdome see *Mad Max: Beyond Thunderdome*
Biddle, Adrian 24
Biehn, Michael 24, 28, 476, 478, 480
The Big Chill 456
Biggs, R. Christopher 357
Bilbrook, Lydia 377
Bill and Ted's Bogus Journey 56–58
Bill and Ted's Excellent Adventure 55–56
Billings, Dawn Ann 493
Billingsley, Barbara 281
Billy, Michele Ameen 440
Billy the Kid vs. Dracula 142–143, 203
Bilson, Danny 491
Binder, Maurice 64
Bingham, Barbara 225
Binion, Crawford 366
Biolos, Leigh 273
Birch, Frank 153
Birch, Paul 363
Birch, Timothy 472
Birch, Wyrley 315
Birchfield, Cheryl 233
Bird, Minah 152
Bird, Norman 120, 370
Birdsong, Nikki 42
Birkett, Bernadette 125
Birkin, Andrew 370

Birn, Jerry 387
Birnbaum, Bob 365
Birney, David 365
Birney, Frank 104
Biroc, Joseph (Joe) 30, 307, 382
Bischoff, Robert 65
Bishop, Barbara 144
Bishop, Charles 465
Bishop, Edward 499
Bisley, Steve 321
Bissell, Whit 94, 195, 197, 276, 277, 284, 285
The Bite see *Curse II — The Bite*
Bitterman, Shem 249
Bivens, J.B. 252
Bixler, Denise 160
Black, Don 22, 519
Black, Gerry 413
Black, Isobel 508
Black, Karen 28, 30, 527
Black, Shane 388
Black, Stewart 379
"The Black Cat" (film segment) 169
The Blackboard Jungle 463
Blackburn, Clarisse 270
Blackenstein: The Black Frankenstein 209–210
Blackler, George 508
Blackman, Don 59
Blackmer, Sidney 307
Blackmore, Peter 332, 333
Blackshaw, Anthony 201
Blackwell, George 15, 372, 436
Blackwell, R. 388
Blacula 58–59, 210, 276
Blades, Ruben 388
Blahora, Dasha 273
Blair, Isla 145
Blair, Joan 132
Blair, Kevin 224
Blair, Linda 155, 162, 163, 164, 165, 166, 167, 527, 528
Blaisdell, Brad 481
Blaisdell, Paul 30, 363
Blaise, Cynthia 447
Blake, Amanda 238
Blake, Angela 195
Blake, Anne 194
Blake, Arthur 400
Blake, Howard 33, 175
Blake, Madge 47
Blake, Richard 281, 282
Blake, Yvonne 461, 464
Blakely, Colin 437
Blakiston, Caroline 457
Blakley, Ronee 354

Blalack, Robert 527
Blandick, Clara 520
Blaney, Tim 438, 439
Blankfield, Mark 124
Blari, Adam 313
Blass, Everett 284
Blatty, William Peter 162, 164, 165
Blees, Robert 16
Blerk, Patric Van 107
Blessed, Brian 175
Blewitt, David 232
Blezard, John 320
Blick, Hugo E. 48
Blinn, Beatrice 315
Bliss, Lela 331
Blitz, Rusty 210
The Blob (1958) 60–61, 63, 129
The Blob (1988) 63
Block, Irving 281
Block, Larry 259
Blommaert, Susan 373
Blondell, Joan 489
Blondheim, George 23
Blood and Roses 506
Blood from the Mummy's Tomb 64, 122, 346
Blood of Dracula 157–158
Blood of Dracula's Castle 144–145
The Blood on Satan's Claw 173
Blood Sacrifice see *Curse III — Blood Sacrifice*
Bloom, John 49, 131, 147, 153
Bloomfield, John 86, 468
Bloomquist, Tom 155
Blu, Susan 224
The Blue Bird (1940) 65–66
The Blue Bird (1976) 66
"The Blue Danube" (musical composition) 499
Blum, Edwin 258
Blumenfeld, Alan 223
Blumenthal, Herman 516
Blythe, Peter 203
Blythe, Sidney 425
Boa, Bruce 454
Boag, Wally 316
Boam, Jeffrey 411
Bocchicchio, Alfeo 59
Bochner, Hart 466, 467
Bock, Larry 103
Bockner, Martin 240
Bockner, Michael 240
Boddey, Martin 75, 333
Bodeen, DeWitt 72, 74, 75
Bodkin, Craig 282

Bodkin, Tain 212
Body Heat 456
Body Snatchers 288–289
The Body Snatchers (*Collier's* magazine serial and book) 284
Boehm, David 242, 244
Boehm, Susan 234
Boemler, George 425
Boen, Earl 476, 478, 480
Boepple, Beatrice 359
Bogarde, Dirk 120
Bogart, Humphrey 128, 129, 475
Bogart, Keith 250
Bogart, Paul 366
Bogart, Tracy 366
Boggs, Haskell 238
Boggy Creek II: And the Legend Continues... 312
Bohem, Leslie 266, 359
Boht, Margot 146
Boita, Peter 90
Bolder, Cal 203, 204
Boles, John 185
Bolger, Ray 39, 97, 520, 521
Bolin, Nick 209
Boll, Helen 386
Bolling, Claude 64, 32
Bollman, Ryan 79
Bolomet, Patricia 469
Bonacki, Lou 328
Bonanza (TV series) 277
Bond, David 350
Bond, James (character) 23, 224
Bond, Rene 313, 314
Bond, Steve 486, 487
Bond, Tommy 469
Bond, Trevor 334
Bond, Ward 188, 243, 488
Bonham, John 152
Bonilla, Arturo 352
Bonime, Andrew 83
Bonner, Beverly 44
Bonner, William 147
Bonnet, James 61
Bonnie and Clyde 501
Bonus, Vicente 295
The Boogey Man 67
Boogeyman II 67–68
Boorman, Imogen 255
Boorman, John 164, 165
Booth, Nancy 84
Borchers, Donald P. 78
Borde, Mark 252
Borden, Eugene 177
Borge, Rikke 33
Borgnine, Ernest 519
Borher, Corine 527

Borlenghi, Matt 359
Born Free 23
Bornstein, Charles 104, 244, 273, 351
Borris, Clay 39
Boswall, John 362
Boswell, Glen 323
Bottin, Rob 416, 417, 418, 419, 484
Bottoms, Timothy 282
Boucher, Savannah Smith 423
Boudot, Sabrina 392
Boulle, Pierre 380, 381, 382, 383, 384
Boulton, Davis 510
Boulton, Matthew 116, 324
Boushel, Joy 181
Boutross, Thomas F. 311
Bowen, Roger 527
Bower, Antoinette 390, 391
Bower, Dallas 22
Bowers, Lally 148, 239
Bowers, Richard 424
Bowie, David 75
Bowie, Les 148, 201, 203, 342, 398, 404
Bowie Films 140, 345, 404, 436, 437
Bowman, Tom 509
Box, Betty 332, 333
Box, Brian 503
Boxing Helena 513
The Boy Who Cried Werewolf 318
Boyd, David 486
Boyd-Perkins, Eric 117, 436
Boyden, Raymond 67
Boyer, Charles 316
Boyle, Eddie 281
Boyle, Lara Flynn 387
Boyle, Marc 464
Boyle, Peter 210–211
Bracken, Richard 469
Brackenbury, Pat 121
Brackett, Leigh 454
Bracknell, David 506
Bradbury, Ray 406
Braden, Kim 450
Bradford, Greg 527
Bradford, Marshall 195
Bradley, Doug 254, 255, 256
Bradley, Elizabeth 85
Bradley, Jordan 248
Bradshaw, Irene 121
Bradstreet, Charles 192
Brady, Dale 446
Brady, Dorothy 258
Brady, Ed 305
Brady, Scott 241

Braeden, Eric 382
Braga, Brannon 450
Braha, Herb 81, 271
Braham, Lionel 426
Brahm, Hans (John) 425
Brahms, Penny 148, 499
The Brain 309
The Brain That Wouldn't Die 309
Bram Stoker's Dracula 56, 155–157, 216
Branagan, John 364
Branagh, Kenneth 216
Branch, Tom 412
"Brand New Day" (song) 523
Brandenberg, Rosemary 277
Brandner, Gary 271, 273, 274, 275
Brando, Marlon 279, 281, 461
Brandon, Henry 232; *see also* Kleinbach, Henry
Brandon, Peter 123
Brandt, Janet 366
Brandt-Burgoyne, Anita 91
Brandy, Howard 64
Brandy, J.C. 250
Brandy, Mycle 175
Brascia, Dominic 222
Bratcher, Joe 271
Braus, Mortimer 116
Bray, Robert 482
Bray, Thom 267
Brayfield, Douglas 277
Brazzi, Rossano 370
Brealond, Tony 522
Breaux, Marc 239, 240
Bredell, Elwood 189, 336
Bredhoff, Susan 123
Breitenstein, Jochen 67
Bren, Milton H. 489
Brennan, Frederick Hazlitt 242, 244
Brennan, Kevin 90
Brennan, Michael 506
Brennan, Walter 186, 289
Brenner, Dori 123
Brenner, Gordon D. 318
Brenner, Jules 278, 350
Brent, Lynton 302
Breon, Edmond 324, 482
Bresee, Bobbi 235
Bresin, Marty 104
Bresslaw, Bernard 152
Bretherton, David 516
Brett, Anna 121
Brewster, Carol 77
Brewton, Maia 40
Brian, Judith 116

Briant, Shane 208
Brice, Derrick 350
Bricker, Jack 273
Bricker, Randolph K. 250
Bricusse, Leslie 426
The Bride 212–213
Bride of Frankenstein 185–187, 426
Bride of Re-Animator 216, 415
The Brides of Dracula 137, 139–140
Bridges, Alicia 152
Bridges, Jeff 305
Bridges, Lloyd 257, 264
Brierley, Roger 464
Briers, Richard 216
Brigandi, Phil 482
Briggs, Katharine 373
Briley, John 510
Brimble, Nick 214
Brimley, A. Wilford 84, 85, 484
Brincken, William von 131
Bring, Bob 159, 434
Brinton, Ralph 426
Briscoe, Donald 268
Briscoe, Laurie 252
Briskin, Mort 519
Brislane, Mike 446
Brissac, Virginia 231, 337
Britton, Katherine 40
Britton, Tony 310
Broadbent, Jim 468
Broady, Eloise 486
Brocco, Peter 125, 281
Brock, Ian 109
Brock, Phil 261
Brock, Stanley 152
Brockett, Don 349
Broderson, Fred 84
Brodie, Don 158, 209
Brodie, Steve 211, 212, 307
Brodine, Norbert 371, 488, 489
Brodrick, Susan 121
Brody, David A. 102, 103
Broken Arrow (TV series) 203
Broker, Richard 220
Brolin, James 31, 32, 33, 516, 517
Bromberg, Erich 210
Bromberg, J. Edward 131, 292
Bromfield, John 97, 99
Bromley, Sydney 110, 208
Bromwell, Lisa 493, 494
Brooke, Hillary 281
Brooke, Walter 93

Brooks, Elizabeth 271
Brooks, Hugh 307
Brooks, Jack 238
Brooks, Jess Lee 132
Brooks, Joe 241
Brooks, Mel 187, 210, 211
Brooks, Ray 127
Brooks, Rolland M. 519
Brooks, Victor 139, 309
Brophy, Bob 209
Brophy, Edward 319
Bros, Chiodo 104
Brost, Fred 158
Brothers, Joyce 365
Brotherson, Eric 58
Broughton, Bruce 331
Brouwer, Peter 217
Brown, Alfred 429
Brown, Andrea 160
Brown, Blair 123
Brown, Bobie 175
Brown, Clancy 212, 213, 260, 261, 374
Brown, Clarence 35
Brown, David 84, 85
Brown, David Gavin 375
Brown, David Harold 42
Brown, Dwier 265
Brown, Gay 171
Brown, Harry 192
Brown, Hilyard 94, 192
Brown, Jamie 225
Brown, Jennifer 42
Brown, Jimmy 322
Brown, John 126
Brown, Nannette 469
Brown, Pamela 22, 227
Brown, Phil 72, 452
Brown, Ralph 27
Brown, Reb 273
Brown, Rick 511
Brown, Robert (editor) 31
Brown, Robert 171, 372
Brown, Robert, Jr. 369
Brown, Robert Latham 82
Brown, Roger Aaron 418, 440
Brown, Scotty 169
Brown, Thomas 263
Brown, Todd Cameron 43
Brown, Wally 17
Brown, Walter 141
Brown, William F. 522
Brown, William Lyon 372, 437
Browne, Diana 44
Browning, Norman 514
Browning, Ricou 94, 97, 98
Browning, Tod 64, 129, 130
Bruce, Jonathan 395

Bruce, Nigel 65, 435
Bruce, Virginia 291
Bruck, Arnold H. (Arnie) 44, 240
Bruner, Anne 246
Bruno, Richard 259
Bruno the dog 509
Bruns, George 17, 19, 316, 317
Brutsman, Joseph 282
Bryan, Dora 333
Bryan, Peter 139
Bryant, John 423
Bryant, Kurt 474
Bryant, Michael 120
Bryant, Nana 71
Bryant, Todd 22, 447
Bryar, Claudia 195
Brymer 130
Brynner, Yul 516, 517, 518
Bryon, Arthur 335
Buba, Pasquale 102, 349
Buccossi, Peter 261
Buchman, Sidney 257
Buchner, Fern 20
Buck, Pamela 509
Buckler, Hugh 315
Buckley, Gae 166
Buckley, Keith 16
Buckley, Norman 377
Bud the CHUD see *C.H.U.D. II: Bud the CHUD*
Buday, Helen 323
Budd, Roy 432
Buechler, John (Carl) 224, 235, 236, 248, 250, 413, 423, 424, 486, 487
Buff, Conrad 438, 478
Buffy the Vampire Slayer 330
Buford, Gordon 316, 317, 318
Buggy, Niall 254
Bujold, Genevieve 24
Bull, Peter 22, 426
Bulloch, Jeremy 454, 457
Bullock, Walter 65
Bumstead, Henry 238
Bundy, Brooke 356, 357
Bunin, Lou 22
Bunston, Herbert 129
Buono, Victor 381
Burch, Curt 300
Burden, Hugh 64
Burgess, James 165
Burian-Mohr, Chris 52, 244
Burke, Alfred 510
Burke, Billie 488, 489, 520
Burke, Eldon 381
Burke, James 258

Burke, Johnny 89
Burke, Kathleen 294
Burke, Robert John 419
Burkholder, Scott 267
Burman, Bari-Dreiband 427
Burman, Thomas R. (Tom) 75, 247, 297, 427
Burman Studios 277, 444
Burn, Jonathan 64
Burnett, Mary Nancy 298
Burnham, Burnham 273
Burnham, Edward 15
Burnham, Jeremy 207
Burns, George 365, 366, 367
Burns, John Charles 370
Burns, Paul 460
Burns, Paul E. 337
Burns, Robert A. 271, 413
Burns, Stephan W. 319
Burns, Tim 321
Burnside, Henrietta 72
Burr, Cynthia 123
Burr, Jeff 396, 397
Burr, Timothy 225
Burrell, Everett 352
Burress, William 38
Burrill, Timothy 466
Burroughs, Edgar Rice 87, 309, 310
Burroughs, Jackie 184
Burrows, Rosemary 197
Burstyn, Ellen 162, 164
Burton, Jeff 380
Burton, John 315
Burton, Julian 171
Burton, LeVar 450
Burton, Norman 380
Burton, Richard 164, 362
Burton, Robert 195
Burton, Tim 47, 50, 109, 262
Burton, Willie 411
Burtt, Benjamin 408, 410, 411
Burum, Stephen H. 212
Bury, Sean 15
Busby, Jane 457
Busey, Gary 388
Bush, Billy Green 103, 226
Bush, Dick 148, 508
Bush, Grand L. 165, 328
Bush, Jon 509
Bush, Morris 146
Bushelman, John A. 76, 198
Buss, Godfrey 61
Bussieres, Raymond 22
Butcher, Oliver 125
Butkus, Dick 242
Butler, Bill 80, 152, 369
Butler, Cindy 312
Butler, David 88

Butler, Frank 38
Butler, Hugo 425
Butler, Tom 422
Butler, William 352
Butler, William Clarke 224
Butler-Glouner, Inc. 169, 170
Butrick, Merritt 228, 442, 444, 527
Butterworth, Shane 164
Buttram, Pat 43
Byington, Spring 35, 65
Byrne, Eddie 342, 452
Byrne, Michael 411
Byrnes, Burke 82
Byron, Kathleen 508
Byron, Kathryn 335
Byron, Nicholas 482

Cabanne, Christy 336
The Cabinet of Caligari 187
Cabot, Bruce 302
Cabot, Ceil 319
Cabrera, Charley 377
Cacavas, John 149
Cadell, Ava 364
Caglione, John, Jr. 32, 33, 83, 386
Cahall, Robin 306
Cahn, Daniel 109
Cahn, Philip (Phil) 190, 336
Cain, Roger 410
Caine, Henry 194
Caine, Michael 429
Caldinez, Sonny 408
Caldwell, Russ 316
Calico, Ltd. 79
Calker, Darrell 460
Callaghan, Duke 86
Callahan, James T. 353
Callan, Michael 497, 498
Callard, Kay 75
Callaway, Tom 105
Calthrop, Donald 425
Calvet, Corinne 122
Calvin, Henry 39, 40
Calvin, Tony 121
Cambas, Jacqueline 75
Cambern, Donn 234
Cambridge, Ed 57
Cambridge, Godfrey 61, 62
Cameron, Isla 279
Cameron, James 24, 26–27, 29, 476, 478, 480
Cameron, John 108
Cameron, William 349, 352
Camilleri, Terry 56
Camp, Hamilton 259
Camp, Robin 116
Campanella, Frank 259

Campanella, Joseph 519
Campbell, Bill 156
Campbell, Bruce 108, 159, 160, 161, 162, 327, 328
Campbell, Diane 267
Campbell, Doug 527
Campbell, John W., Jr. (aka by pseudonym Don A. Stuart) 482, 484, 486
Campbell, Ken 212
Campbell, R. Wright 171
Campbell, Shawn 282
Campbell, Tisha 314
Campion, Gerald 332
Campisi, Tony 282
Campo, Wally 169, 312
Camroux, Ken 182, 252
Candy, John 314
Candyman 68–69
Candyman: Farewell to the Flesh 69–71
Cane, Charles 97, 307
Cann, David 362
Cannom, Greg 84, 85, 155
Cannon, Dyan 259
Cantamessa, Gene S. 446
Cantarini, Louis 473
Canton, Neil 40, 42, 43
Cantwell, Colin J. 499
Caplin, Cate 486
Capone, Clifford 33
Capote, Truman 279
Capra, Frank 314, 315
Capra, Frank, Jr. 382, 384
Capra, Frank, III 446, 527
Capshaw, Kate 410
Captain Kronos, Vampire Hunter 506
Captain Marvel (radio series) 469
Captain Nemo and the Underwater City 497–499
Captain Sindbad 433
Captive Wild Woman 71
Caramico, Robert 209
Caraway, Jerry 311
Carbone, Anthony 168
Cardi, Pat 384
Cardiff, Jack 64, 65, 87
Cardille, Bill "Chilly Billy" 347, 352
Cardille, Lori 349
Cardos, John 144
Carere, Frank 230
Carewe, Arthur Edmund 127
Carey, Christopher 514
Carey, Harry, Jr. 43, 142, 165, 241
Carey, Leslie I. 94, 97, 100

Carey, Macdonald 301
Carey, Olive 142
Carhart, Timothy 70, 233
Carl, Adam 214
Carleton, Claire 116
Carlin, Fred 518
Carlin, George 56
Carlin, Katie 376
Carlisle, Steve 106
Carlos, Flory 295
Carlson, Jonathan 37
Carlson, Les 181
Carlson, Richard 94, 96, 99, 101, 230
Carlson, Veronica 143–144, 152, 157, 206–207
Carlton, Hope Marie 236, 237, 357
Carlton, Mark 416
Carlton, Rex 144
Carlucci, Lou 361
Carmen, Julie 228
Carmichael, Hoagy 488
Carmichael, Ralph 61
Carmilla (novella) 503, 506
Carney, Art 18, 445
Caron, Leslie 238
Carpenter, Jill 148
Carpenter, John 97, 226, 244, 246, 247, 248, 249, 250, 392, 484, 485, 486, 511, 512
Carpenter, Ken 256
Carpenter, Russell 104, 374
Carpenter, Thelma 522
Carr, Jackie 241, 244
Carr, Larry 195, 221
Carr, Paul 519
Carr, Stephen 460
Carr, Steven E. 396, 397
Carr-Forster, Philippe 67
Carradine, John 67, 71, 133, 135, 142, 144, 145, 186, 190, 191, 192, 211, 212, 271, 272, 289, 292, 339
Carras, Anthony 167, 168, 169
Carras, Nicholas 77, 199
Carras, Robert 122
Carrell, Dany 320
Carrera, Barbara 297
Carrera, Tamara 42
Carreras, Michael 64, 117, 194, 197, 325, 342, 344, 372, 436
Carrey, Jim 52
Carrick, Lloyd 322
Carrie 390, 392, 527
Carrier, Tim 352
Carrillo, Elpidia 388

Carrisosa, Frank 220
Carrol, Ann 363
Carrol, Regina 147
Carrol, Ronn 217
Carroll, Charles 416
Carroll, Edwina 499
Carroll, Gordon 23, 27
Carroll, Leo G. 426
Carroll, Lewis 21, 22, 23
Carroll, Moon 129
Carroll, Ted 153, 175
Carruth, Milton 71, 129, 130, 334, 337
Carson, Charles 180, 425
Carson, Crystal 38
Carson, David 450
Carson, Ganahl 315
Carson, Hunter 282, 283
Carson, John 145
Carter, Ann 74, 89
Carter, Deborah 349
Carter, Eric 426
Carter, Fred 306, 432
Carter, Harry 177
Carter, Helena 281
Carter, Helena Bonham 216
Carter, Jack 171
Carter, Michael 457
Cartlidge, Bill 201
Cartwright, Bob 427
Cartwright, Percy 117
Cartwright, Veronica 23–24, 27, 70, 286
Caruso, Josie 348
Carvalho, Betty 249
Carver, James 393
Carver, Lynne 426
Carvey, Dana 246
Cary, Tristram 64, 404, 407
Casablanca 475
Case, Carroll 142, 203
Case, Justin 523
"The Case of Charles Dexter Ward" (short story) 171, 251, 252, 253
"The Case of M. Valdemar" (film segment) 169
Casella, Martin 385
Casey, Bernie 56, 122
Casey, Gertrude 433
Casey, Katie 67
Casey, Lucille 258
Cash, Renata 208
Cash, Rosalind 122
Cashen, Irina 42
"The Cask of Amontillado" (short story) 169
Caso, Mark 474, 475
Cason, Barbara 164, 268
Cass, David 297

Cassady, Bill 30
Cassady, John 260
Cassidy, Jay 214
Cassidy, Jay Lash 228
Cassidy, Mike 263
Cassie, Alan 410
Castelnuovo-Tedesco, Mario 258, 377
Castle, John 419, 420
Castle, Nick 238, 244
Castle, Roy 126
The Cat and the Canary 231
Cat Girl 75
Cat People 75–76, 193, 274
The Cat People 72–74
Cat-Women of the Moon 76–77, 78
Catacombs 107
Cater, John 15, 16
Cates, Gilbert 365
Cates, Madelyn 125
Cates, Phoebe 241, 242
Cathcart, Daniel B. 114., 238
Cathleen, Charlene 235
Catlin, Victoria 235, 275, 327
Caton, Craig 446
Cattrall, Kim 329, 330, 449
Cavanagh, Paul 116, 324, 325
Cavanaugh, Larry 246
Cavett, Dick 356
Cawthorn, James 309
Cazin, John P. 275
CCH Pounder 419
Ceccatti, Sharon 348
Cecere, Tony 472
Cedar, Larry 84
Cele, Henry 107
Central Park Driver see *Graveyard Shift*
Cerny, David 79
Cervantes, Carlos 275
Cey, Jacques 333
Chaffey, Don 372
Chained Heat 164, 167
Chakiris, George 125
Chalem, Brent 213
Chalk, Gary 182
Challee, William 143
Chamberlain, Richard 239
Chamberlain, Wilt 87, 88
Chambers, John F. 246, 297, 381, 382
Chambers, Michael "Shrimp" 57
Chambers, Stan 31
The Champ 114
Chan, David 472, 474, 475
Chan, George 315

Chan Shen 150
Chancer, Noran 454
Chandler, Eddy 72
Chandler, Estee 278
Chandler, George 158
Chandler, Helen 129, 130
Chandler, John (David) 377, 492
Chandler, Lane 292, 307
Chandler, Vivienne 506
Chandler Group 360
Chandra Kaly Dancers 341
Chaney, Lon, Jr. 131, 133, 135, 147, 189, 190, 191, 192, 251, 252, 337, 338, 339, 341, 342, 371, 524, 525
Chaney, Lon, Sr. 130
Chang, Lia 215
Chantler, David 436
Chapin, Jonathan 249
Chaplin, Jennifer 527
Chapman, Ben 94, 97, 281
Chapman, Joan 330
Chapman, Michael 286, 427
Chapman, Sean 254, 255
Chappelle, Joe 250
Chappelow, T.C. 480
Charbonneau, Patricia 418
Chark, Wallis 307
Charkham, David 499
Charles, Cindy 36
Charles, Gloria 220
Charlesworth, John 426
Charlita 143
Charman, Roy 2
Charney, Jordan 233
Charno, Stu 219
Chase, Carl 28, 47
Chase, Frank 100
Chase, Ken 40
Chase, Steven 61, 62
Chaskin, David 106, 355
Chatfield, Pam 348
Chattaway, Jay 327, 328
Chatto, Tom 400
Chau, Francois 474
Chaves, Richard 388
Chayefsky, Paddy 122
Cheek, Douglas 83
Cheeseman, Ted 302, 304, 435
Chegwidden, Ann 127
Chen, China 219
Cheresnick, Mark 84
Cheshire, Geoffrey 127
Chesney, Peter M. 263, 356, 374
Cheung, George 418
Cheung, Vince 527
Chevaldave, Randolph 225

Chevalier, Catherine 255
Chew, Richard 452
The Cheyenne Social Club 318
Chiang, David 150
Chiao, Roy 410
Chichester, John 513
Chief Big Tree 315
Chilberg, John E., II 444
Child's Play 80–81, 394
Child's Play 2 81–82
Child's Play 3 82–83
"Children of the Corn" (short story) 79
Children of the Corn 78–79
Children of the Corn II 79
Children of the Corn III: Urban Harvest 79–80
Children of the Damned 510–511
Chiles, Lois 103
Chin, Glen 125
Ching, William 232
Chinn, Anthony 408
Chiodo Bros. 105
Chirgwin, Michael 322
Chitty, Eric 506
Chitty Chitty Bang Bang 240
Chivers, Colin 461, 464
Choate, Bennett 469
Chomyn, Chris 377
Chris Walas, Inc. 181
Christian, Claudia 328
Christian, Kurt 431, 432, 433
Christian, Natt 306
Christian, Roger 23
Christie, Helen 506
Christie, Howard 116, 293, 340
Christie, Julie 259
Christine, Virginia 142, 284
Christmas, Eric 36
A Christmas Carol (1938) 425–426
A Christmas Carol (1951) 426, 428
A Christmas Carol (novella) 425, 427
"A Christmas Carol" (song) 427
"Christmas Children" (song) 427
Christopher, Robert 212
Chubalo, George 181
C.H.U.D. 83–84
C.H.U.D. II: Bud the CHUD 84
Church, Peggy 425
Church, Richard 516

Churcher, Melinda 506
Churchill, Marguerite 131
Chuvalo, George 392
Ciannelli, Eduardo 336
Cibelli, Christopher 513
Ciccoritti, Gerard 240
Cichy, Walter R. 175
Cimino, Leonardo 32, 21
Cinderfella 238–239
Cindrich, Reynold 352
Cinema Research Corporation 142, 203
Circus of Horrors 213
Cirillo, Joe 233
Cirino, Chuck 237, 472
Cisar, George 143
Citizen Kane 96
Clair, Jon 80
Clair, Richard 61
Clark, Bobby 284
Clark, Candy 33, 63
Clark, Carroll 17, 19, 39, 302, 433
Clark, Christie 79, 356
Clark, Cliff 337
Clark, Ernest 362
Clark, Fred 344
Clark, Gage 137
Clark, Greydon 147
Clark, James 279
Clark, Mamo 371
Clark, Marlene 61
Clark, Matt 43, 70, 267, 523
Clark, Russell 228
Clarke, Arthur C. 499, 501
Clarke, Charles 331
Clarke, Gary 77
Clarke, Joe 44
Clarke, Justine 323
Clarke, Mae 185
Clarke, Melita 506
Clarke, Mindy 353
Clarke, Robert 211
Clash, Kevin 473, 474
Clatworthy, Robert 72
Claudel, Marcus 311
Claudelle Inglish 397
Claux, Moira 302
Clavell, James 177
Clayton, Curtiss 248
Clayton, Jack 279
Clayton, Kristin 356
Clayton, Melissa 267
Cleaver, Thomas M. 480, 481
Cleese, John 216
Clem, Jimmy 312
Clemens, Brian 121, 261, 431
Clement, Marc 306
Clement, Robert 61

Clemento, Steve 302, 305
Clements, John 120
Clemons, Clarence 56
Clennon, David 484
Cleverdon, Dean 266
Cliff, John 195
Clifford, Jeffrey 322
Clifford, Matt 350
Clive, Colin 185, 186, 319
Clive, E.E. 131, 289
Clooney, George 37
Close, Del 63
Close Encounters of the Third Kind 442, 501
Cloudia 80
Clough, Rodney, Jr. 182
Clunie, Michelle 226
Clure, John 56
Clyde, David 315
Coach (TV series) 94
Coaker, Salami 432
Coates, Bryan 310
Coates, Kathleen 394
Coates, Phyllis 195, 460
Cobb, Ed 169
Cobb, Edmund 30
Cobb, Lee J. 32, 162, 164
Cobb, Ty 35
Cobert, Robert 268, 270
Cochran, Robert 425
Cochrane, Sandy 182
Cockburn, Adam 323
Cockell, Juno Mills 392
Cocoon 84–85
Cocoon: The Return 85–86
Coda, Frank 370
Coe, Peter 191
Cohen, Barney 221
Cohen, David 222
Cohen, Herman 195, 276
Cohen, J.J. 42
Cohen, Jeffrey Jay 40
Cohen, Larry 298, 300, 301, 302, 327, 328
Cohen, Mitchell 490
Cohen, Rob 521
Colcord, Mabel 292
Colcott, Earl 304
Cole, Albert 147
Cole, Ben 275
Cole, George 66, 426, 503
Cole, Jack 258
Cole, Lester 291
Cole, Mark 36
Cole, Stan 39
Coleman, C.C. 315
Coleman, Clarke 125
Coleman, Jerome Daniels 350
Coleman, Tom 36

Coleman, Verena 431
Coles, Barbara 24
Coles, Michael 126, 148, 150
Colgan, Michael 307
Colgan, Valerie 24
Colisimo, Sandy 215
Colley, Don Pedro 381
Colley, Kenneth 454, 457
Collier, Bud 460, 469
Collier, Jim 206
Collier, Lois 71
Collings, David 427
Collins, Eddie 65
Collins, Jack 125
Collins, Jesse 109
Collins, John D. 143
Collins, Michael 64
Collins, Rick 490, 491
Collins, Robert 392
Collins, Stephen 440
Collinson, Madelaine 508, 509
Collinson, Mary 508
Collis, Jack 164
Collister, Peter Lyons 248
Collodni, Joseph G. 393
Colman, Edward 17, 19, 39, 316, 433
Colman, Ronald 315
"The Color Out of Space" (short story) 106, 110, 111
Columbo, Franco 86, 476
Columbus, Chris 241, 242
Colvin, Jack 80
Colwell, K.C. 387, 527
Coma 24
Comar, Richard 439
Combs, Debra 81
Combs, Gary 416
Combs, Jeffrey 413, 415, 492
Comden, Betty 20
Come Back, Little Sheba 519
Comer, Sam 89, 118, 232, 238, 324
Como, Frank 249
Compton, Sharon 122
Conan (character) 176
Conan the Barbarian 86–87, 486
Conan the Conqueror (book) 88
Conan the Destroyer 87–88
Conaway, Curtis 222
Condon, Bill 70
Cone, Bill 375
Cones, Tristam 15, 16
Confessions of a Nazi Spy 296
Conley, Corinne 93
Conlin, Richard 35

Conlon, Tim 392
A Connecticut Yankee 88–89
A Connecticut Yankee in King Arthur's Court 89–90
A Connecticut Yankee in King Arthur's Court (book) 88
Conners, Julie 92
Connery, Sean 260, 261, 262, 411, 413
Connolly, Bobby 520
Connor, Kenneth 498
Connor, Kevin (director) 309, 310
Connors, Chuck 498, 499
Connors, Kevin (actor) 377
Conquest of the Planet of the Apes 382, 383–384
Conrad, Eddy 489
Conrad, Jack 271
Conrad, Jan 334
Conrad, Michael 59
Conrad, Rich 480
Conrad, Rick 515
Conrad, Sid 305
Conried, Hans 365, 434
Conroy, Burt 518
Conroy, Jarlath 349
Conselman, William 88
Considine, John W., Jr. 319
Considine, Tim 433
Constable, Bill 126
Constable, David A. 305
Constantine, Eddie 300
Converse, Cleo 208
Conville, David 201
Conway, Gary 195
Conway, Gerry 87
Conway, Lyle 63, 314, 523
Conway, Richard 468, 497
Conway, Russ 293
Conway, Tim 434
Conway, Tom 72
Coogan, Jackie 122
Cook, Caroline 188
Cook, Clyde 116
Cook, Elisha 58; *see also* Cook, Elisah, Jr.
Cook, Elisha, Jr. 252
Cook, Jill 386
Cook, Myron 30
Cook, Paul 370
Cook, Peter 466
Cook, Phil 58, 229, 230
Cook, Randall William 386, 501
Cook, Willis R. 77
Cooke, Caroline 524
Cooke, Jennifer 223
Cooke, Malcolm 175, 306, 466

Cooke, Wendy 84
Cooksey, Danny 478
Cookson, Peter 243
Cool Breeze 59
Coontz, Bill 199
Coop, Denys 120
Cooper, Alice 223, 360
Cooper, Charles 447
Cooper, Dorree 263, 266
Cooper, Gary 21
Cooper, George A. 143, 309
Cooper, George Lane 47
Cooper, Jack 491
Cooper, Jackie 461, 464, 465, 468
Cooper, Merian C. 302, 306, 435, 436
Cooper, Tamar 363
Cooper, Ted 482, 495
Cooper, Wilkie 334, 372, 497
Cooper, Willis 187
Copeland, Stewart 261
Copeman, Michael 181, 184
Copley, Peter 404
Coppin, Tyler 322
Coppola, Christopher 155
Coppola, Francis Ford 155, 157, 216
Coppola, Marc 155
Coppola, Roman 155
Corado, Gino 191
Corbin, Barry 104
Corby, Ellen 35
Corby, Francis 38
Corcoran, Brian 39
Corcoran, Donna 35
Corcoran, Kevin 39, 43, 159
Cordell, Cathleen 350
Corden, Henry 116
Cordero, Laurencio "Chob" 388
Cording, Harry 291
Cordio, Carlo Maria 106
Cordova, Fred 133
Corey, Jeff 87, 190, 331, 365, 381, 460
Corey, Phil 282
Corff, Robert 227
Corian, Anthony 145
Corigliano, John 123
Corliss, Tom 21
Corman, Avery 365
Corman, Catherine 214
Corman, Roger 99, 111, 167, 168, 169, 170, 171, 173, 174, 200, 214, 215, 251, 252, 253, 271, 272, 312, 363, 364, 480, 481, 514
Cornell, Arthur J. 178

Cornell, Ellie 248, 249
Cornell, Pamela 427
Cornfield, Stuart 181
Cornthwaite, Robert 482, 483, 518
Correll, Charles 444
Corri, Nick 354
Corrigan, D'Arcy 426
Corrigan, Kevin 165
Corrigan, Lloyd 71, 231
Corrigan, Ray "Crash" 71
Corrington, John William 384
Corrington, Joyce Hooper 384
Corseaut, Aneta 61, 62
Corso, Marge 170
Cort, Bud 282
Cortez, Stanley 369
Cory, Phil 21, 329
Coscarelli, D.A. (Don) 54, 375, 376, 377
Coscia, Marcello 379
Cosmo, James 260
Cossins, James 64
Costello, Don 257
Costello, George 476
Costello, Lou 116, 192, 293, 341
Costello, Ward 159
Cotonaro, Tommy 281
Cotten, Joseph 15, 208
Cotter, Allan 390
Cotterill, Ralph 273
Cottingham, Sterline 182
Cotton, Joan 178
Cotton Comes to Harlem 62
Cottrell, William 307
Couch, Lionel 64, 150, 437
Coufos, Paul 184
Coulouris, George 64
Coulter, Winston 311
Count Basie 238
Count Down — Son of Dracula see *Son of Dracula* (1974)
Count Dracula and His Vampire Bride see *The Satanic Rites of Dracula*
Count Yorga, Vampire 60, 92–93
Countess Dracula 157, 506
"Courage" (song) 520
Courage, Alexander 444, 446, 468
Court, Hazel 170–173, 194–195, 325, 327, 370, 371
Court, Ken 24
Courtland, Jerome 158
Courtney, Chuck 142

Cousar, James 209
Cousins, Julie 61
Cove, Kenneth 201
Cowan, David 78
Cowan, Jerome 72, 331
Cowan, Will 71
Cowell, June 509
Cox, Alfred 110, 139, 173, 197, 342
Cox, Brian 323
Cox, Courteney 85
Cox, Frank 22
Cox, Freddie 22
Cox, Larry 224
Cox, Morgan B. 72
Cox, Penney Finkelman 263
Cox, Ronny 416, 417
Cox, Tony 125, 237
Coy, Christopher 107
Crabbe, Buster 176, 177
Crabbe, Byron L. 302
Crabtree, Buddy 311
Crabtree, Jeff 311
Craig, Alec 71, 72, 114
Craig, Charles 347
Craig, Daniel 91
Craig, Edwin 47, 255
Craig, Lee 376
Craig, Louis 181
Craig, Michael 497
Craig, Noble 386
Craig, Ron 514
Craig, Wendy 120
Crain, William 58, 122
Crampton, Barbara 413, 414, 415, 492
Crampton, Gerry 212
Crandall, Roger S. 248
Crane, Earl, Sr. 281
Crane, James 335
Crane, Jonathan D. 84
Crane, Richard 499
Cranham, Kenneth 255
Cravat, Nick 297
Craven, Frank 131
Craven, Gemma 239
Craven, James 292
Craven, Wes 354, 356, 359, 360, 361, 362, 469
Crawford, Anne 333
Crawford, David 348
Crawford, Michael 22
Crawford, Terry 268
Crawley, Charles 352
The Creature from the Black Lagoon 94–97
The Creature Walks Among Us 100–102
Creatures the World Forgot 151

Creber, William 381, 382
Creed, Roger 203
Creelman, James 302
The Creeping Unknown see *The Quatermass Xperiment*
Creepshow 102–103
Creepshow 2 103
Cregan, N.R. 21
Crehan, Dorothy 276
Crehan, Joseph 128
Creighton, Sally 482
Cresceman, Vince 93
Crews, Laura Hope 65
Cribbins, Bernard 127, 334, 436
Crichton, Michael 516, 517
Criscuolo, Lou 306
Crisp, Quentin 212
Critters 103–104, 474
Critters 2 104–105
Critters 3 105
Critters 4 105–106
Crockett, Dick 47
Croft, Alyson 492
Crole-Rees, Trevor 15
Cromwell, James 366
Cronenberg, David 181, 420, 421, 422, 423, 424
Cronenberg, Denise 181
Cronenweth, Jordan 122
Cronjager, Henry 320
Cronyn, Hume 84, 85
Crosbie, Annette 239, 240
Crosby, Bing 35, 89
Crosby, Denise 373
Crosby, Floyd 167, 168, 169, 170, 251
Crosby, Harry 217
Cross, Beverly 432
Cross, Harley 182
Cross, Jimmy 30
Crossfire 71
Crothers, Scatman 527
The Crow 109
Crowe, Desmond 216
Crowley, Dermot 457
Crowley, Patrick 419
Crowther, Graeme 412
Cruikshank, Art 319
Cruse and Company 35
Crutchley, Rosalie 64
Cryer, Jon 468
Cudney, Cliff 219
Cuff, John Haslett 240
Cuffling, Bernard 252
Cuka, Frances 427
Cukor, George 66
Culkin, Michael 70
Culley, Cliff 90

Culley, John K. 36
Culliford, James 404
Culp, Steven 226
Culter, Rory 514
Culver, Michael 454
Culver, Roland 258
Cumbuka, Jitu 58, 122
Cummings, Jo B. 43
Cummings, Peg 246
Cummins, Gregory Scott 516
Cummins, Jack 271
Cummins, James 265
Cummins, Juliette 222
Cummins, Martin 225
Cunard, Grace 337
Cundey, Dean 40, 42, 43, 244, 246, 247, 484
Cunha, Richard E. 77, 199
Cunningham, Beryl 379
Cunningham, Christopher 143, 506
Cunningham, Danny 314
Cunningham, Lee 166
Cunningham, Sean S. 217, 226, 264, 266, 267, 268
Cunningham, Susan E. 219
Cura, Carlo 509
Currie, Gordon 396, 397
Currie, Michael 247
Currin, Brenda 83
Curry, Christopher 83
The Curse 106, 112
Curse II — The Bite 106–107
Curse III — Blood Sacrifice 107
Curse IV: The Ultimate Sacrifice 107
The Curse of Frankenstein 194–195, 202, 209, 406
The Curse of the Cat People 74–75
The Curse of the Fly 180–181
The Curse of the Mummy's Tomb 342, 344–345
Curse of the Undead 274
The Curse of the Werewolf 525
Curtis, Alan 292
Curtis, Beatrice 315
Curtis, Billy 281, 460, 482
Curtis, Dan 157, 268, 270, 271
Curtis, David 313
Curtis, Dick 302
Curtis, Donald 292
Curtis, Jamie Lee 244, 246, 390
Curtis, Keene 259
Curtis, Liane 104

Curtis, Robin 444, 446
Curtis, Sonia 214
Curtis, Tony 120
Curtis, Tony (art director) 120
Curtis, William Greg 418
Curtiss, Edward 100, 190, 292
Curtley, Steve 323
Curzon, Jill 127
Cusack, Cyril 362, 363
Cusack, Joan 2
Cushing, Peter 16, 120, 126, 127, 130, 135, 137, 139, 148, 150, 194, 195, 197, 198, 201, 202, 203, 205, 206, 208, 342, 343, 344, 436, 452, 453, 503, 508
Cusimano, Richard 311
Cusinery, Jim 282
Cutell, Lou 210, 263
Cuthbertson, Allan 309, 498
Cutler, Jeff 229
Cutrara, Joel 48
Cutry, Claude 106
Cutter, Murray 520
Cutthroat Island 359
Cypher, Jon 183
Cyphers, Charles 244, 246
Czapsky, Stefan 50, 81

Dabbs, Brenda 310
D'Abo, Olivia 87, 88
Da Costa, Philip 427
Dade, Frances 129
Daggett, Jensen 225
D'Agostino, Albert 72, 74, 130, 378, 482
Da Gradi, Don 19, 316
Daigler, Gary 122
Dailey, Irene 31
Dair, John 48
Dalai (dog) 515
D'Aldia, Tracy 42
Dale, Jim 90–91
Dale, Joan 22
Daleks' Invasion Earth 2150 A.D. 126–127
Dalesandro, James 350
Dallamano, Massimo 379
Dallas (TV series) 62, 148
Dalton, Timothy 175
Daly, Jack 178
Daly, James 380
Daly, Jonathan 434
Daly, Richard 125
Dalya, Jacqueline 371
Dalzell, Archie 312
Damiani, Damiano 32
Damien: Omen II 174, 369–370

The Damned 379
Damon, Gabriel 418
Damon, Mark 167
Dana, Leora 33
Danare, Malcolm 106
Dance, Charles 27
D'Andrea, John 82
Dane, An 301
Dane, Lawrence 109, 420
Danforth, Jim 175
Daniel, Billy 232
Daniel, Rod 277
Danielle, Suzanne 175
Daniels, Anthony 452, 454, 457
Daniels, Danny 410
Daniels, Diane 370
Daniels, Eugene 158
Daniels, Glen 30
Daniels, Lisa 238
Daniels, Mark 68
Daniels, Phil 212
Daniels, Walter 302
Daniels, William 365
Danielson, Dins 373
Danis, Francine 125
Danner, Blythe 518
Danning, Syvil 273
Dano, Royal 236, 266
Danse Macabre (book) 32
Danson, Ted 102
Dante, Crisstyn 359
Dante, Joe 241, 242, 271
Dante, Michael 519
Danza, Tony 36
Danziger, Maia 122
Darabont, Frank 63, 182, 216, 356
Darby, Ken 520
Darby, Kim 250, 278
D'Arcy, Alexander (Alex) 144, 145, 489
D'Arcy, Timothy 166
Darden, Severn 383, 384
Daris, Kenny 241
Dark, John 309, 310
Dark Shadows (TV series) 269
Darkman 108–109
Darkman II: The Return of Durant 109–110
Darkman III 110
Darling, Anne 186
Darling, W. Scott 189
Darling, William 88
Darnell, Deborah 92
Darnell, Vicki 215
Darrin, Diana 30
Daskawisz, Steve 219
D'Auburn, Dennis 315

Daughter of Dr. Jekyll 116, 117, 126
Davalos, Elyssa 319
Davenport, Claire 457
Davenport, Nigel 297
Davey, Bert 309
Davi, Robert 328
David, Bud 519
David, Clifford 56, 165
David, Hal 61, 316
David, Keith 244, 484
David, Mack 232
David, Martha 56
David, Peter 493, 494
David, Pierre 423, 424
David, Thayer 268, 269, 271
David Allen Productions 393, 394
David Miller Creations 361
David Miller Studio 20
Davidson, Ben 86
Davidson, E. Roy 315
Davidtz, Embeth 161
Davies, Craig 416
Davies, Dave 511
Davies, E.R. 359
Davies, Gilbert 400
Davies, Gron 398
Davies, John 416
Davies, Phil 491, 492, 493
Davies, Richard 71
Davies, Rupert 143
Davies, Tessa 64, 212, 314
Davies, Tom 418
Davies, Valentine 331
Davies, William 125
Davis, Bette 159
Davis, Bud 306
Davis, Carl 120, 214
Davis, Carole 329
Davis, Cherry 350
Davis, Frank 37
Davis, Gary 351, 478
Davis, Geena 181
Davis, Gunnis 186
Davis, Jim 147, 148, 203
Davis, Joe W. 444
Davis, Joel 74
Davis, John 388
Davis, John Walter 123
Davis, Kaye 160
Davis, Leon 254
Davis, Marvin Aubrey 39
Davis, Milton, Jr. 36
Davis (Reagan), Nancy 307, 308
Davis, Nathan 387
Davis, Peter S. 259, 261
Davis, Philip 275
Davis, Rod 306

Davis, Roger 268
Davis, Simon 499
Davis, Sonny Carl 492
Davis, Stanton 249
Davis, Steve 106
Davis, Stringer 332, 334
Davis, Traci Dawn 56
Davis, Trevor 194
Davis, Warwick 457
Davison, Bruce 519
Davison, Jon 418
Daw, Jonathan 499
Dawe, Tony 47
Dawn, Doreen 171
Dawn, Jack 114, 377, 425, 520
Dawn of the Dead 348–349
Dawson, Bob 444
Dawson, Frank 65
Dawson, Hal K. 460
Dawson, Kim 472, 475
Day, Bryan 181
Day, Don 84
Day, Ernest 468
Day, Joe 233
Day, John 293
Day, Richard 65, 331
Day, Robert 436
Day, Vera 400
Day of the Dead 349–350
The Day the Earth Stood Still 484
Day the World Ended 99, 363
Dayan, David 235
Dayton, Danny 152
Deacon, Richard 281, 284, 341
A Dead Man Seeks His Murderer see *The Brain*
Deadrick, Vince 411
Deak, Michael S. 397, 493, 494
Deakins, Roger 362
Dean, Ivor 121
Dean, Julie 74
Dean, Margia 398, 460
Deane, Hamilton 129, 153
Dear, William 36
Dearden, Basis 120
Dearing, Dorothy 65
Dearlove, Jac 408
Dearman, Glyn 426
Deary, Tony 322
De Ately, Murray 211
De Bello, Joe 36, 37, 38
DeBenning, Burr 359
Debney, John 106
de Boer, Nikki 393
De Bron, Jack, Jr. 59

De Brulier, Nigel 371
DeBroux, Lee 416
De Camp, Marianne 214
"December the Twenty-Fifth" (song) 427
Deck, Darrell 311
Decker, William L. 490, 491
De Cordoba, Pedro 231
De Corsia, Ted 495
DeCoteau, David 394, 395
DeCuir, John, Jr. 232
Dee, Frances 436
Dee, Ruby 76
Deeter, Jasper 61
Deezen, Ed (Eddie) 104, 527
DeFaria, Christopher 34, 35
De Fina, Ron 511
Defore, Don 243
DeForrest, Kensas 186
DeGrazzie, Doug 386
De Haeck, Hugues 42
DeHay, Alain 464
de Herrera, Nana 429
Dehn, Paul 279, 381, 382, 383, 384
Deighan, Drew 350
De Jesus, Wanda 418
de Juan, Pedro 429
Dekker, Fred 213, 264, 419
Dekker, Thomas 511
de la Bouillerie, Hubert 261
DeLacy, Ralph M. 71
DeLaire, Diane 97
Delamain, Aimee 120
Delaney, Kim 109
Delano, Michael 364
de la Tour, Andrew 212
De Laurentiis, Dino 175, 176, 305, 306
De Laurentiis, Federico 305
DeLaurentiis, Raffaella 86, 87
De Lavallade, Carmen 116
De Leon, Gerry 295
De Leon, Walter 230, 232
Delevanti, Cyril 132
Delgado, Marcel 302
Delgado, Roger 120, 346
Del Genio, Lenny 233
Delia, Russell P. 370
Dell, Charlie 282
Dellos, Dove 166
Delman, Peter 499
Delman, Roxann 77
Delmar, Peter 499
De Marney, Terence 110
Delora, Jennifer 215
Delrich, Hal 159
Delroy, Deni 393
del Ruth, Roy 489

Delsol, Gerald 510
DeLuca, Michael 360
DeLuca, Peppino 379
DeLuca, Rudy 93
DeMarco, Christopher 491
DeMarco, Frank 54
Demarest, William 19–20
DeMay, Janet 54
De Meo, Paul 491
Demetrius and the Gladiators 59
de Metz, Danielle 178, 179
DeMilo, Cardella 209
Deming, Peter 160
de Mora, Robert 164
Demoss, Darcy 223
Dempster, Hugh 194, 426
DeMunn, Jeffrey 63
Demura, Fumio 297
Denberg, Susan 203, 206
Denham, Maurice 332
De Niro, Robert 216, 217
Denison, Leslie 116
Dennehy, Brian 84, 85, 86
Denney, Julie 76
Denning, Richard 94, 96
Dennis, Gill 523
Dennis, John 198
Denny, Reginald 47, 116
Denoue, Thomas F. 394
Denton, Christa 229
Denton, Scot 229
Denver, John 365
De Palma, Brian 300
Depatie, Beth 359
Depew, Gary 79
Depp, Harry 307
Depp, Johnny 354, 360
DeRauch, Micky 372
Deren, Bobby 165
DeRogatis, Al 259
Derr, Richard 295
DeSantis, Tony 439
Des Barres, Michael 120, 235
DeScenna, Linda 42, 427
Deschanel, Mary Jo 501
Desiderio, Robert 366
Design FX Company 374
De Silva, Stany 410
De Simone, Bob 222
Desmond-Hurst, Brian 426
DeSoto, Rosana 449
Destination Inner Space 102
DeSue, Joe 209
Desy, Victor 420
Detective Comics 53
Detitta, George, Jr. 32
De Treaux, Tamara 235
Deutsch, Helen 237

Deutsch, Ron 527
Deutschendorf, Henry J., II 234
Deutschendorf, William T. 234
DeVenney, Scott 446
Devereux, Marie 139
De Vestal, Bob 210
Devi Dja and Her Balinese Dancers 377
Devine, Sophie 279
DeVito, Danny 50
DeVol, Frank 318, 319
DeVorzon, Barry 124, 165
De Vota, Bruno 252
Devry, Elaine 317, 318
Dew, Eddie 72
de Winter, Arione 76
Dewit, Alan 169
de Wolff, Francis 117, 325
De Zarraga, Tony 61, 92
Diamond, Arnold 197, 370
Diamond, Peter 260
Diamond, Ron 76
Diaz, Ken 227
DiCenzo, George 40, 165
DiCicco, Bobby 237, 328
Dick, Keith Joe 235
Dicken, Roger 145
Dickens, Charles 425, 427
Dickey, Paul 230, 232
Dickie, Olga 136
Dickinson, Desmond 320
Dickinson, Dick 133
Dicks, John 454
Dickson, Billy 250
Dickson, Kimberly 184
Die Hard 2 29
Die, Monster, Die! 106, 110–112
Diener, Stephen 356
Dierkes, John 116, 117, 170, 252, 482, 483, 484
Diers, Don 266
Dieterle, William 300
Dietlein, Marsha 351
Dietz, Eileen 164
Diffring, Anton 325, 326, 327
Di Gaetano, Joey 330, 472
Digges, Dudley 289
DiGiacomo, Franco 32
DiLeo, Antone 349
Dilg, Larry 233
Dill, William 226
Dilley, Leslie (Les) 23, 408, 452, 454
Dillman, Bradford 382
Dillon, Brendan 170
Dillon, Carmen 367

Dillon, Constantine 37
Dillon, Costa 36
Dillon, Denny 267
Dillon, Kevin 63
Dillon, Meshell 267
Dilon, Josephine 307
DiLorenzo, Edward 208
DiMaggio, Joe 35
Dimetros, Fiseha 164
"Ding Dong, the Witch Is Dead" (song) 520
Dinga, Pat 167, 168, 169, 170
Di Nove, Denise 50
Dinvale, Mihai 494
di Santo, Byrnadette 376
DiSarro, Al 388
DiSesso, Moe 170, 519
Disney, Walt 17, 19, 23, 39, 240, 433, 459
Dix, Mary Lou 315
Dix, Robert 144, 199, 200
Dixon, James 298, 300, 301
Dixon, Richard 312
Dixon, Robert 222
Dmytryk, Edward 71
Doak, Frank 347
Dobbin, Simon 415
Dobbs, Randolph 210
Dobtcheff, Vernon 411
Dockendorf, David 381
Dr. Black, Mr. Hyde 122
Dr. Heckyl and Mr. Hype 122
Dr. Jekyll and Mr. Hyde (1932) 112–114
Dr. Jekyll and Mr. Hyde (1941) 114–116
Dr. Jekyll and Ms. Hyde 125–126
Dr. Jekyll and Sister Hyde 121–122
Dr. Jekyll's Dungeon of Death 124
Dr. No 402
Dr. Phibes Rises Again 16–17
Dr. Who and the Daleks 126
Dr. Who (character) 126, 127
Doctor X 127–128, 294
"The Doctor's Secret" (story) 128
Dodd, Everett 199
Dodge, Norman B., Jr. 330
Dodson, Mark 242
Dodson, Mary Kay 89
Doerr, Mark 474
Dogans, Ed 476
Dohlen, Lenny Von 155
Dokken 356
Dolan, Charlie 236
Dolan, Dennis 486

Dolan, Michael 426
Dolenz, George 232
D'Oliveira, Damon 438
Domeier, Richard 160
Domela, Jan 89
Dominic, Henry 515
Donaggio, Pino 271
Donaghy, Pip 362
Donahue, Elinor 360
Donahue, Jean 258
Donald, James 404, 407
Donat, Lucas 370
Donati, Danilo 175
Donlan, Yolanda 144
Donlevy, Brian 180, 181, 398, 399, 400, 403, 404, 407
Donner, Clive 40, 152
Donner, Richard 367, 427, 461, 463
Donno, Eddy 282
D'Onofrio, Joseph 473
Donohue, Jack 39
Donovan, King 35, 284
Donovan's Brain 307–309
Donovan's Brain (book) 307, 309
Doody, Alison 411, 413
Doohan, James 440, 442, 444, 446, 447, 449, 450
Doolittle, John 366, 418
DoQui, Robert 416, 419
Dorff, Stephen 229
Dorme, Norman 22, 175
Dorn, Lu 147
Dorn, Michael 449, 450
Dornisch, William P. 442
Doss, Leonard 177
"Doubleback" (song) 43
Doublin, Anthony 413
Douglas, Josephine 148
Douglas, Kirk 495, 496
Douglas, Melvyn 436
Douglas, Paul 35, 36
Douglas, Sarah 55, 87, 88, 310, 311, 353, 395, 461, 464, 465, 472
Douglas, Shoto von 67
Dourif, Brad 80, 105, 165, 166
Dowd, Judith 370
Dowd, Ross 232
Dowdall, Jim 254
Dowding, Jon 321
Dowe, Don 493
Dowell, Carol 334
Down to Earth 258
Downer, David 322
Downes, Cindy E. 237
Downham, Heather 499

Downing, J. 236
Downs, Cathy 30, 77
Downs, Dermott 158
Downs, Hugh 365
Downs, Johnny 38
Doyle, Chris 472
Doyle, Jim 354
Doyle, Kathleen 288
Doyle, Maxine 307
Doyle, Mike 97
Doyle, Patrick 216
Doyle, Terry 392
Dozier, William 47, 50
Dracula (1931) 64, 129–130, 139, 185
Dracula (1979) 153–155
Dracula (book) 135, 157, 506
Dracula (Spanish version) 130
Dracula: The Love Story 487
Dracula A.D. 1972 148–149, 281
Dracula Has Risen from the Grave 143–144
Dracula, Prince of Darkness 75, 137, 140–142, 143
Dracula Society 149
Dracula Sucks 157
Dracula vs. Frankenstein 147–148
Dracula's Daughter 130–131
Dracula's Dog 158
Dracula's Widow 155
Dragnet (TV series) 313
Drago, Eleonora Rossi 379
Dragon, Carmen 284
Dragoti, Stan 152
Drai, Victor 212
Drake, Anthony 332
Drake, Dodie 312
Drake, Frances 319
Drake, Geoffrey 432
Drake, Larry 108, 109
Drake, Leigh 350
Drake, Oliver 339
Drake, Pauline 519
Draper, Robert 249
Drasin, Richard 519
Dream Quest Images 63, 125, 265, 266, 356, 357, 360, 376, 427, 438, 512
Dreier, Hans 89, 112, 230, 324
Dresden, John 364
Drexler, Doug 386
Dreyfuss, Richard 244
Drier, Moosie 365
Drum, Steve 281
Drumheller, Robert 522
Drummond, Alice 233

Drury, Patrick 64
Dryden, Ernst 315
Dryhurst, Michael 461
Dubay, Ashley 67
Dubensky, Tom 352
Dubin, Joseph S. 495
Dublin, Jessica 491
Dudley, Robert 132
Dudman, Nick 47, 214
Duff, Howard 365
Duff, Norwich 454
Duffell, Bee 404
Duffield, Tom 234
Duffin, Philip 160
Duffy, Jim 84
Duffy, Jo 396, 397
Dugan, Dennis 90, 91, 271
Dugan, Tom 56, 127
Duggan, Andrew 211, 298, 300
Duggan, Terry 499
Duggan, Tom 198
Duggan, Tommy 370, 464
Duguay, Christian 421, 422
Duke, Bill 388
Duke, Patty 35
Duke, Stan 316
Dulac, Arthur 177
Dulany, Caitlin 328
Dullea, Keir 499, 500, 501
Dulo, Jane 366
Dumbrille, Douglas 71
Dumke, Ralph 284
Dunagan, Donnie 188
Dunard, David 360
Dunas, Ronald S. 15
Dunaway, Faye 466, 467
Dunbar, David 131
Duncan, Archie 334
Duncan, Arletta 185
Dune 262
Duning, George 258
Dunlap, Al 158
Dunlap, Paul A. 198, 276
Dunn, Danny 19
Dunn, Emma 188
Dunn, Liam 210, 317
Dunn, Linwood 482
Dunn, Roger 392
Dunna, Bill 359
Dunne, Dominique 385
Dunne, Elizabeth 72
Dunne, Irene 243, 244
Dunsford, John 325
Dunstedter, Eddie 307
The Dunwich Horror 111
DuPont, Michael 320
Dupree, V.C. 225
Du Prez, John 472, 474, 475
Dupuis, Stephan 182

Duquette, Tom 514
Duran, Juan 516
Duran, Lilia 295
Durand, Val 315
Durbin, John 350
Durden, Richard 146
Durkin, Father John 165
Durkin, Patrick 408
Durock, Dick 469, 470, 471, 472
Durrell, William J., Jr. 20
Dutra, Randy 416
Dutton, Charles S. 27
Dutton, Syd 214
Duvitski, Janine 153
Dwan, Isabelle 116
Dworkin, Patty 233
Dwyer, John M. 478
Dwyer, Leslie 110
Dye, Dale 244
Dyer, Elmer 315
Dyer, Olivie 107
Dykstra, John 52, 282, 452, 453
Dyne, Aminata 324
Dysart, Richard 43, 484

Eagle, Charles White 123
Early, David 102, 348
Earthquake 474
"Ease on Down the Road" (song) 523
East, Jeff 461
Eastham, Richard 384
Eastin, Steve 356
Eastman, Kevin 472, 473, 474, 475
Eastman, Lynn 375
Eastman, Marilyn 347
Eastman, Rodney 356, 357
Eastwood, Clint 97, 104
Eatwell, Brian 15, 16
Eberhardt, Norma 137
Ebert, Roger 475
Ebsen, Buddy 521
Eby, David 352
Eccles, Julie 412
Echanove, Josephina 33
Eckel, Tim 256
Eddison, Robert 411
Eddo, Scott 388
Edelman, Randy 36, 234
Edeson, Arthur 184, 289
Edison, Thomas A. 217
Edlund, Richard 27, 213, 214, 227, 233, 385, 386, 408, 501
Edmond, Danielle 28
Edmond, J. Trevor 353
Edmonds, Brian 273

Edmonds, Louis 268
Edmonds, Mike 457
Edmonson, Mike 438
Edmunds, William 191
Edney, Beatie 260
Edouart, Farciot 89, 230, 232, 238
Edwards, Anthony 374
Edwards, Belinda 27
Edwards, Blake 243
Edwards, Edgar 371
Edwards, Edward 416
Edwards, Eric 68
Edwards, Henry 425
Edwards, Mark 64
Edwards, Meredith 333
Edwards, Michael 478
Edwards, Olga 426
Edwards, Sam 158
Edwards, Vince 487, 488
Ege, Julie 150, 151
Eggby, David 321, 512
Ehlers, Corky 183
Ehrin, John 57
Eidelman, Cliff 449, 487
Eirik, Sten 109
Eisele, Robert 109
Eisen, Robert S. 284
Eisenberg, Aron 267, 395
Eisenmann, Ike 158, 159, 442
Eisley, Anthony 147
Ekezian, Harry 294
El Cid 274, 379
El-Shenawi, Ahmed 410
Elcar, Dana 501
Elder, John 140, 201, 203, 208, 345; *see also* Hinds, Anthony
Elek, Katalin 213
Elek, Zoltan 213
Eleniak, Erika 63
Eles, Sandor 201
Elfman, Danny 47, 50, 108, 109, 427
Elias, Jonathan 78
Eliot, Michael 328
Eliott, Marianna 68
Eliscu, Edward 22
Elise, Christine 81, 82, 288
Ellenshaw, Harrison 468
Ellenshaw, Peter 17, 453–454, 495
Ellenstein, Robert 152, 446
Ellerbe, Harry 167, 252
Ellington, Andre 359
Elliot, Peter 306
Elliott, Denholm 408, 410, 411
Elliott, Don 446

Elliott, Jack 365
Elliott, Mary 243
Elliott, Mike 481
Elliott, Paul 224
Elliott, Robert 231
Elliott, Stacey 359
Elliotte, Judith 59
Ellis, Anita 258
Ellis, Berle 352
Ellis, Christopher 120, 279
Ellis, David 512
Ellis, June 404
Ellis, Michael 212
Ellis, William 148
Ellzey, David 82
Elswit, Robert 351
Elton, Ray 332
Eltz, Theodore von 488
Elvira 125, 200
Elwes, Cary 156, 157, 212, 213
Emert, Oliver
Emery, Gilbert 131
Emery, John 257
Emge, David 348, 349
Emhardt, Robert 298, 300
Emmanuel, Takis 431
Emmich, Cliff 246
Emmott, Basil 180
Empire of the Ants 246
The Empire Strikes Back 419, 454–455, 457, 459
Enberg, Dick 259
Enchanted Village, Inc. 297
Endfield, Cy 497
Endore, Guy 319
Enemy from Space see *Quatermass II*
Engel, Roy 363
Engel, Ruth C. 376
Engelberg, Mort 228
Engelen, Paul 47
England, Bryan 225, 230
English, Bradford 250
Englund, Robert 354, 355, 356, 357, 358, 359, 360, 361
en-Meir, Izak 376
Ensign, Michael 80, 125, 233, 265
Epstein, Temi 223
Equus 82
Erham, Kevin 106
Erhart, Thomas O. 370
Erickson, Bill 469
Erickson, Leif 281
Ericson, Helen 65
Ermey, R. Lee 288, 481, 482
Ernsberger, Duke 155
Errickson, Krista 124

Errol, Leon 21, 292
Erwin, John 42
Erwin, Mark 420
Erwin, Stuart 19
Escalante, Henry 94
Escape from New York 481, 485
Escape from the Planet of the Apes 382–383
Escape to Witch Mountain 158–159
Eskra, Donna 82
Essex, Harry 94
Estelita 203
Estevez, Enrique 388
Estrada, Angelina 360
E.T.—The Extraterrestrial 454, 486
Eurythmics 362
Evans, Art J. 227
Evans, Daniel 43
Evans, E. Casanova 42
Evans, Edith 239, 427
Evans, Gene 307, 308
Evans, Herbert 65
Evans, Jimmy 110
Evans, John 47, 468
Evans, Lyn 332
Evans, Maurice 380, 381, 425
Evans, Nicole 392
Evans, Reg 321
Evans, Rex 190
Evans, Roy 121
Evans, Troy 249
Eve, Trevor 153
Everest, Barbara 425
Everhart, Rex 217
Evers, Jason 45, 382
Everton, Deborah 261
Everton, Paul 489
The Evil Dead 159–160, 328
Evil Dead II 160–161, 162
The Evil of Frankenstein 200–203
Ewing, Barbara 143
Ewing, Patrick 165
The Exorcist 32, 162–164, 176, 368, 392, 393, 527
Exorcist II: The Heretic 164–165
The Exorcist III 165–166
Exton, Clive 64
Eyer, Richard 429

Faber, Ron 162
Fabian, Ava 486
Fabin, John 400
Fabrizi, Mario 334
The Factory 275

Fadden, Tom 284
Faga, Gary 440
Fagan, Sean 229
Fahey, Myrna 167
Fahrenheit 451 363
Fairbank, Christopher 28, 48
Fairbanks, Douglas, Jr. 433
Fairbanks, Jay 151
Fairchild, Max 273, 322
Fairfax, Betty 116
Fairman, Blain 24
Faison, Frankie 76
Faison, Matthew 223, 395
Faithfull, Geoffrey 508
Falanga, Nino 429
Falcon, Bruno "Taco" 57
Falk, Gabriella 431
The Fall of the House of Usher 167–168
"The Fall of the House of Usher" (short story) 171
Fallick, Mort 152
Family Ties (TV series) 520
Fann, Al 107, 486
Fann, Junior 42
Fantastic Voyage 26, 495
Fantasy & Film Effects 350
Fantasy II Film Effects 155, 228, 373
Faracy, Stephanie 259
Farago, Joe 476
Faragoh, Francis Edward 184
Fargas, Antonio 275
Farley, Dot 72
Farmer, Suzan 110, 141
Farnum, William 89
Farr, Bobby 309
Farr, Jamie 107, 427
Farrands, Daniel 250
Farrar, Scott 43
Farrell, Charles 503
Farrell, Colin 309
Farrell, Paul 110
Farrell, Sharon 298
Farrell, Terry 256
Farrow, Mia 466
Farwell, Jonathan 515
Fast Times at Ridgemont High 527
"Father Chris'mas" (song) 427
Faulkner, Stephanie 275
Faust, Marty 292
Faustino, Michael 213
Faye, Janine 117, 136, 320
Faye, Julia 89
Faylen, Frank 243
Fazenda, Louise 22

Fazio, Ron 490, 491
Fealy, Margaret 524
The Fearless Vampire Killers 157
Febre, Louis 423
Fee, Melinda O. 356
Feeney, F.X. 214
Fegte, Ernst 460
Feil, Gerald 220
Feinberg, Gregg 70
Feist, Felix 307
Feitshans, Buzz 86
Feitshans, Fred R. (Jr.) 72, 339
Feld, Fritz 319
Felder, Clarence 359
Feldman, Corey 221, 222, 241, 473, 475
Feldman, Jan 124
Feldman, Marty 210
Fell, Norman 84
Fellows, Don 408, 464, 468
Fellows, Robert 89
Felton, Earl 495
Fennell, Albert 121
Fenneman, George 482, 483
Fenner, John 216, 314, 429, 468, 472
Ferber, Dorin 240
Ferguson, Al 116
Ferguson, Frank 192
Ferguson, J. Don 472
Ferguson, Jay 359
Ferguson, Jesse Lawrence 108
Ferguson, Larry 27, 260
Ferguson, Perry 43, 318
Fernandes, Joao 221
Fernandez, Benjamin 86
Ferrara, Abel 288, 289
Ferraro, Ralph 175
Ferrell, Tyra 165
Ferren, Brian 314, 447
Ferrer, Mel 320
Ferrer, Miguel 416
Ferretti, Robert 527
Ferris, Barbara 510, 511
Ferris, Doug 22
Ferry, David 109
Fery, Christian 305
Feuerman, Tod 63
Feuerstein, Allen 446
Fiander, Lewis 121
Fichter, Rick 415
Fidello, Manuel 224
Fiedel, Brad 227, 228, 478
Fiedler, John 434
Field, Logan 5
Field, Mary 291, 331
Field, Virginia 89, 217

Field, Walt Logan 248
Fielder, Pat 137
Fielding, Dorothy 227
Fielding, Edward 291, 324
Fielding, Jerry 279
Fielding, Richard *see* Maxwell, Robert
Fields, Al 72
Fields, Christopher John 28
Fields, Jere 222
Fields, John H. 76
Fields, Rick 514
Fields, Robert 61
Fields, Sidney 116
Fields, Simon 472
Fields, Stanley 294
Fields, Suzanne 175
Fields, W.C. 21
Fierberg, Steven 357
Fiero, John 311
Fierro, Paul 100
Fierstein, Harvey 125
Figg, Christopher 254, 255
Filpi, Carmen 248
Fimple, Dennis 305
The Final Chapter see *Puppet Master 5*
The Final Conflict 370–371
Finan, Tom 374
Finance, Charles 87
Finch, Jon 207, 503
Finch, Peter 316
Fincher, David 27, 29
Findley, Alistair 260
Fine, Harry 503, 506, 508
Fine, Travis 82
Finfer, David 56, 512
Fingado, Diane 515
Finkle, Claudia 275
Finnell, Michael 241, 242, 271
Finneran, Katie 352
Finney, Albert 427, 428
Finney, Jack 284, 286, 289
Finney, Rick 34, 35
Fioritto, Larry 248, 487
Fire, Richard 387
Fish, Nancy 165
Fishburne, Larry 356
Fisher, Carrie 311, 452, 454, 457, 460
Fisher, Diane 65
Fisher, Doris 258
Fisher, George 487
Fisher, Gerry 165, 260, 297
Fisher, Mary Gale 371
Fisher, Sash 404
Fisher, Terence 117, 135, 139, 140, 194, 197, 202, 203, 206, 207, 208, 342, 406

Fisher, Tom 183
Fisher, Tricia Leigh 84
Fishman, Paul 468
Fithian, Ted 71
Fitzgerald, Arthur 106
Fitzgerald, Barry 117
Fitzgerald, Geraldine 386
Fitzgerald, Maggie 150
Fitzgerald, Neil 186, 189
Fitzgibbon, Kitty 473
Fitzpatrick, Amy 282
Fitzpatrick, Ken 268
Five Fingers 431
Five Million Years to Earth
   438; see also *Quatermass*
   III
Fix, Paul 71, 231
Flag, Bob 362
Flaherty, Joe 42
Flaks, Stephen R. 240
Flanagan, Walter 234
Flander, Lewis 16
Flanders, Ed 165
Flash Film Works 361
Flash Gordon 175–176
Flash Gordon (serial) 453
Flash Gordon Conquers the
   Universe (serial) 177
Flash Gordon's Trip to Mars
   (serial) 177
Flato, Richard 178
Flavin, James 231, 302
Flea 42
Fleetwood, David 499
Fleischer, Bruce 87
Fleischer, Charles 42, 354
Fleischer, Dave 469
Fleischer, Max 469
Fleischer, Richard 33, 34,
   87, 495
Fleming, Rhonda 89, 90
Fleming, Victor 114, 242,
   520
Flemyng, Gordon 126, 127
Flesh Gordon 175
Flesh Gordon Meets the Cos-
   mic Cheerleaders 176–177
Flesh + Blood 417
Fletcher, Bramwell 335
Fletcher, Gerry 145
Fletcher, Harold 279
Fletcher, Leno 43
Fletcher, Louise 164, 282,
   283
Fletcher, Robert 444, 446
Flinn, Denny Martin 449
Flint, Sam 307
Flock, Brad 461
Flood, Kevin 204
Flory, Med 118

Flower, Buck 42
Flower, George "Buck" 394
Flowers, Bess 339
Fluegel, Darlanne 374, 423
The Fly (1958) 177–178, 364
The Fly (1986) 181–182
"The Fly" (short story) 178,
   180
The Fly II 182–183
Flynn, Errol 456
Flynn, Joe 19, 316
Flynn, Michael 248
Flynn, Pat 363
Flynn, Peter 515
Flynn, Robert 201
Flynn, Winnie 349
The Fog 484
Fogle, Adeen 314
Foldvary, Leslie 86
Folk, Robert 55
Folse, Marisa 76
Folsey, George 242
Foly, Dan 313
Fonda, Bridget 161, 214, 215
Fonda, Jane 66
Fonda, Peter 215, 518
Fondacaro, Phil 236
Fong, Benson 316
Fong, Brian 316
Fong, Harold 363
Fonseca, Gregg 263
Fontaine, Frank 232
Fonvielle, Lloyd 212
Food of the Gods 183–184
Food of the Gods (book) 106
Food of the Gods, Part 2 184
Foraker, Lois 165
Foran, Dick 336, 337, 341
Forbes, Bryan 239, 240, 400
Forbes, Mary 377
Forbes-Robinson, John 150
"The Forbidden" (short
   story) 68
Forbidden Planet 391
Ford, Francis 185
Ford, Glenn 461, 463
Ford, Harrison 408, 409,
   411, 413, 452, 454, 457,
   458, 459
Ford, John 39
Ford, Mary 77
Ford, Michael 408, 454, 523
Ford, Roy 150
Ford, Wallace 336, 337, 341
Fordney, Alan 316
Fore, Mark 175
Foree, Ken 348, 349
Forges, Robert D. 106
Forman, David 472–473
Forman, Harrison 315

Forney, Don 57
Forrest, Christine 102
Forrest, Frederic 300
Forrest, Irene 415
Forrest, William 143, 281,
   331
Forslund, Constance 511
Forster, Peter 382
Forsyth, Frank 201, 309
Forsythe, John 427
Fort, Fritz 370
Fort, Garrett 129, 130, 184,
   324
Fort Apache 66
48 Hrs. 332
Fosser, William B. 370
Foster, Alan 439
Foster, Craig 67
Foster, David 438, 484
Foster, Eddie 336
Foster, Gary 438
Foster, Preston 127
Foster, Stacie 352
Fotre, Vincent 77
Foulger, Byron 460
Foulk, Robert 316
The Fourth Man 417
Fowlds, Derek 204
Fowler, Brenda 186
Fowler, Gene, Jr. 276
Fowler, Marjorie 383
Fowler, Maurice 464
Fowley, Douglas 77
Fox, Charles 166, 365, 438,
   527
Fox, Colin 184
Fox, Glenn 43
Fox, Michael J. 40, 41, 42,
   43, 44, 277
Fox, Morgan 177
Fox, Neal 37
Fox, Tom 350, 351
Fox, William 370
Foxworth, Robert 369
Foy, Bryan 128
Fraker, William A. 164, 259
Frakes, Jonathan 450
Frame, Philip 93
Frampton, Harry 120
Frampton, Peter 152
France, C.V. 425
France, Larry 484
France, Marie 56
France, Richard 348
Francis, Derek 173, 427
Francis, Freddie 143, 151,
   200, 202, 279, 309
Francis, Jan 153
Francis-Bruce, Richard 323
Franciscus, James 381

Franco, Larry 484
Frank, Fred 187
Frankel, Art 104
Franken, Steve 517
Frankenheimer, John 29
Frankenhooker 215–216
Frankenstein (book) 185,
194, 210, 217
Frankenstein (1931) ii,
184–185, 187, 211
Frankenstein: The True Story
(TV mini-series) 217
Frankenstein — 1970 198–199
*Frankenstein and the Monster
from Hell* 208–209
*Frankenstein Conquers the
World* 217
Frankenstein Created Woman
203–206, 207
Frankenstein Island 211–212
*Frankenstein Meets the Space
Monster* 217
*Frankenstein Meets the Wolf
Man* 190, 202, 525
*Frankenstein Must Be De-
stroyed* 206–207
Frankenstein Unbound
(book) 214
Frankenstein's Daughter
199–200
Frankes, Robin 393
Frankfather, William 282
Frankham, David 169, 178
Franklin, Diane 32, 5
Franklin, Joe 233
Franklin, John 20, 78
Franklin, Pamela 183, 279,
280
Franklyn, William 150, 400,
404
Franz, Arthur 281, 282, 293
Franz, Eduard 482
Fraser, Bill 498
Fraser, David 475
Fraser, Duncan 514
Fraser, Ian 426
Fraser, Richard 377
Fraser, Sally 30
Fraser, Shelagh 452
Fratkin, Stuart 278
Frawley, William 258, 293,
331
Freaks 130
Freda, Bill 514
Freddie 42, 43
*Freddy's Dead: The Final
Nightmare* 360
Frederic, Marc 77, 199
Frederick, Christopher 408
Fredericks, Ellsworth 284

Freeborn, Stuart 22, 454,
457, 464, 499
Freed, Bert 281
Freed, Bill 514
Freed, Reuben 390
Freeman, Bill 44
Freeman, Jeff 166
Freeman, Joan 221, 222
Freeman, Joel 152
Freeman, Kathleen 118, 177,
242, 278
Freeman, Lisa 40
Freeman, Paul 248, 249,
408, 410
Freeman, Yvette 80
Freeman-Fox, Lois 277
Frees, Paul 482
Fremont, Dash 313
French, Edward 103, 449
French, Susan 265
Freulich, Henry 116
Freund, Karl 129, 242, 319,
334
Frewer, Matt 263
Fricker, Brenda 36
Frickert, Joseph 371, 372
Frid, Jonathan 268, 269
Friday the 13th 38, 160,
217–219, 265, 268, 354
*Friday the 13th: The Final
Chapter* 221–222
*Friday the 13th: A New Be-
ginning* 222–223
Friday the 13th, Part II 219
Friday the 13th, Part III
219–221
*Friday the 13th, Part VI:
Jason Lives* 223–224
*Friday the 13th, Part VII —
The New Blood* 224–225,
266
*Friday the 13th, Part VIII:
Jason Takes Manhattan*
225–226
Fridley, Tom 223
Fried, Gerald 137
Friedhofer, Hugo 489
Friedkin, William 162
Friedland, Alicia 313
Friedman, Brent V. 252, 253
Friedman, Louis 300
Friedman, Norman 476
Friedman, Seymour 116
Friel, Cassandra Rachel 360
Friels, Colin 108
Fries, Charles 75
Fright Night 227–228
Fright Night Part 2 228–229
Frisby, Doug 176
Fritsch, Gunther V. 74

Fritz, Ken 476
Froelich, Bill 79
Frohman, Lou 209
From Beyond 414
Frome, Milton 47, 118
Fromin, Troy 376
Frommer, Ben 122
Frost, George 64, 427
Frost, Philip 425
Frost, Sadie 156
Frost, Warren 31
Fry, Gary 493, 494
Fry, Rick 415
Frye, Dwight 129, 153, 185,
186, 187, 188, 289
Frye, Peter 362
Frye, Virgil 122
Fuest, Robert 15–16
Fujimoto, Tak 85, 122
Fujioka, John 518
Full Metal Jacket 482
Fuller, Kurt 234
Fuller, Lisa 214
Fullerton, Carl 219
Fullerton, Fiona 22
Fullilove, Donald 40
Fulton, John P. 130, 131,
133., 186, 190, 238, 289,
291, 292, 334
Fulton, Larry 266
Fung, Willie 315
Funicello, Annette 39, 40,
433
Funk, Greg 352
Funny Girl 501
Furey, John 219
Furlong, Edward 374, 375,
478
Furneaux, Yvonne 342
Furse, Judith 333
Furse, Margaret 427
Furst, Anton 47, 51
Furth, George 365
Futcher, Hugh 404
Future Cop 492
Futureworld 518
Fux, Herbert 208
FX Center 176

Gaba, Marianne 77, 78
Gabbani, Till 495
Gable, Christopher 239
Gabor, Zsa Zsa 356
Gabrielle, Monique 364,
472
Gachman, Dan 137
Gage, Leona 169
Gage, Neva 76
Gahagan, Helen 435, 436
Gaines, George 259

Gains, Courtney 40, 78
Galbraith, Elinor Rose 181
Galbraith, Theresa 177
Gale, Bob 40, 42, 43
Gale, David 413, 414, 415
Gale, John 16
Gale, Lorena 183
Galik, Denise 365
Galili, Hal 464
Gallaudet, John 35
Gallier, Alex 194
Galligan, Zach 241, 242, 513
Gallo, Mario 305
Galtress, Trevor 263
Gamley, Douglas 309
Ganibalova, Valentina Gani-
  lai 66
Ganley, Gail 363
Gant, Richard 226
Garas, Kaz 397, 519
Garay, Joaquin, III 319
Garber, John 438
Garbutt, James 461
Garcia, Rick 301
Gardenia, Vincent 259, 314
Gardner, Arthur 137
Gardner, Brooks 377
Gardner, Caron 201
Gardner, David 390
Gardner, Devin 250
Gardner, Tony 63, 108
Garet, Hank 164
Garfield, James 201
Garfield, Joey 387
Garfield, John D. 431
Gargan, Ed 293
Gargan, Jack 97
Garland, Beverly 363
Garland, Judy 66, 520, 521
Garlick, Stephen 427
Garner, Martin 366
Garnet, Bob 31
Garnett, Tay 89
Garr, Teri 210, 211
Garrett, Grant 116
Garrett, Pat 314
Garrett, Scott 519
Garris, Mick 104, 182
Garson, Arline 268
Garson, Mort 61
Gash, Mark 267
Gaspar, Chuck 164, 233
Gaspard, Ray 311
The Gate 229–230
Gate II 230
Gatehouse, Richard 333
Gates, Bob 311
Gates, Dean 155, 306, 328,
  377
Gates, Larry 284

Gates, Tudor 503, 506, 508
Gator, Linus 175
Gatz, Caatherine 387
Gaunt, Valerie 135, 194
Gausman, Hal 19, 39, 40,
  317
Gausman, Russell A. (R.A.)
  71, 72, 116, 133, 187, 189,
  190, 192, 291, 292, 293,
  336, 337, 341, 524
Gautreaux, David 440
Gavigan, Gerry 452
Gavin, Seth 267
Gavioila, Cassandra 86
Gay, Norman 162
Gaybis, Annie 220
Gaye, Lisa 490, 491
"Gayne Ballet Suite" (musi-
  cal composition) 499
Gaynes, George 123
Gayson, Eunice 197
Gazelle, Wendy 240
Gearren, Leslie Hamilton
  478
Geary, Bud 72
Gee, Caroline 109, 393
Gee, Hazel 320
Gee, Timothy 239
Geer, Lennie 143
Geer, Will 66
Geffen, David 314
Geisinger, Elliott 31
Gelani, Zia 410
Gelbart, Larry 365
Gellow, Janet Ann 189
Gemignani, Rhoda 233
Gemora, Charles 320
Gems, Pam 362
Genghis Khan 56
Gentner, Richard 237
Geoffreys, Stephen 227
George, David 274
George, Frank 143, 400
George, Gil 433
George, John 186
George, Roger 54, 93, 271
George, Wally 166
Geray, Steve 201
Geray, Steven 203
Germain, Michael 246
Gerrard, Charles 129
Gersak, Savina 107
Gershenson, Joseph 97, 293,
  341
Gerson, Betty Lou 177
Gerstad, Harry 47, 519
Gertsman, Maury 72, 100
Geter, Leo 250
Getty, Estelle 329
Gettysburg 106

Getz, John 181, 182
Geyer, Steve 527
Ghadban, Alle 393
Gherardi, Charles 42
The Ghost Breakers 230–231,
  232, 392
Ghost of Frankenstein 133
The Ghost of Frankenstein
  189–190, 192
Ghostbusters 232–234, 392,
  473
Ghostbusters II 234–235
Ghoulies 235
Ghoulies IV 237
Ghoulies Go to College 236–
  237
Ghoulies II 236
Gianopoulos, David 70
The Giant Claw 101
Giardino, Mark 282
Giatti, Ian 366
Gibb, Charles 97
Gibb, Cynthia 438
Gibbel, Ken 478
Gibbons, Carla 376
Gibbons, Cedric 114, 520,
  238, 243, 377, 425
Gibbons, Megan 376
Gibbons, Rodney 422
Gibbs, George 27, 175, 411,
  497
Gibbs, Gerald 400
Gibby, Gwyneth 516
Gibson, Alan 148, 149
Gibson, Brian 385
Gibson, E.B. 302
Gibson, Henry 118, 242
Gibson, Mel 321, 322, 323
Gibson, Sara 427
Gielgud, John 316
Gifford, Alan 499
Gifford, Gloria 246
Gifford, Lauren 492
Giger, H.R. 23, 24, 27, 386,
  396
Gigi 238
Gil, Arturo 237
Gil, Jorge 84
Gil, Miguel A., Jr. 431, 432
Gil, Vince 321
Gilb, Lesley 157
Gilbert, Jody 519
Gilbert, John 249
Gilbert, Ruth 21
Gilbert, Stephen 519
Gilchrist, Stacy 387
Giler, David 23, 24, 27
Gilford, Gwynne 61
Gilford, Jack 84, 85
Gill, Beverly 59

Gill, Bob 429
Gillard, Stuart 475
Gillespie, Arnold 243, 520
Gillespie, Dana 310
Gillespie, John 297
Gillette, Ruth 434
Gillette, Warrington 219
Gilliam, Burton "Bubba"
   43, 481
Gilliam, Stu 122
Gilligan's Island (TV series)
   312
Gillin, Hugh 43
Gilling, John 345
Gillis, Alec 27, 221
Gillis, Ann 499
Gilman, Larry 481
Gilmore, Andrew J. 72, 292
Gilmore, Lowell 377
Gilmore, Peter 15
Gilmore, R.J. 190
Gilpin, Toni 346
Gindes, Mark 152
Ginn, Jeff 63
Ginther, Mark 474
Giorgio, Bill 31
Giorgio, Tony 158
Gish, Sheila 260
Gittens, George 276
Givens, Jack 347
Gladiator (book) 469
Glaser, Bernard 178
Glasgow, William 76
Glass, Everett 482
Glass, Ned 316
Glass, Philip 68, 69
The Glass Slipper 237–238,
   239, 240
Glasser, Albert 30
Glatz, Ilse Von 240
Glazer, Mitch 427
Gleason, Jackie 232
Gleason, James 243, 257, 258
Gleason, Kelly 490, 491
Gleason, Paul 328
Gleeson, Patrick 275
Glenn, Roy E., Sr. 382
Glennon, Bert 21
Glickenhaus, James 45
Gloag, Helena 427
The Glob see *The Blob*
Globus, Yoram 122, 282, 468
The Glory Stompers 267
Glover, Brian 27
Glover, Bruce 513
Glover, Crispin 40, 222
Glover, Danny 36, 388, 390
Glover, John 242, 418, 427
Glover, Julian 404, 407, 411,
   454

Glover, Mrs. 411
Gluck, Dan 446
Glucksman, Ernest D. 118
Glump see *Please Don't Eat
   My Mother*
Glunt, Ruth 175
Glynn, Tamara 249
Glynne, Mary 425
The Goblins 348
Godar, Godfrey 274
Goddard, Charles W. 230,
   232
Goddard, Ian 321
Goddard, Paulette 230, 231,
   392
The Godfather 281
Godfrey, Derek 437
Godfrey, Peter 114
Godfroy, John 221
Godreau, Miguel 123
God's Little Acre 277
Godzilla 97
Goetz, Peter Michael 83,
   306
Gogin, Michael Lee 104
Goins, Jesse 125, 416
Golan, Menahem 122, 282,
   352, 468
Golas, Thaddeus 446
Goldberg, Barry 353
Goldberg, Whoopi 450
Goldblat, Mark 246
Goldblatt, Harold 120, 510
Goldblatt, Mark 271, 388,
   476, 478
Goldblum, Jeff 181, 286
Golden, Sally Anne 218
The Golden Voyage of Sinbad
   431, 432, 433
Goldenberg, Mark 278
Goldenthal, Elliot 27, 52,
   373
Goldin, Daniel 108
Goldin, Joshua 108
Goldin, Ricky Paul 63
Goldman, Danny 210
Goldman, Hal 365
Goldman, Lorry 164
Goldner, Orville 302
Goldoni, Lelia 286
Goldsman, Akiva 52
Goldsmith, Charles 270
Goldsmith, George 78
Goldsmith, Jerry 23, 241,
   242, 367, 369, 370, 380,
   382, 385, 440, 442, 447,
   466, 512
Goldsmith, Joel 328, 514
Goldsmith, Ken 291
Goldstein, Dan 516

Goldstein, Jenette 24, 450,
   478
Goldstein, Robert 165
Goldthwait, Bobcat 427
Goldwyn, Tony 223
Golin, Steve 68
Golitzen, Alexander 97, 100,
   341
Golonka, Arlene 152
Gomez, Thomas 381
Gondek, Beth 391
Gone with the Wind 282
Gonzalez, Carlos 516
Gonzalez, Fernando 310,
   431, 432
Gonzalez, Joseph 215
Gonzalez Gonzalez, Pedro
   316, 319
Good, Maurice 404
Goodan, Miles 277
Goodheart, William 164
Goodkind, Saul 131, 292,
   339
Goodley, Ted 142, 203
Goodman, Joel 221
Goodman, John 83, 244
Goodman, John B. 71, 72,
   133, 190, 292, 339
Goodman, Miles 314, 429
Goodnoff, Irv 252
Goodstein, Robert 519
Goodwin, Fred 106
Goodwin, Gordon 36
Goodwin, Harold 110, 206,
   342, 344
Goodwin, Robin 469
Goodwin, Ron 90, 508, 510
Goodwins, Leslie 339
Goorney, Howard 201
Goosson, Stephen 258, 315
Gordean, William D. 475
Gording, Harry 524
Gordon, Angelica 177
Gordon, Barry 152, 321
Gordon, Bert I. 30–31, 183,
   184
Gordon, Colin 333
Gordon, Debra 349
Gordon, Don 165, 370
Gordon, Douglas 131
Gordon, Flora M. 30
Gordon, Gavin 186
Gordon, Gillian 67
Gordon, Lawrence 124, 387,
   388
Gordon, Leo 252
Gordon, Martin 411
Gordon, Mary 186, 337
Gordon, Philip 476
Gordon, Robert 350

Gordon, Roy 31
Gordon, Stuart 263, 413, 414
Gordon-Levitt, Joseph 36
Gorg, Galyn 418
Gorin, Owen 131
Gorman, Mari 365
Gormenghast (book) 50
Gorney, Walt 217, 219
Gornick, Michael 102, 103, 348, 349
Gorshin, Frank 47
Gortner, Marjoe 183, 184
Gosnell, Raja 278, 331
Goss, Helen 117
Gossett, Cindi 481
Gossett, Lou 35
Goswell, Thomas 139
Gotell, Walter 395
Gottesfeld, Dov 469
Gottfried, Howard 122
Gottlieb, Michael 91, 329
Gough, Michael 47, 50, 52, 135, 223, 251
Gould, Arthur 116
Gould, Brewster 481
Gould, Jay 271
Gould, Lewis 83
Gould, Robert 416
Goulet, Robert 427, 429
Goursaud, Anne 155
Gouw, Cynthia 447
Gover, Michael 461
Governor, Mark 374
Gowans, John D. 440
Gowdy, Curt 259
Gower, Andre 213
Gowland, Gibson 243
Gozier, Bernie 94
Grace, David 352
Gracey, Yale 39
Grady, Ed 79
Graef, Vicki 472
Grafe, Judy 45
Graffeo, Charles M. 442
Graham, C.J. 223
Graham, Frank 307
Graham, Fred 35, 495
Graham, Gerrit 61, 81, 84, 301
Graham, John Michael 245
Graham, John 404
Graham, Marlene 229
Graham, Michael 180
Graham, Paul 387
Graham, Steve 386
Grahn, Nancy Lee 79
Grainer, Ron 334
Grais, Michael 385
Granatelli, Andy 316
Granel, Janine 178

Granger, Bertram 89
Granger, Philip 486
Granke, Anthony 61
Granstedt, Greta 137
Grant, Arthur 64, 143, 145, 173, 203, 206, 345, 404
Grant, Belina 364
Grant, Beth 81
Grant, Bill 164
Grant, Cary 21, 488, 489
Grant, Howard 67
Grant, John 116, 192, 293, 340
Grant, Kathryn 429
Grant, Lawrence 114, 188, 315
Grant, Lee 369
Grant, Micah 486
Grant, Moray 120, 145, 207, 503
Grant, Richard E. 156, 512
Grapewin, Charley 520
Graves, Bryan 212
Graves, Frank 184
Graves, Teresa 152
Graveyard Shift 240
Graveyard Shift II see *The Understudy: Graveyard Shift II*
Gray, Beatrice 133
Gray, Carole 180
Gray, Coleen 75
Gray, Erin 226
Gray, Lauren 376
Gray, Thomas K. 474, 475
Gray, Timothy 359
Gray, William 390
Graysmark, John 175
Graytak, Eugene 166
Greason, Staci 224
The Great Escape 413
The Great John L. (actor) 297
Greaves, Kristoffer 322
Green, Adolph 20
Green, Bruce 36, 222, 223
Green, Danny 429
Green, Dennis 114
Green, Jeremy 103
Green, Joey 164, 265
Green, Nigel 171, 497
Green, Pat 110
Green, Walon 418
Green, Willard 375
Green Hell 341
Greenberg, Adam 476, 478
Greenblatt, Angela 42
Greenblatt, Shon 360
Greene, Angela 518
Greene, Ellen 314

Greene, Stanley 522
Greenfeld, Josh 365
Greenlaw, Verina 171
Greenman, Alvin 331
Greenquist, Brad 373
Greenwald, Stephen R. 32
Greenway, Lee 482
Greenwood, Joan 497
Greenwood, Peter 107
Greenwood, Rosamund 509
Greer, Dabbs 267, 284
Gregg, Bradley 356, 411
Gregory, James 381
Gregory, Kathleen Jordan 106
Gregory, Michael 416
Greist, Kim 83
Gremlins 104, 241–242
Gremlins II: The New Batch 242
Gresham, Gloria 234
Gresley, Margery 197
Gresty, Robert Verner 260
Greville, Edmond T. 320
Greville-Morris, Jeanine 374
Grey, Alexis 490, 491
Grey, Arnold 335
Grey, Eve 425
Grey, Nan 131, 291
Grier, Pam 56
Gries, Jonathan 214, 228
Gries, Tom 307
Grieve, Neil 240
Grifasi, Joe 52
Griffin, Fabus 312
Griffin, Frank 516
Griffin, Lorie 277
Griffin, Robert 276
Griffith, Charles B. 122, 312, 313, 363, 364
Griffith, Hugh 15, 16
Griffith, Jack 312
Griffith, Kenneth 362
Griffith, Peter 245
Griffiths, Lucy 334
Griffiths, Richard 464
Grimes, Rosemary 294
Grimes, Scott 103, 104
Grimsby, Roger 233
Grimshaw, Jim 306, 472
Grimsman, Geoffrey S. 474
Grinde, Nick 38
Gritzus, Ionas 66
Grives, Steven 359
Grodin, Charles 259, 305
Groom, James 139
Gross, Arye 266
Gross, Edan 81, 82
Gross, Frank 192, 291

Gross, Roland 482
Grossman, Abraham 71, 339
Grossman, Eugene 177
Grossman, Ted 408, 411
Grosvenor, Phillip 107
Groundhog Day 427–428
Grove, Richard 161, 423
Grover, Danny 499
Grover, Deborah 229
Grow, Ronald R. 317
Grubb, June S. 311
Grubb, Robert 323
Grubbs, Tom 527
Grummette, Steven 175
Grusin, Dave 259
Gruska, Michele 457
Gruskoff, Michael 210
Grusman, Dorain 227
Guard, Barrie 490
Guastaferro, Vincent 223
Guber, Peter 47, 50
Guedes, Luis 429
Guerin, J.P. 91
Guerra, Castula 478
Guest, Christopher 314
Guest, Lance 246
Guest, Nicholas 397
Guest, Val 96, 144, 398, 399,
    400, 401, 403, 404, 406,
    407
A Guide for the Married Man
    318
Guidery, Wendy 377
Guild, Nancy 293
Guillermin, John 305, 306
Guinness, Alec 427, 452,
    453, 454, 457
Gulager, Clu 350, 351, 355,
    397
Gundlach, Robert 305
Gunn, Moses 32
Gupta, Bandana Das 309
Gurfinkel, David 475
Guterres, Candi 377
Guthridge, John D. 120
Guthrie, Carl E. 198
Guthrie, Red 71
Gutknecht, Robert 482
Guttenberg, Steve 84, 85,
    438
Gutteridge, Martin 260
Guttman, Henry 292
Guy, DeJuan 68
A Guy Named Joe 242–244
Guyler, Deryck 333
Guza, Robert, Jr. 390
Gwenn, Edmund 331
Gwillim, Jack 214, 344
Gwynn, Michael 146, 197,
    509

Gwynne, Anne 191
Gwynne, Fred 373

Haack, Morton 380, 381
Haade, William 258
Haas, Charlie 242
Haber, David M. 213
Hackett, Buddy 316, 317
Hackett, John 169
Hackman, Gene 210, 211,
    461, 463, 465, 466
Haddon, Larry 321
Haden, Sarah 319
Hadlow, Michael 116
Hafenrichter, Oswald 126,
    309, 320
Haffley, Wayne 305
Hagan, Marianne 250
Hagen, Jean 433
Hagen, Julius 425
Haggard, H. Rider 435, 436,
    437
Haggerty, Don 35
Hagman, Larry 61, 62
Hagon, Garrick 48, 452
Hagon, Rex 439
Hahn, Paul 30
Haid, Charles 123
Haiduc, Ion 494
Haim, Corey 514
Haines, Dennis 184
Haines, Richard W. 490
Haines, Richard Haddon
    107
Hairtique 348
Haitkin, Jacques 328, 354,
    355, 423
Halberg, Garry 305
Hale, Creighton 128
Hale, Diana 298
Hales, Gordon 206
Haley, Brian 244
Haley, Jack 520
Haley, Jackie Earle 328
Hall, Alexander 257, 258
Hall, Brian 309
Hall, Charles D. 129, 184,
    186, 289, 371, 489
Hall, David "Buck" 383
Hall, Grayson 268, 270, 271
Hall, Harvey 171, 503, 508
Hall, Huntz 128, 317
Hall, Jerry 47
Hall, Joanna 518
Hall, John 203
Hall, Jon 292
Hall, Justin 83
Hall, Kenneth J. 393
Hall, Kevin Peter 388, 389
Hall, Parnell 83

Hall, Phillip Baker 234
Hall, Porter 331
Hall, Rich 84
Hall, Sam 268, 270, 271
Hall, Shannah 67
Hall, Thurston 65
Hall, Victoria 20
Hall Johnson Choir 315
Hallahan, Charles 484
Hallam, John 175, 310
Haller, Daniel 110, 111, 167,
    168, 169, 170, 251, 312
Halloween 218, 226,
    244–246, 247, 251, 354,
    390, 392, 393, 485, 486
*Halloween: The Curse of
    Michael Myers* 249–251
*Halloween: The Origin of
    Michael Myers see Hal-
    loween 4: The Curse of
    Micheal Myers*
Halloween II 246, 249
*Halloween III: Season of the
    Witch* 247–248
*Halloween 4: The Return of
    Michael Myers* 248–249
Halloween 5 249, 250
Halsey, Brett 97, 178
Halsey, Mary 72
Halsey, Richard 329
Hamill, Mark 452, 454, 457,
    460, 511
Hamilton, Antony 274
Hamilton, Bernie 59
Hamilton, Fenton 298, 300
Hamilton, George 152, 153
Hamilton, John 307, 352
Hamilton, Linda 78, 79,
    210, 306, 307, 476, 478,
    480
Hamilton, Margaret 520,
    521
Hamilton, Murray 31
Hamilton, Neil 47
Hamilton, Roy 76
Hamilton, Suzanna 362
Hamilton, Wendy 146
Hamlin, Larry 108
Hamm, Al 61
Hamm, Sam 47, 50
Hammer, Ben 54
Hammer, Elinor 61
Hammeras, Ralph 88
Hammerstein, David 511
Hammerstein, Oscar 240
Hammond, Les 208
Hamond, Arthur 460
Hamori, Andras 230
Hampton, James 277, 278
Hampton, Janice 360

Hampton, Louise 426
Hampton, Roger 104
Hampton, Sandra 334
Hancock, Lou 160
Hand, Danelle 76
Handl, Irene 333
Handman, David 226
Hands of a Stranger 222,
   320–321
The Hands of Orlac 320
Hands of the Strangler see
   The Hands of Orlac
Handy, Bill 486
Haney, Daryl 224
Hankins, Carol 21
Hanley, Daniel 84, 373
Hanley, Jenny 145, 146, 147
Hanna, Mark 30, 363, 364
Hanna, Robert 150
Hannah, Pace 103
Hannant, Brian 322
Hansen, Paul 92, 93
Hansen, William 519
Hanson, Luke 412
Hanson, Steve 408
"Happiness" (song) 427
Hapy, Marguerite 438
Harben, Hubert 425
Harber, Harry Paul 295
Harburg, E.Y. 520
Hard, Tyler 80
A Hard Day's Night 466
Harder, Richard 446
Harding, Vincent 498
Hardman, Karl 347
Hardman Associates 347
Hardtmuth, Paul 194
Hardwicke, Edward 243
Hardwicke, Sir Cedric 89,
   189, 291, 292, 377
Hardy, J.J. 411
Hardy, Oliver 38
Hardy, Robert 216
Hardy, Sam 302
Hare, Lumsden 114, 435
Hare, Will 40
Hargitay, Mariska 235
Hargitay, Mickey 208
Harkins, John 33
Harlan, Russell 482
Harlin, Renny 29, 357, 359
Harling, W. Frank 289
Harlow, Hugh 201
Harlow, Joel 490, 491
Harper, Robert 102
Harper, Susan 375
Harper, Tess 33
Harrigan, William 289
Harris, Andrew 255
Harris, Anthony 61

Harris, Craig 67
Harris, Cynthia 330
Harris, Danielle 248, 249
Harris, Delmore 142
Harris, Donald 175
Harris, Ed 102
Harris, George 408
Harris, Henry 400
Harris, Jack H. 60, 63
Harris, Julius 328
Harris, Len 197
Harris, M.K. 527
Harris, Marilyn 185
Harris, Michael 30, 89
Harris, Richard A. 281, 478
Harris, Ross 527
Harris, Ted 58
Harris, Theresa 72, 331
Harrison, Anthony 509
Harrison, Evangeline 465
Harrison, Jenilee 107
Harrison, John 102, 349
Harrison, Kathleen 426
Harrison, Linda 84, 85, 380,
   381
Harrison, Philip 152, 438
Harrison, Tony 66
Harrow, Lisa 370
Harryhausen, Ray 372, 429,
   431, 432, 497
Hart, Beverly 447
Hart, Christopher 20
Hart, Eric 248
Hart, Gordon 131
Hart, James (Jim) V. 155,
   157, 216
Hart, John 209
Hart, Richard 103
Hart, Roxanne 260, 366
Harte, Jerry 411, 454
Hartigan, John 221
Hartley, Clabe 493, 494
Hartley, Esdras 128
Hartley, Mariette 93
Hartman, Billy 260
Hartman, Don 258
Hartnell, William 333
Hartner, Rona 494
Hartstone, Christopher 498
Harvey, Don C. 97
Harvey, Edward 75
Harvey, Forrester 114, 291,
   324, 524
Harvey, Harry, Sr. 137
Harvey, Jason 40
Harvey, Jimmy 398
Harvey, Joan 320
Harvey, Morris 425
Harvey, Rolf 181
Harvey, Rupert 103, 105, 359

Harvey, Verna 279
Harwood, Alix 260
Harwood, Bruce 183
Haskell, Peter 81, 82
Haskell, Robert 473
Hasler, Monica 398
Hassel, Danny 357, 359
Hassett, Ray 454
Hastings, Michael 279
Hatch, Eric 488
Hatfield, Hurd 377, 379
Hatley, Marvin 488
Hatton, Rondo 72
Haufrect, Alan 246
Haun, Lindsey 511
The Haunted Palace 170, 171,
   251–252, 253
The Haunting 279
Hauser, Fay 70
Hauser, Ken 55
Hauser, Robert B. 519
Hauser, Wings 55, 516
Hauser's Memory (TV
   movie) 309
Havens, James C. 94
Havlick, Gene 116, 315
Hawdon, Robin 120
Hawkes, Terri 391
Hawkins, Anthony 370
Hawks, Howard 482, 484,
   485, 486
Hawley, Brian 499
Hawley, Lowell S. 39
Haworth, Ted 284
Hay, John M. 472
Hayashi, Henry 475
Hayden, Harry 307
Hayden, Linda 145, 152
Haydn, Richard 210
Hayen, Frank 372
Hayes, Alan 222
Hayes, Debra S. 218
Hayes, Denise 122
Hayes, Helen 317
Hayes, Melvyn 194
Hayes, Terry 322, 323
Hayes, Tubby 437
Haygarth, Tony 153, 212
Hayward, Lillie 433
Hayward, Louis 116
Hayworth, Rita 258
Haze, Jonathan 312, 363
Head, Edith 118, 230, 232,
   238, 257
Healey, Myron 258
Healy, David 466, 506
Healy, Ted 319
The Heap (comic book char-
   acter) 404
Heard, Cordis 8

Heard, John 75, 83
Hearn, Chick 316
Heart, Pauline 150
Heath, Percy 112
Heathcote, Thomas 404, 509
Heaven Can Wait 259
Heaven Can Wait (play) 257, 258
Hebden, Gilly 260
Hebert, Chris 282
Hedaya, Dan 20
Hedden, Rob 225
Hedin, Serene 312
Hedison, Al (David) 177
Heffron, Richard T. 518
Hefti, Neal 47
Heggie, O.P. 186, 187
Heiden, Ira 356, 527
Heinzman, Bill 347
Helfer, Ralph D. 297
Helfrich, Mark 387
Helgeland, Brian 357
Helgenberger, Marg 244
Hellbound: Hellraiser II 255–256
The Hellbound Heart (book) 254
Hellen, Marjorie 77
Heller, Otto 344
Hellman, Bonnie 222
Hello Mary Lou: Prom Night II 391–392
Hellraiser 254–255
Hellraiser III: Hell on Earth 256–257
Helm, Fay 71, 524
Helm, Tiffany 222
Helmer, Richard O. 80
Helmkamp, Charlotte 215
Helpmann, Robert 22
Helton, Percy 232, 331, 495
Heman, Al 302
Hemblen, David 438
Hemingway, Mariel 468
Hemingway, Winston 473
Hempel, Anoushka 146
Hemsley, Sherman 152
Hemson, Joyce 141
Hench, John 495
Henderson, Don 452
Henderson, Saffron 182
Hendrickson, Lance 478
Hendrie, Chris 227
Hendriksen, Lance 24, 27, 476
Hendry, Ian 510
Heneker, David 117
Henenlotter, Frank 44, 45, 215, 216

Henesy, David 268
Henley, Drewe 452
Henley, Kaleb 43
Henn, Carrie 24
Hennessey, Peter 75
Hennessy, Jill 419
Hennesy, Dale 384
Henreid, Paul 164
Henriksen, Lance 267, 369
Henrikson, Linda 47
Henry, Bill 307
Henry, Buck 259
Henry, Charlotte 21–22, 38
Henry, Gloria Lynne 377
Henry, Max 482
Henschell, Todd 396, 397
Henson, Brian 429, 523
Henson, Elizabeth 22
Henson, Frank 153
Henson, Jim 472, 474
Henson, Nicky 152
Henteloff, Alex 446
Hepburn, Audrey 244
Hepburn, Katharine 116
Herbeck, Bobby 472
Herbert, Charles 177
Herbert, Holmes 112, 189, 289, 292
Herbert, Leon 28
Herbert, Martin 362
Herbert, Percy 372, 400, 497
Herbert, Victor 38, 39, 4
"Herbert West — Re-anima-tor" (short story) 413, 414
Herbertson, Scott 527
Herbie Goes Bananas 318–319
Herbie Goes to Monte Carlo 318
Herbie Rides Again 317–318
Herd, Richard 491
Here Comes Mr. Jordan 257–258
Herek, Stephen 103
Herman, Gary 86
Hernandez, Nicholas 352
Hernandez, Robert 30
Heroux, Claude 420
Herrin, Kym 233
Herrmann, Bernard 298, 300, 301, 414, 429, 431, 497, 519
Herschel, David 67
Hertford, Whitby 359
Hertz, Ralph 21
Hervey, Jason 214
Herz, Michael 490, 491
Herzbrun, Bernard 94, 116, 192, 293
Herzog, John 391

Herzog, Werner 157
Hess, David 469
Hess, Jon 514
Hessey, Russ 286
Hessler, Gordon 431
Heston, Charlton 64, 122, 380, 381
Hewitt, Henry 426
Hewitt, Jean 144
Hewitt, Pete 56
Hewitt, Shawn 181
Hewlett, Brian 171
Hewlett, David 422
Hey, Virginia 322
Heylen, Syd 322
Heymann, Werner R. 371, 489
Heyward, Louis M. 15, 16
Heywood, Anne 309
Hibbs, Gene 281
Hibler, Christopher 316
Hice, Fred 416
Hickey, William 393
Hickman, Bob 94, 97
Hickman, Howard 128
Hickox, Anthony 256, 513
Hickox, James D.R. 79, 256, 513
Hickox, Sid 128
Hicks, Catherine 80, 446
Hicks, Dan (Danny) 108, 160
Hicks, Grant 362
Hicks, Russell 65
Hicks, Seymour 425
Hickson, Joan 333
Higgins, Anthony 212, 408
Higgins, Clare 254, 255
Higgins, Deirdre 267
High School Hellcats 199
Highlander 259–261
Highlander 2: The Quickening 261–263
Hilbert, Tina Louise 46
Hildreth, Rick (Rock) 312
Hill, Arthur 518
Hill, Clayton 348
Hill, Debra 244, 246, 247, 250
Hill, Frankie 222
Hill, James 497
Hill, Matt 475
Hill, Michael, J. 84, 373
Hill, Teresa 396, 397
Hill, Walter 24, 27
Hiller, Colette 24
Hillmann, Alfred 60
Hillyer, Lambert 130
Hilton, Arthur 76
Hilton, James 315

Hinchley, Tommy 480
Hindle, Art 286
Hinds, Anthony 135, 139, 140, 143, 145, 194, 197, 200, 201, 398, 400
Hinds, Samuel S. 71, 131, 435
Hines, David 499
Hines, Karen 184
Hines, Robert 254
Hingle, Pat 47, 50, 52, 53
Hird, Thora 279, 398
Hirsch, Paul 102, 452, 454
Hirsch, Tina 241
Hirschfeld, Gerald 210
His Majesty O'Keefe 207
Hiser, Tim 411
Hitchcock, Alfred 300, 385
Hitchcock, Keith 65, 116
Hittleman, Carl K. 142, 203
Hively, George 220
Hixon, John P. 311
Hoag, Judith 472
Hoagland, Ellsworth 230
Hoax, Clair 481
Hobart, Rose 112, 113
Hobbes, Halliwell 112, 257; see also Hobbs, Halliwell
Hobbs, Halliwell 131, 292
Hobson, I.M. 156
Hobson, Valerie 186
Hochstatter, Zoran 364, 472
Hodder, Kane 224, 225, 226, 264, 267
Hodge, Jim 366
Hodgeman, Edwin 323
Hodges, Jonathon 327
Hodges, Michael (screen-writer) 369
Hodges, Mike (director) 175
Hodges, Tom 104
Hodgkinson, Janet 182
Hodgson, Gaynor 427
Hodgson, Leyland 189, 524
Hodgson, William Hope 472
Hoenig, Michael 63, 229
Hoesli, John 499
Hoey, Dennis 190
Hoffenstein, Samuel 112
Hoffman, Basil 152
Hoffman, Joe 221
Hoffman, Michael 213
Hoffman, Morris 276
Hoffman, Paul 307
Hofman, Maury 30
Hofues, John 311
Hogan, Hulk 242
Hogan, Jeff 349
Hogan, Robert 517

Hohl, Arthur 294, 295
Holbrook, Hal 102
Holcombe, Harry 158
Holden, Gloria 131
Holden, Jan 4
Holden, Lansing C. 435, 436
Holden, William 368
Holdren, Judd 30
Holdridge, Lee 54
Hole, Fred 24, 457, 523
Holland, Anthony 365
Holland, Erik 234, 327
Holland, John 292
Holland, Tom 80, 227, 228
Hollander, Adam 245
Hollander, Frederick 257
Hollander, Howard 519
Holliday, Polly 241
Hollier, Emery 76
Holliman, Earl 232
Hollingsworth, John 135, 194, 325, 398
Hollis, John 461, 454, 464
Hollis, Tommy 233
Holloway, Sterling 47, 65
Hollywood Optical Systems 105
Hollywood Special Effects 327
Holm, Arwen 370
Holm, Barnaby 370
Holm, Ian 23
Holm, Sonia 332
Holman, Harry 127
Holman, Rex 158, 447
Holmes, Barbara 349
Holmes, Ernie 227
Holmey, Erick 86
Holscher, Walter 116
Holsopple, Theobold (Ted) 117, 177, 320
Holt, Jack 72
Holt, Seth 64
Holton, Mark 277, 278
Holton, Nigel 516
Holzer, Hans 32
Holzman, Daniel 298
Homburg, Wilhelm Von 234
Home Alone 242
Hondo 274
Honess, Peter 260, 298
Honey, Bert 320
Honey, I Blew Up the Kid 264
Honey, I Shrunk the Kids 20, 263–264
Hong, Alison 125
Hood, Don 76
Hood, Gavin 107

Hood, Noel 194
Hooks, Robert 444
Hooper, Ewan 143
Hooper, Tobe 282, 385, 406
Hootkins, William 47, 175, 408, 452, 468
Hoover, Elva Mai (Elva May) 230, 464
"Hop-Frog" (short story) 173
Hope, Bob 230, 231, 392
Hope, William 24, 255
Hopkins, Anthony 156, 157
Hopkins, Miriam 112
Hopkins, Stephen 359, 388
Hopkins, Telma 491, 492, 493
Hopper, Hedda 131, 488
Hopper, William 128
Hora, John 241, 242, 271
Horan, James 423
Hordern, Michael 22, 239, 426
Horery, Bob 323
Horgan, Patrick 201
Horger, Jack 122
Horger, John C. 384
Horino, Tad 57
Hornblow, Arthur, Jr. 230
Horne, Derek 22
Horne, Lena 522
Horner, James 24, 84, 85, 263, 442, 444
Horner, Yvonne 372
Horning, William A. 520
Horror of Dracula 22, 135–137, 139, 151, 194
The Horror of Frankenstein 207
The Horror Show 266–267
Horrors of the Black Museum 53, 223
Horsley, David S. 293
Horsley, John 333
Horton, Edward Everett 21, 257, 258, 315
Horton, Peter 78
Hoskins, Raymond 427
Hotte, Paul 125
Hotton, Donald 282
Houck, Doris 258
Hough, John 158, 159, 274, 508
Houghton, Don 148, 149, 150
Houlihan, Terrence M. 350
The Hound of Florence (story) 433, 434
The Hour of the Dragon (book) 88

House 264–266, 267
House, Don 97
*The House at the End of the
World* see *Die, Monster,
Die!*
House IV 267–268
House of Dark Shadows
268–270, 271
House of Dracula 133–135,
192, 526
*The House of Dracula's
Daughter* 158
House of Frankenstein 133,
190–192, 202, 525
House of Fright see *The Two
Faces of Dr. Jekyll*
House of Whipcord 152
The House on the Borderland
(book) 472
*The House That Dripped
Blood* 506
House II: The Second Story
266
House III see *The Horror
Show*
Houseman, John 427, 429
Hove, Anders 105
Howard, Barbara 222
Howard, Ben 309
Howard, Clint 84
Howard, John 210, 315
Howard, Lisa K. 307
Howard, Rachel 220
Howard, Rance 80
Howard, Robert E. 86, 87,
88, 176
Howard, Ron (effects man)
508
Howard, Ronald (actor) 344
Howard, Tom 499
Howard, Trevor 461
Howard A. Anderson Com-
pany 320
Howarth, Alan 246, 247,
248, 249, 376, 444
Howarth, Kristine 153
Howerton, Charles 122
Howitt, Peter 410, 411, 464
Howland, Olin 128; *see also*
Howlin, Olin
Howland, Robert 350
Howlett, Noel 404, 426
Howley, Janice 509
Howlin, Olin 61, 62
The Howling 271–272, 454
The Howling I (book) 274,
275
Howling II (book) 273
*Howling II ... Your sister Is a
Werewolf* 273

The Howling III 273–274
The Howling III (book) 273
*Howling IV: The Original
Nightmare* 274–275
Howling V: The Rebirth 275,
276
Howling VI: The Freaks
275–276
Hoy, Bob 59
Hoy, Renata 77
Hoy, Robert 97
Hoyt, John 175
Hsu, Victor 365
Hubbard, Geoff 388
Hubbard, John 337, 371
Huckabee, Cooper 106
Hudgins, Joseph 175
Hudson, Ernie 233, 234
Hudson, Gary 423
Hudson, Larry 100
Hudson, Rock 101
Hudson, William 30
Huebsch, Edward 116
Huehes, Marjorie 438
Huey Lewis and the News
40
Hughes, Barnard 365
Hughes, Brendan 275, 486
Hughes, Cooper 83
Hughes, John 331
Hughes, Miko 37, 361
Hughes, Prince A. 227
Hughes, Raymond 523
Hughes, Roddy 426
Hughes, Stuart 184
Hughes, William 30
Huguely, Jay 226
Huke, Bob 309
Hulce, Tom 216
Humanoids from the Deep
102
Humbert, George 488
Hume, Alan 309, 310, 466,
497
Hume, Marjorie 194
Humphries, Barry 273
Humpoletz, Paul 412
Hungry Pets see *Please Don't
Eat My Mother*
Hunt, Allan 319
Hunt, Helen 491, 492, 493
Hunt, J. Roy 435
Hunt, Jimmy 281
Hunt, John 107
Hunt, Marsha 148
Hunt, Marsha A. 273
Hunt, Martita 139
Hunt, Neil 124
Hunt, William Dennis 175,
177

Hunter, C. Roy 129, 184
Hunter, Heather 215
Hunter, Holly 244
Hunter, Ian 114
Hunter, Kim 380, 381, 382
Hunter, Ross 316
Hunter, Russell 145
Hunter, Shaun 42
Hunter, Virginia 258
Huntley, Anne 103, 264, 354
Huntley, Kelly 314
Huntley, Raymond 342, 343
Hurd, Gale Anne 24, 476
Hurlbut, William 185
Hurley, Craig 513
Hurndall, Richard 120
Hurst, Brandon 65, 89, 191,
324
Hurst, David 333
Hurst, Paul 294, 489
Hurst, Ralph S. 519
Hurt, John 23–24, 214, 362
Hurt, William 123
Hurwitz, Tom 103
Hussey, Olivia 316
Huston, Anjelica 20
Huston, Craig 259
Huston, John 384
Hutchence, Michael 214
Hutcheson, David 201
Hutchinson, Josephine 188
Hutchinson, Tim 260
Hutton, Ian 37
Hutton, Rif 80
Hutton, Robert 238
Huyck, Willard 410, 411
Huyette, Page 487
Hyams, Eddie, Jr. 71
Hyams, Leila 294
Hyams, Peter 501, 502
Hyatt, Robert 331
Hyde, Roy 145, 345, 404,
503
Hyde, Vern 160
Hyde-White, Alex 411
Hyde-White, Wilfrid 365
"Hyde's Got Nothing to
Hide" (song) 124
Hytower, Roy 387
Hytten, Olaf 116, 189, 191,
524

I, Claudius (TV series) 91
I, Monster 120–121
I Dream of Jeannie (TV se-
ries) 62
"I Found a New Friend"
(song) 319
"I Hate People" (song) 427
"I Like Life" (song) 427

"I Love the Nightlife" (song) 152
I Married a Monster from Outer Space 61
I Walked with a Zombie 348
I Was a Teenage Frankenstein 195–197, 277
I Was a Teenage Werewolf 197, 276–277
Iacovelli, John 263
Ibbetson, Paul 23
Ickes, John 43
Ievins, Edgar 44, 45, 215
"If I Only Had a Heart" (song) 520
"If I Were King" (song) 520
Ihnen, Wiard 65
"I'll Begin Again" (song) 427
I'll Cry Tomorrow 519
"I'll Get By (As Long as I Have You)" (song) 243
Illusion Arts 214
Image Engineering 224, 357
Iman 449
Imi, Tony 239
Impert, Margie 271
Impey, Betty 400
Imrie, Celia 216, 260
Indiana Jones and the Last Crusade 411–413
Indiana Jones and the Temple of Doom 410–411, 413
Industrial Light & Magic 40, 42, 43, 84, 85, 234, 244, 385, 411, 442, 445, 446, 449, 450, 459, 478
Inez, Frank 221
Information International 516
Ingham, Barrie 126
Ingham, Robert E. 370
Ingle, John 418
Ingold, Larry 43
Ingram, Donna Patrice 522
Ingram, Joan 332
The Innocents 279, 280
The Innocents (play) 279
Inns, Garth 260
Inscoe, Joe 473
Introvision International, Inc. 161
Introvision Systems International 108
Invaders from Mars (1953) 281–282
Invaders from Mars (1986) 282–283
Invasion Earth 2150 A.D. see *Daleks' Invasion Earth 2150 A.D.*

Invasion of the Body Snatchers (1956) 237, 248, 284–286, 404, 485
Invasion of the Body Snatchers (1978) 286–288
Invasion of the Saucermen 277
Invasion U.S.A. 396
Invisible Agent 292
The Invisible Man 289–291, 293
The Invisible Man (book) 291, 293
The Invisible Man Returns 291
The Invisible Man's Revenge 292–293
The Invisible Woman 291, 293
Ireland, John 309, 310
Irene 489
Ironside, Michael 261, 263, 391, 392, 420, 421, 514
Irvine, Irina 227
Irvine, Paula 376
Irvine, Richard 331
Irvine, Thomas 476
Irving, David 84
Irving, George 132, 294
Irving, Louis 273
Irving, Penny 152
Irving, Richard 331
Irwin, Boyd, Sr. 315
Irwin, Jennifer 229
Irwin, Mark 63, 181, 228, 361, 418, 420
Irwin, Nate 484
Isaacks, Levie 79
Isaacs, David 330
Isaacs, Frank 55
Isbell, John C. 76
Ishida, James 42
Ishioka, Eiko 155
The Island of Dr. Moreau 287, 296–298, 299
The Island of Dr. Moreau (book) 294, 298
Island of Lost Souls 287, 294, 295, 307, 325
Island of the Alive see *It's Alive III: Island of the Alive* 298
Israel, Betty 330
Isreal, Neal 301
It, the Terror from Beyond Space 23, 106, 481
It Came from Outer Space 96, 97
It Lives Again 300–301
It's About Time see *Amityville 92: It's About Time*

It's Alive 298–300
It's Alive III: Island of the Alive 301–302
Itzkowitz, Howard 440
Ivens, Terri 493, 494
Iversen, Portia 282
Ives, Douglas 333
Ivey, Dana 20
Ivins, Perry 188
Ivory, James 379
Iwerks, Ub 495

Jablow, Michael 429
Jack of Swords see *Trancers 4: Jack of Swords*
Jackson, Clinton 522
Jackson, Dan 497
Jackson, David 64
Jackson, Freda 110, 139
Jackson, Gordon 398, 427
Jackson, Inigo 508
Jackson, Jocelyn 75
Jackson, Kate 271
Jackson, Mary 165
Jackson, Michael 21, 239, 519, 520, 522, 523
Jackson, Roosevelt 209
Jackson, Thomas 127
Jackson, Tony 499
Jacobs, Allan 152
Jacobs, Andre 107
Jacobs, Arthur P. 380, 382, 383, 384
Jacobs, Michael 249
Jacobs, Seama 365
Jacobsen, Tom 249
Jacobson, Dean 82
Jacobson, Scott 330
Jacoby, Billy 54
Jacoby, Pat 215
Jacoby, Scott 486, 487
Jacques, Hattie 426
Jacquet, Jeffrey 159
Jaeckel, Richard 319
Jaeger, Frederick 411
Jaeger, Kabi 214
Jaffe, Charles 449
Jaffe, Herb 227, 228
Jaffe, Nicole 316
Jaffe, Sam 315
Jaffe, Shirley 145
Jaffe, Steven-Charles 182
Jaffe, Taliesin 501
Jagger, Bianca 84
Jaggs, Allan 383
Jahraus, Donald 243
Jake the Dog 357
Jakoby, Don 282
Jakubowicz, Alain 282
James, Allan 461

James, Anthony 159
James, Brion 267, 423
James, Clifton 464
James, Don 240
James, Graham 64, 207
James, Harri 397
James, Henry 279
James, Jocelyn 254
James, Kyle 307
James, Peter 279
James, Richard 372
James, Ron 67
James, Sidney 400
James, Steve 309
Jameson, Joyce 169
Jameson, Susan 120
Jamison, Peter 418
Janes, Hurford 197
Janiger, Robert 486
Janis, Conrad 365
Janovitz, Walter 142
Janowitz, Walter 125
Janssen, Else 131
Janssen, Kathryn 233
Jarre, Maurice 212, 213, 323, 324
Jarrott, Charles 316
Jarvis, Jeff 438
Jarvis, Martin 145
Jason, Bob 438
Jason, Peter 511
Jason, Sybil 65
Jason Goes to Hell: The Final Friday 226–227
Jason Lives see *Friday the 13th, Part VI: Jason Lives*
Jason Takes Manhattan see *Friday the 13th, Part VIII: Jason Takes Manhattan*
Javier, Maria Delia 122
Jaws 97
Jay, Ernest 194
Jay, Griffith 71, 336, 337, 339
Jayston, Michael 22
Jeakins, Dorothy 210
Jeavons, Colin 204
Jeeves, M. Kan 84
Jefers, Megan 123
Jefferies, Philip 297, 383
Jefferson Starship 329
Jefford, Barbara 506
Jeffrey, Peter 15, 16
Jeffries, Brad 40
Jeffries, Lionel 197, 398
Jeffries, Oliver 130
Jekyll and Hyde ... Together Again 124–125
Jenkins, Eric 122
Jenkins, Megs 279
Jenkinson, Chris 412

Jenks, Frank 30
Jenks, Si 488
Jennings, Gordon 89, 232, 294
Jennings, Tom 323
Jenson, Sasha 236, 248
Jergens, Adele 258, 293
Jersey, William 61
Jesse James Meets Franken-stein's Daughter 203, 204
Jessop, Clytie 279
Jevne, Jack 488, 489
The Jewel of the Seven Stars (book) 64, 346
Jewell, Isabel 315
Jewell, Robert 127
Jewett, Thomas 424
Jillian, Ann 39, 40
Job, Ann 328
Jocelyn, June 30, 31
Jockinsen, John 359
Joel, Deborah 255
Johann, Zita 335
Johansen, David 427
John, Tim 125
John and Rosalind (musical duo) 152
John-Jules, Danny 314
Johnny Belinda 308
Johns, Glynis 332, 333
Johns, Mervyn 362, 426
Johns, Milton 454
Johnson, Arnold 366
Johnson, Arte 152, 153
Johnson, Ben 36
Johnson, Brad 244
Johnson, Brett 282
Johnson, Brian 22–24, 145
Johnson, Carlton 522
Johnson, D.G. 78
Johnson, Dale 160
Johnson, E. 388
Johnson, Fred 139, 194
Johnson, Kenneth 438
Johnson, Laurie 300, 301
Johnson, Lorimer 188
Johnson, Louis 522
Johnson, Michael 506
Johnson, Monica 124
Johnson, Noble 231, 302, 305, 315, 335, 435
Johnson, Pat E. 472, 474, 475
Johnson, Payne 65
Johnson, Reginald Vel 233
Johnson, Rita 257
Johnson, Sandy 245
Johnson, Shelly 474
Johnson, Steve 227, 275, 353, 357, 386

Johnson, Sunny 122
Johnson, Van 243
Johnston, Joanna 42, 43, 411
Johnston, Joe 263, 457
Johnston, John 236
Johnston, John Dennis 125
Johnston, Katie Jane 449
Johnston, Oliver 173
Johnstone, Babs 315
Johnstone, Joan 508
Joint, Alf 468
Jolley, Stanford 252
Jolly, Arthur 490, 491
Jolson, Al 258
The Jolson Story 258
Jones, Al 59
Jones, Andras 357
Jones, Andrew R. 37
Jones, Anne 322
Jones, Barry 238
Jones, Carolyn 20, 284
Jones, Charlie 37, 38
Jones, Claude Earl 415
Jones, Dean 316, 317, 318, 434
Jones, Dean (effects) 480, 515
Jones, Duane 347, 486
Jones, Freddie 150, 152, 206
Jones, Grace 87
Jones, Griffith 332
Jones, Grover 371
Jones, Hank 317, 434
Jones, Herb 311
Jones, James Earl 86, 164, 452, 454, 457
Jones, John G. 34, 35
Jones, Ken 375
Jones, Kenneth V. 173, 309
Jones, Mark 454
Jones, Michael Steve 244
Jones, Morgan 363
Jones, Norman 15
Jones, Quincy 522
Jones, Rachel 155
Jones, Renee 223, 481
Jones, Richard 85
Jones, Robert (art editor) 121, 372, 436
Jones, Robert C. (editor) 259
Jones, Robert J., Jr. 370
Jones, Sam 175, 176
Jones, Simon 331
Jones, Stanley 314
Jones, Tommy Lee 52
Jones, William Starr 515
Joo, Chua Kah 410
Jordan, Charles 72
Jordan, John 499

Jordan, June 376
Jordan, Leslie 226
Jordan, Marsha 92
Jory, Victor 77
Joseph, Allen (Al) 93, 460
Joseph, Jackie 241, 242, 312
Joseph, Robert 265
Josephson, Rick 228
Jourdan, Louis 157, 469, 472
Journey to the Center of the Earth 496
Journey to the 7th Planet 296
Jovan, Slavitza 233
Joy, Robert 33
Joyce, Dorothy 65
Joyner, C. Courtney 395, 492
Judd, Edward 437
Judgment Day see *Terminator 2: Judgment Day*
Juhl, Jerry 429
Jules, Maurice 59
Julia, Raul 20, 214
Juliano, Lenny 364
Jung, Calvin 416
The Jungle Book 240
Jungle Captive 72
Jungle Woman 71–72
Junkin, John 309
Juran, Nathan 429
Jurassic Park 517
Justice, Bill 39
Juttner, Christian 159
Jympson, John 314

Kaczenski, Chester 277
Kaethler, Paul 465
Kagel, Jim 221
Kagen, David 223
Kahan, Steve 513
Kahler, Wolf 408
Kahn, Barbara 472
Kahn, Brigitte 454
Kahn, Karen 51
Kahn, Madeline 210
Kahn, Michael 244, 385, 407, 410
Kahn, Sheldon 232, 234
Kaitan, Elizabeth 224
Kalbus, Terrie 375
Kalipha, Stefan 412
Kaliz, Armand 489
Kalmes, Nadine 124
Kalmus, Natalie 89
Kamal, Jon Rashad 440
Kamen, Michael 260
Kaminski, Janusz 481
Kandel, Aben see Langtry, Kenneth
Kane, Bob 47, 50, 52, 53

Kane, Carol 20, 427, 429
Kane, Charles 281
Kane, Eddie 335
Kane, Jayson 265
Kania, Cynthia 223
Kanig, Frank 249
Kann, Lilly 75
Kaper, Bronislau 237
Kaplan, Elliot 183
Kaplan, Marvin 3, 118
Kaplan, Wendy 249
Karanj, Nizwar 410
The Karate Kid 475
Karen, James 282, 283, 350, 351, 385
Karlan, Richard 341
Karlen, John 268, 269, 271
Karlin, Fred 516
Karloff, Boris ii, 110, 111, 116, 130, 135, 170, 185, 186, 187, 188, 190, 191, 198, 207, 335, 336, 341, 342, 399
Karlovitz, Katie 102
Karlson, Karl 61
Karlson, Phil 519, 520
Kartalian, Buck 313, 380
Kasdan, Lawrence 407, 454, 456, 457
Kasem, Casey 233
Kaset, Harold 429
Kash, Daniel 24
Kastner, Elliott 63
Katch, Kurt 341, 524
Katims, David 220
Katon, Rosanne 527
Katsuragi, Mayako 490
Katt, William 265, 267
Katz, A.L. 79
Katz, Brent 32
Katz, Erica 32
Katz, Fred 312
Katz, Gloria 410, 411
Katz, Lee 128
Katz, Virginia 70
Kaufman, Cristen 40
Kaufman, Lloyd 490, 491
Kaufman, Maurice 15, 398
Kaufman, Philip 286, 287, 288, 407
Kaufman, Robert 152
Kaun, Bernhard 128
Kay, Hadley 464
Kaye, Tom 44
Kazanjian, Howard 407, 457
Keal, Anita 32
Keane, Edward 307
Kearney, Cheryal 385
Kearney, John 124
Keast, Paul 195

Keaton, Michael 47, 49, 50, 52
Keays-Byrne, Hugh 321
Keefer, Don 102
Keegan, Kari 226
Keehne, Chuck 158, 317, 318, 433
Keehne, Virginia 282
Keen, Bob 68, 254, 255, 256, 260, 513
Keen, Geoffrey 120, 145
Keen, Noah 384
Keesee, Oscar 295
Keesee, Peyton 295
Kehoe, Patrick 305, 446
Keir, Andrew 64, 127, 141, 404, 407
Keith, David 106
Keith, Hardy 527
Keith, Paul 267
Keith, Randal 493
Keith, Woody 415
Kellams, Phillip G. 349
Kellard, Bill 32
Kellaway, Cecil 291, 336, 433
Kelleher, Tim 240, 475
Keller, Walter E. 30, 74
Kellerman, Sally 316, 321
Kelley, Barry 316
Kelley, DeForest 440, 442, 443, 444, 446, 447, 449
Kelley, W. Wallace 118
Kelljan, Bob (Robert) 59, 60, 92, 93
Kelly, Dawn Carver 124
Kelly, John 509
Kelly, Lesley 240, 392
Kelly, Patsy 489
Kelly, Robyn 177
Kelter, Jerie 223
Kelton, Roger 235
Kemeny, John 229
Kemp, Roger 464
Kemp, Valli 16–17
Kemper, Victor 365
Kempson, Rachel 180
Kendall, Kenneth 309
Kendall, Merelina 362
Kendrick, Florina 156
Keney, Terry 288
Kenion, Geoffrey 121
Kennaway, James 120
Kennedy, Byron 321, 322
Kennedy, Douglas 231, 281
Kennedy, George 103, 316, 480
Kennedy, Kathleen 42, 43, 241, 242, 244
Kennedy, Ken 311

Kenney, Jack 198
Kensit, Patsy 66
Kent, Peter 413
Kent, Stapleton 307
Kent, Ted J. 94, 185, 187, 189, 524
Kenton, Erle C. 133, 189, 190, 294
Kenworthy, Michael 63, 351
Kenyon, Charles 324
Keogh, Barbara 15
Keramidas, Harry 40, 42, 43, 78
Kern, David 301, 327, 328
Kern, Robert J. 35
Kerner, Bruce M. 476
Kernerman, Doron 181
Kernohan, Roxanne 104, 105, 364
Kerns, Sandra 84
Kerr, Deborah 279, 280
Kerr, Donald 72, 116
Kerr, Frederick 185
Kerr, John 168
Kerrigan, J.M. 495, 524
Kershner, Irvin 418, 454, 456
Kerwin, Brian 306
Kessler, Debora 224
Kessler, Kenneth 490
Kesten, Stephen F. 33
Ketchum, David 152
Kevan, Jack 94, 97, 100
Key, Alexander 158, 159
Key, Janet 148, 503
Key, Janey 362
Keyes, Evelyn 257
Keys, Anthony Nelson 135, 140, 194, 197, 203, 206, 345, 404
Keys, Larry "Big Mo" 438
Keywan, Alicia 438
Khachaturian, Aram 499
Khambatta, Persis 440
Khojayan, Shirak 312
Khopler, Bill 312
Kiam, Omar 489
Kibbe, Gary B. 419
A Kid in King Arthur's Court 91–92
Kidder, Margot 31, 33, 461, 464, 465, 468
Kidman, Nicole 52
Kidnie, James 230
Kieffer, Dorothy 317
Kiel, Richard 118
Kier, Udo 157
Kiernan, William 116, 258
Kiersch, Fritz 78
Kiesser, Jan 227

Kiger, Robby 78
Kilar, Wojciech 155
Kilburn, Terry 426
Killer Tomatoes Eat France 38
Killer Tomatoes Strike Back! 37–38
Kilmer, Val 52, 53
Kimball, Bruce 147
Kimball, Russell 307
Kimball, Ward 39
Kimberley, Maggie 346
Kimmell, Dana 220
Kimmins, Kenneth 282
A Kind of Loving 334
Kindlon, David 46, 349
King, Adrienne 217, 219
King, Andrea 209
King, Chuck 30
King, Ivan 508
King, Joe 102
King, Larry 165, 233
King, Leslie 486, 487
King, Leslie T. 21
King, Mabel 522
King, Peggy 341
King, Rob Wilson 220, 469
King, Sandy 511
King, Stephen 32, 69, 78, 79, 102, 103, 254, 373, 374
King, Wright 380
King Kong (1933) 302–304, 435, 436
King Kong (1976) 305–306
King Kong Lives 306–307
King of the Khyber Rifles 396
King Solomon's Mines (book) 436
Kingsford, Guy 131
Kingsley, Dorothy 35, 36
Kingsley, James 59
Kingston, Claude 194
Kingston, Kiwi 201, 202
Kinmont, Kathleen 248, 415
Kinnaman, Melanie 222
Kinnear, Roy 145, 427
Kinney, Tiffany 164
Kinnoch, Ronald *see* Barclay, George
Kinski, Klaus 157
Kinski, Nastassia 75, 76
Kirby, Terrence 78
Kirchen, Basil 15
Kirek, Milos 370
Kirk, Joe 192
Kirk, Tommy 17, 19, 39, 40, 433, 434, 435
Kirkpatrick, Bruce 349
Kirkpatrick, T.K. 250
Kirksey, Van 59

Kirschner, David 80, 81, 82
Kirshoff, Steve 219, 349
Kirzinger, Ken 225
Kiser, Terry 224, 330
Kiser, Virginia 385
Kish, Joseph 178, 284
Kissel, William 380
Kitchen, Michael 148
Kitorsser, Martin 219, 221, 222
Klaff, Jack 452
Klar, G. Howard 349
Klastorin, Michael 43
Klatt, Paul 281
Klein, Ray 366
Kleinbach, Henry 38, 39; *see also* Brandon, Henry
Kleinow, Peter 161
Kligher, Michael 125
Kline, Richard H. 305, 384, 440
Klugman, Shawn 364
Knaggs, Skelton 133, 292
Kneale, Nigel 97, 181, 248, 398, 399, 400, 403, 404, 406
Knickrehm, Janice 250
Knight, Andy 384
Knight, Don 469
Knight, Eddie 206
Knight, Felix 38
Knight, Sandra 199, 200
Knight, Tonga 469
Knight, Tuesday 357
Knoll, John 450
Knopf, Edwin H. 237
Knotts, Don 445
Knowles, Patric 190, 524
Knox, Alexander 116
Knox, Elyse 337, 338
Knox, Mickey 214
Knox, Terence 79
Knue, Michael N. 264, 357
Kober, Marta 219
Kobs, Dorothy 218
Koch, Howard W., Jr. 142, 198, 203, 259
Koch, Jay 42
Koch, Norma 281
Koch, Pete 481
Koenekamp, Fred J. 31
Koenig, Raymond 58, 59
Koenig, Walter 440, 442, 444, 446, 447, 449, 450
Kogan, Milt 122
Kohlmar, Lee 305
Kohner, Frederick 307
Kolb, Kenneth 429
Kolbert, Katherine 348
Kolker, Henry 319

Kolster, Clarence 184
Komai, Tetsu 294
Koneff, David Allen 256, 513
Konga 53
Konner, Lawrence 449, 468
Konrad, Dorothy 518
Konrad, Tim 43
Koontz, Dean R. 514, 515, 516
Koop, C. Everett 165
Korman, Harvey 319
Korman, Irene 376
Kornbau, Karen 235
Kortman, Robert 294
Kosana, George 347
Kosslyn, Jack 30, 31
Kossoff, David 117, 333, 334, 362
Kostal, Irwin 66
Koteas, Elias 472, 475
Kotto, Yaphet 23, 27, 360
Kotzwinkle, William 357
Kounnas, Mark 323
Kovacs, Laszlo 232
Kovacs, Leslie 144
Kowanko, Pete 33
Kozak, Heidi 224
Kozlowski, Linda 511
Kraft, Kendal 352
Kramarov, Savely 501
Kramer, David 321
Kramer, Jeffrey 246
Kramer, Joel 478
Kramer, Larry 316
Kramer vs. Kramer 442
Kranhouse, Jon 223
Krantz, Robert 438
Krasket, Harold 333
Krasner, Milton 189, 291, 292, 381
Kratka, Paul 220
Kraushaar, Raoul 142, 203, 281
Krecmer, Ladislav 273
Kreidt, Martin 408
Krelle, Raquel 237
Kress, Harold F. 114
Kribbe, Gary B. 511
Krick, Howard 438
Krieger, Ed 81
Kriesa, Christopher 423
Kring, R. Timothy 278
Kristel, Sylvia 155
Krog, Tim 67
Kronos 101
Kroopf, Scott 55, 56
Kruger, Mark 70
Kruger, Otto 72, 131
Krumholtz, David 21

Krytmar, Jiri 273
Kubeck, Karen 491
Kubrick, Stanley 394, 453, 454, 482, 499, 501
Kubrick, Vivian 499
Kuehne, Rod 43
Kumar, Barin 486
Kunody, Leonard 281
Kuran, Peter (Pete) 20, 104, 155, 416
Kuri, Emile 19, 39, 433, 495
Kuriloff, Jason 439
Kurtz, Gary 452, 454, 523
Kurtzman, Nicotero and Berger EFX 34, 109, 161, 226, 267, 361, 493
Kuruppu, Dharmadasa 410
Kurz, Ron 219, 220, 221
Kushner, Rubin 376
Kuss, Richard 512
Kutry, Claude 106
Kuynetzoff, Adia 190
Kwouk, Bert 180
Kybartas, Sandy 391
Kyle, David 245

Labatt, Susan 160
LaBelle, Kimberley 56
LaBelle, Rob 361
Labyorteaux, Patrick 236
Lacey, Bruce 334
Lacey, Catherine 346
Lachman, Stanley 30
Lack, Stephen 420
Lacouter, Jacques 211
Lacroix, Michael 181
Lacy, Jerry 268
Lacy, Ronald 408
Laczko, William Andrew 349
Ladanyi, Andrea 230
Ladd, Alan, Jr. 453
Lader, Anton M. 510
Lady, Steph 216
The Lady and the Doctor see *The Lady and the Monster*
The Lady and the Monster 307
Lady Dracula 157
Lady Frankenstein 207–208
Laemmle, Carl, Jr. 129, 185, 289, 334
LaFayette, John 480
Lafferty, Marcy 440
Lafia, John 81
La Fleur, Art 63, 491, 492
Lagola, Charles 328
Lahr, Bert 520
Laidlaw, Ethan 302
Laird, Jenny 509

Laird, Peter 472, 473, 474, 475
Lake, Arthur 488
Lake, Don 439
Lala 514
Lalande, Guy 125
LaLanne, Jack 166
Lamarr, Lucille 116
Lamb, Charles 404
Lambert, Christopher 260, 261, 262
Lambert, Jack 141, 232
Lambert, Mary 373, 374
Lambert, Paul 380
Lambert, Ryan 213
Lamble, Lloyd 400
Lamont, Charles 116, 293, 340
Lamont, Duncan 201, 203, 404
Lamont, Harry 133
Lamont, Michael 24
Lamour, Dorothy 103
Lampert, Zohra 165
Lampkin, Charles 84
Lampson, David 93
Lancaster, Bill 484
Lancaster, Burt 207, 297, 299
Lanchester, Elsa 186, 238, 519
Land of Oz (book) 523
The Land That Time Forgot 309–310
Landau, Richard 198, 398
Landey, Clayton 356
Landfield, David 118
Landham, Sonny 388
Landi, Michael 165
Landis, Carole 371, 489
Landis, John 108, 384
Landis, Monte (Monty) 210, 333
Landman, Hanie 142
Landman, Jeffrey 249
Landon, Hal, Jr. 56, 57
Landon, Laurene 301, 327, 328
Landon, Michael 276, 277
Landres, Paul 137
Lane, Dick 434
Lane, Mike 198
Lane, Rosemary 128
Lane, Rusdi 370
Lane, Vicky 72
Laneuville, Eric 152
Lanfranchi, Damien 212
Lang, Charles 128, 230
Lang, Harold 398
Lang, Judy 92

Lang, Walter 65
Langan, Glenn 30, 128
Langan, John 128
Langdon, Sue Ane 527
Lange, Harry 454
Lange, Hope 355
Lange, Jessica 305, 306
Lange, Samuel M. 488
Langedijk, Jack 109
Langelaan, George 177, 178, 180, 181
Langella, Frank 153, 154
Langen, Todd W. 472, 474
Langenkamp, Heather 354, 356, 361
Langhurst, Henry 333
Langley, Faith 307
Langley, Noel 426, 520
Langlois, Yves 422
Langtry, Kenneth 195
Lansbury, Angela 377
Lansford, Carney 36
Lansing, Ernest 331
Lantieri, Michael 227, 386, 446
Lapis, Joe 94
Larange, Stewart 523
Larch, John 31
La Riana 524
Larkin, Bob 223
Larkin, Linda 527
Larkin, Sheena 125
Larrecq, Henry 484
Larrinaga, Mario 302
Larroquette, John 76, 123, 444, 445
Larsen, Lance 175
Larsen, William 259
Larson, Darrel 518
Larson, Gary 55
Larson, Lauritz 176
Larson, Philip 268
Larsson, Paul 323
La Rue, Eva 236
Lasalle, Richard 320
LaSardo, Robert 439
Laser, Louise 215
LaShelle, Joseph 276
Lashly, James 244
Lassick, Sydney 107
Laszlo, Andrew 385, 447
Laszlo, Ernest 232
The Latent Image 347
Latham, Philip 141
Lathrop, Philip 124
Latimer, Jonathan 489
Laughton, Charles 294, 295, 307
Launer, S. John 276
Laurel, Stan 38

Laurel and Hardy 39, 40
Laurence, Ashley 254, 255, 256
Laurie, Piper 523
Lauritzen, Nickie 248
Lauter, Ed 305
Lavelle, Bradley 255
La Vigne, Emile 284
Law, Don 306
Law, John Phillip 431
Lawford, Peter 377, 379
Lawner, Mordecai 234
Lawrence, Billy 509
Lawrence, Delphi 325
Lawrence, Hap 123
Lawrence, Jeremy 104
Lawrence, Jody 116
Lawrence, Marjie 120
Lawrence, Tim 234
Lawrence, Tom 438
Lawrence, Viola 257, 258
Lawson, Arthur 309
Lawson, Christyne 436
Lawson, Dennis 452, 454, 457
Lawson, Gerald 437
Lawson, Mary 425
Lawson, Richard 59, 385
Laxton, Julian 107
Lazare, Carol 181
Lazarus, Paul N., III 516, 518
Lea, Petra 32
Leachman, Cloris 210, 211, 319
Leah, Michael 328
Leahy, Eugene 194
Leake, Damien 260
Leakey, Philip (Phil) 75, 135, 194, 197, 398, 400
Lealand, David 146
Leapman, Jackie 506
Lear, Norman 232
Lease, Maria 147
LeBeau, Becky 364
Lebor, Stanley 175, 468
LeBorg, Reginald 71, 339
LeBron, Larry 122
Leddy, Arthur D. 133
Lederer, Charles 482
Lederer, Francis 137, 139, 295, 296, 297
Lederer, Richard 164
Ledwell, L.W. 311
Lee, Ann Marie 182
Lee, Bernard 208, 309
Lee, Brandon 109
Lee, Christopher 107, 117, 120, 130, 135, 137, 139, 140, 143, 145, 148, 150, 151, 155,

157, 159, 194, 195, 207, 242, 273, 320, 325, 327, 342, 343, 436, 437
Lee, Damian 184, 513
Lee, Dana 353
Lee, Danny 319
Lee, David 171
Lee, Jason Scott 42, 236
Lee, John 75
Lee, Margaret 379
Lee, Michele 316, 317
Lee, Penelope 173, 461
Lee, Rosanna 152
Lee, Rowland 187
Lee, Sondra 32
Lee, Stephen 236, 418
Lee-Thompson, Peter 165
Leeper, Trish 439
Leer, Hunter Von 246, 493
Lees, John 24, 468
Lees, Robert 192, 293
Leeves, Jane 331
Le Fanu, J. Sheridan 503, 506, 508
LeFevre, Ned 97
LeFleur, Art 125
Legend, Johnny 80
The Legend of Boggy Creek 311
The Legend of Hell House 251, 279
The Legend of the 7 Golden Vampires 150–151
Legere, Phoebe 490, 491
Legion (book) 165
Legler, Steve 271
Le Gros, James 376
Lehman, Ari 218
Lehmann, Olga 497
Leider, Jerry 125
Leigh, Janet 35
Leigh, Joy 427
Leigh, Susanna 152, 506
Leighton, Jan 527
Leitch, Christopher 278
Leitch, Donovan 63
Leiterman, Richard 514
Leith, Virginia 309
LeMaire, Charles 177
LeMat, Paul 39
LeMay, John D. 226
LeMesurier, John 90, 334
Lemkow, Tutte 408
Lemmo, James 328
Lemmons, Kasi 68
Lemora: A Child's Tale of the Supernatural 157
Lemshed, Bruce 322
Lenard, Mark 440, 444, 446, 449

Lenard, Melvyn 117
Lenehan, Nancy 125
Leningrad Kirov Ballet 66
Lennox, Annie 155
Lenny, Bill 135, 334
Lens, Terry 510
Lenz, Abigail 353
Lenz, Kay 265
Leon, Connie 524
Leon, Valerie 64
Leonard, Harry M. 177
Leonard, Sheldon 293
Leondopoulos, Jordan 162
Leone, Sergio 235
Leonetti, John R. 82
Leonetti, Matthew F. 36, 385
Leong, Al 56
Leong, James L. 305
Leong, Page 234
LePage, Brent 245
LeParmentier 452
Lerios, Cory 82
Lerner, Fred 248
Lerner, Ken 165, 418
Lerner, Michael 328
LeRoy, Mervyn 520
Lerpae, Paul 232
Les Brown and His Band of Renown 118
Lesnie, Andrew 322
Lesson, Michael 124
Lester, Buddy 118
Lester, Jeff 446
Lester, Kathy 375
Lester, Ketty 58
Lester, Richard 334, 463, 465, 466
Levay, Sylvester 329
Leven, Boris 281
Leven, Mel 39
Levenson, Dode B. 79
Lever, Reg 427
Levey, Bill 209
Levey, William A. 209
Levin, Darlene 20
Levin, Maureen Sue 20
Levin, Pete 328
Levine, Jeff 357
Levine, Jerry 277
Levine, Ken 330
Levinsky, Sheri 223
Levinson, Art 329
Levinson, Mark 277
Levy, Jefery 235, 236
Levy, Jules V. 137
Levy, Marty 42
Levy, Peter 359, 388
Levy, Robert L. 91
Lewin, Albert 22, 377

Lewis, Edward 66
Lewis, Fiona 16
Lewis, Forrest 19, 434
Lewis, Garrett 155, 213, 438
Lewis, George J. 293
Lewis, Herman 383
Lewis, Huey 40
Lewis, Jerry 118, 119, 120, 232, 238, 476
Lewis, Jerry Lee 468
Lewis, Louise 276
Lewis, Vera 30, 128
Lewnes, Pericles 490, 491
Lewslie, Avril 197
Lewthwaite, Bill 362, 497
Lewton, Val 72, 74, 348, 400
Ley, Margot 498
Liapis, Peter 235, 237
Liberty, Richard 349
Licht, Daniel 34, 35, 79
Lieberman, Frank 334
Lieberman, Rick 416
Lierley, Hal 178
Lifeforce 406
"Ligeia" (short story) 173
Ligeti, Gyorgy 499
Light and Motion Corporation 392
Lighton, Louis D. 21
Lili 238
Liljedahl, Marie 379
Lill, Denis 48
Lime, Yvonne 199, 276
Lin, Traci 22
Lincoln, Lar Park 224, 266
Linden, Edward (Eddie) 302, 304
Linden, Jennie 126
Lindfors, Viveca 102, 165
Lindholm, Kirsten 508
Lindsay, Delia 146, 147
Lindsay, Raymond 184
Lindsly, Chuck 104
Lineback, Richard 222
Linero, Jeanie 259
Ling, Barbara Yu 150
Ling, Lai 145
Link, John F. 387
Linson, Art 427
Linton, John K. 516
Linville, Larry 84
The Lion in Winter 501
Lipinski, Eugene 412, 464
Lippert, Robert L. 180
Lipsius, Dhani 248
Liska, Stephen 444
Liss, Bennett 527
Liss, Ted 80
Liston, Ian 454
Litel, John 128, 292

Lithgow, John 501
Little, Caryl 506
Little, Dwight H. 248
Little, Thomas 65, 331
"Little Girl Lost" (*Twilight Zone* episode) 385
The Little Mermaid 314
Little Shop of Horrors 314
The Little Shop of Horrors 122, 312–313
Littlefield, Lucien 258
Littlewood, Harry 370
Lively, Gerry 79, 256, 353, 487, 513
Livingston, Harold 439
Livingston, Jerry 232
Livingstone, Russell 252
Llosa, Luis 516
Lloyd, Art 38
Lloyd, Christopher 20, 36, 40, 42, 43, 444, 445
Lloyd, Doris 116, 189, 190, 292, 524
Lloyd, Harold, Jr. 199, 200
Lloyd, Hugh 334
Lloyd, Jeremy 152
Lloyd, Julie 366
Lloyd, Kathleen 300
Lloyd, Michael 236
Lloyd, Rollo 186
Lloyd-Pack, Charles 325
Locatell, Carol 222
Locher, Felix 199
Locise, Nicholas 427
Lock, Peter 427
Locke, Samus 298
Locke, Sondra 519
Locker, Phil 387
Lockhart, Gene 331, 426
Lockhart, June 84, 426
Lockhart, Kathleen 426
Locklear, Heather 472
Lockwood, Gary 499
Lockwood, Margaret 239, 240
Lockyer, Malcolm 126
Lodge, Andrew 309
Lodge, Jean 171
Lodge, Roger 364
LoDuca, Joe 159, 160, 161
Loeb, Joseph, III 277, 278
Loeb, Lee 116, 340
Loftus, Bryan 499
Loftus, Cecilia 65
Logan, Bob 166
Logan, Bruce 499
Logan, James 116
Logan, John 278
Logan, Kathryn Miles 222
Logan, Kristopher 395

Logan, Laurie V. 387
Logan, Pat 352
Logan, Phyllis 362
Logan, Ricky Dean 42, 360
Logan's Run 82, 306
Lom, Herbert 379, 497
Lomas, Raoul 78
Lombard, Michael 373
Lombard, Paty 387
Lombardo, Tony 125
Lommel, Ulli 67
London, James 490, 491
London, Julie 71
London, Tom 307
Lone, John 305
Long, Keny 305
Long, Sarah 509
"Long Tall Sally" (song) 388
Longaker, Rachel 365
Longden, John 400
Longhurst, Graham 255, 260
Longhurst, Sue 506
Longo, Tony 36
Loo, Richard 315
"Look at Me" (song) 318
Lookinland, Todd 66
Loomis, Nancy 244
Loomis, Rod 54, 56
Lopez, Gerry 86
Lopez, Julio 94
Lopez, Sal 353
Lord, Rosemary 121
Lords, Traci 364
Lorey, Dean 226
Lorinz, James 215
Lormer, Jon 102
Lorre, Peter 169, 170, 292, 319, 320, 495
Lost Horizon (1937) 314–316
Lost Horizon (1973) 316
Lottman, Evan 162
Lou Bunin Puppets 22
Louanne 365, 366
Loudon, Carolyn 219
Loughery, David 447
Loughlin, Lori 33, 34
Loughran, Derek 352
Louie, John 241
Louis, Jean 258, 316
Louis, John 365
Louis, Justin 391
Love, Bessie 510
Love, Lucretia 122
Love, Nicholas 67
Love, Suzanna 67
Love at First Bite 152–153
The Love Bug 316–317, 319
"Love Song for a Vampire" (song) 155

Lovecraft, H.P. 106, 110, 111, 171, 251, 252, 253, 413, 414, 415
Lovegrove, Arthur 117
Lovejoy, Ray 24, 47, 499
Lovell, Marilyn 93
Lovell, Mike 499
Low, Andrew 437
Low, Warren 232, 519
Lowe, Edward T. 133, 190
Lowe, Heather 384
Lowell, Mark 307
Lowery, Carolyn 68
Lowery, Robert 339
Lowitz, Siegfried 309
Lowry, Lynn 76
Lowry, Morton 377
Loy, Myrna 89
Lozoff, Joshua Bo 473
Lucas, George 176, 407, 409, 410, 411, 413, 441, 452, 453, 454, 456, 457, 459, 460
Lucas, Marcia 452, 457
Lucas, Paul 495
Lucas, Robert 350
Lucht, Darlene 252
Luckinbill, Laurence 447, 449
Lucky, Joseph P. 52, 478
Lucy, Arnold 112
Ludden, Allen 518
Ludvikova, Hana 273
Ludwig, Adam 420, 439
Luff, William 425
Lugosi, Bela 129, 130, 135, 139, 157, 188, 189, 190, 192, 193, 294, 524
Luisi, James 519
Lukas, Paul 231
Lukather, Paul 222, 320
Luke, Keye 241, 242, 292, 319
Lumet, Sidney 521, 523
Lumkin, A.W. 148
Lumley, Joanna 150
Lund, Art 301
Lund, Jana 198, 199
Lundgren, Lyn 313
Lundquist, Steve 37, 38
Lung, Tong 514
Lunghi, Cherie 216
Lupino, Ida 22, 183
Lupton, John 203
Lurking Fear 414
Lusier, Dane 307
Lussier, Patrick 361
Lust for a Vampire 157, 506–508
Lustig, Aaron 108

Lustig, William 327, 328
Lutter, Ellen 219
Lutze, Ric (Rick) 175, 313
"Lux Aeterna" (musical composition) 499
Luxe, Dee 177
Luxford, Bert 260, 508
Lycett, Eustace 17, 39
Lydecker, Theodore 281, 307
Lye, Reg 90
Lyle, Joseph 105
Lynch, David 262
Lynch, Edward 165
Lynch, Paul 390
Lynch, Richard 395, 396, 423, 492
Lynde, Paul 19
Lyndon, Barre 324, 325
Lynley, Carol 61, 62, 276
Lynn, George 195
Lynn, Joe 522
Lynn, Kane W. 295
Lynn, Robert 135, 137, 148
Lyon, Wendy 391, 392
Lyons, Chester 319
Lyons, John 121
Lyons, Stuart 239
Lys, Lya 128
Lysel, Allan 182

Ma, Tzi 418
Maar, Pons 523
Mabray, Stuart 81
Mabry, Moss 305
McAlister, Michael J. 411
Macallister, Patrick 298
McAlpine, Donald 388
Macari, Giuseppe 155
MacArthur, Harold H. 292
McArthur, Steve 43
Macat, Julio 331
McAteer, James 181
Macaulay, Charles 58
McBain, Diane 397
McBride, Donald 257, 258, 489, 490
McBride, Jeri 440
McBride, Tom 219
McCafferty, Dee 438
McCain, Frances Lee 40, 241
McCall, Sean 44
McCalla, Irish 320
McCallany, Holt 28
McCallum, David 217
McCallum, John 332
McCambridge, Mercedes 162, 164
McCann, Chuck 317
McCann, Maria 527

McCardell, James 322
McCarron, Bob 273, 322
McCart, Molly 117
McCarthy, Andrew 329
McCarthy, Dennis 450
McCarthy, Frank 123
McCarthy, Jeff 418
McCarthy, Kevin 236, 237, 271, 284, 285, 286, 287, 288
McCarty, Mary 39
McCary, Rob 317
McCaughry, Brigitte 420
McCausland, James 321
McCharen, David 473
McClellan, Peg 278
McClure, Doug 309, 310
McClure, Marc 40, 43, 461, 464, 466, 468
McCollough, Paul 352
McConnohie, Michael 473
McCord, Kent 353, 354, 388
McCormac, Cynthia 278
McCormack, Patty 374
McCormick, Pat 427, 434
McCorry, Terence 220
McCrane, Paul 63, 416
McCrea, Joel 436
McCrindle, Alex 452
McCrossin, Joseph 244
McCulloch, Andrew 309
McCusker, Mary 125
McDaniel, Etta 132
McDermott, Dylan 331
McDiarmid, Ian 64, 457
McDonald, A.C. 347
MacDonald, Aimi 152
MacDonald, Edmund 291
MacDonald, Hoima 152
MacDonald, J. Farrell 460, 488
MacDonald, Mac 47
MacDonald, Robert 259
McDonald-Peattie, Rose-marie 143
MacDonnell, Colonel 112
MacDonough, Glen 38, 39
McDormand, Frances 108
MacDougall, Roger 333
McDowall, Roddy 227, 228, 380, 381, 382, 383, 384
McDowell, Jay 352
McDowell, Malcolm 75, 450
McDowell, Trevyn 216
McEachin, James 501
McElroy, Alan B. 248
McEnery, John 309
McEnroe, Annie 273
McEveety, Vincent 318
McEvoy, Anne Marie 78

MacEwen, Walter 324
McFadden, Gates 450
McFadden, Thom 356
McGann, Paul 28
McGeagh, Stanley 309
McGee, Jack 331
McGee, Vonetta 58
MacGibbon, Harriet 19
McGiffert, David 305
McGinley, John C. 261
McGinn, Russ 249
McGinnis, Scott 444
McGirr, Joseph 491
McGoohan, Patrick 420
McGovern, Michael 498
MacGowran, Jack 162, 309
McGrath, Doug 244
McGreevey, Michael 434
McGregor, Ken 393
MacGregor, Scott 64, 145, 207, 208, 503
MacGregor-Scott, Peter 52
McGuffie, Bill 127
McGuire, Ida 331
McGuire, Jason 374
McGuire, Michael 124
Machado, Mario 418
McHale, Tony 310
Machette, Anne 56
Macht, Stephen 34, 213, 493, 494
McHugh, David 330
McInerney, Joseph 331
McInnes, Angus 255, 452, 464
McIntire, James 352
McIntire, John 317
McIntyre, Marvin J. 43, 438
Mack, Helen 304, 435
Mackay, Barry 426
Mackay, Michael 214
McKay, Steven 109
McKaye, Patti 116
McKean, Michael 438
McKee, John 35
Mackee, Scott 499
McKelvey, Frank 312
McKenna, James 260
Mackenzie, Evan 236
Mackenzie, Jack (cinematog-rapher) 71
McKenzie, Jack (actor) 454
McKenzie, Mark 125, 487, 513
Mackenzie, Patch 301
MacKenzie, Rock 67
McKern, Leo 333, 367, 368, 370
Mackie, Phil 309
McKim, Josephine 186

McKinney, Bill 43
McKinney, Mira 339
MacKrell, James 277
McKrell, Jim 241, 271
MacLane, Barton 114, 339
McLawhorn, Damian 468
MacLean, Fred 433
McLean, Nick 438
Maclellan, Elizabeth 394
McLeod, Don 271
McLeod, Duncan 56
McLeod, Norman Z. 21, 488
MacLeod, Robert 367
McLoughlin, Bronco 255
McLoughlin, Nancy 223
McLoughlin, Tom 223
McMahon, David 100, 482
McManus, Michael 385
McMillan, Brian 55
McMillan, Roddy 334
McMillan, Toni 332
MacMurray, Fred 17–20, 433
McMurray, Sam 83
McMurry, Gregory L.,
McNab, Michael 360
McNabb, Mark 248
McNamara, Brian 438
McNamara, J. Patrick 56, 376
McNamara, John 30, 137
MacNaughtan, Alan 204
Macnee, Patrick 271, 272, 426
McNeff, Richard 309
MacNichol, Peter 21, 234, 235
McPeters, Brad 43
McPhail, William R. 523
McPherson, John 438
McPherson, Stephen 85
MacQuarrie, Melanie Morse 390
MacQuarrie, Murdock 72, 112
McQueen, Steven (Steve) 61, 62, 413
Macready, Erica 92
Macready, George 92, 93, 258
Macready, Michael 92, 93
McSherry, Rose Marie 182
McShirley, Marjorie (Margie) Stone 42, 43
McTiernan, John 387
MacVicar (Vickers), Martha 71
McWade, Margaret 315
Mad About Men 333
Mad Love 319–320
Mad Max 321–322, 323

Mad Max: Beyond Thunderdome 323–324
Mad Max II 322–323, 417
Maddalena, Julie 78, 486
Maddalena, Marianne 360
Madden, Betty Pecha 54, 55
Madden, Peter 204
Madden, Terry 452
Madden, Tommy 469
Maddi, Mike 221, 422
Maddock, Brent 438
Madoc, Philip 121, 127
Madsen, Harry 522
Madsen, Virginia 68, 261
Maeterlinck, Maurice 65, 66
Magee, Patrick 110, 112, 171
Magenta, Max 57
The Magic Sword 238
Magical Media Industries 224, 236, 237, 250, 357, 360, 423, 424, 487
Magliochetti, Al 215, 226
Magner, Jack 32
Magnificent Seven 151
Magruder, Betsy 476
Maguire, Leonard 64
Maguire, Oliver 454
Mahbay, Judy 391
Maher, Christopher 329
Maher, Joseph 259
Mahin, John Lee 114
Mahoney, Louis 370
Mahoney, Tom 39
Maidment, Terence 372
The Main Course see *Critters 2*
The Main Course see *Critters 2: The Main Course*
Les Mains D'Orlas (book) 319
Mainwaring, Daniel Geoffrey Homes 284
Majestics 152
Major, Mark Anthony 376
Major Dundee 274, 492
Majors, Lee 427
Makan, Moti 410
Make-Up Effects Labs 220
Makeham, Eliot 426
Makin, William J. 128
Mako 86, 87
Malandrinos, Andreas 346
Malcolm, Christopher 260, 454
Maleczech, Ruth 83
Malet, Arthur 210, 245, 259, 366
Maley, Peggy 258
Maliaros, Vasiliki 162
Malick, John Jack 499

Malik, Art 91, 92
Malik, Roger 509
Malikyan, Kevork 411
Malina, Judith 20
Mallard, Grahame 309
Malleson, Clifford 426
Malleson, Miles 135, 139, 309, 426
Malo, Rene 421, 422
Malone, Dorothy 232
Maloney, Jack 306
Maloney, Peter R. 124
Maloney, Peter 484
Malvern, Paul 133, 190
Malyon, Eily 131
Mamoulian, Rouben 112
The Man I Married 296
The Man in Half Moon Street 324–325, 379
The Man in Half Moon Street (play) 325
The Man Who Could Cheat Death 137, 325–327
Manard, Biff 492
Mancini, Don 81, 82
Mancini, Henry 100
Mancini, Ric 233
Mancuso, Frank, Jr. 219, 221
Mandan, Robert 527
Mandel, Howie 242
Mandel, Johnny 158
Mandell, Pamela 464
Mander, Miles 377, 392
Maners, Tana 278
Manfredini, Harry 217, 219, 220, 221, 222, 223, 224, 226, 264, 266, 267, 469
Mangini, Mark 242, 446
Mango, Alec 204, 429
Maniac Cop 327–328
Maniac Cop 2 328
Maniac Cop 3: Badge of Silence 328–329
Manion, Cindy 490
Mankiewicz, Joseph L. 21, 425
Mankofsky, Isidore 59
Mankowitz, Wolf 117
Mankuma, Blu 514
Manley, Stephen 444
Mann, Daniel 519
Mann, Laura 375
Mann, Mark 349
Mann, Stanley 87, 333, 369
Mann, Terrence 103, 104, 105, 106
Mann, Wesley 42
Mannequin 329–330
Mannequin: On the Move 330
Manners, David 129, 335

Manning, Hugh 404
Manoff, Dinah 80, 81
Manos, George J. 259
Manos, Mark 396
Mansano, Roy 282
Mansbridge, John B. 158, 159, 178, 317, 318, 319, 434
Mansfield, Jayne 208
Manson, Mary 180
Manson, Maurice 100
Maraden, Frank 306
Maranda, Andree 490
March, Eve 74
March, Fredric 112, 113, 114, 115
March, Marvin 20
March of the Wooden Soldiers see *Babes in Toyland* (1934)
Marchant, Laurence 499
Marcus, Adam 226
Marcus, Andrew 216
Marcus, Julie 517
Marden, Adriene 460
Marden, Richard 254, 255
Maren, Jerry see Marenghi, Jerry
Marenghi, Jerry 520
Margo 315
Margo, George 333
Margolin, Janet 234
Margolin, Stuart 518
Margolyes, Miriam 314
Margulies, David 233
Margulies, Michael D. 166
Marin, Edwin L. 292, 425
Marin, Jason 40
Marin, Jerry 265
Marion, Paul 232
Marion, Richard 82
Mark, Michael 178, 185, 188, 191, 336
Mark, Tamara 361
Mark of the Vampire 157
Markey, Gene 65
Markham, David 64
Marks, Beau E.L. 387
Marks, Jack 219
Marks, Robert 509
Marla, Norma 117
Marle, Arnold 325, 326
Marley, John 300
Marlow, Tony 335
Marlowe, Jonas 78
Marmorstein, Malcolm 159
Maroney, Kelli 364
Marquand, Richard 457
Marquardt, Paul 520
Marr, Edward (Eddie) 276, 495

Marrero, Ralph 349
Married with Children (TV series) 228
Mars, Keneth 189, 210
Marsh, Carol 22, 135, 137, 426
Marsh, Garry 425
Marsh, Jean 523, 524
Marsh, Keith 127, 145, 427
Marsh, Tiger Joe 158
Marshal, Paula 513
Marshall, Annie 352
Marshall, Bryan 404
Marshall, E.G. 102, 103, 464
Marshall, Ellye 77
Marshall, Frank 42, 43, 241, 242, 244, 385, 407, 408, 411
Marshall, George 230, 231, 232
Marshall, Herbert 177
Marshall, Paula 256
Marshall, Stephen 76
Marshall, Ted 194
Marshall, Tony 276
Marshall, William 58, 59, 60
Marshall, Zena 332
Marshe, Tony 116
Marshek, Archie S. 89, 302
Marston, John 304
The Marsupials see *The Howling III*
Marta, Jack 30
Martel, K.C. 31
Martell, Gregg 178
Martell, Philip 110, 121, 140, 145, 150, 201, 203, 206, 344, 345, 436, 437, 503, 506, 508
Martelli, Carlo 344
The Martian Chronicles (book) 406
Martien, Norman 495
Martin, Dale 416, 418
Martin, Damon 34, 236
Martin, Dean 120, 232
Martin, Derek 201
Martin, Dewey 482, 483
Martin, Douglas Brian 20
Martin, Eugenio 429
Martin, Frederick 499
Martin, George 83
Martin, Ider Cifuentes 516
Martin, Irene 460
Martin, Jim 56
Martin, John Scott 314
Martin, Latesha 68
Martin, Lock 281
Martin, Maggie 236
Martin, Malaika 145

Martin, Mia 150
Martin, Michelle 348
Martin, Nan 356
Martin, Pepper 464
Martin, Robert 45, 215
Martin, Sharlene 225
Martin, Skip 152, 171
Martin, Steve 314
Martin, Steven M. 20
Martin, Strother 434
Martinelli, Susan 349
Martinsen, Dick 490
Martinson, Leslie H. 47
Martone, Elaine 321
Martyn, Larry 370
Martyn, Peter 333
Marvin, Jerry 460
Marx, William (Bill) 59, 92, 93
Mary Poppins 239
Mary Shelley's Frankenstein 216–217
Masche, Jacquelyn 166
Mashita, Nelson 108
Mask, Ace 237, 364, 472
Maskovich, Donald 81
Maslansky, Paul 523
Mason, James 217, 259, 495, 496
Mason, LeRoy 302
Mason, Sydney 94, 97
The Masque of the Red Death 171–173
Massey, Ilona 190, 292
Massie, Paul 117
Masters, Todd 252
Mastrantonio, Mary Elizabeth 157
Masur, Richard 484
Mate, Rudolph 258
Mateos, Julian 431
Mathen, Mahdu 510
Mathers, James 124, 267
Matheson, Chris 55, 56
Matheson, Judy 506, 508
Matheson, Michele 275
Matheson, Muir 19, 426
Matheson, Richard 167, 168, 169, 170
Mathews, Kerwin 429, 430
Mathews, Richard 150
Mathews, Thom 223, 350, 351
Mathie, Marion 143
Mathieson, Muir 120
Matlock, Norman 233
Mattey, Robert A. 39
Matthews, Al 24, 370
Matthews, Christopher 145
Matthews, Dakin 82

Matthews, Francis 141, 197
Matthews, Lester 116, 292
Mattos, Laure 83
Mature, Victor 371
Maude, Beatrice 284
Maugans, Cheri 220
Maus, Rodger 319
Maxey, Caty 46
Maxey, Paul 293
Maxim, John 141, 204, 436
Maxwell, Don 352, 359
Maxwell, Edwin 65
Maxwell, Frank 252
Maxwell, James 201
Maxwell, Kim 349
Maxwell, Paul 24, 411
Maxwell, Robert 460
May, Bradford 109, 213
May, Brian 321, 322, 360
May, Elaine 259
May, Jack 75
May, Jock 139
May, Joe 291
May, Peter 145
May, Roger 387
May, W.H. 194
May, Winston 233
Mayberry, Dick 128
Mayer, Louis B. 114, 116
Mayfield, Les 331
Mayhew, Peter 452, 454, 457
Mayne, Ferdinand (Ferdy) 87, 157, 273, 503
Mayorage, Lincoln 144
Mayweather, Joshua Gibran 70
Mazar, Debi 52, 53
Mazone-Abbott Dancers 341
Mazur, Heather 352
Me: Stories of My Life (book) 116
Me and My Girl (Broadway) 91
Mead, Syd 438
Meaden, Dan 121
Meador, Josh 495
Mear, H. Fowler 425
Meatballs 234
Medalie, Mervyn 437
Meddings, Derek 466
Meddings Magic Camera Company 47
Medeiros, Michael 418
Medwin, Michael 427
Meehan, John 495
Meeker, Ralph 183
Megowan, Don 100
Meheux, Phil 261, 370
Meier, Christian 516
Meier, Ernest 67

Meins, Gus 38
Meisenbach, Kurt 35
Meisle, Kathryn 45
Mejias, Isabele 422
Mel 55
Melato, Mariangela 175
Mele, Nicholas (Nick) 357, 359
Melendez, Ron 79
Melford, Jack 506
Melford, Jill 437
Méliès, Georges 499
Mell, Joseph 276
Mellon, Francis 208
Mellor, Christie 366
Melly, Andree 139
Melniker, Benjamin 50, 469, 472
Melocchi, Vince 81
Melrose, Peter 143
Melton, Gregory 491
Melvin the dog 211
Memoirs of an Invisible Man 438
Menard, Tina 319
Mendez, Raymond A. 102
Mendleson, Anthony 120, 333
Mendoza-Nava, Jamie 311
Menken, Alan 314
Menzies, Mary 168
Menzies, William Cameron 21, 281, 282
Mercer, Marian 365
Mercer, Ray 167, 460
Merchant, Cathy 252
Merck, Wallace 79, 223
Meredith, Burgess 47, 61, 62
Merin, Eda Reiss 233
Merivale, John 289
Meriwether, Lee 47
Merkerson, S. Epatha 478
Merrick, Lynn 258
Merrill, Gary 497
Merrill, Julie 214
Merrill, Tony 307
Merritt, George 120, 400
Merritt, Theresa 522
"Merry Old Land of Oz" (song) 520
Mertin, Janet 307
Mescall, John J. 185, 363
Meshack, Charles C. 81
Messaoudi, Souad 408
Messenger, Charlie 220
Messer, Peter 102
Metcalf, Audrey 61
Metty, Russell 519
Metzler, Jim 79
Metzler, Rick 58

Mey, Gavin 107
Meyer, Breckin 360
Meyer, Mimi 469
Meyer, Nicholas 442, 445, 446, 448, 449
Meyer, Richard C. 178
Meyer, Torben 177, 190
Meyers, Brent 181
Meyjes, Menno 411
Michael, Paul 268
Michael, Ralph 510
Michaels, Julie 226
Michaels, Toby 312
Michelle, Jane 59
Michelson, Denis 242
Michelson, Harold 440
Michettoni, Enio 214
Mickey Mouse Club 40
Middendorf, Tracy 361
Middlemas, Frank 206
Middleton, Charles 176
Middleton, Stuart 204
Midgely, John 254, 255
Midkiff, Dale 373
Midnight 296
The Midwich Cuckoos (book) 508, 511
Mihailoff, R.A. 493
Mikhelson, Andre 510
Mikler, Michael 517
Milan, George 31
Mileham, Mark 509
Miles, Doug 55
Miles, Marc 411
Miles, Will 411
Milford, Gene 315
Milius, John 86
Milland, Ray 158, 159, 170, 208
Millar, Hal 210
Millar, Henry, Jr. 210, 501
Millay, Diana 270
Miller, Allan 444
Miller, Arthur 65
Miller, Beth Ann 278
Miller, Bill 321
Miller, Bruce 349
Miller, David B. 36, 184, 354, 359, 360
Miller, Dean W. 374
Miller, Dick 34, 35, 122, 241, 242, 271, 272, 312, 363, 476
Miller, Frank 418, 419, 499
Miller, Geoff 267
Miller, George 321, 322, 323
Miller, Harvey 124
Miller, Jason 32, 162, 163, 164, 165, 166
Miller, Jeffrey 473

Miller, Jim 20
Miller, Ken 276
Miller, Magda 117
Miller, Martin 333, 510
Miller, Melissa 365
Miller, Murray 364
Miller, Pat 195
Miller, Philip 148
Miller, Randy 109, 256
Miller, Richard 170
Miller, Ron 158, 159, 318
Miller, Selwyn Emerson 125
Miller, Seton I. 257
Miller, Ty 493, 494
Miller, Victor 217, 219, 220, 221
Miller, Virgil 339
Millhauser, Bertram 292
Millican, James 243
Milligan, Spike 22
Millington, James 109
Millkie, Ron 217
Mills, Alec 306
Mills, Frank 302
Mills, Jack 427, 497
Mills, John 407
Mills, Michael John 43
Mills, Robert 439
Milner, Anthony 464
Milrad, Abe 165
Milrad, Josh 54
Miltern, John 315
Milton, Billy 110
Milton, Ernest 22, 75
Mineo, Sal 382
Miner, Michael 416, 418, 419
Miner, Steve (aka Stephen) 51, 217, 219, 220, 264, 512
Mingaye, Don 117, 140, 203, 436
Minor, Bob 59
Minor, Michael 54, 442
Minter, Kelly Jo 359
Minty, Emil 322
Miracle, Irene 393, 515
Miracle on 34th Street (1947) 330–331
Miracle on 34th Street (1994) 331–332
Miranda 332–333
Miranda, Carmen 232
Miranda, Isa 379
Mirelez, Tony 476
Mirisch, Walter 153
Mirkovich, Steve 225, 474
Mirren, Helen 501, 502
Missile to the Moon 77–78, 200
Mistal, Karen 37
Mitamura, Akio 86, 410

Mitchel, Thomas 315
Mitchell, Billy J. 411
Mitchell, Cameron 211, 212
Mitchell, Charlotte 509
Mitchell, David 184, 514
Mitchell, Don 59
Mitchell, James 213, 518
Mitchell, Laurie 77
Mitchell, Mellan 410
Mitchell, Paul 363
Mitchell, Phillip 312
Mitchell, Sean 184
Mitchum, Robert 427
Mitler, Matt 45
Mizzy, Vic 20
Mnoz, Michele 515
Mockridge, Cyril 331
Modean, Jayne 266
Moffat, Donald 484
Mogg, Nann 102
Moldovan, Jeff 493, 494
Molieri, Lillian 10
Molin, Bud 365
Molina, Alfred 408
Moll, Richard 265
Mollin, Fred 224, 225
Mollo, John 23, 452, 454
Molohon, Shirley 258
The Molten Meteor see *The Blob*
Molyneaux, Patrick J. 35
Mondello, Antony 519
Monette, Richard 391
Monkey Planet (book) 380
Monlaur, Yvonne 139, 140
The Monolith Monsters 101
Monoson, Lawrence 222
Monson, Carl 313
The Monster of Piedras Blancas 101
Monster of Terror see *Die, Monster, Die!*
The Monster Squad 102, 155, 213–214, 346, 526
Montaigne, Lawrence 158
Montalban, Ricardo 382, 383, 384, 442, 443, 445
Montanio, Ben 527
Monteros, Rosenda 436
Montes, Lola 307
Montevecchi, Liliane 238
Montez, Paul Felix 215
Montgomery, Lee Harcourt 519
Montgomery, Robert 257, 258
Montoya, Angela 249
Montsash, Henry 194, 197
Monty, Harry 281
Moody, Lynn 59

Moody, Ron 90, 91, 334
Moon, Georgina 120
Moon, Keith 152
Moon, Philip 52
Moon, Travis A. 475
Moorcock, Michael 309
Moorder, Giorgio 465
Moore, Alvy 267
Moore, Arnie 241
Moore, Charles 132
Moore, Del 118, 238
Moore, Dudley 22
Moore, Elizabeth 160
Moore, Frank 184
Moore, Joanne 19
Moore, Matthew 182
Moore, Mavor 420
Moore, Millie 247
Moore, Pauline 185
Moore, Randy 228, 282
Moore, Richard 352
Moore, Ronald D. 450
Moore, Susan 175
Moore, Ted 431, 432
Moore, Terry (creature designer) 311
Moore, Tom 311
Moorhead, Jean 30
Mora, Danny 366
Mora, Philippe 273
Morahan, James 27, 120
Morales, Hector 319
Moran, Eddie 488, 489
Moran, Michael P. 234
Moran, Peggy 336
Moran, Tim 446
Moran, Tony 245
Moranis, Rick 233, 234, 263, 264, 314
Mordant, Edwin 186
More, Camilla 222
More, Carey 222
More, Kenneth 90, 91, 239, 427
More, Ronald D. 450
"More, More, More" (song) 391
More Than Skin Deep 327
Morell, Andre 147, 239, 345, 436, 437
"Morella" (film segment) 169
Moreno, Antonio 94
Moreno, Belita 125, 366
Moreno, Gary 366
Moreno, Jorge 305, 319
Moreno, Rubin 319
Morgan, Charly 214
Morgan, Clive 116, 131
Morgan, Corney 370
Morgan, Dennis 128

Morgan, Ed 364
Morgan, Felicite 67
Morgan, Frank 520
Morgan, Robbi (actress) 217
Morgan, Robert (art director) 67
Morgan, Terence 344
Moriarity, Patrick 132
Moriarty, Michael 301, 302
Moriceau, Norma 322, 323
Morin, Alberto 292
Morison, Tom 160
Morita, Rhett 392
Moroder, Giorgio 75
Moroff, Mike 353
Morphew, Coral 334
Morra, Irene 88
Morrell, Carla 46
Morrell, Carmen 46
Morricone, Ennio 164, 484, 486
Morris, Aubrey 64
Morris, Barboura 252
Morris, Grant 472
Morris, Haviland 242
Morris, Howard 118
Morris, Jack 527
Morris, John 210
Morris, Michael 404, 437
Morris, Oswald 426, 522
Morris, Reg 183
Morris, Robert 203
Morris, Wayne 128
Morrisette, Billy 236
Morriss, Frank 438
Morrissey, Paul 157
Morrow, Jeff 100, 101
Morrow, Mari 80
Morrow, Susan 77
Morse, Fuzzbee 236
Mortimer, John 279
Mortoff, Lawrence 256
Morton, Hugh 404
Morton, Joe 478
Morton, John 175, 454, 464
Moses, Charles A. 198
Moses, Sam 233
Mosley, Bill 352
Moss, Clive 427
Most Dangerous Man Alive 252
Motley 279
Mott, Zachary 352
Motta, Bess 476
Mounds, Melissa 177
Mount, Thom 214
Mountain, Charles 370
The Mouse on the Moon 334
The Mouse That Roared 333–334

The Mouse That Roared (book) 334
Mousseau, Steve 109
Mowbray, Alan 488, 489
Mower, Jack 128
Mowry, Pat 77
Moxey, Hugh 370
Moyer, Tawny 246
Mucci, David 390
Much Ado About Nothing 56
Mudie, Leonard 315, 335
Mueller, Chris 94, 97
Mueller, Maureen 387
Muellerleile, Marianne 107
Muir, David 506
Muir, Domonic 103
Muir, Douglas 426
Muir, Gavin 116, 293
Mulcahy, Russell 260, 261
Mulcaster, Michael 194
Muldowney, Dominic 362
Mulholland, Declan 309
Mullen, Patty 215
Muller, Paul 208
Mulliner, Arthur 324
Mullings, Sharon 486
Mullins, Bartlett 194, 204
Mulshine, Kathy 491
Mulvehill, Charles 155
The Mummy (1932) 334–336
The Mummy (1959) 137, 342–344
The Mummy's Curse 339–340, 341, 342
The Mummy's Ghost 339, 341, 342
The Mummy's Hand 336–337, 341, 342
The Mummy's Shroud 342, 345–346
The Mummy's Tomb 337–338, 341
Munden, Elizabeth 509
Munier, Ferdinand 38, 292
Munns, William (Bill) 209, 469
Munoz, Frank 246
Munro, Alan 20, 359
Munro, Caroline 15–16, 148, 157, 431, 432, 433
Munro, Christa 511
Munro, Lochlyn 493
Munro, Neil 230
The Muppet Christmas Carol 429
Muradian, Gregory 133
Murawski, Bob 161
Murch, Walter 523

Murder in Amityville (book) 32
Murdocco, Vince 177
Murdock, George 447
Murdock, Jack 123
Muren, Dennis 234, 410, 478
Murkey, Ricky 376
Murlowski, John 35
Murphy, Chris 387
Murphy, Dennis 219
Murphy, Donald 129, 199, 200
Murphy, Maurice 243
Murphy, Michael S. (producer) 55
Murphy, Michael (actor) 50
Murphy, Ralph 324
Murphy, Reilly 288
Murphy, Rosemary 519
Murray, Bill 233, 234, 314, 427
Murray, Brian Doyle 234, 427
Murray, David 411
Murray, Don 383, 384
Murray, E.J. 387
Murray, Graeme 183
Murray, James 475
Murray, John T. 315
Murray, Ken 19
Murray, Stephan 22
Murtaugh, Jams 271
Murton, Peter 464
Muscal, Michael 263
Mushroom (dog) 241
Mussorgsky 490
Musumeci-Greco, Enzo 429
Musuraca, Nicholas 72, 74
Mutant 348
Muti, Ornella 175
Myers, Bruce 64
Myers, Ernie 36
Myers, Henry 22
Myers, Kenny 43, 351, 447
Myers, Kim 355
Myers, Ruth 123
Myers, Troy 480
Myhers, John 434, 519
Myhre, John 393
Mylrea, David 183
Myrow, Fred 375, 376, 377
Mysterious Island (1929) 499
Mysterious Island (1961) 497, 498
The Mystery of the Wax Museum 294

Naar, Joseph T. 58, 59
Nadiuska 86

Nadoolman, Deborah 408
Nagel, Conrad 371
Naha, Ed 263
Naish, J. Carrol 71, 147, 190, 191
Naismith, Laurence 427, 509
Naked Gun 38, 125, 167
Nanayakkara, D.R. 410
Nance, Jack 235
Nankin, Michael 229, 230
Nanuzzi, Armando 214
Napier, Alan 47, 72, 89, 170, 291
Napier, Charles 328
Nappil, Malya 372
Narens, Sherry 387
Narita, Hiro 263, 449
The Narrow Margin 34
Nascimbene, Mario 372, 437
Nash, Kevin 474
Nash, Mary 307
Nathan, Jack 15
Nation, Terry 126, 127
National Comics 469
Naughton, David 35
Naulin, John 413
Navarro, George 30
Neal, David 461
Neal, Dylan 392
Nealy, Frances 233
Neame, Christopher 148
Neame, Ronald 426
Neary, Robert 278
Necromancy 79
Necronomicon 414
Needs, James 121, 135, 140, 143, 145, 148, 194, 197, 203, 208, 325, 342, 344, 345, 398, 400, 404, 436, 437, 503
Neeson, Liam 108, 109
Neff, Tom 324
Negley, Howard 192
Negron, Taylor 36
Neil, Noel 469
Neilan, Marshall 312
Neill, Roy William 190
Neill, Sam 370
Neill, Steve 472
Nelkin, Stacey 247
Nelligan, Kate 153, 154
Nelson, B.J. 421, 422
Nelson, Barry 243
Nelson, Connie 147
Nelson, Craig T. 59, 93, 94, 385, 386
Nelson, Dick 30
Nelson, Don 318
Nelson, George R. 386

Nelson, Jessica 125
Nelson, Kenneth 254
Nelson, Lori 97, 99
Nelson, Mark 217
Nelson, Robert 97
Nelson, Shawn 242
Nepomniaschy, Alex 386
Neri, Rosalba *see* Bey, Sara
Nesmith, Otola 524
Ness, Andrew 328
Neuberger, Jan 165
Neumann, Kurt 177, 305
Neumann, Stuart 527
Neumeier, Edward 214, 416, 418, 419
Neuvenheim, Steve 352
Neve, Suzanne 427
Nevedomsky, Leonid 66
Nevil, Steve 271
New, Robert 390
The New Batch see *Gremlins II: The New Batch*
A New Beginning see *Friday the 13th: A New Beginning*
A New Generation see *Amityville: A New Generation*
The New Order see *Scanners II: The New Order*
Newberry, Bill 341
Newbould, Tanya 57
Newcom, James 489
Newcombe, John J. 370
Newcombe, Warren 114, 238, 243
Newell, Mike 64
Newell, Patrick 152
Newington, Joey 43
Newley, Anthony 152
Newman, Alfred 65
Newman, Andrew Hill 330
Newman, David 55, 56, 103, 461, 463, 465
Newman, Laraine 282
Newman, Leslie 461, 464, 465
Newman, Nanette 498
Newman, Phyllis 329
Newsom, David 361
Newton, Eric 252
Ney, Marie 425
Ney, Richard 170
Ng, Walter 482
Ngui, Rex 410
A Nice Girl Like Me 511
Nicholas, Denise 58
Nicholas, P.J. 362
Nicholas, Thomas Ian 91
Nicholls, Anthony 367
Nichols, Dandy 333
Nichols, David B. 184

Nichols, David 469
Nichols, Dudley 435
Nichols, Maurice 208
Nichols, Nichelle 440, 442, 444, 446, 447, 449
Nichols, Paul "Tiny" 318
Nichols, Robert 482, 483
Nichols, Stephen 265
Nichols, Walter 438
Nicholson, Al 369
Nicholson, Bruce 511
Nicholson, Jack 47, 170, 312, 313
Nicholson, James H. 111, 167
Nicholson, Loretta 31
Nicholson, Marty 266
Nicholson, Meredith 77, 199
Nicholson, Sam 247
Nicholson, Tom 124
Nicksay, David 365
Nickson-Soul, Julia 35
Nicolaou, Ted 235
Nicolas, Pedro 295
Nicotero, Gregory 349
Nicova, Leda 72
Nielsen, Hans 309
Nielsen, Leslie 102, 166, 167, 390, 391
Night Court (TV series) 445
Night of Dark Shadows 270–271
Night of the Living Dead (1968) 346–348, 351
Night of the Living Dead (1990) 352–353
Night on Bald Mountain (music) 490
The Nightcomers 279–281
A Nightmare on Elm Street 227, 354, 355, 392
A Nightmare on Elm Street: The Dream Child 359–360
A Nightmare on Elm Street 4: The Dream Master 357–359
A Nightmare on Elm Street Part 2: Freddy's Revenge 355–356
A Nightmare on Elm Street 3: Dream Warriors 356–357
Nilsson, Harry 151
Nilsson, Kjell 322
Nimoy, Leonard 286, 440, 442, 444, 445, 446, 447, 448, 449
Nimoy, Nancy 446
1984 362

Nineteen Eighty-Four 362–363
Nitzsche, Jack 162
Niven, David 152
Nixon, Richard 436
No Down Payment 178
Noble, Robert 57
Noble, Thom 385
Nocturna, Granddaughter of Dracula 158
Noel, Daniele 437
Nolan, Barry 55, 306
Nolet, Michele 125
Nomad, Michael (Mike) 84, 85, 223
Noodlemantra, Oprah 360
Noonan, Kerry 223
Noonan, Tom 213, 418
Norden, Eric 313
Norin, Gus 519
Norman, Monty 117
Norman, Paul 509
Norrington, Steve 523
Norris, Eric 282
Norris, Guy 322
Norris, Palmer 46
Norris, William J. 413
North, Alan 260
North, Alex 519
North, Hope 106
North, Jack 249
North, Noelle 125
North, Sheree 327, 328
North, Virginia 15
Norton, Andre 54, 55
Norton, Arthur 488
Norton, Edgar 112, 131, 188
Norton, Ralph 335
Norton, Rosana 418
Nosferatu (1922) 155, 157
Nosferatu (1978) 157
Nosseck, Ralph 498
Not of This Earth (1956) 363–364
Not of This Earth (1988) 364
"Nothing's Gonna Stop Us Now" (song) 329, 330
Notz, Thierry 214, 480, 515
Novak, Frank 516
Novak, Mickell 371, 372
Nowak, Danny 176
Nowell, Justin 223
Nowell, Tommy 223
Nunez, Miguel 350
Nunez, Miguel A., Jr. 222
Nunez, Tito 439
Nunn, Bill 70
Nupuf, Mason 282
Nurse, Heather 143
Nutter, David 494

The Nutty Professor 118–120, 239
Nuyen, France 384
Nyby, Christian 482, 484
Nye, Ben 47, 177
Nye, Carrie 102

"O Willow Waly" (song) 279
Oakie, Jack 21
Oates, John W. 311
Obalil, Linda 364
O'Bannon, Dan 23–24, 27, 252, 253, 282, 350, 351
Obata, Toshishiro 473, 474
Oberhaus, Tom 476
O'Blath, Carol 300, 395
O'Brian, John 427
O'Brien, Edmond 362
O'Brien, Kenneth 59
O'Brien, Kevin 220, 512
O'Brien, Mariah 250
O'Brien, Richard 175, 434
O'Brien, Willis 302, 304
Obsession 300
O'Byrne, Bryan 152, 527
O'Byrne, Sean 182
Obzina, Martin 131, 133, 190
O'Casey, Ronan 362
O'Conartin, Maureen 224
O'Connell, Arthur 519
O'Connell, Maurice 150
O'Connor, Frank 305
O'Connor, Renee 109
O'Connor, Terrence 440
O'Connor, Una 186, 289
O'Conor, Thomas A. 357
O'Dea, Judith 347
O'Dee, Dusty 56
Odell, David 466
Odney, Laurette 93
O'Doherty, James 46
O'Donnell, Chris 52, 53
O'Donnell, Peter 437
O'Donoghue, Michael 427
O'Donovan, Edwin 259
O'Driscoll, Martha 133
Oehler, Greg 486
Ogden, Mark 56
Ogilvie, George 323
Ogilvy, Ian 397
Oh, Andrew 323
Oh, God! 364–365
Oh, God! Book II 365–366
Oh, God! You Devil 366–367
O'Haco, Jeff 411
O'Halloran, Jack 305, 461, 464
Ohanneson, Jill 55
O'Har, Taras 223

O'Hara, Maureen 331
O'Hara, Pat 178
O'Hare, Michael 83
O'Henry, Marie 122
O'Herlihy, Dan 247, 416, 418, 419
O'Herlihy, Gavan 465
Okada, Daryn 376
O'Keefe, Dennis 489
Okerlund, Gene 166
The Old Dark House 392
Old Dracula 152
"Old Man Moon" (song) 488
Oldfield, Mike 162
Oldfield, Richard 370, 454
Oldman, Gary 155, 157
O'Leary, William 70
Olegario, Frank 410
Oliphant, Tom 195
Oliver! 91, 334, 427, 501
Oliver, Barret 84, 85, 125
Oliver, David 267
Oliver, Edna May 21
Oliver, Jody 45
Oliver, Pita 390
Oliver, Raymond 80
Oliver, Ron 391, 392
Oliver, Ruth 233
Oliveri, Robert 263, 264
Olivier, Laurence 153
Oliviero, Silvio 240
Olson, Brent 236
Olson, James 32, 33
Olson, Jeff 248
Olson, Nancy 17–19
O'Malley, Bingo 102
O'Malley, J. Pat 19, 519
O'Malley, Kathleen 258
O'Malley, Pat 284
O'Malley, The Rev. William 162
O'Mara, Kate 207, 503
O'Meara, C. Timothy 86
Omen, Judd 84, 273
The Omen 65, 309, 367–368, 369, 463
O'Moore, Patrick 116
On the Move see *Mannequin: On the Move*
The One Man Army 246
One Million B.C. 371–372
One Million Years B.C. 372–373
One Night in the Tropics 258
O'Neal, Anne 331
O'Neal, Colette 206
O'Neal, Ron 397
O'Neil, Patrick 212
O'Neill, Amy 263, 264

O'Neill, Gene 83
O'Neill, Jennifer 420
O'Neill, Kevin 155
O'Neill, Remy 486, 487
Onyx, Narda 203, 204
Oppenheimer, Alan 493, 494, 516
Opper, Barry 104, 105
Opper, Don 103, 104, 105, 106
O'Quinn, Terry 35
Orbom, Eric 116
Ordway, Frederick I., III 499
O'Reilly, Kathryn 393
Orend, Jack R. 35
The Origin of Michael Myers see *Halloween: The Curse of Michael Myers*
The Original Nightmare see *Howling IV: The Original Nightmare*
Orlacs Haende 320
Ormsby, Alan 75
Ornitz, Arthur J. 268
O'Rourke, Charles 437
O'Rourke, Heather 385, 386, 387
Ortega, Delia 376
Ortega, Jose Luis 387
Ortega, Ramona 376
Orwell, George 362, 363
Osborn, Lyn 30
Osborne, John 175
Osborne, Kent 144
Osborne, William 125
Oscar, Henry 139
Osco, Bill 175
O'Shannon, Finnuala 150
O'Shea, Oscar 339
Osman, Ahmed 64
Osmond, Hal 332
O'Steen, Sam 32
Ostrer, Bertram 497
Ostwald, Christian 314
O'Sullivan, Maureen 89
Othenin-Girard, Dominique 249
The Other Side see *Poltergeist II: The Other Side*
Otis, Ted 320
O'Toole, Annette 75, 465
O'Toole, Peter 466
Otrin, John 224
Otterson, Jack 187, 189, 291, 292, 336, 337, 524
Ottiano, Rafaela 489
Otto, Barry 273
Ottwell, Taleena 244
Oulton, Brian 332
Our Man Flint 519

Ouspenskaya, Maria 190, 524
Outten, Richard 374
"Over the Rainbow" (song) 520
Overman, Jack 72
Overs, Christine 314
Ovitz, Judy 42
Owen, Cliff 437
Owen, Dickie 346
Owen, Milton 315
Owen, Reginald 426
Owen, Sion Tudor 260
Owen, Yvonne 332
Owens, Gary 316
Owens, Patricia 177, 178
Oz, Frank 314, 457
Ozma of Oz (book) 523
Ozman, Bob 297

Pabian, David 394
Pace, Lloyd 44
Pace, Ralph 472
Pace, Roger 30
Pacey, Peter 412
Pack, Charles Lloyd 136, 197, 400
Pack, Roger Lloyd 362
Pacs, Darryl 499
Pacula, Joanna 513
Padelford, Morgan 495
Page, Gene 58
Page, Geraldine 212, 213
Page, Ken 416
Page, Lawanda 527
Page, Mitchell 36
Page Cavanaugh and His Trio 199
Paget, Debra 169, 252
Paige, Robert 131
Pais, Josh 472, 473
Paiva, Nestor 94, 97, 203
Pak, Tae 473
Palance, Holly 367
Palance, Jack 47, 157
Palange, Inez 371
Palillo, Ron 223
Palk, Anna 279
Pallette, Eugene 488
Pallos, Steven 320
Pallotin, Richard 208
Palmer, Betsy 217, 219
Palmer, Ernest 88
Palmer, Gary 314
Palmer, Gregg 100
Palmer, Maria 201
Palmer, Max 281
Palmer, Michael 516
Palmer, Norman 434
Palmer, Terry 120

Palmisano, Conrad E. 418
Paluzzi, Luciana 498
Pan, Hermes 316
Pandher, Arjun 410
Panga see *Curse III — Blood Sacrifice*
Pangborn, Franklin 489
Pankhurst, Patrick 247
Pankin, Stuart 330
Pankowsky, Raquel 33
Pantanello, Tony 347
Panzer, William N. 260, 261
Paoli, Dennis 236, 288, 413
Paone, Bob 45
Papas, Helen 240
Pappas, Robin 464
Pare, Michael 511
Paredes, Daniel 75
Parfrey, Woodrow 380
Paris, Gerald 509
Parke, MacDonald 333
Parker, Cecil 309
Parker, Daniel 216
Parker, Eddie 190, 292, 337, 338, 341
Parker, Edwin 116
Parker, Ken L. 218
Parker, Lara 270
Parker, Lindsay 104
Parker, Ray, Jr. 232, 234
Parkes, Gerry 439
Parkin, Dean 30
Parks, Catherine 220
Parks, Larry 258
Parmentier, Richard 310, 464
Parr, Bobby 121
Parris, Carl 464
Parrish, Helen 186
Parrish, Julie 118
Parry, Geoff 321
Parsey, Martha 362
Parson, Timothy 208
Parsons, Alibe 24
Parsons, Jack 180
Parsons, Milton 252
Parsons, Steve 184, 273
Part, Michael 91
Partleton, George 203, 345
Partridge, Ross 35
Pascal, Ernest 65
Pascale, Jan 349
Pass, Cyndi 423
Pastell, George 342, 344
Pat Garrett and Billy the Kid 492
Pataki, Michael 93, 152, 248
Pate, Johnny 122
Pate, Michael 273, 274
Patel, Bhasker 410

Paterson, Ian 224, 236
Paterson, Tony 321
Patino, Steven 376
Patric, Jason 214
Patrice, Ann 498
Patrick, Dennis 268
Patrick, John 478
Patrick, Millicent 94, 97, 100, 101
Patterson, Hank 30
Patterson, Jay 473
Patterson, Kenneth 284
Patterson, Rick 37
Patton, Mark 355
Paul, Edna Ruth 159
Paul, Lee 519
Paulin, Scott 277
Paunescu, Oana 493, 494
Paunescu, Vlad 493, 494
Pavia, Ria 68
Pavlon, Jerry 222
Pavlova, Nadia 66
Pavlovitch, Robert 76
Pawlick, Amber 225
Paxton, Bill 24, 476
Payne, Bruce Martyn 275
Payne, James 59
Payne, John 331
Paynter, Robert (Bob) 279, 314, 370, 464, 465
Payson, Keith 397
Peace, J. Stephen 36, 37
Peace, Rock ("Rock") 36, 37, 38
Peacock, David 427
Peake, Mervyn 50
Peaks, John 160
Pearce, Damon 522
Pearl, Daniel 282, 301, 527
Pearson, H.C. 398
Pearson, Jake 124
Pearson, Richard 66
Pearson, Sydney 135, 139
Pearthree, Pippa 511
Peck, Brian 80, 350, 352, 404
Peck, Ed V. 259
Peck, Gregory 367, 368, 369
Peck, J. Eddie 107
Peck, Jim 374
Peckinpah, Sam 284
Pederson, Con 499
Pee Wee's Big Adventure 49
Peel, David 139, 140, 320
Peel, Haley 21
Pefferle, Richard 238
Pei, Edward 275, 515
Peil, Ed, Sr. 186
Pelikan, Lisa 235
Pelkey, Sanita 77

Pellegrino, Frank 184
Pelling, Maurice 127
Pelton, Dale Allan 351
Peluce, Meeno 31
Pember, Ron 309
Pendleton, Austin 438
Penesoff, Stanley 270
Penghlis, Thaao 123
Penhaligon, Susan 309
Penner, Jonathan 34
Penney, John 353
Penniman, R. 388
Pennington, Michael 457
Pennington-Richards, C. 362, 426
Pennock, Christopher 270
Penrose, Charles 332
Pentangelo, Joe 331
The People That Time Forgot 310–311
The People That Time Forgot (book) 310
Pepiot, Ken 388, 512
Peppe, Chris 79
Pepperman, Paul 54, 375
Percy, Lee 413
Pereira, Hal 118, 232, 238
Peretz, Susan 366, 386
Perkins, Elizabeth 331
Perkins, Eric Boyd 344
Perkins, Gil 47, 116
Perkins, Jack 319
Perkins, Jess 418
Perkins, Patricia 76
Perkins, Voltaire 199
Perlberg, William 330
Perle, Rebecca 364
Perreau, Janine 281
Perrello, Hope 393
Perrine, Valerie 461, 463, 466
Perry, Cameron 359
Perry, Felton 396, 416, 418, 419
Perry, Jaime 219
Perry, Peter 144
Perry, Roger 92, 93, 94
Perry, Simon 362
Persaud, Toolsie 346
Pertwee, Carolyn 334
Pertwee, Michael 334
Pes, Carlo 379
Pesce, Frank 328
Pet Sematary 373–374
"Pet Sematary" (song) 373
Pet Sematary II 374–375
Peter Gunn (TV series) 117
Pete's Dragon 90–91
Peterman, Donald (Don) 20, 84, 446

Peters, Barry 31
Peters, Brock 446, 447, 449
Peters, Hans 377
Peters, Jon 47, 50
Peters, Kelly Jean 386
Peters, Luan 506, 508
Peters, Scott 30
Peters, Steve 127
Peters, Virginia 360
Petersen, Curtis 184, 514
Peterson, Cassandra ("Elvira") 124, 125
Peterson, Kristine 105
Peterson, Mark 126
Peterson, Roy E. 80
Petit, Roland 237
Petrie, Daniel 85
Petrie, Doris 422
Petrov, Andrei 66
Petter, Charles 293
Peyton, Robin 56
Pfarrer, Chuck 108
Pfeiffer, Dedee 267
Pfeiffer, Michelle 50
Pfister, Wally 35
Phalen, Robert 245
Phantasm 375–376
Phantasm II 376
Phantasm III: Lord of the Dead 377
The Phantom of the Opera 202
Pharres, Paco 33
Phelps, Buster 65
Phelps, Lee 307
Phelps, Nigel 47
Phelps, Win 318
Philbin, John 78, 350
Philips, Frank 317, 318
Philipson, Adam 68
Phillips, Barney 276
Phillips, Ethan 103
Phillips, Frank 158, 159, 434
Phillips, John 334, 346, 460, 509
Phillips, Kate 60
Phillips, Nicholas 427
Phillips, Samantha 376
Phillips, Shawn 316
Philo, Tim 159
Phinneas D. 43
Phipps, Bill 281
Phipps, Kevin 87
Phipps, Max 322
Phipps, Nicholas 333
Phipps, William 77, 201
Phoenix, River 411
Piazzoli, Roberto D'Ettore 106
Picardo, Robert 242, 271, 366

Pichel, Irving 131, 435, 436, 489
Pickens, Slim 271
Pickrell, Greg 56
The Picture of Dorian Gray 325, 377–379
Pidgeon, Walter 238
Pie, Don 249
Pierce, Bart 159
Pierce, Charles B. 311, 312
Pierce, Chuck 59, 311, 312
Pierce, David 476
Pierce, Jack P. 13, 71, 186, 187, 189, 190, 202, 334, 337, 339, 524
Pierce, Maggie 169
Pierce, Pam 312
Pierce, Scott 357
Pierce, Tony 493
Pierpoint, Eric 282
Pierson, Rex 472
Pieters, Barbara 413
Piffl, John 72
Pigott, Tempe 112, 186
Pike, Kevin 40
Pike, Nicholas 84, 104
Pilato, Joseph 349
Pillow, Mark 468
Pinney, Clay 386, 446
Pinsett, Gordon 58
Piper, Sally 356
Pirkle, Mac 306
Pistone, Martin 446
The Pit and the Pendulum 168–169, 173
Pitofsky, Peter 265
Pitt, Ingrid 2, 94, 157, 437, 503–506, 508
Pittman, Bruce 391
Pittman, Heather 56
Pittman, Ruth 56
Pivar, Ben 71, 336, 337, 339
Pivar, Maurice 71, 185
Piven, Jeremy 125, 126
Pizarro, Artemus 215
Pizer, Larry 330
Planer, Franz 495
Planet of the Apes 380, 381, 501
Plato, Dana 311, 312
Platt, Marc 258
Platten, Jon Richard 249
Players Special Effects 492
Playten, Alice 32
Please Don't Eat My Mother 313–314
Pleasence, Donald 26, 153, 158, 159, 244, 245, 246, 248, 249, 250, 251, 320, 362, 365, 495

Pleshette, Suzanne 365, 366, 434, 435
Ploski, Joe 198
Plowman, Melinda 142
Plowright, Hilda 116
Plumeri, Terry 481
Plummer, Christopher 449
Plummer, Terence 47
Plunkett, Walter 238
Pockett, Christine 437
Poe, Edgar Allan 167, 168, 169, 171, 173, 174, 251, 252
Pogany, Willy 334
Poggi, Lisa Ann 68
Pogue, Charles Edward 181
Poindexter 159
Pointer, Priscilla 356
Pokras, Barbara 84
Polanski, Roman 157
Poledouris, Basil 86, 87, 416, 419
Polglase, Van Nest 435
Polis, Joel 484
Polito, Gene 516, 518
Polito, Jon 260
Polivka, Steven 278
Polizos, Vic 83
Pollard, Bud 21
Pollard, Michael J. 427
Pollard, Snub 331
Pollexfen, Jack 116, 117
Polonsky, Alan 24
Poltergeist 34, 35, 94, 230, 385, 486
Poltergeist II: The Other Side 385–386
Poltergeist III 386–387
Pon, Patrick 252
Ponce, Danny 366
Ponton, Yvan 422
Ponzini, Antony 222
Poole, Anthony 201
Pope, Bill 108, 161
Pope, Natalie 34, 79, 226
Popov, Oleg 66
Porcasi, Paul 302
Porcelli, Claudia 67
Porky's 527
Porro, Joseph 228
Portass, Geoff 255
Portell, Petula 121
Porteous, Emma 24, 362
Porter, Bobby 384
Porter, Brett 449
Portillo, Rose 164
Portney, Charlotte 199
Posey, Stephen L. 222
The Possession see *Amityville II: The Possession*
Post, Don 246, 247

Post, Robert 199
Post, Ted 380
Poster, Thomas W. 515
Postiglione, Giorgio 33
Potter, Charles 312
Potter, Luce 281, 282
Potts, Annie 233, 234
Poudevigne, Gregory 416
Poul, Alan 68
Poulik, Michele 161
Poulton, Raymond 437
Powell, Anthony 411
Powell, Buddy 366
Powell, Clive 510
Powell, Dinny 464
Powell, Eddie (actor) 127, 346
Powell, Edward (composer) 489
Powell, Reg 236
Powell, William 89
Power, John 131
Power, Taryn 432, 433
Power, Tyrone, Jr. 84, 85
Power Rangers 397
"The Power of Love" (song) 40
Powers, Barbara 476
Powers, Mala 75
Powers, Richard 71
Powers, Stefanie 317
Powers, Tom 232, 307
Poynter, Jim 85
Praed, Michael 487
Pratt, Jane 67
Pratt, Roger 47, 216
Pratt, Thomas 128
Pravda, George 206, 208
Prebble, John 497
Precht, Andrew 155
Preclik, Milos 273
Predator 387–388, 516
Predator 2 388–390
Preger, Michael 511
The Premature Burial 169–170
Prescott, Pamela 84
Presley, Elvis 222
Pressfield, Steven 306
Pressman, Michael 474
Preston, Cyndy 392
Preston, David 422
Preston, Mike 322
Preston, Paul 346
Previn, Charles 187, 291, 524
Price, David F. 79, 125, 487
Price, Dennis 22, 151, 207, 508, 509
Price, Karen 469
Price, Peter 171

Price, Vincent 15–17, 167, 168, 169, 170, 171, 173, 174, 177, 178, 192, 251, 291
Prichard, Robert 490
Prickett, Leslie A. 43
Priedel, Peter 509
Priestley, Tom 125, 164, 362
Prince 47
The Princess Bride 157
Prine, Andrew 32, 33
Pringle, Brian 309
Pringle, Irving 516
Pringle, Robert 275
Prinzi, Frank 352
Prior, D. Kerry 377
Prival, Lucien 186
Problem Child 91
Probyn, Brian 149, 208
Procopio, Frank 240
Production Code 114
Prom Night 390–391, 392
Prom Night II see *Hello Mary Lou: Prom Night II*
Prom Night III: The Last Kiss 392
Prom Night IV: Deliver Us from Evil 393
Prophecy 29
Prosky, Robert 242, 331
Prosperi, Federico 106
Provis, George 127
Prowse, David (Dave) 207, 209, 310, 452, 454, 457
Pryor, Nicholas 369
Pryor, Richard 465, 466, 522
Psycho 38, 393, 414
P.T.P. 416
Pugh, Willard 397, 418
Pugsley, Don 81
The Punisher 109
Puppet Master 213, 393–394
Puppet Master II 394–395
Puppet Master III 395–396
Puppet Master IV 396–397
Puppet Master 5 397
Purcell, Bill 416
Purcell, Noel 333
Purdy-Gordon, Carolyn 413
Puri, Amrish 410
Purvis, Jack 452, 454, 457
Pushman, Terrence 210
Putnam, Nina Wilcox 334, 342
Puzo, Mario 461, 463, 464
Pyle, Denver 158, 159
Pyott, Keith 509

Quaid, Randy 217
Quan, Ke Huy 410

Quarry, Robert 16, 92–94
Quarshie, Jugh 260
Quatermass and the Pit (TV series) 406, 407
Quatermass Conclusion (TV series) 407
Quatermass II 400–404
Quatermass III 75, 403, 404–407
The Quatermass Xperiment 193, 248, 398–400
Queen 175, 260, 261
Quennessen, Valerie 86
The Quest for Peace see *Superman IV: The Quest for Peace*
Quezada, Elizabeth 376
Quezada, Roberto A. 376
The Quickening see *Highlander 2: The Quickening*
Quigley, Godfrey 127
Quigley, Juanita 307
Quigley, Lee 461
Quigley, Linnea 350, 351
Quill, Timothy Patrick 161
Quinby, Ripley, III 124
Quinlivan, Joe 155
Quinn, Aidan 216
Quinn, Anthony 231
Quinn, Bill 447
Quinn, Daniel 423, 424
Quinn, Declan 360
Quinn, Fenton 249
Quinn, J.C. 83
Quinn, Vie 21
Quitak, Oscar 197

R/Greenberg 388
Rabe, Vincent J. 327
Rabett, Catherine 214
Rabin, Jack 76, 281
Rabinowitz, Max 315
Rachel, Rachel 501
Rackaukas, Giedra 36
Rade, Nicki 457
Radford, Lynne 362
Radford, Michael 362
Rado, Ivan J. 394
Radon, Peter 32
Rae, John 400
Rae, Ted 184
Raffill, Stewart 330
Raffin, Deborah 422
Ragalyi, Elemer 91
Raggett, Mark 260
Ragsdale, William 227, 228, 330
Raich, Kenneth 252
Raiders of the Living Dead 348

Raiders of the Lost Ark 407–410, 411, 413
Raikes, Robert 400
The Railway Children 82
Raimi, Ivan 108, 161
Raimi, Samuel (Sam) M. 108, 109, 159, 161, 162
Raimi, Theodore 68, 108, 160
Rain, Douglas 499, 501
Rainey, Ford 246
Rains, Claude 257, 289, 290, 291, 293, 524
Rainsbury, Charles 84
Ralph, Jessie 65
Ralston, Gilbert A. 519
Ralston, Kenneth (Ken) 42, 43, 84, 442, 444
Ralston, Vera Hruba 307
Rambaldi, Carlo 23, 87, 306, 307
Ramboldt, Charles 208
Ramirez, Juan 80
Ramis, Harold 232, 233, 234
Rammel, James A. 43
Ramones 373
Ramoundos, Gregory 45
Ramrus, Al 296
Ramsay, Todd 165, 439, 484
Ramsen, Bobby 301
Ramsey, Anne Elizabeth 105
Ramsey, Clark 460
Ramsey, John 83
Ramus, Nick 446
Rand, Patrick 55, 424
Randall, Anne 516, 518
Randall, Dick 208
Randall, Glenn 408, 410
Randall, Stacie 237, 396, 493, 494
Randall, Susan 116
Randall, Tony 242
Randall, Zoe 107
Randel, Tony 34, 255, 256
Randolph, Alice 72, 74
Randolph, Beverly 350
Randolph, Bill 219
Randolph, Jane 73, 192, 193
Randolph, John 259, 305, 382
Randolph, Virginia L. 427
Rankin, Arthur 315
Rape Squad 60
Raphael, Sally Jesse 20
Raposa, Jim 475
Rappaport, David 212
Rasulala, Thalmus 58, 59, 276
Ratchford, Jeremy 392, 439
Rathbone, Basil 169, 188, 436

Rathvon, N. Peter 362
Ratman's Notebooks (book) 519
Rattigan, Jo 258
Rattner, Larry 248
Rattray, Heather 45
Ratzenberger, John 266, 454, 461, 464
The Raven 170–171
Raven, Elsa 31, 40
Raven, Mike 120, 506
Ravich, Rand 70
Ravok, Brian 390
Rawley, James 100
Rawlings, Terry 23, 27, 64
Ray, Allan 482
Ray, Danny 248
Ray, Jimmy 310
Ray, Philip 120, 141, 204
Ray, Stevie-Lyn 177
Raybould, Harry 30
Rayburn, Bill 67
Raymond, Alex 175, 176, 453
Raymond, Paula 144, 145
Raynor, Sheila 110, 367
Razatos, Spiro 327, 328
Rea, Thelma 332
Read, David 22
Reading, Bertice 314
Reading, Tony 306
Reagan, Nancy see Davis (Reagan), Nancy
Re-Animator 219, 413–415
Reardon, Brad 476
Reardon, Michael 427
Rearson, Craig 229, 230
Reason, Rex 100
Reaves, Keanu 57
Rebecca 181
Rebel, Bernard 344
Rebel Without a Cause 277
Rebelo, Hope 275
The Rebirth see *Howling V: The Rebirth*
Recht, Ray 32
The Red Badge of Courage 484
Red Heat 155
Red Sonja 88
Reddington, Ian 260
Redford, J.A.C. 91
Redgrave, Michael 279, 362
Redman, Anthony 261
Redmond, Harry, Jr. 307
Redwing, Rodd 94
Reed, Ben 423
Reed, Donna 377, 379
Reed, Les 103
Reed, Marshall 243

Reed, Michael 14
Reed, Oliver 117, 122, 525
Reed, Ralph 363
Reed, Rex 461
Reed, Walter 460
Reefe, Fred 302
Reel EFX Inc. 221, 222
Rees, John 408
Rees, Yvette 180
Reeve, Christopher 461, 463, 464, 465, 468, 511, 512
Reeve, Spencer 143, 404, 506, 508
Reeves, George 460, 461
Reeves, Keanu 55, 56, 156, 157
Reeves, Perrey 82
Reeves, Richard 143
Reeves, Scott 225
Refalo, Joe 499
Regan, Elizabeth 102
Regehr, Duncan 213
Reicher, Frank 191, 302, 304, 337, 339, 460
Reicher, Hedwigg 131
Reid, Beryl 16
Reid, Elliott 17, 19
Reid, Gaylord 310
Reid, Milton 16, 310
Reidy, Joe 33
Reif, Harry 77, 142, 168, 169, 170, 199, 203
Reilly, Robert 217
Reimbold, Bill 408
Reiner, Carl 365
Reinhart, John K., Jr. 264, 388
Reinhold, Judge 241
Reiniger, Scott H. 348, 349
Reis, Kurt 439
Reiser, Paul 24, 26
Reiss, Ronald R. 475
Reiss, Stuart A. 365, 382
Reitman, Ivan 232, 234, 235
Reitman, Jason 234
Reizenstein, Frank 342
Relph, Michael 120
Remar, James 331, 332
Remick, Lee 367
Remisoff, Nicolai 489
Remsen, Kerry 236
Renard, Ken 164
Renard, Maurice 319
Renay, Liz 209
Renfield, Jon 224
Renie 72
Rennahan, Ray 65, 89
Rennie, Guy 284

Renzetti, Joe 45, 46, 80, 215, 386
Repola, Art 410
Repossessed 37, 164, 166–167
Repp, Stafford 47
"Requiem" (musical composition) 499
Rescher, Gayne 442
Resmukndi, Buster 281
Ressa, Joseph 415
The Resurrected 171, 252–254
Retton, Mary Lou 427
Return from Witch Mountain 159
The Return of Count Yorga 93–94
The Return of Dr. X 128–129
The Return of Dracula 137–139, 296
The Return of Durant see *Darkman II: The Return of Durant*
The Return of Swamp Thing 472
Return of the Fly 178–180
Return of the Jedi 457–460
Return of the Killer Tomatoes 37
The Return of the Living Dead 350–351, 352, 397, 510
Return of the Living Dead Part II 351–352
Return of the Living Dead III 353–354
The Return of the Shaggy Dog (TV movie) 435
Return of the Vampire 157
Return to Boggy Creek 311–312
"Return to Boggy Creek" (song) 311
Return to Oz 523–524
Revell, Graeme 81
The Revenge of Frankenstein 197–198, 202
The Revenge of Michael Myers see *Halloween 5*
Revenge of the Boogeyman 68
Revenge of the Creature 97–99
Revenge of the Nerds 527
Revill, Clive 84
Rex, Roberta 510
Reyes, Ernie, Jr. 474
Reyes, Pia 353
Reynolds, Adeline 132
Reynolds, Cecil 184

Reynolds, Gene 65
Reynolds, Norman 452
Reynolds, Paul 314
Reynolds, Simon 230
Reynolds, Tony 127
Rheume, Dell 286
Rhoades, Barbara 59
Rhodes, Andrew 182
Rhodes, Grandon 97
Rhodes, Hari 383
Rhys-Davies, John 408, 410, 411
Ricci, Christina 20–21
Ricci, Mark 347
Ricci, Rudy 350
Rice, Joan 207
Rice, Milt 284
Rich, Allan 261
Rich, Monica 270
Richard, Eric 370
Richard, Julie 422
Richarde, Tessa 76
Richards, Addison 243
Richards, Dawn 276
Richards, Ethel Robins 82, 152
Richards, Evan 123
Richards, Gwill 298
Richards, Jeff 35
Richards, Kim 158, 159
Richards, Kyle 244
Richards, Paul 381
Richards, Stony 67
Richards, Susan 509
Richards, Ted 482
Richards, Terry 408
Richardson, Edward 75
Richardson, John 24, 261, 310, 367
Richardson, John (actor) 372, 436, 437
Richardson, Lee 165, 182
Richardson, Patricia 83
Richardson, Ralph 22
Richfield, Edwin 400, 404
Richins, Keith 416
Richman, Peter Mark 225, 226
Richmond, Anthony B. 68
Richmond, Bill 118
Richmond, Irene 309
Richmond, Ken 333
Richmond, Ralph 375
Richmond, Tony 152
Richter, Daniel 499
Richter, W.D. 153, 286
Richwood, Frank 388
Ricketts, Tom 188
Riddle, Nelson 47
Ridgely, John 128

Ridley, Emma 523
Ridley, Judith 347
Riedel, Richard 293
Rieva, Gladys 328
Riggins, Terrence 352
Riley, Jack 36, 84
Rilla, Wolf 508, 511
Rimmer, Shane 91, 310, 464
Rinaldi, Joe 39
Rinaldo, Frederic I. 192, 293
Ring, John 32
Ringwood, Bob 47
Ripper, Michael 139, 143, 145, 146, 197, 342, 344, 346, 362, 400
Ripps, Michael 91
Risch, Peter 235
Risher, Sara 361
Riskin, Everett 242, 257
Riskin, Robert 315
Rist, Robbie 473, 475
Ristic, Suzane 182
Ritchie, June 334
Ritter, Joe 490
Ritter, Thelma 331
Ritz, Jim 84
Ritz, Melinda 37
Roach, Daryl 516
Roach, Hal 38, 371, 372, 488, 489
Roach, Hal, Jr. 371
Roach, Pat 87, 90, 408, 410, 412
The Road Warrior 417, 486; see also *Mad Max II*
Roadman, Betty 72
Robbins, Anatole 281
Robbins, Brian 84
Robbins, Cindy 276
Robbins, Gary 439
Robbins, Will 56
Robby the Robot 242
Robert Short Productions, Inc. 84
Roberts, Allan 258
Roberts, Arthur 281, 364
Roberts, Beatrice 190
Roberts, Byron 178
Roberts, Florence 38
Roberts, Irmin 89
Roberts, Leona 65
Roberts, Nicki 397
Roberts, Randy 366
Roberts, Steve 382
Roberts, Tanya 54
Roberts, Tony 33
Robertson, Gordon 439
Robertson, John Forbes 503
Robertson, Kimmy 263
Robertson, R.J. 55, 267, 364

Robertson, Willard 127
Robertson, William Preston 160
Robin Hood: Men in Tights 213
Robins, Oliver 385, 386
Robins, Sheila 509
Robinson, Andrew 254, 493
Robinson, Bernard 135, 139, 143, 206, 325, 342, 345, 400
Robinson, Dewey 65
Robinson, Edward R. 71
Robinson, Frances 114, 291
Robinson, George 71, 116, 130, 131, 133, 187, 190, 293, 337, 340
Robinson, Harry 503, 506, 508
Robinson, Henry Ford 527
Robinson, J. Peter 229, 351, 361
Robinson, Jay 156
Robinson, Joe 117
Robinson, John 403
Robinson, Mabel 522
Robinson, Max 249
Robinson, Peter Manning 105
Robinson, Ruth 315
Robitaille, Ginette 125
Robledo, Rafael H. 109
Robocop 110, 416–418
Robocop 2 418–419
Robocop 3 419–420
Robot Monster 77
Robson, Flora 22
Robson, Mark 72
Robson, May 21
Rocco, Alex 319
Rocco, Mary 218
Roche, Eugene 366
Rock, Kevin 275, 513
"Rock Around the Clock" (song) 463
Rockafellow, Marilyn 360
Rocket to the Moon 77; see also *Cat-Women of the Moon*)
Rockett, Norman 383
Rockow, Jill 221
Rockwell, Jack 132
Rockwell, Rick 37, 38
Rockwell, Sam 473
Rocky 33
Roda, Robert 476
Roddam, Franc 212
Roddenberry, Gene 439, 442, 444, 446, 447, 449, 450

Rodero, Pepe Lopez 86
Rodgers, Agie Guerard 457
Rodgers, Anton 427
Rodgers, Richard 240
Rodine, Alex 518
Rodis-Jamero, Nilo 447, 457
Rodriquez, Charles 522
Roe, Matt 81, 393
Roeg, Nicholas 171
Roehn, Franz 177, 198
Roelofs, Al 158
Roemheld, Heinz 130, 258
Roerick, William 363
Roessell, David 109
Rogan, Beth 497, 498
Roger Corman's Frankenstein Unbound 214–215
Rogers, Charles 38
Rogers, Jean 176
Rogers, Jeffrey 220
Rogers, John 112, 116, 473
Rogers, Liz 93
Rogers, Mark 92
Rogers, Will 89
Rohm, Maria 379
Roisman, Harper 249
Roizman, Owen 20, 162
Rojas, Emmanuel I. 295
"Roland" (TV show host) 131
Roland, Jeanne 344
Rolfe, Charles 332
Rolfe, Guy 212, 213, 395, 396, 397
Rollett, Raymond 194
Rollings, Gordon 464
Rollins, Leslie 331
Rolston, Mark 24, 418, 423
Romano, Carlos 33
Romano, Renato 379
Romanoff, Liz 121
Romans, Cherie 359
Romanus, Robert 252
Romeo and Juliet 501
Romero, Alex 152
Romero, Cesar 47, 50
Romero, Eddie F. 295
Romero, George A. 102, 103, 347, 348, 349, 351, 352, 414
Romero, Ned 79, 267
Ronalds, Lolita 516
Ronne, David 447
Ronzana, Peter 416
Rooney, Wallace 162
Roose, Ronald 449
Roper, Gil 46
Roquette, Suzane 412
Rosado, Carleen 46
Rose, Bernard 68

Rose, Chris 362
Rose, Dan 240
Rose, Earl 61
Rose, Helen 238
Rose, Roger 223
Rose, Ruth 302, 435
Rose, Sherman 137
Rose, Tim 523
Rose, Tim (actor) 457
Rosemary's Baby 368
Rosen, Charles 286
Rosen, Jimmy 21
Rosenberg, Arthur 123
Rosenberg, John 330
Rosenberg, Max J. 126, 127, 309, 310
Rosenberg, Philip 522
Rosenberg, Stuart 31
Rosenblat, Barbara 314
Rosener, George 127
Rosenfarb, Bob 67
Rosenfelt, Scott M. 277
Rosenman, Leonard 381, 384, 418, 446
Rosenstock, Harvey 278
Rosenthal, Laurence 297
Rosenthal, Mark 449, 468
Rosenthal, Rick 246
Rosenthal, Robert 527
Roskilly, Charles 48
Ross, Annie 45, 46, 465, 466
Ross, Arthur 94, 96, 100
Ross, Chelcie 57
Ross, Diana 522, 523
Ross, Gaylen 102, 348, 349
Ross, Gene 248
Ross, Joe E. 316
Ross, Liza 48
Ross, Neil 42, 242
Ross, Ricco 24
Ross, Shavar 222
Ross, Stephen 217
Ross, Ted 181
Ross, Ted (actor) 32, 522
Rossi, Alfred 158
Rossi, Leo 246, 328
Rossiter, Leonard 499
Rossito, Angelo (*Dracula vs. Frankenstein*) 147
Rossitto, Angelo (*Mad Max: Beyond Thunderdome*) 323
Rosson, Edward 152
Rosson, Harold 520
Rossovich, Rick 476
Roth, Christopher 353
Roth, Dan 59
Roth, George 48
Roth, Richard 210
Rothe Caprice 84

Rothman, John 233
Rothman, Marion 296, 381, 382
Rothschild, Elan 423
Rothschild, Gerry 244
Rothschild, Richard Luke 369
Rotundo, Nick 391, 392
Rougas, Michael 276, 440
Roundtree, Richard 35, 327, 328
Roustabout 222
Rowan, Kelly 70, 229
Rowe, Bill 148
Rowe, Clint 247
Rowe, Doug 104
Rowe, Freddie 275
Rowe, Jack 175
Rowland, Elise ("Cricket") 52, 282, 329
Rowlands, Patsy 309
Rowley, Dinah Sue 84
Rowley, Sharon 177
Roy, Deep 523
Roy, Rob 182
Rozsa, Miklos 324, 431
Rub, Christian 71, 131
Ruban, Al 469
Rubenstein, Phil 329, 418
Rubin, Benny 257, 434
Rubin, Bruce 527
Rubin, Jack 77
Rubin, Jennifer 356
Rubin, Murray 233
Rubins, Marybeth 390
Rubinstein, Richard P. 102, 348, 349, 373
Rubinstein, Zelda 385, 386, 387
Ruby, Harry 35
Ruck, Alan 450
Rudd, Paul Stephen 250
Rudin, Scott 20
Rudnick, Paul 20
Rudnik, Oleg 501
Rudy, Reed 527
Ruffner, Benjamin 248
Ruggles, Charles (Charlie) 19, 21
Rugoff, Edward 329, 330
Ruman, Sig 191
Runyon, Jennifer 233
Runyon, Kenneth 427
Ruprecht, David 125
Rush, Don 227
Rushton, Jared 263, 374
Rusk, John 387
Ruskin, Shimen 307
Rusler, Robert 355
Rusoff, Lou 75

Russell, Barbara 349
Russell, Bing 143
Russell, Chuck 63, 356
Russell, Elizabeth 72, 74
Russell, Frank 106
Russell, Gordon 268
Russell, Johnny 65
Russell, Ken 122, 124
Russell, Keri 264
Russell, Kurt 481, 484
Russell, Nipsey 522
Russell, Ray 169
Russell, William 461
Russo, Gus 44
Russo, John A. 347, 350, 352
Russo, Matt 461
Russom, Leon 449
Rutherford, Ann 426
Rutherford, Margaret 332, 333, 334
Ruttenberg, Joseph 114
Ruud, Michael 248
Ryan, Brendan 57
Ryan, John P. 298, 300, 518
Ryan, Meg 33, 34
Ryan, Mitchell 250, 251
Ryan, Natasha 31
Ryan, Pat, Jr. 490
Ryan, Remy 419
Ryan, Robert 231, 498, 499
Ryan, Stephanie 215
Rydbeck, Whitney 223
Ryder, Alfred 158
Ryder, Mark 491, 492, 493
Ryder, Winona 155, 157
Rye, Michael 320
Ryen, Adam 81
Ryerson, Florence 520
Ryerson, Kevin 386

Sabella, Ernie 228
Sacks, Michael 31
Sader, Alan 306
Sadler, William 56, 57
Sadoff, Jay 224
Sadoff, Martin Jay 220
Saenz, Jorge 388
Safan, Craig 357
Sagal, Joey 472
Sager, Ray 392, 393
Sagoes, Ken 356, 357
St. James, Susan 152
St. John, Gina 80
St. John, Marco 222
Saint-Simon, Lucile 320
Saito, James 473
Sakow, Bruce Hidemi 221
Saland, Ellen 31
Saland, Ronald 31
Salata, Paul 35

Sale, Virginia 488
Salenger, Meredith 511
Saletri, Frank R. 209
Salkind, Ilya 461, 463, 465, 466
Salkind Brothers 176
Sallin, Robert 442
Sallis, Crispian 24
Sallis, Peter 145, 334
Salmi, Albert 382
Salomon, Mikael 244
Salsedo, Frank 103
Salten, Felix 433, 434
Salter, Hans J. 94, 131, 189, 190, 291, 292, 336, 337, 339, 524
Salter, Mary 469
Salvati, Sergio 236, 393
Salzedo, Leonard 197
Sambrell, Aldo 431
Samples, Candy 175
Sampson, Donre 249
Sampson, Robert 413
Sampson, Will 386
Samuel, Joanne 321
Samuels, Ted 22, 126, 127
Sand, Paul 278
Sande, Walter 132, 243, 281
Sanders, Beverly 152
Sanders, Cliff 400
Sanders, Cornelia 370
Sanders, George 377, 378, 508
Sanders, Hugh 232
Sanders, Jay O. 36
Sanders, Larry 411
Sanders, Ronald 181, 230, 420
Sanders, Sam 387
Sanders, Shepherd 158
Sanders, Stuart 333
Sandford, Christopher 152
Sandin, Will 245
Sands, Julian 512, 513
Sands, Tibor 33
Sands, Tommy 39, 40
Sandweiss, Ellen 159
Sandy the dog 514
Sanford, Isabel 152
Sangster, Jimmy 135, 139, 194, 197, 207, 325, 342, 506
Sansom, John 140
Sanstorm, R.O.C. 161
Santon, Penny 438
Santos, Gervasio 295
Santos, Hilario 295
Sanz, Jorge 86
Sapag, Edwardo 261
Saperstein, David 84, 85

Saraceni, Gene A. 349
Saraceni, Iva Jean 102
Sarafian, Deren 486
Sarandon, Chris 80, 227, 228, 252, 254
Sarecky, Barney A. 460
Sarno, Robert 273
Sarrazin, Michael 217
Sasdy, Peter 145
The Satanic Rites of Dracula 149–150
Saturday Night Fever 391
Saturday Night Live (TV series) 234
Saunder, George 423
Saunders, Irv 147
Saunders, Russ 316
Saunders, Stuart 334
Savage, Brad 159
Savage, Nick 220, 227
Savage, Tracie 220
Savage Streets 164, 167
Savant, Doug 328
Saville, Victor 114
Savini, Tom 102, 103, 217, 221, 348, 349, 352
Sawalha, Nadim 64, 432
Sawaya, George 47, 321
Sawtell, Paul 72, 116, 177, 178, 339
Saxon, Aaron 170
Saxon, John 354, 356, 361
Sayle, Alexie 212, 411
Sayles, John 271
Saylor, Syd 293
Sayonara 178
Scaife, Hugh 165
Scanlan, Neal 314
Scanner Cop 423–424, 425
Scanners 420–421, 438, 514
Scanners II: The New Order 421–422
Scanners III: The Takeover 422–423
Scanners 4: The Showdown 424–425
Scantlebury, Glen 155
Scared Stiff 231–232
Scargill, Karen 427
Scars of Dracula 145–147, 155, 228
Schachter, Bradley 247
Schaffer, Lauren 492
Schaffner, Franklin 380
Schalman, Tom 263
Scharf, Walter 118, 238, 307, 519
Schayer, Richard 334, 342
Scheer, Philip 195
Scheider, Roy 501

Schell, Maria 461
Schell, Ronnie 152, 434
Schenck, Aubrey 198
Schenck, Earl 243
Schenck, George 518
Schepps, Shawn 476
Scherer, Donna Stamps 104
Scherrer, Paul 79
Schiano, Natasha 67
Schiff, Marty 102, 348
Schifrin, Lalo 31, 32, 159
Schiller, Norbert 137, 198, 482
Schindler, Peter 122
Schindler's List 109
Schirmer, Chason 360
Schliessler, Tobias A. 70
Schlugleit, Eugene 160
Schmidt, Arne 416
Schmidt, Arthur P. 20, 40, 42, 43, 238
Schmidt, Ronn 55, 236, 480
Schmoeller, David 393
Schmoeller, Gary 23, 353
Schnabel, Stefan 155
Schneer, Charles H. 429, 431, 497
Schneider, Gary 490
Schneider, John 106
Schneider, Natasha 501
Schoedsack, Ernest B. 302, 304
Schoelen, Jill 107
Schoenberg, Burt 167
Schoenfeld, Brent 359, 480, 481
Schoengarth, Russell 116, 133, 340
Schofield, Leslie 452
Schon, Kyra 347
Schoolnik, Skip 122, 246
Schoonraad, John 260
Schoppe, James 457
Schow, David J. 105
Schoweiler, John 394, 395
Schrader, Paul 75
Schrage, Lisa 184, 391, 392
Schramm, William 131
Schreck, Max 155, 488
Schroeder, Michael 224
Schrum, Pete 478
Schubert, Bernard 71, 339
Schuler, Fred 33
Schulman, Leo 128
Schulthies, Charles 516
Schultz, Raymond 21
Schumacher, Joel 52, 521
Schumacher, Martha 306
Schunzel, Reinhold 324
Schuylerberke, Mayne 475

Schwab, Lana 166
Schwalm, James D. 80
Schwartz, Howard 47, 518
Schwartz, John 349
Schwartz, Sarah 186
Schwartz, Theo 42
Schwarzenegger, Arnold 86, 87, 88, 388, 417, 476, 477, 478, 479, 480
Schweitzer, Michael 490
Schwiers, Ellen 309
Schwimmer, Rusty 261
Scoble, Lesley 509
Scoby, Robin 454
Scoggins, Tracy 515
Scoppa, Justin 33
Scorsese, Martin 300, 379
Scotford, Sybil 59, 92
Scott, Alex 15, 508
Scott, Allan 64
Scott, Ben R. 386
Scott, Bruce 177
Scott, Cynthia 24
Scott, Deborah L. 40
Scott, Donovan 43
Scott, Elliot 510
Scott, George C. 164, 165
Scott, Harold 139
Scott, John 31, 306
Scott, Kathryn Leigh 268, 269
Scott, Kevin 314
Scott, Linda 517
Scott, Lizabeth 232
Scott, Michael 214
Scott, Michele 201
Scott, Nicola 412
Scott, Randolph 435, 436
Scott, Ridley 23, 27, 29
Scott, Stephen 411
Scott, Tom 319, 383
Scott, Walter (stunt man) 43
Scott, Walter M. (set director) 47, 178, 382
Scott-Taylor, Jonathan 369
Scotti, Vito 317, 319
Scotton, Myrtle 375
Scougall, Adam 323
Scourby, Alexander 433
Scream Blacula Scream 59–60
Screaming Mad George 79, 106, 357, 415
Scrimm, Angus 375, 376, 377
Scrooge (1935) 425
Scrooge (1951) see *A Christmas Carol* (1951)
Scrooge (1970) 426–427, 428

Scrooged 427, 429
Scurfield, Matthew 408
"The Sea Monster" (story idea) 96
Seagrave, Malcolm 375
Seale, Douglas 234
The Search for Spock see *Star Trek III: The Search for Spock*
The Searchers 39
Searle, Ronald 427
Sears, Anthony 472
Sears, Fred 258
Season of the Witch see *Halloween III: Season of the Witch*
Seaton, George 331
Seawright, Roy 371, 488, 489
Seay, James 30, 331
Seberg, Jean 333
The Second Story see *House II: The Second Story*
The Secret of Dorian Gray 379
The Secret of the Ooze see *Teenage Mutant Ninja Turtles II: The Secret of the Ooze*
Secrist, Kim 278
Seddon, Corinna 362
"See the Phantoms" (song) 427
Seedpeople 288
Seely, Joe 359
Segal, Fancine 76
Segal, Zohra 437
Segall, Harry 257, 258, 259
Segall, Pamela 230
Seitz, John 281
Sekine, Tsutomu 491
Selby, David 270, 271
Self, William 482
Selland, Marie 284
Sellars, Elizabeth 346
Selleck, Tom 409
Sellers, Peter 22, 333, 334
Seltzer, David 367, 369
Selznick, David O. 302
Semilian, Julian 423
Semler, Dean 322, 323
Semple, Lorenzo, Jr. 47, 175, 305
Seneca, Joe 63
Senter, Jack 159, 365
"The Sentinel" (short story) 499
Serafine, Frank 386, 438, 444
Serling, Rod 380

Serra, Raymond 473, 474
Serrano, Sandy 527
Sersen, Fred 65, 88, 331
Sessions, Almira 519
Seth, Roshan 410
Sevareid, Susanne 274
The Seven Brothers Meet Dracula see *The Legend of the 7 Golden Vampires*
The Seven Year Itch 101
The 7th Voyage of Sinbad 429–431
Severn, Raymond 243
Severn, Yvonne 243
Sevi, Mark 237, 424
Sewell, Blanche 520
Sewell, George 437
Sexton, Sandra 107
Sexton, Tobe 360
Seyffertitz, Gustav von 188, 435
Seyler, Athene 425
Seymour, Anne 491
Seymour, Dan 158, 178, 341
Seymour, Jane 432, 433
Seymour, Michael 23
Seymour, Ralph 235
Sgueglia, Anthony 366
Shaffer, Henry 165
Shaft 59
Shaftel, Josef 22
Shaggy (dog) 434
The Shaggy D.A. 434–435
The Shaggy Dog 433–434
Shah, Kiran 310, 408
Shaiman, Marc 20
Shaine, Rick 354
Shalikar, Daniel 264
Shalikar, Joshua 264
Sham Unlimited 77, 199
Shamata, Charles 420
Shamroy, Leon 380
Shane 252
Shane, Gene 144
Shane, Maxwell 336
Shaner, John 312
Shaner, John Herman 296
Shanks, Donald L. 249, 250
Shannon, Harry 339
Shannon, Michael J. 464
Shannon, Robert G. 17
Shaphren, Brent 387
Shapiro, Robert 125
Shaps, Cyril 90
Sharkey, Billy Ray 438
Sharp, Don 180, 181
Sharp, Henry 21, 324
Sharp, Rachel 278
Sharp, Thom J. 166
Sharpe, Don 47

Sharpe, Lester 339
Shatner, Melanie 447
Shatner, William 57, 440, 442, 444, 445, 446, 447, 448, 449, 450
Shaughnessy, Alfred 75
Shaver, Helen 31
Shaver, Paul 364
Shaw, Dennis 342
Shaw, Janet 337
Shaw, Martin 431
Shaw, Mary Ellen 375
Shaw, Reta 158
Shaw, Sebastian 457
Shaw, Stan 214
Shaw, Vee King 150
Shaw, Victoria 516
Shawlee, Joan 519
Shawn, Dick 152
Shay, Mildred 314
Shaye, Lin 104, 125, 354
Shaye, Robert 354, 355, 356, 357, 359, 360, 361
Shayne, Konstantin 324
Shayne, Robert 281
She (1935) 435–436
She (1965) 436–437
She (book) 436
She, Elizabeth 275, 276
She and Allan (book) 436
Shea, John 264
Shea, Shannon 446
Shea, Tom 219
Shea, William 112
Shean, Al 65
Sheard, Michael 454
Shearn, Patrick 45
Sheedy, Ally 438
Sheffield, Reginald 324
Shefter, Bert 178
Sheldon, Gene 39, 40
Sheldon, Greg 46
Sheldon, Louis 412
Shellen, Stephen 125
Shelley, Barbara 40, 75, 140, 508
Shelley, Mary Wollstonecraft 184, 185, 189, 194, 207, 210, 217
Shellhammer, Albert 352
Shenson, Walter 333, 334
Shepard, Courtland 178
Shepard, Dodie 449
Shepard, Elaine 488
Shepard, Hilary 423
Shepard, Jewel 350
Shepherd, Elizabeth 173, 174, 369, 370
Shepherd, John 222
Shepherd, Pauline 117

Shepherd, Robert 282
Shepherd, Steve 56
Shepphird, Carol 302
Sher, Anthony 464
Sher, Ken 223
Sheridan, Liz 125
Sheridan, Margaret 482, 483, 484, 484
Sheriff, R.C. 289
"Sheriff of Cochise" (TV series) 99
Sherman, Gary 386
Sherman, George 307
Sherman, Howard 349
Sherman, Richard M. 239
Sherman, Robert B. 239
Sherman, Robert M. 366
Sherman, Vincent 128
Sherrod, John 220, 221
Sherry, Diane 461
Sherwin, Derick 437
Sherwood, John 100, 101
Shewchuk, Steve 438
Shields, Arthur 117, 118, 379
Shields, Sonny 222
Shigeta, James 316
Shih Szu 150
Shimono, Sab 475
Shingleton, Wilfred 279
The Shining 394
Shire, David 366, 438, 501, 523
Shirley, John 468
Shirley, Peg 93
Shirriff, Cathie 444
Shirriff, Cathy 152
Shock Theater (TV) 190, 216
Shockley, William 275
Sholder, Jack 355
Sholem, Lee 460
Shongwe, Dumi 107
Shook, Warner 102
Shoop, Pamela Susan 246
Shor, Dan 56
Shore, Dinah 365
Shore, Howard 181, 420
Shore, Richard 270
Shore, Roberta 433
Shorr, Bill 398
Short, Gertrude 305
Short, Robert 85
Short Circuit 438
Short Circuit 2 438
Shostrom, Mark 160, 355, 376, 377
"Show Me Your Spine" (song) 416
Showacre, David 76
Shuck, John 446, 449
Shue, Elizabeth 42, 43

Shugrue, Robert F. 444
Shuman, Felix 370
Shumway, Lee 292
Shusett, Ronald 27, 306
Shuster, Joe 461, 465, 468, 469
Sibbald, Tony 464
Sibbett, Jane 252, 253
Sibert, Roderick Spencer 522
Sickner, William 339
Sidley, Roberd 252
Sidney, Sylvia 369
Siegel, Don 284, 285, 287, 288, 289, 404, 485
Siegel, Jerry 461, 465, 468, 469
Siegel, Otto 307
Siegler, Marc 359
Siemaszko, Casey 40, 42
Sierra, Gregory 264, 381
Sighvatsson, Sigurjon 68, 69
Sikking, James B. 382, 444
Silla, Felix 265
Silliphant, Stirling 508, 511
Silva, Henry 238
Silver, Erik 265
Silver, Joel 124, 388
Silver, Mark 265
Silver, Michael 226
Silver, Ron 366
Silver, Timothy 22
Silvera, Darrell 72, 74, 482
Silverman, Robert 390, 420
Silvern, Charles 21
Silvestri, Alan 40, 42, 43, 388
Sim, Alastair 426, 428
Sim, Gerald 16, 121, 239
Simmons, Ed 232
Simmons, Paul A. 469
Simmons, Stan 180
Simon, Gayle 416
Simon, Marty 422
Simon, Mayo 518
Simon, Simone 72, 73
Simons, Roger 510
Simonson, Theodore 60
Simpson, Brock 391, 393
Simpson, Claire 83
Simpson, Ivan 291
Simpson, Jonathan 447
Simpson, Peter 390, 391, 392
Simpson, Rick 501
Simpson, Robert 331
Simpson, Tom 372
Sims, Candice 155
Sims, Devin Corrie 487
Sinbad and the Eye of the Tiger 431–433

Sinbad the Sailor 433
Sinclair, Gabriella 84
Sinclair, Ronald 30, 169, 170, 251, 426
Sinden, Donald 333
Sinden, Jeremy 452
Singer, Lori 512
Singer, Marc 54, 515
Singer, Matt 516
Singer, Raymond 81
Singer Midgets 520
Singh, Raj 410
Singleton, Ralph S. 374
Sinutko, Shane 434
Siodmak, Curt (Kurt) 190, 291, 292, 307, 524
Siodmak, Robert 131
Sir Lancelot 74
Sirius Effects 155
Sirlin, Arnie 84
Sirtis, Marina 450
Siskel, Gene 475
Sisters 300
Sisti, Michelan 472, 474
Siteman, Arthur 482
Siter, Tom 155
Skaaren, Warren 47
Skaggs, Jimmie 393
Skeggs, Roy 149, 208
Skerritt, Tom 23, 27, 386
Skinner, Frank 187, 192, 291, 524
Skip, John 359
Skippy (dog) 489
Skipworth, Alison 22
Sklover, Carl 293
Skornarovsky, Vladimir 501
Skotak, Dennis 24
Skotak, Robert 24
Slate, Henry 319, 434
Slater, Christian 449
Slater, Helen 466, 467
Slattery, Page 203
Slattery, Richard X. 317
Slimon, Scott 126
Slingsby, David 322
Slipper and the Rose: The Story of Cinderella 239–240
Sloan, Holly Goldberg 36
Sloan, Ron 222
Sloane, Bart 61
Sloatman, Lala 35
Slocombe, Douglas 407, 410, 411
Slyter, Fred 438
Small, Marya 527
Small, Merrya 393
Smalls, Charlie 522
Smiley, Des 252

Smith, Allison 226
Smith, Bert 6
Smith, Bobbie 427
Smith, Brendan 392, 472, 474
Smith, Brian 509
Smith, Bubba 242
Smith, Bud 75, 108, 162
Smith, C. Aubrey 114
Smith, Charles 243
Smith, Charles Martin 319
Smith, Christine 506
Smith, Dick 123, 162, 164, 177, 268, 386, 420
Smith, Earl E. 311
Smith, Emmett 132
Smith, Frazier 166
Smith, Harry 460
Smith, Herb 438
Smith, Herbert 75
Smith, Howard 348
Smith, Ira N. 32
Smith, Irby 36
Smith, Jack Martin 381, 382
Smith, Kent 72, 73, 74, 316
Smith, Kurtwood 416, 417, 449
Smith, Lee 273
Smith, Leslie 67
Smith, Maddy/Madeline/ Madeleine 145, 208, 209, 503, 506
Smith, Madolyn 501
Smith, Marc 370
Smith, Margaret-Anne 396, 397, 492–493
Smith, Maurice 176
Smith, Melanie 493
Smith, Nicholas C. 155
Smith, Norman 240
Smith, Oliver 254, 255
Smith, Paul (composer) 433, 495
Smith, Paul Gerard (dialogue) 489
Smith, Pete 446
Smith, Robert E. 100
Smith, Scott 108
Smith, Shawnee 63
Smith, Terri Susan 44
Smith, Thorne 488, 489
Smith, Tom 207, 503
Smith, Wendel 391
Smith, William 86, 87, 327, 328
Smith, Willie E. 311
Smith, Wonderful 365
Smithee, Alan (fictitious director and screenwriter name) 266

Smithson, Michael (Mike) 278, 422
Smolinski, Aaron 461
Smothers, Loren 244
Smuin, Michael 155
Smythe Sally 352
Snell, Patsy 498
Snell, Richard 446
Snook, Dan 78
Snowden, Leigh 100, 101
Snyder, Howard 293
Snyder, Michael 446
Snyder, Ray 71, 371
Snyder, Suzanne 351
Snyder, William E. 94
Sobiesk, David 311
Soho, Jerry 110
Soisson, Joel 55, 328
Sokoloff, Vladimir 276
Soldi, Steve 72
Soles, P.J. 244
Solito, Samuel R. 347
Solo, Robert H. 64, 286, 288, 426
Solomon, Ed 55, 56
Solon, Ewen 90, 362
Sommer, Josef 155
Son of Blob see *Beware! The Blob*
Son of Darkness: To Die For II 487–488
Son of Dr. Jekyll 116, 117
Son of Dracula (1943) 131–133
Son of Dracula (1974) 151–152
Son of Flubber 19–20, 318, 434
Son of Frankenstein 187–189
Son of Kong 304–305
Sondergaard, Gale 65, 292
Sonnenfeld, Barry 20
Soo, Jack 159
Soper, Mark 240
Sorel, George 131
Sorel, Ted 45
Sorensen, Michael 439
Sorensen, Fred 408
Sorenson, Heidi 227
Sorenson, Paul 158
Sorrell, Rozlyn 356
Sorrells, Bill 259
Sorvino, Paul 365
Sosalla, David 263
Sound Busters 274
South, Leonard J. 318
Southam, Suzy 78
Southcott, Colin 110, 173
Souther, J.D. 244
Southwick, Brad 79

592 Index

Sowards, Jack B. 442
Sowder, Cindi 235
The Spaceman and King Arthur see *Unidentified Flying Oddball*
A Spaceman in King Arthur's Court see *Unidentified Flying Oddball*
Spadaro, Michele 328
Spader, James 329
Spain, Mark 323
Spalding, Harry 180
Spalding, Thomas 61
Sparks, Ned 22
Spartels, George 323
Spaull, Tom 212
Speaker, Dan 161
Spear, Bernard 127
Spears, Steve J. 322
Speck, Jan 438
Spector, Craig 359
Speed 56
Spellos, Peter 360
Spelman, Sharon 63
Spence, Bruce 322, 323
Spence, Michael 527
Spence, Stephen 314
Spencer, Cleon 464
Spencer, Douglas 482, 483, 484
Spengler, Pierre 461, 463, 465
Spenser, Derek 472
Spenser, Jeremy 309
Sperber, Wendie Jo 40, 43
Sperling, David 67
S.P.F.X., Ltd. 424
Spheeris, Linda 247
Spiegel, Scott 160
Spielberg, Steven 42, 43, 97, 241, 242, 244, 385, 407, 409, 410, 411, 413, 442, 460
Spier, Carol 420
Spila, Otello 379
Spiner, Brent 450
Spink, Justin Mosley 42
Spinks, James 370
Spivak, Murray 302
Spolan, Michael 102
Spooks Run Wild 157
Spotts, George 281
Spradling, Charlie 394
Sprager, Hart 356
Sprague, Chandler 242, 244
Spring, Helen 192, 519
Spring Break 266
Springer, Patricia 366
Sprinkle, Larry 306
Sprotte, Bert 131
Spurlock, Robert 446

Stacy, Eddie 47
Stader, Paul 192
Stadner, Suzan 351
Stafford, Gilbert 32
Stafford, Robert 158
Stahl, Richard 61
Stamp, Terence 461, 464, 465
Stampe, Will 121
Standaart, Gianni 220
Standing, Joan 129
Standord, Jeremy 516
Stanhope, Paul 199
Stanhope, Warren 180
Stanley, David 79
Stanley, Ken 333
Stannard, Roy 508
Stanton, Barry 91
Stanton, Dan 242
Stanton, Don 242, 478
Stanton, Ernie 524
Stanton, Harry Dean 23, 27
Stapleton, James 320
Stapleton, Maureen 84, 85
Star Trek (TV series) 439, 441, 442, 444, 446, 447, 449, 450
Star Trek: Deep Space Nine (TV series) 451
Star Trek: First Contact 452
Star Trek: Generations 450–452
Star Trek: Voyager (TV series) 451
Star Trek — The Motion Picture 439–442
Star Trek II — The Wrath of Khan 442–443, 445
Star Trek III: The Search for Spock 443–446, 486
Star Trek IV: The Voyage Home 445, 446–447
Star Trek V: The Final Frontier 447–449
Star Trek VI: The Undiscovered Country 449–450, 452
Star Wars 106, 207, 311, 409, 441, 452–454, 457, 459, 463
Starbuck, Michele 228
Stargate Films 166
Stark, John 183
Stark, Jonathan 227, 266
Starke, Anthony 37, 166
Starr, Beau 248
Starr, Bruce 67
Starr, Kay 258
Starr, Ringo 151
Stars and Stripes Forever 252

Stateman, Wylie 263
Statham, Patrick 364
Staunton, Anne 331
Stavin, Mary 265, 275
Stavrakis, Taso N. 348, 349
Stay, Richard 248
Steafel, Sheila 404
Steagall, Debra 221
Stearns, Craig 78, 244, 282
Stearns, Michael 384
Stears, John 64, 453
Steedman, Tony 56
Steedman, Trevor 24
Steel, Amy 219, 220
Steel, Charles 195
Steel, Pippa see Steele, Pippa
Steele, Barbara 168
Steele, Don 241
Steele, Gary 512
Steele, Gile 114
Steele, Pippa 503, 506, 508
Steele, Tom 482
Steen, Derek 121
Steenburgen, Mary 43
Steens, Eileen 284
Stefani, Michael 491
Stefanovic, Jasna 393
Steiger, Rod 31, 32
Stein, Herman 97
Stein, Peter 83, 219, 373
Stein, Ronald 169, 251, 252, 363
Steinbach, Victor 501
Steindler, Maureen 387
Steiner, Max 302, 435, 436
Steinfeld, Jake 166
Steinkamp, Frederick 427
Steinkamp, William 427
Steinke, Hans 294
Steinmann, Danny 222
Stelfox, Shirley 362
Steloff, Skip 296
Stensgaard, Yutte 506, 507, 508
Stephen King's Graveyard Shift 241
Stephens, Garn 247
Stephens, Martin 279, 508
Stephens, Nancy 245, 246
Stephenson, Geoffrey 273
Stephenson, Pamela 465, 466
Steranko, Jim 155
Sterland, John 47
Sterling, Jan 362
Sterling, William 22
Stern, Daniel 83
Stern, Philip 240
Stern, Sandor 31

Stern, Stewart 227
Sternad, Rudolph 258
Sterne, David 432
Sterne, Gordon 260
Steven, Carl 263, 444
Stevens, Alex 268
Stevens, Andrew 480, 481
Stevens, Butch (dog) 480
Stevens, Casey 390
Stevens, Craig 116, 117
Stevens, Fisher 438, 439
Stevens, Harvey 367
Stevens, K.T. 77
Stevens, Leith 232
Stevens, Onslow 133, 135
Stevens, Paul 384
Stevens, Ronald Smokey 522
Stevens, Stella 118, 119, 481
Stevens, W.L. 371, 488, 489
Stevens, William 74, 482
Stevenson, Al 104
Stevenson, Bill 81
Stevenson, Edward 74
Stevenson, Michael A. 263, 264
Stevenson, Robert (actor) 482
Stevenson, Robert (director) 17, 19, 316, 317, 434
Stevenson, Robert Louis 112, 114, 117, 121, 124, 125, 126
Stevenson, Tom 524
Steward, Ernest 333
Steward, Karen 374
Stewart, Charles 30
Stewart, Donald 482
Stewart, Douglas 286
Stewart, Edward 522
Stewart, Jim 364
Stewart, M. 37
Stewart, Mary 186
Stewart, Mark 468
Stewart, Marlene 478
Stewart, Mel 415
Stewart, Patrick 450, 451
Stewart, Robert 309
Stewart, Robin 150
Stewart, Roy 508
Steyn, Jennifer 107
Stierman, Vern 311
Stiers, David Ogden 365
Stine, Clifford 100, 340
Sting 212, 213
Stiven, David 322
Stock-Poynton, Amy 56
Stockdale, Carl 315
Stockdale, Kim 82
Stockwell, Guy 298, 300
Stofer, Scott 514
Stoica, Luana 494

Stoker, Austin 384
Stoker, Bram 64, 129, 130, 133, 135, 136, 143, 153, 155, 157, 346, 506
Stoker, Cliff 240
Stokes, Terry 63, 356
Stoler, Shirley 215
Stoll, John 431
Stoltz, Eric 182, 183
Stone, Barry 240
Stone, Christopher 248, 271
Stone, Christopher L. (composer) 376, 377
Stone, Danny 233
Stone, David 242
Stone, Dee Wallace 103
Stone, Ivory 209
Stone, Lewis 35
Stone, Marianne 333, 400, 427
Stone, Michael 35
Stone, Milburn 71, 281, 292
Stone, Oliver 86
Stone, Paddy 426, 427
Stone, Philip 175, 410
Stone, Scott 79
Stone, Wayne 476
Stoneground 148
Stoner, Joy 195
Storey, Lynn 312
Storey, Raymond G. 351
Storm, James 270
Storrs, David 282
Stossel, Ludwig 133
Stothart, Herbert 243, 377, 520
Stott, Wally 497
Stovall, Tom 183
Strader, Paul 301
Stradling, Harry 377
Straight, Beatrice 385
Straight, Clarence 192
Strait, Ralph 247
Strange, Glenn 133, 191, 192, 193, 207, 212, 337
Strange, Richard 47
The Strange Case of Dr. Jekyll and Mr. Hyde (book) 112, 114, 117, 124, 125
"Strange Love" (song) 157, 506, 507
Strassman, Marcia 263, 264
Stratford, Tracy 201
Stratton, John 208
Stratton, Rick 475
Strauss, Johann 499
Strauss, Richard 499
Strawn, C.J. 356
Strawn, Mick 356
Streiner, Gary 347

Streiner, Russell (Russ) W. 346, 350, 352
Stribling, Melissa 135, 137
Strickfadden, Kenneth 184, 210
Stricklyn, Ray 137
Stride, Jon 367
Striepeke, Dan 297, 381, 382
Stripes 234, 427
Stritch, Elaine 85
Strock, Herbert L. 195, 307
Stroheim, Erich von 307
Stroheim, Josef von 30
Stroka, Michael 268
Strom, Florence 178
Strong, Leonard 232
Stross, Raymond 309
Stroucken, Micki 107
Stroud, Don 31, 32
Stroud, Duke 80
Struss, Karl 112, 177, 294
Struycken, Carel 20
Stuart, Alen 464, 519
Stuart, Don A. *see* Campbell, John W., Jr.
Stuart, Donald 289
Stuart, Gloria 289, 290
Stuart, John 197, 342, 400, 461, 509
Stuart, Laird 416
Stubbs, Harry 190, 289, 291, 336, 524
Stubbs, Levi 314
Studio Locations Limited 206
Stumar, Charles 334
Stumpp, William 311
Sturdevant, John 320
Sturgess, Olive 170
Sturgis, Ted 426, 510
Style, Michael 503, 506, 508
Subotsky, Milton 120, 126, 127, 309
Sucher, Henry 71, 337, 339
Suddleson, Dee 220
Sudrow, Penelope 356
Suhrstedt, Timothy (Tim) 55, 103, 277, 329
Sullivan, Barry 365
Sullivan, Charlie 302
Sullivan, Eileen 508
Sullivan, Ernie 110
Sullivan, Frank 242
Sullivan, George 248
Sullivan, Jennifer 224
Sullivan, Owen 370
Sullivan, Sean 499
Sullivan, Sean Gregory 43, 275
Sullivan, Tom 159

Summers, Hope 137
Summers, Neil 416,
Summerscale, Frank 510
Sun, Leland 125
Sundby, Emily 158, 317, 318
Sunderland, Janet 263
Sundfor, Paul 36
Sundin, Michael 523
Sundstrom, Neal 275
Superfly 397
Supergirl 466–468
Superman 461–463
Superman (serial) 469
Superman and the Mole Men
    460–461
Superman II 55, 463–465
Superman III 465–466
*Superman IV: The Quest for
    Peace* 468–469
Surges, Pat 359
Surkin, Eddie 486
Surtees, Bruce 383
Surtees, Robert 316
Survinski, Regis 347
Suschitzky, Peter 454
Suschitzky, Wolf 437
Suskin, Mitch 84
Susskind, Steve 220, 265,
    447
Sutherland, Donald 286,
    287
Sutherland, Kristine 263
Sutherland, Victor 307
Sutton, Gertrude 305
Sutton, John 178, 180, 291
Sutton, Linda Lee 386
Swaby, Paul 314
Swados, Kim 31
Swain, Caskey 222
Swamp Thing 469–472
Swan, Michael 223
Swan Lake (music) 139
Swanson, Kristy 330
Sweeney, Alfred 97
Sweeney, Bob 19
Sweet, Dolph 259
Swenson, Bill 275
Swenson, Bo 107
Swerdlow, Tommy 80
Swift, Chris 223
Swift, Susan 250
Swim, David 67
Swiss Family Robinson 459
The Sword and the Sorcerer
    396
Sydes, Anthony 331
Sydney, Basil 320
Sydow, Max Von 32, 86, 162,
    163, 164, 175
Sylos, Paul 142, 203

Sylvers, Jeremy 82
Sylvester, William 259, 499
Symons, James R. 475
Szwarc, Jeannot 466

Tabet, Sylvia 54, 55
Tablian, Vic 408
Taft, Jerry 298
Taggart, Rita 267
Taggert, Brian 386
Tagliaferro, Pat 223
Tagoe, Eddie 408
Tait, Don 90, 318, 434
Taj Mahal 57
Takacs, Tibor 229, 230
Takei, George 440, 442, 444,
    446, 447, 449
The Takeover see *Scanners
    III: The Takeover*
Talalay, Rachel 356, 357, 360
Talbot, Lyle 469
Talbot, Nita 34, 35, 394
Talbott, Gloria 117, 118
Tales of Terror 169
Tallman, Patricia 161, 352
Tambini, Catherine 67
Tamblyn, Russ 147, 148
Tan, Phil 47
Tandy, Gareth 461
Tandy, Jessica 84, 85
Tanenbaum, James 92
Tann, Philip 410
Tannen, Charles 177
Tannen, Julius 191
Tannen, Terrell 67
Tanner, Joy 393
Tansy 523
Tapert, Robert G. 108, 159,
    160, 161
Tarbuck, Barbara 438
Tarr, Cynthia 366
Tarses, Jay 277
Tartar, Mara 336
Tarzan the Ape Man 89
Tash, Steven 233
Tashlin, Frank 238
Taste the Blood of Dracula
    145
Tate, Reginald 398
Tattersall, Jane 181
Taxi (TV series) 445
Taxi Driver 300
Tayback, Vic 434
Taylor, Bill 214
Taylor, Christopher 34
Taylor, Courtney 392
Taylor, Daniel 472
Taylor, Don 296, 298, 369,
    382
Taylor, Donald 320

Taylor, Dub 43
Taylor, Elizabeth 66
Taylor, Eric 131, 189
Taylor, Femi 457
Taylor, Gilbert (Gil) 153,
    175, 367, 369, 452
Taylor, Grant 404, 407
Taylor, J.O. 302, 304
Taylor, Jack 86
Taylor, Jeannine 217
Taylor, Kimberly 215
Taylor, Lance, Sr. 58
Taylor, Lauren-Marie 219
Taylor, Mark L. 263
Taylor, Meshach 329, 330,
    370
Taylor, Michael 43
Taylor, Peter 509
Taylor, Samuel W. 17, 19
Taylor, Sharon 36
Taylor, William 182
Teal, Ray 18
Teasdale, Verree 489
Tecson, Artemio, B. 295
Teefy, Maureen 466
Teegarden, Jim 43
Teen Wolf 277–278
Teen Wolf (animated TV se-
    ries) 278
Teen Wolf Too 278
Teenage Frankenstein see *I
    Was a Teenage Franken-
    stein*
*Teenage Mutant Ninja Tur-
    tles* 472–474
*Teenage Mutant Ninja Tur-
    tles II: The Secret of the
    Ooze* 474–475
*Teenage Mutant Ninja Tur-
    tles III* 475–476
Teenage Zombies 212
Teixeira, Virgilio 429
Tejada-Flores, Miguel 228
Temple, Shirley 65
Temple-Smith, John 296
Templeton, William P. 362
Tennison, James 312
Tent, Kevin 45, 215
Terechova, Margareta 66
Terhune, William 488
The Terminator 79, 106, 417,
    476–478, 517
Terminator 2: Judgment Day
    210, 375, 478–480
Terror in the Crypt 506
Terror Is a Man 139,
    295–296, 297
The Terror Within 480–481
The Terror Within II
    481–482

Terry, Frank 186
Terry, Gay Partington 490,
  491
Terry, John 252, 253
Terry, Jon 247
Terry, Jonathon 352
Terry, Marty 79
Terry-Thomas 15, 16, 334
Teschner, Peter 376, 415
Tetoni, Charles 249
Tetrick, Harry W. 516
Tettener, John 315
Thalken, Meg 387
Thall, Benj 166
"Thank You Very Much"
  (song) 427
Thatcher, Kirk 242
Thatcher, Torin 429
Thaw, John 16
Thaxter, Phyllis 461
Thayer, Ivy 84
Theiss, Brooke 357
Them 515
Thesiger, Ernest 186, 426
Thibault, Carl 213
The Thief of Damascus 433
The Thing 106, 481,
  484–486, 512
*The Thing from Another
  World* 23, 252, 482–484,
  485, 515
Thiry, Dave 160
This Island Earth 101
Thomas, Bill 39, 316
Thomas, Craig 224
Thomas, Damien 432, 508
Thomas, Dean 17
Thomas, Harry 199, 312,
  460
Thomas, Heather 527, 528
Thomas, James 388
Thomas, Jameson 289
Thomas, Jay 83
Thomas, Jim 387
Thomas, John 183, 388
Thomas, Kathryn Ann 155
Thomas, Leslie 195, 276
Thomas, Lisa 372
Thomas, Llewelyn 67
Thomas, Ralph 333
Thomas, Ramsey 249
Thomas, Roy 87
Thomas, Tommy 42
Thomerson, Tim 124, 491,
  492, 493, 494
Thompson, Brian 228, 476
Thompson, Caroline 20
Thompson, Claude 305
Thompson, Cynthia 364
Thompson, J. Lee 383, 384

Thompson, Joy 390
Thompson, Lea 40, 42, 43
Thompson, Peter 508
Thomson, Alex 16, 27
Thomson, Scott 235
Thor, Larry 30
Thornbury, Bill 375, 377
Thorne, Ken 464, 465
Thorne, Tracy 165
Thorne, William 57
Thornton, Frank 152, 173
Thornton, John 42
Thornton, Ralph 276
Thorpe, Nola 238
Thorsen, Sven Ole 86, 87
Three Blondes in His Life
  296
Three Hits and a Miss 488
The Three Musketeers 466
Thring, Frank 273, 274, 323
Through the Looking Glass
  (book) 23
Through the Portal of Time
  see *Beastmaster 2:
  Through the Portal of Time*
"Thus Spake Zarathustra"
  (musical composition)
  499
THX 1138 453
Thyssen, Greta 295, 296
Tickner, Shane 323
Tierney, Laurence 267
Tierno, Mark 349
Tigar, Keneth 376
Tilden, Leif 472, 474
Tilley, Patrick 310
Tillitt, James 255
Tilly, Meg 288
Tilvern, Alan 314
Tingey, Cynthia 432
Tingwell, Charles 141
Tiomkin, Dimitri 21, 315,
  319, 482
Tippett, Phil 416, 417, 418,
  419, 457
Tipping, Tip 24
Tipton, Brian 446
To Die For 486–487
"To Die For" (musical
  theme) 487
To Die For II see *Son of
  Darkness: To Die For II*
Tobey, Kenneth 99, 241,
  242, 264, 271, 482, 483,
  484, 519, 520
Tobin, Dan 317
Tobolowsky, Stephen 125
Toch, Ernest 230
Tochi, Brian 473, 475
Todd, Ann 65

Todd, Bob 146
Todd, Holbrook N. 117
Todd, Richard 379
Todd, Russell 219
Todd, Sally 199
Todd, Tony 68, 70, 352
Todd Masters Company 275
Tokuno, Dean 387
Toland, Gregg 319
Tolbert, Lloyd L. 42
Tolkan, James 40, 42, 43
The Tomb of Ligeia 111,
  173–174, 370
Tomb of the Cat see *The
  Tomb of Ligeia*
Tomblin, David 367
Tomkins, Alan 454
Tomkins, Leslie 468
Tomlinson, David 316, 332
Toms, Carl 372, 436
Toner, Tom 93
Tonge, Philip 331
Too, Lee Tung 482
Toone, Geoffrey 126
Toop, Carl 24
Topol 175
Topper 488–489
Topper Returns 489–490
Topper Takes a Trip 489
Torbet, Bruce 44
Tordjmann, Fabien 59, 93
Torgl, Mark 490
Torn, Rip 54, 419
Torn Curtain 300
Tornatore, Joe 176
Toro, Antonio 34, 35
Toro, Jorge Luis 83
Torres, Joan 58, 59
Total Recall 417
Toth, Ildiki 267
Toto (dog) 520
Totschek, Jasmine 395
Tottenham, Merle 289
Tough, Michael 390
Touliatos, George 390
Tourneur, Jacques 72
Tovagliei, Enrico 214
Tovey, Roberta 126, 127
Towers, Harry Alan 274, 379
Towler, Jim 176
Towles, Tom 352
Towne, Robert 173
Townley, Toke 146
Townsend, Jill 64
The Toxic Avenger 490
The Toxic Avenger, Part II
  490–491
*Toxic Avenger Part III: The
  Last Temptation of Toxie*
  491

Tozer, Joseph E. 131
Tracy, Lee 127
Tracy, Spencer 114, 115, 116, 243
Trafas, Paul 233
Trainor, Mary Ellen 213 234
Trancers 491–492
Trancers II 492
Trancers III 492–493
Trancers 4: Jack of Swords 493–494
Trancers 5: Sudden Deth 494–495
Trautman, Allan 350, 352
Travelstead, Ted 79
Travers, Henry 289
Travers, Susan 15
Travis, Richard 77
Travis, Ron 255
Travis, Stacey 376
Travis, Tony 177
Traxler, Stephen 155
Trcic, Michael 349
Treas, Terri 214, 267, 480, 481
Tremors 79
Trentini, Peggy 237
Triano, Antonio 307
Triesault, Ivan 339
Triffitt, Nigel 275
Trigger, Sarah 57, 374, 375
Trinidad, Arsenio "Sonny" 108
Tripp, Louis 229, 230
Triska, Jan 501
Troughton, Patrick 146, 194, 208, 367, 369, 432
Troum, Kenn 473, 474
Trowbridge, Charles 336
Trubshawe, Michael 334
Trucco, Eddie 261
True, Andrea 391
Trujillo, Anthony R. 476
Trujillo, Raoul 422
Trumbo, Dalton 242, 244
Trumbull, Douglas 440, 442, 499
Trundy, Natalie 381, 382, 383, 384
Trytel, W. 425
"Tubular Bells" (musical theme) 162, 164
Tucker, Burnell 175, 454
Tufts, Sonny 77
Tufty, Chris 103
Tuke, Simon 249
Tung-Fo, Lee 292
Tuntke, Bill 19
Turco, Paige 474, 475
Turich, Felipe 203

Turich, Rosa 203
Turk, Roy 243
Turman, Glynn 241
Turman, Lawrence 438, 484
The Turn of the Screw (book) 279
Turner, Clive 274, 275
Turner, Frank 182
Turner, John 498
Turner, Lana 114, 115
Turner, Larry 168
Turner, Rick 178
Turner, Stephen 370
Turner, Teddy 153
Turner, Tina 323
Turney, Michael 473
Turpin, Helen 177
Tuttle, Lurene 238
Tuttle, William 152, 210, 238
Twain, Mark 88, 89, 90, 91
20,000 Leagues Under the Sea 34, 495–496
20,000 Leagues Under the Sea (book) 497, 499
Twilight Zone (TV series) 385
Twins of Evil 408, 509
The Two Faces of Dr. Jekyll 117–118
2001: A Space Odyssey 380, 453, 454, 499–501
2010 501–502
Twohy, D.T. (David) 104, 512, 513
Tyler, Betty 116
Tyler, Leon 19
Tyler, Tom 336, 341
Tyler, Walter 118, 317, 324
Tysall, David 91
Tyson, Cicely 66
Tyzack, Margaret 499

Udenio, Fabiana 415, 418
The Ugly Dachshund 435
Ullman, Daniel 497
Ullman, Liv 316
Ulmer, Edgar C. 117
Uncle Was a Vampire 157
The Understudy: Graveyard Shift II 240–241
Underwood, Jay 487
The Undiscovered Country see *Star Trek VI: The Undiscovered Country*
Unidentified Flying Oddball 90–91
Universal City Studios Matte Department 323

Unsworth, Geoffrey 22, 461, 464, 499
Upstairs, Downstairs (TV series) 524
Urban Harvest see *Children of the Corn III: Urban Harvest*
Ure, Mary 120
Urena, Fabio 353
Urioste, Frank J. 33, 87, 416
Urquhart, Robert 194
Ursin, David 104, 249
Ursitti, Susan 277, 278, 527
"U.S. Marshall" (TV series) 99
Usher, Robert 230
Uslan, Michael 50, 469, 472
Ustinov, Tamara 64

Vacano, Jost 416
Vaccaro, Brenda 466
Vadim, Roger 506
Vahanian, Marc 31
Vail, Myrtle 312
Valdez, Georgeana 376
Valentine, Joseph 524
Valentino, Sal 148
Vamos, Thomas 229
Vampira see *Old Dracula*
"Vampira" (song) 152
The Vampire 34
The Vampire Lovers 94, 118, 209, 503–506, 508
Van, Bobby 316
Van, Frankie 293
Van Beers, Stanley 398
Vance, James D. 137
Vance, Marilyn Kay 124
Vanderburg, Charles 312
Van Der Velde, Nadine 103
Vandis, Titos 162, 365
Van Dreelan, John 316
Van Enger, Charles 192
Van er Veer Photo 164
Van Eyck, Peter 309
Van Eyssen, John 135, 400
Van Fleet, Richard 519
Van Haden, Anders 186
Van Hentenryck, Kevin 44, 45
Van Heusen, Jimmy 89
Van Hoorn, Teresa 120
Van Horn, John 147
Vanilla Ice 474
Van Lingen, Thor 351
Vanlint, Derek 23
Van Nuys, Ed 244
Vanorio, Frank 106
Van Ost, Valerie 150
Van Patten, Dick 61, 434, 516

Van Patten, Patricia 319
Van Runkle, Theodora 259
Van Scott, Glory 522
Van Sloan, Edward 129, 131, 185, 335
Van Vogt, A.E. 23
Van Zandt, Billy 440
Van Zandt, Phillip 191, 243
Varnick, Neil P. 71, 337
Vaughan, Dorothy 339
Vaughan, Peter 509
Vaughn, James 487
Vaughn, Robert 84, 465, 466
Vaurinecz, Beata 91
VCE 104
VCE Inc. 155
VCE, Inc./Peter Kuran 34, 155
Veazey, Cindy 217
Veevers, Wally 110, 427, 499
Veilleux, Jim 442
Veith, John 216
Vejar, Harry J. 284
Velez, Josephine 129
Velia, Tania 77
The Vengeance of She 437–438
Veninger, Ingrid 229
Vennera, Chick 481
Ventham, Wanda 506
Ventura, Jesse 166, 388
Venturini, Mark 222, 350
Verardi, Cecilia 219
Vercoutere, Marcel 162
Verdon, Gwen 84, 85
Verdugo, Elena 191
Verhoeven, Paul 416, 417
Verity, Terence 362
Verne, Jules 495, 497, 499
Vernon, Gabor 173
Vernon, John 319
Vernon, Richard 150, 173, 509
Vertal, Susanna 79
Veruschka 212
Vervin, Romuald 181
Vetter, Arlan Jay 397, 493, 494
Vicino, Cindi 84
Vickers, Martha 190, 339, 524
Vickers, Michael 148
Vickery, Courtney 223
Victor, Charles 97, 168
Victor, Henry 335
Victor, Katherine (Kathrin) 212
Victor, Mark 385
Victor-Smith, John 464, 465
Vidale, Thea 125

Vidgeon, Robin 182, 254, 255
Vigran, Herb 293
The Vikings 34, 274
Village of the Damned (1960) 75, 508–510
Village of the Damned (1995) 511–512
Village People 397
Villalobos, Francisco 178
Villasenor, Christopher 234
Villegas, Lucio 186
Villemaire, James 230
Villiers, James 64
Vince, Nicholas 255
Vincent, Alex 80, 81, 82
Vincent, Virginia 137
Vinci, Gerald 210
Vinovich, Stephen 329
Vinson, Helen 307
Virkler, Dennis 52
Virtue, Danny 182
Visaroff, Michael 129
Viskocil, Joe 265
Visual Concept Engineering 416
Vitale, Joseph 89
Vitzin, George 66
Vogan, Emmett 337
Vogel, Darlene 42
Vogel, Paul C. 35
Vogel, Robert 44
Vogel, Tony 370, 408
Vogel, Virgil 293
Voight, Jill 219
Volante, Vicki 144
Voorhees, Debisue 222, 223
Vorkov, Zandor 147
Vosloo, Arnold 109
The Voyage of the Space Beagle (book) 23
Voyage to the Bottom of the Sea (TV series) 178
Vrana, Vlasta 422
Vulich, John 349, 352
Vye, Murvyn 89

Wachner, Sophie 88
Wad, John D. 473
Wade, Brian 223, 446
Wagenheim, Charles 72
Waggner, George 189, 190, 292, 524
Waggner, Pat 312
Wagner, Bruce 356
Wagner, Lou 380, 381, 383
Wagner, Max 281
Wagner, Roy 356
Wagner, Sidney 425
Waites, Thomas 484

Waits, Tom 156
Wakefield, Simon 309, 310
Wakeling, Gwen 65
Walas, Chris 107, 182, 241, 266
Walcott, Gregory 266
Wald, Robert 416
Waldock, Denis 332
Wales, William 33
Walkabout 82
Walken, Christopher 50
Walker, Charles 122
Walker, Graham 322
Walker, Helen 324, 325
Walker, James 362
Walker, Joseph 257, 315
Walker, Matthew 82
Walker, Ray 460
Walker, Robert 61
Walker, Shirley 235
Walker, Vernon 302, 304
Wallace, Andy 499
Wallace, Basil 353
Wallace, Connie 170
Wallace, Dee 271; *see also* Stone, Dee Wallace
Wallace, Edgar 302, 306
Wallace, Jeff 105
Wallace, Jerry 219
Wallace, Marcia 236, 237
Wallace, Scott 82
Wallace, Tommy Lee 32, 228, 244, 247
Waller, Eddy 339
Wallis, Hal 231
Wallis, Peter 153
Wallis, Rit 229
Walmsley, Anna 197
Walsh, Bill 17, 19, 316, 317, 433
Walsh, Edward 92, 93
Walsh, J.T. 331
Walsh, Judy 77
Walsh, Kay 427
Walsh, M. Emmet 103, 382
Walsh, Sally 194
Walsh, Sydney 356, 486
Walshe, Pat 520
Walter, Ernest 66, 510
Walter, Perla 220
Walter, Tracey 47, 87
Walters, Charles 237
Walters, Hugh 362
Walters, James M. 341
Walters, Thorley 141, 203, 206, 207, 310
Walton, Dave 221
Walton, Douglas 112, 186, 377
Walton, Fred 131

Walton, Harry 416
Walton, Tony 522
Waltz, Lisa 374, 375
Wanamaker, Sam 431, 468
Wanger, Walter 284
War of the Colossal Beast 30–31
The War of the Worlds 496
Warbeck, David 508
Warburton, Cotton 17, 19, 317, 318
Ward, Amelita 72
Ward, Burt 47
Ward, Dervis 437
Ward, Katherine 305
Ward, Lawrence 333
Ward, Megan 34, 492, 493
Ward, Olivia 234
Ward, Roger 321
Ward, Simon 206, 466
Ward, Skip 118
Warde, Anthony 339
Warde, Harlan 307
Warden, Jack 259
Wardlow, John 182
Wardlow, Keith 183
Ware, Herta 84, 104, 501
Warford, Jack 122, 312
Warlock 71, 512–513
Warlock, Richard (Dick) 222, 246, 247
Warlock: The Armageddon 513
Warner, Aron 360
Warner, David 367, 447, 449, 474
Warner, H.B. 315, 316, 489
Warner, Jack 398, 426
Warner, Mark Roy 85
Warner, Pamela 222, 355
Warner, Patricia 506
Warner, Richard 346, 509
Warner, Tam G. 160
Warren, Barry 203
Warren, Gene, Jr. 288
Warren, Harry 238
Warren, Jerry 211
Warren, John F. 117
Warren, Kenneth J. 120
Warren, Kimelly Anne 182
Warren, Lesley Ann 240
Warrington, Bill 342, 400
Warschilka, Edward A., Jr. 80, 81, 82, 121, 151, 511
Warwick, Robert 127
Washbourne, Mona 66, 139
Washburn, Beverly 460
Washington, Richard 59
Washington, Vernon 222
Wass, Ted 366

Wasserman, Jerry 182
Wasson, Craig 356
Watanabe, Gedde 242
Watchers 513–514
Watchers (book) 514, 515, 516
Watchers II 481, 514–516
Watchers III 516
Waterbury, Laura 263
Waterman, Dennis 145
Waters, Daniel 50
Waters, Harry, Jr. 40, 42
Waters, Monica 391
Waterstreet, Charles 273
Watford, Gwen 145
Watkin, David 523
Watkin, Pierre 71, 469
Watkins, A.W. 499
Watkins, Sarah Jean 67
Watson, Carol 220, 221
Watson, David 381
Watson, John 75, 309
Watson, Mike 43
Watson, William 301
Watt, Reuben 59
Watts, Robert 410, 411
Watts, Roy 54, 431, 432
Waugh, Fred 486
Waxman, Franz 114, 186, 377, 425
Waxman, Harry 436
Way, Gay 284
Waybill, Fee 56
Waye, Tony 452
Wayne, Billy 293
Wayne, John 436
Wayne, Keith 347
Wayne, Patrick 310, 432, 433
"We Don't Need Another Hero (Thunderdome)" (song) 323
Weatherley, Peter 22, 64, 103, 426
Weatherly, Shawn 34
Weathers, Carl 388
Weatherwax, Paul 97
Weaver, Doodles 488
Weaver, Fritz 102
Weaver, Malcom 408
Weaver, Sigourney 23–29, 233, 234, 285
Webb, Danny 28
Webb, Des 454
Webb, Gregory 394
Webb, Ira S. 71
Webb, Jack 313
Webb, Richard 61, 62, 89
Webb, Roy 72, 74
Weber, Billy 124

Webling, Peggy 184
Webster, Christopher 255
Webster, Ferris 237, 377
Webster, Frank 332
Webster, M. Coates 72
Webster, Patricia 75
Weddle, Vernon 438
Wedlock, Hugh, Jr. 293
Weekend at Bernie's 330
Weekend at Bernie's II 330
Weeks, Donald 194, 400
Weeks, Jimmie Ray 306
Weeks, Michelle 314
Weeks, Stephen 120
Wehling, Robert 97
Weigel, Paul 131
Weigel, Teri 37, 388, 390
Weil, Samuel 490
Weiler, Frederick C. 95
Wein, Len 472
Weinman, Richard 487
Weinrib, Lenny 169
Weintraub, Bruce 75
Weintraub, Jerry 364
Weir, Molly 427
Weisberg, Arthur 124
Weisberg, Brenda 339
Weisman, Matthew 277, 278
Weiss, Chuck 357, 359
Weiss, David 67
Weiss, Michael T. 274
Weiss, Shelly 147
Weisser, Norbert 484
Weissman, Jeffrey 42, 43
Welbourne, Charles S. 94, 97
Welch, Jerry 198
Welch, Raquel 372, 373
Welch, Stephen Kent 37
Welch, Tahnee 84, 85
"Welcome to Munchkin Land" (song) 520
Weldon, Meg 387
Welker, Frank 242
Wellburn, Tim 322
Weller, Peter 416, 417, 418, 419, 420
Welles, Adam 208
Welles, Mel 122, 207, 312, 341
Welles, Meri 312
Welles, Orson 96, 300
Welles, Steve 394
Wellman, William, Jr. 298, 300
Wells, Claudia 40, 41
Wells, David 223
Wells, Dawn 311, 312
Wells, George 35, 36
Wells, H.G. 106, 183, 289,

291, 292, 293, 294, 296, 298, 496
Wells, Jesse 93
Wells, Larry 438
Wells, Veron 322
Welsh, John 197
Wendorff, Leola 312
Wendy, George 125, 265
Wenger, Cliff 297
Wengraff, John 137
Wentworth, Martha 117
Wentworth, Nicholas 379
Wentz, Kip 387
"We're Off to See the Wizard" (song) 520
Wertimer, Stephen 83
Wes Craven's New Nightmare 361–362
West, Adam 47
West, Chandra 396, 397
West, John Stuart 350
West, Kevin 38
West, Vera 187, 336, 339
West Side Story 148
Westbrook, Herbert 279
Westbrook, John 171, 173
Westcott, Helen 116, 117
Westerfield, James 19, 434
Westgate, Murray 422
Westlund, Chris 365
Westmoje, Wally 89
Westmore, Bud 94, 97, 101, 116, 341
Westmore, Perc 128
Westmore, Wally 112, 294, 324
Weston, David 171
Weston, Jack 438
Weston, Jeff 394
Westwood, Patrick 168
Westworld 516–518
Wetherall, Virginia 121
Wetherwax, Michael 397
Whale, James 184, 18, 289, 341
"A Whale of a Tale" (song) 496
Whalen, Michael 77
Whalin, Justin 82
Wheat, Jim 182
Wheat, Ken 182
Wheaton, Amy 106
Wheaton, Will 106
Wheeler, Lyle R. 177, 178
Wheeler, Russ 84
Whelehan, William J. 370
"When You Look for a Dream" (song) 152
Whipp, Joseph 354
Whipple, Sam 125

Whipple, Shonda 282
Whitaker, David 121, 152
Whitaker, Duane 397
Whitaker, Forrest 288
White, Al 42
White, Bruce 362
White, Dan 203
White, Douglas J. 220
White, Gordon 55
White, Jacqueline 243
White, Les 292
White, Merrill 177
White, Morgan B. 248
White, Patrick 249, 510
White, Sheila 90, 91
White, Ted 222
White Zombie 348
Whitecloud, John P. 386
Whitehurst, Derek 145, 207, 208, 503
Whitelaw, Billie 367
Whiteley, Arkie 322
Whiteman, George 305
Whiteman, Peter 208
Whiteman, Russ 195
Whitemore, Hugh 66
Whiting, Margaret 432
Whitlock, Albert J. 75, 164, 522
Whitlock, Denis 145
Whitman, Peter 464
Whitmore, James 380
Whitney, Claire 339
Whitney, Eve 243
Whitney, Grace Lee 440, 446, 449
Whitney, John 243
Whitney, John, Jr. 516
Whiton, James 15
Whitredge, J.R. 74
Whitson-Jones, Paul 121, 171
Whittaker, Ian 260
Whittaker, Ivan 197
Whitthorne, Paul 105
"Who Goes There?" (story) 482, 484, 486
"A Whole Lotta Shakin' Goin' On" (song) 468
Whybrow, Roy 22
Wibberley, Leonard 333, 334
The Wicker Man 173
Wicking, Christopher 64
Wickman, Sven 381
Widen, Gregory 260, 261
Wiederhorn, Ken 351
Wiedlin, Jane 56, 446
Wiend, Dick 222
Wiener, Jack H. 152
Wiesel, Flora 313

Wieternik, Nora 175
Wilbur, Crane 497
Wilbur, George P. 248, 250
Wilcox, Blake 472
Wilcox, Frank 281
Wilcox, John 121, 126, 127, 150, 201
Wilcox, Lisa 357, 359, 360
Wilcox, Sheelah 508
Wilcoxon, Henry 89
Wild, Jeannette 121
Wild, Katy 201
The Wild Angels 215
Wild Jungle Captive see *Jungle Captive*
Wilde, Andrew 362
Wilde, Barbie 255
Wilde, Oscar 377, 379
Wilder, Alan 80, 387
Wilder, Bob 92
Wilder, Gene 210, 211, 466
Wilder, Shane 478
Wilder, Yvonne 93
Wilding, Michael 238
Wiley, David 220
Wiley, Edward 260, 314
Wiley, Ethan 264, 266
Wilke, Robert J. 495
Wilkerson, Guy 252
Wilkins, Jeremy 180
Will Vinton Productions 523
Willard 519
Willat, Boyd 527
Willes, Jean 284
William, Warren 524
William Peter Blatty on The Exorcist: *From Novel to Film* (book) 164
Williams, Alistair 309
Williams, Arnold 59
Williams, Billy 162
Williams, Billy Dee 47, 454
Williams, Chuck 397
Williams, Cindy 61, 62
Williams, Clarence, III 328
Williams, D.J. 425
Williams, Elmo 495
Williams, Esther 243
Williams, Guy 276, 433
Williams, Jack 143
Williams, Jason 175
Williams, Jennifer 55, 512
Williams, Jim Cody 56
Williams, JoBeth 385, 386
Williams, John 153, 244, 407, 410, 411, 452, 454, 457, 461, 463, 468
Williams, Kay 243
Williams, Kelli 527

Williams, Nora 514
Williams, Paul 429
Williams, Rhys 116
Williams, Richard 370
Williams, Robert B. 97
Williams, Robin 466
Williams, Stephanie E. 42
Williams, Steven 226
Williams, Ted 522
Williams, Trevor 270, 518
Williams, Vanessa 68
Williams, Victor 312
Williams, Wade H., III 282
Williamson, Alistair 201
Williamson, Malcolm 139
Williamson, Nicol 165, 523
Willingham, Noble 271
Willis, Austin 333
Willis, Edwin B. 114, 238,
  243, 425, 520
Willis, Matt 243, 292
Willis, Tim 314
Willits, Adam 323
Willman, Noel 437
Willock, Dave 97
Willoughby, George 171
Willoughby, Leueen 370,
  464
Willow 459, 524
Wills, J. Elder 398
Wills, Sherrie 165
Wilmer, Douglas 431, 503
Wilson, Cal 384
Wilson, Charles 128
Wilson, Clarence 305
Wilson, Dale 514
Wilson, Don "The Dragon"
  52
Wilson, Elizabeth 20
Wilson, Freddie 279
Wilson, George 36
Wilson, Harry 116, 199, 200
Wilson, Jim 311
Wilson, Larry 20
Wilson, Lee 181
Wilson, Mak 314, 523
Wilson, Mara 331, 332
Wilson, Marie 38
Wilson, Michael 380
Wilson, Rod 109
Wilson, Ronald 400
Wilson, S.S. 438
Wilson, Scott 165
Wilson, Stuart 475
Wilson, Terry 158, 517
Wilson, Thomas F. 40, 42,
  43
Wilton, Eric 112, 131, 315,
  524
Wiltsie, Melissa 314, 464

Wilyman, Bob 499
Wincenty, Rick 393, 394
Wincott, Jeff 390
Windburn, Jim 244
Windom, William 331, 382
Windsor, Marie 77, 341
Windsor, Romy 274
Windsor, Tammy 312
Winetrobe, Maury 316
Winfield, Paul 442, 476
Wing, Virginia 125
Wingreen, Jason 366
Wingrove, Ian 310, 523
Wingrove, James 323
Winkless, Terence H. 271
Winlaw, Mike 182
Winn, Kitty 162, 164
Winner, Michael 279
Winslet, Kate 91
Winston, Matt 361
Winston, Stan 24, 50, 122,
  282, 388, 476, 478, 522
Winter, Alex 55, 56, 57
Winter, Pauline 120
Winter, Ralph 449
Winter, Terry 427
Winter, Vincent 461
Winters, Ralph E. 305
Winton, Colleen 514
Winwood, Estelle 238, 240
Wirth, Billy 288
Wirth, Sandra 77
Wise, Douglas E. 446
Wise, Ray 416, 469
Wise, Robert 74, 300, 439,
  442, 448
Wisher, William 478
Wisher, William, Jr. 476
Wissner, Gary 472
Witherick, Albert 90
Withers, Googie 332
Witherspoon, John 38
Witley, Wiliam 76
The Wiz 521–523
Wizan, Steve 166
The Wizard of Oz 66, 520–
  521
Wladon, Jean 372
Wolande, Gene 416
Wolcott, E.A. 302
Wolf, Joseph 246, 247
The Wolf Man 190, 524–525
Wolfe, Adam 275, 515
Wolfe, Ian 292
Wolfe, Kedrick 122
Wolff, Ed 178
Wolfit, Donald 320
Wolfson, P.J. 319
Wolman, Harry 313
Wolveridge, Carol 362

The Woman Eater 313
The Wonderful Wizard of Oz
  (book) 520, 521
Wong, Harry D.K. 259
Wong, Phillip 514
Wong, Victor 302, 304, 315
Wong, Vincent 47, 314
Wood, David King 398
Wood, Elijah 42
Wood, James 124
Wood, John 306
Wood, Michael L. 447
Wood, Mike 323
Wood, Natalie 331
Wood, Oliver 56
Wood, Richard 499
Wood-Sharke, Rebecca 222
Woodard, Alfre 427
Woodbridge, George 136,
  141, 197, 333
Woodburn, Eric 279
Woodbury, Joan 186
Woodcock, John 118
Woodcroft, Todd 464
Woodruff, Tom, Jr. 27, 213
Woods, Audrey 15
Woods, Barbara A. 237, 481
Woods, Jack 61
Woodthorpe, Peter 201
Woody, John David 311
Wooley, Harold E. 199
Wooley, Peter 124
Woolf, Edgar Allan 520
Woolsey, Ralph 365
Wordsworth, Richard 197,
  398, 399
Workman, Jimmy 20
Worley, Jo Anne 434
Worlock, Frederic 114
Woronov, Mary 512, 515
Worth, Brian 426
Worth, Lothrop 142, 195,
  203
Worth, Nicholas 59, 108,
  469
Woxholt, Egil S. 497
The Wrath of Khan see *Star*
  Trek II — The Wrath of
  Khan
Wray, Fay 127, 128, 302
Wray, John 127
Wright, Amy 31
Wright, Hilary 476
Wright, Howard 31
Wright, Hugh E. 425
Wright, Jay 67
Wright, John 474
Wright, Julia 121
Wright, Maggie 508
Wright, Marti 514

Wright, Tom 103
Wrightson, Berni 472
Wu, Ju 473
Wu, Vivian 475
Wuhl, Robert 47
Wunderlich, Jerry 162
Wuthering Heights 181
Wyatt, Dale 236
Wyatt, Eustace 324
Wyatt, Jane 315, 446
Wyeth, Katya 508
Wylie, Philip 294, 469
Wymark, Dominic 376
Wynant, H.M. 383
Wyndham, John 508, 511
Wyngarde, Peter 175, 279
Wynkoop, Christopher 233
Wynn, Ed 17, 19, 39, 238, 239
Wynn, Hugh 319
Wynn, Keenan 17, 19, 35, 238, 317, 318, 434, 435
Wynne, Christopher 43
Wynorski, Jim 55, 237, 267, 364, 472
Wynter, Dana 284, 285
Wynters, Sharyn 517
Wyss, Amanda 354, 486, 487

X the Unknown 406
Xanadu 258

Yablans, Irwin 244, 246, 247
Yablans, Mickey 245
Yagher, Kevin 55, 56, 80, 81, 82, 125, 221, 355, 356, 357
Yakim, Moni 416
Yale, Stan 476
Yama, Michael 410
Yamasaki, Kiyoshi 86
Yancy, Emily 58
Yarborough, Barton 189
Yarde, Margaret 425
Yasbeck, Amy 266
Yasuoka, Rikiya 490
Yates, George Worthing 30, 198
Yates, Hayden 364
Yates, Herbert 307
Yeatman, Hoyt 63
Yeaworth, Irvin S., Jr. 60
Yelland, Susan 464

Yiasomi, George 306
Yip, David 410
Yoke-Moon, Lee 510
Yong, Waldemar 294
York, Duke 292, 489
York, Gerald 298
York, Michael 297, 316
York, Sarah 159, 160
York, Susannah 64, 461, 464, 468
York, W. Allen 298
"You Better Come Through" (song) 148
"You Came a Long Way from St. Louis" (song) 341
"You ... You" (song) 427
Young, Aida 143, 145, 372, 436, 437
Young, Burt 32, 33
Young, Chris 513
Young, Christopher 182, 254, 255, 282, 355
Young, Freddie 66
Young, Granville "Danny" 42
Young, Harold 72, 337
Young, Jack H. 30
Young, James 482, 483
Young, Jerry 195
Young, Joan 64
Young, Peter 47, 465, 468
Young, Ray 144
Young, Richard (Ric) 222, 410, 411
Young, Robert Malcolm 158
Young, Roland 488, 489
Young, Sean 125
Young, Victor 89
Young Dracula see *Son of Dracula* (1974)
Young Frankenstein 187, 189, 210–211
The Young Savages 492
Younger, Henry 344
Your Sister Is a Werewolf see *Howling II*
Yuk, Henry 83
Yulin, Harris 234
Yuricich, Richard 56
Yuzna, Brian 263, 353, 413, 415

Zabriskie, Grace 81
Zacherle, John 131, 215, 216
Zall, Andy 366
Zamora, Del 416
Zane, Billy 40, 42, 103
Zane, Lisa 360
Zanuck, Lili Fini 84, 85
Zanuck, Richard D. 84, 85
Zappa, William 322
Zapped 527, 528
Zapped Again 527–528
Zaremba, John 199
Zarou, Stephan 422
Zavod, Allan 273
Zaza, Paul 176, 390, 391, 392, 393
Z'Dar, Robert 327, 328
Zeitlin, Denny 286
Zeller, Gary 420
Zelouf, Susan 106
Zeman, William 484
Zemeckis, Robert 40, 42, 43
Zenda, John 246
Zendar, Fred 495
Zepeda, Jorge 33
Zerner, Larry 220
Zetlin, Barry 79, 224, 236, 487
Ziehm, Howard 175, 176
Ziembiki, Bob 122
Ziesing, Lucinda 67
Ziff, Stuart 63
Ziker, Dick 516
Zilzer, Wolfgang 292
Zimbalist, Al 76, 77
Zimbalist, Stephanie 64, 65
Zimbert, Jonathan, A. 213
Zimm, Maurice 94
Zimmerman, Don 259
Zipson, Alan 15
Zito, Joseph 221
Zittrer, Carl 390
Zorro (TV series) 40
Zorro, the Gay Blade 153
Zuanic, Rod 323
Zuber, Marc 150
Zucco, George 191, 336, 337, 339, 341, 489
Zuchelli, Franca 214
Zuckerman, Alexander 165
Zulu 23
Zuniga, Daphne 182
ZZ Top 43